IMPORTANT

HERE IS YOUR REGISTRATION CODE TO ACCESS MCGRAW-HILL PREMIUM CONTENT AND MCGRAW-HILL ONLINE RESOURCES

For key premium online resources you need THIS CODE to gain access. Once the code is entered, you will be able to use the web resources for the length of your course.

Access is provided only if you have purchased a new book.

If the registration code is missing from this book, the registration screen on our website, and within your WebCT or Blackboard course will tell you how to obtain your new code. Your registration code can be used only once to establish access. It is not transferable.

To gain access to these online resources

1. **USE** your web browser to go to: **www.mhhe.com/brownsp1**

2. **CLICK** on "First Time User"

3. **ENTER** the Registration Code printed on the tear-off bookmark on the right

4. After you have entered your registration code, click on "Register"

5. **FOLLOW** the instructions to setup your personal UserID and Password

6. **WRITE** your UserID and Password down for future reference. Keep it in a safe place.

If your course is using WebCT or Blackboard, you'll be able to use this code to access the McGraw-Hill content within your instructor's online course.

To gain access to the McGraw-Hill content in your instructor's WebCT or Blackboard course simply log into the course with the user ID and Password provided by your instructor. Enter the registration code exactly as it appears to the right when prompted by the system. You will only need to use this code the first time you click on McGraw-Hill content.

These instructions are specifically for student access. Instructors are not required to register via the above instructions.

The **McGraw·Hill** Companies

Higher Education

Thank you, and welcome to your McGraw-Hill Online Resources.

0-07-320413-7 T/A BROWN: SOCIAL PSYCHOLOGY

LMQK-CS5J-7G5G-IU31-59HQ

REGISTRATION CODE

Social Psychology

Jonathon D. Brown
UNIVERSITY OF WASHINGTON

Boston   Burr Ridge, IL   Dubuque, IA   Madison, WI   New York   San Francisco   St. Louis
Bangkok   Bogotá   Caracas   Kuala Lumpur   Lisbon   London   Madrid   Mexico City
Milan   Montreal   New Delhi   Santiago   Seoul   Singapore   Sydney   Taipei   Toronto

Higher Education

SOCIAL PSYCHOLOGY

Published by McGraw-Hill, a business unit of The McGraw-Hill Companies, Inc., 1221 Avenue of the Americas, New York, NY, 10020. Copyright © 2006 by The McGraw-Hill Companies, Inc. All rights reserved. No part of this publication may be reproduced or distributed in any form or by any means, or stored in a database or retrieval system, without the prior written consent of The McGraw-Hill Companies, Inc., including, but not limited to, in any network or other electronic storage or transmission, or broadcast for distance learning.
Some ancillaries, including electronic and print components, may not be available to customers outside the United States.

This book is printed on acid-free paper.

1 2 3 4 5 6 7 8 9 0 WCK/WCK 0 9 8 7 6 5

ISBN   0-07-230796-X

Editor in Chief: *Emily Barrosse*
Publisher: *Beth Mejia*
Executive Editor: *Michael J. Sugarman*
Senior Developmental Editor: *Judith Kromm*
Marketing Manager: *Melissa S. Caughlin*
Managing Editor: *Jean Dal Porto*
Production Service: *Marilyn Rothenberger*
Art Director: *Jeanne Schreiber*
Lead Designer: *Gino Cieslik*
Text Designer: *Kiera Pohl*
Cover Designer: *Gino Cieslik*
Art Manager: *Robin Mouat*
Art Editor: *Katherine McNab*
Photo Research Coordinator: *Natalia C. Peschiera*
Cover Credit: *©José Ortega/images.com*
Media Project Manager: *Alexander Rohrs*
Senior Production Supervisor: *Carol A. Bielski*
Senior Media Producer: *Stephanie George*
Composition: *10/12 Times Roman by Techbooks/GTS–Los Angeles, CA Campus*
Printing: *45# Pub Matte Plus, Quebecor World Versailles Inc.*

Credits: The credits section for this book begins on page C–1 and is considered an extension of the copyright page.

Library of Congress Control Number: 2005927935

The Internet addresses listed in the text were accurate at the time of publication. The inclusion of a website does not indicate an endorsement by the authors of McGraw-Hill, and McGraw-Hill does not guarantee the accuracy of the information presented at these sites.

www.mhhe.com

They all play on the penny whistle, you can hear them blow
if you lean your head out far enough from Desolation Row.

To Margaret, for her friendship, love, and support

About the Author

Jonathon D. Brown received his Ph.D. from UCLA in 1986, and has been at the University of Washington since 1989. He has published dozens of articles on self-esteem and self-enhancement, and has authored a book on the self for the McGraw-Hill series in social psychology. His research has been funded by the National Science Foundation, and he has served as a consulting editor for the *Journal of Personality and Social Psychology* and as a guest editor for the *Journal of Cross-Cultural Psychology*.

Brief Contents

Contents

CHAPTER FOUR

Social Judgment   101

CHAPTER FIVE

The Self   143

CHAPTER SIX

Attitudes and Behavior   194

Preface

Social psychology professors face an embarrassment of riches. Students are fascinated by the topics they encounter and eagerly want to learn them all. But there's so much to know! Expanding like a red giant, social psychology has grown over the past 25 years to include health psychology and law, social cognitive neuroscience and genetics, and cross-cultural research and evolutionary psychology. What's an instructor to do? The field's biggest strength is also its biggest weakness: There is too much interesting material to teach.

Most contemporary textbooks deal with this problem by reducing their coverage of the field. Instead of offering students a comprehensive in-depth survey, their authors cover select topics in a folksy, narrative style supplemented by cartoons, photographs, poems, and jokes. These books are engaging, but I can't help wondering whether we've struck a Faustian bargain. By seeking to entertain, have we compromised the educational experience of our students? I've taught for almost 20 years, and I've yet to meet a student who just loves to light some candles, draw a warm bath, and cozy up on a cold night with a good social psychology text. Maybe I'm wrong, but I think college students want to be educated, not entertained.

The book you are holding represents my attempt to strike a balance between breadth, depth, and interest value. I worked long and hard on this text, striving to make it the most comprehensive yet readable option available. The feedback I have received has been gratifying. One reviewer wrote, "I have been reviewing textbooks for several years, mainly in the areas of Social Psychology, Evolutionary Psychology, and Emotion. I can say right away that this is one of the best written and most comprehensive textbooks I have ever reviewed (or read for that matter)." I hope you will agree.

Distinctive Features

What makes this text different? Aside from the absence of fluff, the theme of the book and an emphasis on the science of social psychology are noteworthy distinctions.

An Overarching Theme

From the beginning, I emphasize that social psychological research is guided by two important assumptions: (1) Subjective perceptions guide behavior, and (2) personality and situational factors combine to influence subjective perceptions. I return to this theme throughout the text, continually stressing that behavior depends on the world as it appears, which in turn depends on a combination of personal and situational factors. Framing the discussion in this way not only provides a unifying scaffold to aid student learning but also shows students how, when, and why various individual difference variables (e.g., personality, gender, culture) influence behavior. For this reason, I have woven these topics into the text where appropriate rather than treating them in special subsections or sidebars.

An Emphasis on Theory

Second, I focus on theories of social behavior. Beginning in Chapter 1, I explain the relation between theory and research, and describe social psychological research as a theory-testing enterprise. Theories then take center stage in Chapter 2, which is entirely devoted to the key theories that shape social psychological research. These theories range from the historical (e.g., Locke and the associationists, Hull and the behaviorists) to the contemporary (e.g., the sociocultural perspective and the field of evolutionary psychology). I return to these theories throughout the text, showing how various lines of current research have their roots in the past. Doing so allows students to see not only how the present builds on the past but also how various lines of contemporary research are joined by virtue of their common heritage.

How Do We Know That?

Third, I present a lot of data. Instead of stating a conclusion and providing a litany of references, I show students the evidence behind each conclusion. Very often, this evidence takes the form of a statistical interaction depicted in a figure. I have found that college students quickly develop the ability to interpret statistical interactions if the data are presented in a consistent, uniform style. For this reason, the text contains numerous bar graphs that maintain a similar format and a guide in Chapter 1 to interpreting and understanding statistical interactions in a factorial design.

Something Old, Something New, Something Borrowed, Something True

Fourth, I present a balanced blend of old and new. For example, when discussing Heider's balance theory, I emphasize its roots in Gestalt psychology, show how it can be used to explain various empirical findings (e.g., similarity and reciprocity), and then discuss its relevance to contemporary research on implicit attitudes. This balance is reflected in the reference list. Of the more than 2,000 references in this text, a third come from sources less than 5 years old, a third from sources less than 15 years old, and a third from sources more than 15 years old. In short, the book gives a balanced look at the field.

This doesn't mean that I have uncritically included every piece of research that's ever been done. Quite the contrary. Rather than simply reporting research findings, I examine them. For example, in Chapter 8 I examine Milgram's claim that his findings illuminate the Holocaust, and in Chapter 12 I examine whether research on the bystander effect means that people are less apt to receive help when many others are present. I believe that students need to see both the merits and limitations of research in order to understand why we continue to examine old topics as well as branching out into new ones.

Writing Style

Finally, I have written this text in a simple, straightforward style, emphasizing clarity over simplicity. I haven't gratuitously included big words to sound smart or technical, but I also don't talk down to students in a way that underestimates their verbal ability and capacity to grow. Some students may need to consult a dictionary on occasion, but I don't regard that as a failing, as long as the vocabulary is appropriate to the topic being discussed.

Pedagogy

In my mind, good pedagogy facilitates learning and does not distract students from this process. My goal in writing this text was to keep students focused on the theories and research of social psychology, in the hope of retaining their interest and enthusiasm. To develop a deep understanding of social psychology, students need nothing more than the right sequence and flow of topics, along with a clear presentation, a few learning aids, and of course, a dedicated teacher.

Chapter Sequence

I have organized the chapters into a sequence that I find most logical and that fits with many other textbooks. After introducing the field, its methods, and it theories (Chapters 1 and 2), I proceed from a discussion of social thinking (Chapters 3–5), to social influence (Chapters 6–10), and then social behavior (Chapters 11–13). I believe it is best to teach the topics in this order, but the book does not require this sequence and instructors are free to follow a different order if they prefer.

Chapter Organization

Each chapter begins with a vignette, followed by a narrative overview of the chapter. The chapters are then divided into major sections (marked by Roman numerals), each ending with a section summary. I have structured the chapter subheadings (marked by capital letters) in an attempt to help students stay informed about where they've been and where they're going. To me, headings function like monkey bars on a playground. If the topics flow naturally from one to the next, students maintain continuity and see the overall picture. Finally, each chapter ends with a bulleted summary that covers all of the key points.

Pedagogical Devices

Aside from a glossary of key terms, I haven't included any modern pedagogical devices. This means there are no boxes or inserts, ancillary photographs, special icons, cartoons, or marginal quotes. Instead, I have opted for a clear, unfettered presentation that emphasizes substance over style. In this sense, the book is something of an anachronism: a meat-and-potatoes entrée in a pine-nuts-and-risotto world. Despite its lack of glitter and glitz, I believe this text provides a satisfying educational experience for all who partake.

Supplemental Materials

For Instructors

The *Instructor's Resource CD-ROM* that accompanies *Social Psychology* includes an Instructor's Manual, PowerPoint slides, and a Test Bank and Computerized Test Bank.

The Instructor's Manual, prepared by Donald Saucier (Kansas State University) outlines each chapter and provides detailed learning objectives and suggested lecture topics. Also included are ideas for classroom activities, student papers, and discussion questions. PowerPoint slides were created for this text by Alisha Janowsky (Southwest Missouri State University).

The Test Bank, written by Julie Kiotas (Pasadena City College), provides a selection of multiple-choice, true–false, and essay questions to assess students' recall of text content as well as their ability to comprehend and apply the concepts presented in the text. All of these questions are available in Microsoft Word format and in EZ Test format.

McGraw-Hill's EZ Test is a flexible, easy-to-use electronic testing program. The program allows instructors to create tests from book specific items. It accommodates a wide range of question types, and instructors may add their own questions. Multiple versions of the test can be created and any test can be exported for use with course management systems such as WebCT, BlackBoard, or PageOut. EZ Test Online is a new service and gives you a place to easily administer your EZ Test–created exams and quizzes online. The program is available for Windows and Macintosh environments.

The Online Learning Center for *Social Psychology* offers a variety of resources for instructors and students. For instructors, the password instructor's center includes a full set of PowerPoint presentation slides, as well as the Instructor's Manual. These resources and others can be accessed at www.mhhe.com/brown1.

For Students

The *Online Learning Center with PowerWeb* provides an online reader for students that includes a number of journal articles selected by Jonathon Brown for use with this text. Instructors can choose to assign any of these articles to enrich and expand students' familiarity with social psychology research.

Acknowledgments

The following individuals helped me write this book by graciously sharing their ideas or data with me. I am very grateful for their generosity.

Joshua Aronson, *New York University*
Diane Berry, *Southern Methodist University*
Robert Bornstein, *Gettysburg College*
Brad Bushman, *University of Michigan*
David Buss, *University of Texas at Austin*
John Cacioppo, *University of Chicago*
Bella DePaulo, *University of Virginia*
John Dovidio, *Colgate University*
Russ Fazio, *Indiana University*
Jonathan Freedman, *University of Toronto*
Rich Gonzales, *University of Michigan*
Judy Hall, *Northeastern University*
Ted Huston, *University of Texas at Austin*
Howard Leventhal, *Rutgers University*

Neil Malamuth, *University of California, Los Angeles*
Norman Miller, *University of Southern California*
John Miyamoto, *University of Washington*
Richard Petty, *Ohio State University*
Dean Pruitt, *State University of New York, Buffalo*
Lee Ross, *Stanford University*
Caryl Rusbult, *University of North Carolina*
Yaacov Trope, *New York University*
Bernard Weiner, *University of California, Los Angeles*
Robert Zajonc, *Stanford University*

In addition, many social psychology instructors reviewed the manuscript for the book. For their thoughtful suggestions and encouragement, I thank the following individuals:

Kelly Anthony, *Wesleyan University*

Jeff Bryson, *San Diego State University*

Keith Campbell, *University of Georgia*

Stuart Fischoff, *California State University, Los Angeles*

Robert D. Johnson, *Arkansas State University*

Donn L. Kaiser, *Southwest Missouri State University*

Saera Khan, *University of San Francisco*

Marc Kiviniemi, *University of Nebraska, Lincoln*

David Lundgren, *University of Cincinnati*

Lisa Matthews, *Texas A&M University*

Joann Montepare, *Emerson College*

Warren Reich, *The Family Center*

Richard M. Ryckman, Emeritus, *University of Maine*

Paul Silvia, *University of North Carolina at Greensboro*

Jacqueline Pope-Tarrence, *Western Kentucky University*

Jonathon D. Brown

Introduction to Social Psychology

Ask people what gives them the greatest joy in life, and most will mention their family, friends, loved ones, and co-workers; ask them to name the greatest source of stress in their lives, and they will probably give you the same answer. Nothing, it seems, is more important to us than our interpersonal relationships. They give meaning to our lives, lead us to laugh and cry, and bring us rapture and despair. It is for these reasons that John Donne's observation "No [hu]man is an island" has achieved the status of a cultural truism. We are, when all is said and done, social beings.

Social psychology is the scientific study of how people perceive, affect, and relate to one another. This definition is quite broad and covers a wide spectrum of human behavior. It includes not only love and friendship but also prejudice and aggression, conformity and persuasion, and cooperation and group conflict. In short, any behavior of a social nature is of interest to a social psychologist.

Social psychology is a relatively young science. The field did not formally begin until the early 1900s, and the vast majority of research has been conducted during the last 50 years. At the same time, the roots of social psychology go back a long time. In some cases, the ideas and insights that set the stage for contemporary research stretch back all the way to the ancient Greeks and Romans. This is not surprising. Ever since the advent of language, people have carefully observed social behavior and have tried to understand themselves and one another.

Most people have not, however, scientifically tested their ideas to see whether these ideas have merit. This is a distinctive feature of social psychology. Unlike other observers of human behavior, social psychologists systematically test their ideas under controlled conditions. This aspect of social psychology distinguishes social psychology from other attempts to understand social behavior.

This book is designed to acquaint you with this research enterprise. It focuses on the manner in which social psychologists take their theoretical ideas and translate them into testable scientific hypotheses. The first part of this chapter introduces the field of social psychology and the topics social psychologists study. Next, you will learn about the nature of science, paying particular attention to the relation between theory and research. Finally, you will learn how to evaluate and interpret scientific findings.

I. The Social Psychological Approach

Like all academic disciplines, social psychologists make some important assumptions about the phenomena they study.

A. Principal Assumptions

1. Interpretations Guide Behavior

The most important assumption social psychologists make is that the meaning people give to their experiences guides their behavior. Within psychology, this position is known as the phenomenological approach or **phenomenology.** Phenomenology comes from a Greek word that means "as it appears." Social psychologists believe that our behavior in any situation depends on how we interpret, construe, appraise, or perceive the situation. It is the world as it appears to the individual that guides behavior.

To illustrate this point, imagine you are riding on a bus and someone bumps into you. How will you react? Very likely, your reaction will depend on the meaning you give to this event. Was it a purposeful act of aggression or an unavoidable accident? Was the other person being careless or was the person unable to walk steadily? Was it entirely the other person's fault or do you share some of the responsibility by not paying close attention to what was happening? Any of these interpretations is plausible, and they will all influence your reaction to the event. You will probably feel angry or afraid if you think you were bumped on purpose, irritated if you think it was a careless accident, sympathetic if you think the other person wasn't able to walk steadily, and apologetic if you think you were at fault. In short, how you feel will depend largely on the meaning you give to the event—on the way you interpret and explain it.

2. Personality and Situational Variables Guide Interpretations

If most events were clear and unambiguous, the importance of subjective construals would be greatly reduced. Everyone would agree on what occurred and why it happened, and everyone would respond accordingly. But this is rarely the case. Most events are ambiguous and open to multiple interpretations. Consequently, it's important to understand what factors influence the meaning we give to the events we encounter.

Generally speaking, the meaning we give to an experience is influenced by two factors—our personality and the situational context in which the event occurs. For our purposes, the term **personality** refers to enduring, consistent, and characteristic patterns of thinking, feeling, and behaving that originate within an individual. This definition captures what most people think of when they think of a person's traits. For example, to say someone is sociable is to say that he or she typically enjoys interacting with others. Personality factors also influence the meaning we give to the situations we are in. In the case of the incident on the bus, it is not unreasonable to assume that hostile people are inclined to believe the act was done on purpose and kind people are apt to believe it was an accident.

Social psychologists do not deny that personality variables like these affect the way people view the world, but they believe that other factors are also important to consider. Such a factor is termed a **situational variable.** This term refers to any factor that provides the context for an event or experience. These variables include the physical environment, any relevant social norms, and the behavior of other people in the situation, as well as more temporary personal factors such as your current mood or level of fatigue. To continue with our example of someone bumping into you, your interpretation will probably be influenced by the other person's appearance and demeanor; by the conditions on the bus (crowded or relatively empty); and even by the temperature, time of day, and whether you are hungry or having a bad day. These factors, in combination with personality, will guide the meaning you give to the situation.

Kurt Lewin (1951) is generally credited with introducing this perspective into the field of social psychology. Lewin believed that people behave in accordance with the perceived world, and that these perceptions are influenced by aspects of the immediate situation (which he called the environment) and the person's more enduring needs, goals, and traits. In more formal terms, Lewin argued that behavior is a function of the person and the environment:

$$B = f(P, E)$$

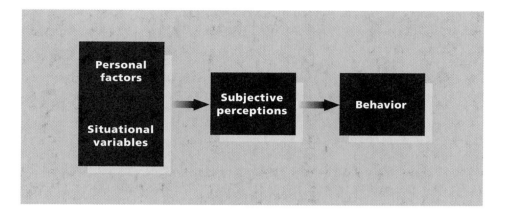

FIGURE 1.1

The Social Psychological Approach to Understanding Social Behavior

The figure shows that (1) personal factors and situational variables combine to influence subjective perceptions and (2) subjective perceptions influence behavior.

Figure 1.1 displays a schematic representation of Lewin's (1951) theory. The figure shows that personal factors and situational variables combine to influence subjective perceptions, and that subjective perceptions guide behavior. These assumptions define the field of social psychology.

3. The Power of the Situation

When studying social behavior, it is easy to overlook the power of the situation and to assume instead that enduring personality forces are more important. Sometimes this is true, but often it is not. In many instances, subtle variations in a situation can profoundly affect how people behave. Consider, for example, a study by Darley and Batson (1973). The participants were seminary students at Princeton University. As they were walking to a classroom to deliver a lecture, they encountered a man slumped in a doorway, head down, eyes closed, not moving. Would these seminary students offer help? One would certainly think so. After all, they were training for the ministry, a profession that emphasizes the importance of good deeds and caring for others. But the experimenters had manipulated a variable in this study. Some students were told they were very late and needed to hurry, others were told they were right on schedule, and a third group was told they were ahead of schedule and had plenty of time.

This situational manipulation proved to have a very powerful effect on whether the students helped the victim or not. As shown in Figure 1.2, a high percentage of students helped when they were not in a hurry, but very few helped when they were in a hurry. In this study, then, a small situational variable had a large effect.

B. Social Psychology versus Other Academic Disciplines

Social psychologists are not the only people who study social behavior. Social behavior is a concern of clinical, personality, and developmental psychologists, and sociologists,

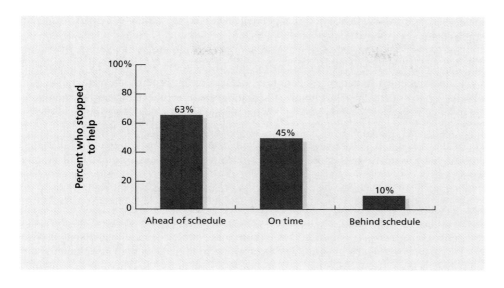

FIGURE 1.2

Percentage of Seminary Students Who Helped a Victim in Distress as a Function of Whether They Believed They Were Late for an Appointment

While walking across campus to deliver a lecture, seminary students encountered a person who needed help. Those who were behind schedule were much less apt to help than were those who were on time or were ahead of schedule. These data show that a small situational variable—whether one is late for an appointment or not—has a large influence on behavior.

Source: Darley and Batson (1973).

cultural anthropologists, and economists also study social interactions. In a large sense, these various disciplines are complementary. They each offer a different perspective on understanding social behavior.

To see how the social psychological approach fits in, let's consider an example from the newspapers. For some years now, the United States has witnessed a dramatic rise in a particular social problem known as road rage. Road rage occurs when a driver engages in reckless, aggressive, or violent behavior because of some perceived slight or transgression. According to a report by the American Automobile Association, there were more than 10,000 incidents of road rage in the United States between 1990 and 1996, resulting in more than 12,000 injuries and 200 deaths. How are we to understand such behavior?

1. Level of Analysis

The anthropologist would focus on cultural factors. As we will see in Chapter 13, the United States is one of the most violent societies on earth. Road rage occurs in other countries, but it is far more likely to happen in the United States. Why? The anthropologist would note that Americans have had a long-standing love affair with the independent, freewheeling cowboy image. The vigilante who takes the law into his own hands is often revered in American literature, songs, and movies. Clint Eastwood has made a career of portraying such characters, and Michael Douglas starred in one such movie, called *Falling Down*. Anthropologists would trace road rage to a cultural legacy that glorifies violence and independence. It is in the nature of Americans to be aggressive.

The field of sociology offers a somewhat different analysis. Although road rage occurs across all levels of American society, it is more likely to be carried out by young males of lower socioeconomic status. Taking note of these facts, a sociologist would ask: What is it about this demographic group that leads to increased incidences of aggression on the highway? In answering this question, a sociologist might emphasize a lack of upward mobility, a sense of economic despair, and social helplessness. These large-scale social forces, the sociologist would argue, explain why road rage is more prevalent among some social groups than among others.

Differences among people are also of interest to personality and clinical psychologists. However, instead of focusing on variables related to social class, personality and clinical psychologists focus on underlying personality dynamics. For example, these theorists would probably note that people who are aggressive or have an antisocial personality disorder are most prone to commit acts of road rage. From this perspective, some people are violent and hostile whereas others are not. To understand who commits violence on the road, we ask, "Which kind of person are you?"

Social psychology offers another perspective. Social psychologists focus on factors in the immediate social situation that influence the meaning people give to the situation. In the case of road rage, some relevant factors to consider are the sense of power that derives from operating a powerful machine; feelings of anonymity that stem from being in a setting where one is likely to be unknown; frustration over traffic, heat, and urban crowding; and even the mere fact that road rage is becoming common and newsworthy. From this perspective, the explanation lies not in what kind of person someone is, but rather in understanding how various situational factors bring out the aggressiveness in people.

2. Methodological Approach

The methods researchers use to gather data also differ among academic disciplines. For the most part, anthropologists examine archival data; sociologists analyze surveys; and personality and clinical psychologists use interviews, questionnaires, and case histories. In contrast, social psychologists most often conduct experimental research in laboratory settings. As we will see in a later section of this chapter, the advantage of laboratory research is that it allows scientists to determine whether one variable causes another. For example, to determine whether heat increases aggression, we could experimentally vary the temperature in a room and measure how aggressively people behave (C. A. Anderson, Deuser, & DeNeve, 1995). Although social psychologists use other methods to supplement the experiment, when they study a problem they use the experimental method by and large. They also tend to perform their experiments in laboratory settings that allow them to control outside sources of variability.

3. Topics in Social Psychology

Having examined how social psychologists think about social behavior, let's take a closer look at the topics they study. To begin, consider the following events:

1. Fifteen years ago, few Americans had ever heard of a double-tall hazelnut latte. It's not that the drink didn't exist, it's that nobody cared to drink it. Things couldn't be more different today. With a coffee stand on virtually every corner, millions of Americans now begin each day by ordering this or a similar beverage. What explains this transformation? How were the buying habits of so many people changed so rapidly?

2. In February 1999, New York City police officers shot and killed a West African immigrant, Amadou Diallo, as he stood on the steps of his apartment building. When later questioned about the incident, the officers testified they believed Diallo was armed and dangerous. In fact, Diallo was holding only his wallet as he attempted to identify himself to the officers. What explains the officers' error? Did they harbor deep-seated prejudices and hatred toward men of African descent, or was this incident simply a tragic case of mistaken identification?

3. On February 1, 2002, the space shuttle *Columbia* exploded 39 miles above the earth, sending all seven crew members to a fiery death. Although accidents are an inevitable part of space travel, this incident bore an eerie resemblance to an earlier tragedy: the explosion of the space shuttle *Challenger* in January 1986. In both cases, inquiries established that faulty decision making on the part of those responsible for ensuring the mission's success contributed to the mission's demise. How could this catastrophe have happened twice? Why would highly trained, intelligent people fail to see the signs of trouble both times?

4. At first, the images out of Iraq's Abu Ghraib prison seemed too bizarre to be real. First released in the spring of 2004 on the CBS television show *60 Minutes,* the photographs showed American soldiers mugging for the cameras in front of naked Iraqi prisoners posed in sexually suggestive positions. Further reports described a carnival-like atmosphere inside the prison, in which U.S. soldiers delighted in the mistreatment and sexual humiliation of their prisoners. Why would U.S. soldiers behave in such a fashion? Were they merely following orders from those in authority (as they claimed during their trial), or did something happen inside the prison that transformed these soldiers, causing them to ignore their training and disregard their own moral compass?

These events differ in many ways, but they all show that people's behavior is shaped by factors in the immediate social situation. Table 1.1 lists other topics you will read about in this book. As you can see, many of these topics concern significant social problems. This is an important aspect of social psychology. Over the years, social psychologists have studied ways to reduce prejudice and discrimination, curb sexual violence, improve the classroom performance of African Americans, promote environmental conservation, and encourage the use of safe sexual practices (Bryan, Aiken, & West, 1999; Dickerson, Thibodeau, Aronson, & Miller, 1992; S. T. Fiske, 1998; Malamuth & Donnerstein, 1984; C. M. Steele, 1997). Social psychologists have made additional contributions in matters of law, health, business, politics, and intergroup conflict (Ellsworth & Mauro, 1998; Kinder, 1998; Pfeffer, 1998; Pruitt, 1998; Salovey, Rothman, & Rodin, 1998). In short, social psychologists study virtually all of the myriad problems that beset contemporary society, and easing these problems is an important goal of social psychological research. We will have the opportunity to review much of this research throughout the text.

TABLE 1.1   Topics in Social Psychology

Chapter 2: Social Psychology's Theoretical Roots
What role do theories play in social psychology?
Where do social psychological theories come from?

Chapter 3: Social Perception
Why are first impressions so important and when do they change?
How do we know when other people are telling the truth or lying?

Chapter 4: Social Judgment
How do we form a complete impression of another person?
How do our explanations for another person's actions influence our behavior toward that person?

Chapter 5: The Self
How does our self-concept develop and change with age?
Why do some people have low self-esteem, and how does low self-esteem influence behavior?

Chapter 6: Attitudes and Behavior
Where do our attitudes come from and what functions do they serve?
How do people respond when they find they have not acted in accordance with their attitudes?

Chapter 7: Persuasion
Are people more persuaded by reasoned arguments or emotional appeals?
Under what conditions are advertisers effective at persuading us to buy their products?

Chapter 8: Social Influence
Why do people often agree to do favors for others even when they don't want to?
Will people obey authority even when they know it is wrong to do so?

Chapter 9: Groups
Do individuals perform better or worse when performing with others?
Do groups make better decisions than individuals working alone?

Chapter 10: Prejudice
How do stereotypes form and can they be changed?
Is intergroup conflict an unavoidable aspect of intergroup relationships?

Chapter 11: Interpersonal Relationships
Why are we attracted to some people but not attracted to others?
What determines whether a couple stays together or breaks up?

Chapter 12: Helping
Are people always egoistic or are they ever capable of acting altruistically?
Are people more apt to receive help in a large group or a small group?

Chapter 13: Aggression
Is aggression inevitable or can it be reduced or eliminated?
Does viewing media violence and pornography increase aggression?

II. The Nature of Science

We have defined social psychology as the *scientific* study of how people perceive, affect, and relate to one another. In order to understand social psychology, then, we need to understand science.

A. What Is Science?

Fortunately, science is easy to understand. It is simply a way of knowing what the world is like. The essence of this method is the integration of logic with systematic and objective observation. Scientists use logic to develop theories and to generate hypotheses. Then they test their hypotheses to see whether those hypotheses are supported.

This combination sets science apart from other ways of learning about the world. Before scientists will accept an idea as true, the idea must pass many hurdles. Scientists are skeptics; they are the proverbial Missourians: "Show me," they say. In science, ideas are presumed to be wrong until they are shown to be true. In this sense, science is the most conservative and, arguably, the surest method for learning about the world.

1. Ways of Knowing

A useful starting point for understanding the nature of science is to consider various ways in which people acquire knowledge (Kerlinger, 1986; McGuire, 1983).

Dogmatism. Dogmatism provides one way of gaining knowledge. Dogma is an idea or set of ideas held to be true because some higher authority says it is true. Dogmatism was very popular during the Middle Ages. Things were true if the Church said they were true. Of course, even today, we learn a great deal about the world in this manner. Much of what children learn comes from what their parents tell them. This is often a very efficient way of learning about the world. If I tell my kids that touching a hot stove will burn them, they are probably better off just taking my word for it rather than testing this idea directly.

Rationalism. Logic and reasoning provide a second way of gaining knowledge. Formally, this method is known as **rationalism.** With rationalism, the acceptance of an idea depends on a careful, logical analysis of the idea's merits. For thousands of years, philosophers have used logic and reasoning to reach tremendous insights into the nature of the world. Descartes's famous dictum "I think, therefore I am" provides the best-known example of this approach.

Because rationalism provides a way of ascertaining truth, it represents an advance over dogmatism. At the same time, logic will not reveal truth if the premise is wrong. For example, suppose you begin with the premise "All dogs have fleas." You would be correct in inferring, then, that the puppy down the street has fleas. After all, if all dogs have fleas and the puppy down the street is a dog, then logic dictates that the puppy down the street must have fleas. The problem is that your premise may be wrong. Maybe not all dogs have fleas; maybe only most dogs have fleas or only some dogs have fleas. In this case, you might incorrectly infer that the puppy down the street has fleas.

The larger point here is that logic is limited because it doesn't provide a way to test assumptions. This may seem like an obvious point, but before the age of science (roughly the 1500s) people didn't think to put their ideas to a test. They merely accepted an idea as true either because someone told them it was true or because a logical analysis indicated that it must be true. Galileo, who is generally regarded as the father of modern science, changed that. He argued that people ought to formally test their ideas to see whether they are true.

Empiricism. The notion that our ideas ought to be tested brings us to the third way of knowing the world—**empiricism.** According to the doctrine of empiricism, an idea is held to be true if and only if it can be observed to be true. Empiricism holds that sensory experience, not reason, is the final arbiter of truth. From this perspective, an idea is not assumed to be true simply because someone said it was true or because a rational analysis indicates that it must be true; instead, an idea is considered true only if it can be shown to be true.

A variant on this theme is known as positivism. The doctrine of **positivism** asserts that an idea is true only if it can be observed to be true by multiple, objective observers. This is a bit different from empiricism. Empiricism requires only that knowledge be acquired through sensory experience. Positivism demands that true knowledge must be gathered through objective procedures that can be repeated and verified by others. In the words of American logician Charles Peirce, "The method must be such that the ultimate conclusion of every [person] shall be the same" (Buchler, 1955).

One way to understand the difference between empiricism and positivism is to consider the manner in which Sigmund Freud developed his theory of psychoanalysis. Freud was an empiricist. He developed his theory by carefully analyzing his own experiences and the experiences of his patients. Freud was not a positivist, however. Neutral observers do not necessarily agree with his observations and the conclusions he drew from them.

Science: Logical Positivism. Modern science combines logic and positivism. Scientists use logic to develop theories and to generate hypotheses about what is likely to be true. Then they test their hypotheses to establish the validity of their ideas. These tests must occur under objective, neutral conditions so that all observers can agree on both the procedures and the findings. Because it combines logic and positivism, modern science has been called logical positivism (Whitehead, 1925).

Summary. There is nothing mysterious about science. It has nothing to do with bubbling beakers or Bunsen burners. Anyone who uses the tools of logic and observation—regardless of whether he or she is a chemist, a nuclear physicist, or a psychologist—is a scientist. A child who reasons, "Stones are stronger than glass. I bet if I throw this rock through the window, the window will break," is using logic. If he then throws the rock through the window to see whether he is right, he is doing science. Although most parents will be angry with the damage he caused, they should also be impressed with the methods he used. He was doing science!

2. Functions of Science

Having introduced the scientific method, let's consider four functions that science serves.

Description. One aim of science is description. Using careful and systematic observation, scientists are able to accurately describe the natural world. This function of science has been fulfilled by compiling the periodic table of elements, cataloging the number of species in the rain forest, and documenting the number of genes on the human genome. Changes in world temperature provide another example. Using sophisticated instruments combined with meticulous observation, scientists have been able to chronicle changing temperature patterns on earth.

Prediction. A second aim of science is prediction. Once we have described a phenomenon, we are often in a position to predict what is apt to happen in the future. With respect to global warming, scientists predict that the seas will rise several feet when the polar ice caps melt, that wheat will be grown in Canada, and that various plant and animal species will be endangered.

Explanation. Description and prediction are important functions of science, but scientists also want to know *why* phenomena occur. This function of science is called explanation. In the case of global warming, we would want to know why it is occurring. In order to answer this question, we need to know what factors affect the temperature of the earth and what changes have taken place on our planet to alter the average temperature.

Control. Control is a final aim of science. In this context, *control* means to gain power over or to take charge of some phenomenon. Most scientists don't simply want to know why global warming is occurring; they also want to be able to stop it from continuing. This is an example of what it means to control a phenomenon.

3. Two Types of Scientific Research

The distinction between explanation and control mirrors the distinction between two different types of scientific research, known as basic research and applied research. The difference between these two types of research lies in their immediate aim. The immediate aim of **basic research** is to understand phenomena; the immediate aim of **applied research** is to achieve some practical benefit. Basic researchers operate at the level of explanation. They want to know why phenomena occur, without regard to whether this knowledge will be used to some practical advantage. In contrast, applied researchers operate primarily at the level of control. They want to use knowledge to improve some aspect of life or solve some problem.

It may seem that applied research is more important than basic research, but this is not necessarily true. Most of the time, applied research is built on basic research. Before we can control a phenomenon, we usually need to understand why it occurs. In the case of global warming, scientists suspect that the overuse of chlorofluorocarbons and the destruction of the rain forests have caused the earth's temperature to rise. Having achieved this understanding, scientists have begun efforts to alter these behaviors and undo the damage that has been done.

Much of the research you will read about in this text falls under the category of basic research. This is because most social psychologists who publish their research findings are basic researchers: They are interested in understanding why people behave as they do in social situations. Other individuals, such as market researchers, political consultants, and health care providers, use the knowledge that basic researchers have generated to effect behavioral change. This is what we mean when we say that applied research builds on basic research.

B. The Scientific Process

Having considered the functions of science and distinguished two kinds of scientific research, let's look more closely at how science is conducted.

1. Hypothesis Generation

Science begins with the identification of a problem or phenomenon of interest. In the domain of social psychology, for instance, we might be interested in the relation between watching violence on television and engaging in aggressive behavior. (We will consider this matter in greater detail in Chapter 13.) After observing or thinking about some aspect of behavior, the scientist forms a **hypothesis,** an educated guess about how two or more variables are related. For example, one might hypothesize that viewing lots of TV violence leads a person to behave aggressively. This hypothesis relates one variable (the amount of violence one watches on TV) with another variable (how aggressively one behaves).

Forming a hypothesis is only the beginning of the process of science. Scientific hypotheses must be stated in such a way that they are capable of being tested. In a general way, hypotheses take the form of an IF:THEN proposition. *If* one watches TV violence, *then* one will behave aggressively. In practice, testable hypotheses most often take the form of an IF:THEN:THAN proposition. *If* viewing violence on television leads to aggression, *then* those who watch lots of TV violence will be more aggressive *than* those who do not watch lots of TV violence. Stated in this way, a hypothesis can be tested to determine whether it is supported.

2. The Role of Theories

Observation provides one way to generate hypotheses. Another, more common approach is to derive a hypothesis from a theory. **Theories** are general principles that explain why two or more variables are related. Less formally, they provide the *why* behind the *what;* they explain why we observe the things we do. Theories are not the same as facts. Facts are the things we observe; they are part of the natural world. Theories are explanations for why we observe what we do; they are human-made and thus not part of the natural world.

Many scientists believe that theory development is the ultimate goal of science (e.g., Braithwaite, 1955; Kerlinger, 1986). By explaining why things occur, theories enable us to control and alter phenomena. This point brings us back to the distinction we made between basic research and applied research. Basic research is concerned primarily with theoretical development and explanation. Once this understanding is reached, we are in a better position to solve applied problems. Within social psychology, the importance of theory development was first emphasized by Kurt Lewin (1951):

> The greatest handicap of applied psychology has been the fact that, without proper theoretical help, it had to follow the costly, inefficient, and limited method of trial and error. Many psychologists working today in an applied field are keenly aware of the need for close cooperation between theoretical and applied psychology. This can be accomplished in psychology, as it has been accomplished in physics, if the theorist does not look toward applied problems with highbrow aversion or with a fear of social problems, and if the applied psychologist realizes that there is nothing so practical as a good theory. (p. 169)

Lewin's point is that theory development normally precedes application. We must understand the world before we can change it.

3. Evaluating Theories

Theories are evaluated according to three criteria: parsimony, breadth, and generativity.

Parsimony. The word *parsimony,* which in general means being careful or economical, refers to the complexity of a theory. In science, theories that are simple and economical are preferred over ones that are complex and cumbersome. This preference for parsimony is known as Occam's razor, in honor of the 14th-century British philosopher William of Occam. Occam argued that complex logic should not be used when simple logic will suffice. Adapting this principle, scientists maintain that if two theories can explain data equally well, the simpler, more parsimonious theory is favored.

Breadth. Breadth is another important property of a theory. The more phenomena a theory can explain, the better the theory. For example, consider Newton's law of gravity. When first proposed, this was a broad theory to explain the attraction of two objects. It explains not only the falling of chalk but also the orbit of the planets around the sun and the rising and falling of the tides. On the surface, these phenomena seem unrelated: What do the orbits of the planets have to do with the falling of chalk? A good theory shows us how seemingly different phenomena can be integrated and understood with only a few principles.

Generativity. A final criterion of a theory is its generativity (or heuristic value). Good theories not only explain or integrate previously observed phenomena but also generate new hypotheses that can be tested. To illustrate, imagine that we notice some irregularity in Jupiter's orbit. On the basis of Newton's law of gravity, we could deduce the existence of a previously undiscovered moon of a specified mass and distance from Jupiter that explains the perturbation. We could then test our ideas by looking for this object. In this manner, a theory would help us discover something we didn't already know.

Summary. To reiterate, good theories are (1) parsimonious, or simple; (2) able to broadly explain much of what we already know to be true; and (3) capable of generating new knowledge and explaining events not yet known. The renowned physicist Stephen Hawking (1988) summarized these points in the following way:

> A theory . . . exists only in our minds and does not have any other reality (whatever that might mean). A good theory . . . must accurately describe a large class of observations on the basis of a model that contains only a few arbitrary elements, and it must make definite predictions about the results of future observations. (p. 9)

4. The Relation between Theories and Hypotheses

So far we've been discussing the nature of theories and the role they play in generating testable hypotheses. Figure 1.3 presents a more complete way of understanding this process. The figure shows that scientific research often begins with a theory. Using deductive reasoning (*deductive* means going from the general to the specific), we deduce a specific hypothesis. We then conduct research to test our hypothesis. On the basis of what we observe, we use inductive reasoning (going from the specific to the general) to modify our theory. In this manner, there is a continuous recycling between theory and research.

To illustrate this process, imagine that I have a general theory that people are imitative creatures ("Monkey see, monkey do"). This is a broad theory about human behavior. For example, it might explain how infants acquire language, why children tend to adopt the political ideology of their parents, and why various fashions and fads sweep the country. It can also explain why viewing violence on television increases aggression. If people are imitative, then they will imitate the violence they see on television and behave aggressively. This is an example of deductive inference or deductive reasoning (i.e., going from the general to the specific).

FIGURE 1.3

The Nature of Scientific Research

Scientific research often begins with a theory. Using deductive reasoning, we then generate a testable hypothesis. Next, we conduct research and, based on our findings, modify our theory using inductive reasoning. In this manner, there is a continuous recycling between theory and research.

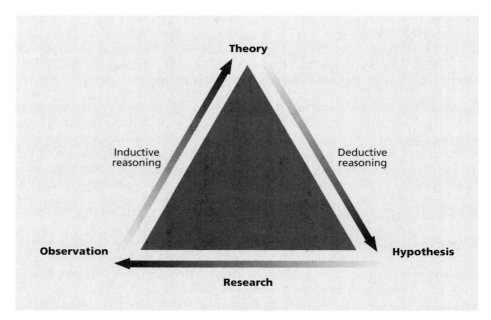

To put my hypothesis in a testable form, I might say, "*If* people imitate what they see, *then* people who watch violence on television will behave more aggressively *than* people who do not." Notice how this statement adheres to the IF:THEN:THAN convention we discussed earlier. Hypotheses stated in this way are capable of being tested. I can conduct a study to determine whether people who watch violence on television behave more aggressively than people who do not. Depending on what I found, I might want to modify my theory. Suppose I found that TV violence affects aggression only among children, not among adults. I would then want to modify my theory to reflect this finding. This would involve the use of inductive reasoning (i.e., going from the specific to the general).

This process of going from theory to hypothesis to observation and back to theory is the essence of scientific research. Scientists continually refine their theories by formulating testable hypotheses. An important (though often overlooked) aspect of this process is that theories themselves are never tested. We test only the hypotheses we have deduced from a theory. To return to our example, children who watch violence on television may behave more aggressively than children who don't, but it may not be because they are imitative. Perhaps viewing violence excites children and they aggress in order to release this arousal or excitement. In this case, my theory predicted the behavior, but the underlying explanation was different from the one I had assumed.

To summarize, when we perform an experiment, we are testing hypotheses, not theories. Theories themselves—ideas about why variables are related—are not directly tested. Instead, we test hypotheses. On the basis of our findings, we use logic and reasoning to refine our theories. This aspect of the scientific process underscores the difference between theories and facts. Unlike facts, theories are never right or wrong; they are simply useful or not useful. And they are always being tested and revised.

Any . . . theory is always provisional: you can never prove it. No matter how many times the results of experiments agree with some theory, you can never be sure that the next time the result will not contradict the theory . . . Each time new experiments are observed

to agree with the prediction, the theory survives and our confidence in it is increased;
but if ever a new observation is found to disagree, we have to abandon or modify the
theory . . . In practice, what often happens is that a new theory is devised that is really
an extension of the previous theory. (Hawking, 1988, p. 10)

C. Types of Research

Having formulated a hypothesis, we are now ready to test it. In science, we use two
types of research for testing hypotheses: correlational research and experimental
research.

1. Correlational Research

With **correlational research,** the experimenter adopts a (fairly) passive role and carefully observes and records the association between two or more naturally occurring
variables. This observation can be accomplished by (1) consulting archival data (such
as police reports of violent crimes), (2) conducting a survey (much like those commonly reported on TV news shows and in newspapers), or (3) simply noticing some
aspect of behavior (e.g., people who have multiple bumper stickers on their car seem
to drive slowly). Regardless of how we gather the information, the key aspect of correlational research is that we are looking for the association between variables that
exist or occur without any manipulation on our part.

To more fully illustrate this approach, imagine that I wish to determine whether
people who drink alcohol are more aggressive than people who do not drink alcohol.
This hypothesis relates two variables: people's drinking habits and their aggressiveness. The easiest way to test my hypothesis is to measure the amount of alcohol people
drink and then measure their belligerence or aggressiveness. Afterward I could plot
the data to determine whether the two variables are related, and assess the strength
of any association using a statistic called a correlation coefficient. Correlation coeffi-
cients range in value from 1.0 (indicating a perfect positive relationship) to 0 (indicating no relationship) to −1.0 (indicating a perfect negative relationship).

Figure 1.4 illustrates these possibilities. Panel 1 shows that a **positive correlation**
occurs when increases in one variable are accompanied by increases in another variable. In our example, a positive correlation would occur if people who drink alcohol
behave more aggressively than people who do not drink alcohol. In Panel 2, we see
a **negative correlation.** This occurs when increases in one variable are accompanied
by decreases in the other variable. In our case, a negative correlation would mean that
people who drink alcohol are less aggressive than people who don't drink alcohol.
Finally, Panel 3 shows what happens when there is no correlation. Here, alcohol
consumption and aggressiveness are completely unrelated.

In terms of the four functions that science serves, the procedures I have described
fall under the categories of description and prediction. By plotting the data, we have
described how the two variables are related. Then, depending on the strength of the
association, we can predict a person's standing on one variable from knowing his or
her score on the other variable. For example, if the data showed a strong positive
correlation, we could predict that a person who drinks frequently will behave more
aggressively than a teetotaler will.

The problem with such a research strategy is that even if we found that the two
variables were positively correlated, we couldn't be sure that drinking alcohol *causes*
aggression. This is because there are three possible explanations for any observed

FIGURE 1.4

Three Possible Relations
between Alcohol
Consumption and
Aggression

Panel 1 shows a positive
correlation: Increases in
one variable are accompa-
nied by increases in the
other variable; Panel 2
shows a negative correla-
tion: Increases in one
variable are accompanied
by decreases in the other
variable; Panel 3 shows no
correlation: Scores on one
variable are unrelated to
scores on the other
variable.

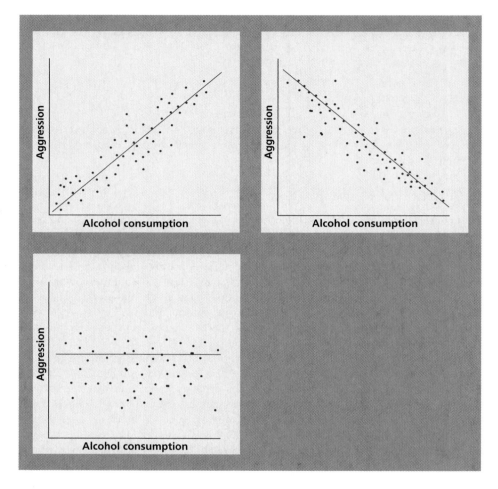

correlation between two variables. One explanation is that the x variable does, in fact, cause the y variable. This is known as the causal hypothesis, because it asserts that x (drinking alcohol) causes y (aggressiveness).

In addition to the causal hypothesis, there are two other explanations for why x and y are correlated. One alternative, known as the reverse causation hypothesis, maintains that instead of x causing y, y causes x. This would occur if a person's aggressive nature influenced his or her drinking habits. This seems quite plausible. People who are angry and ill-tempered might drink to calm themselves down. A final alternative is known as the third variable problem. This problem occurs when a third variable, usually called z, affects x and y, but there is no causal relation between x and y in either direction. Stress is a possible third variable in our example. Stress could lead people to drink and to behave aggressively, but the alcohol doesn't cause aggression and the aggression doesn't lead to drinking. Other plausible third variables are physical pain, problems at work, or a troubled social life. Conceivably, all of these variables could lead people to drink and to behave aggressively.

It's important to note that all three processes can occur: x may cause y, y may cause x, and z may cause both x and y. And therein lies the problem. With correlational research, we don't know which process explains the association between our two variables. In theory, all are equally likely. Unfortunately, this causal uncertainty has an important consequence. Suppose we want to reduce aggression. Prohibitions on alcohol will be effective only if we can establish that drinking alcohol causes aggression.

To summarize, correlational research can establish whether two variables are related, but it cannot tell us whether one variable causes another. Considering this limitation, many students wonder why scientists use correlational research. There are several reasons. First, correlational research is useful for matters of description. Before we undertake a detailed examination of the relation between alcohol and aggression, we might first want to know whether the two variables are related at all. Correlational research is well suited for this purpose.

We also use correlational research because some variables cannot be manipulated. Many variables—such as race, sex, and aspects of personality (e.g., hostility, sociability)—influence social behavior. We cannot randomly assign people to possess these characteristics, so we must study their influence using correlational research.

Third, other variables could be manipulated, but ethical considerations prevent us from doing so. It is important to understand what effect neglect has on children, but it would be unethical to randomly assign some children to be neglected and others to be loved and nurtured. The same holds true for many other variables (e.g., losing your job; being the victim of a violent crime).

Finally, sometimes we just want to be able to predict behavior and are less concerned with understanding why two variables are related. In this case, correlational research is perfectly adequate.

2. Experimental Research

To establish causality, we must turn from correlational research to another form of research, known as **experimental research.** Two aspects of experimental research are critical. The first is called experimental control. Experimental control involves creating two (or more) experimental conditions that vary only with respect to one variable, termed the independent variable. The **independent variable** is the variable the experimenter manipulates. For example, if I conduct an experiment to study the effect of alcohol on aggression in which some **participants** drink alcohol and others do not, alcohol consumption is the independent variable.

The second important aspect of experimental research is random assignment to conditions. With **random assignment,** each person in an experiment has an equal chance of being assigned to any of the various experimental conditions. Random assignment, which can be accomplished simply by flipping a coin, is critical because it allows us to rule out all possible third variables as an explanation for our findings. If we randomly assign a sufficiently large number of people to conditions, the statistical laws of probability ensure that there will be no preexisting differences between our experimental groups.

To continue with our example, imagine that we conduct an experiment in which we randomly assign some people to drink soda spiked with tasteless alcohol and others to drink plain soda pop. Later, we measure how aggressively they behave. Aggression is the dependent variable. The **dependent variable** is the variable the experimenter measures. It is called the dependent variable because we assume that participants' scores on this measure *depend* on which experimental condition they are in. If we find that the people who had drunk alcohol behaved more aggressively than those who hadn't, we would be warranted in concluding that alcohol consumption is one cause of aggression. We would have scientific evidence that x causes y.

This is the power of the experimental method. It permits us to determine whether one variable causes another. It is random assignment to conditions that allows us to reach this conclusion. Experimental control is important, but random assignment to conditions is the essential element of the experimental method. Theoretically, if we have enough participants, random assignment to conditions ensures that the two groups will be equivalent with respect to all possible third variables at the start of the experiment. Just as many people who are under stress will wind up in the "drink alcohol" condition as in the "drink soda pop" condition. Consequently, any effect we find of alcohol cannot be due to preexisting differences in stress. And this is true for all other third variables that affect aggression, because the only difference between the two conditions was whether or not people drank alcohol.

Constructing a situation in which we are able to assign participants to conditions is usually more difficult than merely observing and carefully describing what people do. Why go to the trouble of conducting an experiment? Because only an experiment can establish whether or not two variables are causally related. Before we can control phenomena, we must generally first establish whether a causal relation exists. In order to know whether a causal relation exists, we need to conduct experiments that use random assignment to conditions.

The Need for Multiple Experiments. Experiments give researchers a powerful tool for gaining knowledge, but no single study can tell us everything we want to know. For one thing, knowing that x caused y in a given study doesn't mean that y never causes x. It is entirely possible, for example, that aggressive people drink to calm themselves down. All we know is that this didn't occur in our study, because we randomly assigned participants to drink alcohol or soda pop. In a similar vein, our findings do not rule out the possibility that a third variable influences x and y. Stress may indeed be such a factor, but it couldn't have produced our results, because random assignment to conditions theoretically ensured that the two groups were equal with regard to this factor. By varying only one factor and using random assignment to conditions, we rule out the reverse causation hypothesis and the third variable problem, leaving the causal hypothesis as the only viable explanation for our findings. Our study does not, however, provide evidence that these processes do not occur in other situations.

Single studies are also subject to error. As discussed in a later section of this chapter, chance factors alone may produce the results we observe. For this reason, scientists often repeat their experiments to be certain the findings can be reproduced. If the findings can be replicated, we have greater confidence that the effect truly exists. Ultimately, we may wish to conduct a **meta-analysis** of many studies. With this statistical technique, we pool the results of multiple studies, thereby providing a powerful means for discovering the reliability and strength of an effect.

A third issue to consider is that we still don't know *why* drinking alcohol increases aggression. We're reasonably confident that it does, but we haven't determined what accounts for the effect. Figure 1.5 presents several potential explanations, which scientists call mediators. Perhaps alcohol makes people irritable, and their irritability increases aggression. Maybe alcohol makes people less fearful, reducing a factor that normally inhibits people from behaving aggressively. Or perhaps alcohol impairs people's ability to think of nonaggressive solutions to problems they encounter. Future research is needed to determine which, if any, of these processes explains our findings. (We will review this research in Chapter 13.)

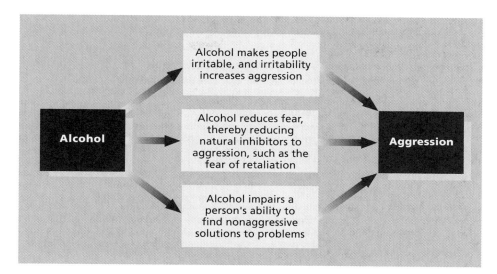

FIGURE 1.5

Three Explanations for Why Drinking Alcohol Might Increase Aggression

Confounding Variables. Sometimes, our results can be explained by a variable we neglected to control. In science, such a variable is called a confounding variable or **confound.** One type of confound occurs when a variable systematically changes along with the independent variable. For example, if we gave the alcohol to the participants in the evening and the soda pop to the participants in the morning, time of day, rather than alcohol consumption, could explain our findings. This type of confound is generally easy to eliminate by making sure that the only difference between the two experimental conditions is the independent variable.

A more serious confound occurs when an unintended consequence of the independent variable influences the dependent variable. To illustrate, imagine that a researcher hypothesizes that people in a good mood are more willing to donate money to a charitable cause than are people in a bad mood. To test this hypothesis, the researcher creates a good mood in some participants by giving them a small gift; other participants do not receive a gift. All participants are then given the opportunity to donate money to a charitable cause. Suppose the researcher finds that those who received the gift were more charitable than those who did not receive the gift. Can we be sure that good moods increase helping? Not necessarily. Receiving a gift may have more than one effect. In addition to making a person feel happy, it might also lead a person to feel obligated to do something nice for someone else. In this case, feelings of obligation represent a potential confound. The effects the researcher attributes to good mood may instead be due to increased feelings of obligation.

The researcher might avoid the possibility of a confound by conducting additional research that induces moods in a variety of ways. He or she might, for example, use pleasant music, agreeable fragrances, humor, and other means of making people happy. If all of these experimental manipulations affect helping behavior in a similar manner, we are confident that good moods affect helping behavior. (Research has, in fact, shown such an effect, and we will discuss this research in Chapter 12.)

D. Where We Conduct Research

Having decided what kind of research to conduct, we must decide where the research is going to be performed. Here we have two choices: the laboratory or the field. A

laboratory is a research setting where the experimenter has control over the kind of events that occur and the sequence in which they occur. A laboratory setting is a pure, ideal world, void of all events that are not directly relevant to the phenomenon under investigation. The advantage of doing research in a laboratory is control: In a laboratory, the experimenter is able to control all extraneous sources of variance.

An example from the physical sciences illustrates this point. Suppose you believe that a pebble and a leaf of equal mass fall to earth at the same rate. Should you test your hypothesis in a blizzard, where wind, snow, and other factors are operating, or in a laboratory setting, where all other factors that affect the rate at which objects fall can be artifically controlled? The obvious answer is a laboratory setting, where you can create a vacuum. By eliminating air resistance, you provide an environment most suitable for testing your hypothesis.

The same principles apply in the social world. Any given piece of social behavior is determined by many factors. For example, numerous factors affect how aggressively people behave; the amount of violence they watch on television may be one of these factors, but it is by no means the only one. If we are interested in testing whether watching violence on television influences aggression, we ought to construct a situation that eliminates, as much as possible, all other variables that affect this behavior. By doing so, we maximize the chances of finding out whether watching TV violence is one of the factors that affects aggression. The reason scientists study phenomena in a laboratory, then, is that it allows them to control other factors that may affect the phenomenon of immediate interest.

Precision and control are the advantages of laboratory research. The disadvantage is artificiality. The laboratory is not realistic or natural. It is purposefully constructed to be artificial and unnatural. Consequently, laboratory studies are not useful for telling us what occurs in the real world. In the real world, pebbles and leaves don't fall at the same speed; if we create a vacuum in a laboratory, they will.

Field settings are used to determine what happens in the real world. A field setting is any naturally occurring environment. Just about any place can serve as a field setting. For example, libraries, public parks, or grocery stores have all been used for research purposes at one time or another. Conducting research in a field setting has an important advantage: Because it is a natural situation, participants in a field study are acting naturally. In fact, they may not even know they are being observed and studied. Unfortunately, field research has an important disadvantage as well: Because the setting is a naturally occurring one, the experimenter will not be able to completely control what goes on during the experiment. This lack of control can obscure important findings.

To illustrate, let's return to our example of an experiment to determine whether people who watch violence on television behave more aggressively than people who don't. To conduct our research in a field setting, we would need to find a place where people are potentially apt to act in an aggressive manner. Elementary school playgrounds and lunchrooms are two such environments. These are real-world settings, and if we find that children who watch lots of TV violence behave more aggressively in these settings than do those who do not watch violence on television, we would be comfortable concluding that the two variables are related in the real world.

The advantage of a field setting is realism. Because it takes place in a naturally occurring environment, field research is realistic. The disadvantage is imprecision. Field research is noisy, meaning that not all sources of variance can be controlled by the experimenter. This noise makes it less likely that we will be able to detect the relations we are interested in discovering.

TABLE 1.2	Four Ways to Examine the Relation between Television Violence and Aggression	

		TYPE OF RESEARCH
Where	**Correlational**	**Experimental**
Field	Visit an elementary school classroom and give the students a questionnaire that assesses how much violence they watch on television. Then observe the number of acts of aggression during the day, and correlate the two scores.	Visit an elementary school and randomly assign some students to watch a violent television program and others to watch a nonviolent program. Then observe how aggressively the participants behave on the playground.
Laboratory	Bring participants into the laboratory for a study regarding the role of punishment in learning. Tell them their task will be to teach another participant some material, and that they will decide how much shock to deliver to the learner whenever the learner gets the wrong answer. Then correlate the amount of shock delivered with an index of how much violence the participant watches on television (as gathered by self-report).	Randomly assign some participants to watch a violent television program and others to watch a nonviolent program. Then have them serve as the teacher in a teacher–learner study, and measure the amount of shock they deliver to the learner.

Because different forms of research have different strengths and weaknesses, whenever possible, researchers like to study a given phenomenon using all of the different approaches. If our results are comparable using divergent methods, we are more confident in our findings. Table 1.2 shows how these various methods could be used to examine the relation between viewing violence on television and aggression.

E. Evaluating Scientific Research

We have been talking about various issues, such as precision, control, realism, and artificiality. A more formal way to think about these issues is with respect to two criteria scientists use to evaluate scientific research. These criteria are known as internal validity and external validity (D. T. Campbell & Stanley, 1966; T. D. Cook & Campbell, 1979).

1. Internal Validity

Internal validity refers to the degree to which our research has clearly established that x caused y. Research that has clearly established that x caused y has high internal validity, and research that has not clearly established that x caused y has low internal validity. By definition, correlational research has low internal validity because it is incapable of identifying a causal relation. Experimental research, if it is carefully conducted, has high internal validity because it is capable of identifying a causal relation between two variables.

Threats to Internal Validity. The use of an experimental design does not, however, guarantee that a study will establish that *x* caused *y*. This is because several factors can undermine the internal validity of our research. These factors stem from the fact that psychological research often takes place in a social context, in which one or more participants interact with an experimenter. The social aspect of the situation introduces some potential problems that are known as threats to internal validity. Although these threats can arise in research of all types, they are particularly important to consider in social psychological research (Kruglanski, 1975).

To illustrate, let's reconsider the hypothesis that drinking alcohol increases aggression. Imagine that we decide to test this hypothesis by conducting a laboratory experiment. We randomly assign some participants to consume drinks with alcohol and others to consume drinks without alcohol. Then we observe how aggressively the participants behave while playing a competitive game in which each is free to give the other aversive bursts of noise as a punishment or deterrent. If we find that the participants who were given alcohol behaved more aggressively during the game than those who were not given alcohol, would we be warranted in concluding that alcohol increases aggression? Unfortunately, no. Several factors may threaten the internal validity of this study.

Demand characteristics are one of these factors. **Demand characteristics** are cues in an experimental setting that lead participants to believe a particular behavior is expected or demanded (Orne, 1962). It isn't far-fetched to think that participants who are given an alcoholic drink and are then placed in a competitive situation might infer that the experiment is concerned with whether drinking affects aggression. This awareness might bias their behavior in one of two ways (S. J. Weber & Cook, 1972). A participant who is being compliant and playing what is known as the *good subject* role might purposely be aggressive in order to confirm the study's (presumed) hypothesis. This threatens internal validity because it would not be the alcohol that is causing the participant's aggression, but the perception of what is expected. Alternatively, a participant might play the *bad subject* role and try to disconfirm the study's hypothesis by being passive or nonviolent. This also threatens internal validity, because the participant's behavior is guided by an attempt to ruin the study rather than by the alcoholic content of the drink.

The desire to present oneself in a positive light introduces another source of bias. Most people like to think of themselves as kind, moral, and psychologically healthy individuals, and many people who take part in an experiment strive to maintain this image, both in their own eyes and in the eyes of other participants or the experimenter. This desire to be perceived as psychologically well adjusted can lead participants to misrepresent themselves or show only their best side (M. J. Rosenberg, 1969). For example, they might be less aggressive in our study than when they drink in a more natural setting. Scientists refer to this bias as **evaluation apprehension.**

There are several ways to minimize threats to internal validity. One way is to prevent participants from knowing which experimental condition they are in. Participants in our study should not know whether they are drinking alcohol or plain soda pop. If they don't know which condition they are in, they cannot systematically bias the results.

In addition, participants should be highly engaged in the experiment so that they are reacting naturally to events and not spending their time wondering what the experimenter wants them to do. The best way to do this is to make sure that the experiment is involving (E. Aronson, Wilson, & Brewer, 1998). If participants are highly involved in an experiment, they are less apt to be speculating about how they are supposed to behave.

A related way to reduce demand characteristics is to divert participants' attention away from the true purpose of the study. This is generally accomplished through the use of deception. For example, you might tell participants that the study is really designed to measure how well people learn under stressful conditions (rather than how aggressive people are when they have been drinking). Because they don't know what the study is really about, their behavior would not be tainted by a desire to act a certain way. This is why we use deception in our research; by diverting participants' attention away from our true purposes, we increase the internal validity of our research.

As you might imagine, the use of deception is a controversial topic. Most social psychologists view deception as a necessary evil. If we are to study social behavior, we need to ensure, as much as possible, that participants are acting naturally and spontaneously without excessive regard for what they think they ought to do. Sometimes this can be accomplished only by deceiving participants about the true nature of the experiment. Most universities have an institutional review board that oversees research and makes sure that all studies involving deception are carried out in ways that preserve participants' dignity and privacy. In addition, participants are given an informed consent form that warns them of any potential injury or discomfort, and they are notified that they are free to withdraw from the study at any time without penalty. Finally, participants are carefully debriefed at the end of the experimental session. During the debriefing session, participants learn about the hypotheses under investigation and the need for deception, and they are given the chance to have their questions answered and their concerns addressed.

Another threat to internal validity, known as **experimenter expectancy effects,** pertains to ways in which experimenters may unwittingly lead participants to confirm their hypotheses (Rosenthal, 1963). For instance, suppose the experimenter inadvertently scowls at participants who get alcoholic drinks and unintentionally smiles at those who receive drinks without alcohol. If our study later finds that participants who drank alcohol were more aggressive than those who did not, the experimenter's behavior, not the alcohol, could have produced this result. This would be a threat to internal validity. The most common solution to this problem is to standardize our procedures so that we treat everyone in the experiment as identically as possible. It is also wise to have our experimenters be unaware of which conditions participants are in. If the experimenters don't know which drinks they are handing out have alcohol in them, they can't systematically bias the findings. Formally, this type of study is known as a **double-blind study,** as neither the participant nor the experimenter knows which condition the participant is in.

2. External Validity

The second criterion we use to evaluate research is called external validity. **External validity** refers to the degree to which our research findings can be generalized to other participants and other settings. Research has high external validity to the extent that the findings apply to other participants and other settings, and low external validity to the extent that the findings apply to only a small set of participants and a small class of situations.

TABLE 1.3 How Random Assignment and Random Sampling Affect Internal Validity and External Validity

	Random Assignment	No Random Assignment
Random Sampling	High internal validity High external validity	Low internal validity High external validity
No Random Sampling	High internal validity Low external validity	Low internal validity Low external validity

Laboratory research tends to be low in external validity. This is because the situation is contrived and artificial. Field research tends to have high external validity. Field research occurs in the real world, so the results are likely to be applicable to other real-world settings.

Sampling Issues and External Validity. Sampling issues have an important effect on external validity. We want our results to generalize to a broad population, but we cannot test everyone. Instead, we opt for using random sampling (sometimes known as random selection). **Random sampling** is a process in which each member of a population has an equal opportunity of being selected to participate in a study. Random sampling is important for external validity. If we randomly select people from a population to be in our study, the characteristics of the sample should mirror the characteristics of the population from which it is drawn. As a result, we feel confident generalizing our findings to the broader population.

Random sampling is not the same as random assignment. Random sampling refers to how we select participants to be in our study; random assignment refers to how the participants we have selected are assigned to experimental conditions. We can have a study without random sampling that uses random assignment, and we can have a study that uses random sampling but doesn't use random assignment. The two are independent. Table 1.3 illustrates this point, showing how each of these issues bears on internal validity and external validity.

In practice, random sampling is rarely used in social psychological research. It is too expensive and impractical. Instead of using a random sample, our participants are typically college students who are enrolled in introductory psychology courses. We assume that these participants are a representative sample of the population at large. Although this assumption is defensible for many (if not most) social psychological phenomena, it is not always justified. College students differ from the rest of the population in important ways (e.g., they are younger, more intelligent, less culturally varied, and generally higher in socioeconomic status). Consequently, it is possible to question the external validity of studies that rely solely on college students (Sears, 1986). As you begin to read social psychological research, you will want to ask yourself whether you think the results apply to other people and to other situations.

Comparing Internal Validity and External Validity. A good way to understand the difference between internal validity and external validity is to consider research showing that saccharine causes cancer in laboratory rats. In these studies, some rats were randomly assigned to drink water that contained a high concentration of saccharine; other rats drank regular water. Later, scientists determined that the rats who drank the water with saccharine were more apt to develop cancerous cells than were rats who drank regular water.

The internal validity of this research is high. Because the two groups of rats were randomly assigned to conditions, they probably differed only in regard to how much saccharine they consumed. As a result, the research clearly established a causal relation between x (saccharine) and y (cancer). Many people question the external validity of the findings, however. They argue that the findings do not apply to other participants (e.g., humans) and to other situations (e.g., this occurs only if you drink water that contains a high concentration of saccharine, not if you drink several diet drinks a day). In formal terms, they accept the internal validity of the findings but question the external validity.

Both their acceptance of the internal validity and their questioning of the external validity are logically defensible. The research clearly established that saccharine can cause cancer in laboratory rats, but it did not clearly show that this will happen to humans using concentrations at lower levels. The warning that accompanies products with saccharine makes this point explicitly. It says, "The use of saccharine has been shown to cause cancer in laboratory animals." Consumers must then decide whether the external validity of this research is sufficiently high to deter them from using the product.

3. When External Validity Is (and Isn't) Important

Many students believe that external validity is more important than internal validity. After all, they argue, if the findings don't generalize, who cares what they are? This argument is reasonable, but it has an important limitation. Experimental studies conducted in laboratory settings are not designed to establish what goes on in the real world. They are designed to help us understand why real-world phenomena occur. In this sense, laboratory experiments are best suited for testing theoretically derived hypotheses. Theories explain why we observe the things we do, and experimental studies conducted in laboratory settings test hypotheses derived from theories.

Mook (1983) illustrated this point by having us consider Harlow's research on emotional development (Harlow & Zimmerman, 1959). Harlow was interested in studying the causes of infant attachment. It is clear that most infants form an attachment to their mothers early in life, but Harlow was interested in understanding why. Why is it that infants become attached to their mothers?

At the time Harlow began his research, the dominant theoretical explanation for infant attachment was a drive-reduction model. We will study the particulars of this model in Chapter 2, but for now we will simply note that the model assumes that infants form attachments to their mothers because they come to associate the mother with hunger reduction. When infants are hungry, their mothers feed them. Food reduces the hunger drive, and the infant comes to associate the mother with drive reduction.

Harlow entertained another idea. His idea was that infant attachment depends on the satisfaction of more psychological needs, such as warmth, contact, and nurturance. From this perspective, infants form an attachment to their mothers not because their mothers reduce their hunger, but because their mothers hold them and cuddle them.

Harlow tested these two competing ideas in an ingenious series of experiments with infant monkeys. Infant monkeys were taken from their mothers and placed in cages with two mother surrogates made out of wire. One of the surrogates was covered with terry cloth and was heated by a small lightbulb from inside. This surrogate, then, provided softness and warmth. The other surrogate was bare and cold. Independently, one of the surrogates was equipped with a nipple that was connected to a supply of milk, whereas the other surrogate provided no nourishment.

The critical question of interest was whether the infant monkeys would form a stronger attachment to the wire surrogate, who provided food (which is what the drive reduction theory predicts), or to the other surrogate, who provided the warm fuzzies (which is what Harlow predicted). Harlow found that the infant monkeys tended to cling to the terry-cloth surrogate, regardless of whether or not this surrogate provided nourishment. Harlow took this as evidence that hunger reduction provides an incomplete explanation for why infants form attachments to their mothers.

If we ask, "How does the external validity of this study stand up?" we would probably conclude, "Not very well." Obviously, humans, let alone monkeys, do not encounter mother surrogates made out of wire and terry cloth. But Harlow was not interested in whether monkeys in the wild run to terry-cloth surrogates. He was interested in whether principles of drive reduction provide an adequate theoretical explanation for why infants form an attachment to their mothers. The study itself is low in external validity, but the insights it provides are important. In fact, along with other research, Harlow's studies changed the way we in the United States think about child-rearing practices. Today we recognize that tenderness, kindness, and warmth are essential to forming a strong infant–caregiver bond.

To summarize, laboratory experiments are not meant to mirror what goes on in the real world. Their purpose is to illuminate why things in the real world happen. Often, this is accomplished by using laboratory experiments to test theoretically derived hyphotheses. Our theories tell us what ought to happen, and we test hypotheses under controlled laboratory conditions to see whether these predictions are correct. We then modify our theory according to what we find. In these cases, the question of interest is not whether the findings themselves occur in the real world, but whether the findings have increased our understanding of real-world phenomena (Berkowitz & Donnerstein, 1982; Mook, 1983).

F. Interpreting Scientific Research

After we have carefully conducted our research, taking special care to maximize internal validity and external validity, we are left with one important task: interpreting our findings.

1. Understanding Statistical Significance

Scientists test hypotheses by asking, "What is the likelihood of getting our results if the only factor operating in the situation was chance?" To illustrate, imagine that you and a friend play 10 hands of gin rummy. One of you wins 8 games and the other wins 2. Should we conclude that the player who won 8 games is a better player? To answer this question, scientists ask, "What is the likelihood of either player winning 8 out of 10 games given that the only factor operating in the situation is chance?" The answer is .088. Approximately 9 times in 100, one player will win 8 of 10 games even when the players are equally matched. By convention, scientists have decided that only outcomes that occur less frequently than 5 times in 100 provide evidence that factors other than chance are operating in the situation. In this case, we would not conclude that one of you is the better player.

TABLE 1.4	Interpreting Mean Differences in Scientific Research	
	BEVERAGE	
	Alcohol	Soda Pop
	3	1
	3	2
	4	2
	4	3
	4	3
	5	3
	5	4
	5	4
	5	5
	5	5
Mean	**4.3**	**3.2**

Note: The data present a hypothetical example of how aggressively people behave after consuming alcohol or soda pop.

The situation is different if one player wins 9 of 10 games. The probability of this happening when only chance factors are operating in the situation is .02, or 2 times out of 100. Since the probability of this outcome is less than 5 times in 100, we conclude that the player who won 9 games is probably better. This is what scientists mean when they say that an effect is **statistically significant.** It means the effect would occur less than 5 times in 100 if the only factor operating in the situation was chance. Note, however, that this doesn't mean that one of you is definitely better than the other. Two times in 100, one player would win as many as 9 out of 10 games even when the players are of equal ability. So we are always making a probabilistic statement in science. Statistical significance in this case means only that one player is probably better than the other.

2. What Mean Differences Mean

Scientific results are often expressed in terms of averages or mean differences. An important part of interpreting scientific research is learning to understand these differences. To illustrate, let's return to our example of alcohol and aggression. Imagine we randomly assign some people to drink alcohol and others to drink soda pop. Later, we measure how aggressive they are when given the chance to punish another person for making a mistake. (For purposes of this example, we will imagine that we are using a 5-point scale of aggressiveness.)

Table 1.4 shows the data for our hypothetical example. The data show that, on average, people who drank alcohol behaved more aggressively (mean = 4.3) than those who drank soda pop (mean = 3.2). The probability of getting data like these, given that the only factor influencing aggression is chance, is less than 5 in 100. Therefore, we conclude that our independent variable (i.e., which beverage participants consumed) affected our dependent variable (aggression). Note, however, that not everyone who drank alcohol was aggressive and that not everyone who drank soda pop was kindhearted. Instead, there is quite a bit of variability. This is almost always true in psychological research. People are different, and we often find a good deal of variability in our dependent variables.

Here's why this is important. Suppose we hear someone say, "Scientists have found that people prefer to affiliate with others who share their attitudes and values." This statement tells us that many people display this preference and that this preference probably isn't due to chance alone. It does not mean that everyone shows this preference. I mention this because many students who take social psychology courses might hear this statement and think, "I don't do that. My best friend and I are completely different." That may well be true. Psychological studies document average tendencies, but they rarely (if ever) demonstrate that everyone does the same thing.

3. Factorial Designs, Main Effects, and Interactions

Much of the research you will read about in this text uses a particular design called a factorial design. In such designs, two (or more) independent variables are varied in the same experiment. For example, imagine that we are still interested in studying aggression. We can conduct an experiment with two independent variables, each with two levels. One variable is whether a person drinks alcohol or soda pop; the other variable is whether or not the person is provoked by a **confederate** (an accomplice of the experiment who pretends to be a regular participant). This sort of design is called a 2 × 2 (read "2 by 2"), because there are two independent variables, each with two levels. When combined, they create four experimental conditions: (1) no provocation/soda pop, (2) no provocation/alcohol, (3) provocation/soda pop, and (4) provocation/alcohol. Our dependent variable will be aggression, as assessed by how much punishment our participants deliver to a person who makes a mistake.

When we analyze data from a factorial design, we look for the presence of main effects and interactions. The term **main effect** refers to how one of our independent variables affects the dependent variable. The term **interaction** refers to the relation between the two variables. Two variables interact (or there is an interaction) if the effect of one variable changes at different levels of the other variable.

Interactions can take different forms, so it will be easier to understand this point if we return to our example. Figure 1.6 presents some hypothetical data from our experiment. Panel 1 shows a single main effect of beverage. Participants who drank alcohol were more aggressive than participants who drank soda pop, and this did not depend on whether or not they were provoked. Panel 2 shows a single main effect of provocation. Regardless of whether they drank alcohol or soda pop, participants who were provoked behaved more aggressively than participants who were not provoked. Panel 3 shows the case where there are two main effects: The main effect of beverage indicates that participants were more aggressive when they drank alcohol, and the main effect of provocation indicates that participants were more aggressive when they were provoked. There was no interaction, because the effects of one variable are the same at each level of the other variable.

The situation changes in the bottom row of Figure 1.6. Now the data do show the presence of an interaction. Panel 4 shows a type of interaction we will call an *only for* interaction. Here, alcohol increased aggression *only* when participants were provoked. In the absence of provocation, participants who drank alcohol were no more aggressive than those who drank soda pop. This pattern signifies the presence of an interaction, because the effect of one variable (beverage) changed at different levels of the other variable (provocation). Panel 5 also shows an interaction, but its form is

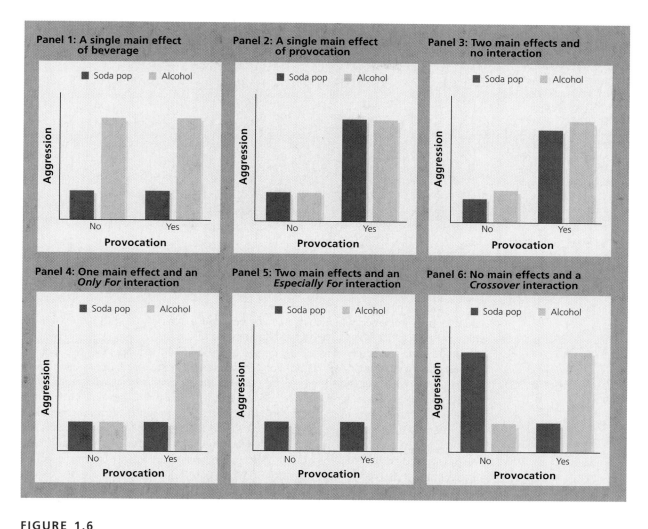

FIGURE 1.6

Illustrating Main Effects and Interactions

In this hypothetical example, participants drank a beverage (either soda pop or alcohol), and were then provoked or not provoked before being given the opportunity to shock a person who made a mistake.

different from the one shown in Panel 4. In Panel 5, we have what we will call an *especially for* interaction. Alcohol increased aggression, *especially* when participants were provoked. Finally, Panel 6 shows a *crossover* interaction. Here, alcohol decreased aggression when there was no provocation but increased aggression when there was provocation.

Because interactions often emerge when we test theoretically derived hypotheses, learning to correctly identify and interpret different interaction patterns will help you understand the research you will read throughout this text. To illustrate, let's return to an issue we discussed earlier in this chapter. We began this chapter by asking you to imagine that someone bumped you on the bus, and then noted that situational

FIGURE 1.7

The "Weapons Effect"

Participants were either provoked or not provoked by a confederate, and were then given the chance to shock the confederate when a gun was present or absent. The data show an interaction effect: High provocation produced more aggression than low provocation, especially when a weapon was present.

Source: Berkowitz and LePage (1967).

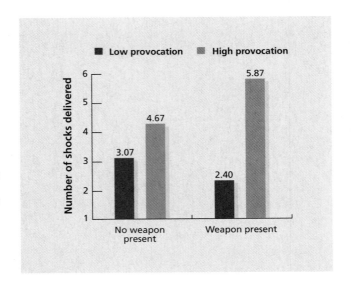

variables can influence whether or not you respond to this event with aggression. A study by Berkowitz and LePage (1967) addressed this issue.

At the time the study was being conducted, Berkowitz was developing a more general theory of aggression. The theory maintains, in part, that aggression is most apt to occur when a person is provoked and situational cues suggest that aggression is an appropriate response to provocation. Berkowitz reasoned that one such situational cue is a gun, because guns are used for aggressive purposes. Building on these ideas, Berkowitz and LePage hypothesized that the presence of a gun increases the likelihood that people will respond to provocation with aggression. An experiment was conducted to test this hypothesis. The participants were male students enrolled in psychology courses at the University of Wisconsin. They were told that the experiment concerned physiological reactions to stressful experiences, and that receiving shock was one such experience. A confederate then delivered mild electric shocks to the participant. In the low-provocation condition, the confederate shocked the participant only once, and in the high-provocation condition, the confederate shocked the participant seven times. Afterward, the roles were reversed and participants were given the opportunity to deliver shocks to the confederate. In one condition, a .38-caliber revolver was lying on the table next to the shock generator; in another condition, the table was empty. These manipulations produced four conditions: (1) low provocation—no weapon present, (2) low provocation—weapon present, (3) high provocation—no weapon present, (4) high provocation—weapon present.

Figure 1.7 shows the number of shocks the participants administered in each of the four conditions. The data show that provocation increased aggression, especially when the weapon was present. Formally, we say that the two variables *interacted.* Aggression in response to provocation was especially severe when a gun was in sight.

This experiment has all the components of a classic piece of social psychological research. Deductive reasoning was used to generate a theoretically relevant hypothesis about the manner in which a situational variable affects behavior. An experiment—conducted under controlled, laboratory conditions and using random assignment to conditions—was then performed to test the hypothesis. Finally, the data were analyzed and their relevance to real-world experiences was considered. In this case, a popular slogan asserts "Guns don't kill people, people kill people." Qualifying this assertion, Berkowitz and LePage's (1967) findings indicate that the presence of weapons can increase aggression among people who have already been provoked.

CHAPTER SUMMARY

- Social psychology is the scientific study of how people think about one another, affect one another, and relate to one another.

- Social psychologists assume that our behavior is guided by the meaning we give to a stimulus or situation. Formally, this perspective is known as the phenomenological approach. According to this approach, subjective perceptions (i.e., the world as it appears) determine behavior.

- Subjective perceptions are influenced by two factors: personality variables (enduring, consistent, and characteristic patterns of thinking, feeling, and behaving that originate within an individual) and situational factors (any factor that provides the context for an event or experience).

- Academic disciplines analyze social behavior in different ways. Anthropologists emphasize cultural factors, sociologists emphasize societal factors, and personality psychologists emphasize internal psychological processes. In contrast, social psychologists emphasize that behavior often depends on factors present in the immediate social situation.

- Social psychologists most often use the experimental method to gather data. Other academic disciplines rely more on surveys, questionnaires, and interviews.

- Science is a way of knowing what the world is like. It combines logic with systematic and objective observation. Scientists use logic to develop theories and to generate hypotheses; then scientists test their hypotheses to see whether they are apt to be true or not.

- Science can be used for four purposes: to describe what occurs, to predict what is apt to occur, to explain why phenomena occur, and to control phenomena.

- The immediate aim of basic research is to understand or explain a phenomenon. The immediate aim of applied research is to achieve some practical benefit. Applied research is most often built on basic research.

- Science begins with a hypothesis. Hypotheses are educated guesses about how two (or more) variables are related. Scientists test their hypotheses to see whether they are likely to be true or not.

- Sometimes hypotheses stem from casual observation, but most often scientists deduce their hypotheses from a theory. Theories are general principles that attempt to explain why two or more variables are related.

- Theories are only tested indirectly and cannot be proved right or wrong. Instead, we use deductive reasoning to derive a testable hypothesis from a theory. We then conduct research to test the hypothesis and use inductive reasoning to modify our theory.

- Theories are evaluated according to three criteria: parsimony (how simple the theory is), breadth (how broad the theory is), and generativity (to what extent the theory generates new hypotheses to be tested). A good theory explains and predicts a broad range of topics using very few principles.

- Correlational research examines the association between naturally occurring variables. The strength of any correlation can be measured by calculating a correlation coefficient. A positive correlation occurs when increases in one variable are accompanied by increases in another variable. A negative correlation occurs when increases in one variable are accompanied by decreases in another variable. Two variables are uncorrelated when scores on one variable are unrelated to scores on the other variable.

- Correlational research can establish whether two variables are related, but it cannot establish whether one variable causes another. This is because there are three explanations for any observed correlation: x causes y; y causes x; and z causes both x and y.

- Experimental research can establish whether one variable causes another. With experimental research, the researcher randomly assigns participants to two (or more) experimental conditions that differ only with respect to one variable, the independent variable.

- A laboratory is a research setting where the experimenter has control over the kind and sequence of events participants are exposed to. A laboratory setting is a pure, ideal world, void of all extraneous influences. Precision and control are the advantages of laboratory research.

- A field setting is any naturally occurring environment. The advantage of a field setting is realism. However, because it is a naturally occurring environment, the researcher cannot completely control all possible factors that influence the phenomenon being studied.

- Internal validity refers to the degree to which our research has clearly identified a causal relation. Research has high internal validity to the extent that it has clearly established that x caused y. Experimental research using random assignment to conditions increases the internal validity of an investigation.

- Several factors can threaten the internal validity of an investigation. These include demand characteristics (cues in an experimental setting that lead participants to believe a particular behavior is expected or demanded), a desire on the part of participants to present themselves in a positive light, and experimenter expectancy effects (unintended behavior on the part of experimenters that lead participants to confirm their hypothesis).

- External validity refers to the degree to which our research findings can be applied to other participants and other settings. Research has high external validity to the extent that the findings hold true for other participants and in other settings. Random (or representative) sampling of participants increases external validity.

- External validity is not always a paramount concern. Scientific research is often intended to test theoretical hypotheses. The best way to test these hypotheses may be to create an artificial situation that does not mirror the real world. Rather than asking whether the findings themselves occur in the real world, it is often more appropriate to ask whether the findings have increased our understanding of real-world phenomena.

- A statistically significant finding is one that would occur less than 5 times in 100 if only chance factors were operating in the situation.

- Scientific findings are often reported in terms of averages (or means). These findings do not indicate that everyone in the sample exhibited the same behavior. Instead, they pertain to the average or modal tendency.

- Factorial designs involve two (or more) independent variables. Such designs yield results of main effects and interactions. A main effect refers to how one of our independent variables affects the dependent variable. An interaction occurs if the effect of one variable changes at different levels of the other variable.

KEY TERMS

social psychology, 2

phenomenology, 2

personality, 3

situational variable, 3

rationalism, 9

empiricism, 10

positivism, 10

basic research, 11

applied research, 11

hypothesis, 12

theories, 12

correlational research, 15

positive correlation, 15

negative correlation, 15

experimental research, 17

independent variable, 17

participants, 17

random assignment, 17

dependent variable, 17

meta-analysis, 18

confound, 19

laboratory, 20

field setting, 20

internal validity, 21

demand characteristics, 22

evaluation apprehension, 22

experimenter expectancy effects, 23

double-blind study, 23

external validity, 23

random sampling, 24

main effect, 28

interaction, 28

confederate, 28

ADDITIONAL READING

Go to the Student Edition of the Online Learning Center for this text (www.mhhe.com/brown) and log in to read the following journal articles, which relate to the content of this chapter:

- Darley, J. M., & Batson, C. D. (1973). From Jerusalem to Jericho: A study of situational and dispositional variables in helping behavior.

- Berkowitz, L., & LePage, A. (1967). Weapons as aggression-eliciting stimuli.

CHAPTER TWO

Social Psychology's Theoretical Roots

It is the theory that decides what we can observe.

Albert Einstein, letter to Werner Heisenberg

Imagine you are a detective working on a complicated case. You have a limited amount of time and resources, so you need to work as efficiently as you can. How will you proceed? Chances are, you will not conduct a random search. Instead, given your intuitions and years of experience, you will follow some leads but not others. Of course, you may encounter some blind alleys and be forced to modify your search, but initially at least, your strategy will be guided by what you expect to find.

In many ways, scientists are like detectives, searching for clues to understand a phenomenon or solve a problem. However, rather than relying on intuition and hunches alone, scientists use theories to guide their search. As discussed in Chapter 1, theories are general principles that have been developed to explain phenomena. Once formed, they influence what we observe and how we make sense of our observations.

In this chapter, you will learn about a number of theories that have influenced social psychological research. These theories, known as grand theories, are very broad and make some important assumptions about human nature. Not all of them were formulated by social psychologists, but all have been used to illuminate the nature of social psychological phenomena.

I. The Present Is Equal to the Sum of the Past

We begin our inquiry at the beginning, by considering a philosophical matter. The question is this: Do we come into the world knowing anything, or is our mind a blank slate? Since the time of the ancient Greeks, philosophers have been divided on this issue. Plato, Descartes, and others maintained that some knowledge is innate and that philosophical training is needed to unlock this knowledge. Aristotle, Locke, and others disagreed, arguing that we are born knowing nothing and acquire knowledge only as we live. John Locke's position on the matter is of particular interest.

> Suppose the mind to be, as we say, white paper, void of all characters, without any ideas; how comes it to be furnished? . . . Whence has it all the materials of reason and knowledge? To this I answer, in one word, from EXPERIENCE: in that, all our knowledge is founded; and from that it ultimately derives itself. (1690, Book 2, Chapter 1)

For Locke, there is nothing in the mind that was not first in the senses (*nihil est in intellectu quod non fuerit in sensu*). Everything known is acquired through experience.

Locke made another, related assumption: If the mind is filled entirely of impressions of the external world, then there must exist an objective world which we passively apprehend with our senses. When we look out the window and see a tree, it is simply because a tree exists. There is nothing active or creative about the act of perception. The mind is a mirror that merely reflects the external world.

> When our senses do actually convey into our understandings any idea, we cannot but be satisfied that there doth something at that time really exist without us, which doth affect our senses . . . and actually produce that idea which we then perceive. (1690, Book 4, Chapter 11)

A. Associationism

At the same time, it is clear that people think of things that they have never experienced through the senses. For example, I might think about a cow with wings, even though I have never seen such a thing. For Locke, thoughts of this sort are understood as elemental sensations linked together: I have seen a cow and I have seen wings, so I can link them together in my mind. This analysis of thought in terms of the compounding of more elemental ideas came to be known as the doctrine of **associationism.**

To further illustrate this approach, let's examine how an associationist would analyze your concept of *house*. An associationist would argue that your concept of house is comprised of smaller elements that combine to form a broader concept. For example, you might think about your bedroom, kitchen, living room, and garage. Each of these rooms is made up of walls, flooring, and furniture. And each of these concepts can be further subdivided into wood, brick, mortar, or molding until finally we have divided as far as we can. From this perspective, your concept of a house is simply the sum of a large number of more elemental ideas linked together through principles of association.

A century after Locke offered his analysis, another British philosopher, James Mill, followed this principle to its logical conclusion. Mill asked, "What does the concept everything mean?" He replied that the term *everything* literally means a mental conglomeration of every thing. When we speak of everything, we are referring to a mental collection of every single thing.

His son, John Stuart Mill, recognized the limitations of this argument. The younger Mill noted that the mind is not capable of holding everything in memory. To account for this fact, he developed a position called *mental chemistry*. According to this view, ideas that are often linked together eventually fuse into one, so that the complex idea is no longer separable into its elemental constituents.

> It is obvious that the complex laws of thought and feeling not only may, but must be generated from simple laws of association. [But when] many impressions or ideas are operating in the mind together, there sometimes takes place a process of a similar kind to chemical combination: [the ideas] melt and coalesce into one another, and appear not as several ideas but as one . . . [In such cases] where separate elements are not consciously distinguishable, complex ideas will be said to result from or be generated by, the simple ideas, but not to consist of them. (Mill, 1843, cited in Boring, 1957, p. 230)

To summarize, associationism holds that people do not have complex ideas innately or holistically. Instead, we are born a blank slate, everything we know is acquired through the senses, and all complex thoughts are comprised of more elemental ideas that are joined through association.

B. Introspectionism

The philosophical approach of Locke and the Mills set the stage for the development of psychology. Most scholars trace the birth of psychology to 1879 when, in Leipzig, Germany, Wilhelm Wundt established the first psychological laboratory. Wundt's approach came to be known by the method he used, **introspectionism.** As practiced by Wundt, introspection entailed systematically analyzing conscious experience into its constituent elements, and discovering the nature and reason for their connection (Boring, 1957). By doing so, Wundt hoped to identify the basic elements of conscious experience.

In a typical investigation, Wundt would expose participants to various stimuli and have them report what they were experiencing. For example, he would give participants a variety of foods to taste and ask them to describe, in as small detail as possible, how the foods tasted. Wundt would then take these reports and attempt to distill the basic elements of sensation. On the basis of his research he concluded that there were four elementary taste sensations: sweet, sour, bitter, and salty. All other tastes were regarded as combinations or blends of these. In a similar manner, four elementary skin sensations were discovered. These were warmth, cold, pain, and pressure; all other sensations of touch were regarded as blends of these four (Woodworth, 1948).

Titchener brought this method of inquiry to the United States. Titchener believed that people needed to be trained before they could attend to the basic elements of a stimulus. For this reason, he used trained research assistants, rather than naive (untrained) participants in his research. He summed up his approach as follows:

> The first object of the psychologist . . . is to ascertain the nature and number of the mental elements. He takes up mental experience, bit by bit, dividing, until he can go no further. When that point is reached, he has found a conscious element. (Titchener, 1896, p. 13)

We can see in this statement how much the introspectionists were influenced by Locke and the associationists. The main difference between introspectionism and the philosophical inquiry that preceded it was the use of multiple observers. Unlike the earlier philosophers who analyzed their own experiences without systematically consulting the experience of others, psychologists carefully analyzed the common experience of multiple observers. Sometimes these observers were untrained, naive participants (as with Wundt's approach) and sometimes they were trained research assistants (as with Titchener's approach). Regardless of how they were trained, the goal was the same: to identify basic units that combine to form psychological life.

C. Behaviorism

> Psychology, as the behaviorist views it, (a) is a purely objective experimental branch of natural science; (b) its theoretical goal is the prediction and control of behavior; (c) introspection forms no essential part of its methods; and (d) it recognizes no dividing line between man and brute. (J. B. Watson, 1913, p. 158)

Introspectionism dominated American psychology for only a relatively brief period of time. In 1913, John Watson published a paper that introduced a new way of doing psychological research. Although Watson agreed with the introspectionists that complex phenomena were comprised of associated elements, he did not believe psychology should study conscious experience. Watson noted that people disagree on what they see, hear, smell, taste, and feel, and there is no way to resolve these disagreements. If psychology was to take its place as an independent science, Watson argued, it must abandon the study of mental life. This approach came to be known as **behaviorism.**

1. Three Key Assumptions

Behaviorism was characterized by three key assumptions (Weiner, 1980).

Positivism. First, by asserting that only behavior should be studied, the behaviorists were adopting the doctrine of positivism. As we noted in Chapter 1, positivism is a methodological doctrine that maintains that only phenomena that can be concretely measured and verified by impartial observers are suitable for scientific analysis. This doctrine leaves out not only sensation and perception but also thoughts, feelings, wishes, dreams, and fantasies. In short, anything that cannot be directly observed is ignored.

Mechanism. The behaviorists adopted a second assumption, known as the doctrine of mechanism. **Mechanism** is an assumption about the nature of psychological life; it asserts that thoughts play no role in directing behavior. Instead, behavior is assumed to be a function of simple stimulus–response bonds (S→R). To illustrate, we might train a pigeon to peck at a particular pattern by giving the pigeon food whenever it pecks in the presence of the pattern. Over time, the pigeon comes to emit the behavior with greater and greater frequency when the stimulus is presented. According to the behaviorist, this occurs because the food (the reinforcer) strengthens the association between the pattern (the stimulus) and the pecking behavior (the response).

Hedonism. A final assumption, **hedonism,** explains why food serves to create these associative bonds. Hedonism is an ancient philosophical doctrine attributed to the Greek philosopher Epicurus (342–270 BCE). It asserts that sensory pleasure is the highest good in life (see also Bentham, 1779/1948). As used by the behaviorists, the doctrine of hedonism asserts that sensory pleasure is reinforcing. Anything that feels good increases the association between a stimulus and a response. In this sense, pleasure provides the glue that connects a response to a stimulus.

2. Mechanism versus Purposivism

Mechanists view the relation between stimuli and responses as direct and immediate. Pigeons (and people) behave as they do simply because certain responses have become attached or conditioned to certain environmental stimuli. In more general terms, we can say that the behaviorists believed that behavior could be fully understood without considering higher-order mental processes (Blumberg & Wasserman, 1995). It is for this reason that the behaviorists studied rats, pigeons, and other animals. It was not merely a matter of convenience; they believed that the laws governing behavior were the same for all animals.

Mechanism contrasts most sharply with what is known as a purposive or goal-directed analysis of behavior. According to a purposive model, behaviors are undertaken in order to achieve some goal (that is, they are undertaken for a purpose). An organism wants or desires something and takes steps to secure or attain it. This emphasis on goal-directed or purposive behavior is completely absent in mechanistic accounts of behavior.

To illustrate these differences, consider a person who thinks, "I'm hungry. I want something to eat," and then walks to the refrigerator and takes out some food. A purposive analysis of behavior would maintain that the thoughts "I'm hungry" and "I want something to eat" led the person to walk toward the refrigerator to get food. The behaviorists would disagree. They would contend that these thoughts did not initiate the behavior. The person walked to the refrigerator simply because that is where the person has found food when hunger arose in the past.

This does not mean that the behaviorists denied the existence of conscious thought. They knew people had thoughts; they just didn't believe these thoughts influenced behavior. They regarded them as epiphenomenal (*epiphenomenal* means "above the phenomena" or "not directly part of the phenomena"). To illustrate this point, let's imagine that we punish a child for stealing food. According to the behaviorist,

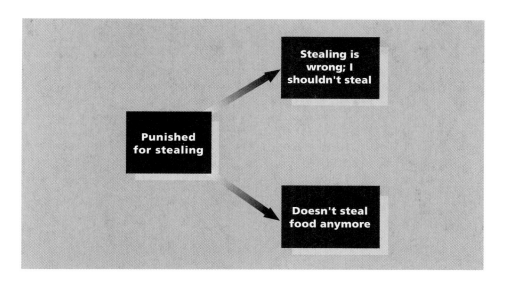

FIGURE 2.1

The Nature of Thought in Behaviorism

Behaviorism contends that being punished for stealing has two independent effects: It leads people to think that stealing is wrong, and it keeps them from stealing in the future. The absence of an arrow connecting the thought to the behavior indicates that the two consequences are viewed as entirely independent. Thoughts occur, but they are epiphenomenal because they do not influence behavior.

punishment produces two independent effects (see Figure 2.1): It leads the child to believe that stealing is wrong, and it reduces the likelihood that the child will steal again. But the thought "Stealing is wrong" is epiphenomenal. People refrain from stealing not because they think stealing is wrong but because they've been punished for stealing in the past. The advantage of this approach is parsimony. As discussed in Chapter 1, good theories are parsimonious: They explain a lot of different things with very few assumptions. Behaviorism is very parsimonious—it uses the same principles to explain the behavior of humans and other animals.

3. Types of Learning

The behaviorists distinguished two types of learning (Hilgard & Marquis, 1940).

Classical Conditioning. Classical conditioning refers to the acquisition of involuntary emotional reactions and behaviors. Classical conditioning was originally conceived as a passive process in which stimuli become associated with one another, either because they resemble one another or because they have appeared together frequently. Pavlov's pioneering work with dogs provides the best example of this process. Prior to feeding his dogs, Pavlov rang a bell. Over time, the dogs began to salivate to the sound of the bell. Through processes of association, the bell had become a conditioned stimulus, capable of evoking the involuntary response of salivating (a conditioned response).

Instrumental Conditioning. A second mechanism of learning, called instrumental conditioning, explains the acquisition of more voluntary behaviors. **Instrumental**

conditioning (also called instrumental learning) is a more active process in which behaviors that meet with reinforcement persist, while those that do not meet with reinforcement perish. Formally, this assumption is known as the **Law of Effect.** According to the Law of Effect, behavior is a function of the consequences it has met with in the past. A behavior that has previously met with positive consequences endures; a behavior that has previously met with negative consequences does not endure.

Thorndike's (1911) research provides the clearest example of this approach. Working in the basement of his research advisor's house, Thorndike placed various animals, usually cats or chicks, in an enclosed box, called a puzzle box. Food was placed outside the box. When the animal made a response that Thorndike had arbitrarily designated to be the correct one, the animal was allowed to escape the box and consume the food.

At first, Thorndike notes, the animal engages in relatively random behavior. At some point, the animal happens to make the response Thorndike arbitrarily chose to be the correct one. The door to the puzzle box is then opened and the animal is allowed to leave the box and consume the food. When the animal is later returned to the box, it tends to emit the correct response sooner than in the initial trial. After many such trials, the animal comes to emit the response immediately upon being placed in the box.

The behaviorist analyzes this behavior in terms of stimulus–response bonds. The reinforcing properties of the food cause the behavior (the response) to become associated with or attached to the puzzle box (the stimulus). When the animal is returned to the box, it emits whatever behavior has been most closely associated with the cues in the environment. In this case, this response is the one Thorndike had earlier labeled as the correct response.

It is important to note that, according to the behaviorist, the animal never makes the correct movements *in order* to get out of the box or *in order* to get the food. That would be too goal-oriented or purposive. Instead, the animal makes the correct response simply because that behavior, more than all others, has come to be most firmly connected to the stimuli in the box via the reinforcing properties of the food. Thorndike (1911) described the process this way:

> The process involved in the learning was evidently a process of selection. The animal is confronted by a state of affairs or, as we may call it, a "situation." He reacts in the way that he is moved by innate nature or previous training to do, by a number of acts. These acts include the particular act that is appropriate and he succeeds. In later trials the impulse to this one act is more and more stamped in. . . The profitless acts are stamped out . . . So the animal finally performs in that situation only the fitting act. Here we have the simplest and at the same time the most widespread sort of intellect or learning in the world. There is no reasoning, no process of inference or comparison; there is no thinking about things, no putting two and two together; there are no ideas—the animal does not think of the box or of the food or of the act he is to perform. (pp. 283–284)

This position may seem odd, but it closely parallels Darwin's ideas about how natural selection shapes physical characteristics Darwin (1859). The process of natural selection is not a purposive one. Random variations occur among individual members of species. Some of these variations prove adaptive: They help the organism to successfully reproduce, so they are selected for and endure. Thus, although natural selection is an active process, it is not goal-directed. Peacocks didn't think, "Gee, if only I could grow a colorful plume, I could attract a mate." Instead, through random variation, some peacocks had more colorful plumes than did others, and peahens happened to find this to be attractive. Ultimately, only peacocks with colorful plumes got to reproduce and pass their colorful genes on to the next generation. The entire process is one of blind chance, not purposive. In the words of Solomon Asch (1952), "Natural selection

. . . produces without purpose the same result that would have been produced had a purposive agent been at work" (p. 97).

The mechanistic view of behavior mirrors the process of natural selection (Skinner, 1990). Just as the theory of natural selection maintains that physical characteristics are shaped by their adaptive consequences, mechanism holds that behavior is shaped by its adaptive consequences. Behaviors that meet with reinforcement are strengthened or repeated; those that do not meet with reinforcement are weakened and extinguished. As Thorndike (1911) noted, there is no reasoning or thinking of any kind. There is only a passive repetition of behaviors that have previously met with positive consequences.

4. Hull's Drive-Reduction Model of Behavior

Clark Hull, an influential Yale psychologist, extended and refined behaviorism during the 1930s and 1940s (C. L. Hull, 1943). The behaviorists had originally assumed that all reinforcers were equally effective. This assumption was called into question when researchers found that food is a more effective reinforcer for a hungry animal than for a thirsty one. To account for this simple fact, behaviorists were forced to include a new construct in their psychology. This construct was called **drive** (Woodworth, 1918). A drive is an internal need that stimulates an organism to act.

The Role of Drive in Hullian Theory. Drive plays two roles in Hull's theory. First, learning (which Hull referred to as the acquisition of a habit) occurs only if a reinforcer reduces a drive. Second, behavior depends on the presence of drive and the strength of the habit that was previously acquired. Formally, this model is represented as:

$$B = D \times H$$
$$\text{Behavior} = \text{Drive} \times \text{Habit}$$

Let's look at an example, so that we are clear about what Hull is saying. Imagine that a hungry animal is walking around and happens upon a spot where there is food. When the animal eats, the food reduces the hunger drive and learning takes place. In Hull's terms, a habit is acquired because the hunger drive is reduced. (Note that no learning would occur, according to Hull, if the animal hadn't been hungry when food was encountered.) Whether this habit is later manifested in behavior depends on whether drive is present. Should the animal experience hunger at a later time, the animal will habitually move toward the spot where food was found.

The Nature of Drives. Two more points about Hull's theory are important to mention. First, Hull extended his theory of drives to include secondary drives. It is evident that stimuli other than food and water can reinforce behavior. Money, for example, is a potent reinforcer, even though it doesn't immediately reduce hunger or thirst. Hull explained this fact by proposing that money is a secondary reinforcer. Money buys food, water, and shelter, so it becomes capable of reinforcing behavior, and the need for money becomes a secondary drive capable of motivating behavior. This prediction led to Harlow's research on infant attachment (Harlow & Zimmerman, 1959). As discussed in Chapter 1, Harlow conducted experiments to determine whether infants become attached to their mothers simply because their mothers reduced their hunger drive.

Hull also believed that drives pool together and can energize a variety of behaviors. For example, an animal that is hungry and thirsty will run faster to food than an animal that is only hungry. In Chapter 13, we will see that this aspect of Hull's theory has been used to explain why stimulants, fear, and other experiences that increase arousal can increase aggression.

D. Summary

> Except for the substitution of action for consciousness, . . . behaviorism was identical with the psychology it was attempting to replace. In fact, the analysis of action corresponded in every detail to the analysis of consciousness. Action, too, was the sum of elementary units. (Asch, 1952, p. 50)

In this section we have covered three different theoretical positions: associationism, introspectionism, and behaviorism. Although there are differences among them, there are important similarities (see Allport, 1955). All assume that (1) the mind is blank at birth, (2) complex phenomena are comprised of smaller elements linked together through principles of association, and (3) people are passive and reactive rather than thoughtful and goal oriented. In short, for these theorists, our psychological lives are completely determined by what has happened to us in the past (the present is equal to the sum of the past).

Although these ideas have never dominated social psychological thinking, they have been influential. For example, as we will see in Chapter 6, advertisers use classical conditioning to sell their products. Cigarettes and beer are paired with sexy models, macho men on horseback, and fun-filled volleyball games on the beach. By doing so, advertisers hope you will come to associate their product with these inherently positive stimuli. Many behaviors are also shaped by instrumental learning. Parents of young children routinely reinforce behaviors they wish to encourage ("You can have a sticker when you clean up your room") and punish behaviors they wish to discourage ("You're grounded because you got a D on your report card"). This selective use of reinforcement molds the child's behavior.

More generally, the theories reviewed in this section have been influential in the way they portray people as rather mindlessly and habitually responding to stimuli in their environment, without thinking too much about what they are doing. Although we might like to think otherwise, it is clear that this sort of mindlessness occurs. Sometimes we act as if we are on autopilot, unthinkingly repeating behaviors that have met with prior reinforcement (Aarts & Dijksterhuis, 2000; Bargh, 1990; Ouellette & Wood, 1998; W. Wood, Quinn, & Kashy, 2002). This is most apt to occur when we've done something many times before, care very little about what we are doing, or are motivated more by efficiency and expediency than by accuracy and understanding. In cases like these, whatever thoughts we have exert only a small influence on our behavior. You will want to keep this perspective in mind as you learn more about social psychological research. (I promise you will be reinforced for doing so.)

II. The Whole Is Greater Than the Sum of the Parts

Behaviorism dominated American psychology for nearly 50 years, but not all psychologists accepted its tenets. In this section, you will study three dissenting theories. All three theories are cognitive, purposive, and holistic. This means they maintain that (1) cognitions play an important role in behavior, (2) behavior is goal oriented and undertaken for a reason, and (3) complex psychological phenomena are more than the sum of their more elemental parts.

A. Tolman's Cognitive Behaviorism

One important dissenter was Edward Tolman (1926, 1932, 1948). Tolman represents a pivotal figure in American psychology. He studied behavior, but he rejected the theoretical assumptions that guided the behaviorist movement.

1. Key Assumptions

Learning Is Cognitive. Tolman's first assumption was that learning is cognitive. When an animal runs a maze, Tolman argued, the animal develops a cognitive map that consists of learning "what-leads-to-what." If needed, the animal then draws on this knowledge to negotiate the maze. By characterizing learning as a cognitive process, Tolman's theory departed in substantial ways from the psychology of behaviorism. The behaviorists championed an S→R psychology. They contended that nothing intervenes between an environmental stimulus (S) and a behavioral response (R). Tolman's insistence that learning was cognitive challenged this assumption and changed the formula from a simple S→R model to an S→O→R model. The O refers to an unobservable, usually cognitive process that takes place within the organism and intervenes between the stimulus and the response. Memory is one such process.

Behavior Is Purposive. Earlier we noted that the behaviorists believed that behavior is never goal directed or purposive. It is initially random and later determined entirely by prior reinforcement histories. In contrast, Tolman believed that behavior is purposive or goal seeking. Cognitions, in the form of memory and expectancies, allow purpose to be expressed. The animal calls on the knowledge it has acquired to get what it wants and needs.

Research on latent learning provides the best illustration of Tolman's position (Blodgett, 1929; Tolman & Honzig, 1930). In this research, two groups of rats are taught to run a maze. During the first four days of training, rats in the "constant reinforcement condition" are given food when they reach the goal box. Those in the "no initial reinforcement condition" run the maze without receiving any reinforcement. On the fifth day of training, all rats receive reinforcement when they reach the goal box.

Figure 2.2 presents a schematic representation of the findings from this investigation. As predicted by the Law of Effect, the rats who receive constant reinforcement initially make fewer errors than do those who find no reinforcement. However, on the day after food is given to the rats who had previously run the maze without finding food, their performance improves dramatically. In fact, they run the maze as efficiently as rats who had been fed in the goal box throughout the experiment. These findings contradict the notion that reinforcement is necessary for learning to occur. This is assumed because the rats in the second group received no food or reinforcement in the goal box during the first few trials. Yet they later ran the maze efficiently, suggesting that they had learned their way through the maze during the nonreinforced trials.

Tolman explained the phenomenon as follows: During the unrewarded trials, the rat forms a cognitive map of the goal box; it learns what happens if it turns left, and it learns what happens if it turns right. When food is later introduced, this learning is manifested in performance. For Tolman, then, learning occurs in the absence of drive reduction but is manifested only in the presence of drive. Note how this differs from Hull, who argued that learning occurs only when a drive is reduced. Tolman disagreed, arguing that the Law of Effect was a principle of performance, not of learning. Reinforcement isn't necessary for learning to occur, Tolman argued, only for translating what has been learned into performance.

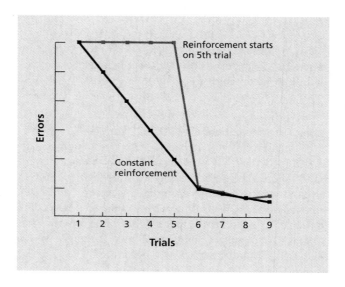

FIGURE 2.2

Tolman's Study of Latent Learning

The performance of rats who received continuous reinforcement gradually improved. In contrast, the rats who did not receive reinforcement until the fifth day showed high error rates until the day after they received food. These findings suggest that learning took place in the absence of reinforcement, but was manifested in behavior only when there was a reason to show what had been learned.

> Our final criticism of the trial and error doctrine is that . . . its fundamental notion of stimulus–response bonds . . . is wrong. Stimuli do not . . . call out responses willy-nilly. Rather, learning consists in the organisms' discovering and refining what all the respective alternative responses lead to. And then, if . . . the consequences of one of these alternatives is more demanded than the other, the organism will tend . . . to select and to perform the response leading to the more demanded-for consequences. (Tolman, 1932, p. 354)

2. Tolman's Legacy

In the 1930s, assumptions about mechanism were so deeply entrenched in American psychology that Tolman's theoretical ideas were viewed as radical. Looking back, Tolman was clearly ahead of his time. Thirty years after Tolman's theory was published, the grip of behaviorism began to wane and cognitively oriented theories began to flourish (Rescorla, 1988).

Social Learning Theory. One of these theories is known as social learning theory (Bandura & Walters, 1963; N. E. Miller & Dollard, 1941). Among other things, social learning theory assumes that (1) people can learn in the absence of reinforcement and (2) expectancies are a critical part of what is learned. For example, if we see another person being punished for stealing, we expect to be punished if we steal. These ideas, which will be discussed in greater detail in Chapter 13, are derived from Tolman's theory. Social learning theory has also been used to explain other social psychological phenomena, such as helping behavior (children learn to be helpful by modeling the behavior of others), and prejudice and discrimination (people imitate negative intergroup attitudes as portrayed by parents, peers, and the media).

Expectancy–Value Models. Tolman's theory also inspired a class of psychological theories known as expectancy–value models of behavior. Such models assume that the choices people make depend on two factors: (1) their subjective expectancy of attaining an outcome, in conjunction with (2) the positive value they place on attaining the outcome and the negative value they place on not attaining the outcome. The idea here is really quite simple. If we want to predict whether a person will apply to graduate school in psychology, we would want to know how likely the person thought it was that she would successfully complete the PhD requirements and the value she places on receiving versus not receiving a PhD.

In an expectancy–value model, these factors are assumed to combine in a multiplicative fashion. This means we multiply (rather than add) the two factors together to determine the strength of an individual's motivation to engage in some behavior. This assumption has an interesting and important consequence. It means that if either factor is set at zero, the goal will not be adopted. If a person sees no possibility that she can successfully complete a PhD program (i.e., if expectancy = 0), she will not apply to graduate school, no matter how much she might value getting a degree. Conversely, if she places absolutely no value on getting the degree (i.e., if value = 0), she will not apply to graduate school no matter how likely she thinks admission would be.

The distinction Tolman drew between learning and performance underlies the expectancy–value model. For Tolman, the behavior of a rat in a maze is determined by what it expects to find and how much it values that outcome. As we will see throughout this text, many of psychology's best-known theories rely on similar principles to explain behavior (Atkinson, 1964; Bandura, 1977; Rotter, 1954; Zuroff & Rotter, 1985).

B. Gestalt Psychology

In formulating his theory, Tolman drew on a school of thought known as **Gestalt psychology** (Koffka, 1935; Köhler, 1929). Gestalt psychology is concerned with how people perceive visual objects. At first, this would seem to have little to do with behavior, but in fact Gestalt psychology has far-reaching implications for behavior. All three of social psychology's most important pioneers—Solomon Asch, Fritz Heider, and Kurt Lewin—received training in Gestalt psychology before emigrating from Germany to the United States. When they settled in America, they used principles of Gestalt psychology to understand social psychological phenomena. For this reason, Gestalt psychology is the most influential perspective we will discuss (Deutsch & Krauss, 1965). The assumptions discussed in the following subsections are particularly important and influential.

1. Perception Occurs in a Field of Interdependent Forces

Earlier we noted that Locke and the introspectionists believed there was a fixed world we passively registered with our senses. The Gestalt psychologists took issue with this claim. They viewed perception as an active process, influenced by a host of contextual and personal variables. Formally, the Gestalt psychologists believed that all psychological experience occurs in a field of interdependent forces. Two entities are interdependent when a change in one creates a change in the other. Figure 2.3 illustrates this principle, showing how the visual perception of an object depends on the surrounding context. The middle (gray) box appears lighter when it is embedded in a dark context than when it is embedded in a light context. Change the context, and you change the way the stimulus is perceived.

FIGURE 2.3

Context Influences
Perception

The gray square looks
lighter when it is set
against a dark background
than when it is set against
a white background.

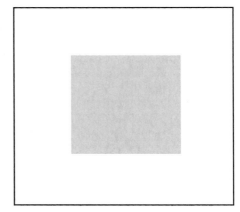

Meaning Is Variable; Context Determines Meaning; Meaning Guides Behavior.
The assumption of interdependence underscores that the meaning of any stimulus is
variable and is determined by the context in which it is embedded. Suppose I ask you
whether the book you are holding is heavy. Your answer will depend on the frame of
reference you use when making your judgment. Undoubtedly, the book will feel heavier
if you've just picked up a feather than if you've just picked up a brick. This is what
Gestalt psychologists mean when they say that perception occurs in a field of interdependent forces that operate as a unified system. These effects are even stronger
when we consider social stimuli. Whether you judge someone to be tall, old, or thin
will depend on who is in the comparison group. The same is true for personality characteristics: Honesty, intelligence, and attractiveness are all comparative judgments,
influenced by contextual factors.

Gestalt psychologists also assume that meaning guides behavior. In Chapter 1 we
noted that this is the hallmark of the phenomenological perspective. Phenomenology
maintains that our behavior depends on the world as it appears, rather than on the
world as it actually exists. Gestalt psychology is very phenomenological. It asserts
that the perceived world, rather than the objective world, guides our behavior.
Throughout the text, we will refer to these principles by saying that meaning is variable, context determines meaning, and meaning guides behavior.

The Whole Is Greater Than the Sum of the Parts. Because perception is characterized by interdependence and is influenced by contextual factors, a stimulus cannot be understood in isolation from its surroundings. This principle underlines the
familiar claim that the whole is greater than (meaning "different from") the sum of
the parts. This maxim can be illustrated most readily with respect to a melody. A
melody is comprised of individual notes (or elements). Yet, if we transpose the melody
to a different octave, we still recognize the melody, even though all of the notes have
changed. On the other hand, if we rearrange all of the notes, the melody is no longer
recognizable even though the elements are still the same. In formal terms, we can say
that a melody is a psychological whole that has its own reality, distinct from the individual elements that make it up. This is why Gestalt psychologists assert that the
whole is *greater than* the sum of the parts.

In social psychology, this assumption has been used to understand the impressions
we form of other people (Chapter 4). From the Gestalt perspective, our impression of

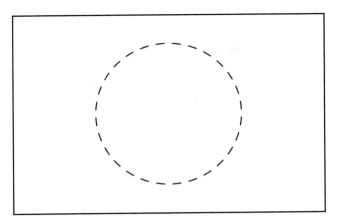

FIGURE 2.4

An Illustration of *Prägnanz*

Even though the stimulus is comprised of a series of arcs, we perceive a complete circle. According to the Gestalt psychologists, this is because perception is organized and oriented toward achieving a certain ideal or end state.

another person cannot be understood simply by combining all that we know about the person. Instead, the whole (our overall impression) is greater than the sum of the parts.

2. Perception Is Directed toward Achieving Order: *Prägnanz*

Gestalt psychologists also assume that some visual displays are simpler or more orderly than are others, and that simple displays are preferred over complex or disorganized ones (Deutsch & Krauss, 1965). The German word **Prägnanz** (literally "precision" or "terseness") refers to the act of perceiving so as to achieve maximum clarity. Figure 2.4 provides an example of this tendency. The figure presents a series of arcs, yet we perceive a unified circle. Our eye fills in the circle because a completed circle makes a better Gestalt.

Perceptual Imbalance Creates Tension That People Are Driven to Reduce. Gestalt psychologists have also considered the origins of *Prägnanz*. According to the Gestalt psychologists, we perceive with maximum clarity because imbalanced or imperfect visual displays are disconcerting and create tension. The brain imposes order on the display as a means of reducing this aversive tension. This is why we automatically fill in the missing pieces and see a unified circle in Figure 2.4. Moreover, this closure is an automatic, structurally determined property of the brain. Much as an electric current jumps a gap in a circuit, so too does the brain automatically bridge the gap to create closure. Woodworth (1948) describes the phenomenon as follows:

> This tendency to close a gap is regarded as revealing a fundamental principle of brain dynamics . . . Tension is built up on both sides of the gap. With the gap present there is a state of unbalanced tensions, but closure brings equilibrium. (p. 130)

Some of social psychology's most important theories proceed from the assumption that *cognitive* imbalance creates an aversive state of tension that people are driven to reduce (Abelson, Aronson, McGuire, Newcomb, Rosenberg, & Tannenbaum, 1968). Other theories assume that people strive to form orderly, coherent impressions in order to better predict and control the social world (e.g., Heider, 1958). Both of these ideas are extensions of Gestalt theories of perception.

Motives, Needs, Wishes, and Desires Cannot Influence Perception. When we say that people strive for perceptual order, we are talking about a form of motivation that is structurally determined. In this context, *structurally determined* means "governed by

FIGURE 2.5

An Illustration of How Expectancies Guide Perception

The same shape that appears to be a B in the first row appears to be a 13 in the second row.

Source: Bruner and Mintern (1955).

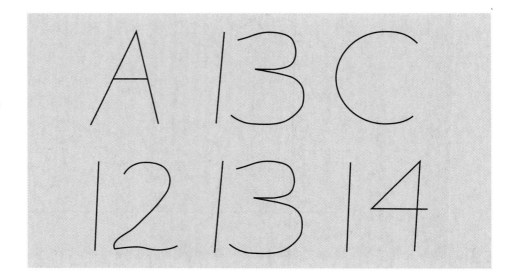

structural components of the brain." Certain end states or relationships among elements are perceived because that is the way our visual apparatus operates. It is the way we process information; it is a direct endowment of the way the human brain is structured. For example, a person in the distance doesn't look unusually small because the brain automatically adjusts for size constancy. This perception is structurally determined.

The Gestalt psychologists believed that although structurally determined factors influence perception, affectively based factors, such as motives, needs, wishes, and desires do not. To continue with the example of size constancy, people can't decide that they *want* to see the person in the distance look small. This would involve motivated misperception, and motivated misperception does not occur within Gestalt psychology.

Expectancies and Schemas Influence Perception. Gestalt psychologists do believe that perception can be influenced by expectancies (Bruner, 1957). To illustrate, consider the image shown in Figure 2.5. The ambiguous middle figure looks like a letter in the first row but a number in the second row. That's because we expect to find a letter amid two other letters, and a number amid two other numbers. The more general point is that just as theories guide a scientist's perception, so too do expectancies guide our perception of objects, people, and events.

> Stimuli . . . do not act upon an indifferent organism. The organism in perception is always in one way or another in a state of expectancy about the environment. It is a truism worth repeating that the perceptual effect of a stimulus is necessarily dependent upon the set or expectancy of the organism. (Bruner & Postman, 1949, p. 206)

Perception is also influenced by hypothetical cognitive structures called **schemas.** Schemas are a type of expectancy, but they are broader. They represent knowledge about a stimulus, person, or event, including information about how things operate or go together (S. E. Fiske & Taylor, 1991; Markus & Zajonc, 1985). Among other things, schemas act as an interpretive structure and guide the meaning we give to a stimulus or an event. To illustrate, whether a kiss on the hand is considered a charming endearment or a lascivious advance depends on the schema we use to interpret the experience. If, on the one hand (no pun intended), we think the person giving the kiss is a refined gentleman, we consider the gesture to be polite and courteous. If, on the other hand, we think the person giving the kiss is a bit of a Lothario, we consider the gesture to be lecherous and licentious. It's the same behavior, but our interpretation depends on our ideas about what the person is like. These ideas comprise a schema and, like expectancies, they guide perception.

3. Summary

Gestalt psychology maintains that (1) psychological phenomena occur in an interdependent field of forces and that, as a consequence, the whole is greater than the sum of the parts; (2) some visual displays are preferred over others and the brain automatically adjusts to perceive with maximum clarity; and (3) expectancies and schemas influence perception, but needs, desires, wishes, and motives do not.

C. Lewin's Field Theory

The next theory we will consider is Lewin's field theory (Lewin, 1935, 1951). Lewin is generally considered the father of modern social psychology because he greatly influenced the way social psychologists think about social behavior and shaped the way they conduct social psychological research.

1. The Psychological Field

Lewin's most fundamental construct is the psychological field, or life space (as he sometimes called it). Lewin used these terms to refer to the perceived world—to the world as it appears to the person. As a phenomenologist, Lewin believed that the meaning we give to the situation determines our behavior. Lewin further believed that the perceived world is determined by a set of interdependent forces involving the person and the environment. These assumptions underlie Lewin's formal statement that behavior (B) depends on both the person (P) and the environment (E): $B = f(P, E)$. In less formal terms, we can say that Lewin believed (1) that behavior is determined by the world as it appears to the individual and (2) that the world as it appears to the individual is determined by a set of interdependent forces involving the person and the environment. These assumptions, which were first introduced in Chapter 1 (see Figure 1.1), came to define the social psychological approach to understanding behavior.

2. Historical Roots

Lewin was a student of the physical sciences, and the roots of his ideas are spelled out in a paper he wrote on Aristotelian and Galilean modes of thought in physics and psychology (Lewin, 1935). Aristotle and Galileo offered very different ideas about why objects behave as they do. Aristotle assumed that objects behave as they do because of their inherent, dispositional properties. These properties were assumed to be fixed and immutable and to operate independently of the surrounding context or situation. For example, fire rises because it has an upward tendency and clay falls because it has a downward tendency. For Aristotle, then, the behavior of an entity is completely determined by the kind of entity it is. The environment, situation, or surrounding context plays a role only insofar as they may disrupt the object's natural inclination or tendency.

In contrast, Galilean physics is dynamic, not static. For Galileo, behavior depends on the situation as a whole—on the relation of the object to the environment. Heavy objects fall not because it is their nature to do so, but because forces of gravity are operating on them. Moreover, both the movement of an object and its actual weight depend on several forces operating on it.

To further illustrate the differences between Aristotle's and Galileo's ideas, imagine we wish to compute the speed of a falling object. In Aristotelian physics, the speed of a falling object is determined entirely by the weight of the object; the heavier the object, the faster it falls. In contrast to this static approach, Galilean physics is more dynamic. It reveals that the speed of a falling object is continually changing at a rate of 32 feet/per second/per second.

The relevance of these ideas to psychological behavior is this: Many early psychological theories adopted the approach of Aristotle. They assumed that people behave as they do because of some inherent, fixed quality. Why is someone aggressive? Because the person possesses an aggressive personality or instinct (McDougall, 1908). This is the psychology that prevailed until Lewin's time, and it is Aristotelian in the sense that it traces behavior to an inherent property or disposition of the person.

In contrast, Lewin championed a Galilean approach to the analysis of psychological behavior. Within this analysis, personality characteristics—properties of objects—are only one of the factors that determine behavior; the dynamics of the situation are also important. Further, to understand behavior we must study the entire situation and examine all of the interdependent forces that influence a person at a given time.

It should be apparent that Lewin's ideas derive from Gestalt psychology. The Gestalt psychologists argued that perception occurs in a field of forces and that all aspects of a situation must be considered in order to understand what is perceived. Lewin broadened this assumption and applied it to behavior. He argued that a person's behavior depends on the perceived situation and that the perceived situation, or life space, depends on all of the interdependent factors that operate in the situation.

3. The Role of Personality Variables

Lewin's emphasis on dynamic interdependence does not mean that personality variables are unimportant. The weight of an object, after all, is determined in part by its mass, and mass is an enduring, inherent, dispositional property. So too do individual differences in personality influence behavior. Extraverts are generally more outgoing than introverts, and meticulous people are generally more fastidious than those who lack conscientiousness. For Lewin, these variables function as specific values in more general laws of behavior.

> Problems of individual differences, of age levels, of personality, of specific situations, and of general laws are closely interwoven. A law is expressed in an equation which relates certain variables. Individual differences have to be conceived of as various specific values which these variables have in a particular case. In other words, general laws and individual differences are merely two aspects of one problem; they are mutually dependent on each other and the study of the one cannot proceed without the study of the other. (Lewin, 1951, p. 243)

One way to think about Lewin's approach is to conceive of personality traits as sensitivities to situational provocation (Marshall, 2003). Consider, for example, what it means to say that someone is a "hostile" person. Commonly, this means the person reacts aggressively to a small affront. In contrast, a "laid-back, mellow, easygoing" person requires much more situational provocation before becoming angry. In Lewin's terms, we can say that a general law holds that provocation produces aggression and that the amount of provocation needed depends on individual differences in trait hostility.

4. Representative Research

Lewin's theoretical ideas represent only one part of his legacy. He also influenced social psychology by championing the use of the experimental method to study complex real-world events under controlled laboratory conditions.

Leadership Styles. One of the best known of Lewin's studies concerned the effectiveness of various leadership styles. With Hitler's domination of Europe increasing, Lewin wondered whether an autocrat leadership style was more effective than a democratic one. To investigate this issue, Lewin, Lippitt, and White (1939) conducted a lab experiment. Groups of 10- and 11-year-old boys gathered after school and were given various tasks to perform (e.g., woodworking). Some of these groups were led by an autocratic leader who dictated what was to be done and who would do it; other groups were lead by a democratic leader who allowed the boys to participate in the decision-making process. Finally, in a third group, known as the laissez-faire condition, the boys were allowed to work on their own without leadership.

Many observations were made, and a great deal of data were collected. On most indices, the democratic group fared best. The importance of this research, however, does not lie in the findings but rather in the approach. Nobody before had thought to use a laboratory experiment to examine a complex psychological issue like this. It just wasn't done. Lewin's decision to study the effectiveness of various leadership styles in this manner was pioneering and very liberating. It opened the door for social psychologists to use the experimental method in laboratory settings to study complex social phenomena.

Level of Aspiration. Another research area of interest concerned the effects of level of aspiration (Lewin, Dembo, Festinger, & Sears, 1944). *Level of aspiration* refers to a standard of performance people set for themselves when undertaking an achievement-oriented activity. A ring toss provides a suitable example. Imagine that you are a participant in a typical experiment. Your task is to toss a ring over a peg. You are first given 10 practice trials to familiarize yourself with the task. Afterward, you are asked to indicate how many of the 10 rings you think will throw over the peg on the next block of trials. Finally, you perform the task and your psychological reactions are examined.

Two findings from level-of-aspiration studies are of especial interest. First, the research showed that feelings of satisfaction or dissatisfaction were determined not solely by the objective outcome but rather by how the outcome compared with the participant's level of aspiration. People felt good if their outcomes matched or exceeded their level of aspiration, and bad if their outcomes fell short of their level of aspiration. This finding, which was first predicted by William James (1890), again demonstrates that it is the perceived world, not the objective world, that guides our behavior. A person who scores low on a task may actually feel better about her performance than does a person who objectively scores higher.

Another interesting point about this research is that people do not simply repeat behaviors that have met with prior reinforcement. Instead, they tend to raise their level of aspiration after they have reached the goal, thereby making the task increasingly more difficult for themselves. The tendency for people to *avoid* repeating behaviors that have met with prior reinforcement runs counter to the Law of Effect. It suggests that people's behavior is not passively driven by the past, but is instead guided by a desire to think favorably about their abilities and to experience feelings of pride.

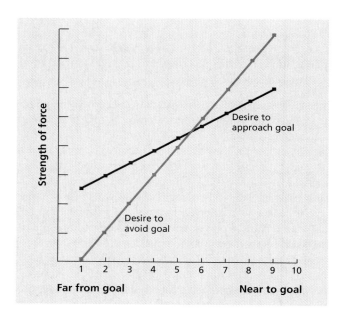

FIGURE 2.6

Strength of Approach and Avoidance Forces in an Approach–Avoidance Conflict

In an approach–avoidance conflict, the same goal has both positive and negative features. Because our desire to avoid the goal's negative features rapidly increases as we near the goal, approach forces dominate when we are far from the goal, but avoidance forces dominate as we near the goal. This asymmetry creates the familiar experience known as cold feet, in which a bride or groom becomes increasingly less certain as the wedding day approaches.

> The law of effect would be truer if it held that a *person*, being rewarded, employs his past successes in whatever way he thinks is likely to bring him satisfaction in the future . . . An individual's past performances often mean little or nothing to him. Only if the [self] would be served thereby, does he engage in a repetition of the successful act. (Allport, 1943, p. 468)

Conflict Situations. Conflict situations provided another fertile area for testing Lewin's ideas. It is customary to distinguish three different conflict situations. In an **approach–approach conflict,** one must choose between two alternatives of near equal attractiveness. For example, a person might want to watch two equally enjoyable TV shows or be forced to choose between two equally attractive universities. In an **avoidance–avoidance conflict,** one must choose between two alternatives that are equally repulsive. For example, a person might be forced to clean the bathroom or take out the trash or be caught between a rock and a hard place. Finally, an **approach–avoidance conflict** occurs when a person must choose whether to undertake an action that has both positive (approach) and negative (avoidance) properties. For example, a child might wish to pet a dog, but at the same time be afraid of being bitten.

Drawing on work in animal learning by N. E. Miller (1944), Lewin believed that approach–avoidance conflicts are difficult to resolve and create psychological tension. The difficulty arises because the strength of the two forces increases at different rates, with the avoidance force increasing more rapidly as we approach the goal (see Figure 2.6). To illustrate, suppose you decide you'd like to take a trip to Europe next year. With the trip still a long time off, your heart is filled with anticipation and joy. The culture, the art, and the food all seem so exciting and inviting. As the trip approaches, you start to become increasingly concerned with the costs, the long airline flight, and the lack of comfort you are apt to encounter in a foreign land. In theoretical terms, we can say that approach forces dominated when you were far from the goal, but avoidance forces dominated when you were near to the goal. This asymmetry explains why many people experience cold feet as their wedding day approaches.

Lewin (1952) used this analysis to study Americans' eating habits during World War II. During this time, the U.S. government wanted Americans to eat cheaper, less-preferred cuts of meat, such as sweetbreads, beef hearts, and kidneys. Lewin conceptualized the situation as an approach–avoidance conflict. Some foods are delicious but expensive; other foods are economical but unsavory. Lewin believed that one way to get people to use less-preferred meats was to increase their public commitment to perform the behavior. To test this idea, Lewin conducted an experiment. In this study, housewives learned why it was important to the war effort for them to start buying less-preferred cuts of meat, and they were given instructions on how to prepare the meats. In the lecture condition, the women passively received this information while listening to a speaker; in the group decision condition, the women received this information while actively participating in a group discussion. Only 3 percent of the women in the lecture condition later reported serving the meats, whereas 32 percent of those in the group decision condition did so. Lewin credited the role of active involvement for producing this difference. For Lewin, actively committing to a new position is a critical element of attitude change. In Chapter 6, we will see that one of Lewin's students, Leon Festinger, incorporated this insight into his own theory of behavior, called cognitive dissonance theory (Festinger, 1957).

D. Summary

In this section we have discussed three cognitive models of behavior. These theories view people as thoughtful, rational, and goal directed. In this sense, they present a portrait that contrasts sharply with the first set of theories we discussed. During psychology's formative years, the two sets of theories were treated as antagonistic to one another, and battle lines were frequently drawn between them. More recently, social psychologists recognize that both theories capture a portion of the truth. Sometimes people are mindless and their behavior is automatic and habitual, and sometimes people are thoughtful and their behavior is deliberate and goal oriented (Chaiken & Trope, 1999; Markus & Zajonc, 1985). The focus has shifted, therefore, away from asking which perspective is right and toward understanding when each type of process operates and what consequences both have for psychological life.

III. Behavior Is Guided by Psychological Needs and Desires

So far we have examined two different kinds of theories. The first assert that complex phenomena are built up of associated elements and that thinking exerts no influence on behavior. The second argue that perception and behavior occur in a field of interdependent forces and that behavior depends on the world as it appears. Missing from these analyses is any mention of the deeper, more emotional side of psychological life. Motivational models of behavior, to which we now turn, redress this omission. These theories argue that often behavior is undertaken in order to satisfy deep-seated and sometimes unconscious motives, needs, wishes, and desires. Such theories are also known as functionalist theories, for they emphasize the functional value of social behavior.

A. Evolutionary Psychology

When reviewing associationism and behaviorism, we noted that these theories assert that people enter the world as blank slates and that their unique lifetime experiences account for their current thoughts and behavior. Evolutionary psychology presents a different perspective on the matter. Instead of asserting that we enter the world knowing nothing and learn only from personal experience, evolutionary psychologists assume that we enter possessing a mind that has successfully solved innumerable adaptive problems humans faced during our ancestral past. The solutions are represented in physical and psychological structures and preferred ways of thinking and behavior.

Many of the adaptive problems our ancestors faced were social psychological in origin. For example, people needed to fight off predators, hunt animals and procure food, and raise children. To solve these problems, people banded together and evolved various ways of thinking and behaving. For example, to live communally, it is necessary to identify freeloaders—people who violate social pacts by taking more than their share or failing to contribute to the common good. As it turns out, people are very adept at making this sort of identification (Tooby & Cosmides, 1992), suggesting that the ability may have evolved over many thousands of years.

1. Modern Skulls House Stone Age Minds

The adaptations that solve problems of survival are ancestral, not modern. For example, snakes and other reptiles have threatened humans for eons, while automobiles have done so for only the past 100 years. For this reason, it is much easier to develop a fear of snakes than a fear of cars, even though the latter pose a greater threat to us today. More generally, the question of whether a particular characteristic is adaptive in the modern world is not relevant to its evolutionary basis. Natural selection occurs very slowly, requiring somewhere between 1,000 and 10,000 generations. Since a human generation is roughly 20 years, somewhere between 20,000 and 200,000 years are needed for changes to spread throughout the human population. Hence, the adaptive structures and behaviors we observe today are ones that helped solve problems our hunter-gatherer ancestors faced over the past 1.8 million years. These adaptations may or may not serve us well in the modern world.

2. Reproductive Success Drives Evolution

Evolution is driven by a single concern: reproductive success. This term refers not to procreation per se, but to the ability to successfully pass one's genes on to future generations. In evolution, it's not enough to simply create a child; one must also raise the child to reproductive age so that it can then procreate and raise its offspring to reproductive age. Many students do not appreciate this fact when learning about evolutionary psychology. They have heard that evolution involves conflict and competition, favoring survival of the fittest. In fact, reproductive success can be enhanced by numerous behaviors that involve cooperation, altruism, and even self-sacrifice (D. M. Buss & Kenrick, 1998). For example, if a father gives his life to save three of his children, he has enhanced his reproductive success, even though he has sacrificed his own life. We will cover this point in greater detail in Chapter 12.

3. Parental Investment Drives Sexual Selection

Many species are marked by large sex differences. For example, male elephant seals typically weigh 4,000 pounds, while female elephant seals weigh a mere 1,000 pounds. If the two sexes faced the same adaptive problems, why are there such pronounced differences? To answer this question, Darwin (1871) devised a second theory of evolution: the theory of sexual selection. Sexual selection occurs through two paths. First, there is intrasexual competition between members of the same sex. Picture two stags locking horns in competition in order to gain access to a female, and you'll get the idea. Second, there is intersexual selection. Here, one member of a sex prefers certain characteristics in a mate, and those who possess this characteristic are more apt to successfully reproduce. Presumably, this is why peacocks have such a brilliant plumage. Peahens favored peacocks with brightly colored plumes, and over time this characteristic became an evolved adaptation.

Trivers (1972) suggested that parental investment is one factor that drives sexual selection. Across species, one sex has a higher parental investment than the other, and the less-investing sex is intrasexually more competitive and intersexually less discerning than is the heavier-investing sex. In most (but not all) species, females shoulder more responsibility for raising the young than do males, so they have greater parental investment. This is certainly true in humans. Women not only incur the burden of internal fertilization, placentation, and gestation but also (in most cases) nurse the child for a period of several years after birth. For this reason, their parental investment is high and they should be cautious about how quickly and frequently they mate, and selective about whom they mate with. Men, in contrast, have a relatively low parental investment. Consequently, they should be willing to mate more frequently and be less discriminating about whom they mate with.

To test these ideas, Schmitt and over 100 colleagues from various countries around the world queried men and women about their sexual preferences (D. P. Schmitt, 2003). More than 16,000 people, representing 52 different countries, were asked to indicate how many sexual partners they desired in the next month. Figure 2.7 presents some of the results from this investigation, grouping the 52 counties into 10 major world regions. As you can see, for every region studied, men indicated a preference for more mates than did women. Evolutionary psychologists believe that these findings stem from sex differences in parental investment. Women have more to lose by making a bad decision, so they are more selective and discriminating than are men (see also D. M. Buss, 1989; D. M. Buss & Schmitt, 1993).

4. Biological Processes Underlie Social Behavior

Along with a wide range of other scientists, evolutionary psychologists have argued that biological processes underlie social behavior. For example, in Chapter 11 you will learn that sex differences in response to stress seem to be influenced by a hormone called oxytocin (Taylor et al., 2000). Other biochemical processes are also being studied, aided by advances in measurement devices. Modern technologies such as positron emission tomography (PET) and functional magnetic resonance imaging (fMRI) are enabling researchers to directly observe the anatomical correlates and, perhaps, causes

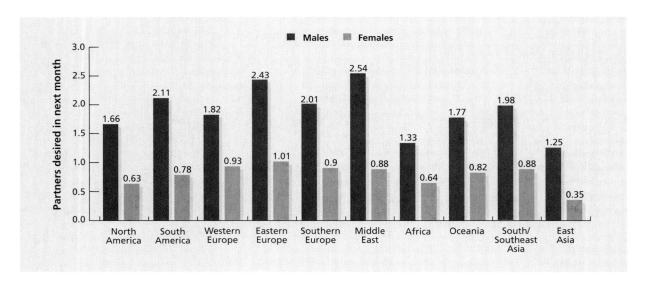

FIGURE 2.7

Desire for Sexual Partners in Various Regions around the World

Across cultures, men desire more sexual partners than do women. According to evolutionary psychologists, these findings provide evidence that sexual preferences were forged millions of years ago.

Source: Adapted from D. P. Schmitt (2003).

of social perception and social behavior (Ochsner & Lieberman, 2001). In the coming years, these technologies will undoubtedly reveal new and exciting insights into the biological bases of social behavior.

5. Summary

Evolutionary psychologists are like astronomers who peer back in time with high-powered telescopes to glimpse the beginning of the universe. Every person alive today is considered to be a well-preserved fossil, carrying all of the mechanisms that enabled people to successfully meet the challenges they faced many thousands of years ago (D. M. Buss & Kendrick, 1998; Tooby & Cosmides, 1992). By carefully documenting what people do today, we gain a glimpse into the behaviors that were adaptive millennia ago.

We will have the occasion to consider this perspective at numerous points throughout this text. In addition to understanding the origins of sexual preferences, we will also use these ideas to understand how we are able to recognize facial expressions of emotion (Chapter 3), the origins of prejudice and group conflict (Chapter 10), altruism (Chapter 12), and aggression (Chapter 13). It will be useful to keep several points in mind when reading about the evolutionary perspective. First, contemporary researchers do not assume that genetically inherited behaviors are inevitable and immutable. Instead, modern proponents of evolutionary psychology emphasize behavioral flexibility and plasticity. The behaviors we see today may be ones that have met with reproductive success in the distant past, but their execution can be overridden or modified.

Another point to keep in mind is that individuals are usually quite unaware that they are acting in ways that maximize their reproductive fitness. For example, in Chapter 12 we will see that people are inclined to give help to those who are genetically similar to themselves (Burnstein, Crandall, & Kitayama, 1994). No one assumes, however, that people consciously calculate the degree of genetic overlap between themselves and another person before deciding whether or not to help. Instead, this decision operates at an unconscious level. After many thousands of years, it has become automatic.

Third, the fact that some behaviors have been forged by natural selection does not mean that all behaviors have been subject to selective pressures. After all, some people like to sing, hum, and whistle while they work, whereas others do not. These behaviors are not relevant to reproductive success, so both types of people exist in the population.

Finally, you should be aware that the evolutionary perspective is quite controversial. Because it uses the past to explain the present, it is ill-suited to making testable predictions about what will occur in the future. Making such predictions is an important function of any theory (see Chapter 1), so this gap limits the theory's usefulness.

B. The Sociocultural Perspective

A glance back at Figure 2.7 reveals a good deal of variability among the 10 regions studied. In all cases, males prefer more mates than females, but the rates vary from region to region. Understanding these differences is the focus of the sociocultural perspective. Whereas evolutionary psychologists look for commonalities among people across a variety of cultures and societies, the sociocultural perspective focuses on the variability we see from culture to culture (A. P. Fiske, Kitayama, Markus, & Nisbett, 1998; D. R. Lehman, Chiu, & Schaller, 2004). It takes as its starting point the observation that most social behaviors are influenced by the customs that operate in a particular cultural context.

Culture is a difficult variable to identify and study. It operates in the background and affects so many things that its influence is often hard to detect. For our purposes, we will define **culture** as a socially constructed and socially transmitted confederation of beliefs, values, goals, norms, traditions, and institutions (A. P. Fiske, 2002). Child-rearing practices, courtship patterns, and beliefs and rituals related to birth and death are examples of some important culturally determined variables. Cultures influence what people believe, what they care about, and how they live their lives.

1. Individualism and Collectivism

Although there are many different ways of parsing cultures, one dimension, individualism–collectivism, has received a great deal of attention within social psychology (Hofstede, 1980; Triandis, 1995). As shown in Table 2.1, individualistic cultures emphasize personal autonomy, self-reliance, and independence. People raised in this cultural context value personal freedom; strive for self-fulfillment; use their own attitudes and interests to guide their behavior; and show qualified respect for authority figures, social institutions, and tradition. In contrast, collectivistic cultures emphasize loyalty to one's group, duty to one's family, and adherence to social traditions and institutions. People raised in this cultural context put the concerns of others ahead of their own and use the behavior and expectations of others to guide their behavior.

TABLE 2.1   Comparing Individualistic and Collectivistic Cultures

Dimension	Individualistic Cultural View	Collectivistic Cultural View
Self	An independent self-view, with a focus on how one is unique and different from others	An interdependent self-view, with an emphasis on commonalities between self and others
Goals	To do one's own thing in an autonomous, self-reliant manner or be better than others through competition	To promote group harmony and put the concerns of others ahead of one's own
Behavioral guides	Personal preferences, attitudes, and values	Social norms and the opinions and expectations of others
Social obligations and duties	Qualified respect for authority figures and social institutions, and relatively little concern for upholding traditions	Great respect for authority figures and social institutions, and a strong desire to uphold tradition

When thinking about these orientations, keep in mind that they are relative, not absolute. People raised in individualistic cultures are capable of putting the interests of others ahead of their own, just as those raised in collectivistic cultures sometimes pursue their own self-interests. Moreover, the two orientations are somewhat independent, with some cultures scoring high on both dimensions and others scoring high on only one (Gelfand, Triandis, & Darius, 1996). For these reasons, the distinction is largely one of emphasis.

2. Comparing Western and East Asian Countries

Nations are political, not social, units, and various cultures and subcultures often coexist within a given nation. This is increasingly true in the United States, for example, as immigration patterns and differential birthrates have transformed a country that was once rather homogenous into a mosaic of different languages, traditions, and ways of understanding the world. For this reason, *culture* is not synonymous with *nationality*.

At the same time, various regions of the world clearly have different cultural traditions. The differences are not always large, and there is variability within nations, but Western countries, such as America, Canada, and the countries of Western Europe, tend to be more individualistic and a bit less collectivistic than the countries of East Asia, such as China, Japan, and Korea (Oyserman, Coon, & Kemmelmeier, 2002). These differences have received a great deal of attention in social psychology over the past 20 years. For example, in Chapter 4 we will see that people raised in Western cultures tend to believe that personality factors are the most important determinants of behavior. "Why do people do what they do?" "Because of the kind of people they are," answer people with a Western cultural background. In contrast, people raised in East Asian countries are more inclined to point to the importance of social roles in determining behavior. They believe that people behave the way they do because of societal expectations and cultural norms. You will have the opportunity to learn about other such differences throughout this text, as the sociocultural perspective provides an important viewpoint on social behavior.

C. Freud's Psychoanalytic Theory

The final theory we will consider is Freud's psychoanalytic theory. This theory is arguably the broadest of all the grand theories. It seeks to explain not only everyday behavior but also abnormal behavior, war, prejudice, and destruction as well as love, humor, and art. Because of its breadth, it is impossible to describe the theory in its entirety. Instead, we will focus on a few themes of particular relevance to social psychology (C. S. Hall & Lindzey, 1957).

1. Psychic Conflict

The evolutionary model underscores that behavior is often driven by deep-seated needs and ancestral desires. The sociocultural model underscores that the expression of these needs and desires is influenced by cultural contexts. This conflict between inner needs and external constraints plays a central role in Freud's theory. According to Freud, behavior represents a compromise between biological needs (which reside in a psychological structure known as the id); societal expectations, morals, and values (which are housed in a psychological structure called the superego); and the ego, which negotiates between the id and the superego while simultaneously avoiding danger in the external world. In short, the ego is engaged in a constant attempt to effect a compromise between needs, ought nots, and better nots.

Societies help people balance these demands by providing them with socially benign ways to satisfy their animalistic urges and needs. As Freud once remarked, "The first human who hurled an insult instead of a stone was the founder of civilization." Freud's point was that social behavior is often a disguised attempt to satisfy needs for sexual gratification and the release of aggressive impulses.

2. Unconscious Processes

The conflict Freud describes is rarely one of which we are consciously aware. Freud likened the mind to an iceberg. Consciousness lies above the water. This is the part we see, but it is not very large or important. The preconscious lies just below the surface. Although this part of the mind is ordinarily hidden, it can be accessed. For example, with effort we can retrieve a memory from our childhood. The largest part of the mind, the unconscious, resides far below the surface. This is the most important part, as it determines almost everything we do. Many social psychologists are now making great use of Freud's division by showing the many ways that unconscious processes guide social perception and behavior.

3. The Mechanisms of Defense

In Freudian theory, the unconscious is more than a repository of inaccessible material. It also houses animal urges, painful memories we prefer not to recall, and unflattering truths about ourselves we wish to avoid confronting. An active force, called **repression,** keeps these forbidden thoughts and desires at bay (Freud, 1933/1964). Repression is an example of what Freud and his daughter, Anna Freud, called a "defense mechanism." These mechanisms help insulate people from psychological pain (Freud, 1894/1962). Contemporary researchers often refer to these tendencies as self-enhancement biases, for we generally use them to cast ourselves in an overly flattering light. For example, people use the defense mechanism of rationalization to avoid thinking of themselves as someone who behaved in a negative manner or brought about a negative outcome. Many of these defense mechanisms also serve to redirect negative feelings we have toward ourselves onto others. Later in this text we will see how such mechanisms contribute to prejudice (Chapter 10) and aggression (Chapter 13).

4. Conservation of Energy

Defending against psychological pain has an important cost. It uses up energy that could better be used for accomplishing more productive goals and tasks. To understand this aspect of Freud's theory, we need to spend a moment talking about the field of physics and the immutable but changeable nature of energy. In 1847, the German scientist Hermann von Helmholtz proposed what is now known as the first law of thermodynamics. This principle states that energy is neither created nor destroyed, but is simply transferred from one state to another.

Freud applied this principle to psychological life, arguing that all psychological activity—thinking, dreaming, perceiving—requires psychic energy. Further, he conceived of humans as closed energy systems. They were born with a certain amount of energy that, like physical energy, can be neither created nor destroyed; it can only be transferred from one state to another.

Needs determine how much free energy exists. When a need arises, energy is invested in a desired object. This investment, known as a **cathexis,** means the energy is no longer available to perform other psychological work. In some cases, a person can become fixated on a desired object, thereby using up a great deal of psychic energy. If you've ever been lovesick or pined for someone who is far away, you have experienced cathexis. You probably weren't able to get your mind off of the person you loved, and this distraction prevented you from doing other things. In the healthy personality, most psychic energy is free and available to do psychological work.

Contemporary social psychologists have used Freud's ideas on conservation of psychic energy to examine a phenomenon known as thought suppression (Wegner, 1994). Thought suppression occurs when people make a conscious effort to not think about something. For example, a dieter might purposefully try not to think of food, or a student anxious about an upcoming exam might actively try to think about something else. Because the total amount of psychic energy is fixed, the energy expended to keep certain thoughts out of awareness is unavailable for other uses.

5. Early Childhood Experiences

Another key aspect of Freud's theory is the notion that early childhood experiences influence adult behavior. Freud believed that the tendencies we display as adults reflect the way we negotiated and resolved childhood conflicts and problems. This aspect of Freud's theory is currently being used to understand the nature of interpersonal relationships. In Chapter 11, you will learn that contemporary researchers known as attachment theorists are exploring how early parent–child interactions affect the way adults interact with their romantic partners.

IV. Concluding Remarks

In this chapter we have covered a great deal of material, spanning hundreds of years. Moreover, the theories we reviewed present conflicting views of behavior, characterizing humans as mindless and habitual, thoughtful and deliberate, or motivated by needs of which they are only dimly aware. Given these divergent positions, it is tempting to ask which theory is right, but this question cannot be answered. As first discussed in Chapter 1, theories, by definition, can never be proved right or wrong. They can only provide a useful way of explaining what we observe and point the way to new observations.

For this reason, it is best to think of the theories discussed in this chapter as complementary rather than competing. An analogy may help you appreciate this point a bit more. Imagine that an alien is sent to earth to discover what the human body is like. The alien has only a limited amount of time to complete its mission, so it decides to interview a physician. The answers it brings back to its home planet will depend a lot on what kind of physician it interviews. A cardiologist would undoubtedly talk about the heart and the circulatory system; a nephrologist would discuss the kidneys and the urinary system; and a neurologist would focus on the brain and the central nervous system. All would impart valuable information, but none would provide a complete, unified portrait.

In a sense, the theories we have covered in this chapter are like medical specialists. Each focuses on one aspect of human functioning, offering important clues about human behavior. Viewing them together gives us a deeper appreciation for the great complexity of human behavior and a keener vantage point for understanding social psychological life.

CHAPTER SUMMARY

- Locke believed that the mind was blank at birth and that principles of association explain the existence of complex ideas. Following in his footsteps, the introspectionists sought to identify the basic elements of consciousness.

- The behaviorists believed that thoughts do not guide behavior and that psychologists need not (and should not) study them.

- Hull believed that learning occurred only when a drive (or need) was reduced and was displayed only when a drive (or need) was present.

- Tolman studied behavior but believed that behavior was cognitive and purposive. Cognitions, in the form of knowledge and expectancies, help the organism attain its goals.

- Gestalt psychologists argued that perception occurs in an interdependent field of forces and that the whole is greater than the sum of the parts. They also believed that perception was guided toward achieving a pleasing end state, and that expectancies and schemas influence perception, but motives, needs, wishes, and desires do not.

- Lewin believed (1) that behavior depends on the perceived world, (2) that the perceived world is determined by a field of interrelated forces that includes the person and the situation, and (3) that behavior is goal directed or purposive.

- The evolutionary perspective argues that natural selection has favored some social behaviors more than others and that the behaviors we see today are ones that met with reproductive success thousands and thousands of years ago.

- The sociocultural perspective argues that cultures influence social behavior. A particularly important distinction exists between individualistic cultures (which emphasize self-reliance) and collectivistic cultures (which emphasize group harmony).

- Freud believed that unconscious conflicts influence psychological life and that various defense mechanisms help people resolve these conflicts.

KEY TERMS

associationism, 36

introspectionism, 36

behaviorism, 37

mechanism, 38

hedonism, 38

classical conditioning, 39

instrumental conditioning, 39

Law of Effect, 40

Drive, 41

Gestalt psychology, 45

Prägnanz, 47

schemas, 48

approach–approach conflict, 52

approach–avoidance conflict, 52

avoidance–avoidance conflict, 52

culture, 57

repression, 59

cathexis, 60

ADDITIONAL READING

Go to the Student Edition of the Online Learning Center for this text (www.mhhe.com/brown) and log in to read the following journal articles, which relate to the content of this chapter:

- Skinner, B. F. (1990). Can psychology be a science of mind?

- Rescorla, R. A. (1988). Pavlovian conditioning: It's not what you think it is.

Social Perception

The Hollywood movie *Catch Me If You Can* (starring Leonardo DiCaprio) is based on the true story of Frank W. Abagnale Jr., a con man, forger, imposter, and escape artist who was the youngest person to ever be on the FBI's most-wanted list. In his short but lucrative career, Abagnale co-piloted a Pan Am jet, masqueraded as the supervising resident of a hospital, practiced law without a license, and even posed as an FBI agent, in the meantime cashing over $2.5 million in forged checks. His exploits came to an end when a flight attendant recognized his face from an Interpol poster. After serving a five-year prison sentence, Abagnale was paroled and joined the FBI, helping officials catch other con men who use the same tricks he had once used.

Abagnale's success as a con artist hinged on his ability to manipulate the impressions other people formed of his character, qualifications, and abilities. Impressions like these arise from social perception. **Social perception** is the study of how we form impressions of other people and how these impressions affect the way we act toward them.

Figure 3.1 shows that three factors influence our first impressions. The first factor involves the person's physical features. People have long assumed that physical qualities provide a window into a person's personality, and the first section of this chapter reviews evidence relevant to this assumption. The second factor involves nonverbal behaviors. In the second section of this chapter you will see that the way people stand, move, and sound influences the inferences we draw about their personality and character. You will also learn that these inferences are not always accurate and that people can misinterpret nonverbal cues. The third factor, cognitive processes, also guides our impressions of other people. Schemas (see Chapter 2) and expectancies act as interpretive filters and impose meaning on the perceptions that reach us. In the third section of this chapter, you will discover how cognitive processes shape your

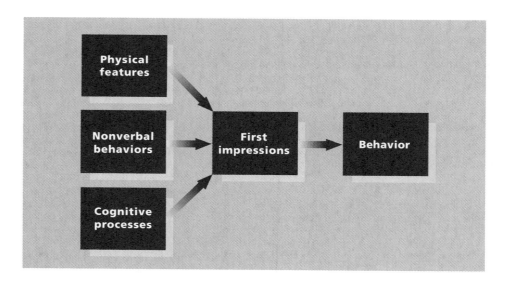

FIGURE 3.1

A Model of the Social Perception Process

The model shows that our impressions of others are influenced by three factors: physical features (e.g., facial attractiveness and emotional expression); nonverbal behaviors (e.g., posture, movements, and tone of voice); and cognitive processes (e.g., prior knowledge, schemas, and expectancies). The model also shows that once they form, first impressions guide our behavior.

impressions of others. Finally, you will see how your impressions affect the way you behave toward other people. In some cases, your own actions lead people to behave in ways that confirm your expectancies about what they are like.

I. Physical Features

Although most of us have been cautioned against making snap judgments about others solely on the basis of their appearance ("You can't judge a book by its cover"), few of us heed this advice. Instead, we rapidly form impressions of other people, often with very limited visual information. Moreover, such judgments tend to be widely shared and often coincide with objective measures. For example, people can reliably judge another person's intelligence after seeing only the person's photograph (Zebrowitz, Hall, Murphy, & Rhodes, 2002). People are especially apt to make snap judgments about another person's warmth. After only a few seconds, we make a decision about whether a person is good-natured and friendly or cold and reserved (Ambady, Hallahan, & Conner, 1999).

One reason we make first impressions so rapidly is that we have preconceptions about what people are like. For example, we may believe that people who have blond hair are fun-loving and carefree, and that people who wear glasses are studious and intelligent. When we encounter people who possess these attributes, our beliefs guide our impression.

Many of these beliefs develop through learning. Either through the media or as a result of their own experiences, people acquire such beliefs as they age and become enculturated and socialized. However, some first impressions also arise independent of learning. Many social psychologists believe that people have an innate, unlearned tendency to interpret certain physical stimuli in specific ways. Two questions are asked when assessing this possibility: (1) Do impressions form at a very early age, before learning has occurred? and (2) Are there cross-cultural similarities in the impressions people form? To illustrate, if people with red hair are universally perceived to be unpredictable and hotheaded, we infer that the link between hair color and perceived temperament is unlearned.

The following section of this chapter will examine evidence that bears on this possibility, focusing on the role of facial attractiveness, facial babyishness, and emotional expression. We will be asking whether social perception is entirely learned or whether people possess an innate tendency to interpret physical qualities in a common manner. These divergent approaches are manifestations of the so-called nature–nurture controversy. Many psychological phenomena can be viewed as arising from either innate, unlearned propensities (nature) or from acquired, learned tendencies (nurture). It is important to understand that all such controversies are characterized by an asymmetry (Pinker, 2002). No one doubts that learning takes place, so the issue is not whether learning occurs; the issue is whether learning is *everything*. Is it true, as John Locke claimed (see Chapter 2), that "there is *nothing* in the intellect that is not first in the senses"? This is the issue to which we now turn.

A. Facial Attractiveness

Two hundred years ago, the German dramatist Friedrich von Schiller remarked that "physical beauty is the sign of an interior beauty, a spiritual and moral beauty" (cited in Dion, Berscheid, & Walster, 1972). Schiller was not alone. Most of us assume that attractive people possess attractive personality characteristics. This **"what is beautiful is good" stereotype** is especially true for judgments of social competence and warmth. Across a variety of age groups, and for both men and women, attractive people are regarded as more socially skilled, friendly, and well-adjusted than are unattractive people (G. R. Adams & Huston, 1975; Eagly, Ashmore, Makhijani, & Longo, 1991; Feingold, 1992a). In fact, about the only positive characteristic that isn't linked to attractiveness is modesty. In this case, attractiveness is a liability, as people assume attractive people are immodest and vain (Cash & Janda, 1984).

Attractive people also enjoy many social benefits. Attractive children are punished less often by their parents and are less apt to be taunted and teased by their peers (Langlois et al., 2000). Attractive adults receive preference in hiring decisions (Cash, Gillen, & Burns, 1977), and earn more money in their jobs (Hammermesh & Biddle, 1994). Attractive criminals even receive more lenient treatment than do unattractive ones (Downs & Lyons, 1991). These findings make it is easy to understand why some groups (e.g., the obese) have attempted to have the equal rights amendment of the Constitution extended to include unattractiveness.

1. Is the Link Between Perceived Attractiveness and Personality Innate?

The "what is beautiful is good" stereotype is undoubtedly influenced by learning. At an early age, children learn that wicked witches are homely and that valorous princes are handsome. Researchers have also found, however, that people have an innate tendency to respond positively to attractive faces. In one study, infants two to three months old looked longer at attractive faces than at unattractive ones (Langlois et al., 1987). In follow-up research, 12-month-old infants displayed more positive emotional reactions to an attractive stranger than to an unattractive stranger and played significantly longer with an attractive doll than an unattractive doll (Langlois, Roggman, & Rieser-Danner, 1990).

Cross-cultural research provides further evidence that the "what is beautiful is good" stereotype has an innate, universal basis. Wheeler and Kim (1997) showed Korean participants photographs of Korean students who varied in terms of their attractiveness. As was true in America, attractive Koreans were judged to be higher in social competence, intellectual ability, psychological adjustment, and sexual interest/warmth than were unattractive people. Attractive Koreans were also evaluated more favorably on two traits that are highly valued among Koreans: integrity and concern for others. These findings suggest that the tendency to respond favorably to attractive faces is innate, and cultural standards influence which qualities attractive people are thought to possess.

2. What Makes a Pretty Face?

Cross-cultural agreement on the "what is beautiful is good" stereotype may surprise you, as many people assume that standards of beauty vary over historical periods and cultures. Standards do shift when it comes to body types. The attractive women featured in paintings by the 17th-century painter Rubens are corpulent in comparison with the gaunt models who grace the covers of contemporary fashion magazines. In contrast, standards of facial beauty are much more consistent across time and cultures, suggesting that they may have an innate basis (Langlois et al., 2000).

The Features of a Pretty Face. To determine how various facial features affect attractiveness, M. R. Cunningham (1986) had male students rate the attractiveness of 50 female faces. By making precise measurements of the size and location of various facial features, Cunningham was able to identify which facial features were linked with perceived attractiveness. Cunningham found that three categories of facial features were linked to judgments of attractiveness. The first category consisted of babyish facial features, such as large, widely spaced eyes; a small nose; and a small chin. A second category comprised mature facial features, including wide cheekbones and narrow cheeks. Expressive facial features, such as a wide smile and large pupils, constituted a third category.

Follow-up research has shown that the attributes Cunningham identified predict attractiveness across cultures. M. R. Cunningham, Roberts, Barbee, Druen, and Wu (1995) had men and women from various racial groups judge the attractiveness of women from a variety of racial and ethnic groups. The data revealed broad agreement on what constitutes an attractive female face. Across the four racial groups, women with large eyes, prominent cheekbones, and large smiles were judged to be more attractive than women who lacked these qualities (see also M. R. Cunningham, Barbee, & Pike, 1990).

Faces with Feminized Features. Qualities that affect perceptions of attractiveness in female faces also affect perceptions of attractiveness in male faces. Perrett and colleagues (1998) prepared computer-generated faces of men and women that had been digitally altered to be more masculine or feminine. When shown these photographs (see Figure 3.2), participants judged the feminized faces to be more attractive than the masculinized faces. They also rated the feminized faces as warmer, more honest, more cooperative, and more apt to be a better parent. This may explain why many teenage heartthrobs, from Ricky Nelson to Jon Bon Jovi, have feminine faces that project a soft, sweet, unthreatening sexuality. It may also explain why both men and women tend to notice attractive women more than attractive men (Maner et al., 2003).

Symmetrical Faces. Have you ever taken a photograph and asked the photographer to get your good side? If so, you've shown an awareness of a simple fact: Faces are not symmetrical. One side is generally more attractive than the other. Of course, individuals differ with regard to facial symmetry, with some people having more symmetrical faces than others. The more symmetrical one's face is, the more attractive one is judged to be (Gangestad & Thornhill, 1997; Grammer & Thornhill, 1994). This effect even extends to twins. Mealey, Bridgstock, and Townsend (1999) found that identical twins could be distinguished according to facial symmetry and that the twin with the more symmetrical face was viewed as more attractive. This finding suggests that people are very sensitive to even minor differences in facial symmetry.

Faces with Average Features. Faces with many average facial features are more attractive than ones with few average facial features (Langlois, Roggman, & Musselman, 1994). To illustrate, Langlois and Roggman (1990) took facial photographs of individuals who varied in attractiveness. The photographs were then scanned and

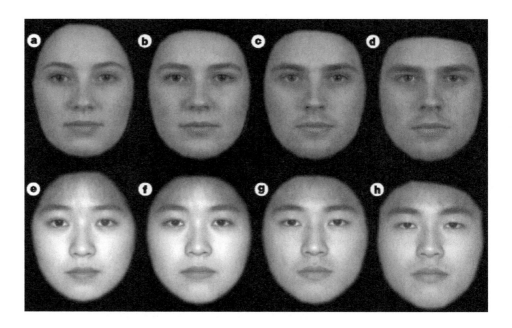

FIGURE 3.2

Feminized and Masculinized Faces of Caucasian and Japanese Men and Women

Within each pair, the face on the left has been digitally feminized and the face on the right has been digitally masculinized. When asked which face they found more attractive, participants preferred the feminized face on the left of each pair. They also believed the person on the left was more trustworthy and warm, suggesting that perceived warmth underlies the preference for feminized faces.

Source: Perrett et al. (1998).

digitized into a computer file, and the digitized values were averaged to form composite photographs (see Figure 3.3). Langlois and Roggman then showed these photographs to a group of college students and asked them to judge the attractiveness of each facial image, using a 1-to-5 scale, with 1 = Very unattractive and 5 = Very attractive. Figure 3.4 shows that the more faces the researchers used to create the facial image, the more attractive the colleges students judged the face to be. These findings support the claim that average facial features are attractive (see also G. Rhodes & Tremewan, 1996).

You should keep two points in mind when considering these results. First, exotic facial features can be attractive. A person with radiant blue eyes can be quite alluring, even though this facial feature is rare. Second, although the word *average* can mean "ordinary" or "typical," it is rare to find a person with many average facial features (Alley & Cunningham, 1991).

3. Why Do People Prefer Attractive Faces?

Two theories have been developed to explain why people prefer attractive faces. An evolutionary model assumes that attractive people are healthier and more fertile than are unattractive people and that, because of this, they were more apt to be chosen as mates and more apt to pass their (attractive) genes on to the next generation (Berry,

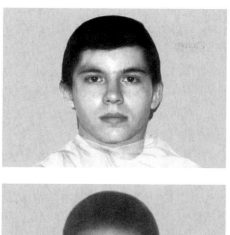

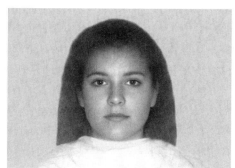

FIGURE 3.3

Faces That Vary in Their
Averageness

Each face has been digitally altered by combining two or more faces to form a composite.

Source: Langlois and Roggman (1990).

2000; D. M. Buss, 1994). From this perspective, our preference for attractive faces evolved over thousands and thousands of years.

We will have more to say about this possibility in Chapter 11 when we discuss the nature of interpersonal relationships. For now, we will simply note that although we assume attractive people are healthier than are unattractive people, there is little evidence that this is the case (Kalick, Zebrowitz, Langlois, & Johnson, 1998). Nor is there evidence that attractive people possess the many wonderful qualities we assume they possess (Feingold, 1992a). In short, although attractive people are perceived to be better than unattractive people, this is not really so (Diener, Wolsic, & Fujita, 1995). These findings pose problems for the evolutionary model.

A second possibility is that we prefer attractive faces simply because they are more aesthetically appealing than unattractive faces. After all, standards of beauty are not entirely arbitrary. Most everyone agrees that colorful sunsets are prettier than gray ones and that snow-capped mountains are more majestic than arid ones, and these

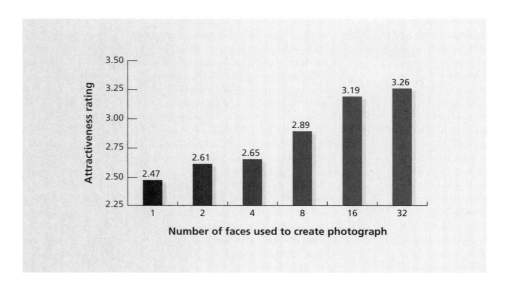

FIGURE 3.4

Judged Attractiveness of Faces Varying in *Averageness*

Attractiveness ratings were higher for photographs comprised of many faces than those comprised of few faces. These findings suggest that "average" facial features are most attractive.

Source: Langlois and Roggman (1990).

preferences bear no relation to reproductive success. Our preference for attractive faces may have a similar aesthetic basis (J. Halberstadt & Rhodes, 2000).

B. Facial Babyishness

Earlier we noted that people with childlike faces are considered more attractive than are people with mature facial features. People with childlike facial features are also presumed to possess childlike personality qualities. To illustrate, Berry and McArthur (1985) had male and female participants view facial photographs of 20 male college students. Afterward, they indicated how kind, warm, honest, naive, and irresponsible they thought each man was. (Notice how these traits are typically associated with immaturity and youth.) Men with babyish facial features were perceived to be kinder, warmer, and more honest and naive than were men with more mature facial features. Follow-up research found that this effect also occurs for women and generalizes across a variety of age, racial, and ethnic groups (Berry & McArthur, 1986; L. Z. McArthur & Berry, 1987; Montepare & Zebrowitz, 1998; Zebrowitz & Collins, 1997; Zebrowitz & Montepare, 1992; Zebrowitz, Montepare, & Lee, 1993).

1. Social Consequences of a Baby Face

Our tendency to assume that people with babyish facial features possess childlike psychological qualities has behavioral consequences. In one study, participants judged the suitability of applicants for several jobs (Zebrowitz, Tenenbaum, & Goldstein, 1991). Baby-faced applicants were favored for jobs requiring warmth and nurturance (e.g., teacher, counselor), whereas mature-faced people were favored for jobs requiring leadership and shrewdness (supervisor, loan officer). Another study investigated how babyish facial features affect courtroom decisions. Using a mock-trial procedure, Berry and Zebrowitz-McArthur (1988) had participants act as judges, sentencing people accused of various crimes. Some of these crimes involved negligent behavior (e.g., failing to report income to the Internal Revenue Service because of poor record keeping), whereas other crimes involved intentional behavior (e.g., evading taxes by falsifying records). Because baby-faced people are viewed as weak and naive, Berry and Zebrowitz-McArthur predicted that they would be less apt to be convicted of an intentional crime than a crime of negligence. This prediction was confirmed. In addition, they found that baby-faced people also received lighter sentences for a negligent offense than for an intentional crime, presumably because people believe they shouldn't be punished for their naiveté.

2. Do Baby-Faced People Really Possess Childlike Personality Traits?

Having read about the link between babyish facial features and perceptions of personality, you may be wondering whether people with babyish facial features actually possess childish personality traits. The best way to test this hypothesis would be to gather ratings of personality by observers who were unaware of the person's facial qualities. Somewhat surprisingly, research has not been conducted in this area. There is, however, evidence that men with babyish facial features regard themselves as being warm and that women with babyish facial features characterize themselves as being physically weak (Berry & Brownlow, 1989). Although the data are not definitive (people may simply apply these stereotypes when judging themselves), they are consistent with the claim that people with babyish facial features possess childlike personality traits.

C. Emotional Expressions in the Human Face

Charles Darwin is best known for his book *On the Origin of Species* (1859), but he wrote another book that has broad significance for social perception. In *The Expression of the Emotions in Man and Animals,* Darwin (1872) asserted that various facial expressions have evolved because they communicate information relevant to the survival of the species. For example, by baring its teeth, a wolf communicates anger and the threat of an attack. Other animals correctly register this emotion and back away. In this manner they avoid fighting and killing one another.

1. Human Displays of Emotion Are Universally Recognized

Darwin believed that facial expressions in humans serve a similar communicative function and that these displays are innate (though modifiable by learning) and universally recognized. To test whether people can reliably recognize emotions from facial expressions, Ekman and colleagues have asked participants to view photographs of people displaying six basic emotional expressions: anger, fear, surprise, disgust, happiness, and sadness (see Figure 3.5). They are then asked to identify the emotion conveyed in each face. People have little trouble identifying which emotion is being expressed, and this agreement occurs across a range of cultures, suggesting that it may have an innate basis (see Ekman, 1972, 1994; Ekman et al., 1987; Frank & Stennett, 2001; Hejmadi, Davidson, & Rozin, 2000).

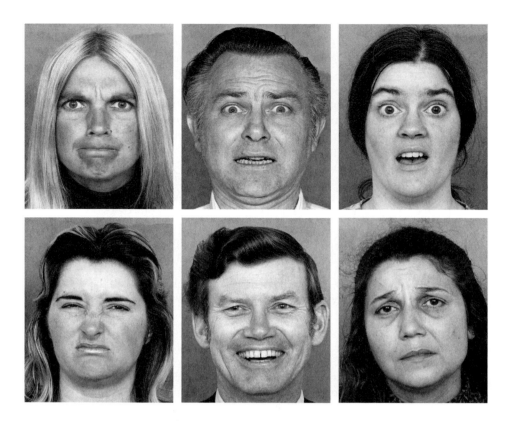

FIGURE 3.5

Six Facial Expressions of Emotion

People in various countries around the world can recognize the emotions being expressed in each face. Top row: anger, fear, surprise. Bottom row: disgust, happiness, sadness.

An investigation by Ekman and Friesen (1971) provided a particularly strong test of this claim. These researchers traveled to a remote village in New Guinea and studied facial recognition of emotions in a visually isolated, preliterate tribe, the South Fore. While listening to an emotion-evoking story (e.g., a father's child has died and he feels sad; a man is looking at something that smells bad), the participants were asked to select a photograph that best represented what the person was feeling. The South Fore had little difficulty with this task, selecting the same emotion photographs that people in literate Western cultures had selected. In a subsequent study, members of the South Fore were asked to show how their faces would look if they were experiencing a variety of emotion-provoking events (e.g., you are angry and about to fight). These expressions were photographed and then shown to Americans. For most of these emotions, the Americans were able to correctly identify the emotional state.

2. Infants Read Facial Expression of Emotion

The universal tendency to recognize facial expressions of emotion suggests that this ability is innate. Research with infants provides further support for this claim. Parent–child communication during infancy occurs largely through nonverbal means, such as facial expressions and vocal tone. By only four months of age, most infants can distinguish various facial expressions of emotion and understand the meaning behind these emotional displays (C. A. Nelson, 1987; Tronick, 1989; Walker-Andrews, 1997).

Campos and colleagues provided a particularly compelling demonstration of this ability (Campos, Barrett, Lamb, Goldsmith, & Sternberg, 1983). In their investigation, 10-month-old infants crawled across a floor that presents a simulated drop-off point (an optical illusion known as the visual cliff). Most infants crossed the visual cliff when their mothers posed a joyful face, but hesitated when their mothers looked angry or fearful. These findings establish that young infants recognize and appreciate the meaning behind various facial displays of emotion.

3. People Are Adept at Recognizing Anger

Recall that Darwin believed that the ability to recognize facial expressions of emotion is adaptive in that it aids survival. Because anger often signals danger, people should be especially adept at recognizing this emotional expression. Hansen and Hansen (1988) found that this is the case. These researchers had participants view a crowd of faces that contained a mixture of happy, angry, or neutral faces. Supporting the claim that people are attuned to identify anger, the participants identified angry faces more quickly and more accurately than faces that were happy or neutral (see also Öhman, Lundqvist, & Esteves, 2001).

Physical Properties of an Angry Face. Another line of research has examined the physical properties of an angry face. Anecdotal evidence suggests that curved, rounded shapes (e.g., the halo of an angel) connote virtue and benign intent, and that angular, pointed shapes (e.g., the face of the devil) connote immorality and malevolent intent. In a test of these links, Aronoff, Barclay, and Stevenson (1988) examined facial masks from various non-Western societies. They found that diagonal, angular, and linear shapes were prominently represented in masks of threatening facial expressions. In a second study, these investigators had participants rate various pairs of geometric shapes, shown in Figure 3.6. Diagonal, angular, and linear shapes were judged to be more threatening (cruel, dangerous); powerful (brave, strong); and active (energetic, excitable) than were less angular, more rounded shapes. This effect was particularly prominent for downward-pointing angular lines, such as those shown in pairs 2, 3, and 4.

Physically Abused Children and Anger Recognition. Although the ability to recognize angry faces may be adaptive for just about everyone, children who are victims of physical abuse seem to be especially attuned to angry faces. In one study, Pollak and Sinha (2002) had eight-year-old children who either were or were not victims of physical abuse view images of a human face displaying one of four emotions: happiness, anger, sadness, or fear. The faces were initially blurred and then became more and more focused until the image could be clearly seen. The children were asked to identify which emotion the person was experiencing, and the investigators recorded the amount of perceptual information that was needed in order to make this recognition.

Figure 3.7 shows some of the findings from this investigation. Although the two groups did not differ in their ability to recognize happiness and fear, physically abused children needed less perceptual information to recognize anger and more information

FIGURE 3.6

Diagonality as a Cue for Anger and Threat

Within each pair, participants judged the diagonal, angular shape on the left to be more threatening than the circular, rounded shape on the right.

Source: Aronoff, Barclay, & Stevenson (1988).

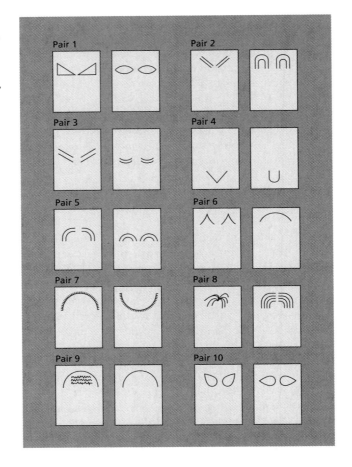

to recognize sadness than did children who were not victims of abuse. This finding makes an important point about facial recognition of anger. Even though this ability seems to have an innate basis, it is also influenced by learning. Children who are abused develop a highly attuned capacity to recognize anger, either because they have seen it all too frequently or because their ability to correctly identify anger helps them avoid further abuse. At the same time, they seem to develop a collateral inability to recognize sadness, perhaps because they are so vigilant for anger that they confuse these two negative emotions (see also Pollak, & Kistler, 2002; Pollak, Cicchetti, Hornung, & Reed, 2000).

D. Section Summary

In this section we have reviewed a variety of evidence suggesting that first impressions have an innate, perceptual basis. Beginning early in life, we prefer to look at attractive faces and believe that attractive people possess culturally valued qualities. We also assume that people with babyish facial features have childlike personalities. Finally, people all over the world are able to recognize facial expressions of emotion, and certain physical properties, such as circularity and angularity, convey emotional

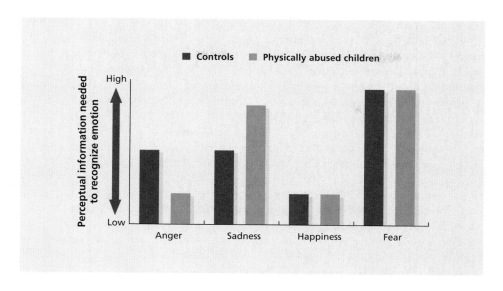

FIGURE 3.7

Perceptual Information Needed to Recognize Four Facial Expressions of Emotion among Physically Abused Children and a Control Group of Nonabused Children

Physically abused children needed less perceptual information to correctly identify anger, but more information to correctly identify sadness. The two groups did not differ in their ability to recognize happiness and fear. These findings suggest that physically abused children have learned to quickly recognize cues associated with anger.

Source: Pollak and Sinha (2002).

information. It is possible to develop separate explanations for each of these findings, but it is more parsimonious (see Chapter 1) to assume that people possess innate tendencies to associate particular psychological qualities with particular facial features.

Does this mean that culture and learning play no role in shaping social perception? Not at all. Cultures determine which qualities a pretty person is thought to possess, and cultures have different norms regarding the events that trigger particular emotions and how these emotions are displayed (Eid & Diener, 2001; Mesquita & Frijda, 1992; J. A. Russell, 1991, 1994; Scherer & Wallbott, 1994). This is undoubtedly one reason why people are most adept at judging facial expressions of emotion for people of their own nationality, region, or culture (Elfenbein & Ambady, 2002). The safest conclusion to be drawn from this research is that although a good deal of social perception is shaped by culture and learning, some aspects of social perception are innate and do not require learning.

II. Nonverbal Behaviors

The movie actor Tom Cruise often walks in a manner that exudes confidence and cockiness. His behavior underscores just how much our impressions of others are influenced by nonverbal communication (DePaulo & Friedman, 1998). **Nonverbal communication** encompasses all the ways people communicate information through nonverbal means. This information is communicated not only through facial expressions but also through (1) kinesic cues (such as body posture and the way people move); (2) paralinguistic cues (including tone of voice, pitch, volume, and rate of speech); and (3) proxemic cues (for example, how far apart people stand when they interact with one another) (Berry, 1991; Borkenau & Liebler, 1992, 1993; Gifford, 1994; Krauss, Freyberg, & Morsella, 2002; Montepare & Zebrowitz-McArthur, 1988).

Movement seems to be particularly important. In an early investigation, Heider and Simmel (1944) had participants watch a brief animated film in which three geometric figures—a large triangle, a smaller triangle, and a circle—move around a large rectangle. When asked to describe what they had seen, very few participants restricted their descriptions to the movement of geometric shapes. Instead, they reported that the large triangle seemed to be an aggressive male who was bullying the feminine circle. Characterizations like these suggest that angular shapes and movements are viewed as aggressive and masculine, and that rounded shapes and movements are viewed as feminine and passive (see also, Berry, Misovich, Kean, & Baron, 1992; Kassin, 1982; Wehrle, Kaiser, Schmidt, & Scherer, 2000).

Aronoff, Woike, and Hyman (1992) followed up these findings by examining how movement and posture convey anger in numerous ballets. Ballets attempt to tell a story through movement and shape, and Aronoff and colleagues hypothesized that diagonal shapes and displays are used more by threatening characters, such as villains and tyrants, than by warmer, more sympathetic characters, such as heroes and lovers (see Figure 3.8). This proved to be the case. Surveying more than 20 different ballets, Aronoff and colleagues found that threatening characters used diagonal poses and movements nearly three times as often as did warm characters, and that warm characters used round poses and movements nearly four times as often as did threatening characters.

FIGURE 3.8

Ballet Movements and Poses That Vary According to Their Angularity and Roundness

A content analysis of 20 ballets revealed that circular poses and movements were used more by heroes than villains, but angular poses and movements were used more by villains than heroes. These findings are consistent with evidence that circular shapes communicate warmth and safety, but diagonal shapes communicate fear and danger.

Source: Aronoff, Woike, and Hyman (1992).

A. Cultural Differences in Nonverbal Communication

Of course, the meaning of many nonverbal behaviors varies from culture to culture (Axtell, 1991). For example, in North America, nodding your head up and down signifies yes and shaking your head from side to side means no. In other parts of the world, such as India and some parts of Africa, these nonverbal behaviors mean just the opposite. Similarly, North Americans indicate agreement by raising a thumb upward while keeping the rest of their fingers in a fist. In Japan, this gesture refers to one's boyfriend and in Iran it conveys an obscenity. Americans traveling abroad need to be mindful of these cultural differences lest they be misunderstood.

Although cultural variation is the rule for many nonverbal behaviors, some nonverbal behaviors are universally understood. Consider eye gaze. In humans and other primates, eye gaze is a universal sign of dominance: Making eye contact signifies power, and averting eye contact conveys submissiveness (Eibl-Eibesfeldt, 1989; Kleinke, 1986). This effect is universal, but culture influences when eye contact is used. In Western cultures, people strive to appear dominant, so they make eye contact when greeting one another. In Eastern cultures, people strive to appear polite and respectful, so they avoid making eye contact when greeting one another. The meaning of eye contact is universal, but rules regarding its display vary across cultures.

B. Gender Differences in Nonverbal Behavior

Even within a culture, people differ in how they display and interpret nonverbal behaviors. Gender differences in nonverbal behavior have received a great deal of attention in the popular press and academic circles. Although the differences are not always large, many studies have found that women are more nonverbally expressive and submissive than are men (J. A. Hall, 1984). For example, compared to men, women tend to smile and nod more during social interactions and are less apt to use eye contact to express social power.

1. Gender Differences in Social Status

Some theorists believe that inequities in social status explain gender differences in nonverbal behavior (e.g., Henley, 1977). According to **social role theory** (Eagly, 1987), gender differences in social roles underlie gender differences in behavior. This theory predicts that gender differences in nonverbal communications of power will be eliminated if status differences are eradicated, and even reversed if women are placed in positions of higher social status than are men.

Research on visual dominance lends some support to this position. When two people are interacting, visual dominance is assessed by calculating the percentage of time people spend looking at a person while they are speaking, relative to the time they spend looking at a person while they are listening. A visual dominance ratio of less than 1.00 (less time spent looking when speaking than when listening) indicates social submissiveness, whereas a visual dominance ratio of 1.00 or more signals high social dominance. Using this index, several studies have found that women generally display less visual dominance than men do (Dovidio & Ellyson, 1985).

To see whether this gender difference depends on differences in social power, Dovidio and colleagues had mixed-sex couples engage in a conversation (Dovidio,

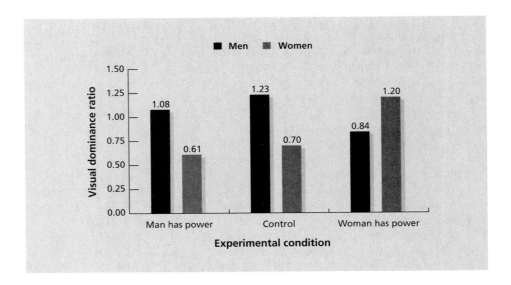

FIGURE 3.9

Visual Dominance, Gender, and Power

Men exhibited more visual dominance when they had power and in the control condition, but women displayed more visual dominance when they had power. These findings suggest that gender differences in visual dominance depend on power.

Source: Dovidio, Ellyson, Keating, Heltman, and Brown (1988).

Ellyson, Keating, Heltman, & Brown, 1988). In one experimental condition, the male was given the power to evaluate the female's performance; in another condition, the female was given the power to evaluate the male's performance; and in a final, control condition, neither partner was explicitly placed in a position of power. Figure 3.9 displays visual dominance ratios as a function of these experimental variations. Replicating prior research, men displayed more visual dominance than women in the control condition and in the condition where they had been placed in a position of power. However, women were more visually dominant than men when they had been given power (see also Dovidio, Brown, Heltman, Ellyson, & Keating, 1988; Snodgrass, 1985, 1992).

Despite the clarity of these findings, power and status differences may not fully explain gender differences in nonverbal behavior. In a more recent study, J. A. Hall and Friedman (1999) videotaped employees of a Boston-area company while they interacted with one another. Women displayed greater signs of nonverbal deference than did men, and this occurred even when women of high status within the organization interacted with men of low status. One conclusion to be drawn from these findings is that power and status differences contribute to, but do not completely explain, gender differences in nonverbal behavior.

2. Gender Differences and Socialization

Why did female executives exhibit deferential nonverbal behaviors when talking to men of lower status? J. A. Hall and Friedman (1999) suggested that this occurred because of socialization practices. Beginning early in life, females are socialized

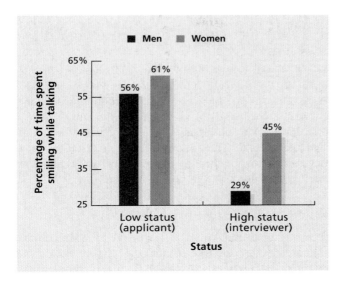

FIGURE 3.10

Frequency of Smiling as a Function of Gender and Social Status

The data show three effects: Low-status applicants smiled more than high-status interviewers; women smiled more than men; and the tendency for women to smile more than men was especially pronounced in the high status (interviewer) condition. Because women were especially sensitive when they didn't need to be, these findings suggest that socialization rather than social roles explains gender differences in deference behavior.

Source: Deutsch (1990).

to be more interpersonally sensitive, attentive, and responsive than are men. These differences manifest themselves in nonverbal behavior and emerge even when women occupy positions of high status usually reserved for men. Unlike social role theory, which predicts that sex differences will disappear once social status is taken into account, the socialization model predicts that sex differences will remain even when men and women occupy similar positions of social status and power.

Deutsch (1990) tested these predictions by examining how often men and women smiled when talking to one another. Previous research had established that women smile more often during conversations than men do (A. G. Halberstadt & Saitta, 1987; J. A. Hall, 1984; LaFrance, Hecht, & Paluck, 2003). To see whether differences in social status account for this effect, Deutsch randomly assigned some participants to act as job applicants (low status) and others to act as job interviewers (high status). She then noted the percentage of time each person smiled during the job interview.

Figure 3.10 shows the data, and three findings are of interest: (1) the low-status applicants smiled more than did the high-status interviewers; (2) women smiled more than men; and (3) women were especially apt to smile more than men when they had high status. The most likely explanation for this finding is that women are socialized to be more interpersonally sensitive than men, and these differences are most apt to manifest themselves when social roles *don't require* interpersonal sensitivity and deference.

C. Accuracy in Sending and Reading Nonverbal Messages

Nonverbal behaviors are used not only to communicate power and status but also to regulate the flow of social interaction. For example, during a conversation, people who have come to the end of their speaking turn gesture less often, speak more softly, and look toward the other person. These nonverbal displays signal that the other person's speaking turn is about to begin. In order to be effective, these nonverbal behaviors must be clearly conveyed and understood. The following section discusses how accurately people send (or convey) information through nonverbal behaviors and how accurately they decode (or receive) information from nonverbal cues.

1. Expressiveness: The Ability to Accurately *Send* Nonverbal Messages

Two factors influence the success of nonverbal communication: The sender's ability to effectively convey information (called **expressiveness**) and the receiver's ability to accurately decode the sender's intent (called **perceptiveness**). Both are important, but the sender's expressiveness plays a more important role than does a receiver's perceptiveness (Kenny & Le Voie, 1984; Snodgrass, Hecht, & Ploutz-Snyder, 1998). Expressive people are lively and animated, and they use their energy to convey information about what they are thinking and feeling. This ability puts us at ease, and we enjoy being in their company (H. S. Friedman, Riggio, & Casella, 1988; Gallaher, 1992; Riggio & Friedman, 1986). In fact, highly expressive physicians have more patients than those who are low in expressiveness (DiMatteo, Hays, & Prince, 1986), and highly expressive teachers receive higher teacher ratings and are more effective than teachers who are low in expressiveness (Abrami, Leventhal, & Perry, 1982; Bernieri, 1991).

2. Perceptiveness: The Ability to Accurately *Read* Nonverbal Messages

Individuals also differ in their ability to accurately read nonverbal cues. Brunswik's (1955) classic model of visual perception provides a context for understanding these effects. Brunswik argued that people use a variety of cues when forming a perception of a visual object. Some of these cues provide valid information about the object's nature, whereas others do not. Brunswik uses the term *cue utilization* to describe the cues people use to form a perceptual judgment and the term *ecological validity* to distinguish cues that provide valid information from those that do not (see also Grahe & Bernieri, 2002; D. J. Reynolds & Gifford, 2001).

Meiran and colleagues applied this model to social perception (Meiran, Netzer, Netzer, Itzhak, & Rechnitz, 1994). These researchers showed participants various photographs of mixed-sex couples seated together and asked them to indicate whether the couples were romantically involved. The pictures varied with respect to how closely the people were sitting to one another, whether or not they were looking at one another, and whether they were dressed alike. To assess ecological validity, Meiran and colleagues examined the correlation between these characteristics and the couple's true romantic status; to assess cue utilization, they examined the correlation between these characteristics and the participants' judgments of the couples' romantic status. The results showed that participants gave disproportionate weight to qualities with low ecological validity. In particular, they believed that the similarity of the couple predicted their relationship status, when in fact it did not. These findings suggest that people who misread nonverbal behaviors pay too much attention to invalid cues (rather than not enough attention to valid cues).

3. Gender Differences in Expressiveness and Perceptiveness

Women are generally more nonverbally expressive than are men, and both men and women have an easier time knowing what women are feeling (DePaulo, 1992; J. A. Hall, 1984; Kring & Gordon, 1998; Rosenthal & DePaulo, 1979). Interestingly, these differences do not arise because women experience emotions more deeply than men. When physiological indicators of emotion such as heart rate, respiration, and skin conductance levels are assessed, men and women do not differ. Nor do women report experiencing emotions more deeply than men (LaFrance & Banaji, 1992). Instead, it appears that women are simply more apt to express the emotions they are feeling.

Women also tend to be more perceptive than men (DePaulo, Epstein, & Wyer, 1993; DePaulo & Friedman, 1998; J. A. Hall, 1978; Zuckerman, Hall, DeFrank, & Rosenthal, 1976). This advantage is most pronounced when it comes to reading facial expressions and is less evident when it comes to reading other forms of nonverbal behavior, such as body movements, posture, and tone of voice (Rosenthal & DePaulo, 1979). To understand these differences, we must first examine how people decide whether someone is telling the truth or not. This is the issue we consider in the next section of this chapter.

D. Detecting Deception

> No mortal can keep a secret. If his lips are silent, he chatters with his fingertips; betrayal oozes out of him at every pore. (Freud, 1905, p. 94)

In January 1998, President Bill Clinton took to the airwaves in an attempt to save his embattled presidency. Sitting calmly and looking relaxed, Clinton stared directly into the camera and denied having had sexual relations with a White House intern, Monica Lewinsky. Millions of Americans watched the declaration, wondering whether Clinton was telling the truth.

Although the stakes are rarely so high, the task TV viewers faced that day is a common one. All of us have occasion to discern who is being truthful and who is not. According to one estimate, people tell two lies per day, doing so in one of every four social interactions (DePaulo, Kashy, Kirkendol, Wyer, & Epstein, 1996). Most of these lies are trivial (e.g., friends smile disingenuously while claiming to adore someone's new outfit), but some are far more consequential (e.g., people lie about their sexual histories to their romantic partners). How good are people at distinguishing those who are being authentic from those who are being phony?

Researchers have developed a variety of strategies for answering this question. In many studies, participants watch videotapes of people expressing a positive or negative reaction to a stimulus, such as a film or another person. Some of these reactions are genuine (the person is smiling while watching a comedy) and others are false (the person is smiling while watching a gory scene of death and destruction). The participants are then asked to decide whether the person's expressions are authentic or fake.

Accuracy rates in these studies are generally modest, averaging around 60 percent (DePaulo, 1994). Since guessing would yield an accuracy rate of 50 percent, it seems that people are barely able to distinguish authentic displays of emotion from inauthentic ones. Moreover, this occurs even when people are highly confident that they know who is being genuine and who is feigning (DePaulo, Charlton, Cooper, Lindsay, & Muhlenbruck, 1997).

These findings run counter to many people's intuitions, leading researchers to wonder whether the findings are valid. For example, in most of the research on detecting deception, people judge the honesty of strangers. Perhaps they are more accurate when judging the truthfulness of their friends and romantic partners. Although some studies have found that this is true (e.g., D. E. Anderson, DePaulo, & Ansfield, 2002; Fleming, Darley, Hilton, & Kojetin, 1990), most have not. People are more confident in their ability to detect the truth from those they are close to, but they are usually no more accurate at detecting their friends' and loved ones' deception than strangers' (DePaulo, 1994; Swann & Gill, 1997).

Perhaps some people are better at detecting deception than others. As you read earlier, women are better able to decode the meanings behind some nonverbal behaviors, and to know what another person is thinking and feeling (Thomas & Fletcher, 2003). Are they also better at detecting deception? Interestingly, the answer is no. In general, women are no more skilled than men at distinguishing truth from lies (DePaulo, 1994; Zuckerman, DePaulo, & Rosenthal, 1981). Here's one way to think about these two findings: If a person is genuinely trying to convey an emotion, women are better at identifying this emotion than are men. However, if the person is feigning an emotion, women are no better than men at detecting this deceit.

1. Formal Training and the Ability to Detect Deception

Are people who have been trained to detect deception more proficient than those who have not received training? Ekman and O'Sullivan (1991) conducted an ambitious study to answer this question. In the first part of the study, student nurses were videotaped while watching one of two films. One film portrayed scenes of natural beauty designed to elicit positive emotion; the other portrayed a gruesome surgical procedure designed to elicit negative emotion. Regardless of which film they were actually watching, the nurses were instructed to act as if they were watching a pleasant scene (under the pretext that a nurse must learn to control negative emotions in order to function effectively in an operating room).

Ekman and O'Sullivan then showed videotapes of the nurses' reactions to people from different occupations, and asked them to determine whether the nurse was truly experiencing positive emotions or was faking. Figure 3.11 shows that only Secret Service agents achieved high levels of accuracy at the task. Federal polygraphers, police officers, judges, and psychiatrists, who are routinely called on to distinguish truth from deception, were no better at judging deception than were ordinary citizens (see also DePaulo & Pfeifer, 1986; Kraut & Poe, 1980). Fortunately, follow-up research paints a more optimistic picture. Ekman, O'Sullivan, and Frank (1999) found that Central Intelligence Agency employees and clinical psychologists with an interest in detecting deception could distinguish truth from lies, suggesting that specialized training can enhance a person's ability to detect deception.

2. Why People Are Unable to Detect Deception

Even the best deception detectors make many errors. Why? For one thing, people are too trusting. Even when told that half the people they are watching are apt to be lying, people estimate that far fewer than half are actually doing so (D. E. Anderson, DePaulo, & Ansfield, 2002; DePaulo, Stone, & Lassiter, 1985; O'Sullivan, 2003).

People also pay attention to the wrong information. Table 3.1 shows the relation between various behaviors and deception (ecological validity in Brunswik's model) and people's judgments about who is lying and who is telling the truth (cue utilization in

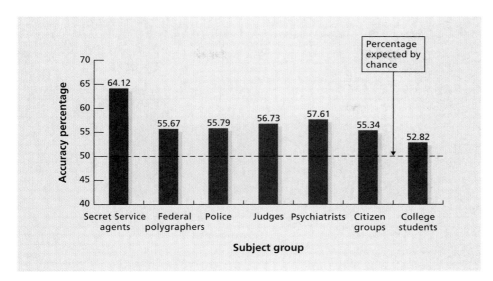

FIGURE 3.11

Accuracy at Distinguishing Truth from Lies

Only Secret Service agents performed at levels that were significantly greater than chance (see dotted line).

Source: Ekman and O'Sullivan (1991).

Brunswik's model). On the one hand, people believe that eye gaze (shifty glances and a failure to make eye contact), smiling, and postural shifts reveal who is lying, when these behaviors are actually unrelated to deception. On the other hand, people do not believe that adaptors such as scratching, grooming, or touching the hair or face signify lying, but actually they do (DePaulo et al., 2003).

Our intuitions are more accurate with respect to auditory cues. We correctly believe that liars hesitate while speaking, talk in high-pitched voices, and make more speech

TABLE 3.1 Behaviors That Reveal Deception

	Do People Assume This Behavior Predicts Deception?	Does This Behavior Predict Deception?
FACIAL CUES		
Eye gaze	✓	
Smiling	✓	
BODY LANGUAGE		
Postural shifts	✓	
Adaptors (e.g., scratching, touching, or grooming behavior)		✓
AUDITORY CUES		
Response latency	✓	
Speech rate	✓	
Speech hesitations	✓	✓
Vocal pitch	✓	✓
Speech errors	✓	✓

Source: DePaulo, Stone, and Lassiter (1985).

FIGURE 3.12

Accuracy at Detecting Deception as a Function of Facial and Body Cues

Participants were least accurate at detecting deception when they only had access to facial cues and were most accurate when they couldn't see the face at all.

Source: Zuckerman, DePaulo, and Rosenthal (1981).

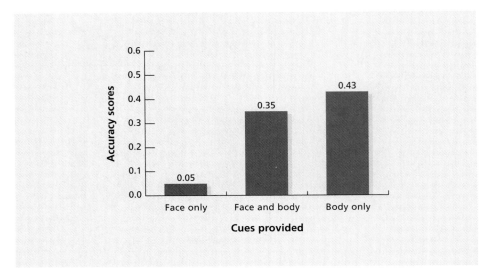

errors than truth tellers (DePaulo et al., 2003; DePaulo, Rosenthal, Rosenkrantz, & Green, 1982; Newman, Pennebaker, Berry, & Richards, 2003; Vrij, Edward, & Bull, 2001). By paying close attention to these auditory cues, you can help improve your ability to detect deception (DePaulo, Lassiter, & Stone, 1982; K. Fiedler & Walka, 1993).

3. Nonverbal Leakage

Research on **nonverbal leakage** provides a framework for understanding why adaptors and some auditory cues reveal deception (Ekman & Friesen, 1969, 1974; Rosenthal & DePaulo, 1979). This framework proposes that deception is most clearly revealed through behaviors that are difficult to control (called leaky behaviors). Facial expressions are relatively easy to control, so they are not very informative about whether or not a person is telling the truth. Body language and posture are intermediate in leakiness. People do have control over their bodily movements, but usually don't think to alter them when telling a lie (Ekman & Friesen, 1974). Finally, auditory cues, such as speech hesitations, vocal pitch, and speech errors constitute the leakiest channels because they are the most difficult to control.

Research on nonverbal leakage has revealed an interesting finding. Because facial expressions are easy to control, people are actually *less* adept at detecting deception when they see a person's face. To illustrate, consider the data shown in Figure 3.12. These data come from a meta-analysis (see Chapter 1) of numerous studies concerning people's ability to detect deception (Zuckerman, DePaulo, & Rosenthal, 1981). In these investigations, participants who had access to facial cues were actually *less* able to distinguish truth from lies than those who did not have access to facial cues. When it comes to catching a liar, then, it is better to ignore the person's face altogether (for related research, see D. J. Reynolds & Gifford, 2001).

There is, however, one exception to this rule. Genuine smiles of enjoyment can be distinguished from feigned ones. A 19th-century French anatomist, Duchenne de Boulogne, first made this observation. Duchenne noted that a facial muscle (the orbicularis oculi) produces crow's-feet wrinkles in a genuine smile but not in a posed smile. Supporting de Boulogne's claim, Ekman and colleagues found that authentic smiles of enjoyment are visibly and physiologically distinct from fake ones (Ekman, Davidson,

& Friesen, 1990; Ekman, Friesen, & O'Sullivan, 1988; Ekman, O'Sullivan, Friesen, & Scherer, 1991), and that people use this information to distinguish true smiles of enjoyment from contrived ones (Frank, Ekman, & Friesen, 1993; Gosselin, Kirouac, & Doré, 1995).

Perhaps you are wondering how these findings square with evidence that a smile doesn't reveal deception. There is an answer. People can easily smile when they lie, so whether they are smiling is not a good indicator of whether they are telling the truth. However, if they do smile, you may be able to distinguish a genuine smile from a feigned one by focusing on the skin around the eyes. If the person has a crinkle around the eyes, he or she is probably genuinely enjoying the moment or telling the truth.

4. Polygraph Tests

If people are usually inefficient at detecting deception, might machines be more accurate? Many people think so. Polygraphs, or lie detectors, are often used in business, government, and legal settings to identify people who are lying. During a polygraph test, respondents are asked a series of questions while physiological indicators of arousal such as breathing rate, heart rate, and skin conductivity are assessed. Allegedly, respondents show greater physiological reactivity when lying than when answering questions truthfully.

Despite their widespread use, the validity of polygraph tests has been questioned (Saxe, Dougherty, & Cross, 1985). The biggest problem is that many people who are telling the truth fail the test, an outcome psychologists call a *false positive*. To illustrate the magnitude of this problem, consider that industry proponents boast a 95 percent accuracy rate for polygraph tests. As Senator Edward Kennedy noted in a congressional debate on the matter, this means that if 1 million people are given the test, 50,000 innocent people will be judged to be lying.

Compounding this problem is the fact that some guilty people pass the exam. In fact, the outcome of the test may simply depend on whether or not the respondent believes the test is valid. Respondents who doubt the test's validity have little difficulty staying calm when questioned about dishonest activities (Saxe, 1994; Saxe, Dougherty, & Cross, 1985). For all of these reasons, the U.S. Congress and state and federal courts have restricted the use of polygraph tests in business and legal settings.

What, then, can we conclude about our ability to detect deception? People are able to detect deception, but there is much room for improvement. Moreover, confidence is unrelated to accuracy and, while formal training helps, even highly accomplished detectors make mistakes. Finally, polygraph machines are not infallible either. Truth, it seems, is often hard to see, and we should all be cautious when deciding who is telling the truth and who is not.

III. Cognitive Processes

To this point, you have learned how various physical factors and nonverbal behaviors influence the judgments you make about other people. These factors are assumed to affect your impressions in a bottom-up fashion. **Bottom-up processing** involves judgments that are based on data rather than on inference. As applied to matters of social perception, this perspective assumes that you directly perceive features of the physical world and that these perceptions directly influence your impressions (Gibson, 1979; McArthur & Baron, 1983).

FIGURE 3.13

Leonardo da Vinici's
Mona Lisa

Our perception of whether
Mona Lisa is smiling or
smirking depends on the
information we have
regarding the type of
person she is. In this case,
our perception represents
a top-down, schema-driven
process.

Credit: Leonardo da Vinci, Mona
Lisa, Louvre, Paris, France. Photo:
Scala/Art Resource.

There is, however, another side to the impression formation process, one that is
more cognitive than perceptual. In **top-down processing,** prior knowledge guides
your perception (Bruner, 1957). What you see depends on what you expect to see.
An easy way to understand these processes is to consider the facial expression in
Leonardo da Vinci's *Mona Lisa* (see Figure 3.13). Is she smiling or is she smirking? The facial expression itself is ambiguous and leaves room for interpretation.
If you knew that Mona Lisa was a happy, carefree woman, you would probably
infer that she is smiling. If, however, you knew she was cynical and rather dour,
you would probably assume that she is smirking. In short, your perception is an
interpretation that depends on what you already know about Mona Lisa's personality and demeanor.

Psychologists refer to such knowledge as a person's schema. As first discussed in
Chapter 2, schemas are hypothetical cognitive structures. They represent organized
knowledge about the world and they influence the way we process information. People have schemas about many different things. For example, you probably have a
schema about baseball. You know the rules of the game, the object of the game, and
the strategies teams use to achieve their goals. Without such a schema, watching a
baseball game would be a welter of confusion. You would wonder what the men were

doing with the stick and how come they were running around. With a schema, it's all comprehensible.

People also use schemas to organize their social world, and three schemas are especially relevant to the impression formation process. **Stereotypes** are schemas about the qualities that characterize members of a social group. To illustrate, according to a common stereotype, people who own Apple computers are nonconforming. Right or wrong, these stereotypes function as schemas and influence the judgments we form about a person. If we meet a person who owns an Apple computer, we assume the person is also an iconoclast. An **implicit personality theory** is another type of schema. It represents the pairing of two or more trait terms. For example, you may believe that extraverts are adventurous or that introverts are studious. A **halo effect** is a special kind of implicit personality theory (W. H. Cooper, 1981). It occurs when we assume that positive traits go together in people. The "what is beautiful is good" stereotype is a halo effect. Once we know that someone is attractive, we assume that he or she possesses other positive attributes and traits.

A. Cognitive Effects of Schemas

Schemas don't have a material existence. They are hypothetical cognitive structures, not anatomical ones. We infer their presence by studying their influence. Three cognitive effects are particularly important: Schemas (1) determine what we notice, (2) guide our interpretation of events, and (3) influence our memory.

1. Schemas Guide Attention

A first consequence of schemas is that they guide our attention. All else being equal, we are especially apt to notice information that fits a schema. If you've ever been on a diet and paid close attention to what other people were eating, you have experienced this effect. Your schema guided your attention.

Schemas can have even more dramatic effects when used repeatedly. People who have highly developed schemas in a domain of expertise automatically notice more schema-relevant details than do novices. When visiting a restaurant, a food critic is apt to pay closer attention to the decor, the service, and the way the meal is presented and prepared than is the average patron. In more general terms, we can say that well-developed schemas allow us to process information more thoroughly, efficiently, and rapidly than we could otherwise do.

Information that violates our expectancies is especially apt to grab our attention. Having been to a restaurant many times, you probably don't notice how the waiter is standing when he takes your order. But you would most certainly pay attention if he had been on stilts or was standing on his head. These behaviors violate your expectations about normal restaurant behavior and consequently command your attention.

2. Schemas Aid Understanding

Schemas also help us understand the world. Earlier we noted how difficult it would be to understand a baseball game if we didn't have a schema for the game itself. The same is true for many other ordinary events. In fact, experiencing the world without a schema is a bit like listening to people speak an unfamiliar foreign language; often times we can't tell where one thought ends and where another begins, and we struggle to make sense of what is being said. We experience no such difficulty, however, once we know the language.

Bransford and Johnson (1972) provided a compelling demonstration of this point. In their study, participants listened while an experimenter read the following passage aloud.

> The procedure is actually very simple. First you arrange items into different groups. Of course, one pile may be sufficient depending on how much there is to do. If you have to go somewhere else due to lack of facilities that is the next step, otherwise, you are pretty well set. It is important not to overdo things. That is, it is better to do too few things at once than too many. In the short run this may not seem important but complications can easily arise. A mistake can be expensive as well. At first the whole procedure will seem complicated. Soon, however, it will become just another facet of life. It is difficult to foresee any end to the necessity for this task in the immediate future, but then one can never tell. After the procedure is completed one arranges the materials into different groups again. Then they can be put into their appropriate places. Eventually they will be used once more and the whole cycle will then have to be repeated. However, that is part of life.

Did you find this passage difficult to understand? Most people do, if they are not given some prior knowledge. In contrast, people told the passage is about washing clothes have little difficulty comprehending it. That's because everything makes sense once your "doing laundry" schema is activated.

Social behaviors are particularly hard to interpret without a schema. Consider that a slap on the back can be viewed as a friendly greeting or an act of aggression. Your interpretation will depend, in large part, on which schema you use to process the event. If you think the backslapper is a jovial, fun-loving type of person, you regard the behavior as a lusty sign of affection; if you think the backslapper is a belligerent bully, you will probably view the behavior as an act of antagonism.

In some cases, schemas can lead us to interpret the same behavior in opposite ways. Suppose you saw a young man helping an elderly woman take her groceries inside. If you think he is an honest young man, you would probably interpret his behavior as an act of helpfulness and like him more. If, however, you think he is disreputable, you would probably construe his behavior as an act of deceit and like him less. In this situation, your schema acted as an interpretive structure, guiding the meaning you give to the event and your emotional reaction (Dunning & Sherman, 1997).

A study by Darley and Gross (1983) shows the power of this effect. These researchers led participants to believe that a fourth-grade student named Hannah probably had high academic ability (positive expectancy condition) or low academic ability (negative expectancy condition). Some participants then watched a videotape of Hannah trying to solve various intellectual problems. The tape was ambiguous with respect to whether it demonstrated high or low ability, as Hannah's performance contained a mixture of success and failure. Finally, all participants rated Hannah's ability in several academic pursuits (e.g., science, mathematics).

Because a mixed performance provides evidence of both high and low ability, we might expect that participants' schemas would be less important after viewing a mixed performance than after viewing no performance at all. In fact, Figure 3.14 shows that just the opposite occurred. Participants' schemas about Hannah's ability had more of an effect in the mixed performance condition. Why? Consider the situation from the participants' point of view. If you were a participant in that condition, you would have seen Hannah struggling to answer a problem. If you thought she had low ability, you would assume she is stymied and that the material is far beyond her capability. If you thought she had high ability, you would assume that she is being appropriately challenged and will eventually prevail. The behavior is the same, but your interpretation depends on what you think about her ability level. This is what we mean when we

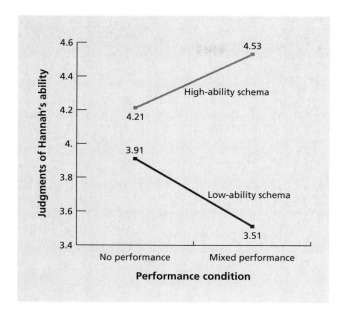

FIGURE 3.14

Judging Hannah's Ability as a Function of Her Task Performance and Beliefs about Her Ability

Participants' schemas shaped their judgments of ability, especially after they had viewed a mixed performance. These data indicate that schemas guide the way we process ambiguous information.

Source: Darley and Gross (1983).

say that our impressions function as schemas, guiding the way we interpret ambiguous information.

3. Schemas Aid Memory

Schemas also improve our memory for information we encounter. In their study, Bransford and Johnson (1972) found that participants who were told the passage they were about to hear was related to washing clothes recalled more than twice as many details of the passage as did participants who listened without knowing what it was about.

Building on these ideas, social psychologists have studied how schemas influence memory for social information. In one such study (Hamilton, Driscoll, & Worth, 1989), investigators instructed participants to form an impression of a person named Bob. Some of the participants were led to believe that Bob was a friendly or an unfriendly person; others were led to believe he was an intelligent or an unintelligent person. Later, all of the participants read a series of 30 sentences describing Bob's behavior. As shown in Table 3.2, some of the behaviors were congruent with the schema, some were incongruent with the schema, and some were unrelated to the schema (i.e., schema-irrelevant). Finally, the participants were asked to recall as many of the behaviors as they could.

Figure 3.15 presents some of the results from this investigation. Two findings are noteworthy. First, schema-congruent and schema-incongruent behaviors were remembered better than were behaviors unrelated to a schema. This finding indicates that memory

TABLE 3.2   Illustration of Research Relating Schema to Memory

		BEHAVIOR		
SCHEMA	Bob went to lunch with a friend	Bob refused to say hello to a co-worker when he passed him in the hall	Bob made the dean's list	Bob failed his written driver's exam 3 times
Friendly	Schema-congruent	Schema-incongruent	Schema-irrelevant	Schema-irrelevant
Unfriendly	Schema-incongruent	Schema-congruent	Schema-irrelevant	Schema-irrelevant
Intelligent	Schema-irrelevant	Schema-irrelevant	Schema-congruent	Schema-incongruent
Unintelligent	Schema-irrelevant	Schema-irrelevant	Schema-incongruent	Schema-congruent

Source: Hamilton et al. (1989).

for schema-relevant information is especially good. The data also show that schema-*incongruent* behaviors were recalled more frequently than were schema-congruent ones (see also Hastie & Kumar, 1979; Stangor & McMillan, 1992).

It is interesting to consider why schema-incongruent information is so memorable. One possibility is that participants are trying to make sense of the inconsistency. In their efforts to form a coherent impression of Bob, they puzzle over the discrepant behavior and attempt to resolve the contradiction. This explanation, first suggested by Solomon Asch (1946), derives from principles of Gestalt psychology. As indicated in Chapter 2, Gestalt psychology assumes that perception is directed toward achieving order and coherence (i.e., toward reaching a good Gestalt), and that people find inconsistency aversive and strive to reduce it. In the present context, people may give inconsistent information a good deal of attention in an attempt to reconcile the

FIGURE 3.15

Memory for Schema-Congruent, Schema-Incongruent, and Schema-Irrelevant Information

Memory was better when participants had a schema than when they did not, and schema-incongruent information was particularly well-remembered.

Source: Hamilton et al. (1989).

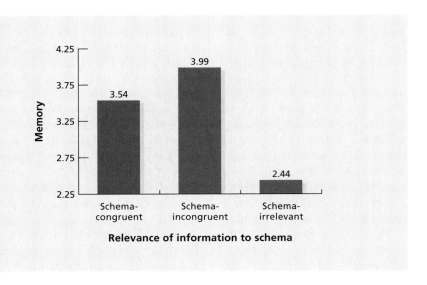

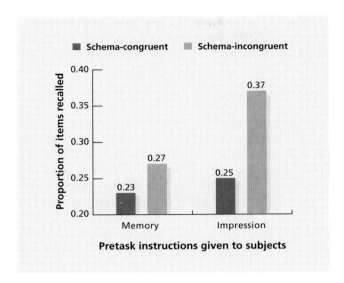

FIGURE 3.16

Memory for Schema-Congruent and Schema-Incongruent Behaviors as a Function of Instructional Set

Schema-incongruent behaviors were especially memorable only when participants were instructed to form an impression of what the person is like. These findings suggest that the greater memorability of schema-incongruent information derives from people's attempts to reconcile the inconsistency with their overall impression.

Source: Wyer and Gordon (1982).

inconsistency with their overall impressions (e.g., why would a smart person fail his driving test three times?). This increased attention leads to increased memory.

This analysis assumes that schema-incongruent information will be especially memorable *only* when participants are attempting to form an impression of what a person is like. Wyer and Gordon (1982) tested this hypothesis by varying the instructions participants received at the outset of their experiment. Some participants were told to form an impression of what the person was like, while others were told simply to remember as much as they could about the person's behaviors. The participants then read a series of behaviors that varied with respect to whether or not they were congruent with the schema they had been given.

Figure 3.16 shows that schema-incongruent information was more memorable *only* when participants had been instructed to form an impression of what the person was like. When participants had been told to simply remember as many behaviors as they could, incongruent behaviors were just as memorable as congruent ones. These findings are consistent with the claim that it is the active attempt to reconcile schema-incongruent information with an overall impression that makes it so memorable (see also Hamilton, Katz, & Leirer, 1980).

In some cases, schematic effects on memory are so strong that they lead people to "remember" things that never happened. To illustrate, imagine that you see a blue-collar worker ordering a drink at a bar. When later asked to recall what the man ordered, you might recall that he ordered a beer, even though he really ordered a glass of wine. These sorts of memory errors (or intrusions, as they are called) occur when people have a well-developed schema for an event. The schema allows us to go beyond the information given, and we wind up confusing what has occurred with what we expected to see (Owens, Bower, & Black, 1979).

B. Schema Activation

Schemas are usually activated in a straightforward way. When you interact with someone you know well, your prior knowledge activates a schema; and when you interact with someone you don't know well, you rely on stereotypes or implicit personality theories. Finally, you may be told what to expect. If your roommate tells you: "My dad is very meticulous, so don't be surprised if he asks you to take off your shoes when you come in the door," you will view this request as an example of cleanliness rather than a religious ritual.

In other cases, schemas are activated by occurrences that have nothing to do with the person you are encountering. Social psychologists call such effects a **priming effect.** A priming effect occurs when a recent experience activates a schema. To illustrate, imagine I tell you I know a person who installed three locks on his apartment door. If you've recently read a story about an increase in local crime, you are likely to view this behavior as quite prudent and reasonable. Conversely, if you've just read a story about paranoia and obsessive-compulsive behavior, you may conclude that the behavior is excessive and rather inappropriate. This example illustrates a priming effect: An extraneous stimulus (a newspaper story) activated a particular schema and, once the schema was activated, you used it to process information.

1. Assimilation Effects Following Schema Activation

In most cases, schema activation produces an assimilation effect. Assimilation effects occur when we interpret ambiguous information to be consistent with the activated schema. An investigation by Srull and Wyer (1979) illustrates this effect. During the first half of the experiment, participants were asked to form three-word sentences from four scrambled words. Half of the participants were given words that, when rearranged, would form sentences conveying hostility (e.g., *leg break arm his*), while the rest of the participants were given words that made up neutral sentences (e.g., *her found knew I*). After engaging in this task, both groups of participants read a story about a character named Donald. In the story, Donald engaged in behaviors that were ambiguous with respect to whether they were motivated by hostility. For example, "Donald refused to pay his rent until his landlord repainted his apartment." This statement could indicate hostility if Donald's apartment had recently been painted, but assertiveness if the apartment had not been painted in a long time despite a promise from the landlord that it would be taken care of. Srull and Wyer hypothesized that participants who had just formed "hostile sentences" would be more apt to interpret Donald's behavior in negative terms than participants who had just formed neutral sentences.

To test their hypothesis, Srull and Wyer had each group of participants rate Donald on a number of negative trait adjectives. Some of these adjectives pertained to hostility (e.g., *hostile, unfriendly*) and others did not (e.g., *boring, selfish*). As you can see in Figure 3.17, Donald was consistently rated more negatively by participants who were primed for hostility than by participants who were not primed for hostility. Srull and Wyer concluded that the scrambled sentences primed different schemas and these schemas influenced the way participants interpreted Donald's behavior (see also Higgins, Rholes, & Jones, 1977).

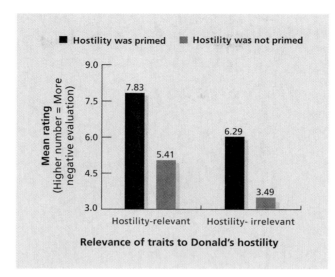

FIGURE 3.17

Priming Effects Influence
Ratings of Hostility

When hostility was primed,
participants rated Donald
more negatively than when
hostility was not primed.
This effect was especially
pronounced for traits
unrelated to hostility,
demonstrating that
activated schemas have
general assimilative effects
on social perception.

Source: Srull and Wyer (1979).

2. Assimilation Effects Following the Unconscious Activation of a Schema

After Srull and Wyer's (1979) findings were published, researchers wondered whether the participants might have guessed that the sentence-fragment task was related to the impression formation task. To examine this issue, Bargh and Pietromonaco (1982) replicated the study using a different priming procedure. In their study, two groups of participants sat at a computer monitor and viewed words related or unrelated to hostility at speeds too fast to allow for conscious recognition. The use of this procedure ensured that participants could not make a connection between the priming manipulation and the rating task. Replicating Srull and Wyer's findings, Bargh and Pietromonaco found that the more hostility-related words participants viewed on the computer, the more negatively they evaluated Donald. Once again, then, the accessibility of a schema guided the participants' interpretation of Donald's behavior.

3. Assimilation Effects for One's Own Behavior

Subsequent research has found that priming effects even influence one's own behavior. Adapting the scrambled-sentence test procedure used by Srull and Wyer (1979), Bargh, Chen, and Burrows (1996) gave participants 30 sets of words to unscramble. Some of the participants worked on words designed to prime politeness (e.g., *respect, honor, considerate, courteous*); some worked on words designed to prime rudeness (e.g., *bold, rude, bother, disturb*); and some worked on a neutral set of words that did not prime either politeness or rudeness. Participants were told to notify the experimenter after they had finished, but when they went to do so, they found him engaged in conversation.

Would participants wait patiently for the conversation to end or rudely interrupt the experimenter to let him know they were finished? Figure 3.18 shows that participants' behavior depended on which schema had recently been activated. Compared to those in the neutral-prime condition, participants in the rudeness-prime condition were more apt to interrupt and those in the politeness-prime condition were less

FIGURE 3.18

Priming Effects on Social Behavior

Compared to participants in the neutral prime condition, participants were more apt to interrupt the experimenter when rudeness had been primed, and less apt to interrupt the experimenter when politeness had been primed.

Source: Bargh, Chen, and Burrows (1996).

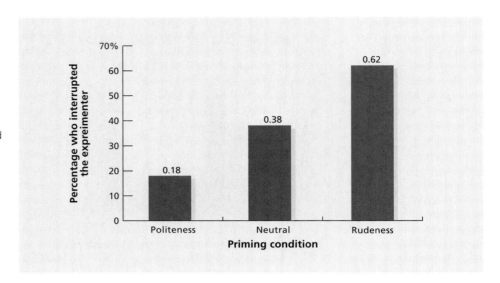

apt to interrupt. These findings establish that priming effects can influence our own behavior (see also Chartrand & Bargh, 1999).

4. Contrast Effects Following Schema Activation

To this point, we have seen that schema activation produces an assimilation effect. If hostility has recently been primed, we interpret ambiguous behaviors to be more hostile than if hostility has not recently been primed. Contrast effects also occur. With a contrast effect, we are less apt to interpret an ambiguous behavior to be consistent with an activated schema. To illustrate, suppose you have recently read a biography of Mother Teresa. If you then read a story about Saddam Hussein, you will probably regard him as more evil than if you had first read a book about Hitler. In cases like these, rather than being assimilated to the activated schema, your judgment is contrasted against the schema.

Research suggests that traits produce assimilation effects but that extreme examples produce contrast effects (DeCoster & Claypool, 2004; Moskowitz & Skurnik, 1999; Stapel, Koomen, & van der Plight, 1997). To illustrate, suppose you see a person solve a puzzle. If the trait term *clever* has recently been primed, you will probably think the person is smart (an assimilation effect). If, however, you have recently been thinking about Albert Einstein, you will probably be less inclined to think the person is smart (a contrast effect). The same thing happens with your own behavior (Dijksterhuis et al., 1998). Thinking about smart people in general tends to improve our performance at a task, but thinking about a particularly smart person, such as Einstein, tends to impair our performance.

C. Overcoming Priming Effects

The research you've been reading about makes it seem as if you are at the mercy of chance events. If a driver happens to cut you off on the way into work, you will interpret a colleague's request to use the copy machine in negative terms and brusquely refuse the person's appeal. This is not always the case, however. For one thing, people possess chronically accessible schemas that can override the influence of recent events. For example, a person who steadfastly believes that people are kind is apt to interpret the request to use the copier in benign terms regardless of which schema has recently been activated (Bargh, Bond, Lombardi, & Tota, 1986; Bargh, Lombardi, & Higgins, 1988). Influences like these are so important that several personality psychologists have built their theory of personality around them (G. A. Kelly, 1955; Lewin, 1935; Mischel, 1973). George Kelly, for example, argued that the way people characteristically interpret events is the most fundamental aspect of their personality, and that these interpretations depend on which schemas the person has developed over the course of his or her lifetime.

We can also deliberately activate or ignore schemas depending on our goals. To illustrate, an employer choosing the best person for the job must be unbiased and unaffected by any schema that just happens to be activated. In situations like these, people are fair-minded and guided by the facts rather than a recently activated schema (Stapel, Koomen, & Zeelenberg, 1998; E. P. Thompson, Roman, Moskowitz, Chaiken, & Bargh, 1994).

IV. Behavioral Confirmation Effects

Imagine you are about to meet someone for the first time when a friend tells you what the person is like. After meeting the person, you find that your friend's description was apt and that this person possessed the qualities described to you. What accounts for your reaction? One possibility is that your friend gave you accurate information and nothing you did influenced the other person's behavior (Jussim, 1989, 1991). There is, however, another, less obvious possibility: Treating your new acquaintance as if he or she was the kind of person your friend described may have forced the person to act in ways that confirmed your expectancy. Social psychologists call this process a **behavioral confirmation effect** (Darley & Fazio, 1980; D. T. Miller & Turnbull, 1986; M. Snyder, 1984).

A. A Four-Stage Model of the Behavioral Confirmation Process

As shown in Figure 3.19, the behavioral confirmation process is comprised of four stages. In the first stage, person A forms an expectancy about person B. This expectancy could be based on firsthand information such as facial features or non-verbal behavior, secondhand information delivered through a third party, or stereotypes that person A may hold. In stage 2, person A acts toward person B on the basis of this expectancy. For example, if person A has heard that person B is snobbish and aloof, person A will be guarded and reserved when speaking with person B. In the third stage, person B responds to person A's behavior. Since person A is acting reserved, person B acts in a cold and unfriendly manner. Finally, person A examines person B's behavior and decides that his or her expectancy has been confirmed. In this manner, person A's expectancy creates a self-fulfilling prophecy: Person A expects person B to be unfriendly and unintentionally behaves in ways that produce the expected behavior.

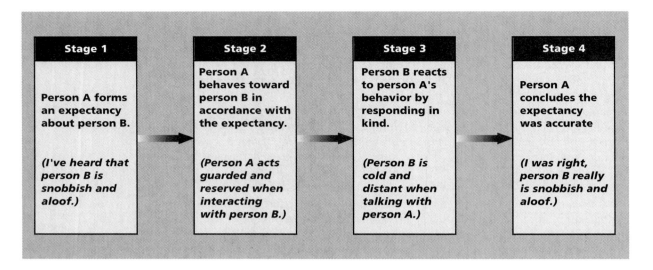

FIGURE 3.19

A Four-Stage Model of the Behavioral Confirmation Processes

Person A expects person B to be snobbish and aloof. Person A then acts toward person B on the basis of this expectancy. Person B reacts to person A's behavior by responding in a similar manner. Person A then concludes that the initial expectancy was correct.

B. Behavioral Confirmation Effects in Action

M. Snyder, Tanke, and Berscheid (1977) first demonstrated behavioral confirmation effects in an experimental setting. These researchers asked previously unacquainted college-age men and women to converse over the telephone. Before the conversation began, the men received a Polaroid snapshot of their telephone partner. The photographs, however, were of completely different women, some of whom were attractive and some of whom were relatively unattractive. After viewing these photographs, the men indicated what they thought their telephone partner would be like by completing a series of rating scales (e.g., How friendly, warm, and sociable do you think your partner will be?). The men then engaged in a 10-minute conversation with their telephone partner.

Stage 1 in the behavioral confirmation process occurs when one person forms an expectancy about another. Snyder and colleagues assumed that their attractiveness manipulation would lead the men to form different expectancies about their conversation partner's personality. This proved to be the case. Consistent with the "what is beautiful is good" stereotype, men who anticipated talking to attractive women expected them to be more sociable, poised, humorous, and socially adept than men expecting to chat with relatively unattractive women.

During stage 2 of the behavioral confirmation process, people act on the basis of their expectancies. To determine whether men's expectancies influenced their behavior, Snyder and colleagues asked participants who were unaware of the experimental conditions to listen to the males' portion of the telephone conversation and rate each man's behavior. As predicted, men who believed they were taking to attractive women were judged to be more outgoing, humorous, and warm on the phone than were men who believed they were talking to unattractive women. Thus, the expectancy they had formed on the basis of the false photographs guided their own behavior.

These behaviors, in term, shaped the women's behavior as well. When judges listened only to the females' portion of the conversation, the women arbitrarily labeled as attractive were judged to be more confident, animated, and outgoing than those arbitrarily labeled as unattractive. Apparently, the women were responding to their conversation partner's behavior. If the man spoke in a warm, unguarded fashion, the woman reciprocated his warmth by also acting open and amiable; however, if he acted cold and aloof, she responded by also acting distant and detached. This constitutes the third stage in the behavioral confirmation process: By altering the way the men behaved, the expectancies created by the attractiveness stereotype produced their own social reality. Finally, although Snyder and colleagues did not ask the males at the end of the experiment whether their expectancies were confirmed (stage 4 in the behavioral confirmation process), subsequent research has found that this occurs (Hilton & Darley, 1985).

Behavioral confirmation effects are not limited to situations in which men talk to attractive or unattractive women. Similar effects are found when women are given expectancies about men's attractiveness (S. M. Anderson & Bem, 1981), and in situations other than get-acquainted conversations. For example, Snyder and Swann (1978) found that participants expecting to play a game with a competitive opponent behaved more competitively than participants expecting to play the game with a cooperative opponent. Moreover, their opponents mirrored the participants' competitiveness or cooperativeness (if someone is being a cutthroat player, you can't afford to be a pushover) and this behavior persisted in future interactions (see also Kelley & Stahelski, 1970; Swann & Snyder, 1980).

The power of these findings may surprise you, but the situations created in these studies are familiar to us all. We all know that our behavior in any social situation is influenced by the actions of the people with whom we interact. You undoubtedly find it easier to be outgoing and friendly when interacting with a warm person than when interacting with someone who is guarded and ill at ease. What we tend not to realize, however, is how much our own behavior shapes the behavior of those around us (E. E. Jones, 1986). Very often, we attribute other people's behavior to dispositional qualities ("That's the kind of person she is"), without considering the extent to which our own behavior has influenced the person's actions. You will read more about this tendency in Chapter 4.

C. Teacher Expectancies and Student Performance

Behavioral confirmation effects have been shown to have important real-world consequences. The most provocative study, published in 1968 by Rosenthal and Jacobson, examined the manner in which teacher expectancies influence student performance. In an elementary school in the South San Francisco area, Rosenthal and Jacobson told teachers that a standardized test of intelligence indicated that some of their students were especially bright and would probably bloom during the academic year. In reality, these researchers had randomly assigned these labels to some students, such that students labeled "likely to bloom" were no more intelligent than students who did not receive this label. However, by the end of the school year, this was no longer the case. Among students in first and second grade, the "bloomers" actually performed better on end-of-the-year standardized intelligence tests than "nonbloomers" did. These results attest to the power of expectancies and the behavioral confirmation process. In this case, an (erroneous) impression that a student was highly intelligent was confirmed.

In subsequent research, Rosenthal identified four ways teacher expectancies affect student performance (Rosenthal, 1987, 1994). First, teachers expecting intellectual growth create a more supportive intellectual climate. They are warmer and more demonstrative toward students they expect to excel. Second, they lavish more attention on such students and challenge them with more difficult material. Third, teachers give high-expectancy students more opportunities to participate in classroom discussions. They call on them more often and give them more time to speak when answering a question. Finally, teachers offer more extensive and detailed feedback to high-expectancy students. These behaviors work together to create better-achieving students, thereby confirming the teacher's expectancies. For these and other reasons, behavioral confirmation effects are more apt to produce overachievement in students than underachievement (Madon, Jussim, & Eccles, 1997; see also, Madon, Guyll, Spoth, Cross, & Hilbert, 2003; Ybarra, Schaberg, & Keiper, 1999).

D. Breaking the Behavioral Confirmation Cycle

Of course, we do not always want expectancies to produce confirming behavior. A common stereotype holds that girls are less suited for math and science than boys are. If, on the basis of this stereotype, teachers treat boys and girls differently, behavioral confirmation effects might contribute to the gender gap in math and science. Fortunately, several factors can combat behavioral confirmation effects. Provided they have the time and ability to be unbiased, expectancy holders are less apt to produce behavioral confirmation effects when they are motivated to form an accurate impression of their conversation partner (Biesanz, Neuberg, Smith, Asher, & Judice, 2001; Darley, Fleming, Hilton, & Swann, 1988; Neuberg, 1989). This suggests that even if they are aware of the stereotype, math and science teachers can avoid producing behavioral confirmation effects if they strive to be fair-minded.

The target of an expectancy can also reduce the power of behavioral confirmation effects (D. M. Smith, Neuberg, Judice, & Biesanz, 1997). In fact, merely being aware that another person has formed a negative expectancy about you may be enough to prevent that expectancy from being confirmed. Hilton and Darley (1985) found that behavioral confirmation effects did not occur when participants knew their conversation partner expected them to be cold and unresponsive. They compensated for the negative expectancy by being especially warm and sociable, and this led their conversation partners to revise their negative expectancy (see also Stukas & Snyder, 2002).

Finally, behavioral confirmation effects are less apt to occur when people have firm ideas about what they are like (Swann & Ely, 1984). To illustrate, suppose you know you are a very gregarious person. Even if you interact with someone who thinks you are shy and retiring, you're unlikely to confirm the expectancy by acting in an introverted fashion. More generally, the more sure of yourself you are, the less susceptible you are to behavioral confirmation effects.

CHAPTER SUMMARY

- Social perception is the study of how we form impressions of other people and how these impressions affect the way we act toward them.

- Three factors influence our impressions: physical features (e.g., facial attractiveness and emotional expression), nonverbal behavior (e.g., body movement and tone of voice), and cognitive processes (e.g., prior knowledge, schemas, and expectancies).

- We form impressions of other people very quickly, and these judgments tend to be shared by others. This is particularly true when we judge another person's warmth.

- A good deal of evidence suggests that our perceptions of other people have an innate basis. Beginning at an early age, and occurring across many cultures: (1) attractive people are assumed to possess pleasing personalities; (2) people with immature facial features are assumed to possess childlike qualities; and (3) people can recognize six basic facial expressions of emotion.

- A great deal of communication occurs nonverbally, and the impressions we form of others are influenced by nonverbal cues.

- Eye gaze is a universal sign of social dominance, and culture influences how it is used during social interactions.

- Men display more visual dominance than women. This occurs in part because of social roles (women are less apt to occupy positions of social power), but women are also socialized to be polite and deferent even when they occupy positions of power.

- The ability to accurately communicate nonverbal information depends on the sender's expressiveness and the receiver's perceptiveness. Both are important, but expressiveness plays a more important role.

- People who misread nonverbal behaviors pay too much attention to factors that have low diagnostic value.

- Woman are more expressive than men and are somewhat more perceptive at reading genuine (as opposed to deceitful) nonverbal behaviors.

- Although we are frequently called on to distinguish truth from lies, few of us are accomplished at this task.

- The ability to detect deception is influenced by nonverbal leakage. Aspects of behavior that are easy to control, such as eye gaze and facial expression, are called nonleaky behaviors. These behaviors don't provide much information about whether a person is telling the truth. Other nonverbal channels, such as vocal pitch and speech hesitations, are more difficult to control. These leaky channels provide valid information about who is telling the truth.

- Formal training can improve a person's ability to detect deception, although even the best detectors make errors.

- Polygraphs detect deception by analyzing physiological changes. Despite their widespread popularity, they are prone to error. Many innocent people are judged to be lying, and some liars are judged to be telling the truth.

- Social perception is influenced by cognitive processes, such as our schemas, stereotypes, and expectancies. These processes influence our impressions in a top-down fashion, by shaping the way we interpret perceptual experiences.

- Priming effects occur when a recent event activates a schema. Priming effects can influence the impressions we form of others, because a schema that just happens to be active guides how we interpret a person's behavior.

- Schemas and expectancies influence how we behave during a social interaction. In some cases, this influence produces a behavioral-confirmation effect (a tendency to unwittingly confirm our expectancies).

KEY TERMS

social perception, 64

"what is beautiful is good" stereotype, 66

nonverbal communication, 75

social role theory, 77

expressiveness, 80

perceptiveness, 80

nonverbal leakage, 84

bottom-up processing, 85

top-down processing, 86

stereotypes, 87

implicit personality theory, 87

halo effect, 87

priming effect, 92

behavioral confirmation effect, 95

ADDITIONAL READING

Go to the Student Edition of the Online Learning Center for this text (www.mhhe.com/brown) and log in to read the following journal articles, which relate to the content of this chapter:

- Ekman, P., Friesen, et al. (1987). Universals and cultural differences in the judgments of facial expressions of emotion.

- Snyder, M., Tanke, E. D., & Berscheid, E. (1977). Social perception and interpersonal behavior: On the self-fulfilling nature of social stereotypes.

CHAPTER FOUR

Social Judgment

Every December, college admissions officers face a daunting task. Hundreds of well-qualified students submit application materials containing a diverse array of information: standardized test scores, GPAs, course load, extracurricular activities, letters of recommendation, and personal statements. Somehow, the admissions officer must combine this information to form an overall impression of the candidate's qualifications and make a decision about whether to admit the applicant to the university.

In this chapter you will study how people make these sorts of decisions. The first part of the chapter examines how we combine and integrate everything we know about a person to form a complete impression. The second section of the chapter examines how we decide why people behave the way they do. The third section of this chapter deals with the social inference process more broadly, examining how people make a wide range of social judgments and decisions.

As you read this material, you may notice that social psychologists have taken different positions regarding people's cognitive abilities. These opposing positions can be understood by examining several metaphors that have guided research in this area (S. T. Fiske & Taylor, 1991). From approximately 1950 to 1965, research was guided by the "consistency seeker" metaphor. This metaphor, which derives from Gestalt psychology, maintains that people strive to form consistent, coherent judgments about their social world. People seek consistency, it is claimed, because inconsistency is aversive (see Chapter 2 for more on this assumption).

A different metaphor, known as the "naive scientist" metaphor, guided research from roughly 1965 to 1980. According to this view, people function as scientists in their day-to-day lives. With diligence and impartiality, they attempt to accurately understand the events they encounter. (In this context, *naive* means "not formally schooled in the tools of science," rather than gullible or innocent.)

From 1980 to 1995, another metaphor gained ascendance. This metaphor, called the "cognitive miser" metaphor, calls attention to the fact that people are not always able or willing to painstakingly process the information they encounter. Consequently, they rely on a number of shortcuts and biases that generally serve them well but sometimes lead them to make judgmental errors.

Current research in social psychology recognizes the validity of all of these different portrayals. Sometimes we strive to maintain consistency among our beliefs, sometimes we carefully strive to uncover the truth, and sometimes we make quick decisions without giving too much thought to the matter. From this perspective, flexibility is the key and all of the opposing viewpoints are applicable in different situations.

I. Forming Complete Impressions

Our impressions of a person commonly contain a variety of information about the person's abilities, traits, values, and beliefs. Our neighbor is good-natured and friendly, but has a childish sense of humor; our boss is dignified and hardworking, but is often impatient and intolerant. How do we combine all of the things we know about a person into a unified impression? This is the area of research to which we now turn.

We will begin by considering two theoretical approaches that have been developed to understand this issue: an elemental model based on principles of learning theory, and a perceptual model based on principles of Gestalt psychology. Each approach has generated important findings, so we will first discuss them separately; later, we will

TABLE 4.1	Likeableness Ratings for Eight Adjectives
Trait	**Likeableness Rating**
Sincere	5.73
Honest	5.55
Thoughtful	5.29
Reasonable	5.00
Ambitious	4.84
Artistic	4.00
Persuasive	3.74
Painstaking	3.45

Source: N. H. Anderson (1968).

attempt to reach some conclusions about which model best explains the impression formation process.

One more word is in order before we begin. In the research to be described, participants are asked to form an impression about another person on the basis of verbal information supplied by the experimenter. For example, participants might be told that Terry is smart, sensitive, reckless, and disrespectful. Participants then indicate their liking for Terry. Admittedly, this is an artificial way of forming an impression of another person. We rarely learn about others based only on verbal information supplied by a third party. It happens from time to time (our roommate describes her brother to us before he comes to visit), but our impressions of others are usually based on firsthand information of the type discussed in Chapter 3.

Although the experimental procedure is artificial, it does have an important advantage. By providing participants with specific information about an individual, researchers are able to control everything participants know about that person and when they know it. These aspects of experimental control, which were discussed in Chapter 1, increase internal validity and help scientists reach causal conclusions about how various types of information affect our impressions of others.

A. Elemental Models

When forming an impression of another person, elemental models assume that we consider each piece of information separately from the others. Everything we know about a person is treated as a distinct fact. Our overall impression is then an algebraic function of the isolated impressions. From this perspective, there is independence, not interdependence. The whole is nothing more than the various elements that make it up.

Elemental models begin by assuming that an evaluative rating can be assigned to each piece of information we have about a person. For purposes of illustration, consider the items presented in Table 4.1. The entries, taken from N. H. Anderson (1968), show the likableness ratings of eight qualities. Each trait was rated on a 6-point scale (0 = Would dislike a person who possessed these qualities; 6 = Would like a person who possessed these qualities). The values are the mean ratings obtained from 100 participants who completed this exercise.

TABLE 4.2	The Additive Model of the Impression Formation Process		
Pat	**Likability Rating**	**Kim**	**Likability Rating**
Sincere	5.73	Honest	5.55
Thoughtful	5.29	Reasonable	5.00
Ambitious	4.84	Artistic	4.00
Persuasive	3.74	Painstaking	3.45
Σ	19.60	Σ	18.00

1. The Additive Model

The simplest elemental model is an additive model. This model assumes that our overall impression of a person can be predicted by summing the evaluative ratings given to each of the individual elements. To illustrate this approach, imagine I describe two people to you: Pat is sincere, thoughtful, ambitious, and persuasive, and Kim is honest, reasonable, artistic, and painstaking. I then ask you which person you like best. Table 4.2 shows that the additive model predicts that you will like Pat more than Kim. This is because the sum of Pat's qualities ($\Sigma = 19.60$) exceeds the sum of Kim's qualities ($\Sigma = 18.00$).

2. The Averaging Model

The additive model assumes that every piece of positive information we have about a person enhances our overall impression. N. H. Anderson (1965a) raised the possibility that an *averaging* model might better capture the impression formation process. With an averaging model, we average, rather than add, all of the information we have about a person to form an overall judgment of liking. The key question of interest here is whether the addition of moderately positive information increases or decreases our liking for a person we already admire. An additive model predicts that adding moderately positive information will increase our liking, but an averaging model predicts that it will not.

Table 4.3 illustrates these divergent perspectives. Terry is described by three positive qualities (sincere, ambitious, and artistic), while Chris is described by just two positive qualities (sincere and ambitious). An additive model predicts that we like Terry (14.57) more than Chris (10.57), while the averaging model predicts that we like Chris (5.29) more than Terry (4.86). In research testing the two models, N. H. Anderson (1965a) found that the averaging model did a better job of predicting how much participants liked another person. This means that if we already think a person has positive qualities, the addition of moderately positive information diminishes, rather than enhances, our liking for the person. In terms of the example shown in Table 4.3, we like a person more when we don't know the person is artistic, even though being artistic is a positive quality.

To summarize, an additive model maintains that any positive quality enhances our liking for a person, whereas the averaging model maintains that minimally positive qualities decrease our liking for a person we already like. Perhaps you are thinking this research is artificial and of little relevance to your own life. Not so. Let's imagine

TABLE 4.3 Comparing an Additive Model and an Averaging Model of the Impression Formation Process

Terry	Likability Rating	Chris	Likability Rating
Sincere	5.73	Sincere	5.73
Ambitious	4.84	Ambitious	4.84
Artistic	4.00		
Σ	14.57		10.57
Average	4.86		5.29

you are on a first date, sharing information about yourself with the other person. Should you disclose every positive quality you have about yourself, no matter how minimally positive it might be? If you think your date uses an additive model, the answer is yes; no matter how minimally positive the quality is, your date will like you more if you bring this quality to his or her attention ("and I always squeeze the toothpaste tube from the bottom."). The averaging model says yes only if your impression is already so low that disclosing this quality makes you look good by comparison. I leave it up to you to decide which of these situations characterizes your usual first date.

3. The Weighted Averaging Model

A final elemental model was proposed by N. H. Anderson and Jacobson (1965; see also N. H. Anderson & Barrios, 1961). This model, known as the weighted averaging model, assumes that important traits receive more weight than do unimportant traits when people combine information about a person to form an overall impression. To calculate our impression, we (1) assign an importance weight to each trait, (2) multiply each trait term by its importance weight, (3) sum these products, and (4) divide this sum by the sum of the importance weights. Formally:

$$\text{Impressions} = [\Sigma(t_k \cdot w_k)] \div \Sigma(w_k)$$

Where t = Trait rating for attribute k, and w = Importance weight given to attribute k.

The formula looks imposing, but it is really quite simple. To illustrate its use, we'll examine how it explains the *primacy effect* in the impression formation process. A primacy effect occurs when information we first learn about a person is more consequential than information we learn at a later time. For example, people express greater liking for a person described as sincere, honest, irresponsible, and phony than a person described as phony, irresponsible, honest, and sincere (note that the latter set of terms is merely the reverse order of the former) (e.g., N. H. Anderson, 1965b; N. H. Anderson & Barrios, 1961; Asch, 1946; Luchins, 1957).

The weighted averaging model explains the effect by assuming that the importance of each trait decreases in a linear fashion, with the first trait being the most important and the last trait being the least important. Table 4.4 illustrates this model. After assigning an importance rating to each trait according to its ordinal position, we multiply each trait rating by its importance weight to derive a weighted sum. We then sum these products, and divide by the sum of the importance weights. In this manner, we can explain why a person described by descending positivity is liked more than a person described by ascending positivity.

TABLE 4.4 A Weighted Averaging Approach to Understanding the Primacy Effect in the Impression Formation Process

	LEON (DESCENDING POSITIVITY)				NOEL (ASCENDING POSITIVITY)		
Trait	Trait Rating	Importance Weighting	Weighted Rating (Trait · Weight)	Trait	Trait Rating	Importance Weighting	Weighted Rating (Trait · Weight)
Sincere	5.73	4	22.92	Persuasive	3.74	4	14.96
Honest	5.55	3	16.65	Ambitious	4.84	3	14.52
Ambitious	4.84	2	9.68	Honest	5.55	2	11.10
Persuasive	3.74	1	3.74	Sincere	5.73	1	5.73
Σ	19.90	10	52.99	Σ	19.90	10	46.31
Weighted average			5.30	Weighted average			4.63

4. Summary of Impression Formation Models

Although different in some respects, the additive, averaging, and weighted averaging models all assume that we combine everything we know about a person into an overall judgment, and that each piece of information exerts an *independent* effect on our overall impression. We call these models elemental models because they assume that the whole is nothing more than the sum (or some other algebraic function) of the parts or elements. These models make no allowance for interpretation or interdependence among the attributes. They simply assume that we combine what we know about a person to form an overall judgment, without giving any thought to how the various bits of information fit together.

B. Asch's Holistic Model

Solomon Asch offered a very different view of the impression formation process. Asch had been trained as a Gestalt psychologist in Germany. When he fled Germany for the United States, he applied principles of Gestalt psychology to matters of social perception. With respect to the impression formation process, Asch (1946) argued (1) that our impressions of others exist as a unified whole, (2) that the meaning we give to each attribute varies as a function of the context in which it is found, and (3) that the whole is greater than the sum of the parts.

To illustrate Asch's holistic approach, imagine that I tell you I know someone who is honest and ambitious. What connotation does the word *ambitious* evoke? Very likely, it calls forth thoughts of diligence, perseverance, and determination. Now suppose I tell you I know someone else who is dishonest and ambitious. Now what does the word *ambitious* mean? In this case, it probably brings to mind someone who is ruthless, driven by greed, and willing to stop at nothing to succeed. The word is the same, but the meaning we give it changes according to the surrounding context the other traits provide (see also D. L. Hamilton & Zanna, 1974; Kunda, Sinclair, & Griffin, 1997; Zanna & Hamilton, 1977).

A more formal way of thinking about these effects is in terms of interdependence. The elementarists assume that the meaning of each trait is independent of the others, but Asch argues that our impressions of others exist as a unified, interdependent whole. Rather than treating each trait as an isolated, separate piece of information, we comprehend the entire person as an indivisible unit. Consequently, the whole is greater than the sum of the parts.

Finally, Asch assumes that this interpretive process is an active, goal-directed one, driven by a desire to form a coherent impression. This assumption derives from the Gestalt principle of *Prägnanz* (see Chapter 2). According to this principle, visual perception is not random and haphazard but is instead directed toward achieving order and simplicity. Asch believed that the same principle operates in the realm of social perception. When forming impressions of others, we strive to reduce inconsistencies and to achieve a pleasing, coherent impression.

This need for order and simplicity is especially important when we confront information that seems contradictory. We could just accept the contradiction, but we don't. We see if we can't somehow make sense of the information, because it would be distressing to form an inconsistent impression:

> We are not content simply to note inconsistencies or to let them sit where they are. The contradiction is puzzling, and prompts us to look more deeply. Disturbing factors arouse a trend to maintain the unity of the impression, to search for the most sensible way in which the characteristics could exist together. (Asch, 1946, p. 285)

1. Asch's Change-of-Meaning Effect

Asch's approach is most clearly revealed in Experiment 1 of his 1946 paper. In this study, participants formed an impression of a person who was described by seven traits. Approximately half of the participants received information about person A and half received information about person B.

Person A: intelligent—skillful—industrious—*warm*—determined—practical—cautious

Person B: intelligent—skillful—industrious—*cold*—determined—practical—cautious

Although the only difference between the two descriptions is the substitution of the word *cold* for the word *warm,* the participants in Asch's study formed very different impressions of person A and person B.

How are we to understand this effect? According to Asch, the words *warm* and *cold* are **central traits** that change the meaning we give to the other characteristics. As shown in Table 4.5, when paired with *warm, intelligent* means "smart"; when

TABLE 4.5	Asch's Change-of-Meaning Hypothesis	
Trait	Meaning of Trait When Paired with *Warm*	Meaning of Trait When Paired with *Cold*
Intelligent	Smart	Devious
Skillful	Competent	Crafty
Industrious	Hardworking	Driven
Determined	Tenacious	Obstinate
Practical	Sensible	Unimaginative
Cautious	Prudent	Timid

paired with *cold, intelligent* means "devious." Similarly, *skillful* means "competent" when it applies to a warm person, but it means "crafty" when it belongs to a cold person. Our understanding of the other traits is likewise transformed by the warm–cold variation. In short, the meaning of these attributes is variable, and the person's warmth (or lack thereof) determines the attribute's meaning. Moreover, once transformed, the attributes form a coherent, consistent package. We view the person as a unified whole, not as a series of disembodied traits.

2. Application to the Real World

The artificial nature of Asch's experimental task raises the question of whether these findings apply in real-world settings. Kelley (1950) conducted an experiment to address this issue. In Kelley's study, college students learned they were about to hear a guest speaker. Prior to the lecture, students read a brief biographical sketch of the speaker. The biographical sketches were alike, except that half of the students were led to believe the speaker was warm and the other half were led to believe he was cold.

After the students had received this information, the speaker entered the classroom and lectured to the class. When he left, the students completed a questionnaire regarding their impressions of him. As Asch's change-of-meaning hypothesis predicts, Kelley found that the "warm" instructor was viewed as more sociable, humorous, popular, considerate, and good-natured than was the "cold" instructor. Moreover, students displayed a behavioral confirmation effect (see Chapter 3), by treating the two instructors differently. Students who believed the instructor was warm participated more in the lecture (e.g., they asked more questions) than those who believed the instructor was cold. In sum, even though the warm–cold designation was entirely arbitrary, the students formed very different impressions of the two instructors and behaved very differently toward them.

3. The Primacy Effect

Because the students in Kelley's (1950) study received the warm–cold information before the lecture began, Kelley's findings constitute a primacy effect. This suggests that first impressions are important not simply because they are weighted more heavily (as the weighted averaging model assumes), but because they affect how we interpret all of the other information we receive. Each new piece of information must somehow fit in with the old as we strive to form a coherent, unified impression.

In this regard, it is interesting to remember a point we first made in Chapter 3: Our judgment about a person's warmth is made rapidly on the basis of very limited information. Once this judgment is reached, it provides a context in which all other information is considered. Of course, we sometimes revise our impressions of others once we get to know them better. But most of the time, our first impressions endure because they shape the way we interpret everything else we know about the person.

4. Not All Traits Are Central Traits

Asch (1946) wondered whether all traits produce such a dramatic alteration in the overall impression. He found that they do not. Substituting the trait pair polite–blunt for warm–cold did not greatly alter the impressions participants formed. Asch concluded that only central traits are important enough to alter the way other traits are viewed. Peripheral traits, such as polite–blunt, are less important and do not exhibit this transformational quality.

TABLE 4.6 Methods Used to Resolve (Apparently) Inconsistent Traits		
Trait Pair	**Inconsistency-Resolving Device**	**Illustration**
Brilliant–foolish	Segregation: Each trait applies to a different aspect of the person's life.	This person is brilliant intellectually but foolish in practical, commonsense matters.
Sociable–lonely	Depth dimension: An outer trait compensates for an inner quality.	This person appears sociable but inwardly is lonely.
Dependent–hostile	Cause–effect: One trait is caused by the other.	People who are dependent develop hostile feelings toward those upon whom they depend.
Cheerful–gloomy	Common source: Both traits arise from a common influence.	This person is very emotional, with extreme highs and lows.
Strict–kind	Means–end: One trait is a means to attaining a desired end.	Parents who care for their children must be strict and set limits.

Source: Asch and Zukier (1984).

Negative traits have been shown to be particularly consequential (S. T. Fiske, 1980; J. G. Klein 1996; Skowronski & Carlston, 1989). A strongly negative quality, such as wicked, is capable of completely dominating the impression we form of another person. This may be because we view this trait as highly important (as a weighted averaging model would predict) or because the negative quality alters the meaning we give to the person's other qualities (as Asch's change-of-meaning approach predicts).

5. Dealing with Inconsistent Information

Situations in which people confront contradictory information about others provide another testing ground for Asch's theory. For example, imagine that we know a person who is peaceful and confrontational. How do we handle such apparent inconsistencies? According to Asch, we resolve the contradiction by altering the meaning of each trait.

A study by Asch and Zukier (1984) illustrates this process. During the first part of the study, participants were told to imagine a person who possessed two potentially conflicting personality traits. They were then asked to briefly describe the person, stating how the two attributes might be related. Table 4.6 shows that participants used a number of devices to resolve the inconsistencies and make the traits fit together.

C. Summary and Integration of the Impression Formation Process

In this section, we have reviewed different models of the impression formation process. Elemental models assume that we treat everything we know about a person as a separate piece of information and somehow combine this independent information to form an overall judgment. In contrast, Asch's holistic model assumes that we strive to make sense of the people we meet by viewing the entire person as an interdependent, unified whole.

Whenever models as different as these are formulated to explain the same phenomenon, we are tempted to ask, "Which one is right and which one is wrong?" Several investigations have, in fact, tried to establish the superiority of one model or the other (e.g., N. H. Anderson & Hubert, 1963; D. L. Hamilton & Zanna, 1974; R. H. Stewart, 1965; Zanna & Hamilton, 1977), but it is doubtful that a definitive test can ever be conducted. As discussed in Chapter 1, theories are never right or wrong; they are only useful or not. In the present case, it is probably best to conclude that each theory offers a useful perspective on the impression formation process.

The advantage of the elemental model is parsimony. Weighted averaging models exist for various judgmental domains (e.g., risk-taking behavior), and the elemental model treats the impression formation process as just another judgmental task. Moreover, weighted averaging models do predict our impressions of others (although this predictive ability doesn't mean the underlying explanation is correct). Finally, elemental models have generated a great deal of research. It is unlikely, for example, that anyone would have thought to pit the averaging model versus an additive model without this theory to guide the search.

However, the elasticity of trait terms poses problems for an elemental model. The elemental model demands that a trait has a single, unwavering meaning, and that a numerical judgment can be assigned to that unchanging trait. In contrast, Asch's model maintains that the meaning of most traits is variable and that context and our desire to reach a coherent impression determine meaning. In short, the fact that the same trait can mean different things is better predicted by Asch's formulation than by the elemental model. Asch's formulation also is better able to explain how inconsistent information affects the impressions we form of others. Rather than simply receiving less weight (as an elemental model predicts), inconsistent information is transformed so as to be consistent with our overall impression. This finding cannot be explained by the elemental approach.

II. Causal Inference

Forming impressions of others often involves an attempt to understand why people do the things they do. To illustrate, suppose we see Sue scold her children in the supermarket. Implicitly, we ask ourselves why. If we decide it's because Sue is impatient, we have come to form an impression of Sue's personality or nature. Social psychologists call these sorts of judgments causal attributions. **Causal attributions** are answers to "why" questions (Weiner, 1985). We observe a behavior and we ask why it occurred: Why did I fail the exam? Why did she lose her keys? Why did he choose to attend Harvard rather than Yale? The answers we give (e.g., I didn't study hard enough; she's absentminded; his parents went to Harvard) are causal attributions. The person's behavior is attributed to a cause.

A. The History of Attribution Theory

Fritz Heider, a German immigrant with training in Gestalt psychology, developed attribution theory in a 1958 book entitled *The Psychology of Interpersonal Relations*. The era in which this book was published was an exciting time of change within the field of psychology. Behaviorism, which had dominated the field for roughly 40 years, was beginning to lose its grip. As discussed in Chapter 2, behaviorism maintained that people are passively driven by their prior reinforcement histories. Heider disagreed with this depiction. He argued that people actively anticipate and interpret events, and that these expectations and interpretations guide their actions (see also G. A. Kelly, 1955).

1. The Naive Scientist Metaphor

In applying his ideas to the study of interpersonal relations, Heider likened people to naive scientists: Much as scientists gather data and rely on logic to interpret their findings, so too do people strive to uncover the true causes for the events they encounter. According to Heider, this search is undertaken because it gives people the ability to better predict and control their environment. If we know why an event has occurred, we are in a better position to anticipate and modify such events in the future. In this sense, Heider believed people are applied scientists (who seek to change phenomena) rather than basic scientists (who seek to understand phenomena):

> If I find sand on my desk, I shall want to find out the underlying reason for this circumstance. I make this inquiry not because of idle curiosity, but because only if I refer this relatively insignificant offshoot event to an underlying core event will I attain a stable environment and have the possibility of controlling it. (Heider, 1958, p. 80)

Causal attributions are very phenomenological (see Chapter 1). They represent our interpretation of events, and they guide our psychological reactions to these events. In fact, people very often respond more to the "why" than to the "what" (Weiner, 1985). Imagine, for example, that a person declines your invitation for a date. How will you feel? Undoubtedly you'll be sad not to get a date, but whether you feel bad about yourself will depend on why you think the person turned you down. If you think it's because the person already has a steady dating partner, you probably will feel better than if you think the person is unattached but not so desperate as to go out with you. In both cases you don't have a date, but how you feel depends largely on why you think you don't have a date. This is why attributions are so important: Rather than being guided by the events we experience (i.e., the what), our psychological lives depend on the attributions we make for these experiences (i.e., the why).

2. Dispositional versus Situational Attributions

When it comes to understanding the causes of social behavior, Heider argued that people make a distinction between dispositional causes and situational causes. A dispositional cause is an enduring, inherent quality of a person, such as the person's character, personality, or ability. To illustrate, if we decide that Chris came late to class because she is lazy and disorganized, we have made a **dispositional attribution** for her behavior.

A situational cause is any factor that isn't dispositional. If we say Chris came late to class because she happened to oversleep or her roommate had taken her car or traffic was bad, we are making a **situational attribution.** Note that these situational attributions can be about Chris (she overslept), about other people (her roommate borrowed her car), or about the environment (traffic was bad), but none refers to an enduring, inherent property of Chris, such as her character or nature.

According to Heider, this distinction between dispositional and situational attributions plays an important role in psychological life. When we observe behavior, we implicitly ask ourselves whether the behavior is caused by a dispositional cause or a situational one. Psychologists do the same thing when they analyze social behavior. In earlier chapters, we discussed Kurt Lewin's assertion that behavior is a function of the person and the environment [B $= f$(P, E)]. Heider's theory builds on Lewin's.

Whereas Lewin's theory is concerned with why people behave the way they do, Heider's theory is concerned with our beliefs about why people behave the way they do. This is why attribution theorists refer to people as naive scientists. They assume that people function as scientists in their attempts to understand whether a person's behavior is due to the person or the situation.

3. Factors That Influence Attributions

In general, three factors influence the attributions we make. The first is information. Like scientists, we consult several important sources of information. We will describe these sources of information momentarily. The second factor is attentional focus. Sometimes the attributions we make are influenced by where our attention happens to be focused. A final factor is motivation. In many circumstances, we are motivated to reach a particular causal conclusion. For example, rather than concluding that we failed an exam because we have low ability, we might console ourselves by deciding that the professor was unclear. In the pages that follow, we will see that each of these factors shapes the attributions people make.

B. Theories of the Attribution Process

Several theories have been developed to explain the manner in which people make attributions. Some of these theories are called normative or prescriptive theories, because they prescribe how people *ought* to make attributions if they are seeking the truth. These theories depict people as naive scientists and emphasize the role of informational factors. Other theories, called descriptive theories of the attribution process, describe how people actually go about making attributions. Rather than emphasizing informational factors, these theories assert that our attributions are also affected by attentional and motivational processes.

1. Kelley's Covariation Model

The first theory we will consider is a normative theory of the attribution process developed by Harold Kelley (1967). Kelley's theory pertains to situations in which we attempt to determine why a person has had a particular reaction to a particular stimulus. To illustrate the theory, let's imagine that Jim tells us he went to Mama Luigi's pizzeria last Saturday night and loved the pizza. The question the naive scientist asks is: What explains Jim's reaction to this stimulus?

According to Kelley, we have three possible answers to this question: (1) It is something about the person (e.g., Jim is a pizza lover); (2) it is something about the stimulus (e.g., Mama Luigi's makes great pizza); or (3) there is some other, more temporary factor pertaining to the situation or the circumstance (e.g., Jim was in a good mood that night or Mama Luigi's got lucky and happened to make one good pizza). Kelley assumes that we consult three sources of information to determine which of these causes most plausibly explains Jim's reaction.

Distinctiveness. The first source of information we consult is distinctiveness. Distinctiveness asks: "Is the person's response to this stimulus different from the person's response to similar stimuli?" In this case, we ask ourselves, "Does Jim usually like pizza?" If he does, his reaction to Mama Luigi's pizza is low in distinctiveness. It's not very distinctive, because he always likes pizza. But if Jim usually doesn't like pizza, then his reaction is highly distinctive. It's unusual for him to like pizza.

SOURCES OF INFORMATION			
Distinctiveness	Consistency	Consensus	Attribution
LOW Jim usually likes pizza, so his positive reaction is not distinctive.	**HIGH** Jim always likes the pizza at Mama Luigi's.	**LOW** No one else likes the pizza at Mama Luigi's.	**PERSON** Jim is a pizza lover.
HIGH Jim usually doesn't like pizza, so his positive reaction is highly distinctive.	**HIGH** Jim always likes the pizza at Mama Luigi's.	**HIGH** Everyone likes the pizza at Mama Luigi's.	**STIMULUS** Mama Luigi's serves great pizza.
HIGH Jim usually doesn't like pizza, so his positive reaction is highly distinctive.	**LOW** Jim has never liked the pizza at Mama Luigi's before.	**LOW** No one else likes the pizza at Mama Luigi's.	**SITUATION** Jim was in a good mood that night; Mama Luigi's got lucky and made one good pizza.

TABLE 4.7 Kelley's Covariation Model of the Attribution Process

Consistency. The second source of information is called consistency information. In contrast to distinctiveness information, which examines the person's reaction to similar stimuli, consistency information asks, "Is the person's reaction to this stimulus consistent over time?" In our example, we want to know whether Jim always likes the pizza at Mama Luigi's or whether he only liked it this one time. If he always likes Mama Luigi's pizza, his positive reaction on Saturday night is high in consistency; if he doesn't usually like Mama Luigi's pizza, his positive reaction is low in consistency.

Consensus. The third source of information is consensus information. Consensus information asks, "How do most people respond to this stimulus?" If many people think Mama Luigi's serves great pizza, there is high consensus for Jim's reaction. If no one else thinks Mama Luigi's serves great pizza, there is low consensus for Jim's reaction.

Table 4.7 shows that the way we answer these questions determines whether we attribute Jim's reaction to him, Mama Luigi's pizza, or some more temporary or situational factor. When distinctiveness is low, consistency is high, and consensus is low, we make a person attribution: We assume that Jim is a pizza lover and that's why he likes the pizza at Mama Luigi's. When all three sources of information are high, we make a stimulus attribution: We decide that Mama Luigi's makes great pizza and that's why Jim likes it. Finally, when distinctiveness is high and consistency and consensus are low, we attribute Jim's reaction to the situation or to circumstance (e.g., Jim was in a good mood that night).

Research testing Kelley's model has found support for these relationships (Försterling, 1992; L. A. McArthur, 1972). When given this information, people make the attributions the theory predicts. Whether people actually search for such information when attempting to explain behavior is less certain. Ultimately, Kelley's research is important not because it so aptly describes the attributional process, but because it so clearly typifies the naive scientist metaphor that guided early research in this area. The

TABLE 4.8 Correspondent Inference Theory

Behavior	Correspondent Inference	Noncorrespondent Inference
Kelsey shares the cake with Chelsea.	Kelsey is kind.	Kelsey's mother forced her to share the cake.
The politician argues for national health care.	The politician believes national health care is a good thing.	The politician is speaking to an audience that supports national health care, and is trying to win votes.
The waiter spills the coffee.	The waiter is uncoordinated.	The coffee pot was too hot to handle.

processes depicted are very logical and require a great deal of time and attention. As we will see momentarily, people do not always follow the formal rules of logic Kelley describes.

2. Correspondent Inference Theory

Around the time that Kelley developed his theory, another theory of the attribution process, known as correspondent inference theory, was being developed (E. E. Jones & Davis, 1965). Like Kelley's theory, **correspondent inference theory** is a normative theory of the attribution process that emphasizes informational factors. The focus of this theory is a bit different from Kelley's, however. Rather than asking what determines a person's reaction to a given stimulus, correspondent inference theory is concerned with understanding the link between behavior and dispositions. Under what conditions does a person's behavior reveal a corresponding disposition rather than the power of some situational factor? To illustrate, imagine that we see Kelsey share her cake with Chelsea. If we decide that this occurred because Kelsey is a kind person, we have made a correspondent inference: We have attributed Kelsey's kind act to a corresponding disposition (kindness). In the language of the theory, then, a correspondent inference occurs when a person's behavior is explained by a corresponding disposition. Table 4.8 presents several examples of correspondent and noncorrespondent inferences.

Before turning to the particulars of this theory, it's important to understand why this issue is worthy of consideration. In the course of social interaction, people are not always who they claim to be. They say things they don't mean (e.g., people agree with us just to be polite), they lie to impress us (e.g., people exaggerate their grade point average or athletic accomplishments), or they conceal their true intentions in order to gain some practical advantage (e.g., employees ingratiate themselves with their bosses in order to get promoted). How are we to know who is being genuine and who is not? This is the issue correspondent inference theory addresses. When can a person's behavior be assumed to accurately reveal the person's true nature? Or, in the language of the theory, under what conditions can we infer that a person's behavior is due to a corresponding disposition?

Three Variables That Influence the Attributions People Make. One variable that correspondent inference theory considers is choice. According to the theory, freely chosen behavior is more revealing of a person's disposition than is coerced behavior. If hostages come on television and denounce the United States, we don't necessarily assume they truly hate America. We recognize that their captors may be forcing them to make this proclamation. In contrast, a person who freely chooses to condemn the United States is assumed to have negative attitudes toward the United States. After all, what other explanation is there? The person was free to do otherwise but spoke against the United States. The person must truly have negative feelings toward America.

The second factor considered by correspondent inference theory pertains to the social appropriateness of behavior. This factor is similar to Kelley's consensus information. Behavior that is at odds with what most people would do in that situation is more revealing of a person's disposition than is behavior that is consistent with what most other people do. For example, we don't necessarily assume that people who pay for their meals at a restaurant are highly principled, law-abiding citizens, because we recognize that most people exhibit this behavior. In contrast, people who fail to pay their bill are apt to be considered dishonest and immoral. Leaving without paying the tab is socially inappropriate behavior and is more revealing of a person's true nature or character than paying the tab is.

The intended consequences of an action are a final variable relevant to correspondent inference theory. Suppose a person chooses to see a science fiction movie rather than a romantic comedy. The behavior was freely chosen, so we assume the person is a science fiction buff. Now assume that the two movies start at different times and are of different lengths, that one is in a small theater while the other is in a large theater, and that one of the theaters serves only buttered popcorn and chocolate raisins while the other offers only caramel corn and nonpareils. Because the two choices have so many nonoverlapping (or noncommon) effects, we aren't certain what the choice reveals about the person. It could mean the person is a science fiction buff, or it could mean the person likes small theaters or buttered popcorn. We can't be sure, because the two choices differ in multiple ways. If, however, a decision involves only a few overlapping consequences, we can identify which corresponding disposition is guiding the choice.

Discounting and Augmenting. These assumptions about the causes of behavior came to be known in terms of discounting and augmenting principles (Kelley, 1972, 1973). According to the **discounting principle,** people discount the extent to which behavior is caused by a dispositional factor when an obvious situational cause is present. When a person sits quietly at a funeral, we don't necessarily assume the person is shy and introverted. The situation provides a plausible explanation for the behavior, and we discount the extent to which the behavior is due to a corresponding disposition.

Now imagine that a person is sitting quietly at a Mardi Gras celebration. Because this behavior is inconsistent with what most people do, we are quick to assume that the person is shy and introverted. This is augmenting. According to the **augmenting principle,** we are especially apt to make a dispositional attribution when a person behaves in a manner that is inconsistent with the requirements of the situation.

An investigation by Trafimow and Schneider (1994) documents these effects. In one portion of this study, participants read a story about a man named Joe who acted very friendly with his co-workers. In one condition, this is all the information participants received. In another condition, participants learned that Joe's boss encourages office camaraderie and promotes only those who exhibit friendly behavior. (Notice how this situation provides a plausible explanation for Joe's affability.) In a third condition, participants read that Joe's boss discourages office camaraderie and tends to promote

FIGURE 4.1

Discounting and Augmenting Effects in Trait Inferences Following Behavior

Participants discounted the causal importance of a trait when a plausible situational cause was present, but augmented the causal importance of a trait when the situation called for behavior that was the opposite of what was expected.

Source: Trafimow and Schneider (1994).

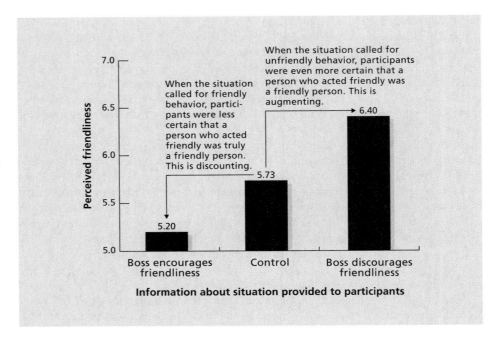

only employees who refrain from exhibiting friendliness in the workplace. (Notice how this situation should lead Joe to behave in a relatively unfriendly manner.) Finally, after receiving this information, participants were asked to decide whether Joe is a friendly person by nature.

Figure 4.1 presents some of the results from this investigation, and the data show evidence of both discounting and augmenting. Discounting is evident when we compare the control condition with the "boss encourages friendliness" condition. When the situation provides a plausible explanation for Joe's amity, participants are less sure he really is a friendly person. Augmenting is apparent when we compare the control condition with the "boss discourages friendliness" condition. Because Joe's friendliness is just the opposite of what one would expect, participants are even more certain that he is a genuinely friendly person.

Discounting and augmenting principles play an important role in people's lives. Far more than you may now realize, you rely on them to determine why people do what they do. You even use these principles to explain your own actions. So keep these principles in mind, because we will have occasion to refer to them throughout the text.

C. Correspondence Bias

Early research in attribution theory depicted people as rational, naive scientists who diligently strive to uncover the true reasons why people behave as they do. As research in this area progressed, it became apparent that people were not as studious as the naive scientist metaphor implies (Nisbett & Ross, 1980; L. Ross, 1977). A study by E. E. Jones and Harris (1967) provided the first hint that this was true. In this study, participants were shown an essay allegedly written by another student. In one condition, the essay supported Fidel Castro's recent takeover of Cuba (pro-Castro essay); in the other condition, the essay opposed Castro's recent takeover of Cuba (anti-Castro

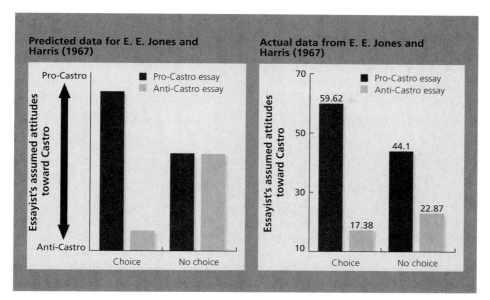

FIGURE 4.2

Assumed Attitudes as a Function of Choice and the Position Taken

The left-hand panel shows the predictions one would make based on E. E. Jones and Davis's (1965) correspondent inference theory. The right-hand panel shows the actual data from a study designed to test the theory. The actual data show that people do make use of situational information, but do not do so as much as the theory predicts.

Source: E. E. Jones and Harris (1967).

essay). In addition, some participants were told that the essay writer had been given no choice as to which position to take, whereas other participants were told the essay writer was free to choose either position. Finally, participants were asked to predict the essay writer's true attitude toward Castro (10 = Very negative; 70 = Very positive). This judgment was intended to assess the extent to which participants drew a dispositional inference from the essayist's behavior.

Before considering the results from this investigation, let's examine the predictions correspondent inference theory makes in this situation. As shown on the left-hand side of Figure 4.2, correspondent inference theory predicts that participants will infer the person's attitude in the choice condition: A person who freely chooses to write a pro-Castro essay must really like Castro and a person who freely chooses to write an anti-Castro essay must really dislike Castro. How could it be otherwise? No one made the person write the essay, so the position taken must reflect the essayist's true attitude. The situation is quite different in the no-choice condition. Here, participants should refrain from making any judgment about the essayist's true attitudes. The behavior was coerced, so it doesn't reveal anything about the writer's attitude. In the language of the theory, the participants should discount the extent to which the position taken reflects the essayist's true attitude, because coercion provides a strong situational explanation.

Inspection of the right-hand side of Figure 4.2 reveals that these predictions were only partially confirmed. In accordance with the theory, participants in the choice condition did infer that a person who wrote a pro-Castro essay had more favorable attitudes toward Castro than a person who wrote an anti-Castro essay. However, this was also true in the no-choice condition. The effect was less pronounced, but even when told the writer had no choice as to which position to argue, participants assumed that a person who wrote a pro-Castro essay had more positive attitudes toward Castro than did a person who wrote an anti-Castro essay. In short, participants gave insufficient weight to whether the essayist was free to choose which side of the issue to argue; they failed to discount as much as they should.

The tendency to underestimate the importance of situational causes and overestimate the importance of dispositional ones is known as the **fundamental attribution**

error (L. Ross, 1977) or the **correspondence bias** (E. E. Jones, 1979, 1990). These terms call attention to the fact that people tend to make dispositional attributions for behavior. In our day-to-day lives, we act as personality psychologists, not social psychologists. We assume that people do what they do because of who they are rather than because of the situational pressures they face. This bias was first described more than 50 years ago by Ichheiser (1943, 1949):

> Instead of saying [that] individual X acted . . . in a certain way because he was . . . in a certain situation, we are prone to believe that he behaved . . . in a certain way because he possessed . . . certain specific personal qualities. (Ichheiser, 1943, p. 152)

1. Theoretical Explanations for the Correspondence Bias

Our tendency to give insufficient emphasis to the situation when explaining people's behavior is influenced by several variables, including perceptual factors (Heider, 1958; Taylor & Fiske, 1975); informational factors (Gilbert & Malone, 1995); and cultural factors (Choi, Nisbett, & Norenzayan, 1999; J. G. Miller, 1984). Two theoretical explanations have been developed to account for the correspondence bias. One model, known as the sequential model, asserts that the attribution process is made up of three stages that vary according to the amount of effort they require (Gilbert, Pelham, & Krull, 1988; E. E. Jones, 1979; Quattrone, 1982). The first stage, called the categorization stage, is automatic and requires little effort. During this stage, people observe and describe behavior. The second stage, termed the characterization stage, is also automatic. Here, people spontaneously make a correspondent dispositional attribution for the behavior they observe. For example, if we see someone sitting quietly, we automatically assume that person is quiet and introverted. In the third stage, the correction stage, we look to the situation to see whether it provides any relevant information. The correction stage, which can lead to either discounting or augmenting, requires effort and occurs only if people are motivated *and* able to give careful thought to the context in which the behavior occurs.

Information-integration models have also been developed to explain the correspondence bias. These models do not assume that dispositional attributions are any less effortful than situational ones. Instead, they assume that the correspondence bias occurs either because dispositional information is ordinarily more noticeable than situational information or because people generally tend to wonder what kind of person someone is rather than what kind of situation the person is in (Krull, 1993; Trope, 1986). In support of this claim, the correspondence bias is reduced or eliminated when situational information is highly salient (Trope & Gaunt, 2000) or when people are explicitly given the goal of inferring the nature of the situation rather than gauging the person's personality or character (Krull & Dill, 1996).

2. Spontaneous Trait Inferences

Despite their differences, the sequential model and the information-integration model accept that, under normal conditions, people tend to assume that a person's behavior is a faithful reflection of the person's nature or character. Uleman and colleagues have provided the clearest evidence that these inferences are made spontaneously, without intention or conscious awareness (Uleman & Moskowitz, 1994; Winter & Uleman, 1984). In one study (Winter, Uleman, & Cunniff, 1985), participants were asked to memorize a list of sentences in which a person performed a given behavior. Table 4.9 presents four examples. Later, during the recall phase of the experiment, the participants

TABLE 4.9 Sample Items from Winter, Uleman, and Cunniff (1985)

	TO-BE-REMEMBERED SENTENCES			
	The tailor carries the old woman's groceries across the street.	The child tells his mother that he ate the chocolates.	The doctor severs the patient's jugular vein during the operation.	The barber loses 20 pounds in six weeks.
MEMORY CUE				
Dispositional	Helpful	Honest	Incompetent	Willpower
Semantic	Clothes	Toys	Medicine	Hair
Action/gist	Assisting	Confessing	Surgery	Dieting

were given several types of memory cues. One cue referred to the disposition that explained the behavior, another cue was semantically related to the person performing the behavior, and a third type of cue described the behavior that occurred.

The key question of interest in this research is how each of these cues influenced participants' memory for the sentences they read. If, as the sequential model assumes, trait inferences are spontaneously made when behaviors are described, we should find that dispositional cues helped participants remember the sentences they read (e.g., the cue *incompetent* reminds the participant of the doctor, because the participant had automatically attributed the doctor's behavior to incompetence when reading the sentence). Figure 4.3 shows that this proved to be the case. Dispositional cues were the most effective memory aid, followed by the action/gist cues, which described the behavior sequence itself. Although there is some disagreement on the matter (D'Agostino, 1991), one interpretation of these findings is that participants spontaneously made trait inferences as they were reading the behaviors. Later, these dispositional cues jogged their memory and helped them remember what they had read (see also Lupfer, Clark, & Hutcherson, 1990; Todorov & Uleman, 2002, 2003).

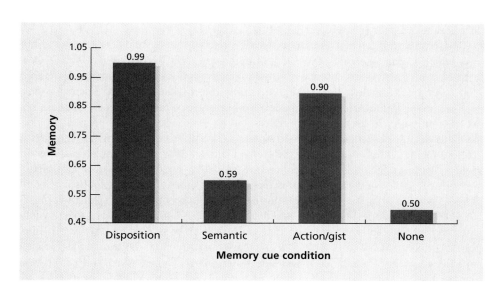

FIGURE 4.3

Memory as a Function of Memory Cue Condition

Dispositional cues were effective memory aids, suggesting that people spontaneously make trait inferences when they observe behavior.

Source: Winter, Uleman, and Cunniff (1985).

To summarize, research on the correspondence bias has found that we sponta-neously make trait inferences from behavior. In a sense, we take behavior at face value. We rather automatically assume, for example, that people who sit quietly are introverts and that people who speak in favor of national health insurance are liberal. For the most part, these assumptions are reasonable. Most of the time, people who sit quietly are introverted and people who espouse liberal causes are liberals. But the sit-uations people find themselves in can also elicit these behaviors, and it is this factor that we often fail to consider.

D. Qualifications to the Correspondence Bias

Although the correspondence bias and the operations that produce it are presumed to be universal, researchers have discovered that the effect is qualified by several impor-tant factors.

1. Cultural Differences in Causal Reasoning

Culture is one factor that qualifies the correspondence bias. In general, East Asians make more use of situational, contextual information when explaining behavior than do Americans (Choi, Nisbett, & Norenzayan, 1999; J. G. Miller, 1984). A study by Morris and Peng (1994, Study 2), illustrates these differences. These researchers examined accounts of murders in American and Chinese newspapers. When describ-ing these crimes, American reporters emphasized the dispositional properties of the murderer (e.g., the perpetrator was a disturbed man who drove himself to personal destruction), whereas Chinese reporters emphasized relationships and other contextual factors (e.g., the perpetrator had difficulty getting along with his superiors and felt isolated from the Chinese community).

These differences in causal reasoning may derive from more fundamental differ-ences in thinking. To understand this claim, we need to revisit a point we first made in Chapter 2: Western cultures tend to be individualistic. They emphasize self-reliance and view the individual as the primary cause of behavior. In contrast, Eastern cultures tend to be collectivistic. They view the individual as part of a broader social context, and emphasize that situational norms, role requirements, and contextual constraints also guide behavior (Markus & Kitayama, 1991).

These traditions have given rise to two different systems of thought: analytic think-ing, which is characteristic of Western cultures, and holistic thinking, which is char-acteristic of East Asian cultures (Nisbett, Peng, Choi, & Norenzayan, 2001; Kim, 2002; Peng & Knowles, 2003). Analytic thinking originated with the ancient Greeks and is similar to the Aristotelian model of physics discussed in Chapter 2. Here, one isolates an entity in an attempt to understand its invariant, inherent properties, inde-pendent of any particular context. In contrast, holistic thinking, which originated in ancient China and is more reminiscent of a Galilean approach, focuses on the entire field of forces that influence an entity in a particular context. Instead of abstracting an entity from its surroundings, as is the case with analytic thought, holistic thought emphasizes the interdependent relationship between an entity and its surroundings.

The holistic mode of thought practiced by East Asians leads them to pay more attention to contextual information than do people from a Western culture. To illus-trate, Masuda and Nisbett (2001) had Japanese and American college students watch an animated film of a fish and other underwater objects. When asked to describe what they had seen, American and Japanese participants were just as likely to mention the

TABLE 4.10	Cultural Differences in Causal Reasoning			
Culture	Tradition	System of Thought	Theory of Behavior	Implications for Causal Inference
Western	Individualistic: Strong beliefs in self-reliance and the power of free will underlie the belief that the individual is the primary agent of behavior.	Analytic: The focus is on classifying the inherent, invariant properties of an object independent of its surrounding context (Aristotelian).	Behavior depends most on the type of person one is.	Focus on dispositions as the cause of behavior leads to a correspondence bias.
East Asian	Collectivistic: Strong beliefs in the importance of maintaining group harmony lead to the belief that behavior is influenced not only by the person but also by situational norms, role requirements, and contextual constraints.	Holistic: The focus is on an object's behavior in a particular context, under the assumption of interdependence (Galilean).	Behavior depends on the interplay between a person's stable dispositions and the properties of the situation.	Attention is given to both dispositions and the relevant features of the situation.

focal fish, but the Japanese participants were more likely than the Americans to mention the context. Later, the Japanese participants showed better memory for contextual information than did the Americans. These findings fit well with other research that has found that, in comparison with Westerners, East Asians seek more information before making a decision (Choi, Dalal, Kim-Prieto, & Park, 2003) and make more use of situational information when explaining behavior (Choi & Nisbett, 1998; Miyamoto & Kitayama, 2002; Norenzayan, Choi, & Nisbett, 2002). Moreover, these differences occur even when cognitive demands are high, suggesting that situational adjustment is a well-learned, automatic process among people from East Asian cultures (Knowles, Morris, Chiu, & Hong, 2001).

Table 4.10 summarizes the research we have reviewed in this section. As you can see, different traditions give rise to different systems of thought, and these modes of thought influence causal inference. As a result, both cultural groups view dispositions as important determinants of behavior, but East Asians give greater weight to contextual, situational factors than do people from Western cultures.

2. Individual Differences in the Correspondence Bias

Table 4.10 shows that the attributions people make depend on their underlying theory of behavior. Although these theories are molded and shaped by culture, individuals also differ within cultures. Dweck and her colleagues have identified one important individual difference (Dweck, Hong, & Chiu, 1993). These researchers have found that some people view traits as stable qualities that can't be modified or developed. These entity theorists, as they are known, tend to pay minimal attention to the situation when describing behavior, focusing instead on the actor's dispositions. Other people believe that traits are malleable and can be cultivated. These incremental theorists give greater weight to situational factors when explaining behavior (Chiu, Hong, & Dweck, 1997).

3. The Actor–Observer Effect

Another factor that limits the generality of the correspondence bias is known as the **actor–observer effect** (E. E. Jones & Nisbett, 1972; D. Watson, 1982). This term refers to the fact that our tendency to make dispositional attributions is more evident when we explain other people's behavior than when we explain our own behavior. When we observe someone acting nervously, we are quick to attribute the person's behavior to a corresponding disposition. In contrast, when we act nervously, we are more apt to point to the situation (e.g., we are about to give an important speech; we had too much coffee to drink).

As with other findings in attributional research, the actor–observer effect was initially thought to depend on informational and perceptual processes. In terms of informational factors, actors have more knowledge of how they have behaved across a diverse range of situations than do observers, and these informational differences can produce the actor–observer effect. To illustrate, students often believe their professors are outgoing and talkative by nature because they see them only in situations that require outgoing, talkative behavior. In contrast, professors often attribute their outgoing classroom behavior to the situation, because they know how quietly they behave in other situations that do not require them to be so loquacious (Robins, Spranca, & Mendelsohn, 1996).

The actor–observer effect is also influenced by perceptual processes (Storms, 1973; S. E. Taylor & Fiske, 1975, 1978). Earlier we noted that Heider, the founder of attribution theory, was trained as a Gestalt psychologist. Drawing on this training, Heider believed that causal attributions are influenced by visual factors. Anything that captures our visual attention tends to be perceived as causal. In the realm of social perception, other people's behavior is more apt to command our attention than is the situation in which the behavior occurs. Consequently, we tend to make dispositional attributions for other people's behavior:

> [A person's] behavior has such salient properties it tends to engulf the field rather than be confined to its proper position as a local stimulus whose interpretation requires the additional data of a surrounding field—the situation in social perception. (Heider, 1958, p. 54)

Divergent visual perspectives can have important consequences. Lassiter and Irvine (1986) showed participants videotaped confessions, in which a suspect confessed to a crime. In one condition, the camera was focused primarily on the suspect; in another condition, the camera was focused primarily on the detective, and in another condition the camera was focused on the suspect and the detective equally. Participants who watched the confession in the suspect-focus condition were less likely to believe the confession was coerced and more likely to believe the suspect confessed because he was guilty.

The Self-Serving Bias in Causal Attribution. A final qualification to the correspondence bias stems from motivational factors. This effect is called the **self-serving attribution bias.** This term refers to the fact that people make dispositional attributions

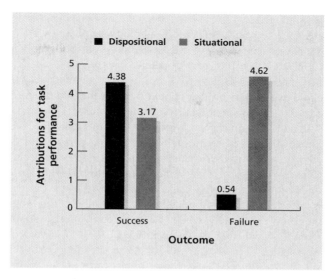

FIGURE 4.4

Attributions to Ability (a Dispositional Factor) and Luck (a Situational Factor) after Success and Failure

The data show a strong self-serving bias in causal attribution: Participants made dispositional attributions for their success and situational attributions for their failures.

Source: M. L. Snyder, Stephan, and Rosenfield (1976).

for their successes but situational attributions for their failures. To illustrate, students rarely cite low intelligence (a dispositional factor) as the cause of a poor exam performance. Instead, they blame a variety of situational factors (e.g., the questions were picky, the professor is disorganized, the book is unclear). Not everyone does this, but most people do (for reviews, see J. D. Brown, 1998; Mezulis, Abramson, Hyde, & Hankin, 2004; Zuckerman, 1979).

M. L. Snyder, Stephan, and Rosenfield (1976) conducted one of the first studies in this area. These investigators had participants succeed or fail at a task and then make attributions for these outcomes to ability (a dispositional factor) or to luck (a situational factor). Figure 4.4 presents some of the results from this investigation. The data show a strong self-serving bias. Success was attributed to dispositional causes more than situational ones, whereas failure was attributed to situational causes more than dispositional ones. The effect is particularly pronounced given failure, indicating that people are especially reluctant to make dispositional attributions for failure.

The self-serving bias is much less apparent when we explain other people's outcomes (Stephan et al., 1976). Consequently, the actor–observer effect occurs only when we make attributions for negative outcomes. To illustrate, when someone cuts us off in traffic, we are rather quick to assume that the person is rude or an incompetent driver. But when we exhibit the very same behavior, we attribute our actions to situational factors, such as poor driving conditions or, a blind spot in our rearview mirror. The reverse is true for positive outcomes: People are more apt to make dispositional attributions for their own positive outcomes than they are for the behavior of others (Schlenker, Hallam, & McCown, 1983). As a result of these tendencies, the self-serving bias qualifies the actor–observer effect (and the correspondence bias). The tendency to make dispositional attributions for behavior occurs when we explain our own successes and other people's failures.

4. A Critical Look at the Correspondence Bias

The tendency to overlook the importance of situational factors when explaining behavior has been one of the most active areas of research in social psychology over the last 30 years. In large part, this is because the effect lies at the heart of the social psychological approach to understanding behavior. As noted in Chapter 1, more than any other discipline, social psychology emphasizes that our behavior is due more to the situational pressures we face than to our enduring dispositional qualities.

Research on the correspondence bias reveals that we are often insensitive to this fact. In our day-to-day lives, we function as personality psychologists, not social psychologists, believing that people do what they do because of who they are rather than because of the situational forces they confront. This belief is one reason people put so much stock in traits when attempting to predict behavior (Kunda & Nisbett, 1986). Suppose you wished to predict whether a person will donate money to a particular charity when asked. What evidence would you use to fashion your prediction? Chances are, you would want to know the person's attitudes toward the cause (does the person support the cause or oppose it?) and the person's general level of generosity (is the person philanthropic or stingy?). You would probably not ask how the request was framed, whether other people in the situation had complied with the request, or whether the temperature in the room was comfortable and fresh cookies were being served. Yet each of these seemingly trivial situational factors has been shown to influence generosity, often exerting at least as much influence as the person's stable dispositions.

It May Be a Bias, But It's Not Necessarily an Error. Our tendency to overlook the power of the situation has been called *the fundamental attribution error* (L. Ross, 1977), but this characterization is not entirely warranted. No one knows why people do what they do, so we can never know whether or not our judgments are in error (Harvey, Town, & Yarkin, 1981; Sabini, Siepmann, & Stein, 2001). Moreover, many events require more than one cause, so discounting isn't always appropriate (McClure, 1998; Morris & Larrick, 1995). For example, a person who commits a violent act may be under severe stress, but even severe strain is unlikely to be sufficiently strong to fully explain the violent act. After all, most people who experience stress are nonviolent, so the situation provides only a partial explanation for the behavior (Reeder, 1993). In such cases, people are warranted in not discounting the causal role of dispositions (Gawronski, 2003a, 2003b; Liu, Karasawa, & Weiner, 1992).

A similar point can be made about the importance of freely chosen behavior. Attribution researchers contend that people should refrain from drawing dispositional inferences from constrained behavior. But this practice is inappropriate only if the behavior would not have occurred in the absence of coercion. To illustrate, suppose a debater is forced to argue that it is healthier to eat your chicken cooked rather than raw. Should we question whether this position reflects the person's true attitude? Attribution researchers argue that since the person had no choice about which position to take, you should not make any assumptions about the person's private attitudes. But this is not so. Almost everyone believes it is better to eat cooked chicken than raw chicken, so the person would probably have taken this position even if not forced to do so. The larger point is that choice should be used as a discounting cue *only* when the behavior would not have occurred in its absence.

In other cases, knowing that a behavior is forced provides important information about the absence of a trait. Suppose we read the following sentence: Billy's mom forced him to clean up his room. The implication here is that Billy would not have cleaned up his room in the absence of coercion, so we would be warranted in inferring that he is messy by nature rather than neat, even though the behavior "cleaning up one's room" connotes a meticulous nature.

Is the Fundamental Attribution Error Really Fundamental? There is also reason to question whether the fundamental attribution error is pervasive. First, the effect itself is rather small in magnitude (Gilbert et al., 1988). People may give insufficient weight to the situation, but they do use situational information when explaining behavior. Moreover, as we have seen, the effect varies across cultures, occurs for some individuals more than others, and rarely occurs when people explain their own negative outcomes. Given these qualifications, the fundamental attribution error doesn't seem all that fundamental.

Nevertheless, the tendency to assume that other people's negative actions are dispositionally caused is of considerable importance. Numerous interpersonal problems involve divergent explanations for behavior. When Pat forgets Chris's birthday, Chris may make a dispositional attribution and accuse Pat of being inconsiderate and self-involved. In contrast, Pat attributes the oversight to situational causes, such as a busy schedule, a misplaced calendar, or a momentary lapse in memory. Schoeneman and Rubanowitz (1985) found that opposing explanations like these abound in letters written to the advice columnists Dear Abby and Ann Landers (see also Farwell & Weiner, 2000). Additional research has found that opposing attributional patterns are commonly found in unhappy marriages (Bradbury & Fincham, 1990) and may even contribute to domestic violence (Holtzworth-Munroe & Hutchinson, 1993) and child abuse (Larrance & Twentyman, 1983). Clearly, the tendency to readily make dispositional attributions for other people's negative actions can have serious social costs.

III. Judgment and Decision Making

What [a] piece of work is a man, how noble in reason, how infinite in faculties.

Shakespeare, Hamlet, *II.2*

As research continued to reveal biases in the way people make causal attributions, a collateral research area developed. This research area examined decision making more broadly by studying how people make a variety of judgments. Instead of viewing people as naive scientists, researchers in this area characterized people as cognitive misers (S. T. Fiske & Taylor, 1991). This metaphor underscores that people's cognitive resources are limited and that judgments and decisions often need to be made very rapidly on the basis of limited information. Consequently, people often use a number of simplifying shortcuts called cognitive heuristics (Kahneman, Slovic, & Tversky, 1982; Tversky & Kahneman, 1974).

Before turning to the specifics of this research, a historical note is in order. One of the individuals most responsible for this research, Daniel Kahneman, received the 2002 Nobel Prize in Economic Sciences. In collaboration with Amos Tversky, Kahneman has spent his career systematically examining how and why people deviate from rational models of decision making and inference (Kahneman, 2003). Kahneman and Tversky's work was based on intuition and is infused with a contagious joy of discovery and innovation. Here's how they described their approach to doing research:

> Our method of research in those early Jerusalem days was pure fun. We would meet every afternoon for several hours which we spent inventing interesting pairs of gambles and observing our own intuitive preferences. If we agreed on the same choice, we provisionally assumed it was characteristic of human kind and went on to investigate its

theoretical implications . . . In a few giddy months, we raced through more than twenty diverse theoretical formulations. (Kahneman & Tversky, 2000, p. x)

In the sections that follow, you will learn about many of the discoveries Kahneman and Tversky made as they explored the gap between "what should be" and "what is."

A. Cognitive Heuristics

Cognitive heuristics are efficient problem-solving strategies that generally yield accurate solutions. For example, medical students are taught to "think horses, not zebras" when diagnosing a patient. This heuristic encourages the doctor to first think of the most obvious cause before considering a more exotic cause (e.g., a patient complaining of fever and chills probably has a cold, not malaria). In most cases, this heuristic is appropriate and saves the physician a lot of time.

1. Representativeness Heuristic

Imagine that a fair coin is flipped 10 times. Which of the following sequences seems more likely?

H H H H H T T T T T

H T H T T H T H H T

When given this problem, most people believe that the second sequence is more probable than the former even though the two sequences are equally probable. Why? According to Kahneman and Tversky, people use the **representativeness heuristic** when making this judgment (Kahneman & Tversky, 1972; Tversky & Kahneman, 1982). This term refers to a tendency to believe that the probability of an occurrence depends on how well it matches our beliefs about what should occur. Because the second sequence seems more random than the first, we judge it to be more probable.

The representativeness heuristic underlies a bias known as the **gambler's fallacy.** This fallacy occurs when people believe that random events are self-correcting. If a flipped coin yields seven heads in a row, people are unduly confident that the eighth trial will produce tails. Tails just seems due. In fact, the probability of tails on any given flip is 0.5, regardless of how many heads have preceded it. A gambler playing roulette may fall prey to this bias by overconfidently betting on red when black has come up many times in a row.

The representativeness heuristic also influences social judgments. Imagine that you are at a party with many artists and few lawyers and are introduced to a person who is wearing a three-piece suit and carries an expensive briefcase. How apt are you to assume the person is a lawyer? Because the person resembles your ideas about what a lawyer is like, you will give insufficient attention to the actual proportion of lawyers at the party and assume the guest is most certainly an attorney. This tendency to make judgments on the basis of representativeness rather than the prevalence of some characteristic in a sample is known as the **base-rate fallacy** (Kahneman & Tversky, 1973).

2. Availability Heuristic

Another heuristic, called the **availability heuristic,** refers to a tendency to make a decision based on the ease with which information comes to mind, with easily retrieved information having a stronger impact than information that is difficult to access (Tversky & Kahneman, 1973). To illustrate, suppose you are asked, "Are there more words in the English language that begin with *k* or more that have *k* as their third letter?" If you're like most people, you find it easier to think of words that begin with *k*, and answer that this is more common. In fact, there are nearly twice as many words with *k* as the third letter (e.g., *joke, make, like*), but these words are not called to mind as readily as those that begin with *k*, so we assume they are less common.

The availability heuristic is a reasonable problem-solving strategy under many circumstances. After all, likely occurrences are encountered more frequently, so their availability provides useful information when making a decision. At the same time, numerous factors that have little to do with the judgment at hand can influence how readily information comes to mind.

Recency. One factor that influences availability is recency. All else being equal, recent information is brought to mind more readily than is temporally distant information. We saw evidence of this in Chapter 3 when we examined how priming manipulations affect the impressions we form of others. Recently encountered information is cognitively available and, once activated, guides our judgments. A similar effect occurs when people assess probabilities. If you ask people how likely you are to die in an earthquake, the estimates you receive will be greater after a highly publicized quake than after a long time has passed since disaster last struck. In fact, even fictional accounts can influence judgment and decision making (Strange & Leung, 1999).

Vividness. Vividness is another factor that influences availability. Vivid and exciting information is brought to mind more readily than is information that is drab and boring. This is one reason why people are unduly influenced by case histories (Nisbett & Ross, 1980). Imagine that you are thinking about buying a car. After extensively researching various models, you settle on a car that has an excellent record. When you tell a friend about your decision, your friend tells you that her cousin bought the same car and had nothing but trouble with it. How influenced will you be by this new piece of information? Logically, you should consider this to be one more piece of evidence pertinent to your decision. But this is not what most people do. Most people give this information undue weight because it is vivid and memorable.

Moods. The word *gloomy* has two meanings: Sometimes it refers to a somber mood and sometimes it refers to a pessimistic outlook. This duality underscores the close connection between feeling and thinking. When we are happy, positive thoughts become more accessible and our interpretation of events and stimuli takes on a rosy glow. When we are sad, we have greater access to negative thoughts and we view the world through a pessimistic lens of cynicism and despair (Bower, 1981; Forgas, 1995; Isen, 1984).

A study by Forgas and Moylan (1987) illustrates these effects. These investigators approached people immediately as they were leaving a happy movie or a sad one. They then asked them to make a variety of judgments regarding various aspects of their own lives (e.g., their expectations about the future and how satisfied they were with the way things were now). Consistent with the notion that mood states activate mood-congruent thoughts, those who had just watched a happy movie evaluated their lives more favorably than those who had just watched a sad movie (see also Mayer,

Gaschke, Braverman, & Evans, 1992; Schwarz & Clore, 1983, 1988; Johnson & Tversky, 1983). Additional research has found that these effects occur for a wide variety of judgments and decisions, even when moods are experimentally induced by listening to happy or sad music, smelling pleasant or unpleasant odors, hypnotic suggestion, or the recall of positive and negative life experiences (Forgas, 1991; Isen, 1984). Of course, people are capable of correcting for this influence if they try hard enough (McFarland, White, & Newth, 2003), but mood-congruent judgments are the rule rather than the exception.

Moods also influence the way we process information. When we are happy, our judgments are based on efficient problem-solving strategies that rely on the heuristics we've been discussing; when we are sad, we are more inclined to take the time to carefully think about our judgments and decisions rather than answering with the first thought that comes to mind (Bodenhausen, Kramer, & Süsser, 1994; Gasper & Clore, 2002; Mackie & Worth, 1989; Park & Banaji, 2000; Ruder & Bless, 2003). As a consequence, happy moods tend to affect easy, simple judgments that require little thought, and sad moods tend to affect complex, difficult judgments that require a great deal of thought (Forgas, 1995).

3. Simulation Heuristic

Closely related to the availability heuristic is the **simulation heuristic.** This term refers to a tendency to judge the probability of a future event on the ease with which it can be imagined. In general, outcomes that are easy to imagine are judged to be more probable than outcomes that are difficult to imagine. For example, suppose you get a C on your next midterm. What will be your grade on the final? Your answer will depend on how readily you can imagine (or simulate) various alternatives. If you can easily imagine yourself buckling down and studying harder, you will be inclined to believe that your grade will improve.

Counterfactual Thinking. The simulation heuristic contributes to an important psychological phenomenon known as **counterfactual thinking.** Counterfactual thinking occurs when people believe that a different outcome would have occurred if different events had taken place. If you've ever thought to yourself, "If only I had studied a little harder, I would have aced that test," you have engaged in counterfactual thinking.

Counterfactual thinking is particularly relevant to situations involving blame and regret (C. G. Davis, Lehman, Wortman, Silver, & Thompson, 1995; D. T. Miller & McFarland, 1986; Niedermeier, Kerr, & Messé, 1999). In general, the easier it is to think of how things could have been different, the worse people feel when things go wrong. Consider the following scenario:

> Mr. Crane and Mr. Tees were scheduled to leave the airport on different flights, at the same time. They traveled from town in the same limousine, were caught in a traffic jam, and arrived at the airport thirty minutes after the scheduled departure time of their flights. Mr. Crane is told his flight left on time. Mr. Tees is told that his flight was delayed, and just left five minutes ago.

When Kahneman and Tversky (1982b) asked people who would feel more upset, almost everyone (96 percent) believed that Mr. Tees would feel worse than Mr. Crane. Why? Because Mr. Tee's flight just left, people assume that he will easily imagine how things could have been different ("If only the driver had made the light on Fifth and Main, I would have made my flight") and will feel worse about missing the flight.

The ease with which an alternative event can be simulated is influenced by several factors (Kahneman & Miller, 1986). For example, actions are easier to undo than are inactions, and rare events are easier to undo than common events (Kahneman & Tversky, 1982a, 1982b). To appreciate this latter effect, read the following two sentences and ask yourself which driver would feel worse (Kahneman & Tversky, 1982b):

> Mr. Adams was involved in a car accident when driving home after work on his regular route.

> Mr. White was involved in a similar accident when driving on a route that he only takes when he wants a change of scenery.

Even though both drivers were involved in an accident, most people (82 percent) believed that Mr. White would feel worse than Mr. Adams, because it is easier for Mr. White to imagine that the accident could have been avoided ("If only I had taken my usual route rather than the scenic route"). Mr. Adams, who took his regular route, is less apt to think about how things could have been different.

Counterfactual thinking also guides people's reactions to their own positive and negative outcomes. An investigation by Medvec, Madey, and Gilovich (1995) provides a particularly engaging demonstration of this effect. These investigators studied the emotional reactions of medalists at the 1992 Summer Olympics. Reasoning that silver medalists would be thinking that they would have won the gold medal if only they had made a slight change in strategy or had tried a little bit harder, Medvec and colleagues predicted that silver medalists (i.e., second-place winners) would actually feel worse than bronze medalists (i.e., third-place winners). To test their ideas, Medvec and colleagues had neutral observers rate each medalist's emotional reactions (as revealed in facial expressions) immediately after the athletic competition ended and later on the medal stand. As predicted, athletes who won a silver medal displayed *less* happiness than did those who won a bronze medal. Presumably, counterfactual thinking underlies these reactions. Because it was easier for the silver medalists to think of ways they could have won, they experienced greater regret and disappointment with their outcome. Undoubtedly, this is one reason why students who just miss earning an A often feel worse about their grades than do students who receive a middle B (Medvec & Savitsky, 1997; see also McMullen & Markman, 2002).

The Psychology of Regret. When examining the manner in which counterfactual thinking influences regret, it is important to distinguish between two types of errors: errors of commission (in which a wrong action is taken) and errors of omission (in which people fail to take an appropriate action). To understand this distinction, consider the following vignette:

> Mr. Paul owns shares in company A. During the past year he considered switching to stock in company B but decided against it. He now finds out that he would have been better off by $1,200 if he had switched to the stock of company B. Mr. George owned shares in company B. During the past year he switched to stock in company A. He now finds out that he would have been better off by $1,200 if he had kept his stock in company B.

When Kahneman and Tversky (1982a) asked respondents who would feel greater regret, 92 percent of them chose Mr. George. According to Kahneman and Miller (1986), this is because it is easier for people to imagine that they hadn't done something they had done than it is to imagine that they had done something they hadn't done. Subsequent research has shown that this is not always the case. Although actions produce greater short-term regret, inaction tends to produce greater long-term regret.

Evidently, when people look back over their lives, regret is greater among those who failed to try than among those who tried and failed (Gilovich & Medvec, 1994, 1995; see also Seta, McElroy, & Seta, 2001).

4. Anchoring and Adjustment

A final heuristic is known as the **anchoring and adjustment heuristic.** When asked to solve a problem, people often begin with an initial judgment (an anchor) and then modify their initial judgment to reach a final decision (adjustment). To illustrate, suppose that you are asked to estimate how many countries there are in the United Nations. As a hint, you're told the number is somewhere between 25 and 250. Now imagine that you're asked the same question, only this time you're told the number is somewhere between 100 and 250. If you're like most people, you will guess a higher number in the latter case than in the former. (Incidentally, the correct answer as of February 2005 is 191.)

Like the other heuristics Kahneman and Tversky identified, the anchoring and adjustment heuristic affects a wide variety of judgments and decisions (for reviews, see Plous, 1993; Tversky & Kahneman, 1974). In fact, we have already seen such an effect when considering the sequential model of the attribution process discussed earlier in this chapter. People begin by making a dispositional attribution and then, if they are willing and able, adjust this attribution on the basis of relevant situational information.

This heuristic can also explain contrast effects in judgment. Suppose you are asked to judge the weight of a paperback book. If you're like most people, you will probably judge the book to be heavier if you have first been asked to judge the weight of a feather than if you first judged the weight of a brick (Helson, 1964). The first object serves as an anchor, and the second object seems heavier or lighter by comparison. Contrast effects also occur when people judge psychological stimuli (Stapel, Martin, & Schwarz, 1998; Wegener & Petty, 1995). For example, when judging the severity of a crime, people rate a crime as more atrocious after evaluating a mild criminal offense than after judging a more heinous act (Pepitone & DiNubile, 1976). In these cases, people's perception of the second stimulus involves an adjustment away from the anchor the first stimulus provides.

B. Judgmental Errors and Biases

Earlier in this chapter we noted that cognitive heuristics allow us to make judgments rather quickly and with little effort. We have also seen that they contribute to several judgmental errors, such as the gambler's fallacy and the base-rate fallacy. In this section, we will examine some additional circumstances in which heuristics lead people astray, causing them to misinterpret or overlook important sources of information when making a decision.

1. Violations of Appropriate Statistical Principles

Insensitivity to Regression Effects. One judgmental bias occurs when people ignore the fact that extreme events tend to be followed by less extreme ones. This statistical phenomenon, known as **regression to the mean,** explains why tall parents tend to have children who are not so tall. If the parents' height is far above the population mean, our best prediction is that their children will be closer to the average height than the parents are. This doesn't mean that tall people have short children, but only that extremely tall people are apt to have children who are shorter than they themselves are.

To use another example, imagine that a high school student has steadily earned a solid 80 average in a certain class. If this student should happen to get a 90 on a

TABLE 4.11	Illustration of Judgments of Covariation	
	BIRD	
	Early	Late
Gets the Worm	16	4
Doesn't Get the Worm	4	1

midterm exam, the best prediction is that the student will get a lower grade than that on the final. That's because the 90 is above the student's mean, so the likelihood is that the next score will be less extreme. In formal terms, we say that the student's score is apt to regress toward the mean.

Regression effects provide an interesting perspective on performance following rewards and punishment. Let's imagine another high school student who has performed poorly on a midterm examination. Her parents decide to punish her by taking her phone privileges away. If her performance improves on her final exam, should her parents conclude that the punishment worked? Not necessarily. If the student's performance was below her average, then the best prediction we can make is that her performance on the next test will improve.

A similar analysis can be applied to a wide range of events and experiences (Nisbett & Ross, 1980). When crime rates are atypically high, cities take steps to reduce them; when sales are unusually low, businesses attempt to boost them. If, later on, crime rates drop and sales rise, we shouldn't automatically assume that the measures have been successful. Because extreme outcomes tend to be followed by less extreme ones, the observed changes may well have occurred even if no steps had been taken. After all, heat waves abate and dry spells end (otherwise they wouldn't be called heat *waves* and dry *spells*).

Misunderstanding Covariation and Correlation. In addition to predicting future performance from past performance, people also commonly determine the association between two or more variables. For example, they may ask themselves: Do blondes really have more fun? Is honesty really the best policy? Do only the good die young? Questions like these involve matters of covariation. To answer them, we must assess the extent to which two (or more) variables go together, or covary. Both the scientist and the naive scientist make use of covariation information when attempting to detect causal relations.

Despite the importance of assessing covariation, research reveals that people often exhibit a bias known as the illusory correlation. An **illusory correlation** occurs when people overestimate the correlation between two or more variables. To see why this occurs, consider the information presented in Table 4.11. Here we are testing the hypothesis that the early bird gets the worm. We have sampled 25 birds and noted whether they are early or late and whether they get a worm or not. Looking at the data, it is tempting to conclude that our hypothesis is confirmed. Sixteen of the 25 birds (64 percent) fall into the early-bird-gets-the-worm cell. Yet the correlation between the two variables is actually 0: 80 percent of early birds get the worm, and 80 percent of late birds get the worm; 80 percent of birds who got a worm were early, and 80 percent of the birds who didn't get a worm were early. In short, an early bird is no more likely to get a worm than a late bird is.

There are several explanations for the illusory correlation (Crocker, 1981; Nisbett & Ross, 1980; Plous, 1993), but the most important seems to be that we base our judgment on only one of the four cells: the confirmatory cell. Instead of looking at all of the information, we notice that there are lots of early birds who get the worm and therefore decide that the two variables are related. But this is an error. We simply have lots of early birds and lots of birds who get worms, so we naturally find many early-bird/get-the-worm pairings. If we look at all four cells, we see that the variables are not related in any systematic way.

Illusory correlations explain why people in Seattle commonly ask: "Why does it always rain on the day I wash my car?" The answer is that it rains a lot in Seattle (a verifiable fact) and that therefore the odds are good that it will rain on a day you wash your car. Another example occurs when people hear of a previously sterile couple who conceive a child after adopting a child (Gilovich, 1991). People tend to think, "This always happens. Right after a couple decides to adopt, they end up having a baby." The availability heuristic can explain this effect. Couples who conceive soon after adopting a baby are noteworthy and therefore unduly influence our judgments. We are less apt to notice and take into account all of the couples who remain unable to conceive after adopting a child (and all the couples who conceive or don't conceive without adopting).

Illusion of Control. Closely related to the illusory correlation is another bias known as the illusion of control. The **illusion of control** occurs when people overestimate the covariation between their own actions and a particular outcome (Jenkins & Ward, 1965; Langer, 1975). Superstitious behaviors provide one example of this bias. Many people believe they can bring about desired outcomes by performing behaviors that bear no logical relationship to the outcome in question. For example, athletes frequently wear the same uniform to each game or event during a winning streak, and many students bring a good-luck charm to a final exam. Although these ritualistic behaviors may well have a calming effect, they are unlikely to cause success or failure.

Langer (1975) noted that superstitious behaviors often occur when people confuse chance events with ones that are determined by skill. For example, gamblers toss the dice softly when hoping for a low number but throw hard when hoping for a high number. In an experimental demonstration of this phenomenon, Langer had male undergraduates play a game of chance with a confederate. In one condition the confederate was well dressed and appeared competent; in the other condition, the confederate was disheveled, acted nervously, and appeared incompetent. During the game, each player picked a card from a deck of cards; the person picking the highest card won. Obviously, winning at this game is entirely determined by chance, and one's odds of winning are no greater when competing against a nervous, awkward opponent than when playing against a highly polished one. Yet participants who played against the nervous opponent wagered more than did those who played against the competent opponent. Langer argued that this occurred because people mistakenly believe they have control over chance events (see also Wohl & Enzle, 2002).

Choice seems to be an especially important component of the illusion of control. In a second study, Langer (1975) had office workers participate in a lottery in which they could win $50 by purchasing a $1 ticket. Half of the workers were simply given a lottery ticket and half were allowed to reach into a container and select a ticket. Several days later, shortly before the lottery, the workers were given the opportunity to sell their ticket back to the experimenter. On average, workers in the no-choice condition were willing to sell their ticket for just under $2, whereas those in the choice condition demanded more than $8. Langer attributed this finding to an illusion of control: People mistakenly believe that choosing the ticket made it more likely that they would win the lottery (see also Tafarodi, Milne, & Smith, 1999). A desire to avoid regret may also underlie the effect (Bar-Hillel & Neter, 1996). People may be reluctant to exchange a lottery ticket they selected because they fear that the ticket they sell will turn out to be the winning ticket. This explanation emphasizes the role of the simulation heuristic and counterfactual thinking (Kahneman & Tversky, 1982a).

2. Choosing a Course of Action

People commonly select a course of action from among a range of alternatives. For example, investors decide which of two stocks to buy, and medical patients choose among various treatment options. In cases like these, we can begin to predict people's behavior by multiplying two factors: (1) the desirability of the outcome and (2) the probability that the outcome will occur. The product, known as the expected-utility of a decision, is a variation on the expectancy-value model (see Chapter 2).

In theory, people should always choose the option with the highest expected utility, as it represents the most rational choice. However, people's actual behavior deviates from this rational approach to decision making. In particular, people tend to be risk averse for gains. They prefer a certain, low payoff option to a low probability-high payoff one (i.e., a bird in the hand is worth two in the bush). In contrast, they are risk-seeking for losses. Instead of accepting a certain, but low cost loss, they gamble on a less certain but potentially more costly alternative (i.e., they will bet the farm to save the barn).

To understand these effects, imagine that you are given a choice between two options, shown under problem 1 in the top half of Table 4.12: Either you will be given $500 or you can play a game of chance in which you have a 25 percent chance of

---

TABLE 4.12   Expected Utility for Two Choice Problems

	Probability	Value	Expected Utility (Probability × Value)	Common Choice
PROBLEM 1: RISK AVERSION FOR GAINS				
Option 1: You win $500.	1.00	$500	$500	Approximately 75% of people choose this option.
Option 2: You have a 25% chance of winning $2,500 (and a 75% chance of winning nothing).	0.25	$2,500	$625	
PROBLEM 2: RISK SEEKING FOR LOSSES				
Option 1: You lose $500.	1.00	−$500	−$500	
Option 2: You have a 25% chance of losing $2,500 (and a 75% chance of losing nothing).	0.25	−$2,500	−$625	Approximately 75% of people choose this option.

Source: Kahneman and Tversky (1979).

winning $2,500 and a 75 percent chance of winning nothing. We compute the expected utility of each outcome by multiplying the probability of the outcome and the dollar value of the outcome.

Even though option 2 has a higher expected utility, approximately 75 percent of people choose option 1 (Kahneman & Tversky, 1979). They avoid the risk of option 2 in favor of the sure gain of option 1. This is what we mean when we say that people are risk-averse for gains. Most people prefer a less attractive but certain outcome over a more attractive but risky alternative.

Interestingly, this occurs only if one of the options is a certain outcome. If asked to choose between two *uncertain* outcomes—for example, a 25 percent chance of winning $2,500 (expected utility = $625) versus a 30 percent chance of winning $2,000 (expected utility = $600)—most people will chose the first option, even though it is a riskier bet. Taken as a whole, we can say that people prefer a sure thing to a bet, but if forced to bet, they will bet on a low-probability/high-payoff alternative more than a high-probability/low-payoff alternative (Kahneman & Tversky, 1979; Tversky & Fox, 1995).

The situation is different when losses are involved. Imagine that you are given another choice to make (see problem 2 in the bottom half of Table 4.12). You can either lose $500 or play a game in which you have a 25 percent chance of losing $2,500 and a 75 percent chance of losing nothing. In this case, about 75 percent of the people will choose option 2, even though the potential cost is greater. This preference is consistent with the claim that people are risk seeking when it comes to losses. They prefer taking a gamble that they will lose nothing over knowing they will surely lose something.

Figure 4.5 presents some of the things we've been discussing, as formalized in a theory known as prospect theory (Kahneman & Tversky, 1979; Tversky & Kahneman, 1992). The S-shaped line in the figure represents a value function. Values above the midpoint represent psychological pleasure and values below the midpoint represent psychological pain. Two effects are of interest. First, the S-shaped line rises and falls steeply at first and then begins to level off, indicating that both gains and losses show

FIGURE 4.5

Hypothetical value function as described by Kahneman and Tversky's prospect theory.

Source: Kahneman & Tversky (1979).

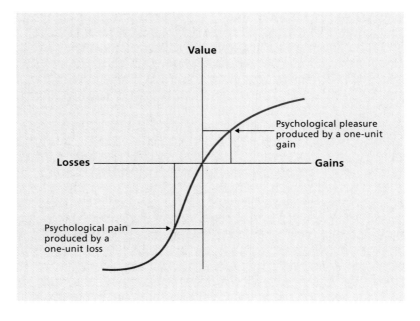

diminished psychological significance. To illustrate, the pleasure produced by a two unit gain is not twice as great as the pleasure produced by a one unit gain, and the pain produced by a two unit loss is not twice as great as the pain produced by a one unit loss. Second, the value function is steeper for losses than for gains, with a one unit loss being approximately equivalent to a two unit gain. Less formally, the pain associated with losing $100 is psychologically equivalent to the pleasure that comes from gaining $200. This explains why people are more risk-seeking for losses than for gains. Losses have a greater emotional impact than gains, so people try especially hard to avoid them.

Although not shown in Figure 4.5, prospect theory make an additional assumption of interest. The theory assumes that events that transform impossibility into possibility, or possibility into certainty, have a greater psychological impact than do events that merely make a possibility more or less likely. To illustrate this "certainty effect," consider several people who have contracted a life-threatening disease. A person who initially believes the disease has no cure will experience a greater rise in elation when learning that the probability of success has jumped to 0.25 than will a person who initially believed the probability of success was 0.25 but now believes it is a 50/50 proposition (even though probabilities rise by 0.25 in both cases). Conversely, a person who learns the probability of success has increased from 0.50 to 0.75 will experience a smaller change in elation than a person who learns the probability of success has increased from 0.75 to 1.0. This is what we mean when we say that events that transform impossibility into possibility (from 0 to 0.25) or from possibility to certainty (from 0.75 to 1.00) have a greater impact than do events that merely make an option more or less probable.

Framing Effects. Because people react differently to gains and losses, the decisions they make depend on how a choice is framed. To better understand this effect, consider the following example, which Tversky and Kahneman (1981) presented to university students:

> Imagine that the United States is preparing for an outbreak of an unusual Asian disease, which is expected to kill 600 people. Two alternative programs to combat the disease have been proposed. The accepted scientific estimate of the consequences of the programs are as follows:
>
> If Program A is adopted, 200 people will be saved.
>
> If Program B is adopted, there is a $\frac{1}{3}$ probability that 600 people will be saved, and a $\frac{2}{3}$ probability than no people will be saved.

The expected utility of both options is equal, but Tversky and Kahneman (1981) found that 72 percent of their participants chose option A. This is expected because the decision is framed in terms of gains (number of people who will be saved), and option A offers a certain outcome. As we have seen, people prefer a certain gain when given the choice.

In a second condition of their study, Tversky and Kahneman had another group of participants choose between two other options:

> If Program C is adopted, 400 people will die.
>
> If Program D is adopted, there is a $\frac{1}{3}$ probability that nobody will die and a $\frac{2}{3}$ probability that 600 people will die.

Notice that the only difference here is that the problem has been reframed: Instead of emphasizing the number of lives that will be saved (a positive frame that focuses on gains), these options emphasize the number of lives that will be lost (a negative frame that focuses on losses). Despite this slight difference, 78 percent of the participants preferred Option D to Option C. This, too, is expected, because the decision is framed in terms of losses, and people prefer a risky but low-cost option (a chance nobody will die) to a safer but costlier option. Although framing effects like these can be reduced when individuals are highly motivated to think carefully about the information being presented (McElroy & Seta, 2003), they can have important real-world consequences. For example, Meyerowitz and Chaiken (1987) found that negatively framed messages were more apt to persuade women to perform breast self-examinations than were positively framed messages (see also Blanton, Stuart, & VandenEijnden, 2001; Rothman & Salovey, 1997).

Temporal Distance. Another factor that influences the subjective value of an outcome is temporal distance. To appreciate the importance of this factor, imagine that you are considering whether to buy one of two raffle tickets. With option A, you have a 70 percent chance of winning $300; with option B, you have a 30 percent chance of winning $700. Which will you choose? Although the two options are equal with respect to their expected utility, your choice may depend on when the raffle is being held. According to Trope and Liberman (2000, 2003), the probability of an outcome is weighted more heavily when an event is in the near future, but the value of an outcome is weighted more heavily when an event is in the distant future. This analysis suggests that you will choose option A if the raffle is being held in the next week or two, but option B if it is being held in the next year or two (Sagristano, Trope, & Liberman, 2002).

The Perils of Too Many Choices. In this section we have been talking about choice. Most of us think choice is a good thing: The more options we have to select from, the more apt we are to make the right choice. This logic helps explain why modern grocery stores have entire aisles devoted solely to various kinds of potato chips, soft drinks, or shampoos. Yet choice is not always beneficial. In some cases, too many choices can undermine satisfaction (B. Schwartz, 2000). This point was illustrated in an investigation by Iyengar and Lepper (2000). Under the guise of a taste test, these investigators presented participants with a sample of Godiva chocolates. Some participants were allowed to choose a sample from among 6 chocolates, whereas others were allowed to choose a sample from among 30 chocolates. A final group was simply given a sample chocolate to taste. Afterward, participants indicated how satisfied they were with the candy they ate. Unsurprisingly, those who were allowed to choose were more satisfied than those who were given no choice. However, among those who were allowed to choose, those in the 6-choices condition expressed greater satisfaction than those in the 30-choices condition. Iyengar and Lepper (2000) concluded that having a choice is a benefit, but having too many choices can be a liability if it leads us to engage in counterfactual thinking (see also Iyengar & Lepper, 1999).

3. Biases in Explaining Events

When considering the past people often view events as predictable or even inevitable: "How could the United States not have foreseen the attack on Pearl Harbor?" or "How could British prime minister Neville Chamberlain have failed to see that his policy of appeasement toward Adolf Hitler was doomed from the start?" A similar logic colors our understanding of more mundane events, such as the stock market ("Many investors on Wall Street were kicking themselves today for not anticipating the recent downturn in the stock market") and interpersonal relationships ("She should have seen he would leave her; the signs were everywhere"). Hindsight, as they say, is 20–20. What seems inevitable looking back is rarely as obvious before we know how things have turned out.

Hindsight Bias: The Past Is More Probable Once It Is Known. Fischhoff (1975) provided an empirical demonstration of this effect. In the first part of the study, participants read a brief description of a little-known historical event: the 19th-century war between the British and the Gurkha of Nepal. Four groups of participants were then given outcome information: They were told either that the British won the war, that the Gurkha won the war, that the war ended in a stalemate, or that the war ended peacefully. A final group of participants received no information about how the war ended. Finally, all participants estimated the probability of the four outcomes, with the participants in the informed groups being asked to answer *as if they did not know* how the war had turned out.

Fischhoff found that participants who had been given outcome information overestimated the likelihood that their known outcome would occur. Furthermore, the participants were unaware that their previous knowledge had influenced their likelihood estimates. This tendency to overestimate the probability that a known outcome would occur is known as the **hindsight bias** (Fischhoff, 1975, 1982; Hawkins & Hastie, 1990). It has been found to influence judgments in a variety of settings, including judgments of physicians who make medical diagnoses (Arkes, Wortmann, Saville, & Harkness, 1981) and perceptions of criminal conduct and liability (Bryant & Brockway, 1997).

The simulation heuristic contributes to the hindsight bias. Knowing what's happened makes the known outcome easier to imagine than any alternative outcome. This account emphasizes that people's explanations for how an event occurred play an important role in their probability judgments. Once we know the outcome, we generate a web of causal explanations that make the outcome seem inevitable ("Obviously the baseball manager should have taken the pitcher out in the eighth inning—he had already thrown 80 pitches and was clearly getting tired"). The key aspect of this account, which Fischhoff (1975) referred to as *creeping determinism,* is people's ability to generate plausible explanations for why the event occurred. If they can't generate a plausible explanation, the hindsight bias doesn't occur. For this reason, outcomes attributed to unforeseeable chance events (e.g., a fluke storm) are not viewed as more probable in hindsight than they actually are (Wasserman, Lempert, & Hastie, 1991). Also, asking people to generate explanations for how other outcomes could have occurred reduces the bias (Arkes, Faust, Guilmette, & Hart, 1988; Slovic & Fischhoff, 1977).

The hindsight bias is also influenced by motivational factors. When it comes to negative outcomes, people often want to believe the outcome was inevitable and unavoidable (Tykocinski, 2001; Tykocinski, Pick, & Kedmi, 2002). This belief relieves them of any sense of personal responsibility and reduces their feelings of regret. Recognizing this, well-intentioned friends will often console a grief-stricken person by saying, "There was nothing anyone could have done."

Explanations and Expectations: The Future Is More Probable Once It Is Imagined. In addition to affecting the perceived likelihood of past events, causal explanations also influence the perceived likelihood of *future* events. When people are asked to consider how an outcome might occur, they come to believe the outcome is more apt to happen. In one investigation (L. Ross, Lepper, Strack, & Steinmetz, 1977),

FIGURE 4.6

Explaining How an Event
Might Have Occurred
Makes the Event Seem
More Probable

Participants who explained
an event subsequently
believed the event was
likely to occur.

Source: L. Ross, Lepper, Strack,
and Steinmetz (1977).

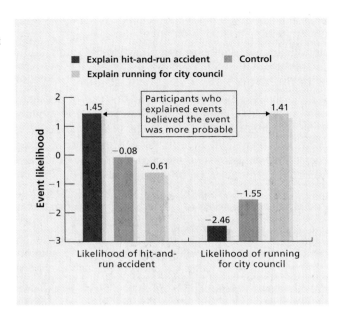

three groups of participants read an actual case history of a psychiatric patient. Participants in a control condition simply read the case history, whereas other participants were told to generate an explanation for why the person's prior behavior might have later led him to either become involved in a hit-and-run accident or become a candidate for city council. Afterward, all participants indicated how likely it was that these two events would occur.

Figure 4.6 presents some of the results from this investigation. The data show that participants who explained how the patient's past might have led him to become involved in a hit-and-run accident subsequently believed that outcome was more likely to occur than did participants who did not explain why such an outcome might transpire. The same was true for participants who explained why the patient might have later run for city council. These findings show that generating an explanation for why an event could occur makes the event's occurrence seem more likely (Koehler, 1991; Sherman, Zehner, Johnson, & Hirt, 1983).

4. Belief Perseverance: Explained Outcomes Resist Disconfirmation

A final research area examines what happens to people's beliefs once they have explained an outcome. To set the stage for this research, let's consider a scene familiar to anyone who has ever watched a courtroom TV show. A jury hears testimony from a witness, only to be told later that the evidence is inadmissible and that they should disregard it. How adept are people at putting aside what they have heard when forming a judgment? Are they really able to revise their beliefs when they learn that the evidentiary basis of those beliefs is faulty?

An investigation by C. A. Anderson and colleagues addressed this issue (C. A. Anderson, Lepper, & Ross, 1980). In the first part of the experiment, participants read evidence regarding a link between risk-taking behavior and success as a firefighter. Some of the participants were led to believe that risk takers make better firefighters, and others were led to believe that risk-taking behavior was an undesirable quality in a firefighter. After receiving this information, participants generated an

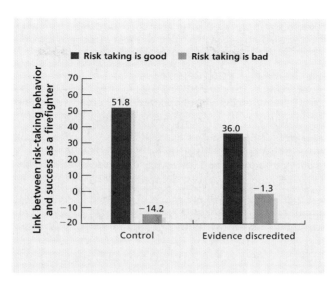

FIGURE 4.7
Belief Perseverance
Effects.

Participants who explained
why two variables were
related continued to
believe the variables were
related even when the
basis of their beliefs had
been discredited.

Source: C. A. Anderson, Lepper,
and Ross (1980).

explanation for the relationship they had been given. Subsequently, some participants were told that the facts they had been given were manufactured and unreliable and that the evidence did not really indicate that one type of firefighter was better than the other; other participants (in a control condition) were not given discrediting information. Finally, participants indicated whether they thought risk takers made better or worse firefighters.

The critical question in this study was whether participants would abandon their beliefs once they knew these beliefs were not based in fact. Figure 4.7 indicates that they did not. Even though they knew the information they had been given was fabricated, the participants continued to believe that the relationship they had explained was valid. C. A. Anderson and colleagues concluded that once a causal explanation has been generated, it survives evidential discrediting. This **belief perseverance effect** explains why people cling to their beliefs even after they learn that the evidence underlying these beliefs is flawed.

Belief perseverance effects even occur when individuals explain their own behavior. L. Ross, Lepper, and Hubbard (1975) led participants in one study to believe they were high or low in empathic ability. Later, they debriefed the participants (see Chapter 1), informing them that the feedback they had received was bogus and bore no relationship to their true ability level. Despite receiving this information, participants who had been given false success feedback continued to believe their ability was higher than did those given false failure feedback (see also Lepper, Ross, & Lau, 1986). These findings suggest that people's judgments and impressions become functionally autonomous from the evidence that created them. Once formed, these beliefs take on a life of their own and are relatively unresponsive to new information.

Findings like these provide an interesting way to integrate material we have covered in this chapter. We started out noting that our impressions of others are often influenced by a primacy effect. Once formed, these judgments affect the way we process information, including the causal attributions we make for the behaviors we observe. Once a causal explanation is reached, we continue to judge the person according to it even if the basis for that explanation has been discredited (or, more commonly, forgotten). Ultimately, we may like or dislike a person without even being able to remember why we feel the way we do.

C. Social Prediction

Of all the judgmental tasks people face, none is as complex or consequential as predicting another person's behavior. We may ask: "Can I trust Zak to keep a secret?" "If I lend Sara my car, will she return it in time for me to get to work?" or "If I join a study group, can I count on the other members to pull their weight?" People make predictions like these every day, often without thinking too much about it. But these judgments are very complex. Not only do we need to identify the person's relevant dispositional qualities (e.g., Sara's conscientiousness), but we must also integrate this information with knowledge of the situation, including features that are apt to be known with only limited certainty (e.g., whether or not the traffic is bad).

So how adept are we at predicting other people's behavior? When researchers have examined this question, two findings have emerged: People are able to predict another person's behavior with some degree of accuracy, but they are overconfident in that the accuracy they attain falls below the accuracy they expect to achieve (Dunning, Griffin, Milojkovic, & Ross, 1990; Griffin, Dunning, & Ross, 1990). We do better when we are asked to predict how people we know well will behave in familiar situations, but familiarity alone does not ensure accuracy or eliminate overconfidence (Gill & Swann, 2004; Swann, 1984; Swann & Gill, 1997). In fact, people even overestimate their ability to predict their own behavior. When Stanford undergraduates were asked to predict whether they would join a sorority or fraternity, become involved in a romantic relationship, or declare a major during the coming academic year, they expressed a great deal of confidence in their forecasts. The predictions came true more often than not, but they were not as accurate as the participants expected them to be (Vallone, Griffin, Lin, & Ross, 1990).

D. Summary of Judgment and Decision Making

In this section we have reviewed a good deal of evidence indicating that people use a variety of heuristics when making social judgments and decisions. These heuristics are often appropriate, but their use can also lead to a variety of predictable errors. Before we conclude this section, we need to address several additional issues.

First, we should acknowledge that many of the experimental tasks we have studied stack the deck in favor of revealing judgmental errors. When participants are given information in an experiment, it is reasonable for them to assume that they are supposed to use it (Schwarz, Strack, Hilton, & Naderer, 1991). This factor undoubtedly contributes to the hindsight bias and to the belief perseverance effect. It is also the case that participants in an experiment are rarely motivated to think carefully about the problems they are asked to solve. Although high involvement does not guarantee accuracy, biases can be reduced when people are motivated to be accurate (Harkness, DeBono, & Borgida, 1985; Pelham & Neter, 1995; Tetlock & Kim, 1987).

It's also important to consider why psychologists study errors in thinking at all. The reason is that we can learn a great deal about how people solve problems by focusing on instances in which problem-solving goes awry. This approach is also followed by those who study visual phenomena. Optical illusions are entertaining, but their scientific value lies in revealing ways in which our visual apparatus operates.

Another reason to focus on errors in thinking is that they are often highly consequential. Many fatal accidents, such as plane crashes and industrial disasters, involve judgmental errors. Erroneous beliefs have also put our planet in jeopardy and have led to the endangerment of many species. As Gilovich (1991) notes, the rhinoceros is endangered because people believe their horns can improve sexual potency, and the Chinese green-haired turtle is almost extinct because the Taiwanese believe it can cure cancer. Clearly, judgmental errors and mistaken beliefs can have important costs.

Finally, by understanding judgmental errors, we are in a better position to correct them. In fact, although they are not eliminated, biases and errors can be reduced when people are simply made aware of them (Ginossar & Trope, 1987; Stapel, Martin, & Schwarz, 1998; Wegener & Petty, 1995). Formal statistical training provides even greater improvements in judgmental accuracy (D. R. Lehman, Lempert, & Nisbett, 1988; Nisbett, Fong, Lehman, & Cheng, 1987). These efforts do not ensure that people will never err when making a decision, but they do offer a safeguard against the problems that arise when people are unaware that their judgments may be erroneous.

CHAPTER SUMMARY

- Elemental models of the impression formation process assume that people treat everything they know about a person as independent, isolated pieces of information and combine this information to form an overall judgment. From this perspective, the whole is equal to the sum (or some other algebraic function) of the parts.

- According to Solomon Asch, people strive to form consistent, coherent social perceptions, and everything we know about a person exists in a state of interdependence. From this perspective, the whole is greater than the sum of the parts.

- Causal attributions are answers to "why" questions. Attributions are influenced by information, motivation, and attention.

- When making attributions, people distinguish between dispositional causes (inherent, enduring properties of a person) and situational causes (anything that isn't a dispositional cause).

- When an obvious situational cause is present, we discount the role of a dispositional factor; when a person behaves in a manner that is inconsistent with the requirements of the situation, we augment the role of a dispositional factor.

- People tend to make dispositional attributions for behavior, a tendency known as the fundamental attribution error or the correspondence bias.

- Several factors qualify the fundamental attribution error. The effect is more apt to occur in Western cultures than in East Asian ones, and people who believe that traits are stable and unchanging are more apt to commit the error than are those who believe traits are malleable and modifiable. Moreover, the actor–observer effect reveals that people are more apt to make dispositional attributions for other people's behavior than for their own, and the self-serving bias reveals that people are more apt to make dispositional attributions for their own successes than for their own failures.

• People often rely on cognitive heuristics when making judgments. These heuristics are shortcuts that usually work well but can sometimes lead us astray.

KEY TERMS

primacy effect, 106	correspondence bias, 118	counterfactual thinking, 128
central traits, 107	actor–observer effect, 122	anchoring and adjustment heuristic, 130
causal attributions, 110	self-serving attribution bias, 122	regression to the mean, 130
dispositional attribution, 111	cognitive heuristics, 126	illusory correlation, 131
situational attribution, 111	representativeness heuristic, 126	illusion of control, 132
correspondent inference theory, 114	gambler's fallacy, 126	hindsight bias, 137
discounting principle, 115	base-rate fallacy, 126	belief perseverance effect, 139
augmenting principle, 115	availability heuristic, 126	
fundamental attribution error, 117	simulation heuristic, 128	

ADDITIONAL READING

Go to the Student Edition of the Online Learning Center for this text (www.mhhe.com/brown) and log in to read the following journal articles, which relate to the content of this chapter:

• Tversky, A., & Kahneman, D. (1981). The framing of decisions and the psychology of choice.

• Iyengar, S., & Lepper, M. R. (2000). When choice is demotivating: Can one desire too much of a good thing?

The Self

In her book *Black, White, and Jewish: Autobiography of a Shifting Self,* Rebecca Walker (2001) details her lifelong search to find herself. Rebecca is the daughter of Alice Walker, a highly acclaimed African American novelist and author of *The Color Purple,* and Melvyn Leventhal, a white Jewish lawyer who was an activist in the civil rights movement of the 1960s. Her parents divorced when Rebecca was eight, and she found herself shuttled between two worlds, confused about who she was and unable to define herself. Her book describes her often painful search for self-discovery:

> Late one night during my first year at Yale, a WASP-looking Jewish student strolls into my room through the fire-exit door. He is drunk, and twirling a Swiss Army knife between his nimble, tennis-champion fingers. "Are you really black and Jewish?" he asks, slurring his words, pitching forward in an old raggedy armchair my roommate has covered with an equally raggedy white sheet. "How can that be possible?"
>
> . . . after he leaves through the (still) unlocked exit door, I sit for quite a while in the dark.
>
> Am I possible? (p. 25)

Not everyone experiences as much confusion about his or her identity as Rebecca Walker has experienced, but we all journey to discover and define ourselves. In this chapter we examine this journey by considering the nature of the self. We begin by exploring the origins of self-awareness, paying particular attention to whether it is a uniquely human capacity. We then consider the nature of the self-concept, focusing on how people answer the question "Who am I?" Here we will also examine whether people know what they are really like. Next, we will explore the process by which people regulate and control their behavior. Finally, we will examine the role that self-relevant processes play in psychological health and well-being.

I. The Nature of the Self

It is almost certain that people everywhere have a concept of self. The ways in which they think about themselves differ, of course, but people have long been aware of their own existence and have thought about what they are like (Jaynes, 1976).

A. The Origins of Self-Awareness

George Herbert Mead was one of the first scholars to consider how self-awareness arises. Mead was a sociologist, with interests in a theory known as symbolic interactionism (Charon, 2001). Symbolic interactionism is concerned with understanding the socialization process. How is culture acquired and perpetuated? How do people come to adopt the values, standards, and norms of the society into which they are born? In short, how are individuals transformed from asocial creatures at birth into socialized beings?

Mead (1934) believed that socialization is synonymous with self-development and occurs when individuals imagine how they appear from another person's point of view. To illustrate, imagine that a very young child is scribbling on the walls with a crayon. Because the child is not yet able to ask, "I wonder what Mom and Dad would think of my behavior?" the child is not acting with reference to self and is not acting in a socialized manner. As the child matures, this perspective-taking ability develops ("I bet Mom and Dad wouldn't be happy with what I'm doing to the wall"). According to Mead, this capacity to imagine how we appear in the eyes of others constitutes the emergence of self and heralds the beginning of the socialization process.

Mead wondered how the perspective-taking ability develops. He asked, "How can an individual get outside himself . . . in such a way as to become an object to himself?" (1934, p. 138). Mead believed that symbolic communication in the form of language was the key to understanding the "essential problem of selfhood." He based his analysis on Darwin's theory of the evolution of emotional expressions (Darwin, 1872). In Chapter 3 we noted that various emotional states are associated with specific bodily and facial expressions, and that Darwin believed that these expressions communicate information about what an animal is likely to do. In this sense, nonverbal gestures (as Mead called them) constitute a form of communication; they let other animals know what is about to occur.

Communication in lower animals is largely instinctive. An angry wolf doesn't ask itself, "How can I let this other wolf know I'm angry?" It instinctively bares its teeth and communicates the internal state. Humans also communicate through instinctive facial expressions (Ekman, 1993), but these displays represent only a small portion of human communication. More commonly, people communicate symbolically, using language and gestures. In order to do so, Mead argued, they must adopt the perspective of another person and imagine how their actions will be regarded by that person.

To illustrate, suppose I want you to know that you are welcome in my home. How can I communicate this information to you? According to Mead, I need to put myself in your shoes and ask myself, "What behavior or gesture on my part would let you know you are welcome here?" After engaging in this process, I might conclude that opening up my arms in the form of a hug would do the trick. In this fashion, the need to communicate with symbols forces individuals to adopt the perspective of others and creates the self.

It is important to note the strong emphasis Mead gave to social interaction in his analysis of self-development. In the absence of social interaction, symbolic communication wouldn't be necessary and the self would not develop through the perspective-taking process Mead describes. This doesn't mean that we are always acting in a self-conscious and socialized fashion, however. Sometimes we are wholly unaware of ourselves. For example, if we are walking along, mindlessly humming a tune, we are not acting with reference to self. Only when something happens that causes us to become the object of our own attention (e.g., someone calls our name) are we swept out of our unsocialized reverie back into the self-conscious state that is socialized behavior.

At the same time, once the perspective taking ability has developed, people can act in a self-conscious fashion even when no one is around. This is the case because people can mentally represent others and imagine how their behavior would appear in another person's eyes. In the movie *Cast Away,* Tom Hanks displayed this tendency with a volleyball he named Wilson.

1. Visual Self-Recognition in Nonhumans

Believing that only humans communicate with language, Mead believed that only humans develop self-awareness. In an ingenious series of experiments, Gallup (1977) tested this hypothesis by seeing whether chimpanzees could recognize themselves in a mirror. Mirror recognition, Gallup argued, implies a rudimentary self-concept, as the animal must know the image in the mirror is his or hers.

In an initial investigation, Gallup exposed chimpanzees to a full-length mirror and recorded their behavior over a 10-day period. Initially, the animals responded to the mirror image as if it were another chimpanzee. Gradually, this behavior was replaced by activities of a distinctively self-directed nature. For example, while looking into the mirror, some chimpanzees began to groom parts of their body that could not be seen directly and pick material out of their teeth. Gallup argued that this switch in behavior indicated that the chimpanzees had come to recognize that the animal in the mirror was their own reflection.

Subsequent research provided even stronger support for this assertion. In a follow-up investigation, Gallup (1977) anesthetized the chimpanzees and, while they were unconscious, painted the uppermost portion of their eyebrow with a tasteless, odorless red dye. The dye was applied so that it was visible to the chimpanzees only when they viewed themselves in a mirror. Upon awakening, the animals were again exposed to their mirror image, and the number of behaviors they directed to the spot where the dye had been applied was recorded. In comparison with their earlier behavior, Gallup found that the chimpanzees were over 25 times more likely to touch the spot where the dye had been applied when they saw their reflection in the mirror. Moreover, this increased activity did not occur among a control group of chimpanzees that had not received prior exposure to their mirror image. These findings imply that the experimental group had earlier learned to recognize themselves in a mirror and were aware that the red-stained image in the mirror was that of their own face.

Other experiments have replicated this basic finding and tested whether other animals possess self-awareness. This research has found that orangutans and dolphins are also capable of self-recognition (Marino, Reiss, & Gallup, 1994; Meddin, 1979; Povinelli, Rulf, Landau, & Bierschwale, 1993; Reiss & Marino, 2001). For reasons not yet known, gorillas, despite being highly similar to humans, do not pass the mirror-recognition test.

Gallup's findings challenge Mead's assertion that self-awareness is a uniquely human capacity (but see Heyes, 1994). But what of Mead's more specific claim that self-awareness arises only in the context of social interaction? Must one have the opportunity to view oneself from the perspective of another before one can develop a concept of self? Gallup (1977) conducted additional research to test this idea. He repeated his earlier experiments using chimpanzees who had been reared in isolation, without ever having seen another chimpanzee. If, as Mead claimed, social interaction is necessary to the development of self, chimpanzees who have never had the opportunity to view themselves through the eyes of others should fail to recognize themselves in the mirror. This is precisely what occurred. The chimpanzees reared in isolation showed no signs of self-recognition. Only after three months of social interaction did they begin to recognize themselves in the mirror. Although alternative explanations for these results can be generated (e.g., being reared in isolation may have created a general cognitive deficit), the data are in accordance with Mead's claim that the opportunity to adopt the perspective of others is critical to the development of self.

2. Visual Self-Recognition in Infants

A modified version of the facial mark test (sans anesthesia!) has been used to assess self-recognition in infants. This research has generally found that visual self-recognition emerges during the first year of life (Lewis & Brooks-Gunn, 1979). By 12 months of age, most infants show signs of recognizing themselves when seeing themselves in a mirror or when watching themselves on videotape. This may well be a conservative estimate of when self-awareness arises. Some research suggests that self-awareness exists in a rudimentary form during the first few days of life (e.g., Butterworth, 1992; Meltzoff, 1990; Neisser, 1988).

B. Components of the Self-Concept

Although infants possess self-awareness, they do not yet possess a sophisticated **self-concept.** This term refers to people's ideas about who they are and what they are like. Before reading further, take a moment to consider what you would tell another person about yourself if you wanted that person to know what you were really like. Feel free to include aspects of your personality, background, physical characteristics, hobbies, things you own, people you are close to, and so forth. In short, anything that helps the person know what you are really like. More than a century ago, William James (1890) decided that people's answers to the question "Who am I?" fall into three categories. With a few modifications (Brewer & Gardner, 1996), James's ideas are still pertinent today.

1. Material Self

The first category James considered includes physical objects that people designate as *my* or *mine.* This category, termed the material self, not only includes our bodies (e.g., a person speaks of *my arms* or *my legs*) but also people we care deeply about (my children), possessions (my car), places (my hometown), and the products of our labors (my painting). Considering its breadth, it's important to establish a means of identifying whether a given entity is part of this **extended self.** James believed we can make this determination by examining our emotional investment in the entity. If we respond in an emotional way when the entity is praised or attacked, the entity is apt to be part of the self. Everyday experience gives testimony to James's intuitions. Parents, for example, glow with pride when a teacher praises their child's behavior and cringe with embarrassment when their child acts boorishly in a restaurant or grocery store. It's almost as if they themselves have done something good or bad.

People's possessions evoke similar emotional reactions. Many car owners react with anger (and often rage) when their cars are damaged, even when the physical damage is only slight. This reaction suggests that the accident is experienced as a personal affront. In a similar manner, people who lose possessions in a natural disaster often go through a grieving process akin to the process people go through when they lose a loved one (Belk, 1988).

Further evidence that possessions are part of the self comes from a series of experiments by Beggan (1992). In an initial study, participants were shown a variety of inexpensive objects (e.g., a key ring, a plastic comb, playing cards). They were then given one object and told it was theirs to keep. Later, participants evaluated their object more favorably than the objects they didn't receive. Follow-up research suggests that this mere-ownership effect stems from a desire to feel good about ourselves. In general, once something becomes ours, we imbue it with value and use it to promote feelings of self-worth.

This tendency even extends to letters of the alphabet. When asked to judge the pleasantness of various letters, people show enhanced liking for the letters that make up their own name, particularly their own initials (Greenwald & Banaji, 1995; J. T. Jones, Pelham, Mirenberg, & Hetts, 2002; Nuttin, 1985, 1987). This effect has been observed in a variety of cultures (Hoorens & Todorova, 1998; Kitayama & Karasawa, 1997) and may even influence important life decisions. Pelham, Mirenberg, and

Jones (2002) found that people are more likely to live in cities or choose occupations that match their name or initials. For example, people named Jack are disproportionately likely to live in Jacksonville, Florida, and people named Harvey are disproportionately likely to own a hardware store (see also Gallucci, 2003; Pelham, Carvallo, DeHart, & Jones, 2003).

2. Social Self

The social roles people occupy are also part of the self-concept (Deaux, Reid, Mizrahi, & Ethier, 1995). Included among these social identities are vocations (e.g., plumber), avocations (e.g., snowboarder), and informal social categories (e.g., jock). Our identifications with various groups are also part of the social self. These collective identities, which include our nationality (e.g., American), religious identities (e.g., Catholic), and racial and ethnic identities (e.g., African American) are routinely mentioned when people describe themselves, and are capable of producing very strong emotions (Luhtanen & Crocker, 1992; E. R. Smith & Henry, 1996; J. C. Turner, Oakes, Haslam & McGarty, 1994).

Even relatively trivial associations can generate a lot of emotion. After an important sports victory, it is not uncommon to see fans spilling onto the field chanting "We're number one." Cialdini and associates coined the term *basking in reflected glory* (*BIRGing*) to describe such reactions, noting that the use of the personal pronoun *we* implies that the victory is experienced in a personal way (Cialdini et al., 1976). In contrast, people frequently distance themselves from a loser by saying "*They* lost" when the team they were rooting for tastes defeat (Hirt, Zillmann, Erickson, & Kennedy, 1992; C. R. Snyder, Lassegard, & Ford, 1986).

Of course, people cannot always so easily dismiss their identification with a group, leading them to experience negative emotions when the group they associate themselves with does something blameworthy. The collective guilt many Germans feel for the atrocities their forebears committed during World War II provides a dramatic illustration of this effect. Even though they had nothing to do with the Holocaust, they feel a sense of personal responsibility and remorse (Doosje, Branscombe, Spears, & Manstead, 1998).

3. Spiritual Self

James's final category, the spiritual self, refers to people's understanding of their psychological qualities. One's perceived abilities, attitudes, emotions, opinions, and traits are what James had in mind here. Some of these identities are rather general (e.g., "I am honest"), but most are contextualized: They depend on the situation we are in or the person we are with. Figure 5.1 illustrates this point, showing how a hypothetical person might think of herself in relation to various people, situations, and activities. For example, she thinks of herself as diligent at work, tender with her spouse, and playful with her nephews.

C. Cultural Differences in the Self-Concept

James (1890) believed that spiritual identities are the most important aspect of the self-concept, and research supports his contention (Gaertner, Sedikides, & Graetz, 1999). At the same time, cultures also differ in the importance people attach to their perceived psychological qualities (A. P. Fiske, Kitayama, Markus, & Nisbett, 1998;

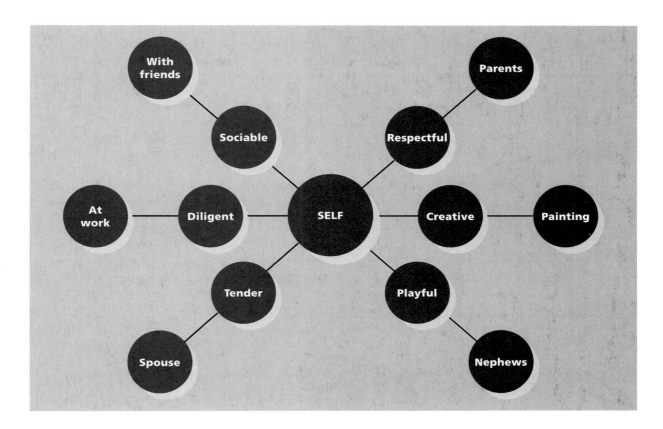

FIGURE 5.1

The Contextualized Nature of Self-Knowledge

The figure shows that thoughts about ourselves are linked to particular relationships, situations, and activities.

Markus & Kitayama, 1991; Triandis, 1989). As we note throughout this text, Western countries (e.g., the United States, Canada, and Western European countries) are individualistic—people raised in these cultures tend to develop an independent self-view that stresses the importance of their distinctive personal qualities. When describing their most important attributes, individualists mention their emotions, attitudes, and beliefs. In contrast, East Asian countries (e.g., China, Japan, Korea) tend to be more collectivistic. The emphasis on collectivism leads people to develop an interdependent self-view, highlighting ways in which they are linked to one another by virtue of their shared social identities. When describing their most important attributes, collectivists mention their social roles, group memberships, and other people who are part of their extended self (Cousins, 1989; Trafimow, Triandis, & Goto, 1991; Wang, 2001).

D. Self-Complexity

Former president Lyndon Johnson once described himself as "a free man, an American, a United States Senator, a Democrat, a liberal, a conservative, a Texan, a taxpayer, a rancher, and not as young as I used to be nor as old as I expect to be" (cited in Gergen, 1971). Not everyone's self-concept is this detailed, however. Some people think of themselves in lots of different ways, whereas others think of themselves in only a few different ways. Linville (1985, 1987) coined the term *self-complexity* to refer to such differences. People who think of themselves in many different ways are high in self-complexity, and those who think of themselves in relatively few ways are low in self-complexity.

People who are low self-complexity seem to experience more extreme emotional reactions to positive and negative events. To illustrate, suppose you are a single-minded lawyer. Your entire life revolves around your law practice. If you win a case, you will feel ecstatic; if you lose a case, you may feel devastated. Now consider the situation if you think of yourself as a hardworking lawyer but also as an understanding friend, a loving spouse, a caring parent, and so on. Because you have so many identities, your performance as a lawyer won't have such a strong emotional impact on you (see also Dixon & Baumeister, 1991; Niedenthal, Setterlund, & Wherry, 1992; C. M. Steele, 1988, Thoits, 1983).

Although multiple identities may generally be healthy, they may also get us into trouble. The problem, as William James noted, is that we cannot be all the things we would like to be:

> I am often confronted by the necessity of standing by one of my empirical selves and relin-
> quishing the rest. Not that I would not, if I could, be both handsome and fat and well-
> dressed, and a great athlete, and make a million a year, be a wit, a *bon-vivant*, and a
> lady-killer, as well as a philosopher, a philanthropist, statesman, warrior and African
> explorer, as well as a "tone-poet" and saint. But the thing is simply impossible. The mil-
> lionaire's work would run counter to the saint's; the *bon-vivant* and the philanthropist
> would trip each other up; the philosopher and the lady-killer could not well keep house
> in the same tenement of clay. (James, 1890, pp. 309–310)

The point here is that each additional identity can be a burden as well as a blessing. Ultimately, it depends on whether the identities fit well with one another. We hear often in modern society about role conflict. Women, for example, are expected to be wage earners, wives, mothers, educators, athletes, chauffeurs, doctors, and more. These multiple social identities may create conflict. Women may also experience friction among their various personal identities. After the birth of a child, they may experience a conflict between a desire to be nurturing and a desire to be ambitious. An investigation of women pursuing a career in the sciences illustrates the problem. Settles (2004) found that women who experienced a conflict between their identity as a woman and their identity as a scientist reported more depression, lower self-esteem, and less satisfaction with their lives than did women who did not perceive a conflict between these two identities. Whether more is better, then, is likely to depend on whether the fit among the various identities is good (see also Donahue, Robins, Roberts, & John, 1993; Woolfolk, Novalany, Gara, Allen, & Polino, 1995).

II. Sources of Self-Knowledge

Having examined how individuals answer the question "Who am I?" we can now consider the sources of these answers. In other words, we can ask: How do we know what we are like?

A. Physical World

The physical world provides us with some information about ourselves. For example, if you want to know how tall you are, you can measure your height; if you want to know how strong your muscles are, you can go to a health club and record how many pounds you can lift. In these cases, you are using the physical world to gain knowledge of yourself.

Though useful as a source of self-knowledge, the physical world is limited in two important respects. First, many personal attributes are not anchored in physical reality. Suppose you want to know how kind you are. You can't simply get out a yardstick and measure your kindness. The same is true if you want to know how clever or sincere you are. A physical basis for gaining knowledge in these domains (and many others) is lacking.

Even when the physical world does provide some basis for learning about yourself, the knowledge it provides is rarely the knowledge you are after. Knowing your height doesn't really tell you whether or not you are tall. You need to know how tall other people are, on average. The same is true when it comes to knowing how strong you are or how smart you are. These attributes, like most others, are meaningful only in comparative terms. To say someone is talented is to say he or she is more talented than most other people are.

B. Social World

1. Social Comparison Processes

Recognizing that the physical world provides only limited information, Festinger (1954) developed **social comparison theory.** According to this theory, we gain knowledge of ourselves by comparing ourselves with others (Suls & Miller, 1977; Suls & Wills, 1991). To illustrate, in order to know whether or not you are strong, you have to compare your strength with that of other people. But who should you choose to compare yourself with? Festinger believed that people strive to know the truth about themselves and will therefore compare themselves with those who are similar to them. In this context, *similar* means "similar on dimensions relevant to the attribute being assessed." For example, I would best be able to tell how strong I am by comparing myself with other middle-aged men. Comparing my strength with that of women or children is less informative, because they are generally too different from me when it comes to physical strength.

People tend to compare themselves with others who are similar to them, but they do not always do so (J. V. Wood, 1989). People also compare themselves with those who are better off than they (a process called *upward comparison*) and with those who are worse off than they (a process called *downward comparison*) (R. L. Collins, 1996; Goethals & Darley, 1977; Wills, 1981). This occurs because the need for accurate self-knowledge is not the only motive that drives social comparison processes (Helgeson & Mickelson, 1995). People engage in upward comparison in an attempt to inspire and improve themselves (e.g., if they can do it, I can do it), and they engage in downward comparison in an attempt to console themselves (e.g., I may be poor, but at least I have a roof over my head, unlike some people) (Taylor & Lobel, 1989).

Social Context and Self-Descriptions. People are not always free to choose their comparison targets. Sometimes they are forced to compare themselves with others who are part of the social situation. Ordinarily, this makes people think of themselves in ways that distinguish them from others. For example, when McGuire and McGuire (1981, 1988) asked children to describe themselves, 27 percent of very tall or very short children spontaneously mentioned their height, but only 17 percent of children of average height did so. Similar results were found for weight, hair color, and birthplace. The more distinctive the attribute, the more likely children were to use it to describe themselves (see also Nelson & Miller, 1995; von Hippel, Hawkins, & Schooler, 2001).

Distinctiveness also influences the salience of group identities (J. C. Turner, Hogg, Oakes, Reicher, & Wetherell, 1987). For example, an American is more apt to be thinking of his national identity when he is in Rome, Italy, than when he is in Rome, Georgia, because his nationality is distinctive when he is in a foreign land. The salience of group identities is also influenced by group size. Almost by definition, minority groups tend to be statistically distinctive (in part, this is what it means to be a minority). Because of this distinctiveness, minority group members are more apt to think about their group identity than are majority group members (Brewer, 1991; Mullen, Migdal, & Rozell, 2003; B. Simon & Hamilton, 1994).

These effects have important implications for people with bicultural identities. Many Americans today were born in another country or have parents who were. Labels such as Asian American, African American, and Mexican American highlight this biculturalism. Such people often live a bicultural life. They "act American" when they are with their friends but behave in a more traditional Old World fashion when they are with their family and neighbors. They also think about themselves differently in different cultural contexts. For example, M. Ross, Xun, and Wilson (2002) found that Chinese-born Canadian college students were more apt to mention their collective identities when describing themselves in Chinese than when describing themselves in English. These findings underscore that subtle variations in social context can influence how people with a bicultural identity think of themselves (see also Phinney, 1990; Trafimow, Silverman, Fan, & Law, 1997).

Social Context and Self-Evaluations. The social context also influences how people evaluate themselves. This phenomenon can be observed in virtually all U.S. grocery stores, whose checkout stands are lined with magazines that depict thin fashion models in provocative poses. Typically, exposure to these images produces a contrast effect: Women evaluate themselves more negatively after viewing images of attractive female models, particularly when men are present (Cash, Cash, & Butters, 1983; Henderson-King, Henderson-King, & Hoffman, 2001).

A similar effect occurs when it comes to self-perceptions of ability. Before reading about this research, decide how you would answer the following question: Do you think you would feel smarter if you were attending a university with very smart students or a university with students who were not so smart? To answer this question, Marsh, Kong, and Hau (2000) interviewed more than 7,000 students attending various schools in Hong Kong. The schools varied in their academic excellence, enabling the researchers to determine how these variations influence students' perceptions of their academic ability. Contrast effects occur if students attending low-achieving schools evaluate themselves more positively than do those attending high-achieving schools. The data displayed in Figure 5.2 provide evidence for this effect. At every level of actual ability, students attending low-achieving schools evaluated themselves more positively than did students attending medium- or high-achieving schools (see also Bachman & O'Malley, 1986; J. A. Davis, 1966; Marsh & Hau, 2003; Marsh & Parker, 1984). Informally, this effect is known as the frog pond effect, because it suggests that people feel like big fish in a little pond.

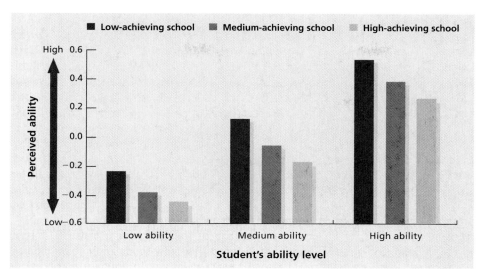

FIGURE 5.2

The Frog Pond Effect in the Classroom

At every level of ability, students who attended low-achieving schools thought they were smarter than students who attended high-achieving schools. These findings suggest that people evaluate their ability by comparing themselves with others in their immediate social surroundings.

Source: Marsh, Kong, and Hau (2000).

Not all research shows evidence of a contrast effect in self-evaluations, however. Under some conditions, people show an assimilation effect: They evaluate themselves more positively when they compare themselves with others who are exemplary on some dimension (Mussweiler, 2003). Sometimes this occurs when people believe the comparison attribute can be modified. For example, if you think you can improve your soccer skills, you will probably be inspired when you compare yourself with a world champion (Lockwood & Kunda, 1997; Major, Testa, & Blysma, 1991; Stapel & Koomen, 2000; S. E. Taylor & Lobel, 1989).

Psychological closeness also influences when assimilation effects occur. To illustrate, in one investigation, my colleagues and I led female participants to believe they would be having a get-acquainted conversation with another woman (J. D. Brown, Novick, Lord, & Richards, 1992). Prior to the conversation, they were shown a picture of what the other woman (allegedly) looked like. Some participants saw a very attractive woman, and others saw a woman who was relatively unattractive. To vary psychological closeness, some participants were led to believe that they shared the same birthday with the woman in the photograph; participants in a control condition were not given this information. Finally, participants rated their own attractiveness.

My colleagues reasoned that the shared birthday manipulation would lead participants to feel psychologically connected to the woman in the photograph (Cialdini & De Nicholas, 1989; Finch & Cialdini, 1989; D. T. Miller, Downs, & Prentice, 1998) and that these feelings of relatedness would lead participants to assimilate to the woman's attractiveness. The data shown in Figure 5.3 confirm these predictions. Although the usual contrast effect was found in the control condition (participants viewing the attractive woman rated themselves as less attractive than did participants viewing the unattractive woman), assimilation effects occurred in the shared-birthday condition (participants rated themselves as more attractive when viewing the attractive woman than when viewing the unattractive woman). These findings establish that assimilation effects occur when people compare themselves with a person who is part of their extended self (see also Brewer & Weber 1994; Broemer & Diehl, 2004; Gardner, Gabriel, & Hochschild, 2002; McFarland & Buehler, 1995; Pelham & Wachsmuth, 1995).

FIGURE 5.3

Assimilation and Contrast Effects in Self-Evaluations of Attractiveness

The data show a contrast effect in the control condition, but an assimilation effect in the shared-birthday condition. These findings indicate that people assimilate to the characteristics of others when they feel psychologically connected to them.

Source: J. D. Brown, Novick, Lord, and Richards (1992).

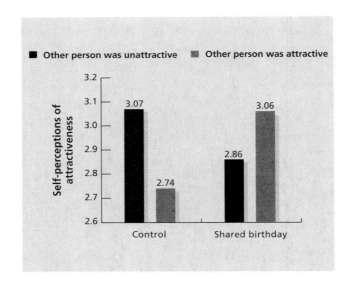

2. Reflected Appraisals

Social relationships influence the self-concept in another important way. Sometimes people learn about themselves by imagining how they appear in the eyes of others. For example, suppose I tell a joke and nobody laughs. I might reasonably infer that I have don't have a very good sense of humor. The **reflected appraisal model** describes this process (Cooley, 1902; Kinch, 1963). As shown in Figure 5.4, this process is comprised of three components: (1) What other people actually think of us (the actual appraisals of others), (2) our perception of these appraisals (our perceived appraisals), and (3) our own ideas about what we are like (our self-appraisals). The model assumes that actual appraisals determine perceived appraisals and that perceived appraisals determine self-appraisals. As an example, the model assumes (1) that if other people think you are attractive (actual appraisal), (2) you will become

FIGURE 5.4

The Reflected Appraisal Model

In this model, what other people think of us (actual appraisals) influences our self-appraisals indirectly, via perceived appraisals.

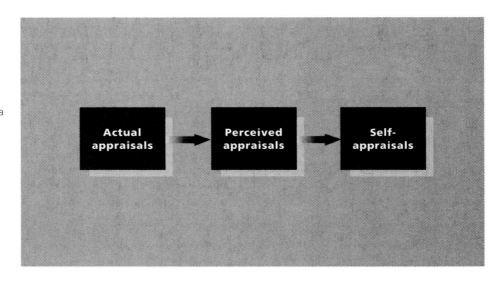

aware of this (perceived appraisal) and (3) start to think you are attractive (self-appraisal).

A great deal of research has tested the model shown in Figure 5.4 (for reviews, see Felson, 1993; Kenny & DePaulo, 1993). In general, this research has turned up only limited support for the reflected appraisal model. First, contrary to the model, people are not very good at knowing what any particular individual thinks of them. In part, this is because communication barriers and social norms limit the information we receive from others (Felson, 1993). This is especially true when the feedback would be negative. People adhere to the dictum "If you don't have anything nice to say about someone, don't say anything at all" and thus rarely give one another negative feedback, so people rarely conclude that other people dislike them or evaluate them negatively.

A different problem clouds the interpretation of the association between perceived appraisals and self-appraisals. These variables are highly correlated (Kenny & DePaulo, 1993; Shrauger & Schoeneman, 1979), but the causal association between them is unclear. The reflected appraisal model assumes that perceived appraisals determine self-appraisals (e.g., if we think other people think we are clever, then we think we are clever), but the reverse causal sequence is also possible (e.g., if we think we are clever, we assume other people think so, too). Although correlational studies provide an imperfect test of this issue, the association between perceived appraisals and self-appraisals seems to occur because people assume that others see them as they see themselves (Felson, 1993).

These findings suggest some important qualifications to the reflected appraisal model. As originally conceived, the model assumed that people see themselves as others see them. Person A forms an opinion about person B, and person B pliantly registers this opinion and incorporates it into her self-concept. This sequence may accurately characterize matters in childhood (Frome & Eccles, 1998), but it appears to be less relevant later in life. People are simply not as passive as the model assumes. They strategically decide whose eyes to look into, and they selectively interpret the image they see reflected in those eyes. For this reason, people usually believe that others see them as they see themselves or wish to be seen.

Thinking about Others Activates Self-Views. Of course, the fact that support for the reflected appraisal model is limited doesn't mean we are never influenced by the perceived judgments of others. Clearly, a disapproving glance from a spouse or a friend can make us feel bad about ourselves. In an engaging study, Baldwin and colleagues demonstrated this effect experimentally (Baldwin, Carrell, & Lopez, 1990). In this investigation, graduate students in psychology were asked to evaluate their research ideas after viewing (at levels below conscious awareness) the scowling face of their advisor or the approving face of a fellow student. Those exposed to the disapproving face subsequently evaluated their work more negatively than did those exposed to the approving face (see also Baldwin, 1994; Hinkley & Andersen, 1996).

It is especially noteworthy that the students in Baldwin's research were not consciously aware they had viewed an approving or disapproving face, even though seeing these faces affected the way they thought about themselves. This finding is consistent with evidence that even stimuli we're not paying attention to can activate particular self-views (Bargh, 1982; Strauman & Higgins, 1987). You might, for example, catch a glimpse of someone who reminds you of your mother. Then, without even realizing it, you might start seeing yourself through her eyes and thinking of yourself from her point of view (Andersen & Chen, 2002).

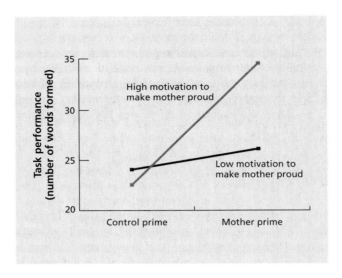

FIGURE 5.5

Task Performance after Thinking about Someone We Care to Please

The priming manipulation had no effect among participants who weren't motivated to please their mother, but it did increase performance among those who were motivated to make their mother proud of them. These findings show that the mental activation of another person can influence people's behavior.

Source: Fitzsimons and Bargh (2003).

Research by Fitzsimons and Bargh (2003) suggests that you might even start behaving differently. These investigators first had participants indicate whether or not they were motivated to make their mother proud. Some indicated that they were motivated, and others indicated that they weren't. Several weeks later, the participants all came to a laboratory and completed a priming task. Half we asked to think about their mother, and half were asked to think about other things (e.g., the route they take to school). Finally, all of the participants were given a test of their verbal ability, in which they were asked to generate as many unique words as they could in five minutes. Fitzsimons and Bargh predicted that thinking about their mother would facilitate the performance of participants who wanted to please their mother but would have little effect on the performance of participants for whom this goal was of lesser importance. Figure 5.5 shows exactly this effect. This finding reveals that merely thinking about another person can alter people's behavior (see also Shah, 2003a, 2003b).

C. Psychological World

Processes of a personal nature also influence the way people think about themselves.

1. Introspection

Introspection occurs when people peer inward and directly consult their attitudes, feelings, and motives. Suppose, for example, I want to know whether I'm a sentimental person. I can look inward and ask myself how I feel during weddings, tear-jerker movies, and other occasions relevant to sentimentality. If I feel soft and warm on these occasions, I will conclude that I am a sentimental person. Although intro-spection doesn't always yield accurate self-knowledge (T. D. Wilson & LaFleur, 1995), people learn a good deal about themselves by directly examining their thoughts, feelings, and intentions (Andersen, 1984; Andersen & Ross, 1984; Sedikides & Skowronski, 1995; T. D. Wilson & Dunn, 2004).

2. Self-Perception Processes

In addition to looking inward, we can also gain self-knowledge by examining our behavior. This process lies at the heart of Bem's (1972) **self-perception theory.** According to this theory, people learn about themselves by making attributions for their behavior. To illustrate, suppose you ask me whether I like classical music. If I am an ardent fan of this type of music, I would immediately answer yes. But sup-pose my feelings are not so passionate or well defined. To answer this question I might recall that I frequently listen to classical music while driving in my car. So I answer, "Yes, I like classical music." After all, what other reason can there be? No one makes me listen to it, so I must like it.

Notice that this inference process involves the principle of discounting (as dis-cussed in Chapter 4). We use situational information to infer the presence or absence of a dispositional cause. If my car radio receives classical music stations only, then the situation provides a plausible explanation for my behavior and I discount the role of a dispositional factor (in this case, that I like classical music). But if I can hear all kinds of music in my car, then the situation cannot explain why I listen to classical music and I infer the presence of a dispositional cause (i.e., that I am a fan of clas-sical music).

Notice that an outside observer would have reached a similar conclusion. You will also infer I like classical music if you know I frequently choose to listen to it:

> To the extent that internal cues are weak, ambiguous, or uninterpretable, the individual is functionally in the same position as an outside observer, an observer who must necessarily rely upon those same external cues to infer the individual's inner states. (Bem, 1972, p. 2)

This equivalence is a hallmark of Bem's theory. The theory assumes that people acquire self-knowledge by passively observing their own behavior and drawing log-ical conclusions about why they behaved as they did, much as an outsider would do. This assumption distinguishes self-perception processes from introspection. Only you can introspectively examine your attitudes, feelings, and motives; with self-perception, we indirectly infer our attitudes, feelings, and motives by analyzing our behavior.

Many students are skeptical when they are first introduced to self-perception theory. They assume they know why they feel, think, and act the way they do without resorting to the inferential process Bem describes. Although this may generally be true, social psychological research has provided support for self-perception theory.

Self-Perception of Attitudes. One line of research has examined how self-perception processes influence attitudes. According to Bem, people with poorly defined or weak attitudes use their behavior to infer their attitudes. Chaiken and Baldwin (1981) tested this prediction by first identifying two groups of participants: Those with firmly held attitudes toward environmental issues and those with weakly held attitudes toward environmental issues. Later, all participants completed a questionnaire asking them to indicate how often they performed various behaviors related to the environment. Using

FIGURE 5.6

Attitude Strength and the Self-Perception of Attitudes

Questionnaires designed to elicit pro- or anti-environment answers had no effect on people with strong attitudes but did affect participants with weak attitudes. This finding supports self-perception theory's claim that people with weakly held attitudes use their behavior to infer their attitude.

Source: Chaiken and Baldwin (1981).

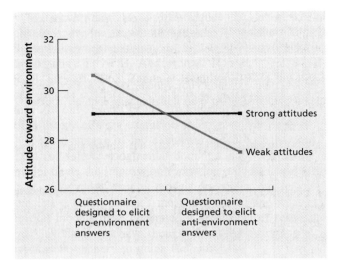

a device developed by Salancik and Conway (1975), Chaiken and Baldwin framed the questions in such a way that respondents were apt to conclude they had positive attitudes toward the environment or negative attitudes toward environment. For example, participants in the pro-environment condition were asked whether they frequently litter (most said no), whereas those in the anti-environment condition were asked whether they occasionally litter (most said yes).

After completing the questionnaires, the respondents rated their attitudes toward the environment. Self-perception theory predicts that people with weak or poorly defined attitudes toward the environment will use their prior behavior to infer their attitudes. Figure 5.6 shows that this prediction was confirmed. Whereas people with firmly held attitudes toward the environment were unaffected by which questionnaire version they received, people with weakly held attitudes expressed more positive attitudes toward the environment when their prior behavior suggested they had a positive attitude than when their prior behavior suggested they had a negative attitude (see also Albarracín & Wyer, 2000; Zanna, Olson, & Fazio, 1980).

Self-Perception of Motivation: The Overjustification Effect. Many parents give their children stickers, candy, or other rewards for playing the piano, doing their homework, or cleaning up their room. Although these rewards are given with the best of intentions, self-perception theory tells us that they may have a hidden cost. When the children ask themselves why they are engaging in the activity, they might conclude it is because of the external rewards they receive rather than any intrinsic interest. In more formal terms, receiving a reward can lead people to discount the extent to which the behavior is performed for intrinsic reasons.

The negative effects of external rewards were first demonstrated by Lepper, Greene, and Nisbett (1973). In this study, nursery school children were allowed to play with felt-tip markers. Three experimental conditions were created. Children in the expected-reward condition were told they would receive a reward (in the form of a special certificate) if they drew with the markers. Children in the unexpected-reward condition also received a reward for playing with the markers, but they were not told ahead of time that they would receive it. Finally, children in a control condition neither expected nor received an award for playing with the markers.

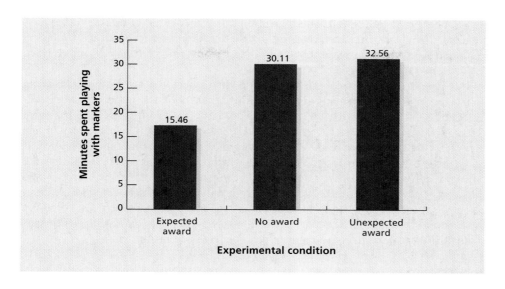

FIGURE 5.7

The Overjustification Effect

Children who earlier had received an expected reward for playing with felt-tip markers subsequently showed less interest in the markers than did children who received either an unexpected reward or no reward at all. These findings document that expected rewards can undermine intrinsic motivation.

Source: Lepper, Greene, and Nisbett (1973).

Several days later, the children were brought back into the laboratory and were given the opportunity to play with a number of attractive toys, including the felt-tip markers. No rewards were mentioned or administered during this phase of the experiment. To measure intrinsic interest, the researchers noted the amount of time the children spent playing with the markers during this free period. Consistent with the claim that external rewards can dampen intrinsic motivation, the data shown in Figure 5.7 reveal that the children in the expected-reward condition spent less time playing with the markers during the second stage of the experiment than did children in the other two conditions (for related research, see Boggiano & Main, 1986; Higgins, Lee, Kwon, & Trope, 1995). One explanation for this finding is that the reward undermined the children's interest through a self-perception process. The reward led children to discount the extent to which their original behavior (playing with the markers) was due to their intrinsic interest.

Fortunately, external rewards do not always undermine intrinsic motivation. Deci (1975) noted that external rewards contain two components. On the one hand, they can function as a bribe and reduce freedom by coercing people to behave in ways they normally would not. On the other hand, they can provide important information about the quality of one's efforts and accomplishments (as when a person receives a reward for trying hard or for turning in an exemplary performance). Rewards appear to undermine intrinsic interest only when the controlling aspect of the reward is more prominent than its informational value (Ryan, Mims, & Koestner, 1983). This means that rewarding someone for a job well done does not necessarily diminish the person's enthusiasm for performing the task (R. Eisenberger, Armeli, & Pretz, 1998;

R. Eisenberger, Rhoades, & Cameron, 1999). The same is true of praise. Verbal reinforcement heightens enjoyment when it is sincere and promotes choice and autonomy but dampens enthusiasm when it is controlling and conditional (Assor, Roth, & Deci, 2004; Henderlong & Lepper, 2002).

It is interesting to consider this distinction with respect to a reading program being conducted in Tifton, Georgia. This town has undertaken a quest to become the Reading Capital of the World (www.readingcapital.com). To achieve this aim, the town offers monetary rewards to citizens who read. The program is a huge success in that the town's inhabitants are reading much more than they did before the program was initiated. The question arises, however, as to whether rewarding people in this manner will undermine their intrinsic enjoyment of reading. The developers of this program think not. They note that the rewards are given only when readers demonstrate competency. To receive a reward, the reader must pass a comprehension test for every book he or she reads. Because these rewards convey information about performance standards, they are unlikely to dampen people's enthusiasm for reading.

Self-Perception of Emotion. So far we have seen that self-perception theory applies to attitudes and motivation. The theory has also been used to explain emotional experience. According to Schachter's **two-factor theory of emotion,** emotional experience is comprised of two factors: physiological arousal and a cognitive interpretation, attribution, or label (Schachter, 1964; Schachter & Singer, 1962). Ordinarily, people have little difficulty identifying why they feel the way they do. For example, the sound of a dentist's drill leads most people to feel dread, anxiety, and fear. On other occasions, however, the eliciting stimulus is less obvious. Suppose you wake up one day feeling uneasy. Undoubtedly, you will look to the situation to see if it provides a suitable explanation. If you have an exam that day, you're apt to conclude that you're nervous; if your boyfriend or girlfriend is coming to visit, you may decide that you're excited. In terms of Schachter's theory, you attribute the arousal you feel to a cause in the manner described by Bem's self-perception theory.

A classic experiment by Schachter and Singer (1962) showed that people sometimes use the behaviors of others to label their own emotional states. The participants in this study were led to believe that the experimenters were testing how a vitamin supplement affects vision. All participants then received a shot. In one condition, the shot was a placebo and had no physiological effects. In another condition, the shot contained epinephrine (a drug that causes arousal, such as increased heart rate and accelerated breathing). Some of the participants who received the epinephrine were correctly told that the drug would produce various side effects (increased pulse rate, mild heart palpitations), whereas other participants were not told about the drug's true side effects. These variations resulted in three conditions: (1) a no arousal/placebo condition, (2) an informed-arousal condition, and (3) an uninformed-arousal condition.

After receiving their shots, the participants were escorted to another room while the experimenter prepared the vision test. A confederate who allegedly had also received the injection was waiting in the room. In one condition, the confederate acted euphoric and ebullient. He made silly airplanes out of questionnaires and joyously shot baskets with wadded-up balls of paper. In the other condition, the confederate acted agitated and upset. He complained about having to participate in psychology experiments and angrily ripped up the questionnaires he had been given.

Several minutes later, the participants were asked to indicate how they were feeling (euphoric or angry), allowing Schachter and Singer to determine whether the confederate's behavior influenced the participants' own emotional states. Recall that

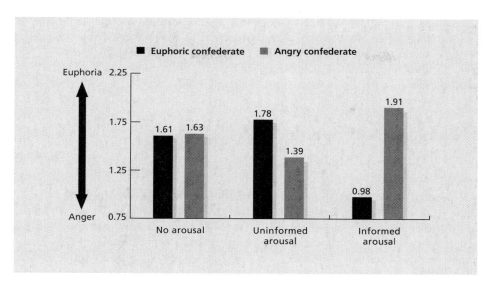

FIGURE 5.8

Schachter's Two-Factor Theory of Emotion

The data show that the theory was supported in the no arousal/placebo condition and in the uninformed arousal condition, but not in the informed arousal condition. These findings provide qualified support for the claim that emotional states are comprised of two factors: Physiological arousal and a cognitive label.

Source: Schachter and Singer (1962).

Schachter's theory maintains that emotional experience is comprised of two factors: physiological arousal and a cognitive label. Participants given a placebo were not experiencing any physiological arousal, so they should not have been searching for a cognitive label and should not have been affected by the confederate's behavior. Participants given epinephrine were experiencing arousal, but some of these participants were correctly informed that the shot they were given would make them feel excited and aroused. Since these participants already had an explanation for what they were feeling, they, too, should have been unaffected by the confederate's behavior. The key prediction, then, was that only participants who were experiencing *unexplained* arousal (i.e., those in the uninformed-arousal condition) would be influenced by the confederate's behavior.

The data shown in Figure 5.8 provide some support for these predictions. As expected, participants in the no-arousal placebo condition were unaffected by the confederate's behavior, and those in the uninformed-arousal condition felt better when the confederate was happy than when the confederate was angry. These findings support the contention that people who experience unexplained arousal look to the situation to label their emotional experience. The data in the informed-arousal condition do not conform to the experimental predictions, however. These participants should have been unaffected by the confederate's behavior, but they felt angry when the confederate was euphoric, and euphoric when the confederate was angry. These results indicate that factors other than self-perception processes influence emotional states (Reisenzein, 1983).

Misattribution of Arousal. Because people do not always know why they feel the way they do, they can be led to misattribute the true causes of their emotional states. This misattribution of arousal can have some interesting consequences. For example, one investigation found that college students were more likely to cheat on a test if they had been told a drug they had been given would produce symptoms of anxiety than if they had been told the drug would relax them (Dienstbier & Munter, 1971). Why did this occur? Most people experience anxiety and arousal when they contemplate committing an immoral act. Even though all participants had been given a placebo, the participants in the anxiety-producing-drug condition could easily believe that the anxiety they were feeling was due to the pill they had been given rather than to any compunction about cheating. This misattribution of arousal made it easier for them to cheat (see also Batson, Engel, & Fridell, 1999; Storms & Nisbett, 1970; Valins, 1966).

III. Do People Know What They Are Really Like?

Self-perception theory highlights that people don't always know why they feel and behave the way they do. But what about their traits and abilities? Do people know, for example, how intelligent they really are, or how attractive, kind, and honest? Most people think they do, but social psychological research shows that people generally think they are better than they really are (J. D. Brown, 1991, 1998; Taylor & Brown, 1988, 1994a, 1994b).

A. The Better-Than-Most Effect

Suppose you randomly sample a group of people and ask them: "Compared to most other people, how intelligent are you?" Logically, half of the people should say they are more intelligent than most other people, and half should say they are less intelligent than most other people. But this is not what happens. Instead, most people say they are more intelligent than most other people. Moreover, this **better-than-most effect** occurs for a wide variety of personality traits and abilities. People think they are more caring than others (Epley & Dunning, 2000; White & Plous, 1995); more deserving than others (Diekmann, Samuels, Ross, & Bazerman, 1997); more insightful than others (Pronin, Kruger, Savitsky, & Ross, 2001); and fairer than others (Messick, Bloom, Boldizar, & Samuelson, 1985). They also believe they drive better than others (Svenson, 1981); are happier than others (Lykken & Tellegen, 1996); and have more satisfying interpersonal relationships than do others (Buunk & van den Eijnden, 1997; Van Lange & Rusbult, 1995). This bias even includes members of our extended self, as people believe their friends, family, and fellow group members are also better than most other people (J. D. Brown, 1986; J. D. Brown & Kobayashi, 2002).

Naturally, people don't think they're good at everything. Many people concede that they can't juggle, program a computer, or bake a soufflé, and this admission leads them to believe they are below average in these activities (Kruger, 1999). When people do concede that they don't have a certain attribute, they tend to dismiss the attribute as inconsequential or view it as something they can acquire with practice (J. D. Brown, 1991; J. D. Brown, Dutton, & Cook, 2001; Elliot et al., 2000).

1. Is the Better Than Most Effect Limited to Western Cultures?

Most of the research on the better-than-most effect comes from Western cultures, raising the possibility that people from countries with a more interdependent, collectivistic focus may not show the effect. To examine this issue, J. D. Brown and Kobayashi (2002) conducted a study in America and Japan. College students at Osaka University and the University of Washington were asked to evaluate themselves, most other

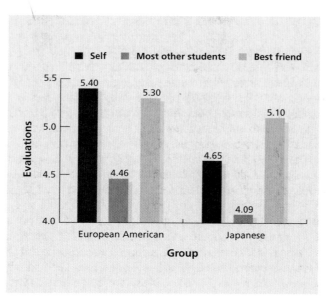

FIGURE 5.9

The Better-Than-Most Effect in America and Japan

Students in America and Japan regarded themselves and their best friend more positively than they regarded most other students at their university. This finding is consistent with the claim that the better-than-most effect is a universal phenomenon.

Source: J. D. Brown and Kobayashi (2002).

students at their university, and their best friend on a variety of traits and abilities (e.g., competent, friendly, and well-liked). Figure 5.9 shows the findings. Although the Japanese students were generally more modest than the Americans, they were just as apt to regard themselves and their best friend more positively than they regarded most other students at their university. Moreover, the more important the trait, the greater the gap between self, best friends, and most other people. Along with other research, these findings suggest that the better-than-most effect is a general, universal phenomenon (Kobayashi & Brown, 2003; Kurman, 2001; Kurman & Sriram, 1997; Sedikides, Gaertner, & Toguchi, 2003).

One other aspect of these data merits comment. Figure 5.9 shows that only the Japanese participants rated their best friends more positively than they rated themselves. This finding fits with other evidence that people from collectivistic cultures have a broad extended self that incorporates others, leading them to glorify their family, friends, and fellow group members (Hetts, Sakuma, & Pelham, 1999).

2. Do People Think They Are Biased?

Considering that the better-than-most effect is so extensive, you might think people are aware that they are biased. Not so. Most of us steadfastly deny that we are biased in any way, believing instead that other people are biased. For example, when discussing politics, we believe our opinions are well supported by facts but that other people's opinions are driven by ideology (Robinson, Keltner, Ward, & Ross, 1995). We also believe that our judgments are less distorted by greed, self-aggrandizement, or personal gain than are other people's judgments (D. T. Miller & Ratner, 1998; Pronin, Lin, & Ross, 2002; Pronin, Gilovich, & Ross, 2004).

B. Egocentric Biases

In his landmark research with children, the Swiss psychologist Jean Piaget noted that young children are very egocentric (Piaget, 1929). They tend to believe the world

FIGURE 5.10

Memory for Words
Referenced to Oneself
or Rated According to
Other Properties

Words rated according to
their self-relevance were
more memorable than
were words rated accord-
ing to nonself-relevant
features.

Source: T. B. Rogers, Kuiper, and
Kirker (1977).

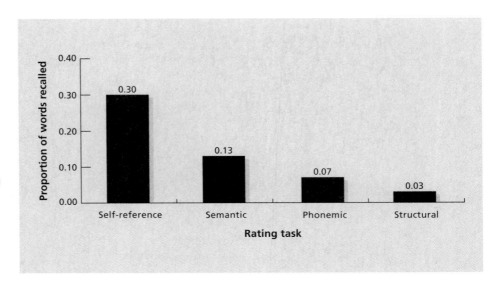

revolves around them and that everyone shares their perspective. Although Piaget
believed people grow out of this tendency as they age, more recent research suggests
that this is not always the case. Rather than viewing themselves as one actor in an
ensemble, people tend to believe they are the lead actor in a play written especially
for them.

1. Self-Relevant Information Is Especially Noticeable and Memorable

Have you ever been at a party and heard your name mentioned from across a crowded
room? This familiar experience, known as the cocktail-party effect, shows that people are highly attuned to self-relevant information. They are especially apt to notice
such information and to process it efficiently and deeply (Markus, 1977). These effects
were demonstrated in an investigation by T. B. Rogers, Kuiper, and Kirker (1977). In
the first part of the experiment, participants were asked to answer one of four questions about a series of words. Some of the words were judged for their self-relevance
(e.g., Does *honest* describe you?); some were judged according to their semantic properties (e.g., Does *kind* mean the same as *nice*?); some were judged according to their
phonemic features (e.g., Does *shy* rhyme with *sky*?); and some were judged according to their structural properties (e.g., Is the word *rude* printed in lowercase letters?).
After making these judgments, participants were unexpectedly asked to recall as many
of the words as they could remember.

Figure 5.10 shows that words referenced to the self produced the highest rates of
recall, indicating that people's ideas about themselves function as a powerful memory
aid. Numerous investigations have subsequently replicated this **self-reference effect**
(Greenwald & Banaji, 1989; S. B. Klein & Kihlstrom, 1986). You might want to keep
this point in mind the next time you study for an exam. If you can relate the material
to your own life, you will be able to remember it better. This will be particularly true
if you also generate your own ideas and examples. In group settings, people show
better memory for their own actions than for the actions of others (M. Ross & Sicoly,
1979), and better memory for statements they have uttered than for statements other
people have voiced (Greenwald, 1981).

2. Egocentric Social Judgments

Heightened attention to and memory for our own attributes and behaviors produces a number of predictable biases. For example, people tend to give themselves too much credit for things. When husbands and wives are asked how often they do various household chores (e.g., wash the dishes, take out the garbage), each accepts more responsibility than he or she is given by the other (M. Ross & Sicoly, 1979; S. C. Thompson & Kelley, 1981), and each believes his or her allocations of responsibility are fair but the other spouse's are biased (Kruger & Gilovich, 1999).

People also use themselves as a reference point when judging others (Beauregard & Dunning, 1998; Klar & Giladi, 1999; Kruger, 1999; Kruger & Burrus, 2004). For example, when asked to predict how other people would feel in a particular situation, our predictions are heavily influenced by what we think we would feel (Van Boven & Loewenstein, 2003). Often this produces a **false-consensus effect:** a tendency for people to believe that their own tendencies, preferences, and values are shared by others to a greater degree than is usually the case (L. Ross, Greene, & House, 1977). The false-consensus effect is most evident when we judge the commonness of our negative qualities or behaviors (Mullen et al., 1985). For example, if you speed on the freeway or cheat on your income tax, you probably exaggerate the number of people who do likewise. No such bias exists when we do something meritorious or consider our positive qualities. Here, we exhibit a **false-uniqueness effect,** believing our virtues and assets are rare and distinctive (J. D. Campbell, 1986; Marks, 1984; Suls & Wan, 1987). To continue with this earlier example, if you think you are a safe driver and scrupulous when filling out your taxes, you will probably underestimate how many other people are similarly honorable.

3. Negative Effects of Egocentrism: The Spotlight Effect

Egocentrism isn't always a good thing. Many students get anxious when called on to answer a question during a lecture. They feel like everyone's eyes are on them and that everyone will remember if they make a mistake. Dubbing this tendency the *spotlight effect,* Gilovich and colleagues have shown that people overestimate (1) how harshly they will be judged for making a mistake, (2) how conspicuous their absence will be from a group or meeting, and (3) how much attention people pay to their appearance (Gilovich, Kruger, & Medvec, 2002; Gilovich, Medvec, & Savitsky, 2000; Savitsky, Epley, & Gilovich, 2001; Savitsky, Gilovich, Berger, & Medvec, 2003). In a nutshell, we think everyone is watching us, but they're not: They're watching themselves. Keep this in mind the next time you feel like you're having a bad hair day. Chances are, fewer people than you think are noticing.

C. Unrealistic Optimism

Judgments of the future provide another realm in which to test the accuracy of people's beliefs. Most people are optimistic (Tiger, 1979). They believe that lots of good things will happen to them and that their future will be bright and sunny. Whether this optimism is warranted is difficult to say. No one can foretell the future, so there's no way to know whether people's beliefs are accurate. We can, however, ask people to compare their future with other people's futures. If people consistently claim that their futures will be brighter than those of their peers, there is evidence for unrealistic optimism. After all, most people can't have a happier life than most other people.

Research adopting this approach has found consistent evidence for unrealistic optimism (for a review, see Weinstein & Klein, 1995). Most people believe they are more likely than their peers to experience a wide variety of pleasant events, such as having a gifted child, owning their own home, or living past the age of 80 (Weinstein, 1980). Conversely, most people believe they are less likely than their peers to experience a wide variety of negative events, such as being involved in an automobile accident (Robertson, 1977); being a crime victim (Perloff & Fetzer, 1986); or becoming ill (Weinstein, 1982, 1984). Since not everyone's future can be rosier than that of their peers, the optimism people exhibit seems illusory.

This does not mean, however, that people's judgments of the future are unaffected by reality (Gerrard, Gibbons, & Bushman, 1996; Kruger & Burrus, 2004; van den Velde, van der Pligt, & Hooykaas, 1994). For example, smokers acknowledge that they are at greater risk for lung disease than are nonsmokers. At the same time, they underestimate their comparative risk, believing they are less likely to get cancer than are most other smokers (Gibbons, Gerrard, Lando, & McGovern, 1991). It is in this sense, then, that people are overly optimistic.

D. How Do People Maintain Positive Self-Views?

To this point we have seen that people have views of themselves that are a bit too good to be true. Considering all the feedback we get in life, how is this possible? In other words, how are the majority of people able to believe that they are kinder, more loyal, and more sincere than their peers? Several processes conspire to sustain these beliefs.

1. Self-Serving Definitions of Traits

Perhaps the most important process people use to maintain a positive self-view is to define qualities in self-serving ways. Consider, for example, what it means to be athletic. Does it mean that you have good hand–eye coordination? That you can run very far without getting tired? That you can bench-press your weight? All of these examples, and more, are indicative of athleticism, but none is necessary or defining. This uncertainty opens the door for individuals to define athleticism in ways that cast themselves in a favorable light (Dunning, 1993; Kunda & Sanitioso, 1989). People who think they are agile and quick define athletic ability in terms of balance and speed; those who are rather brawny and thick define athletic ability in terms of power and strength. In this manner, each claims to be more athletic than the other.

This effect is most evident for ambiguous traits (Dunning, Meyerowitz, & Holzberg, 1989; Felson, 1981). Imagine that you tell a friend you really like his new hair style, even though you don't like it much at all. Are you being kind or phony? The behavior itself is ambiguous and can be defined either way. If you're like most people, you'll call it an act of kindness when you say it, but phoniness when someone else says it. In so doing, you maintain a positive self-view and continue to believe you are better than others.

2. Selective Exposure to Favorable Feedback

People also maintain their positive self-views by selectively exposing themselves to positive feedback. For example, students more enthusiastically seek feedback about their abilities when they expect it to be positive than when they expect it to be negative

(J. D. Brown, 1990; Sachs, 1982; Sedikides, 1993). A similar tendency occurs in the social domain. Most people associate with others who like them, not with those who don't like them. Think about your friends for a moment. Don't you think they have many positive qualities? Chances are, they think the same way about you (otherwise they wouldn't be your friends). Choosing to interact with people who like and admire us ensures that most of the interpersonal feedback we receive is positive.

3. Biased Social Comparison

People also use social comparison processes to develop and maintain positive views of themselves. One way they do this is by strategically choosing targets of comparison. If I compare my athletic ability with that of most Nobel laureates, I'm apt to conclude that I am pretty athletic. If I compare my intellectual ability with most professional athletes, I'm likely to conclude that I am pretty smart. Had I reversed the targets of these comparisons, I would undoubtedly have come to some very different conclusions about myself.

4. Cognitive Factors That Promote Positive Self-Views

Finally, various cognitive processes promote positive self-views. Most people uncritically accept positive self-relevant feedback but carefully scrutinize and refute negative self-relevant feedback (Ditto & Lopez, 1992; Ditto, Scepansky, Munro, Apanovitch, & Lockart, 1998; Kunda, 1990; Liberman & Chaiken, 1992; Pyszczynski & Greenberg, 1987). They also show better memory for their strengths rather than their weaknesses (Kuiper & Derry, 1982); recall their past in ways that allow them to believe they have many good qualities and are continually improving (Conway & Ross, 1984; Klein & Kunda, 1993; Sanitioso, Kunda, & Fong, 1990); and introspect about themselves in ways that guarantee they will find that they possess many positive attributes but few negative ones (Sedikides, 1993).

Self-serving attributions are another factor that help people maintain positive self-views. As first discussed in Chapter 4, individuals tend to take credit for their successes but deny responsibility for their failures (for reviews, Mezulis, Abramson, Hyde, & Hankin, 2004; Zuckerman, 1979). For example, students tend to attribute their successes to high ability but to excuse their failures by citing external factors (e.g., "I received a low test grade because the test was unclear") or less central aspects of the self (e.g., "I received a low test grade because I studied the wrong material"). By denying that negative outcomes are due to one's enduring character, abilities, or traits, individuals are able to hold on to their self-enhancing beliefs even when confronted with negative feedback.

5. Self-Handicapping

Occasionally, individuals will even work to obscure the informational value of negative feedback. Berglas and Jones (1978) coined the term *self-handicapping strategies* to refer to situations in which people erect barriers to their own success. A student who doesn't study for an exam may be exhibiting self-handicapping behavior. Although the behavior makes success less likely, it protects and promotes a positive self-view. Failure is blamed on low effort instead of low ability, and success, should it occur, is viewed as providing even greater evidence for high ability. After all, only a veritable genius could succeed when saddled with the impediment of insufficient preparation.

IV. Self-Regulation of Behavior

Chances are, you know people who work really hard at what they do. They always try their best and rarely give up. When the going gets tough, these people get going. You probably also know people who aren't like that at all. They're content to settle for second best or are easily frustrated when encountering difficulties. Differences like these stem from the way people regulate their own behavior.

A. Goals and Expectancies

Self-regulation begins when people adopt a goal. Goals represent the cognitive representation of an intention. For example, we might want to lose 10 pounds, plan on taking a vacation, or strive to get into graduate school. As first noted in Chapter 2, goals can be understood by applying an expectancy–value framework (Atkinson, 1964; Rotter, 1954; Tolman, 1932, 1948). Expectancy–value models assume that two factors influence what we choose to do: (1) our perceived likelihood of success and (2) the value we place on attaining or not attaining the goal. A person who believes she can climb Mount Rainier and values the experience will probably be highly motivated to give it a try.

1. Self-Efficacy Beliefs

Expectancies of success are influenced by a number of self-relevant beliefs, including **self-efficacy beliefs** (Bandura, 1997). This term refers to people's belief in their ability to successfully perform some action. For example, if you think you can begin an exercise program or give your car a tune-up, you have high self-efficacy beliefs in those areas and will probably attempt these tasks. Conversely, if you doubt your ability to succeed at these tasks, you will probably be reluctant to invest the effort in trying.

People with high self-efficacy beliefs generally adopt more difficult goals and work longer and harder to attain them than do those with low self-efficacy beliefs. They are not, however, necessarily more able; they only think they are. The classic children's book *The Little Engine That Could* illustrates these differences. The little blue engine that ultimately carried the toys over the mountain to the waiting children had high self-efficacy beliefs ("I think I can; I think I can"). Even though many of the other trains were bigger and stronger, they doubted their ability to make the trek over the mountain and didn't bother trying.

2. Defensive Pessimism

High self-efficacy beliefs are usually beneficial, but not everyone benefits by them. In fact, I had a friend in college who used to exasperate me. Before every test, she would tell me how nervous she was and how bad she was going to do. Invariably, she would then proceed to set the curve for the test by getting the highest score. The first few times this happened, I figured my friend was just trying to save face in case she did poorly on the test. But as I got to know her better, I realized this strategy of expecting the worst was an important part of her success.

Norem (2001; Norem & Cantor, 1986) coined the term **defensive pessimism** to describe my friend's behavior. Despite having a history of success in achievement situations, defensive pessimists doubt their ability to succeed in the future. Instead of imagining themselves doing well, they imagine worst-case scenarios and dwell on all the ways things could go wrong. This does not mean that defensive pessimists adopt a passive what's-the-use attitude, however. In fact, just the opposite is true. Focusing on potential problems prods defensive pessimists to make sure these calamities don't occur. This is the key component to making defensive pessimism work. Defensive pessimists feel anxious when they approach a performance situation. To quell their anxiety, they painstakingly work through all the ways things could go wrong, and then cover their bases by taking active steps to avoid these pitfalls. In this manner, imagining the worst motivates the defensive pessimist to work harder and perform better.

3. Personal Goal Orientations

Goals can be conceived at different levels of abstraction (Powers, 1973; Vallacher & Wegner, 1987). Some goals are specific and concrete (e.g., I want to lose five pounds); others are broad and abstract (e.g., I want to be a healthier person). The same task can be relevant to more than one goal. For example, you may be reading this passage to learn the material, do well on a test, or prepare for graduate school. Generally speaking, goals conceived in broad terms assume greater value than do goals conceived in specific terms. At the most general level, people's goals center on who they want to be or what they want to become. For example, a person might be striving to be independent or even to be a good person. Personal goals like these are often the most highly valued goals in life (Emmons, 1986; Klinger, 1977; Little, 1981; Zirkel & Cantor, 1990).

Mastery versus Performance Goals. When it comes to an achievement-related activity, such as doing schoolwork or training for an athletic event, two broad goals are important. Sometimes people pursue mastery goals: They focus on acquiring skills or mastering a task as a means of improving themselves. Other times they adopt performance goals: They focus on demonstrating competence relative to others (Ames & Ames, 1984; Dweck & Leggett, 1988; Harackiewicz & Sansone, 1991; Nicholls, 1984). Although certain tasks promote one or the other orientation, most tasks can be approached from either perspective. For example, one person might want to learn five new words each week to improve his vocabulary, whereas another person might want to learn five new words each week in order to improve his performance on the verbal section of the GRE.

Different situations can also foster one goal or the other. Teachers who grade on a curve or employers who pay only on commission tend to instill performance goals rather than mastery goals (Flink, Boggiano, & Barrett, 1990; Ryan & Deci, 2000). At the same time, people also differ in their chronic tendencies to favor one goal over the other. Table 5.1 presents some sample items from a scale developed to assess different goal orientations (Amabile, Hill, Hennessey, & Tighe, 1994). The first five items measure mastery goals, and the second five assess performance goals. Most people score a bit higher on mastery than on performance, but the gap between these orientations varies.

How do these differences influence our behavior? People who approach a task with a mastery orientation usually enjoy themselves more than do those who adopt performance goals (Lepper & Henderlong, 2000; Rawsthorne & Elliot, 1999; Van Yperen, 2003). They also tend to persist longer and perform better, especially when obstacles to success are encountered (Grant & Dweck, 2003; VandeWalle, Brown, Cron, & Slocum, 1999). When confronting setbacks and disappointments, people bent on

TABLE 5.1 Sample Items from a Scale Used to Measure Individual Differences in Goal Orientations

	Never or Almost Never True of Me	Rarely True of Me	Sometimes True of Me	Always or Almost Always True of Me
1. I enjoy tackling problems that are completely new to me.	1	2	3	4
2. I enjoy trying to solve complex problems.	1	2	3	4
3. The more difficult the problem, the more I enjoy trying to solve it.	1	2	3	4
4. I want my work to provide me with opportunities for increasing my knowledge and skills.	1	2	3	4
5. What matters most to me is enjoying what I do.	1	2	3	4
6. I believe there is no point in doing a good job if nobody else knows about it.	1	2	3	4
7. I am strongly motivated by the grades I earn.	1	2	3	4
8. To me, success means doing better than other people.	1	2	3	4
9. I prefer having someone set clear goals for me in my work.	1	2	3	4
10. I am strongly motivated by the recognition I can earn from other people.	1	2	3	4

Source: Amabile Hill, Hennessey, and Tighe (1994).

demonstrating their competence become upset and quit. Fearing that their incompetence will be revealed, they no longer wish to work on the task. People with a mastery orientation show a different reaction. Instead of viewing setbacks as threats to be avoided, they view them as challenges to be overcome.

Dweck and Leggett (1988) have shown that these different reactions depend, in part, on attributional principles, first discussed in Chapter 4. For a person with a performance goal, effort and ability are negatively correlated: The higher your ability, the less hard you should have to try. Consequently, trying hard is threatening because it signals low ability. In contrast, people with a mastery orientation see a positive correlation between effort and ability. The harder you try, the more you are cultivating competence. For these individuals high effort doesn't pose a threat; it represents an opportunity to become more skilled and competent.

These goals seem to be shaped by the theories people hold about the nature of intelligence. People who typically adopt performance goals hold an *entity* theory of intelligence. They view intelligence as a fixed, immutable quality. Intelligence is something you either have or don't have (like blue eyes), and your goal in an achievement setting is to demonstrate that you have it. People who typically adopt mastery goals hold an *incremental* theory of intelligence. They view intelligence as a fluid, malleable quality that can be developed and cultivated. This perspective leads them to enter achievement situations with the goal of increasing their ability level by becoming more proficient and skilled.

Approach versus Avoidance Goals. Performance goals are less detrimental when they represent an attempt to demonstrate competence rather than to avoid demonstrating incompetence (Barron & Harackiewicz, 2001; Elliot & Church, 1997; Van Yperen, 2003). To understand this effect, we need to consider that goals can take two directions. Approach goals represent movement toward a desired state (striving for success), whereas avoidance goals represent movement away from an undesired state (trying not to fail). This distinction, which has long been used to explain behavior in achievement settings (Atkinson, 1964), illuminates how performance goals affect performance (Elliot & McGregor, 2001). People motivated to demonstrate their competence perform better than those who are motivated to avoid demonstrating incompetence. In fact, performance-approach goals can be as beneficial as mastery goals if they lead people to work especially hard to demonstrate their ability.

Higgins (1998, 1999) has used this distinction to develop a wide-ranging theory of motivation. The theory begins by assuming that people vary with respect to their general motivational orientation. Some people adopt a promotion focus in life, motivated by a desire to grow and attain desired outcomes. Other people adopt a prevention focus, driven by concerns with safety and protection, and a desire to avoid experiencing negative outcomes. Both approaches can lead to success, but people enjoy engaging in activities that fit their particular style. For example, people with a promotion focus prefer creative tasks with an element of risk, whereas people with a prevention focus prefer familiar activities with clearly defined guidelines for success (Friedman & Förster, 2001). These differences also influence how people feel when they succeed or fail. Whereas people with a promotion focus are elated when they succeed and dejected when they fail, people with a prevention focus are relieved when they succeed and worried when they fail (Higgins, Shah, & Friedman, 1997).

4. Goal Activation

In the research we've been discussing, people consciously select a goal and deliberately strive to attain it. Behavior is not always this intentional, however. Sometimes we have done something so many times before that our behavior is habitual and we don't even consciously think about what we are doing. For example, stepping onto a tennis court may automatically activate a goal of winning in someone who has played competitively for many years (Aarts & Dijksterhuis, 2000).

Bargh (1990) has even argued that people may usually be unaware of why they are pursuing a task or activity. Building on themes first espoused by the behaviorists (see Chapter 2), Bargh contends that various features of the environment, such as its physical properties or the behavior of others, automatically activate goals and guide behavior without cognitive awareness or intervention. One experiment used a priming procedure to test these ideas (Bargh, Gollwitzer, Lee-Chai, Barndollar, & Trötschel, 2001). During the first part of the experiment, participants worked on a word-search puzzle in which they looked for various words among a large matrix of letters. Participants in the achievement-prime condition were told to look for words that related to success (e.g., achieve, master, strive, win), and participants in a neutral-prime condition were asked to find words unrelated to achievement (e.g., carpet, ranch, river, shampoo). Afterward, both groups of participants worked on three more puzzles with themes unrelated to achievement. Bargh and colleagues predicted that the words in the achievement-prime condition would activate achievement goals and enhance task performance. This proved to be the case. Even though they were unaware that achievement goals had been unconsciously primed, participants in the achievement-prime condition subsequently outperformed those in the neutral-prime condition. Along with other research, these findings establish that goals can be activated in the absence of conscious awareness (Fishbach, Friedman, & Kruglanski, 2003; Shah, Friedman, & Kruglanski, 2002; Shah & Kruglanski, 2002, 2003).

B. Self-Presentation

Social situations are often ones with important goals. When we are on a job interview or first date, we are motivated to put our best foot forward and make a positive impression. In situations like these, we are engaging in self-presentational behavior. **Self-presentation** involves any behavior intended to create, modify, or maintain an impression of ourselves in the minds of others.

Because much of our time is spent in the company of other people, self-presentation is a pervasive feature of social life. It is also very important. Our success at leading others to believe we possess various characteristics has a profound influence on who we marry, who our friends are, and whether we get ahead at work (Hogan & Briggs, 1986). Undoubtedly, this is one reason why people spend billions of dollars a year on cosmetics and other personal-appearance products, and engage in behaviors that enhance their appearance to others but simultaneously jeopardize their own physical well-being, such as overexposure to the sun or excessive dieting (Fredrickson & Roberts, 1997; Leary, Tchividijian, & Kraxberger, 1994). In extreme cases, concerns with creating a desirable impression can underlie such self-destructive habits as cigarette smoking, substance abuse, and risky sexual practices (Bryan, Aiken, & West, 1999; K. A. Martin & Leary, 1999; Sharp & Getz, 1996).

1. Why Do People Engage in Self-Presentation?

Perhaps the most basic question we can ask with regard to self-presentational behavior is: Why do people bother to do it at all? In other words, why do we work so hard to lead people to see us in one way or another?

Facilitate Social Interaction. One function of self-presentation is to define a given social situation (Goffman, 1959). Most social interactions are strongly governed by roles. Each person has a role to play, and the interaction proceeds smoothly when these roles are enacted effectively. For example, airline pilots are expected to be poised and dignified. As long as they convince their passengers that they possess these qualities, their passengers remain calm and behave in an orderly fashion. Imagine, for example, how unsettling it would be if your airline pilot acted like the character Kramer on the television show *Seinfeld*.

Gain Material and Social Rewards. People also strive to create impressions of themselves in the minds of others in order to gain material and social rewards (or avoid material and social punishments). Being promoted at work depends on our ability to be perceived as productive and responsible. In a similar vein, being liked hinges on our ability to convince others that we are likable and thus worthy of their affections.

In many situations, it is beneficial to be seen as both likable and competent. For example, job offers are extended to applicants who are perceived as highly competent and pleasant to be around. Unfortunately, it is not always easy to simultaneously display both of these qualities. On the one hand, blowing your own horn may convince people that you are competent, but it rarely leads people to like you. On the other hand, modesty can instill liking, but it rarely instills a perception of competence. For this reason, people are forced to balance these self-presentational strategies (Schlenker, 1980). Women have a particularly difficult time achieving this compromise, because they risk being perceived as too masculine if they strive to appear competent and too ineffectual if they appear too modest and likable (Rudman, 1998).

Self-Construction. A final reason we try to create impressions of ourselves in the minds of others is to construct a particular identity for ourselves (Baumeister, 1982; Gollwitzer, 1986). Here, self-presentational behavior serves a more private, personal function. By convincing others that we possess some quality or attribute, we are better able to convince ourselves.

Although distinct, the three functions often go together. For example, airline pilots project an air of dignity because doing so (1) makes the plane ride go smoother; (2) helps them retain their jobs; and (3) leads them to think of themselves as dignified people, which in turn makes them feel good about themselves.

2. Individual Differences in Self-Presentation

Although everyone engages in self-presentation, people vary with respect to how concerned they are with their public image and with the kinds of impressions they try to convey. Before reading further about these differences, complete the scale shown in Table 5.2. When you are finished, return to the text and learn more about this issue.

M. Snyder (1974) developed the scale shown in Table 5.2 to measure the degree to which people monitor and control their behavior in public situations. People who score high on the scale (termed high self-monitors) regard themselves as highly flexible people who strive to be the right person for every occasion. When entering a social situation, they try to discern what the model or prototypic person would do in that situation. They then use this knowledge to guide their behavior. Low self-monitors adopt a different orientation. They regard themselves as highly principled people who value consistency between who they are and what they do. When entering a social situation, they use their attitudes, beliefs, and feelings to guide their behavior. Instead of striving to be the right person for the situation, they strive to be themselves in social settings (Rowatt, Cunningham, Druen, 1998).

Self-monitoring influences a wide-range of social behaviors (M. Snyder, 1979, 1987). For example, in comparison with low self-monitors, high self-monitors are more attracted to careers that emphasize the importance of public behavior, such as acting, sales, and public relations. Friendship patterns are also influenced by differences in self-monitoring. High self-monitors tend to have many different friends, each suitable for a different activity. For example, they play sports with one friend, go to the theater with another, and talk politics with yet another. This pattern allows them to be a different person in different situations. In contrast, low self-monitors have fewer friends and engage in multiple activities with each friend. They are more inclined to play sports, go to the theater, and talk politics with the same friend. This pattern is conducive to being the same person in all situations.

TABLE 5.2 The Self-Monitoring Scale

Please answer each of the following items true or false by circling T (for true) or F (for false).

T   F   1. I find it hard to imitate the behavior of other people.

T   F   2. My behavior is usually an expression of my true inner feelings, attitudes, and beliefs.

T   F   3. At parties and social gatherings, I do not attempt to do or say things that others will like.

T   F   4. I can only argue for ideas which I already believe.

T   F   5. I can make impromptu speeches even on topics about which I have almost no information.

T   F   6. I guess I put on a show to impress or entertain people.

T   F   7. When I am uncertain how to act in a social situation, I look to the behavior of others for cues.

T   F   8. I would probably make a good actor.

T   F   9. I rarely seek advice of my friends to choose movies, books, or music.

T   F   10. I sometimes appear to others to be experiencing deeper emotions than I actually am.

T   F   11. I laugh more when I watch a comedy with others than when alone.

T   F   12. In a group of people I am rarely the center of attention.

T   F   13. In different situations and with different people, I often act like very different persons.

T   F   14. I am not particularly good at making other people like me.

T   F   15. Even if I am not enjoying myself, I often pretend to be having a good time.

T   F   16. I'm not always the person I appear to be.

T   F   17. I would not change my opinions (or the way I do things) in order to please someone else or win their favor.

T   F   18. I have considered being an entertainer.

T   F   19. In order to get along and be liked, I tend to be what people expect me to be rather than anything else.

T   F   20. I have never been good at games like charades or improvisational acting.

T   F   21. I have trouble changing my behavior to suit different people and different situations.

T   F   22. At a party I let others keep the jokes and stories going.

T   F   23. I feel a bit awkward in company and do not show up quite so well as I should.

T   F   24. I can look anyone in the eye and tell a lie with a straight face (if for a right end).

T   F   25. I may deceive people by being friendly when I really dislike them.

Note: To determine your score, give yourself 1 point if you answered true to items 5, 6, 7, 8, 10, 11, 13, 15, 16, 18, 19, 24, and 25, and 1 point if you answered false to items 1, 2, 3, 4, 9, 12, 14, 17, 20, 21, 22, and 23. Then add up your total score. Scores of 12 or less are characteristic of a low self-monitor; scores of 13 or more are characteristic of a high self-monitor.

Source: M. Snyder (1974).

C. Exercising Self-Control

Every year, millions of people around the world make New Year's resolutions, vowing to lose weight, save money, or simply make more time for friends and family. Keeping these resolutions is a matter of exercising self-control, and self-control is one of the most important skills a person can have (Tangney, Baumeister, & Boone, 2004). Other animals initiate action, but humans seem uniquely able to control their behaviors. Indeed, Freud (1930) believed that the ability to delay gratification was the hallmark of the well-functioning personality. Supporting Freud's contention, research has shown that this ability measured at age four predicts behavioral adjustment and scholastic performance more than 10 years later (Mischel, Shoda, & Peake, 1988; Shoda, Mischel, & Peake, 1990). In this section, you will learn about three components of self-control: The ability to suppress unwanted thoughts, the ability to control one's emotions, and the ability to resist temptation. Finally, we will focus on situations in which our efforts at self-control fail.

1. Mental Control

If you've ever tried not to think about something, you probably discovered a curious (and annoying) fact. The harder you try to put the thought out of your mind, the harder it is to quit thinking about it. Dieters, for example, frequently report that they can often think of little else but food. A similar malady afflicts those who resolve to quit drinking or smoking, or get over a broken heart. In short, the more we try not to think about something, the more preoccupied with that something we seem to become (Wenzlaff & Wegner, 2000).

Wegner's ironic process theory of mental control explains this paradox (Wegner, 1989, 1994). This theory asserts that mental control consists of two processes. First, the person makes a concerted effort to suppress an unwanted thought. For example, a dieter might actively try not to think about a luscious piece of chocolate cake that is in the refrigerator. This effortful process is accompanied by a more automatic process that checks periodically to see if the forbidden thought has been successfully suppressed. Wegner refers to this latter process as an ironic monitoring process because it inadvertently brings the unwanted thought to mind every time it checks. Being automatic, the monitoring process requires less cognitive resources than does the effortful suppression process. This state of affairs means that people will be less successful at suppressing unwanted thoughts when they are fatigued, under pressure, or overwrought (Wegner & Erber, 1992).

Wegner and his colleagues have discovered another feature of thought suppression. People who actively suppress a thought experience a rebound effect when suppression is lifted. To illustrate, Wegner, Schneider, Carter, and White (1987) asked participants to think aloud for a certain amount of time. Some participants were initially told, "Try *not* to think of a white bear," whereas other participants were told, "Try to think of a white bear." In both conditions, the participants were instructed to ring a bell whenever thoughts of a white bear entered their mind. After five minutes had elapsed, the instructions were reversed: Those initially told to suppress the thought were told to express it, and those initially told to express the thought were told to suppress it.

Figure 5.11 shows the number of times participants rang the bell in each of these four experimental conditions. It is apparent that participants who initially suppressed thoughts of a white bear and then were told to think about it thought about white

FIGURE 5.11

Rebound Effects Following Thought Suppression

Participants who initially tried to suppress thoughts of a white bear thought about a white bear even more once suppression had been lifted. These findings suggest that thought suppression can sometimes produce a rebound effect.

Source: Wegner, Schneider, Carter, and White (1987).

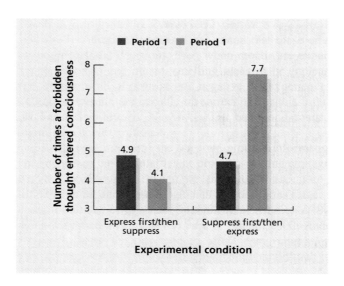

bears the most. This rebound effect carries some disturbing consequences for those engaged in mental control. Although people may initially succeed at keeping unwanted thoughts from coming to mind, they may experience a resurgence of those thoughts once their vigilance wanes. Fortunately, the effect does not occur under all circumstances and is rather short-lived (A. E. Kelly & Kahn, 1994; Liberman & Förster, 2000; Wegner & Gold, 1995; Wegner et al., 1987).

2. Emotional Regulation: Hiding One's Feelings

In addition to controlling their thoughts, people also try to regulate their emotions. Familiar sayings like "Stay cool," "Don't wear your heart on your sleeve," and "Keep your emotions in check" emphasize the importance our culture places on this ability. Emotional regulation doesn't come without a cost, however. Concealing what we feel requires energy and creates stress. In one investigation, J. M. Richards and Gross (2000) instructed some participants to hide their feelings while viewing photographs of gruesome scenes (e.g., graphic pictures of accident victims). Compared to participants who were not told to hide their feelings, those who did exhibited higher levels of physiological arousal and poorer memory for what they had seen. These findings support the claim that emotional suppression is a psychologically demanding task that requires psychological energy (see also Gross & Levenson, 1993; Muraven & Baumeister, 2000; Muraven, Tice, & Baumeister, 1998; J. M. Richards & Gross, 1999).

3. Behavioral Control: Resisting Temptation

That emotional suppression is psychologically demanding comes as no surprise to anyone who has ever tried to resist temptation. The simple fact is that choosing not to do something is often more effortful than deciding to do it. A study by Baumeister, Bratslavsky, Muraven, and Tice (1998) illustrates this point. Most of the participants in this study signed up for an experiment involving a taste test. Upon entering the laboratory, they saw two plates: one filled with freshly baked chocolate chip cookies, the other full of radishes. Half of the participants were told they could eat the cookies

FIGURE 5.12
Persistence at a Puzzle after Resisting Temptation

Participants who resisted cookies exhibited less persistence than did control participants or those who resisted radishes. Because most people find cookies more tempting than radishes, these findings suggest that resisting temptation is draining and leaves less energy available for other tasks.

Source: Baumeister, Bratslavsky, Muraven, and Tice (1998).

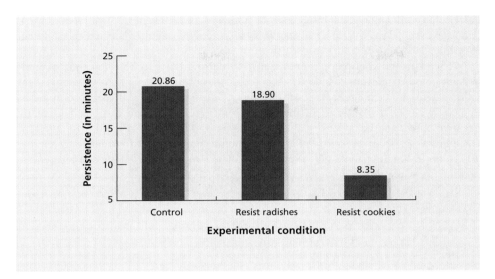

but not the radishes, while the other half were told they could eat the radishes but not the cookies. After a five-minute taste test, all of these participants (and another group who never participated in the taste test at all) worked on a difficult set of puzzles. Figure 5.12 shows how long participants in the three conditions persisted at this task. It is evident that participants who resisted tempting cookies quit the task sooner than did participants in the other two conditions. Apparently, the effort required to resist the cookies left participants with little energy for the puzzle task.

4. Self-Awareness and Self-Regulation

Many of the problems that currently plague modern society—alcoholism, domestic violence, drug use, drunk driving, excessive gambling, smoking, and unsafe sexual practices—reflect, to some extent, people's inability to control themselves. These problems arise when people focus on the immediate, short-term benefits of a behavior rather than its long-term consequences (Baumeister, Heatherton, & Tice, 1994; Trope & Fishbach, 2000). A night of partying with friends might bring immediate delight but will create problems down the road if homework goes undone. Successful self-regulation occurs when higher-order goals and desires (e.g., a desire to save money and act responsibly) override or supersede lower-order impulses and desires (a desire to own a new stereo or take a vacation).

Because forgoing immediate pleasures requires effort, our ability to do so is compromised by factors that deplete our psychological resources. For example, we find it difficult to maintain proper health habits when we are under stress, tired, or sad (Tice, Bratslavsky, & Baumeister, 2001). Self-awareness also plays a role in this process. Building on ideas discussed by Mead (1934), Duval and Wicklund (1972) argued that self-awareness leads people to compare their current behavior with a relevant standard. In effect, when people become aware of themselves, they ask themselves, "Is where I am now where I want to be?" If their behavior is falling short of their standards, they experience distress and act in ways to reduce the discrepancy. In this manner, self-awareness usually aids self-regulation, leading people to act in more responsible, socially appropriate ways (Carver & Scheier, 1981, 1998). For example, in comparison with people who are not self-aware, people who are self-aware are more honest (Beaman, Klentz, Diener, & Svanum, 1979; Diener & Wallbom, 1976); less aggressive (Carver, 1975); and less likely to stereotype others (Macrae, Bodenhausen, & Milne, 1998).

What happens when people aren't able to narrow the gap between their present behavior and a relevant standard? According to self-awareness theory, people deal with this dilemma by reducing self-awareness. Although this can be accomplished in healthy, positive ways (e.g., meditation or exercise), it can also lead to many negative habits and behaviors, such as overeating and excessive drinking (Baumeister, Heatherton, & Tice, 1994; Heatherton & Baumeister, 1991; Moskalenko & Heine, 2003). For example, people may turn to alcohol as a means of reducing self-awareness, particularly when things are going poorly in life (J. G. Hull, Levenson, Young, & Sher, 1983). Nearly 1,000 years ago, the Persian poet Omar Khayyam described the experience in this way:

> I drink not from mere joy in wine nor to scoff at faith—no, only to forget myself for a moment, that only do I want of intoxication, that alone.

Unfortunately, by reducing self-awareness, alcohol contributes to many socially inappropriate behaviors, such as domestic violence, date rape, and unsafe sexual practices (J. G. Hull, 1981; J. G. Hull et al., 1983; MacDonald, Zanna, & Fong, 1996).

In extreme cases, the need to escape self-awareness may even lead to suicide. According to Baumeister (1990), suicide occurs when negative experiences, such as a business failure or the breakup of an important interpersonal relationship, lead to an intense state of heightened self-awareness. When other efforts to eliminate this aversive state fail to bring relief, people begin to contemplate suicide. For these people, suicide represents a last-ditch attempt to escape an acute state of self-awareness.

V. The Self and Well-Being

Traditionally, psychologists have focused on understanding dysfunction and treating psychological disorders (Myers & Diener, 1995). This emphasis is appropriate, given the amount of human suffering these maladies create, but it has led to a neglect of the healthier side of psychological life. This imbalance is increasingly being redressed by a new movement devoted to the study of positive psychology (Seligman & Csikszentmihalyi, 2000; Sheldon & King, 2001). The way people think and feel about themselves is an important aspect of psychological well-being, and this section will focus on three relevant phenomena: happiness, personal fulfillment, and self-esteem.

A. Subjective Well-Being: How Happy Are You with Your Life?

People have long pondered the question "What makes a life good?" Although different cultures emphasize different things (e.g., piety, civic duty, honor), most agree that happiness is one component of the good life. The right to happiness was given prominence in the Declaration of Independence ("life, liberty, and the pursuit of happiness"), and people around the world frequently mention "to be happy," when asked what they want out of life (Diener, 1984, 1994, 2000).

Psychologists use the term **subjective well-being** to refer to people's assessments of their own happiness and life satisfaction. Subjective well-being consists of four components: positive emotions, negative emotions, judgments about one's life as a whole, and judgments about satisfaction with specific aspects of life, such as work, leisure time, friends, and family (Diener, Scollon, & Lucas, 2004). The role of positive and negative emotions is of particular interest. Although we tend to think of happiness and sadness as opposites (i.e., if one feels happy, one can't feel sad), research shows that this is not always the case (D. Watson & Tellegen, 1985). For example, when moving out of their dormitory at the end of the school year, many college students reported feeling excited about summer vacation yet also sad to leave their friends behind (J. T. Larsen, McGraw, & Cacioppo, 2001). More generally, when looking over our lives, we make somewhat independent assessments of the amount of joy and pleasure we feel, and the amount of sadness and worry (Bradburn, 1969; Lucas, Diener, & Suh, 1996). Happiness is associated with a tendency to experience more positive than negative emotion, but a person doesn't have to completely avoid sadness in order to feel happy. Moreover, it is the frequency of this balance, not the intensity of emotions, that is critical (Diener, Sandvik, & Pavot, 1991). Happy people are frequently more happy than sad, but they do not necessarily report feelings of intense rapture or euphoria.

1. The Advantages of Being Happy

Happiness is associated with a wide variety of positive outcomes. Compared to unhappy people, happy people are more creative, sociable, and energetic, and more caring, helpful, and involved in community affairs (Lyubomirsky, King, & Diener, in press). They also appear to live longer. Danner, Snowdon, and Friesen (2001) studied handwritten autobiographies of 180 Catholic nuns, composed when the nuns were in their early 20s. Each sister was asked to write a short sketch of her life at the time she entered a convent, and these autobiographies were later coded for the presence of positive emotional content. Figure 5.13 shows that women who expressed the most positive emotion lived nearly seven years longer than those who expressed the least positive emotion. It is especially notable that these effects appeared more than 50 years after the essays were written.

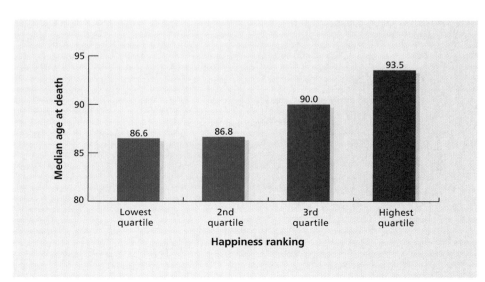

FIGURE 5.13

Happiness and Longevity

Nuns who wrote positively toned autobiographies in their early 20s lived longer than those whose autobiographies were less positive.

Source: Danner, Snowdon, and Friesen (2001).

2. Do External Events Create Enduring Happiness?

Happiness depends, as nature shows,
less on exterior things than most suppose.

William Cowper, 1731–1800

Suppose someone gave you a million dollars. How happy do you think that would make you feel, and how long would you feel that way? Now suppose you were seriously injured in a car accident. How unhappy do you think that would make you feel, and how long would you feel that way? If you're like most people, you believe events of this type will have a sharp and enduring influence on your general level of happiness (Gilbert, Pinel, Wilson, Blumberg, & Wheatley, 1998; T. D. Wilson, Wheatley, Meyers, Gilbert, & Axsom, 2000). But this is usually not the case. Although dramatic events cause short-term changes in happiness, their influence tends to wane rather quickly and people soon find themselves feeling pretty much as they felt before.

An investigation by Brickman, Coates, and Janoff-Bulman (1978) provides the best-known evidence for this effect. These investigators interviewed three groups of people: lottery winners, accident victims (who were either paraplegic or quadriplegic), and a control group of people who had recently encountered neither good fortune or misfortune. Among other things, the groups were asked: "How happy are you now (at this point in your life)?" "How happy were you in the recent past?" and "How happy do you expect to be in a couple of years (0 = Not at all; 5 = Very much)?" Figure 5.14 shows the results, and several findings are of interest: First, the lottery winners (some of whom had just won a million dollars or more) were no happier than the control group. Second, although the accident victims were currently less happy than the lottery winners and the controls, their happiness ratings fell above the scale midpoint of 2.5, suggesting that they did not feel terribly unhappy in an absolute sense. Finally, all three groups expected to be equally happy in the future. Apparently, when it comes to happiness, remarkable events can have rather unremarkable consequences (see also Dijkers, 1997).

FIGURE 5.14

Happiness Ratings for Accident Victims, Lottery Winners, and Controls

The data show that (1) lottery winners do not report greater happiness than controls; (2) accident victims, while less happy than the other two groups, are still quite happy; and (3) all three groups expect to be very happy in the future.

Source: Brickman, Coates, and Janoff-Bulman (1978).

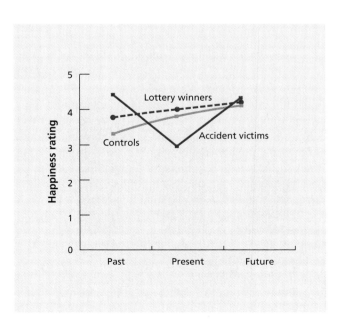

This conclusion is tempered by two considerations (Lucas, Clark, Georgellis, & Diener, 2003). First, there is variability. On average, external events don't alter happiness, but some people do experience enduring change. Second, negative events tend to produce greater and more enduring changes than positive ones. Nevertheless, the fact remains that external events rarely produce lasting changes in happiness. Various factors explain why this is so:

- The events themselves serve as an anchor against which other events are evaluated (Helson, 1964; Parducci, 1984; R. H. Smith, Diener, & Wedell, 1989). People who win the lottery suddenly find that ordinary events now bring them less pleasure than before, while victims of misfortune take greater joy in everyday experiences they once overlooked or took for granted.
- People get accustomed to extreme events (Brickman & Campbell, 1971). Over time, the extraordinary becomes ordinary and we find ourselves accommodating to the changes these experiences wrought in our lives. From this perspective, people are on a "hedonic treadmill," destined to eventually return to their own level of happiness (Kahneman, 1999).
- Other events of a more mundane nature take place, and their immediacy affects our happiness (T. D. Wilson, Wheatley, et al., 2000). For example, people who are out of work still feel happy when they fall in love, and people who fall in love still feel unhappy when their favorite baseball team loses the World Series.
- Social comparison processes operate (Diener & Fujita, 1997; Hagerty, 2000; Stouffer, Suchman, DeVinney, Starr, & Williams, 1949). Middle-class people who win a million dollars in a lottery no longer compare their wealth with members of the middle class. Instead, they raise their comparison group and begin to evaluate themselves relative to other wealthy people, thereby making themselves seem less wealthy by comparison (i.e., the so-called keeping-up-with-the-Joneses effect).
- In a related vein, people's aspirations climb with their attainments. Having money leads us to want more expensive things, so we wind up being no happier with what we have (Solberg, Diener, Wirtz, Lucas, & Oishi, 2002).

3. National Wealth and Happiness

We can see many of these processes at work when we examine the association between a nation's wealth and its subjective well-being. For an economist, these two variables are very nearly one and the same. The higher the nation's purchasing power, the more satisfied the nation's citizens should be. Social psychological research reveals that the picture is more complicated than this. Table 5.3 shows the per capita income of various countries around the world, and the percentage of people who claimed to be more satisfied than dissatisfied with their lives (Diener & Biswas-Diener, 2002). It is apparent that rich countries tend to be happier than poor countries, but does this mean that money buys happiness? Not necessarily. As we learned in Chapter 1, correlations can't establish causation, and rich nations differ from poor ones in a great many ways. Most notably, they are more democratic, allow people greater freedom and human rights, are more educated, and have lower crime rates. Although some of these differences might reasonably be regarded as consequences of affluence, there is no way to tell whether money per se buys happiness. Moreover, there are some notable exceptions. People in Portugal are happier than those in Japan, even though the Portuguese make roughly half the money. This, too, suggests that money does not guarantee happiness.

TABLE 5.3 National Income and Well-Being

Country	Per Capita Income (1990)	Percentage above Neutral in Life Satisfaction
United States	17,945	85
Canada	16,362	90
Switzerland	15,887	89
Japan	15,105	72
Sweden	13,986	87
France	13,918	72
Netherlands	13,281	92
New Zealand	11,363	84
Ireland	9,637	88
Russia	7,741	28
Portugal	7,478	76
Mexico	6,253	83
Bulgaria	5,208	33
Hungary	4,645	52
Brazil	3,882	72
South Africa	3,068	56
Romania	2,043	57
Bangladesh	1,510	63
China	1,493	72
India	1,282	67
Nigeria	978	71

Note: Correlation between income and well-being = 0.54.
Source: Diener and Biswas-Diener (2002).

Another way to address this issue is to see whether economic growth produces corresponding increases in subjective well-being. The United States provides a suitable example. Income in the United States has increased dramatically since World War II. In 1988, the adjusted wealth of the lowest fifth of Americans surpassed the median income in 1955 (Diener & Biswas-Diener, 2002). Despite this remarkable rise in purchasing power, Figure 5.15 shows that Americans are no happier now than they were 60 years ago. In fact, by some indicators, things are worse: Divorce rates have skyrocketed, depression rates have risen, and suicide rates have climbed as well (Myers, 2000). The same is true in Japan and other industrialized countries that have experienced dramatic economic growth without seeing a comparable rise in happiness.

Finally, we can examine the correlation between income and happiness within a country. If we look at very poor countries, such as India, we find that wealth matters a lot. People who have almost nothing are less happy than people who are better off (Biswas-Diener & Diener, 2001). But if we look at wealthier countries, such as America, we find that income matters very little (Diener, Diener, & Diener, 1995). Within these wealthier countries, people with lots of money aren't noticeably happier than those without lots of money (Diener, Sandvik, Seidlitz, & Diener, 1993). Taken together, the findings point to a simple conclusion: Money buys happiness if it means meeting our basic needs for food, shelter, and safety; beyond this, it doesn't matter much at all.

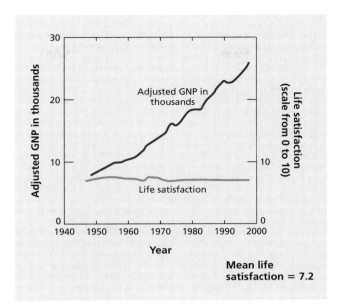

FIGURE 5.15

Ratings of Life Satisfaction and Adjusted Income in America over a 60-Year Period

Although adjusted income has risen steadily in the past 60 years, life satisfaction has remained constant. These findings support the claim that money doesn't buy happiness.

Source: Diener and Seligman (2004).

4. The Happy Personality

If external events don't determine happiness, is happiness a trait? The answer seems to be yes. In a study of identical twins, Lykken and Tellegen (1996) found that one twin's happiness was the best predictor of the other twin's happiness. This finding suggests that happiness has a strong genetic component. In fact, there is even evidence that chimpanzees display heritable differences in happiness (A. Weiss, King, & Enns, 2002). In general, happy people tend to be high in extraversion, low in neuroticism, and very agreeable (DeNeve & Cooper, 1998; Heller, Watson, & Ilies, 2004).

This doesn't mean, however, that happiness exists apart from life circumstances. Instead, people inclined toward happiness behave in ways that promote ongoing feelings of happiness (Headey & Wearing, 1989). First, they make "happy lifestyle choices." For example, they are more apt to get married and stay married; spend time with friends; and take care of themselves by eating a healthy diet, exercising, and sleeping a proper amount (Lucas et al., 2003; Magnus, Diener, Fujita, & Pavot, 1993; Seidlitz & Diener, 1993). Happy people also tend to be religious, involved in their community, and inclined to serve others rather than thinking only of themselves (Myers, 2000). Third, people with a happy disposition interpret events in positive ways (Brief, Butcher, George, & Link, 1993; Lyubomirsky, 2001). In colloquial terms, they are optimistic and easygoing, and they don't sweat the small stuff. Finally, people with a happy disposition focus on the good rather than the bad. They tend to remember more positive than negative events in their lives, and they base their judgments of life satisfaction on the positive ones (Diener, Lucas, Oishi, & Suh, 2002; Seidlitz & Diener, 1993; Updegraff, Gable, & Taylor, 2004). In effect, they count their blessings and are grateful for what they have (Emmons & McCullough, 2003).

B. Personal Growth and Fulfillment

Happiness is not the only thing people want out of life (L. A. King & Napa, 1998; Ryff, 1989). People also aspire to fulfill their potential and to develop a sense of purpose and meaning in their lives. Meeting these goals often brings people joy and satisfaction, but happiness and fulfillment are not the same thing (Ryan & Deci, 2001). In fact, many people are happy but unfulfilled (Compton, Smith, Cornish, & Qualls, 1996; Keyes, Shmotkin, & Ryff, 2002; McGregor & Little, 1998).

1. Need Satisfaction and the Pursuit of Meaningful Goals

Many theorists, including some of psychology's most famous figures, such as Erik Erikson (1959), Abraham Maslow (1968), and Carl Rogers (1961), have sought to identify basic human needs that, when satisfied, lead to a sense of personal fulfillment (sometimes called self-actualization). Following in this tradition, self-determination theory (Ryan & Deci, 2000) contends that people have three fundamental psychological needs: competence (a need to believe they are effective at what they do), autonomy (a need to believe their behavior is freely chosen and under their control), and relatedness (a need to connect with others and to have intimacy and warmth in their lives). According to the theory, people feel satisfied when these needs are met, and dissatisfied when these needs aren't met (Sheldon & Elliot, 1998; Sheldon, Ryan, & Reis, 1996).

Only some of the things people choose to do in life satisfy these needs (Sheldon & Elliot, 1998). Consider a person who has pursued a career in medicine. If, on the one hand, this desire stems from a genuine attempt to help others (relatedness) or an intrinsic interest in curing disease (autonomy and competence), it is apt to produce a strong sense of personal fulfillment and imbue the person's life with meaning. If, on the other hand, pursuing a career in medicine is viewed simply as a way of making money or pleasing one's parents, it is unlikely to prove fulfilling and may even undermine well-being (Carver & Baird, 1998; Kasser & Ryan, 1993, 1996; Sheldon, Ryan, Deci, & Kasser, 2004; Srivastava, Locke, & Bartol, 2001).

2. Doing for Doing's Sake

Reaching our goals is not the only way to feel fulfilled. We can also feel good about pursuing our goals, even when we have yet to reach them. In part, this is because our feelings depend more on whether we are moving toward a certain goal than how far we are from it (Carver & Scheier, 1990; Hsee & Abelson, 1991; Hsee, Salovey, & Abelson, 1994). In less formal terms, we can say that the journey is often more important to people than the destination. Suppose you decide to take up the piano. You can feel a sense of fulfillment after learning a few simple tunes (e.g., "Twinkle, Twinkle, Little Star"), even though you are not yet very accomplished. As long as you believe that you are improving, you will likely feel satisfied about your progress.

In fact, sometimes we are better off not even asking ourselves whether we are improving or not. On the basis of interviews with people engaged in activities without any discernible extrinsic value (e.g., rock climbing, playing chess), Csikszentmihalyi (1975) concluded that people experience a transcendent flow experience when they become so immersed in an activity that they no longer are self-conscious about why they are doing it or what they are trying to attain. In effect, they become lost in the experience for the sheer pleasure it brings. When this occurs, people feel at one with the experience and cease to notice external stimuli or the passage of time. This experience is similar to one that professional athletes describe as "being in the zone." Despite the distractions that come from performing in front of thousands of screaming fans, these athletes report being calm and completely focused on the task at hand, seemingly oblivious to all that surrounds them. In such moments, people experience a euphoric sense of fulfillment and purpose. Fortunately, one needn't be a world-class athlete to reap these rewards. Anyone who becomes absorbed in an activity can experience flow (K. W. Brown & Ryan, 2003; Csikszentmihalyi, 1975, 1990; Omodei & Wearing, 1990).

3. The Benefits of Perceived Control

Among the numerous psychological needs people have, the need to feel in control of one's life is given particular prominence. Numerous theorists believe that this need emerges at a very early age and is a principal motive governing human behavior (e.g., deCharms, 1968; R. W. White, 1959). In support of this conjecture, people who believe they are in control of their lives are generally more satisfied with their lives than are those who believe they lack control (Rodin, 1986; Rotter, 1954; Taylor & Brown, 1988).

A classic study by Langer and Rodin (1976) documented the importance of perceived control. This field experiment was conducted in a Connecticut nursing home. One group of the elderly residents was given sympathetic care but little decision-making power over day-to-day events. Members of another group were encouraged to make choices about how to spend their time and arrange their lives, and were given responsibilities and duties to fulfill. The results were dramatic: Over a three-week period, only 21 percent of the residents in the control group showed improvement in functioning, whereas 93 percent of those in the group that was allowed to make choices also. Moreover, 18 months later, mortality rates differed between the two groups: Whereas 30 percent of the residents in the control group had passed away, only 15 percent of those in the experimental group had died. Along with many other findings, these results suggest that beliefs in personal control are generally beneficial (Taylor, Kemeny, Reed, Bower, & Gruenewald, 2000).

In extreme cases, people who lack control may succumb to **learned helplessness.** The term comes from studies with laboratory dogs. In these studies, dogs first exposed to inescapable electrical shocks later displayed passivity when exposed to escapable electrical shocks (Maier, Seligman, & Solomon, 1969). Instead of taking action (such as crossing over to the other side of the room), they listlessly accepted their fate, choosing to endure the shock rather than trying to escape it. People who believe that nothing they do makes any difference may be displaying a form of learned helplessness (Seligman, 1975).

C. Self-Esteem

No discussion of psychological well-being would be complete without considering the nature of self-esteem. Its importance varies a bit from culture to culture, but self-esteem is a key component of life satisfaction and happiness in virtually every nation around the world (Diener & Diener, 1995). It is no wonder, then, that self-esteem is also one of psychology's most popular constructs.

1. Three Ways the Term *Self-Esteem* Is Used

Although self-esteem is part of everyday language, the term is used in three different ways.

Global Self-Esteem. Sometimes the term *self-esteem* is used to refer to a personality variable that captures the way people generally feel about themselves. Researchers call this form of self-esteem global self-esteem or trait self-esteem, because it is relatively enduring across time and situations. In this book we will use the term *self-esteem* in this global sense of general feelings of love or affection people have for themselves, no different in kind from the love or feelings of affection they have for others. High self-esteem is characterized by a general fondness or love for oneself; low self-esteem is generally characterized by mildly positive or ambivalent feelings toward oneself. In extreme cases, low-self-esteem people dislike or hate themselves, but true self-loathing occurs only in people who are clinically depressed (Baumeister, Tice, & Hutton, 1989).

Feelings of Self-Worth. The term *self-esteem* is also used to refer to momentary emotional states, particularly those that arise from a positive or negative outcome. This is what people mean when they speak of experiences that bolster their self-esteem or threaten their self-esteem. For example, a person might say her self-esteem was sky-high after getting a big promotion, or a person might say his self-esteem was really low after a divorce. Following William James (1890), we will refer to these emotions as *feelings of self-worth*. Feeling proud or pleased with ourselves (on the positive side) or humiliated and ashamed of ourselves (on the negative side) exemplifies feelings of self-worth.

Self-Evaluations. Finally, the term *self-esteem* is used to refer to the way people evaluate their specific abilities and attributes. For example, a person who doubts his ability in school is sometimes said to have low academic self-esteem, and a person who thinks she is popular is said to have high social self-esteem. In a similar vein, people speak of having high self-esteem at work or low self-esteem in sports. The terms *self-confidence* and *self-efficacy* have also been used to refer to these beliefs, and some people equate self-confidence with self-esteem.

2. The Origins of Global Self-Esteem

Now that we have some idea of what we mean by self-esteem, we can ask where global self-esteem comes from. Three perspectives have been developed to address this question:

1. *Affective models.* Some theorists believe that self-esteem is an emotion that develops early in life in response to heritable, temperamental factors and the nature of the parent–child relationship (J. D. Brown, 1993, 1998; Deci & Ryan, 1995; Kernis, 2003; Neiss, Sedikides, & Stevenson, 2002). Children who feel unconditionally loved and valued develop high self-esteem, and children who feel unloved or loved conditionally develop low self-esteem. These feelings normally arise in the first year of life and persist across the lifespan (Trzesniewski, Donnellan, & Robins, 2003).

2. *Cognitive models.* Other theorists take a different view on the origins of self-esteem. They argue that self-esteem arises from a rational, judgmental process in which people survey their various characteristics, weight them by their importance, and somehow combine this information to arrive at a decision about themselves (Coopersmith, 1967; Harter, 1986; Marsh, 1990). This approach, which assumes a great deal of cognitive sophistication and maturity, assumes that self-evaluations determine global self-esteem. High self-esteem comes from believing you have many important qualities and can do many things well.

3. *Sociocultural models.* A related perspective on self-esteem assumes that cultures dictate what's important and that people who believe they possess

culturally valued qualities develop high self-esteem (Heine, 2003; Solomon, Greenberg, & Pyszczynski, 1991). For example, if your culture (or subculture) values intelligence, you will develop high self-esteem if you think you are smart, but low self-esteem if you think you lack intelligence.

Each of these perspectives enjoys support. One way to integrate them is to assume that self-esteem develops early in life, as the affective model suggests, and then influences how people evaluate themselves, with high-self-esteem people believing they possess many culturally valued qualities (J. D. Brown, 1998; J. D. Brown, Dutton, & Cook, 2001; J. D. Brown & Marshall, 2003).

3. The Self-Enhancement Motive

Whatever its origins, people strive to feel good about themselves. Within psychology, this desire is known as the **self-enhancement motive.** This term refers to the fact that people try to build, maintain, and enhance their feelings of self-worth. They want to feel proud of themselves rather than ashamed of themselves. Culture shapes the motive's expression and the importance people attach to its pursuit (Heine, Lehman, Markus, & Kitayama, 1999), but its existence is universal (J. D. Brown, 2003; Kurman, 2001; Sedikides, Gaertner, & Toguchi, 2003). This point was eloquently made by the Pulitzer Prize–winning anthropologist Ernest Becker (1968), who wrote:

> The fundamental datum for our science is a fact that at first seems banal, or irrelevant: it is the fact that—as far as we can tell—*all organisms like to "feel good" about themselves* . . . Thus in the most brief and direct manner, we have a *law* of human development. (p. 328)

A great deal of research in social psychology attests to the self-enhancement motive's power (J. D. Brown, 1998). Of particular interest is evidence that this need can be satisfied in a variety of more or less interchangeable ways (C. M. Steele, 1988; Tesser, Crepaz, Beach, Cornell, & Collins, 2002). For example, a student who has just failed an important exam can restore feelings of self-worth by focusing on his athletic prowess, artistic ability, or social skills (J. D. Brown & Smart, 1991). Alternatively, he can bask in the reflected glory of another person's accomplishments (Cialdini et al., 1976; Tesser, 1988), or simply remind himself that he holds many fine values in life and is generally a good person (C. M. Steele, 1988).

Why do people strive to feel good about themselves? First, it makes them happy. It simply feels better to feel proud of ourselves rather than to feel ashamed of ourselves. Second, people are more open and less defensive when they are feeling good about themselves, and this helps them deal more effectively with the demands of life (Bonanno, Field, Kovacevic, & Kaltman, 2002; Raghunathan & Trope, 2002; D. A. K. Sherman, Nelson, & Steele, 2000). Ultimately, feelings of self-worth may even allay concerns about our own mortality. Terror management theory proposes that the awareness of death fills people with existential terror (Pyszczynski, Greenberg, Solomon, Arndt, & Schimel, 2004). To quell this anxiety, people build feelings of self-worth by convincing themselves that they are good, moral, deserving people.

Although all people strive to feel good about themselves, people differ with regard to their contingencies of self-worth (Crocker & Wolfe, 2001). Some people derive self-worth from their achievements, whereas other people derive self-worth from their interpersonal relationships, appearance, or religious faith. Regardless of where these feelings come from, problems can arise if people spend too much time attending to their self-enhancement needs (Crocker & Park, 2004; Ryan & Brown, 2003). Rather than doing things they enjoy, people bent on boosting their self-worth may undertake activities for extrinsic rewards and praise. Although these activities may promote feelings of self-worth, their influence is apt to be fleeting.

One way to think about these issues is to consider a child who is making mud pies. The squishing of mud between the fingers, and the sheer joy that comes from that experience, make the child feel good about himself or herself. These feelings are not produced by thinking one is a good mud pie maker. Making mud pies is process oriented—the joy comes from creating and manipulating; evaluating oneself is outcome-oriented—it is a judgment about whether one is good at something. Only "doing for the sake of doing" is apt to build enduring self-esteem.

4. Measuring Global Self-Esteem

You probably know someone you think has high self-esteem and someone you think has low self-esteem. Your intuitions are probably based on what each person says and does. Psychologists also rely on these cues to measure self-esteem.

Self-report measures. The Rosenberg (1965) self-esteem scale is one of the most widely used instruments for measuring self-esteem in research settings. This scale, which is shown in Table 5.4, was developed to assess global self-esteem. It focuses on people's general feelings toward themselves, without referring to any specific quality or attribute. Half the items are worded in a positive direction ("On the whole,

---

TABLE 5.4 The Rosenberg Self-Esteem Scale

Please indicate your level of agreement with each of the following statements by circling one number on the rating scale that best describes the way you feel about yourself.

	Strongly Disagree	Disagree	Agree	Strongly Agree
1. At times I think I am no good at all.	0	1	2	3
2. I take a positive view of myself.	0	1	2	3
3. All in all, I am inclined to feel that I am a failure.	0	1	2	3
4. I wish I could have more respect for myself.	0	1	2	3
5. I certainly feel useless at times.	0	1	2	3
6. I feel that I am a person of worth, at least on an equal plane with others.	0	1	2	3
7. On the whole, I am satisfied with myself.	0	1	2	3
8. I feel I do not have much to be proud of.	0	1	2	3
9. I feel that I have a number of good qualities.	0	1	2	3
10. I am able to do things as well as most other people.	0	1	2	3

To compute your score, first reverse your answers to items 1, 3, 4, 5, and 8 (0 = 3)(1 = 2)(2 = 1)(3 = 0). Then sum your answers to all 10 items. A score of 22 is average with American samples.

Source: Rosenberg (1965).

I am satisfied with myself"); the other half are worded in a negative direction ("All in all, I am inclined to feel that I am a failure").

Many other self-report instruments are available. Some of these assess the way people evaluate themselves in various aspects of life (Marsh, 1990). Included are items pertaining to one's (perceived) physical abilities, appearance, problem-solving abilities, social skills, peer relationships, opposite-sex relationships, and emotional stability. Harter (1986) has developed a similar scale for children, with subscales assessing (perceived) scholastic competence, athletic competence, social acceptance, physical appearance, and behavioral conduct. Scales of this type focus on the third meaning of *self-esteem* we discussed earlier—they assume that people have different self-esteem levels for different attributes, situations, and activities. Typically, these scales also include a separate subscale to measure global self-esteem.

Indirect Measures of Self-Esteem. Self-report measures of self-esteem are widely used and possess a high degree of validity. But they are not without problems. For example, they may be compromised by self-presentational concerns, as people may misrepresent themselves in order to impress the experimenter or fellow participants (Baumeister, Tice, & Hutton, 1989). Defensive processes may also influence self-report measures of self-esteem. People who score high on self-report measures of self-esteem may be lying to themselves by claiming to feel better about themselves than they really do (Paulhus & Reid, 1991).

In an effort to overcome these problems, researchers have developed indirect measures of self-esteem that do not rely on verbal reports (Bosson, Swann, & Pennebaker, 2000; Jordan, Spencer, Zanna, Hoshino-Browne, & Correll, 2003). Rather than measuring a person's explicit level of self-esteem, these indirect measures assess implicit self-esteem. One widely used approach assesses the speed with which people associate themselves with various positive and negative concepts (Greenwald & Banaji, 1995; Greenwald & Farnham, 2000). People who find it easy to associate themselves with positive concepts have high implicit self-esteem, and those who find it difficult to do so have low implicit self-esteem. People's scores on this measure are only weakly related to their expressed level of self-esteem, suggesting that different aspects of self-esteem are being measured.

5. Are There Different Types of High Self-Esteem?

The lack of an association between direct and indirect measures of self-esteem raises the possibility that there are different types of high self-esteem: genuine or authentic high self-esteem versus pseudo or inauthentic high self-esteem. The former, characterized by high scores on both explicit and implicit measures, refers to feelings of self-love that are stable and secure, and that are not contingent on any particular quality or performance (J. D. Brown, 1998; Deci & Ryan, 1995; Kernis, 2003). People with this form of self-esteem are comfortable with themselves and do not feel the need to boast excessively or outdo others.

In contrast, other people possess inauthentic self-esteem. They claim to love themselves (high explicit self-esteem) but are unconsciously beset by self-doubts and emotional ambivalence (low implicit self-esteem) (Jordan et al., 2003; Tracy & Robins, 2003). This type of self-esteem is unstable and gives rise to anger and defensiveness (Kernis & Waschull, 1995). In extreme cases, people with this form of self-esteem may possess a narcissistic personality disorder. The term *narcissism* comes from a mythical Greek character, Narcissus, who fell in love with his reflection while staring in a pool and subsequently perished from his self-absorption. Narcissism is characterized by an exaggerated sense of self-importance and entitlement, and a tendency to exploit others for personal gain.

Earlier we noted that most people think of themselves in very positive terms, suggesting that many people possess subclinical levels of narcissism (Emmons, 1987; Raskin & Terry, 1988; Rhodewalt & Morf, 1998). The question arises as to whether this is a benefit or a liability. Although there is evidence on both sides of the matter, it appears that positive self-evaluations are generally beneficial, provided that the degree of distortion is not too extreme. People who (1) think they are somewhat better than they really are, (2) exaggerate their ability to bring about desired outcomes, and (3) are overly optimistic about their future are happier, have more satisfying friendships and romantic relationships, are more productive and creative in their work, and are better able to cope and grow with life's challenges than are people with more realistic self-views (Taylor & Brown, 1998, 1994a, 1994b). Of course, it's not good to think you're too wonderful, because this may irritate those around you or lead you to pursue activities for which you are ill-suited (Baumeister, Heatherton, & Tice, 1993; Colvin & Block, 1994; Colvin, Block, & Funder, 1995; Heatherton & Vohs, 2000; John & Robins, 1994). Instead, it is best to have self-views that are just a bit more positive than reality warrants (J. D. Brown, 1991; Taylor, Lerner, Sherman, Sage, & McDowell, 2003).

6. What Is Self-Esteem Good For?

Self-esteem has received a lot of attention in the past 20 years and has been touted as a cure for a variety of social ills, including juvenile delinquency, drug use, teen pregnancy, and criminal behavior. These claims are exaggerated. Self-esteem isn't a panacea. In fact, self-esteem is essentially uncorrelated with everything you really are (Baumeister, Campbell, Krueger, & Vohs, 2003; J. D. Brown, 1998). On average, people who are attractive, intelligent, successful, and rich don't have higher self-esteem than people who lack these qualities. Yet self-esteem is highly correlated with what people think they are like, and high-self-esteem people believe they are smarter, more attractive, and more successful than do low-self-esteem people. Thus, although having high self-esteem doesn't help people succeed, it does help them feel better about the level of success they attain (J. D. Brown & Marshall, 2001).

Self-esteem plays a particularly important role when people encounter negative feedback, such as academic failure, athletic defeat, or interpersonal rejection. Low-self-esteem people react to failure very differently than high self-esteem people do. Failure or rejection makes low-self-esteem people feel humiliated and ashamed of themselves; it makes them think they are worthless, unloved, and bad. Failure and rejection do not have this effect on high-self-esteem people. High-self-esteem people feel sad and disappointed when they fail, but they do not feel humiliated. They do not take failure as personally as do low-self-esteem people.

An investigation by (J. D. Brown & Dutton, 1995) illustrates these effects. In this study, high-self-esteem and low-self-esteem participants were led to experience success or failure at a test that allegedly measured an important intellectual ability. After learning how they had done, they completed two mood scales. One of the scales assessed very general emotional responses to success and failure (happy, sad, unhappy, glad). The other scale assessed feelings of self-worth (proud, pleased with myself, ashamed, humiliated).

The left-hand panel in Figure 5.16 displays the results for the four general emotions. Here we can see that participants felt sadder after they had failed than after they had succeeded, and this was just as true of high-self-esteem participants as of

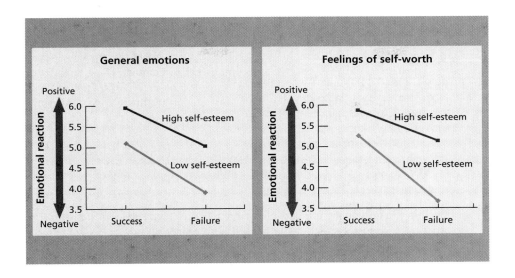

FIGURE 5.16

Self-Esteem and Emotional Reactions to Success and Failure

After succeeding or failing at a test of their verbal ability, participants indicated how they felt in general (left-hand panel) and how they felt about themselves (right-hand panel). Both self-esteem groups felt sad and unhappy when they failed (left-hand panel), but low self-esteem participants felt especially bad *about themselves* when they failed (right-hand panel).

Source: J. D. Brown and Dutton (1995).

low-self-esteem participants. In other words, self-esteem did not influence how happy or sad participants felt when they succeeded or failed. The situation is different when we look at how participants felt *about themselves* after learning they had succeeded or failed. On the right-hand panel of Figure 5.16 we do find an effect of self-esteem. Low-self-esteem participants felt proud of themselves when they succeeded, but humiliated and ashamed of themselves when they failed. This was much less true of the high-self-esteem participants. How they felt about themselves didn't depend so much on whether they had just succeeded or failed.

The findings from this investigation make several points. It seems that low-self-esteem people take failure very personally. It humiliates them and makes them feel ashamed of themselves. High-self-esteem people do not show this effect; failure makes them sad, but it does not make them feel bad about themselves.

There's another way to look at the findings. Low-self-esteem people's feelings toward themselves are conditional. If they succeed, they feel good about themselves; if they fail, they feel bad about themselves (see also Baldwin & Sinclair, 1996). This is a precarious approach to emotional life. Low-self-esteem people feel that they're only as good as their latest outcome. The comedian David Letterman aptly describes the experience:

> Every night you're trying to prove your self-worth. It's like meeting your girlfriend's family for the first time. You want to be the absolute best, wittiest, smartest, most charming, best-smelling version of yourself you can possibly be. That's how I feel every night I go down there to the Ed Sullivan theater. If I can make these 500 people enjoy the experience, and have a higher regard for me when I'm finished, it makes me feel like

an entire person . . . How things go for me every night is how I feel about myself for the next 24 hours. (quoted in *Parade* magazine, May 26, 1996, p. 6)

High-self-esteem people don't live this way. How they feel about themselves doesn't depend on whether or not they have just accomplished something. Their feelings of self-worth are solid and steady; they don't swing from one extreme to another. This may well be the primary value of having high self-esteem: It allows you to fail without feeling bad about yourself.

CHAPTER SUMMARY

- Species other than humans are capable of recognizing themselves in a mirror, but experience in social situations is needed before they will do so.

- William James believed that people's answer to the question "Who am I?" fall into three categories: the material self, the social self, and the spiritual self. The material self consists of all of the tangible objects that carry the designation *my* or *mine*. The social self consists of our social roles, and the people and groups we refer to as *ours*. The spiritual self consists of our psychological self, perceived abilities, attitudes, traits, and habits.

- People learn about themselves by consulting the physical world, by comparing themselves with others and looking at themselves through other people's eyes, and by examining their thoughts and feelings and making attributions for their own behavior.

- Most people have overly positive views of themselves. They think they are better than their peers and believe their future will be brighter than most other people's. A variety of processes contribute to the development and maintenance of these beliefs. In particular, people define traits in ways that emphasize their perceived strengths, seek feedback more vigorously when they think it will be good rather than bad, and compare themselves with others in ways that make them look good by comparison.

- People's beliefs about their ability to successfully perform some action are called self-efficacy beliefs. In general, people with high self-efficacy beliefs adopt more difficult goals and work longer and harder to attain them than do those with low self-efficacy beliefs.

- Self-presentation refers to any attempt to create, maintain, or modify our impression in the minds of other people. People engage in self-presentation to regulate social interaction, to obtain material and social rewards, and to construct a desired identity for themselves.

- High self-monitors are social chameleons. They enjoy being different people in different situations, and they play many roles. In contrast, low self-monitors think of themselves as highly principled individuals who cherish being true to themselves in various situations.

- Successful self-control requires psychological resources. People who refrain from thinking about some topic, conceal their emotions, or resist temptation are left in a psychologically weakened state.

- Happiness is partly heritable, and people with a disposition to be happy interpret experiences in positive ways that maintain ongoing feelings of happiness.

- Personal fulfillment involves the satisfaction of three basic needs: competency, autonomy, and relatedness. Beliefs in personal control are particularly important, because people who feel they are in control of their lives are most apt to feel fulfilled.

- The term *self-esteem* has been used in three ways: *Global self-esteem* refers to enduring feelings of affection for oneself; *feelings of self-worth* refers to more or less momentary reactions to positive or negative events; and *self-evaluations* refer to the way people appraise their specific attributes and abilities.

- Psychologists disagree about how self-esteem develops. Whereas some believe that self-esteem forms early in life in response to temperamental factors and interpersonal relationships, others believe that self-esteem develops later in life as individuals acquire the cognitive ability to make a sophisticated judgment about their worth as a person

- Self-esteem plays its most important role when people confront negative feedback, such as academic failure, athletic defeat, or interpersonal rejection. These experiences make low-self-esteem people feel bad about themselves, but this is much less true for high-self-esteem people.

KEY TERMS

self-concept, 147

extended self, 147

social comparison theory, 151

reflected appraisals model, 154

introspection, 156

self-perception theory, 157

two-factor theory of emotion, 160

better-than-most effect, 162

self-reference effect, 164

false-consensus effect, 165

false-uniqueness effect, 165

self-efficacy beliefs, 168

defensive pessimism, 168

self-presentation, 172

subjective well-being, 178

learned helplessness, 185

self-enhancement motive, 187

ADDITIONAL READING

Go to the Student Edition of the Online Learning Center for this text (www.mhhe.com/brown) and log in to read the following journal articles, which relate to the content of this chapter:

- Gilovich, T., Medvec, V. H., & Savitsky, K. (2000). The spotlight effect in social judgment: An egocentric bias in estimates of the salience of one's own actions and appearance.

- Baumeister, R. F., Bratslavsky, E., Muraven, M., & Tice, D. M. (1998). Ego depletion: Is the active self a limited resource?

CHAPTER SIX

Attitudes and Behavior

How do you feel about same-sex marriages? Are you in favor of them or against them? How about the United Nations? Do you support this organization or oppose it? What about stem cell research, national health insurance, or the development of alternative fuel sources? Do you care strongly about these issues, or are they of little importance to you?

Questions like these focus on your attitudes. Attitudes represent people's likes and dislikes: the issues they support and embrace, and those they condemn and reject. The study of attitudes once dominated the field of social psychology, leading one commentator to call attitudes "the keystone in the edifice of American social psychology" (Allport, 1935, p. 198). Although the field is more diversified now, the study of attitudes continues to occupy a central role (Eagly, 1992; Eagly & Chaiken, 1993, 1998). Issues that were addressed during the formative years of the discipline are currently being reexamined with new methods and new theoretical advances. Throughout this chapter, we will see how the old and the new combine to enrich our understanding of the nature of attitudes.

The chapter is divided into five sections. The first section deals with the nature of attitudes—what they are and how they can be measured. The second section of this chapter covers the origins of attitudes, discussing how attitudes arise and why they are resistant to change. The third section focuses on the cognitive consequences of attitudes. Attitudes, like schemas, bias the way we process information, often leading us to see more support for our position than actually exists. Attitudes also guide our behavior, and the fourth section of this chapter examines the links among thoughts, feelings, and actions. Finally, we consider behaviors that run counter to attitudes. People don't always act in accordance with their attitudes, and they deal with hypocrisy and inconsistency in a number of ingenious ways.

I. What Is an Attitude?

A. Definitional Issues

Attitudes are evaluative reactions to people, issues, or objects. "I like Sue," "I'm against the logging of old growth forests," and "I prefer vanilla ice cream" are examples of attitudes. All of these statements refer to an evaluative (positive or negative) reaction to some person, issue, or object. Attitudes do not have a physical reality. They are hypothetical mediating variables. We infer that people hold attitudes by observing their reactions to various stimuli (called attitude objects). In this sense, attitudes are an O in an S→O→R (stimulus, organism, response) model of behavior. They are intervening mental structures that guide our responses to attitude objects.

Three types of attitudes are of particular interest to social psychologists: attitudes toward social issues (e.g., abortion, gun control); attitudes toward specific individuals (e.g., Fidel Castro, your next door neighbor), and attitudes toward social groups (e.g., Americans, Democrats). The study of prejudice focuses on attitudes toward social groups; a topic we will discuss at greater length in Chapter 10.

Although people don't hold attitudes toward everything, and some people are more prone to evaluate than others are (Jarvis & Petty, 1996; Tormala & Petty, 2001), evaluation is a fundamental human activity. When people are asked to describe various objects, evaluation (good–bad) emerges as the most important judgment they make (Osgood, Suci, & Tannenbaum, 1957). Moreover, such judgments tend to be made very rapidly, often without conscious intention or effort (Bargh, Chaiken, Govender, &

Pratto, 1992; W. A. Cunningham, Johnson, Gatenby, Gore, & Banaji, 2003; Duckworth, Bargh, Garcia, & Chaiken, 2002; Fazio, Sanbonmatsu, Powell, & Kardes, 1986). Many psychologists believe this propensity developed because it provided an evolutionary advantage: People who reached a quick decision about a person's or an animal's friendliness fared better than those who took a long time to make such a judgment or failed to do so altogether (e.g., Fazio, Blascovich, & Driscoll, 1992; Katz, 1960; M. B. Smith, Bruner, & White, 1956).

Attitudes are similar to values, but there is a difference. Unlike attitudes, which always refer to a particular attitude object, **values** are broader, more abstract ideals and goals (Feather, 1995; Rokeach, 1968; S. H. Schwartz & Bilsky, 1987, 1990). Freedom, dignity, beauty, and truth are examples of various values that people hold in life. Attitudes and values are related in that our attitudes allow us to express our broader values. For example, a person who values the sanctity of human life might oppose abortion on demand (Verplanken & Holland, 2002).

Attitudes are also related to schemas (see Chapter 2). Like schemas, attitudes affect the way people process information. In many respects, it is possible to think of attitudes as evaluative schemas (Allport, 1935; Bartlett, 1932; Eagly & Chaiken, 1993). The key difference is that attitudes are always evaluative, whereas schemas do not necessarily incorporate an evaluative component.

B. Tricomponent Model of Attitudes

Attitudes are commonly assumed to be comprised of three components: beliefs, feelings, and actions (Breckler, 1984; Breckler & Wiggins, 1989). The first component, beliefs, refers to all of the knowledge one has about an attitude object. For example, one person might believe that nuclear power offers a cheap, efficient form of energy, whereas another might believe that nuclear power is highly dangerous. Feelings are the second component of an attitude. A teenage boy might experience a rush of excitement when a sleek new car races by, whereas a parent might respond to the same stimulus with feelings of apathy or scorn. Action or behavior is the final component of an attitude. Attitudes are generally (though not always) associated with behavioral tendencies. Positive attitudes are joined with approach tendencies, and negative attitudes are linked to withdrawal and avoidance. For example, a person who likes fantasy epics is more apt to have seen all three *Lord of the Rings* films than someone who doesn't enjoy this genre of film.

Figure 6.1 shows that this approach to understanding attitudes contains two additional assumptions of importance. The first assumption is that the three components fit together. This assumption originates in Gestalt theories of perception and is representative of the consistency seeker metaphor discussed in Chapter 4. According to this perspective, people strive to maintain consistency among these various attitude elements. It feels odd to say "Betty has many negative qualities; I feel uncomfortable when I'm around her, and I seek out her company every chance I get." Inconsistencies like these create psychological tension, which people are driven to avoid and reduce (Festinger, 1957; Heider, 1958).

Figure 6.1 also reveals that attitudes can originate from any of the three components. With many attitudes, beliefs are primary. We first learn something about an attitude object, and this knowledge leads us to feel good or bad toward the object and approach or avoid it. For example, after examining a politician's voting record, we might form a positive attitude toward the politician and cast our vote accordingly. This very rational approach to understanding attitude formation does occur, but it is by no

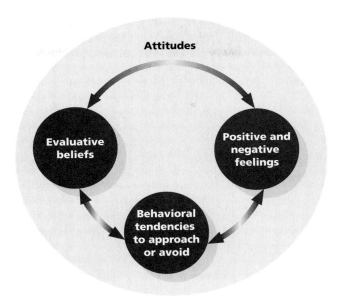

FIGURE 6.1

Tricomponent Theory of Attitudes

Attitudes consist of three correlated components: evaluative beliefs, positive and negative feelings, and behavioral tendencies to approach or avoid an attitude object.

means the only way attitudes can be formed. As we will see in a later section of this chapter, feelings and behavior can also be primary in the formation of attitudes.

C. Measuring Attitudes

Earlier we noted that attitudes are hypothetical cognitive structures without a physical basis. How, then, can we measure attitudes? Several strategies have been devised.

1. Self-Report Measures

The most common approach to measuring attitudes uses a self-report format, in which respondents express their attitudes through verbal or written means. One of the earliest attempts to create such a method was outlined by Louis Thurstone in a 1928 paper entitled "Attitudes Can Be Measured." The Thurstone procedure begins by assembling a large pool of statements that express varying levels of favorableness and unfavorableness toward an attitude issue. The items are then shown to a panel of judges who assign a scale value to each item according to its favorability or unfavorability. The scaled items are then presented to respondents who select items with which they agree. Finally, an attitude score is formed by calculating the mean or median value for all such items. The top section of Table 6.1 presents an illustration of this approach. (Note that respondents don't see the scale values when making their choices.)

Because it requires an initial scaling procedure, the Thurstone method is rather time-consuming and cumbersome. In 1932, Renis Likert devised an attitude scale that overcame these problems. The Likert scale is illustrated in the middle section of Table 6.1, using portions of a scale designed by Batson and Ventis (1982) to measure religious attitudes. Like Thurstone, Likert began by selecting a number of statements relevant to an attitude issue. However, instead of then presenting these issues to a panel of judges to be sorted and rated, Likert simply asked respondents to indicate their level of agreement with each item using a multiple-choice format. After reversing the

TABLE 6.1 Three Ways to Measure Attitudes Toward Religion Using Self-Report Scales

THURSTONE SCALE

Please place a checkmark next to all statements with which you agree.

Scale Value

0.2	___	I believe the church is the greatest institution in America today.
2.0	___	I believe the church provides most of the leaders for every movement for social welfare.
3.8	___	I like our church for it gives young people a change to have some fun and yet it is religious.
5.3	___	I don't believe church-going will do anyone any harm.
8.6	___	I feel the chruch is petty, always quarreling over matters that have no interest or importance.
9.4	___	I feel the chruch is bound hand and foot by money interests and cannot practice the religion of Jesus.
11.0	___	I think the church is a parasite on society.

Source: R. C. Peterson and Thurstone (1933/1970), pp. 22–23.

LIKERT SCALE

Please circle one number next to each item to indicate your level of agreement with that item.

	Strongly Disagree	Disagree	Neither Agree nor Disagree	Agree	Strongly Agree
1. My religious beliefs are what really lie behind my whole approach to life.	1	2	3	4	5
2. I try hard to carry my religion over into all my dealings in life.	1	2	3	4	5
3. Although I am a religious person, I refuse to let religious considerations influence my everyday affairs.	1	2	3	4	5
4. Although I believe in my religion, I feel there are many more important things in my life.	1	2	3	4	5

Source: Batson and Ventis (1982).

SEMANTIC DIFFERENTIAL SCALE

Place an X above each line to indicate your attitude toward **Americans.**

bad	___ ___ ___ ___ ___ ___ ___ ___ ___	good
undesirable	___ ___ ___ ___ ___ ___ ___ ___ ___	desirable
unpleasant	___ ___ ___ ___ ___ ___ ___ ___ ___	pleasant
foolish	___ ___ ___ ___ ___ ___ ___ ___ ___	wise

Source: Osgood, Suci, and Tannenbaum (1957).

scoring for negatively worded items (items 3 and 4 in Table 6.1), a final attitude score is found by summing these responses.

A third type of self-report attitude scale is known as the semantic differential scale (Osgood, Suci, & Tannenbaum, 1957). This scale focuses on people's feelings toward an attitude object. The bottom section of Table 6.1 illustrates this approach. As with the Likert scale, an attitude score is derived by assigning numbers to each of the nine response options and then summing across the items. Several aspects of this procedure are noteworthy. First, it focuses on feelings rather than beliefs. Second, because there is no need to generate and test statements pertaining to the specific attitude being measured, this procedure is convenient and expedient. Third, the generic nature of this method makes it easy to compare different attitudes. In theory, the semantic differential scale can be used to compare people's feelings toward any attitude object.

2. Surveys and Opinion Polls

Regardless of how the questions are phrased, self-report measures provide a fast and cost-effective way of gauging people's attitudes. The ease and efficiency with which such questions can be asked makes self-report measures exceedingly common. In fact, they are the staple of national polling services that inundate the news media as elections near. Perhaps you've wondered how these polls are able to accurately represent national attitudes from small samples. The first trick is to use representative sampling (see Chapter 1). Here, the pollster determines the demographic characteristics of the population being studied (e.g., 60 percent of all voters are married) and then ensures that this division characterizes the sample being polled (e.g., 60 percent of all sample respondents will be married).

The second trick is to ensure that the sample size is adequately large. Interestingly, the number of people needed in the sample is probably less than you realize. A statistic known as the sample margin of error ($1/\sqrt{N}$) reveals that we can be 95% certain that with a sample of 1,200 respondents, the true population result falls within 3% (in either direction) of our sample result. To illustrate, suppose 65% of all registered American voters intend to vote for the incumbent in the next election. Ninety-five percent of the time, a poll conducted with 1,200 representative voters will show that the range of support for the incumbent lies between 62 and 68%. This is what pollsters mean when they say their polls are accurate with a margin of error of ± 3.

Of course, proper sampling alone does not guarantee accuracy. The poll questions, too, must be worded fairly. Unfortunately, this is not all that easy to do. As we saw in Chapter 4, subtle changes in wording or question framing can profoundly affect the decisions people make. The same is true with attitude questionnaires. The manner in which questions are worded can strongly influence how people express their attitudes (Schuman & Presser, 1981; Schwarz, 1999; Schwarz, Groves, & Schuman, 1998; Sudman, Bradburn, & Schwarz, 1996; Tourangeau & Rasinski, 1988). Consider the following two questions:

Do you think the United States should *allow* public speeches against democracy?

Do you think the United States should *forbid* public speeches against democracy?

Even though the two questions are mirror images of the other, when Rugg (1941) posed this question to a sample of Americans, 46 percent of the respondents replied that we should not forbid such speeches, but only 25 percent indicated that we should allow them. A replication of this research in the 1980s produced a comparable pattern of findings, although people were generally more tolerant of dissent than they were in the 1940s (Schuman & Presser, 1981).

The response options people are given also affect their expressed attitudes. To illustrate, Schwarz and Hippler (1995) had Germans evaluate six politicians. All respondents were given an 11-point scale, with verbal endpoints "Don't think very highly" and "Think very highly." Half of the participants were given a scale from −5 to +5 and half were given a scale from 0 to 10.

−5	−4	−3	−2	−1	0	1	2	3	4	5
Don't think very highly								Think very highly		

0	1	2	3	4	5	6	7	8	9	10
Don't think very highly								Think very highly		

Even though the verbal endpoints were the same, the politicians were rated more favorably among participants who used the −5 to +5 scale than among participants who used the 0 to 10 scale. Presumably this occurred because the −5 endpoint was viewed as more negative than the 0 endpoint (for related research, see Haddock & Carrick, 1999; Salancik & Conway, 1975; Schwarz, Hippler, Deutsch, & Strack, 1985; Schwarz, Knäuper, Hippler, Noelle-Neumann, & Clark, 1991; Winkielman, Knäuper, & Schwarz, 1998). Considering that public opinion polls not only reflect but also shape public sentiment, the implications of this finding are substantial. By including very negative values in the rating scale, shrewd political operatives can increase the favorability rating of their candidate.

Another factor that influences responses to attitude polls is question order. Much as our first impression of a person influences the way subsequent information is interpreted, so too do initial questions in a questionnaire affect the way later questions are construed. This effect was first illustrated by Hyman and Sheatsley (1950), who posed the following questions to Americans in 1948:

1. Do you think the United States should let Communist newspaper reporters from other countries come in and send back to their papers the news as they see it?
2. Do you think a Communist country like Russia should let American newspaper reporters come in and send back to America the news as they see it?

Only 36 percent of Hyman and Sheatsley's respondents said yes to question 1 when that question preceded question 2, yet 73 percent of the respondents agreed to question 1 when it followed question 2. There are several explanations for this finding, but the most likely is that people who had first indicated that American reporters should be allowed into Communist countries felt that it was only fair that Communist reporters also be allowed into America.

Schwarz and Bless (1992) have outlined a theoretical model to explain effects such as these. Their model begins by noting that evaluative judgments consist of two processes: a representation of the object being judged, and a standard or frame of reference against which the object is evaluated. Imagine that I hand you an object and ask you whether or not it is heavy. Your judgment will depend on your perception of the object's weight and your ideas about the weight of other objects. Schwarz and

Bless argue that the same processes operate to shape people's attitudes. If I ask you whether or not you are liberal, your answer depends on your own beliefs relative to what you think other people believe.

The model explains why previous questions often produce contradictory effects (Stapel & Schwarz, 1998). Imagine you are filling out a survey about how safe schools are today. If the question is preceded by a reminder of violence in schools (e.g., Do you recall the Columbine shooting in Littleton, Colorado?), you will probably think schools are less safe than in years gone by. This is an assimilation effect, as your judgment of the safety of schools is altered in the direction of the violence at Columbine. But now suppose you are asked how safe a given school is. If you use Columbine High School as a frame of reference, you will probably show a contrast effect and judge any given school to be relatively safe. In short, the same piece of information can produce an assimilation effect when a broad, general attitude is assessed (how safe are schools, in general) but a contrast effect when a narrow, specific instance is judged (how safe is any given school).

These opposing tendencies can explain a curious fact about people's attitudes toward a variety of issues. Although Americans distrust Congress in general, they do not distrust their own representative. In a similar vein, members of minority groups often report high levels of discrimination against their group but relatively low levels of personal discrimination.

To summarize, minor changes in wording and context can alter people's self-reported attitudes. Although these effects are especially pronounced among people with indifferent or weak attitudes (Chaiken & Baldwin, 1981; Hippler & Schwarz, 1986; Lavine, Huff, Wagner, & Sweeney, 1998), even people with strongly held attitudes are susceptible to these influences (Bassili & Krosnick, 2000; Krosnick & Schuman, 1988). It would be incorrect, however, to view these effects as merely contaminants in the attitude measurement process; instead they serve as another reminder that meaning is variable and context determines meaning.

3. Supplemental Attitude Measures

Aside from the methodological factors discussed in the preceding subsection, several other factors limit the validity of self-report measures. The desire to present oneself in a socially desirable manner is probably the most important factor to consider. When asked to express their attitudes toward various issues, people may shade their answers in order to appear more moral, tolerant, or caring than they are in reality. This problem is especially acute when the issues under consideration are highly personal or contentious. For this reason, it is especially difficult to gauge people's true attitudes when it comes to matters of sexuality and prejudice.

Numerous attempts have been made to overcome people's tendency to give socially desirable answers to self-report questions. One strategy relies on a device known as the bogus pipeline (E. E. Jones & Sigall, 1971). Participants are connected to an imposing machine that allegedly measures heart rate and blood pressure, and are told that the device can accurately detect their true attitudes toward an issue or a person. The physiological apparatus doesn't really work, but merely telling people that the truth can be detected is sufficient to increase (though not ensure) the honesty of their responses (Roese & Jamieson, 1993; Tourangeau, Smith, & Rasinski, 1997). Other supplemental attitude measures include indirect measures and physiological measures.

Indirect Measures. Indirect measures of attitudes disguise the true purpose of the attitude scale (Fazio & Olson, 2003). One such measure, called the implicit association test (Greenwald, McGhee, & Schwartz, 1998), assesses the extent to which people readily associate various attitude objects with other positively or negatively valued stimuli (see https://implicit.harvard.edu/implicit). In a typical investigation of attitudes toward presidential candidates, participants were asked to simultaneously classify pictures of George W. Bush and Al Gore, and pictures of pleasant and unpleasant stimuli, such as flowers and spiders (Greenwald, Nosek, & Banaji, 2003). Participants who found it easier to pair Bush with pleasant pictures and Gore with unpleasant ones were said to have a favorable implicit attitude toward Bush. The opposite was true for those who found it easier to pair Gore with pleasant stimuli and Bush with unpleasant stimuli. In Chapter 10, we will examine how procedures like these are used to identify people who are prejudiced toward minority groups.

Physiological Measures of Attitudes. Although attitudes do not have a physical basis, they do have some measurable physiological manifestations. Facial expressions, for example, change in response to positive and negative stimuli. The brow is furrowed when people think about or view negative stimuli, and the cheeks and eyes are raised when people think about or view positive stimuli. By measuring these changes, researchers are able to detect people's underlying attitudes toward various attitude objects (Cacioppo, Bush, & Tassinary, 1992; Cacioppo, Petty, Losch, & Kim, 1986). A related assessment approach examines electrical activity in the brain. People display a reliable increase in brain-wave activity when novel or evaluatively inconsistent stimuli are encountered. Charting these changes helps researchers assess whether people automatically categorize attitude objects as good or bad (Cacioppo, Crites, Bernston, & Coles, 1993; Cacioppo, Crites, & Gardner, 1996; Crites, Cacioppo, Gardner, & Bernston, 1995).

D. Further Issues Regarding the Nature of Attitudes

1. Attitudes as a Bidimensional Concept

Most people assume that attitudes lie on a continuum ranging from extremely negative to extremely positive. Challenging this assumption, Cacioppo, Gardner, and Bernston (1997) have suggested that people's positive and negative reactions to an attitude object are at least somewhat independent. This conceptual scheme, which is shown in Table 6.2, leads to the identification of four different types of attitudes. Attitudes characterized by an absence of positive and negative feelings are classified as indifferent. Positive attitudes are characterized by strong positive feelings and weak negative ones, whereas negative attitudes are characterized by strong negative feelings and weak positive ones. Finally, ambivalent attitudes are characterized by strong

TABLE 6.2   Bidimensional Approach to Understanding Attitudes

| | | Positive Evaluation | |
		Weak	Strong
Negative Evaluation	Weak	Indifference	Positive attitude
	Strong	Negative attitude	Ambivalence

positive and strong negative feelings. (The word *ambivalent* means "two valences" rather than apathetic or indifferent.)

Ambivalent attitudes are particularly common toward behaviors that compromise one's health and well-being. To illustrate, most smokers know that smoking isn't good for them, and many express guilt about smoking and a desire to quit. However, they derive joy from smoking and believe it calms them down. In short, they hold ambivalent attitudes toward smoking. This ambivalence has an important consequence: The more conflicted smokers are about smoking, the more they want to quit (Lipkus, Green, Feaganes, & Sedikides, 2001; see also Newby-Clark, McGregor, & Zanna, 2002; Priester & Petty, 1996, 2001).

2. Attitude Strength and Attitude Importance

When thinking about the nature of attitudes, it's also important to consider that they differ not only with respect to whether they are positive or negative but also with respect to their strength and importance (Petty & Krosnick, 1995). When people care a great deal about an issue (e.g., abortion or human rights), their attitudes are typically strong and extreme. In contrast, when people are less concerned about an issue (e.g., zoning laws or campaign finance reform), their attitudes are usually weaker and less polarized (Boninger, Krosnick, & Berent, 1995; Krosnick, Boninger, Chuang, Berent, & Carnot, 1993). As you might expect, strongly held attitudes tend to be more stable and more consequential than weakly held ones (Bizer & Krosnick, 2001), and people who hold strong attitudes are more apt to try to persuade others to adopt their point of view (Visser, Krosnick, & Simmons, 2003).

II. Origins of Attitudes

Having discussed various ways in which attitudes can be measured, we are ready to consider how they arise. To set the stage for this discussion, let's review the tricomponent model of attitudes shown in Figure 6.1. The figure shows (1) that attitudes consist of three correlated components (beliefs, feelings, and behavior); (2) that any one of these components can be primary in the formation of an attitude; and (3) that once an attitude is formed, pressures toward consistency operate to make these components match one another.

A. Emotional Theories of Attitude Formation

The first class of theories we will consider are called **emotional theories of attitude formation.** There are several such theories, but all assume that emotions are primary in the formation of attitudes, and that attitudes arise independent of beliefs.

1. Learning Theory Accounts of Attitude Formation

Learning theory provides one example of an emotional theory of attitude formation. Recall from Chapter 2 that learning theory assumes that thoughts play no role in guiding behavior. Thoughts occur, but they are epiphenomenal. These assumptions are consistent with the notion that attitudes arise independent of beliefs.

Instrumental Learning of Attitudes. Some attitudes are acquired through instrumental learning. Consider your attitudes toward sharing and stealing. Chances are, you have a positive attitude toward the former and a negative attitude toward the latter. Why? In large part, it's because you have been reinforced for holding these attitudes. You received positive reinforcement when you shared and were punished when you took something that didn't belong to you. You may also have witnessed another person being rewarded for sharing or punished for stealing. Because learning also takes place through observation and modeling (Bandura & Walters, 1963), these vicarious experiences can influence attitude formation.

Verbal agreement from another person constitutes another form of reinforcement. We are gratified when another person agrees with us and displeased when he or she disagrees with us. To see whether verbal reinforcement influences attitudes, Insko and Cialdini (1969) conducted a field experiment (see Chapter 1). Participants were called on the phone and asked their opinions about an issue of the day (pay TV). Using random assignment to conditions, the researchers reinforced some participants for expressing positive attitudes toward pay TV (the experimenter said "Good" whenever participants expressed support for the issue and "Humph" in a disapproving manner whenever they expressed opposition). Other participants received the opposite reinforcement schedule (they were reinforced for making negative statements, not positive ones). Finally, the researchers assessed the participants' attitudes toward pay TV. They found that respondents who were selectively reinforced for expressing positive opinions toward pay TV subsequently expressed more positive attitudes toward the issue than did those who were reinforced for expressing negative opinons. Moreover, the participants were not aware of the power of the reinforcement. When asked later, few of the participants indicated that they had noticed the subtle reinforcement they had received.

Classical Conditioning of Attitudes. Instrumental learning of attitudes occurs when a behavioral or verbal response is selectively reinforced. Attitude formation can also occur through principles of classical conditioning (Staats & Staats, 1958; Walther, 2002; Zanna, Kiesler, & Pilkonis, 1970). Unlike instrumental learning, classical conditioning does not require an initial response. Advertisers often rely on principles of classical conditioning to sell their wares. Sunny skies, sex appeal, friendship, and excitement are paired with soft drinks, cigarettes, deodorants, and cars. Why? Because the advertisers hope that the good feelings elicited by these intrinsically positive stimuli will transfer to the products they are selling (see Figure 6.2). Notice how the aim

FIGURE 6.2

Classical Conditioning of Attitudes

Attractive models in advertisements evoke positive feelings, and these feelings are transferred to the product being advertised.

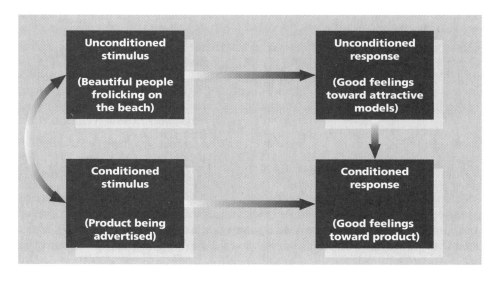

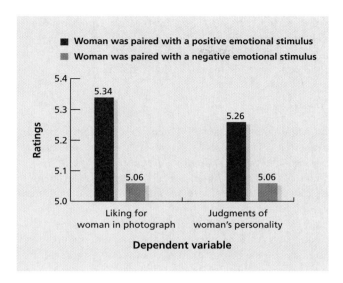

FIGURE 6.3

Classically Conditioned Attitudes

Participants formed more positive attitudes toward a woman and believed she had a more pleasing personality when, through classical conditioning, she was associated with a positive emotional stimulus rather than a negative emotional stimulus. These findings suggest that classically conditioned feelings can precede and cause the formation of beliefs.

Source: Krosnick, Betz, Jussim, and Lynn (1992).

here is to affect people's attitudes without affecting their beliefs. People don't think, "If I smoke brand X cigarettes, I will learn how to ride a horse like a macho cowboy." They simply form a positive attitude toward the product on the basis of the product's emotional association with other, inherently pleasant stimuli. Of course, once the attitude is formed, pressures toward consistency will lead people to think the product also has many positive features (e.g., "I think the hard pack best protects my smokes") and purchase it. But these beliefs were not primary in the formation of the attitude; they came after the attitude had already been formed.

Classical conditioning of attitudes works best when unfamiliar or novel stimuli are involved (Cacioppo, Marshall-Goodell, Tassinary, & Petty, 1992; Staats & Staats, 1958). It even works when people are unaware that the unconditioned stimulus has occurred at all. Krosnick, Betz, Jussim, and Lynn (1992, Study 2) had participants view slide photographs of a woman engaged in various activities. Immediately preceding these slides were other slide photographs, which appeared for only 9 milliseconds (less than 0.01 second). For some participants, these slides depicted positive emotional scenes (e.g., a pair of kittens, a child with a doll), whereas for other participants, the slides depicted negative emotional scenes (e.g., a bloody shark, a skull).

Afterward, participants indicated how much they thought they would like the woman in the photographs and then rated her personality on a variety of scales (e.g., honest–dishonest, polite–rude, successful–unsuccessful). Figure 6.3 shows how powerful classical conditioning effects can be. Even though the slides were presented at exposure times too fast to be consciously recognized, participants formed more positive attitudes toward the woman when she was paired with positive emotional slides than when she was paired with negative emotional slides (Murphy & Zajonc, 1993; Niedenthal, 1990; M. A. Olson

& Fazio, 2001). Notice also that participants who saw the positive emotional slides described the woman's personality more positively than did those who saw the negative emotional slides. These findings suggest that these beliefs were a consequence of the liking participants felt toward the person, rather than a cause of that liking.

2. The Mere Exposure Effect

Another way attitudes can be acquired independent of beliefs is through a process known as the **mere exposure effect.** The mere exposure effect refers to the fact that the more often we are exposed to a neutral stimulus, the more we like it. You've probably experienced this effect with songs you've heard on the radio. The more familiar the song becomes, the more you like it. There are limits, of course, but familiarity generally breeds liking (not contempt).

The effect was demonstrated by Zajonc (1968). In initial research, Zajonc examined the correlation between liking for various words and the frequency with which these words appear in the English language. For example, university students rated how much they liked various trees, fruits, vegetables, and flowers. Zajonc found that frequently used words (e.g., elm, apple, corn, and rose) were liked more than were relatively rare words (e.g., acacia, mango, parsnip, and cowslip). Although correlational data like these cannot establish that frequency causes liking, they do show that frequency and liking are related.

Zajonc turned to an experimental design to determine whether mere exposure causes liking. In several experiments, participants were shown novel stimuli, such as Chinese ideographs. Some ideographs were shown many times, whereas others were displayed relatively infrequently. Later, participants indicated their liking for these stimuli. Zajonc found that participants liked the ideographs they had seen many times more than the ones they had seen infrequently, leading him to conclude that liking for a novel stimulus increases merely as a result of repeated exposure. Subsequent research has found strong support for this claim (R. F. Bornstein, 1989). Although researchers aren't entirely sure why mere exposure increases liking, they suspect that familiarity induces a general positive mood and, through principles of classical conditioning, this positive mood becomes associated with the stimulus that produced it (Harmon-Jones & Allen, 2001; Monahan, Murphy, & Zajonc, 2000; Winkielman & Cacioppo, 2001; Zajonc, 2001).

Earlier we noted that learning can create attitudes even when people aren't aware of the reinforcement they have received (in instrumental learning) or the unconditioned stimulus they have experienced (in classical conditioning). R. F. Bornstein and D'Agostino (1992) conducted an investigation to see whether mere exposure also produce attitudes without awareness. They found clear evidence that it can. In fact, stimuli shown repeatedly at 5 milliseconds produced a stronger mere exposure effect than did stimuli shown at 500 milliseconds, indicating that the mere exposure effect is actually more powerful when subliminal stimuli are used.

Several points should be kept in mind when evaluating this research. First, although mere exposure effects occur with mildly negative stimuli (Zajonc, Markus, & Wilson, 1974), they do not occur with highly negative stimuli. Being exposed repeatedly to a noxious stimulus will probably not make you like it more. Second, there is a risk of oversaturation. After about 25 exposures, people begin to get bored and liking may even decrease (R. F. Bornstein, 1989). For this reason, exposure effects tend to be stronger with complex visual stimuli than with very simple ones (R. F. Bornstein, Kale, & Cornell, 1990). This may explain why repeatedly hearing a formulated pop song eventually drives us to distraction (the so-called Barry Manilow effect). Finally, the effect also works in reverse. Just as familiarity leads to liking, so too does liking lead to a subjective sense of familiarity. The more we like something, the more certain we are that we have encountered it before (Garcia-Marques, Mackie, Claypool, Garcia-Marques, 2004; Monin, 2003).

3. Subliminal Perception and Attitude Formation

So far we have seen that attitudes can be formed independent of beliefs. This can occur through instrumental learning, classical conditioning, and mere exposure. Moreover, these processes seem to work best when people are unaware that they are operating. Does this mean that attitudes are easily conditioned and that people are at the mercy of forces occurring outside conscious awareness?

This question first gained prominence during the late 1950s. While patrons at a drive-in theater in New Jersey were watching a movie, messages were flashed urging them to drink Coca-Cola and eat popcorn. Although these messages appeared at recognition rates too fast to be consciously recognized, Coca-Cola sales allegedly jumped 18 percent and popcorn sales supposedly increased by a whopping 58 percent. Coming during the height of the cold war, these findings evoked images of mind control, fueling speculation that Americans could be brainwashed by everything from the Russians to rock and roll.

In fact, the researcher who conducted this study later admitted to fabricating the data to boost sales (see Weir, 1984). Subsequent research has found that, although short-term behaviors can be affected under certain conditions (Strahan, Spencer, & Zanna, 2002), complex attitudes and behaviors cannot be altered by subliminal stimuli. This conclusion also applies to subliminal self-help tapes that purport to help people lose weight, increase their memory, or boost their self-esteem. Although people believe these tapes are effective, there is no credible evidence that these tapes actually work (Pratkanis, Eskenazi, & Greenwald, 1994).

B. Cognitive Theories of Attitude Formation

Emotional theories of attitude formation emphasize that attitudes can form independent of beliefs. But this is not the only way attitudes form. Our attitudes can also arise from our beliefs. Cognitive theories of attitude formation have been developed to explain this process (N. H. Anderson, 1974; Fishbein & Ajzen, 1975; Wyer, 1974). These theories use an expectancy–value model to understand attitude development (see Chapter 2 for a review of these models).

To illustrate this approach, suppose we wish to predict a person's attitude toward the presidential candidates in the next election. Table 6.3 shows how an expectancy–value model of attitude formation handles this issue. In this example, the voter has first assigned a probability rating that represents his belief that the candidate will bring about the outcome in question. The voter has then placed a value on that outcome (1 = Very low value; 7 = Very high value). (Notice that the value ratings are the same for both candidates, because it's the same voter.) For each candidate, the probability rating is then multiplied by its corresponding value, and the products are summed. In this example, an expectancy–value model predicts that candidate A will be preferred, because this candidate is more apt to bring about outcomes the voter values.

1. Key Features of the Cognitive Approach

The cognitive approach to attitude formation depicts people as making very rational decisions about which attitudes to hold. Often these decisions are influenced by

TABLE 6.3   An Expectancy–Value Model of Cognitively Based Attitudes

| | CANDIDATE A | | | CANDIDATE B | | |
Issue	Expectancy That the Candidate Will Bring the Outcome About	Value Placed on Outcome	Weighted Rating (Expectancy × Value)	Expectancy That the Candidate Will Bring the Outcome About	Value Placed on Outcome	Weighted Rating (Expectancy × Value)
Improve schools	0.6	7	4.2	0.5	7	3.5
Clean up environment	0.8	7	5.6	0.4	7	2.8
Preserve Social Security	0.4	4	1.6	0.8	4	3.2
Reduce taxes	0.5	2	1.0	0.6	2	1.2
Sum			12.4			10.7

underlying values. Earlier we noted that values differ from attitudes, in that values are not tied to any specific person, issue, or object. At the same time, attitudes allow us to express our values. In combination with our beliefs, some of the attitudes we hold arise because they give specific form to our more general, abstract values (Bardi & Schwartz, 2003; Feather, 1995; Katz, 1960). A patriotic American may support high tariffs on incoming foreign goods, because these tariffs make foreign products more expensive, leading people to buy American-made products instead.

Cognitive models also assume that people's attitudes serve their self-interest (B. J. Lehman & Crano, 2001). To illustrate, a person without health insurance may favor political candidates who promise to make national health insurance an important goal of their administration. In this case, the person's attitude reflects an interest in bringing about outcomes that provide important self-benefits. Surely this is one reason why candidates who promise to lower taxes can always count on having a solid constituency.

A tendency to favor candidates who share one's values and interests may explain the so-called gender gap in recent elections. It has been estimated that in the 2000 presidential election, 54 percent of women voted for Al Gore, but only 43 percent of men did so (www.feminist.org/Election2000/gendergap_subsets.asp). Eagly and colleagues have suggested that these differences reflect the match between the voters' values and the candidates' positions (Eagly, Diekman, Schneider, & Kulesa, 2003). Women tend to value social compassion and egalitarianism, and vote for liberal candidates who take positions that promote these values (e.g., government-subsidized prescription drugs for the elderly). In contrast, men tend to value self-reliance and competition, and vote for more conservative candidates who take positions that promote these values (e.g., reduced government regulation of business). Each group, then, assesses the match between its values and the candidates' position, and votes for the candidate who best embraces its ideals.

2. Does It Matter Whether Attitudes Are Based on Affect or on Beliefs?

Given that attitudes can be formed through beliefs or through less logical, more emotional means, the question arises as to which of these components of attitudes is more important. Before we answer this question, it will be instructive to examine how these psychological constructs differ. First, they are linked to different areas of the brain (R. J. Davidson, Jackson, & Kalin, 2000; Elliott & Dolan, 1998; Lieberman, 2000). The amygdala is important for emotional processes, and affective preferences are associated with right lateral frontal activation. The hippocampus is important for cognitive judgments, and these reactions are typically associated with activation of the prefrontal cortex. Affect and cognition also differ experientially. We recognize that our cognitive judgments might be in error (e.g., "I think a doughnut has fewer than 100 calories"), but our affective reactions can't be right or wrong (e.g., "I yearn for a Krispy Kreme"). Third, affective reactions to stimuli occur faster than cognitive ones (W. A. Cunningham et al., 2003). Evaluations of an attitude object sometimes occur so fast that we like or dislike something before we even consciously know what that something is. Summarizing these effects, one researcher noted that "preferences need no inferences" (Zajonc, 1980b).

For these and other reasons, affect and cognition are best thought of as two correlated but distinct psychological phenomena. So which is more important? Although there is not perfect agreement on the matter, the evidence favors our hearts over our minds. Compared to the cognitive component, the affective component of an attitude is more closely tied to the overall attitude, is a better predictor of behavior, and is harder to change (Abelson, Kinder, Peters, & Fiske, 1982; Breckler & Wiggins, 1989; D. K. Sherman & Kim, 2002; Simons & Carey, 1998; Stangor, Sullivan, & Ford, 1991). These effects are most clearly illustrated in the political realm. The cognitive model presents a rational approach to understanding voting behavior. If we prefer candidate A to candidate B, it's because candidate A supports the issues we care most about, not because of any emotionally based reason (e.g., that candidate A is taller or more attractive). In fact, the affective component of a political attitude (how the politician makes you feel) is a better predictor of voting behavior than is the cognitive component (Glaser & Salovey, 1998; Marcus, 1988), and the taller candidate has won a disproportionate number of presidential elections since the advent of television (J. Mathews, 1999). We might like to think we are not swayed by such factors, but we are.

T. D. Wilson and his colleagues have conducted another line of research relevant to the cognition–emotion debate (for reviews, see T. D. Wilson, Dunn, Kraft, & Lisle, 1989; T. D. Wilson & Hodges, 1992). Wilson's research is built on the premise that people do not always know why they feel the way they do toward an attitude object (Freud, 1957; Nisbett & Wilson, 1977). Nevertheless, they have little difficulty generating plausible explanations for their feelings. For example, if you were asked why you like your boyfriend or girlfriend, you would probably say it has something to do with the person's personality (e.g., the person's warmth or kindness). In fact, these reasons are imperfectly related to why you feel the way you do. Other reasons, such as the way the person walks, laughs, smells, or gestures may be equally or more important.

Wilson has found that problems can arise when people act on the basis of their beliefs rather than from their hearts. In one investigation, T. D. Wilson, Dunn, Bybee, Hyman, and Rotondo (1984) had college students express their attitudes toward their current dating partner. Half of the participants performed this task after first thinking about why they felt the way they did toward their partner, while the remaining participants simply indicated how they felt without first analyzing why. Approximately nine months later, the experimenters contacted the couples to see if they were still together. The attitudes expressed by partners who did not first analyze their feelings turned out to be a better predictor of whether the couples stayed together than did the attitudes expressed by partners who first thought about why they felt the way they did. Subsequent research has found this effect is strongest when the attitude was originally formed through affective processes rather than cognitive ones (T. D. Wilson, Kraft, & Dunn, 1989). Under these conditions, people are better served by going with their gut feelings rather than thinking too much about why they feel the way they do.

C. Behavior-Based Attitudes

So far we have seen that attitudes can develop through emotional factors (independent of beliefs) or through cognitive factors (in which case beliefs are primary). Behavior can also lead to attitude formation. This process was first illustrated in an experimental context by Janis and King (1954). Janis and King had students deliver and listen to speeches on various topics. Demonstrating the power of behavior, they found that students who delivered the speeches were more apt to form attitudes consistent with the position they espoused than did audience members who passively heard the speeches. Follow-up research (B. T. King & Janis, 1956) showed that this effect occurs only when speakers improvise and devise their own arguments on the issue, suggesting that it is the process of actively taking a stand that produces attitude formation. This may be particularly true when a public commitment is made (Lewin, 1952). It is one thing to espouse a position in the privacy of one's own home, and quite another to publicly commit to a position.

Several processes can explain this tendency. In Chapter 5 we discussed Bem's (1972) self-perception theory. This theory assumes that people infer their attitudes by observing their own behavior. If I publicly advocate national health insurance, I assume that I like it. The process Bem describes is a very passive one. Other researchers have suggested that public behavior influences attitudes through a more active, motivated process. When people publicly commit to an action, they feel pressure to make their attitudes match their actions (Festinger, 1957; Lewin, 1952). We will explore these ideas more fully in a later section of this chapter.

D. Heritable Attitudes

The processes we have been discussing operate throughout a person's lifetime, leading people to acquire attitudes as a result of their unique experiences. In this sense, they fall under the "nurture" category in the familiar nature–nurture debate. Not all attitudes are acquired this way, however. Some attitudes appear to be heritable. In a study with more than 3,000 pairs of twins, N. G. Martin and colleagues (1986) found that identical (monozygotic) twins were more likely than fraternal (dyzygotic) twins to hold comparable attitudes toward issues pertaining to political conservatism, such as the death penalty and racial integration. Other attitudes, such as a liking for jazz music or the value of learning Latin, were also found to be heritable.

Why might this be the case? Tesser (1993) notes that inherited personality variables can influence the attitudes people form. For example, a person who is highly energetic is apt to develop a positive attitude toward sports, just as a person who is quiet and calm is apt to develop a positive attitude toward more sedentary activities, such as card games or reading. Other heritable personality variables, such as intelligence and sociability, can similarly affect the specific attitudes we form. Consequently, although most of our attitudes are shaped by environmental factors, some appear to be inherited to at least some degree (Cleveland, Udry, & Chantala, 2001; McGuire, 1985; J. M. Olson, Vernon, Harris, & Jang, 2001).

III. Cognitive Consequences of Attitudes

Earlier we noted that attitudes function as schemas. Like other schemas, attitudes aid in the processing of information. They influence what we notice, guide our interpretation of events, and affect our memory. Generally speaking, these influences allow people to rapidly make judgments when encountering an attitude object, providing an advantage to those who hold attitudes over those who do not (Fazio et al., 1992).

A. Biased Assimilation Effects

Making rapid, attitude-based decisions is not always advantageous, however. In some cases, people with well-defined attitudes tend to overlook important sources of information when making a decision (Fazio, Ledbetter, & Towles-Schwen, 2000). Attitudes can also bias people's interpretation of events and experiences. If you have ever been at a heated sporting event, you have probably witnessed this effect. When a foul is committed in the NBA, for example, it is quite common for fans to disagree on who was at fault. Was it a charging foul or a blocking foul? It is often difficult to tell, and our perception depends greatly on which team we favor.

Hastorf and Cantril (1954) provided an empirical demonstration of this effect. The situation was this: Princeton and Dartmouth had played a particularly hard-fought football game. Both schools alleged that the other team had played unfairly. One week after the game, Hastorf and Cantril asked students at each university, "Which team do you think started the trouble?" Not surprisingly, students' perceptions were influenced by their school allegiances. Eight-six percent of the Princeton students indicated that Dartmouth had started the trouble, while only 36 percent of Dartmouth students believed this to be the case. Even though they had watched the same game, the students came away with very different interpretations of what they had seen.

Many years after Hastorf and Cantril's pioneering research, C. G. Lord, Ross, and Lepper (1979) set out to discover how attitudes bias people's interpretation of events. In their investigation, students with favorable or unfavorable attitudes toward capital punishment were asked to read two articles that described research on the effectiveness of capital punishment. One of the articles presented evidence that capital punishment effectively deterred serious crimes, and the other presented evidence that capital punishment was an ineffective deterrent. All students read both articles, so all were exposed to conflicting evidence regarding the value of capital punishment.

Given Hastorf and Cantril's work, Lord, Ross, and Lepper expected that students' attitudes toward capital punishment would influence their judgments of the scientific value of the research presented in each essay. Figure 6.4 shows that this was the case. Students with favorable attitudes toward capital punishment believed that the research supporting the use of capital punishment as a deterrent to crime was more scientifically sound than was the research opposing the use of capital punishment. The reverse

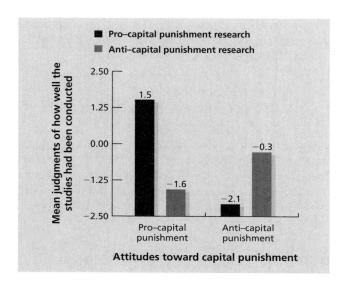

FIGURE 6.4

The Biased Assimilation Effect

Students who favored capital punishment thought the pro–capital punishment research was more convincing than was the anti–capital punishment research, but the opposite was true for students who opposed capital punishment. These findings reveal that attitudes function as schemas, biasing the way people process information.

Source: C. G. Lord, Ross, and Lepper (1979).

was true among students who opposed capital punishment. In short, the very same stimulus was viewed in opposite ways by people with differing attitudes.

The participants were also asked to make written comments regarding each report. Table 6.4 presents a sample of these comments. Looking at these comments, it is easy to see why the two groups had such divergent reactions to the research reports. Evidence that seemed compelling and convincing to one person seemed obviously flawed and specious to another (see also Eagly, Kulesa, Brannon, Shaw, & Hutson-Comeaux, 2000).

Finally, Lord and colleagues assessed how these biased perceptions influenced participants' attitudes. Considering that each participant was exposed to contradictory evidence regarding the effectiveness of capital punishment, we might expect that each participant's attitude would become less extreme. Instead of finding evidence for this type of attitude moderation effect, Lord and colleagues found an attitude polarization effect. When asked to indicate how their attitudes had changed as a result of the materials they had read, proponents of capital punishment reported that they were now more in favor of capital punishment, and opponents reported that they were now less in favor of capital punishment. It's important to understand the significance of this effect. The same evidence that strengthened the convictions of those who support capital punishment also led those who oppose capital punishment to become more entrenched in their position (see also Plous, 1991).

To summarize, the Lord, Ross, and Lepper (1979) findings make three important points. First, they establish that people with different attitudes evaluate the same stimulus in different ways. Second, this occurs largely because people give greater credence to evidence that supports their attitudes and beliefs than to opposing

TABLE 6.4	Attitudes Shape Evidence Validity	
	Proponent of Capital Punishment	Opponent of Capital Punishment
Comments about a pro-deterrence study	It does support capital punishment in that it presents facts showing that there is a deterrent effect and seems to have gathered data properly.	The study was taken only 1 year before and 1 year after capital punishment was reinstated. To be a more effective study they should have taken data from at least 10 years before and as many years as possible after.
Comments about an anti-deterrence study	The evidence given is relatively meaningless without data about how the overall crime rate went up in those years.	There aren't as many uncontrolled variables in this experiment as in the other one, so I'm still willing to believe the conclusion made.

Source: Lord, Ross, and Lepper (1979).

evidence. Finally, as a consequence of these processes, attitudes become more extreme after exposure to inconclusive or mixed evidence.

B. Hostile Media Bias

People don't always see support for their position. Sometimes people with strongly held attitudes believe the evidence is stacked against them. Examples of this tendency can be found in the letters to the editor section of almost every newspaper. Disgruntled conservatives rail against an obvious liberal bias, while annoyed liberals grumble that the coverage is slanted toward a conservative point of view.

Vallone, Ross, and Lepper (1985) conducted a laboratory experiment to investigate the roots of people's perception of media bias. They first identified three groups of students: students with pro-Israel attitudes, students with pro-Arab attitudes, and students with neutral attitudes toward Israel and the Arab nations. Next, they had participants view actual televised accounts of a 1982 incident in the Mideast known as the Beirut massacre, in which a large number of civilians living in refugee camps in Lebanon were killed. Afterward, they indicated whether they thought the television accounts they had viewed were fair or were biased against Israel.

Figure 6.5 shows some of the results from this investigation. It is apparent that students' attitudes strongly shaped their perceptions of media fairness. In comparison with the neutral attitude control group, students with pro-Israel attitudes believed the program was unduly biased against Israel, while students with pro-Arab attitudes believed that the program was heavily slanted toward Israel (see also Giner-Sorolla & Chaiken, 1994).

C. Minimizing Biased Assimilation Effects

The prevalence and importance of the effects we have been discussing have led researchers to look for ways to minimize people's biases. Lord, Lepper, and Preston (1984) considered two possible antidotes. One possibility is to simply instruct people to be fair and impartial in their judgments. This view assumes that biased assimilation

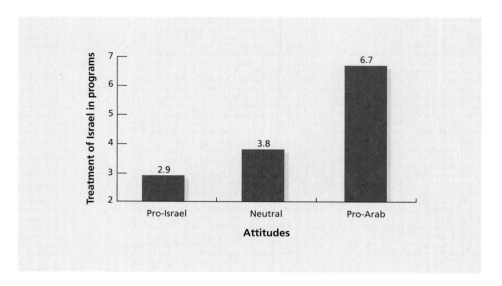

FIGURE 6.5

Hostile Media Bias

Participants watched television coverage of an incident in the mideast known as the Beirut massacre. In comparison with the judgments of participants with neutral attitudes, participants with pro-Israel attitudes believed the TV coverage was slanted against Israel, whereas participants with pro-Arab attitudes believed the coverage was slanted toward Israel. (Higher numbers indicate that the coverage was biased toward Israel.)

Source: Vallone, Ross, and Lepper (1985).

effects can be reduced merely by reminding participants that they might be biased. Another strategy involves actively encouraging participants to see the evidence from the other side's viewpoint. This approach, termed the consider-the-opposite strategy, assumes that it's not enough to simply tell participants they should be unbiased. Instead, participants need to be given a particular strategy for overcoming their potential biases.

Lord and colleagues (1984) tested these two corrective strategies in a replication of the C. G. Lord, Ross, and Lepper (1979) study on capital punishment. There were three experimental conditions. Some participants were in the control condition and, just as in the original study, no correction instructions were provided. Other participants were in the be-unbiased condition; these participants received the following instructions prior to reading the capital punishment essays:

> We would like you to be as objective and unbiased as possible in evaluating the studies you read. You might consider yourself to be in the same role as a judge or juror asked to weigh all of the evidence in a fair and impartial manner.

A final group of participants was in the consider-the-opposite condition; these participants received the following instructions prior to reading the capital punishment essays:

> Ask yourself at each step whether you would have made the same high or low evaluation had exactly the same study produced results on the other side of the issue.

The data displayed in Figure 6.6 show that urging people to be fair and impartial did not reduce the assimilation bias. Instead, the assimilation bias was eliminated only

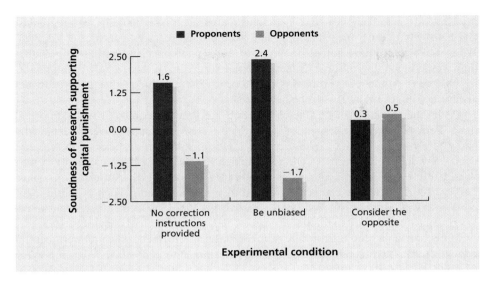

FIGURE 6.6

Interventions Designed to Reduce Biased Assimilation Effects

Telling participants they should be impartial did not reduce the assimilation bias, but urging them to consider the opposite did eliminate the bias.

Source: C. G. Lord, Lepper, and Preston (1984).

when participants were told to consider how they would have evaluated the study had the findings supported the position opposite their own (see Mussweiler, Strack, & Pfeiffer, 2000, for related research).

D. Summary of Attitude Bias

In this section, we have seen that people's attitudes strongly bias the way they interpret information. Most often, these biases lead people to see greater support for their position than would be seen by a neutral observer. Far from being of little consequence, these biases can exacerbate conflicts between opposing parties and constitute barriers to peaceful settlements. The good news is that biases resulting from strongly held attitudes can be reduced if people are counseled to view the evidence from the opposition's point of view.

IV. Attitudes and Behavior

People generally act in accordance with their attitudes. For example, people who prefer Pepsi to Coke tend to buy more Pepsi than Coke, and people who favor a particular presidential candidate usually vote for that candidate come election time. Attitudes do not, however, always guide behavior. Pepsi lovers sometimes buy Coke, and people who favor particular candidates don't always bother to vote. Inconsistencies between attitude and behavior occur for a number of reasons. In this section of the chapter, you will study some of these factors and consider the complexities of the attitude–behavior relation.

A. Early Investigations of the Attitude–Behavior Relation

Research in this area was initiated by a Stanford sociologist named Richard LaPiere. In the mid 1930s, LaPiere and a young Chinese couple took an automobile trip around the United States. They visited 251 establishments, such as restaurants, campgrounds, and hotels. With only one exception, they were offered service at each establishment. When LaPiere returned home, he wrote to these establishments and asked whether they would be willing to serve Chinese people. Surprisingly, the overwhelming majority said they would not. From this, LaPiere (1934) concluded that people do not always act in accordance with their attitudes.

Critics quickly noted that LaPiere's research was beset by numerous methodological flaws. Perhaps the people responding to LaPiere's survey weren't the same people who had offered service to the Chinese couple a few months earlier; perhaps the respondents were simply trying to discourage visitations by the Chinese by avowing that they would refuse service; or perhaps their attitudes had changed in the months since LaPiere and the Chinese couple had visited their establishments. Each of these possibilities, as well as others (C. G. Lord, Lepper, & Mackie, 1984), could have led LaPiere to erroneously conclude that attitudes cannot be used to predict behavior.

Many social psychologists were somewhat surprised, then, when a more careful review of the literature reached a conclusion similar to LaPiere's. After surveying 47 studies that had examined the correlation between attitudes and behavior, Wicker (1969) determined that attitudes were generally "unrelated or only slightly related to overt behaviors" (p. 65). This conclusion led many researchers to question whether attitudes were a useful scientific construct.

Around the same time, a similar debate was brewing in the field of personality (S. J. Sherman & Fazio, 1983). In 1968, Mischel examined whether traits predict behavior and concluded that they often do not (Mischel, 1968). Like Wicker, Mischel argued that the power of long-standing dispositions and attitudes is often swamped by subtle situational factors. In short, several researchers argued that neither attitudes nor personality could usefully predict how people behave in any given situation.

Looking back, it seems evident that these concerns were exaggerated. Attitudes (and personality traits) do predict behavior in many situations, and these effects are often sizable. In a more recent meta-analysis of the relevant literature, Kraus (1995) found that "attitudes significantly and substantially predict future behavior" (p. 58). By Kraus's calculations, 60,983 additional studies reporting no correlation would be needed to challenge this conclusion.

That there is a general correspondence between attitudes and behavior does not mean that all attitudes predict behavior in all situations. After all, most of us can think of times we have not acted in accordance with our attitudes, so it's clear that people are not always true to their convictions. Social psychologists have pursued several different strategies in their attempts to understand when (and why) attitudes predict behavior (Zanna & Fazio, 1982).

B. Situational Factors That Influence When Attitudes Predict Behavior

One factor to consider in studying the attitude–behavior relation is that not all situations allow for the expression of attitudes. Although a therapist may have a negative attitude toward a client, professional ethics prevent the therapist from acting on the basis of his or her beliefs. In a similar vein, federal laws prohibit people with negative attitudes from exhibiting discrimination. In more general terms, we can say that some situations are relatively strong and provide clear guidelines for how people are to behave, whereas other situations are relatively weak and give people greater behavioral freedom (M. Snyder & Ickes, 1985). All else being equal, attitudes will be more closely linked to behavior in the latter situation than in the former. The correspondence between attitudes and behavior is even stronger when individuals are allowed to choose which type of situation to enter (DeBono & Snyder, 1995).

1. Matching Levels of Specificity

Another factor that influences the association between attitudes and behavior is the match between the breadth of the attitude and the breadth of the behavior. Fishbein and Ajzen (1974, 1975; Ajzen & Fishbein, 1977) contend that attitudes predict behavior only when the specificity of the attitude matches the specificity of the behavior. Imagine, for example, that someone claims to have a positive attitude toward the environment. Should we then expect this person to always recycle his or her aluminum cans? Not necessarily. Attitudes toward the environment are too broad, Fishbein and Ajzen argue, to predict a behavior as specific as recycling. To predict this specific behavior, we must measure the person's attitude toward recycling aluminum cans.

To test Fishbein and Ajzen's prediction, Weigel, Vernon, and Tognacci (1974) administered a survey of attitudes toward environmental issues to a sample of citizens. Four types of items were represented on the survey. Some items measured very general attitudes toward environmental issues (e.g., the importance of living in harmony with nature); some items assessed more specific attitudes toward air and water pollution; some items measured attitudes toward conservation of natural resources and land use; and some items focused on the respondent's more specific attitude toward the Sierra Club, a well-known environmental group. Later, the respondents were called on the telephone and asked if they would be willing to donate money or volunteer their time to work for the Sierra Club. Only people's specific attitudes toward the Sierra Club predicted their willingness to volunteer their time and money to support this environmental group. These findings support the claim that attitudes predict behavior when both constructs are measured at a comparable level of specificity (see also A. R. Davidson & Jaccard, 1979).

2. Aggregating across Behaviors

Even though general attitudes don't always predict specific behaviors, they may predict multiple behaviors. To illustrate, let's reconsider a person who has a positive attitude toward the environment. Although this general attitude might not allow us to predict any specific behavior (e.g., whether the person carpools to work), it might enable us to predict whether the person generally acts in an environmentally responsible manner.

Weigel and Newman (1976) examined this issue. To begin, they administered a general survey of attitudes toward the environment to residents of a New England town. Three months after the surveys had been returned, the respondents were contacted and offered opportunities to participate in a variety of organized ecology projects. These projects included signing petitions opposing offshore drilling or the construction of nuclear power plans; picking up litter along the roadside; and recycling bottles, cans, and paper goods each week for eight weeks.

Weigel and Newman hypothesized that general attitudes would predict a general tendency to behave in an environmentally friendly manner. This proved to be the case. Attitudes toward the environment were not highly related to any specific behavior, but they were highly related to a composite index formed by summing across the various behaviors. Along with other research (e.g., Fishbein & Ajzen, 1974), these findings make an important point about the nature of attitudes. If a friend tells you he likes Latin music, you may not be able to predict with certainty whether he likes Tito Puente. You can, however, predict with some certainty that your friend generally owns quite a few CDs from this genre (and probably thinks Ricky Martin is an imposter).

C. Which Attitudes Predict Behavior?

Some attitudes are more apt to influence behavior than other attitudes are. Attitude strength and attitude importance are probably the two most important factors to consider here. Earlier in this chapter, we noted that some of our attitudes are very important to us whereas others are relatively unimportant. In general, strong and important attitudes are more apt to guide behavior than are weak and unimportant ones (Krosnick, 1988).

The effects of attitude strength and attitude importance depend, in part, on attitude accessibility (Krosnick, 1989). Attitude accessibility refers to how readily an attitude comes to mind when an attitude object is encountered or considered. Some attitudes are highly accessible and apt to guide behavior, whereas other attitudes are less accessible and unlikely to guide behavior (Fazio, 1986; 1990; Fazio & Williams, 1986).

Attitude accessibility is usually measured using a response-time analysis. Researchers ask respondents a series of questions about their attitudes toward various topics and record the time it takes them to answer these queries. Attitudes that are expressed relatively quickly are considered more accessible than attitudes that are expressed rather slowly. Fazio and Williams (1986) used this procedure to assess voting behavior in the 1984 presidential election between Ronald Reagan and Walter Mondale. Several months before the November election, selected voters indicated their attitudes toward the two presidential candidates. After they had cast their votes on election day, they were contacted again and asked how they had voted. Consistent with the claim that attitude accessibility affects the attitude–behavior relation, highly accessible attitudes were better predictors of voting behavior than were less accessible attitudes.

The accessibility of an attitude is affected by a number of factors beyond attitude strength and attitude importance. Recency of activation is one factor to consider. As was true with schemas, attitudes that have recently been primed are more accessible than are attitudes that have not recently been primed (Fazio, Powell, & Herr, 1983). Another relevant factor is frequency. Frequently expressed attitudes are more accessible and more apt to guide behavior than are attitudes that are infrequently expressed (Fazio, Chen, McDonel, & Sherman, 1982).

Direct experience with an attitude object also influences attitude accessibility. Some attitudes are formed rather passively. For example, even though most of us have never actually met a sumo wrestler or an astronaut, we have attitudes about these social groups. These attitudes are formed indirectly, through the media. Other attitudes, such as our attitudes toward professors and physicians, are acquired through direct personal experience. In general, attitudes formed through direct personal experience are more cognitively accessible and more apt to guide behavior than are attitudes formed through indirect experience (Fazio & Zanna, 1981; S. J. Sherman et al., 1982).

Attitude accessibility may be a particularly important factor to consider when more than one attitude is relevant to guide behavior. For example, a person might have both a positive attitude toward ice cream and a positive attitude toward a healthy heart and a trim waistline. In these cases, the stronger, more important, and more accessible attitude will probably be the one to guide behavior.

D. Attitudes Predict Behavior in Some People More Than in Others

Finally, attitudes are more apt to guide behavior in some people than in others. In Chapter 5 we discussed M. Snyder's (1979) work on self-monitoring. High self-monitors regard themselves as highly pragmatic and flexible people who strive to be the right person for every occasion. When entering a situation, they do what the model person in the situation would do. Low self-monitors adopt a different orientation. They regard themselves as highly principled people who value consistency between who they are and what they do. When entering a situation, they look inward and use their attitudes, beliefs, and feelings to guide their behavior. Because they value being true to themselves, low self-monitors are more likely to act on the basis of their attitudes than are high self-monitors (M. Snyder, 1982; M. Snyder & Swann, 1976). This appears to be particularly true when attitudes are accessible and available to guide behavior (M. Snyder & Kendzierski, 1982).

E. Theory of Reasoned Action

The variables we have been considering up to this point have involved rather spontaneous behaviors, in which the behavioral expression of an attitude occurs without much planning or forethought. Attitudes also influence long-term, deliberate actions, such as when people decide to go to graduate school or take up golf. In the 1970s, Fishbein and Ajzen (1974, 1975) developed a theory of reasoned action to explain behavior in situations such as these (see also Ajzen & Fishbein, 1977, 1980). The theory, which is shown in Figure 6.7, makes several important assumptions.

First, the theory of reasoned action assumes that attitudes typically arise from a rational process in which a person's beliefs about an attitude object are weighted by

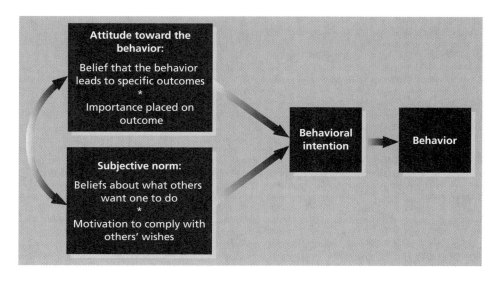

FIGURE 6.7

Fishbein and Ajzen's Theory of Reasoned Action

The theory maintains that behavioral intentions directly influence behavior, and that behavioral intentions are influenced by attitudes and subjective norms.

the perceived importance of that outcome. For example, if I think gun control laws will save lives and I value saving lives, I will have a positive attitude toward gun control laws. These assumptions reflect the cognitive approach to understanding attitude formation. The model also assumes that attitudes and behavior must be measured at the same level of specificity. General attitudes predict broad behaviors, and specific attitudes predict specific behaviors. The validity of these assumptions was reviewed earlier in this chapter.

The model further assumes that attitudes influence behavior only indirectly, via their influence on behavioral intentions. This assumption underscores that people are not always free to act on the basis of their attitudes. A person with a positive attitude toward eating healthy foods may wind up dining at a restaurant that serves only unhealthy meals. In this case, the person is unable to act in accordance with his or her attitudes. Similarly, a student with negative attitudes toward calculus might wind up taking the class because it is required. Attitudes don't predict behavior under these conditions because the behavior is constrained by other factors.

You may have noticed that the model of reasoned action does not include a direct link from attitudes to behavior. Attitudes influence intentions, and intentions influence behavior, but attitudes do not affect behavior directly. Support for this assumption comes from a study of blood donor behavior. Bagozzi (1981) found that (1) attitudes toward giving blood predicted people's intentions to give blood; (2) that intentions to give blood predicted whether or not people gave blood; and (3) that once behavioral intentions were taken into account, attitudes did not directly predict blood donor behavior. These findings support the attitude→intention→behavior sequence (but see also Bentler & Speckart, 1979).

The model of reasoned action makes an additional assumption. As shown in Figure 6.7, the model assumes that attitudes are not the only factor that influences behavioral intentions. Behavioral intentions are also influenced by subjective norms. In the context of the theory, the term *subjective norms* refers to our beliefs about how others would like us to behave, in conjunction with our desire to comply with these beliefs. Imagine that a high school student is attending a party where drinking is involved. Even though the student might personally hold negative attitudes toward drinking, the student might believe that the other people at the party want him or her to drink heavily. This belief, in conjunction with the student's motivation to comply with these (perceived) norms, will influence whether or not the student intends to drink (Terry & Hogg, 1996; Trafimow & Finlay, 1996).

The theory of reasoned action has been widely tested and supported in dozens of studies (for reviews, see Ajzen, 1988; Sheppard, Hartwick, & Warshaw, 1988). It has proved particularly useful in understanding behaviors of personal or social significance, such as safe sexual practices (Albarracín, Johnson, Fishbein, & Muellerleile, 2001; Cochran, Mays, Ciarletta, Caruso, & Mallon, 1992; Reinecke, Schmidt, & Ajzen, 1996); organ donation (Borgida, Conner, & Manteufel, 1992); seatbelt use (Stasson & Fishbein, 1990); and breast self-examination in women (Meyerowitz & Chaiken, 1987) and testicle self-examination in men (Steffen, 1990).

1. The Theory of Planned Behavior

The theory of reasoned action is most applicable when people are free to act on their intentions. To explain behaviors that are not entirely under one's control, Ajzen (1985, 1988) developed an extension of the theory called the theory of planned behavior. This revision includes an additional construct, termed perceived behavioral control. Similar to Bandura's (1977) self-efficacy beliefs (see Chapter 5), perceived behavior control captures the extent to which people believe they are capable of acting in accordance with their intentions. To illustrate, a smoker might have a negative attitude toward smoking and believe that his friends and family would like him to quit. But if he also believes that he is incapable of kicking the habit, he will probably not even bother to try. The addition of this construct has helped the theory explain the link between attitudes and behavior in a variety of situations (Ajzen & Madden, 1986; Armitrage & Conner, 2001; Borgida, Conner, & Manteufel, 1992; Madden, Ellen, & Azjen, 1992).

2. Unintended Behavior

Both the theory of reasoned action (which focuses on behaviors that are volitional) and the theory of planned behavior (which also explains behaviors that are not entirely under one's control) apply to situations in which people consciously intend to perform some action. Not all behavior is intentional, however. People frequently act mindlessly or habitually, without giving too much thought to why they are doing what they are doing (Langer, 1975). In situations like these, prior behavior emerges as a better predictor of future behavior than do attitudes (Bentler & Speckart, 1979; Ouellette & Wood, 1998; W. Wood, Quinn, & Kashy, 2002).

In some cases, people find themselves doing things they neither intended nor wanted to do. Such behaviors may be especially frequent during adolescence and young adulthood. Having unprotected sex or drinking to excess are examples of such behaviors. Peer pressure is perhaps the most salient feature of these situations. Adolescents often experience enormous pressures to conform to the behavior of others, even though they may personally oppose such behaviors. The construct of subjective norms takes this pressure into account, but only in situations where people willfully alter their behavior to please others.

F. Summary of the Attitude–Behavior Relation

Early researchers argued that attitudes are poor predictors of behavior. Subsequent research has offered a more optimistic view. People do frequently act on the basis of their attitudes, and these effects are often substantial. At the same time, some attitudes are better predictors of behavior than others are, and some people are more likely to act in accordance with their attitudes than others are. Finally, it's important to understand that people are not always free to act in accordance with their attitudes, either because there are competing attitudes in the situation, because there are situational norms and other situational pressures, or because not all behaviors are under their control. For all of these reasons, attitudes sometimes fail to predict people's actions. In the next section of this chapter, you will learn how people cope with situations in which they do not behave in accordance with their attitudes.

V. From Behavior to Attitudes: Cognitive Dissonance Theory

One needn't be a cynic to recognize that people frequently act hypocritically. They believe it's best to carpool, but they drive to work alone; they know they should exercise, but they all too frequently find themselves watching television or surfing the Web instead. The manner in which people deal with situations like this is the subject of one of social psychology's most important theories, cognitive dissonance theory (Festinger, 1957).

A. Theoretical Assumptions

Cognitive dissonance theory is a cognitive consistency theory with roots in Gestalt psychology. As discussed in Chapter 2, Gestalt psychologists assume that perception is guided toward achieving a simple, pleasing end state in which visual stimuli fit well with one another. Visual consistency is sought, because imbalance creates tension which people are driven to reduce.

1. Cognitive Inconsistency Creates Cognitive Dissonance

Festinger (1957) extended the Gestalt psychologists' ideas to incorporate psychological processes other than visual ones. He argued that people also seek cognitive consistency, and that cognitive inconsistency creates an aversive state of arousal that people are driven to reduce. This aversive state of arousal, called **cognitive dissonance,** arises when two or more cognitions are inconsistent, or dissonant, with one another.

In this context, *inconsistent* means that one cognition does not follow logically from the other. Suppose that a person believes that politicians always tell the truth. If one day the person learns that the president of the United States has lied under oath, the person will experience cognitive dissonance. That's because the two cognitions don't fit together. The belief that politicians always tell the truth is inconsistent with the knowledge that the president lied.

Dissonance often arises when people behave in ways that are inconsistent with their own attitudes. For example, consider a father who believes it is wrong to scold his children. If one day he yells at his children, he will experience cognitive dissonance. This will occur because his behavior (yelling at his children) is inconsistent with his attitude (parents shouldn't scold their children).

2. Three Ways to Reduce Cognitive Dissonance

There are three ways to reduce cognitive dissonance. One way is to change the behavior. In this case, the father could stop yelling at his children. Now the cognition "I don't scold my children" is consistent with the cognition "Parents shouldn't scold their children." Another way to reduce cognitive dissonance is to change the attitude. In this case, the parent could convince himself that yelling at children is a good thing, not a bad thing. (Spare the yell, spoil the child.) A third way to reduce cognitive dissonance is to add a cognition. For example, the parent could either dismiss the transgression as inconsequential or justify his behavior by thinking that although it is generally bad to yell at one's children, sometimes you have to do it to keep them from getting hurt. In this manner, he rationalizes or excuses what he has done (L. Simon, Greenberg, & Brehm, 1995).

Let's look at another example. Most smokers are well aware that smoking has been linked to a variety of life-threatening illnesses, including emphysema, lung cancer, and heart disease. This knowledge arouses cognitive dissonance. To reduce this dissonance, they can (1) quit smoking; (2) change their attitude (e.g., decide that smoking isn't bad for them); or (3) add a cognition (e.g., tell themselves a few cigarettes a day can't hurt you or remind themselves that their Uncle Leo smoked two packs a day and lived to be 94). Quitting is unquestionably the best choice, but it's also the most difficult; many people who try to quit fail to do so. How do these people cope with their cognitive dissonance? Gibbons, Eggleston, and Benthin (1997) found that many smokers who had tried to quit smoking only to relapse decreased their perceptions of the risks associated with smoking. In essence, they reduced dissonance by deciding that smoking really isn't all that bad for you.

B. Historical Perspective

No theory in social psychology has been the subject of as much research or controversy as cognitive dissonance theory. There are several reasons for this. First, the theory was one of the first psychological theories to hold that cognitions have motivational properties. Believing that human behavior was determined in much the same way as the behavior of lower animals, most previous theorists had presumed that all behavior stemmed from a desire to satisfy basic physiological needs (food, water, sex, and the absence of pain). By asserting that cognitions also had motivational properties, Festinger argued for a uniquely human motivation, thus breaking with this tradition. In 1957, this was quite liberating and exciting.

The theory also gained popularity because it was able to explain a broad range of behavior. Moreover, many of its predictions ran counter to common sense, so they were quite startling. These predictions were often exactly opposite the ones made by the learning theory model. In fact, cognitive dissonance theorists reveled in revealing the limitations of a strict learning theory analysis. They argued that, rather than being the passive creatures learning theorists painted them to be, people actively justify and rationalize their behavior so that it makes sense to them.

C. Illustrative Research

Cognitive dissonance theory has spawned hundreds of investigations. Many of the relevant studies have become classics in the field because they were performed with great creative flair and produced unexpected findings. The topics of these studies tend to fall into four categories: (1) attitude change following attitude-discrepant behavior; (2) attitude change following high effort expenditure; (3) behavior change following hypocritical behavior; and (4) postdecision dissonance reduction.

1. Attitude Change Following Attitude-Discrepant Behavior

Early tests of cognitive dissonance theory had people perform a behavior that ran counter to their initial attitude. The theory then predicted that under certain conditions, people would change their attitudes to make them consistent with their behavior. The key variable of interest is the extent to which people believe they have received sufficient justification for performing the behavior. If people are given a good reason, such as a high monetary reward to perform the action, they have received sufficient justification and do not need to change their attitude. They can simply add the cognition that they did what they did for the reward or money. If people are not given sufficient justification, they will have to reduce dissonance by changing their attitude to match their behavior.

Festinger and Carlsmith (1959). Predictions related to sufficient justification for attitude-discrepant behavior were first tested in an experiment conducted by Festinger and Carlsmith (1959). In this study, male undergraduates at Stanford University signed up for an experiment entitled "Measures of Performance." The experimental task was exceedingly boring. Among other things, the participants were asked to turn a peg a quarter turn clockwise, put their hand down, and then repeat this activity for 30 minutes. This meaningless, monotonous activity was designed to ensure that all participants developed a negative attitude toward the experimental task.

After they had completed this task, the experimenter told them the experiment was really concerned with how expectancies affect performance, and that they had been in the no-expectancy condition. Other participants, the experimenter explained, were in a positive expectancy condition and were led to believe the task was actually very interesting and enjoyable. At this point, three experimental conditions were created. Participants in a control condition were sent into a waiting room and were given no additional information. In two other conditions, the experimenter became very fidgety and concerned that something was wrong. He explained that the next participant had arrived but that his experimental assistant had not. This was a problem because the next participant was supposed to be in the positive expectancy condition, and the assistant was supposed to tell her the task would be fun and interesting.

The experimenter then asked the participant whether he would be willing to tell the next participant that the experiment was fun and interesting. In one condition the experimenter offered the participant $1 to tell this lie, and in another condition he offered the participant $20. All participants acceded to this request. Later, after the experiment had supposedly ended, all three groups of participants completed a questionnaire indicating how interesting and enjoyable they thought the experimental task was. This was the measure of the participants' attitude toward the experimental task.

Learning theory maintains that the more you reward a person for engaging in an activity, the more positive his or her attitude toward that activity should be. Consequently, the theory predicts that participants in the $20 condition would express more positive attitudes toward the task than would participants in the other two conditions. Cognitive dissonance theory makes a different prediction. For participants in the $20 and $1 conditions, the cognition "I just told someone that this task is fun and interesting" is inconsistent with the cognition "This task is in fact dull and boring beyond tears." This inconsistency creates cognitive dissonance according to the theory. One way to reduce dissonance is to change the behavior. But in this case the behavior is irrevocable; the participant has clearly told the next participant that the task is interesting, so he can't readily convince himself that he said it was boring.

Another way to reduce dissonance is to add a cognition by justifying your actions. In this case, a participant could say: "Yes, I told the next participant that the task was fun and interesting even though I believe that it's boring, but I got paid $20 to say it." Adding this cognition provides sufficient justification for the behavior and reduces dissonance. Participants in the $1 condition don't have this option. One dollar does not provide sufficient justification (or at least provides less than $20), so they can't completely reduce dissonance by adding this cognition. According to the theory, then, the only method left to reduce dissonance is to change their attitudes. These participants must decide that the task was pretty interesting after all. This reduces dissonance, because the cognition "I told the next participant the task was fun and interesting" is now consistent with the cognition "I think the task was fun and interesting."

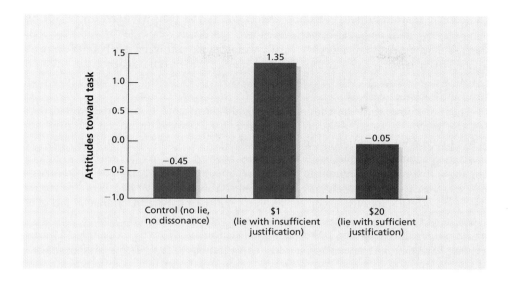

FIGURE 6.8

Attitudes Toward a Boring Experimental Task as a Function of the Payment Received

Participants given $1 to say that a dull task was interesting subsequently developed more positive attitudes toward the task than did control participants or those who received a $20 payment. These data support the claim that small rewards sometimes produce greater liking for an activity than do large rewards.

Source: Festinger and Carlsmith (1959).

In sum, cognitive dissonance theory predicts that participants in the $1 condition will subsequently come to have more positive attitudes toward the task than will participants in the other two conditions. Figure 6.8 shows that these predictions were confirmed. When asked to indicate how much they enjoyed the experimental task, participants who received $1 indicated that they liked the task more than did participants who received $20 or those who never told another participant the experiment was interesting. According to Festinger and Carlsmith, this occurred because telling another participant a boring task is interesting created cognitive dissonance and, having little justification for what they had done, participants in the $1 condition were forced to change their attitude toward the task in order to reduce their psychological discomfort (see also Zimbardo, Weisenberg, Firestone, & Levy, 1965).

E. Aronson and Carlsmith (1963). Let's look at another classic dissonance study. Suppose you wanted someone to develop a negative attitude toward some activity or issue. How would you go about instilling it? Learning theorists would maintain that the most effective way to create a negative attitude is to punish it severely. The more severe the punishment, the more negative the person's attitude will be. Cognitive dissonance theory makes a different prediction. Just as small rewards can sometimes produce more liking for a task than do large rewards, mild punishment can create greater disliking for an activity than severe punishment.

This effect was demonstrated in an experiment by E. Aronson and Carlsmith (1963). The participants were preschool children (approximately four years of age). They were brought into a playroom filled with several toys. After they indicated how much they liked each toy, they were instructed not to play with their second most favorite toy.

Children in the mild threat condition were told "If you play with this toy, I will be annoyed," whereas children in the severe threat condition were told "If you play with this toy, I would be very angry . . . and I would think you were a baby." The experimenter then left the room for 10 minutes, during which time none of the children played with the forbidden toy. Afterward, the children indicated again how much they liked the various toys.

Thirty-six percent of the children in the mild threat condition decreased their liking for the toy, whereas none of the children in the severe threat condition did so. Why? According to cognitive dissonance theory, the cognition "I like this toy" is inconsistent with the cognition "I'm not playing with it." This inconsistency creates cognitive dissonance. Children in the severe threat condition can reduce the dissonance by justifying their avoidance. They think, "Yes, I'm not playing with this attractive toy, but that's because I will be severely punished if I do." Children in the mild threat condition have less justification for avoiding the toy, so they reduce the dissonance by deciding they don't like the toy all that much. Now the cognition "I'm not playing with that toy" is consistent with the cognition "I don't like it all that much."

The findings from the E. Aronson and Carlsmith (1963) study parallel the fable of the fox and the sour grapes. When the fox can't reach the grapes, he decides they are sour. For cognitive dissonance theorists, this occurs because the cognition "Those grapes are sweet" is inconsistent with the cognition "I can't have them." To reduce dissonance, the fox decides the grapes aren't sweet after all.

2. Effort Justification and Attitude Change

Military boot camp is said to be one of the most demanding experiences a person can go through. For weeks, recruits endure physical, emotional, and mental agony. Why, then, do many recruits end up having a positive attitude toward the experience? According to cognitive dissonance theory, people do not want to think they have suffered for nothing, so they convince themselves their suffering has been worthwhile.

Effort justification occurs in a variety of contexts. Many high school students spend a lot of time and money preparing for their senior prom, only to find that the experience does not live up to their expectations. How do they deal with this discrepancy? Looking back, they frequently come to believe the experience was worthwhile and enjoyable. To do otherwise would be to admit that they wasted their time and money for nothing, and most people do not want to believe they do such things. In a similar vein, many fraternities and sororities require new members to go through an initiation, and the more severe the initiation, the more new members seem to like the group (E. Aronson & Mills, 1959). Therapy patients also show greater improvement when therapy is highly effortful than when it is less effortful, even when the effort is unrelated to any known mode of improvement (Axsom, 1989; Axsom & Cooper, 1985; Axsom & Lawless, 1992). Presumably, this occurs because people feel the need to justify the effort they have devoted to the therapy.

3. Hypocrisy and Behavior Change

If you're like most people, you probably think it's a good idea to save electricity and gasoline. At the same time, you don't always turn off the lights when you leave home, or bike or walk to school instead of drive your car. In short, you sometimes act inconsistently with your beliefs. So far, we have seen that people deal with inconsistencies like these by justifying their behavior or by changing their attitudes. In an applied setting, E. Aronson and his colleagues have identified conditions in which participants use the third mode to dissonance reduction—changing their behavior. In these investigations, the participants are first led to behave hypocritically. Then they are given the opportunity to rectify their hypocrisy by acting in accordance with their attitudes.

To illustrate, Stone, Aronson, Crain, Winslow, and Fried (1994) studied ways to promote safe sexual practices. The participants were heterosexually active students between the ages of 18 and 25. At the start of the experiment, these participants were asked to prepare a persuasive speech regarding the importance of condom use as a means of preventing the transmission of AIDS. Some of the participants were told they would publicly deliver the speech to a group of high school students (high commitment), whereas others were told that they would simply prepare a speech but not deliver it (low commitment). Within each of these two groups, half of the participants were asked to think about times they had failed to use condoms when having sexual intercourse (reminded of inconsistency), whereas the other half were not asked to think about this matter (not reminded of inconsistency). At the end of the experiment, all of the participants were given the opportunity to buy condoms with the money they had earned for participating in the study.

Stone and his colleagues reasoned that participants who had been publicly hypocritical and were reminded of this inconsistency would experience the most cognitive dissonance. To reduce this dissonance, these participants would be especially apt to purchase condoms when given the opportunity to do so. Figure 6.9 shows that these predictions were confirmed. Participants who had made a public commitment to recommend condom use and had acknowledged failing to use condoms in the past purchased more condoms than did participants in the other experimental conditions. In other research, hypocrisy has been used to promote recycling and water conservation, even when other, less effortful

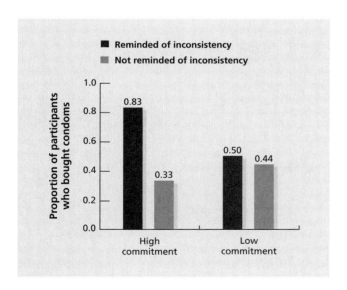

FIGURE 6.9

Proportion of Participants Who Bought Condoms after Behaving Hypocritically

Participants who made a public commitment to use condoms and were reminded that they had failed to do so in the past were most apt to buy condoms when given the chance. Cognitive dissonance theorists claim this is because public commitment and private inconsistency created the most dissonance, which participants reduced by changing their behavior to match their attitude.

Source: Stone, Aronson, Crain, Winslow, and Fried (1994).

means of dissonance reduction are available (Fried & Aronson, 1995; Dickerson, Thibodeau, Aronson, & Miller, 1992; Stone, Wiegand, Cooper, & Aronson, 1997).

4. Postdecision Dissonance Reduction

Did you ever have to make up your mind?
To pick up on one and leave the other behind.
It's not often easy, it's not often kind.
Did you ever have to make up your mind?
John Sebastian, (Alley Music Corporation and Trio Music Co., 1965, 1966)

John Sebastian's lyrics remind us that making decisions is often difficult. Living with our decisions can also bring problems. According to cognitive dissonance theory, dissonance arises whenever a person is forced to choose between two alternatives of near equal attractiveness. This is because the cognition "Alternative X has many desirable features" is inconsistent with the cognition "I won't be enjoying those features because I chose alternative Y." To reduce this dissonance, the theory predicts that people will enhance the features of the chosen alternative and devalue the features of the unchosen alternative immediately after making the choice. This effect is known as postdecision dissonance reduction (Frenkel & Doob, 1976; Knox & Inkster, 1968).

Figure 6.10 shows a schematic representation of postdecision dissonance reduction. To illustrate, imagine that you are deciding whether to attend one of two concerts, featuring either the Backstreet Boys or *NSYNC. Immediately before you decide, the

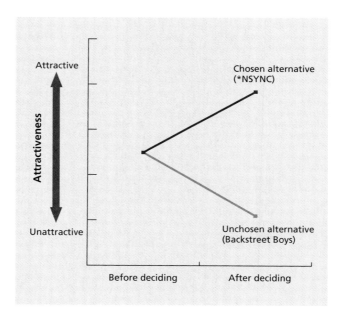

FIGURE 6.10

Postdecision Dissonance Reduction

In this hypothetical example, a person is initially deciding whether to attend a concert by two equally attractive bands: the Backstreet Boys or *NSYNC. Dissonance arises immediately after the person makes a choice, because the person will not be enjoying the positive features of the unchosen alternative. To reduce dissonance, the person increases the attractiveness of the chosen alternative (*NSYNC) and decreases the attractiveness of the unchosen alternative (Backstreet Boys).

two concerts are equally attractive to you, making it difficult to choose. Now suppose you decide to buy tickets for the *NSYNC concert. Immediately afterward, you will reduce dissonance by exaggerating the positive value of the chosen concert (Justin Timberlake is so cool) and denigrating the virtues of the unchosen alternative (Nick Carter is over the hill).

Interestingly, people are often unaware of the extent to which postdecision dissonance reduction operates. Gilbert and Ebert (2002) allowed participants to choose a poster from a variety of prints by famous painters. Some were told their choices were irrevocable; others were told they were free to change their minds in the next month if they so desired. Although most people prefer the opportunity to change their minds, participants who were not given this chance subsequently expressed greater liking for their poster than did those whose choices were modifiable. In this situation, then, choice can be detrimental. When we're told we'll have to make do with what we have, postdecision dissonance reduction helps us convince ourselves we did the right thing (see also Iyergar & Lepper, 2000).

D. Boundary Conditions

So far, we have seen that cognitive dissonance theory can be applied to a wide range of situations. Like all theories, however, cognitive dissonance theory applies only under some conditions. Scientists call these conditions boundary conditions, because they place boundaries on a theory's range of application. The most important boundary condition for cognitive dissonance theory is choice (Linder, Cooper, & Jones, 1967). Inconsistent behavior and decision making produce attitude change only when people believe their behavior was freely chosen. For example, suppose someone puts a gun to my head and forces me to say that Cleveland is a nicer city than Seattle. Even though I don't happen to believe that's true, I won't change my attitude. I can add the cognition "I said it, but I had no choice. The person held a gun to my head." The absence of choice provides sufficient justification for my actions, so no attitude change occurs.

A second, somewhat less important boundary condition is known as foreseeable negative consequences. Cognitive dissonance is most likely to produce attitude change when people feel personally responsible for bringing about a negative outcome (B. E. Collins & Hoyt, 1972; Scher & Cooper, 1989). If I tell my children, "Eat your brussels sprouts. They're yummy," I don't necessarily change my attitude toward brussels sprouts. That's because I justify my inconsistency by saying I did it for my children's own good. Although cognitive dissonance can produce attitude change in the absence of foreseeable negative consequences (Harmon-Jones, Brehm, Greenberg, Simon, & Nelson, 1996), it is most apt to do so when people believe their actions have a negative effect on them or somebody else (R. W. Johnson, Kelly, & LeBlanc, 1995).

E. Self-Perception Theory: A Counter Explanation

With its emphasis on a uniquely human form of motivation and its quirky predictions tested in dramatic fashion, cognitive dissonance theory captivated the hearts of American social psychologists. Not everyone was impressed, however. In 1965, Daryl Bem offered a much simpler explanation for the effects dissonance theorists had reported. As first discussed in Chapter 5, self-perception theory assumes that people learn about themselves by observing their behavior and making an appropriate inference about why they did what they did. Bem introduced the theory as a counterpoint to cognitive dissonance theory. Instead of assuming that inconsistency creates an aversive state of arousal that people are driven to reduce, Bem argued that many times people change their attitudes simply by looking at their behavior in the situational context in which it occurs. More formally, they use principles of discounting and augmenting, and make an attribution for their own behavior (see Chapter 4). If the situation provides a suitable explanation for their behavior, they discount the role of a dispositional factor; if the situation does not provide a suitable explanation for their behavior, they make a dispositional attribution to explain why they have done what they have done.

1. Applying Self-Perception Theory

To illustrate Bem's thinking, let's reconsider the results of the Festinger and Carlsmith (1959) study. The participants in the two experimental conditions (the $1 condition and the $20 condition) have just told someone that the experimental task is fun and interesting. Broadly speaking, there are two reasons to say such a thing: The participant actually believes the task is fun and interesting (a corresponding dispositional attribution) or anything else (a situational attribution). Participants in the $20 condition can attribute their behavior to a high monetary reward, so they discount the extent to which a dispositional cause is present. For participants in the $1 condition, this situational attribution is less plausible, so they assume that they must really think the task is interesting.

A similar analysis applies to the forbidden toy study (E. Aronson & Carlsmith, 1963). According to Bem, the children in this study implicitly ask themselves, "Why aren't I playing with that toy?" In the severe punishment condition they answer, "Because if I do I'll be severely punished." But in the mild punishment condition, the threat of punishment does not provide a compelling explanation for avoiding the toy. So they conclude, "I guess I don't find this toy all that attractive after all; otherwise, I'd be playing with it."

Finally, the same logic can be used to explain postdecision dissonance reduction. If I have just chosen to attend a concert by *NSYNC than one by the Backstreet Boys, it must be because I think *NSYNC is better. After all, what other reason can there be? No one forced me to do it (i.e., I had high choice), so I must think *NSYNC is the better band. Otherwise, I would have chosen to see the Backstreet Boys.

To summarize, cognitive dissonance theory and self-perception theory often make similar predictions. Both theories assume that people will change their attitudes when they have insufficient justification for engaging in an attitude-discrepant manner. The theories differ with respect to why this attitude change occurs. For cognitive dissonance theory, arousal (i.e., psychological discomfort or tension) is a key theoretical construct. Cognitive inconsistency creates arousal, tension, and discomfort, and people take some action to reduce this uncomfortable state. Arousal plays no role in self-perception theory. People simply examine their behavior in the context in which it occurs and draw an appropriate inference about why they did what they did. If the situation provides a compelling explanation (e.g., if there is sufficient justification), people discount the role of their own attitudes. If the situation does not provide a compelling explanation, people assume they must feel differently about the attitude object and subsequently they change their attitude.

2. Comparing the Two Theories

When two theories offer competing explanations for the same effect, the theory that makes the fewest assumptions is preferable. Formally, this is known as the principle of parsimony (see Chapter 1). In this case, self-perception theory makes fewer assumptions than does cognitive dissonance theory. Self-perception theory does not assume that individuals experience an internal motivational state of arousal. The theory says that people simply look at their behavior in the context in which it occurs and draw an appropriate inference, much as an objective, uninvolved (and nonaroused) observer would. Because it doesn't assume the presence of an aversive state of arousal, self-perception theory is simpler. If both theories were equally valid, self-perception theory would be preferred.

One way to think about these differences is that self-perception theory assumes that there is nothing special about being a participant in a study. If I said to you, "I just heard someone say a task was interesting, and he only received a dollar to say it," you would probably think, "Well, he must think it's interesting. What else could it be?" But if I told you the person received a lot of money to say what he did, you wouldn't be so sure he really thought the task was interesting. This is precisely what we do when we see a celebrity spokesperson selling a product in an advertisement. When Whoopi Goldberg tells us to drink milk, we don't necessarily assume that she's a big milk drinker. We apply principles of discounting and remind ourselves that she gets paid a lot of money to say "Got Milk?"

3. Critical Research

J. Cooper, Zanna, and Taves (1978) conducted an experiment to determine whether arousal influences attitude change in the typical cognitive dissonance study. In this study, participants who initially opposed pardoning Richard Nixon wrote an essay supporting his pardon. Some participants wrote the essay under conditions of low choice (i.e., they were led to believe they had to write the essay as part of the experiment), whereas other participants wrote the essay under conditions of high choice (i.e., they were told they didn't have to write the essay if they didn't want to, but that the experimenter would very much appreciate it if they did).

Prior to writing the essay, the participants ingested a drug as part of an ostensibly unrelated experiment on memory. All participants were told that the drug produced no side effects, but this was really true for only one-third of the participants (i.e., those in a placebo control condition). The remaining participants were either given a tranquilizer (which reduces arousal) or a stimulant (which increases arousal). After the participants completed the essay, the researchers assessed their attitudes toward Richard Nixon's pardon. Since all participants initially opposed the pardon, favorable attitudes demonstrate attitude change.

Figure 6.11 shows the predictions the two theories make under these conditions. Because arousal plays no role in self-perception theory, the theory predicts that high-choice participants will change their attitudes more than low-choice participants (simply because the situation provides no plausible explanation for why they have written an essay supporting the pardon of Richard Nixon), and this will not depend on how much physiological arousal the participants are experiencing. Cognitive dissonance theory makes a different prediction. Although it also predicts that high-choice participants will change their attitudes more than low-choice participants, it hypothesizes that this will also depend on how much arousal these participants are experiencing. This is the case because cognitive dissonance theory believes that participants in the high-choice condition are changing their attitudes in order to reduce the arousal

FIGURE 6.11

Comparing Self-Perception Theory and Cognitive Dissonance Theory

Both theories predict that high-choice participants will show greater attitude change than will low-choice participants, but only cognitive dissonance theory predicts that this will also depend on how much physiological arousal participants are experiencing.

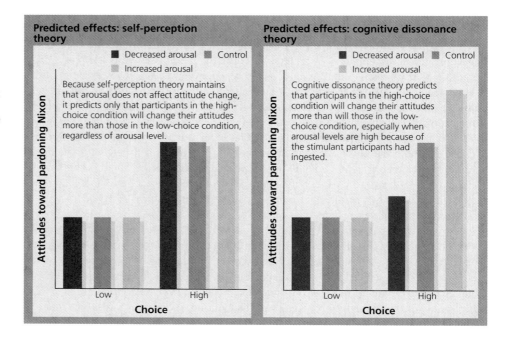

they are experiencing. Participants given a tranquilizer will experience less emotional arousal than those given a placebo, so they will have less of a need to change their attitudes. In contrast, participants given a stimulant will experience more arousal than those who are given a placebo, so they will have an even greater need to change their attitudes to reduce their discomfort.

Figure 6.12 shows the actual data from this investigation. Notice that, as both theories predict, attitude change was generally greater in the high-choice condition than in the low-choice condition. Notice also that, in the high-choice condition, the tranquilizer reduced the amount of attitude change and the stimulant increased the amount of attitude change. In other words, the more aroused participants felt after writing a counterattitudinal essay under conditions of high choice, the more attitude change they showed. Since only cognitive dissonance theory argues that arousal drives attitude change, these findings are more consistent with it than with self-perception theory.

4. Summary

Along with other research (Croyle & Cooper, 1983; C. M. Steele, Southwick, Critchlow, 1981), the findings from the J. Cooper, Zanna, and Taves (1978) experiment support the claim that arousal plays a role when individuals advocate a position that is contrary to their initial attitude. It's important to note, however, that this effect would not have occurred had participants been told about the drug's side effects. If they had known the drug would make them relaxed or hyper, they would have attributed their arousal to the drug rather than to their inconsistency, and they would not have felt the need to change their attitudes to make themselves feel better (Zanna & Cooper, 1974).

It's also important to note that these findings do not mean that self-perception processes never influence attitude change. Quite often, people look at their behavior

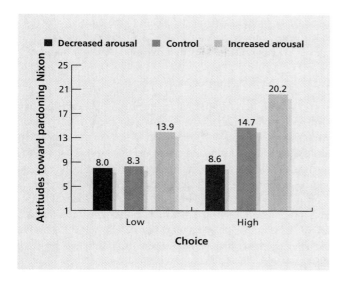

FIGURE 6.12

Attitudes toward Pardoning Richard Nixon as a Function of Choice and the True Side Effects of a Drug

The data show two effects of interest: First, the drug's effect was stronger in the high-choice condition than in the low-choice condition. Second, within the high-choice condition, participants given a tension-inducing drug showed a lot of attitude change, and participants given a relaxing drug showed relatively little attitude change. These findings provide stronger support for cognitive dissonance theory than for self-perception theory.

Source: J. Cooper, Zanna, and Taves (1978).

and infer their attitudes, motives, and feelings. Fazio, Zanna, and Cooper (1977) attempted to identify when cognitive dissonance occurs and when self-perception occurs. They argued that self-perception processes determine attitude change when we act in a manner that is not too discrepant from our initial position, and that cognitive dissonance determines attitude change when we do something that's very discrepant from our initial position. Insofar as people rarely act in ways that are terribly discrepant from what they believe, self-perception processes tend to occur much more frequently than cognitive dissonance.

F. What Creates Arousal?

In addition to exploring whether physiological arousal influences attitude change in the manner specified by cognitive dissonance theory, researchers have also examined the origins of arousal. Several theoretical positions have been offered over the years.

1. Festinger: Cognitive Inconsistency Creates Arousal

According to Festinger's (1957) original theory, cognitive inconsistency creates arousal. This inconsistency arises whenever two cognitions don't go together. For example, if you think all NASCAR racers are uncouth, you will experience cognitive dissonance if you learn that your favorite driver has an extensive collection of fine art. As noted earlier, this position is rooted in Gestalt theories of perception. Much as people find incongruous visual displays to be disconcerting, so too do they presumably experience arousal whenever two cognitions are inconsistent with one another.

2. Aronson: Inconsistency with Self-Image Creates Arousal

E. Aronson (1968, 1992) amended Festinger's initial statement by proposing that one of the cognitions must be self-relevant. Dissonance arises, Aronson argued, only when people behave in ways that run counter to their self-image or to the person they want to be. If, for example, you didn't want to live a long life, then the cognitions "I smoke" and "Smoking is bad for my health" wouldn't create dissonance. Similarly, if you think of yourself as a liar and a scoundrel, then the cognitions "I think this task is boring" but "I just lied and said it was interesting" wouldn't create any arousal whatsoever. According to Aronson, then, people with a positive opinion of themselves experience dissonance when they act in a negative manner, but people with a negative opinion of themselves experience cognitive dissonance when they act in a positive manner (see also Swann, 1990).

3. Schlenker: The Public Appearance of Inconsistency Creates Arousal

Other theorists have suggested that people experience dissonance when they publicly behave in a hypocritical manner (Schlenker, 1982; Schlenker, Forsyth, Leary, & Miller, 1980; Tedeschi, Schlenker, & Bonoma, 1971). From this perspective, the public appearance of inconsistency creates arousal, which people reduce by publicly changing their attitudes so as to appear consistent in the eyes of others. Private inconsistency is thought to be quite tolerable and to create little arousal, and people do not need to privately change their attitudes in order to feel better.

4. Cooper and Fazio: Foreseeable Negative Consequences Create Arousal

Inconsistency has played a central role in each of the preceding explanations. J. Cooper and his colleagues (Cooper & Fazio, 1984; Fazio & Cooper, 1983) have offered a very different perspective on the matter. These researchers contend that "dissonance is not motivated by inconsistency at all, but by the production of undesired consequences" (Scher & Cooper, 1989, p. 900). Early in life, people learn that it is wrong to willingly bring about a negative outcome. Through processes of classical conditioning, they come to experience arousal whenever they feel personally responsible for producing a negative consequence to themselves or to others. They reduce this arousal by justifying what they have done or by changing their attitude toward the behavior in question.

5. Steele: Self-Image Threat Creates Arousal

C. M. Steele's self-affirmation theory also strays from Festinger's theory. Dismissing the role of inconsistency entirely, Steele (1988; C. M. Steele & Spencer, 1992) argues that cognitive dissonance arises whenever people say or do something that suggests they are incompetent or immoral. They can reduce this dissonance either by altering their attitude or by engaging in some irrelevant self-affirming experience.

Steele's theory sounds similar to Aronson's, but there are two important differences. First, inconsistency plays a key role in Aronson's theory, but not in Steele's theory. To illustrate, suppose you think you are bad at math and do poorly on a math test. Whereas Aronson predicts that this outcome will not create arousal (because it matches your self-image), Steele predicts it will (because failure makes you feel bad

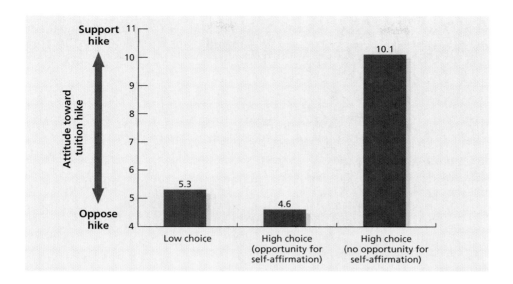

FIGURE 6.13

Attitudes toward a Tuition Hike as a Function of Choice and an Opportunity for Self-Affirmation

All of the participants wrote an essay supporting a tuition hike at their university. Only participants who freely chose to write the essay *and* were given no opportunity to affirm a positive self-image subsequently expressed positive attitudes toward a tuition hike. These data suggest that people can tolerate inconsistency if they are able to remind themselves that they are a good person in general.

Source: C. M. Steele and Lui (1983).

about yourself). The two theories are also distinguished when it comes to how people cope with arousal. According to Aronson, in order to reduce arousal people must resolve the inconsistency that gave rise to the dissonance. In Steele's theory, people don't need to resolve the inconsistency in order to reduce dissonance. They can reduce arousal simply by reminding themselves that they are generally a good person.

Steele conducted an experiment to test this idea (C. M. Steele & Lui, 1983). All of the participants in the experiment wrote essays supporting a tuition hike at their university, a position that was inconsistent with their true attitudes. As in many cognitive dissonance studies, some participants wrote the essay under conditions of low choice and other participants wrote the essay under conditions of high choice. Typically, we should find that high-choice participants change their attitudes but that low-choice participants do not. A third condition was added to this basic procedure, however. In this condition, participants wrote the essay under conditions of high choice but were then given the opportunity to restore a positive self-image by reminding themselves that they hold many fine values in life. Finally, attitudes toward a tuition hike were measured.

The researchers predicted that inconsistency would produce attitude change only among high-choice participants who were not given an opportunity to affirm a positive self-image. The data displayed in Figure 6.13 support this prediction. The data show that participants who willingly wrote an essay supporting a tuition hike changed their attitudes only if they did not have an opportunity to reestablish a positive self-image through other means. If they were allowed to first affirm their self-image, they showed no more attitude change than did participants who wrote the essay under conditions of

TABLE 6.5 Comparing Various Theories of Cognitive Dissonance

Theorist	Explanation	Does Arousal Play a Role?	Does Inconsistency Play a Role?	Do People Need to Resolve the Particular Inconsistency That Created Dissonance?	Do Private Attitudes Change?
Festinger	Inconsistency between any two cognitions creates an aversive state of arousal that people are driven to reduce.	Yes	Yes	Yes	Yes
Bem	People look at their behavior in the context in which it occurs and draw an appropriate inference about why they acted as they did.	No	Yes	Yes	Yes
Aronson	Inconsistency between a self-relevant cognition and a behavior creates an aversive state of arousal that people are driven to reduce.	Yes	Yes (but one of the cognitions must be self-relevant)	Yes	Yes
Schlenker	People don't want to be hypocritical, so they attempt to negotiate a more positive social identity with themselves and their audience.	Yes	Yes (but only public inconsistency; private inconsistency is tolerable)	Yes	Not necessarily
Cooper and Fazio	People have been punished for willingly bringing about foreseeable negative outcomes. The punishment gives rise to anticipatory anxiety, which people are driven to reduce.	Yes	No	Yes	Yes
Steele	People are motivated to maintain a global image of adequacy. This image is challenged when they behave in a hypocritical fashion, and they restore the positive image by engaging in self-affirmation (independent of whether it involves resolving the specific inconsistency).	Yes	No	No	Yes

low choice. These findings suggest that people can tolerate a good deal of inconsistency as long as they are able to view themselves in generally positive terms.

6. Comparing the Various Theories of Cognitive Dissonance

Table 6.5 compares the various theories we've been discussing. Each offers a unique perspective on the conditions that generate arousal or produce attitude change. It is apparent that cognitive dissonance theory has evolved a great deal over the years.

From its origins as a cognitive consistency theory, cognitive dissonance theory has been transformed into a self-enhancement theory (Greenwald & Ronis, 1978). Inconsistency creates arousal only if it reflects poorly on oneself, and inconsistency produces attitude change only if one is unable to restore a positive self-image through other means. Viewed in this way, cognitive dissonance theory and the research it inspired provide further testament to the ingenious and myriad ways people actively work to maintain high feelings of self-worth.

CHAPTER SUMMARY

- Attitudes are evaluative reactions to people, issues, and objects. They consist of evaluative beliefs, affective preferences, and behavioral tendencies.

- Emotional theories of attitude formation assert that attitudes arise independent of beliefs. They can be acquired through instrumental conditioning, classical conditioning, observational learning, or the mere exposure effect.

- Cognitive theories of attitude formation adopt an expectancy–value framework and assume that our attitudes are based on a rational analysis of the pros and cons associated with various positions.

- Attitudes are more likely to predict behavior when (1) the attitude and the behavior are measured at comparable levels of specificity, (2) the attitude is strong and accessible, and (3) people care a lot about maintaining consistency between their attitudes and their behavior.

- The theory of reasoned action asserts that attitudes and subjective norms influence behavioral intentions, and behavioral intentions influence behavior.

- According to cognitive dissonance theory, people experience an aversive state of tension when they hold two inconsistent cognitions. Often this state of tension arises when they fail to act in accordance with their attitudes. To reduce cognitive dissonance, people can (1) change their behavior, (2) change their attitude, or (3) justify their behavior by adding a cognition.

- Several theories offer refinements of cognitive dissonance theory. These theories disagree with regard to whether arousal instigates attitude change and, if so, whether arousal arises from inconsistency between any two cognitions.

KEY TERMS

attitudes, 195

values, 196

emotional theories of
attitude formation, 203

mere exposure effect, 206

cognitive dissonance, 222

ADDITIONAL READING

Go to the Student Edition of the Online Learning Center for this text (www.mhhe.com/brown) and log in to read the following journal articles, which relate to the content of this chapter:

- Bornstein, R. F., & D'Agostino, P. R. (1992). Stimulus recognition and the mere exposure effect.

- Festinger, L., & Carlsmith, J. M. (1959). Cognitive consequences of forced compliance.

Persuasion

The Internet isn't what it used to be. What began as a commercial-free forum for transmitting information has morphed into a highly commercialized medium that pelts users with a constant barrage of advertisements and appeals. Pop-up ads commandeer our browsers, spam chokes our e-mail inboxes, and many Web sites feature a continuous stream of commercials and ads. Of course, the Internet isn't the only medium that has been commercialized. Entire channels on cable television are devoted to selling products, and infomericals masquerade as entertainment. Even our schools are no longer a haven from persuasive appeals. Children all across America regularly watch *Channel One News,* a program that includes 2 minutes of advertising for every 12 minutes of content. In short, we live in an age of propaganda (Pratkanis & Aronson, 2001). More than ever before, we are bombarded with persuasive messages, as advertisers, politicians, and special interest groups attempt to persuade us to buy their wares or adopt their point of view.

In this chapter, we will consider theoretical models of the attitude change process (i.e., persuasion). These models tend to fall into three camps. Some theories emphasize that attitude change is a passive process in which people are swayed by factors largely unrelated to the issues at hand. The first perspective we will consider in this chapter is largely (though not entirely) of this variety. In the second section of this chapter, we will review theories that conceive of attitude change as an active, thoughtful process. This perspective assumes that attitude change occurs when people give careful consideration to the merits of the arguments they receive. In the third section of this chapter, we will consider dual-process models of persuasion. These theories adopt a middle ground, arguing that persuasion is sometimes passive and mindless and other times active and mindful. Finally, we will see how these models have been used to promote healthy behaviors, such as the practice of safe sex, smoking cessation, and the use of sunscreen and seatbelts.

I. The Yale Communication and Attitude Program

Persuasion has always been a central concern in social psychology, but interest in the topic accelerated greatly following World War II. During the war, Carl Hovland, a Yale psychologist, served as the director of the U.S. Army's Information and Education Division. Hovland was charged with promoting troop morale, and although his work identified numerous factors that influenced persuasion, it did not reveal why various factors worked as they did (Hovland, Lumsdaine, & Sheffield, 1949). After the war, Hovland committed himself to understanding the dynamics of attitude change. Funded by a large grant from the Rockefeller Foundation, he founded an extensive program to study persuasion, known as the Yale Communication and Attitude Program (Hovland, Janis, & Kelley, 1953).

A. Theoretical Assumptions

Although Hovland and his colleagues did not propose a formal theory of attitude change, their approach was heavily influenced by Clark Hull's learning theory (see Chapter 2). This is not surprising. Hovland had received his Ph.D. under Hull's direction, and he continued to be guided by Hull's theory when he turned his attention from the study of verbal learning (his dissertation topic) to the study of attitude change.

TABLE 7.1 Comparing Hull and Hovland

	Hull	Hovland
Nature of the phenomenon	Behaviors are motor habits.	Attitudes are implicit verbal habits.
Laws of behavior	Behaviors are acquired through processes of reinforcement.	Attitudes are acquired through processes of reinforcement.
Behavior change	To change a habit you must provide the organism with an incentive or reinforcement.	To change someone's attitude you must provide the person with an incentive or reinforcement.
Nature of reinforcement	Reinforcement must involve the reduction of a drive or need.	Reinforcement must involve the reduction of a drive or need.

1. The Three-Stage Model of Message Learning

Hovland's background in verbal learning led him to develop a *message learning* approach to attitude change. According to this approach, a message must be learned before an attitude can be changed. The process of learning a persuasive message was divided into three stages: attention, comprehension, and retention. The idea here is quite simple: A persuasive message can be learned only if a person attends to it, comprehends it, and retains it. These stages apply to learning situations of all types. For example, to learn the material presented in this paragraph, you must read it (attention), understand it (comprehension), and remember it (retention). The same is true when you receive a persuasive appeal. If I were trying to convince you that exercising every day does you more harm than good, you would need to attend to my message, understand what I was saying, and remember it.

2. The Three-Step Model of Attitude Acquisition

Attention, comprehension, and retention determine whether a persuasive message is learned, but reinforcement determines whether attitude change occurs. This is where Hull's influence is most apparent. In Chapter 2, we noted that Hull believed that behaviors are acquired through reinforcement, and that reinforcers must reduce a drive if learning is to occur. Table 7.1 shows that Hovland adopted (and adapted) these assumptions in his attempt to understand attitude change.

First, Hovland conceived of attitudes as verbal habits, no different in principle from motor habits. You *think* them, but the thought is an implicit, covert, verbal statement. To illustrate, suppose you have a positive attitude toward flossing your teeth after every meal. According to Hovland, this attitude is an implicit verbal statement. When you think about your attitude, you (silently) say, "I favor flossing after every meal." Treating attitudes and thoughts this way is consistent with positions held by other behaviorists, such as B. F. Skinner (1990).

The second assumption, which follows from the first, is that the laws of learning govern the acquisition of attitudes. Some attitudes are acquired through processes of association (classical conditioning), but most are acquired as a function of reinforcement (instrumental learning). Reinforcement in Hullian psychology always involves drive reduction, so Hovland assumed that the attitudes we hold today are ones that have reduced a need in the past. In order to change someone's attitude, then, you need to provide that person with an incentive that reduces some need (or promises to reduce some need).

An analogy may help clarify the theoretical underpinnings of Hovland's approach to attitude change. Consider the behavior of a rat at a choice point in a maze. As the rat moves along the maze, it makes little movements to the left and little movements to the right. Initially, these movements are randomly determined. Now suppose you provide reinforcement when the rat turns left instead of right. Over time, turning left will become habitual. The rat consistently turns to the left whenever the choice point is revisited, because that behavior has met with prior reinforcement. If you later want to change the rat's behavior, you need (1) to return the rat to the choice point, (2) give it a nudge in the new direction, and (3) provide stronger reinforcement to the new location than the rat has found in the prior location. It's just that simple.

Hovland believed that attitude change in humans is equally simple. Imagine that you want to convince a conservative friend of yours (who typically "turns" to the right) to become more liberal (by "turning" to the left). According to Hovland, you must (1) return the person to the choice point by asking her to reconsider her position; (2) present your alternative position; and (3) give her a greater incentive to adopt your position than she has previously received for being a conservative. With time, the new reinforced response will become dominant and the person's attitude will have changed. In Hovland's words:

> We assume that opinions, like other habits, will tend to persist unless the individual undergoes some new learning experiences. Exposure to a persuasive communication which successfully induces the individual to accept a new opinion constitutes a learning experience in which a new verbal habit is acquired. . . . When presented with a given question, the individual now thinks of and prefers the new answer suggested by the communication to the old one held prior to exposure to the communication. (Hovland et al., 1953, p. 10)

3. Types of Incentives

Because incentives are needed to change attitudes, the nature of incentives becomes a critical variable to consider in models of attitude change. Several types of incentives were discussed by Hovland and his associates.

Tangible Rewards. Tangible reinforcers, such as food or water, are one important type of incentive. All else being equal, the more food and water you offer someone for holding a particular attitude, the more likely the person is to adopt that attitude. Money is another kind of tangible reward. Money is a secondary reinforcer and, as such, is functionally equivalent to food and water. Consequently, the more money you give someone for holding a particular attitude, the more apt he or she should be to hold that attitude. This prediction—the more money you offer someone, the more likely they will be to adopt a new attitude—inspired the Festinger and Carlsmith (1959) study we discussed in Chapter 6.

Fear Reduction. Fear reduction is another important incentive. Anything that reduces an organism's fear is reinforcing. Rats, for example, are reinforced for performing behaviors that terminate a painful or frightening stimulus. Hovland and his colleagues believed that attitudes are also strengthened by fear-reducing messages. Imagine that you are afraid of getting gum disease. Any message that assures you that flossing after ever meal will help you avoid gingivitis is reinforcing.

Social Needs. Members of the Yale program also assumed that people have psychological needs as well as physical needs. First, people want to be right. Anything that leads people to believe they will be doing the right thing if they change their attitude satisfies this need and serves as a reinforcer. This desire to be right is not cognitively mediated. It's not that people think, "That makes a lot of sense to me; I guess I'll change my attitude." Such thinking would emphasize higher-order cognitive activity as a determinant of attitude change—an O in an S→O→R (Stimulus→Organism→Response) model (see chapter 2). But this is not an S→O→R model; it's an S→R model. Being right is merely a reinforcer, no different from food or water. It serves merely to glue or connect the new response (attitude) to the stimulus (question).

Another important psychological need is the need for social approval. Simply put, people want to be liked. If we are told that people we admire will like us if we adopt a particular attitude, their approval serves as a reinforcer. Again, this is because being liked in the past has been reinforcing. This process explains why people adopt the attitudes of the various groups to which they belong.

The desire to be like someone is a third psychological need relevant to persuasion. Here we adopt an attitude because we wish to think of ourselves as having a particular attribute or as being similar to someone we admire. Advertisers often use this incentive to sell products. A popular commercial some time ago for a sports drink featured basketball star Michael Jordan accompanied by the slogan "Be like Mike." We don't necessarily think we are doing the right thing for our bodies by purchasing this product, and we certainly don't believe that Michael Jordan is going to become our friend if we drink it. Instead, we are persuaded because we want to be like Michael Jordan. This is the third type of social influence that members of the Yale program considered.

B. Empirical Findings

The Yale program was exceptionally prolific at generating research. Its members conducted and published dozens of investigations. Because of the great volume of research these psychologists produced, it is possible here to discuss at length only a few effects of interest. As an organizing framework, researchers considered three independent variables: the source, the message, and the audience. In less formal terms, the Yale program considered the question "Who (source) said what (message) to whom (audience)?"

1. Source Characteristics

Much of the Yale program's early work was devoted to understanding what makes for an effective source (see Kelman, 1958). This issue is of considerable theoretical and practical importance. Advertisers spend billions of dollars each year in an effort to persuade us to buy their products. These persuasive appeals are often delivered by people who represent the company's interests. What aspects of a spokesperson are associated with the ability to persuade?

Source Credibility. Aristotle considered source characteristics of persuasion more than 2,000 years ago and focused on the speaker's credibility:

> Persuasion is achieved by the speaker's personal character when the speech is so spoken as to make us think him credible. We believe good men more fully and more readily than others; this is true generally whatever the question is, and absolutely true where exact certainty is impossible and opinions are divided. *Rhetoric* (355, BCE)

Empirical research provides strong support for Aristotle's insights (Eagly & Chaiken, 1993; Petty & Wegener, 1998; Pornpitakpan, 2004). All else being equal, a source of high credibility is more persuasive than a source of low credibility. The mechanism here, or the incentive, is the desire to be right. We are more persuaded by credible sources because we assume they know what they are talking about and we want to be right.

The credibility of a source is affected by two factors: expertise and trustworthiness. The effects of expertise are easy to understand: The more certain we are that a person knows what she is talking about, the more apt we are to be persuaded by her message. Imagine, for example, that someone comes on TV to tell you that she is a pediatrician and that, when her children get sick, she gives them ibuprofen to reduce their fever and relieve their aches and pains. Chances are, you would find this appeal persuasive. A pediatrician is an expert when it comes to caring for children, and assuming you want to do the right thing for your children, you should do what she does.

Source expertise matters most when an extreme position is being advocated (E. Aronson, Turner & Carlsmith, 1963; Bochner & Insko, 1966). Suppose that a person tells you that it is perfectly fine to be a couch potato who gets no exercise at all. This is a pretty extreme position, and you will probably find it to be more persuasive if it comes from a Nobel Prize–winning cardiologist than from your neighborhood grocer.

Expertise is not the only factor that affects source credibility. Trustworthiness is also important. Not surprisingly, sources we trust are more apt to persuade us than are sources we distrust. Trustworthiness depends in part on self-interest. When someone stands to gain in some way from the position he is taking, his persuasiveness is undermined. Think back to the pediatrician who is trying to convince you to use ibuprofen. Wouldn't you be less persuaded if you knew she was being paid to sell you ibuprofen? In contrast, your level of persuasion would increase if you knew she worked for a rival aspirin company and still was trying to convince you that ibuprofen was best.

Although not considered by the Yale group, attributional principles of discounting and augmenting can explain why self-interest undermines a source's credibility. Recall from earlier discussions (Chapter 4) that discounting occurs when a plausible situational factor leads us to discount a dispositional attribution. Broadly speaking, there are two reasons why someone would tell you a given product is best. One reason is that the person actually thinks the product is best; another is that the person has some other motive. When a person stands to gain by touting the benefits of a product, we are less sure the person truly thinks the product is great (discounting); when a person stands to lose a great deal by extolling the virtues of a product, we are even more sure the person truly thinks the product is great (augmenting). Formally, our attributions about the communicator's motives influence our judgments of the communicator's trustworthiness (Eagly & Chaiken, 1975; Eagly, Wood, & Chaiken, 1978; Fein, 1996; Fein, Hilton, & Miller, 1990; Tripp, Jensen, & Carlson, 1994; W. Wood & Eagly, 1981).

Intention to persuade is another factor that influences the trustworthiness of a source. We tend to be suspicious of people when we know they are trying to change our minds, and our suspicion weakens their persuasive impact (Brock, 1965). For this reason, overheard persuasion attempts are particularly effective (Brock & Becker, 1965;

Walster & Festinger, 1962). When we just happen to hear someone advocating a particular position, we discount the extent to which his or her proclamations are motivated by self-interest or stem from an intent to deceive us. We are then more apt to trust that person's claims and to be persuaded by them. Advertisers often use this gambit when they present commercials of two people talking, and they cast the audience in the role of an eavesdropper (e.g., "Let's listen in and hear what people are saying about the new flu remedy, FeelBetterFast Syrup").

Suspicions of personal gain are especially apt to erode the persuasibility of untrustworthy sources. Walster, Aronson, and Abrahams (1966) had junior high school students read variations on a persuasive message in which a person argued that courts should have more or less power to discipline criminals. The two opposing positions were allegedly held by a prosecutor (trustworthy condition) or a criminal currently serving jail time (untrustworthy condition). After reading these remarks, the students were asked to indicate how much authority they thought the courts should have. The trustworthy source (the prosecutor) was equally persuasive in both conditions, but the untrustworthy source (the criminal) was persuasive only when he argued a position that ran counter to his own self-interest (i.e., when he said courts should have more power).

Source Likability. The persuasiveness of a source also depends on how likable the source is. Although exceptions occur (Zimbardo, Weisenberg, Firestone, & Levy, 1965), likable sources tend to be more persuasive than unlikable sources. Likable sources tend to be (1) physically attractive (Chaiken, 1979); (2) of good character (Eagly & Chaiken, 1975); (3) similar to us (Berscheid, 1966; Brock, 1965); or (4) famous (Kahle & Homer, 1985; Tripp, Jensen, & Carlson, 1994). Fashion models such as Cindy Crawford and Christie Brinkley are very effective communicators because they are beautiful and famous. Numerous figures from the world of sports, such as Joe Montana and Tiger Woods, also reap enormous endorsement contracts because they are highly effective spokespersons for various companies. This is true even when the product being sold is unrelated to the person's area of expertise. For example, Andre Agassi encourages us to buy cameras. We don't believe that Andre is an expert when it comes to taking photographs, but his celebrity status and attractiveness make him an effective spokesman nonetheless.

Occasionally, advertisers get very savvy and combine credibility and liking. A few years ago, there was a commercial with a handsome man in a white doctor's coat who said, "I'm not a doctor, but I play one on TV, and when I get a headache I take brand XYZ." This commercial attempts to influence us in two ways. The white lab coat establishes the source's credibility, and the actor's attractiveness and celebrity status enhance his likability.

Sleeper Effect. Although high-credibility sources are more apt to persuade us than are sources who lack credibility, this effect tends to diminish over time. In fact, as time passes, the persuasive impact of a low-credibility source increases, an effect known as the **sleeper effect** (Kumkale & Albarracín, 2004). A study by Hovland and Weiss (1951) illustrates this effect (see also Hovland, Lumsdaine, & Sheffield, 1949). Hovland and Weiss had college students read a variety of messages. Some of the messages were attributed to sources of high credibility (e.g., "The *New England Journal of Medicine* argued that antihistamines should be sold without a doctor's prescription"); other messages were attributed to sources of low credibility (e.g., a popular picture magazine made the same claim). The students then indicated their agreement with the position advocated in the message, both immediately after reading the reports and four weeks later.

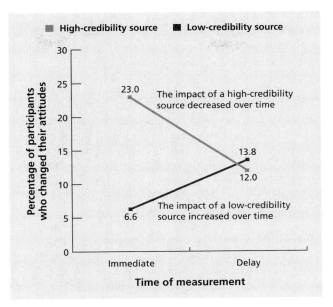

FIGURE 7.1

Source Credibility, Time of Measurement, and the Ability to Persuade

The impact of a high-credibility source *decreased* over time, but the impact of a low-credibility source *increased* over time. This latter tendency has been dubbed the sleeper effect.

Source: Hovland and Weiss (1951).

Figure 7.1 presents some of the data from this investigation. Several aspects of the data are noteworthy. First, looking only in the immediate measurement condition, we see that a high-credibility source was more effective than a low-credibility source. This is the usual communicator credibility effect. Four weeks later, however, this effect had disappeared. Now, the two communicators were equally effective. This occurred because the persuasive impact of the high-credibility source decreased over time, while the persuasive impact of the low-credibility source increased over time.

The declining impact of the high-credibility source is easy to understand, because many persuasive appeals weaken over time. But why should the impact of a low credibility source increase over time? Hovland and Weiss (1951) invoked principles of dissociation to explain this sleeper effect. According to this explanation, the message and the source are initially associated (or joined) in memory at the time the message is received. Over time, the message becomes dissociated from the source and we can't remember whether the message came from a low-credibility source or a high-credibility source. As a consequence, the persuasive impact of the message increases.

To test this idea, Kelman and Hovland (1953) added a condition to the study Hovland and Weiss (1951) had conducted. During the delayed testing session, half of the students were reminded who had been the source of the message they received earlier; the other students did not receive this reminder. Kelman and Hovland found that the sleeper effect occurred only when participants had not been reminded who was the source of the communication. This result, they argued, provided support for the notion that the sleeper effect occurs because the source and message become dissociated with the passage of time (see also T. D. Cook, Gruder, Hennigan, & Flay, 1979; Gruder, et al., 1978).

Subsequent research has found that the timing of the credibility cue is another important consideration. Testing a hypothesis first set forth by Gruder and colleagues (1978), Pratkanis, Greenwald, Leippe, and Baumgardner (1988) had participants read a persuasive message. Some participants learned before they read the passage that the message they were reading was authored by a low-credibility source; other participants received this information only after they read the passage. Attitudes were then measured immediately after the passage had been read and six weeks later. The sleeper effect occurred only when the credibility cue was given after the message was read. When the low-credibility cue was given before the passage was read, the message did not become more persuasive over time. (In a later section of this chapter, we will consider the reason why this occurred.)

2. Message Characteristics

To this point, we have been considering how source characteristics affect attitude change. Researchers have also examined the effectiveness of various message characteristics. In general, this research suggests that no one characteristic or set of characteristics is reliably persuasive. A strategy that is effective in some situations is ineffective in others. In more formal terms, we can say that interactions, rather than main effects, are the rule. The effectiveness of any given message characteristic depends on other relevant factors.

One-Sided versus Two-Sided Appeals. In trying to persuade someone, is it best to only state your position or to also acknowledge opposing views? Suppose, for example, that you were trying to persuade some adolescents to avoid smoking. Should you only discuss the reasons why smoking is bad, without mentioning all of the factors that lead people to smoke, or should you mention both sides of the issue? The answer to this question is that it depends on whether your audience is initially sympathetic to your position (Crowley & Hoyer, 1994; Hovland, Lumsdaine, & Sheffield, 1949). When the audience is already leaning toward your side (i.e., when you're preaching to the choir), a one-sided argument is more effective than a two-sided argument. The reverse is true, however, when the audience is initially opposed to your position. Under these circumstances, a two-sided message is more effective than a one-sided one. These effects are not always large (M. Allen, 1991), but they have been found in a variety of settings.

Visual Appeals versus Printed Messages. When constructing your antismoking ads, you might also want to consider whether visual appeals are more effective than printed messages. Here again, the answer is "It depends." In this case, it depends on the complexity of the material you are presenting. Visual messages are more effective than printed messages when the material is simple or easy to understand, but printed messages are more effective than visual messages when the material is complex or difficult to understand (Chaiken & Eagly, 1976, 1983).

Emotion or Reason. Another issue to consider is whether you should base your appeal on logical grounds ("Statistics shows that smoking will increase your risk for cancer, emphysema, and heart disease") or emotional grounds ("Smoking smells bad, and gives you wrinkles and yellow teeth"). As you might expect, neither strategy is always best. Instead, it depends on how the attitude was formed. Emotional appeals work best when the attitude is based on feelings and emotion, but cognitive appeals work best when the attitude is based on beliefs and information.

To illustrate, Fabrigar and Petty (1999) first created positive attitudes toward a fictional marine animal called a lemphur. Half of the participants read an affectively based passage designed to create good feelings toward the animal; the remaining participants read a dry, factual account of the animal that highlighted the animal's intelligence and usefulness. Afterward, the investigators attempted to change the participants' attitudes: Half of the participants received an affectively based passage that presented a graphic depiction of an incident in which a lemphur brutally attacked and

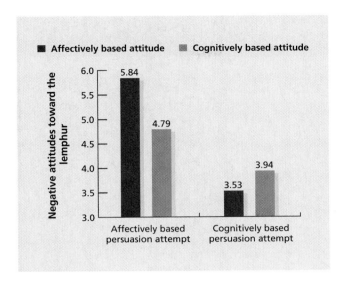

FIGURE 7.2

Affective–Cognitive Matching Effects in Persuasion

An affectively based persuasion attempt was more effective at changing affectively based attitudes, but a cognitively based persuasion attempt was more effective at changing cognitively based attitudes. These findings demonstrate an affective–cognitive matching effect: Persuasive appeals tend to be most effective when the nature of the appeal matches the basis of the attitude.

Source: Fabrigar and Petty (1999).

ate a swimmer; the other half read a factual account of the animal's unpredictable temperament in the wild and its adverse effects on the fishing industry. Finally, the researchers gathered attitudes toward the animal.

Figure 7.2 shows some of the results from this investigation. In the figure, higher numbers indicate more negative attitudes toward the lemphur, so they indicate attitude change from the initially positive attitude. Although the affectively based persuasion attempt was more effective at changing affectively based attitudes than cognitively based ones, the reverse was true for the cognitively based persuasion attempt. In short, the data show a matching effect: Appeals are most effective when their tone matches the manner in which the attitude was initially formed (see also Edwards, 1990; Edwards & von Hippel, 1995; Huskinson & Haddock, 2004).

Message Order Effects. Every four years, the Republican and Democratic parties hold their national conventions to select their respective candidates for president. By agreement, the two parties alternate which convention is held first. In half of the election years the Republicans go first, and in the other half the Democrats go first. The conventions are designed to persuade Americans to vote for their party's candidate, so the question arises as to whether it is advantageous to go first (primacy effect) or last (recency effect).

N. Miller and Campbell (1959) addressed this question in the context of a simulated jury decision. Arguments for the plaintiff and defendant were condensed, and half of the participants heard the plaintiff's case first and the other half heard the defendant's case first. Miller and Campbell included two other variables of

TABLE 7.2 Message Order Effects in Persuasion

			EXPERIMENTAL CONDITION				
1	Case 1	Case 2	One-week delay	Decision		The two cases were presented without a delay between them, but a one-week delay occurred between the time the last case was presented and the jury's decision.	Primacy effect: Participants were more persuaded by the first argument they heard.
2	Case 1	One-week delay	Case 2	Decision		The two cases were presented with a one week delay between them, and the jury's decision was made immediately after the second case was received.	Recency effect: Participants were more persuaded by the second argument they heard.
3	Case 1	Case 2	Decision			The two cases were presented without a delay between them, and no delay occurred between the last case and the jury's decision.	No effect: Jury decisions did not differ as a function of presentation order.
4	Case 1	One-week delay	Case 2	One-week delay	Decision	The two cases were presented with a one week delay between them, and the jury's decision was made one week after the second case was received.	No effect: Jury decisions did not differ as a function of presentation order.

Source: N. Miller and Campbell (1959).

interest: the time between the two cases (the cases were heard with either no delay between them or a one-week delay between them) and the time between the conclusion of the evidence and the jury's decision (either immediate or a one-week delay).

Table 7.2 summarizes the procedure and the results of this investigation. The table shows that primacy effects occurred in the first condition. When the cases were presented without any delay between them, and attitudes were measured one week after the second case was received, participants were more persuaded by the first case they read. Recency effects occurred in condition 2. When there was a one-week delay between the time the two cases were read, and attitudes were measured immediately after the second case was read, the second case was more persuasive than the first. Conditions 3 and 4 showed neither a primacy nor a recency effect.

Returning to the question of whether either political party gains by holding its convention first or last, the answer appears to be no. The situation is most like row 4 in Table 7.2. There is a delay between the two conventions, and a substantial delay between the conventions and the election in November. Under these conditions, neither party benefits from being first or last.

3. Audience Characteristic

Earlier we noted that the members of the Yale program built their research around the question of "Who said what to whom?" We have considered the who (the source) and the what (the message), but we have not yet considered the whom (the audience). The search for audience variables was guided by the notion that some people are more easily influenced than others are. This general tendency to yield to or to resist persuasion was referred to as a person's persuasibility (Janis & Field, 1956).

Originally, three personality variables were thought to affect a person's persuasibility: Intelligence (people of low intelligence were thought to be more easily persuaded than were people of high intelligence), self-esteem (low self-esteem people were thought to be more easily persuaded than were high self-esteem people), and gender (females were thought to be more easily persuaded than were men). Although there is evidence to support each of these predictions, it is modest in magnitude and narrow in scope (for reviews, see Eagly & Carli, 1981; McGuire, 1985; N. Rhodes & Wood, 1992). The predicted differences are not always found, and even when reliable effects are found, their size is usually small.

McGuire (1968, 1985) offered an explanation for these inconsistent and modest effects. He argued that audience variables have different effects at different stages of the attitude change process, and that these effects tend to cancel one another out. High intelligence, for example, increases the likelihood that a message will be understood and remembered but decreases the likelihood that the person will yield to the position advocated in the message. As a consequence of these opposing tendencies, people of moderate intelligence are expected to be most easily led (see N. Rhodes & Wood, 1992, for evidence relevant to this position).

Persuasibility and Age. Age is another variable that has been linked to persuasibility. It is widely believed that older people are less apt to change their attitudes than adolescents or young adults are (you can't teach an old dog new tricks). Research generally supports this characterization, and two explanations have been offered to explain why it occurs (Alwin, Cohen, & Newcomb, 1991; Krosnick & Alwin, 1989). One explanation, termed the impressionable years hypothesis, asserts that late adolescence and early adulthood are uniquely impressionable years in which people are particularly susceptible to attitude change. Another explanation, termed the lifelong openness hypothesis, maintains that people are equally open to attitude change throughout their lives, but younger people experience more instability in their lives than do older people and this explains why their attitudes are less stable.

Tyler and Schuller (1991) tested these competing hypotheses by examining people's attitudes toward the government as a function of their age and their experience with government agencies. They found evidence for the lifelong openness model. Young people's attitudes toward the government were more apt to change, but this seemed to be because they had greater contact with government agencies. When the amount of contact was taken into account, older people's attitudes changed as much as those of younger people. These findings suggest that the greater instability young people show is not due to any unique psychological properties of adolescence, but instead arises because young people's experiences are more novel and variable.

Audience Characteristics and Message Content. Many advertisers tailor their message to a particular audience. Consider, for example, how automobile companies sell their products. Volvo highlights safety, Cadillac stresses comfort, and Pontiac promotes excitement. The assumption here is that these appeals will effectively persuade some people but not others. Research on self-monitoring and persuasion illustrates the value of varying message content according to the intended audience. As discussed in Chapter 5, high self-monitors are attuned to the social appropriateness of their behavior and strive to cultivate a desirable public identity in social settings. Low self-monitors, in contrast, regard themselves as highly principled people who strive to remain true to themselves in social situations (see M. Snyder, 1979, 1987, for reviews).

M. Snyder and DeBono (1985) examined how these differences influence people's reactions to persuasive appeals. In one of their studies, participants heard one of two descriptions of a shampoo. An image-oriented description emphasized that the shampoo makes your hair look great; a quality-oriented description emphasized that the shampoo excels at cleaning your hair. The participants then indicated how interested they were in using the shampoo. Because high self-monitors are highly concerned with their social image, Snyder and DeBono hypothesized that they would be more influenced by the image-laden description than by the quality-oriented ad. The reverse pattern was predicted for low self-monitors, who value substance over style. Figure 7.3 reveals strong support for these predictions. High self-monitors were more willing to try the shampoo when they believed it would leave their hair looking great, but low self-monitors were more willing to try the shampoo when they believed it would leave their hair healthy and clean (see also DeBono, 1987; DeBono & Harnish, 1988; DeBono & Packer, 1991).

Culture and Message Content. The effectiveness of a message also depends on the cultural context. In one study, Han and Shavitt (1994) analyzed magazine ads in America (an individualist culture) and Korea (a collectivistic culture). As expected,

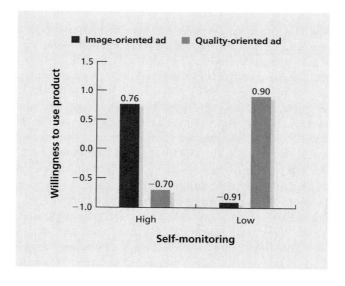

FIGURE 7.3

Self-Monitoring, Message Content, and Persuasibility

Participants heard one of two advertisements for a shampoo. One of the advertisements was very image-oriented ("Using this shampoo will leave your hair looking great"), and the other emphasized the shampoo's quality ("Using this shampoo will give you healthy hair"). As expected, image-conscious high self-monitors were more influenced by the image-oriented advertisement, but value-conscious low self-monitors were more influenced by the advertisement that focused on the product's quality.

Source: M. Snyder and DeBono (1985).

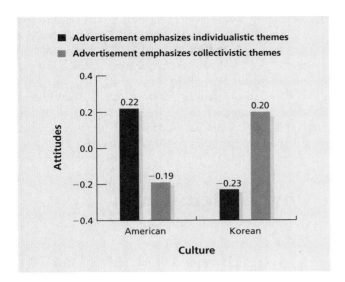

FIGURE 7.4

Culture and the Persuasiveness of Individualistic and Collectivistic Appeals

American college students were more persuaded by individualistic ads than by collectivistic ads, but Korean college students were more persuaded by collectivistic ads than by individualistic ones.

Source: Han and Shavitt (1991).

advertisements that emphasized self-reliance, improvement, and competition ("You, only better") were more common in America than in Korea, whereas advertisements that emphasized family harmony and social acceptance (e.g., "The dream of prosperity for all of us") were more common in Korea than in America (see also Aaker, Benet-Martínez, & Garolera, 2001).

Han and Shavitt (1994) conducted a second study to see whether these differences affect the persuasiveness of various messages. During the first part of the experiment, American and Korean college students read advertisements for various products. Some of these advertisements emphasized individualistic themes, and some emphasized collectivistic themes. Students then indicated how desirable they found the products. The data displayed in Figure 7.4 show that message content and culture interacted to affect persuasion. Among American college students, advertisements that focused on individualistic themes were more persuasive than were ads that focused on collectivistic themes. The opposite was true for Korean college students. These findings provide further evidence that messages are rarely universally effective. What works for some people doesn't work for others, and what's effective in some cultures is ineffective in other cultures (see also Aaker & Schmitt, 2001; Evans & Petty, 2003).

C. The Legacy of the Yale Communication and Attitude Program

Having reviewed a good deal of research inspired by the Yale Communication and Attitude Program, it is appropriate to step back and evaluate this research effort. First, Hovland's group paved the way for almost all subsequent work on persuasion. In this sense, the research had very high heuristic value. The theoretical yield was not as strong, however. As noted at the beginning of this chapter, the Yale group was strongly influenced by Hull's theory yet did not propose its own formal theory of attitude change. This atheoretical stance is apparent in the research the Yale investigators conducted. Many studies were conducted, but few had a strong theoretical basis. Instead, the research tended to be effect-driven rather than theory-driven.

Perhaps the Yale program's most enduring legacy is methodological. The research effort was systematic, and researchers conducted multiple investigations testing specific hypotheses under controlled laboratory conditions. The great volume of studies these researchers produced set the standard for other research efforts to follow.

II. Perceptual/Cognitive Models of Attitude Change

With its emphasis on message learning, it may seem as if the Yale approach was a cognitive approach. This is not so. Message learning is viewed as a necessary but not sufficient cause of attitude change. Ultimately, attitude change requires incentives that are sufficiently strong to overcome prior habit tendencies. These incentives are largely derived from Hull's theory of behavior. Also, the Yale approach does not portray the message recipient as an active information processor. In the message learning model, people do not actively transform, construe, or interpret the persuasive messages they encounter; they passively receive and register them. In short, although the Yale approach sounds cognitive, it regards attitude change as a passive, mindless process.

A. Asch's Model of Attitude Change

Solomon Asch (1948) took issue with the theoretical assumptions of the message learning approach. Applying principles of Gestalt psychology, Asch argued that people do not passively register the messages they receive but actively transform them, and the meaning they give to these messages determines whether attitude change occurs. Asch's approach builds on the three tenets of Gestalt psychology we discussed in Chapter 2: Meaning is variable; context determines meaning; meaning guides behavior.

Asch used his model of attitude change to understand communicator likability effects. As noted earlier, likable communicators are generally more persuasive than unlikable communicators. Learning theorists explain this phenomenon in terms of transfer of affect. According to this explanation, the liking we feel for the communicator comes to be associated with the message the communicator is advocating. If we like the communicator, we like the message; if we dislike the communicator, we dislike the message. The process is extremely passive, not at all unlike the manner in which Pavlov's dogs learned to salivate to the sound of a bell.

Asch had a different explanation for why likable communicators are more persuasive. He argued (1) that the meaning of any message is variable and depends on the context in which it is found; (2) that the liking we feel for the communicator provides the context and alters the meaning of the message; and (3) that the meaning we give to the message guides attitude change. From this perspective, it is not that we evaluate an unchanged message more favorably when it is linked to a liked communicator; it is, rather, that our liking for a communicator alters the meaning of the message itself. Messages mean something different when they are attributed to likable communicators than when they are attributed to disliked communicators, and this alteration in meaning determines attitude change.

Asch illustrated his perspective by replicating a study by Lorge (1936). Lorge presented participants with various statements referring to political and economic issues of the day. For example, some participants read "I hold it that a little rebellion now and then is a good thing, and as necessary in the political world as are storms in the physical." Half of the participants were told that the statement was authored by the Communist leader Vladimir Lenin; the other half were told that Thomas Jefferson had penned the statement. After receiving this information, the participants indicated their agreement with the passage. Lorge found that participants agreed with the passage more when they thought Jefferson had said it than when they thought Lenin had said it. Invoking principles of association to explain this communicator likability effect, Lorge argued that the liking we feel for Jefferson transfers to the statement he purportedly authored. (Jefferson was, in fact, the author of this statement.)

Asch repeated this study but also had participants indicate what the term *rebellion* meant. He found that participants in the two conditions had very different ideas. When attributed to Lenin, rebellion brought to mind images of revolution and bloodshed, anarchy and injustice; when attributed to Jefferson, rebellion brought to mind images of debate and democracy, an honest, fair airing of ideas, and gentle winds of change sweeping the land. This is precisely what Asch meant when he said that our liking for the communicator alters the communicator's message. Most everyone agrees that bloodshed is bad and gentle winds of change are good. The liking we feel for the communicator influences which of those two connotations comes to mind when we consider the word *rebellion,* and the connotation or meaning we give to the message determines attitude change (see also Zanna & Hamilton, 1977).

It is important to appreciate the contrast between Asch's approach and the one favored by Lorge and other psychologists with roots in behaviorism. Learning theory paints a very passive portrait of people and maintains that our feelings of affection are blindly transferred from one object to another. Asch's theory asserts that people are actively trying to make sense of their world. In the present case, it assumes that people (implicitly) ask themselves: "Why would Thomas Jefferson advocate rebellion? What could he possibly have meant? He was a good man, so he probably meant something related to democracy and fairness." People's agreement with the statement, then, is a function of the meaning they give to it. It's not mindless and passive; it's thoughtful and rational.

A similar analysis can be used to explain other findings we have discussed. Earlier in this chapter we noted that the sleeper effect does not occur if the low credibility cue is given before the message is read. Asch would say this is because the meaning of the message changes when the low-credibility cue is given first. The message now seems less convincing, less compelling, and consequently less persuasive. And when the persuasive impact of the message no longer increases over time, it's not because of principles of dissociation, it's because the very meaning of the message (the object of judgment) was altered by the credibility cue and was unpersuasive to begin with. This explanation is very different from the one favored by learning theorists and those who followed in this tradition (see also G. L. Cohen, 2003).

B. Social Judgment Theory

Inspired by Asch's work and influenced by the cognitive revolution that began to dominate American psychology, Hovland and his group eventually developed a more cognitively oriented theory of attitude change called **social judgment theory** (Sherif & Hovland, 1961). Published just after Hovland's death, this theory was advanced to explain a finding that appeared in some of Hovland's earlier research. Several investigations had found that people's attitudes affect whether or not they think other attitude positions are fair. Positions that lie close to one's own view are judged to be fair and impartial, while messages that fall far from one's own view are judged to be unfair and propagandistic (Hovland, Harvey & Sherif, 1957; Hovland & Weiss, 1951; see also Kelman & Eagly, 1965).

1. Latitudes of Acceptance and Rejection

Sherif and Hovland (1961) relied on principles of psychophysics to explain when a persuasive message will be viewed as fair or propagandistic. They argued that a person's existing attitude functions as an anchor or reference point, and that this anchor serves to bias and distort the meaning given to other attitude positions. Attitudes that fall near one's existing attitude are said to lie within one's latitude of acceptance and are subject to assimilation effects. Assimilation effects occur when attitudes are judged to be closer to one's own point of view and are viewed as being reasonable, fair, and cogent. The situation is different for messages that fall far from one's existing attitude. These messages are said to lie within one's latitude of rejection and are subject to contrast effects. Contrasts effects occur when the message is regarded as being far away from one's own position and is perceived to be unreasonable, unfair, and unconvincing. Finally, Sherif and Hovland proposed that people have a latitude of noncommitment that includes positions they neither accept nor reject. This aspect of the theory has received comparatively little attention and will not be discussed further.

Notice how social judgment theory incorporates principles of Gestalt psychology. The meaning of a persuasive communication is variable. Your own position provides the context in which the message is understood. Messages that lie close to your own position are assimilated into the context (i.e., they are viewed as similar to your own attitude), and ones that fall far from your own position are subject to contrast effects (i.e., they are viewed as dissimilar to your own attitude). Finally, meaning guides attitude change.

Hovland, Harvey, and Sherif (1957) conducted one of the first tests of the theory in a study of prohibition. This issue was quite timely and involving for the participants, because efforts were under way to overturn prohibition in the participants' home state of Oklahoma. At the start of the investigation, Hovland and his colleagues administered an attitude scale. On the basis of the responses they received, they classified participants as having either pro-alcohol views, anti-alcohol views, or moderate views that fell between these two extremes.

During the second part of the investigation, all three groups of participants were asked to evaluate the fairness of nine attitudinal positions. These positions, shown in Table 7.3, varied from favoring prohibition to opposing prohibition. After reading each statement, the participants indicated how fair they thought the statement was and whether or not they agreed with it. As expected, participants who opposed prohibition regarded the anti-prohibition statements to be the fairest, those who favored prohibition judged the pro-prohibition statements to be the fairest, and those with moderate views showed no preference either way. These findings are consistent with the claim that our own attitude influences how fair other attitudes are judged to be.

TABLE 7.3 Attitudinal Statements Used by Hovland, Harvey, and Sherif (1957)

1. Since alcohol is the curse of mankind, the sale and use of alcohol, including light beer, should be completely abolished.

2. Since alcohol is the main cause of corruption in public life, lawlessness, and immoral acts, its sale and use should be prohibited.

3. Since it is hard to stop at a reasonable moderation point in the use of alcohol, it is safer to discourage its use.

4. Alcohol should not be sold or used except as a remedy for snake bites, cramps, colds, fainting, and other aches and pains.

5. The arguments in favor and against the sale of alcohol are nearly equal.

6. The sale of alcohol should be so regulated that it is available in limited quantities for special occasions.

7. The sale and use of alcohol should be permitted with proper state controls, so that the revenue from taxation may be used for the betterment of schools, highways, and other state institutions.

8. Since prohibition is a major cause of corruption in public life, lawlessness, immoral acts, and juvenile delinquency, the sale and use of alcohol should be legalized.

9. It has become evident that man cannot get along without alcohol; therefore, there should be no restriction whatsoever on its sale and use.

2. Factors That Determine Latitude Width

Because the meaning of a persuasive message depends on whether it falls inside or outside of one's latitude of acceptance, a critical issue for social judgment theory is to identify the factors that influence latitude width. Two factors were proposed. The first is the extremity of the person's position. Compared to people with moderate views, people with extreme views have narrower latitudes of acceptance and broader latitudes of rejection. The personal relevance of the issue is another important factor to consider. Sherif and Hovland argued that the more important or personally relevant an issue is to a person, the narrower will be the person's latitude of acceptance and the broader will be the person's latitude of rejection. Sherif and Hovland referred to this tendency as ego involvement, but most contemporary researchers use the terms *personal involvement, personal importance,* or *personal relevance* (B. T. Johnson & Eagly, 1989, 1990; Petty & Cacioppo, 1990).

The manner in which personal involvement affects latitude width is easy to illustrate. When people have a high personal stake in an issue and when the issue is something they care deeply about, they tend to be relatively intolerant of dissenting opinions. In the theory's terms, they have a narrow latitude of acceptance and a broad latitude of rejection. But when people do not care deeply about an issue and it's not something that affects them personally, they tend to be rather broad-minded about dissenting opinions. They have a large latitude of acceptance and a narrow latitude of rejection.

3. Discrepant Communications and the Dynamics of Attitude Change

Social judgment theory sheds light on an interesting issue. Suppose you wanted to change someone's attitude. How extreme should your advocacy be? Should you advocate a position that lies far from the person's existing view, in hopes of achieving partial movement toward your position, or should you play it safe and advocate a position that lies very near to the person's present view, settling for whatever change you could effect?

Social judgment theory provides an answer to this question. Recall that people view messages that fall within their latitude of acceptance as fair and compelling, whereas they view those that fall within their latitude of rejection as biased and lacking in cogency. Accordingly, you want your message to fall just inside the person's latitude of acceptance, without crossing over into the person's latitude of rejection. If you succeed, your message will be subject to an assimilation effect and will be seen as fair-minded and credible; if you fail, your message will be subject to a contrast effect and will be viewed as unfair and unconvincing.

Figure 7.5 illustrates these principles as a function of personal involvement. If the person is highly involved in the issue (see the solid line in Figure 7.5), you'll need to be conservative in your recommendations because the person's latitude of acceptance is narrow. If, however, the person is not highly involved in the issue (see the dotted line in Figure 7.5), you can afford to advocate a more extreme position because the person's latitude of acceptance is broad. In short, the more important an issue is to your audience, the less extreme your advocacy should be (Hovland & Pritzker, 1957).

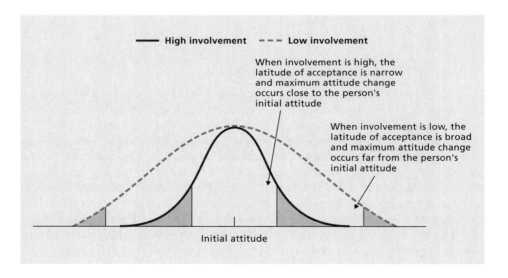

FIGURE 7.5

Predictions Social Judgment Theory Makes about Attitude Change as a Function of Involvement

Under each curve, the shaded areas show the person's latitude of rejection and the areas without shading show the person's latitude of acceptance. When involvement is high (solid line), the person's latitude of acceptance is narrow and maximum attitude change occurs close to the person's initial attitude. When involvement is low (dotted line), the person's latitude of acceptance is broad and maximum attitude change occurs far from the person's initial attitude.

4. Summary of Social Judgment Theory

Drawing on principles of Gestalt psychology, social judgment theory asserts that people's existing attitudes influence the way they perceive a persuasive communication, and the way people perceive a persuasive communication determines whether or not attitude change occurs. If the advocated message falls within our latitude of acceptance, it is subject to an assimilation effect. We think to ourselves, "That seems fair to me; I can agree with that." Under these circumstances, attitude change in the direction of the communication is apt to occur. If, however, the advocated message falls within our latitude of rejection, it is subject to a contrast effect. In this case we think, "That's absurd; I can't agree with that." Under these conditions, attitude change in the direction of the communication is unlikely to occur. Finally, the more important the issue is to us—the more involved we are—the smaller our latitude of acceptance is and the broader our latitude of rejection.

As is true with a number of theories of attitude change, empirical support for social judgment theory is mixed. On the one hand, there is evidence that people who are highly involved in an issue consider opposing arguments to be weaker and show less attitude change than do those who are less involved (Eagly, 1967; Edwards & Smith, 1996; Hovland et al., 1957). These findings are consistent with the claim that people who are highly involved in an issue have a narrow latitude of acceptance and a broad latitude of rejection. There is less evidence, however, that perceptual processes of assimilation and contrast underlie these effects, or that extreme (i.e., highly discrepant) messages are more apt to persuade uninvolved people than involved ones (Eagly & Telaak, 1972).

C. Resistance to Persuasion

Social judgment theory assumes that persuasion is determined by what people think about the message they receive, rather than the message itself. It's important to appreciate how fundamentally different this is from the learning theory approach first advocated by Hovland and his colleagues. Instead of assuming that thoughts play no role in attitude change (as a simple S→R model asserts), the way people think about the messages they receive was now viewed as a critical aspect of the attitude change process.

In the late 1950s and early 1960s, other research offered additional evidence that attitude change is often driven by the thoughts a person is having about a persuasive message. Much of this research was designed to identify factors that make people resistant to persuasion. Research on two-sided appeals provides the starting point for this research effort. Earlier we noted that two-sided appeals are effective when the audience is initially opposed to your position. Although not discussed at the time, two-sided appeals affect persuasion in another way: They make people who are sympathetic to your position more resistant to future persuasive communication attempts.

An investigation by Lumsdaine and Janis (1953) illustrates this effect. This study was conducted at the start of the cold war. During the first part of the investigation, high school students listened to a communication arguing that the Soviet Union would not be able to develop large numbers of atomic bombs in the near future. Half of the students heard a one-sided message, in which only arguments supporting this position were presented; the remaining students heard a two-sided message, in which both supporting and opposing arguments were presented. Some of the opposing arguments were refuted and others were not, but the communication always favored the conclusion that the Soviets were incapable of developing atomic weapons.

One week after hearing one of these two messages, students were exposed to another communication in which it was argued that the Soviets were, in fact, on the brink of developing atomic bombs. Agreement with this new argument constituted the critical dependent variable. The data showed that students who had initially heard the two-sided message were less likely to agree with this new position than were those who initially heard the one-sided message. Lumsdaine and Janis concluded that being exposed to both sides of an issue helps a person resist future persuasive appeals.

Building on these findings, McGuire (1964) developed an **inoculation theory of persuasion.** The model uses a biological analogy to explain how two-sided arguments make people resistant to attitude change. In the medical world, a person who receives a small dose of a virus is immunized or inoculated against developing the disease in the future. This occurs because a small dose of the virus stimulates the body to produce antibodies capable of defending itself against attack. By analogy, McGuire argued that people exposed to a two-sided message are inoculated against future attitude change because exposure to a two-sided message stimulates counterarguments that can later be used to resist attitude change attempts (McGuire & Papageorgis, 1961, 1962; Papageorgis & McGuire, 1961).

It turns out that simply being warned that we're going to hear a persuasive communication can decrease the amount of attitude change we show. Freedman and Sears (1965) told some high school students that they were about to hear a speech arguing that teenagers should not be allowed to drive; other students were not forewarned. Subsequently, all students heard the speech and their attitudes toward teenage driving were assessed. Students who were forewarned were less likely to change their attitudes in response to the communication than were those who were not forewarned.

Presumably, **forewarning effects** occur because people inoculate themselves in the period between the time they learn they are going to hear a persuasive appeal and the time the appeal is delivered. They anticipate arguments the speaker is likely to offer ("I bet he'll say that teens have the highest accident rate of all age groups") and spontaneously generate counterarguments ("That's because teens drive more miles than do people in other age groups").

To test this hypothesis, Chen, Reardon, Rea and Moore (1992) prevented some participants from generating counterarguments during the time they were forewarned and the time they heard a persuasive message. This was accomplished by having the participants perform a demanding cognitive task. If forewarning effects depend on people's ability to spontaneously generate counterarguments, preventing people from generating counterarguments ought to reduce the effects of forewarning. Figure 7.6 shows that this is just what occurred. Forewarning inhibited attitude change only when distraction was low and participants were allowed to think about their attitudes. When distraction was high and participants were prevented from generating counterarguments, it was as if they had not been forewarned at all.

To summarize, research on forewarning effects demonstrates that people are capable of protecting themselves against future attitude change, provided they are not distracted. It's important to note that the critical variable here is not simply whether people are forewarned or not; it's whether they are motivated and able to generate counterarguments in advance of hearing a discrepant communication (Apsler & Sears, 1968; Osterhouse & Brock, 1970; Petty & Cacioppo, 1977, 1979). Presumably, thinking about one's attitude causes the attitude to become strengthened, and this intensification insulates the person against subsequent attitude change (see also Rucker & Petty, 2004; Tesser, 1978; Tormala & Petty, 2002).

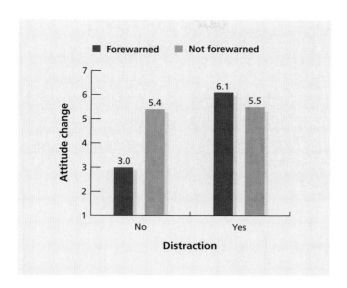

FIGURE 7.6

Forewarning, Distraction, and Persuasion

Participants were either forewarned or not forewarned about an upcoming persuasive appeal. Additionally, some were distracted and some were not. Forewarning reduced attitude change only when participants were not distracted, suggesting that forewarning effects depend on one's ability to generate counterarguments before the appeal is received.

Source: Chen, Reardon, Rea, and Moore (1992).

D. Cognitive Response Theory

The research we've been reviewing suggests that attitude change often depends on the thoughts the person generates about the attitude issue. This process was given prominence in a theory of attitude change known as **cognitive response theory.**

1. Theoretical Assumptions

Cognitive response theory was originally developed as a modification of the Yale approach. The Yale program researchers had maintained that message learning and retention are necessary for attitude change to occur. Yet how much a person learns or remembers about a persuasive message is often not a good predictor of whether or not that person changes his or her attitude (Eagly & Chaiken, 1984, 1993; Petty & Wegener, 1998). In consideration of this finding, Greenwald (1968) proposed that attitude change isn't determined by how well the person learns and remembers a persuasive message, but by the thoughts the person has while receiving the message.

Figure 7.7 presents a more formal description of the theory. The theory assumes that people who receive a persuasive communication actively think about the position being advocated. Some of these thoughts support the position being advocated; others (called counterarguments) oppose it. Additionally, some of these thoughts are mere repetitions of arguments presented in the message itself; other thoughts are entirely original, being either novel or topic-relevant thoughts the person has had before. Finally, the theory assumes that these thoughts (or cognitive responses) determine attitude change, with attitude change occurring when a persuasive appeal evokes more

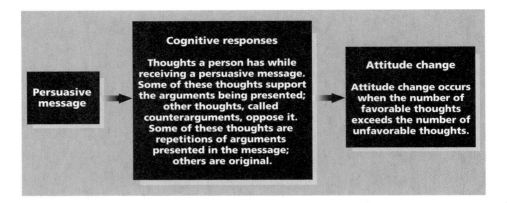

FIGURE 7.7
Cognitive Response Theory of Persuasion

favorable (pro-message) cognitive responses than unfavorable ones. Note, then, that according to the theory, it is the O in an S→O→R model that entirely accounts for attitude change. The external message sets the stage for attitude change, but ultimately what goes on inside the person's head determines whether or not attitude change occurs. All attitude change, the theory contends, occurs as a result of the thoughts the person has while listening to a persuasive appeal.

To illustrate, imagine that a politician is trying to convince you that the United States should eliminate funding for the space station because the money is needed at home. You might be thinking, "I agree that we have many pressing problems here on earth, and that the money spent on the space station could be better used to help solve them." You also might be thinking, "Space exploration is important. Not only do people feel a need to explore the unknown, but space exploration has led to many important discoveries and may eventually help us solve problems here on earth. After all, we wouldn't have Tang if it weren't for the space program." Cognitive response theory assumes that you will change your attitude in the direction advocated by the message only if your pro-argument thoughts outnumber your negative ones.

2. Thought–Listing Technique

Researchers have used a variety of techniques to test cognitive response theory. The most common procedure is to have participants write down or verbalize their thoughts while they are receiving (or immediately after they have received) a persuasive communication (Brock, 1967; Greenwald, 1968). These cognitive responses are then coded as being either favorable (pro-argument), unfavorable (counterargument), or neutral with respect to the attitude issue. Researchers then relate the number of positive and negative thoughts to the amount of attitude change that was produced.

Using these procedures, many investigations have found that people are most apt to change their attitudes when positive thoughts outnumber negative ones (for reviews, see Eagly & Chaiken, 1993; Petty & Cacioppo, 1981, 1986; Petty, Ostrom, & Brock, 1981). Not all investigations find such an effect, however. Sometimes, attitude change is completely unrelated to the thoughts the person is having about the arguments presented in the message. This state of affairs led to the development of more sophisticated models of attitude change.

III. The Dual Process Model of Attitude Change

A. Theoretical Assumptions

1. Two Routes To Attitude Change

Petty and Cacioppo (1981, 1986) developed a dual process model to explain when cognitive responses guide attitude change (see also Chaiken, 1980, 1987). The model assumes that attitude change can occur in two different ways. Sometimes, people change their attitudes in a rational, thoughtful manner. They carefully read or listen to a persuasive communication, think diligently about the merits of the arguments they are receiving, and change their attitudes if they find the arguments cogent and compelling. Petty and Cacioppo have labeled this process the **central route to attitude change,** because here attitude change depends on factors that are central to the quality of the arguments the message contains. When people receive a persuasion communication through the central route, they process information systematically and their thoughts about the quality of the arguments in the message predict attitude change.

People are not always so thoughtful, however. Sometimes they are busy or don't want to devote a lot of attention to considering the merits of a persuasive message. Yet attitude change can still occur under these conditions. People can be swayed by cues such as the attractiveness of the speaker or the length of the arguments in the message. Petty and Cacioppo have labeled this process the **peripheral route to attitude change,** because here attitude change depends on factors that are peripheral to the quality of the arguments in the message itself. When people receive a persuasion communication through the peripheral route, their thoughts about the strength of the message do not predict attitude change. Instead, a variety of extraneous or peripheral factors, such as mere exposure effects, classical conditioning, or various shortcuts and heuristics (e.g., an expert source is always right) determine whether or not attitude change occurs.

2. Factors That Determine Which Route Is Taken: Motivation and Ability

The dual-process model has gone on to identify the factors that determine which route will be taken. The first factor is a motivational factor. If attitude change is to occur through the central route, people must be motivated to give a great deal of thought and attention to understanding the message they are receiving. Although motivation can be influenced by several factors, most research has examined the personal relevance of the issue under consideration, a factor similar to what Sherif and Hovland (1961) called ego involvement.

When personal relevance is high, people care enough to carefully consider the merits of the message they are receiving. If the arguments they receive seem compelling, people change their attitudes; if the arguments they receive seem unconvincing, people don't change their attitudes. Of course, the greater one's involvement, the narrower one's latitude of acceptance. As a consequence, arguments opposed to an initial position are less likely to be considered persuasive when involvement is high (Edwards & Smith, 1996), making attitude change less likely to occur (B. T. Johnson & Eagly, 1989, 1990). Nonetheless, it is still the case that people who are involved in an issue, and care enough to think about a persuasive message, change their minds only if they regard the arguments they receive as convincing. High involvement, then, initiates central route processing, and low involvement initiates peripheral route processing.

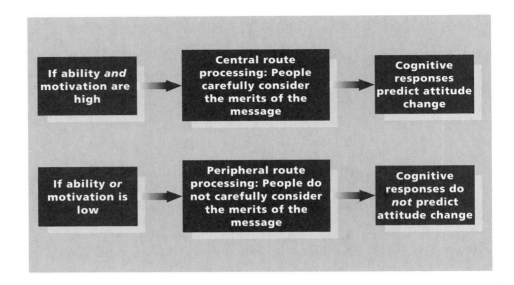

FIGURE 7.8

Dual-Process Model of Attitude Change

When ability *and* motivation are high, people carefully consider the merits of a message, and their cognitive responses predict attitude change. When either ability *or* motivation is low, people do not carefully consider the merits of a message, and their cognitive responses do not predict attitude change.

The ability to think carefully about the merits of a message is the second factor that influences which route is taken. People may be motivated to carefully consider the arguments they are receiving, but they may have difficulty comprehending the message. The arguments may be too complicated, people may be rushed or hurried, or there may be competing sources for their attention. When attitude change occurs under these circumstances, it occurs through the peripheral route rather than the central route, because the merits of the arguments are obscured.

Figure 7.8 summarizes how these two variables combine to influence persuasion. The key point to consider is that the central route is taken relatively infrequently. This is because it occurs only when people are motivated *and* able to think carefully about the information they are receiving. Advertisers seem to recognize this fact. When you are home watching television, you're probably not motivated to carefully attend to a commercial message. Moreover, you're also probably distracted when the commercial comes on (e.g., you are going to the refrigerator to get something to eat). That's why advertisers load up their commercials with peripheral cues. They know you're not thinking a lot about the message itself, so they attempt to persuade you using other means, such as attractive sources or pleasant music.

3. Consequences of Which Route Is Taken

Attitude change can occur through either route, but attitudes changed through the central route are stronger than attitudes changed through the peripheral route. In this context, *stronger* means more enduring, more resistant to attack, and more likely to guide behavior. Attitudes changed through the central route are stronger because they were formed through careful consideration of the merits of the message, rather than through superficial cues, such as the communicator's attractiveness or likability. Why, then, do people ever attempt to persuade us using peripheral cues? In some cases they lack strong arguments, so peripheral cues are all they have at their disposal. In other cases, you're not motivated or able to process the quality of a message, so peripheral cues will be more effective.

B. Empirical Research

Let's look at some of the research the dual-process model of attitude change has inspired.

1. Involvement Moderates the Effects of Argument Quality and Argument Quantity

In one experiment, Petty and Cacioppo (1984) told college students that their university chancellor was considering whether all students should be required to pass a comprehensive written exam in order to graduate. Half of the students were told that the policy would go into effect the following year (high-involvement condition); the other half were told that the policy would go into effect 10 years from then (low-involvement condition).

All students then read a persuasive message that favored instituting senior exams. The messages varied with respect to two factors: argument quality and argument quantity. With respect to argument quality, some students read messages that contained strong and compelling arguments (e.g., "The quality of undergraduate education has improved at schools with the exams"), while other students read messages that contained weak and specious arguments (e.g., "Requiring graduate students but not undergraduates to take the exams is analogous to racial discrimination"). With respect to argument quantity, some messages contained three arguments and others contained nine. After reading one version of the message, students indicated their support for comprehensive senior exams.

Let's examine the predictions the dual-process model makes under these conditions. When involvement is high, the students should be motivated to carefully consider the merits of the arguments they are receiving. Under these conditions, argument quality should affect attitude change, with strong arguments producing more attitude change than weak ones. When involvement is low, the students are not motivated to scrutinize the merits of the arguments they are receiving, so argument quality shouldn't matter. Instead, a peripheral cue, such as the number of arguments in the message, ought to affect attitude change: The more arguments, the more persuasive the message should be. The prediction, then, is that argument *quality* will guide persuasion when involvement is high, but argument *quantity* will drive persuasion when involvement is low.

Figure 7.9 shows that these predictions were confirmed. The left-hand panel shows that argument quality affected persuasion when involvement was high, but had no effect when involvement was low. The right-hand panel shows that argument quantity affected persuasion when involvement was low, but had no effect when involvement was high. This pattern supports the claim that attitude change occurs through the central route when involvement is high and through the peripheral route when involvement is low (see also Petty, Cacioppo, and Goldman, 1981; Petty, Cacioppo, & Schumann, 1983).

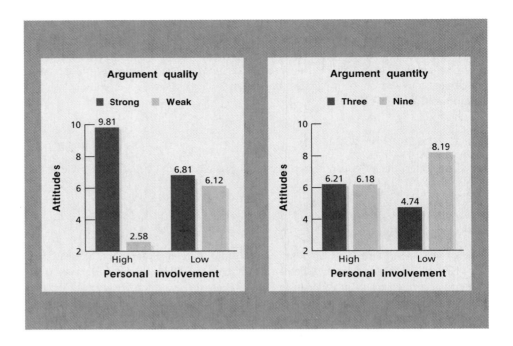

FIGURE 7.9

Personal Involvement, Argument Quality, Argument Quantity, and Attitude Change

The left-hand panel shows that strong arguments produced more attitude change than weak arguments only when involvement was high. When involvement was low, argument quality didn't affect attitude change. The right-hand panel shows that nine arguments produced more attitude change than three arguments only when involvement was low. When involvement was high, argument quantity didn't affect attitude change. This pattern supports the claim that attitude change occurs through the central route when involvement is high and through the peripheral route when involvement is low.

Source: Petty and Cacioppo (1984).

2. Distraction Moderates the Effects of Argument Quality

In the Petty and Cacioppo (1984) study, personal involvement affected participants' motivation to carefully consider a persuasive appeal. Petty, Wells, and Brock (1976) conducted a comparable study to determine how distraction affects attitude change. These researchers argued that distraction makes weak arguments more effective, because even if people are motivated to think about the message, they aren't able to do so when they are distracted. To test these ideas, Petty, Wells, and Brock had college students listen to a persuasive message regarding tuition increases at their university (an issue with high personal relevance). Some of the messages contained strong arguments; others contained weak arguments. In addition, half of the students were distracted during the presentation of the message and half were not distracted. Figure 7.10 shows the results from this investigation. As predicted, argument quality mattered more when distraction was low than when distraction was high, and this occurred because distraction made weak arguments more effective (and strong arguments somewhat less effective). This pattern is consistent with the claim that distraction blocks central route processing and induces peripheral processing.

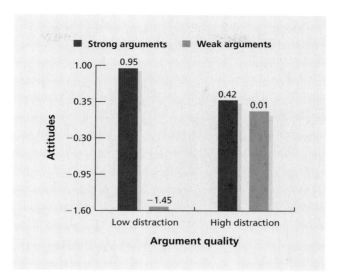

FIGURE 7.10

Attitude Change, Argument Quality, and Distraction

Argument quality had more impact when distraction was low than when distraction was high. This finding suggests that distraction blocks central route processing (and initiates peripheral route processing).

Source: Petty, Wells, and Brock (1976).

3. Mood and Persuasion

Advertisers often try to instill a good mood in their audience when selling their wares. For example, they spruce up their ads with pictures of beautiful beaches, attractive people, and pleasing music. Are these gambits effective? Are people more apt to be persuaded when they are in a good mood than when they are in a bad or neutral mood?

Research in this area indicates that the answer to this question is yes. Across a variety of attitude issues, people are more apt to be persuaded when they are in a good mood than when they are in a bad or more neutral mood. Moreover, this effect is quite general, occurring rather independently of how positive moods are induced. Watching a comedy, eating good food, or sitting in a comfortable and relaxed position have all been shown to increase persuasiveness (Albarracín & Kumkale, 2003; McGuire, 1985).

The dual-process model offers some insight into why people are more apt to be persuaded when they are in a good mood. Bless, Bohner, Schwarz, and Strack (1990) suggest that this occurs because people process information through the peripheral route when they are happy, and consequently are as easily influenced by weak arguments as strong ones. To test their ideas, they first asked college students to write about an important life event. Participants in the happy mood condition were asked to write about a happy life event, and participants in the sad mood condition were asked to write about a sad life event. Afterward, the students listened to a tape-recorded message that announced a fee increase at the student's university beginning next year. For half of the students, 11 strong arguments were used to justify the increase; for the remaining half, 11 weak arguments were used to justify the increase. Finally, students rated their approval for the impending increase.

Bless and colleagues hypothesized that happy moods initiate peripheral route processing and sad moods instigate central route processing. If so, we should expect to find that argument quality had little effect among happy participants but a substantial effect among sad participants. Figure 7.11 reveals just such a pattern. Sad participants were convinced by strong arguments but not by weak ones, but happy participants were just as convinced by weak arguments as they were by strong ones. These findings imply that people process information through the peripheral route when they are happy and through the central route when they are sad (see also Worth & Mackie, 1987).

FIGURE 7.11

Attitude Change, Argument Quality, and Mood

Argument quality affected persuasion when participants were sad, but not when they were happy. These findings suggest that positive moods instigate peripheral route processing and negative moods activate central route processing.

Source: Bless, Bohner, Schwarz, and Strack (1990).

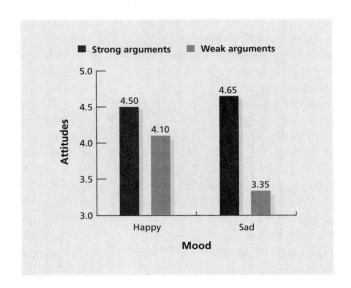

There are several explanations for this effect. Some research shows that happy people are less *willing* to attend to a persuasive message because they fear that doing so will destroy their good mood (Isen, 1984; Wegener, Petty, & Smith, 1995). Other research suggests that happy people are less *able* to attend to a persuasive message because their happy moods distract them and consume a lot of cognitive resources (Mackie & Worth, 1989). Still other research shows that good moods affect persuasion in more than one way. Petty, Schumann, Richman, and Strathman (1993) found that good moods affect persuasion through the peripheral route when involvement is low, but through the central route when involvement is high.

4. Individual Differences: Need for Cognition

So far we have discussed how motivation, ability, and mood states influence whether people process information through the central route or through the peripheral route. A final factor to consider is a personality variable, called need for cognition. Cacioppo and Petty (1982) proposed that people vary with respect to how much they enjoy thinking about problems and issues. Some people like to think a lot and are characteristically in the central mode; other people do not enjoy thinking a lot and are characteristically in the peripheral mode. Table 7.4 presents a scale developed to measure this personality variable.

Although scores on the need for cognition are only weakly related to intelligence, people who score high on the scale do enjoy working on demanding cognitive tasks (for a review, see Cacioppo, Petty, Feinstein, & Jarvis, 1996). Moreover, they tend to process persuasive messages through the central route, and the attitudes they form persist longer, are more resistant to attitude change, and are better predictors of behavior than are the attitudes of people who score low in need for cognition (Cacioppo, Petty, Kao, & Rodriguez, 1986; Cacioppo, Petty, & Morris, 1983; Haugtvedt & Petty, 1992).

C. Summary of the Dual-Process Model

A great deal of theoretical and empirical work has been reviewed in this section. It is apparent that the dual-process model of attitude change enjoys strong support. Numerous investigations have found that there are two routes to attitude change. Sometimes

TABLE 7.4 The Need for Cognition Scale

For each of the statements below, please indicate to what extent the statement is characteristic of you. Please use the following scale:

1 = Extremely uncharacteristic of you (not at all like you)

2 = Somewhat uncharacteristic

3 = Uncertain

4 = Somewhat characteristic of me

5 = Extremely characteristic of me (very much like you)

1. _____ I would prefer complex problems to simple problems.

2. _____ I like to have the responsibility of handling a situation that requires a lot of thinking.

3. _____ Thinking is not my idea of fun.

4. _____ I would rather do something that requires little thought than something that is sure to challenge my intellectual abilities.

5. _____ I try to anticipate and avoid situations where there is a likely chance I will have to think in depth about something.

6. _____ I find satisfaction in deliberating hard and for long hours.

7. _____ I only think as hard as I have to.

8. _____ I prefer to think about small, daily projects to long-term ones.

9. _____ I like tasks that require little thought once I've learned them.

10. _____ The idea of relying on thought to make my way to the top appeals to me.

11. _____ I really enjoy a task that involves coming up with new solutions to problems.

12. _____ Learning new ways to think doesn't excite me very much.

13. _____ I prefer my life to be filled with puzzles that I must solve.

14. _____ The notion of thinking abstractly is not appealing to me.

15. _____ I would prefer a task that is intellectual, difficult, and important to one that is somewhat important but does not require a lot of thought.

16. _____ I feel relief rather than satisfaction after completing a task that requires a lot of mental effort.

17. _____ It's enough for me that something gets the job done; I don't care how or why it works.

18. _____ I usually end up deliberating about issues even when they do not affect me personally.

Scoring: First, reverse your responses to items 3, 4, 5, 7, 8, 9, 12, 16, and 17 (1 = 5)(2 = 4)(4 = 2)(5 = 1). Then add up your scores to all 18 questions. Scores can range from 18 to 90.

Source: Cacioppo, Petty, and Kao (1984).

people process information in a careful, deliberate fashion. When this occurs, attitude change is guided by the perceived merits of the arguments that are presented in the message. Other times, people are not very thoughtful and various peripheral cues, such as source attractiveness and the number of arguments offered to support a conclusion, guide persuasion. Finally, high personal relevance, low distraction, sadness, and high need for cognition promote central route processing, whereas low personal relevance, high distraction, happiness, and low need for cognition promote peripheral route processing.

By specifying the variables that affect which route is operating and identifying the factors that influence persuasion under each route, the dual-process model offers a highly integrative framework for understanding the dynamics of attitude change. In principle, it enables researchers to predict how any given variable will affect persuasion in any given situation. Prediction in the real world is rarely this precise, however. Although laboratory tests of the model provide clear-cut manipulations, matters in real life are usually more complex. For this reason, it is best to think of central and peripheral processing as representing a continuum rather than a dichotomy. People tend to be processing information through one route more than the other, and, as the motivation and ability to process a message increase, persuasion is influenced less by superficial, peripheral cues and more by argument quality.

IV. Persuasion and Health

To this point we have been examining theoretical models of persuasion in an attempt to identify the processes that explain why people change their attitudes in response to persuasive appeals. In this sense, our focus has been on basic research (see Chapter 1). Persuasion also has an applied side, however. Advertisers, politicians, and the government frequently try to change people's attitudes and behavior. In this section, we will consider one of these applications as we explore how persuasion can influence people's health-related attitudes and behavior.

To begin, it's important to note that many of the threats people face to their health today are greatly influenced by lifestyle choices. Smoking, diet, and exercise influence one's susceptibility to heart disease, stroke, and cancer. Similarly, the use of condoms, sunscreen, and seat belts reduces one's susceptibility to sexually transmitted diseases, melanoma, and automobile-related injuries and mortality, respectively. How can we best promote healthy lifestyle choices in people at risk?

A. Message Framing and Health-Promoting Behaviors

One attempt to understand this issue has relied on principles first discussed in Chapter 4. When considering the choices people make in situations involving risk, we noted that people are risk-averse for gains but risk-seeking for losses. Consequently, choices framed in terms of gains are preferred when risk is low, but choices framed in terms of losses are preferred when risk is high.

Using this distinction, Rothman and Salovey (1997) have developed a model to explain when each type of frame will effectively instill proper health habits. They begin by distinguishing two types of health behaviors: prevention and detection. Health-prevention behaviors reduce one's susceptibility to illness or injury. Buckling your seat belt when riding in a car, applying sunscreen while lying on the beach, and using condoms when having sexual intercourse are examples of such behaviors. Health-detection behaviors are

TABLE 7.5   Message Framing and Health-Promoting Behaviors

Behavior	Example	Risk Involved	Most Effective Frame
Prevention	Sunscreen use Exercise Safe sex	Low	Risk is low, so gain frames are best: Emphasize benefits of performing the behavior
Detection	Mammography Prostate exam Stress test	High	Risk is high, so loss frames are best: Emphasize costs of not performing the behavior

somewhat different. Mammograms, prostate examinations, and cholesterol tests allow an illness or condition to be detected, but they don't, in and of themselves, afford any protection from developing the problem. Consequently, health-detection behaviors are riskier than health-prevention behaviors. Because gain frames are more effective when risk is low than when risk is high, Rothman and Salovey believe that gain frames will more effectively persuade people to adopt health-prevention behaviors, but loss frames will more effectively persuade people to adopt health-detection behaviors (see Table 7.5).

Rothman and associates tested these ideas in an experimental study (Rothman, Martino, Bedell, Detweiler, & Salovey, 1999). During the first part of the investigation, the participants read a message about the development of gum disease. Participants in the health-prevention condition read about a mouth rinse that treated gum disease, whereas participants in the health-detection condition read about a mouth rinse that detected the presence of gum disease. Independent of these manipulations, half of the participants read a message that emphasized the benefits of using the rinse (gain frame), and half of the participants read a message that emphasized the dangers of not using the rinse (loss frame). After reading about the mouth rinse, the participants indicated whether they wanted a free sample of the product.

Rothman and colleagues predicted that messages framed in terms of gains would be more effective in the prevention condition, but that messages framed in terms of losses would be more effective in the detection condition. Figure 7.12 provides strong support for these predictions. When prevention was emphasized, participants were more apt to request the product when the message was framed in terms of a gain ("People who use a mouth rinse daily are taking advantage of a safe and effective way to reduce plaque accumulation") than when it was framed in terms of a loss ("People who do not use mouth rinse daily are failing to take advantage of a safe and effective way to reduce plaque accumulation"). In contrast, when detection was emphasized, participants were most apt to request the sample when the message was framed in terms of a loss ("Failing to use a disclosing rinse before brushing limits your ability to detect areas of plaque accumulation") than when it was framed in terms of a gain ("Using a disclosing rinse behavior before brushing enhances your ability to detect areas of plaque accumulation"). Along with other research, these findings establish that message framing effects depend on whether the behavior offers to promote better health or detect an existing health problem (Detweiler, Bedell, Salovey, Pronin, & Rothman, 1999; L. W. Jones, Sinclair, & Courneya, 2003; Lee & Aaker, 2004).

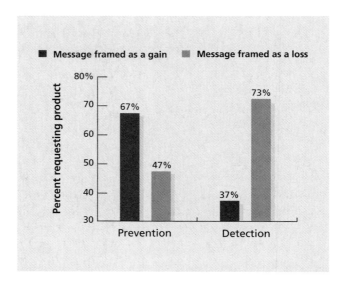

FIGURE 7.12

Message Framing and Persuasion

Messages framed in terms of gains (using this product provides benefits) were more effective when health prevention was emphasized, but messages framed in terms of losses (failing to use this product increases your risk) were more effective when health detection was emphasized.

Source: Rothman, Martino, Bedell, Detweiler, and Salovey (1999).

B. Fear Appeals

The commercial opens with the image of an egg, as a narrator intones, "This is your brain." The egg is then cracked and placed into a sizzling fry pan. "This is your brain on drugs," the narrator continues. "Any questions?" This public service ad is an example of what social psychologists call a fear appeal. Fear appeals are persuasive communications that are designed to frighten people, usually by portraying the seriousness of some behavior in graphic and often morbid detail. Although research in this area is not entirely consistent, fear appeals are generally effective (Eagly & Chaiken, 1993; Janis & Feshbach, 1953; Leventhal, 1970; Witte, 1992). Across a variety of topics (e.g., drug abuse, seat belt use, AIDS prevention), people who receive high-fear messages are more persuaded than are people who receive low-fear messages.

High-fear messages should be accompanied by two assurances in order to achieve long-term behavioral change (Dabbs & Leventhal, 1966; Leventhal, 1970; Mewborn & Rogers, 1979; R. W. Rogers, 1983). First, people need to be assured that the recommended behavior will effectively reduce the risks they are facing (Dad, de Wit, & Stroebe, 2003). Second, people need to be assured that they are capable of performing the recommended behavior. This latter assurance is usually provided by giving people detailed plans of action that specify exactly what they should do (Leventhal, Singer, & Jones, 1965; Leventhal, Watts, & Pagano, 1967). To illustrate, scaring people about the dangers associated with smoking may help them to quit only if we also convince people that quitting smoking will greatly reduce the risks they face (e.g., you can avoid lung cancer, emphysema, and heart disease if you quit smoking now) and then convince them that they are capable of quitting (e.g., you'll use a nicotine patch, carry chewing gum at all times, and avoid restaurants and bars that allow smoking).

C. Overcoming Defensiveness

To be effective, fear appeals must provoke fear without invoking defensiveness. Simply put, people don't want to believe they are at risk for developing an awful disease, and they will defend against this belief by denying their susceptibility if their anxiety and fear become too great (Devos-Comby & Salovey, 2002; Giner-Sorolla & Chaiken, 1997; Liberman & Chaiken, 1992; Sengupta & Johar, 2001).

Applying Steele's (1988) self-affirmation theory (see Chapter 6), D. A. K. Sherman, Nelson, and Steele (2000) demonstrated one strategy for avoiding this pitfall. These investigators had a group of women read a research report linking caffeine consumption to the development of fibrocystic disease, a precursor of breast cancer. Some of the women were heavy coffee drinkers and some were not. Hence, the report posed a greater threat to the former group than to the latter. After reading this article, some of the women were allowed to affirm their self-worth by reminding themselves that they had many fine values, whereas other participants were not given this opportunity. Finally, all of the participants indicated how strong they thought the link was between caffeine consumption and fibrocystic disease, and how important it was for women to reduce their intact of caffeine.

Sherman and colleagues reasoned that, in the absence of any opportunity to affirm their self-worth, heavy coffee drinkers should react to the report defensively by denying its validity. This defensiveness should be reduced, however, following a self-affirmation opportunity. Figure 7.13 shows that these predictions were confirmed. In the absence of the self-affirmation manipulation, coffee drinkers believed the report was less valid than did non–coffee drinkers. These differences were reversed,

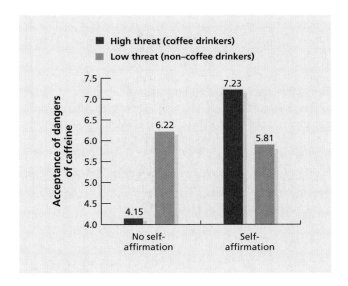

FIGURE 7.13

Self-Affirmation and Defensive Reactions to Threatening Health-Relevant Information

Coffee drinkers defensively denied the validity of a report linking caffeine consumption to fibrocystic disease when they were not given an opportunity to affirm their self-worth by reminding themselves that they possessed many fine values, but accepted the report's validity when they were given an opportunity to affirm their self-worth.

Source: D. A. K. Sherman, Nelson, and Steele (2000).

however, when participants were given the chance to affirm their self-worth. Apparently, defensiveness can be overcome if people are first given the chance to remind themselves that they are generally good, moral, and competent (see also G. L. Cohen, Aronson, & Steele, 2000; Raghunathan & Trope, 2002).

CHAPTER SUMMARY

- Carl Hovland led the Yale Communication and Attitude Program. Hovland believed that attitudes are verbal habits that are acquired and changed through principles of reinforcement. In Hovland's model, message learning sets the stage for attitude change, but attitude change ultimately depends on whether incentives strong enough to break prior habit tendencies are provided.

- Hovland and his colleagues found that numerous factors influence persuasion, including source expertise and likability, the qualities of the message, and the match between the message and the audience's values.

- The impact of a low credibility source increases over time. This effect, termed the *sleeper effect,* occurs only when the low credibility cue is received after the message is received.

- Cultural factors influence persuasion. Advertisements that carry individualistic themes are more prevalent and persuasive in Western cultures than in East Asian cultures. The reverse is true for advertisements that emphasize collectivistic themes.

- Drawing on central tenets of Gestalt psychology, Asch argued that the meaning of any message is variable, and that context determines what the message means. If people change their attitudes, Asch argued, it is because they find the message to be convincing and compelling.

- Social judgment theory assumes that a person's existing attitude serves as a reference point or anchor. Messages close to one's own attitude fall within the latitude of acceptance and are subject to assimilation effects; messages that fall far from one's own attitude lie within the latitude of rejection and are subject to contrast effects. Personal involvement influences latitude width, such that the latitude of acceptance is smaller as involvement increases.

- Cognitive response theory assumes that all attitude change occurs as a function of the thoughts a person has while receiving a persuasive communication. Some of these thoughts support the arguments being presented; others (called counterarguments) oppose it. Some of these thoughts are repetitions of arguments presented in the message; others are original.

- Research testing cognitive response theory has produced mixed results. Under some conditions, people's cognitive responses predict attitude change, but under other conditions they do not.

- The dual-process model of attitude change assumes that there are two routes to attitude change. When people are motivated *and* able to carefully consider the arguments in a persuasive appeal, they process information through the central route and their cognitive responses predict attitude change. When people aren't motivated *or* able to carefully consider the arguments they are receiving, they process information through the peripheral route and their cognitive responses do not predict attitude change.

• Many persuasive appeals target health-relevant behaviors. Messages framed as gains are most effective when health prevention is emphasized, but messages framed as losses are more effective when the focus is on health detection. Fear appeals can also be effective, especially if they provide clear guidelines for action and don't create defensiveness.

KEY TERMS

message learning approach, 240

sleeper effect, 244

social judgment theory, 254

inoculation theory of persuasion, 258

forewarning effects, 258

cognitive response theory, 259

central route to attitude change, 261

peripheral route to attitude change, 261

ADDITIONAL READING

Go to the Student Edition of the Online Learning Center for this text (www.mhhe.com/brown) and log in to read the following journal articles, which relate to the content of this chapter:

• Petty, R. E., & Cacioppo, J. T. (1984). The effects of involvement on responses to argument quantity and quality: Central and peripheral routes to persuasion.

• Han, S., & Shavitt, S. (1994). Persuasion and culture: Advertising appeals in individualistic and collectivistic cultures.

Social Influence

Just after midnight on the morning of September 28, 1997, Boston police were called to a fraternity on the campus of the Massachusetts Institute of Technology. Scott Krueger, an 18-year-old pledge of Phi Gamma Delta, was in an alcohol-induced coma after drinking excessively at a fraternity party. Krueger died three days later, setting off a nationwide examination of the prevalence of binge drinking on college campuses. When asked why so many students drink heavily, one student replied, "When you go to a party, it's not socially acceptable to just sit there and have a couple of drinks. You have to drink as many you can, especially around the time you want to get into a fraternity."

Peer pressure is one of the strongest forces we face in social life (Cialdini & Goldstein, 2004; Cialdini & Trost, 1998). Although we rarely pay a price as severe as the one Scott Krueger paid, we all succumb to the power of social influence. The cars we drive, the clothes we wear, and the music we listen to are all influenced by the tastes, preferences, and behavior of others. In this chapter you will study basic principles of **social influence**—the process by which other people affect your own thoughts, feelings, and actions.

Table 8.1 shows that social influence forms a continuum, depending on the amount of pressure involved. With imitation, we change our behavior to match the behavior of others without feeling any pressure to do so. Conformity is another form of social influence. Here our behavior changes as a result of real or imagined social pressures. Conformity probably explains why so many college students engage in binge drinking: They fear being excluded or ostracized, so they drink to excess even though they know it is bad for their health. Compliance is a third form of social influence. Here our behavior is changed in response to a direct request. If you have ever done something on a dare or bought something you didn't need from an assertive salesperson, you have displayed compliance. Obedience represents a final form of social influence. Here we do what an authority figure tells us to do.

TABLE 8.1 Four Forms of Social Influence

Type of Social Influence	Description	Amount of Pressure
Imitation	Behavior change in the absence of social pressure.	No pressure
Conformity	Behavior change in response to real or imagined social pressure.	
Compliance	Behavior change in response to an explicit request to perform some action.	
Obedience	Behavior change in response to a demand to perform some action.	Extreme pressure

Social influence varies according to how much pressure is involved. Imitation involves no pressure, conformity involves peer pressure, compliance involves an explicit request to perform some behavior, and obedience is a response to a direct order to perform some action.

I. Imitation

Many animals exhibit imitative behaviors ("Monkey see, monkey do"), and people are no exception (R. W. Byrne & Russon, 1998). Infants as young as two days old have been found to mimic adults' facial expressions (Meltzoff & Moore, 1993). Later in life, we smile when others smile, yawn when others yawn, and cough when others cough (Hatfield, Cacioppo, & Rapson, 1994; Neumann & Strack, 2000). Laughter is also contagious. Comedy shows on television almost always have a laugh track, because people tend to laugh more when other people are laughing too.

A. Behavioral Mimicry

Mimicking another person's behavior is sometimes intentional. "Imitation," as the saying goes, "is the sincerest form of flattery," and we can exploit this effect for personal gain. If we are trying to impress a date or curry favor with a boss, we can increase our odds of success by subtly copying that person's movements or imitating his or her facial expressions or tone of voice. We might think people don't benefit by engaging in such behaviors, but they do. Waitresses, for example, receive higher tips when they imitate their customers (van Baaren, Holland, Steenaert, & van Knippenberg, 2003).

Imitation can also occur automatically, without awareness or motive. When we interact with another person, we may unintentionally find ourselves mimicking his or her movements, speech patterns, and expressions. Chartrand and Bargh (1999) provided an experimental demonstration of this effect. They had participants interact separately with two confederates. One of the confederates rubbed his or her face while talking but did not shake his or her foot. The other confederate exhibited the opposite behavior pattern. Figure 8.1 shows that participants mimicked the confederate's behavior. They touched their face more often when interacting with a face-touching confederate, and shook their foot more often when interacting with a foot-shaking confederate.

FIGURE 8.1

Behavioral Mimicry during a Social Interaction

Without being aware that they were doing so, participants imitated the behavior of a confederate during a social interaction.

Source: Chartrand and Bargh (1999).

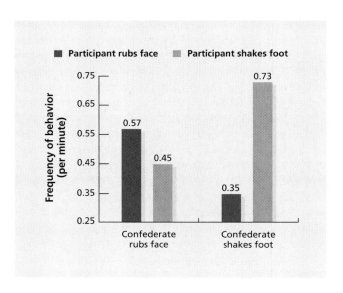

B. Contagion Effects

Imitative behavior can also occur on a larger scale. Every so often, a school, library, or hotel is evacuated after several of its inhabitants report being ill. The syndrome starts when one person complains of rather vague symptoms, such as dizziness or shortness of breath. Other people soon notice that they are having similar problems, and seek medical attention. When environmental engineers scour the building, they are unable to find any physical cause, and when the victims undergo medical testing, no evidence of any physiological illness is found. What is going on? According to one team of researchers, the victims are suffering from a form of contagion known as mass psychogenic illness. (T. F. Jones et al., 2000). Without knowing it, they have mimicked the symptoms of other people.

Behaviors are also subject to contagion effects. Criminologists have long known that copycat crimes follow in the wake of highly publicized crimes. For example, following the September 11, 2001, terrorist attacks, a young man in Tampa, Florida, commandeered an airplane and flew it into a building. Even fictional crimes have been imitated. After viewing a scene depicted in the Clint Eastwood movie *Magnum Force,* two armed men forced the patrons of a convenience store to drink Drano (Leland, 1995).

Imitation can even produce suicide. Two hundred years ago, the German writer Johann Wolfgang von Goethe wrote a novel called *The Sorrows of the Young Werther,* a story of a young man who commits suicide. Suicide rates seemed to rise following publication of the book, prompting some social commentators to wonder whether a highly publicized suicide could prompt people to kill themselves through imitation. The issue was debated until sociologist David Phillips undertook a systematic examination of the issue. Using the period from 1946 to 1968 as his sample, Phillips calculated the occurrence of suicides in the months preceding and following the publication of a suicide in two New York City newspapers.

Figure 8.2 shows that suicide rates rose dramatically following the publication of these stories, and remained elevated for one month afterward. Follow-up analyses established that these effects were matched to the geographic area in which the suicide occurred. For example, if a highly publicized suicide occurred in England, suicide

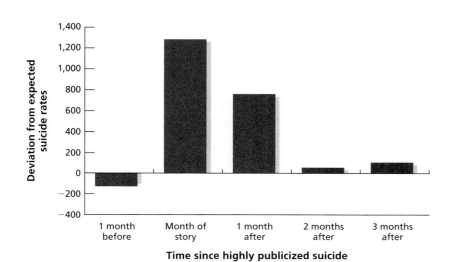

FIGURE 8.2

Suicide as Imitation

Suicides increase in the month after a highly publicized suicide, suggesting that they are affected by imitation.

Source: Phillips (1974).

rates were unusually high in England but not in New York. Moreover, the effect was especially strong among adolescents, a group widely considered to be highly impressionable (Phillips & Carstensen, 1986). In consideration of this evidence, Phillips believes that people tend to imitate suicides reported in the press, with each story resulting in an average increase of 53 suicides.

II. Conformity

Imitation occurs in the absence of social pressure. When we yawn or cough when other people do so, it's not because we feel that we need to imitate these behaviors. In contrast, **conformity** occurs when we change our behavior in response to real or imagined social pressures. In this section, we will examine when and why people conform.

A. Social Norms

If you are like most people, you face the front when riding in an elevator, rise during the playing of the national anthem, and stand back several feet while waiting in line to use an automated teller machine (ATM). Moreover, you probably perform these behaviors without thinking too much about them. That's because your actions are determined by unwritten rules of social conduct called **social norms.**

1. Three Types of Social Norms

Social norms are of three types. First, there are norms specific to particular groups. For example, a ninth-grader attending high school may quickly learn that behaviors acceptable in middle school, such as drinking milk with lunch, are no longer cool. Among other things, social norms influence the choices we make about how to dress, gesture, and speak. Sometimes norms apply to an entire segment of society. Ties and coats were once mandatory attire for many workers, but dress codes have been relaxed in recent years and some companies even have a "casual Friday," allowing workers to wear sports shirts and blue jeans.

Other norms operate in specific cultures or societies. For example, Americans shake hands and look each other in the eye when they greet, while Japanese bow and avoid making eye contact. Similar norms govern other common behaviors, such as gift giving and table manners. In Bolivia, it is customary for dinner guests to show their appreciation by cleaning their plates; in India, this is considered an affront and you should leave food on your plate to signal that the portions were plentiful and generous (Axtell, 1993).

Finally, there are universal rules of conduct. An obvious example is the incest taboo, which forbids sexual relations between family members. In many cultures, this norm has become codified and is now a matter of law. Another universal norm is known as the norm of reciprocity (Gouldner, 1960). This norms dictates that we are "obliged" to return a favor to someone who does a favor for us. Violate this norm and you risk being labeled a freeloader or moocher. The norm of responsibility constitutes a third universal norm (Berkowitz & Daniels, 1963). According to this norm, we have a duty to help those who are worse off than we are, especially if they are not responsible for their plight.

2. Positive Models and Adherence to Norms

Norms generally operate in the background and we tend to notice them only when they are violated. Milgram and Sabini (1978) report an interesting demonstration of this fact. They instructed their research assistants to approach passengers on a subway train and, without offering any reason, ask them to give up their seats. The assistants had great difficulty violating this common norm of courtesy. In fact, many were so uncomfortable they either refused to engage in the behavior or feigned illness to justify their request.

Because norms are often imperceptible, people need to be reminded of them from time to time. Social scientists have used reminders to promote positive social behaviors. For example, water conservation is a concern in California. During one particularly bad drought, citizens were encouraged to take shorter showers and to turn the water off while soaping their bodies. To see whether the presence of a positive role model would increase adherence to this norm, E. Aronson and O'Leary (1982–1983) conducted a field experiment in the men's locker room of the University of California, Santa Cruz. No model was present in the control condition, but in an experimental condition, a confederate modeled the appropriate behavior by turning the water off while he soaped up. In a third condition, two models were present. Compared to those in the control condition, students who viewed the positive models were much more likely to conform to the save-water norm.

3. Negative Models and Adherence to Norms

Under some conditions, even a negative model can increase adherence to a norm. To understand this effect, we need to distinguish two types of norms (Cialdini & Trost, 1998). *Injunctive norms* indicate what behavior is expected or approved of in a given situation. For example, you know you are not supposed to litter by carelessly tossing a soda can out the car window. This is an injunctive norm, because it pertains to what you ought to do. *Descriptive norms* are a bit different. Instead of conveying information about ideal behavior, they provide information about what people actually do. Many people litter peanut shells at a baseball game or leave their candy wrappers in a movie theater because they believe it is acceptable to litter in such places.

Cialdini, Reno, and Kallgren (1990) argued that a negative model can increase compliance with a norm when an injunctive norm is salient. To test this prediction, they conducted a field experiment in a parking lot on the Arizona State University campus. Researchers put a handbill on the windshield of each student's car, and then noted whether students littered this handbill. In one condition (negative model) the students saw another student litter his or her handbill; no model was present in a control condition. One more variable was experimentally manipulated. In one condition, the parking lot was filled with litter and debris, planted by the experimenters (coffee cups, cigarette butts), but in another condition, the litter was swept into a corner and the parking lot itself was clean. Figure 8.3 shows the percentage of participants who littered in each of these conditions. When the parking lot was filled with litter, seeing someone else litter increased littering. However, when the parking lot was clean, seeing someone else litter decreased littering. These findings establish that a negative model can increase conformity when an injunctive norm is salient.

B. Why People Conform

Not only are people usually unaware of social norms but they also fail to appreciate their power and effect. To understand this point, think of a time when you conformed to a group standard. Perhaps you adopted a particular style of dress or espoused a particular belief or point of view. What prompted you to conform? Social psychologists have identified three possible reasons (M. Deutsch & Gerard, 1955; Kelman, 1961).

First, you might have gone along because you thought it was the right thing to do, a process social psychologists call **informational influence.** The need to hold correct judgments or to be right is an important motivator of human behavior, and other people

FIGURE 8.3

Littering and Social Norms

Seeing a confederate litter a parking lot increased littering in a dirty, littered environment, but decreased littering in a clean environment. These findings suggest that a negative model (someone who litters) can have a positive effect under some conditions.

Source: Cialdini, Reno, and Kallgren (1990).

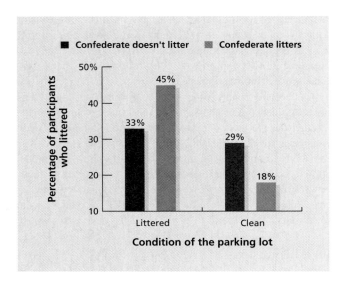

frequently provide useful information about what is right and wrong. For example, suppose you and your friends are discussing the best way to get to a concert in another city. If they know the way better than you do, you will probably drive the route they recommend. In this case, your conformity is motivated by a desire to do what is best or right.

Being right is not the only goal we have in social life. We also want to be accepted and liked, and to avoid being rejected and disliked (Baumeister & Leary, 1995). Often this need leads people to do what other people are doing. For example, to gain acceptance into a particular social group, you may change your hairstyle or your clothing. We will use the term **normative influence** when referring to a process in which people conform in order to win the approval of others, or to avoid their disapproval. Under normative influence we strive not to be accurate but to be liked.

Finally, conformity can be driven by a desire to think of ourselves as being a certain kind of person. Many adolescents who start smoking do so not only because of peer pressure (normative influence) but also because they think it makes them cool and sophisticated. We will use the term **identity influence** when referring to a process in which people conform in order to adopt a particular identity.

In most cases, these three forms of social influence combine to produce conformity. This point was illustrated in an early study by Newcomb (1943). The study was conducted at Bennington College, an elite school located in rural Vermont. The students, all women, came from economically privileged homes and had been raised with traditional, conservative values. In contrast, the faculty at Bennington was quite liberal. Newcomb observed how the women's conservative attitudes changed as a result of their liberal environment. Newcomb found that the women's attitudes became increasingly liberal during their college years, because they were taught to believe liberal policies were better (informational influence), because young women with liberal views became the most popular students on campus (normative influence), and because the students wanted to view themselves as enlightened intellectuals who were sophisticated and urbane (identity influence).

Because they often operate together in real-world settings, it is difficult to know which of the three forms of social influence is dominant in any particular situation. The extent to which behavior occurs in private provides a clue. For example, if a person smokes only when he is with his peers and not when he's alone, we infer that

TABLE 8.2 Why People Conform

Reason for Conforming	Definition and Dominant Motivation	Relevant Personal Variables	Relevant Variables of the Influencing Agent	Does Public Behavior Persist in Private?	Example
Informational influence	Conformity motivated by a desire to be right	Uncertainty, lack of experience	Expertise	Yes: When people are motivated to be right, their private behavior matches their public behavior.	"I wear Nike clothes because I think they are of high quality."
Normative influence	Conformity motivated by a desire to be liked, accepted, and approved	Loneliness; need for approval and attention	Attractiveness of the group	No: If we are conforming only to gain someone's approval, we conform when we are with them but not when we are alone.	"I wear Nike clothes when I go out with friends because they think Nike is hip and they won't let me hang with them if I wear another brand."
Identity influence	Conformity motivated by a desire to think of ourselves as being a certain way	Identity confusion	Role model's desirability	Yes: If we are conforming in order to think of ourselves as having a particular characteristic, we will display the behavior whether we are alone or not.	"I wear Nike clothes because I want to be like Tiger Woods, and he wears Nike clothes."

smoking occurs because of normative influence. In contrast, if a person smokes when he is alone as well as when he is out with his friends, we assume that identity influence is operating (the person thinks smoking makes him sophisticated and mature) or informational influence is operating (the person thinks smoking calms his or her nerves).

Table 8.2 summarizes the three forms of social influence we have distinguished. As you can see, associated with each form are variables pertaining to the person who is being influenced (termed *personal variables*) and to the person or group who is the source of influence (termed the *influencing agent*). Informational influence is most apt to occur when we lack experience or knowledge and other people are considered experts. Normative influence is most apt to occur when we are particularly in need of social approval and other people are highly attractive or desirable (e.g., the most popular kids in school). Finally, identity influence is likely when we are unsure about who we are and other people project a desirable image (such as rock stars or professional athletes).

Keeping these issues in mind, can you think of a time in your life when you didn't know for sure how to behave, were greatly in need of social approval, and were uncertain about the kind of person you wanted to be? For most people, this state of affairs describes adolescence. It is no wonder, then, that teens are highly conforming. During this stage of life, people are particularly dependent and highly vulnerable to social influence.

C. Sherif's Experiment: Conformity in an Ambiguous Situation

Some of social psychology's most important experiments illustrate the principles described in Table 8.2. For example, in 1936, a Turkish emigrant, Muzafer Sherif, was interested in understanding how norms are formed and transmitted across generations. He reasoned that social agreement plays a role. When objective reality is ambiguous, people rely on the judgments of others and a norm emerges through a process of social consensus.

Sherif (1936) conducted an ingenious experiment to test this idea. This research relied on an optical illusion known as the autokinetic effect. When a stationary dot of light is viewed against a dark background, the light appears to move. The perceived movement is illusory. Our brain's natural inclination to compensate for the constant movement of our own eyes is thwarted when the room is completely dark and no frame of reference is available. As a result, the brain mistakes the eye's own movement for object movement (hence the name *autokinetic—auto* meaning "self" and *kinetic* meaning "of or related to motion"). Although most everyone shows this effect, people differ with respect to how much movement they perceive. This gave Sherif an opportunity to test his hypothesis about group consensus.

Imagine yourself as a participant in the experiment. Initially, you are brought into a darkened room. After acclimating a bit to the surroundings, you focus your attention on a dot of light 15 feet away and are asked to estimate how many inches the light is moving. After making your decision, the light disappears and comes back a few seconds later, and you make another estimate. Sherif found that each participant established a personal norm—a standard or reference point pertaining to a particular range of movement—but that this frame of reference differed from one participant to the next. Some participants thought the light was moving a lot (about 10 inches), while others thought it was moving hardly at all (1 or 2 inches). (Remember, the light isn't really moving at all but only appears to be moving.)

A few days later, you return to the laboratory to repeat the experiment, but this time there is another participant who also underwent the task alone. The two of you announce your judgments aloud, so that you can hear what the other participant thinks as well. How will the other participant's perception influence your own? The data displayed in Figure 8.4 provide an answer. Although participants started out with their own opinion, the opinions gradually converged on a group norm. By the end, the participants tended to agree on how much the light had moved.

The ambiguity of the situation is an important aspect of Sherif's research. The participants were viewing an optical illusion in which it was difficult to gauge how far the light appeared to be moving. In this situation, we assume that informational influence

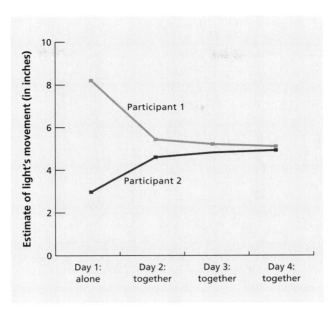

FIGURE 8.4

Sherif's Study of Social Consensus and the Autokinetic Effect

Participants were asked to estimate the movement of a light under two conditions: alone and then with others. Although participants had unique judgments when performing the task alone, the judgments converged toward a group norm when the participants performed the task together. These findings suggest that social norms can form through social consensus.

Source: Sherif (1936).

is operating. Without an external frame of reference, people reasonably relied on the judgments of others. Follow-up research supports this interpretation. Even when tested alone one year after the experiment, participants continued to use the standard established by their group (Rohrer, Baron, Hoffman, & Swander, 1954). It is interesting to note, however, that participants were unaware that they had been influenced by other people. In interviews conducted at the end of the experimental sessions, the majority of participants reported that they had formed their own opinions and were not swayed by other people's opinions.

This finding raises an important point. Most people value independence and do not like to think they are swayed by other people's opinions. This need is strong enough to blind us to the power of social influence. Even when we think we are doing our own thing, we very well may be going along with the crowd. Of course, some people value independence more than others do (C. R. Snyder & Fromkin, 1980), and uniqueness is more highly valued in some cultures than in others (Kim & Drolet, 2003; Kim & Markus, 1999). Nonetheless, we are all susceptible to the power of social influence, particularly when we are placed in a novel, ambiguous situation.

D. Asch's Experiment: Conformity in an Unambiguous Situation

Solomon Asch was not convinced by Sherif's findings. As noted in Chapter 1, Asch was a Gestalt psychologist who fled Germany when Hitler rose to power. Among other things, Gestalt psychologists believe that perception cannot be influenced by motivational factors (see Chapter 2). It would be maladaptive, they argued, if people were free to decide what to see and what not to see. For this and other reasons, Asch believed that Sherif had succeeding in demonstrating conformity only because he had used an ambiguous stimulus. Had he used a more unambiguous standard, Asch contended, people would rely on their own judgments and would not be swayed by the opinions of others.

FIGURE 8.5

Line Judgment Task
Used in Asch's
Conformity Studies

The participants must
identity which of the comparison lines is closest in
length to the standard line.
The task is relatively easy,
and participants made very
few errors when perform-
ing the task alone. But
when placed into a situa-
tion where other people
gave the wrong answer,
participants conformed
about a third of the time.

Source: Asch (1955).

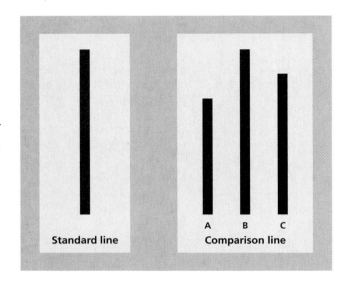

Standard line   A   B   C
                     Comparison line

1. The Experimental Procedure

Asch (1955, 1956) developed an experiment to prove that people would not succumb
to social pressure when judging an unambiguous stimulus. As before, imagine yourself being a participant in this experiment. When you arrive for an experiment on
visual acuity, you find six other people seated in a semicircle around a table. The only
seat open is number 6 (next to the last), so you sit down and listen as the experimenter explains that, on each of 18 trials, he will be showing the group two cards
(see Figure 8.5). The line on the left-hand card serves as a standard, and your task
will be to identify which of the lines on the right-hand card is closest in length to the
line on the left. Finally, you learn that each of the group members will be calling out
his answer in order, going around the table. Unbeknownst to you, the rest of the participants are actually confederates of the experimenter, and they have been trained to
give wrong answers on 12 of the 18 trials.

   The experiment proceeds rather uneventfully at first, with everyone calling out the
correct answer. However, on the third set of lines, all of the participants seated before
you call out the wrong answer. At this point, you confront a dilemma. Should you
rely on your own senses—which tell you the others are wrong, or should you conform to their judgments in order to fit in with the group? Although you probably think
you wouldn't conform, Asch found that almost 75 percent of his participants went
along with the incorrect majority on at least 1 of the 12 critical trials, and 50 percent
went along at least half of the time. Finally, approximately 37 percent of the participants conformed on any given trial.

2. Possible Confounds and Limiting Conditions

The findings in Asch's conformity studies created quite a stir. Many social psychologists were disturbed to learn that individuals readily succumbed to social pressures and
meekly surrendered their own good judgment. Several researchers raised objections
and numerous others made attempts to identify variables that moderate or modify the
effect.

Task Difficulty. One objection to Asch's findings was that the task was harder than it seemed. To examine this possibility, Asch had some participants write down their answers, without expressing their opinions aloud or sharing them with the group. Virtually no one made a mistake under these circumstances, demonstrating that the visual discrimination task was very easy. Because the task was unambiguous, and because behaviors observed in public did not persist in private, we assume that normative influence was operating in Asch's study. Participants publicly went along to avoid appearing different, but they did not privately accept the group's judgments.

The Era. The political and social climate that characterized America in the 1950s may also have played a role in the level of conformity exhibited by the participants in Asch's study. Gripped by the cold war and in the midst of the McCarthy era, Americans were politically conservative and concerned with preserving cultural unity and homogeneity. By the millions, families fled to the suburbs to live in identical houses in identical neighborhoods with identical swing sets and identical school yards. This state of affairs contrasts with the "Do your own thing" mantra of the 1960s and the "Me first" climate of the 1980s. Might Americans be less conforming today than they were in the 1950s? Although conformity has declined a bit over the years, studies done in the 1990s showed similar levels of conformity to those done in the 1950s. (R. Bond & Smith, 1996; Larsen, 1990). It does not seem, therefore, that the findings are specific to any particular era.

The Role of Culture. At several points throughout the text, we have emphasized that some cultures are individualistic and value independence, whereas others are collectivistic and value group harmony. As you might expect, conformity tends to be higher in collectivistic countries than in individualistic ones (R. Bond & Smith, 1996). Don't forget, however, that conformity is high even in countries that are highly individualistic, such as the United States. This suggests that the pressures people face in Asch's line-judgment task are of considerable weight for all.

Gender and Conformity. Only men participated in Asch's original study, leading researchers to wonder whether women would behave differently in this situation. Although the differences are slight, women tend to be a bit more conforming in the situation Asch designed than men are (R. Bond & Smith, 1996; Eagly & Carli, 1981). This is most likely because of socialization: Women are generally taught to be more compromising and accommodating than men are, and this leads them to be slightly more apt to conform, especially on tasks that emphasize stereotypically male abilities and qualities.

3. Contextual Variables That Influence Conformity

The variables we have been reviewing are rather static ones. They pertain to the era, culture, or type of person who conforms. Although some of these variables are important ones to consider, their influence tends to be modest. Variables of a more contextual nature play an even greater role in the situation Asch designed.

The Size of the Majority. Faction size is a contextual variable that appears to influence conformity. In a follow-up study, Asch (1955) examined whether conformity increases with the size of the majority. For example, in variations on the basic line-judgment study, participants performed the task with either just 1 confederate or with

FIGURE 8.6

The Size of the Majority
Affects Conformity

In Asch's research, a
majority of 3 produced just
as much conformity as a
majority of 15.

Source: Asch (1956).

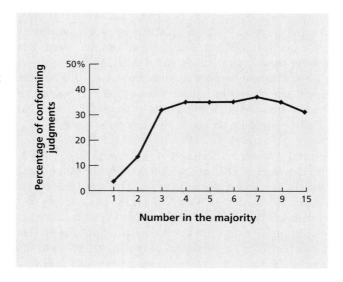

as many as 16 confederates. Figure 8.6 shows that the size of the majority matters, but only up to a point. Once three people are in agreement, conformity is not appreciably increased by the addition of more members.

Faction size is more important when normative influence is operating, as was true in Asch's study, than when informational influence is operating, as was true in Sherif's study (J. D. Campbell & Fairey, 1989). When a task is difficult and people need the judgments of others to help them make a decision, even one person can exert a lot of social influence. The situation is different when people can clearly see what is right and don't need the information other people provide. Under these conditions, people find it much easier to hold fast to their opinion when disagreeing with just one other person than when bucking the opinion of a group of three or more. This is one of the reasons why high school cliques and gangs need to be composed of several members to be effective (Latané, 1981; Latané & Wolf, 1981; Tanford & Penrod, 1984).

The Importance of Unanimity. Asch (1955) also examined whether people are more apt to conform to a unanimous majority than to one that lacks unanimity. In a variation on his original study, Asch had one of the confederates give the right answer on the critical trials. Only 6 percent of the participants conformed under these conditions. Clearly, having an ally in dissent freed participants from the normative pressures they faced and allowed them to remain independent.

In fact, conformity drops dramatically even when a fellow dissenter voices an erroneous judgment (V. L. Allen & Levine, 1969). To illustrate using the example shown in Figure 8.5, suppose the first three confederates announce that C is the correct line and the fourth announces that A is the correct line. Even though A is no more correct than C is, you would probably say that B is the correct line rather than go along with the majority. As long as you are not the only one who disagrees with the majority, you will probably not conform in the situation Asch developed.

The Importance of Importance. A final variable to consider with regard to conformity is task importance. In the studies conducted by Sherif and Asch, participants were making judgments of very little consequence. No one's welfare was at stake, and the participants themselves suffered no negative consequences by caving in to the majority. Perhaps, some researchers suggested, people are less conforming when judgmental errors are made more costly.

R. S. Baron, Vandelo, and Brunsman (1996) conducted an investigation to examine the manner in which task importance affects conformity. Recognizing that most psychology students have heard about Asch's study, Baron and colleagues devised a new method of assessing conformity. They told participants they were measuring the accuracy of eyewitness testimony, and that the participants would view a slide of an alleged perpetrator and then identify the perpetrator from a lineup of several other men. Notice how this is similar to Asch's study, in that participants first view a standard and are then asked to match the standard against several alternatives. Moreover, as in Asch's study, experimental confederates were trained to give wrong answers on several trials, thereby allowing the investigators to see whether participants conformed to the erroneous judgments of others.

Two variables were experimentally manipulated in this study. First, some participants viewed the slides twice and had five seconds to look at them before making a judgment. This made the discrimination task rather easy, creating a situation similar to the one Asch's participants faced. Other participants viewed the photographs only once and were given only half a second to see them. This made the task quite difficult, creating a situation similar to the one Sherif's participants faced. The second variable was the importance of making a correct identification. Some participants were told the task was unimportant and their performance didn't mean anything, whereas others were told the task was quite important and that the person who made the most correct identifications would be eligible to win a $20 prize.

Figure 8.7 shows the rates of conformity in Baron and colleagues' study as a function of these experimental manipulations. When the task was low in difficulty, participants were less apt to conform to the erroneous majority when the task was important than when it was unimportant. This suggests that the participants in Asch's study may have gone along, at least in part, because there was no good reason to dissent. The situation is quite different when the task was difficult. Here, people were more apt to conform when importance was high than when it was low. Apparently, when the task is difficult and the stakes are high, we reasonably err on the side of caution and use the judgments of others as important sources of information.

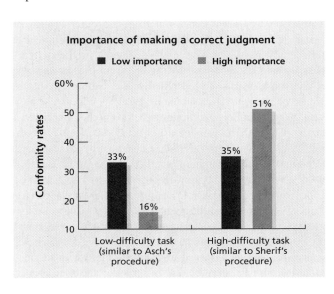

FIGURE 8.7

Conformity, Task Difficulty, and the Importance of Making a Correct Decision

High importance *decreased* conformity when the task was relatively easy (and normative influence was operating), but *increased* conformity when the task was relatively difficult (and informational influence was operating).

Source: R. S. Baron, Vandello, and Brunsman (1996).

What, then, can we conclude from studies of conformity in group settings? First, when a task is difficult, we assume that other people's perceptions and judgments provide useful information, and we use this information to form our own perceptions and judgments. Moreover, the more important it is to be right, the stronger this informational influence is. When a task is easy and we don't need the judgments of others as sources of information, we conform when there is little reason to be right but remain independent when there is reason to be correct.

E. Conformity and Group Decision Making

In Asch's study, participants were entirely free to make their own decisions. This situation contrasts with one in which group members are required to reach a common judgment. For example, several advertising executives might meet to chart a collective marketing strategy. The individuals may have different ideas at the outset, but ultimately they are expected to come to some agreement about a course of action. What role does conformity play in situations like these?

In the 1950s, a group of researchers led by Leon Festinger embarked on an ambitious program of research to answer this question (Festinger, 1950; Festinger & Thibaut, 1951; Schachter, 1951). Festinger noted that groups need to have a uniform outlook on matters of relevance to the group. Pressure toward uniformity, as Festinger called it, derives from two sources. First, to accomplish specific goals, groups must agree on where they are headed and how they are going to coordinate their efforts to reach their destination; this need creates pressures toward uniformity. The second source of pressure is more psychological. Pressures toward uniformity also arise from a need to have a shared view of social reality. According to Festinger, group members need to believe they share the same beliefs, attitudes, and values. Anything that threatens the perception of a shared view threatens group harmony.

1. Reacting to Deviants

Festinger and associates used these assumptions about pressures toward uniformity to generate predictions about communication patterns in small groups (Festinger, 1951; Festinger & Thibaut, 1951). They hypothesized that a dissenter would initially receive a great deal of communication from the other group members as they attempted to persuade him or her to adopt the majority's position. If efforts to sway the dissenter failed, however, Festinger and colleagues predicted that the dissenter would be disparaged and excluded from further group discussions.

Schachter (1951) tested whether the pattern expected by Festinger and colleagues would be particularly pronounced in highly cohesive groups. Cohesiveness refers to how well group members get along with one another and agree about the group's purpose and goals. Although cohesiveness generally has positive consequences for group functioning (Mullen & Cooper, 1994), Schachter hypothesized that cohesive groups are less tolerant of dissent than are noncohesive groups. To test this hypothesis, Schachter began by dividing participants into groups in such a way that half of the groups were highly cohesive and half were not. Each group was then asked to consider the case of "Johnny Rocco," a juvenile delinquent who was awaiting sentence for a minor crime. The group's task was to come to some agreement about how Johnny should be treated by the courts. Each group was composed of five to seven actual members, plus a confederate who had been trained to either disagree with the majority opinion, agree with the majority opinion, or start out disagreeing and then conform to the group's judgment.

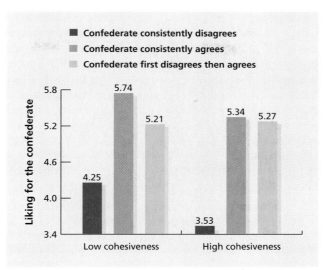

FIGURE 8.8

Liking for Group
Members Who Agree
or Disagree with the
Majority

In Schachter's study, a
confederate who consis-
tently disagreed with the
majority was disliked,
especially when the group
was highly cohesive.

Source: Schachter (1951).

After deciding the case, the participants indicated their liking for everyone in the group. Supporting Schachter's (1951) hypothesis, the data displayed in Figure 8.8 indicate that highly cohesive groups were more disparaging toward a dissenter than were groups that lacked cohesiveness. Subsequent research has found that this is particularly true when disagreement threatens the group's legitimacy or superiority (Matheson, Cole, & Majka, 2003; Scheepers, Branscombe, Spears, & Doosje, 2002). Timing also matters. Dissent is tolerated during the beginning stages of a deliberation, but when it comes time to make a decision, those who refuse to go along with the group tend to be ridiculed and rejected (J. R. Kelly & Karau, 1999; J. R. Kelly & Loving, 2004; Kruglanski & Webster, 1991). This finding explains why the confederate who first disagreed but then relented was not disliked.

2. Group Polarization Effects

So far, we have seen that groups tend to deal harshly with deviants and that group members tend to converge when making a judgment. In the situations we have discussed, group members holding extreme positions have been in the minority. But what happens when moderates and extremists are equal in number? To return to an earlier example, suppose four advertising executives meet to design a new advertising campaign. Two of the members favor a risky but potentially profitable approach, and the other two favor a more cautious, moderate approach. What is the group decision likely to be? Will it be extreme, will it be conservative, or will the group members split the difference and produce a decision that's intermediate and temperate?

A great deal of research has addressed this question, and the answer is now clear: Group judgments tend to be more extreme than the judgments individuals make on their own (Myers & Lamm, 1976). An investigation by Myers and Bishop (1970) demonstrated this **group polarization effect.** Working alone, high school students were initially asked how they felt about various issues pertaining to racial diversity. Later, the students met in small groups to discuss the issues. The groups were composed of members whose prejudice scores were near one another, so that high-prejudiced students interacted with one another and low-prejudiced students

FIGURE 8.9

Racial Tolerance Before
and After Group
Discussion

Groups that were low in
prejudice became more
tolerant of racial diversity
after group discussion,
whereas those that were
high in prejudice became
less tolerant of racial
diversity after discussion.
These tendencies produce
a group polarization effect.

Source: Myers and Bishop (1970).

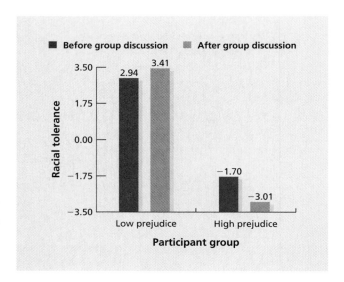

interacted with one another. Finally, each student completed the racial tolerance scale a second time, allowing researchers to determine how group discussion affected their attitudes.

The data presented in Figure 8.9 show a group polarization effect. Following group discussion, groups composed of students scoring low in prejudice became even more tolerant of racial differences and groups composed of highly prejudiced students became even less tolerant of racial differences.

What produces the group polarization effect? Normative influence plays a role (Goethals & Zanna, 1979; Sanders & Baron, 1977). After learning what the group values, individuals adopt those values in order to gain acceptance and avoid rejection. This leads to a polarization effect, because people who initially were only mildly in favor of a course of action come to more fervently support it. This is especially apt to be true when people believe that the extreme judgments reflect well on themselves, suggesting that people adopt extreme views not only because they want to be liked by others but also because they wish to see themselves in a positive light (R. S. Baron & Roper, 1976). Informational influence also operates. In the course of group discussion, individuals learn new arguments in favor of their position, and these arguments serve to strengthen their original opinions (Burnstein & Vinokur, 1977). The more arguments people hear, the more apt their attitudes are to be polarized (Brauer, Judd, & Gliner, 1995; Vinokur & Burnstein, 1974).

Although normative influence and informational influence normally combine to produce the group polarization effect, each is sufficient to produce the effect on its own (Burnstein & Vinokur, 1973; Goethals & Zanna, 1979; Isenberg, 1986). The two processes do, however affect different types of decisions. Normative influence produces the group polarization effect when the decision is value laden and subjective, whereas informational influence produces the group polarization effect when the decision is intellectual and factual (Kaplan, 1988).

One more point about the group polarization effect merits comment: The effect refers to the strengthening of the group's judgment, not the judgments of the individuals themselves (Fraser, Gouge, & Billig, 1971). To illustrate, suppose a group of four people get together. Their initial attitudes on some scale are 9, 9, 3, 3 (group mean = 6). If, following group discussion, the individual attitudes are now 9, 9, 3, 5, the group's decision will have become polarized (group mean = 6.5), despite the fact that three of the four group members didn't change at all and the one who did change moved toward the original group mean, not away from it. More generally, group polarization occurs whenever extremists change their attitudes less than moderates do. This is apt to be especially true when people are discussing issues of high personal importance.

3. Groupthink

In 1961, President John F. Kennedy and his advisers launched an attempt to topple Fidel Castro's regime in Cuba. In a secret mission, Cuban exiles parachuted onto the island to aid rebels in their attempt to stage a coup d'état. The mission at the Bay of Pigs was a disaster. Castro's soldiers were waiting on the beach when the exiles landed, and the operation was widely regarded as a military fiasco. How could Kennedy and his advisers have been so wrong about the mission's possible success? Stupidity is an unlikely answer. Kennedy's advisers were an extremely able group, dubbed the best and the brightest by author David Halberstam (1972). What, then, did lead to such poor decision making?

Before we attempt to answer this question, it will be useful to consider some other highly publicized political and military blunders:

- Pearl Harbor: In the weeks preceding Japan's attack on Pearl Harbor in December 1941, American military commanders received a steady stream of information indicating that an attack somewhere in the Pacific was imminent. Complacent officers dismissed Pearl Harbor as a target, believing it was too secure to be attacked.
- Vietnam War: In the 1960s, President Lyndon B. Johnson and his advisers escalated American involvement in the Vietnam War, despite evidence that the war effort was largely ineffectual and losing popularity at home.
- Iran–Contra affair: In 1985, working under the direction of President Ronald Reagan, Colonel Oliver North and other members of the National Security Council began selling arms to Iran in direct violation of U.S. laws. Further- more, the profits were funneled to right-wing rebels in Nicaragua for use against the left-wing Sandinista government. This policy, too, expressly vio- lated American law. Eventually, the plan was exposed and North and others were convicted of their crimes.
- *Challenger:* In 1986, on an uncommonly cold January morning in Cape Canaveral, Florida, administrators at the U.S. National Aeronautics and Space Administration (NASA) went ahead with the launch of the space shuttle *Challenger,* even though engineers had warned that cold temperatures might cause the O-ring seals in the ship's rocket boosters to fail. Seventy-three sec- onds after liftoff, the *Challenger* exploded, killing all seven crew members, including a New Hampshire high school teacher, Christa McAuliffe. Sixteen years later, the space shuttle *Columbia* suffered a similar fate.

Characteristics of Groupthink. Each of the incidents described on the preceding list may have resulted from a faulty decision-making style called **groupthink** (Janis, 1983; Janis & Mann, 1977). Groupthink occurs when group members become more concerned with maintaining group solidarity than with making a well-thought-out decision. Table 8.3 shows that groupthink is characterized by eight symptoms that fall

TABLE 8.3 Groupthink: Symptoms, Consequences, Causes, and Remedies

Symptoms	Consequences	Causes	Remedies
ILLUSION OF UNANIMITY • Concurrence seeking • Self-censorship • Intolerance of dissent • Mindguards **ILLUSION OF INVULNERABILITY** • Rationalization • Overconfidence **ILLUSION OF INVIOLABILITY** • Unshakable belief in group's morality • Stereotyping of enemies	• Failure to discuss alternatives • Failure to consider expert opinions • Failure to reexamine decisions • Failure to develop contingency plan	• Highly cohesive group • Strong, well-liked leader • Group isolation • Strong external pressures or deadlines	• Leader should refrain from stating a preference • Outside opinions should be sought • Designated dissenter should be appointed • Periodic review of decisions should be scheduled

Source: Janis and Mann (1977).

into three categories. The syndrome begins when a group quickly settles on a course of action. Group members then drum up support for this decision by engaging in a process Janis calls concurrence seeking. Fearing that dissent will rock the boat and alienate them from the group, most group members remain silent (self-censorship). Those who do disagree are told they are being disloyal and need to get on board (intolerance of dissent). Finally, certain group members (called mindguards) insulate the group's leader from hearing anything other than support for the group's policies. Collectively, these tendencies create an illusion of unanimity: a false belief that since no one is voicing an objection, everyone supports the proposed plan. Arthur Schlesinger, one of Kennedy's advisers, describes this process as it applied to the decision to invade Cuba:

> In the months after the Bay of Pigs I bitterly reproached myself for having kept so silent during those crucial discussions in the Cabinet Room, though my feelings of guilt were tempered by the knowledge that a course of objection would have accomplished little save to give me a name as a nuisance. (Schlesinger, 1965, p. 225)

Having decided that everyone supports the group's plan, group members proceed to rationalize and justify their decision. They become overconfident and decide they can't possibly be wrong. These perceptions fuel an illusion of invulnerability. This perception probably pervaded the thinking of the engineers who decided to launch the space shuttle *Challenger* (Moorhead, Ference, & Neck, 1991). At the time of the launch, NASA had flown 55 consecutive missions and had not lost an astronaut since 1967. They had put men on the moon, built and launched the space station Skylab, and succeeded in retrieving failed satellites from orbit and even bringing the crew of *Apollo 13* home safely. Finally, the space shuttle program had become so successful that launches had become almost routine. Given this history of success, no one believed the mission could fail.

Finally, groupthink is characterized by an illusion of inviolability. Group members come to believe that their cause is morally justified—"God is on our side" goes the thinking. This, in turn, leads them to disparage and stereotype the opposition. In the

Iran–Contra affair, Reagan and his advisers flouted the law because they believed they knew what was best for their country.

A recent Senate Intelligence Committee report on the U.S. invasion of Iraq paints a similar picture (http://intelligence.senate.gov/iraqreport2.pdf). In 2003, the United States invaded Iraq on the assumption that Iraq possessed weapons of mass destruction (WMD). The Senate committee concluded that these assumptions were false and that they were largely the product of faulty intelligence gathering and reporting. Summarizing the committee's findings for reporters, committee chairman Senator Pat Roberts stated:

> The committee concluded that the intelligence community was suffering from what we call a collective group-think, which led analysts and collectors and managers to presume that Iraq had active and growing WMD programs. This group-think caused the community to interpret ambiguous evidence, such as the procurement of dual-use technology, as conclusive evidence of the existence of WMD.

Consequences of Groupthink. Being intolerant of dissent and believing they are right and just, group members succumbing to groupthink fail to discuss alternatives or develop contingency plans. They also insulate themselves from outside opinion, further fueling their us-against-the-world mentality.

Causes of Groupthink. Not all groups are susceptible to groupthink. According to Janis, the syndrome is most apt to occur in a highly cohesive group with a strong leader. Once the leader's preference is known, group members become little more than yes-men, offering up nothing but support for the leader's plan. This is especially apt to occur when the group is isolated and under stress to make an important decision.

Remedies. Janis offered several remedies for groupthink. First, leaders should refrain from making recommendations until the group has had the chance to consider various alternatives. Second, an outside member should be sought to provide a more objective perspective on the group's decisions. Third, one group member should be appointed to play devil's advocate. This member should dissent from the group's decision, pointing out flaws in the choice and alternative routes. Finally, the group should schedule periodic reviews of decisions to ensure that the group does not proceed without reassessing its choices.

Empirical Evidence. Groupthink is one of social psychology's best-known theoretical constructs, but it has received only limited empirical support (Aldag & Fuller, 1993; Longley & Pruitt, 1980; McCauley, 1998). In part, this is because it is difficult to simulate a crisis situation in a laboratory setting (J. N. Choi & Kim, 1999). The evidence from case studies of real-world decisions is also mixed (Kramer, 1998; Tetlock, 1998). For every case study supporting the theory, there is another opposing it. For example, Winston Churchill stifled debate when members of his government favored a negotiated peace with Hitler. In this case, preemptive decision making had a positive consequence. In contrast, President Jimmy Carter and his advisers debated at length whether the United States should launch a military mission to free U.S. hostages in Iran in 1980. The plan was ultimately adopted but failed miserably when the helicopters carrying the commandos crashed in the desert. In short, concurrence seeking is no guarantee that decisions will be faulty, and tolerance of dissent is no guarantee that decisions will be wise.

The causes of groupthink are also unclear. Although Janis believed that group cohesiveness was the principal cause of groupthink, the evidence on this point is actually mixed: Some studies find that cohesive groups are more susceptible to groupthink than loosely structured groups are, but others do not (Aldag & Fuller, 1993; Street, 1997). Other factors—such as a need to believe the group is highly competent and efficacious—also appear to play a role, suggesting that groupthink is caused more by arrogance and hubris than by camaraderie (M. E. Turner & Pratkanis, 1998; Whyte, 1998).

Despite limited empirical support, the identification of groupthink has influenced the ways in which decisions are made in political, business, and legal settings. Organizations routinely invite group members to voice oppositions to group decisions, particularly in the initial stages of discussion. The next section of this chapter focuses on how the minority can influence the majority.

F. Minority Influence

Twenty years ago, a few scientists began warning of the perils of global warming. At first, they were dismissed as overzealous environmentalists—Cassandras who wanted only to curb big business. Over time, their viewpoint has become more and more accepted, and most scientists now agree that the earth's temperature is rising.

Moscovici and colleagues have conducted extensive research to examine the process of minority influence. An initial investigation by Moscovici, Lage, and Naffrechoux (1969) illustrates their approach. Instead of confronting participants with an erroneous majority, as Asch had done, Moscovici and colleagues confronted participants with an erroneous minority. The task involved judging the color of various slides, which most people perceive as being blue with some elements of green. In groups of six, four participants were paired with two confederates who maintained that the slides were green. When the confederates were consistent in their judgments, nearly one-third of the real participants reported that at least one slide looked green. Although substantially lower than the percentage of participants who conformed at least once in Asch's study of majority influence, this fraction is still sizable, suggesting that a minority can successfully change people's minds.

1. What Makes a Minority Effective?

Minority members must walk a fine line if they are to be effective in changing the attitude or opinion of the majority. On the one hand, they must be seen as flexible and open-minded; otherwise, their position will be dismissed as fanatical and unreasonable. This can best be achieved by agreeing with the majority on some issues, gaining what one psychologist calls **idiosyncrasy credits** (Hollander, 1958). Idiosyncrasy credits operate like money in the bank. They can be (psychologically) withdrawn when one wants to introduce a dissenting opinion.

Having established their credibility and good intentions, group members holding a minority opinion must then be steadfast and decisive when presenting their opposing point of view. If they appear equivocal or uncertain, the majority will dismiss them as weak and incompetent. Consequently, the most effective minorities are ones that express an unwavering view on the issue at hand (Maass & Clark, 1984; W. Wood, Lundgren, Ouellette, Busceme, & Blackstone, 1994).

2. Do Majority and Minority Influence Operate through the Same Process?

Some researchers believe that majority and minority influence operate through the same process. According to this view, majorities are more influential than minorities simply because there is strength in numbers (Latané, 1981; Latané & Wolf, 1981;

TABLE 8.4 Comparing Majority and Minority Influence

Influence Type	Nature of Conflict	Dominant Type of Influence	Type of Change Produced	Type of Judgment Most Apt to Be Affected
Majority	Will I be rejected if I openly disagree with the group?	Normative	Public agreement/ occasional private acceptance.	Subjective judgment or opinion.
Minority	Am I right?	Informational	Private acceptance, particularly on related issues and judgments.	Objective judgment with a factual basis.

Tanford & Penrod, 1984). Disagreeing with this claim, Moscovici (1980) argued that the two forms of social influence are qualitatively different. The basis for this position resides in the nature of the conflict that disagreement produces. As shown in Table 8.4, when people find themselves disagreeing with a majority point of view, they experience stress because they fear being rejected by the group. Under many circumstances, these normative pressures lead them to publicly agree with the group. This is the situation identified by Asch in his research.

Disagreement with a minority produces a different kind of stress. Lacking the power of normative influence, a statistical minority must exert its influence through informational means. By remaining steadfast in their convictions, members of the minority cause the majority to thoughtfully reconsider whether its position is correct. As a result, minority positions are processed more extensively and produce stronger attitudes than majority positions (Erb, Bohner, Rank, Einwiller, 2002; R. Martin, Hewstone, & Martin, 2003).

Table 8.4 also shows that the two forms of influence differ with respect to the type of change they produce. Whereas majority influence tends to produce public agreement more than private acceptance, minority influence is more apt to actually change people's minds, even when they publicly refrain from endorsing the minority position (W. Wood, et al., 1994). Because of these differences, majority influence is most apt to occur for judgments that are susceptible to normative influence, such as personal opinions, values, and attitudes, whereas minority influence is most apt to occur for judgments that are susceptible to informational influence, such as objective judgments with a factual basis.

A steadfast minority may even be effective when it fails to change the majority's position. Nemeth (1986; Nemeth & Wachtler, 1983) has found that dissenters lead majority members to be more inventive and creative in their decision making. Apparently, being exposed to someone who thinks outside of the box frees group members to see solutions they had overlooked or failed to consider. As a result, groups with a dissenter seem to make more innovative decisions than those without a dissenter. This finding fits well with Janis's recommendation to include a dissenting opinion in every group. Its presence can serve a useful function even if its position is ultimately rejected.

III. Compliance

Anyone who has ever attended a circus, carnival, or state fair is undoubtedly familiar with the masters of influence who populate the midway. Using a variety of techniques, they entice, lure, and ensnare customers to see a show generally lacking in entertainment value. "Step right this way," proclaims the barker. "Hurry, hurry, hurry. The show is about to begin. For just one thin dollar you can watch the alligator boy wrestle the bearded lady." Even though we know we are being hoodwinked, we can't resist being taken in by the pitch.

Such exotic requests are admittedly rare, but we all regularly encounter requests to perform some behavior. Your roommate might ask you to take out the garbage, or a friend might ask you to drive her to the airport. Some of these requests are straightforward, whereas others are more sneaky and sophisticated. This section focuses on the form of social influence known as **compliance.** Compliance occurs when we change our behavior in response to a direct request. By learning a few basic principles, you may avoid becoming an easy mark for a telephone solicitor, a door-to-door peddler, or late-night cable television infomercial.

A. Compliance without Thought

1. The Power of Scripts

In many situations we rely on simple heuristics, or scripts, to guide our reactions to other people's requests. Scripts are like schemas: They tell us what to expect in a social situation. For example, people have a script that says that authority figures have the legitimate power to make a request. When a police officer tells us to move our car, we don't ask why; we assume the request is valid and comply without thinking too much about it.

Another script maintains that people don't ask for help unless they really need it. Langer, Blank, and Chanowitz (1978) demonstrated how this script can be overgeneralized. In their study, a researcher approached students waiting to use a photocopy machine and asked to go first in line. Two variables were experimentally manipulated. The first was the number of copies the researcher needed to make (either 5 or 20). The second was the nature of the request. In one condition, the researcher said simply, "Excuse me. I have 5 (20) pages. May I use the Xerox machine?" In a second condition, the researcher justified the request by adding "because I'm in a rush," and in a third condition, the researcher added "because I have to make some copies." Notice how this final condition really doesn't provide any useful information at all—it simply repeats the information contained in the initial request without providing a rationale for why the person needed to go first.

Figure 8.10 shows the percentage of participants who complied with this request in each of the various experimental conditions. Two effects are of interest. First, it is clear that the request for 20 copies led participants to process the reason behind the appeal. Here, compliance was substantial when a legitimate reason was provided, but low when no reason was provided or when the reason given contained only redundant information. The situation was different when the request was small. Here, compliance increased when a reason was given, even if the reason was a bad one. Langer (1989) refers to such behavior as *mindless,* because people are complying without giving it much thought (see also Folkes, 1985)—they simply agree because they mindlessly assume that any request is a legitimate request.

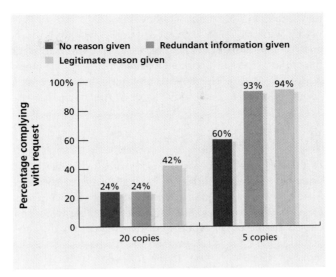

FIGURE 8.10

Percentage of People
Complying with a
Request to Let Another
Person Use the Copier

The legitimacy of a request
had a substantial effect
when the request was
large (20 copies) but not
when the request was
small (5 copies). These
findings suggest that
people mindlessly comply
when the costs are small,
but not when the costs
are large.

Source: Langer, Blank, and
Chanowitz (1978).

Of course, people don't always mindlessly give in to a request. Consider a panhandler. Many people walk by panhandlers without giving them any change because they automatically assume the request isn't legitimate. In order to be effective, a panhandler needs to break through this mindlessness. Santos, Leve, and Pratkanis (1994) conducted a field study showing how such a breakthrough can be achieved. The participants were 289 pedestrians strolling on a wharf in Santa Cruz, California. In each case, they were approached by a female panhandler who asked them for money. There were four experimental conditions. In two conditions, the panhandler made standard requests ("Can you spare any change?" or "Can you spare a quarter?"); in the other two conditions, the requests were unusual ("Can you spare 17 cents?" or "Can you spare 37 cents?"). Only 23 percent of the passersby gave money when standard requests were used, but 37 percent did so when nonstandard requests were used. Santos and colleagues argued that the unusual request interrupted the just-walk-on-by-a-panhandler script, leading people to pay more attention to the request and increasing their compliance.

Other studies provide additional evidence that subtle changes in wording can have important effects on compliance. One study found that people were more apt to give to a charity when the experimenter added "Even a penny will help" (Cialdini & Schroeder, 1976) and another found that adding the question "Can we count on you?" increased compliance with a request to give blood (Lipsitz, Kallmeyer, Ferguson, & Abas, 1989).

2. Liking and Compliance

"Hey, Jonathon," the caller began in a friendly, effusive tone. "It's Mark O'Brien. How ya doing?" I was doing fine, but I was also certain I didn't know anyone named Mark O'Brien, especially someone who would speak to me as if he and I were best friends. "Fine," I replied. "But I don't know anyone named Mark O'Brien. Why are you calling?" As I suspected, Mark and I had never met. Instead, he was with a long-distance telephone company and wanted me to switch my policy. His affability and friendliness were nothing but an insincere marketing ploy.

Are such ploys effective? You bet they are. Tupperware parties have proved enormously successful, because people are more likely to buy a product from someone they like than from someone they don't like. The same is true when it comes to complying with a request. The more familiar we are with the person making the request and the longer that person engages us in conversation, the more apt we are to honor the request (Burger, Soroka, Gonzago, Murphy, & Somervell, 2001; Dolinski, Nawrat, & Rudak, 2001). In general, anything that increases liking increases compliance (Burger, Messian, Patel, del Prado, & Anderson, 2004).

B. Principles of Social Influence

In the early 1970s, a psychology professor, Robert Cialdini, set out to discover the principles of social influence. Taking a leave of absence from his position at Arizona State University, Cialdini went to work for various companies that specialize in sales. He sold encyclopedias, subscriptions for cable television, and raised money for various charitable organizations. His experiences taught him about the nature of influence peddling and the strategies professionals use to make people comply with their requests (Cialdini, 1993). In the following section, you will learn about four of these principles. The first two concern how we judge the value of an object, and the last two concern basic psychological processes that influence compliance.

1. Contrast Effects

The first principle involves perceptual contrast, a term associated with Gestalt psychology. This principle holds that an object's appearance and value are variable and that both factors depend on the surrounding context. For example, a medium piece of pie looks larger when viewed beside two smaller pieces of pie than when viewed beside two larger pieces of pie. Here's how contrast effects can be used as tool of social influence. A number of years ago I was interested in buying a particular house I had seen advertised on a realty company's Web site. I contacted a realtor and asked him to show me the house. He agreed, and he even offered to show me several other houses that were on the way. These houses were absolute dives: ramshackle dwellings being offered at inflated prices. By the time we arrived at the house I wanted to see, it looked palatial by comparison and seemed like an incredible bargain. I didn't know it then, but the realtor had used the principle of psychological contrast to enhance the attractiveness of the house I was interested in buying. By first showing me some houses of lesser quality, he succeeded in augmenting the perceived quality of the only house I had wanted to see.

Clothing stores exploit contrast effects as well. Suppose a man visits an upscale clothing store and tells the clerk he wishes to buy a three-piece suit, a sweater, and a belt. In which order should the items be sold? Clothing stores instruct their salespeople to sell the most expensive item first (the suit), followed by the sweater and finally the belt. Why? Because a $100 sweater doesn't seem so costly in comparison with a $500 suit, and a $50 belt doesn't seem so costly in comparison with a $100 sweater. Car dealers also use this technique. When you are in the process of buying a new car, as soon as you have made the decision to buy, you will be invited to purchase a number of extras: fancy rims, a better stereo system, a sun roof, and cruise control. Each of these items is only a fraction of the cost of a new car, and you will probably think, "Why not? What's another $350 when I've just decided to spend $25,000."

Finally, Figure 8.11 shows how contrast effects can operate in social situations that don't involve compliance strategies.

Dear Mother and Dad,

Since I left for college I have been remiss in writing and I am sorry for my thoughtlessness in not having written before. I will bring you up to date now, but before you read on, please sit down. You are not to read any further until you are sitting down. Okay?

Well, then, I am getting along pretty well now. The skull fracture and the concussion I got when I jumped out the window of my dormitory when it caught on fire shortly after my arrival here is pretty well healed now. I only spent two weeks in the hospital and now I can see almost normally and only get those sick headaches once a day. Fortunately, the fire in the dormitory, and my jump, was witnessed by an attendant at the gas station near the dorm, and he was the one who called the fire department and the ambulance. He also visited me in the hospital and since I had nowhere to live because of the burnt-out dormitory, he was kind enough to invite me to share his apartment with him. It's really a basement room, but it's kind of cute. He is a very fine boy, and we have fallen deeply in love and are planning to get married. We haven't set the date yet, but it will be before my pregnancy begins to show.

Yes, Mother and Dad, I am pregnant. I know how much you are looking forward to being grandparents and I know you will welcome the baby and give it the same love and devotion and tender care you gave me when I was a child. The reason for the delay in our marriage is that my boyfriend has a minor infection which prevents us from passing our premarital blood tests and I carelessly caught it from him. I know that you will welcome him into our family with open arms. He is kind and, although not well educated, he is ambitious.

Now that I have brought you up to date, I want to tell you that there was no dormitory fire. I did not have a concussion or skull fracture. I was not in the hospital. I am not pregnant. I am not engaged. I am not infected, and there is no boyfriend. However, I'm getting a D in American history and an F in chemistry, and I want you to see those marks in their proper perspective.

Your loving daughter,

Sharon

FIGURE 8.11

Perceptual Contrast in Action

Salespeople aren't the only ones who use principles of contrast to their advantage.

Source: Cialdini (1993, p. 14).

2. Scarcity

Stamp collectors, antique dealers, and purveyors of sports memorabilia know that a product's value is determined in part by its availability. The less there is of something, the more valuable that something is judged to be. This is one reason why gold is more valuable than silver. There is less gold in the world than silver, and we use an item's availability to judge its value.

This tendency is not lost on advertisers. Slogans such as "Exclusive limited engagement," "One day only," and "Hurry in—at these prices, these products won't last forever" are designed to increase demand by creating the impression of scarcity in customers' minds. Although many companies make use of this principle, the company that made Cabbage Patch Dolls put it to greatest effect. By purposefully limiting the number of dolls it manufactured, the company increased the value of each doll. Several years later, the maker of Beanie Babies used a similar strategy to increase the sales of its product.

Principles of scarcity also operate in the interpersonal marketplace. In a country-and-western song from the 1970s, Mickey Gilley sang, "Don't the girls all get prettier at closing time?" To test Gilley's hypothesis, Pennebaker and associates (1979) visited several bars in Texas and asked patrons to rate the physical attractiveness of the other patrons at various times during the night. Consistent with Gilley's claim, the perceived attractiveness of members of the opposite sex increased as the night wore on. Further research showed that the perceived increase in attractiveness was not due to the amount of alcohol the patrons had consumed, and that it was especially pronounced among people who were not in a committed relationship (Madey et al., 1996).

Two processes explain why scarcity and value are linked. First, a cognitive explanation maintains that we have simply learned that rare things are more valuable than common things. After all, any given acorn is worth more to a squirrel when acorns are in short supply than when they are plentiful. Motivational processes also operate. According to Brehm (1966), knowing we can't have something creates an aversive psychological state known as **psychological reactance.** People respond to this state by reasserting their freedom, leading them to overvalue the very things they can't have. This principle explains why parents who forbid their child to date a given person often find that their strategy backfires: Feeling that their freedom of choice has been threatened, their child's desire for the forbidden fruit is increased.

Psychological reactance can also be used to sell products. In the 1970s, Dade County, Florida, forbid the use of laundry products that contained phosphates because their use was harming the Everglades. How did Miamians react to this loss of freedom? First, they began to increase their liking for phosphate-based products. Compared to residents of Tampa, who were unaffected by the ban, they viewed phosphate detergents as being more effective in cold water, gentler to clothes, and more powerful on stains. They also began hoarding phosphate-based detergents, traveling to nearby counties to buy and stockpile large amounts of the forbidden product (Mazis, 1975). Clearly, telling people they can't have something is an effective way to increase their desire to have that very thing. This is one reason why movie producers often work to ensure that their movies receive an R rating rather than a PG or PG-13 rating. It piques the interest of young viewers (a desirable target audience, given its size and spending power), who are motivated to see what they're not supposed to see.

3. Psychological Consistency and the Power of Commitment

In Chapter 6, we noted that people strive to maintain harmony between their thoughts, feelings, and actions. We experience psychological tension when we say one thing but do another, so we keep our beliefs, emotions, and behaviors consistent. When it comes to compliance, consistency often takes the form of commitment. Having committed ourselves to a course of action, we feel compelled to complete it. This is why you will probably be invited to take a car out for a test spin when you go to a car dealership. The simple act of sitting in the car and acting as if you owned it increases the odds that you will buy it ("The feel of the wheel will seal the deal"). In a similar vein, companies that sell encyclopedias door-to-door often require their customers to complete the sales agreement themselves. Actively filling out the form increases the buyer's commitment and enhances compliance.

Even academic institutions use the power of commitment to increase enrollment. After receiving notification of admission to one university, my son received a response card to send in along with a check for $100. The letter clearly indicated that the down payment was fully refundable if my son decided to attend a different school and was merely being used to ensure that his spot would stay open should he choose to enroll. I viewed the invitation with a bit of skepticism. Knowing the power of commitment, I recognized the admission committee's attempt to increase enrollment by forcing prospective students to make a behavioral commitment to the university.

Public commitments are especially apt to produce compliance (Lewin, 1952). Many self-help groups, such as those designed to help people lose weight or quit smoking, invite members to stand up and publicly announce their intentions to rid themselves of an unwanted habit. After publicly announcing their intentions, people feel greater pressure to honor their commitments. Although there is some evidence that this sort of commitment is particularly potent in individualistic cultures, such as America and the countries of Western Europe, it also plays a role in collectivistic cultures, such as the countries of East Asia and Eastern Europe (Cialdini, Wosinska, Barrett, Butner, & Gornik-Durose, 1999).

4. The Norm of Reciprocity

If you've ever received a letter from a charitable organization accompanied by a calendar or a set of address labels, you may have wondered, "Why do they give things away? What purpose does it serve?" For the answer, we need to consider a powerful norm that regulates human conduct: the norm of reciprocity. As noted earlier, this norm mandates that people should repay a favor in kind. In effect, we are obliged to do unto others as they have done unto us. Charitable organizations use this obligation to great effect. After receiving a gift (even one as small as a shiny penny), you feel obliged to return the favor by making a contribution (Cialdini, Green, & Rusch, 1992).

This principle was illustrated in a study by D. T. Regan (1971). Working in pairs, male participants rated a series of paintings as part of an alleged experiment of art appreciation. In fact, only one of the participants was a real participant; the other was a confederate. In one condition, the confederate did an unsolicited favor for the real participant: During a short break period, the confederate went to get a Coke for himself and brought back one for the participant as well. In another condition the confederate simply left and returned empty-handed, and in a third condition the experimenter gave both participants Cokes. After the pair had rated all of the paintings, the confederate mentioned that he was selling raffle tickets at 25 cents apiece and asked the participant to buy some. Figure 8.12 shows that participants bought the most tickets from confederates who had previously done them a favor. These results can be explained by the

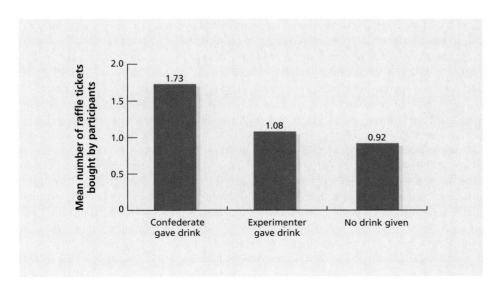

FIGURE 8.12

Reciprocity and Compliance

According to the norm of reciprocity, we feel obliged to help those who have helped us. In this study, participants were more likely to comply with a request to buy raffle tickets when the requester had previously done them a favor.

Source: Regan (1971).

norm of reciprocity: Having received a favor from the confederate, participants felt compelled to return it by buying some of his raffle tickets. Religious groups that once gave books to unsuspecting airport travelers were using the same tactic.

C. Two-Step Influence Techniques

The principles of social influence that Cialdini identified usually operate alone to influence compliance. In some cases, however, they combine to form two-step influence techniques. The first step sets a trap, and the second step snaps it shut. Two-step influence techniques tend to be highly successful, because people are unaware that two different strategies are being used. By learning how they work, you may be better able to avoid falling prey to them.

1. The Foot-in-the-Door Effect

The best known of the two-step influence techniques is the foot-in-the-door effect. With this technique, we start with a request so small that virtually no one would refuse it. Then we proceed to a larger, more consequential request. Like the proverbial traveling salesman, we use the first request to get our foot in the door, allowing us to deliver our second request with greater effectiveness.

The foot-in-the-door effect was first demonstrated experimentally by Freedman and Fraser (1966). These investigators had researchers pose as volunteers for an organization devoted to increasing safety on the highways. In a control condition, the researchers went door-to-door asking homeowners in Palo Alto, California, whether they would be willing to put in their front yard a huge 10-foot-high public service billboard that read DRIVE SAFELY. Only 17 percent of homeowners agreed to this outrageous request. But there was another condition in this study: Two weeks earlier, other homeowners had been approached by a different experimenter and had been asked whether they would be willing to put in their window a tiny three-inch decal that read BE A SAFE DRIVER. Virtually everyone agreed with this modest request. Of the participants who were asked to place the tiny decal in their window, more than 75 percent later agreed to put the huge sign in their yard. Thus, success in the first step of the two-step process produced nearly a fivefold increase in compliance rates. In a second study, the researchers called housewives and asked if they would be willing to allow a team of men to rummage through their cupboards in order to document their use of various household products. Women who had earlier been asked to answer a few questions about household products were more than twice as likely to agree to this request than were those who did not complete an initial questionnaire.

Although the foot-in-the door effect is not always as large as the one found in Freedman and Fraser's study, dozens of follow-up investigations have found that people are more like to comply with a large request to donate their time, money, blood, and other resources if they have first complied with a smaller request (Cialdini & Trost, 1998). Moreover, the effect occurs even when a good deal of time has passed between the first and second request, and even when the second request involves a different issue or task and is delivered by a different requester (Burger, 1999). Finally, the effect is greatest when the second request is large rather than small (Schwarzwald, Bizman, & Raz, 1983). You would be wise to keep these findings in mind the next time you are asked to sign a petition or simply answer a few questions when a telemarketer calls. Chances are, the requester is trying to get a foot in the door so that you will comply with a larger request at some later time.

Several processes produce the foot-in-the-door effect (Burger, 1999). First, self-perception processes operate. When considering whether to comply with the larger request, people reflect on their past behavior and decide they must be the kind of person who accedes to such requests (Bem, 1972; Freedman & Fraser, 1966). For this process to occur, people must not only comply with the initial request, but also make a dispositional attribution for their prior compliance. They will not show the foot-in-the-door effect if they believe they were coerced into complying with the initial request or if they agreed for reasons that have nothing to do with their self-concept (Burger & Guadagno, 2003; Gorassini & Olson, 1995).

Commitment and cognitive consistency also play a role. Having demonstrated their backing for safe driving by displaying the decal, people felt compelled to show their support by displaying the billboard. Doing otherwise would entail abandoning their convictions and abdicating their commitments. In support of this explanation, people who are highly concerned with maintaining consistency are more apt to show the foot-in-the-door effect than are those who are less concerned with maintaining consistency (Cialdini, Trost, & Newsom, 1995; Guadagno, Asher, Demaine, & Cialdini, 2001).

2. Lowballing

An automobile is one of the most expensive items you will purchase in life. Buying a car may also teach you a very expensive lesson about a two-step technique of social influence. Here's how it works: You go to a car dealership and, after a bit of wrangling with the salesperson, settle on a price you are willing to pay for the car of your dreams. As you close the deal with a handshake, the salesperson tells you she must get the manager's approval before the deal is final. A few minutes later she returns, looking crestfallen and somewhat sheepish. "I'm sorry," she says, "but the manager says our agreement price is too low and that we will be losing money at that price. I'm really sorry I screwed up, but there's nothing I can do. The manager has the last word. If you want the car you'll have to pay an extra $1,000."

Now it's your turn to be crestfallen. After all of your hard work, you had your heart set on the car and were excited to take it home. Will you pay the extra $1,000? Before you answer, you might want to know that you are being duped by a common influence technique known as lowballing. The influencing agent starts by throwing you a low ball (a small request) and, after securing your compliance, raises the ante by increasing the cost. Car dealers report that people not only fall prey to lowballing but often wind up paying more for the car than they would have if they had agreed on a slightly higher price to begin with. (The following Web site provides useful tips for avoiding such pitfalls: www.edmunds.com.)

Perhaps you are thinking that lowballing occurs only when people are under stress or are being pressured by a car dealer. Think again. Cialdini, Cacioppo, Bassett, and Miller (1978) used this technique to increase participation in a psychology experiment. These investigators telephoned students and asked them to participate in a study on "thinking processes." Some students were told at the outset that the experiment was being conducted at 7:00 AM; only 24 percent of these students agreed to attend. Other students weren't told about the early-morning starting time until after they had agreed to participate in the study. Of these students, 56 percent agreed to attend. Thus, by first securing the students' commitment, the researchers succeeded in inducing over twice as many to comply with their request.

Commitment is the key to the lowballing effect. Once people agree to a course of action, they feel compelled to complete it. When the deal suddenly becomes more costly (in either time or money), the person feels psychologically bound to continue. Commitment also extends to the salesperson. Having made a deal, you feel obliged to honor your commitment. You may also feel sorry for the salesperson, who seems to be a hapless victim of circumstance rather than a shrewd conspirator of this unscrupulous technique (Burger & Petty, 1981).

Postdecision dissonance reduction also contributes to the effectiveness of lowballing. As discussed in Chapter 6, once people make a decision they enhance the attractiveness of the chosen alternative. After deciding to buy the car, you begin to exaggerate its virtues: It handles like a dream, you love the sunroof, and it gets great mileage on the freeway. Paying a little extra for the car doesn't seem unreasonable, because you now believe its features are better than they were before.

Finally, principles of psychological contrast operate. If you've just agreed to spend $25,000 for a new car, an additional $1,000 doesn't seem so much. For all of these reasons, then, people are highly susceptible to the lowballing procedure, even when they recognize they are being duped.

3. The Door-in-the-Face Effect

The foot-in-the-door technique and lowballing both begin with a small request and follow with a larger, more costly one. Two other techniques take just the opposite approach: They start with a large request and then reduce it. The first of these procedures is known as the door-in-the-face technique. Here we begin with a request so large that virtually no one will comply. We later modify our request and find that people are more willing to accede to the smaller request than they would have been to begin with.

Once again, the effect was experimentally demonstrated by Cialdini and associates (Cialdini, Vincent, Lewis, Catalan, Wheeler, & Darby, 1975). These researchers approached students on campus and asked some of them if they would be willing to work two hours per week for two years at a juvenile detention center. No one complied with this sizable request. The students were then asked if they would be willing to chaperone a group of children from the County Juvenile Detention Center to the zoo, requiring two hours of time on a single afternoon or evening. Half of the students agreed to this request, compared to only 17 percent who agreed when they had not first been asked to consider the larger request. Thus, the door-in-the-face produced a threefold increase in compliance.

Two factors produce the effect. First, the norm of reciprocity operates. The requester has modified his or her initial request, and people feel compelled to reciprocate this concession by compromising as well. Principles of contrast are also at work. The second request seems small in comparison with the initial request, so people are more willing to agree to it.

4. The That's-Not-All Effect

A final two-step technique is known as the that's-not-all effect. Anyone who has ever watched late-night television is familiar with the Popeil pocket fisherman, the Ginzu knife, and the Heartland Record Collection of Rock and Roll Hits from the 1950s. After introducing the product and its price, the announcer declares: "But wait. There's more. Act now and you'll also receive [any number of other products] as a bonus." These bonuses are typically offered for "a limited time only" or are available only when you "call the toll-free number on your screen."

The that's-not-all effect begins with an initial request and then sweetens the deal by throwing in extras (or cutting the price). Like the other strategies we've discussed, it is quite effective. Burger (1986) set up a stand selling various desserts along a college campus walkway. Some participants were told the price of a cupcake and two cookies was 75 cents. Other participants were told the cupcake was 75 cents, but as they were deciding whether to buy it, the researcher announced he or she would add two cookies at no extra price. Only 40 percent of the students purchased the items in the control condition, but 73 percent did so in the that's-not-all condition. Everyone, it seems, loves a bargain, and getting something for nothing or at a reduced price appeals to us all.

The same principles that explain the door-in-the-face effect produce the that's-not-all effect. The person has made a concession by increasing the value of the product, and we feel compelled to reciprocate this generosity by complying with the request. Principles of psychological contrast also operate, because we feel that we are now getting more for our money than we had originally assumed.

5. A Summary of Two-Step Compliance Techniques

Table 8.5 summarizes the various two-step compliance techniques. The table also shows how they can be applied to a single case: selling a vacuum cleaner for $150.

TABLE 8.5 Two-Step Compliance Techniques

	Tactic	Description	Illustration (Selling a Vacuum)	Principles
Start Small, Then Increase	Foot-in-the-door	Start small and, after securing commitment, proceed to a larger request.	Ask to demonstrate how the vacuum works or get the person to agree it is important to have a clean house.	• Self-perception processes • Consistency and commitment
	Lowballing	After securing a commitment to a specified price, increase the price.	Get person to agree to buy the vacuum for $125, then increase the price to $150 when the boss balks at the deal.	• Psychological commitment • Postdecision dissonance reduction • Perceptual contrast
Start Large, Then Decrease	Door-in-the-face	Start large and, after the request is denied, counter with a smaller request.	Ask person to buy a professional rug cleaner for $500. When the person refuses, offer to sell the vacuum for $150.	• Norm of reciprocity • Perceptual contrast
	That's-not-all	After introducing a product, increase the value by decreasing the price or adding extras.	Start with a selling price of $200 and then drop the price to $150 and throw in a floor sweeper for free.	• Norm of reciprocity • Perceptual contrast

Looking over these techniques, it's easy to see why they are so successful. They all rely on basic principles that govern our psychological lives. Being familiar with these strategies can help you avoid succumbing to them. Unfortunately, familiarity alone is no guarantee. You must also be aware the technique is being applied. Those who make their living selling products are masters not only at using these techniques but also at doing so in a way that makes them difficult to detect. Consequently, though knowledge is power, you may very well find yourself succumbing to these influence techniques in the future. For example, you may purchase a new textbook because the publisher has induced a free study guide or is offering free access to the book's Web site. After all, even textbook authors have to make a living!

IV. Obedience to Authority

A final form of social influence is **obedience,** which occurs when we comply with a request from someone who has the legitimate authority to make the request. For example, when a nurse tells us to complete a health form while waiting for the doctor, we automatically do what we are told. We recognize that health care professionals have the right to make certain demands, and we comply with these demands without questioning their authority.

A. Mindless Obedience

In some cases, obedience can be mindless and overgeneralized. In a field experiment by Bickman (1974), participants were stopped on a street corner by a male experimenter. Pointing to a student standing beside a parked car with an expired meter, the experimenter said: "This fellow is overparked at the meter but doesn't have any change. Give him a dime!" In one condition, the experimenter was dressed as a bum, in another condition as a business executive, and in another condition as a firefighter. Participants were much more apt to comply with the request when it came from an authority figure, even though the firefighter's authority was irrelevant to the request itself (see also Bushman, 1984).

B. Milgram's Research

In the late 1950s, while working with Solomon Asch, graduate student Stanley Milgram wondered whether people would conform if doing so injured another person. Milgram decided he first needed a control group to address this issue, so he designed an experiment in which one person, an experimenter, orders another to deliver shocks to a protesting victim. The research Milgram conducted is the most well-known and controversial set of experiments in all of social psychology, and the findings provide a disturbing look at human nature.

1. Experimental Procedure

Imagine being a participant in one of Milgram's studies. You report to a laboratory at Yale University, where you find a somber experimenter dressed in a gray technician's coat and another person who will be participating in the experiment with you. The experimenter explains he is studying how punishment affects learning. One of you will play the role of teacher and the other the role of learner. The teacher will teach the learner a series of word pairs (*blue—box, nice—day*) and deliver shocks of increasing intensity whenever the learner errs. At this point, you and the other person draw slips of paper out of a hat to decide who will be the teacher and who will be the learner. You draw the role of teacher and the other person is assigned the role of learner.

The experimenter then escorts the two of you to another room. He straps the learner into a chair and attaches electrodes to his wrists. Afterward, you accompany the experimenter back to the main room and are seated in front of an imposing "shock generator." The console contains 30 switches, with labels ranging from 15 volts to 450 volts. Beneath these switches are verbal warnings that characterize the strength of these shocks. These warnings vary from "Slight Shock" to "Danger: Severe Shock" and ultimately to a foreboding "XXX" (see the first column of Table 8.6). After being assured that the shocks will be painful but will not cause permanent tissue damage, you are told to give the learner a small shock of 15 volts the first time he makes a mistake and to increase the shock by 15 volts for every subsequent mistake.

The experiment begins uneventfully. You read the first few word pairs to the learner and he answers correctly. Then he makes a mistake and you flip the first switch, believing that you are delivering a shock of 15 volts. Following the fifth mistake, you deliver a shock of 75 volts. Over an intercom, you hear the learner groaning and complaining that the shocks are too painful (see Table 8.6). If you ask the experimenter for guidance or clarification, you hear only one of four replies:

1. "Please continue" or "Please go on."
2. "The experiment requires that you continue."
3. "It is absolutely essential that you continue."
4. "You have no other choice; you must go on."

Now what will you do?

2. Experimental Findings

Most people reading the preceding description predict that they would stop soon after the learner begins to complain (see Milgram, 1974, pp. 27–31). Yet, as Table 8.6 shows, of the 40 participants in this study, very few stopped shocking the learner at this point. Most continued on. Even after the learner complained vigorously of the pain, called attention to a heart condition, and indicated that he no longer consented to being shocked, nearly two-thirds of the participants gave the maximum amount of shock allowed. (Of course, the drawing was rigged and the whole experiment was a well-choreographed charade. The "learner" was a confederate of the experimenter, and was never shocked at all.)

Why did participants continue to administer shocks? Were they sadistic monsters who reveled in inflicting torture and abuse? The evidence suggests otherwise. Although some personality variables predict who obeys and who does not (Blass, 1991), most participants were willing to administer shocks strong enough to inflict severe pain. Moreover, the participants were ordinary citizens living in New Haven, Connecticut; many had respectable jobs, and some were highly religious and active in civic affairs. Nearly all of the participants were visibly shaken throughout the procedure, and most pleaded with the experimenter to call a halt to the proceedings. Yet few refused to follow the experimenter's commands.

Instead of trying to identify an "obedient personality type," Milgram believed that the participants' behavior could best be explained by the type of situational pressures

TABLE 8.6 Shock Levels and the Learner's Schedule of Protests in one of Milgram's Studies of Obedience to Authority

	Learner's Scripted Remarks	Number of Participants Who Stopped
SLIGHT SHOCK		
15 volts		
30 volts		
45 volts		
60 volts		
MODERATE SHOCK		
75 volts	Ugh!	
90 volts	Ugh!	1
105 volts	Ugh! (*Louder*)	
120 volts	Ugh!! Hey, *this* really hurts.	
STRONG SHOCK		
135 volts	Ugh!!	
150 volts	Ugh!!! Experimenter! That's all. Get me out of here. I told you I had heart trouble. My heart's starting to bother me now. Get me out of here, please. My heart's starting to bother me. I refuse to go on. Let me out.	6
165 volts	Ugh! Let me out! (*Shouting*)	
180 volts	Ugh! I can't stand the pain. Let me out of here! (*Shouting*)	1
VERY STRONG SHOCK		
195 volts	Ugh! Let me out of here. Let me out of here. My heart's bothering me. You have no right to keep me here! Let me out! Let me out of here! Let me out! Let me out of here! My heart's bothering me. Let me out! Let me out!	
210 volts	Ugh! Experimenter! Get me out of here. I've had enough. I won't be in the experiment anymore.	
225 volts	Ugh!	
240 volts	Ugh!	
INTENSE SHOCK		
255 volts	Ugh! Get me out of here.	
270 volts	(*Agonized scream*) Let me out of here. Let me out of here. Let me out. Do you hear? Let me out of here.	2
285 volts	(*Agonized scream*)	
300 volts	(*Agonized scream*) I absolutely refuse to answer anymore. Get me out of here. You can't hold me here. Get me out. Get me out of here.	1
EXTREME INTENSITY SHOCK		
315 volts	(*Intensely agonized scream*) I told you I refuse to answer. I'm no longer part of this experiment.	1
330 volts	(*Intense and prolonged agonized scream*) Let me out of here. Let me out of here. My heart's bothering me. Let me out, I tell you. (*Hysterically*) Let me out of here. Let me out of here. You have no right to hold me here. Let me out! Let me out! Let me out! Let me out of here! Let me out! Let me out!	1
345 volts	(*Silence*)	
360 volts	(*Silence*)	
DANGER: SEVERE SHOCK		
375 volts	(*Silence*)	1
390 volts	(*Silence*)	
405 volts	(*Silence*)	
420 volts	(*Silence*)	
XXX		
435 volts	(*Silence*)	
450 volts	(*Silence*)	26

Source: Milgram (1974, Experiment 5, pp. 56–57).

they faced. As a symbol of authority, the experimenter commands respect. He appears to be responsible and reasonable, and the experiment's goal seems appropriate and important. People have been taught to respect such figures, and participants see no reason why they shouldn't trust a scientist. In addition, the procedure unfolds gradually, with each shock being just a bit more intense than the last. Without realizing it, participants become caught up in the experience and find themselves behaving in ways they wouldn't ordinarily do.

3. Contextual Variables That Influence Obedience

Milgram conducted a great number of experiments to better understand people's behavior in the situation he constructed. Several factors that seemed relevant turned out to make little difference. For example, women were just as apt to deliver the maximum shock as men were, and conducting the study in a broken-down building did not produce any less obedience than when the study was conducted at Yale University. Other factors did make a difference—as shown in Figure 8.13, three factors affected whether participants obeyed the experimenter's commands. The first is the perceived legitimacy of the request: For obedience to be high, participants must believe the person giving the order is fully authorized to do so. Obedience dropped dramatically when the experimenter's legitimacy was challenged by a second experimenter who presented an opposing view (Experiment 15); when two participants openly defied the experimenter (Experiment 17); and when the orders were given by a fellow participant who did not possess the authority to issue the commands (Experiment 13). The second factor of importance is the immediacy of the command and the deed. Obedience was high when the authority figure was near and the victim far away, but low if the authority figure delivered the command by telephone (Experiment 7) or if the participant had to place the victim's hand directly on the shock plate (Experiment 4). The final factor to consider is the extent to which the participant bears direct responsibility for the deed. Obedience was especially high when participants functioned as "bureaucrats," passively

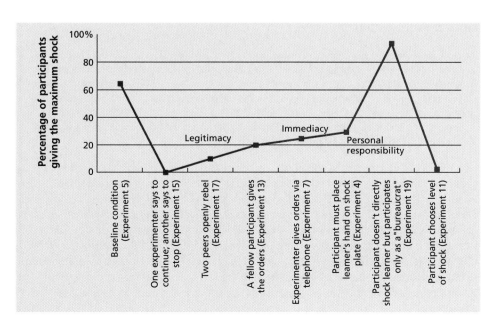

FIGURE 8.13

Percentage of Participants Who Delivered the Maximum Shock in Milgram's Studies of Obedience to Authority

The data show that participants were most likely to inflict harm when the command was legitimate and immediate, and they could inflict pain from a distance without feeling a sense of personal responsibility.

Source: Milgram (1974).

recording the amount of shock given by a fellow participant (Experiment 19), and especially low when participants had to decide for themselves how much shock to administer (Experiment 11).

To summarize, Milgram found that people were especially apt to obey an experimental command to harm another person when the command was legitimate and immediate, and they could inflict pain from a distance without feeling a sense of personal responsibility. The situation is not unlike that of a bombardier who flies a mission during a war. On the orders of his superiors, he drops a bomb miles above its intended target. Does this mean bombardiers feel no guilt or remorse for what they have done? Not at all. Milgram's participants were clearly uncomfortable inflicting harm on another person, and soldiers at war are no different. Still, the ability to inflict harm on another is maximized when it can be justified and done as we will see in Chapter 13, from a distance.

4. Controversial Issues Surrounding Milgram's Research

In the years following its publication, Milgram's research attracted a tremendous amount of attention. Some social scientists were disturbed by Milgram's experimental method (Baumrind, 1964; A. G. Miller, 1986). These critics argued that Milgram had breached normal ethical considerations governing laboratory research by leading people to believe they were capable of committing extreme acts of violence. In his defense, Milgram (1974) noted that 84 percent of the participants later indicated they were glad to have participated in the study, and that only 1 percent regretted having volunteered. Still, the scientific community responded to Milgram's studies by curtailing this type of deception, and Milgram's research could be not conducted today.

The external validity of Milgram's findings also drew attention. Though people are rarely called on to shock others under seemingly legitimate conditions, Milgram argued that his findings were applicable to a wide variety of real-world settings. He was particularly enthusiastic about generalizing his results to the Holocaust. Noting that ordinary people were rather easily led to commit immoral acts in the name of following orders, Milgram argued that his findings explained why so many Germans killed Jews during World War II:

> Obedience, as a determinant of behavior, is of particular relevance to our time. It has been reliably established that from 1933 to 1945 millions of innocent people were systematically slaughtered on command. Gas chambers were built, death camps were guarded, daily quotas of corpses were produced with the same efficiency as the manufacture of appliances . . . The Nazi extermination of European Jews is the most extreme instance of abhorrent immoral acts carried out by thousands of people in the name of obedience. (Milgram, 1974, pp. 1–2)

Milgram's account is emblematic of a situationist view of behavior favored by social psychology. Rather than assuming that the Holocaust was committed by bad people, Milgram's account assumes it was perpetuated by ordinary people facing extraordinary pressures. Echoing this perspective, Zimbardo (1974) claimed that "evil deeds are rarely the product of evil people acting from evil motives, but are the product of good bureaucrats simply doing their job" (p. 566). Even the Germans embraced this perspective. During the Nuremberg trials following the war, Adolf Eichmann, a man responsible for the deaths of thousands of Jews, asserted that he was simply following orders. He and other Germans portrayed themselves not as hateful and violent

TABLE 8.7   Key Differences between Milgram's Study and the Holocaust

Volunteer to inflict damage	In Milgram's research, participants did not sign up for an experiment on "shocking another human being." Many Germans, especially those in positions of power within the Nazi Party, volunteered for the job.
Hatred for the victim	In Milgram's research, participants did not know the victim and harbored no hatred for him. Germans had hated Jews for centuries.
Informed consent	In Milgram's research, the learner agreed to be shocked. Although he later retracted his consent, he initially agreed to receive shocks. In the Holocaust, Jews did not consent to the treatment they received.
Actual physical damage	In Milgram's research, the participants were told that although the shocks were painful, they would not cause any permanent tissue damage. In the Holocaust, German soldiers knew they were causing great harm.
Rebellion	In Milgram's research, obedience dropped to 0 when two peers rebelled. Many Germans aided Jews and rebelled, but this did not stop the killing.

but rather as dutiful civil servants who were only doing their job. This "obedience alibi" led one writer to characterize the atrocities as representing a "banality of evil" (Arnedt, 1965), carried out with efficiency rather than enmity.

Not everyone accepts Milgram's thesis that most Germans were merely following orders. In an award-winning book entitled *Hitler's Willing Executioners,* Harvard professor Daniel Goldhagen (1996) notes that many Germans eagerly volunteered for service in the German army. This was not true in Milgram's research. Milgram's participants volunteered for an experiment on learning and suddenly found themselves in a situation very different from the one they expected. Milgram's analysis also ignores the social conditions that existed in Germany prior to and during the war. At this time, Germany was in economic decline and searching for a convenient scapegoat. The Jews were vilified and subjected to discrimination. In fact, Germans had hated Jews for centuries. Economic pressure and long-term hatred did not exist in Milgram's laboratory.

Table 8.7 summarizes a number of other important differences between Milgram's experiment and the Holocaust. For example, in Milgram's experiment, participants watched as the learner consented to be shocked. Although the learner later withdrew his approval, he clearly participated on his own accord. This was not true of Germany's Jews. The participants in Milgram's studies were also told that although the shocks were painful, they would not cause any permanent damage. This, too, fails to mirror the situation in Germany when Jews were rounded up and slaughtered. Finally, obedience in Milgram's studies dropped to zero when peers rebelled (see again Figure 8.13, Experiment 17). Many Germans aided Jews, but this did not stop other Germans from attempting to exterminate them.

We can appreciate these differences by considering the actions of Reserve Police Battalion 101, a unit of the German Order Police (Goldhagen, 1996; Mandel, 1998).

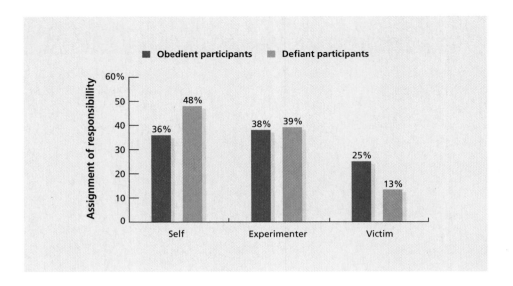

FIGURE 8.14

Responsibility Ratings in Milgram's Studies on Obedience to Authority

When asked, "Who was responsible for shocking the confederate?" obedient participants were less apt to hold themselves accountable for their actions than were disobedient ones, but they were not more apt to blame the experimenter. Instead, obedient participants blamed the victim. These findings undercut Milgram's claim that obedient participants believed they were merely following orders.

Source: Milgram (1974).

In Józefów, Poland on July 13, 1942, the battalion's commander, Major Wilhelm Trapp, told his troops he had received orders to carry out a mass killing of Jews. His soldiers were to collect the Jews in the market square, take them in small groups to the outskirts of town, and shoot them there at close range. Unlike Milgram's authority figure, Trapp was not impassive but was visibly upset about this order. He also told his men that those who did not "feel up to the task of killing Jews" could be assigned to other duties. Despite this option, only 2 percent of the 500 men stepped forward and asked to be reassigned. The rest carried out the execution of more than 1,500 Jews. It is doubtful, then, whether these soldiers were reluctantly following orders.

As it turns out, the obedience alibi may not even apply to Milgram's own participants. At the end of several of his studies, the experimenter asked participants: "How much is each of us responsible for the fact that this person was given electric shocks against his will?" (Milgram, 1974, p. 203). If obedient participants believed they were only following orders, they should be more apt than defiant participants to blame the experimenter. The data displayed in Figure 8.14 indicate that this was not the case. What distinguished obedient participants from those who rebelled was not the extent to which they held the experimenter accountable for what happened, but the extent to which they excused themselves and blamed the victim. This finding suggests an interpretation different from the one Milgram favored: Rather than merely following orders, participants justified their behavior by disparaging the enemy, concluding that the learner deserved the treatment they inflicted on him. In Chapter 13, you will learn that this is a common behavior among perpetrators of violence.

5. Epilogue

Stanley Milgram conducted social psychology's most well-known set of experiments. His findings revealed an alarming tendency for ordinary people to commit violence under the shroud of legitimacy. Whether these findings are due to obedience or to some other factor, the fact remains that they provide a disturbing view of human nature and an exceptionally vivid testament to the power of the experimental situation Milgram created.

CHAPTER SUMMARY

- Social influence is the study of how our thoughts, feelings, and actions are influenced by others.

- Imitation occurs when we mimic the behavior of other people, without feeling any pressure to do so. Although most imitation is harmless, imitation can also have negative consequences, producing mass psychogenic illness, copycat crimes, and suicide.

- Conformity occurs when we change our behavior in response to real or imagined social pressures. People can conform because of a desire to be right (informational influence), a desire to be liked (normative influence), or a desire to establish a particular identity (identity influence).

- Norms are unwritten rules of social conduct. Some norms apply to specific groups, some apply to particular cultures, and others are universal.

- Sherif studied conformity in an ambiguous situation. He found that people conformed to a group norm, and that this conformity was observed in private as well as in public. Informational influence seems to be operating in this situation.

- Asch studied conformity in an unambiguous situation. He found that people conformed to a group's judgment, but that this conformity occurred only in public, not in private. Normative influence seems to be operating in this situation.

- In Asch's research, a unanimous majority of 3 produced nearly as much conformity as a unanimous majority of 15. However, conformity dropped considerably if even one other person dissented.

- Social influence processes affect group discussions and the decisions that groups make. Dissenters tend to be disparaged and rejected, particularly in highly cohesive groups.

- Groups tend to make more extreme decisions than do individuals working alone. This tendency is called the group polarization effect.

- Groupthink is a group decision-making style characterized by a tendency to value group harmony more than effective decision making. When afflicted by group-think, groups fail to consider alternative options or make contingency plans.

- Group members that hold a minority opinion can influence the majority if they are compromising in general but steadfast on the issue involving dissent.

- Compliance occurs when people accede to another person's request.

- Telemarketers, salespeople, and car dealers use several basic psychological principles to induce compliance in their customers. Two principles—contrast and scarcity—influence how we judge the value of an object; two other principles—cognitive consistency and the norm of reciprocity—refer to basic psychological processes that govern our interactions with others.

- Two-step compliance techniques are particularly effective. The first step sets a trap, and the second step secures compliance. With the foot-in-the-door technique, we follow up an initially small request with a much larger request. With low-balling, we start with a small request and then increase the cost. With the door-in-the-face technique, we follow up an initially large request with a much smaller, more reasonable one. With the that's-not-all effect, we first introduce an offer and then sweeten the pot by throwing in extras or discounting the original price.

- People exhibit obedience when they obey a command from a legitimate authority. Milgram conducted social psychology's most well-known set of experiments. He found that participants were willing to administer high levels of shock to another person simply because the experimenter told them they must.

- Milgram believed his results could explain the behavior of Germans during the Holocaust. Although some Germans were undoubtedly just following orders, others volunteered to inflict harm and continued to do so even when allowed to stop. Moreover, in Milgram's study, obedient participants were not more apt than disobedient ones to say they were merely following orders. Instead, they were more apt to blame the victim for the treatment they inflicted on him.

KEY TERMS

social influence, 275

conformity, 278

social norms, 278

informational influence, 280

normative influence, 280

identity influence, 280

group polarization effect, 289

groupthink, 291

idiosyncrasy credits, 294

compliance, 296

psychological reactance, 300

obedience, 306

ADDITIONAL READING

Go to the Student Edition of the Online Learning Center for this text (www.mhhe.com/brown) and log in to read the following journal articles, which relate to the content of this chapter:

- Chartrand, T. L., & Bargh, J. A. (1996). The chameleon effect: The perception-behavior link and social interaction.

- Milgram, S. (1963). Behavioral study of obedience.

Groups

For eons, humans have survived by banding together in groups. Initially, groups formed to help people hunt and gather food, and to ward off predators and enemies. Later, the advent of farming and herding demanded the creation of more complex groups, with a division of labor and coordinated group efforts. Eventually, groups broadened and evolved from clans and tribes to form the great city states and nations that exist today.

This chapter first discusses the factors that define a group and then explores why people join groups and the functions groups serve. The next section focuses on individual performance in group settings, and the third section examines leadership. Finally, the chapter looks at conflict—situations in which people in groups compete or cooperate.

I. The Nature of Groups

A. What Is a Group?

People gather in many situations, but not all of these congregations qualify as groups. Three factors must be present before a collection of people constitutes a group (Levine & Moreland, 1998). First, there must be a mutual sense of a shared identity—group members must believe they form a unit or are joined in some psychological fashion that creates a subjective sense of "we" or "us." Second, there must be interaction. People must meet from time to time as a group. Increasingly, this can be done over the Internet, as people who regularly frequent chat rooms meet in cyberspace. Finally, there must be interdependence. In this context, interdependence means that the group has a common goal and that one person's outcomes influence another person's outcomes. A baseball team provides a good example. If the shortstop makes a throwing error, the team as a whole suffers the consequences. In sum, we can define a **group** as an interdependent collection of individuals who interact and possess a shared identity.

This definition allows us to distinguish groups from a broader construct known as a social aggregate. A social aggregate consists of a large number of people. Some social aggregates are groups; others are not. For example, under most circumstances, the passengers on a bus do not constitute a group. Although they may interact, their outcomes are not interdependent and they generally do not share a common identity. However, if several of them ride the same bus to work every day, they might form a social group that serves as a form of self-definition. Or if the bus breaks down, forcing the passengers to coordinate their efforts to make repairs, the interdependent nature of the task would create a group.

These examples underscore that the boundaries that distinguish social aggregates from groups are fluid. People's perceptions of what constitutes a group are also variable. The extent to which a collection of individuals is judged to form an integrated unit, or entity, is termed *group entitativity* (D. T. Campbell, 1958; D. L. Hamilton & Sherman, 1996). A group high in entitativity is one that is judged to be a single, meaningful entity. The higher a group's entitativity, the more we assume the group's members share a unified identity. To illustrate, suppose we learn that one group member is honest. If the group's entitativity is high, we tend to assume that other group members are honest as well (Crawford, Sherman, & Hamilton, 2002, McConnell, Sherman, & Hamilton, 1994, 1997).

Lickel and colleagues (2000) investigated factors that influence group entitativity. These investigators had college students rate 40 social aggregates (e.g., members of a rock band, residents of a retirement home) along several dimensions. For example, they

TABLE 9.1   Four Types of Groups That Vary in Entitativity

Category Label	Examples	Description
Intimacy groups	Families Romantic couples	Small size High levels of interaction Long duration
Task-oriented groups	People attending a support group Members of a sports team	Small size High levels of interaction Moderate duration
Social categories	Americans Doctors	Large size Moderate levels of interaction Long duration
Loose associations	People who live in the same neighborhood Students attending a university	Large size Low levels of interaction Moderate duration

Source: Lickel et al. (2000).

rated how important the group was, how often the group members interacted, and how similar to one another the members were. In addition, they indicated the group's entitativity by rating the degree to which the people qualified as a group. Table 9.1 shows that four categories emerged from this analysis. The groups with the highest entitativity ratings were *intimacy groups,* such as families and romantic couples. *Task-oriented groups,* such as support groups or sports teams, comprised the second category. A third type, labeled *social categories,* included various social identities, such as American or doctor. The final category was labeled *loose associations.* Included here were people who live in the same neighborhood or attend the same university.

B. Why Join a Group?

If you're like most people, you belong to several groups. Some of these are formal organizations (perhaps you belong to a sorority or fraternity, or a church or synagogue), while others are more informal (perhaps you have formed a study group that meets to discuss social psychology). If you think about it, you probably joined these groups for a variety of reasons.

1. Functions of Groups

Groups Help Us Achieve Goals.   You may have joined a group with a specific goal in mind. For example, if you want to play lead guitar, you need to form a rock band with a bass player, drummer, and rhythm guitar player. Groups can also help us achieve our goals by providing information. Many college freshman join groups to learn about campus life and help them adjust to their new experience. In both of these examples, groups serve an instrumental function: Joining a group helps people achieve a goal or objective they wouldn't be able to attain on their own.

Groups Provide Companionship. People also join groups for companionship. Although people differ in their desire for company, everyone needs to affiliate with others (Baumeister & Leary, 1995). Joining groups is one way we satisfy this need. By joining groups, we get to know people and make friends. Evolutionary psychologists believe that companionship served an instrumental function. By banding together, people were more likely to survive and successfully reproduce.

Groups Are Important Aspects of Self-Identity. Finally, we join groups to help define ourselves. In Chapter 5 we noted that our self-concept includes not only ourselves but also our loved ones, our possessions, and the groups to which we belong. Some group memberships are ascribed (our ethnic and racial heritage are set at birth), but others are attained when people choose to join various organizations, clubs, and groups. For many people, the church they attend or their political affiliation represents an important aspect of their identity. People often carry this identity with them throughout life. Many students, for example, join alumni associations and sport automobile license plates that announce their alma mater.

Group identities serve two purposes (Bettencourt & Sheldon, 2001; Brewer, 1991; J. C. Turner, & Onorato, 1999; Vignoles, Chryssochoou, & Breakwell, 2000). First, by highlighting our connection with others, they satisfy a need for belonging and social inclusion ("I'm a member of Group X"). Second, by highlighting our dissimilarity from others, they satisfy a need for uniqueness and social distinctiveness ("I'm not a member of Group Y"). According to Brewer's optimal distinctiveness theory, people attempt to satisfy the dual needs for belonging and uniqueness by joining moderately sized, tight-knit groups of high social status (Pickett & Brewer, 2001; Pickett, Silver, & Brewer, 2002). Being a member of a moderately sized, high-status group satisfies our need for uniqueness, and being a member of a tight-knit group satisfies our need to belong.

2. Sex Differences in the Motivation to Join Groups

Women tend to have stronger affiliative needs than men and are more apt to seek out the company of others, especially under periods of stress (S. E. Taylor, Klein, et al., 2000). Are women also more likely than men to join groups? Research suggests that they are not (Forsyth, 1999). Men and women do, however, tend to join different sorts of groups for different reasons. Women tend to join small, informal, intimate groups that satisfy their need to belong, whereas men tend to join larger, more formal, more structured groups that help them achieve their goals (Baumeister & Sommer, 1997). These differences are rarely large. Moreover, task-oriented groups frequently provide companionship and intimacy groups regularly adopt various goals to accomplish, so the difference is mainly one of emphasis. A bridge club, for example, meets for both instrumental reasons (so people can play bridge) and for social reasons.

In fact, most groups fulfill all three functions: goal attainment, companionship, and social identity. To illustrate, people who join political parties typically do so for instrumental reasons (e.g., to elect candidates); for friendship (e.g., group members often become close friends); and for social identity (for many people, political affiliation is a central part of their self-concept). Undoubtedly, groups are so attractive because they help people fulfill many important goals of social life.

C. Steps to Joining a Group

Many college campuses have a rush week—a period when students decide which sorority or fraternity they will join. This process is characterized by a number of stages

(Moreland & Levine, 1982). During the investigation stage, prospective members seek information about which groups best fulfill their needs and goals, and existing group members evaluate the attractiveness of potential candidates and recruit the ones they regard as most desirable. This period of investigation culminates when a group issues an invitation to join and a recruit accepts.

The second stage involves socialization, a period when new members learn the norms and customs of the group and the group changes to accommodate the newcomers' needs. There is a good deal of give and take during this period of adjustment, although new recruits tend to adapt their behavior to match the group's, rather than vice versa. Groups do, however, evolve over time, and each new member has the potential to alter the group's direction and customary behavioral patterns.

After a period of adjustment and accommodation, the group enters a period of maintenance. Here, new members have been fully absorbed into the group and the group functions as a cohesive unit. Of course, this stage is not always reached. In some cases a new member quits after repeatedly failing to fit in with the group.

D. Roles and Norms

Although groups come in all shapes and sizes, they can be characterized according to their roles and norms. *Roles* describe the position people occupy within a group. For example, many groups have a leader or secretary, a president, or a chief executive officer. *Norms* refer to expectations about how members are supposed to behave. Some of these norms are role-specific (leaders should be demanding), whereas others refer to the group as a whole (members are expected to support one another).

Groups function most effectively when members fulfill one of two roles (Benne & Sheats, 1948). Task-oriented members push the group toward meeting its goals and ensure that the group stays on track. Emotion-focused members are more concerned with promoting and maintaining harmony among group members. Instead of directly moving the group forward, these members instill a sense of camaraderie and companionship.

Both roles are needed, but people rarely play both roles at once. Instead, there is a tendency to choose one role or the other: Those who opt for being directive are rarely accommodating, and those who opt for being conciliatory are rarely assertive. Traditionally, the sexes have differed with regard to which role they adopt. Men have been more apt to adopt an instrumental role, and women have been more apt to assume a socioemotional role. In a later section of this chapter, we will discuss these differences in greater depth and examine their effect on leadership ability.

II. Individual Performance in a Group Setting

If you're like most students, you have joined a study group to prepare for an examination, taken a test in a crowded roomful of students, and participated in a group project in which each student is responsible for a different part of a group task. The manner in which your performance is affected by these situations is one of social psychology's oldest research areas. In the following section, you will learn to identify the conditions that determine when the presence of other people helps or hinders your performance. To foreshadow, the effects depend on (1) whether the task is easy or difficult and (2) whether your efforts and contributions can be easily identified and compared with the efforts and contributions of others.

A. Social Facilitation

The story begins in 1898, when a French scientist, Norman Triplett, noticed that bicycle riders posted faster times when racing with others than when racing alone. Diminished air resistance was commonly thought to explain the effect. Like geese flying in formation, the first rider breaks the air current for the others, creating less resistance and allowing them to go faster. Triplett wondered whether social factors might also be operating. He theorized that competition might energize individuals and thereby improve their performance. To test his idea, he conducted one of social psychology's first experiments by having children spin a fishing line with other children or alone. On average, the children performed this task more quickly when they performed in the presence of others than when performing the task alone, leading Triplett to conclude that the presence of others improves task performance (Triplett, 1898).

Follow-up research found that the presence of others enhances performance regardless of whether the other people are active co-participants (termed coactors) or passive observers (an audience). The effect even occurs in other species. Chickens, for example, eat more when other chickens are around than when they are alone (Zajonc, 1980a). Not all situations produce this effect, however. In some circumstances, the presence of others impairs performance, such that humans and animals perform these tasks better when they are alone than when others are present (Pessin, 1933). Whenever scientists uncover inconsistent findings like these, they search for variables that determine when one or the other effect occurs.

1. The Effects of Task Difficulty

In 1965, Zajonc found a variable that determines whether the presence of others improves task performance. In his **social facilitation theory,** Zajonc argued that the presence of others enhances performance on familiar or well-learned tasks but impairs performance on difficult or poorly learned tasks. In formulating his prediction, Zajonc drew on principles of drive theory (C. L. Hull, 1943; Spence, 1956). As discussed in Chapter 2, this theory argues that behavior is a multiplicative function of two factors: drive and habit strength. As drive increases, strongly acquired habits (known as dominant responses) are more apt to be displayed. Building on this framework, Zajonc argued that the presence of others creates arousal and that this arousal increases the likelihood that a dominant response will be exhibited. When a task is easy, familiar, or well learned, the dominant response is usually correct and the presence of others enhances performance. When a task is difficult, novel, or poorly learned, the dominant response is usually incorrect and the presence of others impairs performance. This theory, which is illustrated in Figure 9.1, can explain why professional golfers (like Tiger Woods) perform best when they are in front of a large audience, while weekend duffers (like me) perform more poorly when others are around (Zajonc & Sales, 1966).

2. What Produces Arousal?

Having formed his social facilitation theory, Zajonc (1965, 1980a) went on to consider why the presence of others creates arousal. He argued that other people are inherently unpredictable and that this unpredictability makes us more alert whenever they are around. From this perspective, other people don't need to do anything unusual or odd in order to create arousal. They need only be present. Because it maintains

FIGURE 9.1

Zajonc's (1965) Model of
Social Facilitation

The presence of others
creates arousal, and
arousal facilitates performance on easy tasks but
impairs performance on
difficult tasks.

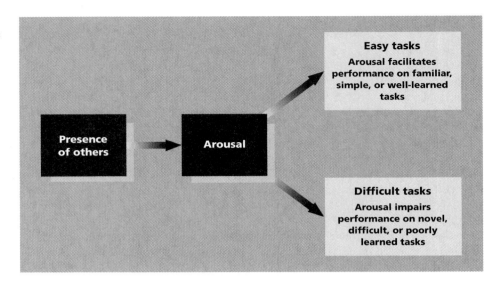

that the mere presence of others is sufficient to produce arousal, this hypothesis is known as the **mere presence hypothesis.**

Although there is evidence that people become aroused when performing a task in front of others (Blascovich, Mendes, Hunter, & Solomon, 1999), not everyone accepts Zajonc's claim that the mere presence of others creates arousal. Instead, some theorists have suggested that the presence of other people produces arousal only if we are concerned that they are evaluating us (C. F. Bond & Titus, 1983; Cottrell, 1972; Henchy & Glass, 1968).

Markus (1978) conducted a study to test these competing hypotheses. Participants were told they were going to take part in an experiment that required them to wear some unfamiliar clothing. All participants were then taken to a waiting room and told to take off their shoes and socks (easy task) and put on a pair of large socks, over-sized tennis shoes, and an ill-fitting lab coat (difficult task). An experimental assistant, hiding behind a one-way mirror, secretly recorded the amount of time it took participants to complete these tasks. Three experimental conditions were created to determine whether the mere presence of others is sufficient to enhance performance on easy tasks and impair performance on difficult tasks. In one condition, participants were alone; in an inattentive-audience condition, a confederate was situated in a corner of the room, facing away from the participant, busily engaged in repairing a piece of machinery for use in another experiment; and in an attentive audience condition, another participant (actually a confederate) attentively observed the participants as they changed their clothes. The key question of interest was whether the mere presence of another person (represented by the inattentive-audience condition) would improve performance at an easy task but impair performance at a difficult task.

Figure 9.2 shows that it did. Compared to those who performed the task alone, participants who performed the task in front of an inattentive audience took less time to doff their own shoes and socks and more time to don unfamiliar, ill-fitting clothing. Supporting Zajonc's social facilitation theory, this pattern suggests that the mere presence of others creates arousal.

Perhaps you noticed that the effect is somewhat stronger in the attentive audience condition. This suggests that an evaluating audience creates even more arousal than an

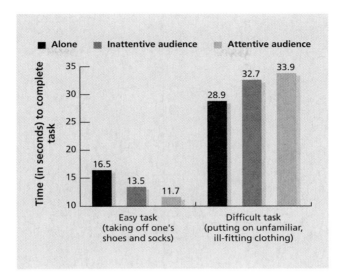

FIGURE 9.2
Social Facilitation Effects

In support of Zajonc's mere presence hypothesis, even an inattentive audience enhanced performance at an easy task but impaired performance at a difficult task.

Source: Markus (1978).

inattentive one. Other factors might produce still more arousal. For example, we would probably be even more tense and nervous if the other person was moving around a lot and distracting us, or if we feared being physically punished for making a mistake (R. S. Baron, 1986; E. E. Jones & Gerard, 1967). These factors do not, however, negate Zajonc's claim that the mere presence of others is sufficient to aid our performance at easy tasks but disrupt our performance at difficult tasks (see B. H. Schmitt, Gilovich, Goore, & Joseph, 1986, for further evidence relevant to this point).

Animal studies provide even clearer evidence that the mere presence of others creates arousal. Zajonc believed that social facilitation effects occur in many species besides humans. He claimed that whenever a member of the same species is around, drive is increased and performance improves on easy tasks but declines on difficult tasks. To test this idea, Zajonc, Heingartner, and Herman (1969) had a group of cockroaches run one of two mazes. One maze was very easy; the other was quite difficult. While running the mazes, the cockroaches were either alone or in the presence of other roaches. (This was accomplished by building a Plexiglas viewing area, where other roaches were placed.) Figure 9.3 shows the results. Keeping in mind that lower numbers mean faster or better performance, the data offer strong support for Zajonc's model: The presence of an audience improved performance at an easy task but impeded performance at a difficult task. Since it is unlikely that these cockroaches feared being evaluated, these data provide solid evidence that the mere presence of others creates arousal.

B. Social Loafing

In the typical social facilitation study with humans, each person's performance is individually identifiable and capable of being evaluated. Not all tasks are of this type, however. For example, if a car gets stuck in a snow bank and a group of citizens gathers to push it out, it is generally not possible to know who's pushing hardest. In situations like these, people sometimes exhibit **social loafing:** They exert less effort when working with others than when working alone (Karau & Williams, 1993; Latané, Williams, & Harkins, 1979; Shepperd, 1993; K. D. Williams & Karau, 1991).

FIGURE 9.3

Social Facilitation Effects among Cockroaches

In support of Zajonc's mere presence hypothesis, the data show that the presence of an audience improved cockroaches' performance at an easy task, but impeded their performance at a difficult task.

Source: Zajonc, Heingartner, and Herman (1969).

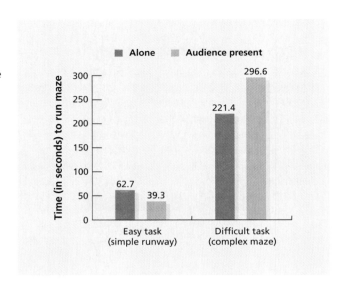

The effect was first demonstrated in the 1880s by Max Ringelmann, a French agriculturist (Kravitz & Martin, 1986). Ringelmann was studying the performance of workers as they either pulled or pushed a wooden cart. He had people try the task alone and then in groups of various sizes, much as a team of oxen might pull a load. Using a dynamometer, Ringelmann was able to calculate the amount of force being applied to the object. He found that individuals working in groups produced less force than individuals who worked alone. For example, a three-person group produced a combined force that was 15 percent less than three times the force an individual produced when working alone. Ringelmann attributed this outcome to a coordination loss, assuming that his participants were not working together efficiently. Social loafing may also have played a role (Ingham, Levinger, Graves, & Peckham, 1974). A variety of research has found that while working on physical tasks that do not require coordinated efforts, such as shouting, clapping, and pumping air, and on cognitive tasks, such as brainstorming or puzzle solving, people exert less effort in a group than when alone (for a review, see Karau & Williams, 1993). Individuals even remember less when working in a group setting than when working alone (Weldon & Bellinger, 1997).

1. What Causes Social Loafing?

Several factors produce social loafing. First, people don't try hard when they doubt whether their efforts will improve the group's performance or when they doubt whether a good performance on the part of the group will lead to a desired outcome (Shepperd & Taylor, 1999). For example, suppose you are part of a business team trying to land an important corporate account. You may withhold effort if you think no one listens to your ideas or if you think even good ideas are unlikely to win the account. In contrast, social loafing is reduced when people believe their contributions matter (Sanna, 1992; Shepperd, 1993).

The potential for self-evaluation also influences whether or not social loafing occurs. Two factors are involved here. First, your efforts need to be identifiable. If you can't identify your contribution to a group project, you can't evaluate your own performance. Second, some standard or basis for comparison must exist. Simply knowing what you've contributed isn't enough; you need a standard to determine whether your contribution is large or small.

A study by Szymanski and Harkins (1987) illustrates how identifiability combines with performance standards affect social loafing. The participants in this study signed up in groups of four for an experiment on "brainstorming" in groups. Every time they thought of a use for a common household object—a box—they wrote it down on a piece of paper and slid it down a tube for the experimenter to collect. To manipulate identifiability, half of the participants were told that the experimenter could identify each person's ideas, while the other half were told that all of the ideas would be pooled and that there would be no way of knowing how many ideas each person contributed. Independently, three additional conditions were created. Some participants were told they would learn how other participants had performed on the task (evaluation standard provided), some were told they would not learn how others had performed on the task (evaluation standard not provided), and some were given no information either way (control condition).

Figure 9.4 shows that social loafing occurred in the control condition and when no evaluation standard was provided, as here participants generated fewer uses when they thought their answers would be pooled than when they thought their answers were individually identified. In contrast, no social loafing occurred when an evaluation standard was available. In this condition, participants who believed their answers would be pooled worked just as hard as those who believed their answers were identifiable. These findings establish that people will not loaf when they are given some means of assessing their own performance (see also Harkins & Jackson, 1985; Harkins & Szymanski, 1988; K. D. Williams, Harkins, & Latané, 1981).

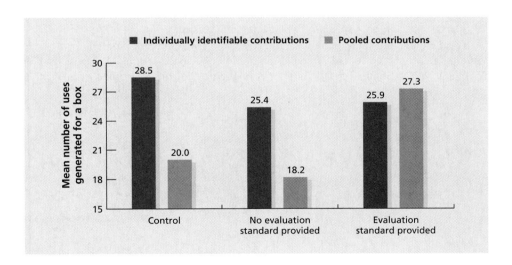

FIGURE 9.4

Social Loafing, Identifiability, and Evaluation

Social loafing occurred in the control condition and when no evaluation standard was provided. Here, participants generated fewer uses when they believed their contributions were pooled than when they believed their contributions were individually identifiable. In contrast, social loafing did not occur when an evaluation standard was provided, as participants in the pooled conditions worked just as hard as those whose efforts could be identified.

Source: Szymanski and Harkins (1987).

2. Variables That Moderate Social Loafing Effects

When learning about research on social loafing, many students think to themselves: "I don't do that. If I'm in a group where other people are slacking off, I work even harder to make up for their laziness." Although no one enjoys being taken advantage of (Kerr, 1983), there are conditions under which people exhibit social compensation—they work even harder when other group members are not pulling their weight. This is most apt to occur when a task is important or personally meaningful (K. D. Williams & Karau, 1991). In fact, social loafing effects are reduced when people care a great deal about whether the group succeeds or fails.

Individuals also differ in how likely they are to slack off. Although the effects are small, women are less likely to exhibit social loafing than men are, and people from Eastern cultures are less apt to exhibit social loafing than people from Western cultures are (Karau & Williams, 1993; Kugihara, 1999). Presumably, this occurs because women show greater concern for maintaining group harmony than men do, and because people from Eastern cultures have a more collectivistic orientation than people from Western cultures have.

C. Integrating Social Facilitation Research and Social Loafing

Earlier we noted that the presence of others impairs performance on difficult tasks. Although this is usually the case, the presence of others can sometimes enhance our performance at a difficult task. Imagine, for example, that you are going to publicly sing a very challenging song. Chances are, you'd be more nervous singing alone in front of an audience than singing along with a large choir. That's because the presence of others can calm us, especially when a task is difficult.

The fact that in some situations there is safety in numbers has led theorists to develop an integrated model of social facilitation and social loafing (J. M. Jackson & Williams, 1985; Sanna, 1992). As shown in Figure 9.5, the key variable is whether

FIGURE 9.5

An Integrated Model of Social Facilitation and Social Loafing

When performances can be identified and evaluated, the presence of others creates arousal, which improves performance at easy tasks but impairs performance at difficult tasks. When performances cannot be identified and evaluated, the presence of others relaxes us, which impairs performance at easy tasks but improves performance at difficult tasks.

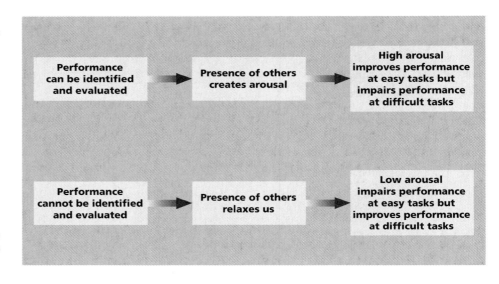

our performance can be identified and evaluated. When it can, the presence of others creates arousal. This arousal aids our performance on easy tasks (social facilitation) but impairs our performance on difficult tasks (social impairment). When our performance is pooled and cannot be identified or evaluated, we relax when others are around. This can lead to a poor performance when the task is easy (social loafing) but may improve our performance when the task is difficult. This latter effect, a type of social comfort, occurs because we worry less about making a mistake when others are around to share the responsibility.

Sanna (1992) tested this model. The participants in Sanna's study were asked to solve easy or difficult problems related to creativity. Some of the participants solved the problems while working alone, some worked with others but believed their performance could be evaluated, and some worked with others and believed their performance could not be evaluated. Figure 9.6 shows that, for easy tasks, the presence of others improved performance when performances could be identified and evaluated (social facilitation) but impaired performance when performance could not be identified and evaluated (social loafing). When a task was difficult, the presence of others impaired performance when performances could be identified and evaluated (social impairment) but improved performance when performances could not be identified and evaluated (social comfort).

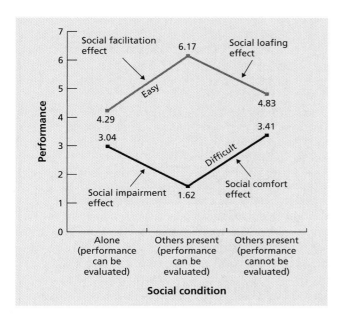

FIGURE 9.6

Social Facilitation, Social Loafing, and Task Difficulty

When a task is easy, the presence of others improves our performance on an easy task if our performance can be identified and evaluated (social facilitation) but impairs our performance if our performance cannot be identified and evaluated (social loafing). When a task is difficult, the presence of others impairs our performance when our performance can be identified and evaluated (social impairment) but improves our performance when our performance cannot be identified and evaluated (social comfort).

Source: Sanna (1992).

III. Evaluating Group Performance

So far, we have been discussing how individuals perform in a group setting. A related question of interest is whether groups perform better than individuals. Folk wisdom provides opposing views on the matter. Sometimes we hear that "two heads are better than one" and other times we hear that "too many cooks spoil the broth." So which is it? The answer, as you might imagine, depends on several factors (Kerr & Tindale, 2004).

A. Task Type

The type of task is the first factor to consider (Steiner, 1972). An *additive task* is one in which the group product is the sum of all of the group members' contributions. When Girl Scouts sell cookies, the total money earned represents the pooled contribution of all of the members of a troop. Similarly, the amount of noise fans generate at a basketball game is an additive task. With an additive task, groups are generally better than individuals working alone. If you are having a charity drive, you will probably raise more money if you have many solicitors going door-to-door than if you have just a few. This is true even though any given individual might have worked harder if he or she had been solely responsible for the outcome.

Most social loafing studies use additive tasks. Consequently, the group's performance generally exceeds the performance of individuals working alone. Recall that Ringelmann found that three people working together to push or pull a wooden cart produced a force that was approximately 2.85 times as much as the force produced by one person working alone. Although this is less than the amount expected if all three people worked up to their potential, it is still far greater than the force exerted by just one person.

A *conjunctive task* is one in which the group's performance depends on the individual with the poorest performance. When a team of surgeons is operating, the entire operation can be jeopardized if one physician makes a mistake. The same is true in many business settings. If the person in charge of ordering a product fails to order the correct amount, the company as a whole suffers. Because you're only as strong as your weakest link on a conjunctive task, groups generally perform worse than do individuals working alone. This occurs even though social loafing tends to be minimized on conjunctive tasks (Messé, Hertel, Kerr, Lount, & Park, 2002).

Finally, a *disjunctive task* is one in which the group's success can be determined by just one group member. If you and your friends are sitting around trying to think of a theme for your next party, all you need is one person to come up with a good idea. Because only one good idea is needed, groups generally outperform individuals on disjunctive tasks (Laughlin, Zander, Knievel, & Tan, 2003). This is not always the case, however. One problem that arises is that the most talented group members aren't always able to persuade the rest of the group that their ideas should be adopted. As we saw in Chapter 5, people exaggerate their own virtues and assume that their ideas are better than everyone else's. Because of the better-than-most effect, the best ideas are not always embraced by the group as a whole.

B. Brainstorming

Research on brainstorming reveals other reasons why groups don't always outperform individuals on disjunctive tasks. Brainstorming was developed by an advertising executive, Alex Osborn, who believed it was easier to tone down a wild idea than create a new one (Osborn, 1957). With Osborn's procedure, individuals gather in a group setting and are instructed to express whatever ideas come to mind, without censoring themselves. Other group members are urged to build on these ideas and to refrain from judging them as good or bad until after the brainstorming session has been completed. Later, the group members evaluate and refine the ideas that were generated during the initial session.

Within a short time, many political, educational, and business organizations embraced brainstorming as an effective technique for getting their members to think creatively. Confidence in the technique proved to be unfounded, however. Although brainstorming is an effective way for individuals to generate creative ideas, it is not particularly effective in a group setting (Diehl & Stroebe, 1987, 1991; Mullen, Johnson, & Salas, 1991). In fact, individuals who brainstorm in a group usually generate ideas that are less creative and innovative than those who brainstorm alone. Why? For one thing, people are reluctant to suggest zany, creative ideas in a group setting, fearing they will appear foolish or be ridiculed. Second, as in a typical social loafing setting, people may assume that others will carry the load and thereby reduce their own effort. Third, people have to wait their turn to speak in a group. This may cause them to become distracted, forget their original idea, or lose interest (Nijstad, Stroebe, & Lodewijkx, 2003). Although steps can be taken to alleviate these problems (Offner, Kramer, & Winter, 1996; Oxley, Dzindolet, & Paulus, 1996), individuals who brainstorm together rarely produce better ideas than do individuals who brainstorm alone. Nevertheless, people continue to believe that brainstorming in groups is effective, in part because they enjoy the process more (Paulus, Dzindolet, Poletes, & Camacho, 1993; Stroebe, Diehl, & Abakoumkin, 1992).

C. Information Exchange in Group Settings

The Supreme Court of the United States has nine justices. Presumably, the justices share their knowledge during their deliberations, producing a legal decision that is more informed than one produced by any given individual working alone. Unfortunately, group decisions don't always work this way. Instead of sharing the unique information each member possesses, group members tend to discuss information everyone already knows. This tendency to focus the discussion on shared information undermines the effectiveness of group decisions.

To illustrate this problem, consider the information presented in Table 9.2. Here, a committee of three people has gathered to bestow a teaching award. In the first example, all three members have access to the same information. They all know that candidate A has three positive qualities and that candidate B has four positive qualities. Logically, they should choose candidate B, and this is usually what occurs. Now consider the situation in the second example. All three committee members know three positive things about candidate A but only two positive things about candidate B. If each were making a decision alone, this information pattern would lead them to select candidate A. However, if they were to pool their information, they would learn four positive things about candidate B and conclude that this candidate is superior. Research suggests that this rarely occurs. Instead of sharing unique information, group members tend to discuss the information they have in common (Stasser & Titus, 1985; Winquist & Larson, 1998). Moreover, this occurs even with highly consequential decisions, such as those made by a medical team (Larson, Christensen, Abbott, & Franz, 1996; Larson, Christensen, Franz, & Abbott, 1998).

TABLE 9.2 Shared and Unshared Information

EXAMPLE 1: SHARED INFORMATION

	CANDIDATE A			CANDIDATE B	
Knowledge Possessed by Committee Member 1	Knowledge Possessed by Committee Member 2	Knowledge Possessed by Committee Member 3	Knowledge Possessed by Committee Member 1	Knowledge Possessed by Committee Member 2	Knowledge Possessed by Committee Member 3
Accessible office hours	Accessible office hours	Accessible office hours	Personable	Personable	Personable
Considerate of alternative viewpoints	Considerate of alternative viewpoints	Considerate of alternative viewpoints	Well-organized lectures	Well-organized lectures	Well-organized lectures
Articulate	Articulate	Articulate	Cares about learning	Cares about learning	Cares about learning
			Knowledgeable about subject matter	Knowledgeable about subject matter	Knowledgeable about subject matter

EXAMPLE 2: UNSHARED INFORMATION

	CANDIDATE A			CANDIDATE B	
Knowledge Possessed by Committee Member 1	Knowledge Possessed by Committee Member 2	Knowledge Possessed by Committee Member 3	Knowledge Possessed by Committee Member 1	Knowledge Possessed by Committee Member 2	Knowledge Possessed by Committee Member 3
Accessible office hours	Accessible office hours	Accessible office hours	Personable	Personable	Personable
Considerate of alternative viewpoints	Considerate of alternative viewpoints	Considerate of alternative viewpoints	*Well-organized lectures*	*Cares about learning*	*Knowledgeable about subject matter*
Articulate	Articulate	Articulate			

The tendency to discuss things everyone already knows stems, in part, from a desire for social approval. We like others who validate our own views and attitudes, so we like people who discuss information we have more than those who bring up information we don't have (Wittenbaum & Bowman, 2004; Wittenbaum, Hubbell, & Zuckerman, 1999; Wittenbaum & Park, 2001). Fortunately, this problem can be avoided if everyone is aware that each group member has expertise with respect to some issues but not others (Stasser, Stewart, & Wittenbaum, 1995; Stewart & Stasser, 1995) and if the group is encouraged to make a critical decision rather than a consensual one (Postmes, Spears, & Cihangir, 2001). Groups are also more likely to discuss unshared information in the latter stages of a discussion and when the information is particularly important or diagnostic (J. R. Kelly & Karau, 1999).

IV. Leadership

When evaluating the effectiveness of a group's performance, no subject is more important than the issue of group leadership. Whether it's the manager of a sports team, the chief executive officer of a large corporation, or a military officer leading troops into battle, leaders are held responsible for the group's successes and failure. Although there are many ways to describe it, we will define **leadership** as a reciprocal relationship in which an individual exerts social influence over cooperating individuals to promote the attainment of group goals. The word *reciprocal* requires some elaboration. In this context, the word calls attention to the fact that the relationship between leader and follower is bidirectional. Leaders clearly influence their followers, but followers also influence their leaders (Hollander, 1993).

The use of the term *cooperating individuals* also deserves mention. Leadership entails power, but power alone does not constitute leadership. Dictators who rule their countries through fear and intimidation are not displaying leadership. Instead, leadership occurs only when subordinates willingly follow a course a leader has charted. In the words of Harry Truman, "A good leader has the ability to get other people to do what they don't want to do, and like it" (cited in Forsyth, 1999, p. 341).

A. The Emergence of Leadership: Who Shall Lead?

Leaders emerge whenever individuals gather in a group setting to solve a problem or reach a goal. Sometimes individuals thrust themselves into positions of leadership by actively lobbying for the position; other times they are quietly chosen by other group members to lead the group. In both cases, people's ideas about who *should* lead influence who *does* lead.

1. Implicit Theories of Leadership

Social psychologists refer to beliefs about who should lead as people's implicit theories of leadership. These theories represent our ideas about the psychological qualities that good leaders should possess (Kenney, Schwartz-Kenney, & Blascovich, 1996; R. B. Lord & Maher, 1991). First, leaders are expected to possess task-relevant qualities associated with action and purpose. They need to have a clear vision of the group's goals and be determined, influential, and resourceful in their commitment to attain those goals. Second, leaders should be caring and compassionate. They should be aware of group members' feelings and attentive to their needs. Good leaders are also expected to possess particular skills, talents, and abilities. Intelligence is important, but expertise in a particular area is often a more significant factor. Finally, a good leader should be charismatic. Webster's dictionary defines charisma as "a personal magic of leadership, arousing . . . loyalty or enthusiasm for a public figure" (www.m-w.com). No single factor makes a person charismatic. John F. Kennedy's charisma was derived from his vitality, charm, and intelligence; Franklin Roosevelt's charisma was derived from his earnestness, quiet manner, and fortitude.

2. Demographic Variables That Predict Leadership Emergence

Beyond the psychological qualities represented in people's implicit theories of leadership, several demographic variables also play a role (Forsyth, 1999). For example, leaders are often physically distinctive. They tend to be taller, heavier, and older than their subordinates. Height is particularly important, as people tend to associate height with power. Undoubtedly, this is one reason why the taller of the two presidential candidates usually wins the popular vote. Gender also matters. All else being equal, men are more apt to be selected as leaders than women are. Group participation also matters. People who talk a lot during group discussions are more apt to lead than are those who remain quiet (Mullen, 1991). Even the manner in which people position themselves plays a role. People who sit at the head of a table are more apt to be selected to lead than are those who sit in the middle.

B. Leadership Style

Leaders differ in many respects, but two aspects of leadership style are particularly important. First, leaders differ with respect to their dominant goal. Some leaders are task-oriented; they are primarily concerned with making sure the group meets its goals, and they pay relatively little attention to the needs and feelings of their subordinates. Other leaders are more relationship-oriented. Rather than focusing solely on the bottom line, relationship-oriented leaders are concerned with building solidarity, promoting group morale, and maintaining group harmony.

The manner in which leaders attempt to motivate their followers also varies. Some leaders, called transactional leaders, appeal directly to the self-interest of their subordinates. They reward their subordinates for meeting specified objectives, and punish or refrain from rewarding them when they fall short of meeting their goals. This type of leadership is common among sales managers, who dole out incentive bonuses and promotions according to performance. Often such leaders are rather aloof, intimidating, or domineering. Other leaders adopt a more accessible, transformational style (Bass, 1998; Burns, 1978). In comparison with transactional leaders, transformational leaders are generally more charismatic and innovative. Instead of strictly emphasizing the attainment of performance standards, transformational leaders empower their subordinates by allowing them to specify their own goals and by encouraging them to develop their full potential.

C. Leadership Effectiveness: What Makes a Leader Great?

History books contain biographies of key individuals who have distinguished themselves as uncommonly effective leaders. Hannibal, Gandhi, Mao Zedong, and Susan B. Anthony are just some of the great leaders we encounter throughout history. What made these individuals so effective? Even historians are unsure. Some people believe that leadership is an innate quality—a skill a person possesses at birth. Others argue that leadership is an ability that can be acquired and honed. As with most such matters, support for both sides can be found, suggesting that the truth lies somewhere between these extremes.

1. Natural Leaders: The Great Person Theory

In the spring of 1963, the Reverend Martin Luther King Jr. led a march on the nation's capital. Standing before a sea of nearly 400,000 faces, King delivered his "I Have a Dream" speech, uniformly regarded as one of the most stirring political addresses of modern times. King's ability to arouse the passions of his followers and energize his constituents to fight for change without resorting to violence established him as the leader of the civil rights movement. Certainly, King possessed all of the qualities of a great leader. He was charismatic, had a clear vision of where he wanted his followers to go, and was a man of uncommon gentleness and intelligence.

King's story exemplifies one view of leadership: the notion that leaders are great people who are destined to rule under many circumstances. This "great person" theory of leadership was first put forth by Thomas Carlyle (1841) and later elaborated by Sir Francis Galton (1869/1952). Although early reviews of the literature provided only limited support for this view (Mann, 1959; Stogdill, 1948), more recent research has found evidence that effective leaders do possess particular traits (Albright & Forziaati, 1995). For example, they tend to be intelligent (Simonton, 1985); sociable and empathic (Hogan, Curphy, & Hogan, 1994); and highly motivated (D. G. Winter, 1987). These findings lend support to the view that many great leaders, especially those who wielded power without having a formal constituency, were able to effect change largely because of their inherent abilities.

2. Situational Theories of Leadership

Leadership effectiveness also depends on the situation. Leaders who face difficult, stressful circumstances are better able to demonstrate their excellence than are leaders who preside over calm, tranquil times. Consider presidential greatness. Simonton (1987) found that five situational variables predict presidential greatness in the United States: the length of the president's term in office, the number of war years the president served in office, whether there was a scandal during his tenure in office, whether the president was a war hero before coming to office, and whether the president was assassinated while in office. In a similar vein, McCann (1992) found that our most esteemed presidents have all faced a crisis of some sort. Presidents who preside over periods of national calm have a much more difficult time demonstrating their excellence.

Another determining factor is the zeitgeist, or the spirit of the time. The historian Arthur Schlesinger (1986) notes that America has undergone a series of 30-year shifts in its political climate, alternating between periods of public purpose and private interest. The former phase is characterized by idealism, passion, and a willingness to sacrifice for the common good (e.g., the World War II era); the latter is characterized by self-indulgence, materialism, and a persistent pursuit of personal gratification (e.g., the Roaring Twenties). Presidents who serve during eras of self-sacrifice are more apt to be considered great than are those who serve during periods of self-indulgence.

3. Interactional Models of Leadership

A third perspective maintains that leadership effectiveness depends on the interaction between the qualities of the leader and the situational needs of the group. According to this view, a person who is an effective leader in one situation may be ineffective

FIGURE 9.7

Two Great Leaders with Different Leadership Styles

Vince Lombardi was a no-nonsense football coach in an era when athletes had respect for authority. Phil Jackson, a modern basketball coach, is a "Zen master" who leads by listening to his players and satisfying their individual needs.

in another. To illustrate this position, consider the two coaches shown in Figure 9.7. Vince Lombardi was a highly successful coach in the National Football League. By all accounts, he was a stern taskmaster who led by stridently exhorting his players to submerge their individualism for the greater good of the group. This leadership style worked well in the 1950s and early 1960s, when players were loyal to their team and respectful of authority. It is questionable whether such a leadership style would succeed in the present era. Today's athletes are well-paid superstars who are used to having their own way. Phil Jackson is a highly effective basketball coach in today's world. Jackson is a "Zen master" who has led the Chicago Bulls and the Los Angeles Lakers to numerous world championships by inspiring his players to rise above their egoistic concerns for the higher good of the team. Clearly, a coaching style that works in one era or situation may not work in another.

The notion that leadership effectiveness depends on both the person and the situation forms the heart of Fiedler's (1967, 1978) **contingency theory of leadership.** This theory assumes that leadership effectiveness depends on two factors: leadership style and situational control. The first factor, leadership style, concerns the extent to which the leader is task-oriented or relationship-oriented. As noted earlier, some leaders are relatively inattentive to the emotional needs of the group, whereas others are concerned with maintaining group harmony.

The second factor in Fiedler's model is situational control, a term that refers to the amount of control the leader has over the group. Three factors combine to determine situational control. The first concerns the nature of the relationship between the leader and its members. Some leaders have a good rapport with the group's members, and some do not. The second factor refers to the amount of power the leader wields. Some leaders have a lot of power, whereas others have relatively little power. The third factor pertains to the structure of the task. In some situations, the group's task is very clear and highly structured. For example, an organization deciding where to

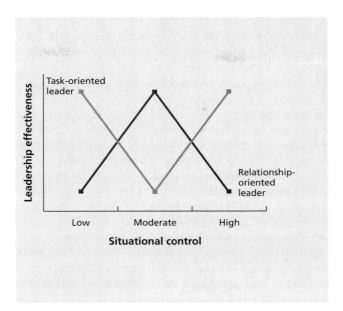

FIGURE 9.8

Fiedler's Contingency Model of Leadership

The model maintains that task-oriented leaders are most effective when situational control is high or low, but that relationship-oriented leaders are most effective when situational control is moderate.

hold its next convention is facing a highly structured task. In other situations, the group's task is ambiguous and unstructured. For example, a corporation that meets to discuss how to boost profits is facing a rather ambiguous task, in that there are many possibilities to consider.

As shown in Figure 9.8, Fiedler believes that task-oriented leaders are most effective when situational control is either very high or very low. In the former case, the group is already functioning effectively, so a relationship-oriented leader isn't needed. In the latter case, the group is adrift and needs a task-oriented leader to provide strong direction to get it back on course. Relationship-oriented leaders are most effective at moderate levels of situational control, because they are needed to produce group cohesion and promote group harmony. Although contradictory findings have been reported, the research generally supports Fiedler's model, especially when situational control is high (Peters, Hartke, & Pohlmann, 1985; Stroebe & Garcia, 1981). Under these conditions, task-oriented leaders tend to outperform relationship-oriented leaders.

4. Adaptive Leadership

Whatever their leadership style, great leaders must adapt themselves to the situations they face. Former New York major Rudolph Giuliani exemplifies this point. During most of his term, Giuliani was known as a hard-nosed reformer who came to power promising to reduce crime in New York City. Although he alienated many of his constituents, Giuliani succeeded in reducing crime and corruption in New York, earning himself a reputation as an efficient, no-nonsense politician. All of this changed on September 11, 2001. When terrorists attacked the World Trade Center, Giuliani appeared on television to calm and soothe a troubled nation. In a moment's time, he was transformed from being a heartless bureaucrat to a warm, gentle source of solace and comfort. Interestingly, President George W. Bush experienced almost the opposite transformation. Known as an affable, hands-off administrator, Bush suddenly became a more hardened president who vowed to rid the world of evil. The same event that softened Giuliani hardened Bush. These men understood that, to lead effectively, leaders must adapt to the circumstances they face.

D. Gender Differences in Leadership Style and Effectiveness

A common stereotype maintains that women are more focused on relationships than men are. Are women also more apt to be relationship-oriented leaders than men? Research is mixed on this point (Eagly & Johnson, 1990). No gender differences have been found in field studies of naturally appointed leaders. For example, in organizational settings, women who naturally rise to positions of leadership are no less task-oriented leaders than men are. Laboratory research provides a somewhat different picture. When groups are created and men and women are appointed to be leaders, women tend to be more relationship-oriented than men. The bottom line? Women who seek leadership roles are just as task-oriented as men are, but women who are arbitrarily chosen to lead tend to be less task-oriented than men.

Even though women who seek positions of power are just as task-oriented as men are, they are less likely to be chosen to lead (Goktepe & Schneier, 1989). Nowhere is this disparity more apparent than in the business world. Although women commonly occupy many middle-management positions, few of the top 100 corporations on the Forbes list have women as their chief executive officers (www.forbes.com/2001/03/28/0327women.html). This state of affairs is changing, but the fact remains that many women face a "glass ceiling": an invisible barrier that prevents them from reaching pinnacles of success in organizational settings (Eagly, Johannesen-Schmidt, & van Engen, 2003; Morrison & Von Glinow, 1990; Morrison, White, & Van Velsor, 1987).

Does this barrier reflect true differences in leadership effectiveness? In other words, are women less effective as leaders than men are? The answer is no. Following a comprehensive review of the literature, Eagly, Karau, and Makhijani (1995) concluded that men and women are equally effective when it comes to leadership. There are, however, differences in terms of the situations in which male and female leaders excel. Men are more effective than women when the situation calls for a take-charge approach and task-oriented skills; women are more effective than men when the situation calls for conciliation, consensus, and relationship-oriented skills (see also W. Wood, 1987). These findings fit well with the notion that leadership effectiveness depends on the fit between the personal characteristics of the leader and the type of situation the leader confronts.

Before leaving this topic, we need to consider one other important issue. In many instances, the judgment of a leader's effectiveness is subjective. If people are unhappy with a leader or believe someone else could have performed better, they may give the leader a negative rating despite a positive performance. Research shows that women are more apt than men to receive such negative ratings. Even though women are more apt than men to possess qualities associated with strong leadership, they are less apt to be viewed as being effective leaders (Eagly, Johannesen-Schmidt, & van Engen, 2003). Eagly and Karau's (2002) role congruity theory provides a context for understanding this effect. According to this theory, people resent those who violate social norms of appropriate behavior. Since women are expected to be accommodating and demure rather than assertive and independent, women who lead with a task-oriented style tend to be disliked and are evaluated negatively (Butler & Geis, 1990; see also

Heilman, Wallen, Fuchs, & Tamkins, 2004; Rudman, 1998; Rudman & Glick, 1999). Both sexes display this tendency, so it is not as if only men judge strong women harshly. We will consider these issues in greater detail in Chapter 10 when we discuss prejudice and sexism.

V. Social Dilemmas

The world's population is expected to swell to 8 billion people by 2025. This population explosion will greatly tax the earth's natural resources. Food, water, and clean air are replenishable commodities, provided that people use these resources responsibly. In the summer of 2002, delegates from more than 100 countries traveled to Johannesburg, South Africa, to discuss these and related issues at the United Nations' World Summit on Sustainable Development. The key question under consideration: How can governments ensure that individual nations cooperate to share the earth's resources?

The situation being discussed at the World Summit on Sustainable Development illustrates a class of social situations known as a **social dilemma.** In a social dilemma, two or more interdependent parties face a conflict between maximizing their own interests or sacrificing for the benefit of the group as a whole. It's a dilemma, because even though each party is better off pursuing a noncooperative course of self-interest, the group suffers if everyone chooses that option. To illustrate, although each country would benefit by using more than its fair share of natural resources, if everyone does so the earth's resources will be depleted. Consequently, nations must learn to put long-term collective interests above their own short-term interests.

Social dilemmas occur frequently in social life. Consider the situation facing taxpayers. Although each individual is better off not paying taxes, the country cannot provide needed services if everyone pursues this strategy. The same situation faces a commuter. Most everyone enjoys the privacy and convenience of driving alone, but if no one takes mass transit the freeways become so clogged no one can get to work. In each of these situations, the rational pursuit of self-interest can result in collective disaster.

A. Resource Dilemmas

One type of social dilemma involves the sharing of a common resource. Resource dilemmas come in two forms: commons dilemmas and public goods dilemmas.

1. Commons Dilemma

A **commons dilemma** is a situation in which individuals must decide how much of a shared commodity to use. The name was coined by Hardin (1968), who illustrated this dilemma using a group of villagers who share a pasture (the town common). If the villagers allow each of their cows to graze for a limited amount of time, the pasture will replenish itself and sustain the village for years. But if individuals get greedy and fatten up their cows by taking more than their fair share, the pasture will be picked dry and perish. The Pacific Northwest today is facing a commons dilemma. In recent years, excessive fishing has led to dwindling levels of salmon in the waters of the Pacific Northwest. If this trend continues, the salmon population will be threatened to the point of extinction and no one will be able to make a living fishing.

2. Public Goods Dilemma

A second type of resource dilemma is known as a **public goods dilemma.** A public good is a service or commodity that can be provided only if people contribute their resources (e.g., time or money) to its provision. However, provided enough people contribute, even those who do not contribute can enjoy the commodity. Public television provides a good example. If enough people subscribe, the station can produce quality programming that even nonsubscribers can enjoy. But if too many people fail to subscribe, the station won't have enough money to stay on the air and everyone will suffer. Blood banks provide another example. The blood is available to everyone, but individual donations are needed to replenish the supply. If people use the supply and never donate, the supply will disappear. Finally, social loafing is a type of public goods dilemma (Kerr, 1983). As discussed earlier, social loafing occurs when individuals reduce effort when working on a collective project. In a public goods dilemma, people loaf or free-ride by failing to contribute their resources to a collective group project.

3. Comparing the Two Dilemmas

Although the commons dilemma and the public goods dilemma are similar, they differ in an important respect. In a commons dilemma, people decide how much of a shared commodity they will use; in a public goods dilemma, people decide how much of their own resources they will donate to a public project. These differences lead people to act more cooperatively in a commons dilemma than in a public goods dilemma (Brewer & Kramer, 1986; van Dijk & Wilke, 2002). People view a commons dilemma as a gain ("How much should I take?") but a public goods dilemma as a loss ("How much must I give?"). Because people are more sensitive to losses than to gains (see Chapter 4), they are less willing to contribute their fair share of resources to a group than to refrain from taking more than their fair share of a group commodity.

4. Resolving Resource Dilemmas

Resource dilemmas are not easily resolved. According to one estimate, approximately one-third of all individuals cooperate when confronted with a resource dilemma (Komorita & Parks, 1995). Several factors influence this rate. In general, these factors fall into two camps: structural solutions that impose cooperation, and psychological factors that encourage cooperation.

Structural solutions operate by making noncompliance more costly than compliance (Messick & Brewer, 1983; Van Vugt, 2001). For example, laws can be enacted and regulatory agencies created to ensure abidance with these laws. The Environmental Protection Agency (EPA) illustrates this solution. Founded in 1970, the EPA promotes conservation of the earth's natural resources and monitors compliance with existing regulations. Citizen watchdog groups serve a similar function. Drivers are encouraged to call a hotline number whenever they see a car with only one passenger using the high-occupancy vehicle lane. Structural solutions are effective, but they are costly because resources must be invested to ensure compliance.

Installing a leader with the authority to demand compliance represents another structural solution. Under most circumstances, people resist this option, especially when facing a public goods dilemma (van Dijk, Wilke, & Wit, 2003; Van Vugt, Jepson, Hart, & De Cremer, 2004). People resent being told what to do, especially if they are told how much of their own resources they must contribute to a common purpose.

TABLE 9.3 A Questionnaire for Determining One's Social Value Orientation

Imagine that you and another person have worked on a project together. The boss has given you the opportunity to decide how much each of you should receive in compensation. Choose from one of the three choices below.

	OPTION		
	A	B	C
Your Pay	$14	$13	$13
Your Partner's Pay	$12	$13	$10

Several psychological variables also influence how people behave when confronting a resource dilemma. Before considering these variables, let's examine what needs to happen in order for people to act cooperatively during a resource dilemma. Pruitt and Kimmel (1977) used an expectancy–value model (see Chapter 2) to analyze this issue. They argued that cooperation occurs when individuals (1) place a high value on the collective outcome and (2) trust that others will also behave cooperatively. As with all expectancy–value models, both variables must be greater than zero in order for behavior to occur. In the present case, this means that people must value the group outcome *and* believe that others can be trusted to cooperate. Keep these points in mind as you learn more about the variables that influence how people behave when confronting a resource dilemma.

Social Value Orientation. The first variable we will consider is a personality variable known as one's social value orientation (De Dreu, Weingart, & Kwon, 2000; Messick & McClintock, 1968; Parks, 1994; Van Lange & Kuhlman, 1994). You can calculate your social value orientation by competing the brief questionnaire in Table 9.3.

Did you choose option A? If so, you would be classified as being an individualist, because the first option gives you the most money. If you chose option B, you would be classified as a cooperative person or someone with a prosocial orientation, because option B is the fairest distribution. Finally, if you chose option C, you would be designated as having a competitive orientation, because option C maximizes your advantage over your partner.

As you might expect, people with a prosocial orientation act more cooperatively when confronting a resource dilemma than do those with an individualistic or competitive orientation. In part, this is because prosocial individuals value group outcomes more than do those with an individualistic or competitive orientation. Trust is also important (Allison & Kerr, 1994). People with a prosocial orientation are more trusting of other people and view the situation in moral terms. Instead of asking themselves whether they can take advantage of others in this situation, they ask themselves whether they can rely on others to be honest (Van Lange & Kuhlman, 1994).

Early childhood experiences are thought to contribute to the development of a prosocial orientation (Van Lange, Otten, De Bruim, & Joireman, 1997). Children from large families who grow up with caring, self-sacrificing parents tend to develop a more prosocial orientation than do children who grow up in small families with parents who are less giving.

Group Identity. Situational variables can produce a temporary prosocial orientation. One such variable is a strong group identity. People are more apt to cooperate when they strongly identify with their group than when their group identification is weak (Kramer & Brewer, 1984; Wit & Kerr, 2002). Having a strong group identity leads people to increase the value they place on the group outcome. The pop song "We Are the World" provides an excellent example of this effect. By emphasizing the degree to which we are all citizens of the world, this song raised money used to alleviate famine and drought in Africa. The song's success stemmed, in part, from its ability to instill a collective group identity in its audience, leading people to take responsibility for the suffering in Africa rather than viewing the situation as someone else's problem.

Culture. Another important factor is culture. Although the effects are not always large, individuals from collectivistic cultures tend to be more cooperative than individuals from individualistic ones (Arunachalam, Wall, & Chan, 1998; Parks & Vu, 1994). This occurs because people from collectivistic cultures place greater value on a group outcome and are more trusting that others will do the same.

Communication. Finally, individuals are more apt to cooperate when they can communicate with one another than when communication is prevented (G. Bornstein, 1992; Bouas & Komorita, 1996; Kerr & Kaufman-Gilliland, 1994). Talking the situation through creates a common group identity and leads people to trust that others will be more cooperative. This latter factor seems to be particularly important. During the course of group discussion, people extract commitments from other group members to sacrifice for the public good. In turn, these commitments lead people to be more cooperative.

B. The Prisoner's Dilemma

In a resource dilemma, individuals must learn to manage resources for a common good. If everyone cooperates, everyone wins; if no one cooperates, nobody wins. In another type of conflict situation, two or more interdependent parties compete against one another, and one party's loss is the other party's gain. By way of illustration, consider the relationship that exists between sellers and buyers. In a capitalistic system, sellers want to get us much as they can for their wares. In opposition, buyers want to pay as little as possible for the seller's goods. The two parties must compromise to resolve this dilemma. Otherwise, neither gets what the other has.

Psychologists study this type of conflict situation using a device known as the **prisoner's dilemma.** The dilemma takes its name from the following scenario: Two partners in crime are picked up by the police for questioning. The police have only enough evidence to convict them of a relatively minor offense, but if they can get one criminal to testify against the other, they can convict one of them of a more serious crime. The police separate the prisoners during questioning and offer each of them the following choices:

1. If both maintain their innocence to a serious crime, each receives a 1-year sentence for the minor charge.
2. If both confess and plead guilty to the serious crime, each receives a 5-year sentence.
3. If only one confesses to the serious crime, the one who confesses goes free and the one who doesn't serves a 10-year sentence.

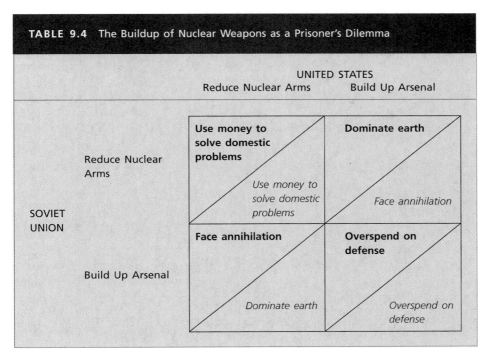

TABLE 9.4 The Buildup of Nuclear Weapons as a Prisoner's Dilemma

	UNITED STATES	
	Reduce Nuclear Arms	Build Up Arsenal
SOVIET UNION — Reduce Nuclear Arms	**Use money to solve domestic problems** / *Use money to solve domestic problems*	**Dominate earth** / *Face annihilation*
SOVIET UNION — Build Up Arsenal	**Face annihilation** / *Dominate earth*	**Overspend on defense** / *Overspend on defense*

The United States' outcomes are shown in boldface; the Soviet Union's outcomes are shown in italics.

Can you see the dilemma here? If you were one of the prisoners, you should confess and hope your partner doesn't. That way you go free. However, if you both confess, each of you serves 5 years in jail, so you might be tempted to remain silent. But if you do so and your partner confesses, you go to jail for 10 years. So what will you do: Keep quiet or squeal? Most individuals tend to confess in this situation. They accept the moderate sentence because they mistrust their partner to remain silent.

Although few of us will ever face the prisoner's dilemma, the situation it presents is not as artificial as it may seem. Consider the buildup of nuclear arms in the cold war era. As shown in Table 9.4, the United States and the Soviet Union would clearly have benefited if they had trusted one another to reduce their stockpiling of nuclear weapons. However, if one country failed to cooperate, it gained a tremendous advantage over the other. As a consequence, each country built a large store of nuclear weapons, diverting resources that could have been used for more humanitarian purposes.

1. Resolving the Prisoner's Dilemma

In experimental situations, the prisoner's dilemma is usually played over a number of trials, allowing individuals to accumulate points or other resources. This strategy allows researchers to study patterns of cooperation, in hopes of identifying the most effective way to resolve such dilemmas.

Reciprocity. Reciprocity is one way to resolve the prisoner's dilemma (Axelrod, 1984). People who begin by cooperating and then match their partner's responses on subsequent trials achieve the greatest benefits. This tit-for-tat strategy has also been shown to be an effective way for resolving other social dilemmas.

FIGURE 9.9

The Acme–Bolt Trucking Game

Playing the role of a trucking company executive, participants earn points by driving their truck from a starting point to their destination as quickly as possible. The quickest route is the one-lane road in the middle, but only one truck can pass on the road at any time. To maximize their profits, each company must cooperate with the other. In some versions of the study, some of the participants were given gates they could use to block the other company's progress on the one-lane road.

Source: Deutsch and Krauss (1960).

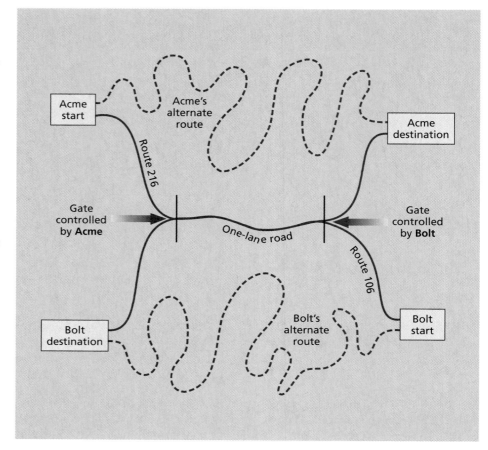

Threat Capacity. At various times throughout the cold war, the United States and the Soviet Union were belligerent, each asserting superiority and threatening to annihilate the other. Is threat an effective way to resolve social dilemmas? An early investigation by Deutsch and Krauss (1960) addressed this issue. Participants were asked to imagine that they were in charge of a trucking company. One person was chosen to head a company called Acme and the other to head a company called Bolt. Their task was to transport merchandise to a destination. For each of 20 trips, they received 60 cents minus expenses. Expenses were calculated at 1 cent per second, so if a trip took 35 seconds to complete, the participant would receive 25 cents (60 − 35). If the trip took longer than 60 seconds, the participant would lose money.

Figure 9.9 shows that the quickest route to the specified destination was a one-lane road in the middle. However, this road was so narrow that it could be used by only one truck at a time. Consequently, the participants had to either cooperate or use the much longer alternate route, which cost them 10 cents on each trip. Three experimental conditions were created. In one condition, neither company could control the road's access. In another condition, known as the unilateral-threat condition, one of the companies was given the power to block the other's access to the road. In a third condition, both companies had roadblocks, so both possessed the capacity to thwart the other from quickly reaching its destination.

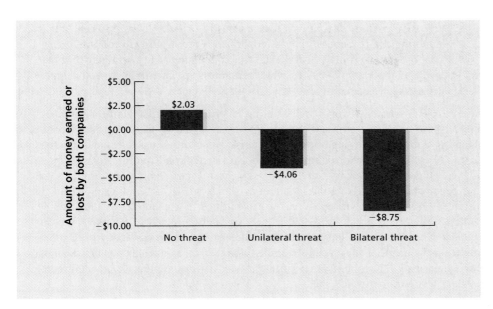

FIGURE 9.10

Threat as an Ineffective Way to Resolve Conflict

In the Acme–Bolt trucking game, each company benefits by using the direct route to their destination, but doing so requires cooperative turn-taking. When either company had the potential to block the other's progress, both received poor outcomes. These findings establish that threat is not an effective way to resolve conflict.

Source: Deutsch and Krauss (1960).

How did these variations influence the amount of money participants won? Figure 9.10 provides the answer. The participants in the control condition made a modest profit. After a few trials, they worked out a system that allowed one company to use the road while the other one waited for its turn. The situation was quite different when threat was available. When one company could unilaterally close the road down, the other company retaliated by parking its truck on the road, thereby blocking the other company's progress. As a consequence, neither company made a profit. What about when both companies had control of the gate? Would parity force the two companies to cooperate and resolve the impasse? Inspection of Figure 9.10 indicates that it did not. Instead of resolving their differences and making money, bilateral threat capacity led both companies to become even more combative, resulting in a considerable loss of money. Clearly, threat potential was not an effective means of forging an agreement in this context.

Communication. Verbal communication was forbidden in the original version of the Acme–Bolt trucking game. Following up their research, Deutsch and Krauss (1962) found that the losses in the threat conditions were reduced slightly when the two sides were allowed to discuss the situation. Unfortunately, the effect was very modest, in large part because communication did not promote trust. Instead of reassuring one another that they would behave cooperatively, the two companies became bellicose and threatened to destroy one another.

2. The Graduated and Reciprocated Initiative in Tension Reduction (GRIT)

Fortunately, communication can promote cooperation if used effectively. Osgood (1962, 1979) formulated such a strategy known as the **graduated and reciprocated initiative in tension reduction (GRIT).** The GRIT model involves the following steps:

- One party makes a general announcement stating its intention to reduce conflict through cooperation and inviting the other side to cooperate (Lindskold, Han, & Betz, 1986).

- This party pursues alternatives that are costly or risky to its position, thereby countering the perception that its concessions are a ploy (Komorita, 1973).
- If the other party fails to cooperate, the cooperative party retaliates but then resumes cooperative behavior while reiterating its intentions to find a mutually satisfactory agreement (Lindskold, Betz, & Walters, 1986).

The GRIT strategy works by fostering interpersonal trust while simultaneously establishing one's strength and resolve. Announcing one's intention to cooperate and showing goodwill by doing so first ease tension and promote understanding; reciprocating exploitive behavior demonstrates one's strength and reinforces the impression that a mutually satisfactory agreement must be reached. Although the GRIT model has been primarily tested in the laboratory (Lindskold, 1978; Lindskold & Han, 1988; Pruitt, 1998), it also operates in real-world settings. For example, in 1958 the Soviet Union unilaterally announced that it was discontinuing all atmospheric testing of nuclear weapons and called on all other nuclear powers to do likewise. The Soviets added, however, that they would resume testing if other nuclear powers did not follow their lead. These and other initiatives led to the signing of a comprehensive nuclear test ban treaty in 1963.

C. Bargaining and Negotiation

The GRIT strategy represents an attempt to resolve a dispute through negotiation. **Negotiation** can be defined as the process by which two or more interdependent parties attempt to resolve conflicting preferences (L. Thompson, 1990a). Although negotiations can produce mutually beneficial agreements, they do not always do so. All too frequently, labor disputes and divorce proceedings become rancorous, underscoring the difficulty people have in successfully resolving their differences. Numerous factors undermine people's attempts to forge mutually beneficial agreements.

1. Fixed-Pie Perception in Negotiation

One problem in negotiation is that people frequently fail to see the potential for a mutually beneficial agreement. Instead of searching for compatible interests, they view the situation in competitive terms and assume that their interests are directly opposed to their partner's interests. This perception is known as the fixed-pie perception in negotiation (L. Thompson & Hastie, 1990). Follett (1942) provided a colorful illustration of this problem using a story of two sisters who quarrel about an orange. After much discussion, the sisters decide to split the orange in half. One sister then squeezes the juice out of her portion of the orange, drinks it, and throws the peel away. The other squeezes the juice out of her portion of the orange but then throws the juice away and uses the peel in a cake she is baking. Obviously, the sisters would have been better off if they had seen the potential for an integrative agreement: One sister gets all the juice, and the other gets the entire peel. Instead, they fell prey to the fixed-pie (or in this case fixed-cake) perception and failed to see the more profitable outcome.

Reaching a mutually beneficial, integrative agreement requires a skill known as logrolling. With logrolling, negotiators make trade-offs among issues, such that each party gets what it wants on its most important issue in exchange for making concessions on issues of lesser importance. Experimental studies of logrolling generally have participants engage in a simulated negotiation. To illustrate, consider the information presented in Table 9.5. The table presents a hypothetical negotiation between a

TABLE 9.5 Payoff Schedules and Agreements in a Simulated Integrative Bargaining Situation between a Prospective Tenant and Landlord

Move-In Date	Tenant	Landlord	Rent	Tenant	Landlord	Security Deposit	Tenant	Landlord	Furniture	Tenant	Landlord
Immediately	*100*	*500*	$700	*500*	*100*	None	*300*	*100*	Unfurnished	*100*	*300*
Two weeks	*200*	*200*	$800	*200*	*200*	1 month's rent	*200*	*200*	Partially furnished	*200*	*200*
One month	*500*	*100*	$900	*100*	*500*	1½ months' rent	*100*	*300*	Fully furnished	*300*	*100*

COMPROMISE AGREEMENT

	Tenant	Landlord
Move in two weeks	200	200
$800 rent	200	200
1 month's security	200	200
Partially furnished	200	200
Total points won	800	800

INTEGRATIVE AGREEMENT

	Tenant	Landlord
Move in immediately	100	500
$700 rent	500	100
1 month's security	200	200
Partially furnished	200	200
Total points won	1,000	1,000

Note: Payoff schedules are in italics. Bargainers see only their own payoff schedule, and are told to earn as many points for themselves as possible.

landlord and a prospective tenant. Four issues are under consideration: move-in date, rent, security deposit, and furniture. The payoff schedules (in italics) indicate how important each issue is to the two parties. Move-in date is the most important issue for the landlord (500 points for immediate move-in), while rent is the most important issue for the tenant (500 points for $700 rent). Each party sees only its own payoff schedule and is instructed to earn as many points as possible.

The bottom half of Table 9.5 shows two potential agreements. If the two parties compromise on all four issues (left-hand side), they will each achieve a total of 800 points. If, however, they engage in logrolling (the tenant agrees to move in immediately in exchange for a lower monthly rent—see the right-hand side) they will achieve 1,000 points.

Being held accountable for one's decisions reduces fixed-pie perceptions (De Dreu, Koole, & Steinel, 2000), and the ability to identify compatible interests and achieve integrative solutions can be acquired with training (Neale & Northcraft, 1986; L. Thompson, 1990b). At the same time, logrolling can succeed only if people faithfully communicate their interests to one another during the negotiation process (L. Thompson & Hrebec, 1996). Sometimes, one party mistakenly assumes that its preferences and values are known by the other party (Vorauer & Claude, 1998). In other cases, people willfully misrepresent their interests in order to gain a competitive edge (O'Connor & Carnevale, 1997). To illustrate, consider a situation in which a husband and wife are negotiating how to spend a Saturday night. Both want to eat at an Italian restaurant, but they disagree over which movie to see. The husband wants to see a melodramatic tear-jerker about a lonely woman who finally finds her one true love, and the wife wants to see an action thriller in which two men destroy three alien worlds. (I never said they were a typical couple!) If the man falsely claims to want Chinese food for dinner, he can see the movie he wants by logrolling: I'll compromise on dinner and eat Italian if you'll come see the movie I want. Even though he wanted Italian food all along, by feigning interest in Chinese food, he was able to have his movie and dinner too.

2. Negotiation Beliefs

When people enter into a negotiation, they have ideas about what is likely to happen (Bazerman & Neale, 1992). Sometimes these ideas are accurate, and sometimes they are not. For example, people think a deadline will hurt their negotiation outcomes, even though moderate deadlines tend to produce more satisfying settlements (D. A. Moore, 2004). People also believe they will behave more competitively when negotiating with a competitive partner, but they actually tend to become more cooperative (Diekmann, Tenbrunsel, & Galinsky, 2003).

The goals and expectancies people bring to a negotiation also matter. High goals have a paradoxical effect: Although they tend to produce better outcomes, they also lead to less satisfaction with the outcome a person actually attains (Galinsky, Mussweiler, & Medvec, 2002). Imagine that you are bargaining with a loan officer at your university for a financial package. If you enter the negotiation expecting to get an all-expenses-paid tuition-free offer, you will probably get a better deal than another student who had merely hoped to get $1,000 per year at 10 percent interest. At the same time, you are apt to be less satisfied with your package than the other student is, because the offer you receive will probably fall short of your expectations whereas the other student's offer will exceed his or her expectations.

Perceptions of fairness also influence how satisfied people are with negotiated outcomes. Consistent with research first discussed in Chapter 5, most people are self-serving in their perceptions of fairness: They believe they are fairer than others when allocating resources, and more deserving than others when receiving resources (Babcock, Loewenstein, Issacharoff, & Camerer, 1995; Diekmann, Samuels, Ross, & Bazerman, 1997; Messick, Bloom, Boldizar, & Samuelson, 1985; L. Thompson & Loewenstein, 1992). Needless to say, these biases undercut both the odds of achieving a mutually beneficial settlement and people's satisfaction with whatever outcome they end up attaining.

3. Negotiation across Cultures

In today's global economy, with so many multinational corporations, negotiations are increasingly being conducted across cultures. The potential for cultural misunderstandings is great, because different cultures adopt different approaches to a negotiation situation (Gelfand et al., 2001; Gelfand et al., 2002; Volkema, 2004). In individualistic cultures, negotiations tend to follow an adversarial model that emphasizes competition and an attitude of "All's fair in love and war." In contrast, individuals from collectivistic cultures adopt a more harmonious approach to negotiations that emphasizes fairness and cooperation, and a concern for joint benefits. How do these differences affect negotiations across cultures? Research in this area is just beginning, but cross-cultural negotiations tend to produce fewer mutually beneficial agreements than do negotiations within cultures (Adair, Okumura, & Brett, 2001; Brett & Okumura, 1998; Chen, Mannix, & Okumura, 2003).

4. Suspicion, Mistrust, and the Reactive Devaluation Effect

> Yet there remains another wall. This wall constitutes a psychological barrier between us, a barrier of suspicion, a barrier of rejection; a barrier of fear, of deception . . . A barrier of distorted and eroded interpretation of every event and every statement.
>
> *President Anwar al-Sadat, statement made before the Israeli Knesset, Jerusalem,*
> *November 29, 1977*

In 1977, Egyptian president Anwar al-Sadat made an unprecedented journey to Israel. Sadat came on a mission of peace, offering to end generations of war between Israelis and Egyptians. Speaking before the Israeli Knesset, Sadat noted the formidable psychological barriers that stood in the way of making peace between two countries who had fought for so long.

Sadat's speech underscored that parties to a negotiation frequently assume their opponents are trying to take advantage of them and have only their own interests at heart (Morris, Larrick, & Su, 1994). According to L. Ross and Stillinger (1991), suspicion of this type produces a barrier to conflict resolution known as the **reactive devaluation effect.** This term refers to the fact that negotiators tend to believe that concessions offered by the opposition are unfairly disadvantageous to one's own side (Curhan, Neale, & Ross, 2003).

Ma'oz, Ward, Katz, and Ross (2002, Study 2) studied this tendency in the context of the search for peace in the Mideast. These investigators had Israeli Jews and Israeli Arabs read a proposal for an interim end to the fighting in the Mideast. Half of the participants were told that the proposal was offered by Israel; the other half were told (correctly) that the proposal was offered by the Palestinians. All participants then indicated how favorable they thought the proposal was to Israel and to the Palestinians. Two factors were therefore varied in this study: who proposed the plan (US or THEM)

FIGURE 9.11

Reactive Devaluation
Effects

The data show that people
believe peace proposals
unfairly favor the opposition, and this is particularly
true when the proposal is
allegedly offered by the
opposition.

Source: Ma'oz, Ward, Katz, and
Ross (2002).

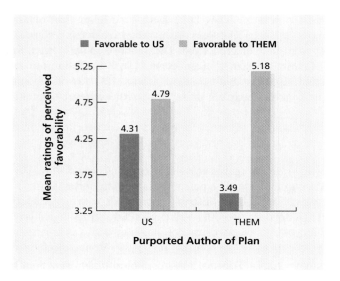

and who the plan appeared to favor (US or THEM). For the Israeli Jews, *US* refers
to Israel and *THEM* refers to the Palestinians; for the Israeli Arabs, *US* refers to the
Palestinians and *THEM* refers to Israel.

Figure 9.11 presents some of the findings from this investigation. Two effects are
of interest. First, there is a general tendency to believe that all proposals favor THEM
more than US. Second, this tendency is particularly pronounced when people
believe the opposition has authored the proposal. A plan considered moderately advantageous to one's cause when offered by one's own group is viewed as highly
disadvantageous to one's cause when offered by a group one opposes. In short, the
general tendency to believe agreements are biased against us is especially pronounced
when the agreement is offered by the opposition.

The reactive devaluation effect poses a serious impediment to peace in the Mideast.
A proposal that is viewed as reasonable when offered by one's own side is viewed as
unfair when offered by the opposition. Undoubtedly, the suspicion and enmity from
generations of ill will between the disputants contributes to this bias. But the data also
make a more fundamental point about the nature of psychological life. As we have
seen throughout this text, meaning is variable and context determines meaning. The
same agreement settlement can mean very different things depending on whether we
have positive or negative attitudes toward the people who proposed it (Curhan, Neale,
& Ross, 2004).

5. Group Negotiations

So far, we have been discussing situations in which individuals negotiate with one
another. Groups also take part in negotiations, as when union members negotiate with
management (Bazerman, Mannix, & Thompson, 1988; L. Thompson, Mannix, &
Bazerman, 1988). In general, the more people involved in a negotiation, the more
contentious the negotiation is. The effect is nearly linear: Individuals are more cooperative than small groups, and small groups are more cooperative than large groups
(Allison, McQueen, & Schaerfl, 1992; Brewer & Kramer, 1986; Insko, Schopler,
Hoyle, Dardis, & Graetz, 1990; Wildschut, Insko, & Gaertner, 2002). Several factors

contribute to this effect. First, people distrust large groups, assuming that strength lies in numbers. Consequently, they expect to be exploited when they negotiate with a group and are reluctant to concede even basic points of agreement. People in groups also believe that other group members want them to behave competitively, and this perception emboldens them to seek a more advantageous agreement for their side. Finally, people in a group situation are generally more anonymous and less identifiable than are people who negotiate alone. Since accountability leads people to find mutually beneficial solutions to problems, the lack thereof leads people to be less conciliatory.

Bornstein (1992) offers an interesting perspective on the problems this group-size effect poses. He notes that the very factors that lead people to resolve an intragroup social dilemma can fan the flames of intergroup distrust. Consider a country that anticipates going to war in the near future. The citizens face a public goods dilemma. They want to win the war, but they do not want to sacrifice their own resources to do so. The nation's leaders can counter the citizens' reluctance by creating a superordinate group identity in the nation's citizenry, best accomplished by emphasizing the us-versus-them nature of the international conflict. Unfortunately, viewing the opposition as the enemy minimizes the likelihood that war can be averted through peaceful negotiations. In short, the very processes that resolve the internal social dilemma exacerbate the external conflict.

CHAPTER SUMMARY

- A group is an interdependent collection of individuals who interact and possess a shared identity.

- Groups generally serve three functions: They help people achieve their goals, they provide companionship and acceptance, and they give people a sense of identity.

- Women and men are equally likely to join groups, but women tend to join groups for companionship, whereas men tend to join groups to achieve specific goals.

- The mere presence of others creates arousal sufficient to improve performance at an easy task but to impair performance at a difficult task.

- Social loafing occurs when individuals withhold effort when working in a group setting. It can be eliminated if people's outputs are capable of being identified and evaluated.

- Groups generally perform better than do individuals working alone on additive and disjunctive tasks, but not on conjunctive tasks.

- Individuals who brainstorm together produce ideas that are no more innovative and creative than individuals who brainstorm alone.

- When making a group decision, individuals tend to share information they all know rather than to discuss unshared information they alone may know.

- Leadership is a transactional relationship in which an individual exerts social influence over cooperating individuals to promote the attainment of group goals.

- Although great leaders possess some shared personality traits, leadership effectiveness often depends on the match between the leader's style and the group's needs.

- Women who naturally rise to positions of leadership are as task-oriented and effective as men are.

- A situation in which two or more interdependent individuals face a conflict between maximizing their own interests or sacrificing their interests for the group's benefit is called a social dilemma. A commons dilemma occurs when individuals decide how much of a shared resource they will use; a public goods dilemma occurs when individuals must donate some of their own resources to a public project.

- Social dilemmas are easier to resolve when people value the collective outcome more than their own outcomes and trust that others do the same.

- In a prisoner's dilemma, cooperation produces the best collective outcome, but cooperating with a competitive partner brings personal disaster.

- Reciprocity and communication are effective ways to resolve the prisoner's dilemma; threat is not as effective.

- In a negotiation, two or more interdependent parties agree on a solution. Negotiations are often undermined by suspicion and a fixed-pie perception that a mutually beneficial solution can't be reached.

KEY TERMS

group, 317

social facilitation theory, 324

mere presence hypothesis, 322

social loafing, 323

leadership, 331

contingency theory of leadership, 334

social dilemma, 337

commons dilemma, 337

public goods dilemma, 338

prisoner's dilemma, 340

graduated and reciprocated initiative in tension reduction (GRIT), 343

negotiation, 344

reactive devaluation effect, 347

ADDITIONAL READING

Go to the Student Edition of the Online Learning Center for this text (www.mhhe.com/brown) and log in to read the following journal articles, which relate to the content of this chapter:

- Szymanski, K., & Harkins, S. G. (1987). Social loafing and social evaluation with a social standard.

- Ma'oz, I., Ward, A., Katz, M., & Ross, L. (2002). Reactive devaluation of an "Israeli" vs. "Palestinian" peace proposal.

On August 10, 1999, Buford O. Furrow, a white supremacist living in the greater Los Angeles area, went on a shooting rampage. Furrow initially targeted the Simon Wiesenthal Center, an educational institute dedicated to combating bigotry and anti-Semitism. Finding security at the center too stringent, the 39-year-old mechanic changed his plans and stalked a Jewish community center in the San Fernando Valley section of the city, wounding five. Later, he killed a Filipino American mail carrier and fled to Las Vegas, where he scoured the phone book looking for synagogues to assault. With a smile on his face, Furrow later admitted that his actions were designed to "wake up America to kill Jews."

Unfortunately, Furrow's story is not an isolated incident. In the year preceding his attack, three European American men tied an African American man, James Byrd Jr., to the back of a pickup truck and dragged his body down a rural Texas road until he was decapitated. Later that year, three men brutally tortured and murdered a homosexual, Matthew Shepard, allegedly because one of the men thought Shepard was making a pass at him.

Though admittedly less extreme, many other, more subtle forms of prejudice and discrimination are commonplace in America. Compared to whites, members of minority groups are more likely to be stopped and questioned by police (a procedure known as racial profiling) and are less likely to receive home loans from banks and mortgage companies (a procedure known as redlining). Discrimination also affects women. Women have difficulty ascending to high levels of business administration (the glass ceiling effect), and earn roughly 80 cents for every dollar men earn (Bureau of Labor Statistics, *Highlights of Women's Earnings in 2003,* Department of Labor.)

In this chapter we will study prejudice, focusing on five issues. First, we will examine the nature of prejudice—what it is and how it is measured. We will then explore the origins of prejudice. Here you will see that prejudice has many causes, including social, situational, and personal factors. Third, we will consider how prejudice is displayed, with a focus on understanding the activation and application of stereotypes. Next, we will examine prejudice from the perspective of its victims. Finally, we will address the most important question we can ask about prejudice: How can it be reduced or eliminated?

When considering these issues, it is important to remember that social psychology is the study of normal (nonpathological) populations. Accordingly, the type of prejudice being studied is most often subtle or mild. On the one hand, this emphasis is entirely appropriate. Most people do not harbor deep-seated hatred toward others or engage in malicious forms of discrimination. At the same time, questions of external validity arise. It is unclear whether the findings from social psychological research can explain the intense hatred that motivated the actions of Buford Furrow, or the men who killed James Byrd Jr. and Matthew Shepard.

I. The Nature of Prejudice

A. Defining Prejudice

Prejudice is a negative attitude directed toward a group and its members. It is both a collective (group) phenomenon and an individual (personal) one. Individuals harbor prejudice against other individuals, but their attitudes depend on the other individuals' group membership. In fact, group membership is the defining feature of prejudice. **Racism** is a particular form of prejudice. It refers to negative attitudes toward a person based solely on the person's race. Similarly, **sexism** refers to negative attitudes toward a person based solely on the person's gender.

Like other attitudes, prejudice consists of three correlated components. The cognitive component, which psychologists call stereotypes (see Chapter 3), consists of the beliefs we hold about members of a social group. In most cases, these beliefs are derogatory (e.g., the French are rude; the elderly are bad drivers), but they can also be positive (e.g., Asian Americans are good at math and science). The behavioral component, known as **discrimination,** refers to a tendency to behave negatively toward a person solely because of the person's membership in a certain group. For example, a math teacher who rarely calls on female students to answer a question is displaying discrimination. Finally, prejudice includes feelings toward a group and its members. These feelings are almost always negative (e.g., anti-Semites hate Jews). Somewhat unfortunately, the affective aspect of a prejudicial attitude is called prejudice. To avoid confusion, I will use the term *prejudice* to refer to the attitude itself, and the term **prejudiced feelings** when referring specifically to the affective component.

In most cases, people are prejudiced against groups of which they are not a member. In the literature, such groups are called *outgroups,* and the groups to which we belong are called *ingroups*. Much of the research on prejudice has examined the different way people treat ingroup members and outgroup members, showing substantial evidence of **ingroup favoritism:** a tendency to treat and evaluate ingroup members more favorably than outgroup members.

Prejudice is usually directed against minority group members. In the present context, the word *minority* refers to being socially disadvantaged rather than being statistically rare. For example, women make up more than 50 percent of the population, yet they are considered a minority group because they are discriminated against and are less powerful than men. Similarly, African Americans comprise a statistical majority in some American cities, but they are a minority group because they do not enjoy the social privileges and advantages of European Americans. Of course, minority groups also harbor prejudice against the majority and against other minority groups (Shelton, 2000; Stephan et al., 2002). Although our focus will be on understanding prejudice from the majority's perspective, we will also consider how prejudice manifests itself among minority group members.

B. The Changing Face of Prejudice

By many indications, prejudice and discrimination in the United States have declined in the last 60 years (Schuman, Steeh, Bobo & Kyrsan, 1997). Not so long ago, African Americans were barred from attending public universities and faced restrictions on where they could sit in restaurants, movie theaters, and buses. It is almost impossible to imagine these limits being imposed today, attesting to the dramatic changes that have occurred. Stereotypes of African American have also changed, and these shifts generally represent a more tolerant, positive view (Madon et al., 2001).

Even people's attitudes toward prejudice itself have changed. Throughout most of American history, prejudice toward minority group members was condoned and socially sanctioned. This is no longer the case. Bigotry and intolerance are now viewed as inappropriate, and blatant prejudicial attitudes and remarks meet with censure rather than acceptance. When the baseball pitcher John Rocker voiced prejudicial attitudes in a magazine article, he was widely condemned. Moreover, many people feel bad

FIGURE 10.1

Facial Prominence in Magazine Photographs of European American and African American Men and Women

In magazine photographs, faces of European Americans and men were more prominently featured than were faces of African Americans and women. Because facial prominence signals social dominance, these differences reflect subtle forms of racism and sexism.

Source: Zuckerman and Kieffer (1994).

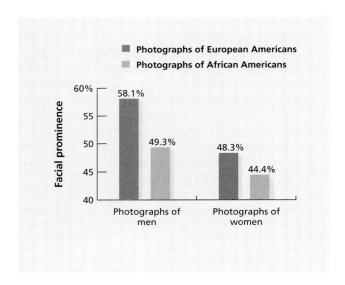

when they realize they have displayed prejudice or acted in a discriminatory manner, and their guilt motivates them to be more tolerant and fair-minded (Devine & Monteith, 1993; Dunton & Fazio, 1997; Fazio & Hilden, 2001; Monteith & Walters, 1998; Swim & Miller, 1999).

Despite these changes, prejudice still exists, usually manifesting itself in more subtle and covert ways than in days gone by (Gaertner & Dovidio, 1986; McConahay, 1986; Sears & Funk, 1990, 1991). For example, many European Americans support the abstract principle of racial equality but are reluctant to vote for African American candidates for elective offices. A similar shift has occurred in attitudes toward women. Fewer men now claim that a woman's place is in the home, but many still believe it is wrong for a woman to take a job away from a man, even when both are equally qualified (Swim, Aikin, Hall, & Hunter, 1995).

Research by Zuckerman and Kieffer (1994) shows just how subtle contemporary prejudice can be. These researchers examined photographs of European American and African American men and women in several popular magazines. For each photograph, the researchers measured whether the face was featured or whether the entire body was shown. Figure 10.1 shows the relative prominence given to the face in these photographs, and two findings are of interest: Facial prominence was greater for European Americans than for African Americans, and was greater for men than for women (see also D. Archer, Iritani, Kimes, & Barrios, 1983; Mullen, 2004). Because facial prominence conveys social dominance, these photographs appear to represent a subtle form of "face-ism." By prominently depicting the faces of European Americans and men, these photographs communicate the perception that these groups are more powerful than African Americans and women.

C. Measuring Prejudice

Changing social norms complicate efforts to measure prejudice. People who claim to be tolerant may actually harbor negative attitudes toward minority groups. An investigation by Judd and colleagues illustrates the problem (Judd, Park, Ryan, Brauer, & Kraus, 1995). These investigators asked European American and African American

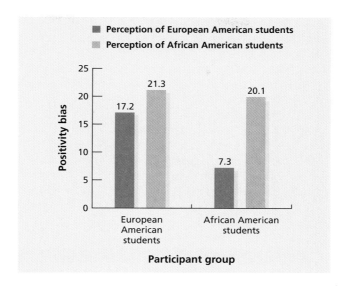

FIGURE 10.2

Ingroup Favoritism and Race

When asked to evaluate European Americans and African Americans, European American students were egalitarian, but African American students displayed ingroup favoritism.

Source: Judd, Park, Ryan, Brauer, and Kraus (1995).

college students to evaluate most other European American and African American college students on a number of positive and negative attributes. Figure 10.2 shows the ratings each group received, with higher numbers signifying more positive evaluations. As you can see, the European American students were very egalitarian: They gave equal evaluations to European American and African American students. The African American students, however, showed ingroup favoritism. They evaluated African American students more positively than they evaluated European American students.

What are we to make of these findings? Should we conclude that European American students are far less prejudiced than African American students? Perhaps. But it's also possible that the European American students were reluctant to express prejudice toward African Americans. Having been socialized to be fair-minded, they refrained from characterizing African Americans in negative terms. In support of this possibility, the European American students admitted to feeling less positively toward African Americans than toward European Americans. Dovidio and Gaertner (1998; Gaertner and Davidio, 1986) use the term **aversive racism** to refer to the genuine desire to be nonprejudiced, accompanied by negative feelings (e.g., anger, fear, resentment) toward minority groups. It is aversive in that people wish they didn't have the negative feelings they do in fact have.

1. Implicit Measures of Racial Prejudice

Like other self-report questionnaires, the scale used by Judd and colleagues (1995) measures people's explicit attitudes. **Explicit attitudes** are ones people consciously access and report. As such, they are subject to bias: If people are unable or unwilling to access their real attitudes, their responses will not reflect their true thoughts and feelings. To overcome the potential limitations associated with explicit attitudes, researchers have developed measures that assess people's implicit attitudes. **Implicit attitudes** are not accessible to consciousnesses and cannot be measured by self-report. Instead, they are inferred using more indirect methods (W. A. Cunningham, Preacher, & Banaji, 2001; Fazio & Olson, 2003; Greenwald & Banaji, 1995).

One approach to measuring implicit attitudes uses a semantic priming task developed by Meyer and Schvaneveldt (1971). With this procedure, participants make

FIGURE 10.3

Implicit Prejudice

For both European American and African American participants, seeing a member of another race facilitated the classification of negative trait adjectives but impeded the classification of positive trait adjectives. These findings suggest that both racial groups harbor unconscious prejudice.

Source: Fazio, Jackson, Dunton, and Williams (1995).

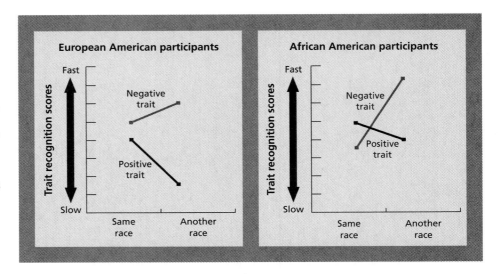

judgments about a target word after first being exposed to a preceding word, called the prime. The typical finding is that judgments are made more easily when the prime is semantically related to the target word than when the prime is unrelated. For example, decisions concerning the word *nurse* are made more rapidly and efficiently when this word is preceded by the word *doctor* than when it is preceded by the word *butter*.

Fazio, Jackson, Dunton, and Williams (1995) adapted this semantic priming technique to study racial attitudes. The African American and European American participants in this study saw a number of trait adjectives (e.g., attractive, dislikable) and were asked to decide as quickly as possible whether each item had a positive connotation or a negative connotation. The time taken to make these judgments was then recorded. Prior to making each judgment, the participants viewed faces of either an African American or a European American student. The priming pictures appeared quickly and were immediately followed by the trait adjective.

Fazio and colleagues argued that if prejudiced attitudes are activated automatically, viewing members of another race ought to speed up the recognition of negative traits but slow down the recognition of positive traits. As you can see in Figure 10.3, the data supported the researchers' predictions. For both European Americans and African Americans, seeing a member of another race facilitated the classification of negative traits but impeded the classification of positive traits. These data suggest that both groups have implicit negative attitudes toward members of the other race (see also Dovidio, Kawakami, Johnson, Johnson, & Howard, 1997; Greenwald, McGhee, & Schwartz, 1998; Perdue, Dovidio, Gurtman, & Tyler, 1990; Perdue & Gurtman, 1990; Wittenbrink, Judd, & Park, 1997, 2001).

2. Behavioral Measure of Prejudice and Discrimination

Prejudice can also be assessed using behavioral measures. In some experiments, participants are given an opportunity to help another person (usually a confederate of the experimenter) who is either African American or European American. The usual finding is that people are more apt to help members of their own race than members of another race (Crosby, Bromley, & Saxe, 1980).

Discrimination is especially apt to surface when people are able to justify their prejudice (D. L. Frey & Gaertner, 1986; Gaertner & Dovidio, 1977). M. L. Snyder, Kleck, Strenta, and Mentzer (1979) asked participants to watch a comedy videotape in one of two rooms. For some participants, the same videotape was playing in both rooms; for other participants, a different videotape was playing in each room. In addition, another person was already seated in each room. The person in one room was physically handicapped, and the person in the other room was not physically handicapped. Snyder and colleagues reasoned that although many people feel uncomfortable being near physically disabled people, they do not wish to discriminate against them. Consequently, they will not avoid contact with the disabled unless they are given a way of justifying their avoidance. In this experiment, the participants in the different-tapes-are-playing-in-each-room condition are given just such an opportunity. By being interested in whichever videotape the physically handicapped person is not watching, participants can avoid the physically disabled person without appearing to be prejudiced. The prediction, then, is that participants will avoid the handicapped person in the different-tapes condition but not in the same-tapes condition. The data revealed just such a pattern. Whereas 58 percent of the participants sat with the disabled person when the same videotape was playing in each room, only 17 percent did so when a different videotape was playing. Along with other research, these findings indicate that people exhibit discrimination when it can be disguised, rationalized, or excused (e.g., Beal, O'Neal, Ong, & Ruscher, 2000; Dovidio & Gaertner, 2000; Hodson, Dovidio, & Gaertner, 2002; Monin & Miller, 2001).

Prejudice and discrimination also surface when people have been threatened or attacked by an outgroup member. To illustrate, Sinclair and Kunda (2000) had male participants apply for a simulated job. The participants then received either positive or negative feedback from a supervisor who was either male or female. Finally, participants evaluated the supervisor's competence. Figure 10.4 shows that male participants who received a positive evaluation did not display sexism, but that male participants who received a negative evaluation did. These findings suggest that sexism is normally suppressed unless individuals are provoked or otherwise frustrated and thwarted (see also Sinclair & Kunda, 1999).

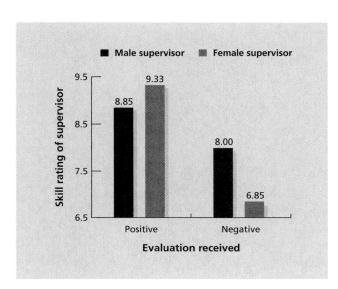

FIGURE 10.4

Sexism Following Threat

Male participants who were evaluated positively showed no sexism, but those who were evaluated negatively rated the female supervisor less favorably than the male supervisor.

Source: Sinclair and Kunda (2000).

3. Relation between Different Measures of Prejudice

So far we have seen that prejudice can be assessed with explicit attitude measures such as self-report questionnaires, and implicit measures such as a semantic priming task. Perhaps you are wondering how these various measures of prejudice are related. Explicit attitudes and implicit attitudes tend to be correlated, but the relationship between them is rarely strong (Dovidio et al., 1997; Fazio et al., 1995; Greenwald et al., 1998; McConnell & Leibold, 2001; von Hippel, Sekaquaptewa, & Vargas, 1997; Wittenbrink et al., 1997, 2001).

The lack of a strong correlation between these two measures suggests that they capture somewhat different aspects of prejudicial attitudes. The question, then, is: Which measure provides the better predictor of behavior—explicit attitudes or implicit attitudes? Interestingly, the answer seems to be "It depends" (see Figure 10.5). Explicit measures predict behaviors that are deliberate, conscious, or easily controlled, such as verbal behaviors, evaluations, and thoughtful judgments. In contrast, implicit measures predict behaviors that are spontaneous, unconscious, or less easily controlled, such as nonverbal behavior or snap judgments (Fazio et al., 1995; T. D. Wilson, Lindsey, & Schooler, 2000).

An investigation by Dovidio and colleagues (1997, Experiment 3) illustrates these relations. In this experiment European American participants' attitudes toward African Americans were assessed using both explicit and implicit measures. Afterward, the participants interacted with a European American and an African American interviewer. Later, the participants evaluated the interviewers and the two interviewers provided information about how the participants had behaved during the interview.

An interesting pattern of results emerged. Scores on the explicit, self-report measure predicted how the participants evaluated the two interviewers. Participants who scored high on an explicit measure of prejudice were especially apt to evaluate the African American interviewer less favorably than the European American interviewer. The implicit measure of prejudice did not predict these conscious evaluations. It did, however, predict the participants' nonverbal behavior during the interview. Participants who scored high on implicit measures of prejudice avoided making eye

FIGURE 10.5

Relation between Different Measures of Prejudice and Different Types of Behavior

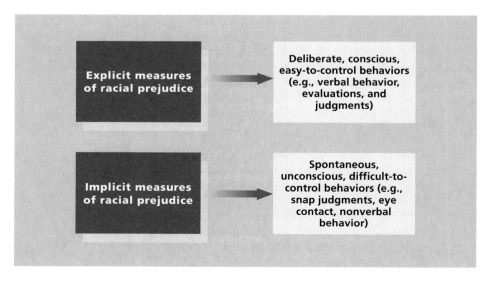

contact with the African American interviewer and appeared more ill at ease during the conversation.

These differences may explain why interracial interactions sometimes produce mis-understandings (Dovidio, Kawakami, & Gaertner, 2002). When looking back on their behavior, European Americans consider their controllable actions, which are guided by their explicit attitudes. To the extent that these attitudes are positive, they believe they behaved in a friendly and warm manner. In contrast, African Americans base their judgments of interaction quality on the European American's nonverbal behavior, which is controlled by their implicit attitudes. Since many people still harbor implicit prejudice, these nonverbal behaviors are generally less friendly and warm, leading to disagreements: European Americans believe the interaction was amicable, but African Americans believe it was tense.

II. Origins of Prejudice

Prejudicial attitudes arise from numerous sources, with economic, political, and personal forces all playing a role. This section presents four major approaches to understanding the origins of prejudice: (1) realistic group conflict theory, which maintains that prejudice arises because groups compete for finite resources; (2) motivational models, which assert that people develop prejudice because it makes them feel better about themselves; (3) learning theory approaches, which maintain that people learn to be prejudiced; and (4) personality theories, which strive to understand why some people are more prejudiced than others.

A. Realistic Group Conflict Theory

For decades now, negotiators have tried to forge a peace agreement between Israelis and Palestinians. The key issue is an exchange of land for peace. If Israel agrees to give up portions of Jerusalem and to dismantle settlements in the Gaza Strip, the Palestinians will agree to discontinue acts of terrorism. This proposal exemplifies an important theory of prejudice known as **realistic group conflict theory** (D. T. Campbell, 1965). Realistic group conflict theory proposes that prejudice arises when groups compete for scarce resources. These resources can include material goods (e. g., land, oil, water) or less tangible commodities (e. g., good schools and safe neighborhoods). The use of the word *realistic* in the theory underscores that competition for these resources is real and that intergroup hostility has at least some rational basis. In the extreme case of war, one group threatens another's actual existence.

Americans' attitudes toward the Japanese illustrate this effect. During World War II, Japan posed a realistic threat to America, and anti-Japanese sentiment developed rapidly following the bombing of Pearl Harbor. Several years later, American autoworkers found their livelihood threatened by an influx of well-built, inexpensive foreign cars, many of which were made in Japan. Here again, the negative attitudes many autoworkers developed toward the Japanese can be understood as arising from a realistic appraisal of competition and conflict.

To summarize, realistic group conflict theory assumes that prejudice arises when people compete for scarce resources. The theory makes two important predictions. First, it predicts that people who are realistically threatened or disadvantaged are more prejudiced than people who are not realistically threatened or disadvantaged;

second, it predicts that prejudice will be eradicated if there are enough resources to go around. The next subsection of this chapter examines these predictions.

1. Supporting Evidence: The Robbers Cave Experiment

The importance of group conflict was demonstrated in a landmark experiment by Sherif, Harvey, White, Hood, and Sherif (1961). The experiment took place at a boys' summer camp, located at the Robbers Cave State Park in Oklahoma. All of the boys were of a similar age (11 or 12) and came from stable, Protestant, middle-class homes. Completely unaware that they were part of an experiment on group relationships, the boys were divided into two groups prior to the start of camp and were taken in separate buses to different locations. They lived apart during this first stage of the experiment, and each group quickly developed a sense of cohesion and solidarity. They selected names for themselves (in one camp session, one group chose the name Rattlers and the other chose the name Eagles) and began engaging in numerous group activities. Flags were created with group symbols, and T-shirts were emblazoned with the group names.

One week later, the boys were brought together. To see whether group conflict creates intergroup tension, Sherif and colleagues had the two groups participate in a series of competitive activities in which victory for one group came at the expense of the other. For example, the counselors arranged a tournament of games, such as a tug-of-war, and only the winners enjoyed a cookout that night. After a few days, hostility between the groups developed, resulting in name-calling and petty acts of violence. Each group began to see the other as "the enemy," and tensions ran high whenever the groups were together. On the basis of these findings, Sherif and colleagues concluded that realistic group conflict is one cause of prejudice.

In a subsequent phase of the experiment, the researchers attempted to reduce prejudice by having the groups interact in social situations that did not involve competition. These encounters did not reduce the enmity between the groups. If anything, they served only to fan the flames of distrust, as the two groups repeatedly taunted and ridiculed each other. Fortunately, a final phase of the experiment did reduce prejudice. Sherif and colleagues arranged for a series of cooperative group activities, in which success demanded that the two groups work together as one. For example, a truck broke down miles from camp, and the two groups had to unite in order to get it started. After a while, these collaborative activities reduced prejudice and led to a feeling of oneness among all camp members. A later section of this chapter discusses how these findings have guided efforts to reduce prejudice in America's schools.

2. Opposing Evidence: Prejudice Occurs in the Absence of Realistic Conflict

Sherif and colleagues' research showed that prejudice can arise when groups compete for finite resources, but this does not mean that people are prejudiced only against those who constitute a realistic threat to their welfare or way of life. For one thing, the perception of conflict is more important than any realistic competition. If members of a group believe their status or safety is threatened by another group, they may develop hostility toward that group even though no actual threat exists.

People also engage in social comparison processes when evaluating their groups. In some cases, they may feel they are relatively disadvantaged in comparison to some other group. This perception, known as **relative deprivation** (Stouffer, Suchman, DeVinney, Starr, & Williams, 1949), may have played a role in the urban riots that occurred in America in the 1960s. Despite the fact that prejudice and discrimination were declining during this period, many African Americans were angry that they were still disadvantaged in comparison with the privileges European Americans enjoyed. This perception of relative deprivation fueled frustration and civil unrest.

Another problem with realistic group conflict theory is that it assumes that people are only prejudiced against those who pose a realistic threat to their well-being. Yet sometimes people inappropriately blame others for their troubles or hardships. This form of prejudice is known as **scapegoating.** In the years following World War I, Germany was in economic decline; inflation was rampant and unemployment was prevalent. When Hitler seized power, he told the Germans that the Jews were responsible for the country's plight and that Germany's problems would be solved by isolating and eliminating Jews. Unable to defend themselves against these attacks, the Jews served as a convenient scapegoat as Hitler consolidated power (Berkowitz, 1962).

A classic investigation by Hovland and Sears (1940) documented another instance of scapegoating. These researchers examined the association between the sale of cotton (an index of economic prosperity) and the lynching of African Americans in several southern states during the early part of the 20th century. A significant negative association was found, indicating that violence toward African Americans was linked with lower prices of cotton. Although a reanalysis of the data has suggested that the size of the effect is smaller than originally believed, a modest relationship between these variables does exist (Green, Glaser, & Rich, 1998; Hepworth & West, 1988).

Scapegoating and realistic group conflict are related, but there is an important difference: With realistic group conflict, the target of prejudice constitutes an actual threat to one's welfare; with scapegoating, the target of prejudice does not pose an actual threat to one's welfare, but simply serves as a convenient whipping boy. Research on scapegoating tells us, then, that realistic group conflict need not be evident in order for prejudice to occur.

Research on **symbolic prejudice** provides further evidence that self-interest and realistic conflict are not necessary features of prejudice. Symbolic prejudice is directed toward any group that is viewed as posing a threat to one's values or worldview. To illustrate, many people oppose government funding of AIDS research because they consider AIDS to be a lifestyle disease that people can choose to avoid (Pryor, Reeder, & McManus, 1991). The conflict here is not over tangible resources such as food, water, and land, but over ideals, values, and a way of life. People's attitudes toward school busing programs in the 1970s provide a good way to understand how symbolic prejudice differs from realistic group conflict. At that time, many cities were sending schoolchildren across town to achieve racial integration. Realistic group conflict theory predicted that parents whose children were directly affected would have more extreme attitudes toward school busing than parents whose children were not directly affected. Although there is some evidence that this occurred (Bobo, 1983), people's attitudes toward busing did not depend solely on whether they were directly affected by the program. Instead, opposition represented a more diffuse, general antagonism toward any program that would alter the status differential between European Americans and African Americans (Sears, Hensler, & Speer, 1979; see also Nier, Mottola, & Gaertner, 2000).

To summarize, realistic group conflict certainly contributes to prejudice, but prejudice can arise even when groups do not compete for tangible resources. Unfortunately, this means that even if there were enough land, enough oil, and enough food to go around, prejudice would probably not be eliminated.

B. Motivational Models

The limitations of realistic group conflict theory have led researchers to search for other factors that contribute to prejudice. Motivational factors have been shown to play an important role. Although there are several motivational models, all assume that people exhibit prejudice because it makes them feel better about themselves.

1. Social Identity Theory

One motivational model is Tajfel's **social identity theory** (Tajfel & Turner, 1986). This theory assumes that people want to feel good about themselves and that one way they achieve this goal is by believing that the groups they belong to are somehow better than the groups to which they do not belong (Aberson, Healy, & Romero, 2001; Oakes & Turner, 1980; Rubin & Hewstone, 1998). Notice how this theory incorporates aspects of social identity and the extended self, first articulated by William James (1890). As discussed in Chapter 5, our self-concept includes other people and our memberships in various social groups, and we feel better when these aspects of the extended self are praiseworthy or meritorious. Believing the groups we belong to are somehow special or advantaged gives us a heightened sense of self-worth.

Tajfel tested his ideas using a procedure known as the **minimal group paradigm** (Billig & Tajfel, 1973; Tajfel, Billig, Bundy, & Flament, 1971). After reading reports of Sherif's research on competition and prejudice, Tajfel wondered how much competition was needed to produce prejudice. To examine this issue, he first created a nondiscrimination baseline condition void of all psychological significance. Participants were arbitrarily assigned to groups and had no contact with other participants, either within or between groups. Later, he intended to add variables to this bare-bones situation in order to identify factors needed to create prejudice.

For example, in one study (Billig & Tajfel, 1973) a coin was flipped and participants were randomly placed into two groups: group X and group W. The participants were then shown a payoff matrix similar to the one displayed in Table 10.1, and were asked to allocate money to other group members identified only by their group label. Notice that each option represents a unique pattern of outcomes. Participants who select option A are choosing to maximize the ingroup's relative advantage over the outgroup; participants who pick option B are opting to distribute the resources equally; and participants who select option C are choosing to maximize the ingroup's benefits.

TABLE 10.1 Sample Allocation Matrix Used in Tajfel's Minimal Group Paradigm

		CHOICE	
	A	B	C
Payoff for ingroup member	12	15	18
Payoff for outgroup member	9	15	21
Ingroup − Outgroup	+3	0	−3

Source: Tajfel, Billig, Bundy, and Flament (1971).

Notice also that participants are not competing for scarce resources: Option B allows them to split the pot equally, and options A and C give them the chance to have more or less than the outgroup.

Billig and Tajfel found that participants most often chose option A over the other alternatives. Even though this cost the ingroup money in absolute terms, participants preferred to maximize their group's advantage over the outgroup. In subsequent research, participants have been asked to evaluate members of their own group or an outgroup. Here again, participants consistently evaluated their ingroup members in more glowing terms than they evaluated members of the outgroup. This type of ingroup favoritism does not occur for every trait, but it is a general effect (Brewer, 1979; K. J. Reynolds, Turner, & Haslam, 2000).

To summarize, even in a minimal group situation, when division into groups is arbitrary and people never compete for scarce resources, people discriminate in favor of their own group. On the basis of these findings, Tajfel concluded that group favoritism does not require any kind of competition or conflict. Instead, it arises whenever individuals are categorized into social groups (Brewer & Brown, 1998). Bear in mind, however, that ingroup favoritism does not imply outgroup derogation. Tajfel's research shows that people favor their own groups, but this research has not shown that people placed into groups on an arbitrary basis develop hostility and hatred toward outgroup members. Instead, they simply favor their own group in situations where they are forced to choose (Brewer, 1999; Mummendey, Otten, Berger, & Kessler, 2000).

2. Prejudice as Self-Enhancement

Social identity theory assumes that ingroup favoritism makes people feel better about themselves. Lemyre and Smith (1985) conducted an experiment to test this hypothesis. In this study, participants were arbitrarily divided into two groups: the Red group and the Blue group. The participants were then asked to allocate resources using pay-off matrixes similar to those shown in Table 10.1. Some participants allocated resources between an ingroup member and an outgroup member, some participants distributed resources between two ingroup members, and other participants apportioned resources among two outgroup members. A fourth group of participants was not given an opportunity to allot any resources. Finally, all participants completed a variety of scales designed to measure their feelings of self-worth. Lemyre and Smith predicted that participants who had been categorized into groups and given the opportunity to display ingroup favoritism would feel especially good about themselves. Figure 10.6 shows that this prediction was confirmed. Participants in the ingroup–outgroup allocation condition who were given a chance to display ingroup favoritism felt better about themselves than did participants who were not given this opportunity. Other research has found that people who strongly identify with an ingroup derive pleasure when an outgroup suffers misfortune or hardship (Leach, Spears, Branscombe, & Doosje, 2003). Evidence like this supports the claim that ingroup favoritism serves a self-enhancement function (Fein & Spencer, 1997; Maass, Cadinu, Guarnieri, & Grasselii, 2003).

3. Prejudice and the Denial of Death

In his award-winning book *The Denial of Death,* Ernest Becker (1973) argued that the capacity to contemplate one's own death creates existential terror in people and that a great deal of psychological life is devoted to managing this terror. Building on this work, J. Greenberg, Solomon, and Pyszczynski (1997) have argued that one way

FIGURE 10.6

Feelings of Self-Worth after Ingroup Favoritism

Participants who were given the chance to exhibit ingroup favoritism felt best about themselves. These data are consistent with the claim that discrimination and prejudice serve to enhance feelings of self-worth.

Source: Lemyre and Smith (1985).

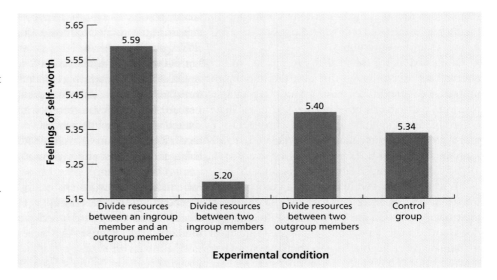

people cope with existential terror is by denigrating outgroups. This gives people a sense that their view of the world is correct and imbues them with a sense of superiority. J. Greenberg and colleagues (1990) designed an experiment to test this hypothesis. During the first part of the experiment, Christian participants completed a series of questionnaires. For participants assigned to the mortality-salient condition, one of the questionnaires asked participants to contemplate their death and to describe how they thought they would feel as they were dying. Participants in a control condition did not complete this task. During the next part of the experiment, participants read about another participant they were going to meet. In one condition, the other person indicated that he was Christian; in another condition, the other participant indicated that he was Jewish. Finally, the participants indicated how much they thought they would like the person they were going to meet.

Terror management theory asserts that thoughts of one's own death create existential terror and that people manage this anxiety by convincing themselves that their view of the world is the correct one to hold. As applied to the experimental situation created by Greenberg and colleagues, the theory predicts that participants who have recently contemplated their death will be especially approving of someone who shares their worldview and especially disparaging of someone whose worldview differs from theirs. The data in Figure 10.7 reveal just such a pattern. After thinking and writing about their death, these Christian participants indicated greater liking for a Christian and less liking for a Jew. Terror management theory assumes that this pattern represents an attempt to reduce the anxiety occasioned by the thoughts of one's death (see also Castano, Yzerbyt, Paladino, & Sacchi, 2002; Solomon, Greenberg, & Pyszczynski, 2000).

4. Reverse Favoritism: The Black-Sheep Effect

Ingroup favoritism is the rule, but sometimes people enhance their feelings of self-worth by derogating an ingroup member. This occurs when an ingroup member does something particularly reprehensible or blameworthy. For example, suppose someone from your university defected to a foreign country that is an enemy of the United States. Chances are you would soundly condemn the individual as a traitor. By derogating the

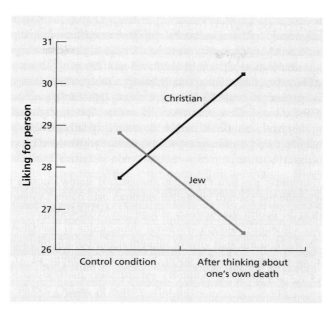

FIGURE 10.7

Mortality Salience and Prejudice

After contemplating their own death, Christian participants expressed greater liking for a Christian and less liking for a Jew. These findings suggest that prejudice may manage the existential terror produced by an awareness of one's own death.

Source: Greenberg et al. (1990).

proverbial black sheep, you repair your group's tarnished identity and maintain a positive self-image (Branscombe, Wann, Noel, & Coleman, 1993; Eidelman & Biernat, 2003; Marques, Robalo, & Rocha, 1992).

C. Social Learning

Realistic group conflict and motivational models provide two ways to understand the development of prejudice. Prejudice can also be learned. Via the media and interactions with parents and peers, people learn various stereotypes. After all, few of us have ever met an Italian mobster, but most of us have a pretty clear stereotype of this social group, having seen movies like *The Godfather* and television shows like *The Sopranos*. Unfortunately, media portrayals of minority group members have long been negatively skewed. In films, television, and music videos, women are too often depicted as seductresses and African American males are portrayed as aggressive and sexually abusive. Other minority groups are simply ignored. Asians and Latinos comprise a substantial proportion of the population in America, but they rarely appear in films and on television. Although this situation is changing, there is no doubt that people learn negative stereotypes from media depictions.

Learning influences the development not only of stereotypes but also of prejudiced feelings. During the cold war, American schoolchildren were taught to fear and hate the Russians. Now that the Soviet Union no longer exists and Russians pose less of a threat to the United States, these attitudes have softened. This example highlights the interplay between realistic group conflict and learning theory. For many years, the Soviet Union posed a threat to America, and this led to the development of prejudice. This prejudice was then transmitted from generation to generation through social norms and social communication (Brauer, Judd, & Jacquelin, 2001; Crandall, Eshleman, & O'Brien, 2002; Lyons & Kashima, 2003; Schaller, Conway, & Tanchuk, 2002; M. S. Thompson, Judd, & Park, 2000; Wigboldus, Semin, & Spears, 2000).

D. Individual Difference Approaches

Archie Bunker is one of the most recognizable television characters of all time. In the hit comedy show *All in the Family*, Archie (played by Carroll O'Connor) consistently spewed invectives toward a wide variety of social groups: women, homosexuals, Jews, Catholics, Polish Americans, African Americans, and so on. In short, Archie was a bigot who hated just about everyone who wasn't just like him. Although fictional, the Archie Bunker character calls attention to the fact that some people are more prejudiced than others. Our final theory of prejudice examines the origins of these differences.

1. The Authoritarian Personality

Seeking to understand the strong anti-Semitism that characterized Germany during Hitler's regime, a group of researchers set out in the 1940s to describe the characteristics of a person who is prejudiced against many social groups (Adorno, Frenkel-Brunswik, Levinson, & Sanford, 1950). Table 10.2 describes key aspects of this profile, which is known as the authoritarian personality. Among other things, the authoritarian personality is characterized by a rigid adherence to conventional values, hero worship, and a tendency to think in categorical (black-and-white) terms.

Although the scale used to measure the authoritarian personality was devised more than 50 years ago, it continues to predict attitudes toward contemporary issues and concerns. For example, people who score high in authoritarianism express punitive attitudes toward gays and lesbians, drug users, the homeless, and people who are HIV positive (Haddock, Zanna, & Esses, 1993; B. E. Peterson, Doty, & Winter, 1993; Whitley, 1999). Authoritarians even express negative attitudes toward people who are overweight (Crandall & Biernat, 1990).

TABLE 10.2 Characteristics of the Authoritarian Personality

Factor	Description	Sample Items
Conventionalism	Rigid adherence to conventional, middle-class values	Obedience and respect for authority are the most important virtues children should learn.
Authoritarian submission	Submissive, uncritical, and idealized attitude toward moral authorities of the ingroup	Every person should have complete faith in some supernatural power whose decisions he obeys without question.
Authoritarian aggression	Tendency to condemn, reject, and punish people who violate conventional values	Most of our social problems would be solved if we could somehow get rid of the immoral, crooked, and feebleminded people.
Superstition and stereotypy	The belief in mystical determinants of the individual's fate; the disposition to think in rigid categories	People can be divided into two classes: the weak and the strong.

Source: Adorno, Frenkel-Brunswik, Levinson, and Sanford (1950).

What factors lead to the development of this personality type? Inspired by Freudian theory, Adorno and his colleagues assumed that high authoritarianism arises from conflicts in early childhood brought on by a domineering father and a punitive mother. More modern theorists have suggested that social learning plays a more important role, as prejudiced parents model and inculcate prejudicial attitudes in their children (Altemeyer, 1988). Despite these different emphases, both theoretical camps assume that an intolerance toward those who threaten conventional values arises early in life and characterizes attitudes toward a great many social groups.

2. Religion and Prejudice

> Some people say the only cure for prejudice is more religion; some say the only cure is to abolish religion. (Allport, 1954, p. 444)

Are religious people more or less prejudiced than nonreligious people? Arguments can be mustered for both conclusions. On the one hand, most major religions preach tolerance and compassion, and exhort their followers to treat people with kindness, dignity, and respect. On the other hand, religion plays a key role in much of the violence and hatred that exists in this world: Muslims and Jews war in the Middle East; Protestants and Catholics battle in Northern Ireland; and Sikhs and Hindus fight in India.

Given these contradictory perspectives, it is not surprising that research reveals a somewhat complicated picture between religion and prejudice (Hunsberger, 1995). Although there is little evidence that religious people are less prejudiced than nonreligious people, whether they are more prejudiced than nonreligious people depends on what we mean by the word *religious*. If we look simply at church attendance and a superficial adherence to religious teachings, we find that religious people are slightly more prejudiced than nonreligious people (Allport & Ross, 1967). This association is stronger if we examine religious fundamentalism. As you might imagine, the belief that there is one true set of religious teachings that must be aggressively defended against nonbelievers and infidels predicts greater prejudice, intolerance, and hatred (Altemeyer & Hunsberger, 1992). Finally, people who are open to exploring diverse points of view regarding religious and existential matters are no more prejudiced than are nonreligious people (Batson, Schoenrade, & Ventis, 1993).

3. Political Conservatism, Individualism, and Prejudice

Another correlate of prejudice is political conservatism. In general, conservatives are resistant to change and strongly endorse Protestant virtues, particularly individualism and self-reliance (Jost, Glaser, Kruglanski, & Sulloway, 2003). This leads many conservatives to believe that the socially disadvantaged are responsible for their plight in life and need only to work hard in order to overcome obstacles and improve their condition (Farwell & Weiner, 2000; Zucker & Weiner, 1993). In some cases, these beliefs fuel prejudice toward minority group members, especially those viewed as behaving in ways that contradict the central tenets of individualism (Sears & Henry, 2003). Table 10.3 presents some items from a scale designed to assess these attitudes (McConahay, Hardee, & Batts, 1981). People who score high on this modern racism scale, believe that discrimination is no longer a problem and that African Americans (and other minority groups) do not deserve any special treatment.

It is interesting to relate these attitudes to an issue facing industrialized nations today. Many of these countries were once homogeneous with respect to ethnicity, race,

TABLE 10.3   Sample Items from the Modern Racism Scale

	Disagree				Agree
1. Discrimination against blacks is no longer a problem in the United States.	1	2	3	4	5
2. Members of ethnic minorities often exaggerate the extent to which they suffer from racial inequality.	1	2	3	4	5
3. More and more, blacks use accusations of racism for their own advantage.	1	2	3	4	5
4. A primary reason that ethnic minorities tend to stay in lower paying jobs is that they lack the motivation required for moving up.	1	2	3	4	5
5. The desire of many ethnic minorities to maintain their cultural traditions impedes the achievement of racial equality.	1	2	3	4	5

Source: McConahay (1986).

and religion. This is no longer the case, as immigration patterns and war have transformed numerous countries into a hodgepodge of diverse cultural groups. People differ with respect to whether cultural diversity should be encouraged or discouraged. Conservatives generally believe that minority groups should assimilate to the dominant, majority culture. In the United States, this preference is expressed by opposing programs that allow people of different backgrounds to celebrate and retain their heritage (e.g., bilingual education). Many liberals and minority groups believe these calls for a color-blind society amount to little more than veiled prejudice. By demanding that minority groups conform to a European American ideal, these attitudes imply that diversity is a liability in need of correction (Bonilla-Silva, 2003; Monteith & Spicer, 2000; Richeson & Nussbaum, 2004; Wolsko, Park, Judd, & Wittenbrink, 2000).

4. Social Dominance Orientation

The link between conservatism and prejudice is also influenced by people's beliefs about the inevitability and desirability of group differences (Pratto, Sidanius, Stallworth, & Malle, 1994; Sidanius, Pratto, & Bobo, 1996). Social dominance orientation is a general tendency to believe that social groups are inherently unequal, and that more able and favored groups should dominate over less capable and less fortunate ones. Table 10.4 presents portions of a scale used to measure this individual difference variable. As you can see, those who score high on the scale believe that social inequality is justified and even desirable, and tend to oppose social programs designed to rectify social inequality, such as affirmative action, increased rights for immigrants, and universal health care.

The nature of social dominance orientation is still being explored. Although it is sometimes treated as a personality variable that operates independent of the situation (Pratto et al., 1994), scores on the scale correlate highly with social status. This means that people in dominant social positions believe social hierarchies are more necessary and desirable than do those who do not enjoy positions of privilege (Guimond,

TABLE 10.4 Sample Items from the Social Dominance Orientation Scale

1. Some groups of people are simply inferior to other groups.

2. In getting what you want, it is sometimes necessary to use force against other groups.

3. It's OK if some groups have more of a chance in life than others.

4. To get ahead in life, it is sometimes necessary to step on other groups.

5. If certain groups stayed in their place, we would have fewer problems.

6. It is probably a good thing that certain groups are at the top and other groups are at the bottom.

Source: Pratto, Sidanius, Stallworth, and Malle (1994).

Dambrun, Michinov, & Duarte, 2003). This suggests that social dominance orientation is a reaction to having social power, not a stable personality variable: People who possess status and power adopt this orientation to convince themselves that they truly deserve their social privilege.

III. Stereotypes and Prejudice

At the outset of this chapter we noted that prejudice is an attitude that consists of three correlated components: cognitions, emotions, and behavioral tendencies. Stereotypes are the cognitive component of prejudice. They consist of people's beliefs about the qualities that characterize members of social groups. For example, statements like "The British are stoic" or "Italians are hot-blooded" represent stereotypes. We also hold stereotypes about various professions (e.g., "Librarians are shy"), social groups ("Baby boomers are vain"), and racial and ethnic groups ("The Chinese are mathematical"). In this section, we will examine the nature of stereotypes: their consequences, development, function, and control.

A. The Nature of Stereotypes

Stereotypes are overgeneralizations about people (Lippmann, 1922). When we say "White men can't jump," we are making a sweeping generalization about a large group of people. Since there is always variability within groups, stereotypes are never completely accurate. At the same time, they may contain a kernel of truth (Allport, 1954; Ashton, & Esses, 1999; Judd & Park, 1993; Jussim, 1991, 1993; Swim, 1994). For example, a common stereotype holds that men are more aggressive than women. This stereotype is largely accurate: Across a range of indicators, men generally are more aggressive than women (Eagly & Steffen, 1986). It is also the case, however, that many men are passive and many women are violent. We err when we ignore variations and apply stereotypes too broadly.

By definition, stereotypes involve a tendency to underestimate the variability among outgroup members. Rather than seeing outgroup members as individuals, we tend to think they are all alike. A belief that people of other races all look alike provides a dramatic illustration of the **outgroup homogeneity bias.** Devine and Malpass (1985) had African American and European American participants study faces of African American and European American males. Later, the participants were shown a larger number of faces and were asked to identify which faces they had seen earlier. Both European Americans and African American showed better memory for faces of their own race than for faces of the other race. One explanation of this effect is that people homogenize members of races other than their own, failing to notice each person's unique features (see also Anthony, Cooper, & Mullen, 1992; Bothwell, Brigham, & Malpass, 1989).

The outgroup homogeneity effect occurs for psychological qualities as well (Ostrom & Sedikides, 1992). For example, when asked to estimate the percentage of people who are characterized by a given trait, we make higher estimates for an outgroup than for an ingroup (Judd, Park, Ryan, Brauer, & Kraus, 1995; B. Park & Rothbart, 1982). We are also more apt to base our behavioral predictions on the behavior of an outgroup member than the behavior of an ingroup member. To illustrate, suppose you observe a person select one of several movies to attend. If you were then asked to predict which movie another person would choose, you would be more apt to assume the same choice would be made if both people were outgroup members than if they were ingroup members (Quattrone & Jones, 1980).

The outgroup homogeneity effect was initially thought to depend on unfamiliarity with the outgroup (Linville, Salovey, & Fischer, 1986). Subsequent research has shown, however, that familiarity alone cannot explain this effect (Huddy & Virtanen, 1995). Instead, it appears that motivational processes also contribute to this bias, as people enhance their feelings of self-worth by viewing their own group as more unique and diverse than outgroups.

B. A Cognitive Model of Stereotype Formation

Like other aspects of prejudice, stereotypes arise from many sources. Cultural and social learning factors certainly play a role, in that many stereotypes are transmitted from generation to generation via word of mouth and through the media. Motivational factors are also relevant. **Projection** occurs when we unconsciously assume that other people possess the undesirable qualities we fear that we possess. For example, people who believe they lack sophistication may accuse computer programmers of being nerds (Rucker & Pratkanis, 2001).

Cognitive processes also influence the development of stereotypes. A cognitive approach makes three important assumptions: Stereotypes (1) arise from normal, cognitive processes and are an inevitable consequence of the way people perceive the world; (2) help people process information quickly and efficiently and can be adaptive and functional; and (3) are activated automatically whenever people encounter a member of a social category (S. T. Fiske, 1998; D. L. Hamilton & Sherman,1994; Macrae, Stangor, & Milne, 1994). In the sections that follow, we will examine the evidence for each of these assumptions.

1. The Role of Categorization in Stereotype Formation

A cognitive model of stereotype formation maintains that stereotypes arise from a normal cognitive process known as categorization. Categorization involves distinguishing and grouping entities on the basis of shared characteristics. This clustering process begins at an early age and is a fundamental feature of the way people learn and process information. We learn, for example, to distinguish pens from paper, tables from chairs, and rain from snow. Associated with each of these categories is a set of distinctive features. We may believe that raindrops are largely alike, but that no two snowflakes are the same. Some of these beliefs are accurate; some are not.

Our thoughts about members of social groups also follow a similar course. Throughout our lives, we learn to distinguish various social categories: males and females, professors and students, artists and engineers. Each of these social categories is accompanied by a distinctive set of characteristics. We may believe that professors are absentminded and students are overworked. Some of our beliefs regarding social categories are accurate; some are not. One way to think about the categorization process is in terms of a judgment of covariation. As discussed in Chapter 4, these judgments describe the relation between two or more variables. Stereotypes, such as "Rednecks are hot-tempered" or "Hippies are laid-back," are a type of covariation judgment. They describe an apparent association between two variables or characteristics.

When discussing this judgmental process in Chapter 4, we noted that people tend to overestimate the degree to which two variables are correlated, a bias known as illusory correlation. One factor that affects this bias is distinctiveness. An illusory correlation is more apt to occur when two variables are highly noticeable, rare, or distinctive. This tendency may explain why people have negative stereotypes of minority groups. Most minority groups are statistically rare and distinctive, and negative behaviors, such as criminal acts of violence, are also uncommon and conspicuous. The combination of these factors may give rise to an illusory correlation, leading people to exaggerate the extent to which minority group members commit violent crimes (D. L. Hamilton, 1979; D. L. Hamilton & Gifford, 1976). This is especially apt to occur when we already have preconceptions of how two variables fit together (D. L. Hamilton & Rose, 1980).

Limits to the Cognitive Model. The cognitive model of stereotype formation has proved very useful and has generated a great deal of research (for reviews, see S. T. Fiske, 1998; D. L. Hamilton & Sherman, 1994; Macrae & Bodenhausen, 2000), but it has an important limitation. It can explain how stereotypes form, but it has difficulty explaining why most of our stereotypes of outgroups are negative. After all, acts of heroism are also rare, yet few people think minority group members are particularly heroic. For this and other reasons, the safest conclusion to be drawn from cognitive studies of stereotype formation is this: Categorization processes and illusory correlations contribute to the development of stereotypes, but other processes, such as realistic group conflict and the need to feel good about ourselves, also play a role.

Adding Motivation to the Cognitive Model. S. T. Fiske, Cuddy, Glick, and Xu (2002) have argued that two factors determine when stereotypes will be positive and when they will be negative. The first factor, competition, captures the extent to which a group poses a threat to one's own group. The second factor, social status, is a social structural variable that refers to whether a group has achieved a high degree of social success. As shown in Table 10.5, combining these variables yields four types of social stereotypes. First, low-status groups that pose a threat are perceived to be incompetent and cold, and these groups generally evoke feelings of anger and contempt. In contrast, low-status groups that pose no threat are regarded as incompetent but warm, and these groups frequently evoke feelings of pity and compassion. High-status groups that pose a threat are viewed as competent but cold. These groups typically evoke feelings of envy and are often targeted as scapegoats. Finally, high-status groups that pose no threat are regarded in uniformly positive terms.

TABLE 10.5 Social Structural Model of Prejudice				
	LOW STATUS		HIGH STATUS	
	High Competition	Low Competition	High Competition	Low Competition
EXAMPLE	Unskilled foreign immigrants Working women	Elderly The disabled Traditional housewife	Jews Germans Japanese	Ingroup
COMMON STEREOTYPES	Incompetent, cold	Incompetent, warm	Competent, cold	Competent, warm
PREVALENT EMOTION	Anger, contempt	Pity, compassion, sympathy	Envy	Liking

Source: S. T. Fiske, Cuddy, Glick, and Xu (2002).

2. Cognitive Consequences of Stereotypes

In addition to considering how stereotypes arise, cognitive models also consider the functions stereotypes serve. Most cognitive theorists adopt a functional approach, arguing that stereotypes allow people to process information rapidly and efficiently (S. T. Fiske, 1998; Macrae, Milne, & Bodenhausen, 1994). From this perspective, stereotypes function as schemas. They influence what we notice, how we interpret what we see, what we remember, and how we explain what we see (Allport, 1954).

Stereotypes Influence Interpretation. In February 1999, New York City police officers shot and killed a West African immigrant, Amadou Diallo, when they mistakenly assumed a wallet he was holding in his hand was a gun. Although numerous factors contributed to this tragic incident, stereotypes may have played a role. A common cultural stereotype holds that African Americans are more aggressive and violent than European Americans. Like other stereotypes, this belief influences the way people process ambiguous information. To illustrate, in one early investigation, Duncan (1976) had European American participants watch a staged interaction between a European American actor and an African American actor. During the interaction, one of the actors appeared to shove the other. Thirteen percent of the participants characterized the shove as a violent act when the European American actor exhibited the behavior, whereas 73 percent of the participants made this judgment when the African American actor exhibited the behavior. Since many European Americans believe that African Americans are violent, these findings show that stereotypes guide the way we interpret various behaviors. In a replication of this research with sixth-grade children, Sagar and Schofield (1980) found that both European Americans and African Americans displayed this tendency, suggesting that the stereotype develops at an early age and is held by African Americans as well as by European Americans.

Could this stereotype explain why New York City police offers mistakenly shot Amadou Diallo? To answer this question, Correll, Park, Judd, and Wittenbrink (2002) had European American participants play a video game that required them to quickly identify whether a person was holding a weapon or some other object (e.g., an aluminum can, a cell phone). If the object was a weapon, the participants were to shoot the man by pressing a button labeled "shoot." If the object was not a weapon, the participants

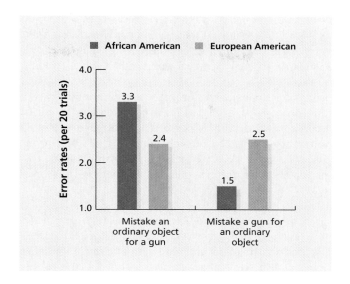

FIGURE 10.8

Weapon Misidentification and Race

While playing a video game, European American participants quickly judged whether an object being held by a man was an ordinary household object or a weapon. Participants were more apt to assume that an ordinary object was a weapon when it was in the hands of an African American man than when it was in the hands of a European American man, and that a weapon was an ordinary object when it was in the hands of a European American man than when it was in the hands of an African American man.

Source: Correll, Park, Judd, and Wittenbrink (2002).

were to press another button labeled "don't shoot." In some cases the person holding the object was a European American, whereas in other cases he was an African American.

The key question of interest was whether the participants were more apt to mistake an ordinary object for a weapon when it was in the hands of an African American. Figure 10.8 provides strong evidence that they did (see also Greenwald, Oakes, & Hoffman, 2003; B. K. Payne, 2001; B. K. Payne, Lambert, & Jacoby, 2002). Follow-up research found that stereotypes, not prejudiced feelings, underlie this effect (Judd, Blair, & Chapleau, 2004). Rather than being due to hatred, fear, or other negative emotions, the effect stems from the belief that weapons are more apt to be found in the hands of African Americans than in the hands of European Americans.

The weapon misidentification effect establishes that common cultural stereotypes can have dangerous consequences. Although the effects of stereotypes are rarely this consequential, they are pervasive. Suppose I tell you I have a friend who is aggressive. What image do you have of this person? As Solomon Asch's research showed (see Chapter 4), traits like these can be interpreted in more than one way. Depending on contextual cues, *aggressive* can mean either "assertive" or "violent." Our stereotypes provide important contextual information (Dunning & Sherman, 1997; Kunda, Sinclair, & Griffin, 1997). If I tell you my aggressive friend is a lawyer, you will probably assume he is assertive; if I tell you my aggressive friend is a truck driver, you will probably conclude he is violent. By providing contextual cues, stereotypes influence the way we interpret everything else we know about a person.

This effect can also bias our evaluations of group members. Biernat, Manis, and Nelson (1991) showed that people apply different standards when judging men and women. For example, when considering whether a person is athletic, we apply lower standards when judging a woman than when judging a man ("You throw a ball pretty well—for a girl"). Just the opposite occurs when considering whether a person is accomplished at turning a house into a home ("You've done a great job with this place—for a guy"). As a consequence of shifting standards, it's easier for people to be viewed as possessing qualities that are uncharacteristic of their group rather than ones that are characteristic of their group (Biernat, 2003; Biernat & Kobrynowicz, 1997; Biernat & Vescio, 2002). The rock band The Offspring provided a colorful example of this effect in their hit song "Pretty Fly (for a White Guy)."

Stereotypes Influence Attributions. Like schemas and expectancies, stereotypes also influence the attributions we make for other people's behavior. In general, dispositional attributions are more apt to be made for behaviors that fit a stereotype than for ones that don't fit a stereotype. This effect is readily observed when we examine the attributions people make for performance on sex-linked tasks (Rosenfield & Stephan, 1978; Swim & Sanna, 1996). When a man succeeds on a stereotypically masculine task, people assume it's because of high ability; when a woman succeeds on the same task, people assume she got lucky or tried especially hard, or that the task was very easy. Just the opposite pattern occurs for stereotypically feminine tasks. Here, people assume that women succeed because of high ability but that men succeed because of extra effort or good fortune.

Stereotypes influence attributions in another manner. Dispositional attributions are especially apt to be made for the positive outcomes of ingroup members and negative outcomes of outgroup members (Chatman & von Hippel, 2001; Hewstone, 1990; Islam & Hewstone, 1993; L. J. Jackson, Sullivan, & Hodge, 1993). For example, when an ingroup member rises from poverty to make a million dollars, we cite the person's character and ability as likely causal factors. When an outgroup member performs the very same feat, we say the person got lucky or had extra help. The opposite pattern occurs when negative outcomes are involved. We make situational attributions for the negative outcomes of ingroup members and dispositional attributions for the negative outcomes of outgroup members. Pettigrew (1979) has termed this attributional asymmetry the ultimate attribution error, noting that the bias can be especially troublesome when minority group members are helped by affirmative action programs. People readily assume that the beneficiaries of such programs did not succeed on their own and are undeserving of their accomplishments.

Stereotypes even shape the way we describe behavior. When an ingroup member does something meritorious, we describe the event in terms of a dispositional quality. When an outgroup member does the same thing, we describe the behavior in concrete terms. To illustrate, suppose we see Kim hold the door open for another person. If Kim is an ingroup member, we say "Kim was helpful." If Kim is an outgroup member, we merely say "Kim held the door open for another person." The opposite tendency occurs if the behavior is negative. If we see someone failing to hold a door open, we are more apt to describe the behavior as "rude" when it was performed by an outgroup member than by an ingroup member (Maass, Salvi, Arcuri, & Semin, 1989). This intergroup linguistic bias is fueled by a desire to boost our feelings of self-worth (Maass, Ceccarelli, & Rudin, 1996).

C. Stereotype Activation, Application, and Control

Some stereotypes, such as "African Americans are musical" and "White men can't jump," are heard so commonly that they have become permanent fixtures of American culture. Even people who disavow the accuracy of these stereotypes readily admit to being aware of them (Devine, 1989; Devine & Elliot, 1995). An interesting question arises as to whether people who personally reject negative stereotypes can successfully avoid using them when encountering an outgroup member.

1. Devine's Activation–Application Model

Devine (1989) has addressed this issue. Along with other theorists, Devine assumes that forming an impression of another person involves a two-step process (Brewer, 1988; Fiske & Neuberg, 1990). During the first stage, stereotypes associated with the person's category membership are activated. During the second stage, these stereotypes may or may not be applied. If we are unwilling *or* unable to think more carefully about what the person is like, we rather mindlessly apply the stereotype. If, however, we are willing *and* motivated to think carefully about what the person is like, we consider the person's unique qualities and attributes and do not apply automatically the stereotype. To illustrate, when meeting an elderly person, we might initially assume that the person's cognitive abilities are limited and that their memory is poor. If, however, we take the time to know the person better, we might conclude that their mind is nimble and their memory superb.

Devine has used the activation–application model to understand individual differences in racial prejudice. As shown in Figure 10.9, Devine assumes that, regardless

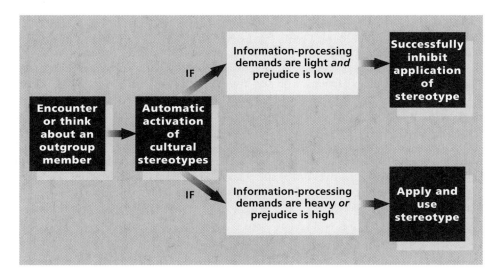

FIGURE 10.9

Devine's Model of Stereotype Activation and Application

The model maintains that, regardless of one's personal level of prejudice, stereotypes are automatically activated whenever one encounters or thinks about an outgroup member. If prejudice is low *and* processing demands are light, these stereotypes are inhibited and are not applied. If, however, prejudice is high *or* processing demands are heavy, these stereotypes are applied.

Source: Devine (1989).

of one's level of prejudice, stereotypes are activated automatically when people encounter or think about an outgroup member. If information-processing demands are light (e.g., people have a lot of time to make a decision or are not attending to more than one stimulus at the time), low-prejudice people (who are motivated to be fair-minded) will successfully inhibit the use of automatically activated stereotypes. If, however, information-processing demands are heavy, even low-prejudice people will be unable to inhibit the use of stereotypes.

Devine's model of stereotype activation and application has stimulated a great deal of research. The model's predictions have not always been supported, however. For example, although even fair-minded people are aware of negative cultural stereotypes, they tend to be less aware of these stereotypes than highly prejudiced people are (Gordijn, Koomen, & Stapel, 2001). Moreover, negative stereotypes are not automatically activated in low-prejudiced people whenever they think about an outgroup member (Lepore & Brown, 1997), and they are not necessarily applied when information-processing demands are heavy (Fazio & Dunton, 1997; Kawakami, Dion, & Dovidio, 1998). Finally, even prejudiced people can be trained to ignore or suppress stereotypes when thinking about outgroup members (Kawakami, Dovidio, Moll, Hermsen, & Russin, 2000). In short, stereotype activation is not always automatic, and stereotype application is not inevitable (Blair, 2002).

2. Motivation to Control Prejudice

Having established that stereotype activation and application are not inevitable, researchers have turned their attention to understanding factors that influence when stereotypes come to mind (Kunda & Spencer, 2003). One fruitful line of research has focused on identifying the motivation behind prejudiced and unprejudiced reactions (Dunton, & Fazio, 1997; Plant & Devine, 1998). Table 10.6 shows a scale designed to measure two distinct motivations. The first four items assess the extent to which a person is intrinsically motivated to avoid prejudice. People who score high on this scale truly want to be fair-minded and egalitarian, and they try hard not to judge people by their group memberships. The next four items assess extrinsic reasons to avoid prejudice. People who score high on this scale fear being evaluated negatively if they display prejudice, and they work hard to suppress prejudice to avoid public censure and disapproval. Because the two scales are uncorrelated, a person who is intrinsically motivated to avoid prejudice may or may not be extrinsically motivated to avoid prejudice. People who want to be unprejudiced for purely personal reasons (high intrinsic/low extrinsic motivation) tend to be the most unbiased (Amodio, Harmon-Jones, & Devine, 2003; Devine, Plant, Amodio, Harmon-Jones, & Vance, 2002).

D. Stereotypes and Sexism

Cognitive models of stereotyping assume that stereotypic beliefs underlie prejudiced feelings and discrimination. Having learned that some group is characterized by negative qualities, we come to develop an antipathy toward its members and discriminate against them. Although this logical sequence can occur, it doesn't characterize all forms of prejudice. In some cases, prejudiced feelings are primary and people justify their negative feelings by assuming that a group has many negative qualities (Allport, 1954; Jussim, Nelson, Manis, & Soffin, 1995). In other cases, stereotypes and prejudice are largely unrelated. For example, many anti-Semites concede that Jews are

TABLE 10.6   Motivation to Respond without Prejudice Scales

INTERNAL MOTIVATION TO AVOID PREJUDICE

1. I attempt to act in nonprejudiced ways toward Black people because it is personally important to me.

2. I am personally motivated by my beliefs to be nonprejudiced toward Black people.

3. Because of my personal values, I believe that using stereotypes about Black people is wrong.

4. Being nonprejudiced toward Black people is important to my self-concept.

EXTERNAL MOTIVATION TO AVOID PREJUDICE

5. I try to hide any negative thoughts about Black people in order to avoid negative reactions from others.

6. If I acted prejudiced toward Black people, I would be concerned that others would be angry with me.

7. I attempt to appear nonprejudiced toward Black people in order to avoid disapproval from others.

8. I try to act nonprejudiced toward Black people because of pressure from others.

Source: Plant and Devine (1998).

competent and hardworking, yet they still dislike them. For these and other reasons, stereotypes and prejudiced feelings are not always closely associated (Dovidio, Brigham, Johnson, & Gaertner, 1996).

People's attitudes toward women illustrate the complex relation between stereotypes, prejudiced feelings, and discrimination. The first words uttered in a delivery room generally announce the child's sex ("It's a girl"), and this information immediately shapes how an infant is treated and perceived. One study found that parents of one-day-old girls were more apt than parents of one-day-old boys to use words like *beautiful, cute,* and *pretty* when describing their infants (Rubin, Provenzano, & Luria, 1974). Similar characterizations persist throughout life. Across a variety of age groups and nationalities, women are perceived to be warmer, more affectionate, more understanding, and more supportive than men, and men are perceived to be more confident, capable, ambitious, and objective than women (Broverman, Vogel, Broverman, Clarkson, & Rosenkrantz, 1972; J. E. Williams & Best, 1982). Both men and women endorse these characterizations, indicating that the sexes largely agree when it comes to judging what men and women "are like."

1. Two Types of Sexism: Hostile Sexism and Benevolent Sexism

When I was recruited as a policewoman in 1971, the only things they would let women do were menial jobs and paper-shuffling. They thought women were weak, and just gave us gentle work, and this really got me thinking. All of the things people do to overprotect women are really just ways of looking down on them.

Kim Kang Ja, police chief, Seoul, South Korea
(New York Times, *February 8, 2003, p. A4)*

Because interpersonal qualities of warmth and caring are highly valued, women are generally evaluated more positively than are men (Eagly & Mladinic, 1989). This does not necessarily imply a lack of prejudicial feelings, however. Glick and Fiske (1996, 2001) have argued that sexism can take two forms. **Hostile sexism** is characterized by a belief that women are incompetent, overly emotional, and manipulative. This form of sexism is clearly negative. In contrast, **benevolent sexism** is positive in tone. It is characterized by a belief that women are pure creatures who should be pampered, protected, and placed on a pedestal. Although the characterizations associated with benevolent sexism appear to be positive, they imply that women are weak and need to be coddled and thus restrict women from occupying positions of power, leadership, and privilege.

Table 10.7 presents a scale used to measure hostile and benevolent sexism. Although men score much higher than woman on the hostile sexism items, the two sexes do not differ much on the benevolent sexism items (Glick & Fiske, 1996). Interestingly, women score especially high in benevolent sexism in countries with restrictive codes of sexual conduct (Glick et al., 2000). Glick and Fiske believe this is because benevolent sexism offers women some protection from the hostile sexism they endure in these cultures.

2. Prejudice, Gender Roles, and Gender Stereotypes

Benevolent sexism may also serve to justify and perpetuate a division of labor in contemporary societies. Despite the large-scale integration of women into the workforce, many occupations are still highly sex-typed. For example, women make up more than 95 percent of all dental hygienists and secretaries, while men make up more than 95 percent of all carpenters and auto mechanics (U.S. Bureau of Labor Statistics, 1998). One explanation for the persistence of sex-typed occupations is that people believe that success in certain jobs requires qualities assumed to be more typical of one sex than of the other. For example, nurses are expected to be nurturant and caring, women are believed to be more nurturant and caring than are men, and most nurses are women; commercial airline pilots are expected to be unemotional and brave, men are believed to be less emotional and more courageous than are women, and most commercial airline pilots are male (Cejka & Eagly, 1999). In this manner, gender stereotypes both reflect and preserve the division of labor in our society (Eagly, 1987; Eagly & Steffen, 1984; Eagly & Wood, 1999; W. Wood & Eagly, 2002).

Several studies document the pervasiveness of occupational sex-typing. In one investigation, Lippa and Connelly (1990) asked men and women to rate their preference for each of 70 occupations that varied in terms of their masculinity and femininity. Using only these occupational ratings, Lippa and Connelly were able to successfully classify 90 percent of the participants as being male or female. This finding indicates that men and women are strongly attracted to careers that emphasize qualities associated with their gender. Furthermore, sexism is especially apt to surface when women seek to occupy roles thought to require stereotypically masculine qualities. Eagly (2000) has suggested that as long as women do "women's work," prejudice is minimized. But when a woman attempts to cross gender lines and do "a man's job," prejudice arises. Importantly, this occupational sex-typing is not limited only to men. Many women also disparage another woman who attempts to crash a male-dominated occupation or role, in part because the woman is displaying the masculine qualities associated with that role (Eagly, Makhijani, & Klonsky, 1992; Glick, Diebold, Bailey-Werner, & Zhu, 1997; Heilman, Wallen, Fuchs, & Tamkins, 2004; Rudman, 1998; Rudman & Glick, 1999; Rudman & Kilianski, 2000).

TABLE 10.7   The Ambivalent Sexism Inventory

Below are a series of statements concerning men and women and their relationship in contemporary society. Please indicate the degree to which you agree or disagree with each statement using the scale below.

0	1	2	3	4	5
disagree strongly	disagree somewhat	disagree slightly	agree slightly	agree somewhat	agree strongly

1. No matter how accomplished he is, a man is not truly complete as a person unless he has the love of a woman.	0	1	2	3	4	5
2. Many women are actually seeking special favors, such as hiring policies that favor them over men, under the guise of asking for "equality."	0	1	2	3	4	5
3. In a disaster, women ought to be rescued before men.	0	1	2	3	4	5
4. Most women interpret innocent remarks or acts as being sexist.	0	1	2	3	4	5
5. Women are too easily offended.	0	1	2	3	4	5
6. People are not truly happy in life without being romantically involved with a member of the opposite sex.	0	1	2	3	4	5
7. Feminists are seeking for women to have more power than men.	0	1	2	3	4	5
8. Most women have a quality of purity that few men possess.	0	1	2	3	4	5
9. Women should be cherished and protected by men.	0	1	2	3	4	5
10. Most women fail to appreciate fully all that men do for them.	0	1	2	3	4	5
11. Women seek to gain power by getting control over men.	0	1	2	3	4	5
12. Every man ought to have a women whom he adores.	0	1	2	3	4	5
13. Men are incomplete without women.	0	1	2	3	4	5
14. Women exaggerate problems they have at work.	0	1	2	3	4	5
15. Once a woman gets a man to commit to her, she usually tries to put him on a tight leash.	0	1	2	3	4	5
16. When women lose to men in a fair competition, they typically complain about being discriminated against.	0	1	2	3	4	5
17. A good woman should be set on a pedestal by her man.	0	1	2	3	4	5
18. Many women get a kick out of teasing men by seeming sexually available and then refusing male advances.	0	1	2	3	4	5
19. Women, compared to men, tend to have a superior moral sensibility.	0	1	2	3	4	5
20. Men should be willing to sacrifice their own well being in order to provide financially for the women in their lives.	0	1	2	3	4	5
21. Feminists are making unreasonable demands of men.	0	1	2	3	4	5
22. Women, as compared to men, tend to have a more refined sense of culture and good taste.	0	1	2	3	4	5

Note: To calculate scores on the benevolent sexism subscale, average your responses to items, 1, 3, 6, 8, 9, 12, 13, 17, 19, 20, and 22; to calculate scores on the hostile sexism scale, average your responses to items 2, 4, 5, 7, 10, 11, 14, 15, 16, 18, and 21.
Source: Glick and Fiske (1996).

The case of Ann Hopkins provides a graphic example of occupational sexism. Hopkins was a top accountant at Price Waterhouse, one of the most prestigious accounting firms in the United States. Despite being highly productive, well liked by her clients, and generally regarded as aggressive, hardworking, and ambitious, she was denied partnership. Her supervisors complained that she lacked interpersonal skills and that she could correct this shortcoming by walking, talking, and dressing in a more feminine manner. In short, Hopkins was denied partnership because she was not acting in ways people expect women to act. Hopkins filed a lawsuit alleging sex discrimination against Price Waterhouse and won. Price Waterhouse then appealed the verdict to the U.S. Supreme Court. The Court upheld the original verdict, relying on social psychological evidence that women who fail to display stereotypically feminine qualities are often targets of prejudice and discrimination (S. T. Fiske, Bersoff, Borgida, Deaux, & Heilman, 1991). Although Hopkins won her case, the verdict did not put an end to occupational sexism. Recently, the brokerage firm Morgan Stanley reached a $54 million settlement in a sex discrimination case involving a bond saleswoman who contended she was denied promotion because she was a woman (www.eeoc.gov/press/7-12-04.html).

IV. Victims of Prejudice

Overt acts of prejudice and discrimination have declined since the civil rights movement of the 1960s. While this is certainly true, it would be naive to suggest that racial, ethnic, and social minorities no longer confront prejudice in their lives. They still do, often with devastating consequences (Gibbons, Gerrard, Cleveland, Wills, & Brody, 2004; Kessler, Mickelson, & Williams, 1999; Mellor, 2003; Swim, Hyers, Cohen, & Ferguson, 2001). In this section we will examine prejudice from the victim's perspective, with an eye toward understanding how victims cope with prejudice and discrimination.

A. Identity Maintenance

In every culture around the world, ethnic and racial minorities face a predicament. Should they try to blend in and assimilate to the dominant culture, or should they retain their unique identity and preserve their racial or national heritage? Historically, assimilation was the norm. Upon entering the United States, many 20th-century immigrants changed their names, studiously tried to lose their accents, and altered their mannerisms and styles of dress in an attempt to become more Americanized. This state of affairs has changed a lot over the past 50 years. Beginning with the Black Pride movement of the 1960s, racial, ethnic, and other social minorities such as gays and lesbians have been encouraged to celebrate their differences and retain their unique identities rather than hide them. By doing so, they would transform America into a mosaic of cultural pluralism rather than a homogenized melting pot.

Efforts to maintain cultural identity appear to be meeting with success. Most minority group members now evaluate their collective identity in positive terms (Crocker, Luhtanen, Blaine, & Broadnax, 1994; Phinney, 1990), and many report a personal level of self-esteem that is comparable to or exceeds that of European Americans (Gray-Little & Hafdahl, 2000; Twenge & Campbell, 2002; Twenge & Crocker, 2002). This finding is somewhat surprising when one considers that many minorities are subjected to prejudice and discrimination.

Several explanations have been offered to explain why minority group members often report having high self-esteem. First, it is possible that minority group members have high *explicit* self-esteem, but low *implicit* self-esteem. In support of this possibility, Livingston (2002) found that African Americans who reported experiencing a lot of discrimination showed high levels of explicit ingroup favoritism but low levels of implicit ingroup favoritism. This suggests that prejudice and discrimination may adversely affect unconscious self-relevant attitudes (see also Mendoza-Denton, Downey, Purdie, Davis, & Pietrzak, 2002). Another possibility is that group pride insulates people from discrimination and prejudice. Although people who identify strongly with their group are more inclined to believe they are being discriminated against (Major, Quinton, & Schmader, 2003; Operario & Fiske, 2001; Sellers & Shelton, 2003), they also tend to be less adversely affected by discrimination (Branscombe, Schmitt, & Harvey, 1999; Sellers & Shelton, 2003). This suggests that group pride is a resilience factor that offsets the negative effects of prejudice and discrimination.

The attributions minority members make for discrimination may also protect their feelings of self-worth. Under some conditions, minority group members attribute negative outcomes to discrimination (Crocker & Major, 1989; Crocker, Voelkl, Testa, & Major, 1991; Major et al., 2002; Major, Kaiser, & McCoy, 2003; Stangor, Swim, Van Allen, & Sechrist, 2002). For example, if they fail to be promoted at work or receive a poor grade on an essay, they may believe that the outcome was due to prejudice rather than to the quality of their performance. Attributing negative outcomes to external factors may, in turn, protect their feelings of self-worth (Crocker et al., 1991; Major, Kaiser, & McCoy, 2003). Unfortunately, attributions to discrimination can also reflect poorly on an individual, because people disapprove of individuals who evade personal responsibility for a negative outcome (Kaiser & Miller, 2001).

B. Test Performance in Achievement Settings: The Role of Stereotype Threat

On average, African Americans and Latinos score lower than European Americans on standardized tests of intelligence and achievement, such as IQ tests and the Scholastic Aptitude Test (SAT). There are many possible explanations for this effect, including lack of family support, impoverished social conditions, and, perhaps, genetic factors (Herrnstein & Murray, 1994). Factors in the immediate testing situation may also play a role (C. M. Steele, 1992, 1997, 2004; C. M. Steele & Aronson, 1995). When African American students perform an intellectual task, they fear being judged by the negative cultural stereotype that African Americans lack intelligence. In turn, this fear, or **stereotype threat,** creates anxiety and leads to poor task performance (Blascovich, Spencer, Quinn, & Steele, 2001; see also O'Brien, & Crandall, 2003).

The phenomenon was first demonstrated in a series of experiments by C. M. Steele and Aronson (1995). In one study, African American and European American students at Stanford University took a test that measured their verbal ability. Half of the participants were asked to record their race on a questionnaire prior to taking the test, and half were not. Steele and Aronson reasoned that making race salient would activate stereotype threat in African American students and undermine their performance. Figure 10.10 shows support for this hypothesis. After adjusting the scores for pre-existing differences in verbal ability, Steele and Aronson found that African Americans who indicated their race performed worse on the task than African Americans who

FIGURE 10.10

Stereotype Threat and Test Performance

African Americans per-formed just as well as European Americans in the control condition but performed more poorly than European Americans when they had first been asked to think about their race. These findings sug-gest that African Ameri-cans may sometimes suffer from stereotype threat in achievement-relevant situations.

Source: C. M. Steele and Aronson (1995).

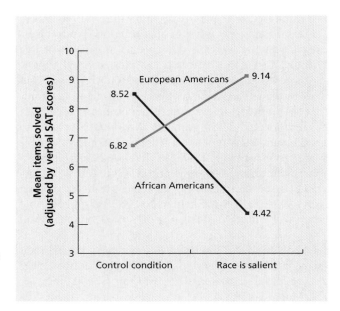

did not indicate their race. The opposite tended to occur among European Americans, although the effect was not significant. Although these findings do not establish that stereotype threat explains racial differences in achievement, they do show that African Americans suffer performance impairments when race is a salient factor (Sackett, Hardison, & Cullen, 2004).

1. Who's Susceptible to Stereotype Threat?

Stereotype threat primarily affects students who identify strongly with doing well in school. If success means very little to a student, the student won't be vulnerable to stereotype threat. Because good students care most about doing well, this means that stereotype threat will have its greatest effect on the most promising students (Pronin, Steele, & Ross, 2004; Schmader, 2002). Moreover, stereotype threat can occur even when students have substantial confidence in their own ability to succeed. The stereotype applies to the group, not to the individual, and a student needn't accept the stereotype in order to be susceptible to its negative effects. It is simply the fear of being judged by the stereotype that undermines performance. (J. Aronson et al., 1999; C. M. Steele, 1997).

Finally, you don't have to be African American to suffer from stereotype threat. The phenomenon can occur for any group that is characterized by a negative stereo-type. For example, common stereotypes maintain that European Americans are inferior to Asians in science and engineering and inferior to African Americans in athletic ability. Consistent with Steele's theory of stereotype threat, research has found that the task performance of European Americans suffers in these areas when they are reminded of these stereotypes (Stone, Lynch, Sjomeling, & Darley, 1997).

2. Stereotype Threat among Women

Women consistently score lower on standardized tests of math ability than do men (Benbow, Lubinski, Shea, & Eftekhari-Sanjani, 2000), and this fact is a common

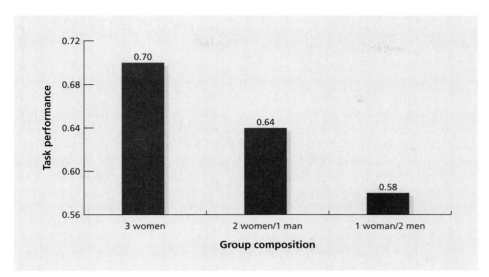

FIGURE 10.11

Task Performance and
Group Composition

Women performed more
poorly on a math test
when they were in the
statistical minority. These
data suggest that minority
status can heighten iden-
tity salience and identity
salience, in turn, can
undermine performance via
stereotype threat.

Source: Inzlicht and Ben-Zeev
(2000).

social stereotype. Consequently, women are susceptible to stereotype threat in math when their gender identity is salient (R. P. Brown & Josephs, 1999; Quinn & Spencer, 2001; Shih, Pittinsky, & Ambady, 1999; Spencer, Steele, & Quinn, 1999). An investigation by Inzlicht and Ben-Zeev (2000) highlights just how easily this can occur. These investigators had women take a math test in three-person groups. In one condition the groups were comprised of all women, in another condition there were two women and one man, and in another condition there was one woman and two men. On the basis of evidence that minority status influences identity salience (see Chapter 5), Inzlicht and Ben-Zeev predicted that stereotype threat would be most apt to undermine the performance of women in the one-woman/two-men condition. The data displayed in Figure 10.11 indicate that these predictions were confirmed. Apparently, simply being in the minority was sufficient to active stereotype threat (see also Sekaquaptewa & Thompson, 2003; M. Thompson & Sekaquaptewa, 2002).

Inzlicht and Ben-Zeev's findings have important implications for current efforts to improve the educational performance of women in engineering, math, and the sciences. According to a report by the National Science Foundation (1998), women constitute only 35 percent of undergraduate students enrolled in physics, math, and computer science courses, and less than 20 percent of those enrolled in engineering classes. Being surrounded by men might undermine women's performance in these courses, leading them to avoid taking such classes in the future. This possibility lends support to those who advocate single-sex educational environments. (A more detailed discussion of these issues can be found in a report by the American Association of University Women Educational Foundation, 1998.)

3. Reducing Stereotype Threat

Fortunately, several steps can be taken to reduce the negative effects of stereotype threat. First, stereotype threat can be attenuated by the presence of positive role models (Marx, & Roman, 2002; McIntyre, Paulson, & Lord, 2001). Apparently, being reminded that other people have persevered inspires minority students to rise above the stereotype and perform their best. Stereotype threat is also reduced when students are encouraged to view intelligence as a malleable quality that can be cultivated, rather than a fixed capacity one either does or does not possess (J. Aronson, Fried, & Good, 2002; Good, Aronson, & Inzlicht, 2003).

C. Disidentification and Disengagement

Ultimately, stereotype threat can lead minority students to disengage from educational pursuits and disidentify with academic achievement (Pronin et al., 2004; Schmader, Major, & Gamrzow, 2001; C. M. Steele, 1997). Disidentification occurs when students no longer care about doing well in school. In effect, they no longer base their feelings of self-worth on their academic performance. Disidentification can also lead people to belittle the importance of education and disparage those who continue to strive for academic excellence. Peer pressure being what it is, these attitudes can affect entire communities, leading scores of children to devalue the importance of education and disengage from educational pursuits.

A study by Osborne (1995) illustrates the nature of these effects. Osborne examined the correlation between self-esteem and academic performance in European American and African American students as they made the transition from middle school to high school. The left-hand panel of Figure 10.12 shows the results for the European American students. Grade level had little effect here. In contrast, the right-hand panel of Figure 10.12 shows a different effect for African American students. As they made the transition to high school, their self-esteem became increasingly

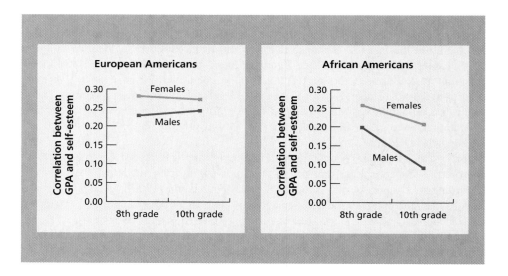

FIGURE 10.12

Disidentification among African American Students

The left-hand panel shows that, among European American students, the correlation between grade point average (GPA) and self-esteem remained constant from 8th grade to 10th grade. The right-hand panel shows that, among African American students, the correlation declined, especially among African American males. These finding suggest that African American students disidentify with educational attainments as they get older.

Source: Osborne (1995).

independent of their performance in school. This was especially true for African American boys, suggesting that this group is especially apt to disidentify with academic performance. This process further fuels the negative cultural stereotype that African Americans lack academic proficiency, perpetuating a vicious cycle of underachievement (Major, Spencer, Schmader, Wolfe, & Crocker, 1998; Schmader et al., 2001).

D. Affirmative Action Programs

One way to keep people interested in school is to apply lower performance standards to minority groups. This approach plays a role in some affirmative action programs. As you probably know, affirmative action programs attempt to redress years of institutionalized discrimination against minority groups by giving them special consideration in a variety of areas, such as the issuing of government contracts. These programs are quite controversial, and college admission decisions have been a lightning rod for this debate. In 1978, the U.S. Supreme Court ruled that admission decisions that rely on quotas or set-asides are illegal, even though they are designed to provide racial and ethnic balance in academic settings (*Regents of the University of California* v. *Bakke,* 1978, Citation 438 U.S. 265, Docket 76–811). Many universities have struggled to remain within the bounds of this law while still promoting diversity on their campuses, arguing that a diverse student body gives students a better educational experience (Orfield, 2001; www.umich.edu/~urel/admissions/legal/index.html).

The manner in which affirmative action programs affect the individuals who benefit from them is also a topic of debate. The expectation is that the beneficiaries of affirmative action will be better off having enjoyed this advantage. In contrast, some theorists have argued that students who receive special consideration from affirmative action programs might ultimately be ill-served, because they do not achieve success on their own terms (S. Steele, 1990).

One way to resolve the different positions on affirmative action is to assume that the programs are beneficial as long as people believe that merit played some role in the selection process. In one study that tested this hypothesis, women were assigned to play the role of a leader in a three-person group (R. P. Brown, Charnsangavej, Keough, Newman, & Rentfrow, 2000). In the control condition, assignment to the leadership role was allegedly determined by a flip of a coin. In the affirmative action/quota condition, the participants were told they were chosen to lead simply because the experimenters needed to balance the numbers of men and women, and they had already had too many male leaders. In the affirmative action/merit condition, the researchers told the participants that not enough women had signed up, so the most qualified woman in the group had been selected to be the leader.

After being assigned to one of the three conditions, the participants completed a problem-solving task. Figure 10.13 shows the number of problems these women solved in each of the three experimental conditions. It may be seen that the participants in the affirmative action/quota condition performed more poorly than did participants in the other two groups. These findings suggest that affirmative action programs have negative effects only if people believe they received preferential treatment without regard to merit (see also M. E. Turner & Pratkanis, 1994).

It's important to underscore that findings like those illustrated in Figure 10.13 do not mean that affirmative action programs do more harm than good. After all,

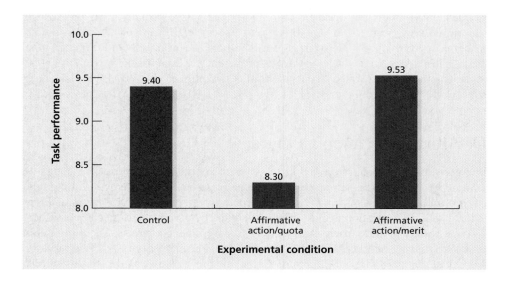

FIGURE 10.13

Affirmative Action and Test Performance

Women chosen to lead a group simply because of their gender (affirmative action/quota condition) performed more poorly than did control participants or women who believed merit played a role in their selection as group leaders. These findings indicate that affirmative action programs have detrimental effects on task performance only if their beneficiaries believe they were given preferential treatment regardless of merit.

Source: R. P. Brown Charnsangavej, Keough, Newman, & Rentfrow (2000).

disadvantaged students admitted to prestigious universities are able to enjoy an educational experience they might not otherwise have had. Racial and ethnic diversity also enrich the intellectual climate of a university and thereby promote a higher learning experience for all students, regardless of race or ethnicity (Crosby, Iyer, Clayton, & Downing, 2003). In short, instead of suggesting that affirmative action programs should be abolished, the data point out that steps should be taken to ensure that those who are chosen by race or gender remain motivated to succeed by believing that competence played a role in their selection. In addition, minority group members should receive assurances that they are capable of performing at high levels of achievement and that their teachers and employers are confident in their ability to succeed (Cohen, Steele, & Ross, 1999; Harber, 1998).

V. Reducing Prejudice

When studying the nature of prejudice, no issue is more important than a consideration of how it can be reduced. Over the years, many different approaches have been tried. For the most part, these approaches fall into two camps: One approach attempts to alleviate prejudice by changing the way people *think* about minority groups members; the other attempts to reduce prejudice by altering the way people *behave* toward minority group members.

A. Cognitive Models of Prejudice Reduction

Imagine that you meet a prejudiced person who believes that woman are ineffective leaders, that Jews lack athletic ability, and that Japanese Americans are unpatriotic. Now suppose you tell that person that Margaret Thatcher ruled Britain with an iron fist, that Mark Spitz won seven gold medals in the 1972 Olympics, and that the most highly decorated combat unit in World War II was composed entirely of Japanese Americans. Would this knowledge lead them to change their opinions and feelings toward these minority groups?

Unfortunately, the answer appears to be no. Instead of altering beliefs, knowledge of exceptional cases generally leads people to mentally create a subtype (Allport, 1954; Kunda & Oleson, 1995; Z. Richards & Hewstone, 2001; R. Weber & Crocker, 1983). Believing in exceptions to the rule allows people to retain their stereotypic beliefs even when confronted with disconfirming evidence. In fact, the more exceptional the case, the easier it is to dismiss. For this reason, it is often more effective to change stereotypes by exposing people to many moderate counterexamples rather than to a few extreme ones (Kunda & Oleson, 1997). To illustrate, suppose a teenage boy's parents don't want him consorting with skateboarders because they think skateboarders are bad students. Rather than bringing one exceptionally bright skateboarder home for dinner, the teenager should have his parents meet a group of skateboarders who, though not brilliant, all get decent grades (R. Weber & Crocker, 1983; Wilder, Simon, & Faith, 1996).

Regrettably, even this strategy may fail to produce lasting tolerance. Henderson-King and Nisbett (1996, Study 2) conducted an investigation showing that a single negative instance is capable of undoing whatever benefits exemplary counterexamples provide. In their research, European American college students were asked to interview an African American student (actually a confederate). Three experimental conditions were then created. Prior to the interview, some of the participants witnessed another African American student (also a confederate) acting in a rude and hostile manner; participants in a second experimental group witnessed a European American student (also a confederate) acting in a rude and hostile manner; and participants in a control condition saw neither type of behavior. Finally, all of the European American participants conducted an interview with an African American confederate, and the amount of time they spent talking was recorded. As shown in Figure 10.14, European American participants who had previously seen an African American person act in a rude manner spent the least amount of time interviewing another African American. A single negative instance was sufficient to trigger stereotypes, prejudice, and discrimination (see also Kunda, Davies, Adams, & Spencer, 2002).

B. Behavioral Models of Prejudice Reduction

In a landmark decision issued in 1954, the U.S. Supreme Court ruled that forced segregation of schools, in which African Americans were required to attend all–African American schools, violated an individual's constitutional right to equal protection under the law (*Brown* v. *Board of Education*). In reaching their "separate is not equal" ruling, the court echoed arguments prepared by social scientists (for a review, see S. W. Cook, 1984, 1985). These scientists presented evidence that forced segregation fostered feelings of inferiority in African American children and compromised their educational experience. They also argued that racially integrated schools would

FIGURE 10.14

The Negative Effects of a Negative Instance

European American participants avoided talking to an African American after witnessing another African American student exhibit rude behavior. These findings suggest that a single negative instance can activate stereotypes and produce discrimination.

Source: Henderson-King & Nisbett (1996).

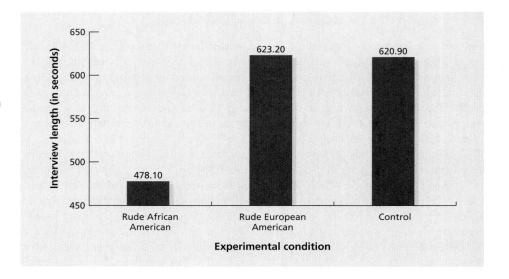

improve the academic performance of African American children and lead to better interracial relations.

1. Desegregation and the Contact Hypothesis

The *Brown* ruling set in motion widespread efforts to reduce prejudice and discrimination by legislation, culminating in the Civil Rights Act of 1964. Among the many programs that emanated from this legislative effort, none was more controversial than the forced busing of schoolchildren to achieve racial integration. Under this program, many African American children were bused to predominantly European American schools and many European American students were bused to predominantly African American schools. Despite achieving some success (S. W. Cook, 1984, 1985), the promise of this program was never fully realized (Gerard, 1983; Schofield, 1979; Schofield & Francis, 1982). Moreover, the program was enormously controversial and sparked civil unrest and disobedience, as many European American families either refused to send their children to inner-city schools or fled to the suburbs to avoid having to do so. Forty years after the program was launched, it was abandoned.

2. Four Conditions Needed for Contact to Reduce Prejudice

With the benefit of hindsight, it is easy to see why forced integration failed to achieve racial harmony. As first discussed by Allport (1954), interracial contact is apt to reduce prejudice only when certain conditions are met. Table 10.8 summarizes these conditions. First, the participants must be of equal status. In terms of schooling, this means they should be of comparable background, status, and ability. This condition was rarely met in the forced integration of schooling, as poor inner-city African American children were often placed into classrooms with European Americans who had enjoyed a privileged background and a better education.

The second condition is interdependence. This means the participants must work toward a common goal, with everyone contributing to the group's success. Earlier we noted that Sherif and his colleagues (1961) were able to reduce prejudice at the Robbers Cave Boy's Camp by having the campers work toward a common goal. For

TABLE 10.8 Conditions Needed before Interracial Contact Will Reduce Racial Prejudice	
Condition	Explanation
Equal status	The participants must be equal in background, status, and ability.
Cooperative interdependence	The participants must work toward a common goal, with the success of the group depending on everyone's performance.
Pleasant interactions	The atmosphere must be friendly rather than hostile.
Supporting social norms	Parents and other authority figures must actively support integration rather than being ambivalent or working to undermine it.

Sources: Allport (1954); S. W. Cook (1985).

example, the campers had to cooperate in order to repair a broken truck. This sort of cooperative interdependence reduces prejudice by creating a superordinate identity, in which the group members begin to think of themselves as forming one large group rather than two separate groups (Dovidio, Gaertner, Niemann, & Snider, 2001; Dovidio, Gaertner, & Validzic, 1998; Gaertner, Mann, Murrell, & Dovidio, 1989; Gaertner et al., 1999). Unfortunately, this condition is rarely present in a classroom situation. Most classrooms are competitive arenas in which children vie for grades and for the teacher's attention.

The final two conditions are related to one another. Pleasant interactions are needed if contact is to reduce prejudice, and unless authority figures actively support interracial contact, contact will serve only to exacerbate tension and enmity. Anyone who witnessed the forced busing of schoolchildren can tell you that these conditions were rarely met. There was considerable resistance on the part of parents, and considerable civil unrest and tension. In many cases, armed soldiers were called out to escort African American children into formerly segregated all-white schools. Thus, the interactions were rarely pleasant and community support was rarely strong.

In short, the conditions surrounding the forced integration of schools were not conducive to racial harmony. The schoolchildren were not of equal status and they did not work cooperatively toward a common goal. Moreover, the interactions were often strained and undermined by parents, politicians, school administrators, and community leaders. It is no wonder, then, that these programs failed to achieve their stated aims.

C. The Jigsaw Classroom

Fortunately, other programs have fared better in reducing prejudice (Ensari & Miller, 2002; Pettigrew, 1997). Drawing on the principles discussed in Table 10.8, E. Aronson and his colleagues developed a program for use in the classroom (E. Aronson, Blaney, Stephan, Sikes, & Snapp, 1978). This program, called the Jigsaw Classroom, involves a cooperative learning task in which students work together on a group project. Each student in a small, racially integrated group is given one piece of information needed for success. When the pieces are combined, the group succeeds. To illustrate, in one study, fifth-grade students in a racially integrated classroom were studying biographies of great Americans. The researchers created a biography of newspaper magnate Joseph

Pulitzer. The biography was made up of six paragraphs. One focused on his ancestry, another on his early life, another on his success in the newspaper business, and so forth. Each paragraph described a different part of Pulitzer's life, but no paragraph contained information about his entire life.

The students were then placed into six-person groups, and each student was given one paragraph. In this manner, each group had access to the entire biography of Joseph Pulitzer, but each student had only one-sixth of the story. After receiving their paragraphs, the students were told to master the information in their paragraph and then teach it to the others in their group. They were also informed that each person would be tested on his or her knowledge of Pulitzer's entire life. The name Jigsaw Classroom was chosen for this program because each student has one piece of a puzzle and success requires that they work cooperatively to form the bigger picture. Compared to a control group of students who worked in a traditional classroom environment, students in the Jigsaw Classroom developed greater liking for their fellow students, enjoyed school more, and learned as much or more.

D. Integrated Sports Teams

In April 1947, Branch Rickey, the general manager of the Brooklyn Dodgers, shocked the world of sports by announcing that Jackie Robinson, an African American, was joining the Brooklyn Dodgers. Heretofore, African Americans played baseball in a separate league. No matter how accomplished they were, they were barred from playing in the major leagues. As you might imagine, Robinson's entry into major league baseball met with widespread opposition. Despite having a stellar season with the Dodgers and leading them to the World Series, Robinson was routinely taunted, bullied, and threatened with bodily harm and death. Throughout it all, he comported himself with dignified restraint and grace. Eventually, he came to earn the respect of his teammates, those he played against, and the nation at large.

Racially integrated athletic teams are now the rule rather than the exception, and in most cases the different racial groups get along well. Pratkanis and Turner (1994) have suggested that racial integration has succeeded in professional sports because team sports satisfy most of the criteria of the contact hypothesis (see Table 10.8). By definition, team sports are a cooperative endeavor, as the players must work together to achieve success. Sports teams also provide equal status contact among the players, as the members are typically of equal caliber. And, at least while the team is winning, the interactions are generally pleasant and the support from others (owners and fans) is usually high. For these reasons, integrated athletic teams often promote racial harmony.

CHAPTER SUMMARY

- Prejudice is a negative attitude toward a group and its members. It is made up of three components: stereotypes, prejudiced feelings, and discrimination.

- People tend to favor groups they belong to over ones to which they don't belong. This tendency is known as ingroup favoritism.

- Levels of prejudice have changed a lot over the past 60 years. Laws have been enacted to outlaw discrimination, and people no longer think it is appropriate to harbor negative attitudes toward outgroups. Nevertheless, prejudice still exists in a more modern form. This form of prejudice is expressed in more disguised, socially appropriate ways.

- When it comes to prejudice, consciously accessible attitudes (known as explicit attitudes) predict behaviors that are easily controlled, and unconsciously accessible attitudes (known as implicit attitudes) predict behaviors that are more difficult to control.

- According to realistic group conflict theory, prejudice arises because groups compete for scarce resources. Although conflict is sufficient to produce prejudice, it is not necessary. Numerous lines of research show that people have prejudiced attitudes even when group conflict does not exist.

- Motivational models maintain that prejudice serves a self-enhancement function. In support of this assumption, people exhibit prejudice under minimal group conditions; feel better about themselves after displaying ingroup favoritism; and show more prejudice after suffering a blow to their feelings of self-worth.

- Prejudice can also be taught and transmitted through media depictions and cultural stereotypes.

- Some people are more prejudiced than others. The authoritarian personality is characterized by rigid adherence to conventional values, hero worship, and a tendency to think in categorical terms.

- Stereotypes are overgeneralized beliefs about a group and its members. As a consequence of overgeneralization, we tend to think outgroup members are all alike. This tendency is known as the outgroup homogeneity bias.

- According to cognitive models, stereotypes develop though a normal cognitive process of categorization. This approach can explain why people hold many stereotypes, but it cannot explain why most stereotypes are negative.

- Stereotypes have several cognitive consequences: they bias our interpretation of ambiguous information, leading us to see what we expect to see, and they influence the attributions we make for other people's behavior.

- Stereotypes are difficult to suppress, and even well-intentioned people may apply stereotypes when they lack the ability to keep them from coming to mind.

- Stereotypes of women are not always negative. However, even positive stereotypes can constitute a form of sexism if they imply that women need to be protected and pampered.

- Stereotype threat occurs when individuals fear their performance at some task will confirm a negative cultural stereotype.

- Affirmative action programs are most beneficial if their recipients believe that competency played a role in the treatment they received.

- Cognitive models of prejudice reduction attempt to reduce prejudice by changing people's beliefs. Unfortunately, people often subtype exceptional cases, enabling them to retain their stereotypic beliefs even when confronted with disconfirming evidence.

- Behavioral models of prejudice reduction attempt to reduce prejudice through social interaction. Interaction can be effective if the participants are of equal status, work toward a common goal in a pleasant environment, and receive the support of authority figures such as parents and teachers.

KEY TERMS

prejudice, 352

racism, 352

sexism, 353

discrimination, 353

prejudiced feelings, 353

ingroup favoritism, 353

aversive racism, 355

explicit attitudes, 355

implicit attitudes, 355

realistic group conflict
theory, 359

relative deprivation, 360

scapegoating, 361

symbolic prejudice, 361

social identity theory, 362

minimal group
paradigm, 362

outgroup homogeneity
bias, 370

projection, 370

hostile sexism, 378

benevolent sexism, 378

stereotype threat, 381

ADDITIONAL READING

Go to the Student Edition of the Online Learning Center for this text (www.mhhe.com/brown)
and log in to read the following journal articles, which relate to the content of this chapter:

- Correll, J., Park, B., Judd, C. M., & Wittenbrink, B. (2002). The police officer's dilemma:
  Using ethnicity to disambiguate potentially threatening individuals.

- Steele, C. M., & Aronson, J. (1995). Stereotype threat and the intellectual test performance
  of African Americans.

CHAPTER ELEVEN

Interpersonal Relationships

TABLE 11.1 Popular Songs Expressing Themes of Unconditional Caring and Love

"I'll Be There" (Holland-Dozier-Holland, 1966, Stone Agate Music-BMI, Publisher)	Now if you feel that you can't go on Because all of your hope is gone And your life is filled with much confusion Until happiness is just an illusion And your world around is crumbling down, Darlin' reach out, reach out for me I'll be there with a love that will shelter you I'll be there with a love that will see you through.
"Bridge Over Troubled Water" (Paul Simon, 1969, Charing-Cross)	When you're weary, feeling small, When tears are in your eyes, I will dry them all. I'll take your part, when darkness comes and friends just can't be found. Like a bridge over troubled water, I will lay me down.
"You've Got a Friend" (Carole King, 1971, Colgems-Emi, Inc.)	When you're down and troubled, and you need some love and care And nothing, nothing is going right. Close your eyes and think of me, and soon I will be there To brighten up, even your darkest night. You just call out my name, and you know wherever I am, I'll coming running to see you again. You've got a friend.
"Lean on Me" (Bill Withers, 1972)	Lean on me, when you're not strong, and I'll be your friend, I'll help you carry on.
"I'll Be There for You" (Theme from Friends) (Danny Wilde & Phil Solem)	So no one told you it was gonna be this way. Your job's a joke, you're broke, your love life's DOA. It's like you're always stuck in second gear. When it hasn't been your day, your week, your month, or even your year I'll be there for you, when the rain starts to pour; I'll be there for you, like I've been there before.
"Make You Feel My Love" (Bob Dylan, 1997, Special Rider Music)	When evening shadows and the stars appear, And there is no one to dry your tears, I could hold you for a millions years, And make you feel my love.
"All You Wanted" (Michelle Branch, 2001, Warner Bros.)	If you want to, I can save you, I can take you away from here So lonely inside, so busy out there, and all you wanted was somebody who cares.

Every few years, the airwaves are filled with a familiar type of song, in which a narrator promises to provide unconditional care to a friend or loved one (see Table 11.1). The songs are popular because they speak to a basic human need: the need to connect emotionally with others and to be comforted when times are rough (Baumeister & Leary, 1995). How basic is this need? When people of various ages are asked what will make them happy and content, the item that tops the list is fulfilling interpersonal relationships (Berscheid & Peplau, 1983). This preference is well advised. People who have satisfying interpersonal relationships are happier and healthier than those who do not. When all is said and done, people who need people *are* the luckiest people in the world.

In this chapter, we will examine interpersonal relationships. We will begin by exploring the nature of **affiliation,** the desire to seek the company of others. Next we will consider friendship, noting that only a few variables are needed to understand why we like the people we like. Finally, we will examine romantic relationships. As you might imagine, love is more complex than friendship, and numerous factors determine why we are romantically attracted to another person and whether that relationship flourishes or perishes.

I. Affiliation

Have you ever noticed that people often congregate when disaster strikes? Consider the response to the September 11, 2001, terrorist attacks on the World Trade Center and the Pentagon. For months afterward, New Yorkers assembled on street corners and in parks to swap stories and comfort one another. The same thing happens following a natural disaster. After floods, earthquakes, or tornadoes, citizens come out of their houses to huddle together until calm is restored.

A. Affiliation and Stress

The informal gatherings that occur in times of disaster suggest that people are motivated to affiliate when they are afraid or under stress. Schachter (1959) conducted a series of studies to examine this hypothesis. In an initial experiment, he led female undergraduates to believe they were going to receive some shocks. Participants in the high-fear condition were told that the shocks would be very painful, whereas participants in the low-fear condition were told the shocks would be very mild. Then, while the experimenter was allegedly getting the shock equipment ready, all participants were given the opportunity to wait either alone or with other participants. Schachter reasoned that if people affiliate when they are afraid, the desire to wait with others should be stronger in the high-fear condition than in the low-fear condition. The results confirmed this hypothesis: Nearly two-thirds of those in the high-fear condition chose to wait with others, whereas only one-third of those in the low-fear condition did so. Follow-up research found that this occurred only when the people in the waiting room were about to undergo the same experience. This finding led Schachter (1959) to conclude, "Misery doesn't just love any kind of company; it loves only miserable company!" (p. 24).

1. Why Do People Affiliate When They Are Afraid?

Although several factors lead people to affiliate when they are afraid (Hill, 1987), Kulik and associates have shown that information exchange is especially important. When people are afraid or are feeling stressed, they seek advice from others to calm themselves. To illustrate, Kulik and Mahler (1989) allowed hospital patients awaiting a surgical procedure to choose from among three types of roommates. One roommate was undergoing a completely different procedure that did not involve surgery; another roommate was about to undergo an identical or highly similar surgical procedure; and a third roommate had already undergone an identical or highly similar surgical procedure. The vast majority of patients chose to room with a patient who had already undergone a similar procedure, presumably because they wanted to learn what the procedure was like so they would know what to expect (see also Kulik, Moore, & Mahler, 1993).

A follow-up study found that rooming with a postoperative patient has beneficial effects (Kulik, Mahler, & Moore, 1996). In this study, men awaiting coronary bypass surgery were randomly assigned to room with a preoperative patient or a postoperative one. Patients who awaited surgery with a postoperative patient handled the surgery better than those who waited with a preoperative patient. They needed fewer medications to calm themselves down before surgery, suffered fewer complications during surgery, and were released from the hospital more quickly.

2. Gender Differences in Affiliation

Women tend to be more affiliative than men, particularly during periods of stress (Belle, 1987; Tamres, Janicki, & Helgeson, 2002). In a provocative article, S. E. Taylor and colleagues have speculated that this tendency may have an evolutionary basis (S. E. Taylor et al., 2000). Historically, women have borne the major responsibility for nurturing offspring and ensuring their survival. Consequently, they have evolved a strategy for dealing with stress different from the one men have evolved. Whereas men are inclined to directly confront a stressor—either by fighting it or fleeing from it (the familiar fight-or-flight reaction)—women respond to stress by tending to their young and affiliating with other women because there is safety in numbers. Taylor and associates have gone on to speculate that this tend-and-befriend response may be influenced by the pituitary hormone, oxytocin. When secreted under conditions of stress, oxytocin enhances relaxation and promotes maternal and affiliative behaviors (e.g., grooming). Naturally, this doesn't mean that men are unconcerned with the care of their young, nor does it imply that men don't affiliate under stress (Geary & Flinn, 2002). Instead, there is simply a greater tendency on the part of women to affiliate under stressful conditions, and this tendency may have a biological basis (S. E. Taylor et al., 2002).

B. Social Support and Well-Being

A tendency to seek the company of others is adaptive. Research in the area of **social support** has shown that friends can be good medicine. For example, people who frequently interact with others are happier, healthier, and better able to handle the challenges of life than are those who are more socially isolated (Salovey, Rothman, & Rodin, 1998). Social support also helps people cope with illness itself. Cancer patients feel better when they have support from others, and caretakers of the ill and elderly suffer less psychological distress when they are embedded in a strong web of friends and family (Gilbar, 2002; S. E. Taylor & Dakof, 1988).

Most important, people with high levels of social support live longer than those who are without this resource (for reviews, see S. Cohen, Underwood, & Gottlieb, 2000; House, Landis, & Umberson, 1988). In a landmark investigation, Berkman and Syme (1979) studied 4,775 Alameda County, California, residents over a nine-year period. People who scored high on an index of social integration (consisting of marital status, contact with family and friends, involvement in group activities, and religious attendance) lived longer than those who were more socially isolated. These findings held true across racial, ethnic, and socioeconomic groups. Another study found that socially active men were two to three times less likely to die within 9 to 12 years than were more socially isolated men of similar age (House, Robbins, & Metzner, 1982).

In fact, social isolation was as predictive of mortality as other known risk factors, such as high cholesterol, inactivity, and smoking (see also Blazer, 1982).

1. Understanding the Link between Social Support and Well-Being

Why do socially active people enjoy better health? Although research in this area is correlational and cannot establish causality, several possible explanations exist. First, people who are socially active tend to take better care of themselves than do those who are more socially isolated (S. Cohen, 1988). For example, they are more apt to exercise, eat right, and seek help when medical problems arise. Second, people generally feel better when they are with others than when they are alone and, as first noted in Chapter 5, positive moods promote physical health (Danner, Snowdon, & Friesen, 2001). Third, social support affects basic biological processes that influence health. Compared to people with low levels of social support, those with high levels of social support have lower blood pressure, better endocrine functioning, and higher immune system functioning (Uchino, Cacioppo, & Kiecolt-Glaser, 1996). These diverse pathways may explain why people with high levels of social support are less susceptible to a wide range of diseases, including cancer, heart disease, and various infectious diseases such as colds and the flu (S. Cohen, Tyrrell, & Smith, 1991). Finally, when people do get sick, those who enjoy high levels of social support recover faster than those who lack this resource. In one study, men whose wives visited them often in the hospital recovered more quickly from coronary bypass surgery than did single men or married men whose wives visited only infrequently (Kulik & Mahler, 1989).

2. Measuring Social Support

Psychologists have measured social support in different ways. In some studies it is assessed by calculating a person's involvement in social activities or the number of social contacts a person has. Researchers refer to this variable as a measure of social integration. In other studies, it is assessed by measuring the more subjective perception that one is cared for, loved, and supported. This variable is called perceived support. Although the two variables are correlated, they are not identical (Bolger & Eckenrode, 1991). People can participate in a variety of social activities without feeling they have someone to turn to in times of trouble.

These two aspects of social support also have different consequences (S. Cohen & Wills, 1985; Rook, 1987). Social integration (our involvement in social activities) has a direct effect on physical health, such that socially active people are healthier and live longer than those who are more socially isolated (House et al., 1988). In contrast, the effects of perceived support seem to emerge primarily under periods of stress. When life is going fine, we needn't feel supported in order to function adequately. But when times are tough, those who believe they can turn to others for consolation and strength fare better than those who lack a close, confiding relationship.

Formally, this stress-reducing property of social support is known as a **stress-buffering effect** (Cobb, 1976). Three aspects of social support contribute to this effect (House, 1981). The first, called tangible support, involves the exchange of material goods, such as money, food, or services. For example, if a friend lends you a car when your car is broken or offers to take you to the doctor when you're not feeling well, you have received tangible support. This type of social support has been shown to be particularly beneficial when a natural disaster strikes. Hurricane victims who received tangible support from friends, family, and rescue workers coped better than victims who did not receive this support (Kaniasty & Norris, 1993, 1995; Norris & Kaniasty, 1996).

A second type of social support is known as informational support. Sometimes we get important information from other people, as when we call a friend for advice, join a support group, or simply let a co-worker show us the ropes. In Kulik's studies of patients awaiting surgery, those who chose to room with someone who had already undergone the procedure were seeking this form of social support.

A final aspect of social support is known as emotional support. This is the form of social support pledged in the pop songs we reviewed earlier. Other people are a source of comfort and solace. They make us feel loved and respected, secure and protected, and they give us an outlet to express our own tenderness and compassion. Emotional support appears to be the most important component of perceived support (S. Cohen & Wills, 1985). Under stress, those who feel loved and cared for cope better than those who feel they must go it alone.

Of course, our perceptions of support don't always coincide with what others think (Antonucci & Israel, 1986; Coriell & Cohen, 1995; Cutrona, 1989). Suppose a friend comes to you with a problem. Even if you try your best to be compassionate and supportive, your friend may fail to appreciate your efforts and accuse you of being uncaring. In other situations, well-intending people offer the wrong form of support (Major, Zubek, Cooper, Cozzarelli, & Richards, 1997). In a study of breast cancer patients, Dakof and Taylor (1990) found that women appreciated receiving emotional support from family and friends but did not appreciate receiving informational support. Other studies have found that friends and family members sometimes recoil from giving support to cancer patients (Wortman & Dunkel-Schetter, 1979). Finally, support can sometimes be threatening. Receiving help from others can imply dependency and weakness, and can undermine the recipient's feelings of self-worth (Nadler & Fisher, 1986). For these reasons, support may be most effective when it is subtle and goes unnoticed (Bolger, Zuckerman, & Kessler, 2000; Cutrona, 1989).

Even a pet can be an important source of social support. In a study of more than 1,000 senior citizens, Siegel (1990) found that dog owners were less apt to visit the doctor under periods of high stress than were those who didn't own a dog. Siegel speculated that the companionship a dog provides enabled the elderly to better weather the effects of life stress. Consistent with this claim, another study found that women who worked on a stressful laboratory task were calmer when their pet dog was present than when they were alone or working with a friend (K. M. Allen, Blascovich, Tomaka, & Kelsey, 1991).

3. Marriage and Mortality: What's Good for the Goose Is Even Better for the Gander

Quantity is not the issue when it comes to social support. We needn't have dozens of confidantes to reap the benefits social support provides. Just knowing there is at least one other person we can turn to when times are difficult seems sufficient (Coyne & Delongis, 1986; Reis, Wheeler, Kernis, Speigel, & Nezlek, 1985; Rook, 1987). Research on the advantages of marriage underscores this point. In general, people who are married live longer and enjoy better health than do the unmarried (Burman & Margolin, 1992; Lillard & Waite, 1995; C. E. Ross, Mirowsky, & Goldsteen, 1990; Stroebe, Stroebe, Gergen, & Gergen, 1982; Waite & Gallagher, 2000). This effect is especially pronounced among men. Although married women live somewhat longer than unmarried women, married men live quite a bit longer than unmarried men (Bruce & Kim, 1992; Kiecolt-Glaser & Newton, 2001).

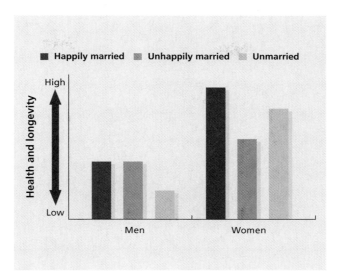

FIGURE 11.1

The Relationship between Marital Status, Marital Quality, Gender, and Health

The data show two effects of interest: (1) Women live longer, healthier lives than men; and (2) men benefit from marriage, regardless of marital quality, but women benefit from marriage only if they are happily married.

To understand this effect, we need to distinguish two terms: marital status (married or single) and martial quality (happily married or unhappily married). Figure 11.1 shows that, for men, marital status is more important than marital quality. This is the case because even unhappily married men benefit from being married. The situation is different for women. Happily married women are better off than unmarried women, but unmarried women are better off than unhappily married women (Orth-Gomer et al., 2000). In short, although both men and women benefit from a happy marriage, only men benefit from an unhappy one. Undoubtedly, this is one reason why women are more apt to dissolve a marriage than men are (Kiecolt-Glaser & Newton, 2001; see also Hill, Rubin, & Peplau, 1976).

4. Adjustment to the Dissolution of a Relationship

Gender differences are also found when we consider how people cope with the dissolution of a relationship. Irrespective of who initiates the breakup, men react more poorly than women to separation and divorce; they also react more poorly to widowhood (Helgeson, 1994; Kiecolt-Glaser & Newton, 2001). For example, following the death of their mate, men are more apt than women to become depressed, get sick, and die within a relatively short time. Although the reasons for these gender differences are not entirely clear, two processes seem to be at work. First, men tend to be less socially active than women, so their involvement in social activities is more affected when their romantic relationship ends. Second, men experience greater losses in intimacy when their romantic relationship dissolves. This loss of intimacy occurs because women's interactions tend to be more intimate than men's. Women share more and disclose more and are generally more supportive and understanding than men are. Moreover, this is true in both same-sex and opposite-sex interactions, and both men and women disclose more when talking to a woman than when talking to a man (Dindia & Allen, 1992; Fritz, Nagurney, & Helgeson, 2003).

An investigation by Reis, Senchak, and Solomon (1985) illustrates this effect. In this investigation, men and women kept a diary of every interaction of 10 minutes or longer they had over a four-day period. Soon after the interaction ended, they

FIGURE 11.2

Relationship Intimacy
among Men and Women

In this study, men and
women kept track of their
interactions over a four-day
period, then rated how
intimate these interactions
were. Interactions that
involved at least one
woman were judged to be
more intimate than inter-
actions between men only.

Source: Reis, Senchak, and
Solomon (1985).

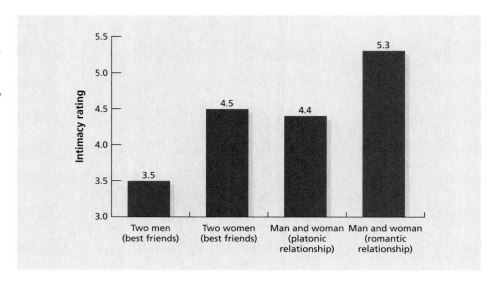

rated how intimate it was on a 7-point scale, ranging from superficial to meaningful
Figure 11.2 shows that even when men talked to their best same-sex friend, their interactions lacked intimacy. In contrast, they were more intimate when interacting with a
woman, particularly if the relationship was a serious, romantic one.

Intimacy, in turn, promotes well-being. People who confide in others and share
their concerns and feelings enjoy better health than do those who keep things to
themselves (Pennebaker, Mayne, & Francis, 1997; Petrie, Booth, & Pennebaker,
1998). This is particularly true under periods of high stress. Following a stressful
experience, such as the loss of a loved one or the breakup of an important relationship, many people join support groups, allowing them to share their thoughts and
feelings with others undergoing similar experiences. Those who do so generally fare
better than those who go it alone (Davison, Pennebaker, & Dickerson, 2000; Pennebaker
& O'Heeron, 1984).

C. Loneliness

Considering how strong is our need to belong and the benefits social ties provide, it
is not surprising that people feel bad when they lack this important resource. Such
feelings are called loneliness. **Loneliness** is a distressing emotional state caused by a
lack of meaningful interpersonal relationships. Although it has been called the common cold of psychological maladies, loneliness can be profoundly disturbing, leading
to alcoholism, physical illness, and even suicide (Hawkley, Burleson, Berntson, &
Cacioppo, 2003; Laudenslager & Reite, 1984; Peplau & Perlman, 1982). It also seems
to be increasing. Rising divorce rates, the breakdown of the nuclear family, and
increasing mobility in modern societies are three factors that, taken together, have
caused loneliness to reach almost epidemic proportions.

Loneliness is not synonymous with being alone. People can feel lonely in a crowd
or perfectly content when they are by themselves (Archibald, Bartholomew, & Marx,
1995; Hawkley et al., 2003; Long, Seburn, Averill, & More, 2003). At the same time,
certain situations are apt to trigger loneliness. If you have ever moved to a new town
or transferred to a new school, you are probably aware that situations like these

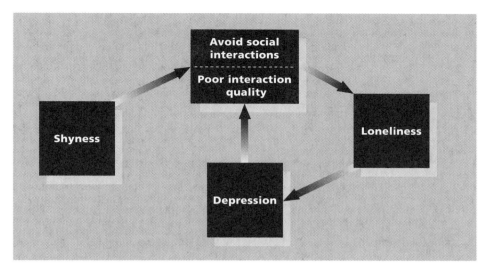

FIGURE 11.3

Shyness, Social Interaction, Loneliness, and Depression

Shyness causes people to avoid social interactions and to interact awkwardly. This, in turn, causes loneliness and depression, which lead to further withdrawal and negative social interactions.

commonly create feelings of loneliness. One study found that nearly three-quarters of freshman felt lonely in their first few weeks of college (Cutrona, 1982). The loss of a close personal relationship also evokes loneliness, sometimes leading to depression, despair, and social withdrawal (Peplau & Perlman, 1982). Finally, social exclusion can trigger loneliness. People feel lonely when they feel left out of a group, ignored, or ostracized (Leary, Springer, Negel, Ansell, & Evans, 1998). For example, finding out that your friends went out for dinner without inviting you is apt to make you feel rejected and lonely.

Even small affronts can create hurt feelings (Buckley, Winkel, & Leary, 2004; Zadro, Williams, & Richardson, 2004). K. D. Williams, Cheung, and Choi (2000) led some computer users to feel left out of a game played over the Internet. Those who were excluded felt worse than those who weren't. A follow-up study found that the emotional pain brought about by this form of exclusion produced measurable neurological consequences similar to those that accompany physical pain (Eisenberger, Lieberman, & Williams, 2003). Apparently, the phrase *hurt feelings* is more than merely metaphoric (MacDonald & Leary, 2005).

For most people, loneliness is a painful but manageable emotion. It comes and goes with the ebb and flow of social life. Other people suffer from chronic feelings of loneliness and report being lonely nearly all the time. In these cases, loneliness occurs along with other personality factors that combine to create a negative, self-defeating pattern (C. A. Anderson & Harvey, 1988; Cacioppo et al., 2000; Russell, Peplau, & Cutrona, 1980). Figure 11.3 shows that the pattern starts with shyness. Shyness, which can begin in early childhood, is characterized by feeling anxious, awkward, and uncomfortable in social situations (Bruch, Gorsky, Collins, & Berger, 1989; Jones, Briggs, & Smith, 1986). This anxiety has two negative interpersonal consequences. First, it leads shy people to avoid social situations, thereby decreasing the quantity of their social contacts. Second, shyness undermines the quality of social interactions, as shy people tend to avoid intimacy through their body language (they fail to make eye contact with their interaction partners); their behavior (they fidget, lack expressiveness, and smile infrequently); and their conversation patterns (they talk less and are less self-disclosing) (DePaulo, Epstein, & LeMay, 1990; Garcia, Stinson, Ickes, Bissonnette, & Briggs, 1991; Meleshko & Alden, 1993). In turn, negative social interactions perpetuate feelings of loneliness and may evoke depression. Unfortunately, this creates further problems: People get sad when interacting with a depressed person, and this further erodes the person's network of social relationships (Coyne, 1976; Joiner, 1994). In this manner, the factors work together to perpetuate poor social interactions and negative feelings. Social skills training may be required to break the spiral (W. H. Jones, Hobbs, & Hockenbury, 1982). By learning to interact more effectively, people can make more friends and reduce their loneliness.

II. Interpersonal Attraction: The Psychology of Friendship

Our desire to affiliate leads us to seek the company of others, but we don't interact with just anyone. Instead, we prefer the company of some people more than that of others. The field of interpersonal attraction studies these interaction preferences. The following section discusses four variables that influence our attraction toward other people: proximity, reciprocity, the personal qualities of other people, and similarity.

A. Proximity

We'll start with a factor that hits close to home: physical distance. All else being equal, we are more attracted to someone who is nearby than to someone who is far away (Hays, 1984; Latané, Liu, Nowak, Bonevento, & Zheng, 1995). The English language reflects this basic fact. The word *close* has two meanings: physically near and emotionally dear.

Liking and proximity are joined in a reciprocal fashion. On the one hand, we are drawn to people we like, so emotional closeness reduces physical distance. On the other hand, physical closeness promotes emotional closeness. Far more than we realize, we tend to like people who are near to us, simply because they are near. Eckland (1968) captured the importance of this **proximity effect** when he quipped, "Cherished notions about romantic love notwithstanding, the chances are about 50/50 that the 'one and only' lives within walking distance."

At least four factors produce the proximity effect. First, and most obviously, opportunities to meet another person increase as the distance between us decreases. We are more apt to meet a person who rides the same bus to work, shops at the same grocery store, and eats at the same restaurants as we do than a person who lives far away. Interestingly, the Internet represents an exception to the proximity effect (Bargh & McKenna, 2004). Cyberspace knows no physical boundaries, so you can just as easily chat with someone from a faraway land as someone from your own hometown. Nevertheless, face-to-face interactions are more common and favor those who are physically near.

Second, motivational processes can explain why we feel close to those who are near. It feels bad to frequently interact with someone we dislike, so we try to appreciate the person's good qualities rather than focusing on his or her faults (Klein & Kunda, 1992). Perhaps you experienced this effect when meeting your college roommate. Knowing that you would be spending a lot of time together motivated you to view the person in a positive light. In fact, we become fond of people we simply anticipate meeting, presumably because we want to have an enjoyable interaction (Berscheid, Graziano, Monson, & Dermer, 1976; Darley & Berscheid, 1967).

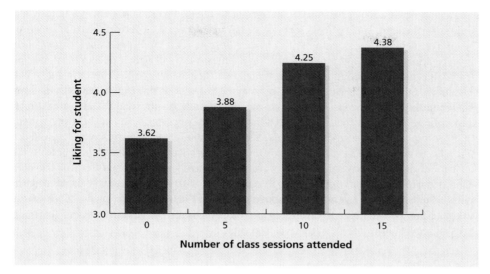

FIGURE 11.4

Liking and the Mere Exposure Effect

Students expressed greater liking for a fellow student who attended class frequently than one who attended only infrequently. These data show that the more times we see someone, the more we like him or her.

Source: Moreland and Beach (1992).

Third, the mere exposure effect (Zajonc, 1968) can explain why we feel close to those who are nearby. As discussed in Chapter 6, this effect refers to the relationship between familiarity and liking. The more times we are exposed to a stimulus, the more we like that stimulus. Seeing the same people in our neighborhoods, schools, or places of business renders them more familiar and heightens our affections for them. Moreland and Beach (1992) conducted a clever demonstration of the mere exposure effect. These researchers arranged to have a female undergraduate attend class on various occasions. The woman did not draw attention to herself in any way, except to walk into class, sit down, and walk out. At the end of the academic term, the rest of the students were shown the woman's picture and asked to indicate how much they liked her. Illustrating the importance of the mere exposure effect, Figure 11.4 shows that liking for the student increased with familiarity. The more class sessions she attended, the more her fellow students liked her.

Finally, the costs of social interaction can also explain why we are attracted to people who are nearby. Suppose you want to go to a movie with a friend, and you are driving. You can choose to ask someone who lives nearby or someone who lives far away. If you like the two people equally, you will probably choose the person who is nearby, because the costs of interacting with that person are lower. However, you might be willing to drive clear across town for someone who is especially desirable to you.

Your preferences can be explained by a general theory of interpersonal attraction known as **social exchange theory** (Blau, 1964; Homans, 1961). Social exchange theory adopts an economic model of human behavior and analyzes interpersonal relationships in terms of market demands. The theory makes two important assumptions. First, people bring to the interpersonal marketplace certain goods they can exchange. These goods include tangible qualities (e.g., a fancy car); personal qualities (e.g., good looks); or social status (e.g., a good family name). Second, people keep track of what they are giving and receiving in an interpersonal relationship—and they seek a bargain. In essence, they strive to get as much as they can for the goods they have to offer. Because it is less costly to interact with someone who is nearby, social exchange theory predicts that you will like those who are near to you more than those who are far away.

A final point about proximity is important to make. Physical distance is not always the issue. Instead, the critical issue is *functional distance,* a term that refers to how often you actually cross paths with another person. This point was made in an early investigation by Festinger, Schachter, and Back (1950). These researchers studied friendship patterns among military veterans and their wives. At the time the study was conducted, the couples were living in housing projects at the Massachusetts Institute of Technology in Boston. Attesting to the importance of physical distance, Festinger and colleagues found that people in adjacent units were more apt to become friends than were people in more distant units. Yet functional distance also played a role. People who lived near the stairwells were more apt to become friends with people in the apartment directly above them than were those who lived in the middle of a corridor. This occurred because couples who lived near the stairwells frequently crossed paths with couples who lived one flight above them. The lesson here is clear: If you want to make lots of friends, a good first step would be to rent an apartment near the mailbox or secure an office near the water cooler.

B. Reciprocity

Another way to make friends is to be a friend. Although there are exceptions, people generally like those who like them (Vonk, 2002). This is known as the **reciprocity principle.** In fact, if you want to know whether Brittany likes Whitney and you have just one question to ask, ask Whitney whether she likes Brittany. If she does, the odds are good that Brittany likes her back.

Why do we like people who like us? The most probable explanation is that we find their liking to be rewarding. People want to feel that they are desirable, lovable, and sought after, and the attentions and affections of another person satisfy this need. Changes in liking seem to be particularly consequential. E. Aronson and Linder (1965) had female college students engage in a series of get-acquainted conversations with another person (who was actually an experimental accomplice). Following the first few conversations, the students "happened" to overhear their partner talking to the experimenter. Using random assignment to conditions, half of the participants heard that the other person liked them and half heard that the other person didn't like them. Later, after several additional conversations, the participants received further information about the other person's (apparent) liking for them. Finally, they were asked how much they liked the person they had interacted with.

Figure 11.5 shows that participants expressed more liking for a person who first evaluated them negatively and later evaluated them positively (Column 1) than for a person who consistently evaluated them positively (Column 2). This finding suggests that we are especially fond of someone when we believe we have earned that person's respect once he or she got to know us better. In a complementary vein, consistently negative feedback (column 3) led to greater liking than did feedback that turned from positive to negative (column 4). Apparently, we particularly dislike someone who used to like us but rejected us after getting to know us better (see also J. D. Brown, Farnham, & Cook, 2002; Buckley, Winkel, & Leary, 2004).

1. Playing Hard to Get

E. Aronson and Linder's (1965) data document that people are especially fond of another person when they think they have won the person's affections. This effect is relevant to a well-known ploy for piquing another person's romantic interest, known

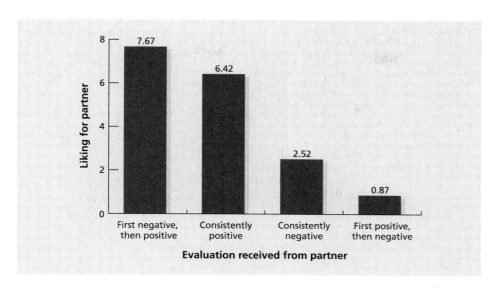

FIGURE 11.5

Liking for Another Person Who Evaluates Us Positive or Negatively

In this study, participants interacted with another person on multiple occasions. Participants were especially fond of someone who disliked them at first but later liked them after getting to know them better (see column 1), and especially disapproving of someone who liked them at first but later disliked them after getting to know them better (see column 4). This finding suggests that changes in evaluation are particularly powerful, especially changes that go from good to bad.

Source: E. Aronson and Linder (1965).

as playing hard to get. With this tactic, we appear to be disinterested in a person who likes us. Presumably, behaving as if we are unattainable will make the person like us even more.

The strategy of playing hard to get rests on sound theoretical principles. For example, cognitive dissonance theory (see Chapter 6) maintains that we come to value goals we work hard to attain (E. Aronson & Mills, 1959; Festinger, 1957). To the extent that this is so, a person who plays hard to get should be liked more than one who is immediately accessible. Psychological reactance theory can also explain why we are drawn to people whose affections are difficult to secure (J. W. Brehm, 1966). As discussed in Chapter 8, psychological reactance is an aversive psychological state that arises when people think their freedom of choice is limited. Because people commonly react to these restrictions by reasserting their desire for the forbidden object, people may be especially drawn to those who make themselves unavailable by playing hard to get.

Despite these compelling theoretical reasons, there is little experimental evidence that playing hard to get is an effective interpersonal strategy (S. S. Brehm, 1992). More often than not, people who fail to reciprocate our affections draw our ire rather than arouse our desire. We are, however, drawn to people who are hard for everybody else but us to get. This point was made in an investigation by Walster, Walster, Piliavin, and Schmidt (1973). In their study, male students participated in an investigation of dating preferences. The participants viewed the profiles of several women, and then decided which one they wished to date. Allegedly, each woman had already

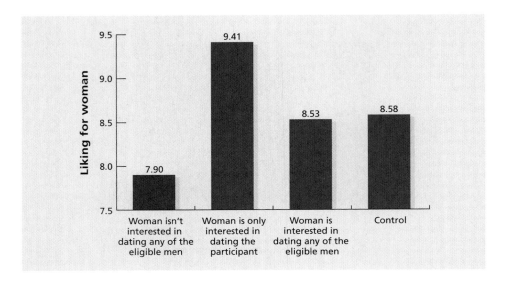

FIGURE 11.6

Yearning for the Discerning

After participating in a simulated dating study, male participants indicated how much they liked various women who varied with respect to how much they liked the eligible men. Participants were especially interested in a woman who expressed a great deal of interest in dating the participant but not in dating anyone else. This finding suggests that we are especially drawn to someone who selectively likes only us.

Source: Walster, Walster, Piliavin, and Schmidt (1973).

received information about all of the eligible men and had formed opinions about them. In the uniformly-hard-to-get condition, the woman indicated that she did not find any of the available men to be very desirable. In the selectively-hard-to-get condition, the woman indicated that she found only the participant himself to be a desirable date, but felt that the rest of the men were undesirable. In the uniformly-easy-to-get condition, the woman indicated that she found all of the men, including the participant, to be desirable. Finally, in a control condition, no preferences were stated either way. Figure 11.6 shows that participants expressed the greatest interest in dating the woman who seemed to like only them. This finding suggests that being discerning but not rejecting is a highly effective interpersonal strategy (see also Landy & Aronson, 1968).

2. Self-Verification Theory

So far we have seen that we like people who like us, and this is especially true when we win the person over after the person gets to know us better and the person is selective and choosy rather than simply liking everyone in general. These conditions allow us to attribute the person's liking to our own good qualities rather than to some other factor. But what about people who are not so fond of themselves? For example, do people with low self-esteem prefer others who dislike them?

Swann's self-verification theory makes just such a prediction (Swann, 1990, 1996). This theory assumes that we feel more comfortable and secure when we interact

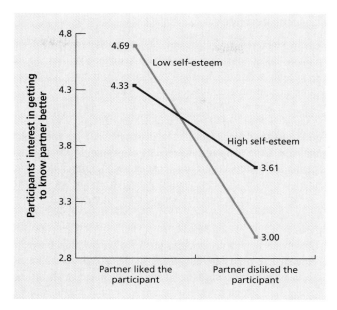

FIGURE 11.7

Interest in Getting to Know Someone Who Likes Us or Dislikes Us

Participants were more interested in getting to know someone who liked them than someone who disliked them, and this was particularly true among low-self-esteem partici- pants. These data argue against the claim that people who feel bad about themselves seek others who dislike them.

Source: Bernichon (1999).

with people who see us as we see ourselves. Consequently, the theory predicts that high-self-esteem people like people who like them, but that low-self-esteem people like people who dislike them (McNulty & Swann, 1984). Bernichon (1999) conducted a study to test this hypothesis. In this study, college students with varying levels of self-esteem interacted with another student in the context of a get-acquainted discus- sion. Using random assignment to conditions, half of the participants later learned that the other person liked them and half learned that the other person did not like them. Afterward, the students indicated how interested they were in getting to know the other person better.

Figure 11.7 shows some of the results from this investigation. It is apparent that people preferred to interact with someone who liked them more than with someone who disliked them, and this was no less true among low-self-esteem people than it was among high-self-esteem people. If anything, low-self-esteem people were actu- ally more drawn to someone who liked them than were high-self-esteem people. Along with other research (Bernichon, Cook, & Brown, 2003), these findings provide little evidence that low-self-esteem people prefer to interact with someone who dislikes them. Instead, reciprocity is the rule: We like people who like us.

C. Personal Qualities of a Likable Person

You'd be hard-pressed to find someone more likable than Tiger Woods. Whether he is pitching products, making the rounds on the talk-show circuit, or playing an excit- ing round of golf, Tiger is one of the most appealing celebrities of our day. Tiger's likability is no mystery: He is competent and attractive, and he has a warm, pleasing manner. In short, he has all the qualities of a likable person (N. H. Anderson, 1968; Folkes & Sears, 1977). In this section, you will learn how these variables affect liking (N. L. Collins & Miller, 1994).

1. Competence

The first factor we will consider is competence. Although extremely competent people can be off-putting at times (E. Aronson, Willerman, & Floyd, 1966), we are drawn to people who are talented and accomplished. There is one catch, however. Under some conditions, another person's accomplishments can be threatening and make us feel bad about ourselves in comparison. According to Tesser's self-evaluation maintenance model, this occurs when the other person excels at something we wish to be good at too (Tesser, 1988). To illustrate, if your roommate is a talented concert pianist and you have aspirations to be a musician, you may envy your roommate's achievements. If, however, you don't aspire to be a musician, you can take pride in your roommate and bask in the reflected glory of his or her accomplishments (see Chapter 5).

Tesser's model is a self-enhancement model. It assumes that people seek relationships that make them feel good about themselves and avoid relationships that make them feel bad about themselves. The model therefore predicts that people will choose to be friends with those who perform worse than they do in domains of high personal relevance, but better than they do in domains of low personal relevance. For example, a person who cares a lot about his athletic ability and little about his intellectual ability will probably prefer a friend who is less coordinated but more intelligent than he is (Tesser, Campbell, & Smith, 1984). Beach and Tesser (1995) have applied these ideas to the study of close personal relationships. They believe that husbands and wives often arrange matters so that each spouse excels in domains of low importance to the other. This arrangement allows people to have their cake and eat it too: They outperform their mate in areas about which they care deeply, but they bask in the reflected glory of their mate's accomplishments in areas about which they care very little (Beach et al., 1998; Beach et al., 1996). Of course, negative comparisons can't always be avoided. In these cases, partners who feel especially close to their mate console themselves by focusing on the strength of their relationship (Lockwood, Dolderman, Sadler, & Gerchak, 2004).

2. Attractiveness

In a popular shampoo commercial, a woman pleads, "Don't hate me because I'm beautiful." Although beauty can create envy, the model's worries are largely unfounded. The more attractive a person is, the more attracted we are to him or her. In part, this is because good-looking people are aesthetically pleasing. Through processes of classical conditioning, we come to associate the person with feeling good and develop an overall liking for him or her. We also assume that attractive people have pleasing personalities. As first discussed in Chapter 3, people believe in the stereotype that what is beautiful is good (Dion, Berscheid, & Walster, 1972). Across age groups and cultures, and for both men and women, attractive people are viewed as more socially skilled, friendly, and well-adjusted than are unattractive people (G. R. Adams & Huston, 1975; Eagly, Ashmore, Makhijani, & Longo, 1991; Wheeler & Kim, 1997). Although there is little evidence that attractive people actually possess these characteristics, we believe they do and therefore seek their company (Feingold, 1992a).

People may also seek the company of attractive others because they can gain in social status by having beautiful friends. Before we review the research in this area, ask yourself this: Do you think other people will judge you more positively if you are linked to highly attractive people versus unattractive people? This question was addressed in an investigation by Sigall and Landy (1973). Male and female participants saw a photograph of a man and a woman seated together. In one condition the

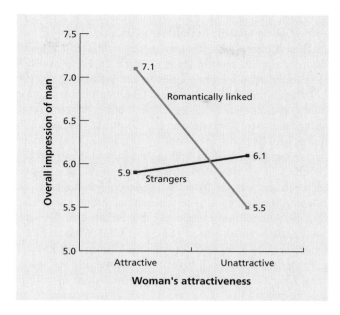

FIGURE 11.8

The Social Benefits of Having a Beautiful Girlfriend

After viewing a photograph of a man and a woman, participants formed a more favorable impression of a man who had an attractive girlfriend than one who had an unattractive girlfriend. The woman's attractiveness had no effect when the man and woman were strangers to one another.

Source: Sigall and Landy (1973).

woman was stylishly dressed and looked very attractive; in another condition she wore no makeup, an unattractive wig, and ill-fitting clothes. Half of the participants were led to believe that the man and woman were strangers who just happened to be sitting together, whereas the other half were led to believe they were romantically involved. Afterward, the participants indicated their overall impression of the man. Consistent with the notion that people gain socially by associating with beautiful people, Figure 11.8 shows that the man was judged most favorably when he was romantically linked to an attractive woman. Follow-up research has found that a similar, though weaker tendency characterizes same-sex friendships (Kernis & Wheeler, 1981).

3. Gender Differences in Interpersonal Attraction

The preference for attractive interaction partners is a general one. It occurs for platonic relationships as well as for romantic ones, and for same-sex friendships as well as for mixed-sex friendships. The effect is strongest, however, when heterosexual men seek a romantic partner. For example, when asked what qualities they desire in a mate, men rate physical attractiveness more highly than women do (D. M. Buss & Kenrick, 1998; Sprecher, Sullivan, & Hatfield, 1994). In contrast, women value a mate's status, earning potential, and education more highly than men do (Feingold, 1992b; Li, Bailey, Kenrick, & Linsenmeier, 2002). In short, many men view women as "sex objects," while many women view men as "success objects."

Social exchange theory can explain gender differences in interpersonal attraction. In most societies, men occupy positions of higher status and wealth than women do. Consequently, they are able to exchange their social status for a woman's attractiveness. Women, in contrast, have traditionally held positions of lower social status and wealth. Consequently, they trade their attractiveness to acquire these commodities (Gangestad, 1993). These trade-offs can explain why wealthy, older men are sometimes seen with young, attractive women (and why wealthy, older women are sometimes seen with young, attractive men) (Caporael, 1989). As one observer wryly noted, "A proposal of marriage in our society tends to be a way in which a man sums up his social attributes and suggests to a woman that hers are not so much better as to preclude a merger or partnership" (Goffman, 1952, p. 456).

Evolutionary psychologists offer a related perspective on gender differences in interpersonal attraction (Berry, 2000; D. M. Buss & Schmitt, 1993). These theorists agree that people's choices are influenced by principles of social exchange, but they do not believe cultural factors alone determine the value that is placed on many characteristics. Instead, they believe that evolutionary forces have shaped the value that men place on youth and attractiveness and that women place on wealth and status. Drawing on work by Darwin (1871) and Trivers (1972), the evolutionary argument begins by noting that men and women face different challenges when it comes to passing along their genes to the next generation. Men can father many children and do not bear the burden of giving birth or nursing the young. Consequently, they value a mate with characteristics suggesting high reproductive potential. Because attractiveness signals health and is correlated with youth, men seek young, attractive women (Singh, 1993). Women face a different challenge. They can bear only a limited number of children and invest heavily in each child's care, carrying the child until birth and then nursing for some time afterward. As a result, they look for a mate who has resources and is willing to share them to shoulder this responsibility. This imperative leads women to seek mates who have wealth and high status.

If these preferences have an evolutionary basis, they should be found in various cultures around the world. To test this hypothesis, D. M. Buss (1989) examined more than 10,000 respondents from 33 countries located on six continents and five islands. Among other things, the respondents were asked how important or desirable would it be for a mate to have "good financial prospects" and "good looks." Across the various cultures, men valued good looks more than women did, and women valued good financial prospects more than men did. Gays and lesbians also express these preferences, providing further evidence that the preferences may be biological in origin (Bailey, Gaulin, Agyei, & Gladue, 1994). The only exception comes when we consider casual sexual encounters (e.g., a one-night stand). Under these circumstances, attractiveness is less important to men than to women (Kenrick, Groth, Trost, & Sadalla, 1993; D. P. Schmitt, Couden, Baker, 2001).

The "men seek youth and beauty, and women seek wealth and status" effect shapes courtship rituals. When placing a personal ad in the newspaper or on the Internet, men are more apt than women to highlight their wealth and status and to request attractiveness, whereas women are more apt than men to mention their attractiveness and to seek wealth and status (Koestner & Wheeler, 1988). These preferences also influence people's self-evaluations (Roney, 2003). Men evaluate their own desirability as a romantic partner less favorably after being exposed to other men of high status and dominance, whereas women evaluate their desirability as a romantic partner less favorably after being exposed to highly attractive women (Gutierres, Kenrick, & Partch, 1999).

Finally, it should be noted that these sex differences obscure some important main effects. Both men and women value partners who are kind, trustworthy, sincere, and dependable (Feingold, 1990; Fletcher, Tither, O'Loughlin, Friesen, & Overall, 2004; Hanko, Master, & Sabini, 2004; Jensen-Campbell, Graziano, & West, 1995; Sprecher & Regan, 2002). So it isn't the case that men care only about youth and beauty and that women care only about wealth and status. It is simply that the two sexes weigh these qualities differently, possibly as a result of evolutionary forces.

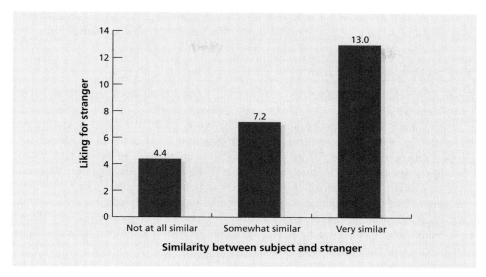

FIGURE 11.9

Liking for People Who Are Like Us

The data show that similarity increases liking in a near linear fashion. The more similar we are to another person, the more we like him or her.

Source: Byrne (1961).

D. Similarity

Perhaps you have heard these two adages: "Birds of a feather flock together" and "Opposites attract." The former argues that people like those who are like them, whereas the latter asserts that people prefer to affiliate with those who are not like them. So which is it? Do we like others who are like us or do we look for friends and mates that complement our qualities? Overwhelmingly, the evidence favors the power of similarity in attraction. With regard to almost all psychological and physical characteristics, people like those who are like them. Undoubtedly, this is one reason why the word *like* has two meanings: "similar to" and "fond of."

Byrne (1961) initiated experimental research in this area. In this study, participants were led to believe they were about to meet a fellow student. The participants then received some information about the other student's hobbies, political attitudes, background, and interests. Depending on which condition they were in, participants learned that they and the other student were very similar, somewhat similar, or not at all similar. After receiving this information, the participants indicated how much they liked the person and how much they thought they would enjoy working with the person. The two scores were combined to yield an index of interpersonal attraction. As shown in Figure 11.9, participants expressed greater liking for a student who was "just like them" than for one who was not at all like them. Along with other findings, these data establish that we like those who are like us (see also Newcomb, 1961).

Dissimilarity is also important. In a replication and extension of Byrne's research, Rosenbaum (1986) found that differences and dissimilarities matter more to people than convergences and similarities do. Rather than liking people who are like us, Rosenbaum's research suggested that we dislike people who are different from us. This finding led Byrne and his associates to propose that attraction is a two-step process (Byrne, Clore, & Smeaton, 1986). First, when choosing friends, dates, or spouses, we eliminate from consideration people who are too dissimilar from us. Having then reduced the potential pool of eligible people to include only those who are at least moderately similar to ourselves, we use similarity to make our final choices.

In this scheme, dissimilarity is more important during the initial stage of a relationship and similarity is more important during the latter stages of a relationship.

1. Theoretical Explanations

Multiple psychological processes seem to underlie the similarity/dissimilarity effect. First, similarity is reinforcing (Byrne, 1971; Byrne & Clore, 1970). Learning that another person shares our opinions, attitudes, tastes, and hobbies is validating and makes us feel good about ourselves. It is also generally more pleasant to interact with people who agree with us than with those who challenge our tastes and values. Through principles of classical conditioning, these good feelings translate into increased liking for the person whose tastes and preferences mirror our own. Third, we assume that people who are similar to us like us, and reciprocity leads us to like them back (Condon & Crano, 1988). Fourth, we assume that people who are like us have many other positive qualities and attributes, and these cognitive judgments promote liking (Montoya & Horton, 2004).

Finally, principles of cognitive consistency operate. To appreciate their role, we need to examine an important social psychological theory called **balance theory.** This theory was developed by Fritz Heider (1958), one of social psychology's most important figures. Like Festinger's theory of cognitive dissonance (see Chapter 6), balance theory incorporates principles of Gestalt psychology (see Chapter 2). Gestalt psychologists argue (1) that people strive to form coherent, consistent impressions and (2) that inconsistency creates tension that people are driven to reduce. Applying these principles, Heider's balance theory asserts that people's interpersonal relationships are driven by a desire for harmony and balance.

Balance theory begins by distinguishing between two kinds of relations: unit relations and sentiment relations. Unit relations pertain to whether two entities (people, objects, attitudes) are joined or belong together. A father and his son share a unit relation, whereas a father and an unrelated child in another town typically do not. Two entities can also be joined by situational factors. For example, two Americans who meet while vacationing in Europe often feel a special bond. Finally, unit relations also occur within individuals. For example, we feel connected to our possessions; our actions; and our emotions, attitudes, opinions, and beliefs (Abelson, 1986).

Sentiment relations refer to feelings of liking or disliking. Liking is represented as a positive sentiment relation, and disliking is represented as a negative sentiment relation. According to Heider, sentiment and unit relations tend toward a balanced state, meaning they "fit together without stress" (Heider, 1958, p. 180). For most of us, this means we like things we are connected with and dislike things we are disconnected with. It is also true that we wish to be connected with things we like and disassociated from things we don't like.

Heider illustrated his theory with a device known as a P-O-X triad. The triad involves three elements: two people (P and O) and an attitude object (X). Figure 11.10 shows eight such triads, representing the relationship between You (P), your new college roommate (O) and you and your roommate's attitudes toward hip-hop music (X). The arrows signify unit relationships, and the plus and minus signs indicate sentiment relationships, which represent liking or disliking.

The first two pairs show why similarity leads to liking. In the first pair, you and your roommate like the same kind of music. The relationship is balanced when you like your roommate (left-hand column) but imbalanced when you don't (right-hand column). Why? Psychologically, you *should* like someone who likes what you like.

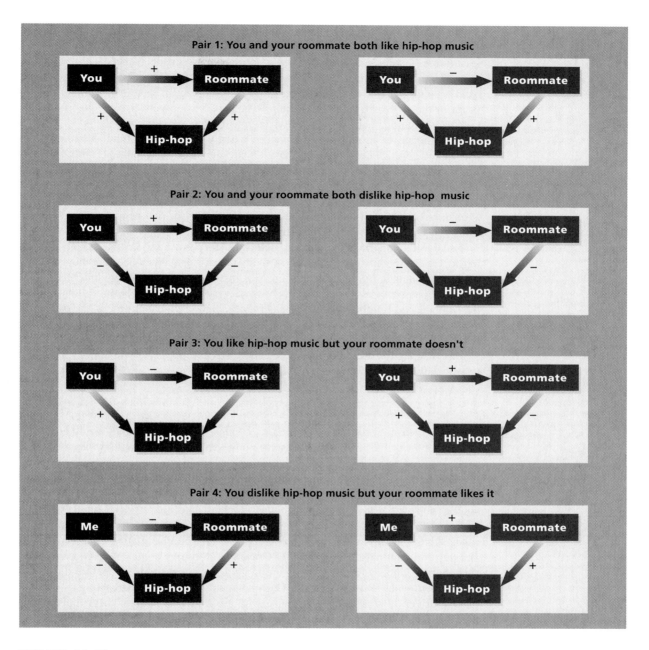

FIGURE 11.10
Heider's Balance Theory

After all, if you like the same things, what's not to like? The second pair shows an analogous situation. Here, you and your roommate both dislike hip-hop music. Since you both dislike the same thing, the relationship is balanced when you like your roommate (left-hand column) but imbalanced when you don't (right-hand column).

The third and fourth pairs depict situations involving dissimilarity. In the third pair, you like hip-hop music but your roommate doesn't. Assuming tastes in music are at least somewhat important to you, the relationship would be balanced if you dislike your roommate (left-hand column) but imbalanced if you like your roommate (right-hand column). In the final pair, you dislike hip-hop music but your roommate likes it. As in the third pair, the relationship is balanced when you dislike your roommate (left-hand column) but imbalanced when you like your roommate.

In summary, relationships are balanced when we like people who share our tastes and values and dislike people who don't share our tastes and values. Heider's theory has been tested and supported under a variety of conditions (Abelson et al., 1968). The theory can also explain a number of commonsense observations. For example, consider the saying "My enemy's enemy is my friend." In Figure 11.10, this situation is captured by the left-hand panel in pair 2. In this triad, two people who dislike the same thing like each other (see also E. Aronson & Cope, 1968).

Finally, it's important to note that Heider's theory is a motivational model. According to Heider, people seek balance in their interpersonal lives because they find imbalance to be disturbing and distressing. For instance, if you suddenly find that a good friend of yours supports a political cause you very much oppose, you will try to alter this imbalanced relationship by either (1) reevaluating your opinion of the cause, (2) attempting to change your friend's mind, or (3) changing how you feel about your friend. In a related manner, the model's constructs are joined in a reciprocal fashion. Just as we long to be connected to the people we like, so too do we long to like those to whom we are connected.

2. Similarity and Marriage

Have you ever noticed that many married couples seem so alike they could almost be brother and sister? If so, your observations are well supported by psychological research. Studies of married couples find substantial partner resemblance for physical characteristics (e.g., height and weight); demographic variables (e.g., ethnicity, race, and socioeconomic standing); cognitive abilities (e.g., word fluency, inductive reasoning, and verbal ability); and attitudes, hobbies, and interests (D. M. Buss, 1984; Galton, 1869/1952; Gruber-Baldini, Schaie, & Willis, 1995). These effects, known as **assortative mating,** may have a biological basis. Assortative mating effects are found among lower animals (e.g., Shine, O'Connor, LeMaster, & Mason, 2001), and married couples who share many genes are more apt to have children than are those who share fewer genes (Rushton, 1988). One explanation for assortative mating is that people are driven to reproduce with those who are highly similar to them, maximizing the survival of their own genetic structure.

Married couples are also similar when it comes to attractiveness (Feingold, 1988; Kalick & Hamilton, 1986). This finding presents something of a paradox. Although people prefer to interact with attractive people, they wind up married to someone who is similar to them in attractiveness. How are we to account for this effect? One possibility is that similarity is a more important determinant of attraction than attractiveness is. When the two variables clash, similarity wins. This account assumes that people purposefully seek a person whose attractiveness matches their own. In fact, there is scant evidence that this occurs. Although people take their own attractiveness into account when seeking a romantic partner, both men and women seek mates whose attractiveness far exceeds their own (Berscheid, Dion, Walster, & Walster, 1971; Folkes, 1982). For this reason, principles of social exchange seem to provide a better explanation for the matching effect in attractiveness. People aspire to find mates of high attractiveness, but unless they have some comparable quality to offer in exchange (such as their own attractiveness or wealth and status), they end up only being able to attract a mate whose attractiveness matches their own.

3. Limits to the Similarity Effect

Although similarity matching is the rule when it comes to attitudes, abilities, physical characteristics, and demographic variables, it exerts a much weaker effect when it comes to personality variables. In fact, for some personality variables, opposites attract. For example, a dominant person who enjoys taking charge of things is happiest interacting with a person who is more submissive and passive (Dryer & Horowitz, 1997). In this case, the two personality variables complement each other. Moreover, too much similarity can be boring: We don't always like people who are just like us, and many of us like variety and seek partners who possess qualities we believe we lack (Herbst, Gaertner, & Insko, 2003; Novak & Lerner, 1968). It's also important to note that similarity matching occurs at a very broad level. Consider height: Although a very tall man is unlikely to marry a very short woman, a moderately tall man may marry a moderately short woman. For this reason, people don't necessarily wind up with someone who is just like them.

Lykken and Tellegen (1993) have even gone so far as to suggest that our selection of a marriage partner is unlawful and random. This provocative conclusion is based, in part, on the marital choices made by identical twins. Identical twins commonly like the same things. For example, they dress similarly, furnish their houses similarly, and even enjoy the same type of leisure activities, such as vacation spots. Yet their spouses are no more alike than are the spouses of nonidentical (fraternal) twins. Nor are identical twins particularly fond of their twin's spouse. In short, identical twins tend to like the same things, except when it comes to who they marry. Building on Rosenbaum's (1986) research, Lykken and Tellegen (1993) argued that mate selection is a two-stage process. During the first stage, we eliminate from consideration people who are highly dissimilar from ourselves. Having then reduced our list of partners to roughly 50 percent of the population, we fall in love with whoever happens to be available when we are ready to fall in love. They liken the whole process to a choice of what to eat for dinner. Although we can reliably predict which restaurants people frequent, we cannot predict which meal they will select once they look over the menu.

III. The Nature of Love

Perhaps we should not be surprised to find that love is hard to explain. After all, poets, playwrights, philosophers, and novelists have sought to understand love for thousands of years, often with only limited success. Social psychological research on the topic began less than 50 years ago, so there is still much work to be done. Nonetheless, research has succeeded in identifying the key features of love and the factors that influence whether it endures or dies.

A. What Is Love?

Defining our terms is a first step in studying any phenomenon. Unfortunately, love is a particularly difficult concept to define. It's not that no one has an opinion; it's that everyone has his or her own ideas about love and a consensus has yet to develop

FIGURE 11.11

Liking and Loving

The figure shows that liking and loving are related as overlapping sets. As a result, there are people we like but don't love, people we love and like, and people we love but don't like.

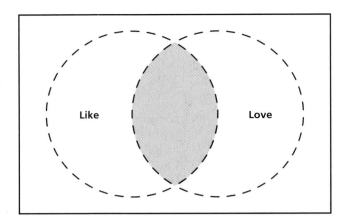

(S. S. Brehm, 1992; Fehr & Russell, 1991). You will appreciate the problem if you think about the people you love. Chances are, you love them all in different ways. The love you feel for your parents is undoubtedly different from the love you feel for your siblings, and the love you feel for your best friend is different from the love you feel for your romantic partner. This complexity increases greatly if we consider that some people also profess to love not only their jobs, pets, possessions, and activities but also abstract entities such as beauty, God, or freedom.

1. Liking and Loving

Despite these obstacles, there is widespread agreement that "loving" and "liking" are qualitatively different phenomena. While it is true that loving involves more affection than liking, love is not simply "a lot of liking" (Rubin, 1973). As shown in Figure 11.11, one way to think about the relation between these two constructs is to treat them as overlapping sets (Sternberg, 1987). The area on the far left represents people we like but don't love, the hatched area in the middle represents people we like and love, and the area on the far right represents people we love but don't like. The fact that we can love people without liking them provides strong evidence that love is not merely "more liking."

2. Different Kinds of Love

Love can also take many forms (Berscheid & Walster, 1978). **Companionate love** is a deep, abiding attachment, characterized by feelings of caring, affection, and respect. Companionate love develops slowly, as people gradually share more and more of themselves with each other. Although it is commonly found among same-sex friends and relatives, people also feel companionate love for their romantic partners. Indeed, in the most successful marriages, people regard their spouse as their best friend.

In contrast, **passionate love** is a more intense emotional state, involving sexual desire, feelings of ecstasy, and perhaps anguish. Passionate love develops rather quickly and may seem to be largely out of one's control. The word *passionate* has its roots in a Latin word that means "capable of suffering," and people commonly speak of being lovesick or swept off their feet. Although passionate love is not necessarily a deeper form of love than companionate love, it is more varied. It is accompanied by physiological sensations (butterflies in stomach, increased heart rate) and is manifested cognitively (preoccupation with the other person); emotionally (feelings of euphoria, contentment, and sometimes despair); and behaviorally (a strong desire to remain near the beloved).

As you can see, arousal is one of the key features of passionate love. Unlike the slow-burning flame of companionate love, passionate love is characterized by high energy, excitement, and wildly fluctuating emotions. The importance of arousal in the experience of passionate love was highlighted by Berscheid and Walster (1974). Drawing on Schachter's (1964; Schachter & Singer, 1962) two-factor theory of emotion (see Chapter 5), Berscheid and Walster argued that passionate love occurs when we (1) experience physiological arousal and (2) attribute this arousal to a beloved. In most cases, the arousal we experience is a direct result of something the other person has done. For example, our heart skips a beat when our partner looks into our eyes or we experience shortness of breath when our partner touches our hand. Less commonly, arousal can originate from some other source and intensify our romantic feelings for another person. To illustrate, suppose you decide to take a date to an amusement park, and the two of you ride the roller coaster together. At the end of the ride, you will probably find that your heart is racing, your skin is flushed, and you are short of breath. As a result of this arousal, your romantic interest in your partner may increase.

This possibility was tested in a field experiment by Dutton and Aron (1974). These investigators had a male and female experimenter conduct an interview with male participants as they walked across one of two bridges in Vancouver, British Columbia. For participants in the low-arousal condition, the interview took place on a stable wooden bridge situated low to the ground above a shallow body of water. For participants in the high-arousal condition, the interview took place on a wobbly suspension bridge that swayed precariously from side to side 230 feet above a raging river. The experimenters gave participants their phone number when the interview was over, and told them to call if they were interested in learning more about the experiment. Among the men who had been interviewed by a woman, those in the high-arousal condition were more apt to call her than were those in the low-arousal condition. Dutton and Aron argued that this occurred because the men had misinterpreted their arousal. Instead of realizing they were aroused because they were standing high above a gorge, they assumed their arousal was due to the attraction they felt toward the interviewer, and they called her in hopes of establishing a relationship.

Subsequent research has clarified the nature of the arousal effect. First, there is evidence that the attraction men felt in this situation arose from fear reduction, not misattribution (Kenrick & Cialdini, 1977; Kenrick, Cialdini, & Linder, 1979). Frightened as they crossed a raging river, the men may have felt calmed by the woman's presence. Through principles of classical conditioning, this comfort translated into greater liking for the woman. Second, subsequent research suggests that the effect depends on the woman's attractiveness: Arousal increases our attraction to an attractive member of the opposite sex, but decreases our attraction to an unattractive member of the opposite sex (Istvan, Griffitt, & Weidner, 1983). Third, these effects occur even when people are aware of why they feel aroused (Foster, Witcher, Campbell, & Green, 1998). These qualifications suggest that the misattribution process discussed by Berscheid and Walster (1974) plays only a minor role in the arousal–attraction link. Instead, as in Zajonc's (1965) social facilitation model (see Chapter 9), it appears that arousal intensifies our dominant responses. Arousal heightens our attraction toward attractive romantic partners but lessens our attraction toward unattractive romantic partners.

3. What's Love Got to Do with It?

Although marriages are still arranged in many parts of the world, most Americans are free to marry whomever they choose. If the divorce rate is any indication, they do not

FIGURE 11.12

Percentages of Men And Women Who Said They Would Not Marry a Person They Didn't Love

Sources: The 1967 data are adapted from Kephart (1967); the remaining data are adapted from Simpson, Campbell, and Berscheid (1986).

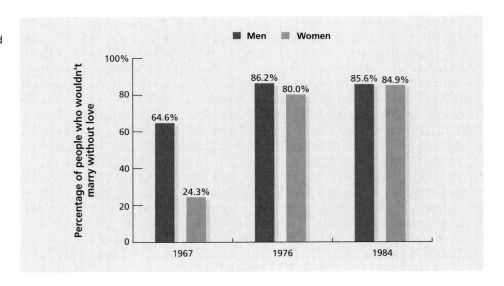

always choose wisely. In a later section of this chapter we will consider the factors that influence whether a relationship endures or dissolves. For now, we will consider only people's ideas about the role love plays in the matter.

Figure 11.12 presents data relevant to this issue. At various times over a 20-year period, researchers have asked college students the following question: "If a man (woman) had all the other qualities you desired, would you marry this person if you were not in love with him (her)?" Figure 11.12 shows the proportion of men and women who said they would not marry without love. As you can see, men have consistently said they wouldn't marry unless they were in love, while more and more women have come to adopt this position. Undoubtedly, the increase in economic opportunities available to women accounts for the change. Now that most women are capable of supporting themselves, they no longer need to settle for a loveless marriage.

4. Cultural Differences in The Experience of Love

If most Americans marry only when they are in love, why do so many marriages fail? One possibility is that they marry for the wrong type of love. Passionate love is quicker to develop than is companionate love, so it dominates in the early stages of a relationship. Blinded by passion, lovers see only the good aspects of their relationship, believing that love conquers all. Alas, passionate love burns out more quickly than does companionate love, and its euphoria and optimism invariably give way to a steadier, more realistic view of the relationship and its problems and possibilities.

People in other parts of the world seem to appreciate this fact. Although passionate love is a common human experience (Jankowiak, 1995), cultures differ in regard to the importance they attach to it. When choosing a mate, people from collectivistic countries, such as India, Pakistan, and Thailand, generally place less importance on romantic love than do people in individualistic countries, such as Australia, England, and the United States (K. L. Dion & Dion, 1988, 1993a, 1993b; R. V. Levine, Sato, Hashimoto, & Verman, 1995). They also give greater weight to a potential mate's character and background rather than his or her attractiveness and personality. Finally, they pay more attention to the wishes of their parents. Does this mean couples in

TABLE 11.2 Sternberg's Theory of Love

Relationship Type	Intimacy	Passion	Commitment	Description
Nonlove	−	−	−	A superficial, relationship void of intimacy, passion, or commitment
Liking	+	−	−	Intimacy without passion or commitment
Infatuation	−	+	−	Passion without intimacy or commitment
Empty love	−	−	+	Commitment without intimacy or passion
Romantic love	+	+	−	Intimacy and passion without commitment
Companionate love	+	−	+	Intimacy and commitment without passion
Fatuous love	−	+	+	Passion and commitment without intimacy
Consummate love	+	+	+	Intimacy, passion, and commitment

Source: Sternberg (1986).

collectivistic cultures never experience passion? Not at all. It simply means that passion isn't the only consideration. After conducting research in the People's Republic of China, R. L. Moore (1998) concluded that

> young Chinese do fall deeply in love and experience the same joys and sorrows of romance as young Westerners do. But they do so according to standards that require . . . [them to] sacrifice personal interests for the sake of the family [and avoid] fleeting infatuations [and] casual sexual encounters. (p. 280)

5. The Components of Love

Sternberg (1986) created a theory of love that synthesizes some of the themes we've been discussing. According to this theory, relationships can be understood in terms of three elements: intimacy, passion, and commitment; *intimacy* refers to feelings in a relationship that foster closeness and connectedness; *passion* refers to strong feelings of sexual desire and a desire to merge with the other person; *commitment* refers to a motivation to maintain the relationship over time. Table 11.2 shows that these three elements combine to form eight different types of relationships:

1. The first, which Sternberg calls nonlove, is a superficial relationship characterized by none of the three elements.
2. The second, liking, involves intimacy without passion or commitment. This type of liking often develops among people who work together or share some common background or interest.

3. The third type, infatuation, occurs when we experience passion in the absence of intimacy and commitment. Some students experience this type of relationship during spring break, when they find themselves romantically involved with a person they do not know well.

4. Empty love is the fourth type of relationship. Here, there is a commitment to remain together but no passion or intimacy. Many couples experience these feelings of emptiness in the years leading up to a divorce.

5. The fifth type of relationship is known as romantic love. Here, there is intimacy and passion, but no commitment. If you are currently in a satisfying romantic relationship but have no plans to remain with that person in the years ahead, you are probably experiencing romantic love.

6. Companionate love involves intimacy and commitment without passion. This is the type of love that develops between two close friends who are not romantically involved.

7. Fatuous love occurs when there is passion and commitment but no intimacy. If you are currently in a committed, sexually gratifying relationship, but feel that you and your partner don't connect emotionally, you are experiencing what Sternberg calls fatuous love.

8. The final relationship, termed consummate love, involves all three elements. Here, partners are emotionally intimate, passionate about each other, and committed to maintaining the relationship. This is the type of ideal relationship to which almost everyone aspires: a romantic partner for life who is also one's best friend.

B. Individual Differences in Relationship Orientations

So far, we have been reviewing the nature of love without regard to individual differences. But people also differ in how they approach a romantic relationship. Some people are eager to get close and fall in love rather easily; others are wary and more reluctant to take the plunge.

1. Styles of Love

Drawing on classical literature and interviews with several hundred respondents, J. A. Lee (1977) identified six styles of love. These styles, presented in Table 11.3, refer to the attitudes people hold toward love and the way they approach a romantic relationship. *Eros* refers to a romantic love style, guided by a quest for a perfect, ideal lover. *Ludus* refers to a relatively playful love style, in which love is treated as a game that is not to be taken too seriously. The ludic lover prefers to keep relationships relatively shallow rather than letting them develop too deeply. The third style, *storge,* is a form of companionate love. The storgic lover values intimacy and mutual sharing, and prefers to take things slow in order for these feelings and behaviors to develop. Practicality is the key element of the fourth love style, *pragma.* Pragmatic lovers make thoughtful decisions about whom to love, basing their decisions on whether or not the person fulfills certain criteria. *Mania* is the fifth love style. Manic lovers metaphorically want to consume their lovers and frequently experience extreme ups and downs. *Agape* is the final love style. Agapic lovers are self-sacrificing, putting their lover's needs ahead of their own. In general, men tend to be more ludic than women, and women tend to be more storgic, manic, and pragmatic than men. The two sexes do not differ on the other two love styles (Hendrick & Hendrick, 1986, 1991).

TABLE 11.3	J. A. Lee's Six Love Styles and Sample Items Used to Measure Them	

Love Style	Description (J. A. Lee, 1973)	Sample Items Used to Measure Love Style (Hendrick & Hendrick, 1986)
Eros	A love style characterized by the search for a perfect, ideal, "one-and-only" love	I feel that my lover and I were meant for each other. My lover fits my ideal standards of physical beauty/handsomeness.
Ludus	A permissive and promiscuous love style in which love is treated as a playful game, and relationships are relatively shallow and short-lived	I try to keep my lover a little uncertain about my commitment to him/her. I enjoy playing the "game of love" with a number of different partners.
Storge	A love style based on a slowly developing affection and companionship, with gradual self-disclosure and an expectation of long-term commitment	The best kind of love grows out of a long friendship. Love is really a deep friendship, not a mysterious, mystical emotion.
Pragma	A love style based on practicality and demographic compatibility	I consider what a person is going to become in life before I commit myself to him/her. An important factor in choosing a partner is whether or not he/she will be a good parent.
Mania	An obsessive, jealous, emotionally intense love style, characterized by preoccupation with the beloved and a need for repeated reassurance of being loved	When I am in love, I have trouble concentrating on anything else. Sometimes I get so excited about being in love that I can't sleep.
Agape	An altruistic, self-sacrificing love style in which the person gives without expectations to receive	I would rather suffer myself than let my lover suffer. I would endure all things for the sake of my lover.

Sources: The descriptions are adapted from J. A. Lee (1973); the sample items are adapted from Hendrick and Hendrick (1986).

2. Romantic Love as an Attachment Bond

Bowlby's attachment theory provides another perspective on different styles of loving. Bowlby (1969, 1973) was concerned with the attachment bonds that form between infants and their caregivers (usually their mothers). He concluded that these bonds serve a paradoxical function: By becoming securely attached, infants feel confident enough to leave their mothers and explore the world. Although Bowlby's ideas have received widespread support, subsequent research using a procedure known as the "strange situation" has shown that not all infants form a secure attachment (Ainsworth, Blehar, Waters, & Wall, 1978). In this situation, an infant is brought into a laboratory with his or her mother. After a few minutes, the mother suddenly leaves and a stranger takes her place. The child's emotional reaction to this abrupt separation is then recorded. Several minutes later, the mother returns, and the infant's emotional reaction to her reappearance is noted.

Table 11.4 shows that infants display three different responses to this situation. Securely attached infants exhibit some distress when the mother leaves, but are easily

TABLE 11.4 Three Infant Attachment Styles and Their Manifestation in Adulthood

Attachment Style	Behavior Displayed in Infancy in Response to Separation from Mother	Associated Parenting Style	Presumed Manifestation in Adulthood
Securely attached	Distressed when mother leaves but comforted when she returns	Responsive, consistent, dependable	Capable of forming close love relationships and a willingness to trust and depend on others
Insecure-avoidant	Exhibits little distress when the mother leaves and shows little interest in her when she returns	Cold, uninvolved, unresponsive	Fear of getting close to others, accompanied by a cynical view of relationships and distrust of others
Insecure-anxious	Greatly distressed when mother leaves and not easily consoled upon her return	Inconsistent parenting style	Tendency to form insecure love relationships, characterized by feelings of jealousy and fear of abandonment

consoled upon her return. According to Ainsworth et al., this form of attachment arises when parents are consistently responsive to their infant's needs. Insecure infants show one of two patterns. Insecure-avoidant children exhibit little distress when their mother leaves and show little interest in her when she returns. This pattern is produced by a cold, uninvolved, unresponsive parenting style. Having learned that their mother won't be available when needed, insecure-avoidant infants suppress their desire for warmth and affection. Insecure-anxious infants are highly distraught when their mother leaves and are not easily consoled when she returns. This type of attachment style is thought to be the result of inconsistent parenting, leaving infants unsure of whether their mother will be available when needed.

According to Hazan and Shaver (1987, 1994) the attachment style we form in childhood influences the types of romantic relationships we form in adulthood. The last column in Table 11.4 describes this influence. Securely attached adults are comfortable getting close to a romantic partner and believe they can depend on their partner to be available when needed. Insecure-avoidant adults have difficulty getting close to a partner, are cynical about love, and are distrusting of others. Insecure-anxious adults tend to form insecure romantic relationships and are prone to feelings of abandonment. They readily fall in love but doubt whether their partners love them in return. Consequently, they feel unfulfilled, worry that they will be abandoned, and exhibit extreme jealousy and possessiveness.

In the years since Hazan and Shaver offered their theory, many investigations have examined how different attachment styles influence various aspects of psychological life (for a review, see Hazan & Shaver, 1994). In general, the results have supported the theory. Compared to those with an insecure attachment style, securely attached people

- Have more satisfying and enduring love relationships (Brennan & Shaver, 1995; N. L. Collins & Read, 1990; Kirkpatrick & Hazan, 1994; Klohnen & Bera, 1998; Simpson, 1990).
- Are more apt to describe their parents as having a warm marriage and as being supportive and warm toward them (N. L. Collins & Read, 1990; Diehl, Elnick, Bourbeau, Labouvie-Vief, 1998; Feeney & Cassidy, 2003; Levy, Blatt, & Shaver, 1998).
- Have more positive views of themselves, are more trusting of others, and more apt to believe in the possibility of true love (N. L. Collins & Read, 1990; Diehl et al., 1998; Feeney & Noller, 1990; Hazan & Shaver, 1987; Mikulincer, 1998).
- Experience less distress when undergoing a stressful experience (Fraley & Shaver, 1998; Rholes, Simpson, & Oriña, 1999), including the dissolution of a relationship (D. Davis, Shaver, & Vernon, 2003).
- Ask for social support when they need it and provide support to their partner when their partner needs it. In contrast, insecure-avoidant people don't ask for help and are reluctant to give it when requested; insecure-anxious people ask for help but give less effective help when their partner requests it, in part because they are controlling and overbearing (N. L. Collins & Feeney, 2000; Feeney & Collins, 2001; Fraley & Shaver, 1998; Rholes, Simpson, Campbell, & Grich, 2001; Rholes, Simpson, & Oriña, 1999; Simpson, Rholes, & Nelligan, 1992; Simpson, Rholes, & Phillips, 1996).

3. Can Attachment Styles Change?

I thought love was only true in fairy tales,
And then for someone else but not for me.
Love was out to get me, that's the way it seemed.
Disappointment haunted all my dreams.
Then I saw her face. Now I'm a believer.
Not a trace of doubt in my mind.
I'm in love, I'm a believer, I couldn't leave her if I tried.

Neil Diamond, 1965

Hazan and Shaver (1987, 1994) argued that attachment styles are formed in childhood and persist into adulthood. In this sense, they are similar to personality variables that people carry with them from relationship to relationship. Although there is evidence that attachment styles are stable during childhood and adolescence (Fraley, 2002), they are subject to change in adulthood. For example, Kirkpatrick and Hazan (1994) found that 30 percent of a sample of respondents changed attachment styles over a four-year period (see also Davila, Burge, & Hammen, 1997). Moreover, one's current attachment style was a better predictor of relationship satisfaction than was one's previous attachment style. Rather than being a stable aspect of our personality that inevitably shapes our relationships, these findings suggest that attachment styles change as a consequence of the relationships we form (Baldwin & Fehr, 1995; Baldwin, Keelan, Fehr, Enns, & Rangarajoo, 1996; Bartholomew, 1994; W. L. Cook, 2000; Davila, Karney, & Bradbury, 1999; Davila & Cobb, 2003; Davila & Sargent, 2003; Simpson, 1990; Simpson, Rholes, Campbell, & Wilson, 2003). Like the narrator in Neil Diamond's hit song "I'm a Believer," people can go from an insecure attachment style to a securely attached one.

IV. The Developmental Course of Romantic Relationships

Romantic relationships don't exist in an unchanging state. They are dynamic rather than static, and they develop, unfold, grow, and change. In the final section of this chapter, we will examine the developmental course of romantic relationships, beginning with the biological bases of romantic attraction and ending with a consideration of why marriages succeed or fail.

A. Falling in Love

1. Love at First Sight

> Where both deliberate, the love is slight:
> Who ever loved, that loved not at first sight?
>
> *Christopher Marlowe, from* Hero and Leander

Many people have caught a glimpse of someone across a crowded room and felt their pulse race, their palms sweat, and their heart pound. Instantly, they knew they were in love. Although love doesn't always begin this way, scientists suspect that these feelings may have a neurobiological basis. In a series of papers, H. Fisher and colleagues have hypothesized that romantic attraction activates pockets of the brain with high concentrations of receptors for the neurotransmitter dopamine (H. Fisher, Aron, Mashek, Li, & Brown, 2002; Fisher, Aron, Mashek, Li, Strong, et al., 2002). Dopamine is a chemical messenger that plays a role in addiction, craving, and euphoria. Our experience of falling head-over-heels in love with someone may stimulate the release of this neurotransmitter, explaining why people who are smitten experience heightened energy, reduced need for sleep or food, and impaired concentration. From this perspective, falling in love is a high, not unlike the exhilaration produced by some narcotics.

2. The Odor of Ardor

Every year, people spend billions of dollars on deodorant, cologne, lotion, after-shave, and perfume. In most cases, people buy these products to disguise their own odor, replacing it with a more redolent fragrance. Principles of classical conditioning operate here. Perfumes (a positive, unconditioned stimulus) evoke a favorable response, and over time we come to associate positive feelings with the person who wears the perfume. These effects are so powerful that many years after a relationship has ended, the scent of a favorite perfume can trigger a powerful wave of longing and romantic desire.

People's natural body odors may also play a role in romantic attraction. These odors are called pheromones. The term comes from the Greek words *pherei,* "to carry," and *hormon,* "to excite" (Karlson & Luscher, 1959). Although animal studies have long shown that pheromones affect mating behaviors in a wide range of species, their influence in human mating has only recently been investigated. At this point, the evidence regarding the role pheromones play in human mating is unclear, but this will undoubtedly be an important area of research in the years ahead (Filsinger, Braun & Monte, 1985; Kohl, Atzmueller, Fink, & Grammer, 2001).

TABLE 11.5 Ten Strategies Used to Initiate a Romantic Relationship with a Member of the Opposite Sex

Category	Example	All Participants	Men	Women
Talk in person	We stayed up all night talking about personal things.	94.1	91.2	97.6
Touching	We held hands and kissed.	63.8	69.4	57.3
Ask directly	I asked the other person out on a date.	62.7	77.6	45.2
Talk on the phone	We talked on the phone for four hours.	53.5	51.0	56.5
Passive	I let the other person do all the work.	50.2	40.1	62.1
Flirting	I flirted with my body language.	36.9	33.3	41.1
Manipulate setting	I played romantic music and lit some candles.	33.6	33.3	33.9
Present self well	I was charming and sweet.	22.5	32.0	11.2
Nonverbal	I made a point of looking deeply into his/her eyes.	20.3	19.0	21.8
Gift-giving	I brought flowers.	21.0	25.9	15.3

Note: Gender differences emerged for the five underlined categories.
Source: Clark, Shaver, and Abrahams (1999).

3. Initiating a Relationship

In every relationship, the partners can tell a story of how they met. Most of the time, one partner develops an interest in the other and conveys this interest in hopes of having his or her affections reciprocated. To see how this process develops, C. L. Clark, Shaver, and Abrahams (1999) asked college students to describe the strategies they had used in the past to initiate a romantic relationship. Table 11.5 presents the 10 most frequently mentioned strategies. The most common strategy was to talk with the other person about matters of a personal nature. As we will see momentarily, this strategy is an excellent way to build intimacy. Other common strategies including touching, asking the person out on a date, and talking on the phone.

Not all romantic overtures meet with success. Part of the problem is that people tend to overestimate the extent to which they are communicating their interest in a potential romantic partner (Vorauer, Cameron, Holmes, & Pearce, 2003). We think our intentions are obvious, but they can be overlooked. Misunderstandings can also occur. Men too readily assume that a woman who shows an interest in them desires a sexual relationship, even when her interest is only to establish a friendship (Abbey, 1982, 1987). In Chapter 13 we explain that misunderstandings like these can have serious consequences involving date rape or other forms of sexual coercion (Muehlenhard, 1988).

4. Becoming Intimate

Most people who seek a romantic relationship hope to become intimate with their partner. But what is intimacy? The word comes from the Latin word *intimatus,* which means "to make the innermost known." Thus, intimacy involves sharing our innermost thoughts and feelings with others, even though it may be painful to do so. Intimacy demands vulnerability: To be truly intimate with another person, we must be willing to reveal things we would rather keep secret. Disclosure alone, however, does not create intimacy. Intimacy also involves the perception that the listener is responding positively to our disclosures. In more formal terms, we can say that "intimacy involves feeling understood, validated, cared for, and closely connected with another person" (Reis & Shaver, 1988, p. 385).

Of course, relationships don't ordinarily begin with such intimacy. Instead, intimacy emerges gradually over time. As they get to know one another, people increasingly reveal more about themselves and learn more about their partner (Altman & Taylor, 1973). Disclosure occurs at two parallel levels: breadth and depth. As we become intimate, we share a broader range of topics and discuss them in a more personal, emotional manner.

5. Becoming One: Turning "You and Me" into "We"

As you and your partner share more and more of yourself with each other, the boundaries that separate you may begin to dissolve and you may create a merged identity that incorporates the other person. Aron, Aron, Tudor, and Nelson (1991) referred to this aspect of closeness as a kind of interconnectedness. According to these researchers, intimacy and closeness emerge as the boundaries that separate self from other blur. Aron, Aron, and Smollan (1992) developed a measure to test this hypothesis. As shown in Figure 11.13, participants examine a series of pictures in the form of a Venn diagram and choose the one picture that best describes their romantic relationship. In accordance with their predictions, the longer two people have been together and the more satisfied they are with their relationship, the more apt they are to choose overlapping circles to describe their relationship. Follow-up studies have found that people who are led to describe their relationship using the pronoun *we* (e.g., We like to go to the theater) feel warmer toward their partner than do those who begin sentences with *He and I* or *She and I* (Fitzsimons & Kay, 2004). Apparently, thinking of your relationship as a single unit both reflects and promotes relationship closeness (Mashek, Aron, & Boncimino, 2003).

B. Satisfaction and Commitment

When studying interpersonal relationships, no questions are more important than "Are we happy?" and "Should we stay together?" At first glance, these questions seem redundant: If we're happy, we should stay together; if we're unhappy, we should split up. However, things are rarely so simple. Most of us know couples who split up even though they seemed to get along very well, and couples who remain together even though they seem to have an unsatisfying relationship. This occurs because the factors that influence relationship satisfaction (i.e., how favorably a person evaluates a romantic relationship) are not the same ones that influence relationship commitment (i.e., the extent to which a person intends to maintain the relationship and feels psychologically attached to it) (Fehr, 1988, 1999; Kelley, 1983).

1. Kelley and Thibaut's Interdependence Model

Using principles of social exchange, Kelley and Thibaut (1978; Thibaut & Kelley, 1959) developed a model to explain the processes that determine relationship satisfaction

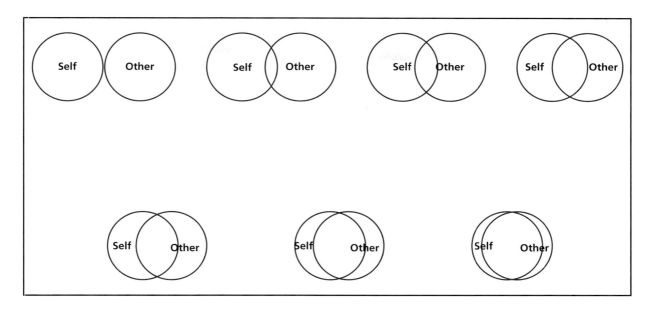

FIGURE 11.13

The Inclusion of Other in the Self (IOS) Scale

Using this method, partners in a romantic relationship are asked to pick the pair of circles that best describes their relationship. The more satisfied couples are with their relationship, the more apt they are to choose the overlapping circles.

Source: Aron, Aron, and Smollan (1992).

and relationship commitment. The model is made up of three constructs. The first, termed the **outcome level (OL),** is a benefits/costs ratio comprised of the things we think we are getting out of a relationship relative to what we think are putting into the relationship. Benefits include love and affection, material goods, and status; costs include loss of freedom, disapproval from others, money, and the time and energy required to make a relationship work (Sedikides, Oliver, & Campbell, 1994). **Comparison level (CL)** is the second construct in the model. This term refers to the minimum outcome level we find satisfactory in a relationship. The final construct in the model is called one's **comparison level of alternatives (CL_{alt}).** This term refers to the outcome value we think we could obtain in our best alternative relationship (including being in no relationship at all).

According to Kelley and Thibaut (1978), satisfaction with a relationship depends on the match between outcome level and comparison level. We are satisfied if our benefits/costs ratio meets or exceeds the minimum level we find satisfactory ($OL \geq CL$), and dissatisfied if our benefits/costs ratio falls below the minimum level we find satisfactory ($OL < CL$). Commitment to a relationship depends on the match between our outcome level and our comparison level of alternatives. Commitment is high if we think our current outcomes meet or exceed the outcomes we could get in an alternative relationships ($OL \geq CL_{alt}$) and low if we think our current outcome level is less than what we could get in alternative relationships ($OL < CL_{alt}$).

FIGURE 11.14

Rusbult's Investment Model of Interpersonal Relationships

The model shows that three factors (benefits, costs, and comparison level) influence relationship satisfaction, and relationship satisfaction, the quality of alternative relationships and investments predict relationship commitment. Finally, relationship commitment predicts relationship stability.

Source: Rusbult (1980).

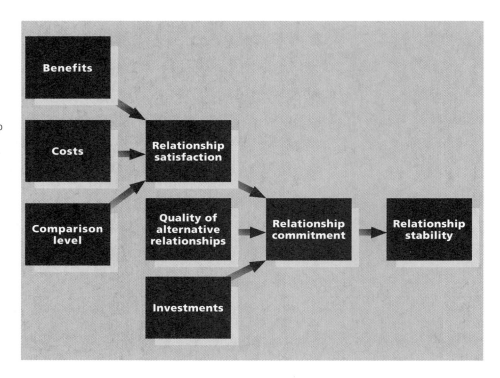

2. Rusbult's Investment Model

Building on Kelley and Thibaut's model, Rusbult (1980, 1983) developed an investment model of interpersonal relationships (see Figure 11.14). In agreement with Kelley and Thibaut, Rusbult's model holds that relationship satisfaction is determined by three factors: benefits, costs, and comparison level. Relationship commitment is also thought to be influenced by three factors: relationship satisfaction, the perceived quality of alternative relationships, and **investments.** This last term refers to all of the things that would be lost if the relationship were dissolved. These investments can include tangible goods, (e.g., a house, a pet, or mutual friends) and intangible things (e.g., the energy one has spent working on the relationship, the years one has devoted to the relationship, or the emotional well-being of one's children). According to the model, relationship commitment is strong when investments are high and relatively weak when investments are low. Finally, relationship commitment determines relationship stability. This term refers to whether couples actually decide to remain together or split up.

Rusbult (1983) tested the model over a one-year period, comparing people who remained in a relationship, left a relationship, or were left by their relationship partner. Figure 11.15 shows an intriguing pattern of results. Looking only at benefits and costs, we can see that people who stayed with their partner experienced more benefits and fewer costs than did those whose relationships ended. Notice also that this pattern is the same for those who were left by their partner as those who left their partner. The other three variables show a different pattern. Here, we see that people who left a relationship differ from those who stayed or were left behind, with leavers reporting greater alternatives, fewer investments, and a lower commitment to the relationship. Taken together, these findings support the claim that a decision to leave a relationship depends more on alternatives, investments, and commitment than on benefits and costs.

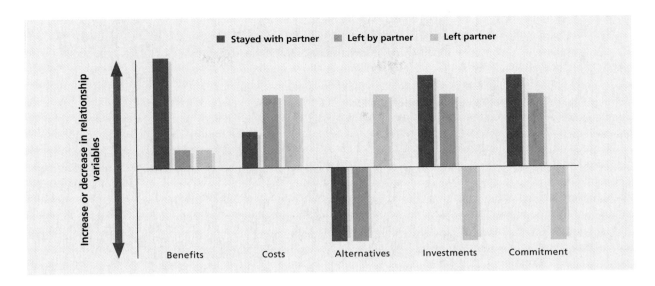

FIGURE 11.15

A Test of Rusbult's Investment Model

The data show that benefits and costs distinguished people who stayed with their partner from those who were left by their partner or left their partner, and that alternatives, investments, and commitment distinguished those who left their partner from those who stayed with their partner or were left by their partner. These findings underscore that a decision to leave a relationship depends less on the balance of benefits and costs and more on the perceived availability of alternative relationships and low investments.

Source: Rusbult (1983).

Subsequent research has found a similar pattern of results with older adult couples (Rusbult, Johnson, & Morrow, 1986a) and with gay and lesbian couples (Duffy & Rusbult, 1986; Kurdek, 1991, 1992). In a particularly important test of the theory, Rusbult and Martz (1995) interviewed women who had sought refuge in a shelter for battered women. As predicted by the model, women with large investments and few economic alternatives were more apt to return to an abusive husband than were women who felt they had invested little in the relationship or had more attractive alternatives elsewhere. These data illuminate the reasons why some women become trapped in abusive relationships. Rather than being satisfied in their relationship, these women remain committed because they see few alternatives and believe they have already invested heavily in the relationship.

3. Equity Theory

In the two models we've been discussing, satisfaction and commitment are determined only by one's own outcomes. For example, a husband is satisfied if his benefits/costs ratio exceeds his comparison level, and is committed to the relation if he has invested a lot in the relationship and sees few alternative relationships. Theoretically, his wife's satisfaction and commitment don't enter into the equation.

Equity theory challenges this theoretical assumption (J. S. Adams, 1963; Walster, Walster, & Berscheid, 1978). Like other social exchange theories, equity theory argues that people keep track of what they give to a relationship and get from it. Equity

TABLE 11.6 Illustration of Equity Theory

	Ken's Benefits/Costs	Barbie's Benefits/Costs
Relationship 1: equal but inequitable	$\dfrac{4}{2} = 2.0$	$\dfrac{4}{1} = 4.0$
Relationship 2: equitable but unequal	$\dfrac{3}{2} = 1.5$	$\dfrac{6}{4} = 1.5$

theory goes on to maintain that people also keep track of their partner's benefits and costs, and that people prefer equitable interpersonal relationships. An equitable relationship is one in which one person's benefits/costs ratio equals the other person's benefits/costs ratio. Less formally, an equitable relationship occurs when there is a balance between what people put into a relationship and what they get out of it.

Equity is not the same as equality. *Equality* occurs when people receive the same benefits; *equity* occurs when people receive the same balance of benefits to contributions. Consider the data shown in Table 11.6. Here I have given two relationship partners, Ken and Barbie, some arbitrary values for their benefits/costs ratio. Relationship 1 is equal (because both partners receive the same benefits) but not equitable (because Ken puts twice as much into the relationship as Barbie). Relationship 2 is equitable (the balance of benefits/costs is the same for both partners), but unequal (because Barbie receives twice as much from the relationship as Ken).

Equity theory makes some interesting predictions about these relationships. Because the theory assumes that people seek and are most satisfied with equitable relationships, it predicts that both partners will prefer relationship 2 over relationship 1, even though each of their benefits/costs ratio is greater in relationship 1. The theory also makes some predictions about how Ken and Barbie will feel when they find themselves in an inequitable relationship, such as the one described in relationship 1. According to the theory, inequity creates psychological discomfort of two types: Ken will feel angry because he is being underbenefited (receiving less than he deserves), and Barbie will feel guilty because she is being overbenefited (receiving more than she deserves). To alleviate their distress, Ken is apt to withhold his future contributions and Barbie is likely to make reparations by giving more to the relationship.

Equity theory has received some empirical support (Hatfield, Utne, & Traupmann, 1979; Walster, Walster, & Berscheid, 1978), but research has also revealed some important qualifications. First, people tend to overestimate their own contributions to a relationship (M. Ross & Sicoly, 1979). Second, even when partners do agree on the contributions each makes to a relationship, people believe their own contributions are more valuable than their partner's (P. C. Regan & Sprecher, 1995). Third, people who are underbenefited feel more distressed and are more likely to leave an inequitable relationship than are people who are overbenefited (Katzev, Warner, & Acock, 1994; Sprecher, 2001a, 2001b). This last finding is particularly important. Inequity feels bad, but people are more apt to leave a relationship when they feel they are being taken advantage of than when they think they are getting more than they deserve. Although this narrows equity theory's power, it doesn't negate the central point the theory makes: Our own satisfaction and commitment to a relationship are affected by what our partner is giving and getting.

4. Exchange versus Communal Relationships

In this section, we have reviewed three social exchange theories: Kelley and Thibaut's interdependence model, Rusbult's investment model, and equity theory. All three maintain that people keep track of what they are contributing to a relationship and what they are getting back, with an eye toward receiving a favorable return on their investments. Although some types of relationships operate according to principles of social exchange, you can probably think of many relationships in your life that aren't characterized by such a strict benefits/costs analysis. M. S. Clark and Mills (1979, 1993) agree. They have suggested that there are two types of relationships: **exchange relationships** and **communal relationships.** The former are governed by principles of social exchange, in which we give benefits with the expectation of receiving a comparable benefit in the near future. In contrast, partners in a communal relationship pledge only to be responsive to each other's needs, without expecting a benefit to be repaid in kind. Instead of saying "I'll cook dinner, if you'll wash the dishes," partners in a communal relationship say "I'll be a loving, caring partner to you, if you'll be a loving, caring partner to me." Whether communal relationships exclude all elements of social exchange is unclear (Batson, 1993), but there is little doubt that many relationships, such as those between parent and child, and husband and wife, include communal elements.

C. Relationship Longevity

No relationship, no matter how healthy, exists in a state of perpetual bliss. Sooner or later, couples confront difficulties and must find a way to iron out their differences. This section examines factors that influence whether marriages succeed or fail. Although much of the material also applies to less committed romantic relationships, we will focus on marriage because it has been the subject of extensive research and because it has sizable effects on health and well-being.

1. The Trajectory of Marriage

We'll begin our look at relationship longevity with some sobering statistics. Although most people marry in their lifetime, a sizable number of marriages end in divorce. Current estimates in America place the divorce rate for first marriages at just over 50 percent, with the divorce rate for second marriages being somewhat higher (Karney & Bradbury, 1995). Half of all divorces occur in the first seven years of marriage, and approximately one-third occur in the first five years (National Center for Health Statistics, 1991).

Even couples who don't divorce experience substantial declines in satisfaction. Kurdek (1999) studied 93 couples over a 10-year period, gathering annual reports of relationship satisfaction. Figure 11.16 shows a steady decline in marital quality for both husbands and wives. Three periods are characterized by marked change. Marital quality declines rapidly after the first year (when the honeymoon is over), during the fourth year (when many couples have their first child), and during the eighth year (the so-called seven-year itch). At the same time, it's also worth noting that couples

FIGURE 11.16

Declines in Marital Quality over the First 10 Years of Marriage

The data show that, for both husbands and wives, marital satisfaction scores declined steadily throughout the first 10 years of marriage, with the steepest drops occurring during the first, fourth, and eighth years of marriage.

Source: Kurdek (1999).

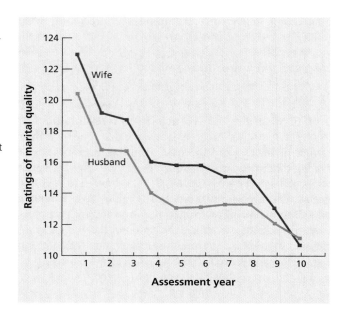

are reporting relatively high levels of satisfaction. The scale used to measure satisfaction had a maximum value of 151, so the satisfaction levels being reported are much closer to "very satisfied" than to "very dissatisfied."

The data displayed in Figure 11.16 don't distinguish happily married couples from unhappily married ones, leaving open the possibility that only unhappy couples experience declines in satisfaction. A study by Huston and associates examined this issue (Huston, Caughlin, Houts, Smith, & George, 2001). Beginning two months after their wedding and continuing throughout the first two years of their marriage, 152 newlyweds were interviewed and asked a series of questions about their relationship. Among other things, the couples were asked how much love and affection they expressed and received when interacting with their mate. The couples were then contacted annually over the next 11 years, allowing Huston and colleagues to examine changes in love and affection during the first two years of marriage for four types of couples: happily married couples, unhappily married couples, couples who divorced early (before their 7th anniversary) and those who divorced late (after being married at least 7 years).

Figure 11.17 presents some of the key findings from this investigation. First, notice that all four groups experienced declines in love and affection over the first two years of marriage. Second, as one might expect, this deterioration is steeper in couples that divorced (dotted lines) than in those that remained married (solid lines). Third, this deterioration rate *doesn't* distinguish happily married couples from unhappily married ones. Looking only at the solid lines in Figure 11.17, we can see that happily married couples start out with greater love and affection than do unhappily married ones, and they maintain this difference throughout the first two years of marriage. Fourth, if we focus only on couples who divorced (the dotted lines in Figure 11.17), we can see that couples who divorced late started out with greater love and affection than did those who divorced early. In fact, as newlyweds, late-divorcing couples showed as much love and affection as did couples who remained happily married. Collectively, these findings indicate that marital dissolution is best

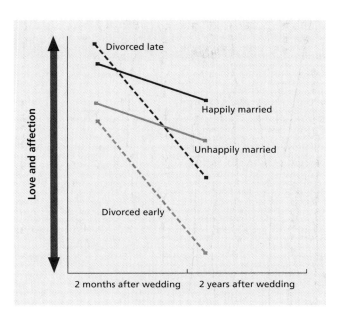

FIGURE 11.17

Marital Satisfaction and Marital Status

The data come from a 13-year study of marital stability. Beginning two months after their wedding and continuing throughout the first two years of marriage, 152 couples reported how much love and affection they expressed and received when interacting with their partner. These reports were then used to predict marital outcomes 11 years later. The data show five effects of interest: (1) all groups experienced declines in love and affection during the first two years of marriage; (2) couples who divorced experienced steeper declines in love and affection across the first two years of marriage than did those who remained married; (3) among couples who stayed married, initial levels of love and affection were higher among those who were happily married than among those who were unhappily married, and this effect remained constant throughout the first two years of marriage; (4) compared to couples who divorced early, couples who divorced late began with higher levels of love and affection; and (5) couples who divorced late started out with levels of affection that were at least as high as couples who stayed together.

Source: Huston, Caughlin, Houts, Smith, and George (2001).

predicted by declines in affection rather than the amount of affection present at the start of a marriage, whereas the reverse is true when predicting satisfaction in intact marriages.

Although not shown in Figure 11.17, Huston et al. (2001) also found that positive relationship factors, such as love and affection, were greater predictors of marital status and satisfaction than were negative relationship factors, such as the presence of arguments or conflict. The authors conjectured that couples who have a warm, loving relationship are better able to handle conflict and strife than are those whose relationship is cold and uncaring. For this reason, having romantic dinners, exchanging special favors and gifts, and sharing exciting, mutually enjoyable activities are important aspects of a happy marriage (Aron, Norman, Aron, McKenna, & Heyman, 2000). The warmth and affection these activities create enable couples to withstand threats to their relationship.

TABLE 11.7 A Typology for Understanding How Couples Cope with Conflict

	Active	
	EXIT Threatening to end the relationship, or engaging in abusive acts such as yelling or hitting.	**VOICE** Openly discussing matters with the partner, changing behavior in such a manner as to solve the problem, or obtaining advice from a friend or therapist.
Destructive to Relationship		Constructive to Relationship
	NEGLECT Avoiding discussion of critical issues, reducing interdependence with the partner, or nagging the partner about unrelated matters.	**LOYALTY** Optimistically waiting for conditions to improve or defending the partner in the face of criticism.
	Passive	

Source: Rusbult, Zembrodt, and Gunn (1982).

2. Coping with Conflict: The Right and Wrong Ways to Argue

Although the presence of conflict does not in and of itself condemn a marriage to fail, the way couples deal with disagreements and arguments does play an important role in marital satisfaction and longevity. Rusbult, Zembrodt, and Gunn (1982) have provided a useful way of understanding this issue. As shown in Table 11.7, these researchers have identified four ways of coping with conflict that differ with respect to whether they are active or passive and constructive or destructive to the relationship. *Voice* is an active, constructive approach to dealing with conflict. It involves an active attempt to resolve differences, either through negotiation and compromise or by seeking a solution from an outside party. *Loyalty* is a passive, constructive approach to conflict. Here, the partner attempts to preserve the relationship by optimistically waiting for troubles to pass or by smoothing things over. *Neglect* is a passive, destructive strategy. Neglectful partners withdraw from conflict, either by refusing to confront the problem or by bringing up unrelated issues. The final strategy, *exit,* is an active, destructive approach. It involves berating one's partner and threatening to leave if the problem isn't solved.

Using this typology, Rusbult, Johnson, and Murrow (1986b, 1986c) found that couples who are happy and satisfied with their relationship use constructive problem-solving strategies of voice and loyalty, rather than destructive problem-solving strategies of neglect and exit. Gender differences were also found. Women were more apt to engage in active problem-solving strategies than men were. This tendency is one of the oldest and most well-established findings in research on marital interactions (Terman et al., 1938). Known as the wives-demand/husbands-withdraw pattern, it leads to a consistent gender difference in martial complaints: Husbands complain that their wives nag and criticize them, and wives complain that their husbands ignore them and withdraw from them (Christensen & Heavy, 1990; Vogel & Karney, 2002). The pattern is particularly destructive in relationships in which the wife is verbally more dominant than the husband (Swann, Rentfrow, & Gosling, 2003).

3. Conflict Styles and Marital Longevity

Conflict styles do more than affect marital satisfaction; they also predict who stays together and who divorces. Gottman and Levenson (1992; Levenson & Gottman, 1983, 1985) pioneered much of the research in this area. In a typical study, these researchers bring couples (often newlyweds) into a laboratory and have them discuss a problem of ongoing concern in their marriage for 15 minutes. While they are speaking, the experimenters videotape the conversation and collect a variety of physiological measures, such as heart rate and respiration rate. The videotapes are then coded at a later date, and the behaviors exhibited by the couples, along with measures of physiological arousal, are used to predict marital stability over several years.

Research using this procedure has found that the manner in which couples discuss problems in their marriage predicts whether they stay together or get divorced (Gottman, 1993; Levenson & Gottman, 1983, 1985; Levenson, Carstensen, & Gottman, 1994). The findings vary from one study to the next, but couples who divorce generally (1) use destructive rather than constructive problem-solving strategies; (2) exhibit more negative emotion during the conversation; (3) display less affection toward their partner; (4) are less nonverbally supportive of their partner (e.g., they are less apt to nod approvingly while their partner speaks and more apt to roll their eyes in derision); and (5) are more physiologically aroused during the interaction than are couples who remain married (see also Kiecolt-Glaser, Bane, Glaser, & Malarkey, 2003; Kiecolt-Glaser & Newton, 2001; Kiecolt-Glaser et al., 1996). As before, gender differences occur for some of these variables. Most notably, wives tend to be conflict-engaging and husbands tend to be conflict-avoiding (Gottman & Levenson, 1992).

It is important to appreciate the meaning of Gottman and Levenson's findings. Although it is hardly surprising that couples who belittle one another are more distressed than those who support one another, it is surprising that these behaviors manifest themselves so clearly in a laboratory setting during a simple 15-minute conversation. One would expect couples in such a setting to be on their best behavior. Yet distressed couples seem incapable of disguising their maladaptive behavioral patterns for even a short time, even though they know they are being scrutinized and evaluated. Second, it's important to bear in mind that these are averages; not all unhappy couples display all of the negative behaviors, nor do all happy couples refrain from displaying some of these behaviors. In consideration of this fact, Gottman and Levenson (1992) have speculated that marital stability is best predicted by the ratio of positive to negative behaviors that occur during the 15-minute interaction. Couples likely to stay together display nearly five times as many positive behaviors as negative behaviors. These findings provide further evidence that the presence of positive behaviors is at least as important to marital stability as the absence of negative ones (see also Carrère, Buehlman, Gottman, Coan, & Ruckstuhl, 2000; Gottman, 1994a, 1994b; Gottman, Coan, Carrère, & Swanson, 1998).

4. Negative Attributions and Interpretations

Unhappy couples exhibit other destructive tendencies. When their partner does something that displeases them, they make a dispositional attribution (Bradbury & Fincham, 1990; Holtzworth-Munroe & Jacobson, 1985). For example, if one partner does less than his or her share of the housework, an unhappily married spouse will assume that this is because the partner is inconsiderate and uncaring rather than stressed or overworked. Once these attributional patterns develop, they affect other aspects of relationship functioning. Partners who make relationship-harming attributions tend to exhibit destructive problem-solving styles and, collectively, these processes further erode marital satisfaction and stability (Bradbury, Beach, Fincham, & Nelson, 1996; Bradbury & Fincham, 1992; Karney & Bradbury, 2000).

As troubles mount and the bond between them weakens, unhappy relationship partners can begin to feel unloved and underappreciated. These perceptions create more problems. For example, instead of turning to their partner for love and understanding when they are under stress, insecure partners tend to belittle their mate and disparage the relationship. This leads the other partner to withdraw further and to retaliate for the bad behavior (Murray, Billavia, Rose, & Griffin, 2003; Murray, Griffin, Rose, & Billavia, 2003). Ultimately, distressed couples can find themselves trapped in a negative spiral that sows the seeds of further misunderstanding and conflict.

5. Relationship-Enhancing Strategies and Relationship Commitment

So far we have seen that distressed couples exhibit a variety of behaviors that undermine the stability of their marriage. But what about happy couples? Do they simply refrain from displaying these negative behaviors or do they act in more positive ways that contribute to the stability of their marriage? The answer depends, in part, on their level of commitment to the relationship. In an extensive program of research with dating couples and spouses, Rusbult and colleagues have shown that people who are strongly committed to maintaining their relationship engage in behaviors that actively promote the stability of the relationship. For example, in comparison with noncommitted partners, committed partners

- Are more apt to use constructive, rather than destructive problem-solving strategies (Rusbult, Verette, Whitney, Slovik, & Lipkus, 1991).
- Are more apt to make relationship-enhancing attributions (Yovetich, Rusbult, 1994).
- Tend to think in terms of "us, we, and ours," rather than "me, my, or mine" (Agnew, Van Lange, Rusbult, & Langston, 1998).
- Are more willing to put their partner's interests ahead of their own (Van Lange, Rusbult, Drigotas, Arriaga, & Witcher, 1997).
- Forgive their partner for making a transgression (Finkel, Rusbult, Kumashiro, & Hannon, 2002).
- Are faithful and loyal to their partner (Drigotas, Safstrom, & Gentilia, 1999).

6. Relationship-Enhancing Behaviors and Relationship Commitment

> Love to faults is always blind,
> Always is to joy inclined,
> Lawless, winged, and unconfined,
> And breaks all chains from every mind.
>
> *William Blake*

Rusbult and associates have also identified behaviors that promote commitment to a relationship. According to Drigotas and Rusbult (1992), commitment to a relationship is fostered by feelings of dependency. Dependency arises from the perception that one's current relationship is extremely satisfying and better than any other relationship one could have. In less formal terms, if you think you and your partner have the best relationship in the world, you will be committed to maintaining it. From this perspective, there are two ways to build your commitment: You can enhance the value of your current relationship, or you can denigrate the value of alternative relationships.

Viewing One's Relationship through Rose-Colored Glasses. In considering how romantic partners view one another, one possibility is that they are accurate, seeing both the virtues and the flaws of their partner. The British poet William Blake suggested another possibility: that love is blind and people see only the good in those they love. So which is it—truth or illusion? The bulk of the evidence favors illusion. People who are satisfied and committed to their relationship view their romantic partners in unrealistically positive terms. They evaluate their partners more positively than their partners evaluate themselves, and they evaluate their partners more positively than their partners are evaluated by other people, including close friends. Even when they acknowledge a fault in their partner, they put a positive spin on it ("Oh, he's not stubborn; he's just strong-willed") (Murray & Holmes, 1993, 1997, 1999; Murray, Holmes, Bellavia, Griffin, & Dolderman, 2002; Murray, Holmes, Dolderman, & Griffin, 2000; Murray, Holmes, & Griffin, 1996a, 1996b).

Happy couples also regard their *relationship* in unrealistically favorable terms. For example, they believe their relationship has improved, even when there is no objective evidence that this is so (Frye & Karney, 2002; Karney & Frye, 2002; Sprecher, 1999). They also believe their love is stronger than other people's love, that the problems that beset other people's relationships, such as poor communication skills or incompatible interests, pose little threat to their own relationship, and that they are more apt to remain together than are other couples (Buunk & van der Eijnden, 1997; Fowers, Lyons, & Montel, 1996; Fowers, Lyons, Montel, & Shaked, 2001; Murray & Holmes, 1997; Van Lange & Rusbult, 1995). Moreover, this **relationship superiority bias** occurs across cultures (Endo, Heine, & Lehman, 2002) and is especially pronounced among people who are highly committed to their relationship (Rusbult, Van Lange, Wildschut, Yovetich, & Verette, 2000).

The correlation between commitment and the relationship superiority bias can be interpreted in different ways. On the one hand, being involved in an above-average relationship could foster commitment. After all, if one's relationship is extraordinarily good, one will want to maintain it. On the other hand, commitment may lead people to think their relationship is especially wonderful. If you feel highly committed to your relationship, you may feel better if you think it's especially wonderful. Instead of assuming that the relationship superiority bias gives rise to commitment, this explanation assumes that commitment gives rise to a relationship superiority bias.

FIGURE 11.18

The Relationship Superiority Bias under Threat

Participants who were strongly committed to their relationship were more apt to exhibit the relationship superiority bias, especially when their relationship had been threatened. This finding suggests that the relationship superiority bias represents a motivated attempt to see one's relationship in highly positive terms.

Source: Rusbult, Van Lange, Wildschut, Yovetich, and Verette (2000).

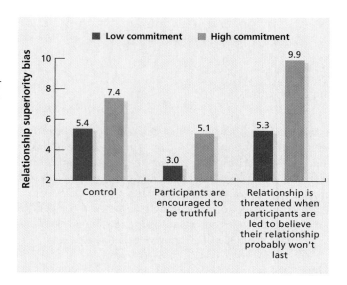

To investigate these possibilities, Rusbult and colleagues recruited a group of college students who were currently involved in a dating relationship (Rusbult et al., 2000). After indicating how committed they were to their relationship, the participants were asked to compare their relationship with other people's under one of three conditions: Some participants were given no specific instructions, some were told to be as truthful and accurate as possible, and some were told that the investigators were especially interested in these comparisons because research had shown that romantic relationships in college tend to be somewhat unsatisfying and short-lived. Presumably, this information poses a threat to the relationship. If the relationship superiority bias stems from a motivated tendency to believe one's relationship is especially wonderful, people who are strongly committed to their relationship should be particularly apt to show the bias when their relationship has been threatened. The data displayed in Figure 11.18 support the motivational interpretation. Participants who were highly committed to their relationship believed that their relationship was much better than other people's, especially after their relationship had been threatened by the knowledge that it might not last. These findings suggest that people are motivated to see their relationship in highly positive terms as a means of bolstering their commitment.

Denigrating Alternatives. Dependency and commitment to a relationship can also be enhanced by denigrating the attractiveness of alternative relationships. After all, if you don't find other relationship partners to be enticing, you're likely to stay committed to your current partner (Broemer & Diehl, 2003; Buunk, Oldersma, & de Dreu, 2001). Lydon and colleagues conducted an investigation to determine whether committed partners devalue the attractiveness of alternative relationships (Lydon, Meana, Sepinwall, Richards, & Mayman, 1999). In one experimental condition, college students currently involved in heterosexual dating relationships signed up for an experiment designed to test a campus-based dating service. They were then shown a picture of a person of the opposite sex. In the high-threat condition, participants were told that this person had seen their picture and found them to be highly attractive and desirable as a dating partner. In the low-threat condition, participants were given no information one way or another about the other person's interest in them. Finally, the participants indicated how desirable they found the person to be.

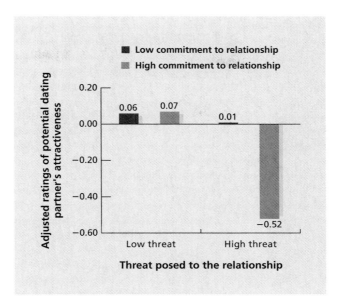

FIGURE 11.19

Commitment, Threat, and the Desirability of Alternative Dating Partners

The data show that people in a committed relationship denigrate the attractiveness of alternative relationship partners when these partners pose a threat to their relationship.

Source: Lydon, Meana, Sepinwall, Richards, and Mayman (1999).

Figure 11.19 presents some of the findings from this study. The scores were computed by subtracting the participants' ratings from those made by single, unattached college students who had also participated in the experiment. As you can see, commitment had virtually no effect in the low-threat condition but a sizable effect in the high-threat condition. The negative value for the high-commitment participants in the high-threat condition is particularly noteworthy. This value shows that when the other person posed a threat to their dating relationship, participants who were highly committed to maintaining their relationship viewed the person as much less attractive than did unattached students. Along with other research, these findings suggest that people who are happy with their current relationship devalue the attractiveness of alternative relationships as a means of fostering their dependency and maintaining their commitment (Bazzini & Shaffer, 1999; D. J. Johnson & Rusbult, 1989; Lydon, Fitzsimons, & Naidoo, 2003; R. S. Miller, 1997; Simpson, Gangestad, & Lerma, 1990).

7. A General Model of Interpersonal Relationships

In this section we have examined the nature of interpersonal relationships, with an eye toward understanding why some relationships survive when others don't. Figure 11.20 presents a model of relationship functioning that integrates many of the topics we have covered (Wieselquist, Rusbult, Foster, & Agnew, 1999). The model is reciprocal, which means we can enter at any point and move forward or backward (P. J. E. Miller & Rempel, 2004). For purposes of illustration, we'll start at the far left-hand side, representing the point at which Jack becomes dependent on his relationship with Jill. *Dependence,* defined as the perception that the relationship provides desired benefits one can't enjoy with anyone else, builds Jack's commitment to maintain his relationship with Jill. His commitment then gives rise to a host of relationship maintenance behaviors, such as the use of constructive problem-solving strategies, willingness to sacrifice, and a tendency to think in terms of "us and ours" rather than "I or mine." These behaviors instill trust in Jill, leading her to value the relationship more and building her dependence. The cycle then continues as Jill's dependence

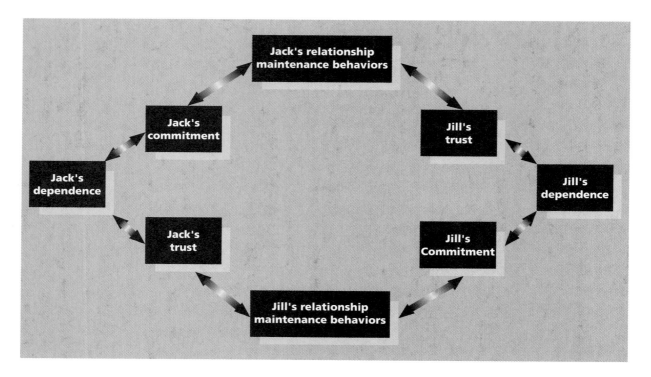

FIGURE 11.20

A Reciprocal Model of Relationship Functioning

Source: Wieselquist, Rusbult, Foster, and Agnew (1999).

promotes her own commitment, leading her to display relationship maintenance behaviors of her own. Unless something happens to weaken one partner's dependence, the couple should continue to experience a stable, satisfying union.

CHAPTER SUMMARY

- People affiliate when they're afraid, because they want the emotional comfort other people provide and because they want information about what's going to happen.

- Women are more apt to affiliate under stress than men are. This may be due to the influence of the hormone oxytocin.

- Social relationships provide many health benefits. People who are socially active are less susceptible to a variety of illnesses and live longer than those who are more socially isolated. The perception that one is loved and cared for is particularly important under periods of high stress.

- Men and women benefit from marriage, but men benefit more. This is because a bad marriage has positive effects on men's health but a negative effect on women's health.

- Loneliness is a common but painful experience. It can arise even when we are surrounded by other people, and is especially likely to occur when we have entered a new situation or lost an important relationship. When accompanied by shyness, loneliness can undermine the quantity and quality of one's social relationships and lead to depression.

- People feel emotionally close to those who are physically near. There are numerous reasons for this: (1) opportunities to meet are increased; (2) it's less costly to interact with someone who is close; and (3) mere exposure effects operate to increase our liking for someone we often see.

- According to the principles of reciprocity, we like people who like us. This is just as true of low-self-esteem people as of high-self-esteem people.

- Likable people tend to be competent, warm, and attractive.

- When seeking a mate, men place more importance on youthfulness and attractiveness than do women, and women place more importance on status and wealth than do men. These preferences occur in various cultures around the world, suggesting that they may have an evolutionary basis.

- According to Heider's balance theory, we feel best when we are joined with things we like and disassociated from things we don't like. In the world of interpersonal relationships, this leads us to like people who like what we like. Dissimilarity also plays a role, especially during the early stages of a relationship.

- Married couples tend to be alike. This effect, known as assortative mating, occurs for physical characteristics, personality, attitudes, background, and socioeconomic status.

- *Liking* and *loving* are distinct phenomena. There are people we like but don't love, people we like and love, and people we love but don't like.

- Companionate love is a slowly developing, deep attachment, characterized by feelings of caring, affection, and respect. Passionate love is a more intense emotional state, involving sexual desire, feelings of ecstasy, and perhaps anguish.

- People all over the world experience passionate love, but people in Western cultures place greater emphasis on it when choosing a marriage partner than do people in Eastern cultures.

- The attachment relationship children form with their parents may influence the romantic relationships they form later in life. Securely attached children go on to form more stable and fulfilling romantic relationships than do children with an insecure attachment style.

- Many romantic relationships follow a common path, in which people gradually disclose more of themselves over time. Eventually, people begin to think in terms of "us and we" rather than in terms of "I and me."

- Social exchange models assume that romantic relationship operate according to economic principles of supply and demand. People are satisfied with their relationships when they believe they are getting more out of them than they are putting into them, and they are committed to their relationships when they have invested a lot in their relationship and believe alternative relationships would be less satisfying.

- Equity theory argues that our partner's outcomes influence our own relationship satisfaction and commitment.

- Most couples experience declines in satisfaction during the first few years of marriage. These declines are steeper among couples who divorce, but do not differ between happily married and unhappily married couples.

- The way couples cope with conflict in their marriage is a good predictor of marital satisfaction and stability. Poorly functioning couples (1) use destructive rather than constructive problem-solving strategies, (2) exhibit more negative emotion when speaking with their partner, (3) display less affection toward their partner, and (4) are less nonverbally supportive of their partner.

- Well-functioning couples tend to see their relationship through rose-colored glasses. They view their partner in highly positive terms and believe their relationship is better than other people's relationships. People who are dependent on a relationship and highly committed to it are especially apt to show these biases.

KEY TERMS

affiliation, 395	assortative mating, 414	equity theory, 429
social support, 396	companionate love, 416	exchange relationships, 431
stress-buffering effect, 397	passionate love, 416	communal relationships, 431
loneliness, 400	outcome level (OL), 427	relationship superiority bias, 437
proximity effect, 402	comparison level (CL), 427	
social exchange theory, 403	comparison level of alternatives (CL$_{alt}$), 427	
reciprocity principle, 404	investments, 428	
balance theory, 412		

ADDITIONAL READING

Go to the Student Edition of the Online Learning Center for this text (www.mhhe.com/brown) and log in to read the following journal articles, which relate to the content of this chapter:

- Huston, T. L., Caughlin, J. P., Houts, R. M., Smith, S. E., & George, L. J. (2001). The connubial crucible: Newlywed years as predictors of marital delight, distress, and divorce.

- Murray, S. L., Holmes, J. G., & Griffin, D. W. (1996). The self-fulfilling nature of positive illusions in romantic relationships: Love is not blind, but prescient.

CHAPTER TWELVE

Helping

TABLE 12.1 Different Types of Helping

Type of Helping	Characteristics	Examples
Everyday acts of kindness	Common, short-lived, low-cost	• Taking a sick friend to the doctor's • Helping a stranded motorist change a flat tire • Making a charitable contribution
Extraordinary acts of bravery or heroism	Uncommon, short-lived, high-cost	• Rushing into a burning building to save a child • Agreeing to donate a kidney • Saving Jews during the Holocaust
Volunteerism	Common, sustained, moderate-cost	• Performing community service (e.g., working for Meals on Wheels) • Donating blood • Building houses for Habitat for Humanity

Bill Gates, Andre Agassi, Oprah Winfrey, and Steven Spielberg have all enjoyed enormous success in their chosen fields. They have also been enormously generous. They have all given away millions of dollars of their own money and used their celebrity status to raise millions more to help those in need of assistance. Although extraordinary in their magnitude, these gifts are hardly unique. Every year, millions of people donate their time and money to help those less fortunate than themselves. These contributions take many forms, from giving a homeless person pocket change to giving blood at a blood bank. Whatever the specific behavior, all such acts are intended to alleviate the distress of others.

In this chapter, we will study the nature of helping behavior. Helping is one type of prosocial behavior. Prosocial behaviors are voluntary actions undertaken to benefit another person. Sharing, kindness, compliments, and displays of affection are all prosocial acts intended to make other people feel better. **Helping** is a prosocial behavior intended to alleviate another person's distress.

Table 12.1 shows that helping can take many forms. Most acts of helping are rather ordinary. We comfort a friend who is feeling down or give a neighbor a ride to the store. These actions are common, occur for a limited time, and involve little in the way of personal sacrifice. Less commonly, helping can involve extraordinary acts of bravery or heroism. A person might rush into a burning house to save a trapped child, or offer to donate a kidney to a loved one or complete stranger. Finally, helping can be more sustained and time-consuming. For example, many people volunteer for community service by building homes in poverty-stricken areas, donating blood through the Red Cross, or serving as aides at a local hospital. Although each type of helping is unique and is influenced by different factors, all of them share an important feature: They aim to improve the welfare of someone in a state of distress.

The first part of this chapter deals with the origins of helping. Here, we will examine why people help and consider whether people are innately helpful. We will then explore the relation between emotions and helping. Here, we explain that our decision to help another person often depends on our emotional reaction to the person's situation and the mood we happen to be in when a need for help is encountered. The next section examines helping in an emergency situation, with a particular focus on whether the presence of other people inhibits us from helping someone who needs assistance. Finally, we will study volunteerism, focusing on personality variables and demographic factors that influence who is most apt to help, as well as on programs that are designed to promote community service and volunteerism.

I. Why Do People Help?

On October 11, 2001, a two-year-old boy wandered onto a four-lane highway in Eufaula, Alabama. Anita Bowden Brown, a 34-year-old administrative assistant, spotted the toddler while riding as a passenger along the road. Instructing the driver of her vehicle to pull over, Brown jumped out of the car and raced across the highway to rescue the boy as speeding cars smashed into one another just feet from where the boy had been standing.

Every year, the Carnegie Hero Fund Commission acknowledges individuals who have demonstrated heroic bravery while attempting to save the life of another person (www.carnegiehero.org). What compels people to exhibit such valor? Why do people help others even when helping entails a substantial personal cost? This question has intrigued moral philosophers for thousands of years. Many philosophers, such as Jeremy Bentham and Thomas Hobbes, endorse a philosophical doctrine of **egoism.** According to this doctrine, people always act out of self-interest. They may help others, but ultimately their behavior is undertaken in order to benefit themselves. Other philosophers, such as Auguste Comte and Adam Smith, disagree. While not denying that people often act out of self-interest, these philosophers contend that people are also capable of acting altruistically. **Altruism** occurs when people act to benefit another person without regard to whether they will derive any sort of personal benefit. The phrase *without regard* merits particular attention. Altruism does not demand that one suffer some loss or that one derive no personal benefit. It requires only helping without regard for how one's actions will affect one's own well-being.

A. Cost/Benefit Analysis of Helping

A cost/benefit analysis provides one way to think about helping behavior. According to this approach, people help when the perceived benefits of helping outweigh the perceived costs. Let's begin by looking first at some potential benefits of helping.

1. Benefits of Helping

In Chapter 8 we noted that human behavior is guided by a norm of reciprocity (Gouldner, 1960). This norm is embodied in the familiar saying "If you scratch my back, I'll scratch yours." As applied to situations involving helping, this saying highlights that helping can be motivated by an implicit covenant of reciprocity. If I do something for you, you'll feel obligated to do something in return for me. One benefit of helping, then, is that people who give help are apt to receive help in the future.

Helpful people may also receive material rewards. For example, people who make charitable contributions of money, clothing, or furniture are able to take a deduction on their income tax. Social rewards also accrue to those who are helpful. At an early age, children are rewarded for engaging in a variety of prosocial behaviors, such as sharing, cooperating, and helping those who are in need of assistance (Eisenberg, 1992). Over time, these rewards become internalized (R. F. Weiss, Buchanan, Altstatt, & Lombardo, 1971). Consequently, people feel good about themselves and experience joy and happiness when they help others. (J. D. Fisher, Nadler, Hart, & Whitcher, 1981; C. E. Schwartz & Sendor, 1999; Williamson & Clark, 1989).

2. Costs of Helping

If helping only entailed benefits, everyone would do it. But helping is also costly. Generally speaking, the costs of helping fall into four categories. Some involve the expenditure of material goods such as money or clothing, as in giving change to a panhandler or blankets to a homeless person. Other costs are physical. Giving blood, for example, can be painful and leave you weakened and feeling dizzy. In extreme cases, helping can involve the risk of injury or even death. The costs of helping can also be psychological. People sometimes feel embarrassed to help. They may feel incompetent or simply reluctant to be the center of attention. Finally, helping can be inconvenient, taking time and effort.

The importance of time as a cost of helping was demonstrated in one of social psychology's most provocative studies (Darley & Batson, 1973). As first discussed in Chapter 1, the participants in this study were seminary students. As they were walking across campus to deliver a lecture on the parable of the Good Samaritan, they encountered a man slumped in a doorway. Some of the participants had been told they were late for the lecture and needed to hurry, others were told they were on time, and still others were told they were running well ahead of schedule. These variations had a large influence on helping. When they weren't in a hurry, nearly two-thirds of the seminarians helped the victim; when they were in a hurry, only 10 percent offered assistance. Clearly, time is an important consideration when people decide whether or not to help.

3. Attributions of Responsibility and the Decision to Help

Imagine that you are walking out of class one day when two students approach you and ask to borrow your class notes. One student explains that she missed class because she was bedridden with the flu; the other says she missed class because the weather was nice and she wanted to spend the day at the beach. Which student are you more likely to help? If you're like most people, you will be more apt to help the student who claimed to have the flu. Why? According to Weiner, we feel little sympathy for people who are responsible for their plight, and this lack of sympathy leads us to withhold aid (Schmidt & Weiner, 1988; Weiner, 1980b).

Attributions of responsibility also influence how willing people are to support various social causes. For many years, certain social afflictions—such as obesity, alcoholism, drug addiction, and gambling—were viewed as character disorders, largely under personal control. Recently, it has been claimed that these maladies have a genetic basis and that the afflicted are victims of these problems and should not be held accountable for their plight. Do attributions of responsibility affect people's willingness to help? To answer this question, Weiner, Perry, and Magnusson (1988) had participants indicate how responsible they thought people were for various

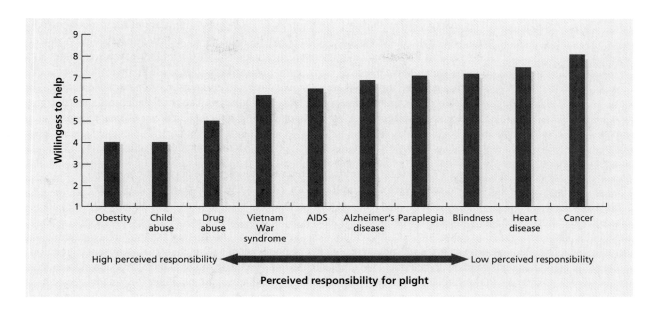

FIGURE 12.1

Attributions of Responsibility and Helping

The more responsible victims were held to be for their plight, the less willing participants were to give money to help.

Source: Weiner, Perry, and Magnusson (1988).

illnesses and conditions, and how likely they would be to donate money to fight the cause. As shown in Figure 12.1, participants were quite willing to give money to fight afflictions viewed as largely out of one's personal control (e.g., blindness, heart disease, cancer) but relatively unwilling to donate money to fight afflictions viewed as largely under a person's control (e.g., obesity, child abuse, drug abuse). These findings establish that attributions of responsibility affect decisions to help (Weiner, 1993).

4. Costs of Not Helping

Finally, we must also consider the costs of not helping. These costs are most obviously related to the victim. If we fail to help, the victim is likely to suffer. But potential helpers also incur costs if they fail to help. For example, we might feel guilty or ashamed of ourselves for falling short of a high moral standard. We might also feel upset and distressed to know that someone else is suffering. In a later section of this chapter, we will see that helping is often undertaken to avoid experiencing negative emotions like these.

B. Evolutionary Models of Helping

So far, we have been discussing factors that influence helping in the immediate situation in which it occurs. Evolutionary models contend that helping behavior has also been shaped by hundreds of thousands of years of human history, and that the costs and benefits are ancient ones rather than modern ones. To understand this argument, we need to understand how contemporary researchers think about the process of natural selection. In its original form, Darwin's theory of natural selection emphasized competition for scarce resources and survival of the fittest individual. Since many acts of heroism involve placing one's own life in danger, it is difficult to see how self-sacrificing behavior could ever be advanced by principles of natural selection. Yet people in every culture around the world frequently sacrifice their time and energies to help others, suggesting that acts of helping may have an evolutionary basis.

1. Theoretical Processes

In the 1960s, several scientists offered resolutions to the apparent contradiction between survival and self-sacrificing behavior (for reviews, see Hoffman, 1981; E. O. Wilson, 1975). Three mechanisms were identified. The first, known as **kin selection,** builds on Darwin's original theory by maintaining that natural selection operates at the level of the gene, not the individual (Dawkins, 1976). From this perspective, anything that enhances the reproductive success of one's genes is selected for. Because we share our genes with relatives, we can increase our "inclusive fitness" by helping our kin survive (Hamilton, 1964). Consider a father with three children. Since he shares one-half of his genes with each child, he can maximize his genetic fitness by sacrificing his own life for theirs. More formally, Hamilton's rule maintains that helping will occur when $rb - c > 0$, where r = Relatedness of two individuals, b = Benefits to the recipient, and c = Costs to the benefactor. To demonstrate this formula's application, if the recipient of helping is a sibling ($r = 0.5$), the benefit to the sibling must be more than twice the cost of helping. If the recipient is an aunt, uncle, grandparent, nephew or niece ($r = 0.25$), the benefit must be more than four times the cost of helping (and so on).

A second mechanism is known as **reciprocal "altruism"** (Trivers, 1971, 1985). The term calls attention to something we noted earlier in this chapter: People who give help are more apt to receive it. Hundreds of thousands of years ago, the earth was a dangerous place and people often needed assistance. If helpful people were more apt to receive help because they were more apt to offer it, they would have a reproductive advantage and their helpfulness would be passed along to successive generations. Note, however, that the term *altruism* makes the label of this process a misnomer (Krebs & Miller, 1985). Because the probability of helping depends on the probability of receiving future assistance, reciprocal "altruism" is egoistic. The mechanism would more appropriately be termed a model of reciprocal egoism (hence the use of quotation marks above).

The third mechanism is known as **group selection.** Eons ago, most humans lived in small, nomadic hunting and gathering groups. If groups with many helpful people were more apt to survive, and helpers were allowed to mate more freely than nonhelpers, genes favoring helpfulness would be selected for in the overall population. Over hundreds and thousands of years, a willingness to help others would have become a basic human trait.

2. Tests of the Evolutionary Model

Evolutionary models of helping hinge on two testable propositions: (1) People can identify those who are genetically similar to them, and (2) people are more willing to help those who are genetically similar to them than those who are genetically dissimilar.

Can People Detect Genetic Similarity? Experimental studies have shown that several animal species recognize genetic similarity. For example, in the sweat bee, guard bees are more apt to allow genetically similar bees to enter the nest than bees that are genetically dissimilar (L. Greenberg, 1979). The evidence that humans can also detect genetic similarity is less direct, but there is reason to believe they can (for reviews, see Porter, 1987; Rushton, 1989). For example, infants can distinguish their mother's voice from the voice of other women within the first day of life, and mothers recognize their infant's smell after only a few hours of contact. Later in life, people tend to form closer bonds with those who are genetically similar to them. For example, friends are more genetically similar to one another than are acquaintances or nonfriends, and married couples are more genetically similar to one another than are romantically involved but unmarried couples. Although alternative explanations can be generated for each of these findings (Economos, 1989), an ability to detect genetic similarity is certainly one possibility.

Do People Help Those Who Are Genetically Similar to Them? The evidence supporting the proposition that people help those who are genetically similar to them is fairly plentiful. Anthropological studies show that in countries around the world, people are more apt to help close family members and kin than those who are less genetically similar to them (Essock-Vatale & McGuire, 1985). Moreover, identical twins (who share 100 percent of their genes) are more apt to help each other than fraternal twins (who share 50 percent of their genes) are (Segal, 1984). These findings lend credence to the maxim "Blood is thicker than water" (Neyer & Lang, 2003; Webster, 2003).

The tendency to help blood relatives is particularly strong when the costs and benefits of helping are high. To illustrate, Burnstein, Crandall, and Kityama (1994) asked college students to decide who they would help under one of two conditions. In the everyday-helping condition, participants were simply asked to do a small favor for another person (e.g., pick up an item at the store). In this situation, the costs and benefits of helping are low. In the life-or-death condition, participants were asked to consider which person they would save if a building were on fire and they could save only one person. Here, the costs and benefits of helping are large. Finally, those in need of help were described as being either (1) young or old, (2) healthy or unhealthy, and (3) genetically similar (e.g., close relative) or genetically dissimilar (e.g., distant cousin or acquaintance).

Figure 12.2 shows some of the data from this investigation. Panel A shows that although participants were generally more inclined to help a close relative than a distant relative or acquaintance, genetic similarity played a stronger role in a life-or-death situation than in a more mundane one. This makes sense from an evolutionary perspective. When the costs and benefits of helping are rather low, we are about as willing to help a stranger as we are to help a close blood relative. In contrast, when the costs and benefits of helping are high, we are much more willing to help a close blood relative than we are to help a distant blood relative or a stranger.

Panel B shows the findings for the age and health of the recipient. Before reviewing the findings, let's consider why the nature of the helping situation should matter here. According to a universal norm of responsibility, people should help those who are unable to help themselves (Berkowitz & Daniels, 1963). Under ordinary circumstances, this norm leads us to help the elderly and frail more than the young and able-bodied. But in life-or-death situations, helping the elderly and frail is disadvantageous, because their reproductive potential is limited. Accordingly, when danger is present and the costs and benefits of helping are high, we should be less willing to save the elderly and frail and more apt to save the young and able-bodied. Panel B shows just

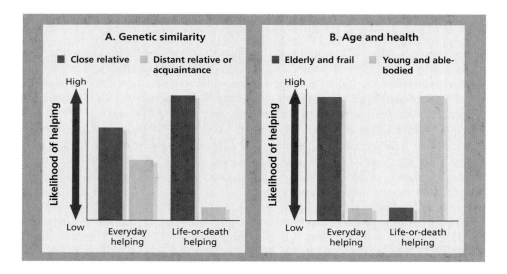

FIGURE 12.2

Testing the Evolutionary Model of Helping

Panel A shows that genetic similarity plays a rather small role in everyday helping situations, but a large role in situations involving life-or-death decisions. Panel B shows that people will help those who are unable to help themselves in everyday helping situations, but they help the young and healthy in life-or-death situations. These findings suggest that when the costs and benefits of helping are high, people take a person's reproductive potential into account when deciding whether or not to help.

Source: Burnstein, Crandall, and Kitayama (1994).

such a pattern. In everyday helping situations, we help the elderly and frail more than the young and able-bodied; but in life-or-death situations, we help the young and able-bodied more than the elderly and frail.

II. Situational Influences on Helping

Every need for helping takes place in a particular context, and these contextual features influence whether help ultimately occurs. This section discusses three important situational influences on helping: our emotional reactions to a person in need, the nature of the relationship between the helper and the person needing help, and our moods at the time a helping decision is made.

A. Emotional Reactions to a Person in Need

The commercial opens with a panoramic view of a desolate, arid land. Sitting amid abject poverty, a starving child with a plaintive expression stares listlessly into the camera. The child seems to be looking directly at you, begging for your help. Finally, a toll-free number appears on the screen as a narrator announces that you can feed the child for a year for only a few cents a day.

How would this commercial make you feel? If you're like most people, it is apt to evoke two distinct, though related, emotional reactions (Batson, 1987; Eisenberg et al., 1988; Gruen & Mendelsohn, 1986). The first, **personal distress,** is an egoistic emotion characterized by feelings of alarm, discomfort, and uneasiness. Simply put, seeing a starving child upsets us and makes us feel uncomfortable. The second emotional reaction, **sympathy,** is an other-directed emotion characterized by feelings of concern, compassion, and tenderness. Here we feel warmth and genuine affection for a person who so clearly needs our help.

1. The Developmental Course of Personal Distress and Sympathy

Feelings of personal distress develop earlier in life than do feelings of sympathy (Hoffman, 1981). In fact, even newborns become distressed when they encounter another infant who is upset or suffering. Simner (1971, Experiment 1) had three-day-old infants listen to one of three sounds. Some infants heard the sound of another infant crying, some heard the sound of a comparable synthetic noise, and some heard no noise at all. Simner then measured the likelihood that the infants themselves would begin to cry. As shown in Figure 12.3, infants were nearly three times more likely to cry when hearing the sound of another infant's cry than when hearing a comparable synthetic noise or no noise at all. Subsequent research has found that this tendency occurs during the first day of life and that it does not occur when infants hear their own tape-recorded cry (G. B. Martin & Clark, 1982; Sagi & Hoffman, 1976). Taken together, these findings suggest that humans possess an innate capacity to feel distressed when others are distressed.

Unlike the capacity for personal distress, which seems to be present at birth, sympathy develops as people mature. In one study, researchers had mothers keep track of their infant's reactions to other people's distress over a one-year period (Zahn-Waxler, Radke-Yarrow, Wagner, & Chapman, 1992). Among the reactions they chronicled were feelings of personal distress, sympathy, and behavioral efforts to intervene on the behalf of the victim or alleviate the victim's suffering. For example, if another child fell off the merry-go-round and cried in pain, the mothers noted whether their

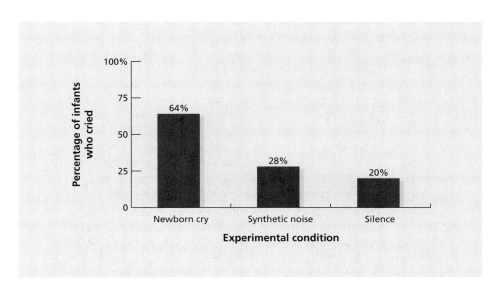

FIGURE 12.3

Infants Cry More When They Hear Another Infant Cry

Newborns were more apt to cry when hearing the sound of another infant's cry than when hearing synthetic noise or no noise at all. These findings suggest that the capacity to feel another person's distress develops very early in life and may even be innate.

Source: Simner (1971).

FIGURE 12.4

Developmental Changes
in Helping Reactions

In response to seeing
another person in distress,
feelings of personal distress
declined in frequency over
the second year of life,
while feelings of sympathy
and prosocial behavior
increased.

Source: Zahn-Waxler, Radke-
Yarrow, Wagner, and Chapman
(1992).

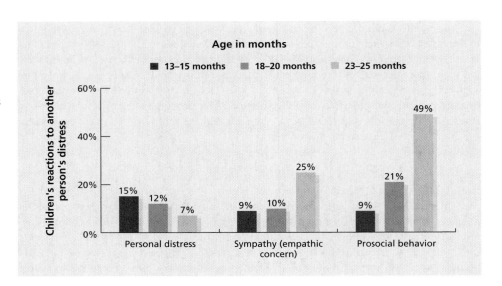

own child began to cry (personal distress), expressed sorrow or concern for the other child (sympathy), or took aims to help (e.g., rushed over to see if the other child was alright). Figure 12.4 shows the developmental changes that occurred with regard to these reactions. Notice that feelings of personal distress declined in frequency during the second year of life but that feelings of sympathy and prosocial behaviors increased in frequency during this period. It is particularly noteworthy that the youngest children displayed prosocial behaviors less than 10 percent of the time, while the oldest children did so almost half of the time.

2. The Empathy–Altruism Hypothesis

As they age, people continue to experience feelings of personal distress and sympathy when they encounter another person in need of help. Moreover, both emotions are capable of motivating helping behavior. The motives for helping may differ, however. According to Batson (1987), when feelings of personal distress dominate, helping is egoistically motivated, driven by a desire to relieve one's own discomfort rather than a desire to alleviate the other person's suffering. In contrast, when sympathy dominates, helping is altruistic, driven by a genuine desire to relieve the other person's distress rather than a desire to relieve one's own distress.

To better understand these predictions, imagine that you are walking down the street and come upon a disheveled person slumped in a doorway. Your reaction might be either of two types. First, you might feel alarmed and uncomfortable. In this case, you might help to alleviate your own discomfort. Alternatively, you might feel sympathetic and compassionate. In this case, you might help primarily to relieve the other person's distress. Of course, helping when you feel sympathy might also make you feel better, but making yourself feel better was not your primary aim.

What determines which emotion dominates? Batson believes that **empathy** is the key factor to consider. Empathy involves the capacity to take the perspective of another person; to put yourself in another person's shoes and view the situation from his or her point of view. According to Batson, when people are being empathic, sympathy dominates over feelings of personal distress, and helping is altruistic (see the top row of Table 12.2). In contrast, when people are not being empathic, feelings of

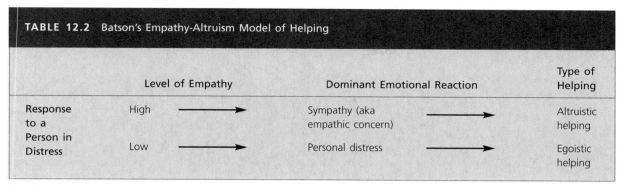

TABLE 12.2 Batson's Empathy-Altruism Model of Helping

	Level of Empathy		Dominant Emotional Reaction		Type of Helping
Response to a Person in Distress	High	⟶	Sympathy (aka empathic concern)	⟶	Altruistic helping
	Low	⟶	Personal distress	⟶	Egoistic helping

Note: Empathy determines how we feel when we encounter a person in a state of need, and our dominant emotional reaction determines the type of helping that occurs.

personal distress dominate over sympathy, and any helping that occurs is egoistic (see the bottom row of Table 12.2).

Experimental Tests of Batson's Model. Batson and colleagues have conducted dozens of investigations to test the empathy–altruism model of helping (for a review, see Batson, 1987). Many of these studies use a similar procedure in which participants are asked to observe, over closed-circuit television, another person receiving mild electric shocks while working at some task. (Participants are unaware that the whole procedure is staged and no shocks are actually being delivered.) The researchers manipulate two variables. The first is empathy. Participants in the low-empathy condition are instructed to be objective and impartial and to watch the proceedings with an air of detachment. Participants in the high-empathy condition are told to imagine themselves in the worker's shoes and to experience what the worker is experiencing. The second variable pertains to when participants can leave. All participants learn that the worker will be completing 10 trials, but some participants are told they have to observe only 2 of the trials. This condition is known as the easy-escape condition, because participants can easily escape any distress they are feeling by leaving the experiment. Other participants are not given this opportunity. They are told they must watch all 10 trials, so no escape is possible.

Once the experiment begins, the first two trials pass uneventfully. However, at this point the learner becomes very distraught and confesses that he or she had a traumatic experience with shock as a child and doesn't want to continue. The experimenter then asks the participant whether he or she would be willing to trade places and receive the shocks in the role of the worker. This willingness constitutes the primary measure of helping.

Let's look at what Batson's model predicts in this situation. Participants in the low-empathy condition should be experiencing high levels of personal distress, and any helping that occurs should be egoistically motivated. When they can't escape the situation, the only way to relieve their distress is to offer to trade places with the worker and take the shock themselves. However, when it is easy to escape the situation, they can leave the experiment, much as a person might decide to change the channel when a starving child appears on the television screen with an appeal for help. The first prediction, then, is that participants in the low-empathy condition will help when they can't escape but not when they can escape. A different pattern is predicted for participants in the high-empathy condition. Presumably, these participants are feeling sympathy for the

FIGURE 12.5

Predicted Rates of Helping by Batson's Empathy–Altruism Model

When empathy is low, people are expected to help when they can't escape but not when they can. In contrast, when empathy is high, people are expected to help even when escape from the situation is easy. According to Batson, this occurs because low empathy leads to egoistic helping and high empathy leads to altruistic helping.

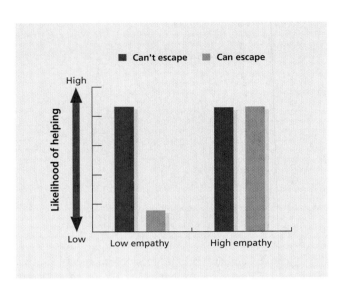

worker and are primarily motivated to alleviate the worker's distress rather than their own. Whether they can escape or not has no bearing on this issue, so they should help as much when they can escape the situation as when they can't escape the situation.

Figure 12.5 shows these predicted effects, and several investigations have produced this same pattern of findings (Batson, Duncan, Ackerman, Buckley, & Birch, 1981; Batson, O'Quin, Fultz, Vanderplas, & Isen, 1983; Coke, Batson, & McDavis, 1978; Toi & Batson, 1982). Participants who are being empathic feel sympathetic toward the victim and help even when they can easily escape the situation, whereas those who are not being empathic experience high levels of personal distress and help only when escape is difficult. In consideration of these findings, Batson believes that empathy produces a form of altruistic motivation in which alleviating the other person's distress is our primary goal.

Challenges to Batson's Findings. Batson's research has clearly established that empathy promotes helping even when escape is easy, but whether or not this helping is altruistic remains the source of some debate. At least four issues have been raised:

- People who empathize with a victim feel sadder than those who remain detached, and they help in order to alleviate their own sorrow rather than to promote the other person's welfare (Cialdini et al., 1987; Schaller & Cialdini, 1988).
- People who are empathic anticipate feeling particularly guilty if they fail to help someone they care about, so they help in order to avoid feelings of remorse and regret (Dovidio, 1984).
- Because they view the situation from the other person's perspective, people who are empathic help because they feel particularly joyful when the other person's situation improves (K. D. Smith, Keating, & Stotland, 1989).
- High empathy produces a form of psychological merging, whereby self and other are seen as a single psychological unit. Consequently, helping the other person is a disguised form of egoistic helping (Cialdini, Brown, Lewis, Luce, & Newberg, 1997; Maner et al., 2002).

Batson and others have conducted research to address each of these alternative explanations (e.g., Batson et al., 1988; Batson et al., 1989; Batson et al., 1991; Batson et al., 1997; Schroeder, Dovidio, Sibicky, Mathews, & Allen, 1988). Still, the possibility that helping is egoistically motivated persists (Maner et al., 2002), and the safest conclusion to be drawn from this research is that empathy promotes helping even when escape is easy and the costs of helping are high, and that this type of helping may be altruistically motivated (M. H. Davis, 1983; Eisenberg & Miller, 1987).

B. Whom Do We Help?

Because empathy promotes helping, any factor that influences empathy influences the likelihood that helping will occur. Similarity is one such factor. People find it easier to empathize with those who are similar to themselves, and people are more apt to help those who are similar to them versus those who are dissimilar (Dovidio, 1984). People are also more apt to help ingroup members versus outgroup members (Feldman, 1968), except that both men and women tend to help women more than men (Piliavin & Unger, 1985).

Interpersonal attraction also affects helping. Not surprisingly, people help those they like more than those they dislike. Consequently, factors that influence interpersonal attraction influence helping. For example, people are more apt to help an attractive person versus an unattractive one (Benson, Karabenick, & Lerner, 1976).

In most situations, people are also more apt to help a friend versus a stranger (Amato, 1990; Williamson & Clark, 1989). There are exceptions to this general rule, however. Helping can sometimes imply superiority on the part of the helper and dependency on the part of the recipient (Nadler & Fisher, 1986; Schneider, Major, Luhtanen, & Crocker, 1996). For this reason, people are sometimes reluctant to help their family, friends, and loved ones, particularly if the need is slight and helping would damage the recipient's feelings of self-worth.

C. Mood States and Helping

In addition to being influenced by factors related to empathy, decisions about whether or not to help are also guided by relatively momentary factors. How we happen to be feeling at the time help is needed is one such factor. Interestingly, both positive and negative moods promote helpfulness under certain conditions.

1. Happiness and Helping

Imagine it's a beautiful day. The sun is shining and you are feeling relaxed and unfettered, when a stranger approaches you and asks you to fill out a survey. Will you help? M. R. Cunningham (1979) found that you probably will. In a study conducted during the summer and winter in Minneapolis, Minnesota, Cunningham found that passersby were more apt to stop to fill out a survey on a sunny, temperate day, than on a cloudy, inclement one. Follow-up research conducted in the greater Chicago area found that restaurant patrons tipped more generously on sunny days than on cloudy ones. Cunningham reasoned that people are in better moods on nice days and that a positive mood leads to more helping.

Other investigations have also found that people in a good mood are especially beneficent. Finding a dime in a phone booth, receiving a gift, eating fresh-baked cookies, smelling a pleasing fragrance, and imagining a trip to Hawaii have all been shown to increase helping by promoting happiness (for a review, see Carlson, Charlin, & Miller, 1988).

Three explanations have been offered to account for this effect. First, positive moods prime positive thoughts, and people in a good mood look more favorably on opportunities to help (Isen, 1984). Second, positive moods increase sociability and a concern for others (M. R. Cunningham, 1988). Finally, people help to maintain their happiness (Isen & Levin, 1972; Isen & Simmonds, 1978). Being aware that helping feels good, people help as a means of prolonging their positive mood. In support of this explanation, researchers have found that happy people do not help more than do those in a neutral mood when helping is costly or threatens to destroy their good mood.

2. Sadness and Helping

So far we have seen that people feel better when they help another person. In some circumstances, people exploit this relation between helping and happiness to improve their moods when they are sad. You have probably experienced this effect firsthand. Recall a time when you were feeling blue. Perhaps a friend or parent advised you to do something nice for someone as a way to make yourself feel better. If so, the person's advice was built on solid social psychological principles (Carlson & Miller, 1987).

The mood-elevating properties of helping lie at the heart of Cialdini's negative state relief model of helping (Cialdini & Kenrick, 1976). According to the model, sad people are helpful only when they believe helping will improve their mood. To test this prediction, Manucia, Baumann, and Cialdini (1984) led participants to believe they were taking part in a study testing the effects of a memory drug called Mnemoxine. In one condition, participants were told that the drug tended to "fix" a person's mood, such that whatever mood a person was in when ingesting the drug would be chemically preserved until the drug wore off. Participants in a control condition were not given this information. Several minutes after ingesting the drug (which was actually a placebo), the alleged memory task began. Some participants were asked to reminisce about a happy experience, some were asked to reminisce about a sad experience, and a third group was asked to recall a neutral mood experience. These variations comprised the mood manipulations. Finally, as the participants were leaving the experiment, a confederate appeared and asked the participants whether they would be willing to make some phone calls to help collect information for blood donors.

Figure 12.6 shows the percentage of participants in each condition who agreed to help with this task. The data reveal two important effects: (1) Happy participants helped more than participants in a neutral mood, regardless of whether or not their mood was "fixed," but (2) sad participants helped more than participants in a neutral mood only when they believed helping could improve their mood. These findings suggest that mood improvement influences helping decisions when people are sad, but not when they are happy.

3. Helping and the Self-Image

Success and failure can prompt benevolence much as happiness and sadness do (Isen, Horn, & Rosenhan, 1973). They do so through different means, however (Cunningham, Steinberg, & Grev, 1980; Weyant, 1978). Success makes people feel happy and competent, and these factors promote generosity and helpfulness. In contrast, failure creates sadness and deflates feelings of self-worth, and people help in order to repair their negative moods and restore a positive self-image (J. D. Brown & Smart, 1991).

People who are embarrassed or are feeling guilty because they have harmed someone are also more helpful than those who are not embarrassed or feeling guilty

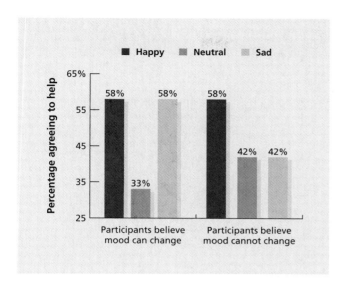

FIGURE 12.6

Moods and Helping as a Function of Whether Moods Can Change

Before being given the chance to help in a blood drive, participants were placed into a happy, sad, or neutral mood, and told their mood could or could not change for a while. The data show that (1) happy participants helped more than participants in a neutral mood regardless of whether their moods could change, but (2) sad participants helped more than participants in a neutral mood only when they believed helping could improve their mood. These findings suggest that mood improvement motivates helping when people are sad.

Source: Manucia, Baumann, and Cialdini (1984).

(Apsler, 1975; Carlsmith & Gross, 1969; Regan, Williams, & Sparling, 1972). A field experiment by Regan, Williams, and Sparling (1972) illustrates this point. A male confederate stopped a female passerby and asked her if she would use his camera to take his picture. Just as the woman was about to snap the picture, the camera would break. In a control (no-guilt) condition, the confederate assured the woman it was not her fault, but in the guilt condition, the confederate blamed the woman for breaking his camera. Several minutes later, the participants crossed paths with another confederate whose groceries were falling out of her shopping bag. Although only 15 percent of the participants in the control condition helped, 55 percent of those in the guilt condition did so. Subsequent research has replicated this effect and provided evidence that people who feel guilty do not help more if they are given an alternative opportunity to restore a positive self-image (Cialdini, Darby, & Vincent, 1973; McMillen, 1971).

4. Summary of Moods and Helping

Table 12.3 summarizes the points we have been reviewing in this section. The table shows that different moods and self-relevant experiences promote helping through a variety of means (Cunningham, Shaffer, Barbee, Wolf, & Kelley, 1990). Happiness and success prime positive thoughts, increase social concern and sociability,

TABLE 12.3 Mood, Self-Relevant Experiences, and Helping	
Mood and Self-Concept Variables	**Reasons Why Variable Promotes Helping**
Happiness	• Primes positive thoughts and interpretations • Increases social concern and sociability • Creates a desire for mood maintenance
Sadness	• Creates a desire for mood improvement
Success	• Creates happiness • Instills self-confidence and perceived competence
Failure	• Creates sadness • Produces a need for self-image repair
Embarrassment and guilt	• Creates sadness • Generates a need to restore a positive self-image

instill confidence, and promote mood maintenance strategies. Sadness, failure, embarrassment, and guilt create needs for mood improvement and self-image restoration.

III. Helping in an Emergency

At 3:20 AM on March 13, 1964, a 28-year-old bar manager, Catherine (Kitty) Genovese, parked her car on a tree-lined street in a residential section of Queens, New York. While she was walking to her nearby apartment, a man came out of the shadows and grabbed her. Genovese screamed, "Oh my God, he stabbed me!" and lights turned on in an adjacent apartment building. When a man opened a window and shouted, "Let that girl alone," the attacker shrugged his shoulders and walked away. As Genovese lay sobbing in the street, the lights flickered off. A few minutes later, the assailant returned, stabbing her repeatedly. Genovese cried out, "I'm dying! I'm dying!" and again lights flickered on and the assailant left. Finally, bleeding badly, Genovese staggered to her feet and attempted to enter her apartment building. Seeing she was still alive, the attacker returned, sexually assaulted her, and then stabbed her again. By the time the police were called at 3:50, Genovese was dead, a victim of a random act of violence by a complete stranger.

In the aftermath of this incident, 38 people admitted they had heard Kitty Genovese's screams or had witnessed part of the attack, which lasted more than 30 minutes. Many also reported being aware that many of their neighbors were at their windows watching. Yet aside from a man who yelled at the assailant, no one intervened. Why? At the time this incident occurred, the dominant explanation centered on apathy and alienation: People in large cities had become hardened to the fate of their fellow citizens. They didn't care anymore whether their neighbors lived or died.

Two New York social psychologists, John Darley and Bibb Latané, wondered whether certain social psychological processes might also have played a role. They reasoned that so many people may have failed to help precisely because so many people witnessed the attack. They used the term **bystander effect** to refer to the possibility that the presence of other people inhibits helping.

A. Decision–Making Model of Emergency Intervention

Building on the idea of the bystander effect, Darley and Latané went on to propose a formal model of emergency intervention (Darley & Latané, 1968; Latané & Darley, 1970; see also Dovidio, Piliavin, Gaertner, Schroeder, & Clark, 1991). Figure 12.7

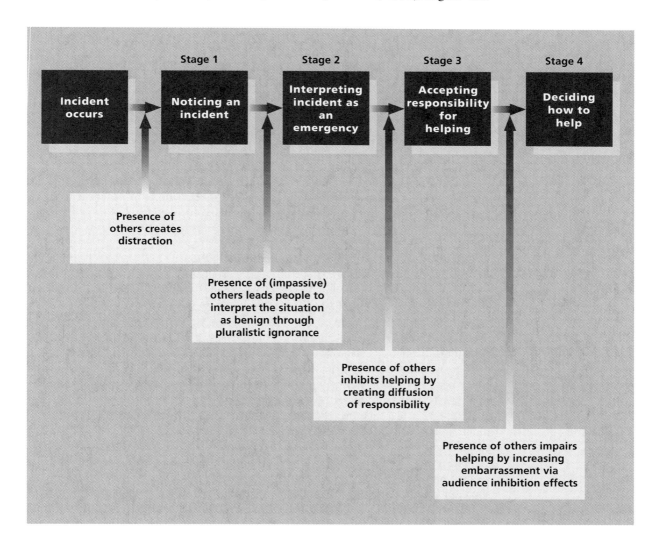

FIGURE 12.7

Decision-Making Model of Emergency Intervention

The model shows that bystanders must make several decisions before they will provide aid to a victim. At each stage, the presence of others makes it less likely that people will decide to help.

shows that the model involves four decision-making stages and that, at each stage, the presence of other people can interfere with the likelihood that helping will occur.

1. Stage 1: Noticing a Potential Emergency

Noticing that something has happened is the first step in the decision-making model of emergency intervention. Anything that distracts us or diverts our attention can block this step. For example, people may be busy or preoccupied and fail to notice that an emergency has occurred (Darley & Batson, 1973; K. E. Mathews & Canon, 1975). The presence of other people may also create a distraction. In large cities full of noise and crowds, people may overlook a potential emergency because they are experiencing stimulus overload (Milgram, 1970). In order to cope with the hustle and bustle of the city, they tune out other people and keep to themselves. This may explain why people in densely populated urban areas are generally less helpful than those in less populated rural areas (Amato, 1983; Steblay, 1987).

2. Stage 2: Deciding It Is an Emergency

Once people notice that an event has occurred, they must decide whether it is an emergency that requires some form of intervention. The less ambiguous the situation is, the more likely people are to construe it as an emergency. For example, screams and cries for help are particularly apt to promote helping, because these cues clearly indicate that an emergency has taken place (Clark & Word, 1972).

How does the presence of other people influence this stage of the decision-making model? When a situation is ambiguous, we use the reactions of others to help us decide what is happening. If everyone else appears unconcerned, we will probably conclude that nothing is amiss. If, in contrast, other people appear alarmed, we will probably decide that an emergency is taking place.

This effect was demonstrated in an experiment by Latané and Darley (1968). Male students were invited to participate in a discussion of campus life at a large urban university. As they were completing a questionnaire, smoke began to fill the room. The situation was somewhat ambiguous, because the smoke was odorless and did not clearly indicate the presence of a fire. Latané and Darley created three experimental conditions to see whether social factors influenced participants' interpretations of this ambiguous situation. The participants were either alone, with two other participants, or with two confederates of the experimenter who had been coached to remain calm and to act as if nothing were wrong. This condition was designed to determine whether participants would fail to act if other people appeared unconcerned.

Figure 12.8 presents the percentage of participants in each condition who left the room in order to tell the experimenter something was wrong. As predicted, 75 percent of the participants who were alone left the room to get the experimenter, but only 10 percent of those who waited with the unconcerned confederates did so. Presumably, seeing that other people in the situation were calm led these participants to decide the situation wasn't serious and didn't require any action.

Figure 12.8 shows one more effect of interest. Only 38 percent of the participants who waited with two other participants left to get help. **Pluralistic ignorance** provides one explanation for this behavior. Pluralistic ignorance occurs when people misread one another's behavior and assume that their thoughts and feelings are unique. Many students have experienced this effect in a large lecture hall. After listening to the professor, they are confused or have questions that require clarification. However, they are reluctant to raise their hand because they are embarrassed to admit they are

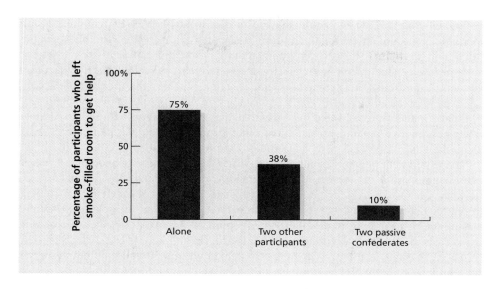

FIGURE 12.8

Behavior in an Ambiguous Situation as a Function of Bystander Reactions

As participants were filling out a questionnaire, an odorless smoke began to fill the room. Participants were more likely to leave the room to alert the experimenter when they were alone than when they were with others. Presumably, this occurred because participants relied on the behavior of others to decide whether or not the situation was an emergency.

Source: Latané and Darley (1968).

perplexed, so they wait to see whether anyone else asks a question. Unfortunately, other students are doing the same thing, so everyone concludes that he or she is the only one who is confused and no one asks for clarification.

Pluralistic ignorance may have influenced the behavior of the participants in Latané and Darley's (1968) study. Very likely, all of the participants were confused when smoke began to fill the room. Before registering their concern, they looked around to see whether anyone else was alarmed. Nobody wanted to be the first to look concerned, so everyone stayed calm and looked unperturbed. This led most participants to conclude that their concerns were unfounded and that nothing was amiss. Consequently, they failed to take action.

3. Stage 3: Accepting Responsibility

Noticing an incident and recognizing that it is an emergency do not guarantee that helping will occur. People must also accept responsibility for helping by deciding it is up to them to do something. Here again, the presence of other people poses a barrier to helping. When people know others are around, they may decide that they don't have to help because other people will help or have already done so. This **diffusion-of-responsibility effect** may have influenced Kitty Genovese's neighbors. As they looked out their windows, they saw many of their neighbors doing the same thing. They may have then decided that they didn't need to intervene directly or call the police, because other people would do so.

Darley and Latané (1968) conducted an experiment to test the diffusion-of-responsibility hypothesis. Participants arrived at a laboratory and were escorted into individual rooms. Each was told that he or she would be taking part in a group discussion concerning personal problems associated with college life, and that the discussion would take place over an intercom to avoid the embarrassment that can arise in face-to-face interactions. Finally, the participants were told that the intercom system allowed only one person to speak at a time and that the experimenter could not hear what was being said. The size of the group was experimentally manipulated. The participants were told that they were having a conversation with either just one other person, two other people, or five other people. In fact, the participants were alone the entire time and the conversations were prerecorded.

The experiment began uneventfully, as participants heard the prerecorded voice of one (or more) students presenting their personal problems. Suddenly, one of the participants became distressed. Growing increasingly loud and incoherent, the student began to stammer and cry out for help, complaining that he was having a seizure and was afraid he was going to die. Panel A in Figure 12.9 shows the percentage of participants who left the interview room to help the victim. As you can see, 85 percent of the participants in the two-person group helped when they believed they were the only ones who knew the seizure was taking place. In contrast, only 62 percent of the participants helped when they thought one other person was available to help (three-person group), and only 31 percent helped when they believed four other people were available to help (six-person group). In short, as the number of perceived bystanders increased, the likelihood that any given person would help decreased.

Panel B in Figure 12.9 shows how much time elapsed before participants provided help. It is also apparent that help was provided more slowly when participants thought other people were available to help. When participants believed many others were available to help, they hesitated before acting, waiting nearly three minutes to see whether someone else would take charge. In contrast, they reacted rather quickly (within the first minute) when they thought they were the only one available to help, and within the first two minutes when they thought only one other person was available to help.

Finally, panel C shows the probability that the victim would have received help from at least one person. Clearly, these values don't vary much across conditions. Thus, although it is the case that any given person is less likely to help when others are around, the likelihood that at least one person will take action is constant. This means that a victim is just as apt to receive help when many bystanders are present as when very few are present. Keep in mind, however, that help will be provided less quickly when many bystanders are present. Since time is often of the essence in an emergency situation, delays can have serious consequences.

Not everyone is affected equally by diffusion of responsibility in an emergency. For example, in a group situation, a leader is more apt to take action than are subordinate group members (Baumeister, Chesner, Sanders, & Tice, 1988). People who are trained to help in emergency situations, such as firefighters or nurses, are also less apt to hesitate before helping (Cramer, McMaster, Bartell, & Dragma, 1988; Shotland & Heinold, 1985). Finally, the diffusion-of-responsibility effect is less apt to occur when an emergency situation is unambiguous and people are identifiable rather than anonymous. Consequently, if you ever find yourself needing help, it's a good idea to make it very clear that help is needed and to single individuals out, either by calling their name or by looking them directly in the eye (Clark & Word, 1972; Shotland & Stebbins, 1980).

4. Stage 4: Deciding How to Help

Deciding how to help is the final step in Darley and Latané's model. Here, we have two choices: to help directly or to help indirectly by alerting someone else that help

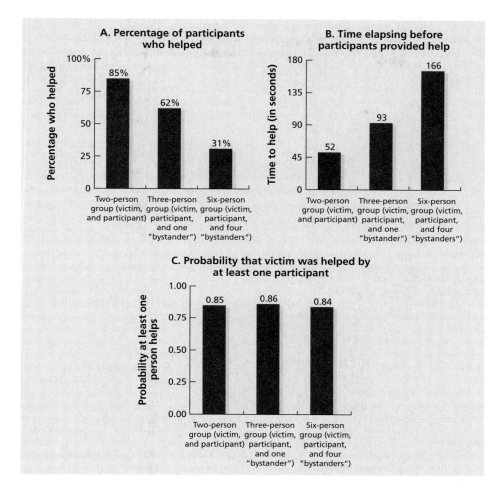

A. Percentage of participants who helped

Percentage who helped

- Two-person group (victim, and participant): 85%
- Three-person group (victim, participant, and one "bystander"): 62%
- Six-person group (victim, participant, and four "bystanders"): 31%

B. Time elapsing before participants provided help

Time to help (in seconds)

- Two-person group (victim, and participant): 52
- Three-person group (victim, participant, and one "bystander"): 93
- Six-person group (victim, participant, and four "bystanders"): 166

C. Probability that victim was helped by at least one participant

Probability at least one person helps

- Two-person group (victim, and participant): 0.85
- Three-person group (victim, participant, and one "bystander"): 0.86
- Six-person group (victim, participant, and four "bystanders"): 0.84

FIGURE 12.9

Helping and Group Size

Panel A shows that any given individual is more apt to help when a group is small than when a group is large. Panel B shows that helping occurs more quickly in small groups than in large ones. Panel C shows that the likelihood of receiving help is not influenced by group size.

Source: Darley and Latané (1968).

is needed. The presence of others can affect our decision here as well. If people aren't sure how to provide help, they may be reluctant to help when others are around for fear of being embarrassed or viewed as being incompetent. Given the current legal climate, people may also be afraid of being sued if they make a mistake when they come to another person's aid. For this reason, many states have enacted Good Samaritan laws that protect those who offer help in an emergency. Here's an excerpt from a California law:

> In order to encourage people to participate in emergency medical services training programs and to render emergency medical services to others, no person who in good faith renders emergency care at the scene of an emergency shall be liable for any act or omission.
>
> *Section 1767, Article 4, Chapter 130, California Health and Safety Code*

B. Summary of Helping in Emergencies

Darley and Latané's decision-making model of emergency intervention stimulated a good deal of research and received a good deal of empirical support. The research also exemplified the social psychological approach to understanding behavior. Drawing inspiration from a dramatic, real-world incident, Darley and Latané systematically showed that helping is influenced by subtle situational factors such as group size and the reactions of other people. Does this mean these factors explain the behavior of the 38 New Yorkers who stood by the night Kitty Genovese was brutally murdered? Not necessarily. Other factors, such as fear or an unwillingness to get involved may have also played a role. More generally, there is simply no way to know why people behaved the way they did that night. Darley and Latané's research shows only that group size could have played a role.

It is also important to note that apathy is not always observed in emergency situations. One need only think of the heroic efforts of countless citizens in the wake of the September 11, 2001, terrorist attacks to appreciate the extent to which people are willing to get involved when their help is needed. These heroes included not only officials charged with preserving public safety—such as police, firefighters, and medical personnel—but also ordinary citizens who found themselves caught up in extraordinary circumstances. For example, many occupants of the World Trade Center helped others to escape, thereby delaying their own escape and imperiling their own lives. More dramatically, passengers aboard United Airlines Flight 93 rushed the cockpit, causing the plane to crash in the Pennsylvania countryside. Clearly, people are capable of rising to the occasion when their help is needed, even in situations involving danger, uncertainty, and confusion.

IV. Volunteerism

Since the 1980s, government services for the needy have been cut, and the private sector has been called on to shoulder more of the responsibility for taking care of the sick, elderly, and poor. This shift in responsibility has been accompanied by specific initiatives and programs aimed at increasing volunteerism. For example, President George H. W. Bush signed the National and Community Service Act of 1990, incorporating the Points of Light Foundation and the Commission on National and Community Service, and President Bill Clinton signed the National and Community Service Trust Act, providing funding for AmeriCorps and Learn and Serve America. Recently, efforts to motivate individuals to volunteer have become global in scope. The United Nations General Assembly declared 2001 the International Year of Volunteers and passed a resolution to "promote the contribution that volunteerism can make to the creation of caring societies" (annex III, article 54, p. 24).

In the United States, this call for **volunteerism** has been answered. In 2001, 83.9 million Americans volunteered at least some amount of time and services, in total representing the equivalent of more than 9 million full-time employees at a value of $239 billion (www.independentsector.org). This section examines the types of people who are most apt to volunteer and the various factors that promote volunteerism.

A. Who Helps?

1. Demographic Variables

Although many people volunteer for community service, some types of people are more apt to volunteer than others are. In the United States, people who are well educated, religious, and of high socioeconomic status are more helpful than are people who lack these qualities (U.S. Bureau of Labor Statistics, www.bls.gov.cps). Volunteers are also more apt to be of middle age (between 35 and 54 years of age), to be married, and to have children under the age of 18.

2. Personality Variables

Personality variables also influence helping and volunteerism. Not surprisingly, helpful people tend to be empathic and sympathetic, to believe they are responsible for the welfare of others, and to believe they are capable of making a difference (Aquino & Reed, 2002; Carlo, Eisenberg, Troyer, Switzer, & Speer, 1991; Eisenberg et al., 2002; Penner & Finkelstein, 1998; Staub, 1974). Interestingly, these qualities appear to be partly heritable, as identical twins have been found to share many of these personality traits (M. H. Davis, Luce, & Kraus, 1994; Rushton, Fulker, Neale, Nias, & Eysenck, 1986; Zahn-Waxler, Robinson, & Emde, 1992).

3. Motives for Helping

In 1942, at just 12 years of age, Samuel Oliner was herded along with his family into a ghetto for Jews in Poland. When his family was later sent to a death camp, Samuel escaped with the aid of a Christian woman he barely knew. After the war, Oliner settled in America and became a sociology professor. Eventually, he and his wife (also a Holocaust survivor) set about to study the qualities that distinguished rescuers from nonrescuers (Oliner & Oliner, 1988). On the basis of interviews with more than 400 rescuers (and a matched sample of 126 nonrescuers), the Oliners identified three motives that led people to help in this situation.

First, more than one-half of the rescuers (52 percent) helped because they felt a strong sense of social responsibility. When asked why they had helped, these rescuers emphasized the importance of duty to their church or a desire to live up to the expectations of others. Another 11 percent helped because of moral outrage. These individuals viewed the Germans as depraved and thought no human being should suffer the treatment they were inflicting on the Jews. Finally, 37 percent helped out of empathic concern. These individuals felt sorry for those being victimized, and their compassion compelled them to help despite the obvious costs and risks.

Omoto and Snyder (1995) found a similar pattern of results in a study of AIDS volunteers. On the basis of extensive interviews, these investigators identified five motives that lead people to volunteer. As shown in Table 12.4, some people help for relatively altruistic reasons (e.g., community concern), whereas others volunteer for relatively egoistic concerns (e.g., personal growth, self-enhancement). Interestingly, those whose motives were egoistic were more apt to continue helping over a two-year period than were those who volunteered for more altruistic reasons. Omoto and Snyder speculated that being an AIDS volunteer requires strength and personal sacrifice, and people who volunteer for altruistic reasons are more apt to become disillusioned than those who volunteer for more egoistic reasons.

4. Gender Differences in Helping Behavior

When asking the question "Who helps?" it is important to keep in mind that helping can occur in a variety of ways and that a person who helps in one situation may not be helpful in another. For example, a person who brings meals to the elderly may not donate blood. Similarly, a person who rushes to give a stricken citizen cardiopulmonary resuscitation (CPR) may not give change to a homeless person.

TABLE 12.4   Motivations to Volunteer to Help People with AIDS

COMMUNITY CONCERN
- To help members of the gay community
- Because of my concern and worry about the gay community

VALUES
- Because of my humanitarian obligation to help others
- Because I consider myself a loving and caring person

GAIN UNDERSTANDING
- To learn more about how to prevent AIDS
- To learn about how people cope with AIDS

PERSONAL DEVELOPMENT
- To meet new people and make new friends
- To challenge myself and test my skills

SELF-ENHANCEMENT
- To feel better about myself
- To feel less lonely

Source: Omoto and Snyder (1995).

Research on gender differences in helping underscores this point. Men and women tend to be equally helpful, but they help in different ways (Eagly & Crowley, 1986). Men help more than women in situations involving danger and the risk of personal injury (e.g., rushing into a burning building to rescue a child), whereas women help more than men in situations involving the provision of care (e.g., bringing soup to a homebound elderly person). These differences undoubtedly reflect the power of socialization. Men are generally raised to be courageous and chivalrous, whereas women are brought up to be caring and nurturant. Given these differences, it is not surprising that men help more when danger is a factor and that women help more when it is not.

5. Cultural Differences in Helping Behavior

Cultural differences in helping behavior provide further evidence that people can be socialized to be helpful. At various points throughout this text, we have noted that cultures vary along an important dimension of individualism–collectivism. Helpfulness is among the behaviors influenced by this distinction. Whereas people in individualistic cultures are taught to look out for themselves, people in collectivistic cultures are taught to be more concerned with their neighbors and fellow citizens.

An investigation by J. G. Miller and colleagues shows the influence of these differences (J. G. Miller, Bersoff, & Harwood, 1990). These investigators asked Americans and Indian Hindus to read a story about a person who failed to help someone. Afterward, the participants indicated whether they thought the person was obligated to help. Two factors were varied: First, either the recipient's need was extreme (a need for mouth-to-mouth resuscitation), moderate (a need for psychological support before surgery) or minor (directions to a store). Second, the nature of the relationship between the person needing help and the person who failed to provide it was varied. Either parents refused to help their children, an adult refused to help a friend, or an adult refused to help a stranger.

Before presenting the results of this investigation, let's take a moment to consider the predictions. India is a collectivistic culture and people feel obligated to help others. In contrast, America is an individualistic culture and people feel less of an obligation to help. How might these differences affect helping? When the need is great or the relationship close and dependent (e.g., parent–child), these differences should be slight because the situation is strong and calls for helping. In contrast, when the need is minor and the people are strangers, cultural differences should be substantial, because helping in these situations is more or less discretionary.

Figure 12.10 shows just such a pattern. Cultural differences were slight when the need was extreme or the relationship was close, but they were rather substantial when

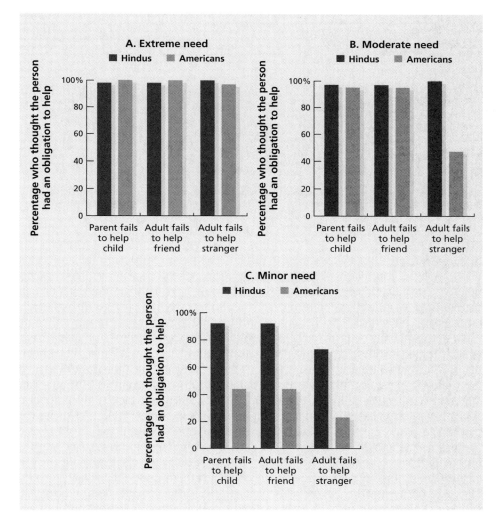

FIGURE 12.10

Percentage of Participants Saying the Person Had an Obligation to Help

When asked how obligated people are to help in various situations, Indian Hindus replied that people have an obligation to help even in situations of low need from a stranger. In contrast, Americans saw little need to help someone who had a minor need, or a stranger who had a moderate need.

Source: J. G. Miller, Bersoff, and Harwood (1990).

TABLE 12.5 Percentage of People Who Stopped to Help a Stranger in Various Cities around the World

City, Country	Percentage Who Helped
Rio de Janeiro, Brazil	93
San Jose, Costa Rica	91
Lilongwe, Malawi	86
Calcutta, India	83
Vienna, Austria	81
Madrid, Spain	79
Copenhagen, Denmark	78
Shanghai, China	77
Mexico City, Mexico	76
San Salvador, El Salvador	75
Prague, Czech Republic	75
Stockholm, Sweden	72
Budapest, Hungary	71
Bucharest, Romania	69
Tel Aviv, Israel	68
Rome, Italy	63
Bangkok, Thailand	61
Taipei, Taiwan	59
Sofia, Bulgaria	57
Amsterdam, Netherlands	54
Singapore, Singapore	48
New York, United States	45
Kuala Lampur, Malaysia	40

Note: Underlined entries represent countries with a tradition of *simpatia* (in Spanish) or *simpatico* (in Portuguese). People in these countries were especially helpful.

Source: R. V. Levine, Norenzayan, and Philbrick (2001).

the need was minor or the relationship distant. This occurred because Indian Hindus felt an obligation to help in all situations, whereas Americans felt very little obligation to help when the need was not severe. These findings highlight that even though the norm of social responsibility operates in all cultures, it is stronger in some cultures than in others (see also J. Baron & Miller, 2002).

Of course, feeling obligated to help doesn't mean that people always act on the basis of their responsibilities. To see whether obligations to help translate into actual helping, Levine and colleagues staged several "helping incidents" in various cities around the world (R. V. Levine, Norenzayan, & Philbrick, 2001). For example, a person with a hurt leg accidentally dropped some packages and needed help picking them up, or a person who was apparently blind needed help crossing the street. Table 12.5 shows the percentage of people who offered help in various cities around the world. Three findings are of interest. First, New York City wound up near the bottom of the list, indicating that people there were not very helpful. Second, on average, collectivistic countries (e.g., Taiwan, Singapore) were no more helpful than were individualistic ones (e.g., Austria, Denmark). Levine and colleagues reasoned that this occurred because people in collectivistic cultures are socialized to help ingroup members, but they are not necessarily expected to help strangers (see also L'Armand, & Pepitone, 1975). Third, Spanish and Latin American countries did help more than other countries. These countries have a tradition of *simpatia* (in Spanish) or *simpatico* (in Portuguese), which teaches concern for others and carries with it an implicit obligation to be friendly, polite, and helpful toward strangers. The underlined values in Table 12.5 show that such countries were, in fact, generally more helpful (Mean = 83 percent) than were countries that do not have this tradition (Mean = 66 percent) (see also Feldman, 1968).

B. Learning to Help

Cultural values are transmitted through a socialization process in which people learn to be helpful. Even within cultures, learning influences who is helpful and who is not (Eisenberg, Fabes, Schaller, Carlo, & Miller, 1991; Grusec, 1982).

1. Rewards and Punishments

Children who receive social praise for helping ("I'm proud of you for sharing with your friend") are more apt to help in the future than are those who are not rewarded (Rushton & Teachman, 1978). Material rewards such as money, special privileges, or candy are generally less effective in encouraging children to help, particularly if these rewards are excessive. As discussed in Chapter 5, people who receive a large payment for performing some action often attribute their behavior to the inducement rather than to any enduring disposition. Consequently, children who receive large rewards for helping are unlikely to view themselves as being "a helpful person," and this undermines their helpfulness.

Punishing a child for refusing to help can also promote helping, but the effects here are modest. Instead of punishing children when they fail to help, it is generally better to ask them to consider how they would feel if no one helped them or to focus on how bad the victim feels. This latter strategy is called moral induction. By alerting children to the negative consequences of their behavior, parents can help their children develop a more caring attitude toward those less fortunate than themselves (see also Batson et al., 2003).

2. Social Learning

In addition to rewards, social factors also contribute to the development of helpfulness. Parents who spend a lot of time with their children and encourage them to be emotionally expressive tend to raise children who care about others and are helpful (Eisenberg, 1992; Koestner, Franz, & Weinberger, 1990). Children also learn to be helpful by observing helpful models (Rushton, 1982). Parents are particularly important role models: Helpful, caring parents tend to raise helpful, caring children. Rosenhan (1970) studied people who participated in the civil rights movement during the 1950s and 1960s. Rosenhan found that "freedom riders" had parents who preached the importance of compassion and demonstrated their own concern by helping others. Similarly, Piliavin and Callero (1991) found that blood donors often know a family member or close friend who has given blood and has served as a positive model.

Parents are not the only role models children observe. Teachers, athletic coaches, and other adults also influence helping by serving as helpful models (Rushton, 1975; Sarason, Sarason, Pierce, Shearin, & Sayers, 1991). Even media figures are influential. On November 7, 1991, basketball star Earvin "Magic" Johnson Jr., announced that he

FIGURE 12.11

Percentage of Participants Who Agreed to Volunteer to Help an AIDS Victim before and after Magic Johnson's Disclosure That He Was HIV-Positive

Females were unaffected by Magic's announcement that he was HIV-positive, but volunteerism among males increased dramatically after his announcement and remained high four and half months later.

Source: Penner and Fritzshce (1993).

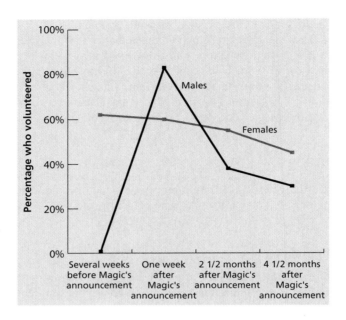

had tested positive for HIV. The announcement stunned the nation, as AIDS and HIV were relatively unknown at the time, and Johnson was one of the nation's most beloved superstars. Johnson made the announcement with uncommon courage, dignity, and maturity, choosing to emphasize the good he could do with his celebrity status rather than his own personal tragedy: "It's God's way. He is now directing me to become a teacher, to carry the message about AIDS to everyone. . . . I think I can spread the message about AIDS better than almost anyone. I'm a super-strong person, physically and emotionally (1991, p. 25)."

More than 13 years after making his announcement, Magic Johnson continues to be an advocate for AIDS awareness and prevention. His story has inspired millions, but has it served to recruit people to volunteer to help people with AIDS? Research by Penner and Fritzshce (1993) provides some answers. Just weeks before Johnson made his disclosure, these investigators had conducted a study in which they asked college students how willing they were to help an HIV-positive person. Taking advantage of a natural event, the investigators then repeated their study at three more time intervals: one week after Johnson's disclosure, two and a half months after his disclosure, and four and a half months after his disclosure. Figure 12.11 presents some of the data from this study. Two effects are apparent. First, Johnson's announcement had little effect on the volunteerism of female participants. Among males, however, there was a dramatic increase in volunteerism one week after Johnson's announcement. Although the rates of volunteerism declined in the months ahead, they remained far above the level found during the initial assessment period. These findings show that a positive role model can increase volunteerism rates.

Former president Jimmy Carter and his wife, Rosalynn, provide further evidence that role models can increase volunteerism. Every year since 1984, the Carters have helped to build homes in poverty-stricken areas as members of an organization called Habitat for Humanity (www.habitat.org). The public's response to this well-publicized effort has been dramatic: Many people who had never volunteered before have followed the Carters' lead.

C. Service Learning: "Required" Volunteerism

Many high schools, colleges, and universities now require students to do volunteer work or other forms of community service before graduation. Clearly, these programs benefit the community, but what effect do they have on the volunteers? For example, are people who are required to help more or less likely to help in the future? Unfortunately, the answer to this question is not yet known, because the programs have not been in place long enough to provide enough data on the matter. We can, however, make some informed guesses on the basis of the things we have learned throughout this chapter (Piliavin, 2003; Steinke, Fitch, Johnson, & Waldstein, 2002).

First, let's consider the potential benefits to the individual. People who volunteer are apt (1) to gain a newfound perspective for the plights of others, and (2) to develop a sense of community and compassion with those who are worse off than themselves. In turn, these insights should foster empathy and sympathy. Second, many volunteers will experience joy in helping and heightened feelings of self-worth and competence. These emotions should also foster further helping. Finally, volunteers should experience changes in their self-concept. Thinking of oneself as the type of person who volunteers contributes to further helping (Penner, 2002).

Of course, requiring people to help does pose some problems. People who are forced to volunteer may come to resent their involvement or attribute their helpfulness to external factors rather than a true desire to help. Several steps can be taken to avoid these problems (Stukas, Snyder, & Clary, 1999; Werner & McVaugh, 2000). First, people should be given a choice of service options. By choosing which volunteer effort to pursue, people will experience a sense of freedom and efficacy. Second, it would be wise to match the type of helping activity with the motives and personality of the volunteer (Clary et al., 1998). For example, people who are highly emotional and easily distressed should not be required to work in a hospital setting, and people who require excitement and stimulation should not be required to stuff envelopes for a charitable organization. Finally, efforts should be taken to ensure that the interactions are pleasant and that helping is identifiable and publicly acknowledged. Working in a cold organizational setting with the sense that nobody knows or appreciates one's efforts will undermine one's desire to help in the future.

D. The Volunteer Experience

Many of the themes discussed in the preceding paragraphs are touched on by volunteers who reflect on their experience. In conjunction with *Parade* magazine, State Farm Insurance sponsors the National Youth Service Day, in which millions of young people participate in a variety of community service projects (www.ysa.org/nysd). Here's how two volunteers recently described their experience:

> I began volunteering really as a way to help myself—people told me that whenever you reach out to someone, it helps you feel better. Helping others is an integral part of who I am now. (Jason Crowe, *Parade,* March 30, 2003, p. 18)

> Find something you like to do and think of ways it can help someone else. If you like to read, do it in a day-care center. It's also good to volunteer with friends and people you know—it will be more fun than you think. Volunteering has made me a much better person. I've learned not to judge people so quickly. And not to take things for granted. (Jeremy Drummond, *Parade,* March 30, 2003, p. 18)

When reading these testimonials, you may have noticed that they emphasize the joy and sense of personal fulfillment that arise from being a volunteer. More formally, they underscore that egoistic concerns are often of paramount importance in helping situations. Perhaps this is as it should be. Helping brings people many personal rewards, and it is doubtful whether so many people would help if this weren't the case. Thus, although we might prefer that people act without regard for self-benefit, our capacity to feel joy when helping another person may be the single most important motive for helping. Without it, there would be a lot less helping and a lot more people in need.

CHAPTER SUMMARY

- Helping is a prosocial behavior intended to alleviate another person's distress. Helping can involve everyday acts of kindness; extraordinary acts of bravery; or sustained, committed volunteerism.

- According to the philosophical doctrine of egoism, people always act out of self-interest. According to the doctrine of altruism, people sometimes help others without regard to whether they will derive any sort of personal benefit.

- Decisions to help can be understood as a cost/benefit analysis. The benefits of helping include material and social rewards, a greater likelihood of receiving help in the future, and feelings of pride and happiness. The costs of helping include expenditure of time and money, pain and inconvenience, and potential embarrassment.

- Before deciding whether to help, people consider why help is needed. Help is more apt to be provided to people who are not responsible for their plight.

- Evolutionary models of helping argue that natural selection favored helpfulness as a basic human trait, because it increased a person's inclusive fitness through kin selection, their personal survival through reciprocal "altruism," or because groups with many helpful members were more apt to survive and helpfulness was rewarded with reproductive opportunities. Although it is not possible to test these assumptions directly, research suggests that humans may be able to detect genetic similarity and are more apt to help those who are genetically similar to them, especially when the costs and benefits of helping are high.

- Emotional responses to a person in need often take two forms. Feelings of personal distress are an egoistic emotional reaction, characterized by feelings of alarm, discomfort, and uneasiness. Sympathy is an other-oriented emotional reaction, characterized by feelings of concern, compassion, and tenderness. Feelings of personal distress arise early in life, whereas feelings of sympathy develop more slowly.

- Empathy is a cognitive capacity to take the perspective of another person. According to Batson's empathy–altruism hypothesis, when empathy is low, feelings of personal distress dominate and helping is motivated by an egoistic concern to reduce one's own distress. In contrast, when empathy is high, sympathy dominates and helping is motivated by an altruistic desire to reduce the victim's distress.

- People are most apt to help those who are similar to them, attractive, and a friend or family member.

- Happiness promotes helping by triggering positive cognitions, increasing social concern, and instigating a desire to maintain pleasant feelings. Sadness promotes helping as a means of repairing a negative mood.

- Following the tragic murder of Kitty Genovese, Darley and Latané developed a model of bystander intervention in an emergency helping situation. The model proposes that bystanders make several decisions when deciding whether to help during an emergency and that, at each stage, the presence of other people inhibits the likelihood that help will be offered. Among other things, this occurs because of pluralistic ignorance and diffusion of responsibility.

- Millions of Americans volunteer for community service. In general, volunteers tend to be well educated, religious, high in socioeconomic status, and married with young children.

- People can learn to help, as result of early childhood experiences, the provision of rewards and punishments, and the presence of helpful models.

- Many schools now require some form of volunteerism as a requirement of graduation. These programs are apt to produce positive benefits if people are allowed to choose which project they pursue, and helping is identifiable and publicly acknowledged.

KEY TERMS

helping, 444

egoism, 445

altruism, 445

kin selection, 448

reciprocal "altruism," 448

group selection, 448

personal distress, 451

sympathy, 451

empathy, 452

bystander effect, 459

pluralistic ignorance, 460

diffusion-of-responsibility effect, 461

volunteerism, 464

ADDITIONAL READING

Go to the Student Edition of the Online Learning Center for this text (www.mhhe.com/brown) and log in to read the following journal articles, which relate to the content of this chapter:

- Darley, J. M., & Latané, B. (1968). Bystander intervention in emergencies: Diffusion of responsibility.

- Omoto, A. M., & Snyder, M. (1995). Sustained helping without obligation: Motivation, longevity of service, and perceived attitude change among AIDS volunteers.

CHAPTER THIRTEEN

Aggression

TABLE 13.1   Crimes in America

- One murder every 32 minutes.
- One violent crime every 6 seconds.
- One robbery every 55 seconds.
- One assault every 7 seconds.
- One rape/sexual assault every 2 minutes.
- 56 women are victimized by an intimate every hour.
- A teenager is victimized every 19 seconds.
- A child is abused and/or neglected in America every 35 seconds.
- Every 19 seconds a violent crime is committed against a person at work or on duty.
- 3 people become victims of stalking every minute.

Source: National Center for Victims of Crime, www.ncvc.org/ncvc/AGP.Net/Components/documentViewer/Download.
aspxnz?DocumentID=33522.

In the time it takes you to read this chapter, dozens of Americans will be assaulted, raped, or murdered, and numerous children will be abused or neglected (see Table 13.1). As alarming as these statistics are, they represent only a fraction of the aggressive and violent acts that occur throughout the world every day. Terrorism, political oppression, and wars plague international relations, and hate crimes, gang violence, and school-related shootings attest to the immediacy of violence at home. Although violent crimes in America are currently declining (www.ojp.usdoj.gov/bjs/homicide/hmrt.htm), aggression continues to be an all-too-common feature of human interaction.

This chapter examines social psychological approaches to aggression. Social psychologists define **aggression** as behavior intended to physically or psychologically harm another person. Table 13.2 shows that aggression can be physical or verbal, and can be directed at a person's body, property, or reputation. Though they differ in kind and severity, all of these types of aggression have in common an intention to harm another person.

The first part of this chapter is devoted to understanding the origins of aggression. Here, we examine whether people are innately aggressive or whether aggression is entirely learned. The second section of this chapter deals with the dynamics of an aggressive episode. Here we look at personality variables and situational factors that influence whether people become angry when they are provoked and whether they aggress when they are angry. Section three considers the link between media-violence

TABLE 13.2 Types of Aggression		
		FORM OF AGGRESSION
Type of Aggression	Direct	Indirect
Physical	Assault, bullying	Vandalism, destruction of property
Verbal	Insult, teasing	Harming a person's reputation by spreading malicious rumors or gossiping

and aggression. There is currently much debate as to whether violent movies, television shows, video games, and song lyrics contribute to the violence in American society, and the third section of this chapter examines the evidence regarding this issue. We will then explore aggression among intimates, with a particular focus on school violence and sexual abuse. Finally, we will consider programs designed to curb aggression.

Before we begin our survey of aggression, we need to define some terms. First, we need to distinguish two forms of aggression: hostile aggression and instrumental aggression (Feshbach, 1964). **Hostile aggression** is fueled by anger and is usually a reaction to some form of provocation. Crimes of passion and retaliatory rage epitomize this form of impulsive aggression. The ultimate aim of a hostile aggressor is to inflict injury on another person, with little concern for any personal cost or benefit.

Instrumental aggression occurs when people aggress to attain a desired goal. Competitive athletics provides a convenient framework for thinking about this form of aggression. For example, hockey players routinely check one another into the boards, as a means of stealing the puck or preventing their opponent from scoring a goal. This act of aggression may or may not be accompanied by anger, but it is primarily undertaken as a means to an end: The object is to win the game, and harming one's opponent is instrumental to attaining that objective.

Not all acts of aggression can easily be classified as hostile or instrumental (Bushman & Anderson, 2001a). For example, why did boxer Mike Tyson bite the ear of his opponent, Evander Holyfield, during their heavyweight boxing fight in 1997? Did Tyson simply lose his composure and act impulsively, or did he deliberately try to stop a fight he was most certainly going to lose? There's simply no way to know. Despite this uncertainty, the distinction between hostile and instrumental aggression remains important. For one thing, the legal system views crimes committed in the heat of passion differently from calculated, cold-blooded ones. Moreover, people prone to commit acts of hostile aggression are not necessarily prone to commit acts of instrumental aggression (Dodge & Coie, 1987). Finally, the physiological correlates of the two types of aggression differ: Intense physiological arousal is more often a feature of hostile aggression than of instrumental aggression (Hubbard et al., 2002).

Finally, it is important to distinguish aggression from violence. The difference is one of severity, with violence representing a severe form of aggression (C. A. Anderson & Bushman, 2002). Bosses who berate or intimidate their employees are being aggressive; spouses who physically abuse their partner are being violent. Another way of looking at these terms is to note that all acts of violence are aggressive, but not all acts of aggression are violent.

I. The Origins of Aggression

Observers of human nature have long debated the origins of aggression. Some have argued that aggression is part of human nature and that society functions to regulate and channel our instinctive, aggressive impulses. Others have argued that people are inherently good and act aggressively only because of restrictive social forces. Still others maintain that people are neither good nor bad and that experience and learning entirely determine whether people act aggressively or peacefully.

Building on these themes, psychologists have developed their own theories of aggression. At present, there is now agreement that people possess an innate capacity to behave aggressively but that social factors and learning greatly influence when, how, and even whether aggression is expressed. In this section, we will review theory and research that support this conclusion.

A. Freud's Instinct Theory of Aggression

We will begin by considering the views of Sigmund Freud, who maintained that aggression is innate—present at birth and influential throughout life. Freud came to this conclusion relatively late in his career. After surveying the carnage and destruction that occurred during World War I, he concluded that people are compelled to aggress by an instinctive, unconscious desire to end their own lives and return to an inanimate state (Freud, 1932/1963). Freud called this death instinct *Thanatos* and assumed it was opposed by a life-sustaining drive, called *Eros*. Eros redirects Thanatos, such that people aggress against others rather than harming themselves. In the Freudian perspective, aggression against others is necessary and inevitable because it keeps people from harming (and even killing) themselves.

Unfortunately, the need to aggress can only be temporarily satisfied. Freud believed that, like other drives, aggression decreases in strength after being expressed and then builds slowly over time until it must be satisfied again. Moreover, the longer it goes unfulfilled, the greater will be the expression of aggression when it inevitably erupts. For this reason, Freud believed that people must periodically release their aggressive energy.

In the field of aggression, Freud's claim is known as the **catharsis hypothesis.** According to the catharsis hypothesis, aggressive drive is reduced by engaging in or witnessing aggressive behavior. The word *catharsis* comes from a Greek word that means "to cleanse or purge". In Freud's view, exhibiting or viewing aggression allows aggressive needs to be released, thereby temporarily reducing the need to aggress. Societies must therefore provide people with socially acceptable outlets for expressing their aggressive impulses.

As you might imagine, many aspects of Freud's theory are controversial, and much of what he said lacks scientific confirmation. Nevertheless, his ideas have stimulated a good deal of research, and we will review evidence relevant to his theory at various points throughout this chapter.

B. Evolutionary Models of Aggression

Freud was not the only theorist to believe that aggression is an instinctive tendency. Evolutionary psychologists hold this belief as well.

1. Lorenz's Ethological Model of Aggression

The Nobel Prize–winning ethologist Konrad Lorenz is one such theorist. Lorenz is best known for his work on imprinting in birds, but he also wrote about the origins of aggression (Lorenz, 1966). Like Freud, Lorenz believed that humans possess an aggressive instinct that can be channeled but not eliminated. Unlike Freud, he did not believe this instinct represented a desire to defend against self-destructive tendencies or to return to an inanimate state. Instead, drawing on an extensive array of literature on animal behavior, Lorenz held that intraspecies aggression evolved to prevent other animals from encroaching on one another's territory, thereby guaranteeing that a species spreads out across all inhabitable land.

Though he dismissed the notion that aggression springs from a death instinct, Lorenz agreed with Freud that aggressive needs build over time and must be expressed. In fact, he believed that if aggression is suppressed for too long, it will spontaneously erupt without any provocation. He also agreed with Freud that societies must provide people with appropriate outlets for releasing these needs, lest aggression be released in socially destructive ways.

2. Inhibitors of Aggression

Even if aggression is innate, it need not be violent. In the animal world, intraspecies aggression rarely ends in excessive physical harm or murder. Instead, it ends when the weaker member of the species surrenders and relinquishes its territorial rights. To aid this process, Lorenz noted that animals have evolved particular appeasement gestures that signal submission. Vanquished opponents instinctively display these signs of submission, and victors instinctively recognize their meaning and refrain from committing further aggression (see also Lore & Schultz, 1993). For example, when defeated, wolves turn their head away from their opponent, offering the vulnerable, arched side of their neck.

Humans also possess natural inhibitors of aggression. For example, seeing fear in another person's eyes serves to inhibit further aggression. Unfortunately, our advanced weaponry renders these natural inhibitors ineffective. When dropping a bomb from several miles above a target, a bombardier doesn't visually confront the enemy. In this sense, the familiar saying "Guns don't kill people, people kill people" should be amended. Weapons that enable people to kill from a distance—such as guns, hand grenades, and bombs—increase violence by circumventing the natural inhibitors to aggression that have evolved in humans.

C. Gender Differences in Aggression

In most societies, males commit the vast majority of violent crimes. For example, they commit more than 80 percent of all murders and aggravated assaults in America (www.ojp.usdoj.gov/bjs/homicide/gender.htm). Moreover, violent crimes are most often committed by young, unmarried males who lack social status and monetary resources. Noting the parallels between these patterns and aggression in the animal world, M. Wilson and Daly (1985; Daly & Wilson, 1988) have suggested that the "young male syndrome" is a vestige of our evolutionary past, in which males competed to gain physical access to sexually available females. Of course, modern men are not like elks, locking horns in a mating ritual. Instead, they fight for status and resources that can be used to obtain mates.

The evolutionary model may even explain the onset of war. Mesquida and Wiener (1999) showed that countries are most apt to engage in war when the ratio of young males (ages 15 to 29) to older men is particularly high. Under these conditions, competition for mates is especially intense and young males are eager to fight for scarce resources.

1. Biological Factors

Biological factors contribute to the greater aggression men display (Maccoby & Jacklin, 1974). Men produce more testosterone than women, and testosterone is linked to aggression in animals and humans (Archer, 1988, 1991). In a study of prison inmates, Dabbs, Carr, Frady, and Riad (1995) found that men with high testosterone levels were more apt to be serving time for violent crimes, and were more confrontational and argumentative with prison authorities than were those with relatively low levels of testosterone. A follow-up study uncovered a similar, albeit less violent, pattern among college fraternities. Dabbs, Hargrove, and Heusel (1996) found that fraternities composed of men with high levels of testosterone were more rambunctious, cruder, and less academically successful than were fraternities comprised of men with low levels of testosterone.

2. Socialization and Gender Roles

If biology were the only factor to consider, we should find that men are always more aggressive than women. This is not the case, however. Gender differences are greatly attenuated when people are provoked or have reason to believe that aggression is appropriate (Bettencourt & Kernahan, 1997; Bettencourt & Miller, 1996). Moreover, although men are more apt to directly inflict physical injury and harm, women are more apt to indirectly inflict psychological and social harm through manipulation, exclusion, or malicious gossip (Björkqvist, Lagerspetz, & Kaukiainen, 1992; Crick, Casas, & Mosher, 1997; Lagerspetz & Björkqvist, 1994; Österman et al., 1998).

In consideration of these findings, many psychologists believe that gender differences in aggression primarily reflect different socialization practices rather than biological differences (e.g., Bandura, 1973; Eagly & Steffen, 1986). Beginning at an early age, boys are taught that direct aggression is appropriate and even desirable, whereas girls are taught that aggression is inappropriate and should be suppressed. Being discouraged from engaging in direct aggression, females then resort to aggressing in more indirect ways.

D. Cultural Differences in Aggression

Cultural differences in aggression provide further evidence that socialization shapes the expression of aggression. Aggression and violence show a great deal of cultural variation (M. H. Bond, 2004). Figure 13.1 reveals that homicide rates vary widely across countries. Although most industrialized countries (e.g., Canada, France, Germany, and Japan) are relatively peaceful, some, such as the United States, are relatively violent. Variations exist even within cultures. Many groups, such as the Amish, live very peacefully in the United States, and violent crimes are much more apt to be committed by people of lower socioeconomic status than by those who live comfortably or are well-off.

1. Cultures of Honor

A variety of factors influence rates of aggression across nations and within a given country. Poverty, ethnic and racial diversity, and the accessibility of firearms all play a role. Cultural attitudes are also relevant. Violent cultures tend to emphasize personal achievement and encourage competition among their citizens, whereas nonviolent cultures champion harmony and promote cooperation (Bonta, 1997).

Many violent cultures also endorse the importance of maintaining honor and status, particularly among men. In these "cultures of honor," men are taught to use aggression to preserve their reputation and protect their possessions. Several Latin American countries and the countries of southern Europe are characterized by this type of machismo.

2. A Subculture of Honor in the United States

The American South also possesses a culture of honor (Nisbett & Cohen, 1996). In earlier times, the southern economy was based on herding, and men relied on force to protect themselves and their property from rustlers. Consequently, it became

FIGURE 13.1

Homicide Rates in Various Countries Around the World (1997–2000)

Source: World Health Organization, www3.who.int/whosis/menu.cfm?path=whosis,mort&language=english.

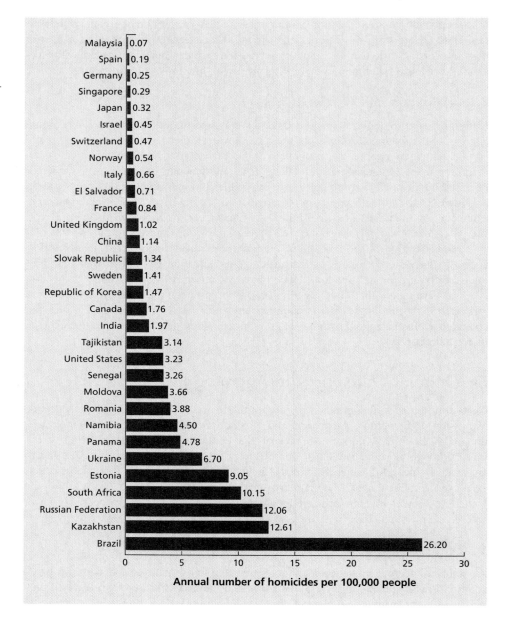

Country	Rate
Malaysia	0.07
Spain	0.19
Germany	0.25
Singapore	0.29
Japan	0.32
Israel	0.45
Switzerland	0.47
Norway	0.54
Italy	0.66
El Salvador	0.71
France	0.84
United Kingdom	1.02
China	1.14
Slovak Republic	1.34
Sweden	1.41
Republic of Korea	1.47
Canada	1.76
India	1.97
Tajikistan	3.14
United States	3.23
Senegal	3.26
Moldova	3.66
Romania	3.88
Namibia	4.50
Panama	4.78
Ukraine	6.70
Estonia	9.05
South Africa	10.15
Russian Federation	12.06
Kazakhstan	12.61
Brazil	26.20

Annual number of homicides per 100,000 people

important to develop a reputation for toughness—as someone who shouldn't be messed with, because retributive violence would ensue. Although the economic conditions that gave rise to these norms are no longer prevalent, the attitudes they spawned are still part of the southern legacy. For example, southern regions of the U.S. have higher homicide rates than do those of the North, but only for homicides committed during an argument or quarrel, where reputations are at stake (D. Cohen, 1998). Moreover, although they do not express greater approval than Northerners for violence in general, Southerners are more apt than Northerners to endorse violence for protecting oneself from insults and threats to self, family, or property and

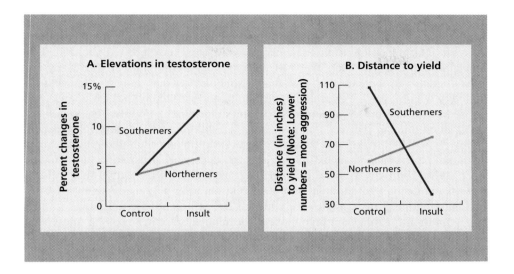

FIGURE 13.2

Southern and Northern American Men's Reactions to an Insult

While walking down a narrow hallway, southern and northern men were insulted by a confederate who refused to yield. In comparison with northern men, southern men responded to this
insult with increased testosterone (panel A) and more aggression toward a second confederate
(panel B). These data are consistent with the claim that the American South is characterized by a
culture of honor.

Source: D. Cohen, Nisbett, Bowdle, and Schwarz (1996).

to be accepting of a person who has committed a crime of honor (D. Cohen &
Nisbett, 1997).

Cohen and colleagues conducted a series of experiments to examine these tendencies under controlled laboratory conditions (D. Cohen, Nisbett, Bowdle, & Schwarz,
1996). One study involved northern and southern students attending the University of
Michigan. In this study, a male participant was walking through a narrow hallway when
a confederate of the experimenter came toward him, refusing to yield. After bumping
into the participant, the confederate insulted him, using a vulgar epithet. Finally, the participant encountered another confederate farther down the hallway. Figure 13.2 shows
that this affront had a greater effect on southern men than on northern men. In comparison to men in a control condition who had not been bumped or insulted, southern
men experienced greater rises in testosterone (panel A) and were less apt to yield to the
second confederate walking down the hall (panel B) than were northern men. These
findings are consistent with the claim that southern men are especially apt to become
aggressive when their masculinity is challenged or their reputation is impugned.

E. Learning to Aggress

Cultural variations in levels of aggression demonstrate that aggression is substantially
influenced by learning. Although some socialization is explicitly taught and verbally
reinforced, a good deal of socialization occurs through observation. After watching
how adults behave, children model this behavior and act in a similar way.

The modeling of aggression was illustrated in one of social psychology's best-known experiments. Bandura, Ross, and Ross (1961) had young children (approximately 4.5 years of age) watch as an adult played with a toy known as a Bobo doll. This inflatable doll bounces back up when held to the floor or punched. Three experimental conditions were created. One-third of the children saw an adult play with the doll very aggressively. For example, the adult punched the doll, sat on it, and hit it on the head with a mallet, shouting "Sock him in the nose . . .," "Hit him down . . .," and "Throw him in the air." Another group of children saw an adult play nonaggressively with a different toy, and in a control condition no adult was present. Later, after the experimenter had led the children to experience frustration, the children were allowed to play with the Bobo doll. Consistent with the notion that children learn by imitation, the children who had seen the adult play aggressively with the doll behaved much more aggressively toward the doll than did children in the other two conditions. Moreover, this tendency extended to other toys in the room, suggesting that the children had learned a more general behavior pattern (see also Bandura, Ross, & Ross, 1963).

So do children always imitate aggression? Fortunately, the answer is no. It depends on whether they believe that aggression will go unpunished. In a replication of the Bobo doll study, Rosekrans and Hartup (1967) had young children watch an adult model play aggressively with the toy. The experimenter verbally approved of the adult's behavior in one condition (e.g., "Good for you! I guess you really fixed him that time!") but disapproved of the adult's behavior in another condition ("Don't do that, or I won't let you play anymore"). The experimenter showed inconsistent reinforcement in a third condition, praising the model half of the time for playing aggressively and criticizing the model half of the time. Finally, a fourth group of children never saw the adult play with the doll at all.

Figure 13.3 shows how aggressively the children played with the doll when they were later given the chance. It is clear that children did not imitate aggression when it met with consistent punishment and were only moderately aggressive when the model received both reinforcement and punishment. These findings suggest that

FIGURE 13.3

The Influence of Rewards and Punishment on the Modeling of Aggressive Behavior

Children imitated an aggressive model only if the model received at least some reinforcement for being aggressive. These data suggest that children imitate aggression only if they believe they will not be punished for doing so.

Source: Rosekrans and Hartup (1967).

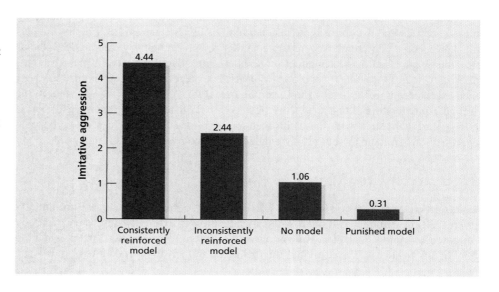

children imitate aggression only if they believe that aggression is appropriate and will not meet with censure or punishment.

II. Acts of Aggression

> Murders result from little ol' arguments over nothing at all. Tempers flare. A fight starts, and somebody gets stabbed or shot. I've worked on cases where the principals had been arguing over a 10 cent record on a juke box, or over a one dollar gambling debt from a dice game. (Dallas homicide detective, cited in Mulvihill, Tumin, & Curtis, 1969, p. 230)

Acts of aggression usually arise in response to provocation. Spouses argue when one suspects the other of being unfaithful, drivers become irate when another vehicle refuses to allow them to change lanes, and schoolchildren tussle when one accuses the other of cheating at kickball. In these cases, something happens to incite a person and an ensuing chain of events leads to aggressive behavior. This section details how these acts of aggression unfold and describes personality variables and situational factors that influence the course of aggression.

A. Provocation

Figure 13.4 shows that an aggressive episode begins with some sort of provocation. Typically, this involves (1) a physical assault on a person's body or property; (2) a psychological affront, as when one person threatens another person's dignity or reputation; or (3) some experience that produces frustration. Frustration is a psychological state that arises when we are prevented from attaining an expected goal or reward. Its role as an instigator of aggression was highlighted in a classic program of research known as the **frustration–aggression hypothesis** (Dollard, Doob, Miller, Mowrer, &

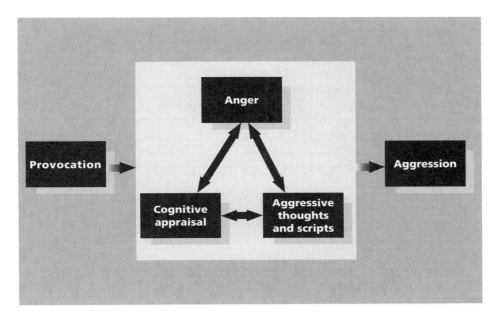

FIGURE 13.4

Stages in an Aggressive Episode

The figure shows that provocation produces aggression via three internal variables that are joined in a reciprocal fashion, such that the activation of one factor increases the activation of other factors.

Sears, 1939). According to this hypothesis, frustration *always* produces aggression and aggression is *always* the result of frustration.

Although it generated a great deal of research and attention, the frustration–aggression hypothesis turned out to be too simplistic. For one thing, even though frustration can produce aggression (A. H. Buss, 1966), it doesn't always do so. If your two-year-old niece drops a piece of cake she was bringing you to eat, you may laugh at the situation or even feel sorry for the toddler rather than becoming upset and scolding her. In addition, aggression can result from factors other than frustration. For example, people behave aggressively when they are tired or overheated, and this is not because they are prevented from attaining an anticipated goal. For these and other reasons, researchers now believe that frustration is simply one factor that can produce aggression (Berkowitz, 1989).

B. Cognition and Emotion

The movement away from the simple frustration–aggression hypothesis represented an awareness that cognitive and emotional variables intervene between provocation and aggression. In terms of material first discussed in Chapter 2, it was a switch from an S →R model of behavior applicable to lower animals and humans, to a more sophisticated, S →O →R model that includes uniquely human elements. To illustrate, if you take food away from a hungry animal, it will probably snarl at you and prepare to attack. This type of aggression is automatic and reflexive. People can also respond to provocation in an impulsive, automatic way, but as they mature they learn to give some thought to what has occurred. As a consequence, cognitions play a key role in the unfolding of an aggressive episode.

1. Cognitive Appraisal and Anger

First, people ask themselves whether the provoking incident is relevant to their well-being or sense of self-worth. As we saw earlier, men from the American South were more apt than those from the North to perceive a bumping in the hallway as an affront to their honor and masculinity.

Attributions of intent provide another type of cognitive appraisal. Once people have decided that provocation is relevant to their well-being, they ask themselves why it has occurred. In general, people experience more anger when they judge provocation to be intentional or arbitrary rather than accidental or justified (Dodge & Coie, 1987; Weiner, 1985). Suppose that another driver prevents you from changing lanes and you miss your exit on the freeway. If you think the other driver's behavior was a deliberate attempt to put you down, you are apt to be furious and react with aggression. In contrast, you will be far less angry if you think the other driver's behavior was an oversight or you were at fault for not signaling early enough.

2. Aggressive Thoughts and Scripts

Figure 13.4 shows that aggression is also fueled by the thoughts that come to mind when we are upset (Berkowitz, 1990). Everyone has ideas about how to react to provocation. "Count to 10" and "Turn the other cheek" are two common sayings that inhibit aggression, whereas "Stand up for yourself" and "Show them who's boss" are two common sayings that promote aggression. These behavioral scripts promote or discourage the expression of aggression in response to provocation.

Fear of retaliation also dampens aggressive impulses. We may be filled with rage and believe that aggression is appropriate, but we may refrain from aggressing if we worry about the consequences. This is one reason why people rarely yell at their boss. They understand they will lose their job, so they keep their anger in check.

The relation between aggressive thoughts and aggressive feelings plays a key role in Berkowitz's cognitive neoassociation model of aggression (Berkowitz, 1990). According to this model, aggressive thoughts and anger are joined in a reciprocal fashion (see the double-headed arrows in Figure 13.4). Anger activates aggressive thoughts, and aggressive thoughts activate anger. This relationship explains why the presence of aggressive stimuli, such as a gun, can increase anger and aggressive behavior. As first discussed in Chapter 1, Berkowitz and LePage (1967) found that people who were provoked were more aggressive toward another person when a gun was present than when it was absent. Presumably, this "weapons effect" occurred because the gun activated aggressive thoughts, and aggressive thoughts fueled anger and fed aggressive impulses (see also, C. A. Anderson, Benjamin, & Bartholow, 1998; Carlson, Marcus-Newhall, & Miller, 1990; Lindsay & Anderson, 2000).

C. Individual Differences in Aggression: The Role of Hostility

When considering the dynamics of an aggressive episode, it is important to bear in mind that some people are generally more aggressive than others are. Figure 13.4 helps us understand why this is so. **Hostility** is the propensity for an individual to become angry and act aggressively. Hostile people tend to become angry with very little provocation, appraise events in hostile terms, and readily generate aggressive thoughts when they are mad, believing that aggression is an appropriate and effective response to provocation (K. B. Anderson, Anderson, Dill, & Deuser, 1998; Bushman, 1996; Dill, Anderson, Anderson, & Deuser, 1997; Lindsay & Anderson, 2000; Marshall, 2003). Table 13.3 presents a scale that is widely used to measure hostility (A. H. Buss & Perry, 1992). By completing the scale, you can calculate your level of hostility.

1. The Origins of Hostility

Several personality variables can produce hostility in people. For example, some hostile people are narcissistic and defensive. They tend to be easily hurt when they believe they are being criticized, ignored, or rejected, and they respond with anger and retaliatory aggression (Bushman & Baumeister, 1998; Twenge & Campbell, 2003). In other cases, people who are highly competitive and achievement-oriented become hostile when they experience frustration or encounter incompetence in others (T. Q. Miller, Smith, Turner, Guijarro, & Hallet, 1996). Rumination can also produce hostility (Rusting & Nolen-Hoeksema, 1998). Instead of distracting themselves or releasing their anger in a healthy way, some people brood about things. Doing so makes them even angrier and more likely to aggress. People who are impulsive, thrill-seeking, or concerned with the immediate consequences of their actions also tend to be aggressive (Joireman, Anderson, & Strathman, 2003).

Finally, people who are cynical or distrusting of others become aggressive when they assume others are intentionally trying to harm them (Crick & Dodge, 1994; Dodge, 1980; Dodge & Coie, 1987). Dodge and associates have most fully explored this aspect of hostility by studying the attributions people make for provoking behaviors.

TABLE 13.3   Buss-Perry Aggression Scale

The following statements describe a variety of feelings, behaviors, and beliefs. Please indicate the extent to which each statement is characteristic of you, using the following scale as your guide: 0 (extremely uncharacteristic) to 5 (extremely characteristic).

1. Some of my friends think I am a hothead	0	1	2	3	4	5	Anger
2. I flare up quickly but get over it quickly.	0	1	2	3	4	5	Anger
3. I have trouble controlling my temper.	0	1	2	3	4	5	Anger
4. When frustrated, I let my irritation show.	0	1	2	3	4	5	Anger
5. I sometimes feel like a powder keg ready to explode.	0	1	2	3	4	5	Anger
6. Sometimes I fly off the handle for no good reason.	0	1	2	3	4	5	Anger
7. <u>I am an even-tempered person</u>.	0	1	2	2	4	5	Anger
8. When people are especially nice to me, I wonder what they want.	0	1	2	3	4	5	Hostility
9. I wonder why sometimes I feel so bitter about things.	0	1	2	3	4	5	Hostility
10. I am suspicious of overly friendly strangers.	0	1	2	3	4	5	Hostility
11. I am sometimes eaten up with jealousy.	0	1	2	3	4	5	Hostility
12. At times I feel I have gotten a raw deal out of life.	0	1	2	3	4	5	Hostility
13. I sometimes feel that people are laughing at me behind my back.	0	1	2	3	4	5	Hostility
14. Other people always seem to get the breaks.	0	1	2	3	4	5	Hostility
15. I know that "friends" talk about me behind my back.	0	1	2	3	4	5	Hostility
16. If I have to resort to violence to protect my rights, I will.	0	1	2	3	4	5	Physical aggression
17. I have become so mad that I have broken things.	0	1	2	2	4	5	Physical aggression
18. Once in a while, I can't control the urge to strike another person.	0	1	2	3	4	5	Physical aggression
19. I have threatened people I know.	0	1	2	3	4	5	Physical aggression
20. Given enough provocation, I may hit another person.	0	1	2	3	4	5	Physical aggression
21. <u>I can think of no good reason for ever hitting a person</u>.	0	1	2	3	4	5	Physical aggression
22. If somebody hits me, I hit back.	0	1	2	3	4	5	Physical aggression
23. There are people who pushed me so far that we came to blows.	0	1	2	3	4	5	Physical aggression
24. I get into fights a little more than the average person.	0	1	2	3	4	5	Physical aggression
25. I tell my friends openly when I disagree with them.	0	1	2	3	4	5	Verbal aggression
26. I can't help getting into arguments when people disagree with me.	0	1	2	3	4	5	Verbal aggression
27. When people annoy me, I may tell them what I think of them.	0	1	2	2	4	5	Verbal aggression
28. I often find myself disagreeing with people.	0	1	2	3	4	5	Verbal aggression
29. My friends say that I'm somewhat argumentative.	0	1	2	3	4	5	Verbal aggression

Note: To calculate your score, first reverse the scoring for the two underlined items (0 = 5, 1 = 4, 2 = 3, 3 = 2, 4 = 1, 5 = 0). Then add up the items that comprise each of the four subscales. The following figures show the means for men and women on the various scales.

	Males	Females
Anger	17.0	16.7
Hostility	21.3	20.2
Physical aggression	24.3	17.9
Verbal aggression	15.2	13.5
Total	77.8	68.2

Source: A. H. Buss and Perry (1992).

In one study, aggressive and nonaggressive boys watched a videotape in which one child provoked another (Dodge, 1980). Afterward, the boys were asked to describe what had happened and what they would do if this had happened to them. Compared to nonaggressive boys, chronically aggressive boys were twice as apt to assume that provocation was intentional and to generate an aggressive response to the problem. Similar results have been found with girls (Crick, Grotpeter, & Bigbee, 2002) and with women who have sought counseling for child abuse (Graham, Weiner, Cobb, & Henderson, 2001). A tendency to interpret ambiguous behaviors in hostile terms is known as the **hostile attribution bias** (Nasby, Hayden, & DePaulo, 1979).

2. The Stability of Hostility

Whatever its origins, hostility endures once it forms. Although almost everyone becomes less aggressive as they age, the relative rank-ordering of individuals remains fairly constant: Aggressive children grow up to become aggressive adolescents, and aggressive adolescents grow up to be aggressive adults (Huesmann, Eron, Lefkowitz, & Walder, 1984). To explain the stability of hostility, Huesmann and Eron (1984) have suggested that aggression starts when children are unable to generate nonaggressive solutions to problems and begin using aggression in response to provocation (see also Crick & Ladd, 1990). Their aggressiveness then invites ridicule and rejection from others, further fueling aggressive tendencies. Over time, this cycle leads to more aggressive interactions and more interpersonal problems. From this perspective, aggressive people unwittingly provoke others and create aversive social conditions that perpetuate their aggressiveness (Hodges & Perry, 1999).

This self-defeating cycle of violence may explain why aggression runs in families. In general, aggressive people tend to marry aggressive spouses and raise aggressive children (Huesmann et al., 1984). According to one report, nearly one-half of all inmates in state prisons have a parent or other close relative who has also been incarcerated (*New York Times,* August, 21, 2002, p. 1).

Undoubtedly, environmental factors contribute to this tendency. As we have seen, children model aggressiveness. Those who observe aggression, who are reinforced for behaving aggressively, and who are the object of aggression by others tend to develop hostility and aggressiveness (Bandura, 1973). Genetic factors are also implicated. Identical (monozygotic) twins are more similar in their level of aggressiveness than are fraternal (dyzygotic) twins, and the aggressiveness of adopted children is more similar to the aggressiveness of their biological parents than to their adopted parents. On the basis of these findings, some researchers now believe that nearly 50 percent of the variance in aggressiveness can be explained by heritable, biological factors (Miles & Carey, 1997; Rushton, Fulker, Neale, Nias, & Eysenck, 1986).

D. Situational Influences on Aggression

Even mellow, laid-back people have a breaking point—a point at which they become angry and potentially aggressive. This breaking point is often precipitated by situational factors. Physical discomfort is one such factor. The more uncomfortable people are, the more irritable they become and the more apt they are to react to provocation with anger and aggression. Pain, overcrowding, air pollution, smoke, unpleasant odors, loud noises, and fatigue have all been shown to produce discomfort and increase aggression (Geen, 1998).

1. Heat and Aggression

> I pray thee, good Mercutio, let's retire;
> The day is hot, the Capulets abroad,
> And, if we meet, we shall not 'scape a brawl,
> For now, these hot days, is the mad blood stirring.
>
> *Shakespeare,* Romeo and Juliet

Heat also produces discomfort, and people have long noticed an association between heat and aggression. The hotter it is, the more uncomfortable people are and the more aggressively they behave. This relation is reflected in the English language, in that the words *temper* and *temperature* share a common origin.

Archival data provide ample evidence for the strength and generality of the relation between heat and aggression (C. A. Anderson, 1989; C. A. Anderson & DeNeve, 1992; C. A. Anderson, Deuser, & DeNeve, 1995). Within the United States, (1) the incidence of violent crimes is higher in cities with high average temperatures than in those with low average temperatures (C. A. Anderson, 1987; C. A. Anderson & Anderson, 1996); (2) more violent crimes are committed during the summer than during the rest of the year (C. A. Anderson, 1987); and (3) more violent crimes are committed during hot years than during years that are more comfortable and cool (C. A. Anderson, Bushman, & Groom, 1997). The effect even extends to the world of sports: Batters are more apt to be hit by a pitch when baseball games are played on hot days than when they are played on cooler days (Reifman, Larrick, & Fein, 1995).

The relation between heat and aggression is not linear. Instead, aggression increases with heat up to a point, but beyond this point, people become lethargic and passive, and aggression levels off or declines (R. A. Baron, 1972; Bell, 1992; Cohn & Rotton, 1997). Rotton and Cohn (2000) recently provided an interesting analysis of this issue. They examined reports of aggravated assaults in Dallas, Texas during a two-year period, keeping track of whether the crime occurred during daylight hours (9:00 AM–8:59 PM) or during the evening hours (9:00 PM–8:59 AM).

Figure 13.5 shows some of the findings from this investigation. Looking first at the pattern during the daylight hours, we see evidence of a curvilinear relation: Aggravated assaults increased with temperature until the temperature reached 95 degrees Fahrenheit, at which point they leveled off and even declined a bit. The pattern during the nighttime was different. Because nighttime temperatures rarely rise above 95 degrees, the relation appears linear. Assaults rise slowly until the nighttime temperature hits 75 degrees, at which point they increase dramatically. These findings show that although intense heat reduces aggression, people are most aggressive when nighttime temperatures provide no relief from the heat of a summer day.

2. Arousal

Heat makes people irritable in part by increasing arousal. Arousal is a rather vague psychological construct that concerns the amount of tension, nervousness, or energy an organism is experiencing. Numerous factors besides heat increase arousal, including fear, caffeine, fatigue, sexual interest, and even laughter and exercise.

Arousal affects aggression in several ways. First, it increases discomfort, making people more sensitive to provocation. Arousal can also influence aggression by impairing people's ability to generate nonaggressive solutions to problems. Finally, arousal can intensify people's emotional reactions and increase the amount of anger they are feeling.

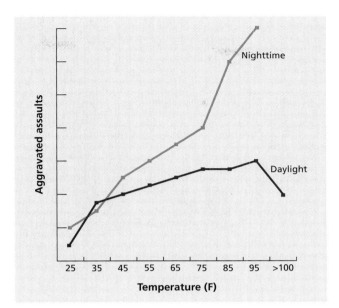

FIGURE 13.5

Aggravated Assaults in Dallas, Texas as a Function of Temperature and Time of Day

The data show that the relation between daytime assaults and temperature is curvilinear: Violent crimes increase up to a point (about 95°) and then decrease. In contrast, the relation between nighttime assaults and temperature is linear: The warmer it is at night, the more assaults there are. The rise is especially dramatic when the nighttime temperature remains above 75°.

Source: Rotton and Cohn (2000).

This last route plays an important role in **excitation transfer theory** (Zillman, 1978). According to this theory, arousal generated from one stimulus can spill over and intensify a person's emotional reaction to a different stimulus. Imagine that you have been drinking coffee while up all night cramming for an exam (in a course other than social psychology, I hope). Now imagine that you are driving to school when you get behind a very slow-moving driver who is going to make you late. How will you react? Fatigued from lack of sleep, hyper from the coffee, and nervous about your upcoming exam, your arousal level is high. Very likely, the arousal you feel will intensify your negative reaction to this frustration, increasing the likelihood of an aggressive response.

Research by Zillman, Katcher, and Milavsky (1972) illustrates these effects in an experimental setting. In this experiment, participants were first either provoked or not provoked by an experimental confederate. Later, some of the participants were asked to ride an exercise bike as part of an ostensibly unrelated experiment. Finally, all of the participants were given the chance to shock the confederate as part of an alleged experiment on punishment and learning. The level of shock the participants believed they were administering to the confederate for making a mistake constituted the measure of aggression. (In fact, no shock was actually administered.)

Figure 13.6 presents the key results from the experiment. Notice first that there was little aggression in the absence of any provocation. However, participants were aggressive when they were provoked, especially if they had just ridden an exercise bike. According to excitation transfer theory, this occurred because the arousal generated by exercise intensified the anger participants were feeling in response to provocation.

3. Self-Awareness and Its Absence

In June 2002, a riot broke out in Moscow following a World Cup soccer match in which Russia was beaten by Japan, 1–0. Dozens of people were injured and two were killed as thousands of vodka-sodden fans went on a violent rampage, overturning cars,

FIGURE 13.6

Arousal and Aggression

Exercise-induced arousal did not influence aggression when provocation was low, but did heighten aggression when provocation was high. These findings support the claim that arousal from irrelevant sources intensifies aggressive responses.

Source: Zillman, Katcher, and Milavsky (1972).

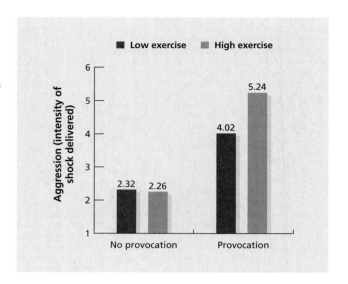

flinging bottles, and breaking store windows near Red Square. Mob violence of this sort is hardly limited to European soccer fans: Following the 1992 verdict in the Rodney King case, in which four police officers were acquitted of using excessive violence, hundreds of citizens took to the streets of Los Angeles setting bonfires, looting stores, and physically assaulting fellow citizens.

A French social scientist, Gustave Le Bon, provided one of the first attempts to understand acts of mob violence in his influential book *The Crowd: A Study of the Popular Mind* (Le Bon, 1895/1995). According to Le Bon, individuals lose their sense of individuality when they become immersed in a group, and this lack of self-awareness leads them to act in aggressive, antisocial ways. One need only think of the images of hooded and cloaked Ku Klux Klan lynch mobs in the United States to appreciate Le Bon's argument. Stripped of their individuality, people can become swept up in a contagion of antisocial behavior, leading to a frenzy of violence.

Festinger, Pepitone, and Newcomb (1952) coined the term **deindividuation** to refer to the psychological state that arises when individuals lose self-awareness as a consequence of being submerged in a group. Over the years, the causes of deindividuation have been expanded to include other factors that reduce individuality and self-awareness, such as anonymity and the absence of accountability (Postmes & Spears, 1998; Zimbardo, 1969).

Deindividuation can lead to aggression in two ways. First, the energy and emotion of a group situation increases arousal, feeling anger and impairing people's ability to formulate nonaggressive solutions to provocation. Second, anonymity and a lack of accountability lead people to believe they can aggress with impunity, thereby relaxing normal inhibitions against aggression. This situation often occurs when looters storm storefronts during a blackout or riot.

4. Social Roles

The images out of the Abu Ghraib prison stunned America and the world. Taken during the Iraqi War and released in the spring of 2004, the photographs showed American soldiers mistreating and humiliating captured Iraqi soldiers and civilians (www.antiwar.com/news/?articleid=2444). In one particularly infamous photo, two American soldiers stood triumphantly in front of a pile of naked Iraqi prisoners. Unfortunately, the mistreatment of the prisoners in the photos was not an isolated event. A report written by Major General Antonio M. Taguba concluded that there were numerous instances of "sadistic, blatant, and wanton criminal abuses" at Abu Ghraib (www.newyorker.com/fact/content/?040510fa_fact).

War is a time of extreme stress, and the abuses at Abu Ghraib might have been due to the extraordinary circumstances the American soldiers faced. A classic social psychological study known as the Stanford prison experiment suggests that less extraordinary factors may also have played a role (Haney, Banks, & Zimbardo, 1973; Haney & Zimbardo, 1998). In an effort to understand the power of institutional environments, researchers created a mock prison in the basement of the psychology building at Stanford University, complete with iron-barred cells and a solitary-confinement closet. An ad was placed in a local newspaper, and 21 men between the ages of 17 and 30 volunteered to participate in a study of prison life. Using random assignment to conditions, the researchers assigned some participants to be prisoners and others to be guards. The guards were given a khaki uniform, a whistle, a police nightstick, and reflecting sunglasses that hid their eyes. The prisoners were clothed in a loose-fitting smock with an identification number, rubber sandals, and an ankle chain.

Although they were given no specific instruction as to how to behave, the mock guards quickly began mistreating the mock prisoners, sadistically harassing and abusing them. The experiment was designed to last two weeks, but the researchers halted it after only six days because conditions inside the prison had deteriorated to the point where the psychological and physical well-being of the mock prisoners was in jeopardy.

How are we to understand the conditions that gave rise to this abuse? It is unlikely that the personalities of the participants were much of a factor. All of the participants had been given psychological tests at the start of the experiment to ensure they were healthy, and random assignment to conditions theoretically ensures that the mock guards were no more hostile by nature than the mock prisoners. This leaves us with three, related explanations: (1) The social roles people play are so powerful that they can override normal psychological tendencies, (2) prisons are dehumanizing institutions that transform normally gentle people into sadistic tormenters, and (3) people take advantage of an opportunity to aggress when they are given the chance. The first two explanations assume that people are naturally gentle and behave aggressively only when they are transformed by circumstances; the third explanation assumes that people possess an aggressive nature that is normally held in check by societal restrictions. Although there is no way to know which process explains the behaviors that occurred in the Stanford prison experiment, it is clear that social roles can release, create, or thwart aggressive impulses.

5. Alcohol and Aggression

In television commercials, people who drink often appear with their friends, gathered together in an atmosphere of frivolity and conviviality. Missing from these commercials is any mention of the strong link between alcohol and aggression. It's not easy to miss this link. Alcohol is implicated in half of all homicides and assaults, and more than 75 percent of all instances of sexual abuse and domestic violence (Murdoch, Pihl, & Ross, 1990; Pedersen, Aviles, Ito, Miller, & Pollock, 2002).

Why is alcohol so destructive? Four explanations have been offered (Bushman, 1997; Bushman & Cooper, 1990; Ito, Miller, & Pollock, 1996). First, studies with laboratory animals suggest that alcohol may have a direct effect on aggression by inhibiting fear and impairing impulse control (Higley, 2001). Second, people who drink tend to believe that alcohol increases aggression, and these expectancies turn into self-fulfilling prophecies as people play the role of the belligerent drunk (Marlatt & Rohsenow, 1980). Third, alcohol reduces self-awareness, and a lack of attention to oneself promotes aggression (J. G. Hull, Levenson, Young, & Sher, 1983). Finally, alcohol increases aggression by limiting people's ability to generate nonaggressive solutions to problems and by leading them to ignore situational cues that normally inhibit aggression (C. M. Steele & Josephs, 1990; Zeichner & Phil, 1979). For all of these reasons, alcohol should not be consumed in situations that have a potential for violence.

III. Media Violence and Aggression

It has been estimated that by the time they finish elementary school, most American children will have seen more than 8,000 murders and 100,000 other acts of aggression (e.g., assaults, rapes) on television (A. C. Huston et al., 1992). When one adds the prevalence of cinematic violence at the movie theater, video games that simulate murder and annihilation, and song lyrics that glorify violence and advocate its use, it is apparent that the average American child is inundated with violent media. In this section, we will look at how this barrage of fictional bloodshed and carnage affects aggressive behavior.

A. Theoretical Reasons Why Viewing Violence Should Increase Aggression

Before we examine evidence pertinent to this question, let's first consider the theoretical issues. Why should media violence affect aggression? Through what processes should viewing violence produce aggression?

- First, viewers may simply imitate the violence they observe. There is some evidence that this occurs. One day after watching the Clint Eastwood movie *Magnum Force,* two gunman imitated a scene from the movie and forced a stereo store owner to drink Drano, a highly toxic and corrosive fluid used to clean clogged drains (Leland, 1995). Such incidents are obviously rare, but they do represent one way in which viewing violence might increase aggression.
- Media violence may also produce aggression through observational learning and modeling (Bandura, 1973). The emphasis here is not on blind imitation, but on the acquisition of a behavior pattern that has previously been seen to produce desirable consequences. For example, in the Bobo doll study discussed earlier in this chapter, children played aggressively with the doll if they had previously seen an adult receive rewards for being aggressive (refer back to Figure 13.3).
- A steady diet of violent television might also increase aggression by altering the way people think about aggression (Huesmann, 1998). Watching lots of violence on television gives people the impression that violence is a common

and socially accepted way of solving problems (Gerbner, Gross, Morgan, & Signorielli, 1994). In part, this is because television shows and movies greatly exaggerate the prevalence of violence. For example, although murders make up less than 0.3 percent of the total crimes committed, they represent almost half of all crimes shown on reality-based police television shows (Oliver, 1994). This differential led one commenter to note:

> About 350 characters appear each night on prime-time TV, but studies show an average of seven of these people are murdered every night. If this rate applied in reality, then in just 50 days everyone in the United States would be killed and the last [person] left could turn off the TV. (Medved, 1995, pp. 156–157)

- TV violence also makes aggressive thoughts more accessible and shapes expectancies about the likelihood that aggression will be successful (Berkowitz, 1984; Bushman, 1998; Bushman & Geen, 1990).
- A steady diet of violence could desensitize people to the pain and suffering of others (Geen, 1981). Most people have a natural inclination to be abhorred by blood, gore, and violence. This natural repulsion is reduced with repeated exposure to violence, thereby circumventing an important inhibitor of aggression.
- Finally, watching media violence could increase aggression by increasing arousal (Berkowitz, 1993; Doob & Climie, 1972; Zillman, 1978). Most violent shows are suspenseful, frightening, action-packed, and exciting. These features increase arousal, and (as we have seen) arousal can promote aggression.

In sum, a variety of processes can explain why exposure to media violence *should* produce aggression. Some of these processes produce short-term effects; others are apt to be more enduring. For example, the greater accessibility of aggressive thoughts and increased arousal are most apt to affect aggression in short-term contexts, whereas beliefs about the prevalence of aggression and its likely consequences are apt to influence aggression in long-term contexts (Huesmann, 1998).

B. Research Regarding Media Violence and Aggression

Three types of studies have been conducted to examine the association between media violence and aggression.

1. Correlational Studies

First, correlational studies have examined the naturally occurring association between the amount of violence a person watches and how aggressively the person behaves. Most of these studies show a similar pattern: Although viewing media violence does not predict aggression among older teenagers and adults, children who watch lots of TV violence behave more aggressively than children who watch little or no TV violence (Eron, 1982; Milavsky, Kessler, Stipp, & Rubens, 1982; National Institutes of Mental Health, 1982; Surgeon General's Scientific Advisory Committee on Television and Social Behavior, 1972). The strength of this correlation varies from study to study, but it is generally of moderate magnitude (Bushman & Anderson, 2001b). Some studies have even found that viewing TV violence at a young age predicts aggression many years later (Huesmann, Moise-Titus, Podolski, & Eron, 2003) although other studies have not found this pattern (Milavsky et al., 1982).

Do these findings mean that TV violence causes aggression? Not necessarily. As first noted in Chapter 1, correlations can never prove causation, because there are always three explanations for any observed correlation. In the present case, viewing violence on television may lead to aggression, but aggressive children might also prefer watching violent TV shows, or it might be that some third variable—such as lack of parental supervision, socioeconomic status, or low intelligence—determines both variables. Tempting as it is to believe otherwise, even strong correlations provide no evidence for causation.

2. Experimental Laboratory Studies

Experimental studies are needed to establish causality. Such studies can be conducted in either a laboratory or a naturally occurring field setting. Laboratory studies of aggression generally have three components. First, using random assignment to conditions, some participants are frustrated or angered, and others are not provoked in any fashion. Independently, some participants are then exposed to violent media, either by watching a violent movie clip or television show, whereas other participants are not exposed to violent media. Finally, all participants are given the chance to engage in some sort of aggressive behavior. Usually, this involves (ostensibly) shocking an experimental confederate who is playing the role of a learner in a teacher–learner procedure. Of course, no one is actually shocked, but the intent to harm is evident.

Research using this design generally finds that viewing violence increases aggression, particularly among participants who score high in hostility and have been angered or frustrated (Bushman, 1995; Geen & Berkowitz, 1967). When considered along with the correlational evidence viewed earlier, many social scientists believe these findings prove that violent media are one cause of aggression and that steps should be taken to reduce people's exposure to fictional depictions of violence on television and in movies (see, e.g., Bushman & Anderson, 2001b).

There is a problem with this conclusion, however. In Chapter 1, we noted that the generalizability of laboratory studies requires scrutiny, because the artificiality of the setting may render the findings inapplicable to real-world contexts. In the case of media violence and aggression, the following concerns have been raised (Freedman, 1984):

- Laboratory studies examine only the short-term effects of violent media, and provide no information about whether any negative effect dissipates quickly over time.
- In the laboratory, aggression is generally sanctioned and may even be encouraged. Participants are told they can set the shock level at any magnitude they desire, and are often told that high levels of punishment facilitate learning.
- Participants in the laboratory do not fear retaliation for acting aggressively. The fear of retaliation is a natural inhibitor of aggression, so laboratory studies may exaggerate the effects of viewing media violence.

3. Experimental Field Studies

To address the potential shortcomings of experimental laboratory studies, some researchers have conducted experimental studies in a field setting. In these studies, participants (usually children) are randomly assigned to view violent or nonviolent television shows for some period (perhaps an hour a day for one week). Their behavior is then observed over the course of the investigation. These studies have found

TABLE 13.4 Summary of Research Linking Media Depictions of Violence and Aggression

Study Type	Findings	Interpretation
Correlational	Children who watch lots of violent TV shows are more aggressive than those who watch little or no TV violence.	Viewing violence on television and aggression are correlated, but the causal direction is unclear.
Laboratory experiments	In a laboratory setting, participants randomly assigned to watch violent media behave more aggressively than those who do not watch violent media, especially if they are high in hostility and have been angered, frustrated, or insulted.	Viewing media violence has demonstrable short-term effects in laboratory settings, particularly for people who are already high in hostility and have been provoked.
Field experiments	In a naturally occurring environment, participants randomly assigned to view media violence do not behave more aggressively than those who do not watch media violence.	The causal effect of media violence in real-world settings has yet to be firmly established.

only weak and inconsistent evidence that violence causes aggression in the real world (for reviews, see Freedman, 1984; W. Wood, Wong, & Chachere, 1991).

4. Summary and Conclusion on Media Violence and Real-Life Aggression

Table 13.4 summarizes the research we've been discussing on media violence and aggression. Correlational studies show that media violence and aggression are linked among children, and laboratory experiments show that media violence can produce aggression, particularly if there is provocation and the individuals are predisposed to behave aggressively. There is not, however, clear and consistent evidence that media violence produces aggression in real-world settings.

In situations like these, when findings are mixed and inconclusive, scientists draw different conclusions about the strength of the evidence. My own interpretation is that media violence contributes little to the aggression we find in America today. The accessibility of handguns and social inequities play a far more important role than cinematic depictions of violence, violent video games, and violence-laden lyrics (Glassner, 1999). Although not everyone agrees with this conclusion (see, e.g., Anderson & Bushman, 2002; Bushman & Anderson, 2001b), even those who believe in the existence of a causal link between media violence and aggression concede that any potential negative influence is relatively modest and apt to occur only among a small subset of young children (e.g., Surgeon General's Scientific Advisory Committee, 1972, pp. 18–19). Given this, perhaps the safest conclusion to be made is that viewing media violence during early childhood may, under some circumstances, incite some children to be more aggressive than their nature or life situation would otherwise dictate.

As it turns out, even the effects of viewing violence in early childhood can be mitigated. Huesmann, Eron, Klein, Brice, and Fischer (1983) found that the correlation between the amount of time spent viewing media violence and aggressive behavior was eliminated if children were reminded that media violence (1) is fictional, (2) doesn't mirror the real-world, and (3) is not condoned. Parents concerned about the negative effects of violence should talk to their children about these issues, ensuring that their children understand that violence is overrepresented on television and is not socially sanctioned (Nathanson, 1999).

IV. Violence among Intimates

No discussion of aggression is complete without considering the nature of the relationship between the aggressor and the victim. In most cases, this relation is an intimate one. Although the media create an impression that violence is often carried out between strangers, the sad fact is that most aggression occurs between people who know one another well.

A. School Violence

> Sticks and stones may break my bones, but names will never hurt me.
>
> *Children's rhyme*

For decades, schoolchildren have been taught that teasing and name-calling are relatively harmless aspects of childhood that can be easily ignored or deflected (Kowalski, 2000). A spate of violence in America's schools has forced parents, educators, and law enforcement officials to revise their thinking. Since 1996, dozens of students have been injured or murdered in an alarming number of school shootings, in which children who are systematically excluded or taunted retaliate with excessive violence. The events that took place at Columbine High School in Littleton, Colorado, provide the most graphic illustration of this pattern. On April 20, 1999, Dylan Klebold and Eric Harris opened fire on their classmates before committing suicide. When their rampage ended, more than 20 people had been injured and 12 students and 1 teacher lay dead. In a videotape the killers made prior to the attack, Klebold and Harris indicated that the incident was partly motivated by retribution against people who had teased, ostracized, and ridiculed them for years (see Leary, Kowalski, Smith, & Phillips, 2003).

The social exclusion Klebold and Harris experienced was extreme, but it is not uncommon. **Bullying** is a persistent pattern of behavior in which one person intentionally abuses another by means of verbal taunts or acts of teasing, physical assaults, deliberate exclusion from social activities, or attempts to sabotage his or her social relationships by spreading malicious gossip and rumors. In a study of Norwegian school children, Solberg and Olweus (2003) found that nearly one-third of the students who were surveyed indicated that they had been bullied in the previous few months, and many of these students reported feeling angry and upset. Of course, few of these children resorted to violence, but teasing, taunting, and social exclusion can precipitate aggression in almost everyone (Coie, Dodge, & Kupersmidt, 1990; Twenge, Baumeister, Tice, & Stucke, 2001).

At the same time, some people are more apt to respond to social exclusion with violence than others are (Georgesen, Harris, Milich, & Young, 1999). People with narcissistic tendencies and a strong sense of entitlement are most apt to become aggressive when they are ridiculed or excluded (Baumeister, Smart, & Boden, 1996; Bushman & Baumeister, 1998; Kirkpatrick, Waugh, Valencia, & Webster, 2002). Feeling belittled, they retaliate in an attempt to reestablish a positive self-image and transform feelings of humiliation and shame into pride (Juvonen & Graham, 2001). The voices on the tape Klebold and Harris left behind provide a chilling illustration of this motive (Twenge & Campbell, 2003). Holding a sawed-off shotgun and staring into the camera, Klebold remarks, "Perhaps now we'll get the respect we deserve."

B. Sexual Violence

Every year, more than 300,000 American women are raped or sexually assaulted (www.ojp.usdoj.gov/bjs/pub/pdf/rsarp00.htm). That averages out to nearly one instance of sexual assault every 2 minutes. Moreover, this statistic most certainly underestimates the amount of sexual violence in America. Many women are reluctant or afraid to report sexual abuse, especially when the assailant is an acquaintance or partner. In this section we consider the causes and consequences of sexual aggression, focusing on instances in which men commit sexual violence against women.

1. The Rape Myth

> Weather's like rape—as long as it's inevitable, you might as well lie back and enjoy it.
>
> *Clayton Williams, 1990, Texas gubernatorial candidate*

The utterly offensive views on rape expressed by Clayton Williams reflect a long-standing tradition on the part of males to condone, trivialize, and excuse acts of sexual aggression against women. Beginning in the 1970s, sociologists (Schwendinger & Schwendinger, 1974), feminists (Brownmiller, 1975), and psychologists (Burt, 1980) began bringing such beliefs to the public's attention. These beliefs, known as **rape myths,** include blaming the victim, absolving the perpetrator, and justifying or minimizing the aggressive nature of rape and sexual violence.

Payne, Lonsway, and Fitzgerald (1998) developed a scale to measure people's endorsement of rape myths. As shown in Table 13.5, the scale consists of seven subscales, representing different aspects of rape myths. All of these beliefs are pernicious, but the first two merit special comment. First, the She Wanted It subscale reflects the belief that women enjoy forcible sex. As we will see momentarily, men prone to sexual aggression are particularly apt to endorse this belief (Malamuth & Check, 1981). The second subscale (She Asked for It), reflects the belief that women who dress provocatively, drink alcohol, or put themselves in dangerous situations are partly responsible if they are sexually assaulted. These beliefs not only exonerate men who commit rape but also prevent women from pressing charges once they have been raped for fear that their reputations will be sullied and their character denigrated.

As you might imagine, men tend to score higher on scales designed to measure rape myths than women do (Payne et al., 1998). Nevertheless, many women also endorse items on the Rape Myths scale, including items on the She Asked for It subscale. Why would women believe that a woman who is raped is partly to blame? One possibility is that this belief stems from a broader tendency known as **belief in a just world** (Lerner, 1980). This term refers to the fact that individuals commonly believe that people get what they deserve in this world, such that good things happen to good people and bad things happen to bad people. When something bad happens to a

TABLE 13.5   Sample Items from the Illinois Rape Myths Scale

Instructions to participants: Read each items and indicate your level of agreement by circling a number to the left of each item.

Subscale	Item	1 2 3 not at all agree	4 5 6 7 very much agree
She Wanted It	Although most women wouldn't admit it, they generally find being physically forced into sex a real "turn-on."	1 2 3	4 5 6 7
	Many women secretly desire to be raped.	1 2 3	4 5 6 7
She Asked for It	If a woman is raped while she is drunk, she is at least somewhat responsible for letting things get out of control.	1 2 3	4 5 6 7
	A woman who dresses in skimpy clothes should not be surprised if a man tries to force her to have sex.	1 2 3	4 5 6 7
He Didn't Mean To	Men don't usually intend to force sex on a woman, but sometimes they get too sexually carried away.	1 2 3	4 5 6 7
	Rape happens when a man's sex drive gets out of control.	1 2 3	4 5 6 7
Not Rape	If a woman doesn't physically fight back, you can't really say that it was rape.	1 2 3	4 5 6 7
	If the rapist doesn't have a weapon, you really can't call it a rape.	1 2 3	4 5 6 7
Rape Is a Trivial Event	If a woman is willing to "make out" with a guy, then it's no big deal if he goes a little further and has sex.	1 2 3	4 5 6 7
	Women tend to exaggerate how much rape affects them.	1 2 3	4 5 6 7
She Lied	A lot of women lead a man on and then they cry rape.	1 2 3	4 5 6 7
	Rape accusations are often used as a way of getting back at men.	1 2 3	4 5 6 7
Deviant Event	Men from nice middle-class homes almost never rape.	1 2 3	4 5 6 7
	It is usually only women who dress suggestively that are raped.	1 2 3	4 5 6 7
	Rape is unlikely to happen in the woman's own familiar neighborhood.	1 2 3	4 5 6 7

Source: Payne, Lonsway, and Fitzgerald (1998).

person, a belief in a just world can lead us to assume that the person played at least some role in bringing the event about, thereby protecting ourselves from the belief that the same event could befall us. Perhaps women who endorse items on the Rape Myths scale do so as a means of reducing their own perceived vulnerability to this often random act of violence.

2. Portrait of a Rapist

Rape myths are cultural stereotypes that are endorsed by a broad segment of the population. Yet most people who hold these attitudes do not commit acts of sexual violence. Based on an extensive program of research, Malamuth and colleagues have concluded that two factors combine to create a propensity to rape (Malamuth, 1986; Malamuth, Check, & Briere, 1986; Malamuth, Linz, Heavey, Barnes, & Acker, 1995).

The first factor, called hostile masculinity, involves attitudes toward women and the use of violence to attain sexual gratification. Men who score high on this measure view women in negative terms, endorse rape myths, and regard the relationship between men and women as being largely adversarial (K. B. Anderson, Cooper, & Okamura, 1997; Leibold & McConnell, 2004). They also feel the need to dominate and control women, and they condone the use of violence to achieve sexual fulfillment. In fact, depictions of forcible sex produce as much sexual arousal in these men as do depictions of consensual sex, a pattern not found with sexually noncoercive men (Abel, Barlow, Blanchard, & Guild, 1977).

The second factor, termed sexual promiscuity, reflects inhibitions to act on aggressive urges. Men who are prone to commit sexual violence have an emotionally detached, noncommittal attitude toward sexual relationships. They began having sex at an early age, have had multiple sexual partners in the past and desire having many more in the future, and view sex as a conquest that involves nothing other than their own sexual gratification. In short, they see women as sex objects whose purpose is to provide them with sexual fulfillment without any expectation that there will be any reciprocal attention to their partner's physical and emotional needs (Dean & Malamuth, 1997; Malamuth et al., 1995).

Finally, it should be noted that not all rape victims are women. Recent events have documented a large number of incidents in which clergymen have sexually violated young boys, and adult men are also victims of homosexual rape. Whether the perpetrators of such crimes subscribe to the same types of beliefs as men who sexually violate women is an important topic for future research.

3. Pornography and Sexual Violence

Pornography—sexually explicit material intended to cause erotic arousal—is big business. Once associated with a fringe market of users who frequented adult bookstores and movie parlors on dimly lit streets in poor parts of town, pornography has gone mainstream and is now estimated by *Forbes* magazine to be a $56 billion global industry (www.forbes.com/2001/05/23/0523sf.html). Its availability on the Internet has proliferated in recent years; in fact, pornographic Web sites are one of the few profitable ventures on the World Wide Web.

Because men are far more apt to purchase and view pornography than women are (Geen, 1998), most researchers have examined whether exposure to pornography influences men's negative attitudes and behavior toward women. To answer this question, we need to distinguish between nonviolent pornography (sometimes called soft porn or erotica) and violent pornography (sometimes called hardcore porn).

Frequent or repeated exposure to nonviolent pornography does affect people's attitudes toward sexual matters (e.g., it can make them more accepting of sex outside of marriage), but it does not increase aggression (Diamond & Uchiyama, 1999; Geen,

FIGURE 13.7

Pornography and
Aggression

After viewing one of three
films, male participants
were given the chance to
shock a female confeder-
ate in an (alleged) investigation of punishment and
learning. Only a violent,
erotic film increased
aggression toward women,
indicating that nonviolent
pornography does not
increase aggression.

Source: Donnerstein (1980).

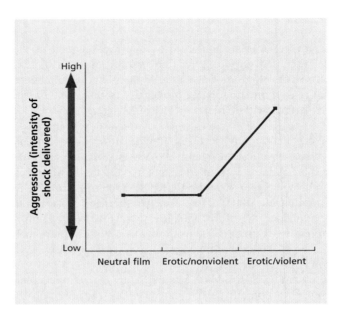

1998; Kutchinsky, 1991). If anything, exposure to nonviolent pornography appears to reduce aggressive tendencies (Geen, 1998).

In contrast, exposure to violent pornography does produce negative consequences. It makes men more accepting of rape myths; increases negative attitudes toward women in general; and may, under certain conditions and for certain men, exacerbate violence toward women (Malamuth, Addision, & Koss, 2002; Malamuth & Check, 1981). An investigation by Donnerstein (1980) reveals these effects. In one condition of this study, male participants were cast in the role of teacher and were instructed to deliver shock to a woman (an experimental confederate) whenever she erred on a learning task. Before the learning task began, the participants viewed one of three films: (1) a neutral film with no sexual content; (2) an erotic, nonviolent film; and (3) an erotic, violent film. Figure 13.7 shows the amount of shock the men administered in each of the experimental conditions. As you can see, only the erotic film that contained violence increased aggression, indicating that violent pornography has serious negative consequences but that nonviolent pornography does not.

In an important follow-up investigation, Donnerstein and Berkowitz (1981) found that the association between violent pornography and aggression depends, in part, on how the violence is portrayed. In this study, male participants were either angered or not angered by their female partner before viewing one of four films: (1) a neutral film with no sexual content; (2) a nonviolent erotic film; (3) a violent erotic film that showed a woman enjoying forcible sex; and (4) a violent erotic film that showed a woman suffering great distress while being violently forced to have sex with a man.

Figure 13.8 shows the amount of shock the men later delivered during the punishment portion of the experiment. First, note again that nonviolent pornography did not increase aggression, even among men who had been angered. Second, notice that violent pornography did increase aggression, but this depended on whether the man

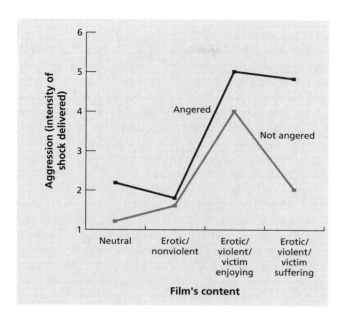

FIGURE 13.8

Pornography, Provocation, and Aggression

As part of an alleged learning study, male participants were given the chance to shock a female confederate (who had either insulted or not insulted them) after watching one of four movies. The data show three effects of interest: (1) nonviolent pornography did not increase aggression toward women; (2) violent pornography that depicted a woman enjoying forcible sex did increase aggression among men, regardless of whether they were angry or not; but (3) violent pornography that depicted the victim suffering led to increased aggression only among men who had been provoked. These data suggest that violent pornography that shows a woman enjoying forcible sex is particularly apt to incite men to be aggressive.

Source: Donnerstein and Berkowitz (1981).

was angered and whether the film offered a realistic (suffering) or unrealistic (rape myth) perspective on forcible sex. Violent pornography that showed a woman enjoying forcible sex promoted aggression in men regardless of whether or not they had been angered. In contrast, violent pornography that showed a woman being distressed by violent sex promoted aggression in men who had been angered but not in men who had not been angered. This finding is consistent with other evidence that pain cues decrease violence if no provocation has occurred (R. A. Baron, 1974; Hartmann, 1969).

It is interesting to consider why violent pornography should have such a deleterious effect. Unlike television shows and movies, most of which are clearly fictional, pornography seems to be realistic. No one but a young child believes that actors are actually killed during a violent movie, but a man inclined to believe that women enjoy forcible sex may believe that an actress who is being victimized in a pornographic movie is actually experiencing sexual gratification. In short, the line between fantasy and reality is blurred in a pornographic film, making the negative effects more severe than with fictional television or movies.

4. Acquaintance Rape

Sexual violence was once thought to occur only among strangers (Muehlenhard & Kimes, 1999). This perception drastically changed in 1982, when, *Ms.* magazine published an article that brought a previously hidden form of rape to the public's attention. This crime, known as acquaintance rape or date rape, occurs when a woman is coerced into having sex by a man she knows well and may even be dating. Although date rape cuts across socioeconomic, racial, and ethnic lines, it appears to be particularly prevalent on college campuses. Estimates vary, but nearly one in five women attending college report having been sexually victimized by a date, friend, or male acquaintance (Brener, McMahon, Warren, & Douglas, 1999; Koss, Gidycz, & Wisniewski, 1987).

In some cases, acquaintance rape stems from miscommunication or different expectations about sexually appropriate conduct (Abbey, 1982). For example, men may believe that a woman who visits them in their dorm room or fraternity house is implicitly agreeing to have sexual relations, even when this is not her intent. Men may also erroneously assume that a woman who is willing to have preliminary sexual contact is also willing to have sexual intercourse. When a woman indicates that she doesn't wish to have greater intimacy, the man ignores her protestations, failing to understand that no means no (Muehlenhard & Hollabaugh, 1988; Muehlenhard & Linton, 1987). These misperceptions appear to be more common when alcohol is consumed (A. M. Gross, Bennett, Sloan, Marx, & Juergens, 2001).

Of course, acquaintance rape is not always the innocent result of miscommunication. Sometimes is it malicious and premeditated. A man may slip a woman a drug or encourage her to drink to excess in hopes of taking advantage of her diminished capacity. Regardless of the circumstances, acquaintance rape is a crime and severe penalties apply whether it is deliberate or the result of miscommunication, and whether or not alcohol and drugs are involved.

5. Domestic Violence

Sexual aggression is not the only type of violence that occurs between men and women. It has been estimated that nearly 2 million American women are physically abused by their husbands or boyfriends every year (Holtzworth-Munroe, 2000). Many men are also physically abused by their wives and girlfriends, although the amount of injury inflicted is far less severe, and female-inflicted violence is often undertaken in self-defense (Archer, 2000).

Jealousy is implicated in many acts of domestic violence (Daly & Wilson, 1998). There is some reason to believe that the nature of this jealousy differs for men and women. Both men and women worry about emotional infidelity in a partner, but men seem to be more troubled by their partner's sexual infidelity than women are (Buss, Larson, Westen, & Semelroth, 1992). This difference, which is not always found (DeSteno, Bartlett, Braverman, & Salovey, 2002; Harris, 2000, 2002, 2003) may reflect differences in evolutionary pressures. Although DNA testing can now be used to establish paternity, men have been unable to ascertain their paternity throughout most of human history. Consequently, they have needed to pay close attention to their partner's sexual infidelity. Alternatively, men may be more bothered by sexual infidelity to ensure that they did not invest their resources in raising another man's child because women are less apt to have casual sex than men are, so sexual infidelity in a woman signals emotional infidelity as well (Nannini & Myers, 2000).

V. Curbing Aggression

To this point we have reviewed social psychological research on the nature of aggression and considered its causes. In this section of the chapter we will consider various strategies that have been used, with varying degrees of success, to curb aggression.

A. Sociocultural Factors

Earlier in this chapter we noted that there are strong cultural differences in incidents of violent crime (refer back to Figure 13.1). These variations suggest that cultures can take steps to inhibit the expression of aggression. The ready availability of guns is surely one factor that makes the United States one of the most violent countries on earth. Most acts of physical aggression involve a weapon, and guns are far and away the most likely weapon to be used during the commission of a violent crime. Limiting the easy access to guns is arguably the most effective way to curb violence in America.

B. Punishment

> If a man put out the eye of another man, his eye shall be put out.
>
> *The Code of Hammurabi, 196*

Throughout recorded history, punishment has been used to deal with acts of aggression. It is generally thought to serve two purposes. First, it serves as a deterrent. Here, the threat of punishment reduces future acts of aggression because people fear reprisal if they are caught. Second, it is used as a form of retribution. Here, punishment is viewed as a means of restoring justice for acts of aggression already committed.

When considering whether or not to use punishment, people's decisions are more often driven by the latter consideration than the former (Carlsmith, Darley, & Robinson, 2002). Believing that it is only fair that those who have committed acts of aggression suffer the consequences of their deeds, people base their decisions more on vengeance than on deterrence. Since the preference for vengeance is a moral matter and not one that can be informed by scientific data, we will forgo discussion of this issue and focus only on whether punishment effectively reduces future aggression.

1. Capital Punishment

In 1972, the U.S. Supreme Court ruled that capital punishment was unconstitutional because it violated a person's constitutional right to equal protection under the law (*Furman* v. *Georgia,* Citation 408, U.S. 238, Docket 2726). Four years later, the court reversed itself (*Gregg* v. *Georgia,* Citation 428, U.S. 153, Docket 74-6257), and 38 of the 50 states now impose the death penalty for some crimes. In 2002, 71 persons in 13 states were executed, with nearly half of them (46 percent) executed in Texas.

Setting aside the issue of whether it is fair or moral for the government to take a person's life, let's examine whether capital punishment effectively deters violent crimes. Figure 13.9 presents data pertinent to this issue. The figure shows homicide rates during periods in which capital punishment was both banned and allowed (R. D. Peterson & Bailey, 1988). Two findings are of interest: (1) States that impose

FIGURE 13.9

Homicide Rates in States That Impose and Do Not Impose the Death Penalty

The data show that states that impose the death penalty have higher (not lower) murder rates than those that do not, suggesting that capital punishment is not an effective deterrent of homicide.

Source: R. D. Peterson and Bailey (1988).

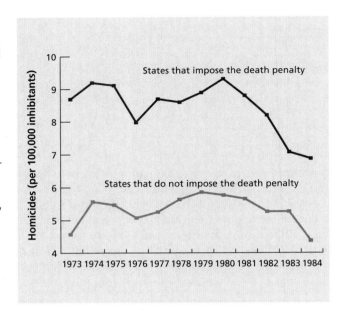

the death penalty have higher (not lower) homicide rates than those who do not impose it, and (2) murder rates did not decline significantly more in states that chose to impose capital punishment than in those that chose not to impose it. On the basis of these and other findings, most social scientists have concluded that the death penalty does not effectively deter violent crimes (R. D. Peterson & Bailey, 1988).

Undoubtedly, the nature of homicide is one reason capital punishment is an ineffective deterrent. Most murderers are driven by passion rather than by a thoughtful consideration of the consequences that await them if they are caught and convicted. Even if this were not the case, the manner in which capital punishment is administered further weakens its effectiveness. For punishment to effectively deter aggression, it must be meted out swiftly and consistently. This is rarely the case when it comes to capital crimes. Many murderers escape detection, and even when they are caught, years pass before they are tried, convicted, sentenced, and executed.

2. Corporal Punishment

> Foolishness is bound in the heart of a child; but the rod of correction shall drive it far from him.
>
> *Proverbs 22:15*

Perhaps less extreme forms of physical punishment are effective. For centuries, parents, teachers, and religious leaders have advocated the use of corporal punishment to curb aggression in children. Is this strategy effective? The answer to this question depends on whether we examine short-term consequences or long-term ones. In the immediate situation, spanking and other, more severe forms of physical punishment do curtail aggressive actions. In the long term, children who are on the receiving end of corporal punishment tend to fare more poorly in life than those who are spared this form of discipline, particularly if the punishment is severe and inflicts injury (Gershoff, 2002).

Why is corporal punishment associated with negative long-term outcomes? First, children who are spanked are less apt to internalize and understand appropriate rules of conduct than are those who are disciplined through other, less physical means. For this reason, parents who use corporal punishment should also take the time to explain why the behavior being punished is undesirable and provide instructions for how the behavior can be avoided in the future.

Another, less tractable problem with corporal punishment is that it tends to produce aggressive children, thereby initiating a cycle of violence that continues into adulthood. Children who receive corporal punishment are not only more apt to use it on their own children but also tend to be more violent toward their spouse. Modeling appears to be the pertinent mechanism (Bandura, 1973). When parents strike their children for acting aggressively, they teach them that violence is an acceptable way to respond to provocation and frustration. The irony, then, is that the very behavior the parents are trying to discourage is reinforced and strengthened.

To summarize, violence begets violence. Consequently, physical discipline should be used sparingly and only as a last resort, when other, less severe forms of discipline have proved ineffective. It should also be mild and accompanied by clear guidelines for behavior (Baumrind, Larzelere, & Cowan, 2002).

C. Catharsis

In the Hollywood movie *Analyze This,* Robert De Niro plays a New York gangster seeking treatment from a psychiatrist (played by Billy Crystal). When the psychiatrist tells De Niro that he should hit a pillow whenever he feels angry, De Niro promptly pulls a pistol out of his pocket and fires several rounds into a pillow. "Feel better?" asks the psychiatrist. "Yeah, I do," De Niro replies.

The movie psychiatrist's advice represents a long-standing tradition in the treatment of aggression, known as the catharsis hypothesis. As discussed earlier in this chapter, the catharsis hypothesis maintains that acting aggressively releases anger and purges aggressive impulses. These beliefs are commonly held by laypeople and professionals alike (Bushman, Baumeister, & Phillips, 2001; Bushman, Baumeister, & Stack, 1999).

For Sigmund Freud, catharsis was not merely desirable but necessary (Freud, 1920/1959, 1932/1963). Freud believed that aggressive impulses increase over time and must be released periodically if people are to maintain psychological health. Otherwise, people are vulnerable to a host of somatic and psychological problems. People who keep their aggression bottled up inside also risk experiencing a dangerous explosion of rage and aggression, which may even turn inward, resulting in suicide. From this perspective, it is better to let off a little steam now and again than to keep anger inside where it is apt to deepen and fester.

1. Direct Catharsis

Catharsis can be achieved in a variety of ways. Direct catharsis occurs when we aggress directly against a person who has provoked us. An investigation by Hokanson and Burgess (1962) examined whether direct catharsis has positive consequences. Half of the participants in this investigation were first provoked by the experimenter, and half were not. Later, some participants were given an opportunity to shock the experimenter as part of an (ostensible) learning task, whereas others were given no such opportunity. Another group of participants in a verbal aggression condition was given the chance to evaluate the experimenter's competence, and participants in a fourth group were allowed to engage in fantasy aggression by writing a story in response to

FIGURE 13.10

Elevations in Systolic Blood Pressure as a Function of Provocation and the Opportunity to Aggress

Provocation increased blood pressure only when participants were not given an opportunity to directly aggress against someone who provoked them. These data support the claim that direct aggression produces a cathartic release of tension.

Source: Hokanson and Burgess (1962).

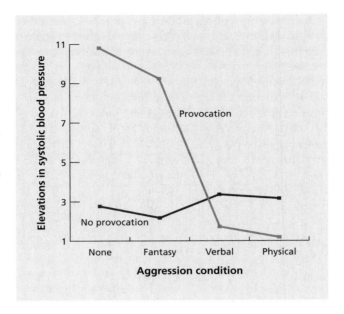

an aggressive picture. Finally, blood pressure readings were taken to determine how upset and aroused participants were feeling.

Figure 13.10 shows some of the results from this investigation. First, notice that in the absence of any provocation, none of the conditions had much of an effect. The situation was different following provocation, however. Here, participants given the chance to verbally or physically aggress were less physiologically upset than were those who were not given the opportunity to release their aggression. In fact, they were as relaxed as those who had never been provoked at all. These findings support the claim that direct aggression produces a cathartic release of tension.

Unfortunately, direct aggression also has some substantial costs. Lashing out against a person who has provoked us can offer a short-term release of aggressive impulses, but the long-term effects are far less positive. As we noted when discussing the effects of corporal punishment, violence begets violence. If we aggress against a person and suffer no negative consequences, we are more apt to aggress against that person in the future. Moreover, we risk becoming embroiled in a more severe situation if the person retaliates. For all of these reasons, direct aggression is an ineffective way to deal with anger and aggressive impulses.

2. Substitute Aggression

In many situations, we are prohibited from aggressing against someone who has provoked us. If our boss criticizes our work, we can't very well respond by hitting him or her or by spewing expletives. In situations like these, people may turn to substitute forms of aggression that offer an indirect form of catharsis.

Displacement is one such behavior. Displacement occurs when we release aggressive drive by aggressing against a person who is not the source of our anger. For example, if you yell at your roommate when you're really mad at your boyfriend or girlfriend, you are exhibiting displacement. There is considerable evidence that people use displacement to release aggressive impulses and that doing so temporarily alleviates aggressive urges (Marcus-Newhall, Pederson, Carlson, & Miller, 2000; N. Miller,

Pederson, Earleywhine, & Pollack, 2003; Pedersen, Gonzales, & Miller, 2000). However, like direct aggression, displacement is not an effective means of dealing with aggressive drive (Baumeister, Dale, & Sommer, 1998). The social costs are too great. Innocent third parties are victimized, and people risk repeating aggression if displaced aggression goes unpunished.

Sublimation constitutes a more appropriate way to handle pent-up aggression. Sublimation occurs when we release aggression in socially acceptable ways. Chopping wood, playing the drums, or taking kickboxing lessons are ways to sublimate aggression. The advantages to sublimation are that no one gets hurt and that society may even benefit. For example, a surgeon may be sublimating aggressive impulses to maul or maim, while providing a much-needed social service. For this reason, Freud believed that sublimation was the most effective way to vent aggressive impulses.

Bushman (2002) conducted a study to see whether sublimation reduces aggression. In this investigation, all participants were first insulted by an experimental confederate. Some participants were then given the chance to hit a punching bag, while other participants did not have this opportunity. Later, when given the chance to deliver aversive bursts of noise to the confederate as part of an (ostensible) reaction-time task, participants in the punching-bag condition were slightly more (not less) aggressive than were participants in the control condition. In short, instead of reducing aggression, sublimation increased it.

One possible explanation for this finding is that the punching bag primed aggressive thoughts and scripts, and these cognitions fed the flames of aggression in the manner specified by Berkowitz's cognitive neoassociation theory (Berkowitz, 1993). Sublimation may more effectively reduce aggression if it is carried out in a manner that does not involve aggression at all (e.g., playing the drums).

3. Dramatic Catharsis

A final form of catharsis involves the vicarious release of aggressive impulses by observing aggression. This account predicts that people who play violent video games or watch violent television shows and movies should behave *less* aggressively than people who are not exposed to violent media. As noted earlier, although it is not entirely clear whether violent media increases aggression, there is no evidence whatsoever that it reduces aggression. Consequently, there is no evidence that dramatic catharsis alleviates aggressive behavior.

4. Summary of the Catharsis Hypothesis

In this section we have reviewed evidence pertaining to the catharsis hypothesis. This evidence can be summarized as follows: People believe in the power of catharsis and often vent their anger instead of holding it in. Although doing so offers immediate psychological and physiological benefits, expressing anger (either directly, indirectly, or vicariously) does not seem to reduce aggressive feelings and behavior over the long term.

Does this mean that the catharsis hypothesis is entirely wrong? Not necessarily. The effects of expressing anger are complex and may be in opposition to one another. For example, if we displace our anger, we may experience an immediate release of aggressive drive (in accordance with the catharsis hypothesis), but a strengthening of a habit because the reduction has reinforced the behavior. Similarly, viewing violence may enable a vicarious release of aggression but may also cognitively prime aggressive thoughts and scripts. These complexities highlight the difficulties in doing experimental research on aggression, while simultaneously calling attention to the need for further investigation.

TABLE 13.6 Components of Interventions to Reduce Aggression

Component	Skills to Be Acquired
Social perspective-taking skills	• Social acuity: ability to accurately read nonverbal behavior • Empathic concern: genuine concern and care for other people's feelings and their well-being
Cognitive/behavioral skills	• Social skills (politeness, control over impulsive behavior, generosity) • Conflict avoidance: ability to anticipate areas of potential conflict and take steps to avert problems before they arise • Conflict resolution: ability to generate and enact nonviolent solutions to problems that arise
Anger management	• Ability to recognize physical cues of anger and to begin relaxation before anger becomes too intense • Acquire strategies designed to keep anger from being expressed (e.g., count to 10; distract instead of ruminate) • Attributional retraining: refrain from assuming hostile intent on the part of others when potential conflicts arise

D. Aggression–Reduction Programs

Finally, we can consider programs expressly developed to curb aggression and antisocial behavior. Such programs have proliferated in recent years, in response to the alarming rate of violence in our society, including our nation's schools (Kazdin, 1987).

Many such programs have been integrated into school curricula. Although various programs exist, they share some common elements (Baldry & Farrington, 2004; Feshbach, 1989; K. S. Frey, 2000; Grossman et al., 1997; Guerra & Slaby, 1990). As shown in Table 13.6, the first component involves the acquisition of two social perspective-taking skills: Social acuity (the ability to accurately read nonverbal behavior in others) and empathic concern (the capacity to experience what another person is experiencing and to care about his or her well-being). The idea here is that violence often occurs when one person misreads the character of a situation or fails to appreciate another person's point of view. By being more sensitive to these matters, we can stop violence before it begins.

The second component is designed to teach various behavioral skills. Many children who are aggressive behave in ways that annoy other children and invite ridicule and rejection. For example, they are rude, selfish, or inattentive to others. By acquiring some basic social skills, they can avoid being provoked by other children and therefore avoid potential conflict.

During this unit children are also taught how to defuse a conflict situation once it begins. Many elementary schools now have conflict managers who roam the playgrounds looking for hot spots that require intervention. Squabbles and arguments are an inevitable feature of playground behavior, but these difficulties can be squelched before they erupt into violence.

A simple apology is a very effective way to resolve a conflict situation (Ohbuchi, Kameda, & Agarie, 1989; Weiner, Amirkhan, Folkes, & Verette, 1987). People are less apt to become aggressive if they believe that the person who provoked them is contrite. For this reason, apologizing for any mistakes we have made can prevent a potentially violent situation from getting out of hand.

A final unit teaches anger management. Here, individuals learn to recognize signs of their own anger and to practice techniques, such as deep breathing or distraction, that will calm them down. Simply counting to 10, thinking of a funny joke, or humming a pleasant tune can effectively reduce aggression, provided we initiate the behavior before our anger becomes too extreme (R. A. Baron, 1976).

Attributional retraining represents another important means of reducing aggression. At the beginning of this book, I asked you to imagine that you were riding on a bus when someone stepped on your toes. I noted that the anger you would feel would depend in large part on why you thought the person stepped on your toes. If you thought it was an unavoidable accident, you would be less angry than if you thought it was done purposefully (Weiner, 1986).

Attributional retraining programs seek to alter the attributions people make when they are provoked. As discussed earlier, aggressive people tend to assume hostile intent on the part of other people. For example, when someone cuts them off in traffic, they assume it was done on purpose rather than by mistake. This assumption of hostile intent feeds their anger and fuels their aggression. By altering the attributions they make for other people's behavior, aggressive people can learn to be less aggressive.

This insight formed the heart of an intervention developed by Hudley and Graham (1993). Using a sample of children nominated by their elementary-school teachers as being highly aggressive, Hudley and Graham taught the children to refrain from assuming that other children intentionally were trying to harm them in situations of ambiguous causality. For example, if they were hit in the head by a ball, they were taught to first consider whether this might be an accident rather than a purposeful act of aggression. At the end of the 12-lesson course, the teachers rated the children's aggressiveness, and this rating was compared to the ratings for children in a control group who never participated in the intervention.

Figure 13.11 shows the results of this intervention. As you can see, children who participated in the attributional retraining program became less aggressive over time, whereas those in the control condition did not.

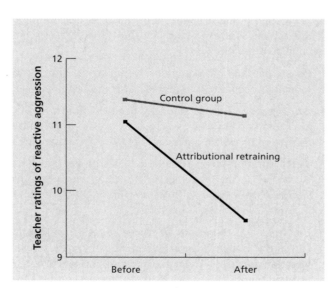

FIGURE 13.11

Attributional Retraining and Anger Management

Students who learned to make benign attributions for potentially provoking situations became less aggressive than did students in a control condition.

Source: Hudley and Graham (1993).

These findings highlight a central tenet of this book: The manner in which we construe, think about, or interpret any act of social behavior influences how we respond. When it comes to aggression, giving other people the benefit of the doubt goes a long way toward reducing violence and promoting positive social interactions.

CHAPTER SUMMARY

- Aggression is any behavior intended to physically or psychologically harm another person. Aggression can be direct or indirect, and physical or verbal. Hostile aggression is fueled by anger and is generally in response to provocation; with instrumental aggression, aggression is a means to an end, undertaken to achieve some other goal. Violence is an especially virulent form of aggression.

- Sigmund Freud believed that aggressive needs are due to a death instinct, which he called Thanatos. This instinct (or drive) continually presses for expression until it is released. From this perspective, aggressive needs can never be completely eliminated; they can only be temporarily satisfied by engaging in aggressive acts.

- Konrad Lorenz also believed that aggression is part of human nature and cannot be eliminated. He did not believe in a death instinct, however. He believed that aggression has evolved to ensure that a species disperses across a broad range of inhabitable land. Animals have evolved appeasement gestures that serve to inhibit aggression, thereby ensuring that aggression doesn't result in excessive violence.

- Men are physically more aggressive than women, committing the vast majority of violent crimes in countries around the world. This difference is due to hormonal and cultural factors.

- Many countries have a culture of honor in which men are taught that aggression is an appropriate response to events that threaten their honor, masculinity, or reputation. Southern regions in the United States seem to be characterized by a culture of honor.

- People can learn to be aggressive by witnessing acts of aggression. This type of modeling occurs only when aggression goes unpunished.

- An aggressive episode generally begins with some sort of provocation. Provocation involves (1) a physical assault; (2) a psychological affront; or (3) some form of frustration, in which a person is blocked from attaining a desired and expected goal.

- The frustration–aggression hypothesis guided much early research on aggression. According to this hypothesis, frustration *always* produces aggression and aggression is *always* the result of frustration. Although influential in its day, the model is now viewed as too simplistic.

- Emotions and cognitions intervene between provocation and aggression. People feel angry when they perceive provocation as a threat and believe it is due to intentional causes. Anger fuels aggression when aggression is thought to be justified, appropriate, and likely to be successful. These factors are related in a reciprocal fashion, such that anger can prime aggressive thoughts and aggressive thoughts can prime anger.

- People differ with respect to how hostile they are. Hostility can arise from a number of sources, including narcissism, competitiveness, a tendency to brood and ruminate, impulsiveness, and a propensity to be critical of others. Once formed, hostility tends to persist across the lifespan, such that aggressive children become aggressive adults. Hostility also seems to be inheritable, as twin studies show that monozygotic (identical) twins are more similar with respect to hostility than are dyzygotic (fraternal) twins.

- Situational factors can bring out the aggressiveness in almost everyone. Factors that cause physical discomfort, such as pain, heat, overcrowding, and fatigue lead people to become short-tempered and aggressive. Arousal increases aggression by producing discomfort, impairing our ability to think of nonaggressive solutions to problems, and intensifying our emotional reaction to provocation. People are also more aggressive when they are immersed in a group setting or otherwise lacking in self-awareness. Finally, alcohol is implicated in many acts of aggression.

- People who watch violent television shows and movies, and play violent video games tend to be more aggressive than people who do not use this form of entertainment, and exposure to media violence causes aggression in laboratory experiments, particularly among people who are hostile and provoked. There is less evidence, however, that exposure to violent media causes aggression in real-world settings.

- Most violence occurs among people who know one another very well. In school settings, people who are taunted, teased, excluded or ostracized can turn to violence as a form of retribution.

- Sexual violence is a major problem in countries across the world. Some of this violence is due to the presence of rape myths that serve to justify and excuse male sexual aggression against women. Men prone to rape have negative attitudes toward women and a promiscuous attitude toward sexual relations.

- Experimental studies conducted in laboratory settings have found that nonviolent pornography does not increase aggression toward women, but violent pornography that depicts a woman enjoying forcible sex promotes aggression toward women, regardless of whether or not a man has been provoked. Finally, violent pornography that depicts a woman being brutalized by forcible sex promotes aggression toward women among men who have been provoked but not among those who have not been provoked.

- Acquaintance (or date) rape is frequently reported on college campuses. In some cases, these incidents stem from miscommunication between a man and a woman. In other cases, date rape is planned and carried out with the use of alcohol or drugs. Regardless of the circumstances, date rape is a serious crime that can land a perpetrator in prison for many years.

- Punishment can be an effective deterrent of aggression provided it is applied swiftly and consistently. Physical punishment has positive, short-term effects, but negative long-term ones. Children who are spanked tend to grow up to be more aggressive toward their own children and toward their spouses.

- Catharsis involves the release of aggressive drive by committing (or witnessing) acts of aggression. Although many people believe it is effective to let off steam now and again, research suggests that catharsis has at least as many negative consequences as positive ones.

- Aggression reduction programs have proliferated in recent years. Many school-based programs teach perspective-taking skills, social skills, and anger management exercises. Giving people the benefit of the doubt is one way to reduce anger and aggression.

KEY TERMS

aggression, 475

hostile aggression, 476

instrumental aggression, 476

catharsis hypothesis, 477

frustration-aggression hypothesis, 483

hostility, 485

hostile attribution bias, 487

excitation transfer theory, 489

deindividuation, 490

bullying, 496

rape myths, 497

belief in a just world, 497

pornography, 499

displacement, 506

sublimation, 507

ADDITIONAL READING

Go to the Student Edition of the Online Learning Center for this text (www.mhhe.com/brown) and log in to read the following journal articles, which relate to the content of this chapter:

- Bandura, A., Ross, D., & Ross, S. A. (1961). Transmission of aggression through imitation of aggressive models.

- Bushman, B. J. (1995). Moderating role of trait aggressiveness in the effects of violent media on aggression.

Glossary

actor–observer effect The tendency to make dispositional attributions for behavior is more evident when we explain other people's behavior than when we explain our own behavior.

affiliation The desire to seek the company of others.

aggression Behavior intended to physically or psychologically harm another person.

altruism The act of helping others without regard to whether one will derive any sort of personal benefit.

anchoring and adjustment heuristic A tendency to make judgments by beginning with an initial estimate (an anchor) and then adjusting this estimate to reach a final decision.

applied research Research undertaken to solve some problem or achieve some practical benefit.

approach–approach conflict Conflict between two equally pleasant alternatives.

approach–avoidance conflict Conflict involving a single choice that has both positive (approach) and negative (avoidance) properties.

associationism A philosophical doctrine maintaining that complex ideas are the sum of smaller, more elemental ideas joined together.

assortative mating A tendency for two people who are married to be similar to each other on a variety of physical and psychological variables.

attitudes Evaluative reactions to people, issues, or objects.

augmenting principle When making attributions, people tend to decide that behavior must be due to a dispositional cause when a person behaves in a manner that is inconsistent with the requirements of the situation.

availability heuristic The tendency to make a decision on the basis of information that readily comes to mind.

aversive racism A genuine desire to be nonprejudiced accompanied by negative feelings toward outgroup members.

avoidance–avoidance conflict Conflict between two equally unpleasant alternatives.

balance theory A social psychological theory that asserts that people strive to maintain cognitive balance in their interpersonal relationships. Balance is maintained when people are associated with things they like and disassociated with things they don't like.

base-rate fallacy A tendency to make likelihood judgments based on representativeness rather than on sample prevalence.

basic research Research undertaken to understand a phenomenon.

behavioral confirmation effect The result that occurs when our expectations about another person lead us to act in ways that confirm our expectancies.

behaviorism A school of psychological thought characterized by three assumptions: (1) psychologists should study only directly observable behavior, (2) thoughts do not influence behavior, and (3) sensory pleasure is reinforcing.

belief in a just world The tendency to blame people for their misfortunes because of the belief that good things happen to good people, and bad things happen to bad people.

belief perseverance effect The tendency for people to cling to their beliefs even after they learn that the evidence underlying these beliefs is flawed.

benevolent sexism The belief that women are pure creatures who should be pampered, protected, and placed on a pedestal.

better-than-most effect The tendency of most people to think they have more positive (and fewer negative) qualities than do most other people.

bottom-up processing The act of basing judgments on data rather than on inference.

bullying A persistent pattern of behavior in which one person intentionally abuses another by means of verbal taunts or acts of teasing, physical assaults, deliberate exclusion from social activities, or attempts to sabotage his or her social relationships by spreading malicious gossip and rumors.

bystander effect The tendency for the presence of other people to inhibit helping.

catharsis hypothesis Hypothesis that states that aggressive needs can be satisfied by exhibiting or witnessing aggression.

cathexis In Freudian theory, psychological energy invested in a desired object.

causal attributions The explanations we make for the events we observe.

central route to attitude change Process that occurs when people are motivated *and* able to think carefully about a message.

central traits Traits capable of completely altering the impression we form of another person, such as a person's warmth.

classical conditioning A process of learning in which two stimuli become associated through similarity or temporal contiguity.

cognitive dissonance An aversive state of arousal that arises when two or more cognitions are inconsistent with one another.

cognitive heuristics Efficient problem-solving strategies that generally yield accurate solutions but can produce judgmental errors.

cognitive response theory Theory that states that all attitude change occurs as a result of the thoughts a person has while receiving a persuasive appeal.

commons dilemma A social dilemma in which individuals must decide how much of a shared commodity to use.

communal relationships Relationships in which members pledge to be responsive to one another's needs without keeping track of whether their own costs match their benefits.

companionate love A deep, abiding attachment, characterized by feelings of caring, affection, and respect.

comparison level (CL) In Kelley and Thibaut's (1978) interdependence model, the minimum outcome level one finds satisfactory.

comparison level of alternatives (CL$_{alt}$) In Kelley and Thibaut's (1978) interdependence model, the outcome level one believes one could obtain in alternative relationships.

compliance A change in behavior in response to a direct request.

confederate In an experiment, an accomplice of the experimenter who pretends to be a regular participant.

confound An uncontrolled variable that affects our dependent variable. Also called a confounding variable.

contingency theory of leadership Theory that states that leadership effectiveness depends on the match

between leadership style and situational control.

correlational research Research undertaken to discover the association between two or more naturally occurring variables.

correspondence bias See *fundamental attribution error.*

correspondent inference An attribution for behavior to a corresponding disposition.

counterfactual thinking A tendency to believe that a different outcome would have occurred if different events had taken place.

culture Socially constructed and socially transmitted confederation of beliefs, values, goals, norms, traditions, and institutions.

defensive pessimism The fear that one is apt to fail despite a strong history of success.

deindividuation A diminished state of self-awareness that can arise when individuals become part of a group.

demand characteristics Cues in an experimental setting that lead participants to believe a particular behavior is expected or demanded.

dependent variable In an experiment, the variable the experimenter measures.

diffusion-of-responsibility effect The belief that we don't need to help in an emergency because other people will do so.

discounting principle When making attributions, people tend to discount the role of a dispositional factor when an obvious situational cause is present.

discrimination A tendency to behave negatively toward a social group and its members.

displacement Aggression directed against a person who is not the source of our anger.

dispositional attribution The tendency to attribute behavior to an enduring, inherent personal quality, such as a person's character, personality, or ability.

double-blind study A study in which neither the participant nor the experimenter knows which condition the participant is in.

drive An internal need that stimulates an organism to act.

egoism A philosophical doctrine that maintains that people always act out of self-interest.

emotional theories of attitude formation Theories that assume that emotions are primary in the formation of attitudes and that attitudes arise independent of beliefs.

empathy The capacity to take the perspective of another person.

empiricism A philosophical school of thought that maintains that truth is acquired through sensory experience.

equity theory A social exchange theory that asserts that people seek and are most satisfied with an interpersonal relationship when their own benefits/costs ratio equals their partner's benefits/costs ratio.

evaluation apprehension Participants' concern about being evaluated or judged during an experiment.

exchange relationships Relationships in which members give with an expectation that they will receive a comparable benefit in the near future.

excitation transfer theory Theory that states that arousal generated from one stimulus can "spill over" and intensify an emotional reaction to a different stimulus.

experimental research Research undertaken to discover whether one variable causes another.

experimenter expectancy effects A process by which experimenters unwittingly lead participants to confirm the experimenters' hypothesis.

explicit attitudes Consciously accessible attitudes that can be misrepresented by self-report.

expressiveness The ability to effectively send nonverbal messages.

extended self Objects, people, and groups that are part of the self-concept.

external validity A standard for evaluating research. Research has high external validity if the findings can be generalized to other participants in other situations.

false-consensus effect The tendency to believe that our opinions and shortcomings are relatively common.

false-uniqueness effect The tendency to believe that our strengths and virtues are rare and distinctive.

field setting Any naturally occurring environment in which scientists conduct research.

forewarning effects People who learn that a person is going to attempt to persuade them are better able to resist attitude change, provided that they are allowed to generate counterarguments before persuasion begins.

frustration-aggression hypothesis Hypothesis that states that frustration *always* produces aggression and aggression is *always* the result of frustration.

fundamental attribution error When making attributions, the tendency to underestimate the importance of situational causes and overestimate the importance of dispositional ones. Also called correspondence bias.

gambler's fallacy The tendency to believe that random events are self-correcting.

graduated and reciprocated initiative in tension reduction (GRIT) A strategy for resolving a mixed-motive dilemma, in which one party announces its intention to cooperate and then behaves cooperatively. If exploited, the party temporarily retaliates, then resumes cooperative behavior.

group polarization effect A tendency for group decisions to be more extreme than the decisions of individuals.

group An interdependent collection of individuals who interact and possess a shared identity.

group selection Mechanism operating as part of natural selection whereby groups with helpful individuals were more apt to survive, and those who helped were rewarded by being allowed to mate more freely.

groupthink A group decision-making style characterized by a tendency to value group harmony more than effective decision making.

halo effect The belief that positive traits go together in people.

hedonism A philosophical doctrine maintaining that sensory pleasure is the goal of life.

helping A prosocial behavior intended to alleviate another person's distress.

hindsight bias A bias that occurs when people overestimate the probability that a known outcome would occur.

hostile aggression Reactive aggression, fueled by anger, whose ultimate aim is to inflict injury on another person.

hostile attribution bias A tendency to assume that provocation is intentional.

hostile sexism The belief that women are incompetent, overly emotional, and manipulative.

hostility The propensity for an individual to become angry and act aggressively.

hypothesis An educated guess about how two or more variables are related.

identity influence Conformity motivated by a desire to think of ourselves as being a certain kind of person.

idiosyncrasy credits Interpersonal credits a minority gains by going along with the majority.

illusion of control A bias that occurs when people overestimate the covariation between their actions and environmental outcomes.

illusory correlation A bias that occurs when people overestimate the correlation between two (or more) variables.

implicit attitudes Unconscious attitudes that are measured indirectly rather than by self-report.

implicit personality theory A schema that represents the pairing of two or more personality traits.

independent variable In an experiment the variable the experimenter manipulates or varies.

informational influence Conformity motivated by a desire to hold correct opinions and do the right thing.

ingroup favoritism A tendency to treat and evaluate ingroup members more favorably than outgroup members.

inoculation effects People who hear a two-sided message are more resistant to persuasion than those who hear a one-sided message.

instrumental aggression Proactive aggression in which aggression is a means to an end.

instrumental conditioning A process of learning in which a response is joined to a stimulus because the response has meet with prior reinforcement. Also called instrumental learning.

interaction A statistical effect that occurs when the effect of one independent variable changes at different levels of another independent variable.

internal validity A standard for evaluating research. Research has high internal validity if it has clearly established that our independent variable (x) caused our dependent variable (y).

introspection A personal process in which we learn about ourselves by accessing and analyzing our thoughts and feelings.

introspectionism A school of psychological thought devoted to identifying the smallest elements of conscious experience.

investments In Rusbult's (1980, 1983) investment model, tangible and intangible things one has put into a relationship that would be lost if the relationship were dissolved.

kin selection An egoistic form of helping in which people help their kin in order to pass along their genes to the next generation.

laboratory A research setting where the experimenter has control over the kind of events that occur and the sequence in which they occur.

law of effect A principle of learning that maintains that behavior is guided by its previous consequences. Behaviors that have met with prior reinforcement persist, and those that have not perish.

leadership A reciprocal relationship in which an individual exerts social influence over cooperating individuals to promote the attainment of group goals.

learned helplessness A state of passivity and resignation that arises when people (and animals) believe they have no control over what happens to them.

loneliness A distressing emotional state caused by a lack of meaningful interpersonal relationships.

main effect A statistical effect that occurs when a single independent variable affects a dependent variable.

mechanism An assumption that thoughts play no role in guiding behavior.

mere exposure effect The fact that the more often we are exposed to a neutral stimulus, the more we like it.

mere presence hypothesis Hypothesis that states that the mere presence of others creates arousal sufficient to enhance performance at easy tasks and impair performance at difficult tasks.

message learning approach An approach to studying persuasion developed by the Yale Communication and Attitude Program that emphasizes that attitudes are verbal habits and are changed through incentives.

meta-analysis A statistical technique used to combine the results of many independent studies.

minimal group paradigm A procedure for testing social identity theory, in which group membership is arbitrary and participants never have any contact with one another.

negative correlation When increases in one variable are accompanied by decreases in another variable.

negotiation The process by which two or more interdependent parties attempt to resolve conflicting preferences.

nonverbal communication Communication that occurs through facial expressions, kinesic cues, paralinguistic cues, and proxemic cues.

nonverbal leakage The revelation of deception through behaviors that are difficult to control (e.g., auditory cues such as speech hesitations, vocal pitch, and speech errors).

normative influence Conformity motivated by a desire to win the approval of others (or avoid their disapproval).

norms See *social norms*.

obedience Compliance to the dictates of an authority figure.

outcome level (OL) In Kelley and Thibaut's (1978) interdependence model, the relative balance of benefits and costs that one obtains in a relationship.

outgroup homogeneity bias A tendency to underestimate the variability among outgroup members.

participants Individuals who participate in psychological research.

passionate love An intense emotional state, involving sexual desire, feelings of ecstasy, and perhaps anguish.

perceptiveness The ability to accurately read nonverbal messages.

peripheral route to attitude change Process that occurs when people are either unmotivated *or* unable to think about the merits of a message. The attitude change is due to factors unrelated to the perceived merits of the message.

personal distress An egoistic emotional reaction to another person's state of need, characterized by feelings of alarm, discomfort, and uneasiness.

personality Enduring, consistent, and characteristic patterns of thinking, feeling, and behaving that originate within an individual.

phenomenology A school of psychological thought that maintains that people's behavior is guided by the world as it appears to them.

pluralistic ignorance A social psychological phenomenon that occurs when people misread other people's behaviors and assume their own thoughts and feelings are unique.

pornography Sexually explicit material intended to cause erotic arousal.

positive correlation When increases in one variable are accompanied by increases in another variable.

positivism A methodological doctrine that asserts that an idea if true only if it can be observed to be true by multiple, objective observers.

Prägnanz A German word that refers to the act of perceiving so as to achieve maximum clarity.

prejudice A negative attitude directed toward a group and its members.

prejudiced feelings Negative feelings toward a group and its members.

primacy effect Effect that occurs when information we first learn affects our judgments more than information acquired at a later time.

priming effect The effect that occurs when recent experiences activate a schema.

prisoner's dilemma A mixed-motives dilemma in which everyone is better off cooperating, but cooperating with a competitive partner brings personal disaster.

projection The unconscious tendency to assume that other people possess the undesirable qualities we fear that we possess.

proximity effect The tendency to feel emotionally close to those who are physically near.

psychological reactance An aversive psychological state that arises when people perceive that their freedom of choice is restricted. People respond to this state by reasserting their freedom, leading to an increased desire for the forbidden object.

public goods dilemma A social dilemma in which individuals must decide how much of their own resources they will donate to a public project.

racism A particular form of prejudice based solely on race.

random assignment Used in an experiment, random assignment to conditions ensures that each subject has an equal chance of being assigned to any of the various experimental conditions.

random sampling A process used to select participants in a study. A sample is random only when each member of a population has an equal chance of being selected to participate.

rape myths Prevalent attitudes and beliefs about the nature of rape that serve to justify and excuse male sexual aggression against women.

rationalism A philosophical school of thought that maintains that truth is acquired through logic and reasoning.

reactive devaluation effect A tendency for a negotiator to believe that concessions offered by the opposition are unfairly disadvantageous to the negotiator's own side.

realistic group conflict theory Theory that states that prejudice arises when groups compete for scarce resources.

reciprocal "altruism" An egoistic form of helping in which people who helped others were more apt to receive help and thereby pass their genes on to the next generation.

reciprocity principle A tendency to like others who like us.

reflected appraisal model A model that describes the process of how we learn about ourselves by imagining how we appear in other people's eyes.

regression to the mean A statistical phenomenon in which extreme events tend to be followed by less extreme ones.

relationship superiority bias A tendency to assume that one's own romantic relationship is better than other people's.

relative deprivation The perception that one is relatively deprived in comparison with other people.

representativeness heuristic A tendency to believe that the probability of an occurrence depends on how well it matches our beliefs about what should occur.

repression In Freudian theory, an active force that keeps painful thoughts from gaining conscious awareness.

scapegoating Blaming other people inappropriately for one's own negative outcomes.

schemas Hypothetical cognitive structures that influence the way we process information.

self-concept People's ideas about who they are and what they are like.

self-efficacy beliefs Beliefs related to one's own ability to perform some action.

self-enhancement motive A universal desire to enhance feelings of self-worth and feel good about oneself.

self-perception theory Theory that maintains that we learn about ourselves by passively observing our own behavior.

self-presentation Any behavior intended to create, modify, or maintain an impression of ourselves in the minds of others.

self-reference effect The tendency of people to easily remember information that they have related to themselves.

self-serving attribution bias Bias that arises when people make dispositional attributions for their success but situational attributions for their failure.

sexism A form of prejudice based solely on gender.

simulation heuristic The tendency to judge the probability of a future event on the ease with which it can be imagined.

situational attribution An attribution to any factor that isn't dispositional— see *dispositional attribution*.

situational variable Any factor that provides the context for an event or experience.

sleeper effect The tendency for the persuasive impact of a low-credibility source to increase over time.

social comparison theory Theory that maintains that we learn about ourselves by comparing ourselves with other people.

social dilemma A situation in which two or more interdependent individuals face a conflict between maximizing their own interests or sacrificing their interests for the group's benefit.

social exchange theory A theory of interpersonal relationships that holds that people have certain goods they bring to the interpersonal marketplace and that they strive to get as much in return for these goods as they can.

social facilitation theory Theory that states that the mere presence of others creates arousal that enhances performance on easy tasks but impairs performance on difficult tasks.

social identity theory Theory that states that people strive to feel good about themselves, and one way they satisfy this goal is by believing that their group is superior to other groups.

social influence The process by which people affect the thoughts, feelings, and behavior of others.

social judgment theory Theory that states that a person's attitude serves as an anchor against which other attitude positions are compared.

social loafing The tendency of people to exert less effort when working with others than when working alone.

social norms Unwritten rules of social conduct.

social perception The study of how we form impressions of other people and how those impressions affect the way we act toward them.

social psychology The scientific study of how people perceive, affect, and relate to one another.

social role theory The theory that gender differences in social roles underlie gender differences in social status and behavior.

social support Our involvement in social activities and our perception that we can count on others for help.

stereotype threat The threat that arises when one fears being judged by a negative stereotype.

stereotypes Schemas and beliefs about the qualities that characterize members of a social group.

stress-buffering effect The tendency for people who enjoy high levels of social support to be better able to withstand stress than people with low levels of social support.

subjective well-being People's assessments of their own happiness and life satisfaction.

sublimation Aggression released in socially acceptable ways.

symbolic prejudice Prejudice directed toward any group that is viewed as violating one's values or worldview.

sympathy An other-directed emotional reaction to another person's state of need, characterized by feelings of concern, compassion, and tenderness.

theories General principles that explain why two or more variables are related.

top-down processing The act of using prior knowledge to guide interpretation of perceptual data.

two-factor theory of emotion A theory that maintains that emotional experience is comprised of two factors: physiological arousal and a cognitive label.

values Broad, abstract ideals that (unlike attitudes) lack a specific referent.

volunteerism Long-term planned helping that usually takes place in an organizational setting.

"what is beautiful is good" stereotype The belief that physically attractive people have pleasing personalities.

References

Aaker, J. L., Benet-Martínez, V., & Garolera, J. (2001). Consumption symbols as carriers of culture: A study of Japanese and Spanish brand personality constructs. *Journal of Personality and Social Psychology, 81,* 492–508.

Aaker, J. L., & Schmitt, B. (2001). Culture-dependent assimilation and differentiation of the self: Preferences for consumption symbols in the United States and China. *Journal of Cross-Cultural Psychology, 32,* 561–576.

Aarts, H., & Dijksterhuis, A. (2000). Habits as knowledge structures: Automaticity in goal-directed behavior. *Journal of Personality and Social Psychology, 78,* 53–63.

Abbey, A. (1982). Sex differences in attributions for friendly behavior: Do males misperceive females' friendliness? *Journal of Personality and Social Psychology, 42,* 830–838.

Abbey, A. (1987). Misperceptions of friendly behavior as sexual interest: A survey of naturally occurring incidents. *Psychology of Women Quarterly, 11,* 173–194.

Abel, G. G., Barlow, D. H., Blanchard, E. B., & Guild, D. (1977). The components of rapists' sexual arousal. *Archives of General Psychiatry, 34,* 895–903.

Abelson, R. P. (1986). Beliefs are like possessions. *Journal for the Theory of Social Behaviour, 16,* 222–250.

Abelson, R. P., Aronson, E., McGuire, W. J., Newcomb, T. M., Rosenberg, M. J., & Tannenbaum, P. H. (Eds.). (1968). *Theories of cognitive consistency: A sourcebook.* Skokie, IL: Rand-McNally.

Abelson, R. P., Kinder, D. R., Peters, M. D., & Fiske, S. T. (1982). Affective and semantic components in political person perception. *Journal of Personality and Social Psychology, 42,* 619–630.

Aberson, C. L., Healy, M., & Romero, V. (2000). Ingroup bias and self-esteem: A meta-analysis. *Personality and Social Psychology Review, 4,* 157–173.

Abrami, P. C., Leventhal, L. & Perry, R. P. (1982). Educational seduction. *Review of Educational Research, 52,* 446–464.

Adair, W. L., Okumura, T., & Brett, J. M. (2001). Negotiation behavior when cultures collide: The United States and Japan. *Journal of Applied Psychology, 86,* 371–385.

Adams, G. R., & Huston, T. L. (1975). Social perception of middle-aged persons varying in physical attractiveness. *Developmental Psychology, 5,* 657–658.

Adams, J. S. (1963). Toward an understanding of inequity. *Journal of Abnormal and Social Psychology, 67,* 422–436.

Adorno, T. W., Frenkel-Brunswik, E., Levinson, D. J., & Sanford, R. N. (1950). *The authoritarian personality.* New York: Harper & Brothers.

Agnew, C. R., Van Lange, P. A. M., Rusbult, C. E., & Langston, C. A. (1998). Cognitive interdependence: Commitment and the mental representation of close relationships. *Journal of Personality and Social Psychology, 74,* 939–954.

Ainsworth, M. D. S., Blehar, M. C., Waters, E., & Wall, S. (1978). *Patterns of attachment: A psychological study of the strange situation.* Mahwah, NJ: Erlbaum.

Ajzen, I. (1985). From intentions to actions: A theory of planned behavior. In J. Kuhl & J. Beckmann (Eds.), *Action control: From cognition to behavior* (pp. 11–39). New York: Springer-Verlag.

Ajzen, I. (1988). *Attitudes, personality, and behavior.* Homewood, IL: Dorsey.

Ajzen, I., & Fishbein, M. (1977). Attitude-behavior relations: A theoretical analysis and review of empirical research. *Psychological Bulletin, 84,* 888–918.

Ajzen, I., & Fishbein, M. (1980). *Understanding attitudes and predicting social behavior.* Englewood Cliffs, NJ: Prentice Hall.

Ajzen, I., & Madden, T. J. (1986). Prediction of goal-directed behavior: Attitudes, intentions, and perceived behavioral control. *Journal of Experimental Social Psychology, 22,* 453–474.

Albarracín, D., Johnson, B. T., Fishbein, M., & Muellerleile, P. A. (2001). Theories of reasoned action and planned behavior as models of condom use: A meta-analysis. *Psychological Bulletin, 127,* 142–161.

Albarracín, D., & Kumkale, G. T. (2003). Affect as information in persuasion: A model of affect identification and discounting. *Journal of Personality and Social Psychology, 84,* 453–469.

Albarracín, D., & Wyer, R. S., Jr. (2000). The cognitive impact of past behavior: Influences on beliefs, attitudes, and future behavioral decisions. *Journal of Personality and Social Psychology, 79,* 5–22.

Albright, L., & Forziati, C. (1995). Cross-situational consistency and perceptual accuracy in leadership. *Personality and Social Psychology Bulletin, 21,* 1269–1276.

Aldag, R. J., & Fuller, S. R. (1993). Beyond fiasco: A reappraisal of the groupthink phenomenon and a new model of group decision processes. *Psychological Bulletin, 113,* 533–552.

Allen, K. M., Blascovich, J., Tomaka, J., & Kelsey, R. M. (1991). Presence of human friends and pet dogs as moderators of autonomic responses to stress in women. *Journal of Personality and Social Psychology, 61,* 582–589.

Allen, M. (1991). Meta-analysis comparing the persuasiveness of one-sided and two-sided messages. *Western Journal of Speech Communication, 55,* 390–404.

Allen, V. L., & Levine, J. M. (1969). Consensus and conformity. *Journal of Experimental Social Psychology, 5,* 389–399.

Alley, T. R., & Cunningham, M. R. (1991). Averaged faces are attractive, but very attractive faces are not average. *Psychological Science, 2,* 123–125.

Allison, S. T., & Kerr, N. L. (1994). Group correspondence biases and the provision of public goods. *Journal of Personality and Social Psychology, 66,* 688–698.

Allison, S. T., McQueen, L. R., & Schaerfl, L. M. (1992). Social decision making processes and the equal partionment of shared resources. *Journal of Experimental Social Psychology, 28,* 23–42.

Allport, G. W. (1935). Attitudes. In C. Murchison (Ed.), *Handbook of social psychology* (pp. 798–844). Worcester, MA: Clark University Press.

Allport, G. W. (1943). The ego in contemporary psychology. *Psychological Review, 50,* 451–478.

Allport, G. W. (1954). *The nature of prejudice.* Cambridge, MA: Addison-Wesley.

Allport, G. W. (1955). *Becoming: Basic considerations for a psychology of personality.* New Haven, CT: Yale University Press.

Allport, G. W., & Ross, J. M. (1967). Personal religious orientation and prejudice. *Journal of Personality and Social Psychology, 5,* 432–443.

Altemeyer, B. (1988). *Enemies of freedom: Understanding right-wing authoritarianism.* San Francisco: Jossey-Bass.

Altemeyer, B. & Hunsberger, B. (1992). Authoritarianism, religious fundamentalism, quest, and prejudice. *The International Journal for the Psychology of Religion, 2,* 113–133.

Altman, I., & Taylor, D. A. (1973). *Social penetration: The development of interpersonal relationships.* New York: Holt, Rinehart, & Winston.

Alwin, D. F., Cohen, R. L., & Newcomb, T. M. (1991). *The women of Bennington: A study of political orientations over the life span.* Madison, WI: University of Wisconsin Press.

Amabile, T. M., Hill, K. G., Hennessey, B. A., & Tighe, E. M. (1994). The work preference inventory: Assessing intrinsic and extrinsic motivational orientations. *Journal of Personality and Social Psychology, 66,* 950–967.

Amato, P. R. (1983). Helping behavior in urban and rural environments: Field studies based on a taxonomic organization of helping episodes. *Journal of Personality and Social Psychology, 45,* 571–586.

Amato, P. R. (1990). Personality and social network involvement as predictors of helping behavior in everyday life. *Social Psychology Quarterly, 53,* 31–43.

Ambady, N., Hallahan, M., & Conner, B. (1999). Accuracy of judgments of sexual orientation from thin slices of behavior. *Journal of Personality and Social Psychology, 77,* 538–547.

American Association of University Women Educational Foundation. (1998). *Separated by sex: A critical look at single-sex education for girls.* Washington, DC: Author.

Ames, C., & Ames, R. (1984). Systems of student and teacher motivation: Toward a qualitative definition. *Journal of Educational Psychology, 76,* 535–556.

Amodio, D. M., Harmon-Jones, E., & Devine, P. G. (2003). Individual differences in the activation and control of affective race bias as assessed by startle eyeblink response and self-report. *Journal of Personality and Social Psychology, 84,* 738–753.

Andersen, S. M. (1984). Self-knowledge and social inference: II. The diagnosticity of cognitive/affective and behavioral data. *Journal of Personality and Social Psychology, 46,* 294–307.

Andersen, S. M., & Bem, S.L. (1981). Sex typing and androgyny in dyadic interaction: Individual differences in responsiveness to physical attractiveness. *Journal of Personality and Social Psychology, 41,* 74–86.

Andersen, S. M., & Chen, S. (2002). The relational self: An interpersonal social-cognitive theory. *Psychological Review, 109,* 619–645.

Andersen, S. M., & Ross, L. (1984). Self-knowledge and social inference: I. The impact of cognitive/affective and behavioral data. *Journal of Personality and Social Psychology, 46,* 280–293.

Anderson, C. A. (1987). Temperature and aggression: Effects on quarterly, yearly, and city rates of violent and nonviolent crimes. *Journal of Personality and Social Psychology, 52,* 1161–1173.

Anderson, C. A. (1989). Temperature and aggression: Ubiquitous effects of heat on occurrence of human violence. *Psychological Bulletin, 106,* 74–96.

Anderson, C. A., & Anderson, K. B. (1996). Violent crime rate studies in philosophical context: A destructive testing approach to heat and southern culture of violence effects. *Journal of Personality and Social Psychology, 70,* 740–756.

Anderson, C. A., Benjamin, A. J., Jr., & Bartholow, B. D. (1998). Does the gun pull the trigger? Automatic priming effects of weapon pictures and weapon names. *Psychological Science, 9,* 308–314.

Anderson, C. A., & Bushman, B. J. (2002). Human aggression. *Annual Review of Psychology, 53,* 27–51.

Anderson, C. A., Bushman, B. J., & Groom, R. W. (1997). Hot years and serious and deadly assault: Empirical tests of the heat hypothesis. *Journal of Personality and Social Psychology, 73,* 1213–1223.

Anderson, C. A., & DeNeve, K. M. (1992). Temperature, aggression, and the negative affect escape model. *Psychological Bulletin, 111,* 347–351.

Anderson, C. A., Deuser, W. E., & DeNeve, K. M. (1995). Hot temperatures, hostile affect, hostile cognition, and arousal: Tests of a general model of affective aggression. *Personality and Social Psychology Bulletin, 21,* 434–448.

Anderson, C. A., & Harvey, R. J. (1988). Discrimination between problems in living: An examination of measures of depression, loneliness, shyness, and social anxiety. *Journal of Social and Clinical Psychology, 6,* 482–491.

Anderson, C. A., Lepper, M., & Ross, L. (1980). Perseverance of social theories: The role of explanation in the persistence of discredited information. *Journal of Personality and Social Psychology, 39,* 1037–1049.

Anderson, D. E., DePaulo, B. M., & Ansfield, M. E. (2002). The development of deception detection skills: A longitudinal study of same-sex friends. *Personality and Social Psychology Bulletin, 28,* 536–545.

Anderson, K. B., Anderson, C. A., Dill, K. E., & Deuser, W. E. (1998). The interactive relations between trait hostility, pain, and aggressive thoughts. *Aggressive Behavior, 24,* 161–171.

Anderson, K. B., Cooper, H., & Okamura, L. (1997). Individual differences and attitudes toward rape: A meta-analytic review. *Personality and Social Psychology Bulletin, 23,* 295–315.

Anderson, N. H. (1965a). Averaging versus adding as a stimulus-combination rule in impression formation. *Journal of Experimental Psychology, 70,* 394–400.

Anderson, N. H. (1965b). Primacy effects in personality impression formation using a generalized order effect paradigm. *Journal of Personality and Social Psychology, 2,* 1–9.

Anderson, N. H. (1968). Likableness ratings of 555 personality trait adjectives. *Journal of Personality and Social Psychology, 9,* 272–279.

Anderson, N. H. (1974). Cognitive algebra: Integration theory applied to social attribution. In L. Berkowitz (Ed.), *Advances in experimental social psychology* (Vol. 7, pp. 1–101). New York: Academic Press.

Anderson, N. H., & Barrios, A. A. (1961). Primacy effects in personality impression formation. *Journal of Abnormal and Social Psychology, 63,* 346–350.

Anderson, N. H., & Hubert, S. (1963). Effects of concomitant verbal recall on order effects in personality impression formation. *Journal of Verbal Learning and Verbal Behavior, 2,* 379–391.

Anderson, N. H., & Jacobson, A. (1965). Effect of stimulus inconsistency and discounting instruction in personality impression formation. *Journal of Personality and Social Psychology, 2,* 531–539.

Anthony, T., Cooper, C., & Mullen, B. (1992). Cross-racial facial identification: A social cognitive integration. *Personality and Social Psychology Bulletin, 18,* 296–301.

Antonucci, T. C., & Israel, B. A. (1986). Veridicality of social support: A comparison of principal and network members' responses. *Journal of Counseling and Clinical Psychology, 54,* 432–447.

Apsler, R. (1975). Effects of embarrassment on behavior toward others. *Journal of Personality and Social Psychology, 32,* 145–153.

Apsler, R., & Sears, D. O. (1968). Warning, personal involvement, and attitude change. *Journal of Personality and Social Psychology, 9,* 162–168.

Aquino, K., & Reed, A., II. (2002). The self-importance of moral identity. *Journal of Personality and Social Psychology, 83,* 1423–1440.

Archer, D., Iritani, B., Kimes, D. D., & Barrios, M. (1983). Face-ism: Five studies of sex differences in facial prominence. *Journal of Personality and Social Psychology, 45,* 725–735.

Archer, J. (1988). *The behavioural biology of aggression.* Cambridge: Cambridge University Press.

Archer, J. (1991). The influence of testosterone on human aggression. *British Journal of Psychology, 82,* 1–28.

Archer, J. (2000). Sex differences in aggression between heterosexual partners: A meta-analytic review. *Psychological Bulletin, 126,* 651–680.

Archibald, F. S., Bartholomew, K., & Marx, R. (1995). Loneliness in early adolescence: A test of the cognitive discrepancy model of loneliness. *Personality and Social Psychology Bulletin, 21,* 296–301.

Arendt, H. (1965). *Eichmann in Jerusalem: A report on the banality of evil* (rev. ed.). New York: Viking Compass.

Arkes, H. R., Faust, D., Guilmette, T. J., & Hart, K. (1988). Eliminating the hindsight bias. *Journal of Applied Psychology, 73,* 305–307.

Arkes, H. R., Wortmann, R. L., Saville, P. D., & Harkness, A. R. (1981). Hindsight bias among physicians weighing the likelihood of diagnoses. *Journal of Applied Psychology, 66,* 252–254.

Armitage, C. J., & Conner, M. (2001). Efficacy of the theory of planned behavior: A meta-analytic review. *British Journal of Social Psychology, 40,* 471–499.

Aron, A., Aron, E., & Smollan, D. (1992). Inclusion of other in the self scale and the structure of interpersonal closeness. *Journal of Personality and Social Psychology, 63,* 596–612.

Aron, A., Aron, E., Tudor, M., & Nelson, G. (1991). Close relationships as including other in the self. *Journal of Personality and Social Psychology, 60,* 241–253.

Aron, A., Norman, C. C., Aron, E. N., McKenna, C., & Heyman, R. E. (2000). Couples' shared participations in novel and arousing activities and experienced relationship quality. *Journal of Personality and Social Psychology, 78,* 273–284.

Aronoff, J., Barclay, A. M., & Stevenson, L. A. (1988). The recognition of threatening facial stimuli. *Journal of Personality and Social Psychology, 54,* 647–655.

Aronoff, J., Woike, B. A., & Hyman, L. M. (1992). Which are the stimuli in facial displays of anger and happiness? Configurational bases of emotion recognition. *Journal of Personality and Social Psychology, 62,* 1050–1066.

Aronson, E. (1968). Dissonance theory: Progress and problems. In R. P. Abelson, E. Aronson, W. J. McGuire, T. M. Newcomb, M. J. Rosenberg, & P. H. Tannenbaum (Eds.), *Theories of cognitive consistency: A sourcebook* (pp. 5–27). Skokie, IL: Rand-McNally.

Aronson, E. (1992). The return of the repressed: Dissonance theory makes a comeback. *Psychological Inquiry, 3,* 303–311.

Aronson, E., Blaney, N., Stephan, C., Sikes, J., & Snapp, M. (1978). *The jigsaw classroom.* Beverly Hills, CA: Sage.

Aronson, E., & Carlsmith, J. M. (1963). The effect of the severity of threat on the devaluation of forbidden behavior. *Journal of Abnormal and Social Psychology, 66,* 156–171.

Aronson, E., & Cope, V. (1968). My enemy's enemy is my friend. *Journal of Personality and Social Psychology, 8,* 8–12.

Aronson, E., & Linder, D. (1965). Gain and loss of self-esteem as determinants of interpersonal attractiveness. *Journal of Experimental Social Psychology, 1,* 156–171.

Aronson, E., & Mills, J. (1959). The effect of severity of initiation on liking for a group. *Journal of Abnormal and Social Psychology, 59,* 177–181.

Aronson, E., & O'Leary, M. (1982–1983). The relative effectiveness of models and prompts on energy conservation: A field experiment in a shower room. *Journal of Environmental Systems, 12,* 219–224.

Aronson, E., Turner, J. A., & Carlsmith, J. M. (1963). Communicator credibility and communication discrepancy as determinants of opinion change. *Journal of Abnormal and Social Psychology, 67,* 31–36.

Aronson, E., Willerman, B., & Floyd, J. (1966). The effect of a pratfall on increasing interpersonal attractiveness.

Journal of Abnormal and Social Psychology, 67, 31–36.

Aronson, E., Wilson, T. D., & Brewer, M. B. (1998). Experimentation in social psychology. In D. T. Gilbert, S. T. Fiske, & G. Lindzey (Eds.), *Handbook of social psychology* (4th ed., Vol. 1, pp. 99–142). New York: McGraw-Hill.

Aronson, J., Fried, C. B., & Good, C. (2002). Reducing the effects of stereotype threat on African American college students by shaping theories of intelligence. *Journal of Experimental Social Psychology, 38,* 113–125.

Aronson, J., Lustina, M. J., Good, C., Keough, K., Steele, C. M., & Brown, J. (1999). When White men can't do math: Necessary and sufficient factors in stereotype threat. *Journal of Experimental Social Psychology, 35,* 29–46.

Arunachalam, V., Wall, J. A., Jr., & Chan, C. (1998). Hong Kong versus U.S. Negotiations: Effects of culture, alternatives, outcome scales, and mediation. *Journal of Applied Social Psychology, 28,* 1219–1244.

Asch, S. E. (1946). Forming impressions of personality. *Journal of Abnormal and Social Psychology, 41,* 258–290.

Asch, S. E. (1948). The doctrine of suggestion, prestige, and imitation in social psychology. *Psychological Review, 55,* 250–276.

Asch, S. E. (1952). *Social psychology.* Englewood Cliffs, NJ: Prentice-Hall.

Asch, S. E. (1955). Opinion and social pressure. *Scientific American, 193,* 31–35.

Asch, S. E. (1956). Studies of independence and conformity: A minority of one against a unanimous majority. *Psychological Monographs, 70* (9, Whole No. 416).

Asch, S. E., & Zukier, H. (1984). Thinking about persons. *Journal of Personality and Social Psychology, 46,* 1230–1240.

Ashton, M. C., & Esses, V. M. (1999). Stereotype accuracy: Estimating the academic performance of ethnic groups. *Personality and Social Psychology Bulletin, 25,* 225–236.

Assor, A., Roth, G., & Deci, E. L. (2004). The emotional costs of parents' conditional regard: A self-determination theory analysis. *Journal of Personality, 72,* 47–88.

Atkinson, J. W. (1964). *An introduction to motivation.* Princeton, NJ: Van Nostrand.

Axelrod, R. (1984). *The evolution of cooperation.* New York: Basic Books.

Axsom, D. (1989). Cognitive dissonance and behavior change in psychotherapy. *Journal of Experimental Social Psychology, 25,* 234–252.

Axsom, D., & Cooper, J. (1985). Cognitive dissonance and psychotherapy: The role of effort justification in inducing weight loss. *Journal of Experimental Social Psychology, 21,* 149–160.

Axsom, D., & Lawless, W. F. (1992). Subsequent behavior can erase evidence of dissonance-induced attitude change. *Journal of Experimental Social Psychology, 28,* 387–400.

Axtell, R. E. (1991). *Gestures: The do's and taboos of body language around the world.* New York: Wiley.

Babcock, L., Loewenstein, G., Issacharoff, S., & Camerer, C. (1995). Biased judgments of fairness in bargaining. *American Economic Review, 85,* 1337–1343.

Bachman, J. G., & O'Malley, P. M. (1986). Self-concepts, self-esteem, and educational experiences: The frog pond revisited (again). *Journal of Personality and Social Psychology, 50,* 33–46.

Bagozzi, R. P. (1981). Attitudes, intentions, and behavior: A test of some key hypotheses. *Journal of Personality and Social Psychology, 41,* 607–627.

Bailey, J. M., Gaulin, S., Agyei, Y., & Gladue, B. A. (1994). Effects of gender and sexual orientation on evolutionarily relevant aspects of human mating psychology. *Journal of Personality and Social Psychology, 66,* 1081–1093.

Baldry, A. C., & Farrington, D. P. (2004). Evaluation of an intervention program for the reduction of bullying and victimization in schools. *Aggressive Behavior, 30,* 1–15.

Baldwin, M. W. (1994). Primed relational schemas as a source of self-evaluative reactions. *Journal of Social and Clinical Psychology, 13,* 380–403.

Baldwin, M. W., Carrell, S. E., & Lopez, D. F. (1990). Priming relationship schemas: My advisor and the Pope are watching me from the back of my mind. *Journal of Experimental Social Psychology, 26,* 435–454.

Baldwin, M. W., & Fehr, B. (1995). On the instability of attachment style ratings. *Personal Relationships, 2,* 247–261.

Baldwin, M. W., Keelan, J. P. R., Fehr, B., Enns, V., & Koh-Rangarajoo, E. (1996). Social cognitive conceptualization of attachment working models: Availability and accessibility effects. *Journal of Personality and Social Psychology, 71,* 94–109.

Baldwin, M. W., & Sinclair, L. (1996). Self-esteem and "If . . . Then" contingencies of interpersonal acceptance. *Journal of Personality and Social Psychology, 71,* 1130–1141.

Bandura, A. (1973). *Aggression: A social learning analysis.* New York: Random House.

Bandura, A. (1977). Self-efficacy: Toward a unifying theory of behavioral change. *Psychological Review, 84,* 191–215.

Bandura, A. (1997). *Self-efficacy: The exercise of control.* New York: Freeman.

Bandura, A., Ross, D., & Ross, S. A. (1961). Transmission of aggression through imitation of aggressive models. *Journal of Abnormal and Social Psychology, 63,* 575–581.

Bandura, A., Ross, D., & Ross, S. A. (1963). Imitation of film-mediated aggressive models. *Journal of Abnormal and Social Psychology, 66,* 3–11.

Bandura, A., & Walters, R. H. (1963). *Social learning and personality development.* New York: Holt, Rinehart, & Winston.

Bardi, A., & Schwartz, S. H. (2003). Values and behavior: Strength and structure of relations. *Personality and Social Psychology Bulletin, 29,* 1207–1220.

Bargh, J. A. (1982). Attention and automaticity in the processing of self-relevant information. *Journal of Personality and Social Psychology, 43,* 425–436.

Bargh, J. A. (1990). Auto-motives: Preconscious determinants of thought and behavior. In E. T. Higgins & R. M. Sorrentino (Eds.), *Handbook of motivation and cognition* (vol. 2, pp. 93–130). New York: Guilford.

Bargh, J. A., Bond, R. N., Lombardi, W. J., & Tota, M. E. (1986). The additive nature of chronic and temporary sources of construct accessibility. *Journal of Personality and Social Psychology, 50,* 869–878.

Bargh, J. A., Chen, M., & Burrows, L. (1996). Automaticity of social behavior: Direct effects of trait construct and stereotype activation on action.

Journal of Personality and Social Psychology, 71, 230–244.

Bargh, J. A., Gollwitzer, P. M., Lee-Chai, A., Barndollar, K., & Trötschel, R. (2001). The automated will: Nonconscious activation and pursuit of behavioral goals. *Journal of Personality and Social Psychology, 81,* 1014–1027.

Bargh, J. A., Lombardi, W. J., & Higgins, E. T. (1988). Automaticity of chronically accessible constructs in person × situation effects on person perception: It's just a matter of time. *Journal of Personality and Social Psychology, 55,* 599–605.

Bargh, J. A., & McKenna, K. Y. A. (2004). The internet and social life. *Annual Review of Psychology, 55,* 573–590.

Bargh, J. A., & Pietromonaco, P. (1982). Automatic information processing and social perception: The influence of trait information presented outside of conscious awareness on impression formation. *Journal of Personality and Social Psychology, 43,* 437–449.

Bar-Hillel, M., & Neter, E. (1996). Why are people reluctant to exchange lottery tickets? *Journal of Personality and Social Psychology, 70,* 17–27.

Baron, J., & Miller, J. G. (2000). Limiting the scope of moral obligations to help: A cross-cultural investigation. *Journal of Cross-Cultural Psychology, 31,* 703–725.

Baron, R. A. (1972). Aggression as a function of ambient temperature and prior anger arousal. *Journal of Personality and Social Psychology, 21,* 183–189.

Baron, R. A. (1974). Aggression as a function of victim's pain cues, level of prior anger arousal, and exposure to an aggressive model. *Journal of Personality and Social Psychology, 29,* 117–124.

Baron, R. A. (1976). The reduction of human aggression: A field study of incompatible responses. *Journal of Applied Social Psychology, 6,* 260–274.

Baron, R. S. (1986). Distraction-conflict theory. Progress and problems. In L. Berkowitz (Ed.), *Advances in experimental social psychology* (Vol. 19, pp. 1–40). New York: Academic Press.

Baron, R. S., & Roper, G. (1976). Reaffirmation of social comparison views of choice shifts: Averaging and extremity effects in an autokinetic situation. *Journal of Personality and Social Psychology, 33,* 521–530.

Baron, R. S., Vandello, J. A., & Brunsman, B. (1996). The forgotten variable in conformity research: Impact of task performance on social influence. *Journal of Personality and Social Psychology, 71,* 915–927.

Barron, K. E., & Harackiewicz, J. M. (2001). Achievement goals and optimal motivation: Testing multiple goal models. *Journal of Personality and Social Psychology, 80,* 706–722.

Bartholomew, K. (1994). Assessment of individual differences in adult attachment. *Psychological Inquiry, 5,* 23–27.

Bartlett, F. C. (1932). *Remembering: A study in experimental and social psychology.* London: Cambridge University Press.

Bass, B. M. (1998). *Transformational leadership: Industry, military, and educational impact.* Mahwah, NJ: Erlbaum.

Bassili, J. N., & Krosnick, J. A. (2000). Do strength-related attitude properties determine susceptibility to response effects? New evidence from response latency, attitude extremity, and aggregate indices. *Political Psychology, 21,* 107–132.

Batson, C. D. (1987). Prosocial motivation: Is it ever truly altruistic? In L. Berkowitz (Ed.), *Advances in experimental social psychology* (Vol. 20, pp. 65–122). New York: Academic Press.

Batson, C. D. (1993). Communal and exchange relationships: What is the difference? *Personality and Social Psychology Bulletin, 19,* 677–683.

Batson, C. D., Batson, J. G., Griffit, C. A., Barrientos, S., Brandt, J. R., Sprengelmeyer, P., & Bayly, M. J. (1989). Negative state relief and the empathy-altruism hypothesis. *Journal of Personality and Social Psychology, 56,* 922–933.

Batson, C. D., Batson, J. G., Slingsby, J. K., Harrell, K. L., Peekna, H. M., & Todd, R. M. (1991). Empathic joy and the empathy-altruism hypothesis. *Journal of Personality and Social Psychology, 61,* 413–426.

Batson, C. D., Duncan, B. D., Ackerman, P., Buckley, T., & Birch, K. (1981). Is empathic emotion a source of altruistic motivation? *Journal of Personality and Social Psychology, 40,* 290–302.

Batson, C. D., Dyck, J. L., Brandt, J. R., Batson, J. G., Powell, A. L., McMaster, M. R., et al. (1988). Five

studies testing two new egoistic alternatives to the empathy-altruism hypothesis. *Journal of Personality and Social Psychology, 55,* 52–77.

Batson, C. D., Engel, C. L., & Fridell, S. R. (1999). Value judgments: Testing the somatic-marker hypothesis using false physiological feedback. *Personality and Social Psychology Bulletin, 25,* 1021–1032.

Batson, C. D., Lishner, D. A., Carpenter, A., Dulin, L., Harjusoloa-Webb, S., Stocks, E. L., et al. (2003). ". . . as you would have them do unto you": Does imagining yourself in the other's place stimulate moral action? *Personality and Social Psychology Bulletin, 29,* 1190–1201.

Batson, C. D., O'Quin, K., Fultz, J., Vanderplas, M., & Isen, A. M. (1983). Influence of self-reported distress and empathy on egoistic versus altruistic motivation to help. *Journal of Personality and Social Psychology, 45,* 706–718.

Batson, C. D., Sager, K., Garst, K., Kang, M., Rubchinsky, K., & Dawson, K. (1997). Is empathy-induced helping due to self-other merging? *Journal of Personality and Social Psychology, 73,* 495–509.

Batson, C. D., Schoenrade, P., & Ventis, W. L. (1993). *Religion and the individual: A social-psychological perspective.* New York: Oxford University Press.

Batson, C. D., & Ventis, W. L. (1982). *The religious experience: A social-psychological perspective.* New York: Oxford University Press.

Baumeister, R. F. (1982). A self-presentational view of social phenomena. *Psychological Bulletin, 91,* 3–26.

Baumeister, R. F. (1990). Suicide as escape from self. *Psychological Review, 97,* 90–113.

Baumeister, R. F., Bratslavsky, E., Muraven, M., & Tice, D. M. (1998). Ego depletion: Is the active self a limited resource? *Journal of Personality and Social Psychology, 74,* 1252–1265.

Baumeister, R. F., Campbell, J. D., Krueger, J. I., & Vohs, K. D. (2003). Does high self-esteem cause better performance, interpersonal success, happiness, or healthier lifestyles? *Psychological Science in the Public Interest, 4,* 1–44.

Baumeister, R. F., Chesner, S. P., Sanders, P. S., & Tice, D. M. (1988). Who's in charge here? Group leaders do lend help in emergencies. *Personality and Social Psychology Bulletin, 14,* 17–22.

Baumeister, R. F., Dale, K., & Sommer, K. L. (1998). Freudian defense mechanisms and empirical findings in modern social psychology: Reaction formation, projection, displacement, undoing, isolation, sublimation, and denial. *Journal of Personality, 66,* 1081–1124.

Baumeister, R. F., Heatherton, T. F., & Tice, D. M. (1993). When ego threats lead to self-regulation failure: Negative consequences of high self-esteem. *Journal of Personality and Social Psychology, 64,* 141–156.

Baumeister, R. F., Heatherton, T. F., & Tice, D. M. (1994). *Losing control: How and why people fail at self-regulation.* San Diego: Academic Press.

Baumeister, R. F., & Leary, M. R. (1995). The need to belong: Desire for interpersonal attachments as a fundamental human motivation. *Psychological Bulletin, 117,* 497–529.

Baumeister, R. F., Smart, L., & Boden, J. M. (1996). Relation of threatened egotism to violence and aggression. The dark side of self-esteem. *Psychological Review, 103,* 5–33.

Baumeister, R. F., & Sommer, K. L. (1997). What do men want? Gender differences and two spheres of belongingness. *Psychological Bulletin, 122,* 38–44.

Baumeister, R. F., Tice, D. M., & Hutton, D. G. (1989). Self-presentational motivations and personality differences in self-esteem. *Journal of Personality, 57,* 547–579.

Baumrind, D. (1964). Some thoughts on the ethics of research: After reading Milgram's "Behavioral study of obedience." *American Psychologist, 19,* 421–423.

Baumrind, D., Larzelere, R. E., & Cowan, P. A. (2002). Ordinary physical punishment: Is it harmful? Comment on Gershoff (2002). *Psychological Bulletin, 128,* 580–589.

Bazerman, M. H., Mannix, E. A., & Thompson, L. L. (1988). Groups as mixed-motive negotiations. *Advances in Group Processes, 5,* 195–216.

Bazerman, M. H., & Neale, M. A. (1992). *Negotiating rationally.* New York: Free Press.

Bazzini, D. G., & Shaffer, D. R. (1999). Resisting temptation revisited:

Devaluation versus enhancement of an attractive suitor by exclusive and nonexclusive daters. *Personality and Social Psychology Bulletin, 25,* 162–176.

Beach, S. R. H., & Tesser, A. (1995). Self-esteem and the extended self-evaluation maintenance model. In M. H. Kernis (Ed.), *Efficacy, agency, and self-esteem* (pp. 145–170). New York: Plenum.

Beach, S. R. H., Tesser, A., Fincham, F. D., Jones, D. J., Johnson, D., & Whitaker, D. J. (1998). Pleasure and pain in doing well, together: An investigation of performance-related affect in close relationships. *Journal of Personality and Social Psychology, 74,* 923–938.

Beach, S. R. H., Tesser, A., Mendolia, M., Anderson, P., Crelia, R., Whitaker, D., et al. (1996). Self-evaluation maintenance in marriage: Toward a performance ecology of the marital relationship. *Journal of Family Psychology, 10,* 379–396.

Beal, D. J., O'Neal, E. C., Ong, J., & Ruscher, J. B. (2000). The ways and means of interracial aggression: Modern racists' use of covert retaliation. *Personality and Social Psychology Bulletin, 26,* 1255–1238.

Beaman, A. L., Klentz, B., Diener, E., & Svanum, S. (1979). Self-awareness and transgression in children: Two field studies. *Journal of Personality and Social Psychology, 37,* 1835–1846.

Beauregard, K. S., & Dunning, D. (1998). Turning up the contrast: Self-enhancement motives prompt egocentric effects in social judgment. *Journal of Personality and Social Psychology, 74,* 606–621.

Becker, E. (1968). *The structure of evil.* New York: George Braziller.

Becker, E. (1973). *The denial of death.* New York: Free Press.

Beggan, J. K. (1992). On the social nature of nonsocial perception: The mere ownership effect. *Journal of Personality and Social Psychology, 62,* 229–237.

Belk, R. W. (1988). Possessions and the extended self. *Journal of Consumer Research, 15,* 139–168.

Bell, P. A. (1992). In defense of the negative affect escape model of heat and aggression. *Psychological Bulletin, 111,* 342–346.

Belle, D. (1987). Gender differences in the social moderators of stress. In R. C. Barnett, L. Biener, & G. K. Baruch

(Eds.), *Gender and stress* (pp. 257–277). New York: Free Press.

Bem, D. J. (1972). Self-perception theory. In L. Berkowitz (Ed.), *Advances in experimental social psychology* (Vol. 6, pp. 1–63). New York: Academic Press.

Benbow, C. P., Lubinski, D., Shea, D. L., & Eftekhari-Sanjani, H. (2000). Sex differences in mathematical reasoning ability at age 13: Their status 20 years later. *Psychological Science, 11,* 474–480.

Benne, K. D., & Sheats, P. (1948). Functional roles of group members. *Journal of Social Issues, 4,* 41–49.

Benson, P. L., Karabenick, S. A., & Lerner, R. M. (1976). Pretty pleases: The effects of physical attractiveness, race, and sex on receiving help. *Journal of Experimental Social Psychology, 12,* 409–415.

Bentham, J. (1948). *An introduction to the principles of morals and legislation.* Oxford: B. Blackwell. (Original work published in 1779).

Bentler, P. M., & Speckart, G. (1979). Attitudes "cause" behaviors: A structural equation analysis. *Journal of Personality and Social Psychology, 40,* 226–238.

Berglas, S., & Jones, E. E. (1978). Drug choice as a self-handicapping strategy in response to noncontingent success. *Journal of Personality and Social Psychology, 36,* 405–417.

Berkman, L. F., & Syme, S. L. (1979). Social networks, host resistance, and mortality: A nine-year follow-up study of Alameda County residents. *American Journal of Epidemiology, 115,* 684–694.

Berkowitz, L. (1962). *Aggression: A social psychological analysis.* New York: McGraw-Hill.

Berkowitz, L. (1984). Some effects of thoughts on anti- and prosocial influences of media events: A cognitive–neoassociation analysis. *Psychological Bulletin, 95,* 410–427.

Berkowitz, L. (1989). Frustration-aggression hypothesis: Examination and reformulation. *Psychological Bulletin, 106,* 59–73.

Berkowitz, L. (1990). On the formation and regulation of anger and aggression: A cognitive-neoassociationistic analysis. *American Psychologist, 45,* 494–503.

Berkowitz, L. (1993). *Aggression: Its causes, consequences, and control.* New York: McGraw-Hill.

Berkowitz, L., & Daniels, L. R. (1963). Responsibility and dependency. *Journal of Abnormal and Social Psychology, 66,* 429–436.

Berkowitz, L., & Donnerstein, E. (1982). External validity is more than skin deep: Some answers to criticisms of laboratory experiments. *American Psychologist, 37,* 245–257.

Berkowitz, L., & LePage, A. (1967). Weapons as aggression-eliciting stimuli. *Journal of Personality and Social Psychology, 7,* 202–207.

Bernichon, T. (1999). *Self-esteem and liking for positive and negative evaluators.* Unpublished research, University of Washington, Seattle, WA.

Bernichon, T., Cook, K. E., & Brown, J. D. (2003). Seeking self-evaluative feedback: The interactive role of global self-esteem and specific self-views. *Journal of Personality and Social Psychology, 84,* 194–204.

Bernieri, F. J. (1991). Interpersonal sensitivity in teaching interactions. *Personality and Social Psychology Bulletin, 17,* 98–104.

Berry, D. S. (1991). Accuracy in social perception: Contributions of facial and vocal information. *Journal of Personality and Social Psychology, 61,* 298–307.

Berry, D. S. (2000). Attractiveness, attraction, and sexual selection: Evolutionary perspectives on the form and function of physical attractiveness. In M. P. Zanna (Ed.), *Advances in experimental social psychology* (Vol. 32, pp. 273–342). New York: Academic Press.

Berry, D. S., & Brownlow, S. (1989). Were the physiognomists right? Personality correlates of facial babyishness. *Personality and Social Psychology Bulletin, 15,* 266–279.

Berry, D. S., & McArthur, L. Z. (1985). Some components and consequences of a babyface. *Journal of Personality and Social Psychology, 48,* 312–324.

Berry, D. S., & McArthur, L. Z. (1986). Perceiving character in faces: The impact of age-related craniofacial changes on social perception. *Psychological Bulletin, 100,* 3–18.

Berry, D. S., Misovich, S. J., Kean, K. J., & Baron, R. M. (1992). Effects of disruption of structure and motion on perceptions of social causality. *Personality and Social Psychology Bulletin, 18,* 237–244.

Berry, D. S., & Zebrowitz-McArthur, L. (1988). What's in a face? Facial maturity and the attribution of legal responsibility. *Personality and Social Psychology Bulletin, 14,* 23–34.

Berscheid, E. (1966). Opinion change and communicator-communicatee similarity and dissimilarity. *Journal of Personality and Social Psychology, 4,* 670–680.

Berscheid, E., Dion, K., Walster, E., & Walster, G. W. (1971). Physical attractiveness and dating choice: A test of the matching hypothesis. *Journal of Experimental Social Psychology, 7,* 173–189.

Berscheid, E., Graziano, W., Monson, T., & Dermer, M. (1976). Outcome dependency: Attention, attribution, and attraction. *Journal of Personality and Social Psychology, 34,* 978–989.

Berscheid, E., & Peplau, L. A. (1983). The emerging science of relationships. In H. H. Kelley, E. Berscheid, A. Christensen, J. H. Harvey, T. L. Huston, G. Levinger, E. McClintock, L. A. Peplau, & D. R. Peterson (Eds.), *Close relationships* (pp. 1–19). New York: Freeman.

Berscheid, E., & Walster, E. (1974). A little bit about love. In T. Huston (Ed.), *Foundations of interpersonal attraction* (pp. 355–381). New York: Academic Press.

Berscheid, E., & Walster, E. (1978). *Interpersonal attraction* (2nd ed.). Reading, MA: Addison-Wesley.

Bettencourt, B. A., & Kernahan, C. (1997). A meta-analysis of aggression in the presence of violent cues: Effects of gender differences and aversive provocation. *Aggressive Behavior, 23,* 447–456.

Bettencourt, B. A., & Miller, N. (1996). Gender differences in aggression as a function of provocation: A meta-analysis. *Psychological Bulletin, 119,* 422–447.

Bettencourt, B. A., & Sheldon, K. (2001). Social roles as mechanisms for psychological need satisfaction within social groups. *Journal of Personality and Social Psychology, 81,* 1131–1143.

Bickman, L. (1974). The social power of a uniform. *Journal of Applied Social Psychology, 4,* 47–61.

Biernat, M. (2003). Toward a broader view of social stereotyping. *American Psychologist, 58,* 1019–1027.

Biernat, M., & Kobrynowicz, D. (1997). Gender- and race-based standards of competence: Lower minimum standards but higher ability standards for devalued groups. *Journal of Personality and Social Psychology, 72,* 544–557.

Biernat, M., Manis, M., & Nelson, T. E. (1991). Stereotypes and shifting standards of judgment. *Journal of Personality and Social Psychology, 60,* 485–499.

Biernat, M., & Vescio, T. K. (2002). She swings, she hits, she's great, she's benched: Implications of gender-based shifting standards for judgment and behavior. *Personality and Social Psychology Bulletin, 28,* 66–77.

Biesanz, J. C., Neuberg, S. L., Smith, D. M., Asher, T., & Judice, T. N. (2001). When accuracy-motivated perceivers fail: Limited attentional resources and the reemerging self-fulfilling prophecy. *Personality and Social Psychology Bulletin, 27,* 621–629.

Billig, M., & Tajfel, J. (1973). Social categorization and similarity in intergroup behavior. *European Journal of Social Psychology, 3,* 27–52.

Biswas-Diener, R., & Diener, E. (2001). Making the best of a bad situation: Satisfaction in the slums of Calcutta. *Social Indicators Research, 55,* 329–352.

Bizer, G. Y., & Krosnick, J. A. (2001). Exploring the structure of strength-related attitude features: The relation between attitude importance and attitude accessibility. *Journal of Personality and Social Psychology, 81,* 566–586.

Björkqvist, K., Lagerspetz, K. M. J., & Kaukiainen, A. (1992). Do girls manipulate and boys fight? Developmental trends regarding direct and indirect aggression. *Aggressive Behavior, 18,* 117–127.

Blair, I. V. (2002). The malleability of automatic stereotypes and prejudice. *Personality and Social Psychology Review, 6,* 242–261.

Blanton, H., Stuart, A. E., & Van den Eijnden, R. J. J. M. (2001). An introduction to deviance-regulation theory: The effect of behavioral norms on message framing. *Personality and Social Psychology Bulletin, 27,* 848–858.

Blascovich, J., Mendes, W. B., Hunter, S. B., & Salomon, K. (1999). Social "facilitation" as challenge and threat.

Journal of Personality and Social Psychology, 77, 68–77.

Blascovich, J., Spencer, S. J., Quinn, D., & Steele, C. (2001). African Americans and high blood pressure: The role of stereotype threat. *Psychological Science, 12,* 225–229.

Blass, T. (1991). Understanding behavior in the Milgram obedience experiment: The role of personality, situations, and their interactions. *Journal of Personality and Social Psychology, 60,* 398–413.

Blau, P. M. (1964). *Exchange and power in social life.* New York: Wiley.

Blazer, D. G. (1982). Social support and mortality in an elderly community population. *American Journal of Epidemiology, 115,* 684–694.

Bless, H., Bohner, G., Schwarz, N., & Strack, F. (1990). Mood and persuasion: A cognitive response analysis. *Personality and Social Psychology Bulletin, 16,* 331–345.

Blodgett, H. C. (1929). *The effect of the introduction of reward upon maze performance of rats.* University of California Publication in Psychology, 4(18), 113–134.

Blumberg, M. S., & Wasserman, E. A. (1995). Animal mind and the argument from design. *American Psychologist, 50,* 133–144.

Bobo, L. (1983). Whites' opposition to busing: Symbolic racism or realistic group conflict? *Journal of Personality and Social Psychology, 45,* 1196–1210.

Bochner, S., & Insko, C. A. (1966). Communicator discrepancy, source credibility, and opinion change. *Journal of Personality and Social Psychology, 4,* 614–621.

Bodenhausen, G. V., Kramer, G. P., & Süsser, K. (1994). Happiness and stereotypic thinking in social judgment. *Journal of Personality and Social Psychology, 66,* 621–632.

Boggiano, A. K., & Main, D. S. (1986). Enhancing children's interest in activities used as rewards: The bonus effect. *Journal of Personality and Social Psychology, 51,* 1116–1126.

Bolger, N., & Eckenrode, J. (1991). Social relationships, personality, and anxiety during a major stressful episode. *Journal of Personality and Social Psychology, 61,* 440–449.

Bolger, N., Zuckerman, A., & Kessler, R. C. (2000). Invisible support and adjustment to stress. *Journal of Personality and Social Psychology, 79,* 953–961.

Bonanno, G. A., Field, N. P., Kovacevic, A., & Kaltman, S. (2002). Self-enhancement as a buffer against extreme adversity: Civil war in Bosnia and traumatic loss in the United States. *Personality and Social Psychology Bulletin, 28,* 184–196.

Bond, C. F., & Titus, L. J. (1983). Social facilitation: A meta-analysis of 241 studies. *Psychological Bulletin, 94,* 265–292.

Bond, M. H. (2004). Culture and aggression—From context to coercion. *Personality and Social Psychology Review, 8,* 62–78.

Bond, R., & Smith, P. B. (1996). Culture and conformity: A meta-analysis of studies using Asch's (1952b, 1956) line judgment task. *Psychological Bulletin, 119,* 111–137.

Bonilla-Silva, E. (2003). *Racism without racists: Color-blind racism and the persistence of racial inequality in the United States.* Lanham, MD: Rowman & Littlefield.

Boninger, D. S., Krosnick, J. A., & Berent, M. K. (1995). Origins of attitude importance: Self-interest, social identification, and value relevance. *Journal of Personality and Social Psychology, 68,* 61–80.

Bonta, B. D. (1997). Cooperation and competition in peaceful societies. *Psychological Bulletin, 121,* 299–320.

Borgida, E., Conner, C., & Manteufel, L. (1992). Understanding living kidney donation: A behavioral decision-making perspective. In S. Spacapan & S. Oskamp (Eds.), *Helping and being helped: Naturalistic studies* (pp. 183–211). Newbury Park, CA: Sage.

Boring, E. G. (1957). *A history of experimental psychology* (2nd ed.). New York: Appleton-Century-Crofts.

Borkenau, P., & Liebler, A. (1992). Trait inferences: Sources of validity at zero acquaintance. *Journal of Personality and Social Psychology, 62,* 645–657.

Borkenau, P., & Liebler, A. (1993). Convergence of stranger ratings of personality and intelligence with self-ratings, partner ratings, and measured intelligence. *Journal of Personality and Social Psychology, 65,* 546–554.

Bornstein, G. (1992). The free-rider problem in intergroup conflicts over step-level and continuous public goods.

Journal of Personality and Social Psychology, 62, 597–606.

Bornstein, R. F. (1989). Exposure and affect: Overview and meta-analysis of research, 1968–1987. *Psychological Bulletin, 106,* 265–289.

Bornstein, R. F., & D'Agostino, P. R. (1992). Stimulus recognition and the mere exposure effect. *Journal of Personality and Social Psychology, 63,* 545–552.

Bornstein, R. F., Kale, A. R., & Cornell, K. R. (1990). Boredom as a limiting condition on the mere exposure effect. *Journal of Personality and Social Psychology, 58,* 791–800.

Bosson, J. K., Swann, W. B., & Pennebaker, J. W. (2000). Stalking the perfect measure of implicit self-esteem: The blind men and the elephant revisited? *Journal of Personality and Social Psychology, 79,* 631–643.

Bothwell, R. K., Brigham, J. C., & Malpass, R. S. (1989). Cross-racial identification. *Personality and Social Psychology Bulletin, 15,* 19–25.

Bouas, K. S., & Komorita, S. S. (1996). Group discussion and cooperation in social dilemmas. *Personality and Social Psychology Bulletin, 22,* 1144–1150.

Bower, G. H. (1981). Mood and memory. *American Psychologist, 36,* 129–148.

Bowlby, J. (1969). *Attachment and loss: Vol. 1. Attachment.* New York: Basic Books.

Bowlby, J. (1973). *Attachment and loss: Vol. 2. Separation: Anxiety and anger.* New York: Basic Books.

Bradburn, N. M. (1969). *The structure of psychological well-being.* Chicago: Aldine.

Bradbury, T. N., Beach, S. R. H., Fincham, F. D., & Nelson, G. M. (1996). Attributions and behavior in functional and dysfunctional marriages. *Journal of Consulting and Clinical Psychology, 64,* 569–576.

Bradbury, T. N., & Fincham, F. D. (1990). Attributions in marriage: Review and critique. *Psychological Bulletin, 107,* 3–33.

Bradbury, T. N., & Fincham, F. D. (1992). Attributions and behavior in marital interaction. *Journal of Personality and Social Psychology, 63,* 613–628.

Braithwaite, R. (1955). *Scientific explanation.* Cambridge: Cambridge University Press.

Branscombe, N. R., Schmitt, M. T., & Harvey, R. D. (1999). Perceiving pervasive discrimination among African Americans: Implications for group identification and well-being. *Journal of Personality and Social Psychology, 77,* 135–149.

Branscombe, N. R., Wann, D. L., Noel, J. G., & Coleman, J. (1993). In-group or out-group extremity: Importance of the threatened social identity. *Personality and Social Psychology Bulletin, 19,* 381–388.

Bransford, J. C., & Johnson, M. K. (1972). Contextual prerequisites for understanding: Some investigations of comprehension and recall. *Journal of Verbal Learning and Verbal Behavior, 11,* 717–726.

Brauer, M., Judd, C. M., & Gliner, M. D. (1995). The effects of repeated expressions on attitude polarization during group discussions. *Journal of Personality and Social Psychology, 68,* 1014–1029.

Brauer, M., Judd, C. M., & Jacquelin, V. (2001). The communication of social stereotypes: The effects of group discussion and information distribution on stereotypic appraisals. *Journal of Personality and Social Psychology, 81,* 463–475.

Breckler, S. J. (1984). Empirical validation of affect, behavior, and cognition as distinct components of attitudes. *Journal of Personality and Social Psychology, 47,* 1191–1205.

Breckler, S. J., & Wiggins, E. C. (1989). Affect versus evaluation in the structure of attitudes. *Journal of Experimental Social Psychology, 25,* 253–271.

Brehm, J. W. (1966). *A theory of psychological reactance.* New York: Academic Press.

Brehm, S. S. (1992). *Intimate relationships* (2nd ed.). New York: McGraw-Hill.

Brener, N. D., McMahon, P. M., Warren, C. W., & Douglas, K. A. (1999). Forced sexual intercourse and associated health-risk behaviors among female college students in the United States. *Journal of Consulting and Clinical Psychology, 67,* 252–259.

Brennan, K. A., & Shaver, P. R. (1995). Dimensions of adult attachment, affect regulation, and romantic relationship functioning. *Personality and Social Psychology Bulletin, 21,* 267–283.

Brett, J. M., & Okumura, T. (1998). Inter- and intracultural negotiations: U.S. and Japanese negotiators. *Academy of Management Journal, 41,* 495–510.

Brewer, M. B. (1979). In-group bias in the minimal intergroup situation: A cognitive-motivational analysis. *Psychological Bulletin, 86,* 307–324.

Brewer, M. B. (1988). A dual process model of impression formation. In T. Srull & R. Wyer (Eds.), *Advances in social cognition* (Vol. 1, pp. 1–36). Mahwah, NJ: Erlbaum.

Brewer, M. B. (1991). The social self: On being the same and different at the same time. *Personality and Social Psychology Bulletin, 17,* 475–482.

Brewer, M. B. (1999). The psychology of prejudice: Ingroup love or outgroup hate? *Journal of Social Issues, 55,* 429–444.

Brewer, M. B., & Brown, R. J. (1998). Intergroup relations. In D. T. Gilbert, S. T. Fiske, & G. Lindzey (Eds.), *Handbook of social psychology* (4th ed., Vol. 2, pp. 554–594). New York: McGraw-Hill.

Brewer, M. B., & Gardner, W. (1996). Who is this "we"? Levels of collective identity and self-representations. *Journal of Personality and Social Psychology, 71,* 83–93.

Brewer, M. B., & Kramer, R. M. (1986). Choice behavior in social dilemmas: Effects of social identity, group size, and decision framing. *Journal of Personality and Social Psychology, 50,* 543–549.

Brewer, M. B., & Weber, J. G. (1994). Self-evaluation effects of interpersonal versus intergroup social comparison. *Journal of Personality and Social Psychology, 66,* 268–275.

Brickman, P., & Campbell, D. T. (1971). Hedonic relativism and planning the good society. In M. H. Appley (Ed.), *Adaptation-level theory: A symposium* (pp. 287–302). New York: Academic Press.

Brickman, P., Coates, D., & Janoff-Bulman, R. (1978). Lottery winners and accident victims: Is happiness relative? *Journal of Personality and Social Psychology, 39,* 917–927.

Brief, A. P., Butcher, A. H., George, J. M., & Link, K. E. (1993). Integrating bottom-up and top-down theories of subjective well-being: The case of health. *Journal of Personality and Social Psychology, 64,* 646–653.

Brock, T. C. (1965). Communicator-recipient similarity and decision change. *Journal of Personality and Social Psychology, 1,* 650–654.

Brock, T. C. (1967). Communication discrepancy and intent to persuade as determinants of counterargument production. *Journal of Experimental Social Psychology, 3,* 269–309.

Brock, T. C., & Becker, L. A. (1965). Ineffectiveness of "overheard" counter-propaganda. *Journal of Personality and Social Psychology, 2,* 654–660.

Broemer, P., & Diehl, M. (2003). What you think is what you get: Comparative evaluations of close relationships. *Personality and Social Psychology Bulletin, 29,* 1560–1569.

Broemer, P., & Diehl, M. (2004). Evaluative contrast in social comparison: The role of distinct and shared features of the self and comparison others. *European Journal of Social Psychology, 34,* 25–38.

Broverman, I. K., Vogel, S. R., Broverman, D. M., Clarkson, F. E., & Rosenkrantz, P. S. (1972). Sex-role stereotypes: A current appraisal. *Journal of Social Issues, 28,* 59–78.

Brown, J. D. (1986). Evaluations of self and others: Self-enhancement biases in social judgments. *Social Cognition, 4,* 353–376.

Brown, J. D. (1990). Evaluating one's abilities: Shortcuts and stumbling blocks on the road to self-knowledge. *Journal of Experimental Social Psychology, 26,* 149–167.

Brown, J. D. (1991). Accuracy and bias in self-knowledge. In C. R. Snyder & D. F. Forsyth (Eds.), *Handbook of social and clinical psychology: The health perspective* (pp. 158–178). New York: Pergamon.

Brown, J. D. (1993). Self-esteem and self-evaluation: Feeling is believing. In J. Suls (Ed.), *Psychological perspectives on the self* (Vol. 4, pp. 27–58). Mahwah, NJ: Erlbaum.

Brown, J. D. (1998). *The self.* New York: McGraw-Hill.

Brown, J. D. (2003). The self-enhancement motive in collectivistic cultures: The rumors of my death have been greatly exaggerated. *Journal of Cross-Cultural Psychology, 34,* 603–605.

Brown, J. D., & Dutton, K. A. (1995). The thrill of victory, the complexity of defeat: Self-esteem and people's emotional reactions to success and failure. *Journal of Personality and Social Psychology, 68,* 712–722.

Brown, J. D., Dutton, K. A., & Cook, K. E. (2001). From the top down: Self-esteem and self-evaluation. *Cognition and Emotion, 15,* 615–631.

Brown, J. D., Farnham, S. D., & Cook, K. E. (2002). Emotional responses to changing feedback: Is it better to have won and lost than never to have won at all? *Journal of Personality, 70,* 127–141.

Brown, J. D., & Kobayashi, C. (2002). Self-enhancement in Japan and America. *Asian Journal of Social Psychology, 5,* 145–167.

Brown, J. D., & Marshall, M. A. (2001). Self-esteem and emotion: Some thoughts about feelings. *Personality and Social Psychology Bulletin, 27,* 575–584.

Brown, J. D., & Marshall, M. A. (2003). *Self-esteem: It's not what we think.* Unpublished manuscript, University of Washington, Seattle, WA.

Brown, J. D., & Smart, S. A. (1991). The self and social conduct: Linking self-representations to prosocial behavior. *Journal of Personality and Social Psychology, 60,* 368–375.

Brown, J. D., Novick, N. J., Lord, K. A., & Richards, J. M. (1992). When Gulliver travels: Social context, psychological closeness, and self-appraisals. *Journal of Personality and Social Psychology, 60,* 717–727.

Brown, K. W., & Ryan, R. M. (2003). The benefits of being present: Mindfulness and its role in psychological well-being. *Journal of Personality and Social Psychology, 84,* 822–848.

Brown, R. P., & Josephs, R. A. (1999). A burden of proof: Stereotype relevance and gender differences in math performance. *Journal of Personality and Social Psychology, 76,* 246–257.

Brown, R. P., Charnsangavej, T., Keough, K. A., Newman, M. L., & Rentfrow, P. J. (2000). Putting the "affirm" into affirmative action: Preferential selection and academic performance. *Journal of Personality and Social Psychology, 79,* 736–747.

Brownmiller, S. (1975). *Against our will: Men, women, and rape.* New York: Simon & Schuster.

Bruce, M. L., & Kim, K. M. (1992). Differences in the effects of divorce on major depression in men and women. *American Journal of Psychiatry, 149,* 914–917.

Bruch, M. A., Gorsky, J. M., Collins, T. M., & Berger, P. A. (1989). Shyness and sociability reexamined: A multi-

component analysis. *Journal of Personality and Social Psychology, 57,* 904–915.

Bruner, J. S. (1957). On perceptual readiness. *Psychological Review, 64,* 123–152.

Bruner, J. S., & Minturn, A. L. (1955). Perceptual identification and perceptual organization. *Journal of General Psychology, 53,* 21–28.

Bruner, J. S., & Postman, L. (1949). On the perception of incongruity: A paradigm. *Journal of Personality, 18,* 206–223.

Brunswik, E. (1955). Representative design and probabilistic theory in a functional psychology. *Psychological Review, 62,* 193–217.

Bryan, A., D., Aiken, L. S., & West, S. G. (1999). The impact of males proposing condom use on perceptions of an initial sexual encounter. *Personality and Social Psychology Bulletin, 25,* 275–286.

Bryant, F. B., & Brockway, J. H. (1997). Hindsight bias in reaction to the verdict in the O. J. Simpson trial. *Basic and Applied Social Psychology, 7,* 225–241.

Buchler, J. (Ed.). (1955). *Philosophical writings of Peirce.* New York: Dover.

Buckley, K. E., Winkel, R. E., & Leary, M. R. (2004). Reactions to acceptance and rejection: Effects of level and sequence of relational evaluation. *Journal of Experimental Social Psychology, 40,* 14–28.

Burger, J. M. (1986). Increasing compliance by improving the deal: The that's-not-all technique. *Journal of Personality and Social Psychology, 51,* 277–283.

Burger, J. M. (1999). The foot-in-the-door compliance procedure: A multiple-process analysis and review. *Personality and Social Psychology Review, 3,* 303–325.

Burger, J. M., & Guadagno, R. E. (2003). Self-concept clarity and the foot-in-the-door procedure. *Basic and Applied Social Psychology, 25,* 79–86.

Burger, J. M., Messian, N., Patel, S., del Prado, A., & Anderson, C. (2004). What a coincidence! The effects of incidental similarity on compliance. *Personality and Social Psychology Bulletin, 30,* 35–43.

Burger, J. M., & Petty, R. E. (1981). The low-ball compliance technique: Task or person commitment? *Journal of*

Personality and Social Psychology, 40, 492–500.

Burger, J. M., Soroka, S., Gonzago, K., Murphy, E., & Somervell, E. (2001). The effect of fleeting attraction on compliance to requests. *Personality and Social Psychology Bulletin, 27,* 1578–1586.

Burman, B., & Margolin, G. (1992). Analysis of the association between marital relationships and health problems: An interactional perspective. *Psychological Bulletin, 112,* 39–63.

Burns, J. M. (1978). *Leadership.* New York: Harper & Row.

Burnstein, E., Crandall, C., & Kitayama, S. (1994). Some neo-Darwinian rules for altruism: Weighing cues for inclusive fitness as a function of the biological importance of the decision. *Journal of Personality and Social Psychology, 67,* 773–789.

Burnstein, E., & Vinokur, A. (1973). Testing two classes of theories about group-induced shifts in individual choice. *Journal of Experimental Social Psychology, 9,* 123–137.

Burnstein, E., & Vinokur, A. (1977). Persuasive argumentation and social comparison as determinants of attitude polarization. *Journal of Experimental Social Psychology, 13,* 315–332.

Burt, M. R. (1980). Cultural myths and supports for rape. *Journal of Personality and Social Psychology, 38,* 217–230.

Bushman, B. J. (1984). Perceived symbols of authority and their influence on compliance. *Journal of Applied Social Psychology, 14,* 501–508.

Bushman, B. J. (1995). Moderating role of trait aggressiveness in the effects of violent media on aggression. *Journal of Personality and Social Psychology, 69,* 950–960.

Bushman, B. J. (1996). Individual differences in the extent and development of aggressive cognitive-associative networks. *Personality and Social Psychology Bulletin, 22,* 811–819.

Bushman, B. J. (1997). Effects of alcohol on human aggression: Validity of proposed explanations. *Recent Developments in Alcoholism, 13,* 227–243.

Bushman, B. J. (1998). Priming effects of media violence on the accessibility of aggressive constructs in memory. *Personality and Social Psychology Bulletin, 24,* 537–545.

Bushman, B. J. (2002). Does venting anger feed or extinguish the flame? Catharsis, rumination, distraction, anger, and aggressive responding. *Personality and Social Psychology Bulletin, 28,* 724–731.

Bushman, B. J., & Anderson, C. A. (2001a). Is it time to pull the plug on the hostile versus instrumental aggression dichotomy? *Psychological Review, 108,* 273–279.

Bushman, B. J., & Anderson, C. A. (2001b). Media violence and the American public. *American Psychologist, 56,* 477–489.

Bushman, B. J., & Baumeister, R. F. (1998). Threatened egotism, narcissism, self-esteem, and direct and displaced aggression: Does self-love or self-hate lead to aggression? *Journal of Personality and Social Psychology, 75,* 219–229.

Bushman, B. J., Baumeister, R. F., & Phillips, C. M. (2001). Do people aggress to improve their mood? Catharsis beliefs, affect regulation opportunity, and aggressive responding. *Journal of Personality and Social Psychology, 81,* 17–32.

Bushman, B. J., Baumeister, R. F., & Stack, A. D. (1999). Catharsis, aggression, and persuasive influence: Self-fulfilling or self-defeating prophecies? *Journal of Personality and Social Psychology, 76,* 367–376.

Bushman, B. J., & Cooper, H. M. (1990). Effects of alcohol on human aggression: An integrative research review. *Psychological Bulletin, 107,* 341–354.

Bushman, B. J., & Geen, R. G. (1990). Role of cognitive-emotional mediators and individual differences in the effects of media violence on aggression. *Journal of Personality and Social Psychology, 58,* 156–163.

Buss, A. H. (1966). Instrumentality of aggression, feedback, and frustration as determinants of physical aggression. *Journal of Personality and Social Psychology, 3,* 153–162.

Buss, A.H., & Perry, M. (1992). The Aggression Questionnaire. *Journal of Personality and Social Psychology, 63,* 452–459.

Buss, D. M. (1984). Marital assortment for personality dispositions: Assessment with three different data sources. *Behavior Genetics, 14,* 111–123.

Buss, D. M. (1989). Sex difference in human mate preferences: Evolution-

ary hypotheses tested in 37 cultures. *Behavioral and Brain Sciences, 12,* 1–49.

Buss, D. M. (1994). *The evolution of desire: Strategies of human mating.* New York: Basic Books.

Buss, D. M., & Kenrick, D. T. (1998). Evolutionary social psychology. In D. T. Gilbert, S. T. Fiske, & G. Lindzey (Eds.), *Handbook of social psychology* (4th ed., Vol. 2, pp. 982–1026). New York: McGraw-Hill.

Buss, D. M., Larsen, R. J., Westen, D., & Semmelroth, J. (1992). Sex differences in jealousy: Evolution, physiology, and psychology. *Psychological Science, 3,* 251–255.

Buss, D. M., & Schmitt, D. P. (1993). Sexual strategies theory: An evolutionary perspective on human mating. *Psychological Review, 100,* 204–232.

Butler, D., & Geis, F. L. (1990). Nonverbal affect responses to male and female leaders: Implications for leadership evaluations. *Journal of Personality and Social Psychology, 58,* 48–59.

Butterworth, G. (1992). Origins of self-perception in infancy. *Psychological Inquiry, 3,* 103–111.

Buunk, B. P., Oldersma, F. L., & de Dreu, C. K. W. (2001). Enhancing satisfaction through downward comparison: The role of relational discontent and individual differences in social comparison orientation. *Journal of Experimental Social Psychology, 37,* 452–467.

Buunk, B. P. & van den Eijnden, R. J. J. M. (1997). Perceived prevalence, perceived superiority, and relationship satisfaction: Most relationships are good, but ours is the best. *Personality and Social Psychology Bulletin, 23,* 219–228.

Byrne, D. (1961). Interpersonal attraction and attitude similarity. *Journal of Abnormal and Social Psychology, 62,* 713–715.

Byrne, D. (1971). *The attraction paradigm.* New York: Academic Press.

Byrne, D., & Clore, G. L. (1970). A reinforcement model of evaluative responses. *Personality: An International Journal, 1,* 103–128.

Byrne, D., Clore, G. L., & Smeaton, G. (1986). The attraction hypothesis: Do similar attitudes predict anything? *Journal of Personality and Social Psychology, 51,* 1167–1170.

Byrne, R. W., & Russon, A. E. (1998). Learning by imitation: A hierarchical approach. *Behavioral and Brain Sciences, 21,* 667–721.

Cacioppo, J. T., Bush, L. K., & Tassinary, L. G. (1992). Microexpressive facial actions as a function of affective stimuli: Replication and extension. *Personality and Social Psychology Bulletin, 18,* 515–526.

Cacioppo, J. T., Crites, S. L., Jr., Bernston, G. G., & Coles, M. G. H. (1993). If attitudes affect how stimuli are processed, should they not affect the event-related brain potential? *Psychological Science, 4,* 108–112.

Cacioppo, J. T., Crites, S. L., Jr., & Gardner, W. L. (1996). Attitudes to the right: Evaluative processing is associated with lateralized late positive event-related brain potentials. *Personality and Social Psychology Bulletin, 12,* 1205–1219.

Cacioppo, J. T., Ernst, J. M., Burleson, M. H., McClintock, M. K., Malarkey, W. B., Hawkley, L. C., et al. (2000). Lonely traits and concomitant physiological processes: The MacArthur Social Neuroscience Studies. *International Journal of Psychophysiology, 35,* 143–154.

Cacioppo, J. T., Gardner, W. L., & Bernston, G. G. (1997). Beyond bipolar conceptualizations and measures: The case of attitudes and evaluative space. *Personality and Social Psychology Review, 1,* 3–25.

Cacioppo, J. T., Marshall-Goodell, B. S., Tassinary, L. G., & Petty, R. E. (1992). Rudimentary determinants of attitudes: Classical conditioning is more effective when prior knowledge about the attitude stimulus is low rather than high. *Journal of Experimental Social Psychology, 28,* 207–233.

Cacioppo, J. T., & Petty, R. E. (1982). The need for cognition. *Journal of Personality and Social Psychology, 42,* 116–131.

Cacioppo, J. T., Petty, R. E., Feinstein, J. A., & Jarvis, W. B. G. (1996). Dispositional differences in cognitive motivation: The life and times of individuals varying in need for cognition. *Psychological Bulletin, 119,* 197–253.

Cacioppo, J. T., Petty, R. E., & Kao, C. F. (1984). The efficient assessment of need for cognition. *Journal of Personality Assessment, 48,* 306–307.

Cacioppo, J. T., Petty, R. E., Kao, C. F., & Rodriguez, R. (1986). Central and peripheral routes to persuasion: An individual difference perspective. *Journal of Personality and Social Psychology, 51,* 1032–1043.

Cacioppo, J. T., Petty, R. E., Losch, M. E., & Kim, H. S. (1986). Electromyographic activity over facial muscle regions can differentiate the valence and intensity of affective reactions. *Journal of Personality and Social Psychology, 50,* 260–268.

Cacioppo, J. T., Petty, R. E., & Morris, K. J. (1983). Effects of need for cognition on message evaluation, recall, and persuasion. *Journal of Personality and Social Psychology, 45,* 805–818.

Campbell, D. T., & Stanley, J. C. (1966). *Experimental and quasi-experimental designs for research.* Chicago: Rand McNally.

Campbell, J. D. (1986). Similarity and uniqueness: The effects of attribute type, relevance, and individual differences in self-esteem and depression. *Journal of Personality and Social Psychology, 50,* 281–294.

Campbell, J. D., & Fairey, P. J. (1989). Informational and normative routes to conformity: The effect of faction size as a function of norm extremity and attention to the stimulus. *Journal of Personality and Social Psychology, 57,* 457–468.

Campos, J. Barrett, K., Lamb, M., Goldsmith, H., & Sternberg, C. (1983). Socioemotional development. In P. H. Mussen (Ed.), *Handbook of child psychology: Vol. 2. Infancy and developmental psychology* (pp. 783–915). New York: Wiley.

Caporael, L. R. (1989). Mechanisms matter: The difference between sociobiology and evolutionary psychology. *Behavioral and Brain Sciences, 12,* 17–18.

Carlo, G., Eisenberg, N., Troyer, D., Switzer, G., & Speer, A. L. (1991). The altruistic personality: In what contexts is it apparent? *Journal of Personality and Social Psychology, 61,* 450–458.

Carlsmith, J. M., & Gross, A. (1969). Some effects of guilt on compliance. *Journal of Personality and Social Psychology, 11,* 240–244.

Carlsmith, K. M., Darley, J. M., & Robinson, P. H. (2002). Why do we punish?: Deterrence and just deserts as motives for punishment. *Journal of Personality and Social Psychology, 83,* 284–299.

Carlson, M., Charlin, V., & Miller, N. (1988). Positive mood and helping behavior: A test of six hypotheses. *Journal of Personality and Social Psychology, 55,* 211–229.

Carlson, M., Marcus-Newhall, A., & Miller, N. (1990). Effects of situational aggression cues: A quantitative review. *Journal of Personality and Social Psychology, 58,* 622–633.

Carlson, M., & Miller, N. (1987). Explanation of the relation between negative mood and helping. *Psychological Bulletin, 102,* 91–108.

Carlyle, T. (1841). *On heroes, hero-worship, and the heroic.* London: Fraser.

Carrère, S., Buehlman, K. T., Gottman, J. M., Coan, J. A., & Ruckstuhl, L. (2000). Predicting marital stability and divorce in newlywed couples. *Journal of Family Psychology, 14,* 42–58.

Carver, C. S. (1975). Physical aggression as a function of objective self-awareness and attitudes toward punishment. *Journal of Experimental Social Psychology, 11,* 510–519.

Carver, C. S., & Baird, E. (1998). The American dream revisited: Is it *what* you want or *why* you want it that matters? *Psychological Science, 9,* 289–292.

Carver, C. S., & Scheier, M. F. (1981). *Attention and self-regulation: A control-theory approach to human behavior.* New York: Springer-Verlag.

Carver, C. S., & Scheier, M. F. (1990). Origins and functions of positive and negative affect: A control-process view. *Psychological Review, 97,* 19–35.

Carver, C. S., & Scheier, M. F. (1998). *On the self-regulation of behavior.* New York: Cambridge University Press.

Cash, T. F., Cash, D., & Butters, J. W. (1983). Mirror, mirror, on the wall . . . ? Contrast effects and self-evaluations of physical attractiveness. *Personality and Social Psychology Bulletin, 59,* 351–358.

Cash, T. F., Gillen, B., & Burns, D. S. (1977). Sexism and "beautyism" in personnel consultant decision making. *Journal of Applied Psychology, 62,* 301–310.

Cash, T. F., & Janda, L. H. (1984, December). The eye of the beholder. *Psychology Today,* pp. 46–52.

Castano, E., Yzerbyt, V., Paladino, M-P., & Sacchi, S. (2002). I belong, therefore, I exist: Ingroup identification, ingroup entitativity, and ingroup bias. *Personality and Social Psychology Bulletin, 28,* 135–149.

Cejka, M. A., & Eagly, A. H. (1999). Gender-stereotypic images of occupations correspond to the sex segregation of employment. *Personality and Social Psychology Bulletin, 25,* 413–423.

Chaiken, S. (1979). Communicator physical attractiveness and persuasion. *Journal of Personality and Social Psychology, 37,* 1387–1397.

Chaiken, S. (1980). Heuristic versus systematic information processing and the use of source versus message cues in persuasion. *Journal of Personality and Social Psychology, 39,* 752–766.

Chaiken, S. (1987). The heuristic model of persuasion. In M. P. Zanna, J. M. Olson, & C. P. Herman (Eds.), *Social influence: The Ontario Symposium* (Vol. 5, pp. 3–39). Mahwah, NJ: Erlbaum.

Chaiken, S. & Baldwin, M. W. (1981). Affective-cognitive consistency and the effect of salient behavioral information on the self-perception of attitudes. *Journal of Personality and Social Psychology, 41,* 1–12.

Chaiken, S., & Eagly, A. H. (1976). Communication modality as a determinant of message persuasiveness and message comprehensibility. *Journal of Personality and Social Psychology, 34,* 605–614.

Chaiken, S., & Eagly, A. H. (1983). Communication modality as a determinant of persuasion: The role of communicator salience. *Journal of Personality and Social Psychology, 45,* 241–256.

Chaiken, S., & Trope, Y. (Eds.). (1999). *Dual-process theories in social psychology.* New York: Guilford.

Charon, J. M. (2001). *Symbolic interactionism: An introduction, an interpretation, an integration* (7th ed.). Upper Saddle River, NJ: Prentice-Hall.

Chartrand, T. L., & Bargh, J. A. (1999). The chameleon effect: The perception-behavior link and social interaction. *Journal of Personality and Social Psychology, 76,* 893–910.

Chatman, C. M. & von Hippel, W. (2001). Attributional mediation of in-group bias. *Journal of Experimental Social Psychology, 37,* 267–272.

Chen, J. D., Reardon, R., Rea, C., & Moore, D. J. (1992). Forewarning of content and involvement: Consequences for persuasion and for resistance to persuasion. *Journal of Experimental Social Psychology, 28,* 523–541.

Chen, Y. -R., Mannix, E. A., & Okumura, T. (2003). The importance of who you meet: Effects of self- versus other-concerns among negotiators in the United States, the People's Republic of China, and Japan. *Journal of Experimental Social Psychology, 39,* 1–15.

Chiu, C.-Y., Hong, Y.-Y., & Dweck, C. S. (1997). Lay dispositionism and implicit theories of personality. *Journal of Personality and Social Psychology, 73,* 19–30.

Choi, I., Dalal, R., Kim-Prieto, C., & Park, H. (2003). Culture and judgment of causal relevance. *Journal of Personality and Social Psychology, 84,* 46–59.

Choi, I., & Nisbett, R. E. (1998). Situational salience and cultural differences in the correspondence bias and actor-observer bias. *Personality and Social Psychology Bulletin, 24,* 949–960.

Choi, I., Nisbett, R. E., & Norenzayan, A. (1999). Causal attribution across cultures: Variation and universality. *Psychological Bulletin, 125,* 47–63.

Christensen, A., & Heavey, C. L. (1990). Gender and social structure in demand/withdraw pattern of marital conflict. *Journal of Personality and Social Psychology, 59,* 73–81.

Cialdini, R. B. (1993). *Influence: Science and practice* (3rd ed.). New York: HarperCollins.

Cialdini, R. B., Borden, R. J., Thorne, A., Walker, M. R., Freeman, S., & Sloan, L. R. (1976). Basking in reflected glory: Three (football) field studies. *Journal of Personality and Social Psychology, 34,* 366–375.

Cialdini, R. B., Brown, S. L., Lewis, B. P., Luce, C., & Neuberg, S. L. (1997). Reinterpreting the empathy-altruism relationship: When one into one equals oneness. *Journal of Personality and Social Psychology, 73,* 481–494.

Cialdini, R. B., Cacioppo, J. T., Bassett, R., & Miller, J. A. (1978). Low-ball procedure for producing compliance: Commitment then cost. *Journal of Personality and Social Psychology, 36,* 463–476.

Cialdini, R. B., Darby, B. L., & Vincent, J. E. (1973). Transgression and altruism: A case for hedonism. *Journal of Experimental Social Psychology, 9,* 502–516.

Cialdini, R. B., & De Nicholas, M. E. (1989). Self-presentation by association. *Journal of Personality and Social Psychology, 57,* 626–631.

Cialdini. R. B., & Goldstein, N. J. (2004). Social influence: Compliance and conformity. *Annual Review of Psychology, 55,* 591–621.

Cialdini, R. B., Green, B. L., & Rusch, A. J. (1992). When tactical pronouncements of change become real change: The case of reciprocal persuasion. *Journal of Personality and Social Psychology, 63,* 30–40.

Cialdini, R. B., & Kenrick, D. T. (1976). Altruism as hedonism: A social developmental perspective on the relationship of negative mood state and helping. *Journal of Personality and Social Psychology, 34,* 907–914.

Cialdini, R. B., Reno, R. R., & Kallgren, C. A. (1990). A focus theory of normative conduct: Recycling the concept of norms to reduce littering in public places. *Journal of Personality and Social Psychology, 58,* 1015–1026.

Cialdini, R. B., Schaller, M., Houlihan, D., Arps, K., Fultz, J., & Beaman, A. L. (1987). Empathy-based helping: Is it selflessly or selfishly motivated? *Journal of Personality and Social Psychology, 52,* 749–758.

Cialdini, R. B., & Schroeder, D. A. (1976). Increasing compliance by legitimizing paltry contributions: When even a penny helps. *Journal of Personality and Social Psychology, 34,* 599–604.

Cialdini, R. B., & Trost, M. R. (1998). Social influence, social norms, conformity, and compliance. In D. T. Gilbert, S. T. Fiske, & G. Lindzey (Eds.), *Handbook of social psychology* (4th ed., Vol. 2, pp. 151–192). New York: McGraw-Hill.

Cialdini, R. B., Trost, M. R., & Newsom, J. T. (1995). Preference for consistency: The development of a valid measure and discovery of surprising behavioral implications. *Journal of Personality and Social Psychology, 69,* 318–328.

Cialdini, R. B., Vincent, J. E., Lewis, S. K., Catalan, J., Wheeler, D., & Darby, B. L. (1975). Reciprocal concessions procedure for inducing compliance: The door-in-the-face technique. *Journal of Personality and Social Psychology, 31,* 206–215.

Cialdini, R. B., Wosinska, W., Barrett, D. W., Butner, J., & Gornik-Durose, M. (1999). Compliance with a request in two cultures: The differential influence of social proof and commitment/ consistency on collectivists and individualists. *Personality and Social Psychology Bulletin, 25,* 1242–1253.

Clark, C. L., Shaver, P. R., & Abrahams, M. F. (1999). Strategic behaviors in romantic relationship initiation. *Personality and Social Psychology Bulletin, 25,* 707–720.

Clark, M. S., & Mills, J. (1979). Interpersonal attraction in exchange and communal relationships. *Journal of Personality and Social Psychology, 37,* 12–24.

Clark, M. S., & Mills, J. (1993). The difference between communal and exchange relationships: What it is and is not. *Personality and Social Psychology Bulletin, 19,* 684–691.

Clary, E. G., Snyder, M., Ridge, R. D., Copeland, J., Stukas, A. A., Haugen, J., et al. (1998). Understanding and assessing the motivations of volunteers: A functional approach. *Journal of Personality and Social Psychology, 74,* 1516–1530.

Cobb, S. (1976). Social support as a moderator of life stress. *Psychosomatic Medicine, 38,* 300–314.

Cochran, S. D., Mays, V. M., Ciarletta, J., Caruso, C., & Mallon, D. (1992). Efficacy of the theory of reasoned action in predicting AIDS-related sexual risk reduction among men. *Journal of Applied Social Psychology, 22,* 1481–1501.

Cohen, D. (1998). Culture, social organization, and patterns of violence. *Journal of Personality and Social Psychology, 75,* 408–419.

Cohen, D., & Nisbett, R. E. (1997). Field experiments examining the culture of honor: The role of institutions in perpetuating norms about violence. *Personality and Social Psychology Bulletin, 23,* 1188–1199.

Cohen, D., Nisbett, R. E., Bowdle, B. F., & Schwarz, N. (1996). Insult, aggression, and the Southern culture of honor: An "experimental ethnography." *Journal of Personality and Social Psychology, 70,* 945–960.

Cohen, G. L. (2003). Party over policy: The dominating impact of group influence on political beliefs. *Journal of Personality and Social Psychology, 85,* 808–822.

Cohen, G. L., Aronson, J., & Steele, C. M. (2000). When beliefs yield to evidence: Reducing biased evaluation by affirming the self. *Personality and Social Psychology Bulletin, 26,* 1151–1164.

Cohen, S. (1988). Psychosocial models of the role of social support in the etiology of physical disease. *Health Psychology, 7,* 269–297.

Cohen, S., Tyrrell, D. A., & Smith, A. P. (1991). Psychological stress and susceptibility to the common cold. *New England Journal of Medicine, 325,* 606–612.

Cohen, S., Underwood, L. G., & Gottlieb, B. H. (Eds.). (2000). *Social support measurement and intervention: A guide for health and social scientists.* London: Oxford University Press.

Cohen, S., & Wills, T. A. (1985). Stress, social support, and the buffering hypothesis. *Psychological Bulletin, 98,* 310–357.

Cohn, E. G., & Rotton, J. (1997). Assault as a function of time and temperature: A moderator-variable time-series analysis. *Journal of Personality and Social Psychology, 72,* 1322–1334.

Coie, J. D., Dodge, K. A., & Kupersmidt, J. B. (1990). Peer group behavior and social status. In S. Asher & J. Coie (Eds.), *Peer rejection in childhood* (pp. 17–59), New York: Oxford University Press.

Coke, J. S., Batson, C. D., & McDavis, K. (1982). Empathic mediation of helping: A two-stage model. *Journal of Personality and Social Psychology, 36,* 752–766.

Collins, B. E., & Hoyt, M. F. (1972). Personal responsibility-for-consequences: An integration and extension of the "forced-compliance" literature. *Journal of Experimental Social Psychology, 8,* 558–593.

Collins, N. L., & Feeney, B. C. (2000). A safe haven: An attachment theory perspective on support seeking and caregiving in intimate relationships. *Journal of Personality and Social Psychology, 78,* 1053–1073.

Collins, N. L., & Miller, L. C. (1994). Self-disclosure and liking: A meta-analytic review. *Psychological Bulletin, 116,* 457–475.

Collins, N. L., & Read, S. J. (1990). Adult attachment, working models, and relationship quality in dating couples. *Journal of Personality and Social Psychology, 58,* 644–663.

Collins, R. L. (1996). For better or worse: The impact of upward social comparisons on self-evaluations. *Psychological Bulletin, 119,* 51–69.

Colvin, C. R., & Block, J. (1994). Do positive illusions foster mental health? An examination of the Taylor and Brown formulation. *Psychological Bulletin, 116,* 3–20.

Colvin, C. R., Block, J., & Funder, D. C. (1995). Overly positive self-evaluations and personality: Negative implications for mental health. *Journal of Personality and Social Psychology, 68,* 1152–1162.

Compton, W. C., Smith, M. L., Cornish, K. A., & Qualls, D. L. (1996). Factor structure of mental health measures. *Journal of Personality and Social Psychology, 71,* 406–413.

Condon, J. W., & Crano, W. D. (1988). Inferred evaluation and the relation between attitude similarity and interpersonal attraction. *Journal of Personality and Social Psychology, 54,* 789–797.

Conway, M., & Ross, M. (1984). Getting what you want by revising what you had. *Journal of Personality and Social Psychology, 47,* 738–748.

Cook, S. W. (1984). The 1954 Social Science Statement and school desegregation: A reply to Gerard. *American Psychologist, 39,* 819–832.

Cook, S. W. (1985). Experimenting on social issues: The case of school desegregation. *American Psychologist, 40,* 452–460.

Cook, T. D., & Campbell, D. T. (1979). *Quasi experiments: Design and analysis issues for field settings.* Skokie, IL: Rand-McNally.

Cook, T. D., Gruder, C. L., Hennigan, K. M., & Flay, B. R. (1979). History of the sleeper effect: Some logical pitfalls in accepting the null hypothesis. *Psychological Bulletin, 86,* 662–679.

Cook, W. L. (2000). Understanding attachment security in family context. *Journal of Personality and Social Psychology, 78,* 285–294.

Cooley, C. H. (1902). *Human nature and the social order.* New York: Charles Scribner's Sons.

Cooper, J., & Fazio, R. H. (1984). A new look at dissonance theory. In L. Berkowitz (Ed.), *Advances in experimental social psychology* (Vol. 17, pp. 229–266). Orlando, FL: Academic Press.

Cooper, J., Zanna, M. P., & Taves, P. A. (1978). Arousal as a necessary condition for attitude change following forced compliance. *Journal of Personality and Social Psychology, 36,* 1101–1106.

Cooper, W. H. (1981). Ubiquitous halo. *Psychological Bulletin, 90,* 218–244.

Coopersmith, S. (1967). *The antecedents of self-esteem.* San Francisco: W. H. Freeman.

Coriell, M., & Cohen, S. (1995). Concordance in the face of a stressful event: When do members of a dyad agree that one person supported the other? *Journal of Personality and Social Psychology, 69,* 289–299.

Correll, J., Park, B., Judd, C. M., & Wittenbrink, B. (2002). The police officer's dilemma: Using ethnicity to disambiguate potentially threatening individuals. *Journal of Personality and Social Psychology, 83,* 1314–1329.

Cottrell, N. B. (1972). Social facilitation. In C. G. McClintock (Ed.), *Experimental social psychology* (pp. 185–236). New York: Holt, Rinehart, & Winston.

Cousins, S. D. (1989). Culture and self-perception in Japan and the United States. *Journal of Personality and Social Psychology, 56,* 124–131.

Coyne, J. C. (1976). Toward an interactional description of depression. *Psychiatry, 39,* 28–40.

Coyne, J. C., & DeLongis, A. (1986). Going beyond social support: The role of social relationships in adaptation. *Journal of Personality and Social Psychology, 54,* 454–460.

Cramer, R. E., McMaster, M. R., Bartell, P. A., & Dragma, M. (1988). Subject competence and minimization of the bystander effect. *Journal of Applied Social Psychology, 18,* 1133–1148.

Crandall, C. S., & Biernat, M. (1990). The ideology of anti-fat attitudes. *Journal of Applied Social Psychology, 20,* 227–243.

Crandall, C. S., Eshleman, A., & O'Brien, L. (2002). Social norms and the expression and suppression of prejudice: The struggle for internalization. *Journal of Personality and Social Psychology, 82,* 359–378.

Crawford, M. T., Sherman, S. J., & Hamilton, D. L. (2002). Perceived entitativity, stereotype formation, and the interchangeability of group members. *Journal of Personality and Social Psychology, 83,* 1076–1094.

Crick, N. R., Casas, J. F., & Mosher, M. (1997). Relational and overt aggression in preschool. *Developmental Psychology, 33,* 579–588.

Crick, N. R., & Dodge, K. A. (1994). A review and reformulation of social information-processing mechanisms in children's social adjustment. *Psychological Bulletin, 115,* 74–101.

Crick, N. R., & Ladd, G. W. (1990). Children's perceptions of the outcomes of social strategies: Do the ends justify being mean? *Developmental Psychology, 26,* 612–620.

Crick, N. R., Grotpeter, J. K., & Bigbee, M. A. (2002). Relationally and physically aggressive children's intent attributions and feelings of distress for relational and instrumental peer provocations. *Child Development, 73,* 1134–1142.

Crites, S. L., Jr., Cacioppo, J. T., Gardner, W. L. & Bernston, G. G. (1995). Bioelectrical echoes from evaluative categorization: II. A late positive brain potential that varies as a function of attitude registration rather than attitude report. *Journal of Personality and Social Psychology, 68,* 997–1013.

Crocker, J. (1981). Judgment of covariation by social perceivers. *Psychological Bulletin, 90,* 272–292.

Crocker, J., Luhtanen, R., Blaine, B., & Broadnax, S. (1994). Collective self-esteem and psychological well-being among White, Black, and Asian college students. *Personality and Social Psychology Bulletin, 20,* 503–513.

Crocker, J., & Major, B. (1989). Social stigma and self-esteem: The self-protective properties of stigmas. *Psychological Review, 96,* 608–630.

Crocker, J., & Park, L. E. (2004). The costly pursuit of self-esteem. *Psychological Bulletin, 130,* 392–414.

Crocker, J., Voelkl, K., Testa, M., & Major, B. (1991). Social stigma: The affective consequences of attributional ambiguity. *Journal of Personality and Social Psychology, 60,* 218–228.

Crocker, J., & Wolfe, C. T. (2001). Contingencies of self-worth. *Psychological Review, 108,* 593–623.

Crosby, F. J., Iyer, A., Clayton, S., & Downing, R. A. (2003). Affirmative action: Psychological data and the policy debates. *American Psychologist, 58,* 93–115.

Crosby, F., Bromley, S., & Saxe, L. (1980). Recent unobtrusive studies of Black and White discrimination and prejudice: A literature review. *Psychological Bulletin, 87,* 546–563.

Crowley, A. E., & Hoyer, W. D. (1994). An integrative framework for understanding two-sided persuasions. *Journal of Consumer Research, 20,* 561–574.

Croyle, R. T., & Cooper, J. (1983). Dissonance arousal: Physiological evidence. *Journal of Personality and Social Psychology, 45,* 782–791.

Csikszentmihalyi, M. (1975). *Beyond boredom and anxiety.* San Francisco: Jossey-Bass.

Csikszentmihalyi, M. (1990). *Flow: The psychology of optimal experience.* New York: HarperCollins.

Cunningham, M. R. (1979). Weather, mood, and helping behavior: Quasi-experiments with the sunshine Samaritan. *Journal of Personality and Social Psychology, 37,* 1947–1956.

Cunningham, M. R. (1986). Measuring the physical in physical attractiveness: Quasi-experiments on the sociobiology of female facial beauty. *Journal of Personality and Social Psychology, 50,* 925–935.

Cunningham, M. R. (1988). Does happiness mean friendliness? The effects of mood and self-esteem on social interaction and self-disclosure. *Personality and Social Psychology Bulletin, 14,* 283–297.

Cunningham, M. R., Barbee, A. P., & Pike, C. L. (1990). What do women want? Facialmetric assessment of multiple motives in the perception of male facial physical attractiveness. *Journal of Personality and Social Psychology, 59,* 61–72.

Cunningham, M. R., Roberts, A. R., Barbee, A. P., Druen, P. B., & Wu, C-H. (1995). "Their ideas of beauty are, on the whole, the same as ours": Consistency and variability in the cross-cultural perception of female physical attractiveness. *Journal of Personality and Social Psychology, 68,* 261–279.

Cunningham, M. R., Shaffer, D. R., Barbee, A. P., Wolf, P. L., & Kelley, D. J. (1990). Separate processes in the relation of elation and depression to helping: Social versus personal concerns. *Journal of Experimental Social Psychology, 26,* 13–33.

Cunningham, W. A., Johnson, W. A., Gatenby, J. C., Gore, J. C., & Banaji, M. R. (2003). Neural components of social evaluation. *Journal of Personality and Social Psychology, 85,* 639–649.

Cunningham, W. A., Preacher, K. J., & Banaji, M. R. (2001). Implicit attitude measures: Consistency, stability, and convergent validity. *Psychological Science, 12,* 163–170.

Curhan, J. R., Neale, M. A., & Ross, L. (2004). Dynamic valuation: Preference changes in the context of face-to-face negotiation. *Journal of Experimental Social Psychology, 40,* 142–151.

Cutrona, C. E. (1989). Ratings of social support by adolescents and adult informants: Degree of correspondence and prediction of depressive symptoms. *Journal of Personality and Social Psychology, 57,* 723–730.

Cutrona, C. E. (1982). Transition to college; Loneliness and the process of social adjustment. In L. A. Peplau and D. Perlman (Eds.), *Loneliness: A sourcebook of current theory, research, and therapy* (pp. 291–309). New York: Wiley.

Dabbs, J. M., Jr., Carr, T. S., Frady, R. L., & Riad, J. K. (1995). Testosterone, crime, and misbehavior among 692 male prison inmates. *Personality and Individual Differences, 18,* 627–633.

Dabbs, J. M., Jr., Hargrove, M. F., & Heusel, C. (1996). Testosterone differences among college fraternities: Well-behaved vs. rambunctious. *Personality and Individual Differences, 20,* 157–161.

Dabbs, J. M., & Leventhal, H. (1966). Effects of varying the recommendations in a fear-arousing communication. *Journal of Personality and Social Psychology, 4,* 525–531.

Dad, E. H. H. J., de Wit, J. B. F., & Stroebe, W. (2003). Fear appeals motivate acceptance of action recommendations: Evidence for a positive bias in the processing of persuasive messages. *Personality and Social Psychology Bulletin, 29,* 650–664.

D'Agostino, P. R. (1991). Spontaneous trait inferences: Effects of recognition instructions and subliminal priming on recognition performance. *Personality and Social Psychology Bulletin, 17,* 70–77.

Dakof, G. A., & Taylor, S. E. (1990). Victims' perceptions of social support: What is helpful from whom? *Journal of Personality and Social Psychology, 58,* 80–89.

Daly, M., & Wilson, M. (1988). *Homicide.* New York: Aldine de Bruyter.

Danner, D. D., Snowdon, D. A., & Friesen, W. V. (2001). Positive emotions in early life and longevity: Findings from the nun study. *Journal of Personality and Social Psychology, 80,* 804–813.

Darley, J. M., & Batson, C. D. (1973). From Jerusalem to Jericho: A study of situational and dispositional variables in helping behavior. *Journal of Personality and Social Psychology, 27,* 100–108.

Darley, J. M., & Berscheid, E. (1967). Increased liking as a result of the anticipation of personal contact. *Human Relations, 20,* 29–40.

Darley, J. M., & Fazio, R. H. (1980). Expectancy confirmation processes arising in the social interaction sequence. *American Psychologist, 35,* 867–881.

Darley, J. M., Fleming, J. H., Hilton, J. L., & Swann, W. B., Jr. (1988). Dispelling negative expectancies: The impact of interaction goals and target characteristics on the expectancy confirmation process. *Journal of Experimental Social Psychology, 24,* 19–36.

Darley, J. M., & Gross, P. H. (1983). A hypothesis-confirming bias in labeling effects. *Journal of Personality and Social Psychology, 44,* 20–34.

Darley, J. M., & Latané, B. (1968). Bystander intervention in emergencies: Diffusion of responsibility. *Journal of Personality and Social Psychology, 8,* 377–383.

Darwin, C. R. (1859). *On the origin of species.* London: Murray.

Darwin, C. R. (1871). *The descent of man and selection in relation to sex.* London: Murray.

Darwin, C. R. (1872). *The expression of the emotions in man and animals.* London: Murray.

Davidson, A. R., & Jaccard, J. J. (1979). Variables that moderate the attitude-behavior relation: Results of a longitudinal study. *Journal of Personality and Social Psychology, 37,* 1364–1376.

Davidson, R. J., Jackson, D. C., & Kalin, N. H. (2000). Emotion, plasticity, context, and regulation: Perspectives from affective neuroscience. *Psychological Bulletin, 126,* 890–909.

Davila, J., Burge, D., & Hammen, C. (1997). Why does attachment style change? *Journal of Personality and Social Psychology, 73,* 826–838.

Davila, J., & Cobb, R. J. (2003). Predicting change in self-reported and interviewer-assessed adult attachment: Tests of the individual difference and life stress models of attachment change. *Personality and Social Psychology Bulletin, 29,* 859–870.

Davila, J., Karney, B. R., & Bradbury, T. N. (1999). Attachment change processes in the early years of marriage. *Journal of Personality and Social Psychology, 76,* 783–802.

Davila, J., & Sargent, E. (2003). The meaning of life (events) predicts changes in attachment security. *Personality and Social Psychology Bulletin, 29,* 1383–1395.

Davis, C. G., Lehman, D. R., Wortman, C. B., Silver, R. C., & Thompson, S. C. (1995). The undoing of traumatic life events. *Personality and Social Psychology Bulletin, 21,* 109–124.

Davis, D., Shaver, P. R., & Vernon, M. L. (2003). Physical, emotional, and behavioral reactions to breaking up: The roles of gender, age, emotional involvement, and attachment style. *Personality and Social Psychology Bulletin, 29,* 871–884.

Davis, J. A. (1966). The campus as a frog pond: An application of the theory of relative deprivation to career decisions of college men. *American Journal of Sociology, 72,* 17–31.

Davis, M. H. (1983). Empathic concern and the muscular dystrophy telethon. *Personality and Social Psychology Bulletin, 9,* 223–229.

Davis, M. H., Luce, C., & Kraus, S. J. (1994). The heritability of

characteristics associated with dispositional empathy. *Journal of Personality, 62,* 369–391.

Davison, K. P., Pennebaker, J. W., & Dickerson, S. S. (2000). Who talks? The social psychology of illness support groups. *American Psychologist, 55,* 205–217.

Dawkins, R. (1976). *The selfish gene.* New York: Oxford University Press.

Deaux, K., Reid, A., Mizrahi, K., & Ethier, K. A. (1995). Parameters of social identity. *Journal of Personality and Social Psychology, 68,* 280–291.

Dean, K. E., & Malamuth, N. M. (1997). Characteristics of men who aggress sexually and of men who imagine aggressing: Risk and moderating variables. *Journal of Personality and Social Psychology, 72,* 449–455.

DeBono, K. G. (1987). Investigating the social-adjustive and value-expressive functions of attitudes: Implications for persuasion processes. *Journal of Personality and Social Psychology, 52,* 279–287.

DeBono, K. G., & Harnish, R. J. (1988). Source expertise, source attractiveness, and the processing of persuasive information: A functional approach. *Journal of Personality and Social Psychology, 55,* 541–546.

DeBono, K. G., & Packer, M. (1991). The effects of advertising appeal on perceptions of product quality. *Personality and Social Psychology Bulletin, 17,* 194–200.

DeBono, K. G., & Snyder, M. (1995). Acting on one's attitudes: The role of a history of choosing situations. *Personality and Social Psychology Bulletin, 21,* 629–636.

deCharms, R. (1968). *Personal causation: The internal-affective determinants of behavior.* New York: Academic Press.

Deci, E. L. (1975). *Intrinsic motivation.* New York: Plenum.

Deci, E. L., & Ryan, R. M. (1995). Human autonomy: The basis for true self-esteem. In M. Kernis (Ed.), *Efficacy, agency, and self-esteem* (pp. 31–49). New York: Plenum.

DeCoster, J., & Claypool, H. M. (2004). A meta-analysis of priming effects on impression formation supporting a general model of informational biases. *Personality and Social Psychology Review, 8,* 2–27.

De Dreu, C. K. W., Koole, S. L., & Steinel, W. (2000). Unfixing the fixed pie: A motivated information-processing approach to integrative negotiation. *Journal of Personality and Social Psychology, 79,* 975–987.

De Dreu, C. K. W., Weingart, L. R., & Kwon, S. (2000). Influence of social motives on integrative negotiation: A meta-analytic review and test of two theories. *Journal of Personality and Social Psychology, 78,* 889–905.

DeNeve, K. M., & Cooper, H. (1998). The happy personality: A meta-analysis of 137 personality traits and subjective well-being. *Psychological Bulletin, 124,* 197–229.

DePaulo, B. M. (1992). Nonverbal behavior and self-presentation. *Psychological Bulletin, 111,* 203–244.

DePaulo, B. M. (1994). Spotting lies: Can humans learn to do better? *Current Directions in Psychological Science, 3,* 83–86.

DePaulo, B. M., Charlton, K., Cooper, H., Lindsay, J. H., & Muhlenbruck, L. (1997). The accuracy-confidence correlation in the detection of deception. *Personality and Social Psychology Review, 1,* 346–357.

DePaulo, B. M., Epstein, J. A., & LeMay, C. S. (1990). Responses of the socially anxious to the prospect of interpersonal evaluation. *Journal of Personality, 58,* 623–640.

DePaulo, B. M., Epstein, J. A., & Wyer, M. M. (1993). Sex differences in lying: How women and men deal with the dilemma of deceit. In M. Lewis & C. Saarni (Eds.), *Lying and deception in everyday life* (pp. 126–147). New York: Guilford.

DePaulo, B. M., & Friedman, H. S. (1998). Nonverbal communication. In D. T. Gilbert, S. T. Fiske, & G. Lindzey (Eds.), *Handbook of social psychology* (4th ed., Vol. 2, pp. 3–40). New York: McGraw-Hill.

DePaulo, B. M., Kashy, D. A., Kirkendol, S. E., Wyer, M. M., & Epstein, J. A. (1996). Lying in everyday life. *Journal of Personality and Social Psychology, 70,* 979–995.

DePaulo, B. M., Lassiter, G. D., & Stone, J. I. (1982). Attentional determinants of success at detecting deception and truth. *Personality and Social Psychology Bulletin, 8,* 273–279.

DePaulo, B. M., Lindsay, J. J., Malone, B. E., Muhlenbruck, L., Charlton, K., & Cooper, H. (2003). Cues to de-

ception. *Psychological Bulletin, 129,* 74–118.

DePaulo, B. M., & Pfeifer, R. L. (1986). On-the-job experience and skill at detecting deception. *Journal of Applied Social Psychology, 16,* 249–267.

DePaulo, B. M., Rosenthal, R., Rosenkrantz, J., & Green, C. R. (1982). Actual and perceived cues to deception: A closer look at speech. *Basic and Applied Social Psychology, 3,* 291–312.

DePaulo, B. M., Stone, J. I., & Lassiter, G. D. (1985). Deceiving and detecting deceit. In B. R. Schlenker (Ed.), *The self and social life* (pp. 323–370). New York: McGraw-Hill.

DeSteno, D., Bartlett, M. Y., Braverman, J., & Salovey, P. (2002). Sex differences in jealousy: Evolutional mechanism or artifact of measurement? *Journal of Personality and Social Psychology, 83,* 1103–1116.

Detweiler, J. B., Bedell, B. T., Salovey, P., Pronin, E., & Rothman, A. J. (1999). Message framing and sunscreen use: Gain-framed messages motivate beach-goers. *Health Psychology, 18,* 189–196.

Deutsch, F. M. (1990). Status, sex, and smiling: The effect of role on smiling in men and women. *Personality and Social Psychology Bulletin, 16,* 531–540.

Deutsch, M., & Gerard, H. B. (1955). A study of normative and informational social influence upon individual judgment. *Journal of Abnormal and Social Psychology, 51,* 629–636.

Deutsch, M., & Krauss, R. M. (1960). The effect of threat upon interpersonal bargaining. *Journal of Abnormal and Social Psychology, 61,* 181–189.

Deutsch, M., & Krauss, R. M. (1962). Studies of interpersonal bargaining. *Journal of Conflict Resolution, 6,* 52–76.

Deutsch, M., & Krauss, R. M. (1965). *Theories in social psychology.* New York: Basic Books.

Devine, P. G. (1989). Stereotypes and prejudice. *Journal of Personality and Social Psychology, 56,* 5–18.

Devine, P. G., & Elliot, A. J. (1995). Are racial stereotypes *really* fading? The Princeton Trilogy revisited. *Personality and Social Psychology Bulletin, 21,* 1139–1150.

Devine, P. G., & Malpass, R. S. (1985). Orienting strategies in differential face

recognition. *Personality and Social Psychology Bulletin, 11,* 33–40.

Devine, P. G., & Monteith, M. J. (1993). The role of discrepancy associated affect in prejudice reduction. In D. M. Mackie & D. L. Hamilton (Eds.), *Affect, cognition, and stereotyping: Interactive processes in intergroup perception* (pp. 317–344). San Diego: Academic Press.

Devine, P. G., Plant, E. A., Amodio, D. M., Harmon-Jones, E., & Vance, S. L. (2002). The regulation of explicit and implicit race bias: The role of motivations to respond without prejudice. *Journal of Personality and Social Psychology, 82,* 835–848.

Devos-Comby, L., & Salovey, P. (2002). Applying persuasion strategies to alter HIV-relevant thoughts and behavior. *Review of General Psychology, 6,* 287–304.

Diamond, M., & Uchiyama, A. (1999). Pornography, rape, and sex crimes in Japan. *International Journal of Law and Psychiatry, 22,* 1–22.

Dickerson, C. A., Thibodeau, R., Aronson, E., & Miller, D. (1992). Using cognitive dissonance to encourage water conservation. *Journal of Applied Social Psychology, 22,* 841–854.

Diehl, M., Elnick, A. B., Bourbeau, L. S., & Labouvie-Vief, G. (1998). Adult attachment styles: Their relations to family context and personality. *Journal of Personality and Social Psychology, 74,* 1656–1669.

Diehl, M., & Stroebe, W. (1987). Productivity loss in brainstorming groups: Toward the solution of a riddle. *Journal of Personality and Social Psychology, 53,* 497–509.

Diehl, M., & Stroebe, W. (1991). Productivity loss in idea-generating groups: Tracking down the blocking effect. *Journal of Personality and Social Psychology, 61,* 392–403.

Diekmann, K. A., Samuels, S. M., Ross, L., & Bazerman, M. H. (1997). Self-interest and fairness in problems of resource allocation: Allocators versus recipients. *Journal of Personality and Social Psychology, 72,* 1061–1074.

Diekmann, K. A., Tenbrunsel, A. E., & Galinsky, A. D. (2003). From self-prediction to self-defeat: Behavioral forecasting, self-fulfilling prophecies, and the effect of competitive expectations. *Journal of Personality and Social Psychology, 85,* 672–683.

Diener, E. (1984). Subjective well-being. *Psychological Bulletin, 95,* 542–575.

Diener, E. (1994). Assessing subjective well-being: Progress and opportunities. *Social Indicators Research, 31,* 103–157.

Diener, E. (2000). Subjective well-being: The science of happiness and a proposal for a national index. *American Psychologist, 55,* 34–43.

Diener, E., & Biswas-Diener, R. (2002). Will money increase subjective well-being? A literature review and guide to needed research. *Social Indicators Research, 57,* 119–169.

Diener, E., & Diener, M. (1995). Cross-cultural correlates of life satisfaction and self-esteem. *Journal of Personality and Social Psychology, 68,* 653–663.

Diener, E., Diener, M., & Diener, C. (1995). Factors predicting the subjective well-being of nations. *Journal of Personality and Social Psychology, 69,* 851–864.

Diener, E., & Fujita, F. (1997). Social comparisons and subjective well-being. In B. Buunk & R. Gibbons (Eds.), *Health, coping, and social comparison* (pp. 329–357). Mahwah, NJ: Erlbaum.

Diener, E., Lucas, R. E., Oishi, S., & Suh, E. M. (2002). Looking up and looking down: Weighting good and bad information in life satisfaction judgments. *Personality and Social Psychology Bulletin, 28,* 437–445.

Diener, E., Sandvik, E., & Pavot, W. (1991). Happiness is the frequency, not the intensity, of positive versus negative affect. In F. Strack, M. Argyle, & N. Schwarz (Eds.), *Subjective well-being: An interdisciplinary perspective* (pp. 119–139). Oxford: Pergamon.

Diener, E., Sandvik, E., Seidlitz, L., & Diener, M. (1993). The relationship between income and subjective well-being. Relative or absolute? *Social Indicators Research, 28,* 195–223.

Diener, E., Scollon, C. N., & Lucas, R. E. (2004). The evolving concept of subjective well-being: The multifaceted nature of happiness. *Advances in Cell Aging and Gerontology, 15,* 187–219.

Diener, E., & Seligman, M. E. P. (2002). Very happy people. *Psychological Science, 13,* 81–84.

Diener, E., & Seligman, M. E. P. (2004). Beyond money: Toward an economy

of well-being. *Psychological Science in the Public Interest, 5,* 1–31.

Diener, E., Suh, E. M., Lucas, R. E., & Smith, H. L. (1999). Subjective well-being: Three decades of progress. *Psychological Bulletin, 125,* 276–302.

Diener, E., & Wallbom, M. (1976). Effects of self-awareness on antinormative behavior. *Journal of Research in Personality, 10,* 413–423.

Diener, E., Wolsic, B., & Fujita, F. (1995). Physical attractiveness and subjective well-being. *Journal of Personality and Social Psychology, 69,* 120–129.

Dientstbier, R. A., & Munter, P. O. (1971). Cheating as a function of the labeling of natural arousal. *Journal of Personality and Social Psychology, 17,* 208–213.

Dijkers, M. (1997). Quality of life after spinal cord injury: A meta-analysis of the effects of disablement components. *Spinal Cord, 35,* 829–840.

Dijksterhuis, A., Spears, R., Postmes, T., Stapel, D. A., Koomen, W., van Knippenberg, A., et al. (1998). Seeing one thing and doing another: Contrast effects in automatic behavior. *Journal of Personality and Social Psychology, 75,* 862–871.

Dill, K. E., Anderson, C. A., Anderson, K. B., & Deuser, W. E. (1997). Effects of aggressive personality on social expectations and social perceptions. *Journal of Research in Personality, 31,* 272–292.

DiMatteo, M. R., Hays, R. D., & Prince, L. M. (1986). Relationship of physicians' nonverbal communication skill to patient satisfaction, appointment noncompliance, and physical workload. *Health Psychology, 5,* 581–594.

Dindia, K., & Allen, M. (1992). Sex differences in self-disclosure: A meta-analysis. *Psychological Bulletin, 112,* 106–124.

Dion, K. L., & Dion, K. K. (1988). Romantic love: Individual and cultural perspectives. In R. J. Sternberg & M. L. Barnes (Eds.), *The psychology of love* (pp. 264–289). New Haven, CT: Yale University Press.

Dion, K. L., & Dion, K. K. (1993a). Individualistic and collectivistic perspectives on gender and the cultural context of love and intimacy. *Journal of Social Issues, 49,* 53–69.

Dion, K. L., & Dion, K. K. (1993b). Gender and ethnocultural comparisons in

styles of love. *Psychology of Women Quarterly, 17,* 463–473.

Dion, K., Berscheid, E., & Walster, E. (1972). What is beautiful is good. *Journal of Personality and Social Psychology, 24,* 285–290.

Ditto, P. H., & Lopez, D. F. (1992). Motivated skepticism: Use of differential decision criteria for preferred and nonpreferred conclusions. *Journal of Personality and Social Psychology, 63,* 568–584.

Ditto, P. H., Scepansky, J. A., Munro, G. D., Apanovitch, A. M., & Lockart, L. K. (1998). Motivated sensitivity to preference-inconsistent information. *Journal of Personality and Social Psychology, 75,* 53–69.

Dixon, T. M., & Baumeister, R. F. (1991). Escaping the self: The moderating effect of self-complexity. *Personality and Social Psychology Bulletin, 17,* 363–368.

Dodge, K. A. (1980). Social cognition and children's aggressive behavior. *Child Development, 51,* 162–170.

Dodge, K. A., & Coie, J. D. (1987). Social-information-processing factors in reactive and proactive aggression in children's peer groups. *Journal of Personality and Social Psychology, 53,* 1146–1158.

Dolinski, D., Nawrat, M., & Rudak, I. (2001). Dialogue involvement as a social influence technique. *Personality and Social Psychology Bulletin, 27,* 1395–1406.

Dollard, J., Doob, L. W., Miller, N. E., Mowrer, O. H., & Sears, R. R. (1939). *Frustration and aggression:* New Haven, CT: Yale University Press.

Donahue, E. M., Robins, R. W., Roberts, B. W., & John, O. P. (1993). The divided self: Concurrent and longitudinal effects of psychological adjustment and social roles on self-concept differentiation. *Journal of Personality and Social Psychology, 64,* 834–846.

Donnerstein, E. (1980). Aggressive erotica and violence against women. *Journal of Personality and Social Psychology, 39,* 269–277.

Donnerstein, E., & Berkowitz, L. (1981). Victim reactions in aggressive erotic films as a factor in violence against women. *Journal of Personality and Social Psychology, 41,* 710–724.

Doob, A. N., & Climie, R. J. (1972). Delay of measurement and effects of film violence. *Journal of Experimental Social Psychology, 8,* 136–142.

Doosje, B., Branscombe, N. R., Spears, R., & Manstead, A. S. R. (1998). Guilty by association: When one's group has a negative history. *Journal of Personality and Social Psychology, 75,* 872–886.

Dovidio, J. F. (1984). Helping behavior and altruism: An empirical and conceptual overview. In L. Berkowitz (Ed.), *Advances in experimental social psychology* (Vol. 17, pp. 361–427). New York: Academic Press.

Dovidio, J. F., Brigham, J. C. Johnson, B. T., & Gaertner, S. L. (1996). Stereotyping, prejudice, and discrimination: Another look. In C. N. Macrae, C. Stangor, & M. Hewstone (Eds.), *Stereotypes and stereotyping* (pp. 276–319). New York: Guilford.

Dovidio, J. F., Brown, C. E., Heltman, K., Ellyson, S. L., & Keating, C. F. (1988). Power displays between men and women in discussions of gender-linked tasks: A multichannel study. *Journal of Personality and Social Psychology, 55,* 580–587.

Dovidio, J. F., & Ellyson, S. L. (1985). Patterns of visual dominance in humans. In S. L. Ellyson & J. F. Dovidio (Eds.), *Power, dominance and nonverbal behavior* (pp. 129–149). New York: Springer-Verlag.

Dovidio, J. F., Ellyson, S. L., Keating, C. F., Heltman, K., & Brown, C. E. (1988). The relationship of social power to visual displays of dominance between men and women. *Journal of Personality and Social Psychology, 54,* 233–242.

Dovidio, J. F., & Gaertner, S. L. (1998). On the nature of contemporary prejudice: The causes, consequences, and challenges of aversive racism. In J. L. Eberhardt & S. T. Fiske (Eds.), *Confronting racism: The problem and the response* (pp. 3–32). Thousand Oaks, CA: Sage.

Dovidio, J. F., & Gaertner, S. L. (2000). Aversive racism and selection decisions: 1989 and 1999. *Psychological Science, 11,* 315–319.

Dovidio, J. F., Gaertner, S. L., Niemann, Y. F., & Snider, K. (2001). Racial, ethnic, and cultural differences in responding to distinctiveness and discrimination on campus: Stigma and common group identity. *Journal of Social Issues, 57,* 167–188.

Dovidio, J. F., Gaertner, S. L., & Validzic, A. (1998). Intergroup bias: Status, differentiation, and a common in-group identity. *Journal of Personality and Social Psychology, 75,* 109–120.

Dovidio, J. F., Kawakami, K., & Gaertner, S. L. (2002). Implicit and explicit prejudice and interracial interaction. *Journal of Personality and Social Psychology, 82,* 62–68.

Dovidio, J. F., Kawakami, K., Johnson, C., Johnson, B., & Howard, A. (1997). On the nature of prejudice: Automatic and controlled processes. *Journal of Experimental Social Psychology, 33,* 510–540.

Dovidio, J. F., Piliavin, J. A., Gaertner, S. L., Schroeder, D. A., & Clark, R. D., III. (1991). The Arousal: Cost-reward model and the process of intervention: A review of the evidence. *Review of Personality and Social Psychology, 12,* 86–118.

Downs, A. C., & Lyons, P. M. (1991). Natural observations of the links between attractiveness and initial legal judgments. *Personality and Social Psychology Bulletin, 17,* 541–547.

Drigotas, S. M., & Rusbult, C. E. (1992). Should I stay or should I go? A dependence model of breakups. *Journal of Personality and Social Psychology, 62,* 62–87.

Drigotas, S. M., Safstrom, C. A., & Gentilia, T. (1999). An investment model of dating infidelity. *Journal of Personality and Social Psychology, 77,* 509–524.

Dryer, D. C., & Horowitz, L. M. (1997). When do opposites attract? Interpersonal complementarity and similarity. *Journal of Personality and Social Psychology, 72,* 592–603.

Duckworth, K. L., Bargh, J. A., Garcia, M., & Chaiken, S. (2002). The automatic evaluation of novel stimuli. *Psychological Science, 13,* 513–519.

Duffy, S. M., & Rusbult, C. E. (1986). Satisfaction and commitment in homosexual and heterosexual relationships. *Journal of Homosexuality, 12,* 1–23.

Duncan, B. L. (1976). Differential social perception and attribution of intergroup violence: Testing the lower limits of stereotyping of Blacks. *Journal of Personality and Social Psychology, 34,* 590–598.

Dunning, D. (1993). Words to live by: The self and definitions of social concepts and categories. In J. Suls (Ed.), *Psychological perspectives on the self* (Vol. 4, pp. 99–126). Mahwah, NJ: Erlbaum.

Dunning, D., Griffin, D. W., Milojkovic, J. D., & Ross, L. (1990). The overconfidence effect in social prediction. *Journal of Personality and Social Psychology, 58,* 568–581.

Dunning, D., Meyerowitz, J. A., & Holzberg, A. D. (1989). Ambiguity and self-evaluation: The role of idiosyncratic trait definitions in self-serving assessments of ability. *Journal of Personality and Social Psychology, 57,* 1082–1090.

Dunning, D., & Sherman, D. A. (1997). Stereotypes and tacit inference. *Journal of Personality and Social Psychology, 73,* 459–471.

Dunton, B. C., & Fazio, R. H. (1997). An individual difference measure of motivation to control prejudiced reactions. *Personality and Social Psychology Bulletin, 23,* 316–326.

Dutton, D. G., & Aron, A. P. (1974). Some evidence for heightened sexual attraction under conditions of high anxiety. *Journal of Personality and Social Psychology, 30,* 510–517.

Duval, S., & Wicklund, R. A. (1972). *A theory of objective self-awareness.* New York: Academic Press.

Dweck, C. S., Hong, Y.-Y., & Chiu, C.-Y. (1993). Implicit theories: Individual differences in the likelihood and meaning of dispositional inference. *Personality and Social Psychology Bulletin, 19,* 644–656.

Dweck, C. S., & Leggett, E. L. (1988). A social-cognitive approach to motivation and personality. *Psychological Review, 95,* 256–273.

Eagly, A. H. (1967). Involvement as a determinant of response to favorable and unfavorable information. *Journal of Personality and Social Psychology, 7* (No. 3, Whole No. 643).

Eagly, A. H. (1987). *Sex differences in social behavior: A social role interpretation.* Mahwah, NJ: Erlbaum.

Eagly, A. H. (1992). Uneven progress: Social psychology and the study of attitudes. *Journal of Personality and Social Psychology, 63,* 693–710.

Eagly, A. H. (2000, August). *Prejudice: Toward a more inclusive definition.* Paper delivered at a Festschrift

Conference, The social psychology of group identity and social conflict: Theory, application, and practice. Cambridge, MA: Harvard University.

Eagly, A. H., Ashmore, R. D., Makhijani, M. G., & Longo, L. C. (1991). What is beautiful is good, but . . . :A meta-analytic review of research on the physical attractiveness stereotype. *Psychological Bulletin, 110,* 109–128.

Eagly, A. H., & Carli, L. L. (1981). Sex of researchers and sex-typed communications as determinants of sex differences in influenceability: A meta-analysis of social influence studies. *Psychological Bulletin, 90,* 1–20.

Eagly, A. H., & Chaiken, S. (1975). An attributional analysis of the effect of communicator characteristics on opinion change: The case of communicator attractiveness. *Journal of Personality and Social Psychology, 32,* 136–144.

Eagly, A. H., & Chaiken, S. (1984). Cognitive theories of persuasion. In L. Berkowitz (Ed.), *Advances in experimental social psychology* (Vol. 17, pp. 267–359). San Diego: Academic Press.

Eagly, A. H., & Chaiken, S. (1993). *The psychology of attitudes.* Orlando, FL: Harcourt, Brace, & Jovanovich.

Eagly, A. H., & Chaiken, S. (1998). Attitude structure and function. In D. T. Gilbert, S. T. Fiske, & G. Lindzey (Eds.), *Handbook of social psychology* (4th ed., Vol. 1, pp. 269–322). New York: McGraw-Hill.

Eagly, A. H., & Crowley, M. (1986). Gender and helping behavior: A meta-analytic review of the social psychological literature. *Psychological Bulletin, 100,* 283–308.

Eagly, A. H., Diekman, A. B., Schneider, M. C., & Kulsea, P. (2003). Experimental tests of an attitudinal theory of the gender gap in voting. *Personality and Social Psychology Bulletin, 29,* 1245–1258.

Eagly, A. H., & Johnson, B. T. (1990). Gender and leadership style: A meta-analysis. *Psychological Bulletin, 108,* 233–256.

Eagly, A. H., Johannesen-Schmidt, M. C., & Van Engen, M. L. (2003). Transformational, transactional, and laissez-faire leadership styles: A meta-analysis comparing women and men. *Psychological Bulletin, 129,* 569–591.

Eagly, A. H., & Karau, S. J. (2002). Role contiguity theory of prejudice toward female leaders. *Psychological Review, 109,* 573–598.

Eagly, A. H., Karau, S. J., & Makhijani, M. G. (1995). Gender and the effectiveness of leaders: A meta-analysis. *Psychological Bulletin, 117,* 125–145.

Eagly, A. H., Kulesa, P., Brannon, L. A., Shaw, K., & Hutson-Comeaux, S. (2000). Why counterattitudinal messages are as memorable as proattitudinal messages: The importance of active defense against the attack. *Personality and Social Psychology Bulletin, 26,* 1392–1408.

Eagly, A. H., Makhijani, M. G., & Klonsky, B. G. (1992). Gender and the evaluation of leaders: A meta-analysis. *Psychological Bulletin, 111,* 3–22.

Eagly, A. H., & Mladinic, A. (1989). Gender stereotypes and attitudes toward men and women. *Personality and Social Psychology Bulletin, 15,* 543–558.

Eagly, A. H., & Steffen, V. J. (1984). Gender stereotypes stem from the distribution of women and men into social roles. *Journal of Personality and Social Psychology, 46,* 735–754.

Eagly, A. H., & Steffen, V. J. (1986). Gender and aggressive behavior: A meta-analytic review of the social psychological literature. *Psychological Bulletin, 100,* 309–330.

Eagly, A. H., & Telaak, K. (1972). Width of the latitude of acceptance as a determinant of attitude change. *Journal of Personality and Social Psychology, 23,* 388–397.

Eagly, A. H., & Wood, W. (1999). The origins of sex differences in human behavior: Evolved dispositions versus social roles. *American Psychologist, 54,* 408–423.

Eagly, A. H., Wood, W., & Chaiken, S. (1978). Causal inferences about communicators and their effect on opinion change. *Journal of Personality and Social Psychology, 36,* 424–435.

Eckland, B. (1968). Theories of mate selection. *Social Biology, 15,* 71–84.

Economos, J. (1989). Altruism, nativism, chauvinism, racism, schism, and jizzum. *Behavioral and Brain Sciences, 12,* 521–523.

Edwards, K. (1990). The interplay of affect and cognition in attitude formation and change. *Journal of Personality and Social Psychology, 59,* 202–216.

Edwards, K., & Smith, E. E. (1996). A disconfirmation bias in the evaluation of arguments. *Journal of Personality and Social Psychology, 71,* 5–24.

Edwards, K., & von Hippel, W. (1995). Hearts and minds: The priority of affective versus cognitive factors in person perception. *Personality and Social Psychology Bulletin, 21,* 996–1011.

Eibl-Eibesfeldt, I. (1989). *Human ethology.* New York: Aldine de Gruyter.

Eid, M., & Diener, E. (2001). Norms for experiencing emotions in different cultures: Inter- and intranational differences. *Journal of Personality and Social Psychology, 81,* 869–885.

Eidelman, S., & Biernat, M. (2003). Derogating black sheep: Individual or group protection? *Journal of Experimental Social Psychology, 39,* 602–609.

Eisenberg, N. (1992). *The caring child.* Cambridge, MA: Harvard University Press.

Eisenberg, N., Fabes, R. A., Schaller, M., Carlo, G., & Miller, P. A. (1991). The relations of parental characteristics and practices to children's vicarious emotional responding. *Child Development, 62,* 1393–1408.

Eisenberg, N., Guthrie, I. K., Cumberland, A., Murphy, B. C., Shepard, S. A., Zhou, Q., et al. (2002). Prosocial development in early adulthood: A longitudinal study. *Journal of Personality and Social Psychology, 82,* 993–1006.

Eisenberg, N., & Miller, P. A. (1987). The relation of empathy to prosocial and related behaviors. *Psychological Bulletin, 101,* 91–119.

Eisenberg, N., Schaller, M., Fabes, R. A., Bustamante, D., Mathy, R. M., Shell, R., et al. (1988). Differentiation of personal distress and sympathy in children and adults. *Developmental Psychology, 24,* 766–775.

Eisenberger, N. I., Lieberman, M. D., & Williams, K. D. (2003). Does rejection hurt? An fMRI study of social exclusion. *Science, 302,* 290–292.

Eisenberger, R., Armeli, S., & Pretz, J. (1998). Can the promise of reward increase creativity? *Journal of Personality and Social Psychology, 74,* 704–714.

Eisenberger, R., Rhoades, L., & Cameron, J. (1999). Does pay for performance increase or decrease perceived self-determination and intrinsic motivation? *Journal of Personality *and Social Psychology, 77,* 1026–1040.

Ekman, P. (1972). Universals and cultural differences in facial expressions of emotion. In J. Cole (Ed.), *Nebraska symposium on motivation, 1971* (pp. 207–283). Lincoln: University of Nebraska Press.

Ekman, P. (1993). Facial expression and emotion. *American Psychologist, 48,* 384–392.

Ekman, P. (1994). Strong evidence for universals in facial expressions: A reply to Russell's mistaken critique. *Psychological Bulletin, 115,* 268–287.

Ekman, P., Davidson, R. J., & Friesen, W. V. (1990). The Duchenne Smile: Emotional expression and brain physiology II. *Journal of Personality and Social Psychology, 58,* 342–354.

Ekman, P., & Friesen, W. V. (1969). Nonverbal leakage and cues to deception. *Psychiatry, 32,* 88–106.

Ekman, P., & Friesen, W. V. (1971). Constants across cultures in the face and emotion. *Journal of Personality and Social Psychology, 17,* 124–129.

Ekman, P., & Friesen, W. V. (1974). Detecting deception from the body or face. *Journal of Personality and Social Psychology, 29,* 288–298.

Ekman, P., Friesen, W. V., & O'Sullivan, M. (1988). Smiles when lying. *Journal of Personality and Social Psychology, 54,* 414–420.

Ekman, P., Friesen, W. V., O'Sullivan, M., Chan, A., Diacoyanni-Tarlatzis, I., Heider, K., et al. (1987). Universals and cultural differences in the judgments of facial expressions of emotion. *Journal of Personality and Social Psychology, 53,* 712–717.

Ekman, P., & O'Sullivan, M. (1991). Who can catch a liar? *American Psychologist, 46,* 913–920.

Ekman, P., O'Sullivan, M., & Frank, M. G. (1999). A few can catch a liar. *Psychological Science, 10,* 263–266.

Ekman, P., O'Sullivan, M., Friesen, W. V., & Scherer, K. R. (1991). Face, voice, and body in detecting deceit. *Journal of Nonverbal Behavior, 15,* 125–135.

Elfenbein, H. A., & Ambady, N. (2002). On the universality and cultural specificity of emotion recognition: A meta-analysis. *Psychological Bulletin, 128,* 203–225.

Elliot, A. J., & Church, M. A. (1997). A hierarchical model of approach and avoidance achievement motivation.

Journal of Personality and Social Psychology, 72, 218–232.

Elliot, A. J., Faler, J., McGregor, H. A., Campbell, W. K., Sedikides, C., & Harackiewicz, J. M. (2000). Competence valuation as a strategic intrinsic motivation process. *Personality and Social Psychology Bulletin, 26,* 780–794.

Elliot, A. J., & McGregor, H. A. (2001). A 2×2 achievement goal framework. *Journal of Personality and Social Psychology, 80,* 501–519.

Elliott, R., & Dolan, R. J. (1998). Neural response during preference and memory judgments for subliminally presented stimuli: A functional neuroimaging study. *Journal of Neuroscience, 18,* 4697–4704.

Ellsworth, P. C., & Mauro, R. (1998). Psychology and law. In D. T. Gilbert, S. T. Fiske, & G. Lindzey (Eds.), *Handbook of social psychology* (4th ed., Vol. 2, pp. 684–732). New York: McGraw-Hill.

Emmons, R. A. (1986). Personal strivings: An approach to personality and subjective well-being. *Journal of Personality and Social Psychology, 51,* 1058–1068.

Emmons, R. A. (1987). Narcissism: Theory and measurement. *Journal of Personality and Social Psychology, 52,* 11–17.

Emmons, R. A., & McCullough, M. E. (2003). Counting blessings versus burdens: An experimental investigation of gratitude and subjective well-being in daily life. *Journal of Personality and Social Psychology, 84,* 377–389.

Endo, Y., Heine, S. J., & Lehman, D. R. (2000). Culture and positive illusions in close relationships: How my relationships are better than yours. *Personality and Social Psychology Bulletin, 26,* 1571–1586.

Ensari, N., & Miller, N. (2002). The outgroup must not be so bad after all: The effects of disclosure, typicality, and salience on intergroup bias. *Journal of Personality and Social Psychology, 83,* 313–329.

Epley, N., & Dunning, D. (2000). Feeling "holier than thou": Are self-serving assessments produced by errors in self- or social prediction? *Journal of Personality and Social Psychology, 79,* 861–875.

Erb, H. -P., Bohner, G., Rank, S., & Einwiller, S. (2002). Processing

minority and majority communications: The role of conflict with prior attitudes. *Personality and Social Psychology Bulletin, 28,* 1172–1182.

Erikson, E. (1959). Identity and the life cycle. *Psychological Issues, 1,* 18–164.

Eron, L. D. (1982). Parent-child interaction, television violence, and aggressive children. *American Psychologist, 37,* 197–211.

Essock-Vitale, S. M., & McGuire, M. T. (1985). Women's lives viewed from an evolutionary perspective. II. Patterns of helping. *Ethology and Sociobiology, 6,* 155–173.

Evans, L. M., & Petty, R. E. (2003). Self-guide framing and persuasion: Responsibly increasing message processing to ideal levels. *Personality and Social Psychology Bulletin, 29,* 313–324.

Fabrigar, L. R., & Petty, R. E. (1999). The role of the affective and cognitive bases of attitudes in susceptibility to affectively and cognitively based persuasion. *Personality and Social Psychology Bulletin, 25,* 363–381.

Farwell, L., & Weiner, B. (2000). Bleeding hearts and the heartless: Popular perceptions of liberal and conservative ideologies. *Personality and Social Psychology Bulletin, 26,* 845–852.

Fazio, R. H. (1986). How do attitudes guide behavior? In R. M. Sorrentino & E. T. Higgins (Eds.), *Handbook of motivation and cognition* (pp. 204–243). New York: Guilford.

Fazio, R. H. (1990). Multiple processes by which attitudes guide behavior: The MODE model as an integrative framework. In M. P. Zanna (Ed.), *Advances in experimental social psychology* (Vol. 23, pp. 75–109). New York: Academic Press.

Fazio, R. H., Blascovich, J., & Driscoll, D. M. (1992). On the functional value of attitudes: The influence of accessible attitudes upon the ease and quality of decision-making. *Personality and Social Psychology Bulletin, 18,* 388–401.

Fazio, R. H., Chen, J., McDonel, E. C., & Sherman, S. J. (1982). Attitude accessibility, attitude-behavior consistency, and the strength of the object-evaluation association. *Journal of Experimental Social Psychology, 18,* 339–357.

Fazio, R. H., & Cooper, J. (1983). Arousal in the dissonance process. In J. T. Cacioppo & R. E. Petty (Eds.), *Social psychophysiology: A sourcebook* (pp. 122–152). New York: Guilford.

Fazio, R. H., & Dunton, B. C. (1997). Categorization by race: The impact of automatic and controlled components of racial prejudice. *Journal of Experimental Social Psychology, 33,* 451–470.

Fazio, R. H., & Hilden, L. E. (2001). Emotional reactions to a seemingly prejudiced response: The role of automatically activated racial attitudes and motivation to control prejudiced reactions. *Personality and Social Psychology Bulletin, 27,* 538–549.

Fazio, R. H., Jackson, J. R., Dunton, B. C., & Williams, C. J. (1995). Variability in automatic activation as an unobtrusive measure of racial attitudes: A bona fide pipeline? *Journal of Personality and Social Psychology, 69,* 1013–1027.

Fazio, R. H., Ledbetter, J. E., & Towles-Schwen, T. (2000). On the costs of accessible attitudes: Detecting that the attitude object has changed. *Journal of Personality and Social Psychology, 78,* 197–210.

Fazio, R. H., & Olson, M. A. (2003). Implicit measures in social cognition research: Their meaning and uses. *Annual Review of Psychology, 54,* 297–327.

Fazio, R. H., Powell, M. C., & Herr, P. M. (1983). Toward a process model of the attitude-behavior relation: Accessing one's attitude upon mere observation of the attitude object. *Journal of Personality and Social Psychology, 44,* 723–735.

Fazio, R. H., Sanbonmatsu, D. M., Powell, M. C., & Kardes, F. R. (1986). On the automatic activation of attitudes. *Journal of Personality and Social Psychology, 50,* 229–238.

Fazio, R. H., & Williams, C. J. (1986). Attitude accessibility as a moderator of the attitude-perception and attitude-behavior relations: An investigation of the 1984 presidential election. *Journal of Personality and Social Psychology, 51,* 505–514.

Fazio, R. H., & Zanna, M. P. (1981). Direct experience and attitude-behavior consistency. In L. Berkowitz (Ed.), *Advances in experimental social psychology* (Vol. 14, pp. 161–202). New York: Academic Press.

Fazio, R. H., Zanna, M. P., & Cooper, J. (1977). Dissonance and self-perception: An integrative view of each theory's proper domain of application. *Journal of Experimental Social Psychology, 13,* 464–479.

Feather, N. T. (1995). Values, valences, and choice: The influence of values on the perceived attractiveness and choice of alternatives. *Journal of Personality and Social Psychology, 68,* 1135–1151.

Feeney, B. C., & Cassidy, J. (2003). Reconstructive memory related to adolescent-parent conflict interactions: The influence of attachment-related representations on immediate perceptions and changes in perception over time. *Journal of Personality and Social Psychology, 85,* 945–955.

Feeney, B. C., & Collins, N. L. (2001). Predictors of caregiving in adult intimate relationships: An attachment theoretical perspective. *Journal of Personality and Social Psychology, 80,* 972–994.

Feeney, J. A., & Noller, P. (1990). Attachment style as a predictor of adult romantic relationships. *Journal of Personality and Social Psychology, 58,* 281–291.

Fehr, B. (1988). Prototype analysis of the concepts of love and commitment. *Journal of Personality and Social Psychology, 55,* 557–579.

Fehr, B. (1999). Laypeople's conceptions of commitment. *Journal of Personality and Social Psychology, 76,* 90–103.

Fehr, B., & Russell, J. A. (1991). The concept of love viewed from a prototype perspective. *Journal of Personality and Social Psychology, 60,* 425–438.

Fein, S. (1996). Effects of suspicion on attributional thinking and the correspondence bias. *Journal of Personality and Social Psychology, 70,* 1164–1184.

Fein, S., Hilton, J. L., & Miller, D. T. (1990). Suspicion of ulterior motive and the correspondence bias. *Journal of Personality and Social Psychology, 58,* 753–764.

Fein, S., & Spencer, S. J. (1997). Prejudice as self-image maintenance: Affirming the self though derogating others. *Journal of Personality and Social Psychology, 73,* 31–44.

Feingold, A. (1988). Matching for attractiveness in romantic partners and same-sex friends: A meta-analysis and theoretical critique. *Psychological Bulletin, 104,* 226–235.

Feingold, A. (1990). Gender differences in effects of physical attractiveness on romantic attraction: A comparison across five research paradigms. *Journal of Personality and Social Psychology, 59,* 981–993.

Feingold, A. (1992a). Good-looking people are not what we think. *Psychological Bulletin, 111,* 304–341.

Feingold, A. (1992b). Gender differences in mate selection preference: A test of the parental investment model. *Psychological Bulletin, 112,* 125–139.

Feldman, R. E. (1968). Response to a compatriot and foreigner who seek assistance. *Journal of Personality and Social Psychology, 10,* 202–214.

Felson, R. B. (1981). Ambiguity and bias in the self-concept. *Social Psychology Quarterly, 44,* 64–69.

Felson, R. B. (1993). The (somewhat) social self: How others affect self-appraisals. In J. Suls (Ed.), *Psychological perspectives on the self* (Vol. 4, pp. 1–27). Mahwah, NJ: Erlbaum.

Feshbach, N. D. (1989). Empathy training and prosocial behavior. In J. Groebel & R. Hindle (Eds.), *Aggression and war: Their biological and social bases* (pp. 101–111). New York: Cambridge University Press.

Feshbach, S. (1964). The function of aggression and the regulation of aggressive drive. *Psychological Review, 71,* 257–272.

Festinger, L. (1950). Informal social communication. *Psychological Review, 57,* 271–282.

Festinger, L. (1954). A theory of social comparison processes. *Human Relations, 7,* 117–140.

Festinger, L. (1957). *A theory of cognitive dissonance.* Evanston, IL: Row Peterson.

Festinger, L., & Carlsmith, J. M. (1959). Cognitive consequences of forced compliance. *Journal of Abnormal and Social Psychology, 58,* 203–211.

Festinger, L., & Maccoby, N. (1964). On resistance to persuasive communications. *Journal of Abnormal and Social Psychology, 68,* 359–366.

Festinger, L., Pepitone, A., & Newcomb, T. (1952). Some consequences of deindividuation in a group. *Journal of Abnormal and Social Psychology, 47,* 382–389.

Festinger, L., Schachter, S., & Back, K. (1950). *Social pressures in informal groups: A study of human factors in housing.* New York: Harper & Brothers.

Festinger, L., & Thibaut, J. (1951). Interpersonal communication in small groups. *Journal of Abnormal and Social Psychology, 46,* 92–99.

Fiedler, F. (1967). *A theory of leadership effectiveness.* New York: McGraw-Hill.

Fiedler, F. (1978). The contingency model and the dynamics of the leadership process. In L. Berkowitz (Ed.), *Advances in experimental social psychology* (Vol. 12, pp. 59–112). New York: Academic Press.

Fiedler, K., & Walka, I. (1993). Training lie detectors to use nonverbal cues instead of global heuristics. *Human Communication Research, 20,* 199–224.

Filsinger, E. E., Braun J. J., & Monte, W. C. (1985). An examination of the effects of putative pheromones on human judgments. *Ethology and Sociobiology, 6,* 227–236.

Finch, J. F., & Cialdini, R. B. (1989). Another indirect tactic of (self-) image management: Boosting. *Personality and Social Psychology Bulletin, 15,* 222–232.

Fincham, F. D., & Bradbury, T. N. (1987). The impact of attributions in marriage: A longitudinal analysis. *Journal of Personality and Social Psychology, 53,* 510–517.

Finkel, E. J., Rusbult, C. E., Kumashiro, M., & Hannon, P. A. (2002). Dealing with betrayal in close relationships: Does commitment promote forgiveness? *Journal of Personality and Social Psychology, 82,* 956–974.

Fischhoff, B. (1975). Hindsight ≠ foresight: The effect of outcome knowledge on judgment under uncertainty. *Journal of Experimental Psychology: Human Perception and Performance, 1,* 288–299.

Fischhoff, B. (1982). For those condemned to study the past: Heuristics and biases in hindsight. In D. Kahneman, P. Slovic, & A. Tversky (Eds.), *Judgment under uncertainty: Heuristics and biases* (pp. 335–354). New York: Cambridge University Press.

Fishbach, A., Friedman, R. S., & Kruglanski, A. W. (2003). Leading us not unto temptation: Momentary allurements elicit overriding goal activation. *Journal of Personality and Social Psychology, 84,* 296–309.

Fishbein, M. & Ajzen, I. (1974). Attitudes toward objects as predictors of single and multiple behavioral criteria. *Psychological Review, 81,* 59–74.

Fishbein, M. & Ajzen, I. (1975). *Belief, attitude, intention, and behavior: An introduction to theory and research.* Reading, MA: Addison-Wesley.

Fisher, H., Aron, A., Mashek, D., Li, H., & Brown, L. L. (2002). Defining the brain systems of lust, romantic attraction, and attachment. *Archives of Sexual Behavior, 31,* 413–419.

Fisher, H., Aron, A., Mashek, D., Li, H., Strong, G., & Brown, L. L. (2002). The neural mechanisms of mate choice: A hypothesis. *Neuroendocrinology Letters, 23* (Supplement 4), 92–97.

Fisher, J. D., Nadler, A., Hart, E., & Whitcher, S. E. (1981). Helping the needy helps the self. *Bulletin of the Psychonomic Society, 17,* 190–192.

Fiske, A. P. (2002). Using individualism and collectivism to compare cultures—a critique of the validity and measurement of the constructs: Comment on Oyserman et al. (2002). *Psychological Bulletin, 128,* 78–88.

Fiske, A. P., Kitayama, S., Markus, H., & Nisbett, R. E. (1998). The cultural matrix of social psychology. In D. T. Gilbert, S. T. Fiske, & G. Lindzey (Eds.), *Handbook of social psychology* (4th ed., Vol. 2, pp. 915–981). New York: McGraw-Hill.

Fiske, S. T. (1980). Attention and weight in person perception: The impact of negative and extreme behavior. *Journal of Personality and Social Psychology, 38,* 889–906.

Fiske, S. T. (1998). Stereotyping, prejudice, and discrimination. In D. T. Gilbert, S. T. Fiske, & G. Lindzey (Eds.), *Handbook of social psychology* (4th ed., Vol. 2, pp. 357–411). New York: McGraw-Hill.

Fiske, S. T., Bersoff, D. N., Borgida, E., Deaux, K., & Heilman, M. E. (1991). Social science research on trial: Use of sex stereotyping research in *Price Waterhouse* v. *Hopkins. American Psychologist, 46,* 1049–1060.

Fiske, S. T., Cuddy, A. J. C., Glick, P., & Xu, J. (2002). A model of (often mixed) stereotype content: Competence and warmth respectively follow from perceived status and competition. *Journal of Personality and Social Psychology, 82,* 878–902.

Fiske, S. T., & Neuberg, S. L. (1990). A continuum of impression formation, from category-based to individuating processes: Influences of information and motivation on attention and interpretation. In L. Berkowitz (Ed.), *Advances in experimental social psychology* (Vol. 23, pp. 1–74). San Diego, CA: Academic Press.

Fiske, S. T., & Taylor, S. E. (1991). *Social cognition* (2nd ed.). New York: McGraw-Hill.

Fitzsimons, G. M., & Bargh, J. A. (2003). Thinking of you: Nonconscious pursuit of interpersonal goals associated with relationship partners. *Journal of Personality and Social Psychology, 84,* 148–164.

Fitzsimons, G. M., & Kay, A. (2004). Language and interpersonal cognition: Causal effects of variations in pronoun usage on perceptions of closeness. *Personality and Social Psychology Bulletin, 30,* 547–557.

Fleming, J. H., Darley, J. M., Hilton, J. L., & Kojetin, B. A. (1990). Multiple audience problem: A strategic communication perspective on social perception. *Journal of Personality and Social Psychology, 58,* 593–609.

Fletcher, G. J. O., Tither, J. M., O'Loughlin, C., Friesen, M., & Overall, N. (2004). Warm and homely or cold and beautiful? Sex differences in trading off traits in mate selection. *Personality and Social Psychology Bulletin, 30,* 659–672.

Flink, C., Boggiano, A. K., & Barrett, M. (1990). Controlling teaching strategies: Undermining children's self-determination and performance. *Journal of Personality and Social Psychology, 59,* 916–924.

Folkes, V. S. (1982). Forming relationships and the matching hypothesis. *Personality and Social Psychology Bulletin, 8,* 631–636.

Folkes, V. S. (1985). Mindlessness or mindfulness: A partial replication and extension of Langer, Blank, and Chanowitz. *Journal of Personality and Social Psychology, 48,* 600–604.

Folkes, V. S., & Sears, D. O. (1977). Does everybody like a liker? *Journal of Experimental Social Psychology, 13,* 505–519.

Follett, M. P. (1942). Constructive conflict. In H. C. Metcalf & L. Urwick (Eds.), *Dynamic administration: The collected papers of Mary Parker Follett* (pp. 30–49). New York: Harper.

Forgas, J. P. (Ed.). (1991). *Emotion and social judgments.* Elmsford, NY: Pergamon.

Forgas, J. P. (1995). Mood and judgment: The affect infusion model (AIM). *Psychological Bulletin, 117,* 39–66.

Forgas, J. P., & Moylan, S. (1987). After the movies: Transient mood and social judgments. *Personality and Social Psychology Bulletin, 13,* 467–477.

Försterling, F. (1992). The Kelley model as an analysis of variance analogy: How far can it be taken? *Journal of Experimental Social Psychology, 28,* 475–490.

Forsyth, D. R. (1999). *Group dynamics* (3rd ed.). Belmont, CA: Wadsworth.

Foster, C. A., Witcher, B. S., Campbell, W. K., & Green, J. D. (1998). Arousal and attraction: Evidence for automatic and controlled processes. *Journal of Personality and Social Psychology, 74,* 86–101.

Fowers, B. J., Lyons, E. M., & Montel, K. H. (1996). Positive marital illusions: Self-enhancement or relationship enhancement. *Journal of Family Psychology, 10,* 192–208.

Fowers, B. J., Lyons, E., Montel, K. H., & Shaked, N. (2001). Positive illusions about marriage among married and single individuals. *Journal of Family Psychology, 15,* 95–109.

Fraley, R. C. (2002). Attachment stability from infancy to adulthood: Meta-analysis and dynamic modeling of developmental mechanisms. *Personality and Social Psychology Review, 6,* 123–151.

Fraley, R. C., & Shaver, P. R. (1998). Airport separations: A naturalistic study of adult attachment dynamics in separating couples. *Journal of Personality and Social Psychology, 75,* 1198–1212.

Frank, M. G., Ekman, P., & Friesen, W. V. (1993). Behavioral markers and recognizability of the smile of enjoyment. *Journal of Personality and Social Psychology, 64,* 83–94.

Frank, M. G., & Stennett, J. (2001). The forced-choice paradigm and the perception of facial expressions of emotion. *Journal of Personality and Social Psychology, 80,* 75–85.

Fraser, C., Gouge, C., & Billig, M. (1971). Risky shifts, cautious shifts, and group polarization. *European Journal of Social Psychology, 1,* 7–30.

Fredrickson, B. L. & Roberts, T. (1997). Objectification theory: Toward understanding women's lived experiences and mental health risks. *Psychology of Women Quarterly, 21,* 173–206.

Freedman, J. L. (1984). Effect of television violence on aggressiveness. *Psychological Bulletin, 96,* 227–246.

Freedman, J. L., & Fraser, S. C. (1966). Compliance without pressure: The foot-in-the-door technique. *Journal of Personality and Social Psychology, 4,* 195–202.

Freedman, J. L., & Sears, D. O. (1965). Warning, distraction, and resistance to influence. *Journal of Personality and Social Psychology, 1,* 262–266.

Frenkel, O. J., & Doob, A. N. (1976). Post-decision dissonance at the polling booth. *Canadian Journal of Behavioural Science, 8,* 347–350.

Freud, S. (1905). Fragments of an analysis of a case of hysteria. *Collected papers* (Vol. 3). New York: Basic Books. (Reprinted in 1959).

Freud, S. (1920/1959). *Beyond the pleasure principle.* New York: Bantam.

Freud, S. (1930). *Civilization and its discontents.* London: Hogarth.

Freud, S. (1932/1963). Why war? In P. Rieff (Ed.), *Freud: Character and culture* (pp. 134–177). New York: Collier.

Freud, S. (1957). Repression. In J. Strachey (Ed. and Trans.), *The standard edition of the complete psychological works of Sigmund Freud* (Vol. 14, pp. 143–158). London: Hogarth Press. (Original work published 1915)

Freud, S. (1962). The neuro-psychoses of defense. In J. Strachey (Ed. and Trans.), *The standard edition of the complete works of Sigmund Freud* (Vol. 3). London: Hogarth Press. (Originally published 1894)

Freud, S. (1964). New introductory lectures on psychoanalysis. In J. Strachey (Ed. and Trans.), *The standard edition of the complete works of Sigmund Freud* (Vol. 22). London: Hogarth Press. (Originally published 1933)

Frey, D. L., & Gaertner, S. L. (1986). Helping and the avoidance of inappropriate interracial behavior: A strategy that perpetuates a nonprejudiced self-image. *Journal of Personality and Social Psychology, 50,* 1083–1090.

Frey, K. S. (2000). Second step: Preventing aggression by promoting social competence. *Journal of Emotional and Behavioral Disorders, 8,* 102–112.

Fried, C. B., & Aronson, E. (1995). Hypocrisy, misattribution, and dissonance reduction. *Personality and Social Psychology Bulletin, 21,* 925–933.

Friedman, H. S., Riggio, R. E., & Casella, D. F. (1988). Nonverbal skill, personal charisma, and initial attraction. *Personality and Social Psychology Bulletin, 14,* 203–211.

Friedman, R. S., & Förster, J. (2001). The effects of promotion and prevention cues on creativity. *Journal of Personality and Social Psychology, 81,* 1001–1013.

Fritz, H. L., Nagurney, A. J., & Helgeson, V. S. (2003). Social interactions and cardiovascular reactivity during problem disclosure among friends. *Personality and Social Psychology Bulletin, 29,* 713–725.

Frome, P. M., & Eccles, J. S. (1998). Parents' influence on children's achievement-related perceptions. *Journal of Personality and Social Psychology, 74,* 435–452.

Frye, N. E., & Karney, B. R. (2002). Being better or getting better? Social and temporal comparisons as coping mechanisms in close relationships. *Personality and Social Psychology Bulletin, 28,* 1287–1299.

Gaertner, L., Sedikides, C., & Graetz, K. (1999). In search of self-definition: Motivational primacy of the individual self, motivational primacy of the collective self, or contextual primacy? *Journal of Personality and Social Psychology, 76,* 5–18.

Gaertner, S. L., & Dovidio, J. F. (1977). The subtlety of White racism, arousal, and the helping behavior. *Journal of Personality and Social Psychology, 35,* 691–707.

Gaertner, S. L., & Dovidio, J. F. (1986). The aversive form of racism. In J. F. Dovidio & S. L. Gaertner (Eds.), *Prejudice, discrimination, and racism* (pp. 61–89). Orlando, FL: Academic Press.

Gaertner, S. F., Dovidio, J. F., Rust, M. C., Nier, J. A., Banker, B. S., Ward, C. M., et al. (1999). Reducing intergroup bias: Elements of intergroup cooperation. *Journal of Personality and Social Psychology, 76,* 388–402.

Gaertner, S. F., Mann, J., Murrell, A., & Dovidio, J. F. (1989). Reducing intergroup bias: The benefits of recategorization. *Journal of Personality and Social Psychology, 57,* 239–249.

Galinsky, A. D., Mussweiler, T., & Medvec, V. H. (2002). Disconnecting outcomes and evaluations: The role of negotiator focus. *Journal of Personality and Social Psychology, 83,* 1131–1140.

Gallaher, P. E. (1992). Individual differences in nonverbal behavior: Dimensions of style. *Journal of Personality and Social Psychology, 63,* 133–145.

Gallucci, M. (2003). I sell seashells by the seashore, and my name is Jack: Comment on Pelham, Mirenberg, and Jones (2002). *Journal of Personality and Social Psychology, 85,* 789–799.

Gallup, G. S. (1977). Self-recognition in primates: A comparative approach in bidirectional properties of consciousness. *American Psychologist, 32,* 329–338.

Galton, F. (1952). *Hereditary genius: An inquiry into its laws and consequences.* New York: Horizon. (Original work published 1869)

Gangestad, S. W. (1993). Sexual selection and physical attractiveness: Implications for mating dynamics. *Human Nature, 4,* 205–235.

Gangestad, S. W., & Thornhill, R. (1997). The evolutionary psychology of extrapair sex: The role of fluctuating symmetry. *Ethology and Human Behavior, 18,* 69–88.

Garcia, S., Stinson, L., Ickes, W., Bissonnette, V., & Briggs, S. R. (1991). Shyness and physical attractiveness in mixed-sex dyads. *Journal of Personality and Social Psychology, 61,* 35–49.

Garcia-Marques, T., Mackie, D. M., Claypool, H. M., & Garcia-Marques, L. (2004). Positivity can cue familiarity. *Personality and Social Psychology Bulletin, 30,* 585–593.

Gardner, W. L., Gabriel, S., & Hochschild, L. (2002). When you and I are "we," you are not threatening: The role of self-expansion in social comparison. *Journal of Personality and Social Psychology, 82,* 239–251.

Gasper, K., & Clore, G. L. (2002). Attending to the big picture: Mood and global versus local processing of visual information. *Psychological Science, 13,* 34–40.

Gawronski, B. (2003a). Implicational schemata and the correspondence bias: On the diagnostic value of situationally constrained behavior. *Journal of Personality and Social Psychology, 84,* 1154–1171.

Gawronski, B. (2003b). On difficult questions and evident answers: Dispositional inference from role-constrained behavior. *Personality and Social Psychology Bulletin, 29,* 1459–1475.

Geary, D. C., & Flinn, M. V. (2002). Sex differences in behavioral and hormonal response to social threat: Commentary on Taylor et al. (2000). *Psychological Review, 109,* 745–750.

Geen, R. G. (1981). Behavioral and physiological reactions to observed violence: Effects of prior exposure to aggressive stimuli. *Journal of Personality and Social Psychology, 40,* 868–875.

Geen, R. G. (1998). Aggression and antisocial behavior. In D. T. Gilbert, S. T. Fiske, & G. Lindzey (Eds.), *Handbook of social psychology* (4th ed., Vol. 2, pp. 317–356). New York: McGraw-Hill.

Geen, R. G., & Berkowitz, L. (1967). Some conditions facilitating the occurrence of aggression after the observation of violence. *Journal of Personality, 35,* 666–676.

Gelfand, M. J., Higgins, M., Nishii, L. H., Raver, J. L., Dominguez, A., Murakami, F., Yamaguchi, S. & Toyama, M. (2002). Culture and egocentric perceptions of fairness in conflict and negotiation. *Journal of Applied Psychology, 87,* 833–845.

Gelfand, M. J., Nishii, L. H., Holcombe, K. M., Dyer, N., Ohbuchi, K-I., & Fukuno, M. (2001). Cultural influences on cognitive representations of conflict: Interpretations of conflict episodes in the United States and Japan. *Journal of Applied Psychology, 86,* 1059–1074.

Gelfand, M. J., Triandis, H. C., & Darius, K-S. C. (1996). Individualism versus collectivism or versus authoritarianism? *European Journal of Social Psychology, 26,* 397–410.

Georgesen, J. C., Harris, M. J., Milich, R., & Young, J. (1999). "Just teasing . . . ": Personality effects on perceptions and life narratives of childhood teasing. *Personality and Social Psychology Bulletin, 25,* 1254–1267.

Gerard, H. B. (1983). School desegregation: The social science role. *American Psychologist, 38,* 869–877.

Gerbner, G., Gross, L., Morgan, M., & Signorielli, N. (1994). Growing up with television: The cultivation perspective. In J. Bryant & D. Zillmann (Eds.), *Media effects* (pp. 17–41). Mahwah, NJ: Erlbaum.

Gergen, K. J. (1971). *The concept of self.* New York: Holt, Rinehart, & Winston.

Gerrard, M., Gibbons, F. X., & Bushman, B. J. (1996). Relation between perceived vulnerability to HIV and precautionary sexual behavior. *Psychological Bulletin, 119,* 390–409.

Gershoff, E. T. (2002). Corporal punishment by parents and associated child behaviors and experiences: A meta-analytic and theoretical review. *Psychological Bulletin, 128,* 539–579.

Gibbons, F. X., Gerrard, M., Cleveland, M. J., Wills, T. A., & Brody, G. (2004). Perceived discrimination and substance abuse in African American parents and their children: A panel study. *Journal of Personality and Social Psychology, 86,* 517–529.

Gibbons, F. X., Gerrard, M., Lando, H. A., & McGovern, P. G. (1991). Social comparison and smoking cessation: The role of the "typical smoker." *Journal of Experimental Social Psychology, 27,* 239–258.

Gibbons, F. X., Eggleston, T. J., & Benthin, A. C. (1997). Cognitive reactions to smoking relapse: The reciprocal relation between dissonance and self-esteem. *Journal of Personality and Social Psychology, 72,* 184–195.

Gibson, J. J. (1979). *The ecological approach to visual perception.* Boston: Houghton-Mifflin.

Gifford, R. (1994). A lens-mapping framework for understanding the encoding and decoding of interpersonal dispositions in nonverbal behavior. *Journal of Personality and Social Psychology, 66,* 398–412.

Gilbar, O. (2002). Parent caregiver adjustment to cancer of an adult child. *Journal of Psychosomatic Research, 52,* 295–302.

Gilbert, D. T., & Ebert, J. E. J. (2002). Decisions and revisions: The affective forecasting of changeable outcomes. *Journal of Personality and Social Psychology, 82,* 503–514.

Gilbert, D. T., & Malone, P. S. (1995). The correspondence bias. *Psychological Bulletin, 117,* 21–38.

Gilbert, D. T., Pelham, B. W., & Krull, D. S. (1988). On cognitive busyness:

When person perceivers meet persons perceived. *Journal of Personality and Social Psychology, 54*, 733–740.

Gilbert, D. T., Pinel, E. C., Wilson, T. D., Blumberg, S. J., & Wheatley, T. P. (1998). Immune neglect: A source of durability bias in affective forecasting. *Journal of Personality and Social Psychology, 75*, 617–638.

Gill, M. J., & Swann, W. B., Jr. (2004). On what it means to know someone: A matter of pragmatics. *Journal of Personality and Social Psychology, 86*, 405–418.

Gilovich, T. (1991). *How we know what isn't so.* New York: Free Press.

Gilovich, T., Kruger, J., & Medvec, V. H. (2002). The spotlight effect revisited: Overestimating the manifest variability of our actions and appearance. *Journal of Experimental Social Psychology, 38*, 93–99.

Gilovich, T. & Medvec, V. H. (1994). The temporal pattern to the experience of regret. *Journal of Personality and Social Psychology, 67*, 357–365.

Gilovich, T. & Medvec, V. H. (1995). The experience of regret: What, when, and why. *Psychological Review, 102*, 379–395.

Gilovich, T., Medvec, V. H., & Savitsky, K. (2000). The spotlight effect in social judgment: An egocentric bias in estimates of the salience of one's own actions and appearance. *Journal of Personality and Social Psychology, 78*, 211–222.

Giner-Sorolla, R., & Chaiken, S. (1994). The causes of hostile media bias. *Journal of Experimental Social Psychology, 30*, 165–180.

Giner-Sorolla, R., & Chaiken, S. (1997). Selective use of heuristic and systematic processing under defense motivation. *Personality and Social Psychology Bulletin, 23*, 84–97.

Ginossar, Z., & Trope, Y. (1987). Problem solving in judgment under uncertainty. *Journal of Personality and Social Psychology, 52*, 464–474.

Glaser, J., & Salovey, P. (1998). Affect in electoral politics. *Personality and Social Psychology Review, 2*, 156–172.

Glassner, B. (1999). *The culture of fear: Why Americans are afraid of the wrong things.* New York: Basic Books.

Glick, P., Diebold, J., Bailey-Werner, B., & Zhu, J. (1997). The two faces of Adam: Ambivalent sexism and polarized attitudes toward women. *Personality and Social Psychology Bulletin, 23*, 1323–1334.

Glick, P., & Fiske, S. T. (1996). The Ambivalent Sexism Inventory: Differentiating hostile and benevolent sexism. *Journal of Personality and Social Psychology, 70*, 491–512.

Glick, P., & Fiske, S. T. (2001). An ambivalent alliance: Hostile and benevolent sexism as complementary justifications for gender inequality. *American Psychologist, 56*, 109–118.

Glick, P., Fiske, S. T., Mladinic, A., Saiz, J. L., Abrams, D., Masser, B. et al. (2000). Beyond prejudice as simple antipathy: Hostile and benevolent sexism across cultures. *Journal of Personality and Social Psychology, 79*, 763–775.

Goethals, G. R., & Darley, J. (1977). Social comparison theory: An attributional approach. In J. Suls & R. L. Miller (Eds.), *Social comparison processes: Theoretical and empirical perspectives* (pp. 259–278). Washington, DC: Hemisphere.

Goethals, G. R., & Zanna, M. P. (1979). The role of social comparison in choice shifts. *Journal of Personality and Social Psychology, 37*, 1469–1476.

Goffman, E. (1952). On cooling the mark out: Some aspect of adaptation to failure. *Psychiatry, 15*, 451–463.

Goffman, E. (1959). *The presentation of self in everyday life.* New York: Doubleday.

Goktepe, J. R., & Schneier, C. E. (1989). Role of sex, gender roles, and attraction in predicting emergent leaders. *Journal of Applied Psychology, 74*, 165–167.

Goldhagen, D. J. (1996). *Hitler's willing executioners: Ordinary Germans and the Holocaust.* New York: Alfred A. Knopf.

Gollwitzer, P. M. (1986). Striving for specific identities: The social reality of self-symbolizing. In R. F. Baumeister (Ed.), *Public self and private life* (pp. 143–159). New York: Springer-Verlag.

Good, C., Aronson, J., & Inzlicht, M. (2003). Improving adolescents' standardized test performance: An intervention to reduce the effects of stereotype threat. *Applied Developmental Psychology, 24*, 645–662.

Gorassini, D. R., & Olson, J. M. (1995). Does self-perception change explain the foot-in-the-door effect? *Journal of*

Personality and Social Psychology, 69, 91–105.

Gordijn, E. H., Koomen, W., & Stapel, D. A. (2001). Level of prejudice in relation to knowledge of cultural stereotypes. *Journal of Experimental Social Psychology, 37*, 150–157.

Gore, S. (1978). The effect of social support in moderating the health consequences of unemployment. *Journal of Health and Social Behavior, 19*, 157–165.

Gosselin, P., Kirouac, G., & Doré, F. Y. (1995). Components and recognition of facial expression in the communication of emotion by actors. *Journal of Personality and Social Psychology, 68*, 83–96.

Gottman, J. M. (1993). A theory of marital dissolution and stability. *Journal of Family Psychology, 7*, 57–75.

Gottman, J. M. (1994a). *Why marriages succeed or fail . . . and how you can make yours last.* New York: Simon & Schuster.

Gottman, J. M. (Ed.). (1994b). *What predicts divorce? The relationship between marital processes and marital outcomes.* Mahwah, NJ: Erlbaum.

Gottman, J. M., Coan, J., Carrère, S., & Swanson, C. (1998). Predicting marital happiness and stability from newlywed interactions. *Journal of Marriage and the Family, 60*, 5–22.

Gottman, J. M., & Levenson, R. W. (1992). Marital processes predictive of later dissolution: Behavior, physiology, and health. *Journal of Personality and Social Psychology, 63*, 221–233.

Gouldner, A. (1960). The norm of reciprocity: A preliminary statement. *American Sociological Review, 25*, 161–178.

Graham, S., Weiner, B., Cobb, M., & Henderson, T. (2001). An attributional analysis of child abuse among low-income African American mothers. *Journal of Social and Clinical Psychology, 20*, 233–257.

Grahe, J. E., & Bernieri, F. J. (2002). Self-awareness of judgment policies of rapport. *Personality and Social Psychology Bulletin, 28*, 1407–1418.

Grammer, K. & Thornhill, R. (1994). Human (Homo sapiens) facial attractiveness and sexual selection: The role of symmetry and averageness. *Journal of Comparative Psychology, 108*, 233–242.

Grant, H., & Dweck, C. S. (2003). Clarifying achievement goals and their impact. *Journal of Personality and Social Psychology, 85,* 541–553.

Gray-Little, B., & Hafdahl, A. R. (2000). Factors influencing racial comparisons of self-esteem: A quantitative review. *Psychological Bulletin, 126,* 26–54.

Green, D. P., Glaser, J., & Rich, A. (1998). From lynching to gay bashing: The elusive connection between economic conditions and hate crimes. *Journal of Personality and Social Psychology, 75,* 82–92.

Greenberg, J., Pyszczynski, T., Solomon, S., Rosenblatt, A., Veeder, M., Kirkland, S., & Lyon, D. (1990). Evidence for terror management theory II: The effects of mortality salience on reactions to those who threaten or bolster the cultural worldview. *Journal of Personality and Social Psychology, 58,* 308–318.

Greenberg, J., Solomon, S., & Pyszczynski, T. (1997). Terror management theory of self-esteem and social behavior: Empirical assessments and cultural refinements. In M. P. Zanna (Ed.), *Advances in experimental social psychology* (Vol. 29, pp. 61–139). New York: Academic Press.

Greenberg, L. (1979). Genetic component of bee odor in kin recognition. *Science, 206,* 1095–1097.

Greenwald, A. G. (1968). Cognitive learning, cognitive response to persuasion, and attitude change. In A. G. Greenwald, T. C. Brock, & T. M. Ostrom (Eds.), *Psychological foundations of attitudes* (pp. 147–170). New York: Academic Press.

Greenwald, A. G. (1981). Self and memory. *The Psychology of Learning and Motivation, 15,* 201–236.

Greenwald, A. G., & Banaji, M. R. (1989). The self as a memory system: Powerful but ordinary. *Journal of Personality and Social Psychology, 57,* 41–54.

Greenwald, A. G., & Banaji, M. R. (1995). Implicit social cognition: Attitudes, self-esteem, and stereotypes. *Psychological Review, 102,* 4–27.

Greenwald, A. G., & Farnham, S. D. (2000). Using the implicit association test to measure self-esteem and self-concept. *Journal of Personality and Social Psychology, 79,* 1022–1038.

Greenwald, A. G., McGhee, D. E., & Schwartz, J. L. K. (1998). Measuring individual differences in implicit cognition: The implicit association

test. *Journal of Personality and Social Psychology, 74,* 1464–1480.

Greenwald, A. G., Nosek, B. A., & Banaji, M. R. (2003). Understanding and using the Implicit Association Test: I. An improved scoring algorithm. *Journal of Personality and Social Psychology, 85,* 197–216.

Greenwald, A. G., Oakes, M. A., & Hoffman, H. G. (2003). Targets of discrimination: Effects of race on responses to weapons holders. *Journal of Experimental Social Psychology, 39,* 399–405.

Greenwald, A. G., & Ronis, D. L. (1978). Twenty years of cognitive dissonance: Case study of the evolution of a theory. *Psychological Review, 85,* 53–57.

Griffin, D. W., Dunning, D., & Ross, L. (1990). The role of construal processes in overconfident predictions about the self and others. *Journal of Personality and Social Psychology, 59,* 1128–1139.

Gross, A. M., Bennett, T., Sloan, L., Marx, B. P., & Juergens, J. (2001). The impact of alcohol and alcohol expectancies on male perception of female sexual arousal in a date rape analog. *Experimental and Clinical Psychopharmocology, 9,* 380–388.

Gross, J. J., & Levenson, R. W. (1993). Emotional suppression: Physiology, self-report, and expressive behavior. *Journal of Personality and Social Psychology, 64,* 970–986.

Grossman, D. C., Neckerman, H. J, Koepsell, T. D., Liu, P. Y., Asher, K. N., Beland, K., et al. (1997). Effectiveness of a violence prevention curriculum among children in elementary school. A randomized controlled trial. *Journal of the American Medical Association, 277,* 1605–1611.

Gruber-Baldini, A. L., Schaie, K., & Willis, S. L. (1995). Similarity in married couples: A longitudinal study of mental abilities and rigidity-flexibility. *Journal of Personality and Social Psychology, 69,* 191–203.

Gruder, C. L., Cook, T. D., Hennigan, K. M., Flay, B. R., Alessis, C., & Halamaj, J. (1978). Empirical tests of the absolute sleeper effect predicted from the discounting cue hypothesis. *Journal of Personality and Social Psychology, 36,* 1061–1074.

Gruen, R. J., & Mendelsohn, G. (1986). Emotional responses to affective displays in others: The distinction

between empathy and sympathy. *Journal of Personality and Social Psychology, 51,* 609–614.

Grusec, J. E. (1982). The socialization of altruism. In N. Eisenberg (Ed.), *The development of prosocial behavior* (pp. 139–166). New York: Academic Press.

Guadagno, R. E., Asher, T., Demaine, L. J., & Cialdini, R. B. (2001). When saying yes leads to saying no: Preference for consistency and the reverse foot-in-the-door effect. *Personality and Social Psychology Bulletin, 27,* 859–867.

Guerra, N. G., & Slaby, R. G. (1990). Cognitive mediators of aggression in adolescent offenders: 2. Intervention. *Developmental Psychology, 26,* 269–277.

Guimond, S., Dambrun, M., Michinov, N., & Duarte, S. (2003). Does social dominance generate prejudice? Integrating individual and contextual determinants of intergroup cognitions. *Journal of Personality and Social Psychology, 84,* 697–721.

Gutierres, S. E., Kenrick, D. T., & Partch, J. J. (1999). Beauty, dominance, and the mating game: Contrast effects in self-assessment reflect gender differences in mate selection. *Personality and Social Psychology Bulletin, 25,* 1126–1134.

Haddock, G., & Carrick, R. (1999). How to make a politician more likable and effective: Framing political judgments through the numeric value of a rating scale. *Social Cognition, 17,* 298–311.

Haddock, G., Zanna, M. P., & Esses, V. M. (1993). Assessing the structure of prejudicial attitudes: The case of attitudes toward homosexuals. *Journal of Personality and Social Psychology, 65,* 1105–1118.

Hagerty, M. R. (2000). Social comparisons of income in one's community: Evidence from national surveys of income and happiness. *Journal of Personality and Social Psychology, 78,* 764–771.

Halberstadt, A. G., & Saitta, M. B. (1987). Gender, nonverbal behavior, and perceived dominance: A test of the theory. *Journal of Personality and Social Psychology, 53,* 257–272.

Halberstadt, J., & Rhodes, G. (2000). The attractiveness of nonface averages: Implications for an evolutionary explanation of the attractiveness of average faces. *Psychological Science, 11*, 285–289.

Halberstam, D. (1972). *The best and the brightest.* New York: Fawcett Crest.

Hall, C. S., & Lindzey, G. (1957). *Theories of personality.* New York: Wiley.

Hall, J. A. (1978). Gender effects in decoding nonverbal cues. *Psychological Bulletin, 85*, 845–857.

Hall, J. A. (1984). *Nonverbal sex differences: Communication accuracy and expressive style.* Baltimore: Johns Hopkins University Press.

Hall, J. A., & Friedman, G. B. (1999). Status, gender, and nonverbal behavior: A study of structured interactions between employees of a company. *Personality and Social Psychology Bulletin, 25*, 1082–1091.

Hamilton, D. L. (1979). A cognitive-attributional analysis of stereotyping. In L. Berkowitz (Ed.), *Advances in experimental social psychology* (Vol. 12, pp. 53–84). New York: Academic Press.

Hamilton, D. L., & Gifford, R. K. (1976). Illusory correlation in interpersonal perception: A cognitive basis of stereotypic judgments. *Journal of Personality and Social Psychology, 12*, 392–407.

Hamilton, D. L., Katz, L. B., & Leirer, V. O. (1980). Cognitive representation of personality impressions: Organizational processes in first impression formation. *Journal of Personality and Social Psychology, 39*, 1050–1063.

Hamilton, D. L., & Rose, T. L. (1980). Illusory correlation and the maintenance of stereotypic beliefs. *Journal of Personality and Social Psychology, 39*, 832–845.

Hamilton, D. L., & Sherman, J. W. (1994). Stereotypes. In R. S. Wyer, Jr., & T. K. Srull (Eds.), *Handbook of social cognition* (Vol. 2, pp. 1–68). Mahwah, NJ: Erlbaum.

Hamilton, D. L., & Sherman, S. J. (1996). Perceiving persons and groups. *Psychological Review, 103*, 336–355.

Hamilton, D. L., & Zanna, M. P. (1974). Context effects in impression formation: Changes in connotative meaning. *Journal of Personality and Social Psychology, 29*, 649–654.

Hamilton, W. D. (1964). The genetical evolution of social behavior: I and II.

Journal of Theoretical Biology, 7, 1–52.

Hammermesh, D. S., & Biddle, J. E. (1994). Beauty and the labor market. *American Economic Review, 84*, 1174–1194.

Han, S., & Shavitt, S. (1994). Persuasion and culture: Advertising appeals in individualistic and collectivistic cultures. *Journal of Experimental Social Psychology, 30*, 326–350.

Haney, C., Banks, C., & Zimbardo, P. (1973). Interpersonal dynamics in a simulated prison. *International Journal of Criminology and Penology, 1*, 69–97.

Haney, C., & Zimbardo, P. (1998). The past and future of U.S. prison policy: Twenty-five years after the Stanford Prison Experiment. *American Psychologist, 53*, 709–727.

Hanko, K., Master, S., & Sabini, J. (2004). Some evidence about character and mate selection. *Personality and Social Psychology Bulletin, 30*, 732–742.

Hansen, C. H., & Hansen, R. D. (1988). Finding the face in the crowd: An anger superiority effect. *Journal of Personality and Social Psychology, 54*, 917–924.

Harackiewicz, J. M., & Sansone, C. (1991). Goals and intrinsic motivation: You can get there from here. In M. Maehr & P. Pintrich (Eds.), *Advances in motivation and achievement* (Vol. 7, pp. 21–49). Greenwich, CT: JAI.

Harber, K. D. (1998). Feedback to minorities: Evidence of a positive bias. *Journal of Personality and Social Psychology, 74*, 622–628.

Hardin, G. J. (1968). The tragedy of the commons. *Science, 162*, 1243–1248.

Harkins, S. G., & Jackson, J. M. (1985). The role of evaluation in eliminating social loafing. *Personality and Social Psychology Bulletin, 11*, 457–465.

Harkins, S. G., & Szymanski, K. (1988). Social loafing and social evaluation with an objective standard. *Journal of Experimental Social Psychology, 24*, 354–365.

Harkness, A. R., DeBono, K. G., & Borgida, E. (1985). Personal involvement and strategies for making contingency judgments: A stake in the dating game makes a difference. *Journal of Personality and Social Psychology, 49*, 22–32.

Harlow, H. F., & Zimmerman, R. R. (1959). Affectional responses in the infant monkey. *Science, 130*, 421–432.

Harmon-Jones, E., & Allen, J. J. B. (2001). The role of affect in the mere exposure effect: Evidence from psychophysiological and individual differences approaches. *Personality and Social Psychology Bulletin, 27*, 889–898.

Harmon-Jones, E., Brehm, J. W., Greenberg, J., Simon, L., & Nelson, D. E. (1996). Evidence that the production of aversive consequences is not necessary to create cognitive dissonance. *Journal of Personality and Social Psychology, 70*, 5–16.

Harris, C. R. (2000). Psychophysiological responses to imagined infidelity: The specific innate modular view of jealousy reconsidered. *Journal of Personality and Social Psychology, 78*, 1082–1091.

Harris, C. R. (2002). Sexual and romantic jealousy in heterosexual and homosexual adults. *Psychological Science, 13*, 7–12.

Harris, C. R. (2003). A review of sex differences in sexual jealousy, including self-report data, physiological responses, interpersonal violence, and morbid jealousy. *Personality and Social Psychology Review, 7*, 102–128.

Harter, S. (1986). Processes underlying the construction, maintenance, and enhancement of the self-concept in children. In J. Suls & A. G. Greenwald (Eds.), *Psychological perspectives on the self* (Vol. 3, pp. 137–181). Mahwah, NJ: Erlbaum.

Hartmann, D. P. (1969). Influence of symbolically model instrumental aggression and pain cues on aggressive behavior. *Journal of Personality and Social Psychology, 11*, 280–288.

Harvey, J. H., Town, J. P., & Yarkin, K. L. (1981). How fundamental is the fundamental attribution error? *Journal of Personality and Social Psychology, 40*, 346–349.

Hastie, R., & Kumar, P. A. (1979). Person memory: Personality traits as organizing principles in memory for behaviors. *Journal of Personality and Social Psychology, 37*, 25–38.

Hastorf, A. H., & Cantril, H. (1954). They saw a game: A case study. *Journal of Abnormal and Social Psychology, 49*, 129–134.

Hatfield, E., Cacioppo, J. T., & Rapson, R. L. (1994). *Emotional contagion.* Cambridge, England: Cambridge University Press.

Hatfield, E., Utne, M. K., & Traupman, J. (1979). Equity theory in intimate relationships. In R. Burgess & T. Huston (Eds.), *Social exchange in developing relationships* (pp. 99–133). New York: Academic Press.

Haugtvedt, C. P., & Petty, R. E. (1992). Personality and persuasion: Need for cognition moderates the persistence and resistance of attitude changes. *Journal of Personality and Social Psychology, 63,* 308–319.

Hawkley, L. C., Burleson, M. H., Berntson, G. G., & Cacioppo, J. T. (2003). Loneliness in everyday life: Cardiovascular activity, psychosocial context, and health behaviors. *Journal of Personality and Social Psychology, 85,* 105–120.

Hawking, S. W. (1988). *A brief history of time: From the big bang to black holes.* New York: Bantam.

Hawkins, S. A., & Hastie, R. (1990). Hindsight: Biased judgments of past events after the outcomes are known. *Psychological Bulletin, 107,* 311–327.

Hays, R. B. (1984). A longitudinal study of friendship development. *Journal of Personality and Social Psychology, 48,* 909–924.

Hazan, C., & Shaver, P. R. (1987). Romantic love conceptualized as an attachment process. *Journal of Personality and Social Psychology, 52,* 511–524.

Hazan, C., & Shaver, P. R. (1994). Attachment as an organizational framework for research on close relationships. *Psychological Inquiry, 5,* 1–22.

Headey, B., & Wearing, A. (1989). Personality, life events, and subjective well-being: A dynamic equilibrium model. *Journal of Personality and Social Psychology, 57,* 731–739.

Heatherton, T. F., & Baumeister, R. F. (1991). Binge eating as escape from self-awareness. *Psychological Bulletin, 110,* 86–108.

Heatherton, T. F., & Vohs, K. D. (2000). Interpersonal evaluations following threats to self: Role of self-esteem. *Journal of Personality and Social Psychology, 78,* 725–736.

Heider, F. (1958). *The psychology of interpersonal relations.* New York: Wiley.

Heider, F., & Simmel, M. (1944). An experimental study of apparent behavior.

American Journal of Psychology, 57, 243–259.

Heilman, M. E., Wallen, A. S., Fuchs, D., & Tamkins, M. M. (2004). Penalties for success: Reactions to women who succeed at male gender-typed tasks. *Journal of Applied Psychology, 89,* 416–427.

Heine, S. J. (2003). Optimal is as optimal does. *Psychological Inquiry, 14,* 41–42.

Heine, S. J., Lehman, D. R., Markus, H. R., & Kitayama, S. (1999). Is there a universal need for positive self-regard? *Psychological Review, 106,* 766–794.

Hejmadi, A., Davidson, R. J., & Rozin, P. (2000). Exploring Hindu Indian emotion expressions: Evidence for accurate recognition by Americans and Indians. *Psychological Science, 11,* 183–187.

Helgeson, V. S. (1994). Long-distance romantic relationships: Sex differences in adjustment and breakup. *Personality and Social Psychology Bulletin, 20,* 254–265.

Helgeson, V. S., & Mickelson, K. D. (1995). Motives for social comparison. *Personality and Social Psychology Bulletin, 21,* 1200–1209.

Heller, D., Watson, D., & Ilies, R. (2004). The role of person versus situation in life satisfaction: A critical reexamination. *Psychological Bulletin, 130,* 574–600.

Helson, H. (1964). *Adaptation-level theory.* New York: Harper & Row.

Henchy, T., & Glass, D. C. (1968). Evaluation apprehension and the social facilitation of dominant and subordinate responses. *Journal of Personality and Social Psychology, 10,* 446–454.

Henderlong, J., & Lepper, M. R. (2002). The effects of praise on children's intrinsic motivation: A review and synthesis. *Psychological Bulletin, 128,* 774–795.

Henderson-King, D., Henderson-King, E., & Hoffman, L. (2001). Media images and women's self-evaluations: Social context and importance of attractiveness as moderators. *Personality and Social Psychology Bulletin, 27,* 1407–1416.

Henderson-King, E. I., & Nisbett, R. E. (1996). Anti-Black prejudice as a function of exposure to the negative behavior of a single Black person. *Journal of Personality and Social Psychology, 71,* 654–664.

Hendrick, C., & Hendrick, S. S. (1986). A theory and method of love. *Journal of Personality and Social Psychology, 50,* 392–402.

Hendrick, C., & Hendrick, S. S. (1991). Dimensions of love: A sociobiological interpretation. *Journal of Social and Clinical Psychology, 10,* 206–230.

Henley, N. M. (1977). *Body politics: Power, sex, and nonverbal communication.* Upper Saddle River, NJ: Prentice-Hall.

Hepworth, J. T., & West, S. G. (1988). Lynchings and the economy: A time-series reanalysis of Hovland and Sears (1940). *Journal of Personality and Social Psychology, 55,* 239–247.

Herbst, K. C., Gaertner, L., & Insko, C. A. (2003). My head says yes but my heart says no: Cognitive and affective attraction as a function of similarity to the ideal self. *Journal of Personality and Social Psychology, 84,* 1206–1219.

Herrnstein, R. J., & Murray, C. A. (1994). *The bell curve: Intelligence and class structure in American Life.* New York: Free Press.

Hetts, J. J., Sakuma, M., & Pelham, B. W. (1999). Two roads to positive regard: Implicit and explicit self-evaluation and culture. *Journal of Experimental Social Psychology, 35,* 512–559.

Hewstone, M. (1990). The "ultimate attribution error"? A review of the literature on intergroup causal attribution. *European Journal of Social Psychology, 20,* 311–335.

Heyes, C. M. (1994). Reflections on self-recognition in primates. *Animal Behavior, 47,* 909–919.

Higgins, E. T. (1998). Promotion and prevention: Regulatory focus as a motivational principle. In M. P. Zanna (Ed.), *Advances in experimental social psychology* (Vol. 30, pp. 1–46). New York: Academic Press.

Higgins, E. T. (1999). Promotion and prevention as a motivational duality: Implications for evaluative processes. In S. Chaiken & Y. Trope (Eds.), *Dual process theories in social psychology* (pp. 503–525). New York: Guilford.

Higgins, E. T., Lee, J., Kwon, J., & Trope, Y. (1995). When combining intrinsic motivations undermines intrinsic interest: A test of activity engagement theory. *Journal of Personality and Social Psychology, 68,* 749–767.

Higgins, E. T., Rholes, W. S., & Jones, C. R. (1977). Category accessibility and impression formation. *Journal of Experimental Social Psychology, 13,* 141–154.

Higgins, E. T., Shah, J., & Friedman, R. (1997). Emotional responses to goal attainment: Strength of regulatory focus as a moderator. *Journal of Personality and Social Psychology, 72,* 515–525.

Higley, J. D. (2001). Individual differences in alcohol-induced aggression: A nonhuman-primate model. *Alcohol Research and Health, 25,* 12–19.

Hilgard, E. R., & Marquis, D. G. (1940). *Conditioning and learning.* New York: Appleton-Century.

Hill, C. A. (1987). Affiliation motivation: People who need people . . . but in different ways. *Journal of Personality and Social Psychology, 52,* 1008–1018.

Hill, C. T., Rubin, Z., & Peplau, L. A. (1976). Breakups before marriage: The end of 103 affairs. *Journal of Social Issues, 32,* 147–168.

Hilton, J. L., & Darley, J. M. (1985). Constructing other persons: A limit on the effect. *Journal of Experimental Social Psychology, 21,* 1–18.

Hinkley, K., & Andersen, S. M. (1996). The working self-concept in transference: Significant-other activation and self change. *Journal of Personality and Social Psychology, 71,* 1279–1295.

Hippler, H. J., & Schwarz, N. (1986). Not forbidding isn't allowing: The cognitive basis of the forbid-allow asymmetry. *Public Opinion Quarterly, 50,* 87–96.

Hirt, E. R., Zillmann, D., Erickson, G. A., & Kennedy, C. (1992). Costs and benefits of allegiance: Changes in fans' self-ascribed competencies after team victory versus defeat. *Journal of Personality and Social Psychology, 63,* 724–738.

Hodges, E. V. E., & Perry, D. G. (1999). Personal and interpersonal antecedents and consequences of victimization by peers. *Journal of Personality and Social Psychology, 76,* 677–685.

Hodson, G., Dovidio, J. F., & Gaertner, S. L. (2002). Processes in racial discrimination: Differential weighting of conflicting information. *Personality and Social Psychology Bulletin, 28,* 460–471.

Hoffman, M. L. (1981). Is altruism part of human nature? *Journal of Personality and Social Psychology, 40,* 121–137.

Hofstede, G. (1980). *Culture's consequences.* Beverly Hills, CA: Sage.

Hogan, R., & Briggs, S. R. (1986). A socioanalytic interpretation of the public and the private selves. In R. F. Baumeister (Ed.), *Public self and private life* (pp. 179–188). New York: Springer-Verlag.

Hogan, R., Curphy, G. J., & Hogan, J. (1994). What we know about leadership: Effectiveness and personality. *American Psychologist, 49,* 493–504.

Hokanson, J. E., & Burgess, M. (1962). The effects of three types of aggression on vascular processes. *Journal of Abnormal and Social Psychology, 64,* 446–449.

Hollander, E. P. (1958). Conformity, status, and idiosyncrasy credits. *Psychological Review, 65,* 117–127.

Hollander, E. P. (1993). Legitimacy, power, and influence: A perspective on relational features of leadership. In M. M. Chemers & R. Ayman (Eds.), *Leadership theory and research* (pp. 29–47). New York: Academic Press.

Holtzworth-Munroe, A. (2000). A typology of men who are violent toward their female partners: Making sense of the heterogeneity in husband violence. *Current Directions in Psychological Science, 9,* 140–143.

Holtzworth-Munroe, A., & Jacobson, N. S. (1985). Causal attributions of married couples: When do they search for causes? What do they conclude when they do? *Journal of Personality and Social Psychology, 48,* 1398–1412.

Holtzworth-Munroe, A., & Hutchinson, G. (1993). Attributing negative intent to wife behavior: The attributions of martially violent versus nonviolent men. *Journal of Abnormal Psychology, 102,* 206–211.

Homans, G. C. (1961). *Social behavior: Its elementary forms.* New York: Harcourt, Brace, & World.

Hoorens, V., & Todorova, E. (1998). The name letter effect: Attachment to self or primacy of own name writing? *European Journal of Social Psychology, 18,* 365–385.

House, J. S. (1981). *Work stress and social support.* Reading, MA: Addison-Wesley.

House, J. S., Landis, K. R., & Umberson, D. (1988). Social relationships and health. *Science, 241,* 540–545.

House, J. S., Robbins, C., & Metzner, H. L. (1982). The association of social relationships and activities with mortality: Prospective evidence from the Tecumseh Community Health Study. *American Journal of Epidemiology, 116,* 123–140.

Hovland, C. I., Harvey, O. J., & Sherif, M. (1957). Assimilation and contrast effects in reactions to communication and attitude change. *Journal of Abnormal and Social Psychology, 55,* 244–252.

Hovland, C. I., Janis, I. L., & Kelley, H. H. (1953). *Communication and persuasion: Psychological studies of opinion change.* New Haven, CT: Yale University Press.

Hovland, C. I., Lumsdaine, A. A., & Sheffield, F. D. (1949). *Experiments on mass communication.* Princeton, NJ: Princeton University Press.

Hovland, C. I., & Pritzker, H. A. (1957). Extent of opinion change as a function of amount of change advocated. *Journal of Abnormal and Social Psychology, 54,* 257–261.

Hovland, C. I., & Sears, R. R. (1940). Minor studies in aggression: VI. Correlations of lynching with economic indicators. *Journal of Psychology, 9,* 301–310.

Hovland, C. I., & Weiss, W. (1951). The influence of source credibility on communication effectiveness. *Public Opinion Quarterly, 15,* 635–650.

Hsee, C. K., & Abelson, R. P. (1991). Velocity relation: Satisfaction as a function of the first derivative of outcome over time. *Journal of Personality and Social Psychology, 60,* 341–347.

Hsee, C. K., Salovey, P., & Abelson, R. P. (1994). The quasi-acceleration relation: Satisfaction as a function of the change of velocity of outcome over time. *Journal of Personality and Social Psychology, 60,* 341–347.

Hubbard, J. A., Smithmyer, C. M. Ramsden, S. R., Parker, E. H., Flanagan, K. D., Dearing, K. F., et al. (2002). Observational, physiological, and self-report measures of children's anger: Relations to reactive versus proactive aggression. *Child Development, 73,* 1101–1118.

Huddy, L., & Virtanen, S. (1995). Subgroup differentiation and subgroup bias among Latinos as a function of familiarity and positive distinctiveness. *Journal of Personality and Social Psychology, 68,* 97–108.

Hudley, C., & Graham, S. (1993). An attributional intervention to reduce peer-directed aggression among African-American boys. *Child Development, 64,* 124–138.

Huesmann, L. R. (1998). The role of social information processing and cognitive schemas in the acquisition and maintenance of habitual aggressive behavior. In R. Geen & E. Donnerstein (Eds.), *Human aggression: Theories, research, and implications for policy* (pp. 73–109). New York: Academic Press.

Huesmann, L. R., & Eron, L. D. (1984). Cognitive processes and the persistence of aggressive behavior. *Aggressive Behavior, 10,* 243–251.

Huesmann, L. R., Eron, L. D., Klein, R., Brice, P., & Fischer, P. (1983). Mitigating the imitation of aggressive behaviors by changing children's attitudes about media violence. *Journal of Personality and Social Psychology, 44,* 899–910.

Huesmann, L. R., Eron, L. D., Lefkowitz, M. M., & Walder, L. O. (1984). Stability of aggression over time and generations. *Developmental Psychology, 20,* 1120–1134.

Huesmann, L. R., Moise-Titus, J., Podolski, C., & Eron, L. D. (2003). Longitudinal relations between children's exposure to TV violence and their aggressive and violent behavior in young adulthood: 1977–1992. *Developmental Psychology, 39,* 201–221.

Hull, C. L. (1943). *Principles of behavior.* New York: Appleton-Century-Crofts.

Hull, J. G. (1981). A self-awareness model of the causes and effects of alcohol consumption. *Journal of Abnormal Psychology, 90,* 586–600.

Hull, J. G., Levenson, R. W., Young, R. D., & Sher, K. J. (1983). The self-awareness reducing effects of alcohol consumption. *Journal of Personality and Social Psychology, 44,* 461–473.

Hunsberger, B. (1995). Religion and prejudice: The role of religious fundamentalism, quest, and right-wing authoritarianism. *Journal of Social Issues, 51,* 113–129.

Huskinson, T. L. H., & Haddock, G. (2004). Individual differences in attitude structure: Variance in the chronic reliance on affective and cognitive information. *Journal of Experimental Social Psychology, 40,* 82–90.

Huston, A. C., Donnerstein, E., Fairchild, H., Feshbach, N. D., Katz, P. A., Murray, J. P., et al. (1992). *Big world, little screen: The role of television in American society.* Lincoln: University of Nebraska Press.

Huston, T. L., Caughlin, J. P., Houts, R. M., Smith, S. E., & George, L. J. (2001). The connubial crucible: Newlywed years as predictors of marital delight, distress, and divorce. *Journal of Personality and Social Psychology, 80,* 237–252.

Hyman, H. H., & Sheatsley, P. B. (1950). The current status of American public opinion. In J. C. Payne (Ed.), *The teaching of contemporary affairs* (pp. 11–34). New York: National Education Association.

Ichheiser, G. (1943). Misinterpretations of personality in everyday life and the psychologist's frame of reference. *Character and Personality, 12,* 145–160.

Ichheiser, G. (1949). Misunderstandings in human relations: A study in false social perception. *American Journal of Sociology, 55,* Part 2, 70.

Igou, E. R., & Bless, H. (2002). Inferring the importance of arguments: Order effects and conversational rules. *Journal of Experimental Social Psychology, 39,* 91–99.

Ingham, A. G., Levinger, G., Graves, J., & Peckham, V. (1974). The Ringelmann effect: Studies of group size and group performance. *Journal of Experimental Social Psychology, 10,* 371–384.

Insko, C. A., & Cialdini, R. B. (1969). A test of three interpretations of attitudinal verbal reinforcement. *Journal of Personality and Social Psychology, 12,* 333–341.

Inzlicht, M., & Ben-Zeev, T. (2000). A threatening intellectual environment: Why females are susceptible to experiencing problem-solving deficits in the presence of males. *Psychological Science, 11,* 365–371.

Isen, A. M. (1984). Toward understanding the role of affect in cognition. In R. S. Wyer, Jr. & T. S. Srull (Eds.), *Handbook of social cognition* (Vol. 3, pp. 179–236). Mahwah, NJ: Erlbaum.

Isen, A. M., Horn, N., & Rosenhan, D. L. (1973). Effects of success and failure on children's generosity. *Journal of Personality and Social Psychology, 27,* 239–247.

Isen, A. M., & Levin, P. F. (1972). Effect of feeling good on helping: Cookies and kindness. *Journal of Personality and Social Psychology, 21,* 384–388.

Isen, A. M., & Simmonds, S. F. (1978). The effect of feeling good on a helping task that is incompatible with good mood. *Social Psychology Quarterly, 41,* 346–349.

Isenberg, D. J. (1986). Group polarization: A critical review and meta-analysis. *Journal of Personality and Social Psychology, 50,* 1141–1151.

Islam, M. R., & Hewstone, M. (1993). Ingroup attributions and affective consequences in majority and minority groups. *Journal of Personality and Social Psychology, 64,* 936–950.

Istvan, J., Griffitt, W., & Weidner, G. (1983). Sexual arousal and the polarization of perceived sexual attractiveness. *Basic and Applied Social Psychology, 4,* 307–318.

Ito, T. A., Miller, N., & Pollock, V. E. (1996). Alcohol and aggression: A meta-analysis on the moderating effects of inhibitory cues, triggering events, and self-focused attention. *Psychological Bulletin, 120,* 60–82.

Iyengar, S., & Lepper, M. R. (1999). Rethinking the value of choice: A cultural perspective on intrinsic motivation. *Journal of Personality and Social Psychology, 76,* 349–366.

Iyengar, S., & Lepper, M. R. (2000). When choice is demotivating: Can one desire too much of a good thing? *Journal of Personality and Social Psychology, 79,* 995–1006.

Jackson, J. M., & Williams, K. D. (1985). Social loafing on difficult tasks: Working collectively can improve performance. *Journal of Personality and Social Psychology, 49,* 937–942.

Jackson, L. J., Sullivan, L. A., & Hodge, C. N. (1993). Stereotype effects on attributions, predictions, and evaluations: No two social judgments are quite alike. *Journal of Personality and Social Psychology, 65,* 69–84.

James, W. (1890). *The principles of psychology* (Vol. 1). New York: Holt.

Janis, I. L. (1967). Effects of fear arousal on attitude change: Recent developments in theory and experimental research. In L. Berkowitz (Ed.), *Advances in experimental social psychology* (Vol. 3, pp. 166–225). New York: Academic Press.

Janis, I. L. (1983). *Groupthink* (2nd ed., revised). Boston: Houghton-Mifflin.

Janis, I. L., & Feshbach, S. (1953). Effects of fear-arousing communications. *Journal of Abnormal and Social Psychology, 48,* 78–92.

Janis, I. L., & Field, P. B. (1956). A behavioral assessment of persuasibility: Consistency of individual differences. *Sociometry, 19,* 241–259.

Janis, I. L., & King, B. T. (1954). The influence of role playing on opinion change. *Journal of Abnormal and Social Psychology, 49,* 211–218.

Janis, I. L., & Mann, L. (1977). *Decision making*. New York: Free Press.

Jankowiak, W. R. (Ed.). (1995). *Romantic passion: A universal experience?* New York: Columbia University Press.

Jarvis, W. B. G., & Petty, R. E. (1996). The need to evaluate. *Journal of Personality and Social Psychology, 70,* 172–194.

Jaynes, J. (1976). *The origin of consciousness in the breakdown of the bicameral mind*. Boston, MA: Houghton-Mifflin.

Jenkins, H. M., & Ward, W. C. (1965). Judgment of contingency between response and outcome. *Psychological Monographs, 79* (1, Whole No. 594).

Jensen-Campbell, L. A., Graziano, W. G., & West, S. G. (1995). Dominance, prosocial orientation, and female preferences: Do nice guys really finish last? *Journal of Personality and Social Psychology, 68,* 427–440.

John, O. P., & Robins, R. W. (1994). Accuracy and bias in self-perception: Individual differences in self-enhancement and the role of narcissism. *Journal of Personality & Social Psychology. 66,* 206–219.

Johnson, B. T., & Eagly, A. H. (1989). Effects of involvement on persuasion: A meta-analysis. *Psychological Bulletin, 106,* 290–314.

Johnson, B. T., & Eagly, A. H. (1990). Involvement and persuasion: Types, traditions, and the evidence. *Psychological Bulletin, 107,* 375–384.

Johnson, D. J., & Rusbult, C. E. (1989). Resisting temptation: Devaluation of alternative partners as a means of maintaining commitment in close relationships. *Journal of Personality and Social Psychology, 57,* 967–980.

Johnson, R. W., Kelly, R. J., & LeBlanc, B. A. (1995). Motivational bases of dissonance: Aversive consequences or inconsistency? *Personality and Social Psychology Bulletin, 21,* 850–855.

Joiner, T. E., Jr. (1994). Contagious depression: Existence, specificity to depressed symptoms, and the role of reassurance seeking. *Journal of Personality and Social Psychology, 67,* 287–296.

Joireman, J., Anderson, J., & Strathman, A. (2003). The aggression paradox: Understanding links among aggression, sensation-seeking, and the consideration of future consequences. *Journal of Personality and Social Psychology, 84,* 1287–1302.

Jones, E. E. (1979). The rocky road from acts to dispositions. *American Psychologist, 34,* 107–117.

Jones, E. E. (1986). Interpreting interpersonal behavior: The effects of expectancies. *Science, 234,* 41–46.

Jones, E. E. (1990). *Interpersonal perception*. New York: W. H. Freeman.

Jones, E. E., & Davis, K. E. (1965). From acts to dispositions: The attribution process in person perception. In L. Berkowitz (Ed.), *Advances in experimental social psychology* (Vol. 2, pp. 219–266). New York: Academic Press.

Jones, E. E., & Gerard, H. B. (1967). *Foundations of social psychology*. New York: Wiley.

Jones, E. E., & Harris, V. A. (1967). The attribution of attitudes. *Journal of Experimental Social Psychology, 3,* 1–24.

Jones, E. E., & Nisbett, R. E. (1972). The actor and the observer: Divergent perceptions of the causes of behavior. In E. E. Jones, D. E. Kanouse, H. H. Kelley, R. E. Nisbett, S. Valins, & B. Weiner (Eds.), *Attribution: Perceiving the causes of behavior* (pp. 79–94). Morristown, NJ: General Learning Press.

Jones, E. E., & Sigall, H. (1971). The bogus pipeline: A new paradigm for measuring affect and attitude. *Psychological Bulletin, 76,* 349–364.

Jones, J. T., Pelham, B. W., Mirenberg, M. C., & Hetts, J. J. (2002). Name letter preferences are not merely mere exposure: Implicit egotism as self-regulation. *Journal of Experimental Social Psychology, 38,* 170–177.

Jones, L. W., Sinclair, R. C., & Courneya, K. S. (2003). The effects of source credibility and message framing on exercise intentions, behaviors, and attitudes: An integration of the Elaboration Likelihood Model and Prospect Theory. *Journal of Applied Social Psychology, 33,* 179–196.

Jones, T. F., Craig, A. S., Hoy, D., Gunter, E. E., Ashley, D. L., Barr, D. B., Brock, J. W., & Schaffner, W. (2000). Mass psychogenic illness attributed to toxic exposure at a high school. *New England Journal of Medicine, 342,* 96–100.

Jones, W. H., Briggs, S. R., & Smith, T. G. (1986). Shyness: Conceptualization and measurement. *Journal of Personality and Social Psychology, 51,* 629–639.

Jones, W. H., Hobbs, S. A., & Hockenbury, D. (1982). Loneliness and social skill deficits. *Journal of Personality and Social Psychology, 42,* 682–689.

Jordan, C. H., Spencer, S. J., Zanna, M. P., Hoshino-Browne, E., & Correll, J. (2003). Secure and defensive high self-esteem. *Journal of Personality and Social Psychology, 85,* 969–978.

Jost, J. T., Glaser, J., Kruglanski, A. W., & Sulloway, F. J. (2003). Political conservatism as motivated social cognition. *Psychological Bulletin, 129,* 339–375.

Judd, C. M., Blair, I. V., & Chapleau, K. M. (2004). Automatic stereotypes vs. automatic prejudice: Sorting out the possibilities in the Payne (2001) weapon paradigm. *Journal of Experimental Social Psychology, 40,* 75–81.

Judd, C. M., & Park, B. (1993). Definition and assessment of accuracy in social stereotypes. *Psychological Review, 100,* 109–128.

Judd, C. M., Park, B., Ryan, C. S., Brauer, M., & Kraus, S. (1995). Stereotypes and ethnocentrism: Diverging interethnic perceptions of African American and White American youth. *Journal of Personality and Social Psychology, 69,* 460–481.

Jussim, L. (1989). Teacher expectations: Self-fulfilling prophecies, perceptual biases, and accuracy. *Journal of Personality and Social Psychology, 57,* 469–480.

Jussim, L. (1991). Social perception and social reality: A reflection-construction model. *Psychological Review, 98,* 54–73.

Jussim L. (1993). Accuracy in interpersonal expectations: A reflection-construction analysis of current and classic research. *Journal of Personality, 61,* 637–668.

Jussim, L., Nelson, T. E., Manis, M., & Soffin, S. (1995). Prejudice, stereotypes, and labeling effects: Sources of bias in person perception. *Journal of Personality and Social Psychology, 68,* 228–246.

Juvonen, J., & Graham, S. (Eds.). (2001). *Peer harassment in school: The plight of the vulnerable and victimized.* New York: Guilford.

Kahle, L. R., & Homer, P. M. (1985). Physical attractiveness of the celebrity endorser: A social adaptation perspective. *Journal of Consumer Research, 11,* 954–961.

Kahneman, D. (1999). Objective happiness. In D. Kahneman, E. Diener, & N. Schwarz (Eds.)., *Well-being: The foundations of hedonic psychology* (pp. 3–25). New York: Russell Sage Foundation.

Kahneman, D. (2003). A perspective on judgment and choice: Mapping bounded rationality. *American Psychologist, 58,* 697–720.

Kahneman, D., & Miller D. T. (1986). Norm theory: Comparing reality to its alternatives. *Psychological Review, 93,* 136–153.

Kahneman, D., Slovic, P. & Tversky, A. (Eds.). (1982). *Judgment under uncertainty: Heuristics and biases.* New York: Cambridge University Press.

Kahneman, D., & Tversky, A. (1972). Subjective probability: A judgment of representativeness. *Cognitive Psychology, 3,* 430–454.

Kahneman, D., & Tversky, A. (1973). On the psychology of prediction. *American Psychologist, 80,* 237–251.

Kahneman, D., & Tversky, A. (1979). Prospect theory: An analysis of decision under risk. *Econometrica, 47,* 263–291.

Kahneman, D., & Tversky. A. (1982a). The psychology of preferences. *Scientific American, 246,* 160–173.

Kahneman, D., & Tversky. A. (1982b). The simulation heuristic. In D. Kahneman, P. Slovic, & A. Tversky (Eds.), *Judgment under uncertainty: Heuristics and biases* (pp. 201–208). New York: Cambridge University Press.

Kahneman, D., & Tversky, A. (2000). Choice, values, and frames. New York: Cambridge University Press.

Kaiser, C. R., & Miller, C. T. (2001). Stop complaining! The social costs of making attributions to discrimination. *Personality and Social Psychology Bulletin, 27,* 254–263.

Kalick, S. M., & Hamilton, T. E., III. (1986). The matching hypothesis reexamined. *Journal of Personality and Social Psychology, 51,* 673–682.

Kalick, S. M., Zebrowitz, L. A., Langlois, J. H., & Johnson, R. M. (1998). Does human facial attractiveness honestly advertise health? Longitudinal data on an evolutionary question. *Psychological Science, 9,* 8–14.

Kaniasty, K., & Norris, F. H. (1993). A test of the social support deterioration model in the context of natural disaster. *Journal of Personality and Social Psychology, 64,* 395–408.

Kaniasty, K., & Norris, F. H. (1995). Mobilization and deterioration of social support following natural disasters. *Current Directions in Psychological Science, 4,* 94–98.

Kaplan, M. F. (1988). The influencing process in group decision making. In C. Hendrick (Ed.), *Group processes. Review of personality and social psychology* (Vol. 8, pp. 189–212). Thousand Oaks, CA, Sage.

Karau, S. J., & Williams, K. D. (1993). Social loafing: A meta-analytic review and theoretical integration. *Journal of Personality and Social Psychology, 65,* 681–706.

Karlson, P., & Luscher, M. (1959). Pheromones: a new term for a class of biologically active substances. *Nature, 183,* 55–56.

Karney, B. R., & Bradbury, T. N. (1995). The longitudinal course of marital quality and stability: A review of theory, method, and research. *Psychological Bulletin, 118,* 3–34.

Karney, B. R., & Bradbury, T. N. (2000). Attributions in marriage: State or trait? A growth curve analysis. *Journal of Personality and Social Psychology, 78,* 295–309.

Karney, B. R., & Frye, N. E. (2002). "But we've been getting better lately": Accuracy and distortion in memories of relationship development. *Journal of Personality and Social Psychology, 82,* 222–238.

Kasser, T., & Ryan, R. M. (1993). A dark side of the American dream: Correlates of financial success as a central aspiration in life. *Journal of Personality and Social Psychology, 65,* 410–422.

Kasser, T., & Ryan, R. M. (1996). Further examining the American dream: Differential correlations of intrinsic and extrinsic goals. *Personality and Social Psychology Bulletin, 22,* 280–287.

Kassin, S. M. (1982). Heider and Simmel revisited: Causal attribution and the animated film technique. *Review of Personality and Social Psychology, 3,* 145–169.

Katz, D. (1960). The functional approach to the study of attitudes. *Public Opinion Quarterly, 24,* 163–204.

Katzev, A. R., Warner, R. L., & Acock, A. C. (1994). Girls or boys? Relationship of child gender to marital instability. *Journal of Marriage and the Family, 56,* 89–100.

Kawakami, K., Dion, K. L., & Dovidio, J. F. (1998). Racial prejudice and stereotype activation. *Personality and Social Psychology Bulletin, 24,* 407–416.

Kawakami, K., Dovidio, J. F., Moll, J., Hermsen, S., & Russin, A. (2000). Just say no (to stereotyping): Effects of training in the negation of stereotypic associations on stereotype activation. *Journal of Personality and Social Psychology, 78,* 871–888.

Kazdin, A. (1987). Treatment of antisocial behavior in children: Current status and future directions. *Psychological Bulletin, 102,* 187–203.

Kelley, H. H. (1950). The warm-cold variable in first impressions of persons. *Journal of Personality, 18,* 431–439.

Kelley, H. H. (1967). Attribution theory in social psychology. In D. Levine (Ed.), *Nebraska Symposium on Motivation* (pp. 192–238). Lincoln: University of Nebraska Press.

Kelley, H. H. (1972). Causal schemata and the attribution process. In E. E. Jones, D. E. Kanouse, H. H. Kelley, R. E. Nisbett, S. Valins, & B. Weiner (Eds.), *Attribution: Perceiving the causes of behavior* (pp. 151–174). Morristown, NJ: General Learning Press.

Kelley, H. H. (1973). The process of causal attribution. *American Psychologist, 28,* 107–128.

Kelley, H. H. (1983). Love and commitment. In H. H. Kelley, E. Berscheid,

A. Christensen, J. H. Harvey, T. L. Huston, G. Levinger, E. McClintock, L. A. Peplau, & D. R. Peterson (Eds.), *Close relationships* (pp. 265–314). New York: Freeman.

Kelley, H. H., & Stahelski, A. J. (1970). The social interaction basis of cooperators' and competitors' beliefs about others. *Journal of Personality and Social Psychology, 16,* 66–91.

Kelley, H. H., & Thibaut, J. W. (1978). *Interpersonal relations: A theory of interdependence.* New York: Wiley.

Kelly, A. E., & Kahn, J. H. (1994). Effects of suppression of personal intrusive thoughts. *Journal of Personality and Social Psychology, 66,* 998–1006.

Kelly, G. A. (1955). *The psychology of personal constructs.* New York: Norton.

Kelly, J. R., & Karau, S. J. (1999). Group decision making: The effects of initial preferences and time pressure. *Personality and Social Psychology Bulletin, 25,* 1342–1354.

Kelly, J. R., & Loving, T. J. (2004). Time pressure and group performance: Exploring underlying processes in the Attentional Focus Model. *Journal of Experimental Social Psychology, 40,* 185–198.

Kelman, H. C. (1958). Compliance, identification, and internalization. *Journal of Conflict Resolution, 2,* 51–60.

Kelman, H. C. (1961). Processes of opinion change. *Public Opinion Quarterly, 25,* 57–78.

Kelman, H. C., & Eagly, A. H. (1965). Attitude toward the communicator, perception of communication content, and attitude change. *Journal of Personality and Social Psychology, 1,* 63–78.

Kelman, H. C., & Hovland, C. I. (1953). "Reinstatement" of the communicator in delayed measurement of opinion change. *Journal of Abnormal and Social Psychology, 48,* 327–335.

Kenney, R. A., Schwartz-Kenney, B. M., & Blascovich, J. (1996). Implicit leadership theories: Defining leaders described as worthy of influence. *Personality and Social Psychology Bulletin, 22,* 1128–1143.

Kenny, D. A., & DePaulo, B. M. (1993). Do people know how others view them? An empirical and theoretical account. *Psychological Bulletin, 114,* 145–161.

Kenny, D. A., & La Voie, L. (1984). The social relations model. In L.

Berkowitz (Ed.), *Advances in experimental social psychology* (Vol. 18, pp. 142–182). Orlando, FL: Academic Press.

Kenrick, D. T., & Cialdini, R. B. (1977). Romantic attraction: Misattribution versus reinforcement explanations. *Journal of Personality and Social Psychology, 35,* 381–391.

Kenrick, D. T., Cialdini, R. B., & Linder, D. E. (1979). Misattribution under fear-producing circumstances: Four failures to replicate. *Personality and Social Psychology Bulletin, 5,* 329–334.

Kenrick, D. T., Groth, G. E., Trost, M. R., & Sadalla, E. K. (1993). Integrating evolutionary and social exchange perspectives on relationships: Effects of gender, self-appraisal, and involvement level of mate selection criteria. *Journal of Personality and Social Psychology, 64,* 951–969.

Kephart, W. (1967). Some correlates of romantic love. *Journal of Marriage and the Family, 29,* 470–479.

Kerlinger, F. N. (1986). *Foundations of behavioral research* (3rd ed.). New York: Holt, Rinehart, & Winston.

Kernis, M. H. (2003). Toward a conceptualization of optimal self-esteem. *Psychological Inquiry, 14,* 1–26.

Kernis, M. H., & Waschull, S. B. (1995). The interactive roles of stability and level of self-esteem: Research and theory. In M. P. Zanna (Ed.), *Advances in experimental social psychology* (Vol. 29, pp. 93–141). Orlando: Academic Press.

Kernis, M. H., & Wheeler, L. (1981). Beautiful friends and ugly strangers: Radiation and contrast effects in perceptions of same-sex pairs. *Personality and Social Psychology Bulletin, 7,* 617–620.

Kerr, N. L. (1983). Motivation losses in small groups: A social dilemma analysis. *Journal of Personality and Social Psychology, 45,* 819–828.

Kerr, N. L., & Kaufman-Gilliland, C. M. (1994). Communication, commitment, and cooperation in social dilemmas. *Journal of Personality and Social Psychology, 66,* 513–529.

Kerr, N. L., & Tindale, R. S. (2004). Group performance and group decision making. *Annual Review of Psychology, 55,* 623–655.

Kessler, R. C., Mickelson, K. D., & Williams, D. R. (1999). The preva-

lence, distribution, and mental health correlates of perceived discrimination in the United States. *Journal of Health and Social Behavior, 40,* 208–230.

Keyes, C. L. M., Shmotkin, D., & Ryff, C. D. (2002). Optimizing well-being: The empirical encounter of two traditions. *Journal of Personality and Social Psychology, 82,* 1007–1022.

Kiecolt-Glaser, J. K., Bane, C., Glaser, R., & Malarkey, W. B. (2003). Love, marriage, and divorce: Newlyweds' stress hormones foreshadow relationship change. *Journal of Consulting and Clinical Psychology, 71,* 176–188.

Kiecolt-Glaser, J. K., & Newton, T. L. (2001). Marriage and health: His and hers. *Psychological Bulletin, 127,* 472–503.

Kiecolt-Glaser, J. K., Newton, T., Cacioppo, J. T., MacCallum, R. C., Glaser, R., & Malarkey, W. B. (1996). Marital conflict and endocrine functioning: Are men really more physiologically affected than women? *Journal of Consulting and Clinical Psychology, 64,* 324–332.

Kim, H. S. (2002). We talk, therefore we think? A cultural analysis of the effect of talking on thinking. *Journal of Personality and Social Psychology, 83,* 828–842.

Kim, H. S., & Drolet, A. (2003). Choice and self-expression: A cultural analysis of variety-seeking. *Journal of Personality and Social Psychology, 85,* 373–382.

Kim, H. S., & Markus, H. R. (1999). Deviance or uniqueness, harmony or conformity? A cultural analysis. *Journal of Personality and Social Psychology, 77,* 785–800.

Kinch, J. W. (1963). A formalized theory of the self-concept. *American Journal of Sociology, 68,* 481–486.

Kinder, D. R. (1998). Opinion and action in the realm of politics. In D. T. Gilbert, S. T. Fiske, & G. Lindzey (Eds.), *Handbook of social psychology* (4th ed., Vol. 2, pp. 778–867). New York: McGraw-Hill.

King, B. T., & Janis, I. L. (1956). Comparison of the effectiveness of improvised versus non-improvised role-playing in producing opinion changes. *Human Relations, 9,* 177–186.

King, L. A., & Napa, C. K. (1998). What makes a life good? *Journal of Personality and Social Psychology, 75,* 156–165.

Kirkpatrick, L. A., & Hazan, C. (1994). Attachment styles and close relationships: A four-year prospective study. *Personal Relationships, 1,* 123–142.

Kirkpatrick, L. A., Waugh, C. E., Valencia, A., & Webster, G. D. (2002). The functional domain specificity of self-esteem and the differential prediction of aggression. *Journal of Personality and Social Psychology, 82,* 756–767.

Kitayama, S., & Karasawa, M. (1997). Implicit self-esteem in Japan: Name letters and birthday numbers. *Personality and Social Psychology Bulletin, 23,* 736–742.

Klar, Y., & Giladi, E. E. (1999). Are most people happier than their peers, or are they just happy? *Personality and Social Psychology Bulletin, 25,* 585–594.

Klein, J. G. (1996). Negativity in impressions of presidential candidates revisited: The 1992 election. *Personality and Social Psychology Bulletin, 22,* 288–295.

Klein, S. B., & Kihlstrom, J. F. (1986). Elaboration, organization, and the self-reference effect in memory. *Journal of Experimental Psychology: General, 115,* 26–38.

Klein, W. M., & Kunda, Z. (1992). Motivated person perception: Constructing justifications for desired beliefs. *Journal of Experimental Social Psychology, 28,* 145–168.

Klein, W. M., & Kunda, Z. (1993). Maintaining self-serving social comparisons: Biased reconstruction of one's past behaviors. *Personality and Social Psychology Bulletin, 19,* 732–739.

Kleinke, C. L. (1986). Gaze and eye contact: A research review. *Psychological Bulletin, 100,* 78–100.

Klinger, E. (1977). *Meaning and void: Inner experience and the incentives in people's lives.* Minneapolis: University of Minnesota Press.

Klohnen, E. C., & Bera, S. (1998). Behavioral and experiential patterns of avoidantly and securely attached women across adulthood: A 31-year longitudinal perspective. *Journal of Personality and Social Psychology, 74,* 211–223.

Knowles, E. D., Morris, M. W., Chiu, C., & Hong, Y. (2001). Culture and the process of person perception: Evidence for automaticity among East Asians in correcting for situational influences on behavior. *Personality and Social Psychology Bulletin, 27,* 1344–1356.

Knox, R. E., & Inkster, J. A. (1968). Post-decision dissonance at post time. *Journal of Personality and Social Psychology, 8,* 319–323.

Kobayashi, C., & Brown, J. D. (2003). Self-esteem and self-enhancement in Japan and America. *Journal of Cross-Cultural Psychology, 34,* 567–580.

Koehler, D. (1991). Explanation, imagination, and confidence in judgment. *Psychological Bulletin, 110,* 499–519.

Koestner, R., Franz, C., & Weinberger, J. (1990). The family origins of empathic concern: A 26-year longitudinal study. *Journal of Personality and Social Psychology, 58,* 709–717.

Koestner, R., & Wheeler, L. (1988). Self-presentation in personal advertisements: The influence of implicit notions of attraction and role expectations. *Journal of Social and Personal Relationships, 5,* 149–160.

Koffka, K. (1935). *Principles of Gestalt psychology.* New York: Harcourt Brace.

Kohl, J. V., Atzmueller, M., Fink, B., & Grammer, K. (2001). Human pheromones: Integrating neuro-endocrinology and ethology. *Neuro-endocrinology Letters, 22,* 309–321.

Köhler, W. (1929). *Gestalt psychology.* New York: Liveright.

Komorita, S. S. (1973). Concession making and conflict resolution. *Journal of Conflict Resolution, 17,* 745–762.

Komorita, S. S., & Parks, C. D. (1995). Interpersonal relations: Mixed-motive interaction. *Annual Review of Psychology, 46,* 183–207.

Koss, M. P., Gidycz, C. A., & Wisniewski, N. (1987). The scope of rape: Incidence and prevalence of sexual aggression and victimization in a national sample of higher education students. *Journal of Consulting and Clinical Psychology, 55,* 162–170.

Kowalski, R. M. (2000). "I was only kidding!": Victims' and perpetrators' perceptions of teasing. *Personality and Social Psychology Bulletin, 26,* 231–241.

Kramer, R. M. (1998). Revisiting the Bay of Pigs and Vietnam decisions 25 years later: How well has the groupthink hypothesis stood the test of time? *Organizational Behavior and Human Decision Processes, 73,* 236–271.

Kramer, R. M., & Brewer, M. B. (1984). Effects of group identity on resource use in a simulated commons dilemma. *Journal of Personality and Social Psychology, 46,* 1044–1057.

Kraus, S. J. (1995). Attitudes and the prediction of behavior: A meta-analysis of the empirical literature. *Personality and Social Psychology Bulletin, 21,* 58–75.

Krauss, R. M., Freyberg, R., & Morsella, E. (2002). Inferring speakers' physical attributes from their voices. *Journal of Experimental Social Psychology, 38,* 618–625.

Kraut, R. E., & Poe, D. (1980). Behavioral roots of person perception: The deception judgments of custom inspectors and laymen. *Journal of Personality and Social Psychology, 39,* 784–798.

Kravitz, D., A., & Martin, B. (1986). Ringelmann rediscovered: The original article. *Journal of Personality and Social Psychology, 50,* 936–941.

Krebs, D. L., & Miller, D. T. (1985). Altruism and aggression. In G. Lindzey & E. Aronson (Eds.), *The handbook of social psychology* (3rd ed., Vol. 2, pp. 1–71). New York: Random House.

Kring, A. M., & Gordon, A. H. (1998). Sex differences in emotion: Expression, experience, and physiology. *Journal of Personality and Social Psychology, 74,* 686–704.

Krosnick, J. A. (1988). The role of attitude importance in social evaluations: A study of policy preferences, presidential candidate evaluations, and voting behavior. *Journal of Personality and Social Psychology, 55,* 196–210.

Krosnick, J. A. (1989). Attitude importance and attitude accessibility. *Personality and Social Psychology Bulletin, 15,* 297–308.

Krosnick, J. A., & Alwin, D. F. (1989). Aging and susceptibility to attitude change. *Journal of Personality and Social Psychology, 57,* 416–425.

Krosnick, J. A., Betz, A. L., Jussim, L. J., & Lynn, A. R. (1992). Subliminal conditioning of attitudes. *Personality and Social Psychology Bulletin, 18,* 152–162.

Krosnick, J. A., Boninger, D. S., Chuang, Y. C., Berent, M. K., & Carnot, C. G. (1993). Attitude strength: One construct or many related constructs? *Journal of Personality and Social Psychology, 65,* 1132–1151.

Krosnick, J. A., & Schuman, H. (1988). Attitude intensity, importance, and certainty and susceptibility to response effects. *Journal of Personality and Social Psychology, 54,* 940–952.

Kruger, J. (1999). Lake Wobegon be gone! The "below-average effect" and the egocentric nature of comparative ability judgments. *Journal of Personality and Social Psychology, 77,* 221–232.

Kruger, J., & Burrus, J. (2004). Egocentrism and focalism in unrealistic optimism (and pessimism). *Journal of Experimental Social Psychology, 40,* 332–340.

Kruger, J., & Gilovich, T. (1999). Naïve cynicism in everyday theories of responsibility assessment: On biased assumptions of bias. *Journal of Personality and Social Psychology, 76,* 743–753.

Kruglanski, A. W. (1975). The human subject in the psychology experiment: Fact and artifact. In L. Berkowitz (Ed.), *Advances in experimental social psychology* (Vol. 8, pp. 101–147). New York: Academic Press.

Kruglanski, A. W., & Webster, D. M. (1991). Group members' reactions to opinion deviates and conformists at varying degrees of proximity to decision deadline and of environmental noise. *Journal of Personality and Social Psychology, 61,* 212–225.

Krull, D. S. (1993). Does the grist change the mill? The effect of the perceiver's inferential goal on the process of social inference. *Personality and Social Psychology Bulletin, 19,* 340–348.

Krull, D. S., & Dill, J. C. (1996). On thinking first and responding fast: Flexibility in social inference processes. *Personality and Social Psychology Bulletin, 22,* 949–959.

Kugihara, N. (1999). Gender and social loafing in Japan. *The Journal of Social Psychology, 139,* 516–526.

Kuiper, N. A., & Derry, P. A. (1982). Depressed and nondepressed content self-reference in mild depressives. *Journal of Personality, 50,* 67–80.

Kulik, J. A., & Mahler, H. I. M. (1989). Social support and recovery from surgery. *Health Psychology, 8,* 21–38.

Kulik, J. A., Mahler, H. I. M., & Moore, P. J. (1996). Social comparison and affiliation under threat: Effects on recovery from major surgery. *Journal of Personality and Social Psychology, 71,* 967–979.

Kulik, J. A., Moore, P., & Mahler, H. I. M. (1993). Stress and affiliation: Hospital roommate effects on preoperative anxiety and social interaction. *Health Psychology, 12,* 119–125.

Kumkale, G. T., & Albarracín, D. (2004). The sleeper effect in persuasion: A meta-analytic review. *Psychological Bulletin, 130,* 143–172.

Kunda, Z. (1990). The case for motivated reasoning. *Psychological Bulletin, 108,* 480–498.

Kunda, Z., Davies, P. G., Adams, B. D., & Spencer, S. J. (2002). The dynamic time course of stereotype activation: Activation, dissipation, and resurrection. *Journal of Personality and Social Psychology, 82,* 283–299.

Kunda, Z., & Oleson, K. C. (1995). Maintaining stereotypes in the face of disconfirmation: Constructing grounds for subtyping deviants. *Journal of Personality and Social Psychology, 68,* 565–579.

Kunda, Z., & Oleson, K. C. (1997). When exception proves the rule: How extremity of deviance determines the impact of deviant examples of stereotypes. *Journal of Personality and Social Psychology, 72,* 965–979.

Kunda, Z., & Nisbett, R. E. (1986). The psychometrics of everyday life. *Cognitive Psychology, 18,* 195–224.

Kunda, Z., & Sanitioso, R. (1989). Motivated changes in the self-concept. *Journal of Experimental Social Psychology, 25,* 272–285.

Kunda, Z., Sinclair, L., & Griffin, D. (1997). Equal ratings but separate meanings: Stereotypes and the construal of traits. *Journal of Personality and Social Psychology, 72,* 720–734.

Kunda, Z., & Spencer, S. J. (2003). When do stereotypes come to mind and when do they color judgment? A goal-based theoretical framework for stereotype activation and application. *Psychological Bulletin, 129,* 522–544.

Kurdek, L. A. (1991). Correlates of relationship satisfaction in cohabiting gay and lesbian couples: Integration of contextual, investment, and problem-solving models. *Journal of Personality and Social Psychology, 61,* 910–922.

Kurdek, L. A. (1992). Relationship stability and relationship satisfaction in cohabitating gay and lesbian couples: A prospective longitudinal test of the contextual and interdependence models. *Journal of Social and Personal Relationships, 9,* 125–142.

Kurdek, L. A. (1999). The nature and predictors of trajectory change in marital quality for husbands and wives over the first 10 years of marriage. *Developmental Psychology, 35,* 1283–1296.

Kurman, J. (2001). Self-enhancement: Is it restricted to individualistic cultures? *Personality and Social Psychology Bulletin, 12,* 1705–1716.

Kurman, J., & Sriram, N. (1997). Self-enhancement, generality of self-evaluation, and affectivity in Israel and Singapore. *Journal of Cross Cultural Psychology, 28,* 421–441.

Kutchinsky, B. (1991). Pornography and rape: Theory and practice? Evidence from crime data in four countries where pornography is easily available. *International Journal of Law and Psychiatry, 14,* 47–64.

LaFrance, M., & Banaji, M. (1992). Toward a reconsideration of the gender-emotion relationship. *Review of Personality and Social Psychology, 14,* 178–201.

LaFrance, M., Hecht, M. A., & Paluck, E. L. (2003). The contingent smile: A meta-analysis of sex differences in smiling. *Psychological Bulletin, 129,* 305–344.

Lagerspetz, K. M. J., & Björkqvist, K. (1994). Indirect aggression in boys and girls. In L.R. Huesmann (Ed.), *Aggressive behavior: Current perspectives* (pp. 131–150). New York: Plenum.

Landy, D., & Aronson, E. (1968). Liking for an evaluator as a function of his discernment. *Journal of Personality and Social Psychology, 9,* 133–141.

Langer, E. J. (1975). The illusion of control. *Journal of Personality and Social Psychology, 32,* 311–328.

Langer, E. J. (1989). Minding matters: The consequences of mindlessness-mindfulness. In L. Berkowitz (Ed.), *Advances in experimental social psychology* (Vol. 22, pp. 137–174). New York: Academic Press.

Langer, E. J., Blank, A., & Chanowitz, B. (1978). The mindlessness of ostensibly thoughtful action. *Journal of Personality and Social Psychology, 36,* 635–642.

Langer, E. J., & Rodin, J. (1976). The effects of choice and enhanced personal responsibility for the aged:

A field experiment in an institutional setting. *Journal of Personality and Social Psychology, 34,* 191–198.

Langlois, J. H., Kalakanis, L., Rubenstein, A. J., Larson, A., Hallam, M., & Smoot, M. (2000). Maxims or myths of beauty? A meta-analytic and theoretical review. *Psychological Bulletin, 126,* 390–423.

Langlois, J. H., & Roggman, L. A. (1990). Attractive faces are only average. *Psychological Science, 1,* 115–121.

Langlois, J. H., Roggman, L. A., Casey, R. J., Ritter, J. M., Rieser-Danner, L. A., & Jenkins, V. Y. (1987). Infant preferences for attractive features: Rudiments of a stereotype? *Developmental Psychology, 23,* 363–369.

Langlois, J. H., Roggman, L. A., & Musselman, L. (1994). What is average and what is not average about attractive faces. *Psychological Science, 5,* 214–220.

Langlois, J. H., Roggman, L. A., & Rieser-Danner, L. A. (1990). Infants' differential social responses to attractive and unattractive faces. *Developmental Psychology, 26,* 153–159.

LaPiere, R. T. (1934). Attitudes vs. actions. *Social Forces, 13,* 230–237.

L'Armand, K., & Pepitone, A. (1975). Helping to reward another person: A cross-cultural analysis. *Journal of Personality and Social Psychology, 31,* 189–198.

Larrance, D. T., & Twentyman, C. T. (1983). Maternal attributions and child abuse. *Journal of Abnormal Psychology, 92,* 449–457.

Larsen, J. T., McGraw, A. P., & Cacioppo, J. T. (2001). Can people feel happy and sad at the same time? *Journal of Personality and Social Psychology, 81,* 684–696.

Larsen, K. S. (1990). The Asch conformity experiment: Replication and transhistorical comparisons. *Journal of Social Behavior and Personality, 5,* 163–168.

Larson, J. R., Jr., Christensen, C., Abbott, A. S., & Franz, T. M. (1996). Diagnosing groups: Charting the flow of information in medical decision-making teams. *Journal of Personality and Social Psychology, 71,* 315–330.

Larson, J. R., Jr., Christensen, C., Franz, T. M., & Abbott, A. S. (1998). Diagnosing groups: The pooling, management, and impact of shared and unshared case information in team-based medical decision making.

Journal of Personality and Social Psychology, 75, 93–108.

Lassiter, G. D., & Irvine, A. A. (1986). Videotaped confessions: The impact of camera point of view on judgments of coercion. *Journal of Applied Social Psychology, 16,* 268–276.

Latané, B. (1981). The psychology of social impact. *American Psychologist, 36,* 343–356.

Latané, B., & Darley, J. M. (1968). Group inhibition of bystander intervention in emergencies. *Journal of Personality and Social Psychology, 10,* 215–221.

Latané, B., & Darley, J. M. (1970). *The unresponsive bystander: Why doesn't he help?* New York: Appleton-Century-Crofts.

Latané, B., Liu, J. H., Nowak, A., Bonevento, M., & Zheng, L. (1995). Distance matters: Physical space and social impact. *Personality and Social Psychology Bulletin, 21,* 795–805.

Latané, B., Williams, K., & Harkins, S. (1979). Many hands make light the work: The causes and consequences of social loafing. *Journal of Personality and Social Psychology, 37,* 823–832.

Latané, B., & Wolf, S. (1981). The social impact of majorities and minorities. *Psychological Review, 88,* 438–453.

Laudenslager, M. L., & Reite, M. L. (1984). Losses and separations: Immunological consequences and health implications. *Review of Personality and Social Psychology, 5,* 285–312.

Laughlin, P. R., Zander, M. L., Knievel, E. M., & Tan, T. K. (2003). Groups perform better than the best individuals on letters-to-numbers problems: Informative equations and effective strategies. *Journal of Personality and Social Psychology, 85,* 684–694.

Lavine, H., Huff, J. W., Wagner, S. H., & Sweeney, D. (1998). The moderating influence of attitude strength on the susceptibility to context effects in attitude surveys. *Journal of Personality and Social Psychology, 75,* 359–373.

Leach, C. W., Spears, R., Branscombe, N. R., & Doosje, B. (2003). Malicious pleasure: Schadenfreude at the suffering of another group. *Journal of Personality and Social Psychology, 84,* 932–943.

Leary, M. R., Kowalski, R. M., Smith, L., & Phillips, S. (2003). Teasing, rejection, and violence: Case studies of the school shootings. *Aggressive Behavior, 29,* 202–214.

Leary, M. R., Springer, C., Negel, L., Ansell, E., & Evans, K. (1998). The causes, phenomenology, and consequences of hurt feelings. *Journal of Personality and Social Psychology, 74,* 1225–1237.

Leary, M. R., Tchividjian, L. R., & Kraxberger, B. E. (1994). Self-presentation can be hazardous to your health: Impression management and health risk. *Health Psychology, 13,* 461–470.

Le Bon, G. (1995). *The crowd: A study of the popular mind.* London: Transaction. (Original work published 1895)

Lee, A. Y., & Aaker, J. L. (2004). Bringing the frame into focus: The influence of regulatory fit on processing fluency and persuasion. *Journal of Personality and Social Psychology, 86,* 205–218.

Lee, J. A. (1977). A typology of styles of loving. *Personality and Social Psychology Bulletin, 3,* 173–182.

Lehman, B. J., & Crano, W. D. (2002). The pervasive effects of vested interest on attitude-criterion consistency in political judgment. *Journal of Experimental Social Psychology, 38,* 101–112.

Lehman, D. R., Chiu, C.-Y., & Schaller, M. (2004). Psychology and culture. *Annual Review of Psychology, 55,* 689–714.

Lehman, D. R., Lempert, R. O., & Nisbett, R. E. (1988). The effects of graduate training on reasoning: Formal discipline and thinking about everyday-life events. *American Psychologist, 43,* 431–442.

Leibold, J. M., & McConnell, A. R. (2004). Women, sex, hostility, power, and suspicion: Sexually aggressive men's cognitive associations. *Journal of Experimental Social Psychology, 40,* 256–263.

Leland, J. (1995, December 11). "Copycat" crimes in New York's subways reignite the debate: Do TV and movies cause actual mayhem? *Newsweek,* p. 46.

Lemyre, L., & Smith, P. M. (1985). Intergroup discrimination and self-esteem in the minimal group paradigm. *Journal of Personality and Social Psychology, 49,* 660–670.

Lepore, L., & Brown, R. (1997). Category and stereotype activation: Is prejudice inevitable? *Journal of Personality and Social Psychology, 72,* 275–287.

Lepper, M. R., Greene, D., & Nisbett, R. E. (1973). Undermining of children's intrinsic interest with extrinsic rewards: A test of the "overjustification" hypothesis. *Journal of Personality and Social Psychology, 28,* 129–137.

Lepper, M. R., & Henderlong, J. (2000). Turning "play" into "work" and "work" into "play": 25 years of research on intrinsic versus extrinsic motivation. In C. Sansone & J. Harackiewicz (Eds.), *Intrinsic and extrinsic motivation: The search for optimal motivation and performance* (pp. 257–307). New York: Academic Press.

Lepper, M. R., Ross, L., & Lau, R. R. (1986). Persistence of inaccurate beliefs about the self. *Journal of Personality and Social Psychology, 50,* 482–491.

Lerner, M. J. (1980). *The belief in a just world: A fundamental delusion.* New York: Plenum.

Levenson, R. W., Carstensen, L. L., & Gottman, J. M. (1994). The influence of age and gender on affect, physiology, and their interrelations: A study of long-term marriages. *Journal of Personality and Social Psychology, 67,* 56–68.

Levenson, R. W., & Gottman, J. M. (1983). Marital interaction: Physiological linkage and affective exchange. *Journal of Personality and Social Psychology, 45,* 587–597.

Levenson, R. W., & Gottman, J. M. (1985). Physiological and affective predictors of change in relationship satisfaction. *Journal of Personality and Social Psychology, 49,* 85–94.

Leventhal, H. (1970). Findings and theory in the study of fear communications. In L. Berkowitz (Ed.), *Advances in experimental social psychology* (Vol. 5, pp. 119–186). San Diego: Academic Press.

Leventhal, H., Singer, R., & Jones, S. (1965). Effects of fear and specificity of recommendation upon attitudes and behavior. *Journal of Personality and Social Psychology, 2,* 20–29.

Leventhal, H., Watts, J. C., & Pagano, F. (1967). Effects of fear and instruction on how to cope with danger. *Journal of Personality and Social Psychology, 6,* 313–321.

Levine, J. M., & Moreland, R. L. (1998). Small groups. In D. T. Gilbert, S. T. Fiske, & G. Lindzey (Eds.), *Handbook of social psychology* (4th ed., Vol. 2, pp. 415–469). New York: McGraw-Hill.

Levine, R. V., Norenzayan, A., & Philbrick, K. (2001). Cross-cultural differences in helping strangers. *Journal of Cross-Cultural Psychology, 32,* 543–560.

Levine, R., Sato, S., Hashimoto, T., & Verma, J. (1995). Love and marriage in eleven cultures. *Journal of Cross-Cultural Psychology, 26,* 554–571.

Levy, K. N., Blatt, S. J., & Shaver, P. R. (1998). Attachment styles and parental representations. *Journal of Personality and Social Psychology, 74,* 407–419.

Lewin, K. (1935). *A dynamic theory of personality: Selected papers.* New York: McGraw-Hill.

Lewin, K. (1951). *Field theory in social science.* New York: Harper & Brothers.

Lewin, K. (1952). Group decision and social change. In G. Swanson, T. Newcomb, & G. Hartley (Eds.), *Readings in social psychology* (Revised ed., pp. 459–473). New York: Henry Holt & Co.

Lewin, K., Dembo, T., Festinger, L., & Sears, P. S. (1944). Level of aspiration. In J. M. Hunt (Ed.), *Personality and the behavioral disorders* (pp. 333–378). New York: Holt.

Lewin, K., Lippitt, R., & White, R. K. (1939). Patterns of aggressive behavior in experimentally created "social climates." *The Journal of Social Psychology, 10,* 271–299.

Lewis, M., & Brooks-Gunn, J. (1979). *Social cognition and the acquisition of self.* New York: Plenum.

Li, N. P., Bailey, J. M., Kenrick, D. T., & Linsenmeier, J. A. W. (2002). The necessities and luxuries of mate preferences: Testing the tradeoffs. *Journal of Personality and Social Psychology, 82,* 947–955.

Liberman, A., & Chaiken, S. (1992). Defensive processing of personally relevant health messages. *Personality and Social Psychology Bulletin, 18,* 669–679.

Liberman, N., & Förster, J. (2000). Expression after suppression: A motivational explanation of postsuppressional rebound. *Journal of Personality and Social Psychology, 79,* 190–203.

Lickel, B., Hamilton, D. L., Wieczorkwska, G., Lewis, A., Sherman, S. J., & Uhles, A. N. (2000). Varieties of groups and the perception of group entiativity. *Journal of Personality and Social Psychology, 78,* 223–246.

Lieberman, M. D. (2000). Intuition: A social cognitive neuroscience approach. *Psychological Bulletin, 126,* 109–137.

Likert, R. (1932). A technique for the measurement of attitudes. *Archives of Psychology, 140,* 1–55.

Lillard, L. A., & Waite, L. J. (1995). 'Til death do us part: Marital disruption and mortality. *American Journal of Sociology, 100,* 1131–1156.

Linder, D. E., Cooper, J., & Jones, E. E. (1967). Decision freedom as a determinant of the role of incentive magnitude in attitude change. *Journal of Personality and Social Psychology, 6,* 245–254.

Lindsay, J. J., & Anderson, C. A. (2000). From antecedent conditions to violent actions: A general affective aggression model. *Personality and Social Psychology Bulletin, 26,* 533–547.

Lindskold, S. (1978). Trust development, the GRIT proposal, and the effects of conciliatory acts on conflict and cooperation. *Psychological Bulletin, 85,* 772–793.

Lindskold, S., Betz, B., & Walters, P. S. (1986). Transforming competitive or cooperative climates. *Journal of Conflict Resolution, 30,* 99–114.

Lindskold, S., & Han, G. (1988). GRIT as a foundation for integrative bargaining. *Personality and Social Psychology Bulletin, 14,* 335–345.

Lindskold, S., Han, G., & Betz, B. (1986). The essential elements of communication in the GRIT strategy. *Personality and Social Psychology Bulletin, 12,* 179–186.

Linville, P. W. (1985). Self-complexity and affective extremity: Don't put all of your eggs in one cognitive basket. *Social Cognition, 3,* 94–120.

Linville, P. W. (1987). Self-complexity as a cognitive buffer against stress-related illness and depression. *Journal of Personality and Social Psychology, 52,* 663–676.

Linville, P. W., Salovey, P., & Fisher, G. W. (1986). Stereotyping and perceived distributions of social characteristics: An application to ingroup–outgroup perception. In J. Dovidio & S. Gaertner (Eds.), *Prejudice, discrimination, and racism: Theory and research* (pp. 165–208). New York: Academic Press.

Lipkus, I. M., Green, J. D., Feaganes, J. R., & Sedikides, C. (2001). The relationship between attitudinal ambivalence and desire to quit smoking among college smokers. *Journal of Applied Social Psychology, 31,* 113–133.

Lippa, R., & Connelly, S. (1990). Gender diagnosticity: A new Bayesian approach to gender-related individual differences. *Journal of Personality and Social Psychology, 59,* 1051–1065.

Lippmann, W. (1922). *Public opinion.* New York: Harcourt Brace.

Lipsitz, A., Kallmeyer, K., Ferguson, M., & Abas, A. (1989). Counting on blood donors: Increasing the impact of reminder calls. *Journal of Abnormal and Social Psychology, 19,* 1057–1067.

Little, B. R. (1981). Personal projects analysis: Trivial pursuits, magnificent obsessions, and the search for coherence. In N. Cantor & J. F. Kihlstrom, (Eds.) *Personality, cognition, and social interaction* (pp. 15–31). Mahwah, NJ: Erlbaum.

Liu, J. H., Karasawa, K., & Weiner, B. (1992). Inferences about the causes of positive and negative emotions. *Personality and Social Psychology Bulletin, 18,* 603–615.

Livingston, R. W. (2002). The role of perceived negativity in the moderation of African-Americans' implicit and explicit racial attitudes. *Journal of Experimental Social Psychology, 38,* 405–413.

Lockwood, P., Dolderman, D., Sadler, P., & Gerchak, E. (2004). Feeling better about doing worse: Social comparisons within romantic relationships. *Journal of Personality and Social Psychology, 87,* 80–95.

Lockwood, P., & Kunda, Z. (1997). Superstars and me: Predicting the impact of role models on the self. *Journal of Personality and Social Psychology, 73,* 91–103.

Long, C. R., Seburn, M., Averill, J. R., & More, T. A. (2003). Solitude experiences: Varieties, settings, and individual differences. *Personality and Social Psychology Bulletin, 29,* 578–583.

Longley, J., & Pruitt, D. G. (1980). Groupthink: A critique of Janis's theory. In L. Wheeler (Ed.,), *Review of Personality and Social Psychology* (Vol. 1, pp. 74–93). Beverly Hills, CA: Sage.

Lord, C. G., Lepper, M. R., & Mackie, D. (1984). Attitude prototypes as determinants of attitude-behavior consis-

tency. *Journal of Personality and Social Psychology, 46,* 1254–1266.

Lord, C. G., Lepper, M. R., & Preston, E. (1984). Considering the opposite: A corrective strategy for social judgment. *Journal of Personality and Social Psychology, 47,* 1231–1243.

Lord, C. G., Ross, L., & Lepper, M. R. (1979). Biased assimilation and attitude polarization: The effects of prior theories on subsequently considered evidence. *Journal of Personality and Social Psychology, 37,* 2098–2109.

Lord, R. B., & Maher, K. J. (1991). *Leadership and information processing: Linking perceptions and performance.* Boston: Unwin-Hyman.

Lore, R. K., & Schultz, L. A. (1993). Control of human aggression: A comparative perspective. *American Psychologist, 48,* 16–25.

Lorenz, K. (1966). *On aggression.* New York: Harcourt, Brace, & World.

Lorge, I. (1936). Prestige, suggestion, and attitudes. *Journal of Social Psychology, 7,* 386–402.

Lucas, R. E., Clark, A. E., Georgellis, Y., & Diener, E. (2003). Reexamining adaptation and the set point model of happiness: Reactions to changes in marital status. *Journal of Personality and Social Psychology, 84,* 527–539.

Lucas, R. E., Diener, E., & Suh, E. (1996). Discriminant validity of well-being measures. *Journal of Personality and Social Psychology, 71,* 616–628.

Luchins, A. S. (1957). Primacy-recency in impression formation. In C. I. Hovland (Ed.), *The order of presentation in persuasion* (pp. 33–61). New Haven, CT: Yale University Press.

Luhtanen, R., & Crocker, J. (1992). A collective self-esteem scale: Self-evaluation of one's social identity. *Personality and Social Psychology Bulletin, 18,* 302–318.

Lumsdaine, A. A., & Janis, I. L. (1953). Resistance to counterpropaganda produced by one-sided and two-sided propaganda presentations. *Public Opinion Quarterly, 17,* 311–318.

Lupfer, M. B., Clark, L. F., & Hutcherson, H. W. (1990). Impact of context on spontaneous trait and situational attributions. *Journal of Personality and Social Psychology, 58,* 239–249.

Lydon, J. E., Fitzsimons, G. M., & Naidoo, L. (2003). Devaluation versus enhancement of attractive alternatives: A critical test using the calibration

method. *Personality and Social Psychology Bulletin, 29,* 349–359.

Lydon, J. E., Meana, M., Sepinwall, D., Richards, N., & Mayman, S. (1999). The commitment calibration hypothesis: When do people devaluate attractive alternatives? *Personality and Social Psychology Bulletin, 25,* 152–161.

Lykken, D. T., & Tellegen, A. (1993). Is human mating adventitious or the result of lawful choice? A twin study of mate selection. *Journal of Personality and Social Psychology, 65,* 56–68.

Lykken, D. T., & Tellegen, A. (1996). Happiness is a stochastic phenomenon. *Psychological Science, 7,* 186–189.

Lyons, A., & Kashima, Y. (2003). How are stereotypes maintained through communication? The influence of stereotype sharedness. *Journal of Personality and Social Psychology, 85,* 989–1005.

Lyubomirsky, S. (2001). Why are some people happier than others? The role of cognitive and motivational processes in well-being. *American Psychologist, 56,* 239–249.

Lyubomirsky, S., King, L., & Diener, E. (in press). Is happiness a strength? An examination of the benefits and costs of frequent positive affect. *Psychological Bulletin.*

Maass, A., Cadinu, M., Guarnieri, G., & Grasselii, A. (2003). Sexual harassment under social identity threat: The computer harassment paradigm. *Journal of Personality and Social Psychology, 85,* 853–870.

Maass, A., Ceccarelli, R., & Rudin, S. (1996). Linguistic intergroup bias: Evidence for in-group-protective motivation. *Journal of Personality and Social Psychology, 71,* 512–526.

Maass, A., & Clark, R. D. III. (1984). Hidden impact of minorities: Fifteen years of minority influence research. *Psychological Bulletin, 95,* 428–450.

Maass, A., Salvi, D., Arcuri, L., & Semin, G. (1989). Language use in intergroup contexts: The linguistic intergroup bias. *Journal of Personality and Social Psychology, 57,* 981–993.

Maccoby, E. E., & Jacklin, C. N. (1974). *The psychology of sex difference.* Stanford, CA: Stanford University Press.

MacDonald, T. K., Zanna, M. P., & Fong, G. T. (1996). Why common sense goes out the window: Effects of alcohol on intentions to use condoms. *Personality and Social Psychology Bulletin, 22,* 763–775.

Mackie, D. M., & Worth, L. T. (1989). Processing deficits and the mediation of positive affect in persuasion. *Journal of Personality and Social Psychology, 57,* 27–40.

Macrae, C. N., & Bodenhausen, G. V. (2000). Social cognition: Thinking categorically about others. *Annual Review of Psychology, 51,* 93–120.

Macrae, C. N., Bodenhausen, G. V., & Milne, A. B. (1998). Saying no to unwanted thoughts: Self-focus and the regulation of mental life. *Journal of Personality and Social Psychology, 74,* 578–589.

Macrae, C. N., Milne, A. B., & Bodenhausen, G. V. (1994). Stereotypes as energy-saving devices: A peek inside the cognitive toolbox. *Journal of Personality and Social Psychology, 66,* 37–47.

Macrae, C. N., Stangor, C., & Milne, A. B. (1994). Activating social stereotypes: A functional analysis. *Journal of Experimental Social Psychology, 30,* 370–389.

Madden, T. J., Ellen, P. S., & Ajzen, I. (1992). A comparison of the theory of planned behavior and the theory of reasoned action. *Personality and Social Psychology Bulletin, 18,* 3–9.

Madey, S. F., Simo, M., Dillowth, D., Tocynski, A., & Perella, A. (1996). They do get more attractive at closing time, but only when you are not in a relationship. *Basic and Applied Social Psychology, 18,* 387–393.

Madon, S., Guyll, M., Aboufadel, K., Montiel, E., Smith, A., Palumbo, P., et al. (2001). Ethnic and national stereotypes: The Princeton Trilogy revisited and revised. *Personality and Social Psychology Bulletin, 27,* 996–1010.

Madon, S., Guyll, M., Spoth, R. L., Cross, S. E., & Hilbert, S. J. (2003). The self-fulfilling influence of mother expectations on children's underage drinking. *Journal of Personality and Social Psychology, 84,* 1188–1205.

Madon, S., Jussim, L., & Eccles, J. (1997). In search of the powerful self-fulfilling prophecy effect. *Journal of*

Personality and Social Psychology, 72, 791–809.

Magnus, K., Diener, E., Fujita, F., & Pavot, W. (1993). Extraversion and neuroticism as predictors of objective life events: A longitudinal analysis. *Journal of Personality and Social Psychology, 65,* 1046–1053.

Maier, S. F., Seligman, M. E. P., & Solomon, R. S. (1969). Pavlovian fear conditioning and learned helplessness. In B. A. Campbell & R. A. Church (Eds.), *Punishment and aversive behavior* (pp. 229–243). New York: Appleton-Century-Crofts.

Major, B., Gramzow, R. H., McCoy, S. K., Levin, S., Schmader, T., & Sidanius, J. (2002). Perceiving personal discrimination: The role of group status and legitimizing ideology. *Journal of Personality and Social Psychology, 82,* 269–282.

Major, B., Kaiser, C. R., & McCoy, S. K. (2003). It's not my fault: When and why attributions to prejudice protect self-esteem. *Personality and Social Psychology Bulletin, 29,* 772–781.

Major, B., Quinton, W. J., & Schmader, T. (2003). Attributions to discrimination and self-esteem: Impact of group identification and situational ambiguity. *Journal of Experimental Social Psychology, 39,* 220–231.

Major, B., Spencer, S., Schmader, T., Wolfe, C., & Crocker, J. (1998). Coping with negative stereotypes about intellectual performance: The role of psychological disengagement. *Personality and Social Psychology Bulletin, 24,* 34–50.

Major, B., Testa, M., & Bylsma, W. H. (1991). Responses to upward and downward social comparison: The impact of esteem-relevance and perceived control. In J. Suls & T. A. Wills (Eds.), *Social comparison: Contemporary theory and research* (pp. 237–257). Mahwah, NJ: Erlbaum.

Major, B., Zubek, J. M., Cooper, M. L., Cozzarelli, C., & Richards, C. (1997). Mixed messages: Implications of social conflict and social support within close relationships for adjustment to a stressful life event. *Journal of Personality and Social Psychology, 72,* 1349–1363.

Malamuth, N. M. (1986). Predictors of naturalistic sexual aggression. *Journal of Personality and Social Psychology, 50,* 953–962.

Malamuth, N. M., Addison, T., & Koss, M. (2000). Pornography and sexual aggression: Are there reliable effects and can we understand them? *Annual Review of Sex Research, 11,* 26–91.

Malamuth, N. M., & Check, J. (1981). The effects of mass media exposure on acceptance of violence against women: A field experiment. *Journal of Research in Personality, 15,* 436–446.

Malamuth, N. M., Check, J. V. P., & Briere, J. (1986). Sexual arousal in response to aggression: Ideological, aggressive, and sexual correlates. *Journal of Personality and Social Psychology, 50,* 330–340.

Malamuth, N. M., & Donnerstein, E. (Eds.). (1984). *Pornography and sexual aggression.* New York: Academic Press.

Malamuth, N. M., Linz, D., Heavey, C. L., Barnes, G., & Acker, M. (1995). Using the confluence model of sexual aggression to predict men's conflict with women: A 10-year follow-up study. *Journal of Personality and Social Psychology, 69,* 353–369.

Mandel, D. R. (1998). The obedience alibi: Milgram's account of the Holocaust reconsidered. *Analyse & Kritik: Zeitschrift für Sozialwissenschaften, 20,* 74–94.

Maner, J. K., Kenrick, D. T., Becker, V., Delton, A., Hofer, B., Wilbur, C. J., & Neuberg, S. L. (2003). Sexually selective cognition: Beauty captures the mind of the beholder. *Journal of Personality and Social Psychology, 85,* 1107–1120.

Maner, J. K., Luce, C. L., Neuberg, S. L., Cialdini, R. B., Brown, S., & Sagarin, B. J. (2002). The effects of perspective taking on motivations for helping: Still no evidence for altruism. *Personality and Social Psychology Bulletin, 28,* 1601–1610.

Mann, R. (1959). A review of the relationships between personality and performance in small groups. *Psychological Bulletin, 56,* 241–270.

Manucia, G. K., Baumann, D. J., & Cialdini, R. B. (1984). Mood influences on helping: Direct effects or side effects? *Journal of Personality and Social Psychology, 46,* 357–364.

Ma'oz, I., Ward, A., Katz, M., & Ross, L. (2002). Reactive devaluation of an "Israeli" vs. "Palestinian" peace proposal. *Journal of Conflict Resolution, 46,* 515–546.

Marcus, G. E. (1988). The structure of emotional response: 1984 presidential candidates. *American Political Science Review, 82,* 737–761.

Marcus-Newhall, A., Pedersen, W. C., Carlson, M., & Miller, N. (2000). Displaced aggression is alive and well: A meta-analytic review. *Journal of Personality and Social Psychology, 78,* 670–689.

Marino L., Reiss, D., & Gallup, G. G., Jr. (1994). Mirror self-recognition in bottlenose dolphins: Implications for comparative investigations of highly dissimilar species. In S. Parker, Mitchell, R., & Boccia, M. (Eds.), *Self-awareness in animals and humans: Developmental perspectives* (pp. 380–391). New York: Cambridge University Press.

Marks, G. (1984). Thinking one's abilities are unique and one's opinions are common. *Personality and Social Psychology Bulletin, 10,* 203–208.

Markus, H. (1977). Self-schemata and processing information about the self. *Journal of Personality and Social Psychology, 35,* 63–78.

Markus, H. (1978). The effect of mere presence on social facilitation: An unobtrusive test. *Journal of Experimental Social Psychology, 14,* 389–397.

Markus, H., & Kitayama, S. (1991). Culture and the self: Implications for cognition, emotion, and motivation. *Psychological Review, 98,* 224–253.

Markus, H., & Zajonc, R. B. (1985). The cognitive perspective in social psychology. In G. Lindzey & E. Aronson (Eds.), *The handbook of social psychology* (3rd ed., Vol. 1, pp. 137–230). New York: Random House.

Marlatt, G. A., & Rohsenow, D. J. (1980). Cognitive processes in alcohol use: Expectancy and the balanced placebo design. In N. K. Mellow (Ed.), *Advances in substance abuse: Behavioral and biological research* (pp. 159–199). Greenwich, CT: JAI.

Marques, J. M., Robalo, E. M., & Rocha, S. A. (1992). Ingroup bias and the "black sheep" effect: Assessing the impact of social identification and perceived variability on group judgments. *European Journal of Social Psychology, 22,* 331–352.

Marsh, H. W. (1990). A multidimensional, hierarchical model of self-concept: Theoretical and empirical justification. *Educational Psychology Review, 2,* 77–172.

Marsh, H. W., & Hau, K-T. (2003). Big-fish-little-pond effect on academic self-concept: A cross-cultural (26-country) test of the negative effects of academically selective schools. *American Psychologist, 58,* 364–376.

Marsh, H. W., Kong, C. K., & Hau, K-T. (2000). Longitudinal multilevel models of the Big-Fish-Little-Pond effect on academic self-concept: Counterbalancing contrast and reflected-glory effects in Hong Kong schools. *Journal of Personality and Social Psychology, 78,* 337–349.

Marsh, H. W., & Parker, J. W. (1984). Determinants of student self-concept: Is it better to be a relatively large fish in a small pond even if you don't learn to swim as well? *Journal of Personality and Social Psychology, 47,* 213–231.

Marshall, M. A. (2003). The traits as situational sensitivities (TASS) model: A more accurate way to predict behavior. *Dissertation Abstracts International: Section B: the Sciences & Engineering. Vol 63(11-B), 5569, US: Universal Microfilms International.*

Martin, G. B., & Clark, R. D., III. (1982). Distress crying in neonates: Species and peer specificity. *Developmental Psychology, 18,* 3–9.

Martin, K. A., & Leary, M. R. (1999). Would you drink after a stranger? The influence of self-presentational motives on willingness to take a health risk. *Personality and Social Psychology Bulletin, 25,* 1092–1100.

Martin, N. G., Eaves, L. J., Heath, A. R., Jardine, R., Feingold, L. M., & Eysenck, H. J. (1986). Transmission of social attitudes. *Proceedings of the National Academy of Sciences, 83,* 4364–4368.

Martin, R., Hewstone, M., & Martin, P. Y. (2003). Resistance to persuasive messages as a function of majority and minority source status. *Journal of Experimental Social Psychology, 39,* 585–593.

Marx, D. M., & Roman, J. S. (2002). Female role models: Protecting women's math test performance. *Personality and Social Psychology Bulletin, 28,* 1183–1193.

Mashek, D. J., Aron, A., & Boncimino, M. (2003). Confusions of self with close others. *Personality and Social Psychology Bulletin, 29,* 382–392.

Maslow, A. (1968). *Toward a psychology of being* (2nd ed.). New York: Van Nostrand.

Masuda, T., & Nisbett, R. E. (2001). Attending holistically versus analytically: Comparing the context sensitivity of Japanese and Americans. *Journal of Personality and Social Psychology, 81,* 922–934.

Matheson, K., Cole, B., & Majka, K. (2003). Dissidence from within: Examining the effects of intergroup context on group members' reactions to attitudinal opposition. *Journal of Experimental Social Psychology, 39,* 161–169.

Mathews, J. (1999). The shrinking field. *Washington Post* (p. C1).

Mathews, K. E., Jr., & Canon, L. K. (1975). Environmental noise as a determinant of helping behavior. *Journal of Personality and Social Psychology, 32,* 571–577.

Mayer, J. D., Gaschke, Y. N., Braverman, D. L., & Evans, T. W. (1992). Mood-congruent judgment is a general effect. *Journal of Personality and Social Psychology, 63,* 119–132.

Mazis, M. B. (1975). Antipollution measures and psychological reactance theory: a field experiment. *Journal of Personality and Social Psychology, 31,* 654–666.

McArthur, L. A. (1972). The how and what of why: Some determinants and consequences of causal attribution. *Journal of Personality and Social Psychology, 22,* 171–193.

McArthur, L. Z., & Baron, R. M. (1983). Toward an ecological theory of social perception. *Psychological Review, 90,* 215–238.

McArthur, L. Z., & Berry, D. S. (1987). Cross-cultural agreement in perceptions of babyfaced adults. *Journal of Cross-Cultural Psychology, 18,* 165–192.

McCann, S. J. H. (1992). Alternative formulas to predict the greatness of U.S. presidents: Personological, situational, and zeitgeist factors. *Journal of Personality and Social Psychology, 62,* 469–479.

McCauley, C. (1998). Group dynamics in Janis's theory of groupthink: Forward and backward. *Organizational Behavior and Human Decision Processes, 73,* 142–162.

McClure, J. (1998). Discounting causes of behavior: Are two reasons better than one? *Journal of Personality and Social Psychology, 74,* 7–20.

McConahay, J. B. (1983). Modern racism and modern discrimination. *Personality and Social Psychology Bulletin, 9,* 544–550.

McConahay, J. B. (1986). Modern racism, ambivalence, and the Modern Racism Scale. In J. F. Dovidio & S. L. Gaertner (Eds.), *Prejudice, discrimination, and racism: Theory and research* (pp. 91–125). Orlando, FL: Academic Press.

McConahay, J. B., Hardee, B. B., & Batts, V. (1981). Has racism declined in America? It depends on who is asking and what is asked. *Journal of Conflict Resolution, 25,* 563–579.

McConnell, A. R., & Leibold, J. M. (2001). Relations among the Implicit Association Test, discriminatory behavior, and explicit measures of racial attitudes. *Journal of Experimental Social Psychology, 37,* 435–442.

McConnell, A. R., Sherman, S. J., & Hamilton, D. L. (1994). On-line and memory-based aspects of individual and group target judgments. *Journal of Personality and Social Psychology, 67,* 173–185.

McConnell, A. R., Sherman, S. J., & Hamilton, D. L. (1997). Target entitativity: Implications for information processing about individual and group targets. *Journal of Personality and Social Psychology, 72,* 750–762.

McDougall, W. (1908). *An introduction to social psychology.* London: Methuen.

McElroy, T., & Seta, J. J. (2003). Framing effects: An analytic-holistic perspective. *Journal of Experimental Social Psychology, 39,* 610–617.

McFarland, C., & Buehler, R. (1995). Collective self-esteem as a moderator of the frog-pond effect in reactions to performance feedback. *Journal of Personality and Social Psychology, 68,* 1055–1070.

McFarland, C., White, K., & Newth, S. (2003). Mood acknowledgment and correction for the mood-congruency bias in social judgment. *Journal of Experimental Social Psychology, 39,* 483–491.

McGregor, I., & Little, B. R. (1998). Personal projects, happiness, and meaning: On doing well and being yourself. *Journal of Personality and Social Psychology, 74,* 494–512.

McGuire, W. J. (1964). Inducing resistance to persuasion. In L. Berkowitz (Ed.), *Advances in experimental social psychology* (Vol. 1, pp. 191–229). San Diego: Academic Press.

McGuire, W. J. (1968). The nature of attitudes and attitude change. In G. Lindzey & E. Aronson (Ed.), *Handbook of social psychology* (2nd ed., Vol. 3, pp. 136–314). Reading, MA: Addison-Wesley.

McGuire, W. J. (1983). A contextualist theory of knowledge: Its implications for innovation and reform in psychological research. In L. Berkowitz (Ed.), *Advances in experimental social psychology* (Vol. 16, pp. 1–47). New York: Academic Press.

McGuire, W. J. (1985). Attitudes and attitude change. In G. Lindzey & E. Aronson (Eds.), *Handbook of social psychology* (3rd ed., Vol. 2, pp. 233–346). New York: Random House.

McGuire, W. J., & McGuire, C. V. (1981). The spontaneous self-concept as affected by personal distinctiveness. In M. D. Lynch, A. A. Norem-Hebeisen, & K. J. Gergen (Eds.), *Self-concept: Advances in theory and research* (pp. 147–171). Cambridge, MA: Balinger.

McGuire, W. J., & McGuire, C. V. (1988). Content and process in the experience of self. In L. Berkowitz (Ed.), *Advances in experimental social psychology* (Vol. 21, pp. 97–144). New York: Academic Press.

McGuire, W. J., & Papageorgis, D. (1961). The relative efficacy of various types of prior belief-defense in producing immunity to persuasion. *Journal of Abnormal and Social Psychology, 62,* 327–337.

McGuire, W. J., & Papageorgis, D. (1962). Effectiveness of forewarning in developing resistance to persuasion. *Public Opinion Quarterly, 26,* 24–34.

McIntyre, R. B., Paulson, R. M., & Lord, C. G. (2001). Alleviating women's mathematics stereotype threat through salience of group achievements. *Journal of Experimental Social Psychology, 39,* 83–90.

McMillen, D. L. (1971). Transgression, self-image, and compliant behavior. *Journal of Personality and Social Psychology, 20,* 176–179.

McMullen, M. N., & Markman, K. D. (2002). Affective impact of close counterfactuals: Implications of possible futures for possible pasts. *Journal of Experimental Social Psychology, 38,* 64–70.

McNulty, S. E., & Swann, W. B., Jr. (1994). Identity negotiation in roommate relationships: The self as architect and consequence of social reality. *Journal of Personality and Social Psychology, 67,* 1012–1023.

Mead, G. H. (1934). *Mind, self, and society.* Chicago: University of Chicago Press.

Mealey, L., Bridgstock, R., & Townsend, G. C. (1999). Symmetry and perceived facial attractiveness: A monozygotic co-twin comparison. *Journal of Personality and Social Psychology, 76,* 151–158.

Meddin, J. (1979). Chimpanzees, symbols, and the reflective self. *Social Psychology Quarterly, 42,* 99–109.

Medvec, V. H., Madey, S. F., & Gilovich, T. (1995). When less is more: Counterfactual thinking and satisfaction among Olympic medalists. *Journal of Personality and Social Psychology, 69,* 603–610.

Medvec, V. H., & Savitsky, K. (1997). When doing better means feeling worse: The effects of categorical cutoff points on counterfactual thinking and satisfaction. *Journal of Personality & Social Psychology, 72,* 1284–1296.

Medved, M. (1995, October). Hollywood's 3 big lies. *Reader's Digest, 147*(882), 155–159.

Meiran, N., Netzer, T., Netzer, S., Itzhak, D., & Rechnitz, O. (1994). Do tests of nonverbal encoding ability measure sensitivity to nonverbal cues? *Journal of Nonverbal Behavior, 18,* 223–244.

Meleshko, K. G. A., & Alden, L. E. (1993). Anxiety and self-disclosure: Toward a motivational model. *Journal of Personality and Social Psychology, 64,* 1000–1009.

Mellor, D. (2003). Contemporary racism in Australia: The experiences of Aborigines. *Personality and Social Psychology Bulletin, 29,* 474–486.

Meltzoff, A. N. (1990). Foundations for developing a concept of self: The role of imitation in relating self to other and the value of social mirroring, social modeling, and self practice in infancy. In D. Cicchetti & M. Beeghly (Eds.), *The self in transition: Infancy to childhood* (pp. 139–164). Chicago: The University of Chicago Press.

Meltzoff, A. N., & Moore, M. K. (1993). Newborn infants imitate adult facial gestures. *Child Development, 54,* 265–301.

Mendoza-Denton, R., Downey, G., Purdie, V. J., Davis, A., & Pietrzak, J.

(2002). Sensitivity to status-based rejection: Implications for African American students' college experience. *Journal of Personality and Social Psychology, 83,* 896–918.

Mesquida, C. G., & Wiener, N. I. (1999). Male age composition and severity of conflicts. *Politics and the Life Sciences, 18,* 181–189.

Mesquita, B., & Frijda, N. H. (1992). Cultural variations in emotions: A review. *Psychological Bulletin, 112,* 179–204.

Messé, L. A., Hertel, G., Kerr, N. L., Lount, R. B., Jr., & Park, E. S. (2002). Knowledge of partner's ability as a moderator of group motivation gains: An exploration of the Köhler Discrepancy Effect. *Journal of Personality and Social Psychology, 82,* 935–946.

Messick, D. M., Bloom, S., Boldizar, J. P., & Samuelson, C. D. (1985). Why we are fairer than others. *Journal of Experimental Social Psychology, 21,* 480–500.

Messick, D. M., & Brewer, M. B. (1983). Solving social dilemmas: A review. *Review of Personality and Social Psychology, 4,* 11–44.

Messick, D. M., & McClintock, C. G. (1968). Motivational basis of choice in experimental games. *Journal of Experimental Social Psychology, 4,* 1–25.

Mewborn, C. R., & Rogers, R. W. (1979). Effects of threatening and reassuring components of fear appeals on physiological and verbal measures of emotion and attitudes. *Journal of Experimental Social Psychology, 15,* 242–253.

Meyer, D. E., & Schvaneveldt, R. W. (1971). Facilitation in recognizing pairs of words: Evidence of a dependence between retrieval operations. *Journal of Experimental Psychology, 90,* 227–234.

Meyerowitz, B. E., & Chaiken, S. (1987). The effect of message framing on breast self-examination attitudes, intentions, and behavior. *Journal of Personality and Social Psychology, 52,* 500–510.

Mezulis, A. H., Abramson, L. Y., Hyde, J. S., & Hankin, B. L. (2004). Is there a universal positivity bias in attributions?: A meta-analytic review of individual, developmental, and cultural differences in the self-serving attributional bias. *Psychological Bulletin, 130,* 711–747.

Mikulincer, M. (1998). Attachment working models and the sense of trust: An exploration of interaction goals and affect regulation. *Journal of Personality and Social Psychology, 74,* 1209–1224.

Milavsky, J. R., Kessler, R. C., Stipp, H. H., & Rubens, W. S. (1982). *Television and aggression: A panel study.* New York: Academic Press.

Miles, D. R., & Carey, G. (1997). Genetic and environmental architecture of human aggression. *Journal of Personality and Social Psychology, 72,* 207–217.

Milgram, S. (1970). The experience of living in cities. *Science, 167,* 1461–1468.

Milgram, S. (1974). *Obedience to authority.* New York: Harper & Row.

Milgram, S., & Sabini, J. (1978). On maintaining urban norms: A field experiment in the subway. In A. Baum, J. E., Singer, & S. Valins (Eds.), *Advances in environmental psychology* (Vol. 1., pp. 9–40). Mahwah, NJ: Lawrence Erlbaum Associates.

Miller, A. G. (1986). *The obedience experiments: A case study of controversy in social science.* New York: Praeger.

Miller, D. T., Downs, J. S., & Prentice, D. A. (1998). Minimal conditions for the creation of a unit relationship: The social bond between birthdaymates. *European Journal of Social Psychology, 28,* 475–481.

Miller, D. T., & McFarland, C. (1986). Counterfactual thinking and victim compensation: A test of norm theory. *Personality and Social Psychology Bulletin, 12,* 513–519.

Miller, D. T., & Ratner, R. (1998). The disparity between actual and assumed power of self-interest. *Journal of Personality and Social Psychology, 74,* 53–62.

Miller, D. T., & Turnbull, W. (1986). Expectancies and interpersonal processes. *Annual Review of Psychology, 37,* 233–256.

Miller, J. G. (1984). Culture and the development of everyday social explanation. *Journal of Personality and Social Psychology, 46,* 961–978.

Miller, J.G., Bersoff, D. M., & Harwood, R. L. (1990). Perceptions of social responsibility in India and in the United States: Moral imperatives or personal decisions? *Journal of Personality and Social Psychology, 58,* 33–47.

Miller, N., & Campbell, D. T. (1959). Recency and primacy in persuasion as a function of the timing of speeches and

measurements. *Journal of Abnormal and Social Psychology, 59,* 1–9.

Miller, N., Pedersen, W. C., Earleywine, M., & Pollock, V. E. (2003). A theoretical model of displaced aggression. *Personality and Social Psychology Review, 7,* 75–97.

Miller, N. E. (1944). Experimental studies of conflict. In J. M. Hunt (Ed.), *Personality and the behavior disorders* (Vol. 1, pp. 431–465). New York: Ronald.

Miller, N. E., & Dollard, J. (1941). *Social learning and imitation.* New Haven, CT: Yale University Press.

Miller, P. J. E., & Rempel, J. K. (2004). Trust and partner-enhancing attributions in close relationships. *Personality and Social Psychology Bulletin, 30,* 695–705.

Miller, R. S. (1997). Inattentive and contented: Relationship commitment and attention to alternatives. *Journal of Personality and Social Psychology, 73,* 758–766.

Mischel, W. (1968). *Personality and assessment.* New York: Wiley.

Mischel, W. (1973). Toward a cognitive social learning reconceptualization of personality. *Psychological Review, 80,* 252–283.

Mischel, W., Shoda, Y., & Peake, P. K. (1988). The nature of adolescent competencies predicted by preschool delay of gratification. *Journal of Personality and Social Psychology, 54,* 687–696.

Miyamoto, Y., & Kitayama, S. (2002). Cultural variation in correspondence bias: The critical role of attitude diagnosticity of socially constrained behavior. *Journal of Personality and Social Psychology, 83,* 1239–1248.

Monahan, J. L., Murphy, S. T., & Zajonc, R. B. (2000). Subliminal mere exposure: Specific, general, and diffuse effects. *Psychological Science, 11,* 462–466.

Monin, B. (2003). The warm glow heuristic: When liking leads to familiarity. *Journal of Personality and Social Psychology, 85,* 1035–1048.

Monin, B., & Miller, D. T. (2001). Moral credentials and the expression of prejudice. *Journal of Personality and Social Psychology, 81,* 33–43.

Monteith, M. J., & Spicer, C. V. (2000). Contents and correlates of Whites' and Blacks' racial attitudes. *Journal of Experimental Social Psychology, 36,* 125–154.

Monteith, M. J., & Walters, G. L. (1998). Egalitarianism, moral obligation, and prejudice-related personal standards. *Personality and Social Psychology Bulletin, 24,* 186–199.

Montepare, J. M., & Zebrowitz, L. A. (1998). Person perception comes of age: The salience and significance of age in social judgments. In M. P. Zanna (Ed.), *Advances in experimental social psychology* (Vol. 30, pp. 93–161). New York: Academic Press.

Montepare, J. M., & Zebrowitz-McArthur, L. (1988). Impressions of people created by age-related qualities of their gaits. *Journal of Personality and Social Psychology, 55,* 547–556.

Montoya, R. M., & Horton, R. S. (2004). On the importance of cognitive evaluation as a determinant of interpersonal attraction. *Journal of Personality and Social Psychology, 86,* 696–712.

Mook, D. G. (1983). In defense of external invalidity. *American Psychologist, 38,* 379–388.

Moore, D. A. (2004). The unexpected benefits of final deadlines in negotiation. *Journal of Experimental Social Psychology, 40,* 121–127.

Moore, D. L., Hausknecht, D., & Thamodaran, K. (1986). Time compression, response opportunity, and persuasion. *Journal of Consumer Research, 13,* 85–99.

Moore, R. L. (1998). Love and limerance with Chinese characteristics: Student romance in the PRC. In V. C. de Munck (Ed.), *Romantic love and sexual behavior* (pp. 251–283). Westport, CT: Praeger.

Moorhead, G., Ference, R., & Neck, C. P. (1991). Group decision fiascoes continue: Space shuttle *Challenger* and a revised groupthink framework. *Human Relations, 44,* 539–550.

Moreland, R. L., & Beach, S. R. (1992). Exposure effects in the classroom: The development of affinity among students. *Journal of Experimental Social Psychology, 28,* 255–276.

Moreland, R. L., & Levine, J. M. (1982). Socialization in small group: Temporal changes in individual-group relations. In L. Berkowitz (Ed.), *Advances in experimental social psychology* (Vol. 15, pp. 137–192). New York: Academic Press.

Morris, M. W., & Larrick, R. P. (1995). When one cause casts doubt on another: A normative analysis of discounting in causal attribution. *Psychological Review, 102,* 331–355.

Morris, M. W., Larrick, R. P., & Su, S. K. (1999). Misperceiving negotiation counterparts: When situationally determined bargaining behaviors are attributed to personality traits. *Journal of Personality and Social Psychology, 77,* 52–67.

Morris, M. W., & Peng, K. (1994). Culture and cause: American and Chinese attributions for social and physical events. *Journal of Personality and Social Psychology, 67,* 949–971.

Morrison, A. M., Von Glinow, M. A. (1990). Women and minorities in management. *American Psychologist, 45,* 200–208.

Morrison, A. M., White, R. P., & Van Velsor, E. (1987). *Breaking the glass ceiling: Can women reach the top of America's largest corporations?* Reading, MA: Addison-Wesley.

Moscovici, S. (1980). Toward a theory of conversion behavior. In L. Berkowitz (Ed.), *Advances in experimental social psychology* (Vol. 13, pp. 209–239). New York: Academic Press.

Moscovici, S., Lage, E., & Naffrechoux, M. (1969). Influence of a consistent minority on the response of a majority in a color preparation task. *Sociometry, 32,* 365–379.

Moskalenko, S., & Heine, S. J. (2003). Watching your troubles away: Television viewing as a stimulus for subjective self-awareness. *Personality and Social Psychology Bulletin, 29,* 76–85.

Moskowitz, G. B., & Skurnik, I. W. (1999). Contrast effects as determined by the type of prime: Trait versus exemplar primes initiate strategies that differ in how accessible constructs are used. *Journal of Personality and Social Psychology, 76,* 911–927.

Muehlenhard, C. L. (1988). Misinterpreted dating behaviors and the risk of date rape. *Journal of Social and Clinical Psychology, 6,* 20–37.

Muehlenhard, C. L., & Hollabaugh, L. C. (1988). Do women sometimes say no when they mean yes? The prevalence and correlates of women's token resistance to sex. *Journal of Personality and Social Psychology, 54,* 872–879.

Muehlenhard, C. L., & Kimes, L. A. (1999). The social construction of violence: The case of sexual and domestic violence. *Personality and Social Psychology Review, 3,* 234–245.

Muehlenhard, C. L., & Linton, M. A. (1987). Date rape and sexual aggression in dating situation: Incidence and risk factors. *Journal of Counseling Psychology, 34,* 186–196.

Mullen, B. (1991). Group composition, salience, and cognitive representations: The phenomenology of being in a group. *Journal of Experimental Social Psychology, 27,* 297–323.

Mullen, B. (2004). Sticks and stones can break my bones, but ethnophaulisms can alter the portrayal of immigrants to children. *Personality and Social Psychology Bulletin, 30,* 250–260.

Mullen, B., Atkins, J. L., Champion, D. S., Edwards, C., Hardy, D., Story, J. E., et al. (1985). The false consensus effect: A meta-analysis of 115 hypothesis tests. *Journal of Experimental Social Psychology, 21,* 262–283.

Mullen, B., & Cooper, C. (1994). The relation between group cohesiveness and performance: An integration. *Psychological Bulletin, 115,* 210–227.

Mullen, B., Johnson, C., & Salas, E. (1991). Productivity loss in brainstorming groups: A meta-analytic integration. *Basic and Applied Social Psychology, 12,* 3–23.

Mullen, B., Migdal, M. J., & Rozell, D. (2003). Self-awareness, deindividuation, and social identity: Unraveling theoretical paradoxes by filling empirical lacunae. *Personality and Social Psychology Bulletin, 29,* 1071–1081.

Mulvihill, D. J., Tumin, M. M., & Curtis, L. A. (1969). *Crimes of violence* (Vol. 11). Washington, DC: U.S. Government Printing Office.

Mummendey, A., Otten, S., Berger, U., & Kessler, T. (2000). Positive-negative asymmetry in social discrimination: Valence of evaluation and salience of categorization. *Personality and Social Psychology Bulletin, 26,* 1258–1270.

Muraven, M., & Baumeister, R. F. (2000). Self-regulation and depletion of limited resources: Does self-control resemble a muscle? *Psychological Bulletin, 126,* 247–259.

Muraven, M., Tice, D. M., & Baumeister, R. F. (1998). Self-control as limited resource: Regulatory depletion patterns. *Journal of Personality and Social Psychology, 74,* 774–789.

Murdoch, D., Phil, R. O., & Ross, D. (1990). Alcohol and crimes of violence: Present issues. *International Journal of Addiction, 25,* 1059–1075.

Murphy, S. T., & Zajonc, R. B. (1993). Affect, cognition, and awareness: Affective priming with optimal and suboptimal stimulus exposures. *Journal of Personality and Social Psychology, 64,* 723–739.

Murray, S. L., Bellavia, G. M., Rose, P., & Griffin, D. W. (2003). Once hurt, twice hurtful: How perceived regard regulates daily marital interactions. *Journal of Personality and Social Psychology, 84,* 126–147.

Murray, S. L., Griffin, D. W., Rose, P., & Bellavia, G. M. (2003). Calibrating the sociometer: The relational contingencies of self-esteem. *Journal of Personality and Social Psychology, 85,* 63–84.

Murray, S. L., & Holmes, J. G. (1993). Seeing virtues in faults: Negativity and the transformation of interpersonal narratives in close relationships. *Journal of Personality and Social Psychology, 65,* 707–722.

Murray, S. L., & Holmes, J. G. (1997). A leap of faith? Positive illusions in romantic relationships. *Personality and Social Psychology Bulletin, 23,* 586–604.

Murray, S. L., & Holmes, J. G. (1999). The (mental) ties that bind: Cognitive structures that predict relationship resilience. *Journal of Personality and Social Psychology, 77,* 1228–1244.

Murray, S. L., Holmes, J. G., Bellavia, G., Griffin, D. W., & Dolderman, D. (2002). Kindred spirits? The benefits of egocentrism in close relationships. *Journal of Personality and Social Psychology, 82,* 563–581.

Murray, S. L., Holmes, J. G., Dolderman, D., & Griffin, D. W. (2000). What the motivated mind sees: Comparing friends' perspectives to married partners' views of each other. *Journal of Experimental Social Psychology, 36,* 600–620.

Murray, S. L., Holmes, J. G., & Griffin, D. W. (1996a). The benefits of positive illusions: Idealization and the construction of satisfaction in close relationships. *Journal of Personality and Social Psychology, 70,* 79–98.

Murray, S. L., Holmes, J. G., & Griffin, D. W. (1996b). The self-fulfilling nature of positive illusions in romantic relationships: Love is not blind, but prescient. *Journal of Personality and Social Psychology, 71,* 1155–1180.

Mussweiler, T. (2003). Comparison processes in social judgment: Mechanisms and consequences. *Psychological Review, 110,* 472–489.

Mussweiler, T., Strack, F., & Pfeiffer, T. (2000). Overcoming the inevitable anchoring effect: Considering the opposite compensates for selective accessibility. *Personality and Social Psychology Bulletin, 26,* 1142–1150.

Myers, D. G. (2000). The funds, friends, and faith of very happy people. *American Psychologist, 55,* 56–67.

Myers, D. G., & Bishop, G. D. (1970). Discussion effects on racial attitudes. *Science, 169,* 778–779.

Myers, D. G., & Diener, E. (1995). Who is happy? *Psychological Science, 6,* 10–19.

Myers, D. G., & Lamm, H. (1976). The group polarization phenomenon. *Psychological Bulletin, 83,* 602–627.

Nadler, A., & Fisher, J. D. (1986). The role of threat to self-esteem and perceived control in recipient reactions to health: Theory development and empirical validation. In L. Berkowitz (Ed.), *Advances in experimental social psychology* (Vol. 12, pp. 81–123). New York: Academic Press.

Nannini, D. K., & Myers, L. S. (2000). Jealousy in sexual and emotional infidelity: An alternative to the evolutionary explanation. *The Journal of Sex Research, 37,* 117–122.

Nasby, W., Hayden, B., & DePaulo, B. M. (1980). Attributional bias among aggressive boys to interpret unambiguous social stimuli as displays of hostility. *Journal of Abnormal Psychology, 89,* 459–468.

Nathanson, A. I. (1999). Identifying and Explaining the Relationship Between Parental Mediation and Children's Aggression. *Communication Research, 26,* 124–143.

National Center for Health Statistics. (1991). Advance report of final marriage statistics: 1988. In *Monthly vital statistics report, 39* (12, Supplement 2, pp. 1–20). Hyattsville, MD: Public Health Service.

National Science Foundation. (1998). *Women, minorities, and persons with disabilities in science and engineering: 1998* (NSF Publication No. 96–311). Arlington, VA: Author.

National television violence study. (Vol. 3). (1998). Santa Barbara: Center for Communication and Social Policy, University of California.

Neale, M. A., & Northcraft, G. B. (1986). Experts, amateurs, and refrigerators: Comparing expert and amateur negotiators in a novel task. *Organizational Behavior and Human Decision Processes, 38,* 305–317.

Neiss, M. B., Sedikides, C., & Stevenson, J. (2002). Self-esteem: A behavioural genetic perspective. *European Journal of Personality, 16,* 1–17.

Neisser, U. (1988). Five kinds of self-knowledge. *Philosophical Psychology, 1,* 35–59.

Nelson, C. A. (1987). The recognition of facial expressions in the first two years of life: Mechanisms of development. *Child Development, 58,* 889–909.

Nelson, L. J., & Miller, D. T. (1995). The distinctiveness effect in social categorization: You are what makes you unusual. *Psychological Science, 6,* 246–249.

Nemeth, C. H. (1986). Differential contributions of majority and minority influence. *Psychological Review, 93,* 23–32.

Nemeth, C. J., & Wachtler, J. (1983). Creative problem solving as a result of majority vs. minority influence. *European Journal of Social Psychology, 13,* 45–55.

Neuberg, S. L. (1989). The goal of forming accurate impressions during social interactions: Attenuating the impact of negative expectancies. *Journal of Personality and Social Psychology, 56,* 374–386.

Neumann, R., & Strack, F. (2000). "Mood contagion": The automatic transfer of mood between persons. *Journal of Personality and Social Psychology, 79,* 211–223.

Newby-Clark, I. R., McGregor, I., & Zanna, M. P. (2002). Thinking and caring about cognitive inconsistency: Does attitudinal ambivalence feel uncomfortable? *Journal of Personality and Social Psychology, 82,* 157–166.

Newcomb, T. M. (1943). *Personality and social change.* New York: Dryden.

Newcomb, T. M. (1961). *The acquaintance process.* New York: Holt, Rinehart, & Winston.

Newman, M. L., Pennebaker, J. W., Berry, D. S., & Richards, J. M. (2003). Lying words: Predicting deception from linguistic styles. *Personality and Social Psychology Bulletin, 29,* 665–675.

Neyer, F. J., & Lang, F. R. (2003). Blood is thicker than water: Kinship orientation across adulthood. *Journal of Personality and Social Psychology, 84,* 310–321.

Nicholls, J. G. (1984). Achievement motivation: Conceptions of ability, subjective experience, task choice, and performance. *Psychological Review, 91,* 328–346.

Niedenthal, P. M. (1990). Implicit perception of affective information. *Journal of Experimental Social Psychology, 26,* 505–527.

Niedenthal, P. M., Setterlund, M. B., & Wherry, M. B. (1992). Possible self-complexity and affective reactions to goal-relevant evaluation. *Journal of Personality and Social Psychology, 63,* 5–16.

Niedermeier, K. E., Kerr, N. L., & Messé, L. A. (1999). Jurors' use of naked statistical evidence: Exploring bases and implications of the Wells effect. *Journal of Personality and Social Psychology, 76,* 533–542.

Nier, J. A., Mottola, G. R., & Gaertner, S. L. (2000). The O. J. Simpson criminal verdict as a racially symbolic event: A longitudinal analysis of racial attitude change. *Personality and Social Psychology Bulletin, 26,* 507–516.

Nijstad, B. A., Stroebe, W., & Lodewijkx, H. F. M. (2003). Production blocking and idea generation: Does blocking interfere with cognitive processes? *Journal of Experimental Social Psychology, 39,* 531–548.

Nisbett, R. E., & Cohen, D. (1996). *Culture of honor: The psychology of violence in the South.* Boulder, CO: Westview Press.

Nisbett, R. E., Fong, G. T., Lehman, D. R., & Cheng, P. W. (1987). Teaching reasoning. *Science, 238,* 625–631.

Nisbett, R. E., & Peng, K., Choi, I., & Norenzayan, A. (2001). Culture and systems of thought: Holistic versus analytic cognition. *Psychological Review, 108,* 291–310.

Nisbett, R. E., & Ross, L. (1980). *Human inference: Strategies and shortcomings of social judgment.* Englewood Cliffs, NJ: Prentice-Hall.

Nisbett, R. E., & Wilson, T. D. (1977). Telling more than we can know: Verbal reports on mental processes. *Psychological Review, 84,* 231–259.

Norem, J. K., (2001). *The positive power of negative thinking: Using defensive pessimism to harness anxiety and perform at your peak.* New York: Basic Books.

Norem, J. K., & Cantor, N. (1986). Anticipatory and post hoc cushioning strategies: Optimism and defensive pessimism in "risky" situations. *Cognitive Therapy and Research, 10,* 347–362.

Norenzayan, A., Choi, I., & Nisbett, R. E. (2002). Cultural similarities and differences in social inference: Evidence from behavioral predictions and lay theories of behavior. *Personality and Social Psychology Bulletin, 28,* 109–120.

Norris, F. H., & Kaniasty, K. (1996). Received and perceived social support in times of stress: A test of the social support deterioration deterrence model. *Journal of Personality and Social Psychology, 71,* 498–511.

Novak, D. W., & Lerner, M. J. (1968). Rejection as a consequence of perceived similarity. *Journal of Personality and Social Psychology, 9,* 147–152.

Nuttin, J. M. (1985). Narcissism beyond Gestalt and awareness: The name letter effect. *European Journal of Social Psychology, 15,* 353–361.

Nuttin, J. M. (1987). Affective consequences of mere ownership: The name letter effect in twelve European languages. *European Journal of Social Psychology, 17,* 381–402.

Oakes, P. J., & Turner, J. C. (1980). Social categorization and intergroup behavior: Does minimal intergroup discrimination make social identity more positive? *European Journal of Social Psychology, 10,* 295–301.

O'Brien, L. T., & Crandall, C. S. (2003). Stereotype threat and arousal: Effects on women's math performance. *Personality and Social Psychology Bulletin, 29,* 782–789.

Ochsner, K. N., & Lieberman, M. D. (2001). The emergence of social cognitive neuroscience. *American Psychologist, 56,* 717–734.

O'Connor, K. M., & Carnevale, P. J. (1997). A nasty but effective negotiation strategy: Misrepresentation of a common-value issue. *Personality and Social Psychology Bulletin, 23,* 504–515.

Offner, A. K., Kramer, T. J., & Winter, J. P. (1996). The effects of facilitation, recording, and pauses on group brainstorming. *Small Group Research, 27,* 283–298.

Ohbuchi, K., Kameda, M., & Agarie, N. (1989). Apology as aggression control: Its role in mediating appraisal of and response to harm. *Journal of Personality and Social Psychology, 56,* 219–227.

Öhman, A., Lundqvist, D., & Esteves, F. (2001). The face in the crowd revisited: A threat advantage with schematic stimuli. *Journal of Personality and Social Psychology, 80,* 381–396.

Oliner, S. P., & Oliner, P. M. (1988). *The altruistic personality: Rescuers of Jews in Nazi Germany.* New York: Free Press.

Oliver, M. B. (1994). Portrayals of crime, race, and aggression in "reality-based" police shows: A content analysis. *Journal of Broadcasting and Electronic Media, 38,* 179–192.

Olson, J. M., Vernon, P. A., Harris, J. A., & Jang, K. L. (2001). The heredity of attitudes: A study of twins. *Journal of Personality and Social Psychology, 80,* 845–860.

Olson, M. A., & Fazio, R. H. (2001). Implicit attitude formation through classical conditioning. *Psychological Science, 12,* 413–417.

Omodei, M. M., & Wearing, A. J. (1990). Need satisfaction and involvement in personal projects: Toward an integrative model of subjective well-being. *Journal of Personality and Social Psychology, 59,* 762–769.

Omoto, A. M., & Snyder, M. (1995). Sustained helping without obligation: Motivation, longevity of service, and perceived attitude change among AIDS volunteers. *Journal of Personality and Social Psychology, 68,* 671–686.

Operario, D., & Fiske, S. T. (2001). Ethnic identity moderates perceptions of prejudice: Judgments of personal versus group discrimination and subtle versus blatant bias. *Personality and Social Psychology Bulletin, 27,* 550–561.

Orfield, G. (2001). *Diversity challenged: Evidence on the impact of affirmative action.* Cambridge, MA: Harvard Graduate School of Education.

Orne, M. T. (1962). On the social psychology of the psychological experiment: With particular reference to demand characteristics and their implications. *American Psychologist, 17,* 776–783.

Orth-Gomer, K., Wamala, S. P., Horsten, M., Schenck-Gustafsson, G. K., Schneiderman, N., & Mittelman, M. A. (2000). Marital stress worsens prognosis in women with coronary heart disease: The Stockholm Female Coronary Risk Study. *Journal of the American Medical Association, 284,* 3008–3014.

Osborn, A. F. (1957). *Applied imagination.* New York: Scribner.

Osborne, J. W. (1995). Academics, self-esteem, and race: A look at the underlying assumptions of the disidentification hypothesis. *Personality and Social Psychology Bulletin, 21,* 449–455.

Osgood, C. E. (1962). *An alternative to war or surrender.* Urbana: University of Illinois Press.

Osgood, C. E. (1979). GRIT for MBFR: A proposal for unfreezing force-level postures in Europe. *Peace Research Reviews, 8,* 77–92.

Osgood, C. E., Suci, C. J., & Tannenbaum, P. H. (1957). *The measurement of meaning.* Urbana: University of Illinois Press.

Osterhouse, R. A., & Brock, T. C. (1970). Distraction increases yielding to propaganda by inhibiting counterarguing. *Journal of Personality and Social Psychology, 15,* 344–358.

Österman, K., Björkqvist, K., Lagerspetz, K. M. J., Kaukiainen, A., Landau, S. F., Frczek, A., & Caprara, G. V. (1998). Cross-cultural evidence of female indirect aggression. *Aggressive Behavior, 24,* 1–8.

Ostrom, T. M., & Sedikides, C. (1992). Outgroup-homogeneity effects in natural and minimal groups. *Psychological Bulletin, 112,* 536–552.

O'Sullivan, M. (2003). The fundamental attribution error in detecting deception: The boy-who-cried-wolf effect. *Personality and Social Psychology Bulletin, 29,* 1316–1327.

Ouellette, J. A., & Wood, W. (1998). Habit and intention in everyday life: The multiple processes by which past behavior predicts future behavior. *Psychological Bulletin, 124,* 54–74.

Owens, J., Bower, G. H., & Black, J. B. (1979). The "Soap opera" effect in story recall. *Memory and Cognition, 7,* 185–191.

Oxley, N. L., Dzindolet, M. T., & Paulus, P. B. (1996). The effects of facilitators on the performance of brainstorming

groups. *Journal of Social Behavior and Personality, 11,* 633–646.

Oyserman, D., Coon, H. M., & Kemmelmeier, M. (2002). Rethinking individualism and collectivism: Evaluation of theoretical assumptions and meta-analyses. *Psychological Bulletin, 128,* 3–72.

Papageorgis, D., & McGuire, W. J. (1961). The generality of immunity to persuasion produced by pre-exposure to weakened counterarguments. *Journal of Abnormal and Social Psychology, 62,* 475–481.

Parducci, A. (1984). Value judgments: Toward a relational theory of happiness. In J. R. Eiser (Ed.), *Attitudinal measurement* (pp. 3–21). New York: Springer-Verlag.

Park, B., & Rothbart, M. (1982). Perception of out-group homogeneity and levels of social categorization: Memory for the subordinate attributes of in-group and out-group members. *Journal of Personality and Social Psychology, 42,* 1051–1068.

Park, J., & Banaji, M. R. (2000). Mood and heuristics: The influence of happy and sad states on sensitivity and bias in stereotyping. *Journal of Personality and Social Psychology, 78,* 1005–1023.

Parks, C. D. (1994). The predictive ability of social values in resource dilemmas and public good games. *Personality and Social Psychology Bulletin, 20,* 431–438.

Parks, C. D., & Vu, A. D. (1994). Social dilemma behavior of individuals from highly individualistic and collectivistic cultures. *Journal of Conflict Resolution, 38,* 708–718.

Paulhus, D. L., & Reid, D. B. (1991). Enhancement and denial in socially desirable responding. *Journal of Personality and Social Psychology, 60,* 307–317.

Paulhus, P. B., Dzindolet, M. T., Poletes, G., & Camacho, L. M. (1993). Perception of performance in group brainstorming: Illusions of group productivity. *Personality and Social Psychology Bulletin, 19,* 78–89.

Payne, B. K. (2001). Prejudice and perception: The role of automatic and controlled processes in misperceiving a weapon. *Journal of Personality and Social Psychology, 81,* 181–192.

Payne, B. K., Lambert, A. J., & Jacoby, L. L. (2002). Best laid plans: Effects of goals on accessibility bias and cognitive control in race-based misperceptions of weapons. *Journal of Experimental Social Psychology, 38,* 384–396.

Payne, D. L., Lonsway, K. A., & Fitzgerald, L. F. (1998). Rape myth acceptance: Exploration of its structure and its measurement using the Illinois Rape Myth Acceptance Scale. *Journal of Research in Personality, 33,* 27–68.

Pedersen, W. C., Aviles, F. E., Ito, T. A., Miller, N., & Pollock, V. E. (2002). Psychological experimentation on alcohol-induced human aggression. *Aggression and Violent Behavior, 7,* 293–312.

Pedersen, W. C., Gonzales, C., & Miller, N. (2000). The moderating effect of trivial triggering provocation on displaced aggression. *Journal of Personality and Social Psychology, 78,* 913–927.

Pelham, B. W., Carvallo, M., DeHart, T., & Jones, J. T. (2003). Assessing the validity of implicit egotism: A reply to Gallucci (2003). *Journal of Personality and Social Psychology, 85,* 800–807.

Pelham, B. W., Mirenberg, M. C., & Jones, J. T. (2002). Why Susie sells seashells by the seashore: Implicit egotism and major life decisions. *Journal of Personality and Social Psychology, 82,* 469–487.

Pelham, B. W., & Neter, E. (1995). The effect of motivation on judgment depends on the difficulty of the judgment. *Journal of Personality and Social Psychology, 68,* 581–594.

Pelham, B. W., & Wachsmuth, J. O. (1995). The waxing and waning of the social self: Assimilation and contrast in social comparison. *Journal of Personality and Social Psychology, 69,* 825–838.

Peng, K., & Knowles, E. D. (2003). Culture, education, and the attribution of physical causality. *Personality and Social Psychology Bulletin, 29,* 1272–1284.

Pennebaker, J. W., Dyer, M. A., Caulkins, R. J., Litowitz, D. L., Ackreman, P. L., Anderson, D. B., et al. (1979). Don't the girls get prettier at closing time: A country and western application to psychology. *Personality and Social Psychology Bulletin, 5,* 122–125.

Pennebaker, J. W., Mayne, T. J., & Francis, M. E. (1997). Linguistic predictors of adaptive bereavement. *Journal of Personality and Social Psychology, 72,* 863–871.

Pennebaker, J. W., & O'Heeron, R. C. (1984). Confiding in others and illness rates among spouses of suicide and accidental-death victims. *Journal of Abnormal Psychology, 93,* 473–476.

Penner, L. A. (2002). Dispositional and organizational influences on sustained volunteerism: An interactionist perspective. *Journal of Social Issues, 58,* 447–467.

Penner, L. A., & Finkelstein, M. A. (1998). Dispositional and structural determinants of volunteerism. *Journal of Personality and Social Psychology, 74,* 525–537.

Penner, L. A., & Fritzsche, B. A. (1993). Magic Johnson and reactions to people with AIDS: A natural experiment. *Journal of Applied Social Psychology, 23,* 1035–1050.

Pepitone, A., & DiNubile, M. (1976). Contrast effects in judgments of crime severity and the punishment of criminal violators. *Journal of Personality and Social Psychology, 33,* 448–459.

Peplau, L. A., & Perlman, D. (1982). Perspectives on loneliness. In L. A. Peplau & D. Perlman (Eds.), *Loneliness: A sourcebook of current theory, research, and therapy* (pp. 1–18). New York: Wiley.

Perdue, C. W., Dovidio, J. F., Gurtman, M. B., & Tyler, R. B. (1990). Us and them: Social categorization and the process of intergroup bias. *Journal of Personality and Social Psychology, 59,* 475–486.

Perdue, C. W., & Gurtman, M. B. (1990). Evidence for the automaticity of ageism. *Journal of Experimental Social Psychology, 26,* 199–216.

Perloff, L. S., & Fetzer, B. K. (1986). Self-other judgments and perceived vulnerability of victimization. *Journal of Personality and Social Psychology, 50,* 502–510.

Perrett, D. I., Lee, K. J., Penton-Voak, I. S., Rowland, D. R., Yoshikawa, S., Burt, D. M., et al. (1998). Effects of sexual dimorphism on facial attractiveness. *Nature, 394,* 884–887.

Pessin, J. (1933). The comparative effects of social and mechanical stimulation on memorizing. *American Journal of Psychology, 45,* 263–270.

Peters, L. H., Hartke, D. D., & Pohlmann, J. T. (1985). Fiedler's contingency theory of leadership: An application of the meta-analysis procedures of Schmidt and Hunter. *Psychological Bulletin, 97,* 274–285.

Peterson, B. E., Doty, R. M., & Winter, D. G. (1993). Authoritarianism and attitudes toward contemporary social issues. *Personality and Social Psychology Bulletin, 19,* 174–184.

Peterson, R. C., & Thurstone, L. L. (1970). *Motion pictures and the social attitudes of children.* New York: Arno Press and the New York Times. (Original work published 1933)

Petrie, K. J., Booth, R. J., & Pennebaker, J. W. (1998). The immunological effects of thought suppression. *Journal of Personality and Social Psychology, 75,* 1264–1272.

Pettigrew, T. W. (1979). The ultimate attribution error: Extending Allport's cognitive analysis of prejudice. *Personality and Social Psychology Bulletin, 5,* 461–476.

Pettigrew, T. W. (1997). Generalized intergroup contact effects on prejudice. *Personality and Social Psychology Bulletin, 23,* 173–185.

Petty, R. E., & Cacioppo, J. T. (1977). Forewarning, cognitive responding, and resistance to persuasion. *Journal of Personality and Social Psychology, 35,* 645–655.

Petty, R. E., & Cacioppo, J. T. (1979). Effects of forewarning of persuasive intent and involvement on cognitive responses and persuasion. *Personality and Social Psychology Bulletin, 5,* 173–176.

Petty, R. E., & Cacioppo, J. T. (1981). *Attitudes and persuasion: Classic and contemporary approaches.* Dubuque, IA: Wm. C. Brown.

Petty, R. E., & Cacioppo, J. T. (1984). The effects of involvement on responses to argument quantity and quality: Central and peripheral routes to persuasion. *Journal of Personality and Social Psychology, 46,* 69–81.

Petty, R. E., & Cacioppo, J. T. (1986). *Communication and persuasion: Central and peripheral routes to attitude change.* New York: Springer-Verlag.

Petty, R. E., & Cacioppo, J. T. (1990). Involvement and persuasion: Tradition versus integration. *Psychological Bulletin, 107,* 367–374.

Petty, R. E., Cacioppo, J. T., & Goldman, R. (1981). Personal involvement as a determinant of argument-based persuasion. *Journal of Personality and Social Psychology, 41,* 847–855.

Petty, R. E., Cacioppo, J. T., & Schumann, D. W. (1983). Central and peripheral routes to advertising effectiveness: The moderating role of involvement. *Journal of Consumer Research, 10,* 135–146.

Petty, R. E., & Krosnick, J. A. (Eds.). (1995). *Attitude strength: Antecedents and consequences.* Mahwah, NJ: Erlbaum.

Petty, R. E., Ostrom, T. M., & Brock, T. C. (Eds.). (1981). *Cognitive responses in persuasion.* Mahwah, NJ: Erlbaum.

Petty, R. E., Schumann, D. W., Richman, S. A., & Strathman, A. J. (1993). Positive mood and persuasion: Different roles for affect under high- and low-elaboration conditions. *Journal of Personality and Social Psychology, 64,* 5–20.

Petty, R. E., & Wegener, D. T. (1998). Attitude change: Multiple roles for persuasion variables. In D. T. Gilbert, S. T. Fiske, & G. Lindzey (Eds.), *Handbook of social psychology* (4th ed., pp. 323–390). New York: McGraw-Hill.

Petty, R. E., Wells, G. L., & Brock, T. C. (1976). Distraction can enhance or reduce yielding to propaganda: Thought disruption versus effort justification. *Journal of Personality and Social Psychology, 34,* 874–884.

Pfeffer, J. (1998). Understanding organizations: Concepts and controversies. In D. T. Gilbert, S. T. Fiske, & G. Lindzey (Eds.), *Handbook of social psychology* (4th ed., Vol. 2, pp. 733–777). New York: McGraw-Hill.

Phillips, D. P. (1974). The influence of suggestion on suicide: Substantive and theoretical implications of the Werther effect. *American Sociological Review, 39,* 340–354.

Phillips, D. P., & Carstensen, L. L. (1986). Clustering of teenage suicides after television news stories about suicide. *New England Journal of Medicine, 315,* 685–689.

Phinney, J. S. (1990). Ethnic identity in adolescents and adults: Review of research. *Psychological Bulletin, 108,* 499–514.

Piaget, J. (1929). *The child's conception of the world.* London: Routledge & Kegan Paul.

Pickett, C. L., & Brewer, M. B. (2001). Assimilation and differentiation needs as motivational determinants of perceived ingroup and outgroup homogeneity. *Journal of Experimental Social Psychology, 37,* 341–348.

Pickett, C. L., Silver, M. D., & Brewer, M. B. (2002). The impact of assimilation and differentiation needs on perceived group importance and judgments of group size. *Personality and Social Psychology Bulletin, 28,* 546–558.

Piliavin, J. A. (2003). Doing well by doing good: Benefits for the benefactor. In C. Keyes & J. Haidt (Eds.), *Flourishing: Positive psychology and the life well-lived* (pp. 227–247). Washington, DC: APA.

Piliavin, J. A., & Callero, P. L. (1991). *Giving blood: The development of an altruistic identity.* Baltimore, MD: Johns Hopkins University Press.

Piliavin, J. A., & Unger, R. K. (1985). The helpful but helpless female: Myth or reality? In V. E. O'Leary, R. K. Unger, & B. S. Wallston (Eds.), *Women, gender, and social psychology* (pp. 149–189). Mahwah, NJ: Erlbaum.

Pinker, S. (2002). *The blank slate: The modern denial of human nature.* New York: Viking.

Plant, E. A., & Devine, P. G. (1998). Internal and external motivation to respond without prejudice. *Journal of Personality and Social Psychology, 75,* 811–832.

Plous, S. (1991). Biases in the assimilation of technological breakdowns: Do accidents make us safer? *Journal of Applied Social Psychology, 21,* 1058–1082.

Plous, S. (1993). *The psychology of judgment and decision making.* New York: McGraw-Hill.

Pollak, S. D., Cicchetti, D., Hornung, K., & Reed, A. (2000). Recognizing emotion in faces: Developmental effects of child abuse and neglect. *Developmental Psychology, 36,* 679–688.

Pollak, S. D., & Kistler, D. J. (2002). Early experience is associated with the development of categorical representations for facial expressions of emotion. *Proceedings of the National Academy of Sciences, 99,* 9072–9076.

Pollak, S. D., & Sinha, P. (2002). Effects of early experience on children's recognition of facial displays of emotion. *Developmental Psychology, 38,* 784–791.

Pornpitakpan, C. (2004). The persuasiveness of source credibility: A critical review of five decades' evidence. *Journal of Applied Social Psychology, 34,* 243–281.

Porter, R. H. (1987). Kin recognition: Functions and mediating mechanisms. In C. Crawford, M. Smith, & D. Krebs (Eds.), *Sociobiology and psychology: Ideas, issues, and applications* (pp. 175–203). Mahwah, NJ: Erlbaum.

Postmes, T., & Spears, R. (1998). Deindividuation and antinormative behavior: A meta-analysis. *Psychological Bulletin, 123,* 238–259.

Postmes, T., Spears, R., & Cihangir, S. (2001). Quality of decision making and group norms. *Journal of Personality and Social Psychology, 80,* 918–930.

Povinelli, D. J., Rulf, A. B., Landau, K. R., & Bierschwale, D. T. (1993). Self-recognition in chimpanzees (*Pan troglodytes*): Distribution, ontogeny, and patterns of emergence. *Journal of Comparative Psychology, 107,* 347–372.

Powers, W. T. (1973). *Behavior: The control of perception.* Chicago: Aldine.

Pratkanis, A. R., & Aronson, E. (2001). *Age of propaganda: The everyday use and abuse of persuasion.* New York: Freeman.

Pratkanis, A. R., Eskenazi, J., & Greenwald, A. G. (1994). What you expect is what you believe (but not necessarily what you get): A test of the effectiveness of subliminal self-help audiotapes. *Basic and Applied Social Psychology, 15,* 251–276.

Pratkanis, A. R., Greenwald, A. G., Leippe, M. R., & Baumgardner, M. H. (1988). In search of reliable persuasion effects: III. The sleeper effect is dead: Long live the sleeper effect. *Journal of Personality and Social Psychology, 54,* 203–218.

Pratkanis, A. R., & Turner, M. E. (1994). Nine principles of successful affirmative action: Mr. Branch Rickey, Mr. Jackie Robinson, and the integration of baseball. *Nine: A Journal of Baseball History and Social Policy Perspectives, 3,* 36–65.

Pratto, F., Sidanius, J., Stallworth, L. M., & Malle, B. F. (1994). Social dominance orientation: A personality variable predicting social and political attitudes. *Journal of Personality and Social Psychology, 67,* 741–763.

Priester, J. R., & Petty, R. E. (1996). The gradual threshold model of ambivalence: Relating the positive and negative bases of attitudes to subjective ambivalence. *Journal of Personality and Social Psychology, 71,* 431–449.

Priester, J. R., & Petty, R. E. (2001). Extending the bases of subjective attitudinal ambivalence: Interpersonal and intrapersonal antecedents of evaluative tension. *Journal of Personality and Social Psychology, 80,* 19–34.

Pronin, E., Gilovich, T., & Ross, L. (2004). Objectivity in the eye of the beholder: Divergent perceptions of bias in self versus others. *Psychological Review, 111,* 781–799.

Pronin, E., Kruger, J., Savitsky, K., & Ross, L. (2001). You don't know me but I know you: The illusion of asymmetric insight. *Journal of Personality and Social Psychology, 81,* 636–656.

Pronin, E., Lin, D. Y., & Ross, L. (2002). The bias blind spot: Perceptions of bias in self versus others. *Personality and Social Psychology Bulletin, 28,* 369–381.

Pronin, E., Steele, C. M., & Ross, L. (2004). Identity bifurcation in response to stereotype threat: Women and mathematics. *Journal of Experimental Social Psychology, 40,* 152–168.

Pruitt, D. G. (1998). Social conflict. In D. T. Gilbert, S. T. Fiske, & G. Lindzey (Eds.), *Handbook of social psychology* (4th ed., Vol. 2, pp. 470–503). New York: McGraw-Hill.

Pruitt, D. G., & Kimmel, M. J. (1977). Twenty years of experimental gaming: Critique, synthesis, and suggestions for the future. *Annual Review of Psychology, 28,* 363–392.

Pryor, J. B., Reeder, G. D., & McManus, J. A. (1991). Fear and loathing in the workplace: Reactions to AIDS-infected co-workers. *Personality and Social Psychology Bulletin, 17,* 133–139.

Pyszczynski, T., & Greenberg, J. (1987). Toward an integration of cognitive and motivational perspectives on social inference: A biased hypothesis-testing model. In L. Berkowitz (Ed.), *Advances in experimental social psychology* (Vol. 20, pp. 297–340). New York: Academic Press.

Pyszczynski, T., Greenberg, J., Solomon, S., Arndt, J., & Schimel, J. (2004).

Why do people need self-esteem? A theoretical and empirical review. *Psychological Bulletin, 130,* 435–468.

Quattrone, G. A. (1982). Overattribution and unit formation: When behavior engulfs the person. *Journal of Personality and Social Psychology, 42,* 593–607.

Quattrone, G. A., & Jones, E. E. (1980). The perception of variability within in-groups and out-groups: Implications for the law of small numbers. *Journal of Personality and Social Psychology, 38,* 141–152.

Quinn, D. M., & Spencer, S. J. (2001). The interference of stereotype threat with women's generation of mathematical problem-solving strategies. *Journal of Social Issues, 57,* 55–71.

Raghunathan, R., & Trope, Y. (2002). Walking the tightrope between feeling good and being accurate: Mood as a resource in processing persuasive messages. *Journal of Personality and Social Psychology, 83,* 510–525.

Raskin, R., & Terry, H. (1988). A principal-components analysis of the Narcissistic Personality Inventory and further evidence of its construct validity. *Journal of Personality and Social Psychology, 54,* 890–902.

Rawsthorne, L. J., & Elliot, A. J. (1999). Achievement goals and intrinsic motivation: A meta-analytic review. *Personality and Social Psychology Review, 3,* 326–344.

Reeder, G. D. (1993). Trait-behavior relations and dispositional inference. *Personality and Social Psychology Bulletin, 19,* 586–593.

Regan, D. T. (1971). Effects of a favor and liking on compliance. *Journal of Experimental Social Psychology, 7,* 627–639.

Regan, P. C., & Sprecher, S. (1995). Gender differences in the value of contributions to intimate relationships: Egalitarian relationships are not always perceived to be equitable. *Sex Roles, 33,* 221–238.

Reifman, A. S., Larrick, R. P., & Fein, S. (1991). Temper and temperature on the diamond: The heat-aggression relationship in major league baseball.

Personality and Social Psychology Bulletin, 17, 580–585.

Reinecke, J., Schmidt, P., & Ajzen, I. (1996). Application of the theory of planned behavior to adolescents' condom use: A panel study. *Journal of Applied Social Psychology, 26,* 749–772.

Reis, H. T., & Shaver, P. (1988). Intimacy as an interpersonal process. In S. Duck (Ed.), *Handbook of personal relationships: Theory, research, and interventions* (pp. 367–389). New York: Wiley.

Reis, H. T., Senchak, M., & Solomon, B. (1985). Sex differences in the intimacy of social interaction: Further examination of potential explanations. *Journal of Personality and Social Psychology, 48,* 1204–1217.

Reis, H. T., Wheeler, L., Kernis, M. H., Spiegel, N., & Nezlek, J. (1985). On specificity in the impact of social participation on physical and psychological health. *Journal of Personality and Social Psychology, 48,* 456–471.

Reisenzein, R. (1983). The Schachter theory of emotion: Two decades later. *Psychological Bulletin, 94,* 239–264.

Reiss, D., & Marino, L. (2001). Mirror self-recognition in the bottlenose dolphin: A case of cognitive convergence. *Proceedings of the National Academy of Sciences, 98,* 5937–5942.

Rescorla, R. A. (1988). Pavlovian conditioning: It's not what you think it is. *American Psychologist, 43,* 151–160.

Reynolds, D. J., Jr., & Gifford, R. (2001). The sounds and sights of intelligence: A lens model channel analysis. *Personality and Social Psychology Bulletin, 27,* 187–200.

Reynolds, K. J., Turner, J. C., & Haslam, S. A. (2000). When are we better than them and they worse than us? A closer look at social discrimination in positive and negative domains. *Journal of Personality and Social Psychology, 78,* 64–80.

Rhodes, G., & Tremewan, T. (1996). Averageness, exaggeration, and facial attractiveness. *Psychological Science, 7,* 105–110.

Rhodes, N., & Wood, W. (1992). Self-esteem and intelligence affect influenceability. *Psychological Bulletin, 111,* 156–171.

Rhodewalt, F., & Morf, C. C. (1998). On self-aggrandizement and anger: A temporal analysis of narcissism and

affective reactions to success and failure. *Journal of Personality and Social Psychology, 74,* 672–685.

Rholes, W. S., Simpson, J. A., Campbell, L., & Grich, J. (2001). Adult attachment and the transition to parenthood. *Journal of Personality and Social Psychology, 81,* 421–435.

Rholes, W. S., Simpson, J. A., & Oriña, M. M. (1999). Attachment and anger in an anxiety-provoking situation. *Journal of Personality and Social Psychology, 76,* 940–957.

Richards, J. M., & Gross, J. J. (1999). Composure at any cost? The cognitive consequences of emotion suppression. *Personality and Social Psychology Bulletin, 25,* 1033–1044.

Richards, J. M., & Gross, J. J. (2000). Emotion regulation and memory: The cognitive consequence of keeping one's cool. *Journal of Personality and Social Psychology, 79,* 410–424.

Richards, Z., & Hewstone, M. (2001). Subtyping and subgrouping: Processes for the prevention and promotion of stereotype change. *Personality and Social Psychology Review, 5,* 52–73.

Richeson, J. A., & Nussbaum, R. J. (2004). The impact of multiculturalism versus color-blindness on racial bias. *Journal of Experimental Social Psychology, 40,* 417–423.

Riggio, R. E., & Friedman, H. S. (1986). Impression formation: The role of expressive behavior. *Journal of Personality and Social Psychology, 50,* 421–427.

Robertson, L. S. (1977). Car crashes: Perceived vulnerability and willingness to pay for crash protection. *Journal of Community Health, 3,* 136–141.

Robins, R. W., Spranca, M. D., & Mendelsohn, G. A. (1996). The actor–observer effect revisited: Effects of individual differences and repeated social interactions on actor and observer attributions. *Journal of Personality and Social Psychology, 71,* 375–389.

Robinson, R. J., Keltner, D., Ward, A., & Ross, L. (1995). Actual versus assumed differences in construal: "Naïve realism" in intergroup perception and conflict. *Journal of Personality and Social Psychology, 68,* 404–417.

Rodin, J. (1986). Aging and health: Effects of the sense of control. *Science, 233,* 1271–1276.

Roese, N. J., & Jamieson, D. W. (1993). Twenty years of bogus pipeline research: A critical review and meta-analysis. *Psychological Bulletin, 121,* 133–148.

Rogers, C. R. (1961). *On becoming a person.* Boston: Houghton Mifflin.

Rogers, R. W. (1983). Cognitive and physiological processes in fear appeals and attitude change: A revised theory of protection motivation. In J. Cacioppo and R. Petty (Eds.), *Social psychophysiology: A sourcebook* (pp. 153–176). New York: Guilford.

Rogers, T. B., Kuiper, N. A., & Kirker, W. S. (1977). Self-reference and the encoding of personal information. *Journal of Personality and Social Psychology, 35,* 677–688.

Rohrer, J. H., Baron, S. H., Hoffman, E. L., & Swander, D. V. (1954). The stability of autokinetic judgments. *Journal of Abnormal and Social Psychology, 49,* 595–597.

Rokeach, M. (1968). *Beliefs, attitudes, and values: A theory of organization and change.* San Francisco: Jossey-Bass.

Roney, J. R. (2003). Effects of visual exposure to the opposite sex: Cognitive aspects of mate attraction in human males. *Personality and Social Psychology Bulletin, 29,* 393–404.

Rook, K. S. (1987). Social support versus companionship: Effects on life stress, loneliness, and evaluations by others. *Journal of Personality and Social Psychology, 52,* 1132–1147.

Rosekrans, M. A., & Hartup, W. W. (1967). Imitative influences of consistent and inconsistent response consequences to a model on aggressive behavior in children. *Journal of Personality and Social Psychology, 4,* 429–434.

Rosenbaum, M. E. (1986). The repulsion hypothesis: On the nondevelopment of relationships. *Journal of Personality and Social Psychology, 51,* 1156–1166.

Rosenberg, M. (1965). *Society and the adolescent self-image.* Princeton, NJ: Princeton University Press.

Rosenberg, M. J. (1969). The conditions and consequences of evaluation apprehension. In R. Rosenthal & R. C. Rosnow (Eds.), *Artifacts in behavioral research* (pp. 280–350). New York: Academic Press.

Rosenfield, D., & Stephan, W. G. (1978). Sex differences in attributions for sex-typed tasks. *Journal of Personality, 46,* 244–259.

Rosenthal, R. (1963). On the social psychology of the psychological experiment: The experimenter's hypothesis as unintended determinant of the experimental results. *American Scientist, 51,* 268–283.

Rosenthal, R. (1987). From unconscious experimenter bias to teacher expectancy effects. In J. Dusek (Ed.), *Teacher expectancies* (pp. 37–65). Mahwah, NJ: Erlbaum.

Rosenthal, R. (1994). Interpersonal expectancy effects: A 30-year perspective. *Current Directions in Psychological Science, 3,* 176–179.

Rosenthal, R., & DePaulo, B. M. (1979). Sex differences in eavesdropping on nonverbal cues. *Journal of Personality and Social Psychology, 37,* 273–285.

Rosenthal, R., & Jacobson, L. (1968). *Pygmalion in the classroom.* New York: Holt, Rinehart, & Winston.

Ross, C. E., Mirowsky, J., & Goldsteen, K. (1990). The impact of the family on health: The decade in review. *Journal of Marriage and the Family, 52,* 1059–1078.

Ross, L. (1977). The intuitive scientist and his shortcomings: Distortions in the attribution process. In L. Berkowitz (Ed.), *Advances in experimental social psychology* (Vol. 10, pp. 173–220). New York: Academic Press.

Ross, L., Greene, D., & House, P. (1977). The false consensus phenomenon: An attributional bias in self-perception and social-perception processes. *Journal of Experimental Social Psychology, 13,* 279–301.

Ross, L., Lepper, M. R., & Hubbard, M. (1975). Perseverance in self-perception and social perception: Biased attributional processes in the debriefing paradigm. *Journal of Personality and Social Psychology, 32,* 880–892.

Ross, L., Lepper, M. R., Strack, F., & Steinmetz, J. (1977). Social explanation and social expectation: Effects of real and hypothetical explanations on subjective likelihood. *Journal of Personality and Social Psychology, 35,* 817–829.

Ross, L., & Stillinger, C. (1991). Barriers to conflict resolution. *Negotiation Journal, 7,* 389–404.

Ross, M., & Sicoly, P. (1979). Egocentric biases in availability and attribution. *Journal of Personality and Social Psychology, 37,* 322–336.

Ross, M., Xun, W. Q. E., & Wilson, A. E. (2002). Language and the bicultural self. *Personality and Social Psychology Bulletin, 28,* 1040–1050.

Rothman, A. J., Martino, S. C., Bedell, B. T., Detweiler, J. B., & Salovey, P. (1999). The systematic influence of gain-and loss-framed messages on interest in and use of different types of health behavior. *Personality and Social Psychology Bulletin, 25,* 1355–1369.

Rothman, A. J., & Salovey, P. (1997). Shaping perceptions to motivate healthy behavior: The role of message framing. *Psychological Bulletin, 121,* 3–19.

Rotter, J. B. (1954). *Social learning and clinical psychology.* Englewood Cliffs, NJ: Prentice-Hall.

Rotton, J., & Cohn, E. G. (2000). Violence is a curvilinear function of temperature in Dallas: A replication. *Journal of Personality and Social Psychology, 78,* 1074–1081.

Rowatt, W. C., Cunningham, M. R., & Druen, P. B. (1998). Deception to get a date. *Personality and Social Psychology Bulletin, 24,* 1228–1242.

Rubin, J. Z., Provenzano, F. J., & Luria, Z. (1974). The eye of the beholder: Parents' views on sex of newborns. *American Journal of Orthopsychiatry, 44,* 512–519.

Rubin, M., & Hewstone, M. (1998). Social identity theory's self-esteem hypothesis: A review and some suggestions for clarification. *Personality and Social Psychology Review, 2,* 40–62.

Rubin, Z. (1973). *Liking and loving: An invitation to social psychology.* New York: Holt, Rinehart, & Winston.

Rucker, D. D., & Petty, R. E. (2004). When resistance is futile: Consequences of failed counterarguing for attitude certainty. *Journal of Personality and Social Psychology, 86,* 219–235.

Rucker, D. D., & Pratkanis, A. R. (2001). Projection as an interpersonal influence tactic: The effects of the pot calling the kettle black. *Personality and Social Psychology Bulletin, 27,* 1494–1507.

Ruder, M., & Bless, H. (2003). Mood and the reliance on the ease of retrieval heuristic. *Journal of Personality and Social Psychology, 85,* 20–32.

Rudman, L. A. (1998). Self-promotion as a risk factor for women: The costs and benefits of counterstereotypical impression management. *Journal of Personality and Social Psychology, 74,* 629–645.

Rudman, L. A., & Glick, P. (1999). Feminized management and backlash toward agentic women: The hidden costs to women of a kinder, gentler, image of middle managers. *Journal of Personality and Social Psychology, 77,* 1004–1010.

Rudman, L. A., & Kilianski, S. E. (2000). Implicit and explicit attitudes toward female authority. *Personality and Social Psychology Bulletin, 26,* 1315–1328.

Rugg, D. (1941). Experiments in wording questions. *Public Opinion Quarterly, 5,* 91–92.

Rusbult, C. E. (1980). Commitment and satisfaction in romantic associations: A test of the investment model. *Journal of Experimental Social Psychology, 16,* 172–186.

Rusbult, C. E. (1983). A longitudinal test of the investment model: The development (and deterioration) of satisfaction and commitment in heterosexual involvements. *Journal of Personality and Social Psychology, 45,* 101–117.

Rusbult, C. E., Johnson, D. J., & Morrow, G. D. (1986a). Predicting satisfaction and commitment in adult romantic involvements: An assessment of the generalizability of the investment model. *Social Psychology Quarterly, 49,* 81–89.

Rusbult, C. E., Johnson, D. J., & Morrow, G. D. (1986b). Determinants and consequences of exit, voice, loyalty, and neglect: Responses to dissatisfaction in adult romantic involvements. *Human Relations, 39,* 45–63.

Rusbult, C. E., Johnson, D. J., & Morrow, G. D. (1986c). Impact of couple patterns of problem solving on distress and nondistress in dating relationships. *Journal of Personality and Social Psychology, 50,* 744–753.

Rusbult, C. E., & Martz, J. M. (1995). Remaining in an abusive relationship: An investment model analysis of nonvoluntary dependence. *Personality and Social Psychology Bulletin, 21,* 558–571.

Rusbult, C. E., Van Lange, P. A. M., Wildschut, T., Yovetich, N. A., & Verette, J. (2000). Perceived superiority in close relationships: Why it exists and persists. *Journal of Personality and Social Psychology, 79,* 521–545.

Rusbult, C. E., Verette, J., Whitney, G. A., Slovik, L. F., & Lipkus, I. (1991). Accommodation processes in close relationships: Theory and preliminary empirical evidence. *Journal of Personality and Social Psychology, 60,* 53–78.

Rusbult, C. E., Zembrodt, I. M., & Gunn, L. K. (1982). Exit, voice, loyalty, and neglect: Responses to dissatisfaction in romantic involvements. *Journal of Personality and Social Psychology, 43,* 1230–1242.

Rushton, J. P. (1975). Generosity in children: Immediate and long term effects of modeling, preaching, and moral judgment. *Journal of Personality and Social Psychology, 31,* 459–466.

Rushton, J. P. (1982). Social learning theory and the development of prosocial behavior. In N. Eisenberg (Ed.), *The development of prosocial behavior* (pp. 77–105). New York: Academic Press.

Rushton, J. P. (1988). Genetic similarity, mate choice, and fecundity in humans. *Ethology and Sociobiology, 9,* 329–333.

Rushton, J. P. (1989). Genetic similarity, human altruism, and group selection. *Behavioral and Brain Sciences, 12,* 503–518.

Rushton, J. P., Fulker, D. W., Neale, M. C., Nias, D. K. B., & Eysenck, H. J. (1986). Altruism and aggression: The heritability of individual differences. *Journal of Personality and Social Psychology, 50,* 1192–1198.

Rushton, J. P., & Teachman, G. (1978). The effects of positive reinforcement, attributions, and punishment on model induced altruism in children. *Personality and Social Psychology Bulletin, 4,* 322–325.

Russell, D., Peplau, L. A., & Cutrona, C. E. (1980). The revised UCLA Loneliness Scale: Concurrent and discriminant validity evidence. *Journal of Personality and Social Psychology, 39,* 472–480.

Russell, J. A. (1991). Culture and the categorization of emotion. *Psychological Bulletin, 110,* 426–450.

Russell, J. A. (1994). Is there universal recognition of emotion from facial expression? A review of the cross-cultural studies. *Psychological Bulletin, 115,* 102–141.

Rusting, C. L., & Nolen-Hoeksema, S. (1998). Regulating responses to anger: Effects of rumination and distraction on angry mood. *Journal of Personality and Social Psychology, 74,* 790–803.

Ryan, R. M., & Brown, K. W. (2003). Why we don't need self-esteem: On fundamental needs, contingent love, and mindfulness. *Psychological Inquiry, 14,* 71–76.

Ryan, R. M., & Deci, E. L. (2000). Self-determination theory and the facilitation of intrinsic motivation, social development, and well-being. *American Psychologist, 55,* 68–78.

Ryan, R. M., & Deci, E. L. (2001). On happiness and human potentials: A review of research on hedonic and eudaimonic well-being. *Annual Review of Psychology, 52,* 141–166.

Ryan, R. M., Mims, V., & Koestner, R. (1983). Relation of reward contingency and interpersonal context to intrinsic motivation: A review and test using cognitive evaluation theory. *Journal of Personality and Social Psychology, 45,* 736–770.

Ryff, C. D. (1989). Happiness is everything, or is it? Explorations on the meaning of psychological well-being. *Journal of Personality and Social Psychology, 57,* 1069–1081.

Sabini, J., Siepmann, M., & Stein, J. (2001). The really fundamental error in social psychological research. *Psychological Inquiry, 12,* 1–15.

Sachs, P. R. (1982). Avoidance of diagnostic information in self-evaluation of ability. *Personality and Social Psychology Bulletin, 8,* 242–246.

Sackett, P. R., Hardison, C. M., & Cullen, M. J. (2004). On interpreting stereotype threat as accounting for African American–White differences on cognitive tests. *American Psychologist, 59,* 7–13.

Sagar, H. A., & Schofield, J. W. (1980). Racial and behavioral cues in Black and White children's perceptions of ambiguously aggressive acts. *Journal of Personality and Social Psychology, 39,* 590–598.

Sagi, A., & Hoffman, M. L. (1976). Empathic distress in the newborn. *Developmental Psychology, 12,* 175–176.

Sagristano, M. D., Trope, Y., & Liberman, N. (2002). Time-dependent gambling: Odds now, money later. *Journal of Experimental Psychology: General, 131,* 364–376.

Salancik, G. R., & Conway, M. (1975). Attitude inference from salient and relevant cognitive content about behavior. *Journal of Personality and Social Psychology, 32,* 829–840.

Salovey, P., Rothman, A. J., & Rodin, J. (1998). In D. T. Gilbert, S. T. Fiske, & G. Lindzey (Eds.), *Handbook of social psychology* (4th ed., Vol. 2, pp. 633–683). New York: McGraw-Hill.

Sanders, G. S., & Baron, R. S. (1977). Is social comparison irrelevant for producing choice shifts? *Journal of Experimental Social Psychology, 13,* 303–314.

Sanitioso, R., Kunda, Z., & Fong, G. T. (1990). Motivated recruitment of autobiographical memories. *Journal of Personality and Social Psychology, 59,* 229–241.

Sanna, L. J. (1992). Self-efficacy theory: Implications for social facilitation and social loafing. *Journal of Personality and Social Psychology, 62,* 774–786.

Santos, M. D., Leve, C., & Pratkanis, A. R. (1994). "Hey buddy, can you spare seventeen cents?" Mindful persuasion and the pique technique. *Journal of Applied Social Psychology, 24,* 755–764.

Sarason, I. G., Sarason, B. R., Pierce, G. R., Shearin, E. N., & Sayers, M. H. (1991). A social learning approach to increasing blood donations. *Journal of Applied Social Psychology, 21,* 896–918.

Savitsky, K., Epley, N., & Gilovich, T. (2001). Do others judge us as harshly as we think? Overestimating the impact of our failures, shortcomings, and mishaps. *Journal of Personality and Social Psychology, 81,* 44–56.

Savitsky, K., Gilovich, T., Berger, G., & Medvec, V. H. (2003). Is our absence as conspicuous as we think? Overestimating the salience and impact of one's absence from a group. *Journal of Experimental Social Psychology, 39,* 386–392.

Saxe, L. (1994). Detection of deception: Polygraph and integrity tests. *Current Directions in Psychological Science, 3,* 69–74.

Saxe, L., Dougherty, D., & Cross, T. (1985). The validity of polygraph testing: Scientific analysis and public controversy. *American Psychologist, 40,* 355–366.

Schachter, S. (1951). Deviation, rejection, and communication. *Journal of Abnormal and Social Psychology, 46,* 190–207.

Schachter, S. (1959). *The psychology of affiliation.* Stanford, CA: Stanford University Press.

Schachter, S. (1964). The interaction of cognitive and physiological determinants of emotional state. In L. Berkowitz (Ed.), *Advances in experimental social psychology* (Vol. 1, pp. 48–81). New York: Academic Press.

Schachter, S., & Singer, J. (1962). Cognitive, social, and physiological determinants of the emotional state. *Psychological Review, 69,* 379–399.

Schaller, M., & Cialdini, R. B. (1988). The economics of empathic helping: Support for a mood management model. *Journal of Experimental Social Psychology, 24,* 163–181.

Schaller, M., Conway, L. G., III., & Tanchuk, T. L. (2002). Selective pressures on the once and future contents of ethnic stereotypes: Effects of the communicability of traits. *Journal of Personality and Social Psychology, 82,* 861–877.

Scheepers, D., Branscombe, N. R., Spears, R., & Doosje, B. (2002). The emergence and effects of deviants in low and high status groups. *Journal of Experimental Social Psychology, 38,* 611–617.

Scher, S., & Cooper, J. (1989). Motivational bases of dissonance: The singular role of behavioral consequences. *Journal of Personality and Social Psychology, 56,* 899–906.

Scherer, K. R., & Wallbott, H. G. (1994). Evidence for universality and cultural variation of differential emotion response patterning. *Journal of Personality and Social Psychology, 66,* 310–328.

Schlenker, B. R. (1980). *Impression management: The self-concept, social identity, and interpersonal relationships.* Monterey, CA: Brooks/Cole.

Schlenker, B. R. (1982). Translating actions into attitudes: An identity-analytic approach to the explanation of social conduct. In L. Berkowitz (Ed.), *Advances in experimental social psychology* (Vol. 15, pp. 193–247). New York: Academic Press.

Schlenker, B. R., Forsyth, D. R., Leary, M. R., & Miller, R. S. (1980). Self-presentational analysis of the effects of incentives on attitude change following counterattitudinal behavior. *Journal of Personality and Social Psychology, 39,* 553–577.

Schlenker, B. R., Hallam, J. R., & McCown, N. E. (1983). Motives and social evaluation: Actor-observer differences in the delineation of motives for a beneficial act. *Journal of Experimental Social Psychology, 19,* 254–273.

Schlesinger, A. M. (1965). *A thousand days: John F. Kennedy in the White House.* Boston: Houghton-Mifflin.

Schlesinger, A. M. (1986). *The cycles of American history.* Boston: Houghton-Mifflin.

Schmader, T. (2002). Gender identification moderates stereotype threat effects on women's math performance. *Journal of Experimental Social Psychology, 38,* 194–201.

Schmader, T., Major, B., & Gramzow, R. H. (2001). Coping with ethnic stereotypes in the academic domain: Perceived injustice and psychological disengagement. *Journal of Social Issues, 57,* 93–111.

Schmidt, G., & Weiner, B. (1988). An attribution-affect-action theory of behavior: Replications of judgments of help-giving. *Personality and Social Psychology Bulletin, 14,* 610–621.

Schmitt, B. H., Gilovich, T., Goore, N., & Joseph, L. (1986). Mere presence and social facilitation: One more time. *Journal of Experimental Social Psychology, 22,* 242–248.

Schmitt, D. P. (2003). Universal sex differences in the desire for sexual variety: Tests from 52 nations, 6 continents, and 13 islands. *Journal of Personality and Social Psychology, 85,* 85–104.

Schmitt, D. P., Couden, A., & Baker, M. (2001). The effects of sex and temporal context on feelings of romantic desire: An experimental evaluation of sexual strategies theory. *Personality and Social Psychology Bulletin, 27,* 833–847.

Schneider, M. E., Major, B., Luhtanen, R., & Crocker, J. (1996). Social stigma and the potential costs of assumptive help. *Personality and Social Psychology Bulletin, 22,* 201–209.

Schoeneman, T. J., & Rubanowitz, D. E. (1985). Attributions in the advice columns: Actors and observers, causes and reasons. *Personality and Social Psychology Bulletin, 11,* 315–325.

Schofield, J. W. (1979). The impact of positively structured contact on intergroup behavior: Does it last under adverse conditions? *Social Psychology Quarterly, 42,* 280–284.

Schofield, J. W., & Francis, W. D. (1982). An observational study of peer interactions in racially mixed "accelerated" classrooms. *Journal of Educational Psychology, 74,* 722–732.

Schroeder, D. A., Dovidio, J. F., Sibicky, M. E., Matthews, L. L., & Allen, J. L. (1988). Empathic concern and helping behavior: Egoism or altruism? *Journal of Experimental Social Psychology, 24,* 333–353.

Schuman, H., & Presser, S. (1981). *Questions and answers in attitude surveys.* New York: Academic Press.

Schuman, H., Steeh, C., Bobo, L., & Krysan, M. (1997). *Racial attitudes in America: Trends and interpretations.* Cambridge, MA: Harvard University Press.

Schwartz, B. (2000). Self-determination: The tyranny of freedom. *American Psychologist, 55,* 79–88.

Schwartz, C. E., & Sendor, M. (1999). Helping others helps oneself: Response shift effects in peer support. *Social Science and Medicine, 48,* 1563–1575.

Schwartz, S. H., & Bilsky, W. (1987). Toward a universal structure of human values. *Journal of Personality and Social Psychology, 53,* 550–562.

Schwartz, S. H., & Bilsky, W. (1990). Toward a theory of the universal content and structure of values: Extensions and cross-cultural replications. *Journal of Personality and Social Psychology, 58,* 878–891.

Schwarz, N. (1999). Self-reports: How the questions shape the answers. *American Psychologist, 54,* 93–105.

Schwarz, N., & Bless, H. (1992). Scandals and the public's trust in politicians: Assimilation and contrast effects. *Personality and Social Psychology Bulletin, 18,* 574–579.

Schwarz, N., & Clore, G. L. (1983). Mood, misattribution, and judgments of well-being: Informative and directive functions of affective states. *Journal of Personality and Social Psychology, 45,* 513–523.

Schwarz, N., & Clore, G. L. (1988). How do I feel about it? The informative function of affective states. In K.

Fiedler & J. Forgas (Eds.), *Affect, cognition, and social behavior* (pp. 44–62). Toronto: C. J. Hogrefe.

Schwarz, N., Groves, R. M., & Schuman, H. (1998). Survey methods. In D. T. Gilbert, S. T. Fiske, & G. Lindzey (Eds.), *Handbook of social psychology* (4th ed., Vol. 1, pp. 143–179). New York: McGraw-Hill.

Schwarz, N., & Hippler, H.-J. (1995). The numeric value of rating scales: A comparison of their impact in mail surveys and telephone interviews. *International Journal of Public Opinion Research, 7,* 72–74.

Schwarz, N., Hippler, H.-J., Deutsch, B., & Strack, F. (1985). Response categories: Effects on behavioral reports and comparative judgments. *Public Opinion Quarterly, 49,* 388–395.

Schwarz, N., Knäuper, B., Hippler, H.-J., Noelle-Neumann, & Clark, L. F. (1991). Rating scales: Numeric values may change the meaning of scale labels. *Public Opinion Quarterly, 55,* 570–582.

Schwarz, N., Strack, F., Hilton, D., & Naderer, G. (1991). Base rates, representativeness, and the logic of conversation: The contextual relevance of "irrelevant" information. *Social Cognition, 9,* 67–84.

Schwarzwald, J., Bizman, A., & Raz, M. (1983). The foot-in-the-door paradigm: Effects of second request size on donation probability and donor generosity. *Personality and Social Psychology Bulletin, 9,* 443–450.

Schwendinger, J. R., & Schwendinger, H. (1974). Rape myths: In legal, theoretical, and everyday practice. *Crime and Social Justice, 1,* 18–26.

Sears, D. O. (1986). College sophomores in the laboratory: Influences of a narrow data base on social psychology's view of human nature. *Journal of Personality and Social Psychology, 51,* 515–530.

Sears, D. O., & Funk, C. L. (1990). Self-interest in Americans' political opinions. In J. Mansbridge (Ed.), *Beyond self-interest* (pp. 147–170). Chicago: The University of Chicago Press.

Sears, D. O., & Funk, C. L. (1991). The role of self-interest in social and political attitudes. In M. P. Zanna (Ed.), *Advances in experimental social psychology* (Vol. 24, pp. 1–91). New York: Academic Press.

Sears, D. O., & Henry, P. J. (2003). The origins of symbolic racism. *Journal of*

Personality and Social Psychology, 85, 259–275.

Sears, D. O., Hensler, C.P., & Speer, L. K. (1979). Whites' opposition to busing: Self-interest or symbolic politics? *American Political Science Review, 73,* 369–384.

Sears, D. O., van Laar, C., Carillo, M., & Kosterman, R. (1997). Is it really racism? *Public Opinion Quarterly, 61,* 16–53.

Sedikides, C. (1993). Assessment, enhancement, and verification determinants of the self-evaluation process. *Journal of Personality and Social Psychology, 65,* 317–338.

Sedikides, C., Gaertner, L., & Toguchi, Y. (2003). Pancultural self-enhancement. *Journal of Personality and Social Psychology, 84,* 60–79.

Sedikides, C., Oliver, M. B., & Campbell, W. K. (1994). Perceived benefits and costs of romantic relationships for women and men: Implications for exchange theory. *Personal Relationships, 1,* 5–21.

Sedikides, C., & Skowronski, J. J. (1995). On the sources of self-knowledge: The perceived primacy of self-reflection. *Journal of Social and Clinical Psychology, 14,* 244–270.

Segal, N. L. (1984). Cooperation, competition, and altruism within twin sets: A reappraisal. *Ethology and Sociobiology, 5,* 163–177.

Seidlitz, L., & Diener, E. (1993). Memory for positive versus negative life events: Theories for the differences between happy and unhappy persons. *Journal of Personality and Social Psychology, 64,* 654–664.

Sekaquaptewa, D., & Thompson, M. (2003). Solo status, stereotype threat, and performance expectancies: Their effects on women's performance. *Journal of Experimental Social Psychology, 39,* 68–74.

Seligman, M. E. P. (1975). *Helplessness: On depression, development, and death.* San Francisco: W. H. Freeman.

Seligman, M. E. P., & Csikszentmihalyi, M. (2000). Positive psychology: An introduction. *American Psychologist, 55,* 5–14.

Sellers, R. M., & Shelton, J. N. (2003). The role of racial identity in perceived racial discrimination. *Journal of Personality and Social Psychology, 84,* 1079–1092.

Sengupta, J., & Johar, G. V. (2001). Contingent effects of anxiety on elaboration and persuasion. *Personality and Social Psychology Bulletin, 27,* 139–150.

Seta, J. J., McElroy, T., & Seta, C. E. (2001). To do or not to do: Desirability and consistency mediate judgments of regret. *Journal of Personality and Social Psychology, 80,* 861–870.

Settles, I. H. (2004). When multiple identities interfere: The role of identity centrality. *Personality and Social Psychology Bulletin, 30,* 487–500.

Shah, J. Y. (2003a). Automatic for the people: How representations of significant others implicitly affect goal pursuit. *Journal of Personality and Social Psychology, 84,* 661–681.

Shah, J. Y. (2003b). The motivational looking glass: How significant others implicitly affect goal appraisals. *Journal of Personality and Social Psychology, 85,* 424–439.

Shah, J. Y., Friedman, R., & Kruglanski, A. W. (2002). Forgetting all else: On the antecedents and consequences of goal shielding. *Journal of Personality and Social Psychology, 83,* 1261–1280.

Shah, J. Y., & Kruglanski, A. W. (2002). Priming against your will: How accessible alternatives affect goal pursuit. *Journal of Experimental Social Psychology, 38,* 368–383.

Shah, J. Y., & Kruglanski, A. W. (2003). When opportunity knocks: Bottom-up priming of goals by means and its effects on self-regulation. *Journal of Personality and Social Psychology, 84,* 1109–1122.

Sharp, M. J., & Getz, J. G. (1996). Substance use as impression management. *Personality and Social Psychology Bulletin, 22,* 60–67.

Sheldon, K. M., & Elliot, A. J. (1998). Not all goals are personal: Comparing autonomous and controlled reasons as predictors of effort and attainment. *Personality and Social Psychology Bulletin, 24,* 546–557.

Sheldon, K. M., & King, L. (2001). Why positive psychology is necessary. *American Psychologist, 56,* 216–217.

Sheldon, K. M., Ryan, R. M., Deci, E. L., & Kasser, T. (2004). The independent effects of goal contents and motives on well-being: It's both what you pursue and why you pursue it. *Personality and Social Psychology Bulletin, 30,* 475–486.

Sheldon, K. M., Ryan, R., & Reis, H. T. (1996). What makes for a good day? Competence and autonomy in the day and in the person. *Personality and Social Psychology Bulletin, 22,* 1270–1279.

Shelton, J. N. (2000). A reconceptualization of how we study issues of racial prejudice. *Personality and Social Psychology Bulletin, 4,* 374–390.

Sheppard, B. H., Hartwick, J., & Warshaw, P. R. (1988). The theory of reasoned action: A meta-analysis of past research with recommendations for modifications for future research. *Journal of Consumer Research, 15,* 325–343.

Shepperd, J. A. (1993). Productivity loss in performance groups: A motivational analysis. *Psychological Bulletin, 113,* 67–81.

Shepperd, J. A., & Taylor, K. M. (1999). Social loafing and expectancy–value theory. *Personality and Social Psychology Bulletin, 25,* 1147–1158.

Sherif, M. (1936). *The psychology of social norms.* New York: Harper and Brothers.

Sherif, M., Harvey, O. J., White, B. J., Hood, W. R., & Sherif, C. W. (1961). *The Robbers Cave experiment: Intergroup conflict and cooperation.* Norman: University of Oklahoma.

Sherif, M., & Hovland, C. I. (1961). *Social judgment: Assimilation and contrast effects in communication and attitude change.* New Haven, CT: Yale University Press.

Sherman, D. A. K., Nelson, L. D., & Steele, C. M. (2000). Do messages about health risks threaten the self? Increasing the acceptance of threatening health messages via self-affirmation. *Personality and Social Psychology Bulletin, 26,* 1046–1058.

Sherman, D. K., & Kim, H. S. (2002). Affective perseverance: The resistance of affect to cognitive invalidation. *Personality and Social Psychology Bulletin, 28,* 224–237.

Sherman, J., Zehner, K. S., Johnson, J., & Hirt, E. R. (1983). Social explanation: The role of timing, set, and recall on subjective likelihood estimates. *Journal of Personality and Social Psychology, 44,* 1127–1143.

Sherman, S. J., & Fazio, R. H. (1983). Parallels between attitudes and traits as predictors of behavior. *Journal of Personality, 51,* 308–345.

Sherman, S. J., Presson, C. C., Chassin, L., Bensenberg, M., Corty, E., & Olshavsky, R. W. (1982). Smoking intentions in adolescents: Direct experience and predictability. *Personality and Social Psychology Bulletin, 8,* 376–383.

Shih, M., Pittinsky, T. L., & Ambady, N. (1999). Stereotype susceptibility: Identity salience and shifts in quantitative performance. *Psychological Science, 10,* 80–83.

Shine, R., O'Connor, D., LeMaster, M. P., & Mason, R. T. (2001). Pick on someone your own size: Ontogenetic shifts in mate choice by male garter snakes result in size-assortative mating. *Animal Behaviour, 61,* 1133–1141.

Shoda, Y., Mischel, W., & Peake, P. K. (1990). Predicting adolescent cognitive and self-regulatory competencies from preschool delay of gratification: Identifying diagnostic conditions. *Developmental Psychology, 26,* 978–986.

Shrauger, J. S., & Schoeneman, T. J. (1979). Symbolic interactionist view of self-concept: Through the looking glass darkly. *Psychological Bulletin, 86,* 549–573.

Sidanius, J., Pratto, F., & Bobo, L. (1996). Racism, conservatism, affirmative action, and intellectual sophistication. A matter of principled conservatism or group dominance? *Journal of Personality and Social Psychology, 70,* 476–490.

Siegel, J. M. (1990). Stressful life events and use of physician services among the elderly: The moderating role of pet ownership. *Journal of Personality and Social Psychology, 58,* 1081–1086.

Sigall, H., & Landy, D. (1973). Radiating beauty: The effects of having a physically attractive partner on person perception. *Journal of Personality and Social Psychology, 28,* 218–224.

Simner, M. L. (1971). Newborn's response to the cry of another infant. *Developmental Psychology, 5,* 136–150.

Simon, B., & Hamilton, D. L. (1994). Self-stereotyping and social context: The effects of relative in-group size and in-group status. *Journal of Personality and Social Psychology, 66,* 699–711.

Simon, L., Greenberg, J., & Brehm, J. (1995). Trivialization: The forgotten mode of dissonance reduction. *Journal of Personality and Social Psychology, 68,* 247–260.

Simons, J., & Carey, K. B. (1998). A structural analysis of attitudes toward alcohol and marijuana use. *Personality* and Social Psychology Bulletin, 24, 727–735.

Simonton, D. K. (1985). Intelligence and personal influence in groups: Four nonlinear models. Psychological Review, 92, 532–547.

Simonton, D. K. (1987). Why presidents succeed: A political psychology of leadership. New Haven, CT: Yale University Press.

Simpson, J. A. (1990). Influence of attachment styles on romantic relationships. Journal of Personality and Social Psychology, 59, 971–980.

Simpson, J. A., Campbell, B., & Berscheid, E. (1986). The association between romantic love and marriage: Kephart (1967) twice revisited. Personality and Social Psychology Bulletin, 12, 363–372.

Simpson, J. A., Gangestad, S. W., & Lerma, M. (1990). Perception of physical attractiveness: Mechanisms involved in the maintenance of romantic relationships. Journal of Personality and Social Psychology, 59, 1192–1201.

Simpson, J. A., Rholes, W. S., Campbell, L., & Wilson, C. L. (2003). Changes in attachment orientation across the transition to parenthood. Journal of Experimental Social Psychology, 39, 317–331.

Simpson, J. A., Rholes, W. S., & Nelligan, J. S. (1992). Support seeking and support giving within couples in an anxiety-provoking situation: The role of attachment styles. Journal of Personality and Social Psychology, 62, 434–446.

Simpson, J. A., Rholes, W. S., & Phillips, D. (1996). Conflict in close relationships: An attachment perspective. Journal of Personality and Social Psychology, 71, 899–914.

Sinclair, L., & Kunda, Z. (1999). Reactions to a Black professional: Motivated inhibition and activation of conflict stereotypes. Journal of Personality and Social Psychology, 77, 885–904.

Sinclair, L., & Kunda, Z. (2000). Motivated stereotyping of women: She's fine if she praised me but incompetent if she criticized me. Personality and Social Psychology Bulletin, 26, 1329–1342.

Singh, D. (1993). Adaptive significance of female physical attractiveness: Role of waist-to-hip ratio. Journal of Personality and Social Psychology, 65, 293–307.

Skinner, B. F. (1990). Can psychology be a science of mind? American Psychologist, 45, 1206–1210.

Skowronski, J. J., & Carlston, D. E. (1989). Negativity and extremity biases in impression formation: A review of explanations. Psychological Bulletin, 105, 131–142.

Slovic, P., & Fischhoff, B. (1977). On the psychology of experimental surprises. Journal of Experimental Psychology: Human Perception and Performance, 3, 544–551.

Smith, D. M., Neuberg, S. L., Judice, N., & Biesanz, J. C. (1997). Target complicity in the confirmation and disconfirmation of erroneous perceiver expectancies: Immediate and longer term implications. Journal of Personality and Social Psychology, 73, 974–991.

Smith, E. R., & Henry, S. (1996). An ingroup becomes part of the self: Response time evidence. Personality and Social Psychology Bulletin, 22, 635–642.

Smith, K. D., Keating, J. P., & Stotland, E. (1989). Altruism reconsidered: The effect of denying feedback on a victim's status to empathic witness. Journal of Personality and Social Psychology, 57, 641–650.

Smith, M. B., Bruner, J. S., & White, R. W. (1956). Opinions and personality. New York: Wiley.

Smith, R. H., Diener, E., & Wedell, D. H. (1989). Intrapersonal and social comparison determinants of happiness: A range-frequency analysis. Journal of Personality and Social Psychology, 56, 317–325.

Snodgrass, S. E. (1985). Women's intuition: The effect of subordinate role on interpersonal sensitivity. Journal of Personality and Social Psychology, 49, 146–155.

Snodgrass, S. E. (1992). Further effects of role versus gender on interpersonal sensitivity. Journal of Personality and Social Psychology, 6249, 154–158.

Snodgrass, S. E., Hecht, M. A., & Ploutz-Snyder, R. (1998). Interpersonal sensitivity: Expressivity or perceptivity? Journal of Personality and Social Psychology, 74, 238–249.

Snyder, C. R., & Fromkin, H. L. (1980). Uniqueness: The human pursuit of differences. New York: Plenum.

Snyder, C. R., Lassegard, M., & Ford, C. (1986). Distancing after group success and failure: Basking in reflected glory and cutting off reflected failure. Journal of Personality and Social Psychology, 51, 382–388.

Snyder, M. (1974). Self-monitoring of expressive behavior. Journal of Personality and Social Psychology, 30, 526–537.

Snyder, M. (1979). Self-monitoring processes. In L. Berkowitz (Ed.), Advances in experimental social psychology (Vol. 12, pp. 85–128). New York: Academic Press.

Snyder, M. (1982). When believing means doing: Creating links between attitudes and behavior. In M. P. Zanna, E. T. Higgins, & C. P. Herman (Eds.), Consistency in social behavior: The Ontario symposium (Vol. 2, pp. 105–130). Mahwah, NJ: Erlbaum.

Snyder, M. (1984). When belief creates reality. In L. Berkowitz (Ed.), Advances in experimental social psychology (Vol. 18, pp. 247–305). Orlando: Academic Press.

Snyder, M. (1987). Public appearances/private realities: The psychology of self-monitoring. New York: W. H. Freeman.

Snyder, M., & DeBono, K. G. (1985). Appeals to image and claims about quality: Understanding the psychology of advertising. Journal of Personality and Social Psychology, 49, 586–597.

Snyder, M., & Ickes, W. (1985). Personality and social behavior. In G. Lindzey & E. Aronson (Eds.), Handbook of social psychology (3rd ed., Vol. 2, pp. 883–947). New York: Random House.

Snyder, M., & Kendzierski, D. (1982). Acting on one's attitudes: Procedures for linking attitude and behavior. Journal of Experimental Social Psychology, 18, 165–183.

Snyder, M., & Swann, W. B., Jr. (1976). When actions reflect attitudes: The politics of impression management. Journal of Personality and Social Psychology, 34, 1034–1042.

Snyder, M., & Swann, W. B., Jr. (1978). Behavioral confirmation in social interaction: From social perception to social reality. Journal of Experimental Social Psychology, 14, 148–162.

Snyder, M., Tanke, E. D., & Berscheid, E. (1977). Social perception and interpersonal behavior: On the self-fulfilling nature of social stereotypes. Journal of Personality and Social Psychology, 35, 656–666.

Snyder, M. L., Kleck, R. E., Strenta, A., & Mentzer, S. J. (1979). Avoidance of the handicapped: An attributional ambiguity analysis. *Journal of Personality and Social Psychology, 37,* 2297–2306.

Snyder, M. L., Stephan, W. G., & Rosenfield, D. (1976). Egotism and attribution. *Journal of Personality and Social Psychology, 33,* 435–441.

Solberg, E. C., Diener, E., Wirtz, D., Lucas, R. E., & Oishi, S. (2002). Wanting, having, and satisfaction: Examining the role of desire discrepancies in satisfaction with income. *Journal of Personality and Social Psychology, 83,* 725–734.

Solberg, M. E., & Olweus, D. (2003). Prevalence estimation of school bullying: The Olweus Bully/Victim questionnaire. *Aggressive Behavior, 29,* 239–268.

Solomon, S., Greenberg, J., & Pyszczynski, T. (2000). Pride and prejudice: Fear of death and social behavior. *Current Directions in Psychological Science, 9,* 200–203.

Spence, K. W. (1956). *Behavior theory and conditioning.* New Haven, CT: Yale University Press.

Spencer, S. J., Steele, C. M., & Quinn, D. M. (1999). Stereotype threat and women's math performance. *Journal of Experimental Social Psychology, 35,* 4–28.

Sprecher, S. (1999). "I love you more today than yesterday": Romantic partners' perceptions of changes in love and related affect over time. *Journal of Personality and Social Psychology, 76,* 46–53.

Sprecher, S. (2001a). A comparison of emotional consequences of and change in equity over time using global and domain-specific measures of equity. *Journal of Social and Personal Relationships, 18,* 477–501.

Sprecher, S. (2001b). Equity and social exchange in dating couples: Associations with satisfaction, commitment, and stability. *Journal of Marriage and the Family, 63,* 599–613.

Sprecher, S., & Regan, P. C. (2002). Liking some things (in some people) more than others: Partner preferences in romantic relationships and friendships. *Journal of Social and Personal Relationships, 19,* 463–481.

Sprecher, S., Sullivan, Q., & Hatfield, E. (1994). Mate selection preferences: Gender differences examined in a national sample. *Journal of Personality and Social Psychology, 66,* 1074–1080.

Srivastava, A., Locke, E. A., & Bartol, K. M. (2001). Money and subjective well-being: It's not the money, it's the motives. *Journal of Personality and Social Psychology, 80,* 959–971.

Srull, T. S., & Wyer, R. B., Jr. (1979). The role of category accessibility in the interpretation of information about persons: Some determinants and implications. *Journal of Personality and Social Psychology, 37,* 1660–1672.

Staats, A. W., & Staats, C. K. (1958). Attitudes established by classical conditioning. *Journal of Abnormal and Social Psychology, 57,* 37–40.

Stangor, C., & McMillan, D. (1992). Memory for expectancy-congruent and expectancy-incongruent information: A Review of the social and social developmental literatures. *Psychological Bulletin, 111,* 42–61.

Stangor, C., Sullivan, L. A., & Ford, T. E. (1991). Affective and cognitive determinants of prejudice. *Social Cognition, 9,* 359–380.

Stangor, C., Swim, J. K., Van Allen, K. L., & Sechrist, G. B. (2002). Reporting discrimination in public and private contexts. *Journal of Personality and Social Psychology, 82,* 69–74.

Stapel, D. A., & Koomen, W. (2000). Distinctness of others, mutability of selves: Their impact on self-evaluations. *Journal of Personality and Social Psychology, 79,* 1068–1087.

Stapel, D. A., Koomen, W., & van der Plight, J. (1997). Categories of category accessibility: The impact of trait concept versus exemplar priming on person judgments. *Journal of Experimental Social Psychology, 33,* 47–76.

Stapel, D. A., Koomen, W., & Zeelenberg, M. (1998). The impact of accuracy motivation on interpretation, comparison, and correction processes: Accuracy × knowledge accessibility effects. *Journal of Personality and Social Psychology, 74,* 878–893.

Stapel, D. A., Martin, L. L., & Schwarz, N. (1998). The smell of bias: What instigates correction processes in social judgments? *Personality and Social Psychology Bulletin, 24,* 797–806.

Stapel, D. A., & Schwarz, N. (1998). The Republican who did not want to become president: Colin Powell's impact on evaluations of the Republican party and Bob Dole. *Personality and Social Psychology Bulletin, 24,* 690–698.

Stasser, G., Stewart, D. D., & Wittenbaum, G. M. (1995). Expert roles and information exchange during discussion: The importance of knowing how knows what. *Journal of Experimental Social Psychology, 31,* 244–265.

Stasser, G., & Titus, W. (1985). Pooling of unshared information in group decision making: Biased information sampling during discussion. *Journal of Personality and Social Psychology, 48,* 1467–1478.

Stasson, M., & Fishbein, M. (1990). The relation between perceived risk and preventive action: A within-subject analysis of perceived driving risk and intentions to wear seatbelts. *Journal of Applied Social Psychology, 20,* 1541–1557.

Staub, E. (1974). Helping a distressed person: Social, personality, and stimulus determinants. In L. Berkowitz (Ed.), *Advances in experimental social psychology* (Vol. 7, pp. 293–341). New York: Academic Press.

Steblay, N. M. (1987). Helping behavior in rural and urban environments: A meta-analysis. *Psychological Bulletin, 102,* 346–356.

Steele, C. M. (1988). The psychology of self-affirmation: Sustaining the integrity of the self. In L. Berkowitz (Ed.), *Advances in experimental social psychology* (Vol. 21, 261–302). New York: Academic Press.

Steele, C. M. (1992, April). Race and the schooling of Black Americans. *The Atlantic Monthly.*

Steele, C. M. (1997). A threat in the air: How stereotypes shape intellectual identity and performance. *American Psychologist, 52,* 613–629.

Steele, C. M. (2004). Not just a test: Why we must rethink the paradigm we use for judging human ability. *The Nation, 278,* 38–41.

Steele, C. M., & Aronson, J. (1995). Stereotype threat and the intellectual test performance of African Americans. *Journal of Personality and Social Psychology, 69,* 797–811.

Steele, C. M., & Josephs, R. A. (1990). Alcohol myopia: Its prized and dangerous effects. *American Psychologist, 45,* 921–933.

Steele, C. M., & Lui, T. J. (1983). Dissonance processes as self-affirmation. *Journal of Personality and Social Psychology, 45,* 5–19.

Steele, C. M., Southwick, L. L., & Critchlow, B. (1981). Dissonance and alcohol: Drinking your troubles away. *Journal of Personality and Social Psychology, 41,* 831–846.

Steele, C. M., & Spencer, S. J. (1992). The primacy of self-integrity. *Psychological Inquiry, 3,* 345–346.

Steele, S. (1990). *The content of our character: A new vision of race in America.* New York: St. Martin's Press.

Steffen, V. J. (1990). Men's motivation to perform the testicle self-exam: Effects of prior knowledge and an educational brochure. *Journal of Applied Social Psychology, 20,* 681–702.

Steiner, I. D. (1972). *Group process and productivity.* New York: Academic Press.

Steinke, P., Fitch, P., Johnson, C., & Waldstein, F. (2002). An interdisciplinary study of service-learning predictors and outcomes among college students. In S. Billig & A. Furco (Eds.), *Service learning: Through a multidisciplinary lens* (pp. 73–102). Greenwich, CT: Information Age Publishing.

Stephan, W. G., Boniecki, K. A., Ybarra, O., Bettencourt, A., Ervin, K. S., Jackson, L. A., McNatt, P. S., & Renfro, C. L. (2002). The role of threats in the racial attitudes of Blacks and Whites. *Personality and Social Psychology Bulletin, 28,* 1242–1254.

Sternberg, R. J. (1986). A triangular theory of love. *Psychological Review, 93,* 119–135.

Sternberg, R. J. (1987). Liking versus loving: A comparative evaluation of theories. *Psychological Bulletin, 102,* 331–345.

Stewart, D. D., & Stasser, G. (1995). Expert role assignment and information sampling during collective recall and decision making. *Journal of Personality and Social Psychology, 69,* 619–628.

Stewart, R. H. (1965). Effect of continuous responding on the order effect in personality impression formation. *Journal of Personality and Social Psychology, 1,* 161–165.

Stodgill, R. M. (1948). Personal factors associated with leadership: A survey of the literature. *Journal of Personality, 25,* 35–71.

Stone J., Lynch, C. I., Sjomeling, M., & Darley, J. M. (1999). Stereotype threat effects on Black and White athletic performance. *Journal of Personality and Social Psychology, 77,* 1213–1227.

Stone, J., Aronson, E., Crain, A. L., Winslow, M. P., & Fried, C. B. (1994). Inducing hypocrisy as a means of encouraging young adults to use condoms. *Personality and Social Psychology Bulletin, 20,* 116–128.

Stone, J., Wiegand, A. W., Cooper, J., & Aronson, E. (1997). When exemplification fails: Hypocrisy and the motive for self-integrity. *Journal of Personality and Social Psychology, 72,* 54–65.

Storms, M. D. (1973). Videotape and the attribution process: Reversing actors' and observers' points of view. *Journal of Personality and Social Psychology, 27,* 165–175.

Storms, M. D., & Nisbett, R. E. (1970). Insomnia and the attribution process. *Journal of Personality and Social Psychology, 16,* 319–328.

Stouffer, S. A., Suchman, E. A., DeVinney, L. C., Starr, S. A., & Williams, R. M. (1949). *The American soldier: Adjustment during Army life* (Vol. 1). Princeton, NJ: Princeton University Press.

Strahan, E. J., Spencer, S. J., & Zanna, M. P. (2002). Subliminal priming and persuasion: Striking while the iron is hot. *Journal of Experimental Social Psychology, 38,* 556–568.

Strange, J. J., & Leung, C. C. (1999). How anecdotal accounts in news and in fiction can influence judgments of a social problem's urgency, causes, and cures. *Personality and Social Psychology Bulletin, 25,* 436–449.

Strauman, T. J., & Higgins, E. T. (1987). Automatic activation of self-discrepancies and emotional syndromes: When cognitive structures influence affect. *Journal of Personality and Social Psychology, 53,* 1004–1014.

Street, M. D. (1997). Groupthink: An examination of theoretical issues, implications, and future research suggestions. *Small Group Research, 28,* 72–93.

Stroebe, M., & Garcia, J. (1981). A meta-analysis investigation of Fiedler's contingency model of leadership effectiveness. *Psychological Bulletin, 990,* 307–321.

Stroebe, W., Diehl, M., & Abakoumkin, G. (1992). The illusion of group effectivity. *Personality and Social Psychology Bulletin, 18,* 643–650.

Stroebe, W., Stroebe, M., Gergen, K. J., & Gergen, M. (1982). The effects of bereavement on mortality: A social psychological analysis. In J. R. Eiser (Ed.), *Social psychology and behavioral medicine* (pp. 527–560). New York: Wiley.

Stukas, A. A., Jr., & Snyder, M. (2002). Targets' awareness of expectations and behavioral confirmation in ongoing interactions. *Journal of Experimental Social Psychology, 38,* 31–40.

Stukas, A. A., Jr., Snyder, M., & Clary, E. G. (1999). The effects of "mandatory volunteerism" on intentions to volunteer. *Psychological Science, 10,* 59–64.

Sudman, S., Bradburn, N. M., & Schwarz, N. (1996). *Thinking about answers: The application of cognitive processes to survey methodology.* San Francisco: Jossey-Bass.

Suls, J., & Miller, R. (Eds.). (1977). *Social comparison processes: Theoretical and empirical perspectives.* Washington, DC: Hemisphere.

Suls, J., & Wan, C. K. (1987). In search of the false-uniqueness phenomenon: Fear and estimates of social consensus. *Journal of Personality and Social Psychology, 52,* 211–217.

Suls, J., & Wills, T. A. (Eds.). (1991), *Social comparison: Contemporary theory and research.* Mahwah, NJ: Erlbaum.

Surgeon General's Scientific Advisory Committee on Television and Social Behavior. (1972). *Television and social behavior* (Report to the Surgeon General, U.S. Public Health Service). Washington, DC: U.S. Government Printing Office.

Svenson, O. (1981). Are we all less risky and more skillful than our fellow drivers? *Acta Psychologica, 47,* 143–148.

Swann, W. B., Jr. (1984). Quest for accuracy in person perception. A matter of pragmatics. *Psychological Review, 91,* 457–477.

Swann, W. B., Jr. (1990). To be adored or to be known? The interplay of self-enhancement and self-verification. In

R. M. Sorrentino & E. T. Higgins (Eds.), *Motivation and cognition* (Vol. 2, pp. 408–448). New York: Guilford.

Swann, W. B., Jr. (1996). *Self-traps: The elusive quest for higher self-esteem.* New York: W. H. Freeman.

Swann, W. B., Jr., & Ely, R. J. (1984). A battle of wills: Self-verification versus behavioral confirmation. *Journal of Personality and Social Psychology, 46*, 1287–1302.

Swann, W. B., Jr., & Gill, M. J. (1997). Confidence and accuracy in person perception: Do we know what we think we know about our relationship partners? *Journal of Personality and Social Psychology, 73*, 747–757.

Swann, W. B., Jr., Rentfrow, P. J., & Gosling, S. D. (2003). The precarious couple effect: Verbally inhibited men + critical, disinhibited women = bad chemistry. *Journal of Personality and Social Psychology, 85*, 1095–1106.

Swann, W. B., Jr., & Snyder, M. (1980). On translating beliefs into action: Theories of ability and their application in an instructional setting. *Journal of Personality and Social Psychology, 38*, 879–888.

Swim, J. K. (1994). Perceived versus meta-analytic effect sizes: An assessment of the accuracy of gender stereotypes. *Journal of Personality and Social Psychology, 66*, 21–36.

Swim, J. K., Aikin, K. J., Hall, W. S., & Hunter, B. A. (1995). Sexism and racism: Old-fashioned and modern prejudices. *Journal of Personality and Social Psychology, 68*, 199–214.

Swim, J. K., Hyers, L. L., Cohen, L. L., & Ferguson, M. J. (2001). Everyday sexism: Evidence for its incidence, nature, and psychological impact from three daily diary studies. *Journal of Social Issues, 57*, 31–53.

Swim, J. K., & Miller, D. L. (1999). White guilt: Its antecedents and consequences for attitudes toward affirmative action. *Personality and Social Psychology Bulletin, 25*, 500–514.

Swim, J. K., & Sanna, L. J. (1996). He's skilled, she's lucky: A meta-analysis of observers' attributions for women's and men's successes and failures. *Personality and Social Psychology Bulletin, 22*, 507–519.

Szymanski, K., & Harkins, S. G. (1987). Social loafing and social evaluation with a social standard. *Journal of Personality and Social Psychology, 53*, 891–897.

Tafarodi, R. W., Milne, A. G., & Smith, A. J. (1999). The confidence of choice: Evidence for an augmentation effect on self-perceived performance. *Personality and Social Psychology Bulletin, 25*, 1405–1416.

Tajfel, H., Billig, M. G., Bundy, R. F., & Flament, C. (1971). Social categorization and intergroup behavior. *European Journal of Social Psychology, 1*, 149–177.

Tajfel, H., & Turner, J. C. (1986). The social identity theory of intergroup behavior. In S. Worchel & W. Austin (Eds.), *Psychology of intergroup relations* (pp. 7–24). Chicago: Nelson-Hall.

Tamres, L. K., Janicki, D., & Helgeson, V. S. (2002). Sex differences in coping behavior: A meta-analytic review and an examination of relative coping. *Personality and Social Psychology Review, 6*, 2–30.

Tanford, S., & Penrod, S. (1984). Social influence model: A formal integration of research on majority and minority influence processes. *Psychological Bulletin, 95*, 189–225.

Tangney, J. P., Baumeister, R. F., & Boone, A. L. (2004). High self-control predicts good adjustment, less pathology, better grades, and interpersonal success. *Journal of Personality, 72*, 271–324.

Taylor, S. E., & Brown, J. D. (1988). Illusion and well-being: A social psychological perspective on mental health. *Psychological Bulletin, 103*, 193–210.

Taylor, S. E., & Brown, J. D. (1994a). Positive illusions and well-being revisited: Separating fact from fiction. *Psychological Bulletin, 116*, 21–27.

Taylor, S. E., & Brown, J. D. (1994b). "Illusion" of mental health does not explain positive illusions. *American Psychologist, 49*, 972–973.

Taylor, S. E., & Dakof, G. A. (1988). Social support and the cancer patient. In S. Spacapan & S. Oskamp (Eds.), *The social psychology of health. The Claremont Symposium on applied social psychology* (pp. 95–116). Thousand Oaks, CA: Sage Publication.

Taylor, S. E., & Fiske, S. T. (1975). Point of view and the perception of causality. *Journal of Personality and Social Psychology, 32*, 439–445.

Taylor, S. E., & Fiske, S. T. (1978). Salience, attention, and attribution: Top of the head phenomena. In L. Berkowitz (Ed.), *Advances in experimental social psychology* (Vol. 11, pp. 249–288). New York: Academic Press.

Taylor, S. E., Kemeny, M. E., Reed, G. M., Bower, J. E., & Gruenewald, T. L. (2000). Psychological resources, positive illusions, and health. *American Psychologist, 55*, 99–109.

Taylor, S. E., Klein, L. C., Lewis, B. P., Gruenewald, T. L., Gurung, R. A. R., & Updegraff, J. A. (2000). Biobehavioral responses to stress in females: Tend-and-befriend, not fight-or-flight. *Psychological Review, 107*, 411–429.

Taylor, S. E., Lerner, J. S., Sherman, D. K., Sage, R. M., & McDowell, N. K. (2003). Portrait of the self-enhancer: Well adjusted and well liked or maladjusted and friendless? *Journal of Personality and Social Psychology, 84*, 165–176.

Taylor, S. E., Lewis, B. P., Gruenewald, T. L., Gurung, R. A. R., Updegraff, J. A., & Klein, L. C. (2002). Sex differences in behavioral and hormonal response to social threat: Reply to Geary and Flinn. *Psychological Review, 109*, 751–753.

Taylor, S. E., & Lobel, M. (1989). Social comparison activity under threat: Downward evaluation and upward contacts. *Psychological Review, 96*, 569–575.

Tedeschi, J. T., Schlenker, B. R., & Bonoma, T. V. (1971). Cognitive dissonance: Private ratiocination or public spectacle? *American Psychologist, 26*, 685–695.

Terman, L. M., Buttenweiser, P., Ferguson, L. W., Johnson, W. B., & Wilson, D. P. (1938). *Psychological factors in marital happiness.* New York: McGraw-Hill.

Terry, D. J., & Hogg, M. A. (1996). Group norms and the attitude-behavior relationship: A role for group identification. *Personality and Social Psychology Bulletin, 22*, 776–793.

Tesser, A. (1978). Self-generated attitude change. In L. Berkowitz (Ed.), *Advances in experimental social psychology* (Vol. 11, pp. 289–338). New York: Academic Press.

Tesser, A. (1988). Toward a self-evaluation maintenance model of social behavior.

In L. Berkowitz (Ed.), *Advances in experimental social psychology* (Vol. 21, pp. 181–227). New York: Academic Press.

Tesser, A. (1993). The importance of heritability in psychological research: The case of attitudes. *Psychological Review, 100,* 129–142.

Tesser, A., Campbell, J., & Smith, M. (1984). Friendship choice and performance: Self-evaluation maintenance in children. *Journal of Personality and Social Psychology, 46,* 561–574.

Tesser, A., Crepaz, N., Beach, S. R. H., Cornell, D., & Collins, J. C. (2000). Confluence of self-esteem regulation mechanisms: On integrating the self-zoo. *Personality and Social Psychology Bulletin, 26,* 1476–1489.

Tetlock, P. E. (1998). Social psychology and world politics. In D. T. Gilbert, S. T. Fiske, & G. Lindzey (Eds.), *Handbook of social psychology* (4th ed., Vol. 2, pp. 868–912). New York: McGraw-Hill.

Tetlock, P. E., & Kim, J. I. (1987). Accountability and judgment processes in a personality prediction task. *Journal of Personality and Social Psychology, 52,* 700–709.

Thibaut, J. W., & Kelley, H. H. (1959). *The social psychology of group*s. New York: Wiley.

Thoits, P. (1983). Multiple identities and psychological well-being. *American Sociological Review, 48,* 174–187.

Thomas, G., & Fletcher, G. J. O. (2003). Mind-reading accuracy in intimate relationships: Assessing the roles of the relationship, the target, and the judge. *Journal of Personality and Social Psychology, 85,* 1079–1094.

Thompson, E. P., Roman, R. J., Moskowitz, G. B., Chaiken, S., & Bargh, J. A. (1992). Accuracy motivation attenuates covert priming: The systematic reprocessing of social information. *Journal of Personality and Social Psychology, 62,* 728–738.

Thompson, L. (1990a). Negotiation behavior and outcomes: Empirical evidence and theoretical issues. *Psychological Bulletin, 108,* 515–532.

Thompson. L. (1990b). The influence of experience on negotiation. *Journal of Experimental Social Psychology, 26,* 528–544.

Thompson, L., & Hastie, R. (1990). Judgment tasks and biases in negotiation.

In B. H. Sheppard, M. H. Brazerman, & R. J. Lewicki (Eds.), *Research in negotiation in organizations* (Vol. 2, pp. 31–54). Greenwich, CT: JAI.

Thompson, L., & Hrebec, D. (1996). Lose-lose agreements in interdependent decision making. *Psychological Bulletin, 120,* 396–409.

Thompson, L., & Loewenstein, G. (1992). Egocentric interpretations of fairness and interpersonal conflict. *Organizational Behavior and Human Decision Processes, 51,* 176–197.

Thompson, L., Mannix, E. A., & Bazerman, M. H. (1988). Group negotiation: Effects of decision rule, agenda, and aspiration. *Journal of Personality and Social Psychology, 54,* 86–95.

Thompson, M., & Sekaquaptewa, D. (2002). The differential effects of solo status on members of high- and low-status groups. *Personality and Social Psychology Bulletin, 28,* 694–707.

Thompson, M. S., Judd, C. M., & Park, B. (2000). The consequences of communicating social stereotypes. *Journal of Experimental Social Psychology, 36,* 567–599.

Thompson, S. C., & Kelley, H. H. (1981). Judgments of responsibility for activities in close relationships. *Journal of Personality and Social Psychology, 41,* 469–477.

Thorndike, E. L. (1911). *Animal intelligence.* New York: Macmillan.

Thurstone, L. L. (1928). Attitudes can be measured. *American Journal of Sociology, 33,* 529–554.

Tice, D. M., Bratslavsky, E., & Baumeister, R. F. (2001). Emotional distress regulation takes precedence over impulse control: If you feel bad, do it! *Journal of Personality and Social Psychology, 80,* 53–67.

Tiger, L. (1979). *Optimism: The biology of hope.* New York: Simon & Schuster.

Todorov, A., & Uleman, J. S. (2002). Spontaneous trait inferences are bound to actors' faces: Evidence from a false recognition paradigm. *Journal of Personality and Social Psychology, 83,* 1051–1065.

Todorov, A., & Uleman, J. S. (2003). The efficiency of binding spontaneous trait inferences to actors' faces. *Journal of Experimental Social Psychology, 39,* 549–562.

Toi, M., & Batson, C. D. (1982). More evidence that empathy is a source of egoistic motivation. *Journal of*

Personality and Social Psychology, 43, 281–292.

Tolman, E. C. (1926). A behavioristic theory of ideas. *Psychological Review, 33,* 352–369.

Tolman, E. C. (1932). *Purposive behavior in rats and men.* New York: Appleton-Century-Crofts.

Tolman, E. C. (1948). Cognitive maps in rats and men. *Psychological Review, 55,* 189–208.

Tolman, E. C., & Honzig, C. H. (1930). *Introduction and renewal of reward, and maze performance in rats.* University of California Publication in Psychology, 4(19), 267.

Tooby, J., & Cosmides, L. (1992). The psychological foundations of culture. In J. Barkow, L. Cosmides, & J. Tooby (Eds.), *The adapted mind: Evolutionary psychology and the generation of culture* (pp. 19–136). New York: Oxford University Press.

Tormala, Z. L., & Petty, R. E. (2001). Online versus memory-based processing: The role of "need to evaluate" in person perception. *Personality and Social Psychology Bulletin, 27,* 1599–1612.

Tormala, Z. L., & Petty, R. E. (2002). What doesn't kill me makes me stronger: The effects of resisting persuasion on attitude certainty. *Journal of Personality and Social Psychology, 83,* 1298–1313.

Tourangeau, R., & Rasinski, K. A. (1988). Cognitive processes underlying context effects in attitude measurement. *Psychological Bulletin, 103,* 299–314.

Tourangeau, R., Smith, T. W., & Rasinski, K. A. (1997). Motivation to report sensitive behaviors on surveys: Evidence from a bogus-pipeline experiment. *Journal of Applied Social Psychology, 27,* 209–222.

Tracy, J. L., & Robins, R. W. (2003). "Death of a (narcissistic) salesman": An integrative model of fragile self-esteem. *Psychological Inquiry, 14,* 57–62.

Trafimow, D., & Finlay, K. A. (1996). The importance of subjective norms for a minority of people: Between-participants and within-participants analyses. *Personality and Social Psychology Bulletin, 22,* 820–828.

Trafimow, D., & Schneider, D. J. (1994). The effects of behavioral, situational, and person information on different attribution judgments. *Journal of Experimental Social Psychology, 30,* 351–369.

Trafimow, D., Silverman, E. S., Fan, R. M. T., & Law, J. S. F. (1997). The effects of language and priming on the relative accessibility of the private self and the collective self. *Journal of Cross-Cultural Psychology, 28,* 107–123.

Trafimow, D., Triandis, H. C., & Goto, S. G. (1991). Some tests of the distinction between the private and the collective self. *Journal of Personality and Social Psychology, 60,* 649–655.

Triandis, H. C. (1989). The self and social behavior in differing cultural contexts. *Psychological Review, 96,* 506–520.

Triandis, H. C. (1995). *Individualism and collectivism.* Boulder, CO: Westview.

Triplett, N. (1898). The dynamogenic factors in pacemaking and competition. *American Journal of Psychology, 9,* 507–533.

Tripp, C., Jensen, T. D., & Carlson, L. (1994). The effects of multiple product endorsements by celebrities on consumers' attitudes and intentions. *Journal of Consumer Research, 20,* 535–547.

Trivers, R. L. (1971). The evolution of reciprocal altruism. *Quarterly Review of Biology, 46,* 35–57.

Trivers, R. L. (1972). Parental investment and sexual selection. In B. Campbell (Ed.), *Sexual selection and the descent of man: 1871–1971* (pp. 136–179). Chicago: Aldine-Atherton.

Trivers, R. L. (1985). *Social evolution.* Menlo Park, CA: Benjamin/Cumming.

Tronick, E. Z. (1989). Emotions and emotional communication in infants. *American Psychologist, 44,* 112–119.

Trope, Y. (1986). Identification and inferential processes in dispositional attribution. *Psychological Review, 93,* 239–247.

Trope, Y., & Fishbach, A. (2000). Counteractive self-control in overcoming temptation. *Journal of Personality and Social Psychology, 79,* 493–506.

Trope, Y., & Gaunt, R. (2000). Processing alternative explanations of behavior: Correction or integration? *Journal of Personality and Social Psychology, 79,* 344–354.

Trope, Y., & Liberman, N. (2000). Temporal construal and time-dependent changes in preference. *Journal of Personality and Social Psychology, 79,* 876–889.

Trope, Y., & Liberman, N. (2003). Temporal construal. *Psychological Review, 110,* 403–421.

Trzesniewski, K. H., Donnellan, M. B., & Robins, R. W. (2003). Stability of self-esteem across the life span. *Journal of Personality and Social Psychology, 84,* 205–220.

Turner, J. C., Hogg, M. A., Oakes, P. J., Reicher, S. D., & Wetherell, M. S. (1987). *Rediscovering the social group: A self-categorization theory.* Oxford England: Basil Blackwell.

Turner, J. C., Oakes, P. J., Haslam, S. A., & McGarty, C. (1994). Self and collective: Cognition and social context. *Personality and Social Psychology Bulletin, 20,* 454–463.

Turner, J. C., & Onorato, R. S. (1999). Social identity, personality, and the self-concept: A self-categorizing perspective. In T. Tyler, R. Kramer, & O. John (Eds.), *The psychology of the social self: Applied social research* (pp. 11–46). Mahwah, NJ: Erlbaum.

Turner, M. E., & Pratkanis, A. R. (1994). Affirmative action as help: A review of recipient reactions to preferential selection and affirmative action. *Basic and Applied Social Psychology, 15,* 43–69.

Turner, M. E., & Pratkanis, A. R. (1998). A social identity maintenance model of groupthink. *Organizational Behavior and Human Decision Processes, 73,* 210–235.

Tversky, A., & Fox, C. R. (1995). Weighing risk and uncertainty. *Psychological Review, 102,* 269–283.

Tversky, A., & Kahneman, D. (1973), Availability: A heuristic for judging frequency and probability. *Cognitive Psychology, 4,* 207–232.

Tversky, A., & Kahneman, D. (1974). Judgment under uncertainty: Heuristics and biases. *Science, 185,* 1124–1131.

Tversky, A., & Kahneman, D. (1981). The framing of decisions and the psychology of choice. *Science, 211,* 453–458.

Tversky, A., & Kahneman, D. (1982). Judgments of and by representativeness. In D. Kahneman, P. Slovic, & A. Tversky (Eds.), *Judgment under uncertainty: Heuristics and biases* (pp. 84–98). New York: Cambridge University Press.

Tversky, A., & Kahneman, D. (1992). Advances in prospect theory: Cumulative representations of uncertainty. *Journal of Risk and Uncertainty, 5,* 297–323.

Twenge, J. M., Baumeister, R. F., Tice, D. M., & Stucke, T. S. (2001). If you can't join them, beat them: Effects of social exclusion on aggressive behavior. *Journal of Personality and Social Psychology, 81,* 1058–1069.

Twenge, J. M., & Campbell, W. K. (2002). Self-esteem and socioeconomic status: A meta-analytic review. *Personality and Social Psychology Review, 6,* 59–71.

Twenge, J. M., & Campbell, W. K. (2003). "Isn't it fun to get the respect that we're going to deserve?" Narcissism, social rejection, and aggression. *Personality and Social Psychology Bulletin, 29,* 261–272.

Twenge, J. M., & Crocker, J. (2002). Race and self-esteem: Meta-analyses comparing Whites, Blacks, Hispanics, Asians, and American Indians and comment on Gray-Little and Hafdahl (2000). *Psychological Bulletin, 128,* 371–408.

Tykocinski, O. E. (2001). I never had a chance: Using hindsight tactics to mitigate disappointment. *Personality and Social Psychology Bulletin, 27,* 376–382.

Tykocinski, O. E., Pick, D., & Kedmi, D. (2002). Retroactive pessimism: a different kind of hindsight bias. *European Journal of Social Psychology, 32,* 577–588.

Tyler, T. R., & Schuller, R. A. (1991). Aging and attitude change. *Journal of Personality and Social Psychology, 61,* 689–697.

Uchino, B. N., Cacioppo, J. T., & Kiecolt-Glaser, J. K. (1996). The relationship between social support and physiological processes: A review with emphasis on underlying mechanisms and implications for health. *Psychological Bulletin, 119,* 488–531.

Uleman, J. S., & Moskowitz, G. B. (1994). Unintended effects of goals on unintended inferences. *Journal of Personality and Social Psychology, 66,* 490–501.

Updegraff, J. A., Gable, S. L., & Taylor, S. E. (2004). What makes experiences satisfying? The interaction of approach-avoidance motivations and emotions in well-being. *Journal of Personality and Social Psychology, 86,* 496–504.

Valins, S. (1966). Cognitive effects of false heart-rate feedback. *Journal of Personality and Social Psychology, 4,* 400–408.

Vallacher, R. R., & Wegner, D. M. (1987). What do people think they're doing? Action identification and human behavior. *Psychological Review, 94,* 3–15.

Vallone, R. P., Griffin, D. W., Lin, S., & Ross, L. (1990). Overconfident prediction of future actions and outcomes by self and others. *Journal of Personality and Social Psychology, 58,* 582–592.

Vallone, R. P., Ross, L., & Lepper, M. R. (1985). The hostile media phenomenon: Biased perception and perceptions of media bias in coverage of the Beirut Massacre. *Journal of Personality and Social Psychology, 49,* 577–585.

van Baaren, R. B., Holland, R. W., Steenaert, B., & van Knippenberg, A. (2003). Mimicry for money: Behavioral consequences of imitation. *Journal of Experimental Social Psychology, 39,* 393–398.

Van Boven, L., & Loewenstein, G. (2003). Social projection of transient drive states. *Personality and Social Psychology Bulletin, 29,* 1159–1168.

van der Velde, F. W., van der Pligt, J., & Hooykaas, C. (1994). Perceiving AIDS-related risk: Accuracy as a function of differences in actual risk. *Health Psychology, 13,* 25–33.

VandeWalle, D., Brown, S. P., Cron, W. L., & Slocum, J. W., Jr. (1999). The influence of goal orientation and self-regulation tactics on sales performance: A longitudinal field test. *Journal of Applied Psychology, 84,* 249–259.

van Dijk, E., & Wilke, H. (2002). Decision-induced focusing in social dilemmas: Give-some, keep-some, take-some, leave-some dilemmas. *Journal of Personality and Social Psychology, 78,* 92–104.

van Dijk, E., Wilke, H., & Wit, A. (2003). Preferences for leadership in social dilemmas: Public goods dilemmas versus common resource dilemmas. *Journal of Experimental Social Psychology, 39,* 170–176.

Van Lange, P. A. M., & Kuhlman, D. M. (1994). Social value orientations and impressions of partner's honesty and intelligence: A test of the might versus morality effect. *Journal of Personality and Social Psychology, 67,* 126–141.

Van Lange, P. A. M., Otten, W., De Bruin, E. M. N., & Joireman, J. A. (1997). Development of prosocial, individualistic, and competitive orientations: Theory and preliminary evidence. *Journal of Personality and Social Psychology, 73,* 733–746.

Van Lange, P. A. M., & Rusbult, C. E. (1995). My relationship is better than—and not as bad as—yours is: The perception of superiority in close relationships. *Personality and Social Psychology Bulletin, 21,* 32–44.

Van Lange, P. A. M., Rusbult, C. E., Drigotas, S. M., Arriaga, X. B., & Witcher, B. S. (1997). Willingness to sacrifice in close relationships. *Journal of Personality and Social Psychology, 72,* 1373–1395.

Van Vugt, M. (2001). Community identification moderating the impact of financial incentives in a natural social dilemma: Water conservation. *Personality and Social Psychology Bulletin, 27,* 1440–1449.

Van Vugt, M., Jepson, S. F., Hart, C. M., & De Cramer, D. (2004). Autocratic leadership in social dilemmas: A threat to group stability. *Journal of Experimental Social Psychology, 40,* 1–13.

Van Yperen, N. W. (2003). Task interest and actual performance: The moderating effects of assigned and adopted purpose goals. *Journal of Personality and Social Psychology, 85,* 1006–1015.

Verplanken, B., & Holland, R. W. (2002). Motivated decision-making: Effects of activation and self-centrality of values on choices and behavior. *Journal of Personality and Social Psychology, 82,* 434–447.

Vignoles, V. L., Chryssochoou, X., & Breakwell, G. M. (2000). The distinctiveness principle: Identity, meaning, and the bounds of cultural relativity. *Personality and Social Psychology Review, 4,* 337–354.

Vinokur, A., & Burnstein, E. (1974). The effects of partially shared persuasive arguments on group induced shifts: A group problem solving approach. *Journal of Personality and Social Psychology, 29,* 305–315.

Visser, P. S., Krosnick, J. A., & Simmons, J. P. (2003). Distinguishing the cognitive and behavioral consequences of attitude importance and certainty: A new approach to testing the common-factor hypothesis. *Journal of Experimental Social Psychology, 39,* 118–141.

Vogel, D. L., & Karney, B. R. (2002). Demands and withdrawal in newlyweds: Elaborating on the social structure hypothesis. *Journal of Social and Personal Relationships, 19,* 685–701.

Volkema, R. J. (2004). Demographic, cultural, and economic predictors of perceived ethicality of negotiation behavior: A nine-country analysis. *Journal of Business Research, 57,* 69–78.

von Hippel, W., Hawkins, C., & Schooler, J. W. (2001). Stereotype distinctiveness: How counterstereotypic behavior shapes the self-concept. *Journal of Personality and Social Psychology, 81,* 193–205.

von Hippel, W., Sekaquaptewa, D., & Vargas, P. (1997). The linguistic intergroup bias as an implicit indicator of prejudice. *Journal of Experimental Social Psychology, 33,* 490–509.

Vonk, R. (2002). Self-serving interpretations of flattery: Why ingratiation works. *Journal of Personality and Social Psychology, 82,* 515–526.

Vorauer, J. D., Cameron, J. J., Holmes, J. G., & Pearce, D. G. (2003). Invisible overtures: Fears of rejection and the signal amplification bias. *Journal of Personality and Social Psychology, 84,* 793–812.

Vorauer, J. D., & Claude, S. (1998). Perceived versus actual transparency in negotiation. *Personality and Social Psychology Bulletin, 24,* 371–385.

Vrij, A., Edward, K., & Bull, R. (2001). Stereotypical verbal and nonverbal responses while deceiving others. *Personality and Social Psychology Bulletin, 27,* 899–909.

Waite, L. J., & Gallagher, M. (2000). *The case for marriage: Why married people are happier, healthier, and better off financially.* New York: Broadway Books.

Walker, R. (2001). *Black, White, and Jewish: Autobiography of a shifting self.* New York: Riverhead Books.

Walker-Andrews, A. S. (1997). Infants' perception of expressive behaviors: Differentiation of multimodal information. *Psychological Bulletin, 121,* 437–456.

Walster, E., Aronson, E., & Abrahams, D. (1966). On increasing the persuasiveness of a low prestige communicator. *Journal of Personality and Social Psychology, 2,* 325–342.

Walster, E., & Festinger, L. (1962). The effectiveness of "overheard" persuasive communications. *Journal of Abnormal and Social Psychology, 65,* 395–402.

Walster, E., Walster, G. W., & Berscheid, E. (1978). *Equity: Theory and research.* Boston: Allyn & Bacon.

Walster, E., Walster, G. W., Piliavin, J., & Schmidt, L. (1973). "Playing hard to get": Understanding an elusive phenomenon. *Journal of Personality and Social Psychology, 26,* 113–121.

Walther, E. (2002). Guilty by mere association: Evaluative conditioning and the spreading attitude effect. *Journal of Personality and Social Psychology, 82,* 919–934.

Wang, Q. (2001). Culture effects on adults' earliest childhood recollection and self-description: Implications for the relation between memory and the self. *Journal of Personality and Social Psychology, 81,* 220–233.

Wasserman, D., Lempert, R. O., & Hastie, R. (1991). Hindsight and causality. *Personality and Social Psychology Bulletin, 17,* 30–35.

Watson, D. (1982). The actor and the observer: How are their perceptions of causality divergent? *Psychological Bulletin, 92,* 682–700.

Watson, D., & Tellegen, A. (1985). Toward a consensual structure of mood. *Psychological Bulletin, 98,* 219–235.

Watson, J. B. (1913). Psychology as the behaviorist views it. *Psychological Review, 20,* 158–177.

Weber, R., & Crocker, J. (1983). Cognitive processes in the revision of stereotypic beliefs. *Journal of Personality and Social Psychology, 45,* 961–977.

Weber, S. J., & Cook, T. D. (1972). Subject effects in laboratory research: An examination of subject roles, demand characteristics, and valid inference. *Psychological Bulletin, 77,* 273–295.

Webster, G. D. (2003). Prosocial behavior in families: Moderators of resource sharing. *Journal of Experimental Social Psychology, 39,* 644–652.

Wegener, D. T., & Petty, R. E. (1995). Flexible correction processes in social judgment: The role of naïve theories in corrections for perceived biases. *Journal of Personality and Social Psychology, 68,* 36–51.

Wegener, D. T., Petty, R. E., & Smith, S. M. (1995). Positive mood can increase or decrease message scrutiny: The hedonic contingency view of mood and message processing. *Journal of Personality and Social Psychology, 69,* 5–15.

Wegner, D. M. (1989). *White bears and other unwanted thoughts.* New York: Viking/Penguin.

Wegner, D. M. (1994). Ironic processes of mental control. *Psychological Review, 101,* 34–52.

Wegner, D. M., & Erber, R. (1992). The hyperaccessibility of suppressed thoughts. *Journal of Personality and Social Psychology, 63,* 903–912.

Wegner, D. M., & Gold, D. B. (1995). Fanning old flames: Emotional and cognitive effects of suppressing thoughts of a past relationship. *Journal of Personality and Social Psychology, 68,* 782–792.

Wegner, D. M., Schneider, D. J., Carter, S. R., & White, T. L. (1987). Paradoxical effects of thought suppression. *Journal of Personality and Social Psychology, 53,* 5–13.

Wehrle, T., Kaiser, S., Schmidt, S., & Scherer, K. R. (2000). Studying the dynamics of emotional expression using synthesized facial muscle movements. *Journal of Personality and Social Psychology, 78,* 105–119.

Weigel, R. H., & Newman, L. S. (1976). Increasing attitude–behavior correspondence by broadening the scope of the behavioral measure. *Journal of Personality and Social Psychology, 33,* 793–802.

Weigel, R. H., Vernon, D. T. A., & Tognacci, L. N. (1974). Specificity of the attitude as a determinant of attitude-behavior congruence. *Journal of Personality and Social Psychology, 30,* 724–728.

Weiner, B. (1980a). *Human motivation.* New York: Holt, Rinehart, & Winston.

Weiner, B. (1980b). A cognitive (attributional)-emotion-action model of motivated behavior: An analysis of judgments of help-giving. *Journal of Personality and Social Psychology, 39,* 186–200.

Weiner, B. (1985). An attributional theory of achievement motivation and emotion. *Psychological Review, 92,* 548–573.

Weiner, B. (1986). *An attributional theory of motivation and emotion.* New York: Springer.

Weiner, B. (1993). On sin and sickness: A theory of perceived responsibility and social motivation. *American Psychologist, 48,* 957–965.

Weiner, B., Amirkhan, J., Folkes, V. S., & Verette, J. A. (1987). An attributional analysis of excuse-giving: Studies of a naïve theory of emotion. *Journal of Personality and Social Psychology, 52,* 316–324.

Weiner, B., Perry, R. P., & Magnusson, J. (1988). An attributional analysis of reactions to stigmas. *Journal of Personality and Social Psychology, 55,* 738–748.

Weinstein, N. D. (1980).Unrealistic optimism about future life events. *Journal of Personality and Social Psychology, 39,* 806–820.

Weinstein, N. D. (1982). Unrealistic optimism about susceptibility to health problems. *Journal of Behavioral Medicine, 5,* 441–460.

Weinstein, N. D. (1984). Why it won't happen to me: Perceptions of risk factors and susceptibility. *Health Psychology, 3,* 431–457.

Weinstein, N. D., & Klein, W. M. (1995). Resistance of personal risk perceptions to debiasing interventions. *Health Psychology, 14,* 132–140.

Weiss, A., King, J. E., & Enns, R. M. (2002). Subjective well-being is heritable and genetically correlated with dominance in chimpanzees (*Pan troglodytes*). *Journal of Personality and Social Psychology, 83,* 1141–1149.

Weiss, R. F., Buchanan, W., Altstatt, L., & Lombardo, J. P. (1971). Altruism is rewarding. *Science, 171,* 1262–1263.

Weldon, M. S., & Bellinger, K. D. (1997). Collective memory: Collaborative and individual processes in remembering. *Journal of Experimental Psychology: Learning, Memory, and Cognition, 23,* 1160–1175.

Wenzlaff, R. M., & Wegner, D. M. (2000). Thought suppression. *Annual Review of Psychology, 51,* 59–91.

Werner, C. M., & McVaugh, N. (2000). Service-learning "rules" that encourage or discourage long-term service: Implications for research and practice. *Michigan Journal of Community Service-Learning, 7,* 117–125.

Weyant, J. M. (1978). Effects of mood states, costs, and benefits on helping. *Journal of Personality and Social Psychology, 36,* 1169–1176

Wheeler, L., & Kim, Y. (1997). What is beautiful is culturally good: The physical attractiveness stereotype has different content in collectivistic cultures. *Personality and Social Psychology Bulletin, 23,* 795–800.

White, J. A., & Plous, S. (1995). Self-enhancement and social responsibility: On caring more, and doing less, than others. *Journal of Applied Social Psychology, 25,* 1297–1318.

White, R. W. (1959). Motivation reconsidered: The concept of competence. *Psychological Review, 66,* 297–335.

Whitehead, A. N. (1925). *Science and the modern world.* New York: Macmillan.

Whitley, B. E., Jr. (1999). Right-wing authoritarianism, social dominance orientation, and prejudice. *Journal of Personality and Social Psychology, 77,* 126–134.

Whyte, G. (1998). Recasting Janis's group-think model: The key role of collective efficacy in decision fiascoes. *Organizational Behavior and Human Decision Processes, 73,* 189–209.

Wicker, A. W. (1969). Attitudes versus actions: The relationship of verbal and overt behavioral responses to attitude objects. *Journal of Social Issues, 25,* 41–78.

Wieselquist, J., Rusbult, C. E., Foster, C. A., & Agnew, C. R. (1999). Commitment, pro-relationship behavior, and trust in close relationships. *Journal of Personality and Social Psychology, 77,* 942–966.

Wigboldus, D. H. J., Semin, G. R., & Spears, R. (2000). How do we communicate stereotypes: Linguistic biases and inferential consequences. *Journal of Personality and Social Psychology, 78,* 5–18.

Wilder, D. A., Simon, A. F., & Faith, M. (1996). Enhancing the impact of counterstereotypic information: Dispositional attributions for deviance. *Journal of Personality and Social Psychology, 71,* 276–287.

Wildschut, T., Insko, C. A., & Gaertner, L. (2002). Intragroup social influence and intergroup competition. *Journal of Personality and Social Psychology, 82,* 975–992.

Williams, J. E., & Best, D. L. (1982). *Measuring sex stereotypes: A thirty-nation study.* Beverly Hills CA: Sage.

Williams, K. D., Cheung, C. K. T., & Choi, W. (2000). Cyberostracism: Effects of being ignored over the internet. *Journal of Personality and Social Psychology, 79,* 748–762.

Williams, K. D., Harkins, S., & Latané, B. (1981). Identifiability as a deterrent to social loafing: Two cheering experiments. *Journal of Personality and Social Psychology, 40,* 303–311.

Williams, K. D., & Karau, S. J. (1991). Social loafing and social compensation: The effects of expectations of co-worker performance. *Journal of Personality and Social Psychology, 61,* 570–581.

Williamson, G. M., & Clark, M. S. (1989). Providing help and desired relationship type as determinants of changes in mood and self-evaluations. *Journal of Personality and Social Psychology, 56,* 722–734.

Wills, T. A. (1981). Downward comparison principles in social psychology. *Psychological Bulletin, 90,* 245–271.

Wilson, E. O. (1975). *Sociobiology: The new synthesis.* Cambridge, MA: Harvard University Press.

Wilson, M., & Daly, M. (1985). Competitiveness, risk-taking, and violence: The young male syndrome. *Ethology and Sociobiology, 6,* 59–73.

Wilson, T. D., Dunn, D. S., Bybee, J. A., Hyman, D. B., & Rotondo, J. A. (1984). Effects of analyzing reasons on attitude-behavior consistency. *Journal of Personality and Social Psychology, 47,* 5–16.

Wilson, T. D., Dunn, D. S., Kraft, D., & Lisle, D. J. (1989). Introspection, attitude change, and attitude-behavior consistency: The disruptive effects of explaining why we feel the way we do. In L. Berkowitz (Ed.), *Advances in experimental social psychology* (Vol. 22, pp. 287–343). New York: Academic Press.

Wilson, T. D., & Dunn, E. W. (2004). Self-knowledge: Its limits, value, and potential for improvement. *Annual Review of Psychology, 55,* 493–518.

Wilson, T. D., & Hodges, S. D. (1992). Attitudes as temporary constructions. In L. L. Martin & A. Tesser (Eds.), *The construction of social judgments* (pp. 37–65). Mahwah, NJ: Erlbaum.

Wilson, T. D., Kraft, D., & Dunn, D. S. (1989). The disruptive effects of explaining attitudes: The moderating effect of knowledge about the attitude object. *Journal of Experimental Social Psychology, 25,* 379–400.

Wilson, T. D., & LaFleur, S. J. (1995). Knowing what you'll do: Effects of analyzing reasons on self-prediction. *Journal of Personality and Social Psychology, 68,* 21–35.

Wilson, T. D., Lindsey, S., & Schooler, T. Y. (2000). A model of dual attitudes. *Psychological Review, 107,* 101–126.

Wilson, T. D., Wheatley, T., Meyers, J. M., Gilbert, D. T., & Axsom, D. (2000). Focalism: A source of durability bias in affective forecasting. *Journal of Personality and Social Psychology, 78,* 821–836.

Winkielman, P., & Cacioppo, J. T. (2001). Mind at ease puts a smile on the face: Psychophysiological evidence that processing facilitation elicits positive affect. *Journal of Personality and Social Psychology, 81,* 989–1000.

Winkielman, P., Knäuper, B., & Schwarz, N. (1998). Looking back at anger: Reference periods change the interpretation of emotion frequency questions. *Journal of Personality and Social Psychology, 75,* 719–728.

Winquist, J. R., & Larson, J. R., Jr. (1998). Information pooling: When it impacts group decision making. *Journal of Personality and Social Psychology, 74,* 371–377.

Winter, D. G. (1987). Leader appeal, leader performance, and the motive profiles of leaders and followers: A study of American presidents and elections. *Journal of Personality and Social Psychology, 52,* 196–202.

Winter, L., & Uleman, J. S. (1984). When are social judgments made? Evidence for the spontaneousness of trait inferences. *Journal of Personality and Social Psychology, 47,* 237–252.

Winter, L., Uleman, J. S., & Cunniff, C. (1985). How automatic are social judgments? *Journal of Personality and Social Psychology, 49,* 904–917.

Wit, A. P., & Kerr, N. L. (2002). "Me versus just us versus us all" categorization and cooperation in nested social dilemmas. *Journal of Personality and Social Psychology, 83,* 616–637.

Witte, K. (1992). Putting the fear back into fear appeals: The extended parallel process model. *Communication Monographs, 59,* 329–349.

Wittenbaum, G. M., & Bowman, J. M. (2004). A social validation explanation for mutual enhancement. *Journal of Experimental Social Psychology, 40,* 169–184.

Wittenbaum, G. M., Hubbell, A. P., & Zuckerman, C. (1999). Mutual enhancement: Toward an understanding of the collective preference for shared information. *Journal of Personality and Social Psychology, 77,* 967–978.

Wittenbaum, G. M., & Park, E. S. (2001). The collective preference for shared information. *Current Directions in Psychological Science, 10,* 70–73.

Wittenbrink, B., Judd, C. M., & Park, B. (1997). Evidence for racial prejudice at the implicit level and its relationship with questionnaire measures. *Journal of Personality and Social Psychology, 72,* 262–274.

Wittenbrink, B., Judd, C. M., & Park, B. (2001). Evaluative versus conceptual judgments in automatic stereotyping and prejudice. *Journal of Experimental Social Psychology, 37,* 244–252.

Wohl, M. J. A., & Enzle, M. E. (2002). The deployment of personal luck: Sympathetic magic and illusory control in games of pure chance. *Personality and Social Psychology Bulletin, 28,* 1388–1397.

Wolsko, C., Park, B., Judd, C. M., & Wittenbrink, B. (2000). Framing interethnic ideology: Effects of multicultural and color-blind perspectives on judgments of groups and individuals. *Journal of Personality and Social Psychology, 78,* 635–654.

Wood, J. V. (1989). Theory and research concerning social comparisons of personal attributes. *Psychological Bulletin, 106,* 231–248.

Wood, W. (1987). Meta-analytic review of sex differences in group performance. *Psychological Bulletin, 102,* 53–71.

Wood, W., & Eagly, A. H. (1981). Stages in the analysis of persuasive messages: The role of causal attributions and message comprehension. *Journal of Personality and Social Psychology, 40,* 246–259.

Wood, W., & Eagly, A. H. (2002). A cross-cultural analysis of the behavior of women and men: Implications for the origins of sex differences. *Psychological Bulletin, 128,* 699–727.

Wood, W., Lundgren, S., Ouellette, J. A., Busceme, S., & Blackstone, T. (1994). Minority influence: A meta-analytic review of social influence processes. *Psychological Bulletin, 115,* 323–345.

Wood, W., Quinn, J. M., & Kashy, D. A. (2002). Habits in everyday life: Thought, emotion, and action. *Journal of Personality and Social Psychology, 83,* 1281–1297.

Wood, W., Wong, F. Y., & Chachere, J. G. (1991). Effects of media violence on viewers' aggression in unconstrained social interaction. *Psychological Bulletin, 109,* 371–383.

Woodworth, R. S. (1918). *Dynamic psychology.* New York: Columbia University Press.

Woodworth, R. S. (1948). *Contemporary schools of psychology* (2nd ed.). New York: Ronald Press.

Woolfolk, R. L., Novalany, J., Gara, M. A., Allen, L. A., & Polino, M. (1995). Self-complexity, self-evaluation, and depression: An examination of format and content within the self-schema. *Journal of Personality and Social Psychology, 68,* 1108–1120.

Worth, L. T., & Mackie, D. M. (1987). Cognitive mediation of positive affect in persuasion. *Social Cognition, 5,* 76–94.

Wortman, C. B., & Dunkel-Schetter, C. (1979). Interpersonal relationships and cancer: A theoretical analysis. *Journal of Social Issues, 35,* 120–155.

Wu, C., & Schaffer, D. (1987). Susceptibility to persuasive appeals as a function of source credibility and prior experience with the attitude object. *Journal of Personality and Social Psychology, 52,* 677–688.

Wyer, R. S., Jr. (1974). *Cognitive organization and change: An information-processing approach.* Mahwah, NJ: Erlbaum.

Wyer, R. S., Jr., & Gordon, S. E. (1982). The recall of information about persons and groups. *Journal of Experimental Social Psychology, 18,* 128–164.

Ybarra, O., Schaberg, L., & Keiper, S. (1999). Favorable and unfavorable target expectancies and social information processing. *Journal of Personality and Social Psychology, 77,* 698–709.

Yovetich, N. A., & Rusbult, C. E. (1994). Accommodative behavior in close relationships: Exploring transformation of motivation. *Journal of Experimental Social Psychology, 30,* 138–164.

Zadro, L., Williams, K. D., & Richardson, R. (2004). How low can you go? Ostracism by a computer is sufficient to lower self-reported levels of belonging, control, self-esteem, and meaningful existence. *Journal of Experimental Social Psychology, 40,* 560–567.

Zahn-Waxler, C., Radke-Yarrow, M., Wagner, E., & Chapman, M. (1992). Development of concern for others. *Developmental Psychology, 28,* 126–136.

Zahn-Waxler, C., Robinson, J. L., & Emde, R. N. (1992). The development of empathy in twins. *Developmental Psychology, 28,* 1038–1047.

Zajonc, R. B. (1965). Social facilitation. *Science, 149,* 269–274.

Zajonc, R. B. (1968). Attitudinal effects of mere exposure. *Journal of Personality and Social Psychology, 9* (No. 2, Pt. 2).

Zajonc, R. B. (1980a). Compresence. In P. B. Paulhus (Ed.), *Psychology of group influence* (pp. 35–60). Mahwah, NJ: Erlbaum Associates.

Zajonc, R. B. (1980b). Feeling and thinking: Preferences need no inferences. *American Psychologist, 35,* 151–175.

Zajonc, R. B. (2001). Mere exposure: A gateway to the subliminal. *Current Directions in Psychological Science, 6,* 224–228.

Zajonc, R. B., Heingartner, A., & Herman, E. M. (1969). Social enhancement and impairment of performance in the cockroach. *Journal of Personality and Social Psychology, 13,* 83–92.

Zajonc, R. B., Markus, H., & Wilson, W. R. (1974). Exposure effects and associative learning. *Journal of Experimental Social Psychology, 10,* 248–263.

Zajonc, R. B., & Sales, S. M. (1966). Social facilitation of dominant and subordinate responses. *Journal of Experimental Social Psychology, 2,* 160–168.

Zanna, M. P., & Cooper, J. (1974). Dissonance and the pill: An attribution approach to studying the arousal properties of dissonance. *Journal of Personality and Social Psychology, 29,* 703–709.

Zanna, M. P., & Fazio, R. H. (1982). The attitude-behavior relation: Moving toward a third generation of research. In M. P. Zanna, E. T. Higgins, & C. P. Herman (Eds.), *Consistency in social behavior: The Ontario symposium* (Vol. 2, pp. 283–301). Mahwah, NJ: Erlbaum.

Zanna, M. P., & Hamilton, D. L. (1977). Further evidence for meaning change in impression formation. *Journal of Experimental Social Psychology, 13,* 224–238.

Zanna, M. P., Kiesler, C. A., & Pilkonis, P. A. (1970). Positive and negative attitudinal affect established by classical conditioning. *Journal of Personality and Social Psychology, 14,* 321–328.

Zanna, M. P., Olson, J. M., & Fazio, R. H. (1980). Attitude-behavior consistency: An individual difference perspective. *Journal of Personality and Social Psychology, 38,* 432–440.

Zebrowitz, L. A., & Collins, M. A. (1997). Accurate social perception at zero acquaintance: The affordances of a Gibsonian approach. *Personality and Social Psychology Review, 1,* 204–223.

Zebrowitz, L. A., Hall, J. A., Murphy, N. A., & Rhodes, G. (2002). Looking smart and looking good: Facial cues to intelligence and their origins. *Personality and Social Psychology Bulletin, 28,* 238–249.

Zebrowitz, L. A., & Montepare, J. M. (1992). Impressions of babyfaced individuals across the life span. *Developmental Psychology, 28,* 1143–1152.

Zebrowitz, L. A., Montepare, J. M., & Lee, H. K. (1993). They don't all look alike: Individuated impressions of other racial groups. *Journal of Personality and Social Psychology, 65,* 85–101.

Zebrowitz, L. A., Tenenbaum, D. R., & Goldstein, L. H. (1991). The impact of job applicants' facial maturity, gender, and academic achievement on hiring recommendations. *Journal of Applied Social Psychology, 21,* 525–548.

Zeichner, A., & Phil, R. O. (1979). Effects of alcohol and behavior contingencies on human aggression. *Journal of Abnormal Psychology, 88,* 153–160.

Zillman, D. (1978). Attribution and misattribution of excitatory reactions. In J. Harvey, W. Ickes, & W. Kidd (Eds.), *New directions in attribution research* (Vol. 2, pp. 335–368). Mahwah, NJ: Erlbaum.

Zillman, D., Katcher, A. H., & Milavsky, B. (1972). Excitation transfer from physical exercise to subsequent aggressive behavior. *Journal of Experimental Social Psychology, 8,* 247–259.

Zimbardo, P. (1969). The human choice: Individuation, reason, and order vs. deindividuation, impulse, and chaos. *Nebraska Symposium on Motivation, 17,* 237–307.

Zimbardo, P. G., Weisenberg, M., Firestone, I., & Levy, B. (1965). Communicator effectiveness in producing public conformity and private attitude change. *Journal of Personality, 33,* 233–255.

Zirkel, S., & Cantor, N. (1990). Personal construal of life tasks: Those who struggle for independence. *Journal of Personality and Social Psychology, 58,* 172–185.

Zucker, G. S., & Weiner, B. (1993). Conservatism and perceptions of poverty: An attributional analysis. *Journal of Applied Social Psychology, 23,* 925–943.

Zuckerman, M. (1979). Attribution of success and failure revisited, or: The motivational bias is alive and well in attribution theory. *Journal of Personality, 47,* 245–287.

Zuckerman, M., Hall, J. A., DeFrank, R. S., & Rosenthal, R. (1976). Encoding and decoding of spontaneous and posed facial expressions. *Journal of Personality and Social Psychology, 34,* 966–977.

Zuckerman, M., & Kieffer, S. C. (1994). Race differences in face-ism: Does facial prominence imply dominance? *Journal of Personality and Social Psychology, 66,* 86–92.

Zuckerman, M., DePaulo, B. M., & Rosenthal, R. (1981). Verbal and nonverbal communication of deception. In L. Berkowitz (Ed.), *Advances in experimental social psychology* (Vol. 14, pp. 1–59). New York: Academic Press.

Zuroff, D. C., & Rotter, J. B. (1985). A history of the expectancy construct in psychology. In J. B. Dusek (Ed.), *Teacher expectancies* (pp. 9–36). Mahwah, NJ: Erlbaum.

Credits

PHOTO

Page 68: Reprinted by permission from *Nature,* Perrett et al, 394, 884–887, © 1998 Macmillan Publishers Ltd.; **69:** Reprinted by permission from Langlois and Roggman, *Psychological Science,* v10.i1, 115–121, Blackwell Publishing Ltd.; **72:** © Paul Ekman 1976–2004; **86:** Leonardo da Vinci, *Mona Lisa,* Louvre, Paris, France. Photo: Scala/Art Resource; **334:** (left) © Bettmann/CORBIS, (right) © Leo Dennis/NewSport/Corbis.

TEXT AND ART

"Desolation Row" by Bob Dylan. Copyright © 1965 by Warner Bros. Inc. Copyright renewed 1993 by Special Rider Music. All rights reserved. International copyright secured. Reprinted by permission.

Fig. 3.6 From "The recognition of threatening facial stimuli" by Arnoff, J., Barclay, A. M., and Stevenson, L. A. in *Journal of Personality and Social Psychology, 54:* 647–655. Copyright © 1988 The American Psychological Association. Reprinted with permission.

Fig. 3.8 From "Which are the stimuli in facial displays of anger and happiness? Configurational bases of emotion recognition" by Arnoff, J., Woike, B. A., and Hyman, L. M. in *Journal of Personality and Social Psychology, 62:* 1050–1066. Copyright © 1992 The American Psychological Association. Reprinted with permission.

Fig. 5.15 From "Beyond money: Toward an economy of well-being" by Diener, E. and Seligman, M. E. P. from *Psychological Science in the Public Interest, 5:*1–31. Copyright © 2004. Reprinted with permission of Blackwell Publishing.

Ch. 6, p. 228 "Did You Ever Have to Make Up Your Mind?" words and music by John Sebastian. Copyright © 1965 EMI Faithful Virtue Music and Alley Music Corporation. All rights for Faithful Virtue Music controlled and administered by EMI April Music Inc. All rights reserved. International copyright secured. Used by permission.

Table 6.1 Likert Scale from *The Religious Experience: A Social-Psychological Perspective* by Batson, C. D. and Ventis, W. L., New York: Oxford University Press, 1982. Reprinted with permission.

Fig. 11.13 From "Inclusion of other in the self scale and the structure of interpersonal closeness" by Aron, A., Aron, E., and Smollan, D. in *Journal of Personality and Social Psychology, 63:* 596–612. Copyright © 1992 The American Psychological Association. Reprinted with permission.

Table 11.1 "I'll Be There" words and music by Holland-Dozier-Holland. Copyright © 1966 EMI Stone Agate Music. All rights for Stone Agate Music controlled and administered by EMI April Music Inc. All rights reserved. International copyright secured. Used by permission.

Table 11.1 "Bridge Over Troubled Water" by Paul Simon. Copyright © 1969 Paul Simon. Used by permission of the Publisher, Paul Simon Music.

Table 11.1 "You've Got a Friend" words and music by Carole King. Copyright © 1971 Colgems-EMI. All rights for Colgems controlled and administered by EMI April Music Inc. All rights reserved. International copyright secured. Used by permission.

Table 11.1 "Lean On Me" words and music by Bill Withers. Copyright © 1972 by Songs of Universal, Inc. All rights reserved. International copyright secured. Used by permission.

Table 11.1 "I'll Be There for You" words and music by Danny Wilde and Phil Solem. Copyright © Warner Brothers Music Corporation. All rights reserved. International copyright secured. Used by permission.

Table 11.1 "Make You Feel My Love" by Bob Dylan. Copyright ©1997 by Special Rider Music. All rights reserved. International copyright secured. Reprinted by permission.

Table 11.1 "All You Wanted" words and music by Michelle Branch. Copyright © Warner Brothers Music Corporation. All rights reserved. International copyright secured. Used by permission.

Ch. 11, p. 423 "I'm a Believer" words and music by Neil Diamond. Copyright © 1966 (renewed), 1978 Stonebridge Music and Foray Music. All rights reserved. International copyright secured. Used by permission.

Name Index

Subject Index